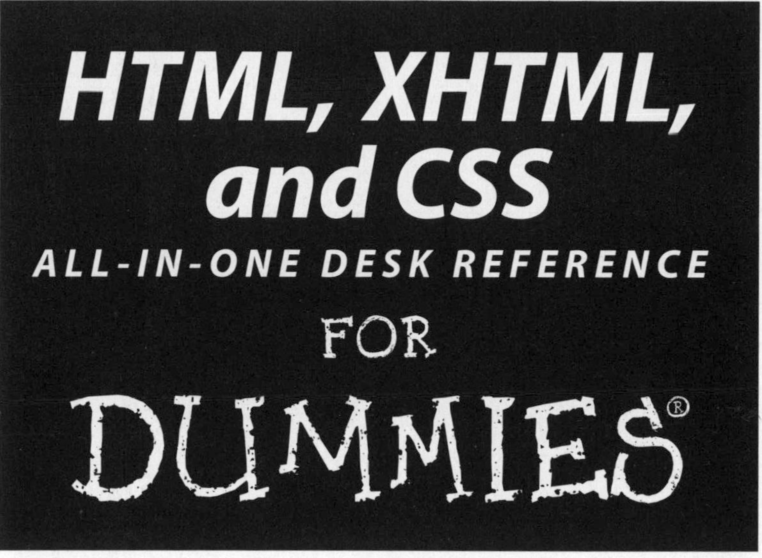

by Andy Harris
and Chris McCulloh

Wiley Publishing, Inc.

HTML, XHTML, and CSS All-in-One Desk Reference For Dummies®

Published by
Wiley Publishing, Inc.
111 River Street
Hoboken, NJ 07030-5774

www.wiley.com

Published by Wiley Publishing, Inc., Indianapolis, Indiana

Published simultaneously in Canada

For general information on our other products and services, please contact our Customer Care Department within the U.S. at 800-762-2974, outside the U.S. at 317-572-3993, or fax 317-572-4002.

For technical support, please visit www.wiley.com/techsupport.

Wiley also publishes its books in a variety of electronic formats. Some content that appears in print may not be available in electronic books.

Library of Congress Control Number: 2008924956

ISBN: 978-0-470-18627-5

Manufactured in the United States of America

10 9 8 7 6 5 4 3 2 1

About the Authors

Andy Harris began his teaching life as a special education teacher. As he was teaching young adults with severe disabilities, he taught himself enough computer programming to support his teaching habit with freelance programming. Those were the exciting days when computers started to have hard drives, and some computers began communicating with each other over an arcane mechanism some were calling the Internet.

All this time Andy was teaching computer science part time. He joined the faculty of the Indiana University/Purdue University — Indianapolis Computer Science department in 1995. He serves as a Senior Lecturer, teaching the introductory course to Freshmen as well as numerous courses on Web development, general programming, and game programming. As manager of the Streaming Media Laboratory, he developed a number of online video-based courses, and worked on a number of international distance education projects including helping to start a computer science program in Tetevo, Macedonia FYR.

Andy is the author of several other computing books, including *Beginning Flash Game Programming For Dummies* and *Game Programming: The L Line*. He invites your comments and questions at `andy@aharrisbooks.net`.

Chris McCulloh has a bachelor's degree in Media Arts and Science from Indiana University/Purdue University — Indianapolis (IUPUI), a certificate in Applied Computer Science from the Computer and Information Science Department (CSCI) at IUPUI, and is a full-time PHP Developer working at CIK Enterprises. He loves to teach, write, and read, and is currently teaching server-side programming for CSCI at IUPUI. He writes a programming-related blog on his Flash game site at `blog.chomperstomp.com`, and maintains a popular Firefox extension located at statusbarcalculator.com.

Dedication

I dedicate the book to Jesus Christ, my personal savior, and to Heather, the joy in my life. I also dedicate this project to Elizabeth, Matthew, Jacob, and Benjamin. I love each of you. **—Andy Harris**

To Julie. **—Chris McCulloh**

Authors' Acknowledgments

Andy would like to thank the following:

Heather, for being amazing even when I'm being . . . an author. Chris, for stepping into a crazy project and performing like a star. Mark Enochs, for listening to my rants and smiling. You are a true friend, and I can't imagine how tough this project would have been without you. Katie Feltman, for being the nicest taskmaster I've ever encountered. Thanks for keeping it positive even when you were dropping the hammer. (Do you have any hammers left? You dropped a lot on this project.) Seriously, I enjoy dreaming up a new project with you, and watching it develop. Jennifer Riggs, for managing my sometimes confused rambling and turning it into something decent. Rodd Mullet, for his technical edit of the manuscript. Jane Harris, for the steady supply of custom tea. I'm getting about 40 pages per gallon now. The many people at Wiley who never meet the author, yet contribute immeasurably to a book like this. Thank you for your contributions. The open-source community, for creating incredible tools and making them freely available for everyone. I'd especially like to thank the developers of Firefox, FireBug, HTML Validator, Web Developer Toolbar, Aptana Studio, Notepad++, PHP, MySQL, phpMyAdmin, Apache, DBDesigner4, jQuery, emacs, VI, and GIMP. Reiner Prokein, for use of his great sprites. Julian Burgess, for use of his tiled background image. The IUPUI computer science family, for years of support on many projects. All my students, current, past, and future, I learn far more from you than the small amount I've given you.

Chris would like to thank the following:

God, for his love, patience, blessings, forgiveness, and Son. But also, for the ability to think logically and communicate ideas through writing (which I enjoy thoroughly). Julie, for the hot delicious scrumptious healthy meals. For making my dresser magically refill itself weekly. For picking up the slack and keeping the house from falling down around us while I worked on this book. But mostly for your love and encouragement. Mom, for teaching me to write. Dad, for having a million books in the house, and reading to me every night when I was little. My editors, for catching all of the mistakes in the places where I forgot what my Mom taught me. Andy Harris, for inspiring me to do more than I ever thought I could do, for (unknowingly) converting me from being a graphics artist into a computer programmer, and for giving me the opportunity to write with one of my favorite authors. Brian, for teaching me QBasic when I was 9.

Publisher's Acknowledgments

We're proud of this book; please send us your comments through our online registration form located at `www.dummies.com/register/`.

Some of the people who helped bring this book to market include the following:

Acquisitions, Editorial, and Media Development

Senior Project Editor: Mark Enochs

Senior Acquisitions Editor: Katie Feltman

Copy Editor: Jennifer Riggs

Technical Editor: Rodd Mullett

Editorial Manager: Leah Cameron

Media Associate Project Manager: Laura Atkinson

Media Development Assistant Producer: Kit Malone

Media Quality Assurance: Angela Denny

Editorial Assistant: Amanda Foxworth

Sr. Editorial Assistant: Cherie Case

Cartoons: Rich Tennant (`www.the5thwave.com`)

Composition Services

Project Coordinator: Lynsey Stanford

Layout and Graphics: Claudia Bell, Alissa D. Ellet, Joyce Haughey, Melissa K. Jester, Shane Johnson, Christine Williams

Proofreaders: Broccoli Information Management, Caitie Kelly

Indexer: Broccoli Information Management

Special Help: Kelly Ewing, Melba Hopper, Jodi Jensen, Laura Miller, Jean Nelson, Blair Pottenger, Nicole Sholly, Rebecca Whitney

---

Publishing and Editorial for Technology Dummies

Richard Swadley, Vice President and Executive Group Publisher

Andy Cummings, Vice President and Publisher

Mary Bednarek, Executive Acquisitions Director

Mary C. Corder, Editorial Director

Publishing for Consumer Dummies

Diane Graves Steele, Vice President and Publisher

Joyce Pepple, Acquisitions Director

Composition Services

Gerry Fahey, Vice President of Production Services

Debbie Stailey, Director of Composition Services

Contents at a Glance

Table of Contents

Book V: Server-Side Programming with PHP................489

Chapter 1: Setting Up Your Server 491

Chapter 2: Generating HTML with PHP 501

Chapter 3: PHP and XHTML Forms 513

Book VII: Into the Future with AJAX 723

Chapter 1: AJAX Essentials 725

Chapter 2: Improving JavaScript with jQuery 739

Chapter 3: Animating with jQuery 759

Introduction

I love the Internet, and if you picked up this book, you probably do, too. The Internet is dynamic, chaotic, exciting, interesting, and useful, all at the same time. The Web is pretty fun from a user's point of view, but that's only part of the story. Perhaps the best part of the Internet is how participatory it is. You can build your own content — for free! It's really amazing. There's never been a form of communication like this before. Anyone with access to a minimal PC and a little bit of knowledge can create his or her own homestead in one of the most exciting platforms in the history of communication.

The real question is how to get there. A lot of Web development books are really about how to use some sort of software you have to buy. That's okay, but it's not necessary. Many software packages have evolved that purport to make Web development easier. Some work pretty well, but regardless what software package you use, there's still a need to know what's really going on under the surface. That's where this book comes in.

You'll find out exactly how the Web works in this book. You'll figure out how to use various tools, but, more importantly, you'll create your piece of the Web. You'll discover:

- **How Web pages are created:** You'll figure out the basic structure of Web pages. You'll understand the structure well because you build pages yourself. No mysteries here.
- **How to separate content and style:** You'll understand the foundation of modern thinking about the Internet — that style should be separated from content.
- **How to use Web standards:** The current Web is pretty messy, but, finally, some standards have arisen from the confusion. You'll discover how these standards work and how you can use them.
- **How to create great-looking Web pages:** Of course, you want a terrific-looking Web site. With this book, you'll find out how to use layout, style, color, and images.
- **How to build modern layouts:** Many Web pages feature columns, menus, and other fancy features. You'll figure out how to build all these things.
- **How to add interactivity:** Adding forms to your pages, validating form data, and creating animations are all possible with the JavaScript language.
- **How to write programs on the server:** Today's Web is powered by programs on Web servers. You'll discover the powerful PHP language and figure out how to use it to create powerful and effective sites.

- **How to harness the power of data:** Every Web developer eventually needs to interact with data. You'll read about how to create databases that work. You'll also discover how to connect databases to your Web pages and how to create effective and useful interfaces.
- **How AJAX is changing everything:** The hottest Web technology on the horizon is AJAX (Asynchronous JavaScript And XML). You'll figure out how to harness this way of working and use it to create even more powerful and interesting applications.

No Experience Necessary

I'm not assuming anything in this book. If you've never built a Web page before, you're in the right hands. You don't need any experience, and you don't have to know anything about HTML, programming, or databases. I discuss everything you need.

If you're reasonably comfortable with a computer (you can navigate the Web and use a word processor), you have all the skills you need.

Great for Advanced Folks, Too!

If you've been around Web development for a while, you'll still find this book handy.

If you've used HTML but not XHTML, see how things have changed and discover the power of the XHTML/CSS combination.

If you're still using table-based layouts, you'll definitely want to read about newer ways of thinking. After you get over the difference, you'll be amazed at the power, the flexibility, and the simplicity of CSS-based layout and design.

If you're already comfortable with XHTML and CSS, you're ready to add JavaScript functionality for form validation and animation. If you've never used a programming language before, JavaScript is a really great place to start.

If you're starting to get serious about Web development, you've probably already realized that you'll need to work with a server at some point. PHP is a really powerful, free, and easy language that's extremely prominent in the Web landscape. You'll use this to have programs that send e-mails, store and load information from files, and work with databases.

If you're messing with commercial development, you'll definitely need to know more about databases. I get e-mails every week from companies looking for people who can create a solid relational database and connect it to a Web site with PHP.

If you're curious about AJAX, you can read about what it is, how it works, and how to use it to add functionality to your site. You'll also read about a very powerful and easy AJAX library that can add tremendous functionality to your bag of tricks.

I wrote this book as the reference I wish I had. If you have only one Web development book on your shelf, this should be the one. Wherever you are in your Web development journey, you can find something interesting and new in this book.

Use Any Computer

One of the great things about Web development is how accessible it can be. You don't need a high-end machine to build Web sites. Whatever you're using now will probably do fine. I built most of the examples in this book with Windows XP and Fedora Core Linux, but a Mac is perfectly fine, too. Most of the software I use in the book is available for free for all major platforms. Similar alternatives for all platforms are available in the few cases when this isn't true.

Don't Buy Any Software

Everything you need for Web development is on the CD-ROM. I've used only open-source software for this book. The CD contains a ton of tools and helpful programs. See Appendix A in the back of this book for a complete listing. Following are the highlights:

- **Aptana:** A full-featured programmer's editor that greatly simplifies creating Web pages, CSS documents, and code in multiple languages.
- **Firefox extensions:** I've included several extensions to the Firefox Web browser that turn it into a thoroughbred Web development platform. The Web Developer toolbar adds all kinds of features for creating and testing pages; the HTML Validator checks your pages for standards-compliance; and the Firebug extension adds incredible features for JavaScript and AJAX debugging.
- **XAMPP:** When you're ready to move to the server, XAMPP is a complete server package that's easy to install and incredibly powerful. This includes the amazing Apache Web server, the PHP programming language, the MySQL database manager, and tons of useful utilities.
- **Useful tools:** Every time I use a tool (such as a data mapper, a diagram tool, or an image editor) in this book, I make it available on the CD-ROM.

There's no need to buy any expensive Web development tools. Everything you need is here, and they're not any harder than the more expensive Web editors.

How This Book Is Organized

Web development today is about solving a series of connected but different problems. This book is organized into eight minibooks based on specific technologies. You can read them in any order you wish, but you'll find that the later books tend to rely on topics described in the earlier ones. (For example, JavaScript doesn't make much sense without XHTML because it's usually embedded in a Web page.) The following describes these eight minibooks:

- **Book I: Creating the XHTML Foundation —** Web development incorporates a lot of languages and technologies, but HTML is the foundation. Here I show you *XHTML,* the latest incarnation of HTML, and describe how it's used to form the basic skeleton of your pages.
- **Book II: Styling with CSS —** In the old days, HTML had a few tags to spruce up your pages, but they weren't nearly powerful enough. Today developers use Cascading Style Sheets (CSS) to add color and formatting to your pages.
- **Book III: Using Positional CSS for Layout —** Discover the best ways to set up layouts with floating elements, fixed positioning, and absolute positioning. Figure out how to build various multicolumn page layouts and how to create dynamic buttons and menus.
- **Book IV: Client-Side Programming with JavaScript —** Figure out essential programming skills with the easy and powerful JavaScript language — even if you've never programmed before. Manipulate data in Web forms and use powerful regular expression technology to validate form entries. Also discover how to create animations with JavaScript.
- **Book V: Server-Side Programming with PHP —** Move your code to the server and take advantage of this powerful language. Figure out how to respond to Web requests; work with conditions, functions, objects, and text files; and connect to databases.
- **Book VI: Databases with MySQL —** Most serious Web projects are eventually about data. Figure out how databases are created, how to set up a secure data server, the basics of data normalization, and how to create a reliable and trustworthy data back end for your site.

- **Book VII: Into the Future with AJAX —** Look forward to the technology that has the Web abuzz. AJAX isn't really a language but rather a new way of thinking about Web development. Get the skinny on what's going on here, build an AJAX connection or two by hand, and read about some really cool libraries for adding advanced features and functionality to your pages.
- **Book VIII: Moving from Web Pages to Web Sites —** This minibook ties together many of the threads throughout the rest of the book. Discover how to create your own complete Web server solution or pick a Web host. Walk through the process of designing a complex multi-page Web site. Discover how to use content management systems to simplify complex Web sites and, finally, to build your own Content Management System with skills taught throughout the book.

Icons Used in This Book

This is a *For Dummies* book, so you have to expect some snazzy icons, right? I don't disappoint. Here's what you'll see:

This is where I pass along any small insights I may have gleaned in our travels.

I can't really help being geeky once in a while. Every so often I want to explain something a little deeper. Read this to impress people at your next computer science cocktail party or skip it if you really don't need the details.

A lot of details are here. I point out something important that's easy to forget with this icon.

Watch out! Anything I mark with this icon is a place where things have blown up for me or my students. I point out any potential problems with this icon.

A lot of really great examples and software are on the CD. Whenever I mention software or examples that are available on the CD, I highlight it with this icon.

What's Next?

Well, that's really up to you. I sincerely believe you can use this book to turn into a top-notch Web developer. That's our goal for you.

Although this is a massive book, there's still more to figure out. If you have questions or just want to chat, feel free to e-mail at `andy@aharrisbooks.net`. You can also visit my Web site at `www.aharrisbooks.net` for code examples, updates, and other good stuff. (You can also visit `www.dummies.com/go/htmlxhtmlcssaiofd` for code examples from the book.)

I try hard to answer all reader e-mails but sometimes I get behind. Please be patient with me, and I'll do my best to help.

I can't wait to hear from you and see the incredible Web sites you develop. Have a great time, discover a lot, and stay in touch! You can contact me at `andy@aharrisbooks.net`.

Book I

Creating the XHTML Foundation

The 5th Wave
By Rich Tennant
FREELANCER NED WILLIS CONSULTS WITH A MEMBER OF HIS TECHNICAL STAFF
©RICHTENNANT

"...and that's pretty much all there is to converting a document to an HTML file."

Contents at a Glance

Chapter 1: Sound HTML Foundations

In This Chapter

- Creating a basic Web page
- Understanding the most critical HTML tags
- Setting up your system to work with HTML
- Viewing your pages

This chapter is your first introduction to building Web pages. Before this slim chapter is finished, you'll have your first page up and running. Creating a basic page isn't difficult, but building pages in a way that grows and expands as you get more sophisticated takes a little foresight. Most of this book uses the XHTML standard. In this first chapter, I show part of an older standard called HTML. HTML is a little bit easier to start with, and everything I show in this chapter translates perfectly to the XHTML you'll use throughout the book.

In this minibook, you discover the modern form of Web design using XHTML. Your Web pages will be designed from the ground up, which makes them easy to modify and customize. As you figure out more advanced techniques throughout this book, you'll take the humble pages you discover in this chapter and make them do all kinds of exciting things.

Creating a Basic Page

Here's the great news: The most important Web technology you need is also the easiest. You don't need any expensive or complicated software, and you don't need a powerful computer. You probably have everything you need to get started already.

No more talking! Fire up a computer and let's build a Web page!

1. **Open a text editor.**

   You can use any text editor you want, as long as it lets you save files as plain text. If you're using Windows, Notepad is fine for now. (Later, I show you some other free alternatives, but start with something you already know.)

Don't use a word processor like Microsoft Word. It doesn't save things in the right format, and all the nifty features, like fonts and centering, don't work right. I promise that you'll figure out how to do all that stuff but without using a word processor. Even the Save as HTML feature doesn't work right. You really need a very simple text editor, and that's it. In Chapter 3 of this minibook, I show you a few more editors that make your life easier. You'll never use Word.

2. **Type the following code.**

   Really. Type it in your text editor so you get some experience writing the actual code. I explain very soon what all this means, but type it now to get a feel for it:

```
<html>
<head>
<!-- myFirst.html -->

<title>My very first Web page!</title>
</head>

<body>

<h1>This is my first Web page!</h1>

<p>
This is the first Web page I've ever made,
and I'm extremely proud of it.
It is so cool!
</p>

</body>
</html>
```

3. **Save the file as `myFirst.html`.**

   It's important that your filename has no spaces and ends with the `.html` extension. Spaces cause problems on the Internet (which is, of course, where all good pages go to live), and the `.html` extension is how most computers know that this file is an HTML file (which is another name for a Web page). It doesn't matter where you save the file, as long as you can find it in the next step.

4. **Open your Web browser.**

   The *Web browser* is the program used to look at pages. After you post your page on a Web server somewhere, your Great Aunt Gertrude uses a Web browser to view your page. You also need one (a browser, not a Great Aunt Gertrude) to test your page. For now, use whatever browser you ordinarily use. Most Windows users already have Internet Explorer installed. If you're a Mac user, you probably have Safari. Linux folks generally have Firefox. Any of these are fine. In Chapter 3 of this minibook, I explain why you probably need more than one browser and how to configure them for maximum usefulness.

5. **Load your page into the browser.**

   You can do this in a number of ways. You can use the browser's File menu to open a local file, or you can simply drag the file from your Desktop (or wherever) to the open browser window.

6. **Bask in your newfound genius.**

   Your simple text file is transformed! If all went well, it looks like Figure 1-1.

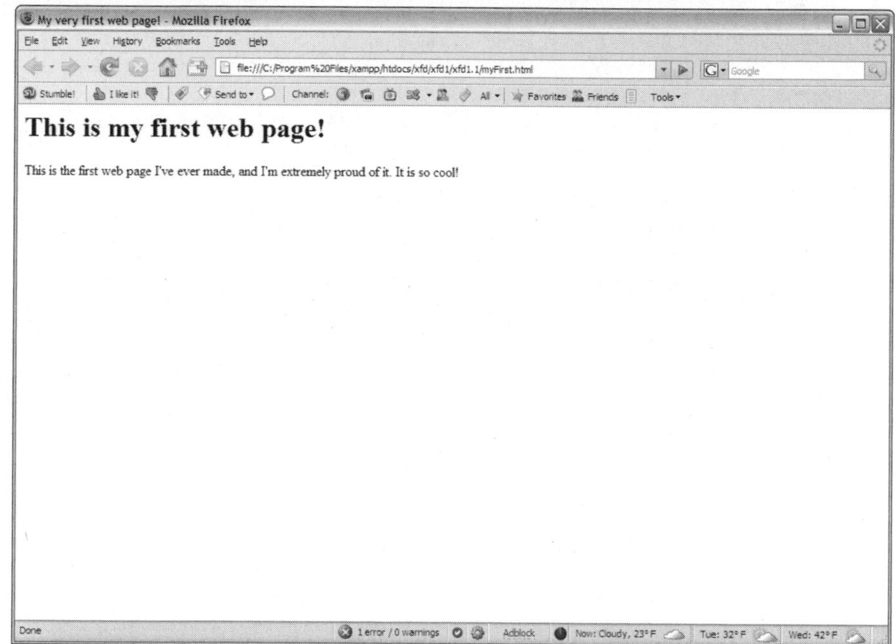

Figure 1-1: Congratulations! You're now a Web developer!

Understanding the HTML in the Basic Page

The page you create in the previous section uses an extremely simple notation — HTML (HyperText Markup Language), which has been around since the beginning of the Web. HTML is a terrific technology for several reasons:

- **It uses plain text.** Most document systems (like word processors) use special *binary encoding schemes,* which incorporate formatting directly into the computer's internal language. This means that a document becomes locked into a particular computer or software. That is, a document stored in Word format can't be read without a program that understands Word formatting. HTML gets past this problem by storing everything in plain text.
- **It works on all computers.** The main point of HTML is to have a universal format. Any computer should be able to read and write it. The plain-text formatting technique aids in this.
- **It describes what documents *mean.*** HTML isn't really designed to indicate how a page or its elements look. HTML is about describing the meaning of various elements (more on that very soon). This has some distinct advantages when you figure out how to use HTML properly.
- **It *doesn't* describe how documents *look.*** This one seems strange. Of course, when you look at Figure 1-1, you can see that the appearance of the text on the Web has changed from the way that text looked in your text editor. Formatting a document in HTML does cause the document's appearance to change. That's not the point of HTML, though. You discover (in Books II and III) how to use another powerful technology — *CSS* — to change the appearance of a page after you define its meaning. This separation of meaning from layout is one of the best features of HTML.
- **It's easy to write.** Sure, HTML gets a little more complicated than this first example, but you can easily figure out how to write HTML by hand without any specialized editors. You only have to know a handful of elements, and they're pretty straightforward.
- **It's free.** HTML doesn't cost anything to use, primarily because it isn't owned by anyone. No corporation has control of it (although a couple have tried), and nobody has a patent on it. The fact that this technology is freely available to anyone is a huge advantage.

Meeting Your New Friends, the Tags

The key to writing HTML code is the special text inside angle braces (<>). These special elements are *tags.* They aren't meant to be displayed on the Web page but offer instructions to the Web browser about the meaning of the text. The tags are meant to be embedded into each other to indicate the organization of the page. This basic page introduces you to all the major tags you'll encounter. (There are more, but they can wait for a chapter or two.) Each tag has a beginning and an end tag. The end tag is just like the beginning, except it has a forward slash (/). For example the entire page begins with an `<html>` tag and ends with `</html>`. Read the `</html>` as "end html." The `<html></html>` combination indicates that everything in the page is defined as HTML code:

✦ **`<html></html>`:** The `<html>` tag is the foundation of the entire Web page. It's the tag that begins the page. Likewise, `</html>` ends the page.

Some books teach you to write your HTML tags all in uppercase letters. This was once a standard, but it is no longer recommended. When you move to XHTML code (which is a slightly stricter form of HTML) in Chapter 2 of this minibook, you'll see that XHTML requires all tags to be entirely lowercase. I'll begin with the standard you use for the rest of this book.

✦ **`<head></head>`:** These tags define a special part of the Web page called the *head* (or sometimes *header*). This part of the Web page reminds me of the engine compartment of a car. This is where you put some really great stuff later, but it's not where the main document lives. For now, the only thing you'll put in the header is the document's title. Later, you'll add styling information and programming code to make your pages sing and dance.

✦ **`<!-- -->`:** This tag indicates a *comment,* which is ignored by the browser. However, a comment is used to describe what's going on in a particular part of the code. All the examples for this book include a comment containing the code's filename. If you want to find out more about any of the code listings in the book, you can just find the appropriate file on the CD-ROM or Web site that accompanies the book.

✦ **`<title></title>`:** This tag is used to determine the page's title. The title usually contains ordinary text. Whatever you define as the title will appear in some special ways. Many browsers put the title text in the browser's title bar. Search engines often use the title to describe the page.

It's not quite accurate to say that the title text always shows up in the title bar because a Web page is designed to work on lots of different browsers. Sure, the title does show up on most major browsers that way, but what about cell phones and Personal Digital Assistants? HTML never legislates what will happen; it only suggests. This may be hard to get used to, but it's a reality. You trade absolute control for widespread capability, which is a good deal.

✦ **`<body></body>`:** The page's main content is contained within these tags. Most of the HTML code and the stuff the user sees is in the body area. If the header area is the engine compartment, the body is where the passengers go.

- **<h1></h1>:** H1 stands for *heading level one.* Any text contained within this markup is treated as a prominent headline. By default, most browsers add special formatting to anything defined as H1, but there's no guarantee. An H1 heading doesn't really specify any particular font or formatting, just the *meaning* of the text as a level one heading. When you find out how to use CSS in Book II, you'll discover that you can make your headline look however you want. In this first minibook, keep all the default layouts for now and make sure you understand that HTML is about semantic meaning, not about layout or design. There are other kinds of headings too, of course, `<h1>` through `<h6>`. `<h2>` indicates a heading slightly less important than `<h1>`, `<h3>` is less important than `<h2>`, and so on.

Beginners are sometimes tempted to make their first headline an `<h1>` tag and then use an `<h2>` for the second and `<h3>` for the third. That's not how it works. Newspapers and books use different kinds of headlines to point out the relative importance of various elements on the page, often varying the point size of the text. You can read more about that in Book II.

- **<p></p>:** In HTML, p stands for the paragraph tag. In your Web pages, you should enclose each standard paragraph in a `<p></p>` pair. You might notice that HTML doesn't preserve the carriage returns or white space in your HTML document. That is, if you press Enter in your code to move text to a new line, that new line isn't necessarily preserved in the final Web page.

  The `<p></p>` structure is one easy way to manage spacing before and after each paragraph in your document.

A few notes about the basic page

Be proud of this first page. It may be simple, but it's the foundation of greater things to come. Before moving on, take a moment to ponder some important HTML/XHTML principles shown in this humble page you've created:

- **All tags are in lowercase.** Although HTML does allow uppercase tags, the XHTML variation you'll be using throughout most of this book requires only lowercase tags.
- **Tag pairs are containers, with a beginning and an end.** Tags contain other tags or text.
- **Some elements can be repeated.** There's only one `<html>`, `<title>`, and `<body>` tag per page, but a lot of the other elements (`<h1>` and `<p>`) can be repeated as many times as you like.
- **Carriage returns are ignored.** In the Notepad document, there are a number of carriage returns. The formatting of the original document has no effect on the HTML output. The markup tags indicate how the output looks.

Some older books recommend using <p> without a </p> to add space to your documents, similar to pressing the Enter key. This way of thinking could cause you problems later because it doesn't truthfully reflect the way Web browsers work. Don't think of <p> as the carriage return. Instead, think of <p> and </p> as defining a paragraph. The paragraph model is more powerful because soon enough, you'll figure out how to take any properly defined paragraph and give it yellow letters on a green background with daisies (or whatever else you want). If things are marked properly, they'll be much easier to manipulate later.

Setting Up Your System

You don't need much to make Web pages. Your plain text editor and a Web browser are about all you need. Still, there are some things you can do to make your life easier as a Web developer.

Displaying file extensions

The method discussed in this section is mainly for Windows users, but it's a big one. Windows uses the *extension* (the part of the filename after the period) to determine what type of file you're dealing with. This is very important in Web development. The files you create are simple text files, but if you store them with the ordinary `.txt` extension, your browser can't read them properly. What's worse, the default setting of Windows hides these extensions from you, so you have only the icons to tell you what type of file you're dealing with. This can cause all kinds of problems. I recommend you have Windows explicitly describe your file extensions. Here's how to set that up:

1. **Open the file manager (My Computer in XP or Computer in Vista.)**

   Use the My Computer window to open a directory on your hard drive. It doesn't matter which directory you're looking at. You just need the tool open.

2. **Choose Tools⇨Folder Options.**

   The Folder Options dialog box appears.

3. **Select the View tab.**

   You see the Folder Options dialog box.

4. **Don't hide extensions.**

   By default, Windows likes to hide the extensions for known file types. However, you're a programmer now, so you deserve to be shown these things. Uncheck the Hide Extensions for Known File Types box, as shown in Figure 1-2.

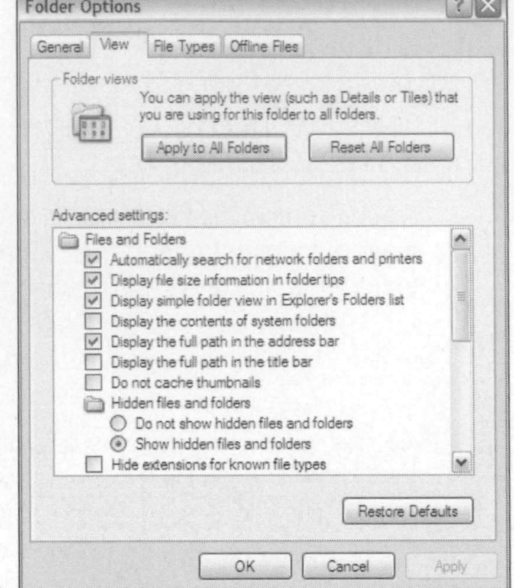

Figure 1-2: Don't hide file extensions (deselect that last check box).

5. **Show the path and hidden folders.**

   I like to be shown my hidden files and folders (after all, they're mine, right?) and I like to have the full path listed. Click the appropriate check boxes to enable these features. You'll often find them to be helpful.

6. **Apply these change to all the folders on your computer by clicking the Apply to All Folders button.**

   This causes the file extensions to appear everywhere, including the Desktop.

Setting up your software

You'll write a lot of Web pages, so it makes sense to set up your system to make that process as easy as possible. I talk a lot more about some software you should use in Chapter 3 of this minibook, but for now, here's a couple of easy suggestions:

- **Put a Notepad icon on your Desktop.** You'll edit a lot of text files, so it's helpful to have an icon for Notepad (or whatever other text editor you use) available directly on the Desktop. That way, you can quickly edit any Web page by dragging it to the Desktop. When you use more sophisticated editors than Notepad, you'll want links to them, too.
- **Get another Web browser.** You may just *love* your Web browser, and that's fine, but you can't assume that everybody likes the same browser you do. You need to know how other browsers will interpret your code. Firefox is an incredibly powerful browser, and it's completely free. If you don't have them already, I suggest having links to at least two browsers directly on your Desktop.

Understanding the magic

Most of the problems people have with the Web come from misunderstandings about how this medium really works. Most people are comfortable with word processors, and we know how to make a document look how we want. Modern applications use WYSIWYG technology, promising that *what you see is what you get.* That's a reasonable promise when it comes to print documents, but it doesn't work that way on the Web.

How a Web page looks depends on a lot of things that you don't control. The user may read your pages on a smaller or larger screen than you. She may use a totally different operating system than you. She may have a dialup connection or may turn off the graphics for speed. She may be blind and use screen-reader technology to navigate Web pages. She may be reading your page on a PDA or a cell phone. You can't make a document that looks the same in all these situations.

A good compromise is to make a document that clearly indicates how the information fits together and makes suggestions about the visual design. The user and her browser can determine how much of those suggestions to use.

You get control of the visual design but never complete control, which is okay because you're trading total control for accessibility. People with devices you've never heard of can visit your page.

Practice a few times until you can easily build a page without looking anything up. Soon enough, you're ready for the next step — building pages like the pros.

Chapter 2: It's All about Validation

In This Chapter

- **Introducing the concept of valid pages**
- **Using a doctype**
- **Introducing XHTML 1.0 Strict**
- **Setting the character set**
- **Meeting the W3C Validator**
- **Fixing things when they go wrong**
- **Using HTML Tidy to automatically clean your pages**

Web development is currently undergoing an important revolution. As the Web matures and becomes more important, it becomes more important to ensure that Web pages perform properly. There is a new call for Web developers to follow voluntary standards of Web development.

Somebody Stop the HTML Madness!

In the bad old days, the Web was a pretty informal affair. People wrote HTML pages however they wanted. Although this was easy, it led to a lot of problems:

- **Browser manufacturers added features that didn't work on all browsers.** People wanted prettier Web pages with colors, fonts, and doodads, but there wasn't a standard way to do these things. Every browser had a different set of tags that supported enhanced features. As a developer, you had no real idea if your Web page would work on all the browsers out there. If you wanted to use some neat feature, you had to ensure your users had the right browser.
- **The distinction between meaning and layout was blurred.** People expected to have some kind of design control of their Web pages, so all kinds of new tags popped up that blurred the distinction between describing and decorating a page.
- **A table-based layout was used as a hack.** HTML didn't have a good way to handle layout, so clever Web developers started using tables as a layout mechanism. This worked, after a fashion, but it wasn't easy or elegant.

- **People started using tools to write pages.** Web pages soon became so ugly that people began to believe that they couldn't do HTML by hand anymore and that some kind of editor was necessary to handle all that complexity for them. The trouble is that although these editing programs introduced new features that made things easier upfront, these tools also made code almost impossible to change without the original editor. Web developers began thinking they couldn't design Web pages without a tool from a major corporation.
- **The nature of the Web was changing.** At the same time, these factors were making ordinary Web development more challenging. Innovators were recognizing that the Web wasn't really about documents but was about applications that can dynamically create documents. Many of the most interesting Web pages you visit aren't Web pages at all, but programs that produce Web pages dynamically every time you visit. This meant that developers had to make Web pages readable by programs, as well as humans.

In short, the world of HTML was a real mess.

XHTML to the rescue

In 2000, the World Wide Web Consortium (usually abbreviated as W3C) got together and proposed some fixes for HTML. The basic plan was to create a new form of HTML that complied with a stricter form of markup, or *eXtensible Markup Language (XML)*. The details are long and boring, but essentially, they came up with some agreements about how Web pages are standardized. Here are some of those standards:

- **All tags have endings.** Every tag comes with a beginning and an end tag. (Well, there are a few exceptions, but they come with their own ending built-in. I'll explain when you encounter the first such tag in Chapter 6 of this minibook.) This was a new development because end tags were considered optional in old-school HTML, and many tags didn't even have end tags.
- **Tags can't be overlapped.** In HTML, sometimes people had the tendency to be sloppy and overlap tags, like this: `<a><b>my stuff</a></b>`. That's not allowed in XHTML, which is a good thing because it confuses the browser. If a tag is opened inside some container tag, the tag must be closed before that container is closed.
- **Everything's lowercase.** Some people wrote HTML in uppercase, some in lowercase, and some just did what they felt like. It was inconsistent and made it harder to write browsers that could read all the variations.
- **Attributes must be in quotes.** If you've already done some HTML, you know that quotes used to be optional — not anymore.

✦ **Layout must be separate from markup.** Old-school HTML had a bunch of tags (like `<font>` and `<center>`) that were more about formatting than markup. These were useful, but they didn't go far enough. XHTML (at least the Strict version covered here) eliminates all these tags. Don't worry, though; CSS gives you all the features of these tags and a lot more.

This sounds like more rules than a strict librarian. Really, they aren't restricting at all because most of the good HTML coders were already following these guidelines or something similar.

There's XHTML, and then there's good XHTML

In old-style HTML, you never really knew how your pages would look on various browsers. In fact, you never really knew if your page was even written properly. Some mistakes would look fine on one browser but cause another browser to blow up.

The whole idea of *validation* is to take away some of the uncertainty of HTML. It's like a spell checker for your code. My regular spell checker makes me feel a little stupid sometimes because I make mistakes. I like it, though, because I'm the only one who sees the errors. I can fix the spelling errors before I pass the document on to you, so I look smart. (Well, maybe.)

It'd be cool if you could have a special kind of checker that does the same things for your Web pages. Instead of checking your spelling, it'd test your page for errors and let you know if you made any mistakes. It'd be even cooler if you could have some sort of certification that your page follows a standard of excellence.

That's exactly how page validation works. You can designate that your page will follow a particular standard and use a software tool to ensure that your page meets that standard's specifications. The software tool is a *Validator.* I show you two different Validators in this chapter, in the section called "Validating Your Page."

The browsers also promise to follow a particular standard. If your page validates to a given standard, any browser that validates to that same standard can reproduce your document correctly, which is a really big deal.

Building an XHTML Document

You create an XHTML document the same way you build ordinary HTML. You can still use an ordinary text editor, but the code is slightly more involved. Take a look at the following code (`template.html` on the CD ROM) to see a bare-bones XHTML document:

```
<!DOCTYPE html PUBLIC "-//W3C//DTD XHTML 1.0 Strict//EN"
    "http://www.w3.org/TR/xhtml1/DTD/xhtml1-strict.dtd">
<html xmlns="http://www.w3.org/1999/xhtml">
<head>
<meta http-equiv="Content-Type" content="text/html;
   charset=utf-8" />
<title></title>
</head>
<body>
<h1></h1>
<p>
</p>

</body>
</html>
```

At first, this new document looks a lot more complicated than the HTML you see in Chapter 1 of this minibook, but it isn't as bad as it seems.

Don't memorize all this!

Before you freak out, don't feel you have to memorize this nonsense. Even people who write books about Web development (um, like me) don't have this stuff memorized because it's too awkward and too likely to change.

Keep a copy of `template.html` on your local drive (I keep a copy on my Desktop) and begin all your new pages with this template. When you start to use a more complex editor (see Chapter 3 of this minibook), you can often customize the editor so that it automatically starts with the framework you want.

You don't have to have all this stuff down cold, but you should understand the basics of what's going on, so the following is a quick tour.

The DOCTYPE tag

The scariest looking new XHTML feature is the `<!DOCTYPE>` tag. This monster is ugly, no doubt about it, but it does serve a purpose. Officially, it's a *document type definition.* Your doctype declares to the world what particular flavor of HTML or XHTML you're using. When you begin your page with the doctype I suggest here, you're telling the browser: "Hey, browser, my page follows the XHTML Strict Guidelines, and if you aren't sure what that is, go to this Web site to get it."

```
<!DOCTYPE html PUBLIC "-//W3C//DTD XHTML 1.0 Strict//EN"
    "http://www.w3.org/TR/xhtml1/DTD/xhtml1-strict.dtd">
```

Many different doctypes are available, but it's really a lot simpler than it seems. In this book, I show you XHTML 1.0 Strict, which is the only doctype you need today. The other variations you might find on the Web (HTML 4.0, Frameset, and Transitional doctypes) are really designed for backwards compatibility. If you're going to go the standards-compliant route, you might as well go whole hog.

It's true that XHTML 1.1 and XHTML 2.0 are on the horizon, but the major psychological barrier is moving from HTML to any form of XHTML Strict. After you make the XHTML Strict leap, you'll find it pretty easy to move on to the other forms of XHTML when they become viable.

The xmlns attribute

The `html` tag looks a little different than the one in Chapter 1 of this mini-book. It has the term `xmlns` after it, which stands for *XML NameSpace.* All this acronym does is help clarify the definitions of the tags in your document:

```
<html xmlns="http://www.w3.org/1999/xhtml">
```

Truthfully, most Web developers don't use the `xmlns` attribute yet. If you leave it out, most browsers work just fine. I include it because the W3C's newest Validator (which was being tested when this book went to press) complains if you don't have it in there. By the time you read this book, that Validator might become the main tool for validation, and I don't want your pages to crash when the `xmlns` attribute becomes a requirement (which looks likely).

The meta tag

The last new and mysterious tag is the funky `meta` tag. `meta` tags have been a part of HTML for a long time. They allow you to describe various characteristics of a Web page:

```
<meta http-equiv="Content-Type" content="text/html;
   charset=utf-8" />
```

The particular form of the `meta` tag you see here defines the character set to use. The `utf` character set handles a number of Western languages well.

The real truth is, if you start with this framework, you'll have everything you need to make official XHTML pages that validate properly.

You validate me

All this doctype and `xmlns` nonsense is worth it because of a nifty program — the *Validator.* The most important is the one at W3C: `http://validator.w3.org`, as shown in Figure 2-1.

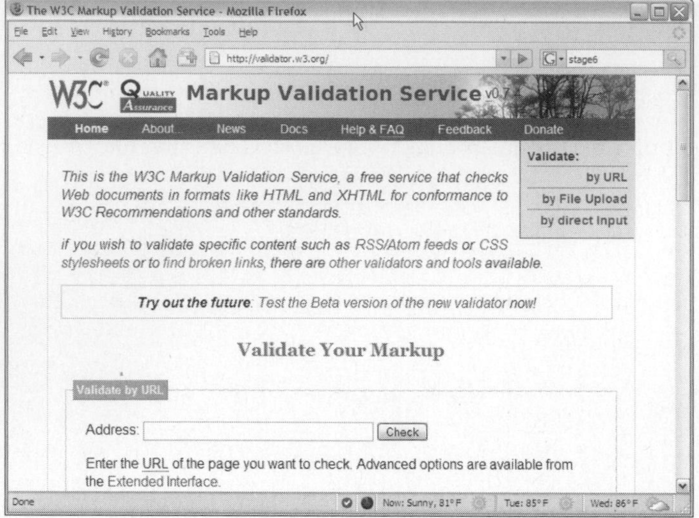

Figure 2-1: The W3C Validator main page isn't exciting, but it sure is useful.

The Validator is actually the front end of a piece of software that checks pages for validity. It looks at your Web page's doctype and sees if the page conforms to the rules of that doctype. If not, it tells you what might have gone wrong.

You can submit code to the Validator in three different ways:

- **Validate by URL.** This option is used when a page is actually hosted on a Web server. Files stored on local computers can't be checked with this technique. Book VIII describes all you need to know about working with Web servers, including how to create your own.
- **Validate by File Upload.** This technique works fine with files you haven't yet posted to a Web server. It works great for pages you write on your computer but you haven't made visible to the world. This is the most common type of validation for beginners.
- **Validate by Direct Input.** The Validator page has a text box you can simply paste your code into. It works, but I usually prefer to use the other methods because they're easier.

Validation might sound like a big hassle, but it's really a wonderful tool because sloppy HTML code can cause lots of problems. Worse, you might think everything's okay until somebody else looks at your page, and suddenly, the page doesn't display correctly.

Validating Your Page

To explain all this, I created a Web page the way Aesop might have done in ancient Greece. Okay, maybe Aesop didn't write his famous fables as Web pages, but if he had, they might have looked like the following code listing:

```
<!DOCTYPE html PUBLIC "-//W3C//DTD XHTML 1.0 Strict//EN"
    "http://www.w3.org/TR/xhtml1/DTD/xhtml1-strict.dtd">
<html xmlns="http://www.w3.org/1999/xhtml">
<head>
<meta http-equiv="Content-Type" content="text/html; charset=iso-8859-1" />

<!-- oxWheels1.html -->

<!-- note this page has deliberate errors!  Please see the text
     and oxWheelsCorrect.html for a corrected version.
-->

</head>
<body>
<title>The Oxen and the Wheels</title>
<h1>The Oxen and the Wheels
<h2></h1>From Aesop's Fables</h2>

<p>
    A pair of Oxen were drawing a heavily loaded wagon along a
    miry country road. They had to use all their strength to pull
    the wagon, but they did not complain.
<p>

<p>
    The Wheels of the wagon were of a different sort. Though the
    task they had to do was very light compared with that of the
    Oxen, they creaked and groaned at every turn. The poor Oxen,
    pulling with all their might to draw the wagon through the
    deep mud, had their ears filled with the loud complaining of
    the Wheels. And this, you may well know, made their work so
    much the harder to endure.
</p>

<p>
    "Silence!" the Oxen cried at last, out of patience. "What have
    you Wheels to complain about so loudly? We are drawing all the
    weight, not you, and we are keeping still about it besides."
</p>

<h2>
They complain most who suffer least.
</h2>

</body>
</html>
```

It looks okay, but there are actually a number of problems. Aesop may have been a great storyteller, but from this example, it appears he was a sloppy coder. The mistakes can be pretty hard to see, but trust me, they're there. The question is how do you find the problems before your users do?

You might think that the problems would be evident if you viewed the page in a Web browser. The Firefox and Internet Explorer Web browsers seem to handle the page decently, even if they don't display it in an identical way. Figure 2-2 shows `oxWheels1.html` in Firefox, and Figure 2-3 shows it in Internet Explorer.

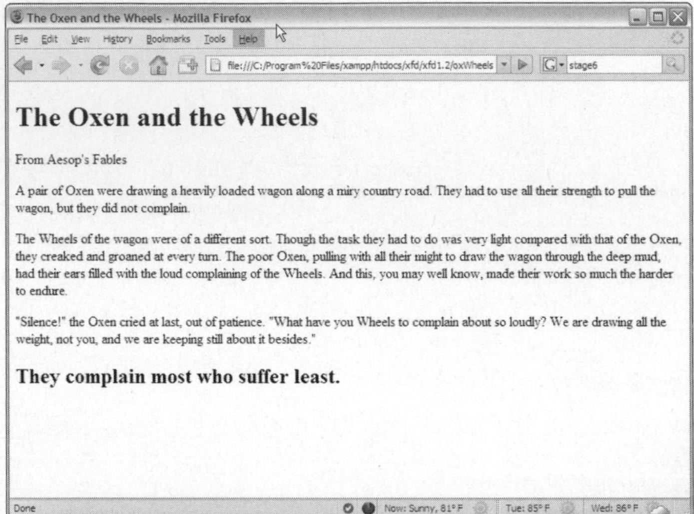

Figure 2-2: oxWheels1.html in Firefox.

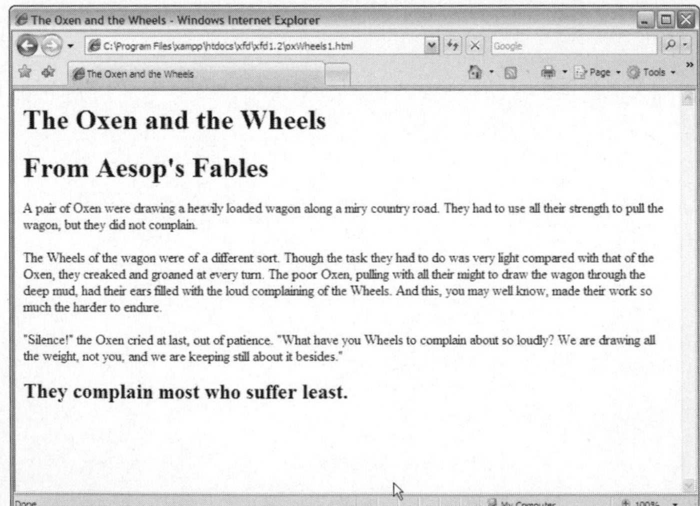

Figure 2-3: oxWheels1.html in Internet Explorer.

Firefox appears to handle the page pretty well, but `From Aesop's Fables` is supposed to be a headline level two, or *H2,* and it appears as plain text. Other than that, there's very little indication that something is wrong.

Microsoft Internet Explorer also tries to display the page, and it also does a decent job. Notice now that `From Aesop's Fables` appears to be a level one header, or H1. That's odd. Still, the page looks pretty good in both the major browsers, so you might assume everything's just fine. That gets you into trouble.

If it looks fine, who cares if it's exactly right? You might wonder why we care if there are mistakes in the underlying code, as long as everything works okay. After all, who's going to look at the code if the page displays properly?

The problem is, you don't know if it'll display properly, and mistakes in your code will eventually come back to haunt you. If possible, you want to know immediately what parts of your code are problematic so you can fix them and not worry.

Aesop visits W3C

To find out what's going on with this page, pay a visit to the W3C Validator at `http://validator.w3.org`. Figure 2-4 shows me visiting this site and uploading a copy of `oxWheels1.html` to it.

Hold your breath and hit the Check button. You might be surprised at the results shown in Figure 2-5.

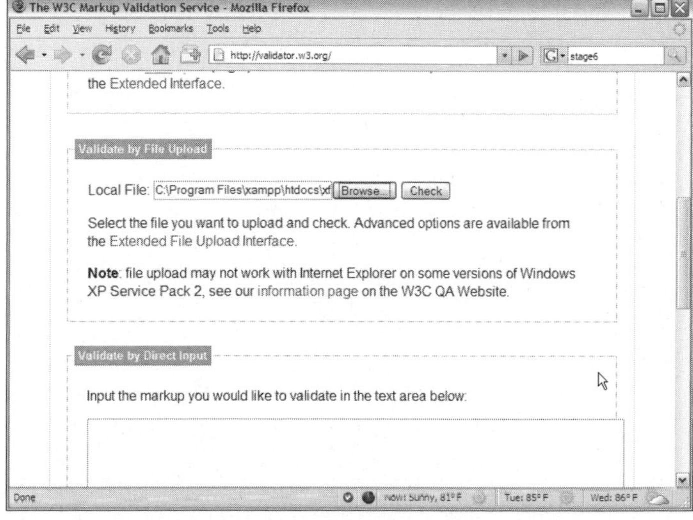

Figure 2-4: I'm checking the oxWheels page to look for any problems.

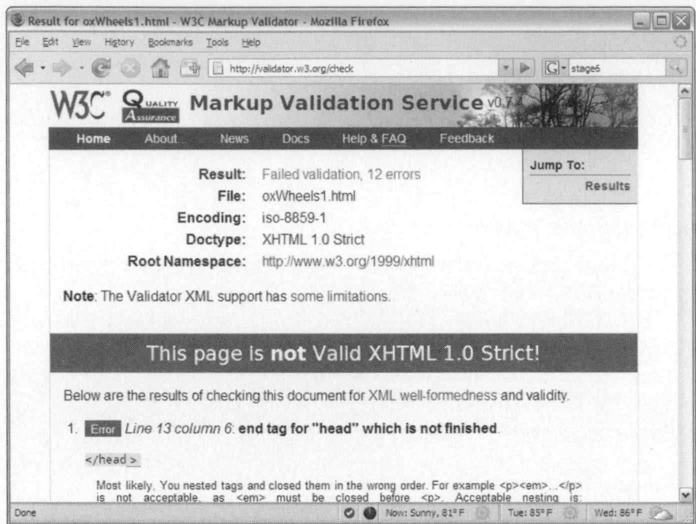

Figure 2-5: Twelve errors? That can't be right!

The Validator is a picky beast, and it doesn't seem to like this page at all. The Validator does return some useful information and gives enough hints that you can decode things soon enough.

Examining the overview

Before you take a look at the specific complaints, take a quick look at the Web page the Validator sends you. The Web page is chock full of handy information. The top of the page tells you a lot of useful things:

- **Result:** This is really the important thing. You'll know the number of errors remaining by looking at this line. Don't panic, though. There are probably fewer errors in the document than the number you see here.
- **File:** This is the name of the file you're currently working on.
- **Encoding:** The encoding is the text encoding you've set. If you didn't explicitly set text encoding, you may see a warning here.
- **Doctype:** This is the doctype extracted from your document. It indicates the rules that the Validator is using to check your page. This should usually say `XHTML 1.0 Strict`.
- **Root Namespace:** If you use the template I give you, you always see the same namespace, and you don't have any surprises.
- **The dreaded red banner:** Experienced Web developers don't even have to read the results page to know if there is a problem. If everything goes well, there's a green congratulatory banner. If there are problems, the banner is red. It doesn't look good, Aesop.

Don't panic because you have too many errors. The mistakes often overlap, so one problem in your code often causes more than one error to pop up. Most of the time, you have far fewer errors than the page says, and a lot of the errors are repeated, so after you find the error once, you'll know how to fix it throughout the page.

Validating the page

The Validator doesn't always tell you everything you need to know, but it does give you some pretty good clues. Page validation is tedious but not as difficult as it might seem at first. Here are some strategies for working through page validation:

- **Focus only on the first error.** Sure, 100 errors might be on the page, but solve them one at a time. The only error that matters is the first one on the list. Don't worry at all about other errors until you've solved the first one.
- **Note where the first error is.** The most helpful information you get is the line and column information about where the Validator recognized the error. This isn't always where the error is, but it does give you some clues.
- **Look at the error message.** It's usually good for a laugh. The error messages are sometimes helpful and sometimes downright mysterious.
- **Look at the verbose text.** Unlike most programming debuggers, the W3C Validator tries to explain what went wrong in something like English. It still doesn't always make sense, but sometimes the text gives you a hint.
- **Scan the next couple errors.** Sometimes, one mistake shows up as more than one error. Look over the next couple errors, as well, to see if they provide any more insight; sometimes, they do.
- **Revalidate.** Check the page again after you save it. If the first error is now at a later line number than the previous one, you've succeeded.
- **Don't worry if the number of errors goes up.** The number of perceived errors will sometimes go up rather than down after you've successfully fixed a problem. This is okay. Sometimes, fixing one error causes others to appear. More often, fixing one error clears up many more. Just concentrate on clearing errors from the beginning to the end of the document.
- **Lather, rinse, and repeat.** Look at the new top error and get it straightened out. Keep going until you get the coveted Green Banner of Validation. (If I ever write an XHTML adventure game, that will be one of the most powerful talismans.)

Examining the first error

Look again at the results for the `oxWheels1.html` page. The first error message looks like Figure 2-6.

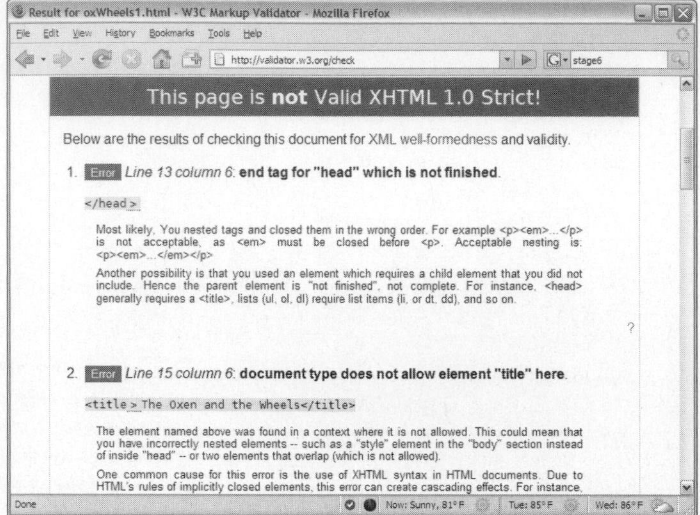

Figure 2-6: It doesn't like the end of the head?

Figure 2-6 shows the first two error messages. The first complains about where the </head> tag is. The second message complains about the <title> tag. Look at the source code, and you see that the relevant code looks like this:

```
<head>
<meta http-equiv="Content-Type" content="text/html; charset=iso-8859-1" />

<!-- oxWheels1.html -->

<!-- note this page has deliberate errors!  Please see the text
     and oxWheelsCorrect.html for a corrected version.
-->

</head>
<body>
<title>The Oxen and the Wheels</title>
<h1>The Oxen and the Wheels
```

Look carefully at the head and title tags, and review the notes in the error messages, and you'll probably see the problem. The <title> element is supposed to be in the heading, but I accidentally put it in the body! (Okay, it wasn't accidental; I made this mistake deliberately here to show you what happens. However, I have made this mistake for real in the past.)

Fixing the title

If the title tag is the problem, a quick change in the HTML should fix this problem. oxWheels2.html shows another form of the page with my proposed fix:

```
<head>
<meta http-equiv="Content-Type" content="text/html; charset=iso-8859-1" />

<!-- oxWheels2.html -->

<!-- Moved the title tag inside the header -->

<title>The Oxen and the Wheels</title>
</head>

<body>
```

Note that I'm only showing the parts of the page that I changed. The entire page is available on the CD-ROM.

The fix for this problem is pretty easy:

1. **Move the title inside the head.**

   I think the problem here is having the `<title>` element inside the body, rather than in the head where it belongs. If I move the title to the body, the error should be eliminated.

2. **Change the comments to reflect the page's current status.**

   It's important that the comments reflect what changes I make.

3. **Save the changes.**

   Normally, you simply make a change to the same document, but I've elected to change the filename so you can see an archive of my changes as the page improves. This can actually be a good idea because you then have a complete history of your document's changes, and you can always revert to an older version if you accidentally make something worse.

4. **Note the current first error position.**

   Before you submit the modified page to the Validator, make a mental note of the position of the current first error. Right now, the Validator's first complaint is on line 13, column 6. I want the first mistake to be somewhere later in the document.

5. **Revalidate by running the Validator again on the modified page.**

6. **Review the results and do a happy dance.**

   It's likely there are still errors, but that's not a failure! Figure 2-7 shows the result of my revalidation. The new first error is on line 16, and it appears to be totally different than the last error. I solved it!

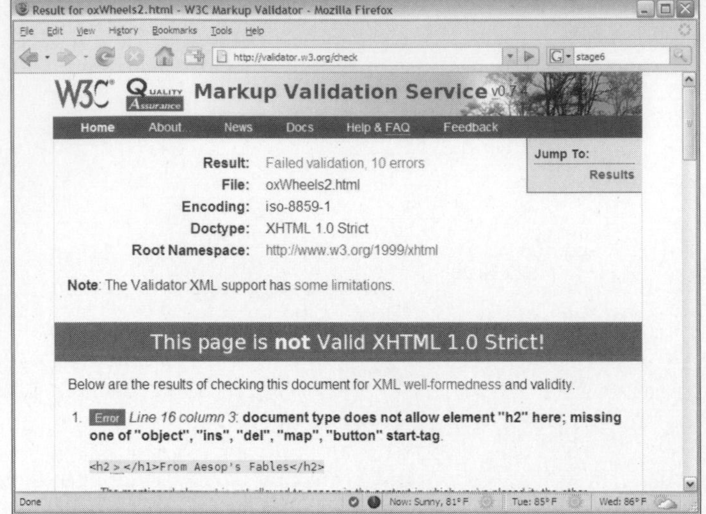

Figure 2-7: Document type does not allow element "h2" here.

Solving the next error

One down, but there are more to go. The next error (shown in Figure 2-7) looks strange, but it's one you'll see a lot.

The `document type does not allow` error is very common. What it usually means is you forgot to close something or you put something in the wrong place. The error message indicates a problem in line 16. The next error is line 16, too. See if you can find the problem here in the relevant code:

```
<body>
<h1>The Oxen and the Wheels
<h2></h1>From Aesop's Fables</h2>
```

After you know where to look, the problem becomes a bit easier to spot. I got sloppy and started the `<h2>` tag before I finished the `<h1>`. One tag can be completely embedded inside another (at least, in many cases), but you can't have tag definitions overlap like I've done here. The `<h1>` has to close before I can start the `<h2>` tag.

This explains why the two main browsers displayed `From Aesop's Fables` differently. It isn't clear whether this code should be displayed in H1 or H2 format, or perhaps with no special formatting at all. It's much better to know the problem and fix it than to remain ignorant until something goes wrong.

The third version — `oxWheels3.html` — fixes this part of the program:

```
<!-- oxWheels3.html -->

<!-- sort out the h1 and h2 tags at the top -->

<title>The Oxen and the Wheels</title>
</head>

<body>
<h1>The Oxen and the Wheels</h1>
<h2>From Aesop's Fables</h2>
```

Checking the headline repair

The heading tags look a lot better, and a quick check of the Validator confirms this fact, as shown in Figure 2-8, which now shows only six errors.

Here's another form of that `document type does not allow` error. This one seems strange because surely `<p>` tags are allowed in the body! The secret to this particular problem is to look carefully at the error message. This document has a lot of `<p>` tags in it. Which one is it complaining about?

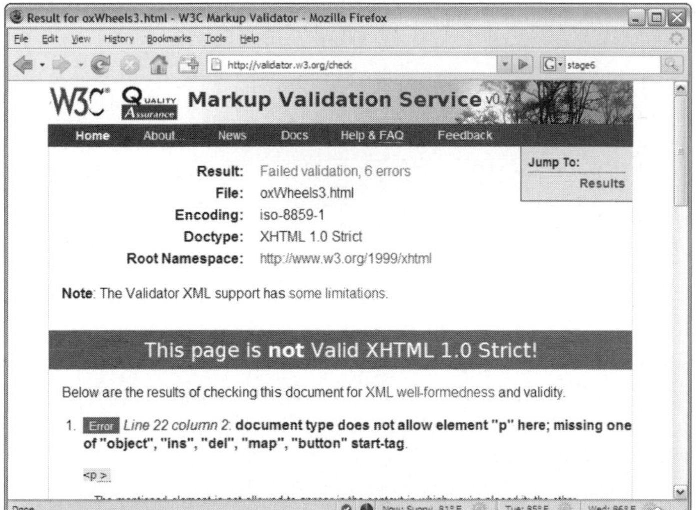

Figure 2-8: Document type doesn't allow "p" here. That's odd.

The complaint is about the `<p>` tag on line 22. Unfortunately, Notepad doesn't have an easy way to know which line you're on, so you just have to count until I show you some better options in Chapter 3 of this minibook. To make things easier, I've reproduced the key part of the code here and highlighted line 22. Try to find the problem before I explain it to you:

```
<h1>The Oxen and the Wheels</h1>
<h2>From Aesop's Fables</h2>

<p>
   A pair of Oxen were drawing a heavily loaded wagon along a
   miry country road. They had to use all their strength to pull
   the wagon, but they did not complain.
<p>

<p>
   The Wheels of the wagon were of a different sort. Though the
   task they had to do was very light compared with that of the
   Oxen, they creaked and groaned at every turn. The poor Oxen,
   pulling with all their might to draw the wagon through the
   deep mud, had their ears filled with the loud complaining of
   the Wheels. And this, you may well know, made their work so
   much the harder to endure.
</p>
```

Aha! Line 22 is supposed to be the *end* of the paragraph, but I somehow forgot the slash character, so the Validator thinks I'm beginning a new paragraph inside the previous one, which isn't allowed. This causes a bunch of other errors, too. Because the Validator can't see the end of this paragraph, it thinks that all the rest of the code is inside this first paragraph. Try changing the `<p>` of line 22 into a `</p>` and see if it works better:

```
<p>
   A pair of Oxen were drawing a heavily loaded wagon along a
   miry country road. They had to use all their strength to pull
   the wagon, but they did not complain.
</p>
```

Figure 2-9 shows the validation results for `oxWheels4.html`.

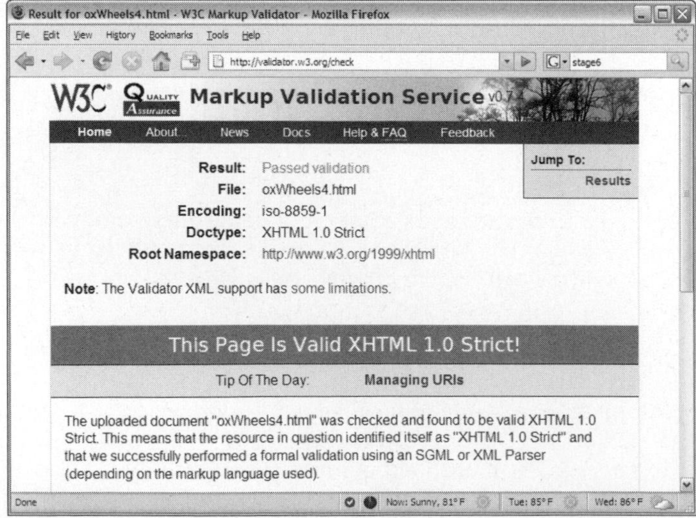

Figure 2-9: Hooray! We have a valid page!

Showing off your mad skillz

Sometimes, that green bar makes little tears of joy run down my cheeks. Congratulations! It's only the second chapter in this minibook, and you're already writing better Web pages than a lot of professionals.

Seriously, a Web page that validates to XHTML Strict is a big deal, and you deserve to be proud of your efforts. The W3C is so proud of you that they offer you a little badge of honor you can put on your page.

Figure 2-10 shows more of the page you get when your page finally validates correctly. You can see a little button and some crazy-looking HTML code.

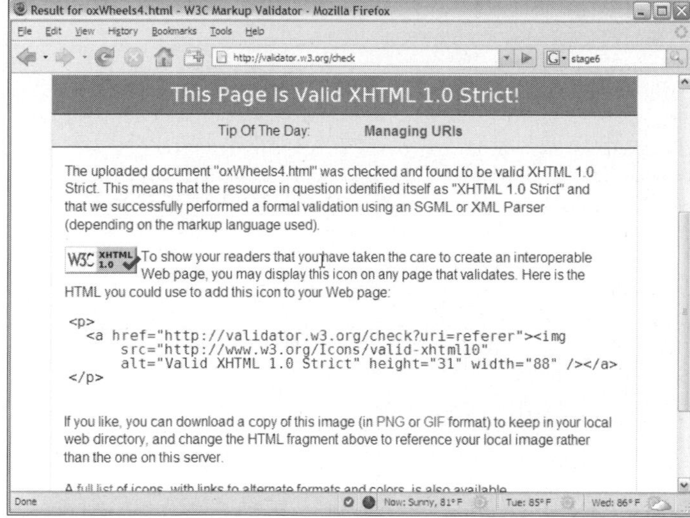

Figure 2-10: The Validator gives you a little virtual badge of honor to show how cool you are.

If you want, you can copy and paste that code into your page. `oxWheels5.html` has that special code added at the end of the body, shown in Figure 2-11.

This little code snippet does a bunch of neat things, such as

- ✦ **Establishing your coding prowess:** Any page that has this image on it has been tested and found compliant to XHTML Strict standards. When you see pages with this marker, you can be confident of the skill and professionalism of the author.
- ✦ **Placing a cool image on the page:** You'll read how to add your own images in Chapter 6 of this minibook, but it's nice to see one already. This particular image is hosted at the W3C site.

✦ **Letting users check the page for themselves:** When the user clicks the image, they're taken directly to the W3C Validator to prove that the page is in fact valid XHTML Strict. Unfortunately, this link works only on pages that are posted to a Web server, so it doesn't work right on a page just sitting on your computer. Scope out Book VIII for suggestions on finding and using a server.

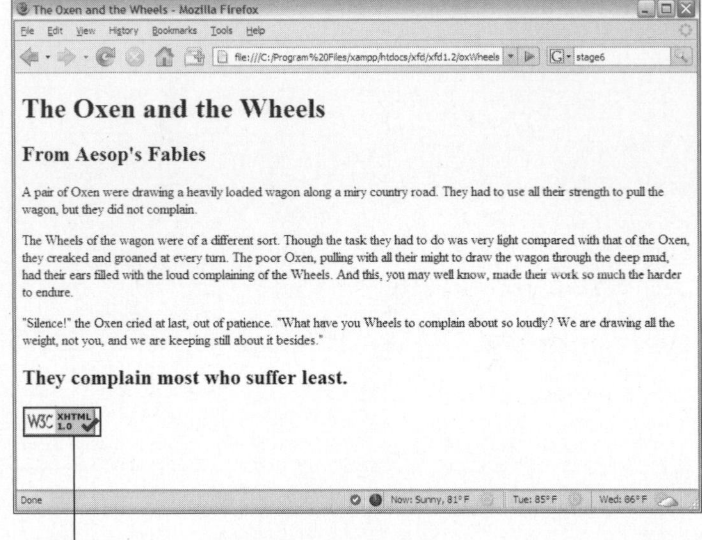

Figure 2-11: Look, I have a medal from the W3C!

Using Tidy to repair pages

The W3C Validator isn't the only game in town. Another great resource — *HTML Tidy* — can be used to automatically fix your pages. You can download Tidy or just use the online version at `http://infohound.net/tidy`. Figure 2-12 illustrates the online version with `oxWheels1.html` being loaded.

Unlike W3C's Validator, Tidy attempts to actually fix your page. Figure 2-13 demonstrates how it suggests how the `oxWheels.html` page should be fixed.

Tidy examines the page for a number of common errors and does its best to fix the errors. However, the result is not quite perfect:

✦ **Tidy adds a new `meta` tag, indicating the page was created by Tidy.** I always get nervous when a program I didn't write starts messing with my pages.

✦ **Tidy tends to choose a sloppier doctype.** If you don't specify otherwise, Tidy checks against XHTML 1.0 Transitional, rather than Strict. This looser definition isn't as stringent. You can (and should) specify the Strict doctype manually in the submission form.

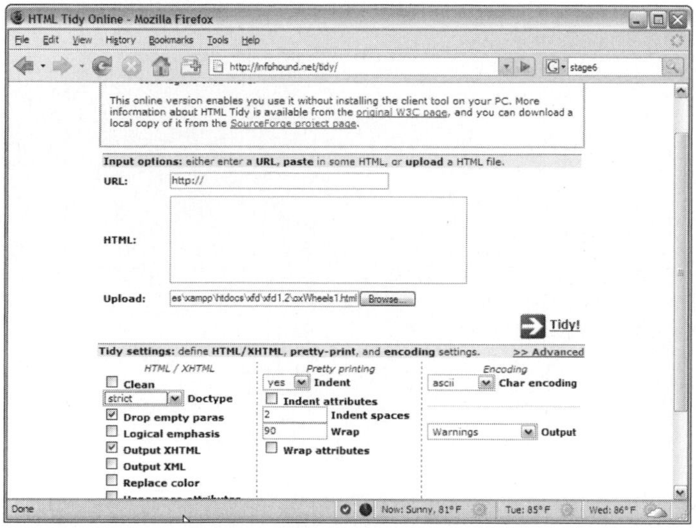

Figure 2-12: HTML Tidy is an alternative to the W3C Validator.

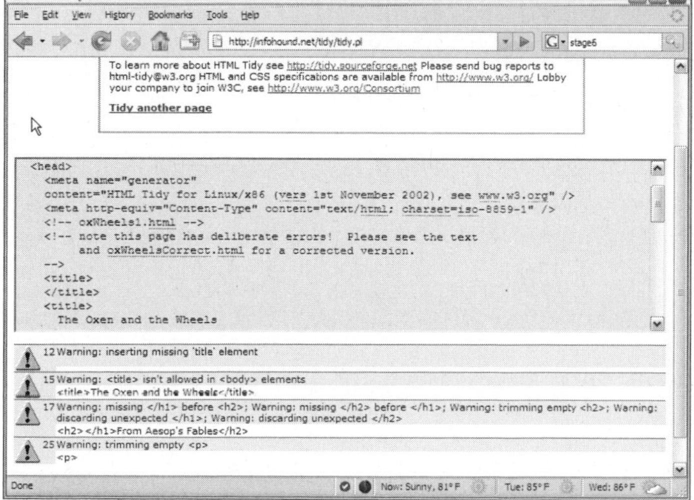

Figure 2-13: Tidy fixes the page, but the fix is a little awkward.

Is validation really that big a deal?

I can hear the angry e-mails coming in. "Andy, I've been writing Web pages since 1998, and I never used a Validator." Okay, it's true. A lot of people, even some professional Web developers, work without validating their code. Some of my older Web pages don't validate at all. (You can run the W3C Validator on any page you want, not just one you wrote. This can be a source of great joy if you like feeling superior to sloppy coders.) When I became more proficient and more prolific in my Web development, I found that those little errors often caused a whole lot of grief down the road. I really believe you should validate every single page you write. Get into the habit now, and it'll pay huge dividends. When you're figuring out this stuff for the first time, do it right.

If you already know some HTML, you're gonna hate the Validator for a while because it rejects coding habits that you might think are perfectly fine. It's a lot harder to unlearn things than it is to learn them in the first place, so I feel your pain. It's still worth it.

After you establish the discipline of validating your pages, you'll find you've picked up good habits, and validation becomes a lot less painful. Experienced programmers actually like the validation process because it becomes much easier and prevents problems that could cause lots of grief later.

- **Tidy got confused by the title.** Tidy correctly diagnosed the title in the wrong place, but it added a blank title, as well as the intended one.
- **Sometimes the indentation is off.** I set Tidy to indent every element, so it is easy to see how things are matched up. If I don't set up the indentation explicitly, I find Tidy code very difficult to read.
- **The changes aren't permanent.** Anything Tidy does is just a suggestion. If you want to keep the changes, you need to save the results in your editor.

I sometimes use Tidy when I'm stumped because I find the error messages are easier to understand than the W3C Validator. However, I never trust it completely. There's really no substitute for good old detective skills and the official W3C Validator.

If you find the W3C Validator and Tidy to be a little tedious to use, look over the HTML Validator extension described in Chapter 3 of this minibook. This handy tool adds both the W3C Validator and Tidy to Firefox and automatically checks every page you visit. It also has Tidy support, so it can even fix most of your errors.

Chapter 3: Choosing Your Tools

In This Chapter

- Choosing a text editor
- Using a dedicated HTML editor
- Comparing common browsers
- Introducing Integrated Development Environments (IDEs)
- Adding important Firefox extensions

Web development is a big job. You don't go to a construction site without a belt full of tools (and a cool hat), and the same thing is true with Web development (except you don't normally need a hard hat for Web development). An entire industry has evolved trying to sell tools that help make Web development easier. The funny thing is that the tools you need might not be the ones that people are trying to sell you. Some of the very best Web development tools are free, and some of the most expensive tools aren't really that helpful.

This chapter tells you what you really need and how to set up your workshop with a lot of great programs that really simplify Web development.

What's Wrong with the Big Boys?

A lot of Web development books are really books about how to use a particular type of software. Microsoft's FrontPage/Express and Macromedia/Adobe Dreamweaver are the two primary applications in this category. These tools are powerful and offer some *seemingly* great features:

- **WYSIWYG editing:** *What you see is what you get* is an idea borrowed from word processors. You can create a Web page much like a word-processing document and use menus, as well as tools, to handle all the formatting. The theory is that you don't have to know any icky codes.
- **Templates:** You can create a template that stays the same and build several pages from that template. If you need to change the template, everything else changes automatically.
- **Site management:** The interaction between the various pages on your site can be maintained automatically.

These sound like pretty good features, and they are. These tools (and the newer replacements, like Microsoft's Expression suite) are very powerful, and they can be an important part of your Web development toolkit. But the same powerful programs introduce problems, such as the following:

- **Code maintenance:** The commercial editors that concentrate on visual design tend to create pretty unmanageable code. If you find there's something you need to change by hand, it's pretty hard to fix the code.
- **Vendor lock-in:** These tools are written by corporations that want you to buy other tools from them. If you're using Dreamweaver, you'll find it easy to integrate with other Adobe applications (like ColdFusion), but it's not as simple to connect to non-Adobe technology. Likewise, Microsoft's offerings are designed to work best with other Microsoft technologies.
- **Cost:** The cost of these software packages keeps going up. Expression Web (Microsoft's replacement for FrontPage) costs about $300, and Dreamweaver weighs in at $400. Both companies encourage you to buy the software as part of a package, which can easily cost more than $500.
- **Complex:** They're complicated. You can take a full class or buy a huge book on how to use only one of these technologies. If it's that hard to figure out, is it really saving you any effort?
- **Code:** You still need to understand it. No matter how great your platform is, at some point, you have to dig into your code. After you plunk down all that money and spend all that time figuring out an application, you still have to understand how the underlying code works because things still go wrong. For example, if your page fails to work on Safari, you'll have to find out why and fix the problem yourself.
- **Spotty standards compliance:** The tools are getting better here, but if you want your pages to comply with the latest standards, you have to heavily edit them after the tool is finished.
- **Display variations:** WYSIWYG is a lie. This is really the big problem. WYSIWYG works for word processors because it's possible to make the screen look like the printed page. After a page is printed, it stays the same. You don't know what a Web page will look like because that depends on the browser. What if the user loads your page on a cell phone or handheld device? The editors tend to perpetuate the myth that you can treat a Web page like a printed document, when in truth, it's a very different kind of beast.

Alternative Web Development Tools

All you really need is a text editor and a Web browser. You probably already have a basic set of tools on your computer. If you read Chapters 1 and 2 of this minibook, you've already written a couple of Web pages. However, the very basic tools that come with every computer might not be enough for serious work. Web development requires a specialized kind of text editor, and a number of tools have evolved that make that job easier.

The things you need to have on your computer

Here's a few things you need that you might not already have on your computer:

- **Line numbers:** Notepad doesn't have an easy way to figure out what line you're on. It's pretty tedious to count lines every time you want to find a problem noted by the Validator.
- **Help features:** It'd be ideal if your editor could help with your code. There are tools that recognize HTML code, help with indentation, and warn you when something is wrong.
- **Macros:** You'll type the same code many times. A program that can record and play keyboard macros can save a huge amount of time.
- **Testing and validation:** It should be easy to test your code in one or more browsers, and there should be an easy way to check your code for standards.
- **Multiple browsers:** As an Internet user, it's fine to have only one browser, but a Web developer needs to know how things look in a couple different environments.
- **Browser features:** You can customize some browsers (especially Firefox) to help you a lot. With the right attachments, the browser can point out errors and help you see the structure of your page.
- **Free and open tools:** The Web is exciting because it's free and open technology. If you can find tools that follow the same philosophy, all the better.

Building a basic toolbox

I've found uses for five main types of programs in Web development:

- **Enhanced text editors:** These tools are text editors, but they're souped-up with all kinds of fancy features, like syntax checkers, code-coloring tools, macro tools, and multiple document interfaces.
- **Browsers and plugins:** The browser you use can make a huge difference. You can also install free add-ons that can turn your browser into a powerful Web development tool.
- **Integrated Development Environments (IDE):** Programmers generally use IDEs, which combine text editing, visual layout, code testing, and debugging tools.
- **Programming technologies:** This book covers all pertinent info about incorporating other technologies, like Apache, PHP, and MySQL. I show you how to install everything you need for these technologies in Book VIII, Chapter 1. You don't need to worry about these things yet, but you

should develop habits that are compatible with these enhanced technologies from the beginning.

✦ **Multimedia tools:** If you want various multimedia elements on your page, you'll need tools to manage them, as well. These could involve graphics and audio editors, as well as full-blown multimedia technologies, like Flash.

Picking a Text Editor

As a programmer, you come to see your text editor as a faithful dog. You spend a lot of time with this tool, so use one that obeys you.

A text editor should save plain text without any formatting at all. You don't want anything that saves colors, font choices, or other text formatting because these things don't automatically translate to HTML.

Fortunately, you have a lot of choices, as the following sections reveal.

Some tools to use when you have nothing else

A text editor may be a simple program, but that doesn't mean they're all the same. Some programs have a history of causing problems for beginners (and experienced developers, too). Because some really great free alternatives are coming up, there's usually no need to use some of these weaker choices.

Just don't use it. Word is a word processor. Even though it can theoretically create Web pages, the HTML code it writes is absolutely horrific. As an example, I created a blank document, wrote "Hello World" in it, changed the font, and saved it as HTML. The resulting page was non-compliant code, was not quite HTML or XHTML, and was 114 lines long. Word is getting better, but it's just not a good Web development tool. In fact, don't use any word processor. They're just not designed for this kind of work.

Windows Notepad

It's everywhere, and it's free. That's the good news. However, Notepad doesn't have a lot of features you might need, like line numbers, multiple documents, or macros. Use it if you're on an unfamiliar machine but try something else if you can. Many people begin with Notepad, but it won't be long until you outgrow its limitations.

Mac TextEdit

Mac also has a simple text editor built in — *TextEdit.* It's pretty similar to Notepad, but it's closer to a word processor than a programmer's text editor. TextEdit saves files in a number of formats. If you want to use it to write Web pages, you must save your files in plain-text format, and you must not use any of TextEdit's formatting features. It's probably best not to use TextEdit unless you really have to.

A noteworthy editor: Notepad++

A number of developers have come up with good text editors. Some of the best are free, such as Notepad++ by Don HO. It's designed for text editing, especially in programming language. Figure 3-1 shows Notepad++ with an HTML file loaded.

Notepad++ has a lot of interesting features. Here are a few highlights:

- **Syntax highlighting:** Notepad++ can recognize key HTML terms and put different types of terms in different colors. For example, all HTML tags are rendered in blue, and text is in black. This makes it easy to tell if you've made certain kinds of mistakes, like forgetting to end a tag. Note that the colors aren't saved in the document. The coloring features are there to help you understand the code.
- **Multiple files:** You'll often want to edit more than one document at a time. You can have several different documents in memory at the same time.

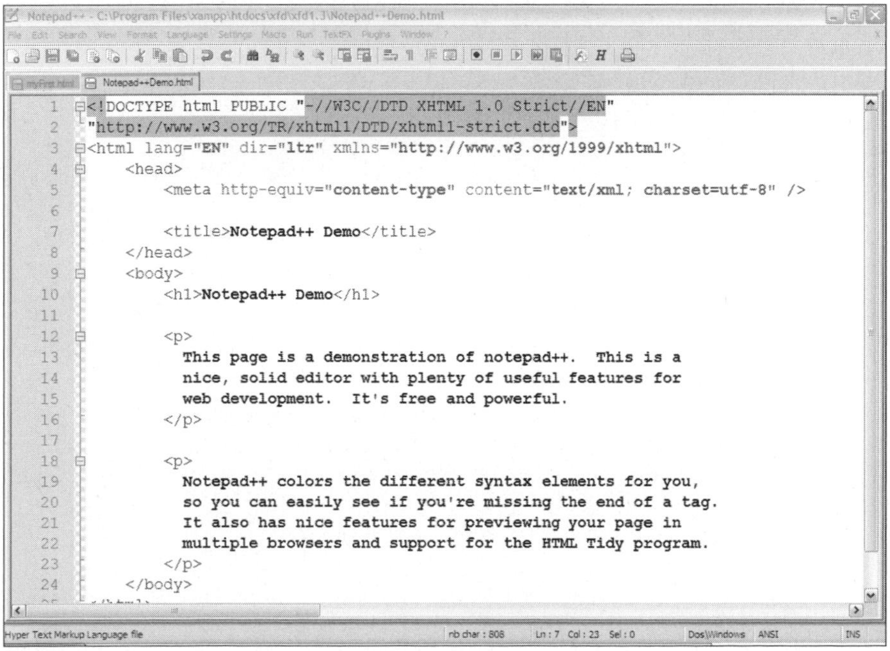
Notepad++ - C:\Program Files\xampp\htdocs\xfd\xfd1.3\Notepad++Demo.html
Notepad++Demo.html
<!DOCTYPE html PUBLIC "-//W3C//DTD XHTML 1.0 Strict//EN"
"http://www.w3.org/TR/xhtml1/DTD/xhtml1-strict.dtd">
<html lang="EN" dir="ltr" xmlns="http://www.w3.org/1999/xhtml">
<head>
<meta http-equiv="content-type" content="text/xml; charset=utf-8" />
<title>Notepad++ Demo</title>
</head>
<body>
<h1>Notepad++ Demo</h1>
<p>
This page is a demonstration of notepad++. This is a
nice, solid editor with plenty of useful features for
web development. It's free and powerful.
</p>
<p>
Notepad++ colors the different syntax elements for you,
so you can easily see if you're missing the end of a tag.
It also has nice features for previewing your page in
multiple browsers and support for the HTML Tidy program.
</p>
</body>
Hyper Text Markup Language file
nb char : 808
Ln : 7 Col : 23 Sel : 0
Dos\Windows
ANSI
INS

Figure 3-1: Notepad++ has many of the features you need in a text editor.

- **Multi-language support:** At the moment, your pages consist of nothing but XHTML. Soon enough, you'll use some other languages, like SQL, CSS, and PHP. Notepad++ is smart enough to recognize these languages, too.
- **Macros:** Whenever you find yourself doing something over and over, consider writing a keyboard macro. Notepad++ has a terrific macro feature. Macros are really easy to record and playback a series of keystrokes. This feature can often save you a lot of work.
- **Page preview:** When you write a page, test it. Notepad++ has shortcut keys built in to let you quickly view your page in Internet Explorer, or *IE,* (Ctrl+Alt+Shift+I) and Firefox (Ctrl+Alt+Shift+X).
- **TextFX:** The open-source design of Notepad++ makes it easy to add features. The TextFX extension (built into Notepad++) allows you to do all sorts of interesting things. One especially handy set of tools runs HTML Tidy on your page and fixes any problems in it.

The old standards: VI and Emacs

No discussion of text editors is complete without a mention of the venerable UNIX editors that are the core of the early Internet experience. Most of the pioneering work on the Web was done in the UNIX and Linux operating systems, and these environments had two extremely popular text-editor families. Both might seem obscure and difficult to modern sensibilities, but they still have passionate adherents, even in the Windows community. (Besides, Linux is more popular than ever!)

VI and VIM

VI stands for *Visual Editor.* That name seems strange now because most developers can't imagine an editor that's *not* visual. Back in the day, it was a very big deal that VI could use the entire screen for editing text. Before that time, line-oriented editors were the main way to edit text files. Trust me, you have it good now. Figure 3-2 shows a variant of VI (called VIM) in action.

VI is a *modal* editor, which means that the same key sometimes has more than one job, depending on the editor's current mode. For example, the I key is used to indicate where you want to insert text. The D key is used to delete text, and so on. Of course, when you're inserting text, the keys have their normal meanings. This multi-mode behavior is baffling to modern users, but it can be amazingly efficient after you get used to it. Skilled VI users swear by it and often use nothing else.

VI is a little too obscure for some users, so there's a number of variants floating around, such as *VIM,* for *VI Improved.* (Yeah, it should be VII but maybe they were afraid people would call it the Roman numeral seven.) VIM is a little friendlier than VI. It tells you which mode it's in and includes modern features like mouse support, menus, and icons. Even with these features, VIM is not intuitive for most people.

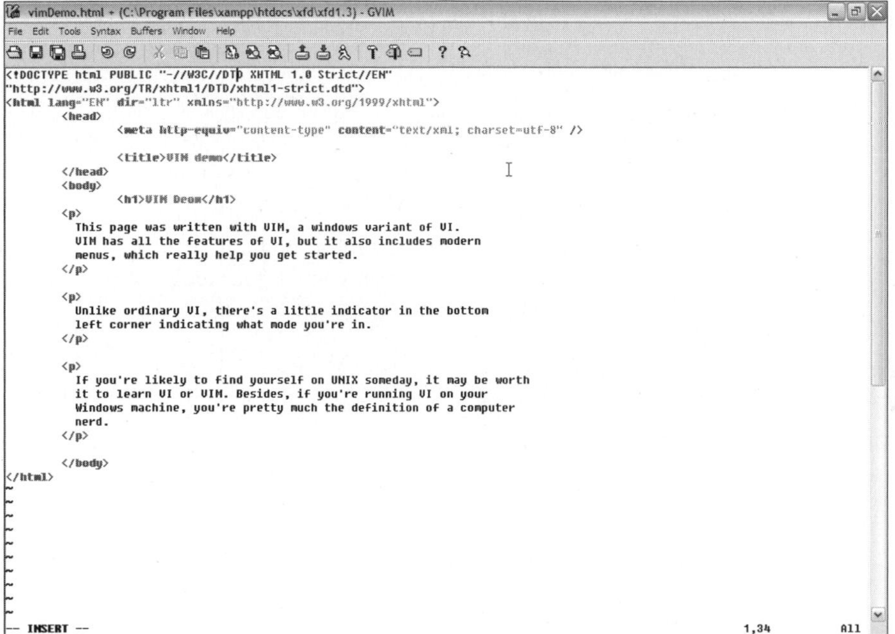

Figure 3-2: VI isn't pretty, but after you know it, it's very powerful.

Versions of VI are available for nearly any operating system being used. If you already know VI, you might enjoy using it for Web page development, as it has all the features you might need. If you don't already know VI, it's probably more efficient for you to start with a more standard text editor, such as Notepad++.

Emacs

The other popular editor from the UNIX world is *emacs.* Like VI, you probably don't need this tool if you never use Linux or UNIX. But also like VI, if you know it already, you probably don't need anything else. Emacs has been a programmer's editor for a very long time, and it has nearly every feature you can think of.

Emacs also has a lot of features you haven't thought of, including a built-in text adventure game and even a psychotherapist simulator. I really couldn't make this stuff up if I tried.

Emacs has very powerful customization and macro features. It allows you to view and edit more than one file at a time. Emacs also has the ability to view and manipulate the local file system, manage remote files, access the local operating system (OS) shell, and even browse the Web or check e-mail without leaving the program. If you're willing to invest in a program that takes some effort to understand, you'll have an incredibly powerful tool in your kit. Versions of Emacs are available for most major operating systems. Emacs is one of the first programs I install on any new computer because it's so powerful. A version of emacs is shown in Figure 3-3.

An enhanced version — *xemacs* — uses standard menus and icons like modern programs, so it's reasonably easy to get started with.

Emacs has an astonishing number of options and a non-standard interface, so it can be challenging for beginners.

Other text editors

Many other text editors are used in Web development. The most important thing is to find one that matches the way you work. If you don't like any of the editors I've suggested so far, here's a few more you might want to try:

- **SynEdit:** This is much like Notepad++ and is very popular with Web developers.
- **Scintilla:** This is primarily a programming editor, but it has nice support for XHTML coding.
- **jEdit:** This is a text editor written in Java. It has nice features and is popular, but some consider it slower than the other choices.

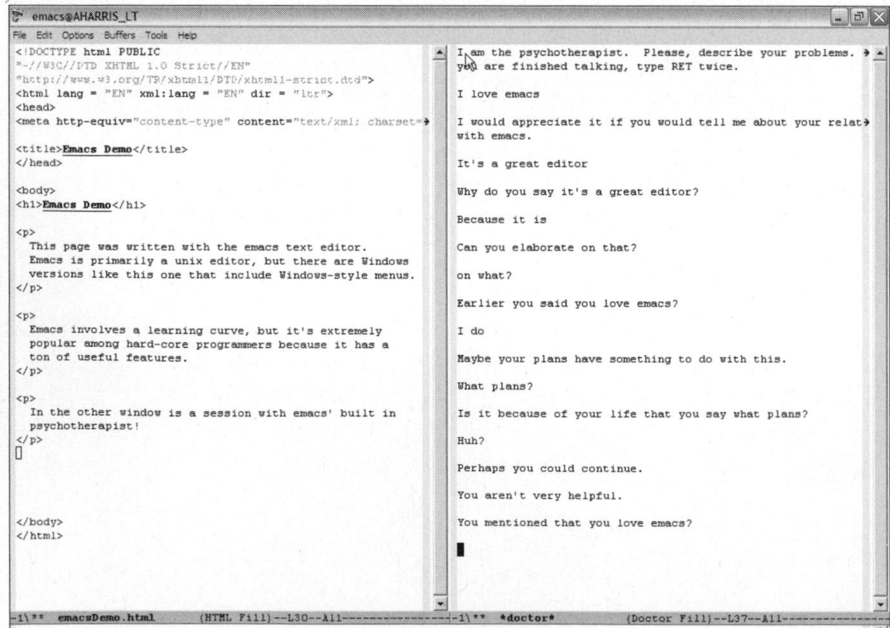

Figure 3-3: Emacs is powerful but somewhat eccentric.

The Web Developer's Browser

Web pages are meant to display in a browser; so, of course, you need browsers for testing. Not all browsers are the same, though, so you need more than one. As of this writing, there are two major browsers and a number of other significant players in the browser world. It's important to know a little about the major browsers, which are discussed later in this section.

A little ancient history

You've probably already noticed that browsers are inconsistent in the way they display and handle Web pages. It's useful to understand how we got into this mess.

Mosaic/Netscape — the killer application

In the beginning, browsers were written by small teams. The most important early browser was *Mosaic* and was written by a team based at the National Center for Supercomputing Applications (NCSA) in Champaign–Urbana, Illinois.

Several of the members of that NCSA team decided to create a completely commercial Web browser. Netscape was born, and it quickly became the most prominent and important browser, with 97-percent market share at the peak of its popularity.

Microsoft enters (and wins) the battle

Microsoft came onto the scene with Internet Explorer (IE). A bitter fight (sometimes called the *Browser Wars*) ensued between Microsoft and Netscape. Each browser added new features regularly. Eventually, entire sets of tags evolved, so a Web page written for IE would not always work in Netscape and vice-versa. Developers had three bad choices: pick only one browser to support, write two versions of the page, or stick with the more limited set of features common to both browsers.

Netscape 6.0 was a technical disappointment, and Microsoft capitalized, earning a nearly complete lock on the browser market. Microsoft's version of standards became the *only* standards because there was virtually no competition. After Microsoft won the fight, there was a period of stability but very little innovation.

Firefox shakes up the world

A new browser rose from the ashes of Netscape (in fact, its original name was Firebird, after the mythical bird that rises from its own ashes). Its name was later changed to Firefox, and it breathed new life into the Web. Firefox has several new features that are very appealing to Web developers:

- **Solid compliance to standards:** Firefox followed the W3C standards almost perfectly.
- **Tabbed browsing:** One browser window can have several panels, each with its own page.
- **Easy customization:** Firefox developers encouraged people to add improvements and extensions to Firefox. This led to hundreds of interesting add-ons.
- **Improved security:** By this time, a number of security loopholes in IE were publicized. Although Firefox has many of the same problems, it has a much better reputation for openness and quick solutions.

Overview of the prominent browsers

The browser is the primary tool of the Web. All your users view your page with one browser or another, so you need to know a little about each of them.

Microsoft Internet Explorer 7

Microsoft Internet Explorer (MSIE or simply IE) is currently the most popular browser on the planet. Before Firefox came along, IE was used by a vast majority of Web users. IE is still extremely prevalent because it comes installed with Microsoft Windows. Of course, it also works best with Microsoft Windows. A version is also available for Macs, but Linux users aren't supported (they don't seem too upset about it, though).

The current version of IE is *Internet Explorer 7,* the first major improvement in IE for years. IE7 features some welcome additions, including tabbed browsing and improved compliance with the W3C standards. Cynics have suggested these improvements are a response to Firefox. Still, IE is a better browser than it has been in a long time.

If you write your code to XHTML 1.0 Strict standards, it almost always displays as expected in IE7.

Older versions of Internet Explorer

The earlier versions of IE are still extremely important because there are so many computers out there that don't have IE7 installed yet.

Microsoft made a version of IE available for programmers to embed in their own software, so a lot of custom browsers are actually IE with a different skin. Most of the custom browsers that are installed with the various broadband services are simply dressed up forms of IE. Therefore, IE is even more common than you might guess because people might be using a version of it while thinking it's something else.

IE6 and earlier versions used Microsoft's own variation of standards. They display old-style HTML well, but these browsers don't comply perfectly with all the W3C standards. Having a version of one of these older browsers around is important so you can see how your pages display in them. If you write standards-compliant code, you'll find that it doesn't work perfectly in these variations. You need to do some tweaking to make some features come out right. Don't panic because they're relatively small details, and I point out the strategies you need as we go.

Checking your pages on IE6 or earlier is necessary. Unfortunately, if you have IE7 or whatever comes next, you probably don't have IE6 anymore. You can't have two versions of IE running on the same machine at once (at least, not easily), so you might need to keep an older machine just for testing purposes.

Microsoft has versions of IE for the Mac OS. Like other early versions of IE, it tends to go its own way and doesn't follow the standards exactly.

Mozilla Firefox

Developers writing standards-compliant code frequently test their pages in Firefox because it has a great reputation for standards compliance. Firefox has other advantages, as well, such as

- **Better code view:** If you view the HTML code of a page, you see the code in a special window. The code has syntax coloring, which makes it easy to read. IE often displays code in Notepad, which is confusing because you think you can edit the code, but you're simply editing a copy.
- **Better error-handling:** You'll make mistakes. In general, Firefox does a better job of pointing out errors than IE, especially when you begin using JavaScript and other advanced technologies.
- **Great extensions:** As you see later in this chapter, Firefox has some wonderful extensions that make Web development a lot easier. These extensions allow you to modify your code on the fly, automatically validate your code, and find out all about what's going on under the hood.

Other notable browsers

Firefox and IE are the big players in the browser world, but they certainly aren't the only browsers you will encounter.

Opera

The Opera Web browser is one of the earliest standards-compliant browsers. It is a technically solid browser but has never been widely used. If you design your pages with strict compliance in mind, users with Opera have no problems accessing them.

Safari

Apple includes a Web browser in all recent versions of the Mac OS. The current incarnation — *Safari* — is an excellent standards-compliant browser. Safari was traditionally designed only for the Mac, but a Windows version has been released recently.

Mozilla

There's still a Mozilla browser, but it has been replaced largely with Firefox. Because Mozilla uses the same underlying engine, it renders code the same way Firefox does.

Portable browsers

The Web isn't just about desktops anymore. Lots of people browse the Web with cell phones, iPhones, and PDAs. These devices often have specialized Web browsers designed to handle the particular needs of the portable computing model. However, these devices usually have tiny screens, small memory capacity, and slower download speeds than their desktop cousins. A portable browser can almost never display a page as it was intended on desktop machines. Portable browsers usually do a good job of making standards-compliant code work, but they really struggle with other types of HTML (especially tables used for formatting).

Text-only browsers

There are browsers that don't display any graphics at all. Some, like Lynx, are intended for the old command-line interfaces. This may seem completely irrelevant today, but they are incredibly fast because they don't display graphics. Auditory browsers read the contents of Web pages. They were originally intended for people with visual disabilities, but they are often used by people without any disabilities, as well. *Fire Vox* is a variant of Firefox that reads Web pages aloud.

The bottom line in browsers

Really, you need to have access to a couple browsers, but you can't possibly have them all. I tend to do my initial development testing with Firefox. I then check pages on IE7 and IE6. I also check the built-in browser on my cell phone and PDA to see how it works there. Generally, if you get a page that gives you suitable results on IE6, IE7, and Firefox, you can be satisfied that it works on most browsers. However, there's still no guarantee. If you follow the standards, your page displays on any browser, but you might not get the exact layout you expected.

Tricking Out Firefox

One of the best features of Firefox is its support for extensions. Hundreds of clever and generous programmers have written tools to improve and alter Firefox's performance. Three of these tools — the HTML Validator, Web Developer toolbar, and Firebug — are especially important to Web developers.

Validating your pages with HTML Validator

In Chapter 2 of this minibook, I explain how important Web standards are and how to use online services such as `http://validator.w3.org` and HTML Tidy online (`http://infohound.net/tidy`). These are terrific services, but it would be even better to have these Validators built directly into your browser. The HTML Validator extension by Marc Gueury is a tool that does exactly that: It adds both the W3C Validator and HTML Tidy to your Firefox installation.

When you have this extension (available on the CD-ROM) running, you have an error count in the footer of every page you visit. (You'll be amazed how many errors are on the Web.) You'll be able to tell immediately if a page has validation errors.

With the HTML Validator, your View Source tool is enhanced, as shown in Figure 3-4.

The View Source tool becomes much more powerful when you run HTML Validator, as follows:

- **Each error is listed in an errors panel.** This is exactly the same error list you see from W3C.
- **Clicking on an error highlights it in the source-code listing.** This makes it easy to see exactly what line of code triggers each error.
- **Complete help is shown for every error.** The Validator toolbar presents much more helpful error messages than the official W3C results.
- **Automated clean-up.** You can click the Clean Up link, and the Validator extension automatically applies HTML Tidy to your page. This can be a very effective way to fix older pages with many errors.

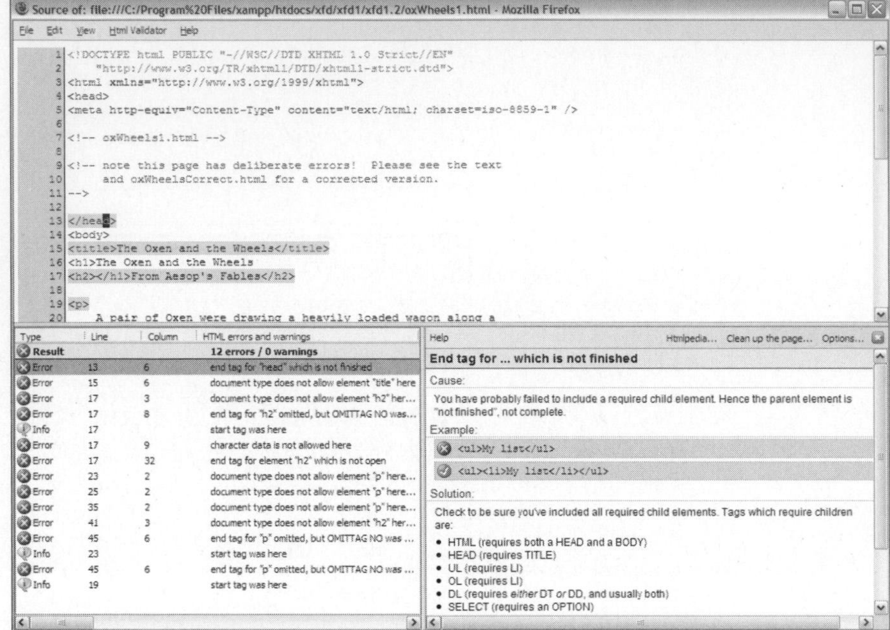

Figure 3-4: The HTML Validator explains all errors in your page.

The HTML Validator tool will revolutionize your Web development experience. It really helps you create standards-compliant sites easily, and it has the added benefit of helping you rapidly discover the level of compliance of any page you visit. (It's fun to feel superior.)

Using the Web Developer toolbar

The Web Developer toolbar by Chris Pederick provides all kinds of useful tools for Web developers. The program installs as a new toolbar in Firefox, as shown in Figure 3-5.

Figure 3-5 shows the Wiley home page with some of the Web Developer toolbar features active. The Edit CSS frame on the left allows me to modify the look of the page in real time, and the thick outlines were added by the toolbar to help visualize the page organization. (I describe these ideas in detail in Books III and IV.)

When you have the Web Developer toolbar activated (use the View➪Toolbars menu command to hide or show it), you can use it to do the following:

- **Edit your page on the fly.** The Edit HTML Entry option on the Miscellaneous menu opens a small text editor on the side of the screen. You can make changes to your HTML here and immediately see the results in the main screen. The changes aren't permanent, but you can save them.

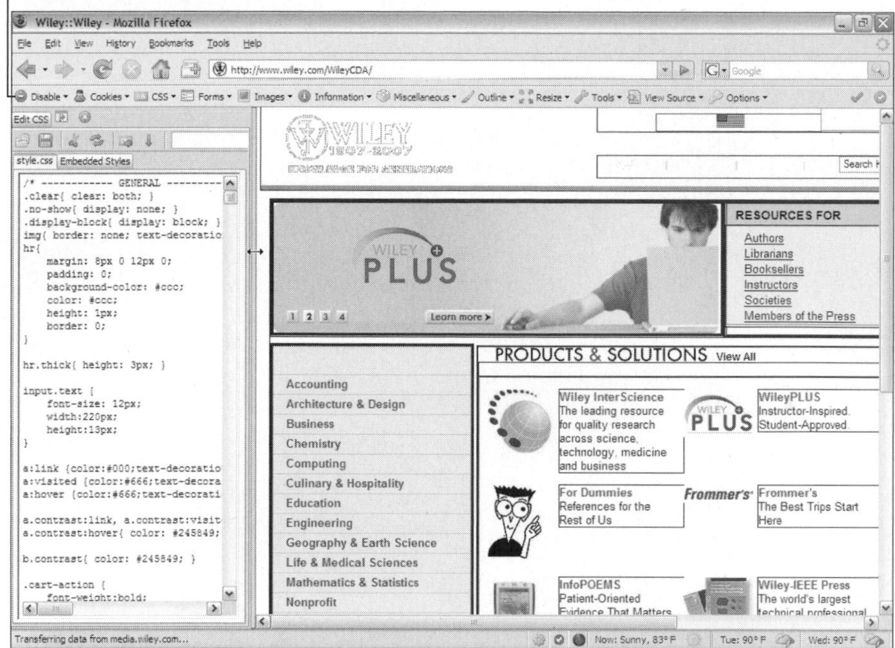

Figure 3-5: The Web Developer toolbar adds several features to Firefox.

- **Validate your pages.** There's a menu command (CSS➪Edit CSS) to validate your page, but the Web Developer toolbar also adds some hotkeys to Firefox so you can instantly send your page to the W3 Validator. Ctrl+Shift+A contacts the W3 Validator and then sends your page directly to it. It's much easier than memorizing the Validator address. This feature alone is worth the download time. You can also do other kinds of validation, check your CSS, or see how well your page conforms to various guidelines for people with disabilities.
- **Manipulate CSS code.** After you define your page with XHTML, use CSS to dress it up. The CSS menu has a number of great tools for seeing how CSS is set up and experimenting with it on the fly. I explain how to use the CSS tools in Books II and III, where I describe CSS.
- **View your page in different sizes.** Not everybody has a huge flat-panel display. It's important to see how your page looks in a number of standard screen resolutions.
- **Get a speed report.** Your Web page may load great on your broadband connection, but how does it work on Aunt Judy's dialup? Web Developer has a tool that analyzes all the components of the page, reports how long each component takes to download over various connections, and suggests ways to improve the speed of your page's download.

The Web Developer toolbar can do a lot more, but those are some of the highlights. The toolbar is a small and fast download, and it makes Web development a lot easier. There's really no good reason to not use it.

Using Firebug

The Firebug extension is another vital tool for Web developers. Firebug concentrates more on JavaScript development rather than pure XHTML development, but it's also useful for XHTML beginners. Figure 3-6 shows the Firebug extension opened as a panel in Firefox.

The *Inspect mode* allows you to compare the HTML code to the output. When you move your mouse over a part of the rendered page, Firebug highlights the relevant part of the code in the other panel. Likewise, you can move the mouse over a code fragment and see the affected code segment. This can be extremely handy when things aren't working out like you expect.

You can view the HTML code as an outline, which helps you see the overall structure of the code. You can also edit the code in the panel and see the results immediately, as you can with the Web Developer toolbar, which I discuss in the previous section. Changes you make in Firebug aren't permanent, but you can copy them to your text editor.

Figure 3-6: Firebug gives a detailed view of your page.

Firebug really shows off when you get to more sophisticated techniques, such as CSS, DOM Manipulation, JavaScript, and AJAX. Although you discover those technologies in Books IV and VII show you how Firebug can be used to aid in these processes.

Using a Full-Blown IDE

You might think I hate dedicated Web page editors, but I don't. I use them all the time for other kinds of programming. The problem is that up until recently, there weren't any real IDEs (Integrated Development Environments) for Web development. Most of the tools try to be visual development tools that automate the design of visual pages, rather than programming environments. They have flaws because Web development is really a programming problem with visual design aspects, rather than a visual design problem with programming underneath.

A couple of IDEs have popped up recently in the open-source community. One tries to be like the commercial tools (and ends up replicating some of their flaws).

Another editor has emerged that seems to be a good compromise between helping you write solid code and growing with you as you get more sophisticated.

Introducing Nvu

One of the most popular HTML IDEs in the open-source community is Nvu (pronounced *en-view*). This editor has a number of editing modes, making it very popular with beginners.

Nvu is available on the CD-ROM that accompanies this book or at `http://nvu.com`.

It defaults to a WYSIWYG mode, like most word processors, as shown in Figure 3-7.

Unlike ordinary word processors, Nvu can show you the code underneath. Figure 3-8 shows the same page with the HTML Tags view enabled.

It might surprise you that there are no `<p>` tags shown in Figure 3-8. Nvu uses the `<br />` tag instead, which means your code won't validate without modification. (I have 11 errors because of the missing `<p>` tags.)

Figure 3-9 demonstrates source mode, which shows the actual source code.

You can modify the code directly in this mode (and you'll need to, if you want the page to validate).

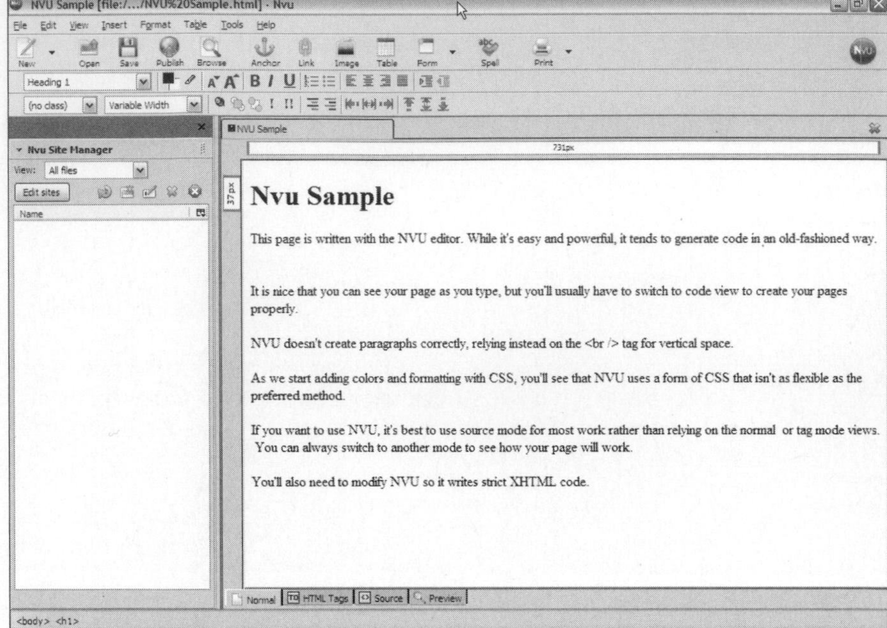

Figure 3-7: Nvu looks a lot like a word processor.

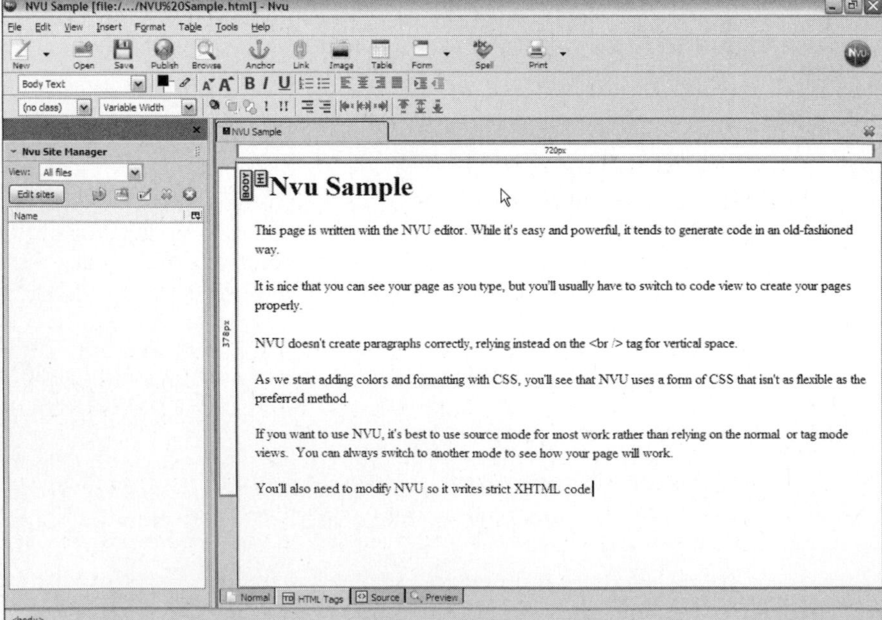

Figure 3-8: HTML Tags view shows which tags are being used.

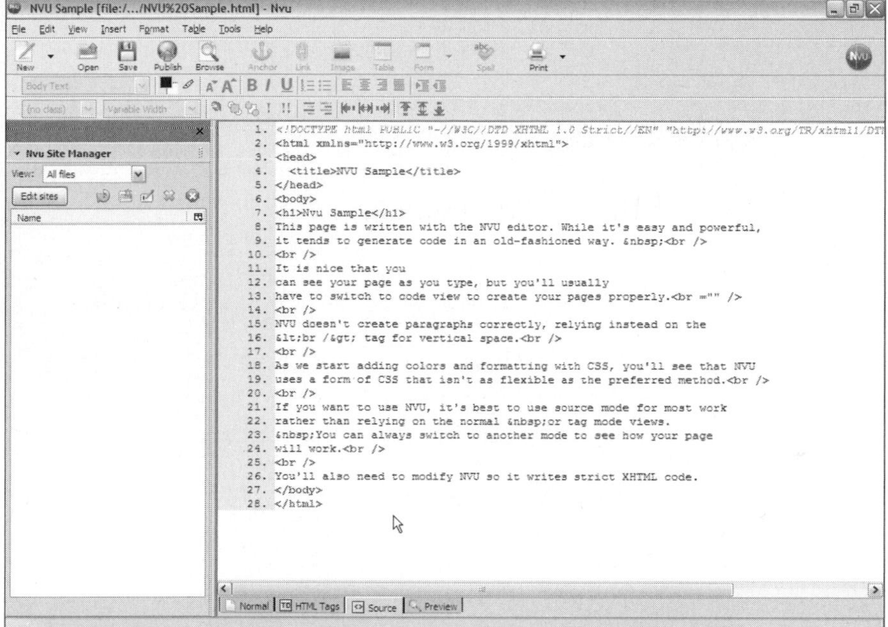

Figure 3-9: This is the code that Nvu generated for the sample page.

Although Nvu has some advantages — especially the spell-checking feature — it encourages bad habits (like most WYSIWYG tools). Because it's safest to use this tool in source mode, you might as well use some other tool that has more features in text mode.

Introducing Aptana

My preferred editor for beginners who intend to become advanced is Aptana (available on the CD-ROM or at `www.aptana.com`). Aptana Studio is a full-blown IDE, based on the popular Eclipse editor. Aptana has a lot of features that make it a good choice for Web developers:

- **Syntax completion:** Aptana has built-in knowledge of HTML (and several other languages). When you start to type HTML code, it recognizes the code and pops up a list of suggestions. Figure 3-10 shows Aptana helping on some HTML code.
- **Automatic ending tags:** As soon as you write a beginning tag, Aptana automatically generates the corresponding end tag. This makes it much less likely that you'll forget an ending tag — one of the most common coding errors.
- **Automatically generated XHTML template:** When you tell Aptana to create an HTML page, it can generate the page template with all the messy doctype stuff built in. (I explain how to customize this feature in the next section.)

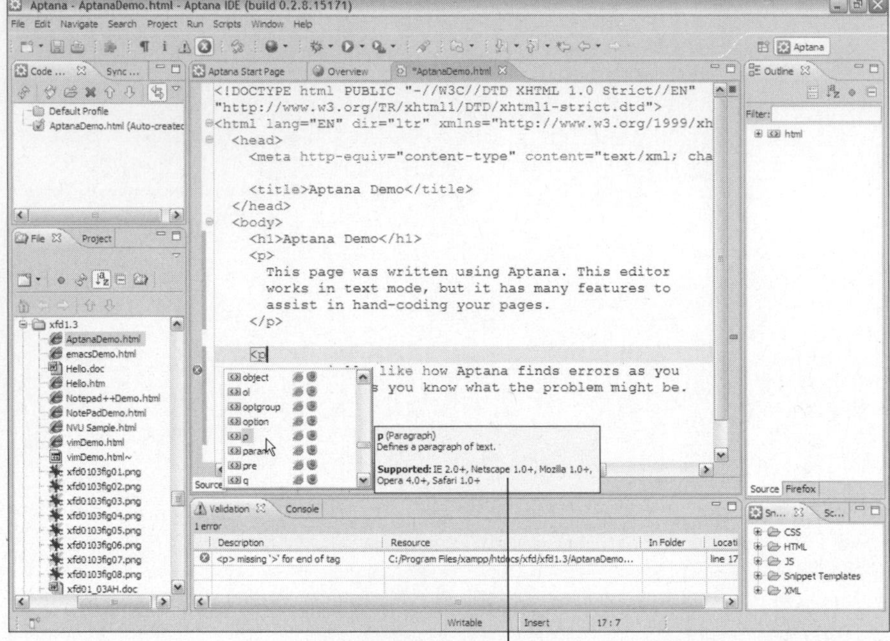

Figure 3-10: Aptana recognizes HTML and suggests code for you.

- **Error detection:** Aptana can look at the code and detect certain errors. Although it isn't a replacement for a Validator, it can be a very handy tool, especially when you begin to write JavaScript code.
- **File management tools:** Aptana makes it easy to work both with the local file system and pages that reside on servers on the Internet.
- **Page preview:** You can preview your page directly within Aptana, or you can view it in your primary browser.
- **Outline view:** This panel displays the page structure as an outline. It helps you see the overall structure of the page. You can also use this panel as a table of contents to quickly get to any particular part of your page in the editor. Figure 3-11 shows the Outline view in action.
- **Advanced features:** When you're ready to try JavaScript and AJAX, Aptana has nice support for these more advanced technologies. The syntax-highlighting features work in CSS, JavaScript, and PHP, just like they do in HTML. This means you can use the same editor for all your Web languages, which is a really great thing.

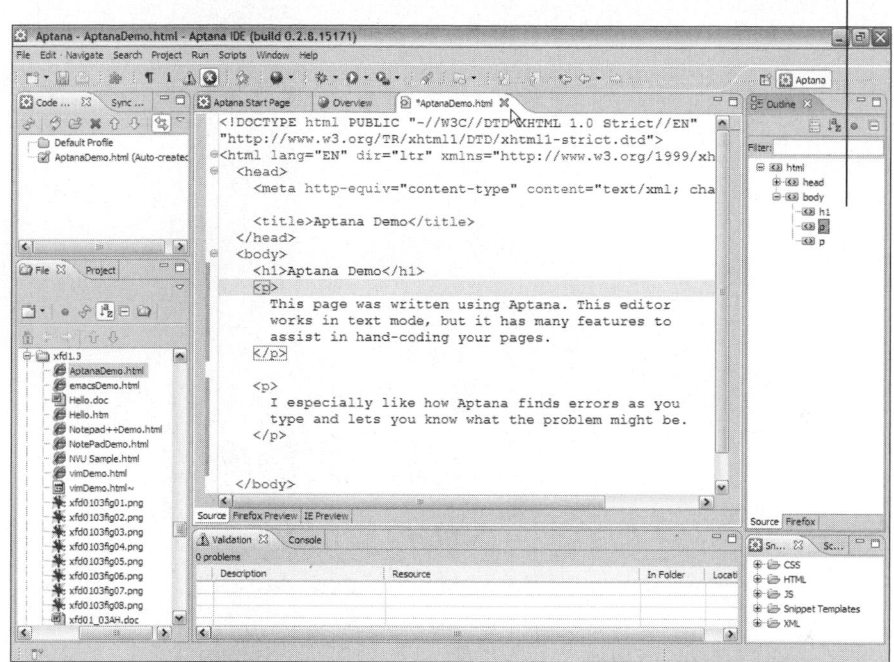

Figure 3-11: The Outline view acts as a table of contents for your page.

Aptana Studio currently comes in two versions. The Community Edition is free and open-source, and the Professional Edition has additional features. I use the Community Edition throughout this book, as it has more than enough features for beginning Web developers.

Customizing Aptana

Aptana is a pretty great editor, but I recommend you change a few settings after you install it on your system.

Getting to the HTML editor preferences

Aptana can be customized in a lot of ways. For now, the only preferences you need to change are in the HTML editor. Choose Windows➪Preferences, and in the Preferences dialog box, expand the Aptana link and select HTML Editor. The dialog box looks like Figure 3-12.

Changing the extension

By default, Aptana saves files with the `.htm` extension. Because this is the extension normally used only by Microsoft servers, I prefer to save pages with `.html`. All Web pages in this book are stored with the `.html` extension.

Enter **.html** in the Default Extension for New HTML Files (Prefix with '.') field to make this change, if you wish.

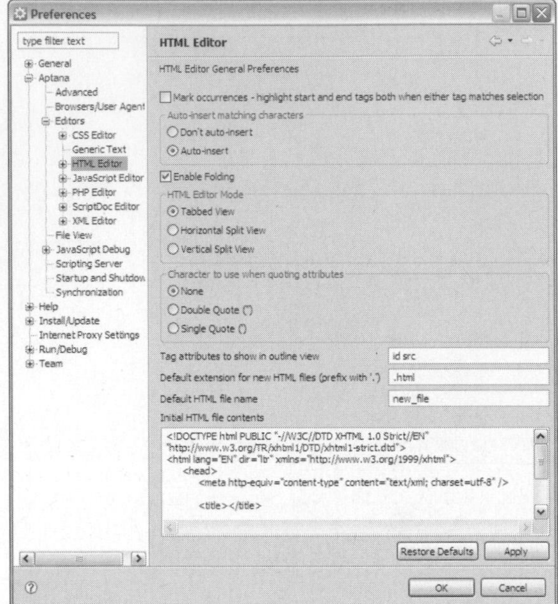

Figure 3-12: Aptana's HTML Editor Preferences dialog box.

Changing the initial contents

When you create a new Web page in Aptana, a basic template appears. This is convenient, but it creates an HTML 4.0 doctype. Open `template.html` in a normal text editor, copy it, and paste it to the provided text area, and your pages will all begin with the standard template.

Changing the view

Aptana allows you to split the screen with your code in one panel and a browser view in another. Every time you save your code, the browser view immediately updates. This is a really good tool, especially for a beginner, because you can get very quick feedback on how your page looks. In the Html Editor Mode section in the Preferences dialog box (see Figure 3-12), you can indicate whether you want the browser preview to be in a separate tab, in a horizontal split screen, or in a vertical split screen. I use tabs because I like to see as much code as possible on-screen. I switch to the preview tab when I need to see how the page looks to the browser.

Chapter 4: Managing Information with Lists and Tables

In This Chapter

- **Understanding basic lists**
- **Creating unordered, ordered, and nested lists**
- **Building definition lists**
- **Building basic tables**
- **Using** `rowspan` **and** `colspan` **attributes**

You'll often need to present large amounts of information organized in some way, and XHTML has some wonderful tools to manage this task. XHTML has three different kinds of lists and a powerful table structure for organizing the content of your page. Figure out how these tools work, and you can manage complex information with ease.

Making a List and Checking It Twice

XHTML supports three types of lists. Unordered lists generally contain bullet points. They're used when the order of elements in the list isn't important. Ordered lists usually have some kind of numeric counter preceding each list item, and definition lists contain terms and their definitions.

Creating an unordered list

All the list types in XHTML are closely related. The simplest and most common kind of list is an *unordered list.*

Looking at an unordered list

Look at the simple page shown in Figure 4-1. In addition to a couple of headers, it has a list of information.

The list of browsers has some interesting visual characteristics:

- **The items are indented.** There's some extra space between the left margin and the beginning of each list item.

- **The list elements have bullets.** That little dot in front of each item is a *bullet.* Bullets are commonly used in unordered lists like this one.
- **Each item begins a new line.** When a list item is displayed, it's shown on a new line.

These characteristics help you see that you have a list, but they're all just default behavior. Defining something as a list doesn't force it to look a particular way, but there is a default view that helps you see that these items are indeed part of a list.

It's important to remember the core idea of XHTML here. You aren't really describing how things *look,* but what they *mean.* As you discover various kinds of listing structures, you'll see that the browsers automatically change what appears on-screen to indicate the various kinds of lists. You can change the appearance later when you figure out CSS, so don't get too tied up in the particular appearance of things. For now, just recognize that HTML (and by extension, XHTML) can build lists and make sure you know how to use the various types.

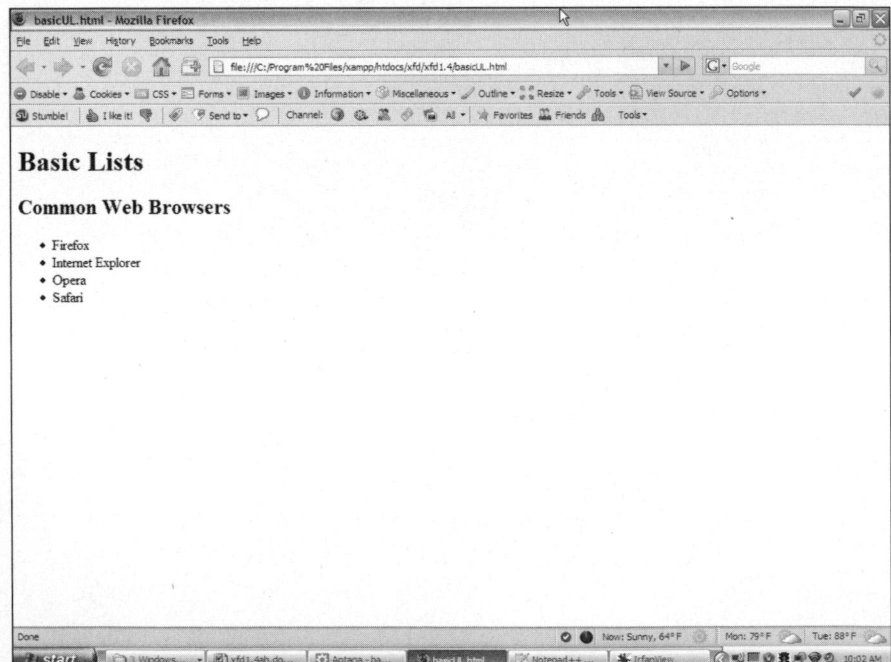

Figure 4-1: An unordered list of Web browsers.

Building an unordered list

Lists are made with two kinds of tags. One tag surrounds the entire list and indicates the general type of list. This first example demonstrates an unordered list, which is surrounded by the `<ul></ul>` pair.

Note that it's common to indent all the code inside the `<ul>` set. The unordered list can go in the main body.

Inside the `<ul></ul>` set is a number of list items. Each element of the list is stored between a `<li>` (list item) and a `</li>` tag. Normally, each `<li></li>` item goes on its own line of the source code, although you can make a list item as long as you want.

Look to Book II, Chapter 4 for information on how to change the bullet to all kinds of other images, including circles, squares, and even custom images.

The code for the unordered list is pretty straightforward:

```
<!DOCTYPE html PUBLIC "-//W3C//DTD XHTML 1.0 Strict//EN"
"http://www.w3.org/TR/xhtml1/DTD/xhtml1-strict.dtd">
<html lang="EN" dir="ltr" xmlns="http://www.w3.org/1999/xhtml">
  <head>
    <meta http-equiv="content-type" content="text/xml; charset=utf-8" />

    <title>basicUL.html</title>
  </head>
  <body>
    <h1>Basic Lists</h1>
    <h2>Common Web Browsers</h2>
    <ul>
      <li>Firefox</li>
      <li>Internet Explorer</li>
      <li>Opera</li>
      <li>Safari</li>
    </ul>

  </body>
</html>
```

Creating ordered lists

Ordered lists are almost exactly like unordered lists. Ordered lists traditionally have numbers rather than bullets (although you can change this through CSS if you want, as you see in Book III, Chapter 3).

Viewing an ordered list

Figure 4-2 demonstrates a page with a basic ordered list — `basicOL.html`.

Figure 4-2 shows another list (like in Figure 4-1), but this time, the items are numbered. When your data is a list of steps or information with some type of numerical values, an ordered list is a good choice.

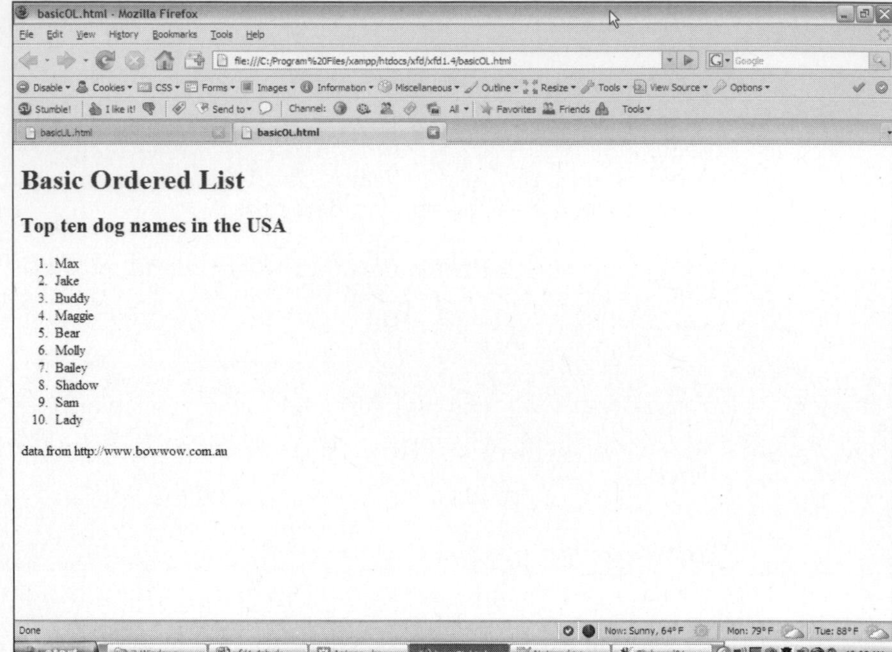

Figure 4-2: A simple ordered list.

Building the ordered list

The code for `basicOL.html` is remarkably similar to the unordered list:

```
<!DOCTYPE html PUBLIC "-//W3C//DTD XHTML 1.0 Strict//EN"
"http://www.w3.org/TR/xhtml1/DTD/xhtml1-strict.dtd">
<html lang="EN" dir="ltr" xmlns="http://www.w3.org/1999/xhtml">
  <head>
    <meta http-equiv="content-type" content="text/xml; charset=utf-8" />
    <title>basicOL.html</title>
  </head>

  <body>
    <h1>Basic Ordered List</h1>
    <h2>Top ten dog names in the USA</h2>
    <ol>
      <li>Max</li>
      <li>Jake</li>
      <li>Buddy</li>
      <li>Maggie</li>
      <li>Bear</li>
      <li>Molly</li>
      <li>Bailey</li>
      <li>Shadow</li>
      <li>Sam</li>
      <li>Lady</li>
    </ol>
```

```
    <p>
      data from http://www.bowwow.com.au
    </p>
  </body>
</html>
```

Note that the only change is the list tag itself. Rather than the `<ul>` tag, the ordered list uses the `<ol>` indicator. The list items are still exactly the same `<li></li>` pairs used in the unordered list.

You don't indicate the item number anywhere. It's automatically generated based on the position of each item within the list. Therefore, you can change the order of the items, and the numbers are still correct.

This is one of those places where it's really great that XHTML is about meaning, not layout. If you specified the actual numbers, it'd be a mess to move things around. All that really matters here is that the element is inside an ordered list.

Making nested lists

Sometimes, you'll want to create outlines or other kinds of complex data in your pages. You can easily nest lists inside each other, if you want. Figure 4-3 shows a more complex list describing popular cat names in the U.S. and Australia.

Figure 4-3 uses a combination of lists to do its work. This figure contains a list of two countries: the U.S. and Australia. Each country has an H3 heading and another (ordered) list inside it! You can nest various elements inside a list, but you have to do it carefully if you want the page to validate.

In this example, there's an unordered list with only two elements. Each of these elements contains an `<h3>` heading and an ordered list. The page handles all this data in a relatively clean way and validates correctly.

Examining the nested list example

The entire code for `nestedList.html` is reproduced here:

```
<!DOCTYPE html PUBLIC "-//W3C//DTD XHTML 1.0 Strict//EN"
"http://www.w3.org/TR/xhtml1/DTD/xhtml1-strict.dtd">
<html lang="EN" dir="ltr" xmlns="http://www.w3.org/1999/xhtml">
  <head>
    <meta http-equiv="content-type" content="text/xml; charset=utf-8" />
    <title>nestedList.html</title>
  </head>

  <body>
    <h1>Nested Lists</h1>
```

```
    <h2>Popular Cat Names</h2>
    <ul>
      <li>
        <h3>USA</h3>
        <ol>
          <li>Tigger</li>
          <li>Tiger</li>
          <li>Max</li>
          <li>Smokey</li>
          <li>Sam</li>
        </ol>
      </li>
      <li>

        <h3>Australia</h3>
        <ol>
          <li>Oscar</li>
          <li>Max</li>
          <li>Tiger</li>
          <li>Sam</li>
          <li>Misty</li>
        </ol>
      </li>
    </ul>
  </body>
</html>
```

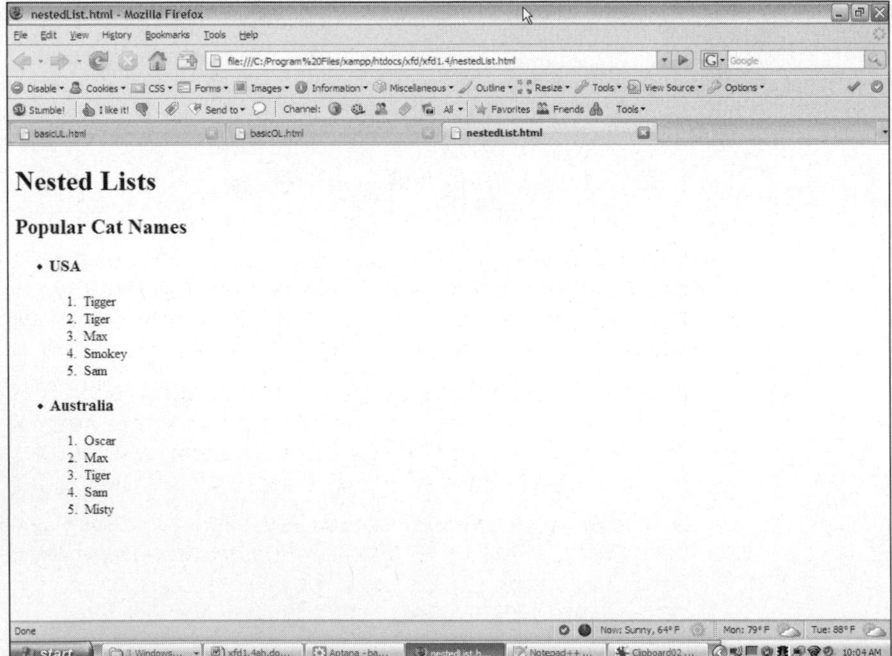

Figure 4-3: An ordered list inside an unordered list!

Here are a few things you might notice in this code listing:

✦ There's a large `<ul>` set surrounding the entire main list.

✦ The main list has only two list items.

✦ Each of these items represents a country.

✦ Each country has an `<h3>` element, describing the country name inside the `<li>`.

✦ Each country also has an `<ol>` set with a list of names.

✦ The indentation really helps you see how things are connected.

Indenting your code

You might have noticed that I indent all the XHTML code in this book. The browsers ignore all indentation, but it's still an important coding habit.

There are many opinions about how code should be formatted, but I use a standard format in this book that serves you well until you can develop your own style.

I generally use the following rules to indent HTML/XHTML code:

✦ **Indent each nested element.** Because the `<head>` is inside the `<html>` element, I indent to indicate this. Likewise, the `<li>` elements are always indented inside `<ul>` or `<ol>` pairs.

✦ **Line up your elements.** If an element takes up more than one line, line up the ending tag with the beginning tag. This way, you know what ends what.

✦ **Use spaces, not tabs.** The `tab` character often causes problems in source code. Different editors format tabs differently, and a mixture of tabs and spaces can make your carefully formatted page look awful when you view it in another editor.

If you are using Aptana (and you really should — see Chapter 3 in this minibook for more information about it), note that Aptana's autoformatting defaults to tabs. From the Window menu, select Preferences. Then find the Aptana⇨Editors panel and select Insert Spaces Instead of Tabs.

✦ **Use two spaces.** Most coders use two or four spaces per indentation level. HTML elements can be nested pretty deeply. Going seven or eight layers deep is pretty common. If you use tabs or too many spaces, you'll have so much white space that you can't see the code.

Aptana defaults to four spaces, but you can change it to two. From the General menu, select Editors then Text Editors, and set Displayed Tab Width to 2.

- **End at the left margin.** If you finish the page and you're not back at the left margin, you've forgotten to end something. Proper indentation makes it easy to see your data structure. Each element should line up with its closing tag.

Building a nested list

If you just look over the code for the nested list, it can look intimidating. It isn't really that hard. The secret is to build the list *outside in:*

1. **Create the outer list first.**

   Build the primary list (whether it's ordered or unordered). In my example, I began with just the unordered list with the two countries in it.

2. **Add list items to the outer list.**

   If you want text or headlines in the larger list (like I did), you can put them here. If you're putting nothing but a list inside your primary list, you may want to put some placeholder `<li>` tags in there just so you can be sure everything's working.

3. **Validate before adding the next list level.**

   Nested lists can confuse the Validator (and you). Validate your code with the outer list to make sure there are no problems before you add inner lists.

4. **Add the first inner list.**

   After you know the basic structure is okay, add the first interior list. For my example, this was the ordered list of cat names in the U.S.

5. **Repeat until finished.**

   Keep adding lists until your page looks right.

6. **Validate frequently.**

   It's much better to validate as you go than to wait until everything's finished. Catch your mistakes early so you don't replicate them.

Building the definition list

One more type of list — the definition list — is very useful, even if it isn't used frequently. The *definition list* was originally designed to format dictionary-style definitions, but it's really useful anytime you have name and value pairs. Figure 4-4 shows a sample definition list in action.

Definition lists don't use bullets or numbers. Instead, they have two elements. *Definition terms* are usually words or short phrases. In Figure 4-4, the browser names are defined as definition terms. *Definition descriptions* are the extended text blocks that contain the actual definition.

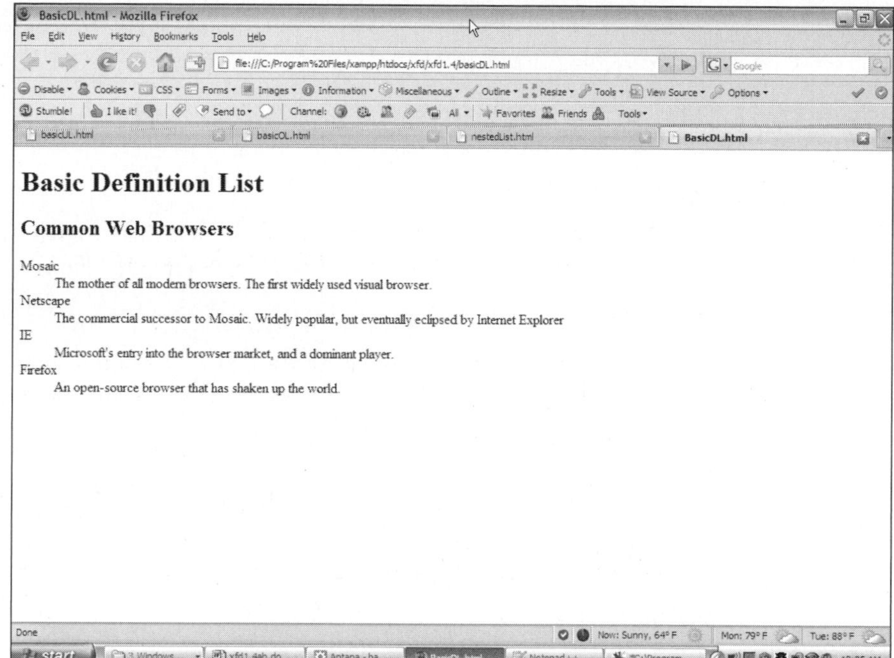

Figure 4-4: A basic definition list.

The standard layout of definition lists indents each definition description. Of course, you can change this layout however you want after you understand CSS in Books II and III.

You can use definition lists any time you want a list marked by key terms, rather than bullets or numbers. The definition list is also useful in other situations, like forms, figures with captions, and so on.

Here's the code for `basicDL.html`:

```
<!DOCTYPE html PUBLIC "-//W3C//DTD XHTML 1.0 Strict//EN"
"http://www.w3.org/TR/xhtml1/DTD/xhtml1-strict.dtd">
<html lang="EN" dir="ltr" xmlns="http://www.w3.org/1999/xhtml">
  <head>
    <meta http-equiv="content-type" content="text/xml; charset=utf-8" />
    <title>BasicDL.html</title>
  </head>

  <body>
    <h1>Basic Definition List</h1>
    <h2>Common Web Browsers</h2>
    <dl>
      <dt>Mosaic</dt>
      <dd>
```

```
          The mother of all modern browsers. The first widely used
          visual browser.
        </dd>

        <dt>Netscape</dt>
        <dd>
          The commercial successor to Mosaic. Widely popular, but
          eventually eclipsed by Internet Explorer
        </dd>

        <dt>IE</dt>
        <dd>
          Microsoft's entry into the browser market, and a dominant
          player.
        </dd>

        <dt>Firefox</dt>
        <dd>
          An open-source browser that has shaken up the world.
        </dd>
      </dl>
    </body>
</html>
```

As you can see, the definition list uses three tag pairs:

- **<dl></dl>** defines the entire list.
- **<dt></dt>** defines each definition term.
- **<dd></dd>** defines the definition data.

Definition lists aren't used as often as they might be, but they can be extremely useful. Any time you have a list that will be a combination of terms and values, a definition list is a good choice.

Building Tables

Sometimes, you'll encounter data that fits best in a tabular format. XHTML supports several table tags for this kind of work. Figure 4-5 illustrates a very basic table.

Sometimes, the best way to show data in a meaningful way is to organize it in a table. XHTML defines a table with the (cleverly named) `<table>` tag. The table contains a number of table rows (defined with the `<tr>` tag). Each table row can consist of a number of table data (`<td>`) or table header (`<th>`) tags.

Compare the output in Figure 4-5 with the code that creates it in `basicTable.html`, for an example:

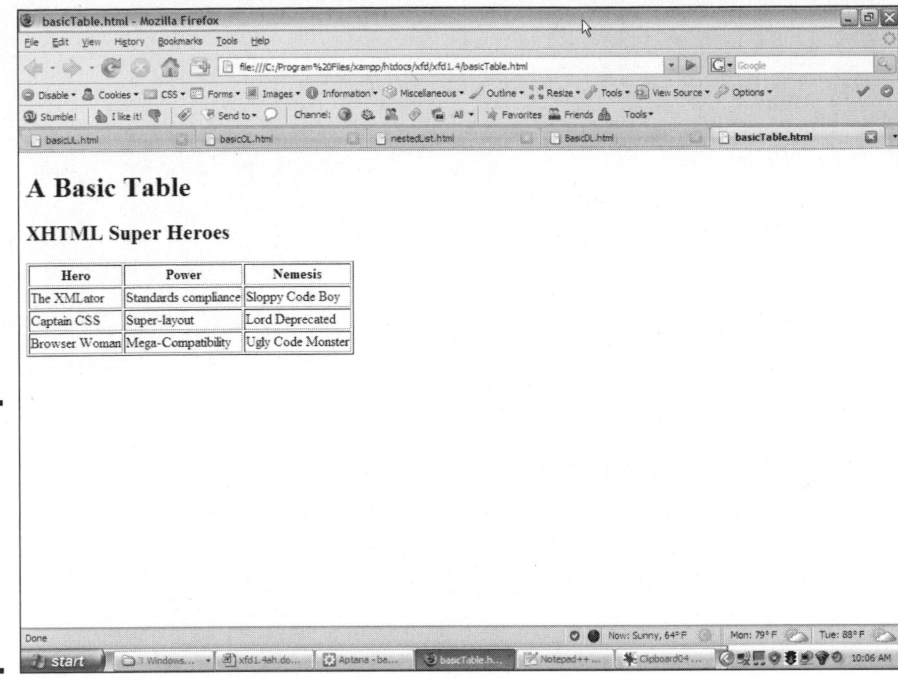

Figure 4-5: Tables are useful for certain kinds of data representation.

```
<!DOCTYPE html PUBLIC "-//W3C//DTD XHTML 1.0 Strict//EN"
"http://www.w3.org/TR/xhtml1/DTD/xhtml1-strict.dtd">
<html lang="EN" dir="ltr" xmlns="http://www.w3.org/1999/xhtml">
  <head>
    <meta http-equiv="content-type" content="text/xml; charset=utf-8" />
    <title>basicTable.html</title>
  </head>

  <body>
    <h1>A Basic Table</h1>
    <h2>XHTML Super Heroes</h2>
    <table border = "1">
      <tr>
        <th>Hero</th>
        <th>Power</th>
        <th>Nemesis</th>
      </tr>

      <tr>
        <td>The XMLator</td>
        <td>Standards compliance</td>
        <td>Sloppy Code Boy</td>
      </tr>

      <tr>
        <td>Captain CSS</td>
        <td>Super-layout</td>
        <td>Lord Deprecated</td>
      </tr>
```

```
      <tr>
        <td>Browser Woman</td>
        <td>Mega-Compatibility</td>
        <td>Ugly Code Monster</td>
      </tr>

    </table>
  </body>
</html>
```

Defining the table

The XHTML table is defined with the <table></table> pair. It makes a lot of sense to indent and space your code carefully so you can see the structure of the table in the code. Just by glancing at the code, you can guess that the table consists of three rows and each row consists of three elements.

In a word processor, you typically create a blank table by defining the number of rows and columns, and then fill it in. In XHTML, you define the table row by row, and the number of columns is automatically determined by the number of elements in each row. It's up to you to make sure each row has the same number of elements.

By default (in most browsers, anyway), tables don't show their borders. If you want to see basic table borders, you can turn on the table's `border` attribute. (An *attribute* is a special modifier you can attach to some tags.)

```
<table border = "1">
```

This tag creates a table and specifies that it will have a border of size `1`. If you leave out the `border = "1"` business, some browsers display a border and some don't. You can set the border value to `0` or to a larger number. The larger number makes a bigger border, like you see in Figure 4-6.

Although this method of making table borders is perfectly fine, I show a much more flexible and powerful technique in Book II, Chapter 4.

It's always a good idea to set a table border because you can't count on browsers to have the same default. Also, note that the border value always goes in quotes. When you read about CSS in Book II (are you getting tired of hearing that?), you discover how to add more complex and interesting borders than this simple attribute allows.

Adding your first row

After you define a table, you need to add some rows. Each row is indicated by a <tr></tr> pair.

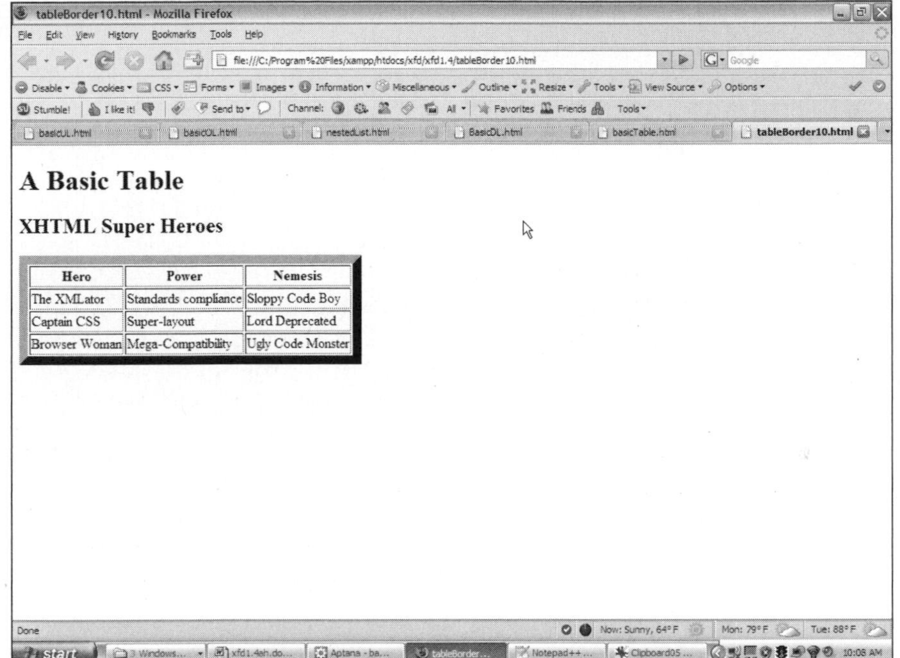

Figure 4-6: I set the border attribute to 10.

Inside the <tr></tr> set, you need some table data. The first row often consists of *table headers*. These are special cells that are formatted differently to indicate they're labels, rather than data.

Table headers have some default formatting to help you remember they're headers, but you can change the way they look. You can change the table header's appearance in all kinds of great ways in Books II and III. Define the table header so when you discover formatting and decide to make all your table headers chartreuse, you'll know where in the HTML code all the table headers are.

Indent your headers inside the <tr> set. If your table contains three columns, your first row might begin like this:

```
<tr>
  <th></th>
  <th></th>
  <th></th>
</tr>
```

Place the text you want shown in the table headers between the <th> and </th> elements. The contents appear in the order they're defined.

Headings don't have to be on the top row. If you want headings on the left, just put a `<th></th>` as the first element of each row. You can have headings at both the top and the left, if you want. In fact, you can have headings anywhere, but it usually makes sense to put headings only at the top or left.

Making your data rows

The next step is to create another row. The data rows are just like the heading row, except they use `<td></td>` pairs, rather than `<th></th>` pairs, to contain the data elements. A three-column table typically has blank rows that look like this:

```
<tr>
  <td></td>
  <td></td>
  <td></td>
</tr>
```

Place the data elements inside the `<td></td>` segments, and you're ready to go.

Building tables in the text editor

Some people think that tables are a good reason to use WYSIWYG (what you see is what you get) editors because they think it's hard to create tables in text mode. You have to plan a little, but it's really quite quick and easy to build an HTML table without graphical tools if you follow this plan:

1. **Plan ahead.**

   Know how many rows and columns will be in the table. It might help to sketch it on paper first. Changing the number of rows later is easy, but changing the number of columns can be a real pain after some of the code has been written.

2. **Create the headings.**

   If you're going to start with a standard headings-on-top table, begin by creating the heading row. Save, check, and validate. You don't want mistakes to multiply when you add more complexity. This heading row tells how many columns you'll need.

3. **Build a sample empty row.**

   Make a sample row with the correct number of `td` elements with one `<td></td>` pair per line. Build one `td` set and use copy and paste to copy this data cell as many times as you need. Make sure the number of `td` pairs equals the number of `th` sets in the heading row.

4. **Copy and paste the empty row to make as many rows as you need.**
5. **Save, view, and validate.**

Be sure everything looks right and validates properly before you put a lot of effort into adding data.

6. **Populate the table with the data you need.**

   Go row by row, adding the data between the `<td></td>` pairs.

7. **Test and validate again to make sure you didn't accidentally break something.**

Spanning rows and columns

Sometimes, you need a little more flexibility in your table design. Figure 4-7 shows a page from an evil overlord's daily planner.

Being an evil overlord is clearly a complex business. From a code standpoint, the items that take up more than one cell are the most interesting. Designing traps takes two mornings, and improving the lair takes three. All Friday afternoon and evening are spent on world domination. Take a look at the code, and you'll see how it works:

```
<!DOCTYPE html PUBLIC "-//W3C//DTD XHTML 1.0 Strict//EN"
"http://www.w3.org/TR/xhtml1/DTD/xhtml1-strict.dtd">
```

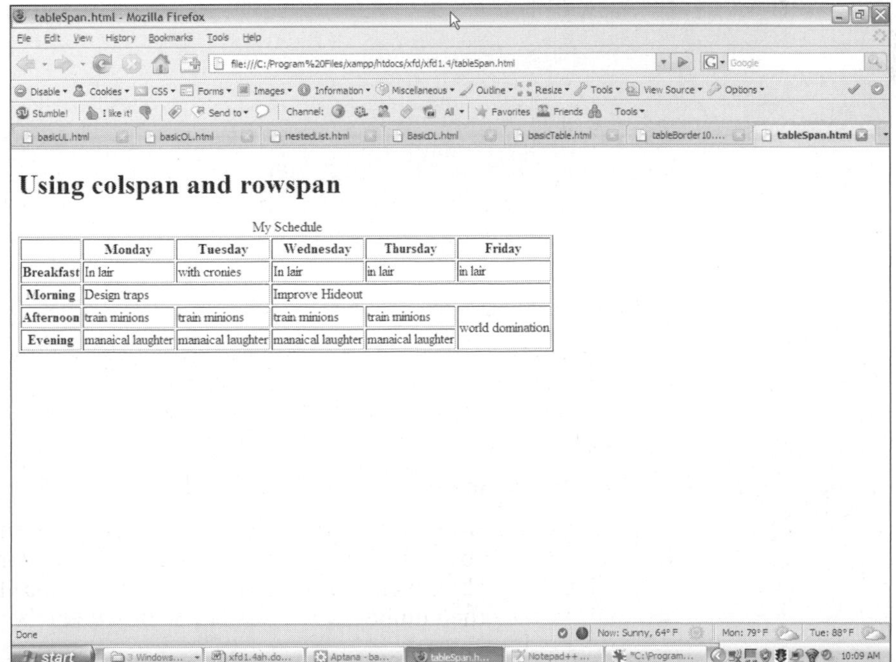

	Monday	Tuesday	Wednesday	Thursday	Friday
Breakfast	In lair	with cronies	In lair	in lair	in lair
Morning	Design traps		Improve Hideout		
Afternoon	train minions	train minions	train minions	train minions	world domination
Evening	manaical laughter	manaical laughter	manaical laughter	manaical laughter	

Figure 4-7: Some of these activities take up more than one cell.

```
<html lang="EN" dir="ltr" xmlns="http://www.w3.org/1999/xhtml">
  <head>
    <meta http-equiv="content-type" content="text/xml; charset=utf-8" />
    <title>tableSpan.html</title>
  </head>

  <body>
    <h1>Using colspan and rowspan</h1>
    <table border = "1">
      <caption>My Schedule</caption>
      <tr>
        <th></th>
        <th>Monday</th>
        <th>Tuesday</th>
        <th>Wednesday</th>
        <th>Thursday</th>
        <th>Friday</th>
      </tr>

      <tr>
        <th>Breakfast</th>
        <td>In lair</td>
        <td>with cronies</td>
        <td>In lair</td>
        <td>in lair</td>
        <td>in lair</td>
      </tr>

      <tr>
        <th>Morning</th>
        <td colspan = "2">Design traps</td>
         <td colspan = "3">Improve Hideout</td>  </tr>
        <tr>
        <th>Afternoon</th>
        <td>train minions</td>
        <td>train minions</td>
        <td>train minions</td>
        <td>train minions</td>
        <td rowspan = "2">world domination</td>
      </tr>

      <tr>
        <th>Evening</th>
        <td>maniacal laughter</td>
        <td>maniacal laughter</td>
        <td>maniacal laughter</td>
        <td>maniacal laughter</td>
      </tr>

    </table>

  </body>
</html>
```

The secret to making cells larger than the default is two special attributes: `rowspan` and `colspan`.

Spanning multiple columns

The morning activities tend to happen over several days. Designing traps will take both Monday and Tuesday morning, and improving the hideout will occupy the remaining three mornings. Take another look at the Morning row, and you'll see how this is done:

```
<tr>
  <th>Morning</th>
  <td colspan = "2">Design traps</td>
  <td colspan = "3">Improve Hideout</td>
</tr>
```

The Design Traps cell spans over two normal columns. The `colspan` attribute tells how many columns this cell will take. The Improve Hideout cell has a `colspan` of `3`.

It's important to note that the Morning row still takes up six columns. The `<th>` is one column wide, like normal, but the Design Traps cell spans two columns and the Improve Hideout cell takes three, which totals six columns wide. If you increase the width of a cell, you need to eliminate some other cells in the row to compensate.

Spanning multiple rows

A related property — `rowspan` — allows a cell to take up more than one row of a table. Look back at the Friday column in Figure 4-7, and you'll see the World Domination cell takes up two time slots. (If world domination was easy, everybody would do it.) Here's the relevant code:

```
<tr>
  <th>Afternoon</th>
  <td>train minions</td>
  <td>train minions</td>
  <td>train minions</td>
  <td>train minions</td>
  <td rowspan = "2">world domination</td>
</tr>

<tr>
  <th>Evening</th>
  <td>maniacal laughter</td>
  <td>maniacal laughter</td>
  <td>maniacal laughter</td>
  <td>maniacal laughter</td>
</tr>
```

The Evening row has only five entries because the World Domination cell extends into the space that would normally be occupied by a `<td>` pair.

If you want to use `rowspan` and `colspan`, don't just hammer away at the page in your editor. Sketch out what you want to accomplish first. I'm pretty good at this stuff, and I still needed a sketch before I was able to create the `tableSpan` code.

Avoiding the table-based layout trap

Tables are pretty great. They're a terrific way to present certain kinds of data. When you add the `colspan` and `rowspan` concepts, you can use tables to create some pretty interesting layouts. In fact, because old-school HTML didn't really have any sort of layout technology, a lot of developers came up with some pretty amazing layouts based on tables. You'll still see a lot of Web pages today designed with tables as the primary layout mechanism.

Using tables for layout causes some problems though, such as

- **Tables aren't meant for layout.** Tables are designed for data presentation, not layout. In order to make tables work for layout, you have to do a lot of sneaky hacks, like tables nested inside other tables or invisible images for spacing.
- **The code becomes complicated fast.** Tables involve a lot of HTML markup. If the code involves tables nested inside each other, it's very difficult to remember which `<td>` element is related to which row of which table. Table-based layouts are very difficult to modify by hand.
- **Formatting is done cell by cell.** A Web page could be composed of hundreds of table cells. Making a change in the font or color often involves making changes in hundreds of cells throughout the page. This makes your page less flexible and harder to update.
- **Presentation is tied tightly to data.** A table-based layout tightly intertwines the data and its presentation. This runs counter to a primary goal of Web design — separation of data from its presentation.
- **Table-based layouts are hard to change.** After you create a layout based on tables, it's very difficult to make modifications because all the table cells have a potential effect on other cells.
- **Table-based layouts cause problems for screen readers.** People with visual disabilities use special software to read Web pages. These screen readers are well-adapted to read tables as they were intended (to manage tabular data), but the screen readers have no way of knowing when the table is being used as a layout technique rather than a data presentation tool. This makes table-based layouts less compliant to accessibility standards.

Resist the temptation to use tables for layout. Use tables to do what they're designed for: data presentation. Book III is entirely about how to use CSS to generate any kind of visual layout you might want. The CSS-based approaches are easier, more dependable, and much more flexible.

Chapter 5: Making Connections with Links

In This Chapter

- Understanding hyperlinks
- Building the anchor tag
- Recognizing absolute and relative links
- Building internal links
- Creating lists of links

The basic concept of the hyperlink is pretty common today, but it was a major breakthrough back in the day. The idea is still pretty phenomenal, if you think about it: If you click a certain piece of text (or a designated image, for that matter), your browser is instantly transported somewhere else. The new destination might be on the same computer as the initial page, or it could be literally anywhere in the world.

Any page is theoretically a threshold to any other page, and all information has the ability to be linked. This is still a profound idea. In this chapter, you discover how to add links to your pages.

Making Your Text Hyper

The hyperlink is truly a wonderful thing. Believe it or not, there was a time when you had to manually type in the address of the Web page you wanted to go to. Not so anymore. Figure 5-1 illustrates a page that describes some of my favorite Web sites.

In Figure 5-1, the underlined words are hyperlinks. Clicking a hyperlink takes you to the indicated Web site. Although this is undoubtedly familiar to you as a Web user, a few details are necessary to make this mechanism work:

- **Something must be linkable.** There must be some text or other element that provides a trigger for the linking behavior.
- **Things that are links should look like links.** This is actually pretty easy to do when you write plain XHTML because all links have a standard (if ugly) appearance. Links are usually underlined blue text. When you can

create color schemes, you may no longer want links to look like the default appearance, but they should still be recognizable as links.

- **The browser needs to know where to go.** When the user clicks the link, the browser is sent to some address somewhere on the Internet. Sometimes, that address is visible on the page, but it doesn't need to be.
- **It should be possible to integrate links into text.** In this example, each link is part of a sentence. It should be possible to make some things act like links without necessarily standing on their own (like heading tags do).
- **The link's appearance sometimes changes.** Links sometimes begin as blue underlined text, but after a link has been visited, the link is shown in purple, instead. After you know CSS, you can change this behavior.

Of course, if your Web page mentions some other Web site, you should provide a link to that other Web site.

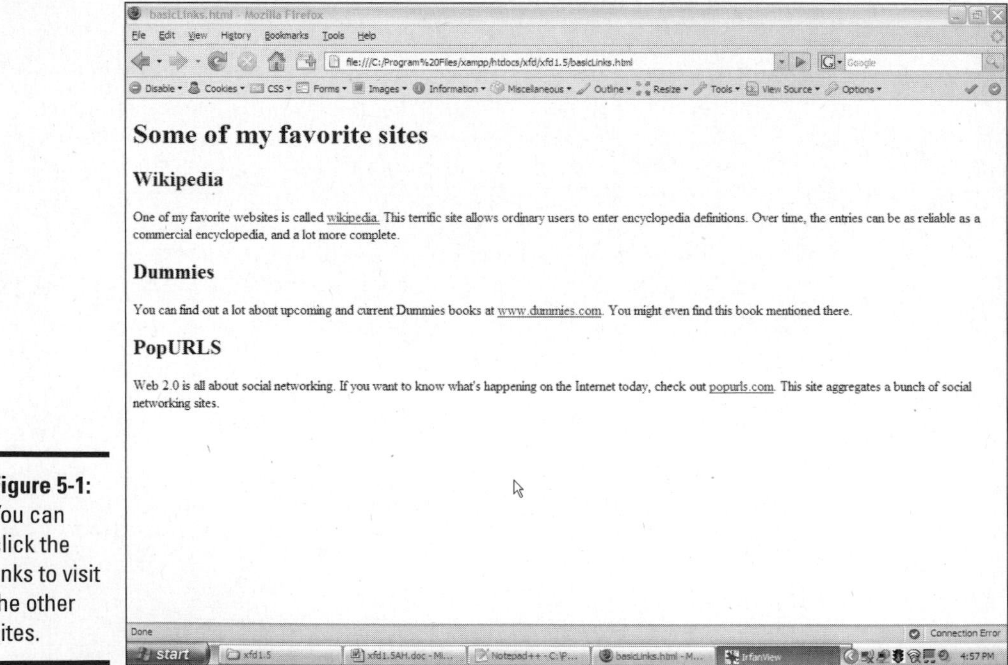

Figure 5-1: You can click the links to visit the other sites.

Introducing the anchor tag

The key to hypertext is an oddly-named tag called the *anchor* tag. This tag is encased in an `<a></a>` set of tags and contains all the information needed to manage links between pages.

The code for the `basicLinks.html` page is shown here:

```
<!DOCTYPE html PUBLIC "-//W3C//DTD XHTML 1.0 Strict//EN"
"http://www.w3.org/TR/xhtml1/DTD/xhtml1-strict.dtd">
<html lang="EN" dir="ltr" xmlns="http://www.w3.org/1999/xhtml">
  <head>
    <meta http-equiv="content-type" content="text/xml; charset=utf-8" />
    <title>basicLinks.html</title>
  </head>

  <body>
    <h1>Some of my favorite sites</h1>
      <h2>Wikipedia</h2>
      <p>
        One of my favorite Web sites is called
        <a href = "http://www.wikipedia.org">wikipedia.</a>
        This terrific site allows ordinary users to enter
        encyclopedia definitions. Over time, the entries
        can be as reliable as a commercial encyclopedia,
        and a lot more complete.
      </p>

      <h2>Dummies</h2>
      <p>
        You can find out a lot about upcoming and current
        Dummies books at <a href = "http://www.dummies.com">
        www.dummies.com</a>. You might even find this
        book mentioned there.
      </p>

      <h2>PopURLS</h2>
      <p>
        Web 2.0 is all about social networking. If you want
        to know what's happening on the Internet today,
        check out <a href = "http://popurls.com">
        popurls.com</a>. This site aggregates a bunch of
        social networking sites.
      </p>
    </ul>
  </body>
</html>
```

As you can see, the anchor tag is embedded into paragraphs. The text generally flows around an anchor, and you can see the anchor code is embedded inside the paragraphs.

Comparing block-level and inline elements

All the tags described so far in this book have been *block-level* tags. Block-level tags typically begin and end with carriage returns. For example, three `<h1>` tags occupy three lines. Each `<p></p>` set has implied space above and below it. Most XHTML tags are block-level.

Some tags are meant to be embedded inside block-level tags and don't interrupt the flow of the text. The anchor tag is one such tag. Anchors never stand on their own in the HTML body. They're meant to be embedded inside block-level tags, like list items, paragraphs, and headings.

Analyzing an anchor

Take another look at the first link. It shows all the main parts of an anchor in a pretty straightforward way:

```
<a href = "http://www.wikipedia.org">wikipedia.</a>
```

- **The anchor tag itself:** The anchor tag is simply the `<a></a>` pair. Note that you don't type the entire word **anchor**, just the **a**.
- **The hypertext reference (`href`) attribute:** Almost all anchors contain this attribute. It's very rare to write `<a` without `href`. The `href` attribute indicates a Web address will follow.
- **A Web address in quotes:** The address that the browser will follow is encased in quotes. See the next section in this chapter for more information on Web addresses. In this example, `http://www.wikipedia.org` is the address.
- **The text that appears as a link:** The user will typically expect to click specially formatted text. Any text that appears between the `<a href>` part and the `</a>` part is visible on the page and formatted as a link. In this example, the word `wikipedia` is the linked text.
- **The `</a>` marker:** This marker indicates that the text link is finished.

Introducing URLs

The special link addresses are a very important part of the Web. You probably already type Web addresses into the address bar of your browser (`www.google.com`), but you may not be completely aware of how they work. Web addresses are technically URLs (Uniform Resource Locators), and they have a very specific format.

Sometimes, you'll see the term *URI* (Uniform Resource Identifier) instead of URL. URI is technically a more correct name for Web addresses, but the term URL has caught on. The two terms are close enough to be interchangeable.

A URL usually contains the following parts:

- **Protocol:** A Web *protocol* is a standardized agreement on how communication occurs. The Web primarily uses HTTP (hypertext transfer protocol), but occasionally, you encounter others. Most addresses begin with `http://` because this is the standard on the Web. Protocols usually end with a colon and two slashes (`://`).
- **Host name:** It's traditional to name your primary Web server `www`. There's no requirement for this, but it's common enough that users expect to type **www** right after the `http://` stuff. Regardless, the text right after `http://` (and up to the first period) is the name of the actual computer you're linking to.
- **Domain name:** The last two or three characters indicate a particular type of Web server. These letters can indicate useful information about the type of organization that houses the page. Three-letter domains usually indicate the type of organization, and two-letter domains indicate a country. Sometimes, you'll even see a combination of the two. See Table 5-1 for a list of common domain names.
- **Subdomain:** Everything between the host name (usually `www`) and the domain name (often `.com`) is the subdomain. This is used so that large organizations can have multiple servers on the same domain. For example, my department Web page is `http://www.cs.iupui.edu`. `www` is the name of the primary server, and this is the computer science department at IUPUI (Indiana University–Purdue University Indianapolis), which is an educational organization.
- **Page name:** Sometimes, an address specifies a particular document on the Web. This page name follows the address and usually ends with `.html`. Sometimes, the page name includes subdirectories and username information, as well. For example, my Web design course is in the N241 directory of my (aharris) space at IUPUI, so its full address is `http://www.cs.iupui.edu/~aharris/n241/index.html`.
- **Username:** Some Web servers are set up with multiple users. Sometimes, an address will indicate a specific user's account with a tilde (~) character. My address has `~aharris` in it to indicate the page is found in my (aharris) account on the machine.

The page name is sometimes optional. Many servers have a special name set up as the default page, which appears if no other name is specified. This name is usually `index.html` but sometimes `home.htm`. On my server, `index.html` is the default name, so I usually just point to `www.cs.iupui.edu/~aharris/n241`, and the index page appears.

Table 5-1 Common Domain Names

Domain	*Explanation*
`.org`	Non-profit institution
`.com`	Commercial enterprise
`.edu`	Educational institution
`.gov`	Governing body
`.ca`	Canada
`.uk`	United Kingdom
`.tv`	Tuvalu

Making Lists of Links

Many Web pages turn out to be lists of links. Because lists and links go so well together, it's good to look at an example. Figure 5-2 illustrates a list of links.

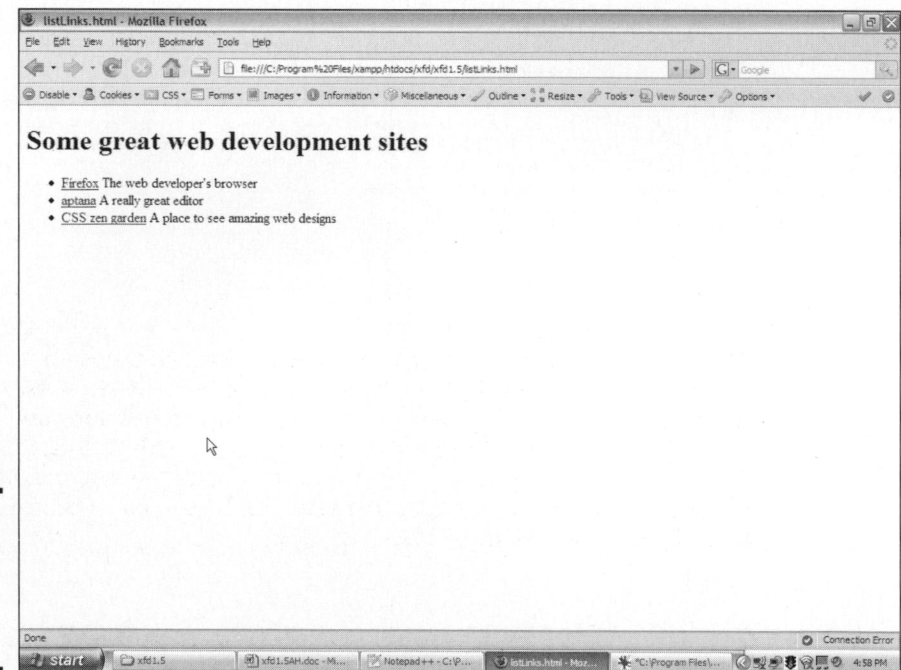

Figure 5-2: It's very common to put links in a list.

There's no new code to figure out in this example, but the page shows some interesting components:

- **The list:** An ordinary unordered list.
- **Links:** Each list item contains a link. The link has a reference (which you can't see immediately) and linkable text (which is marked like an ordinary link).
- **Descriptive text:** After each link is some ordinary text that describes the link. It's very common to write some text to accompany the actual link.

This code shows the way this page is organized:

```
<!DOCTYPE html PUBLIC "-//W3C//DTD XHTML 1.0 Strict//EN"
"http://www.w3.org/TR/xhtml1/DTD/xhtml1-strict.dtd">
<html lang="EN" dir="ltr" xmlns="http://www.w3.org/1999/xhtml">
  <head>
    <meta http-equiv="content-type" content="text/xml; charset=utf-8" />
    <title>listLinks.html</title>
  </head>

  <body>
    <h1>Some great Web development sites</h1>
    <ul>
      <li><a href = "http://getfirefox.org">
          Firefox</a>
          The Web developer's browser</li>
      <li><a href = "http://www.aptana.org">
          aptana</a>
          A really great editor</li>
      <li><a href = "csszengarden.com">
          CSS zen garden</a>
          A place to see amazing Web designs</li>
    </ul>
  </body>
</html>
```

The indentation is interesting here. Each list item contains an anchor and some descriptive text. To keep it all organized, Web developers tend to place the anchor inside the list item. The address sometimes goes on a new line if it's long, with the anchor text on a new line and the description on succeeding lines. I normally put the `<li>` tag at the end of the last line, so the beginning `<li>` tags look like the bullets of an unordered list. This makes it easier to find your place when editing a list later.

Working with Absolute and Relative References

There's more than one kind of address. So far, you've seen only absolute references, used for links to outside pages. There's another kind of reference — a relative reference — used to link multiple pages inside your own Web site.

Understanding absolute references

The type of link used in `basicLinks.html` is an *absolute reference.* Absolute references always begin with the protocol name (usually `http://`). An absolute reference is the complete address to a Web page, just like you'd use in the browser's address bar. Absolute references are used to refer to a site somewhere else on the Internet. Even if your Web site moves (say, from your desktop machine to a Web server somewhere on the Internet), all the absolute references will work fine because they don't rely on the current page's position for any information.

Introducing relative references

Relative references are used when your Web site includes more than one page. You might choose to have several pages and a link mechanism for moving among them. Figure 5-3 shows a page with several links on it.

The page isn't so interesting on its own, but it isn't meant to stand alone. When you click one of the links, you go to a brand-new page. Figure 5-4 shows what happens when you click the market link.

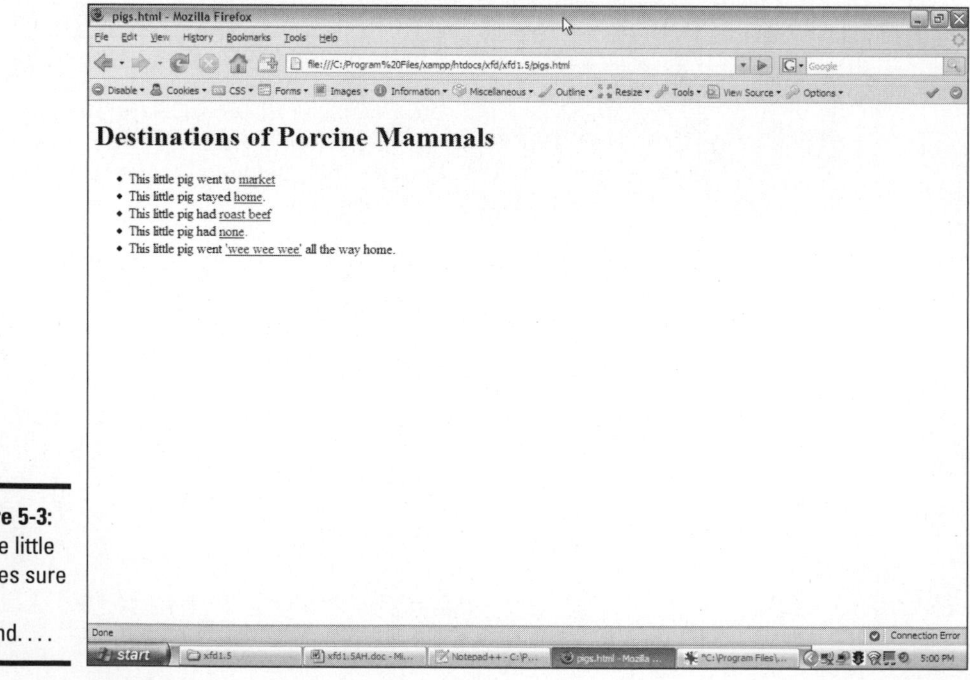

Figure 5-3: These little piggies sure get around. . . .

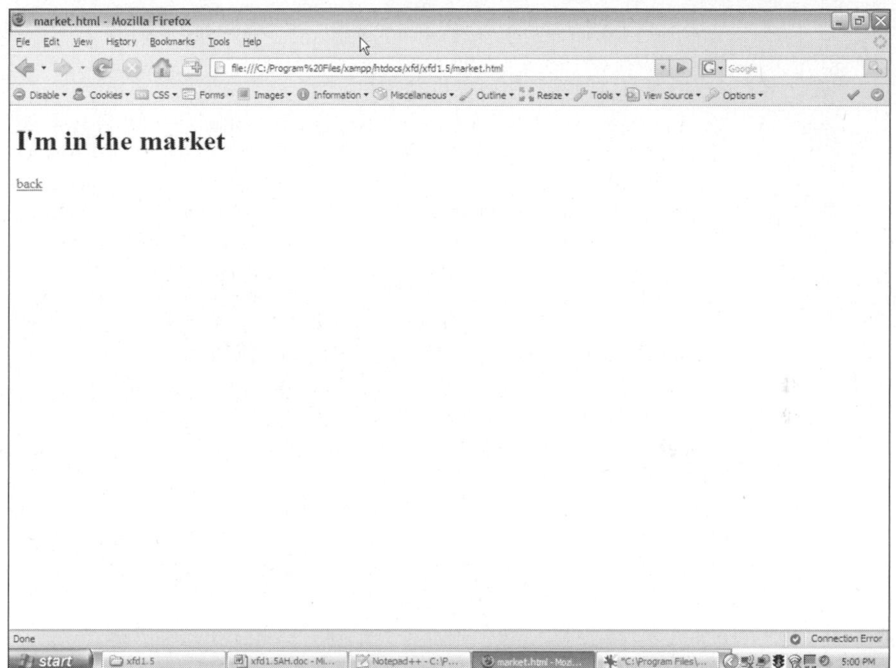

Figure 5-4: The market page lets you move back.

The market page is pretty simple, but it also contains a link back to the initial page. Most Web sites aren't single pages at all, but an interconnected web of pages. The relative reference is very useful when you have a set of pages with interlacing links.

The code for `pigs.html` shows how relative references work:

```
<!DOCTYPE html PUBLIC "-//W3C//DTD XHTML 1.0 Strict//EN"
"http://www.w3.org/TR/xhtml1/DTD/xhtml1-strict.dtd">
<html lang="EN" dir="ltr" xmlns="http://www.w3.org/1999/xhtml">
  <head>
    <meta http-equiv="content-type" content="text/xml; charset=utf-8" />
    <title>pigs.html</title>
  </head>

  <body>
    <h1>Destinations of Porcine Mammals</h1>
    <ul>
      <li>This little pig went to
          <a href = "market.html">market</a></li>
      <li>This little pig stayed
          <a href = "home.html">home</a>.</li>
      <li>This little pig had
          <a href = "roastBeef.html">roast beef</a></li>
      <li>This little pig had
          <a href = "none.html">none</a>.</li>
      <li>This little pig went
          <a href = "wee.html">'wee wee wee'</a>
```

```
        all the way home.</li>
    </ul>
  </body>
</html>
```

Most of the code is completely familiar. The only thing surprising is what's *not* there. Take a closer look at one of the links:

```
<a href = "market.html">home</a>.</li>
```

Note there's no protocol (the `http://` part) and no address at all, just a filename. This is a *relative reference.* Relative references work by assuming the address of the current page. When the user clicks `market.html`, the browser sees no protocol, so it assumes that `market.html` is in the same directory on the same server as `pigs.html`.

Relative references work like directions. For example, if you're in my lab and ask where the water fountain is, I'd say, "Go out into the hallway, turn left, and turn left again at the end of the next hallway." Those directions get you to the water fountain if you start in the right place. If you're someplace else and you follow the same directions, you don't really know where you'll end up.

Relative references work well when you have a bunch of interconnected Web pages. If you make a lot of pages about the same topic and put them in the same directory, you can use relative references between the pages. If you decide to move your pages to another server, all the links still work correctly.

In Book VIII, you discover how to set up a permanent Web server. It's often most convenient to create and modify your pages on the local machine and then ship them to the Web server for the world to see. If you use relative references, it's easy to move a group of pages together and know the links will still work.

If you're referring to a page on somebody else's site, you have to use an absolute reference. If you're linking to another page on your site, you typically use a relative reference.

Chapter 6: Adding Images

In This Chapter

- ✓ **Understanding the main uses of images**
- ✓ **Choosing an image format**
- ✓ **Creating inline images**
- ✓ **Using IrfanView and other image software**
- ✓ **Changing image sizes**
- ✓ **Modifying images with filters**

You have the basics of text, but pages without images are . . . well, a little boring. Pictures do a lot for a Web page, and they're not that hard to work with. Still, you should know some things about using pictures in your pages. In this chapter, you get all the fundamentals of adding images to your pages.

Adding Images to Your Pages

Every time you explore the Web, you're bound to run into tons of pictures on just about every page you visit. Images are typically used in four different ways on Web pages:

- ✦ **External link:** The page has text with a link embedded in it. When the user clicks the link, the image replaces the page in the Web browser. To make an externally linked image, just make an ordinary link (as I describe in Chapter 5 of this minibook) but point toward an image file, rather than an HTML (HyperText Markup Language) file.
- ✦ **Embedded images:** The image is embedded into the page directly. The text of the page usually flows around the image. This is the most common type of image used on the Web.
- ✦ **Background images:** An image can be used as a background for the entire page or for a specific part of the page. Images usually require some special manipulation to make them suitable for background use.
- ✦ **Custom bullets:** With CSS, you can assign a small image to be a bullet for an ordered or unordered list. This allows you to make any kind of customized list markers you can draw.

The techniques you read about in this chapter apply to all type of images, but a couple of specific applications (such as backgrounds and bullets) use CSS. For details on using images in CSS, see Book II, Chapter 4.

Adding links to images

The easiest way to incorporate images is to simply make a link to them. Figure 6-1 shows a page called `externalImage.html`.

The page's code isn't much more than a simple link:

```
<!DOCTYPE html PUBLIC "-//W3C//DTD XHTML 1.0 Strict//EN"
"http://www.w3.org/TR/xhtml1/DTD/xhtml1-strict.dtd">
<html lang="EN" dir="ltr" xmlns="http://www.w3.org/1999/xhtml">
  <head>
    <meta http-equiv="content-type" content="text/xml; charset=utf-8" />
    <title>externalImage.html</title>
  </head>

  <body>
    <h1>Linking to an External Image</h1>
    <p>
      <a href = "shipStandard.jpg">
        Susan B. Constant
      </a>
    </p>
  </body>
</html>
```

Note that the `href` points to an image file, not an HTML page. You can point to any type of file you want in an anchor tag. If the browser knows the file type (for example, HTML and standard image formats), the browser displays the file directly. If the browser doesn't know the file format, the user's computer tries to display the file using whatever program it normally uses to open that type of file.

See Chapter 5 of this minibook for a discussion of anchor tags if you need a refresher.

This works fine for most images because the image is displayed directly in the browser.

You can use this anchor trick with any kind of file, but the results can be very unpredictable. If you use the link trick to point to some odd file format, there's no guarantee the user has the appropriate software to view it. It's generally best to save this trick for very common formats, like GIF and JPG. (If these formats are unfamiliar to you, they are described later in this chapter.)

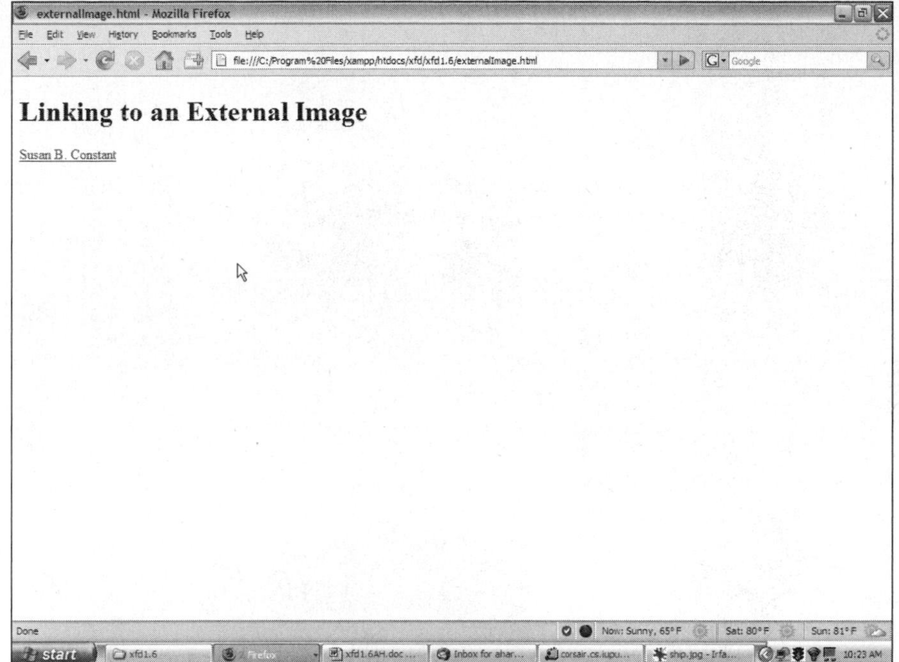

Figure 6-1: This page has a link to an image.

Note that most browsers automatically resize the image to fit the browser size. This means a large image may appear to be smaller than it really is, but the user still has to wait for the entire image to download.

Because this is a relative reference, the indicated image must be in the same directory as the HTML file. When the user clicks the link, the page is replaced by the image, as shown in Figure 6-2.

External links are easy to create, but they have some problems:

- **They don't preview the image.** The user has only the text description to figure out what the picture might be.
- **They interrupt the flow.** If the page contains a series of images, the user has to keep leaving the page to view images.
- **The user must back up to return to the main page.** The image looks like a Web page, but it isn't. No links or other explanatory text in the image indicate how to get back to the Web page. Most users know to click the browser's Back button, but don't assume they all know what to do.

Figure 6-2: The image appears in place of the page.

Adding inline images using the <img> tag

The alternative to providing links to images is to embed your images directly into the page. Figure 6-3 displays an example of this technique.

The code shows how this image was included into the page:

```
<!DOCTYPE html PUBLIC "-//W3C//DTD XHTML 1.0 Strict//EN"
"http://www.w3.org/TR/xhtml1/DTD/xhtml1-strict.dtd">
<html lang="EN" dir="ltr" xmlns="http://www.w3.org/1999/xhtml">
  <head>
    <meta http-equiv="content-type" content="text/xml; charset=utf-8" />
    <title>embeddedImage.html</title>
  </head>

  <body>
    <h1>The Susan B. Constant</h1>
    <p>
      <img src = "shipStandard.jpg"
           height = "480"
           width = "640"
           alt = "Susan B. Constant" />
    </p>

    <p>
```

```
        The <em>Susan B. Constant</em> was flagship of the fleet of three
        small ships that brought settlers to Jamestown, the first successful
        English Colony in the new world.  This is a replica housed
        near Jamestown, Virginia.
      </p>
    </body>
  </html>
```

The image (`img`) tag is the star of this page. This tag allows you to grab an image file and incorporate it into the page directly. The image tag is a one-shot tag. It doesn't end with `</img>`. Instead, use the `/>` characters at the end of the `img` definition to indicate that this tag doesn't have content.

You might have noticed that I italicized *Susan B. Constant* in the page, and I used the `<em>` tag to get this effect. `<em>` stands for *emphasis,* and `<strong>` means *strong emphasis.* By default, any text within an `<em></em>` pair is italicized, and `<strong></strong>` text is boldfaced. Of course, you can change this behavior with CSS.

The image tag has a number of important attributes, which I discuss in the following sections.

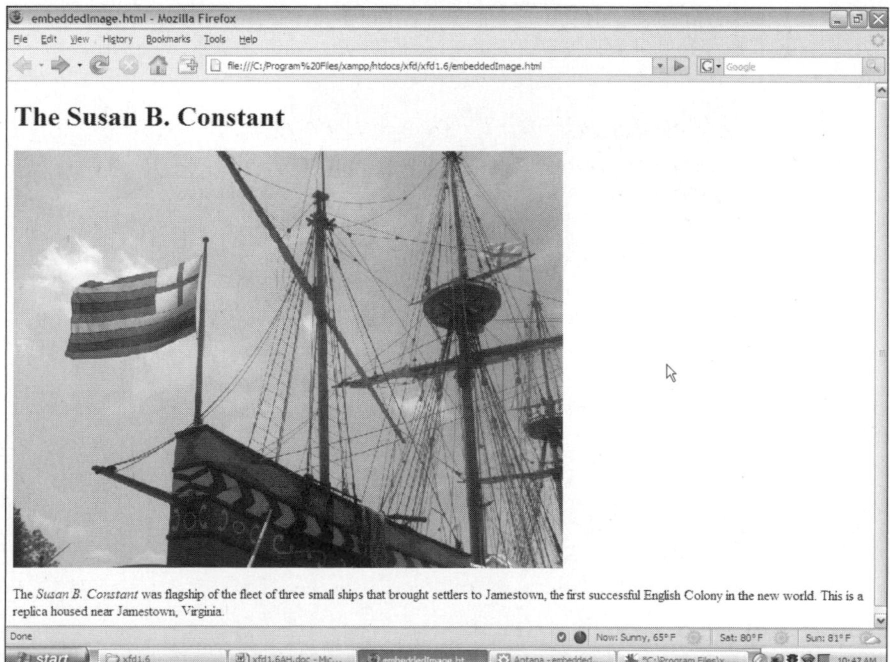

Figure 6-3: The ship image is embedded directly into the page.

src (source)

The `src` attribute allows you to indicate the URL (Uniform Resource Locator) of the image. This can be an absolute or relative reference. Linking to an image on your own system is generally best because you can't be sure an external image will still be there when the user gets to the page. (For more on reference types, turn to Chapter 5 of this minibook.)

height and width

These attributes are used to indicate the size of the image. The browser uses this information to indicate how much space to reserve on the page.

It's tempting to use the `height` and `width` attributes to change the size of the image on the Web page — this is a bad idea. Change the image size with your image editor (I show you how later in this chapter). If you use the `height` and `width` attributes, the user has to wait for the full image, even if she'll see a smaller version. Don't make the user wait for information she won't see. If you use these attributes to make the image larger than its default size, the resulting image has poor resolution. Find the image's actual size by looking at it in your image tool and use these values. If you leave out `height` and `width`, the browser determines the size automatically, but you aren't guaranteed to see the text until all the images have downloaded. Adding these attributes lets the browser format the page without waiting for the images.

alt (alternate text)

The `alt` attribute gives you an opportunity to specify alternate text describing the image. Alternate text information is used when the user has images turned off and by screen readers. Internet Explorer (IE) automatically creates a *ToolTip* (floating text) based on the alternate text.

You can actually add a floating ToolTip to any element using the `title` attribute. This works in all standards-compliant browsers, with nearly any HTML element.

Keep in mind, the `alt` attribute is required on all images if you want to validate XHTML Strict.

Note that the `<img>` tag is an inline tag, so it needs to be embedded inside a block-level tag, like a `<p>` or `<li>`.

Choosing an Image Manipulation Tool

You can't just grab any old picture off your digital camera and expect it to work on a Web page. The picture might work, but it could cause problems for your viewers. It's important to understand a few important ideas about images on the computer. *Digital images* (any kind of images you see on a computer or similar device) are different than the kind of images you see on paper.

An image is worth 3.4 million words!

Digital cameras and scanners are amazing these days. Even moderately priced cameras can now approach the resolution of old-school analog cameras. Scanners are also capable of taking traditional images and converting them into digital formats that computers use. In both cases, though, the default image can be in a format that causes problems. Digital images are stored as a series of dots, or *pixels.* In print, the dots are very close together, but computer screens have larger dots. Figure 6-4 shows the ship image as it looks straight from the digital camera.

My camera handles pictures at 6 megapixels (MP). That's a pretty good resolution, and it sounds very good in the electronics store. If I print that picture on paper, all those dots are very tiny, and I get a nice picture. If I try to show the same picture on the computer screen, I see only one corner. This actual picture came out at 2,816 pixels wide by 2,112 pixels tall. You only see a small corner of the image because the screen shots for this book are taken at 1024 x 768 pixels. Less than a quarter of the image is visible.

Figure 6-4: Wow. That doesn't look like much.

When you look at a large image in most browsers, it's automatically resized to fit the page. The cursor usually turns into some kind of magnifying glass, and if you click the image, you can see it in its full size or the smaller size.

Some image viewers take very large images and automatically resize them so they fit the screen. (This is the default behavior of Windows' default image viewer and most browsers.) The image may appear to be a reasonable size because of this feature, but it'll be huge and difficult to download in an actual Web page. Make sure you know the actual size of an image before you use it.

It's obvious that you need to shrink an image so it's all visible, but there's an even more compelling reason. Each pixel on the screen requires three bytes of computer memory. (A *byte* is the basic unit of memory in a computer.) For comparison purposes, one character of text requires roughly one byte. The uncompressed image of the ship weighs a whopping 17 megabytes (MB). If you think of a word as five characters long, one picture straight from the digital camera takes up the same amount of storage space and transmission time as roughly 3,400,000 words. This image requires nearly three minutes to download on a 56K modem!

In a Web page, small images are often shown at about 320 x 240 pixels, and larger images are often 640 x 480 pixels. If I use software to resample the image to the size I actually need and use an appropriate compression algorithm, I can get the image to look like Figure 6-5.

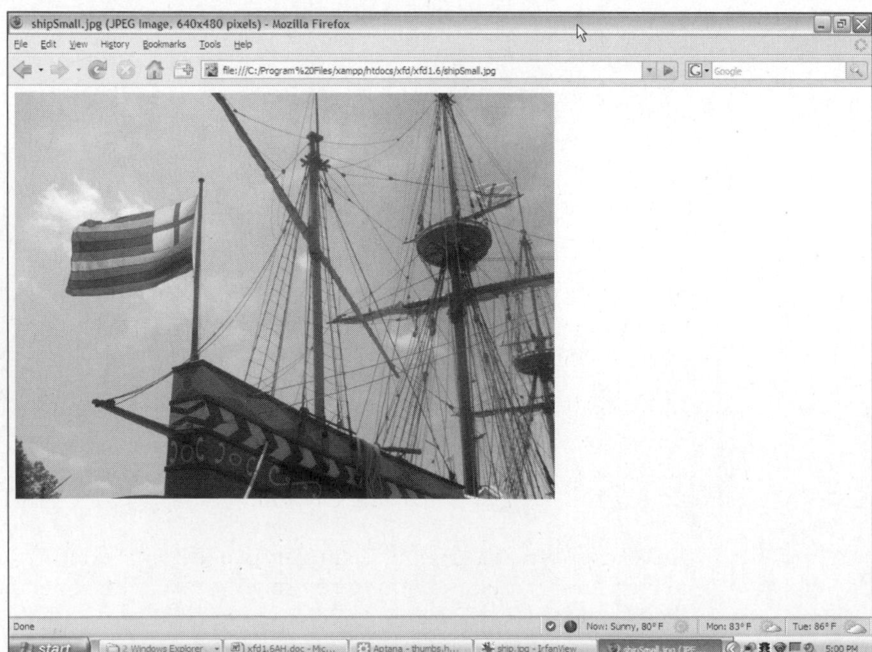

Figure 6-5: The resized image is a lot more manageable.

The new version of the image is the size and file format I need, it looks just as good, and it weighs a much more reasonable 88 kilobytes. That's 2 percent of the original image size.

Although this picture is a lot smaller than the original image, it still takes up a lot more memory than text. Even this smaller image takes up as much transmission time and storage space as 1,600 words! It still takes 10 seconds to download on a 56K modem. Use images wisely.

Images are great, but keep some things in mind when you use them:

✦ **Make sure the images are worth displaying.** Don't use a picture without some good reason because each picture makes your page dramatically slower to access.

✦ **Use software to resize your image.** Later in this chapter, I show you how to use free software to change the image to exactly the size you need.

✦ **Use a compressed format.** Images are almost never used in their native format on the Web because they're just too large. Several formats have emerged that are useful for working with various types of images. I describe these formats in the section "Choosing an Image Format," later in this chapter.

If you're curious how I determined the download speed of these images, it's pretty easy. The Web Developer toolbar (which I mention in Chapter 3 of this minibook) has a View Speed Report option on the Tools menu that does the job for you.

Introducing IrfanView

IrfanView, by Irfan Skiljan, is a freeware program that can handle your basic image manipulation needs and quite a bit more. I used it for all the screenshots in this book, and I use it as my primary image viewer. A copy is included on the CD-ROM that accompanies this book, or you can get a copy at `www.irfanview.net`. Of course, you can use any software you want, but if something's really good and free, it's a great place to start. In the rest of this chapter, I show you how to do all the main image processing jobs with IrfanView, but you can use any image editor you want.

A Web developer needs to have an image manipulation program to help with all these chores. Like other Web development tools, you can pay quite a bit for an image manipulation tool, but you don't have to. Your image tool should have at least the following capabilities:

✦ **Resizing:** Web pages require smaller images than printing on paper. You need a tool that allows you to resize your image to a specific size for Web display.

- **Saving to different formats:** There's a dizzying number of image formats available, but only three formats work reliably on the Web (which I discuss in the next section). You need a tool that can take images in a wide variety of formats and reliably switch it to a Web-friendly format.
- **Cropping:** You may want only a small part of the original picture. A cropping tool allows you to extract a rectangular region from an image.
- **Filters:** You may find it necessary to modify your image in some way. You may want to reduce red-eye, lighten or darken your image, or adjust the colors. Sometimes, images can be improved with sharpen or blur filters, or more artistic filters like canvas or oil-painting tools.
- **Batch processing:** You may have a number of images you want to work with at once. A batch processing utility can perform an operation on a large number of images at once, as you see later in this chapter.

You may want some other capabilities, too, such as the ability to make composite images, images with transparency, and more powerful effects. You can use commercial tools or the excellent open-source program *Gimp,* which is included on the CD-ROM. This chapter focuses on IrfanView because it's simpler, but investigate Gimp (or its cousin *GimpShop,* for people used to Photoshop) for a more complete and even more powerful tool. I use IrfanView for basic processing, and I use Gimp when I need a little more power.

Here are a few free alternatives if you want some other great software to try:

- **XnView:** Similar to IrfanView, allows you to preview and modify pictures in hundreds of formats, create thumbnails, and more.
- **Pixia:** A full-blown graphic editor from Japan. Very powerful.
- **GimpShop:** A version of Gimp modified to have menus like Photoshop.
- **Paint.net:** A powerful Windows-only paint program.

Use Google or another search engine to locate any of these programs.

Choosing an Image Format

Almost nobody uses raw images on the Web because they're just too big and unwieldy. Web images are usually compressed to take up less space. All the different types of image files you see in the computer world (BMP, JPG, GIF, and so on) are essentially different ways to make an image file smaller. Not all the formats work on the Web, and they have different characteristics, so it's good to know a little more about them.

BMP

The BMP format is Microsoft's standard image format. Although it's compressed sometimes, usually it isn't. The BMP format creates very detailed images with little to no compression, and the file is often too large to use on the Web. Many Web browsers can handle BMP images, but you shouldn't use them. Convert to one of the other formats, instead.

JPG/JPEG

The JPG format (sometimes also called JPEG) is a relatively old format designed by the Joint Photographic Experts Group. (Get it? JPEG!) It works by throwing away data that's less important to human perception. Every time you save an image in the JPG format, you lose a little information. This sounds terrible, but it really isn't. The same image that came up as 13MB in its raw format is squeezed down to 1.5MB when stored as a JPG. Most people can't tell the difference between the compressed and non-compressed version of the image by looking at them.

The JPG algorithm focuses on the parts of the image that are important to perception (brightness and contrast, for example) and throws away data that isn't as important (much of the color data is actually thrown away, but the colors are re-created in an elaborate optical illusion).

JPG works best on photographic-style images with a lot of color and detail. Many digital cameras save images directly as JPGs.

One part of the JPG process allows you to determine the amount of compression. When you save an image as a JPG, you can often determine the quality on a scale between accuracy and compression.

Even if you choose 100-percent accuracy, the file is still greatly compressed. The adjustable compression operates only on a small part of the process. Compressing the file too much can cause visible square shadows, or *artifacts.* Experiment with your images to see how much compression they can take and still look like the original.

Keep a high-quality original around when you're making JPG versions of an image because each copy loses some detail. If you make a JPG from a JPG that came from another JPG, the loss of detail starts to add up, and the picture loses some visual quality.

GIF

The GIF format was developed originally for CompuServe, way before the Web was invented. This format was a breakthrough in its time, and it still has some great characteristics.

GIF is a *lossless* algorithm, so potentially no data is lost when converting an image to GIF (compare that to the *lossy* JPG format). GIF does its magic with a *color palette* trick and a *run-length encoding* trick.

The color palette works like a paint-by-number set where an image has a series of numbers printed on it, and each of the paint colors has a corresponding number. What happens in a GIF image is similar. GIF images have a list of 256 colors, automatically chosen from the image. Each of the colors is given a number. A *raw* (uncompressed) image requires 3 bytes of information for each pixel (1 each to determine the amount of red, green, and blue). In a GIF image, all that information is stored one time in the color palette. The image itself contains a bunch of references to the color palette.

For example, if blue is stored as color 1 in the palette, a strip of blue might look like this:

1, 1, 1, 1, 1, 1, 1, 1, 1, 1

GIF uses its other trick — run-length encoding — when it sees a list of identical colors. Rather than store the above value as 1, 1, 1, 1, 1, 1, 1, 1, 1, 1, the GIF format can specify a list of 10 ones. That's the general idea of run-length encoding. The ship image in this example weighs 2.92MB as a full-size GIF image.

The GIF format works best for images with a relatively small number of colors and large areas of the same color. Most drawings you make in a drawing program convert very well to the GIF format. Photos aren't ideal because they usually have more than 256 colors in them, and the subtle changes in color mean there are very few solid blotches of color to take advantage of run-length encoding.

GIF does have a couple of really great advantages that keep it popular. First, a GIF image can have a transparent color defined. Typically, you'll choose some awful color not found in nature (kind of like choosing bridesmaid dresses) to be the transparent color. Then, when the GIF encounters a pixel that color, it displays whatever is underneath instead. This is a crude but effective form of transparency. Figure 6-6 shows an image with transparency.

Whenever you see an image on a Web page that doesn't appear to be rectangular, there's a good chance the image is a GIF. The image is still a rectangle, but it has transparency to make it look more organic. Typically, whatever color you set as the background color when you save a GIF becomes the transparent color.

Creating a complex transparent background, like the statue, requires a more complex tool than IrfanView. I used Gimp, but any high-end graphics tool can do the job. IrfanView is more suited to operations that work on the entire image.

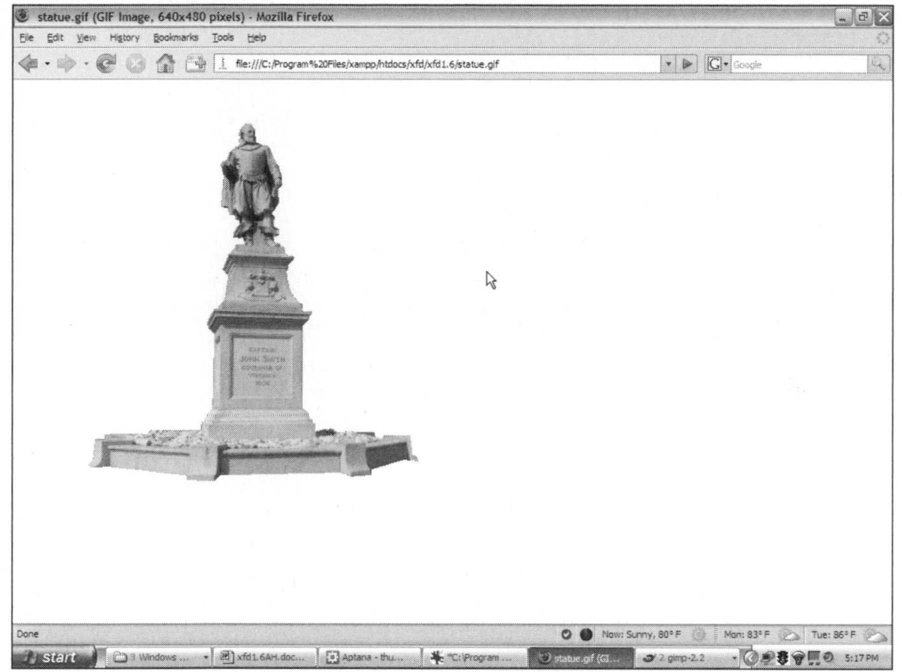

Figure 6-6: This statue is a GIF with transparency.

Another interesting feature of GIF is the ability to create animations. Animated GIFs are a series of images stored in the same file. You can embed information, determining the interval between images. You can create animated GIFs with Gimp, which is included on the CD-ROM.

Animated GIFs were heavily over-used in the early days of the Web, and many now consider them the mark of an amateur. Nobody really thinks that animated mailbox is cute anymore.

For awhile, there were some legal encumbrances regarding a part of the GIF scheme. The owners of this algorithm tried to impose a license fee. This was passed on to people using commercial software but became a big problem for free software creators.

Fortunately, it appears that the legal complications have been resolved for now. Still, you'll see a lot of open-software advocates avoiding the GIF algorithm altogether because of this problem.

PNG

Open-source software advocates created a new image format that combines some of the best features of both JPG and GIF, with no legal problems. The resulting format is *Portable Network Graphics,* or *PNG.* This format has a number of interesting features, such as

- **Lossless compression:** Like GIF, PNG stores data without losing any information.
- **Dynamic color palette:** PNG supports as many colors as you want. You aren't limited to 256 colors like you are in GIF.
- **No software patents:** The underlying technology of PNG is completely open source, with no worries about whether somebody will try to enforce a copyright down the road.
- **True alpha transparency:** The PNG format has a more sophisticated form of transparency than GIF. Each pixel can be stored with an alpha value. *Alpha* refers to the amount of transparency. The alpha can be adjusted from completely transparent to completely opaque.

With all its advantages, you might expect PNG to be the most popular image format on the Web. Surprisingly, it's been slow to catch on. The main reason for this is spotty support for PNG in Internet Explorer (IE). Even the latest version of IE doesn't support PNG's alpha transparency correctly.

Summary of Web image formats

All these formats may seem overwhelming, but it's pretty easy to choose an image format because each format has its own advantages and disadvantages:

- **GIF** is best when you need transparency or animation. Avoid using GIF on photos, as you won't get optimal compression, and you'll lose color data.
- **JPG** is most useful for photographic images, which are best suited for the JPG compression technique. However, keep in mind that JPG isn't suitable for images that require transparency. Text in JPG images tends to become difficult to read because of the lossy compression technique.
- **PNG** is useful in most situations, but be aware that IE doesn't handle PNG transparency correctly. (You sometimes see strange color blotches where you expect transparency.)
- **BMP and other formats** should be avoided entirely. Although you can make other formats work in certain circumstances, there's no good reason to use any other image formats most of the time.

Coming soon — vector formats

Here's another form of image format that will hopefully gain more prominence in the future. All the formats described so far are *raster-based* image formats. This type of image stores an image as a series of dots. *Vector-based* image formats use formulas to store the instructions to draw an image. Certain kinds of images (especially charts and basic line art) can be far more efficient when stored as vector formats. Unfortunately, IE and Firefox support different and incompatible vector formats, so it doesn't look like vector-based images will be a factor soon. Flash also uses vector-based techniques, but this technique requires expensive proprietary software to create vector images and a third-party plugin to use them.

Manipulating Your Images

All this talk of compression algorithms and resizing images may be dandy, but how do you do it?

Fortunately, IrfanView can do nearly anything you need for free. IrfanView has nice features for all the main types of image manipulation you need.

Changing formats in IrfanView

Changing image formats with IrfanView is really easy. For example, find an image file on your computer and follow these steps:

1. **Load the image into IrfanView by dragging the image into IrfanView or using the menu File➪Open command.**
2. **Make any changes you may want to the image before saving.**
3. **Use the File➪Save As command to save the file.**
4. **Pick the image format from the Save Picture As dialog box, as shown in Figure 6-7.**
5. **Save the file with a new filename.**

   Keep the original file and save any changes in a new file. That way, you don't overwrite the original file. This is especially important if you're converting to JPG because each successive save of a JPG causes some image loss.

Figure 6-7: IrfanView can save in all these formats.

Don't use spaces in your filenames. Your files may move to other computers on the Internet, and some computers have trouble with spaces. It's best to avoid spaces and punctuation (except the underscore character) on any files that will be used on the Internet.

Resizing your images

All the other image-manipulation tricks may be optional, but you should *really* resize your images. Although high-speed modems may have no trouble with a huge image, nothing makes a Web page inaccessible to dialup users faster than bloated image sizes.

To resize an image with IrfanView, perform the following steps:

1. **Load the image into IrfanView.**

   You can do this by dragging the image onto the IrfanView icon, dragging into an open instance of IrfanView, or using the menus within IrfanView.

2. **From the Image menu, choose Resize/Resample.**

   You can also use Ctrl+R for this step. Figure 6-8 shows the resulting dialog box.

Figure 6-8: IrfanView's Resize/ Resample Image dialog box.

3. **Determine the new image size.**

A number of standard image sizes are available. 800 x 600 pixels will create a large image in most browsers. If you want the image smaller, you need to enter a size directly in the text boxes. Images embedded in Web pages are often 320 pixels wide by 240 pixels tall. That's a very good starting point. Anything smaller will be hard to see, and anything larger might take up too much screen space.

4. **Preserve the aspect ratio using the provided check box.**

This makes sure the ratio between height and width is maintained. Otherwise, the image may be distorted.

5. **Save the resulting image as a new file.**

When you make an image smaller, you lose data. That's perfectly fine for the version you put on the Web, but you should hang on to the original large image in case you want to resize again.

6. **Resample, rather than resize.**

Resampling is a slower but more accurate technique for changing the image size. This is IrfanView's default behavior, so leave it alone. It's still quite fast on a modern computer. The default (Lanczos) filter is fine, although you can experiment with other filters to get a faster conversion, if you want.

Enhancing image colors

Sometimes, you can make improvements to an image by modifying the colors. The Enhance Colors dialog box on the Images menu gives you a wide range of options, as shown in Figure 6-9.

You can do a surprising number of helpful operations on an image with this tool:

- **Brightness:** When adjusted to a higher value, the image becomes closer to white. When adjusted to a negative value, the image becomes closer to black. This is useful when you want to make an image lighter or darker for use as a background image.

  If your image is too dark or too bright, you may be tempted to use the Brightness feature to fix it. The Gamma Correction feature described later in this section is more useful for this task.

- **Contrast:** You usually use the Contrast feature in conjunction with the Brightness feature to adjust an image. Sometimes, an image can be improved with small amounts of contrast adjustments.

Figure 6-9: You can change several options in the Enhance Colors dialog box.

✦ **Color Balance:** Sometimes, an image has poor color balance (for example, indoor lighting sometimes creates a bluish cast). You can adjust the amount of red, green, and blue with a series of sliders. The easiest way to manage color balance is to look at a part of the image that's supposed to be white and play with the slider until it looks truly white.

✦ **Gamma Correction:** This is used to correct an image that is too dark or too light. Unlike the Brightness adjustment, Gamma Correction automatically adjusts the contrast. Small adjustments to this slider can sometimes fix images that are a little too dark or too light.

✦ **Saturation:** When saturation is at its smallest value, the image becomes black and white. At its largest value, the colors are enhanced. Use this control to create a grayscale image or to enhance colors for artistic effect.

Using built-in effects

IrfanView has a few other effects available that can sometimes be extremely useful. These effects can be found individually on the Image menu or with the Effects browser on the Image menu. The Effects browser (as shown in Figure 6-10) is often a better choice because it gives you a little more control of most effects and provides interactive feedback on what the effect will do. Effects are sometimes called *filters* because they pass the original image through a math function, which acts like a filter or processor to create the modified output.

Figure 6-10: The Effects browser lets you choose special effects.

Here's a run-down of some of the effects and when you would use them:

✦ **None:** Just for comparison purposes, Figure 6-11 shows the ship image with no filters turned on.

I've exaggerated the effects for illustration purposes, but it may still be difficult to see the full effect of these filters on the printed page. The grayscale images in this book are a poor representation of the actual color images. Use the images in this chapter as a starting point, but to understand these filters, you really need to experiment with your own images in IrfanView or a similar tool.

✦ **Blur:** This filter reduces contrast between adjacent pixels. (Really, we could go over the math, but let's leave that for another day, huh?) You might wonder why you'd make an image more blurry on purpose. Sometimes, the blur filter can fix graininess in an image. You can also use blur in conjunction with sharpen (which I cover in just a moment) to fix small flaws in an image. I applied the blur filter to the standard ship image in Figure 6-12.

✦ **Sharpen:** The opposite of blur, the sharpen filter enhances the contrast between adjacent pixels. When used carefully, it can sometimes improve an image. The sharpen filter is most effective in conjunction with the blur filter to remove small artifacts. Figure 6-13 shows the ship image with the sharpen filter applied.

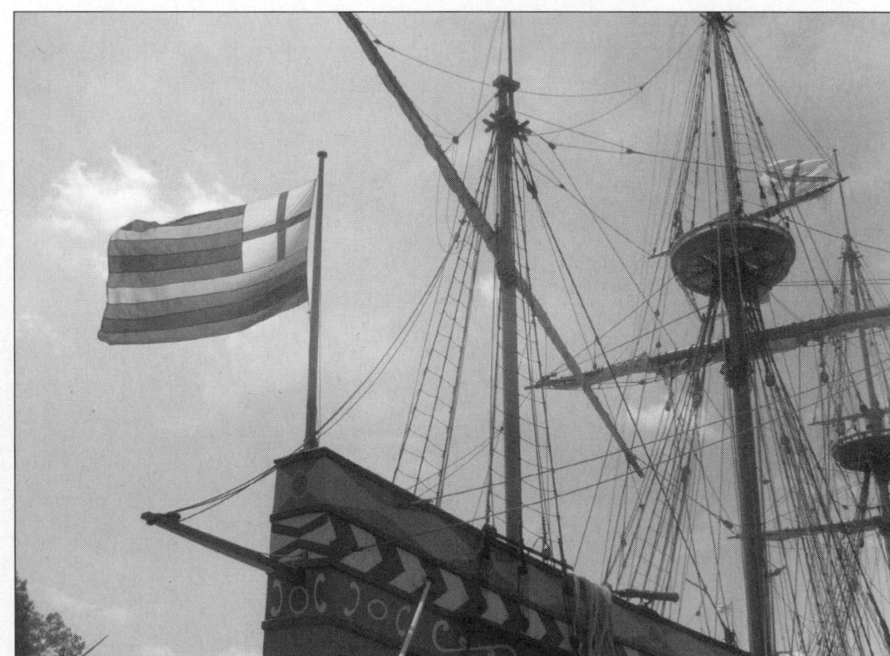

Figure 6-11: Here's the standard ship image, at full-screen resolution.

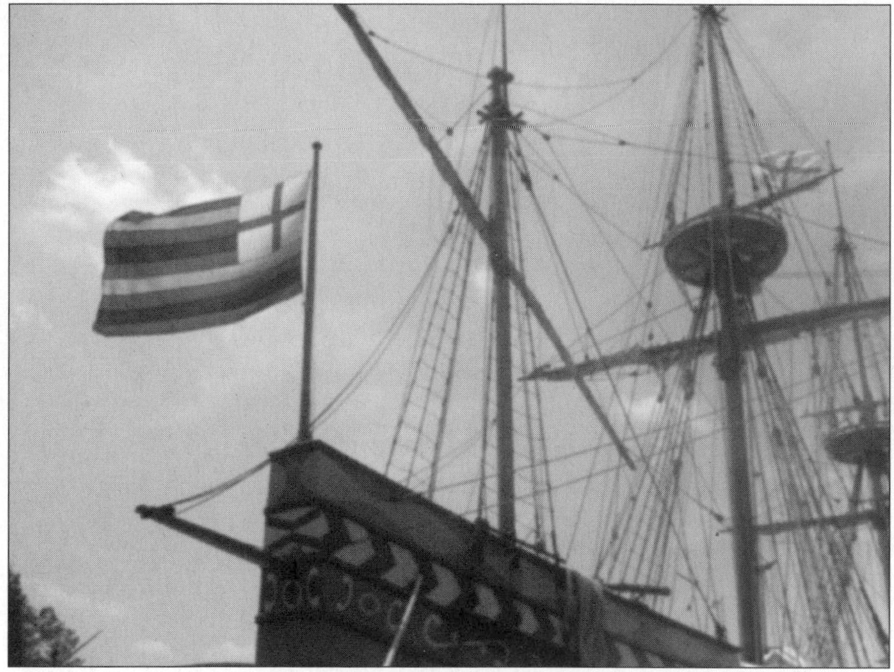

Figure 6-12: The blur filter reduces contrast.

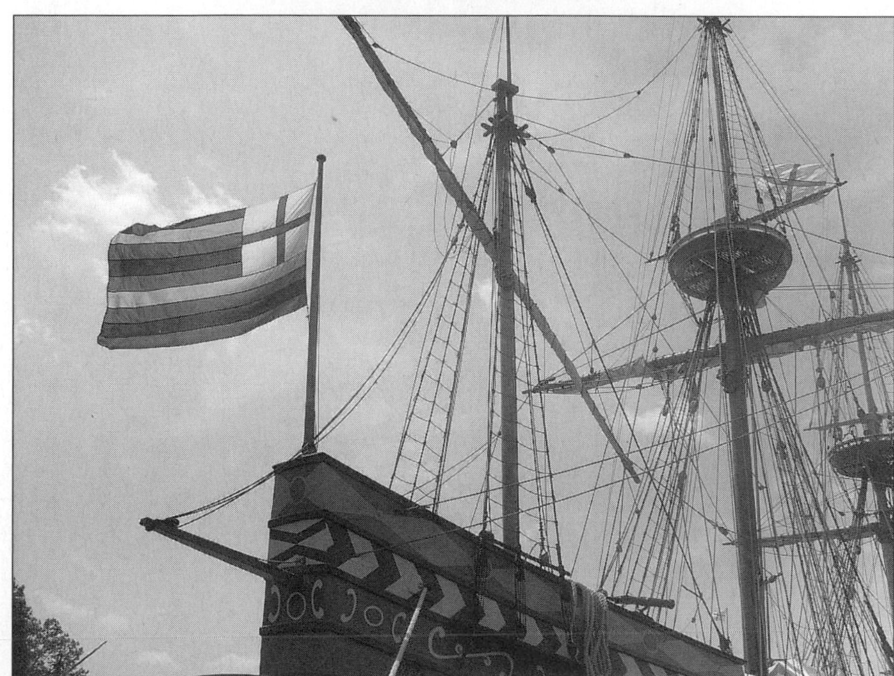

Figure 6-13: The sharpen filter increases contrast.

If you believe crime shows on TV, you can take a blurry image and keep applying a sharpen filter to read a license plate on a blurry image from a security camera. However, it just doesn't usually work that way. You can't make detail emerge from junk, but sometimes, you can make small improvements.

✦ **Emboss:** This filter creates a grayscale image that looks like embossed metal, as shown in Figure 6-14. Sometimes, embossing can convert an image into a useful background image because embossed images have low contrast. You can use the Enhance Colors dialog box to change the gray embossed image to a more appealing color.

✦ **Oil paint:** This filter applies a texture reminiscent of an oil painting to an image, as shown in Figure 6-15. It can sometimes clean up a picture and give it a more artistic appearance. The higher settings make the painting more abstract.

✦ **3D button:** This feature can be used to create an image, like Figure 6-16, that appears to be a button sticking up from the page. This will be useful later when you figure out how to use CSS or JavaScript to swap images for virtual buttons. You can set the apparent height of the image in the filter. Normally, you apply this filter to smaller images that you intend to make into buttons the user can click.

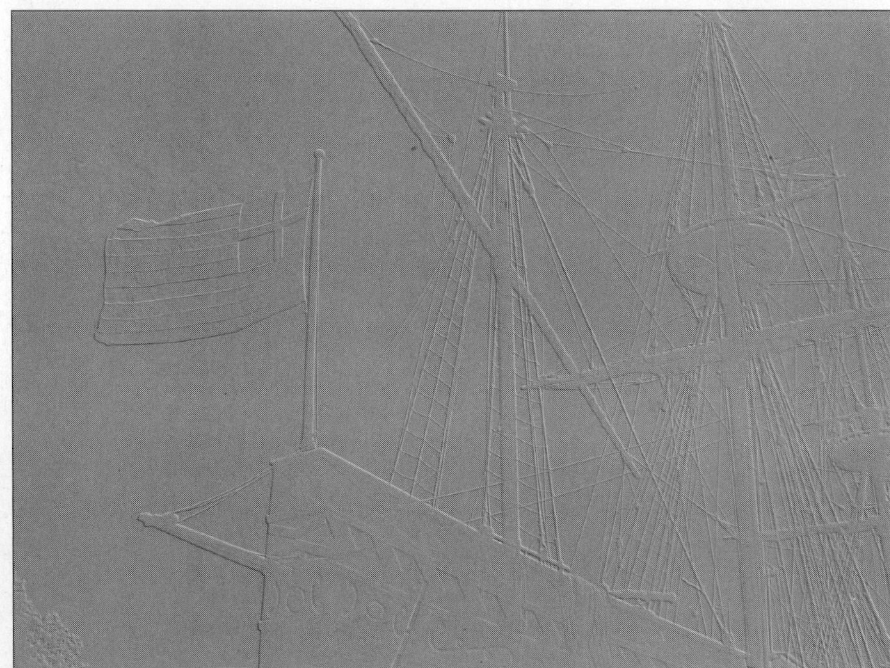

Figure 6-14: Embossing creates a low-contrast 3D effect.

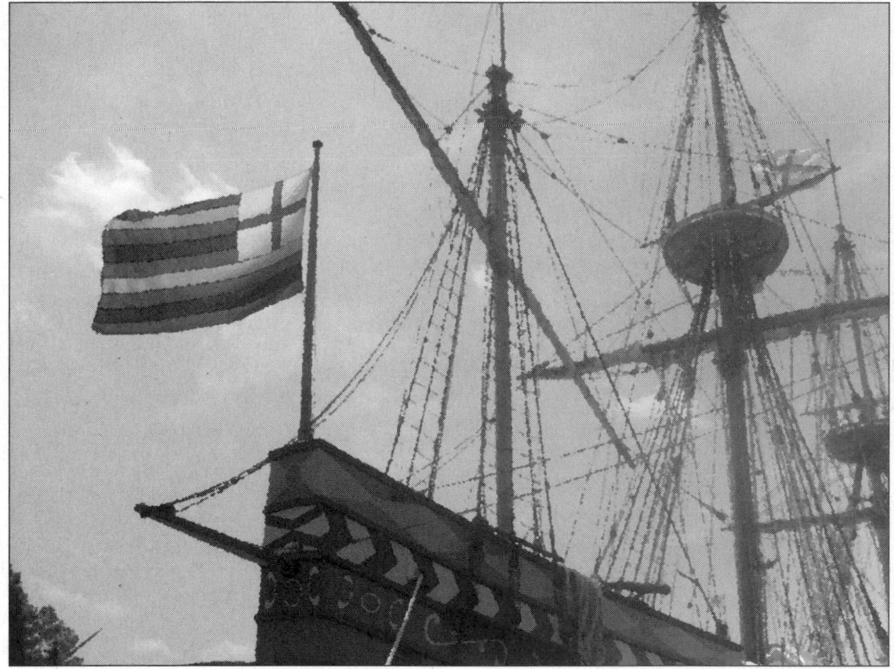

Figure 6-15: Oil painting makes an image slightly more abstract.

Figure 6-16: The image appears to stick up from the page like a button.

- **Red-eye reduction:** You use this filter to fix a common problem with flash photography. Sometimes, a person's eyes appear to have a reddish tinge to them. Unlike the other filters, this one is easiest to access directly from the Image menu. Use the mouse to select the red portion of the image and then apply the filter to turn the red areas black. It's best not to perform this filter on the entire image because you may inadvertently turn other red things to black.

Other effects you can use

Many more effects and filters are available. IrfanView has a few more built in that you can experiment with. You can also download a huge number of effects in the Adobe Photoshop 8BF format. These effects filters can often be used directly in IrfanView and other image-manipulation programs.

Some effects allow you to explode the image, add sparkles, map images onto 3D shapes, create old-time sepia effects, and much more.

If you want to do even more image manipulation, consider a full-blown image editor. Adobe Photoshop is the industry standard, but Gimp is an open-source alternative (included on the CD-ROM) that does almost as much.

Batch processing

Often, you'll have a lot of images to modify at once. IrfanView has a wonderful *batch-processing* tool that allows you to work on several images at once. I frequently use this tool to take all the images I want to use on a page and convert them to a particular size and format. The process seems a little complicated, but after you get used to it, you can quickly and easily modify a large number of images at once.

If you want to convert a large number of images at the same time, follow these steps:

1. **Identify the original images and place them in one directory.**

   I find it easiest to gather all the images into one directory, whether they come from a digital camera, scanner, or other device.

2. **Open the Batch Conversion dialog box by choosing File⇨Batch Conversion — Rename.**

   This Batch Conversion dialog box looks like Figure 6-17.

3. **Find your original images by navigating the directory window in the Batch Conversion dialog box.**

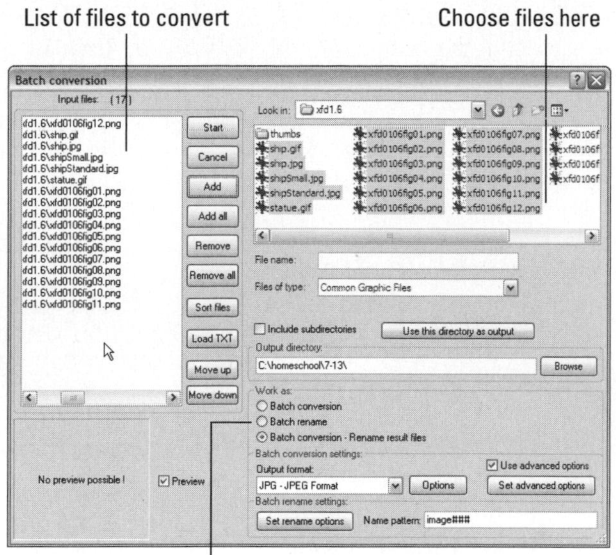

Figure 6-17: IrfanView has a powerful batch conversion tool.

4. **Copy your images to the Input Files workspace by clicking the Add button.**

   Select the images you want to modify and press the Add button. The selected image names are copied to the Input Files workspace.

5. **Specify the output directory.**

   If you want to put the new images in the same directory as the input files, click the Use This Directory as Output button. If not, choose the directory where you want the output images to go.

6. **In the Work As box, choose Batch Conversion — Rename Result Files.**

   You can use this setting to rename your files, to do other conversions, or both. I generally recommend both.

7. **Set the output format to the format you want.**

   For photos, you probably want JPG format.

8. **Change renaming settings in the Batch Rename Settings area if you want to specify some other naming convention for your images.**

   By default, each image is called *image###* where ### is a three digit number. They are numbered according to the listing in the Input Files dialog box. You can use the Move Up and Move Down buttons to change the order images appear in this listing.

9. **Click the Set Advanced Options button to change the image size.**

   This displays the Settings For All Images dialog box, as shown in Figure 6-18.

10. **Specify the new size of the image in the Resize area.**

    Several common sizes are preset. If you want another size, use the given options. I set my size to 320 x 240.

11. **Close the Settings For All Images dialog box and then, back in the Batch Conversion dialog box, press the Start button.**

    In a few seconds, all the new images will be automatically created.

Figure 6-18: Use the Settings For All Images dialog box to resize images in batch mode.

Using Images as Links

Sometimes, you'll want to use images as links. For example, take a look at `thumbs.html`, as shown in Figure 6-19.

This page uses a technique — thumbnail images. A *thumbnail* is a small version of the full-size image. The thumbnail is embedded directly. The user can click it to see the full-size version in the browser.

Thumbnails are good because they allow the user to preview a small version of each image without having to wait for the full-size versions to be rendered on-screen. If the user wants to see a complete image, he can click the thumbnail to view it on its own page.

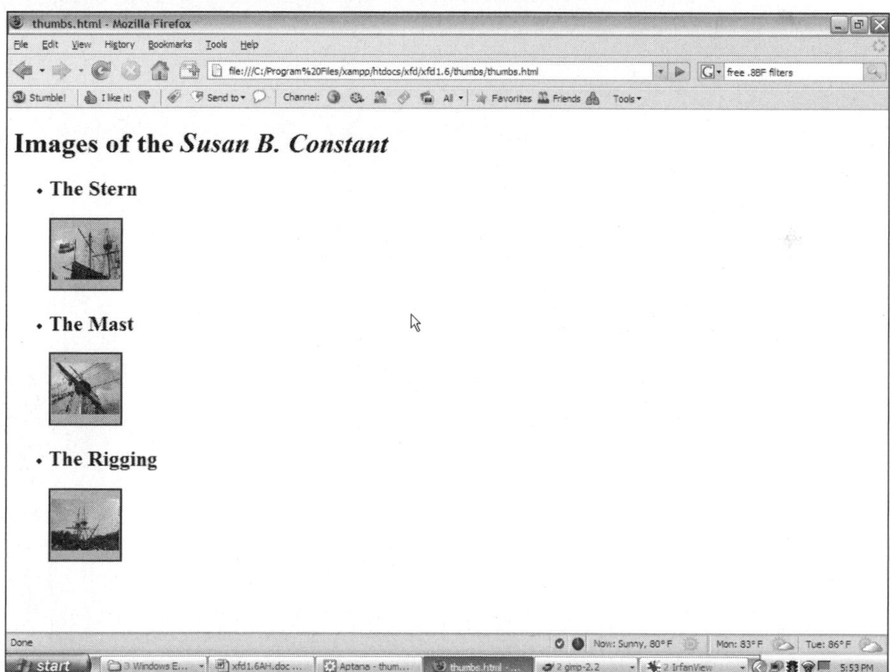

Figure 6-19: Small images can be links to larger images.

Creating thumbnail images

Thumbnails are simply scaled-down versions of ordinary images. Because this process is fairly common, IrfanView comes with a wonderful tool to automate thumbnail creation. To make a batch of thumbnails in IrfanView

1. **Organize your images.**

   Any page that has a large number of images can get confusing. I prefer to organize everything that will be used by a particular page into its own directory. I created a directory, *thumbs,* that will contain `thumbs.html`, all the full-size images, and all the thumbnails. I usually don't find it helpful to have separate directories for images. It's more helpful to organize by project or page than by media type.

2. **Rename images, if necessary.**

   Images that come from a digital camera or scanner often have cryptic names. Your life is a lot easier if your image names are easier to understand. I named my images `ship_1.jpg`, `ship_2.jpg`, and `ship_3.jpg`.

3. **Make any changes you want to the originals before you make the thumbnails.**

   Use the tips described in this chapter to clean up or improve your images before you make thumbnails, or the thumbnails won't represent the actual images accurately.

4. **Open the IrfanView Thumbnails tool by choosing File⇨Thumbnails or by pressing the T key.**

   The Thumbnails tool looks like Figure 6-20.

5. **Select the thumbnails you want to create.**

   Use the mouse to select any images you want to make thumbnails from.

6. **Choose Save Selected Thumbs as Individual Images from the File menu.**

   There are other options, but this gives the behavior you want. The other options create automatic contact sheets, open the batch editor, or create slide shows. These are great things, but for now, you want thumbnails.

7. **Specify the output directory.**

   You can put the thumbnails in the same directory as the originals. The thumbnails have the same name as the originals, but the filenames end with `_t`.

8. **Review the new thumbnail images.**

   You should see a new set of smaller images (default size is 80 x 80 pixels) in the directory.

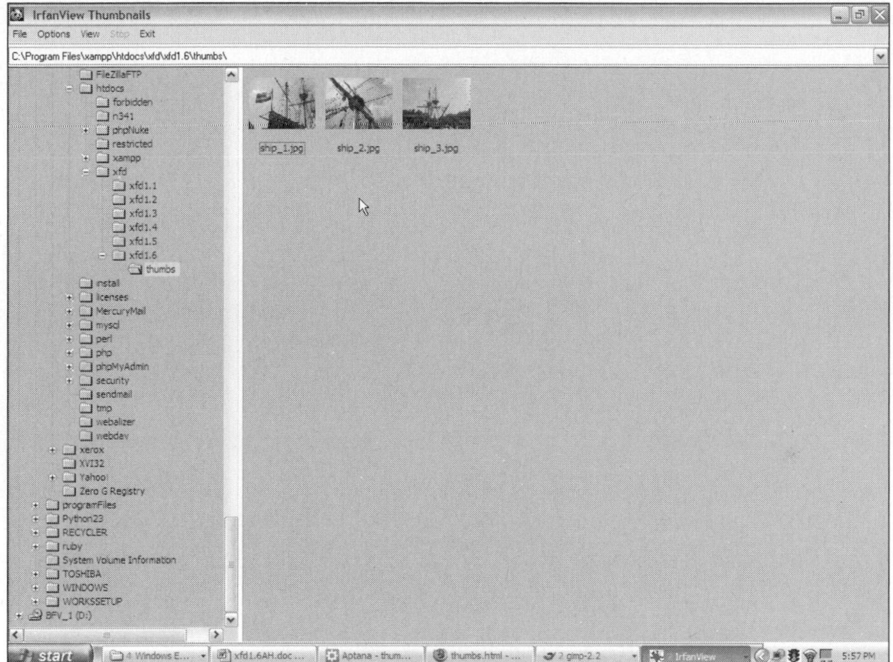

Figure 6-20: IrfanView's Thumbnails tool helps you create thumbnail images.

Creating a thumbnail-based image directory

Now, you have everything you need to build a page like `thumbs.html`. Here's an overview of the code:

```
<!DOCTYPE html PUBLIC "-//W3C//DTD XHTML 1.0 Strict//EN"
"http://www.w3.org/TR/xhtml1/DTD/xhtml1-strict.dtd">
<html lang="EN" dir="ltr" xmlns="http://www.w3.org/1999/xhtml">
  <head>
    <meta http-equiv="content-type" content="text/xml; charset=utf-8" />
    <title>thumbs.html</title>
  </head>

  <body>
    <h1>Images of the <em>Susan B. Constant</em></h1>
    <ul>
      <li>
        <h2>The Stern</h2>
        <a href = "ship_1.jpg">
          <img src = "ship_1_t.jpg"
               height = "80"
               width = "80"
               alt = "ship 1" />
        </a>
      </li>

      <li>
```

```
      <h2>The Mast</h2>
      <a href = "ship_2.jpg">
        <img src = "ship_2_t.jpg"
             height = "80"
             width = "80"
             alt = "ship 2" />
      </a>
    </li>

    <li>
      <h2>The Rigging</h2>
      <a href = "ship_3.jpg">
        <img src = "ship_3_t.jpg"
             height = "80"
             width = "80"
             alt = "ship 3" />
      </a>
    </li>
  </ul>
 </body>
</html>
```

This code looks complicated, but it's really just a combination of techniques described in this chapter. Look over the code and use the indentation to determine the structure.

The page is an unordered list. Each list item contains an H2 headline and an anchor. The anchor contains an image, rather than text. When you include an image inside an `anchor` tag, it's outlined in blue.

The key is to use the thumbnails as inline images inside the page, and the full-size image as the `href` of the anchor. The user sees the small image, but this small image is also a link to the full-size version of the image. This way, the user can see the small image easily but can view the full-size image if she wishes.

Chapter 7: Creating Forms

In This Chapter

- Adding form to your pages
- Creating input and password text boxes
- Building multi-line text inputs
- Making list boxes and check boxes
- Building groups of radio buttons
- Creating buttons

XHTML gives you the ability to describe Web pages, but today's Web isn't a one-way affair. Users want to communicate through Web pages, typing in information, making selections from drop-down lists, and interacting, rather than simply reading. In this chapter, you learn how to build these interactive elements in your pages.

You Have Great Form

There's one more aspect to XHTML that you need to understand — the ability to make forms. *Forms* are the parts of the page that allow some user interaction. Figure 7-1 shows a page with all the primary form elements in place.

The form demo (or `formDemo.html` on the CD-ROM, if you're playing along at home) is an example of all the main form elements in XHTML. In this chapter, you discover how to build all these elements.

You can create forms with ordinary XHTML, but to make them *do* something, you need a programming language. Book IV explains how to use JavaScript to interact with your forms, and Book V describes the PHP language. Use this chapter to figure out how to build the forms and then jump to another minibook to figure out how to make them do stuff. If you aren't ready for full-blown programming yet, feel free to skip this chapter for now and move on to CSS in Books II and III. Come back here when you're ready to make forms to use with JavaScript or PHP.

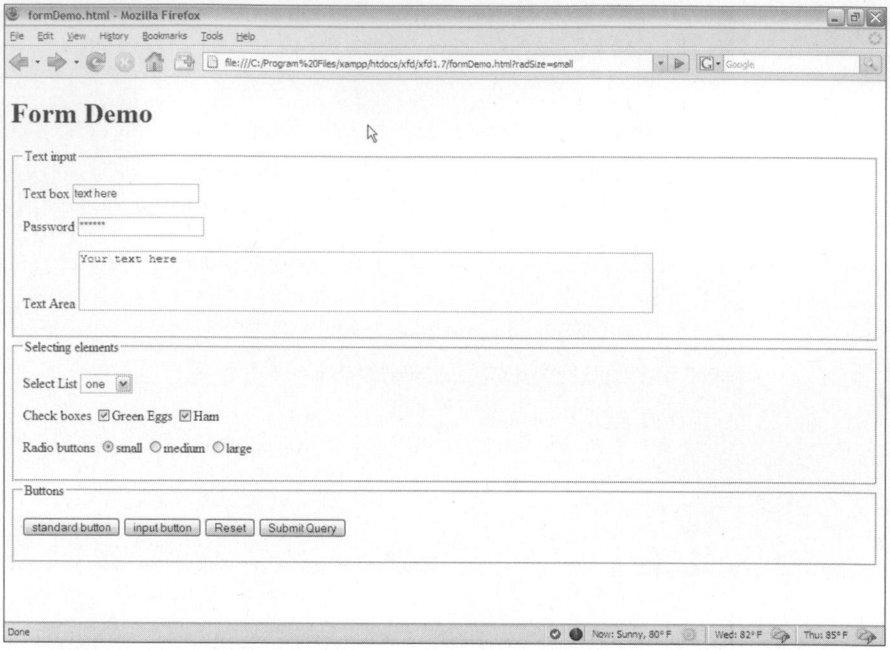

Figure 7-1: Form elements allow user interaction.

The `formDemo.html` page shows the following elements:

- **A form:** A container for form elements. Although the form element itself isn't usually a visible part of the page (like the body tag), it could be with appropriate CSS.
- **Text boxes:** These standard form elements allow the user to type text into a one-line element.
- **Password boxes:** These boxes are like text boxes, except they automatically obscure the text to discourage snooping.
- **Text areas:** These multi-line text boxes accommodate more text than the other types of text boxes. You can specify the size of the text area the user can type into.
- **Select lists:** These list boxes give the user a number of options. The user can select one element from the list. You can specify the number of rows to show or make the list drop down when activated.
- **Check boxes:** These non-text boxes can be checked or not. Check boxes act *independently* — more than one can be selected at a time (unlike radio buttons).
- **Radio buttons:** Usually found in a group of options, only one radio button in a group can be selected at a time. Selecting one radio button deselects the others in its group.

✦ **Buttons:** These elements are used to let the user begin some kind of process. The input button is used in JavaScript coding (which I fully describe in Book IV), whereas the standard and submit buttons are used for server-side programming (see Book V). The reset button is special because it automatically resets all the form elements to their default configurations.

✦ **Fieldsets and legends:** Sometimes, these are used to set off parts of the form. They're optional, but they can add a lot of visual appeal to a form.

Now that you have an overview of form elements, it's time to start building some forms!

Forms must have some form

All the form objects must be embedded inside a `<form></form>` pair. The code for `basicForm.html` illustrates the simplest possible form:

```
<!DOCTYPE html PUBLIC "-//W3C//DTD XHTML 1.0 Strict//EN"
"http://www.w3.org/TR/xhtml1/DTD/xhtml1-strict.dtd">
<html lang="EN" dir="ltr" xmlns="http://www.w3.org/1999/xhtml">
  <head>
    <meta http-equiv="content-type" content="text/xml; charset=utf-8" />
    <title>basicForm.html</title>
  </head>

  <body>
    <h1>A basic form</h1>
    <form action = "">
      <h2>Form elements go here</h2>
      <h3>Other HTML is fine, too.</h3>
    </form>

  </body>
</html>
```

The `<form></form>` pair indicates a piece of the page that may contain form elements. All the other form doohickeys and doodads (buttons, `select` objects, and so on) must be inside a form pair.

The action element indicates what should happen when the form is submitted. This requires a programming language, so a full description of the `action` attribute is in Book IV. Still, you must indicate an action to validate, so for now just leave the `action` attribute null with a pair of quotes (`""`).

Organizing a form with fieldsets and labels

Forms can contain many kinds of things, but the most important elements are the *input elements* (text boxes, buttons, drop-down lists, and the like) and *text labels* that describe the elements. Web developers have traditionally used tables to set up forms, but this isn't really the best way to go because forms aren't really tabular information. XHTML includes some great features to help you describe the various parts of a form. Figure 7-2 shows a page with fieldsets, layouts, and basic input.

A *fieldset* is a special element used to supply a visual grouping to a set of form elements.

The form still doesn't look very good, I admit, but that's not the point yet. Like all the other XHTML tags, the form elements aren't about describing how the table looks, but are about what all the main elements mean. (Here I go again. . . .) You use CSS to make the form look however you want. The XHTML tags describe the parts of the form, so you have something to hook your CSS to. It all makes sense very soon, I promise.

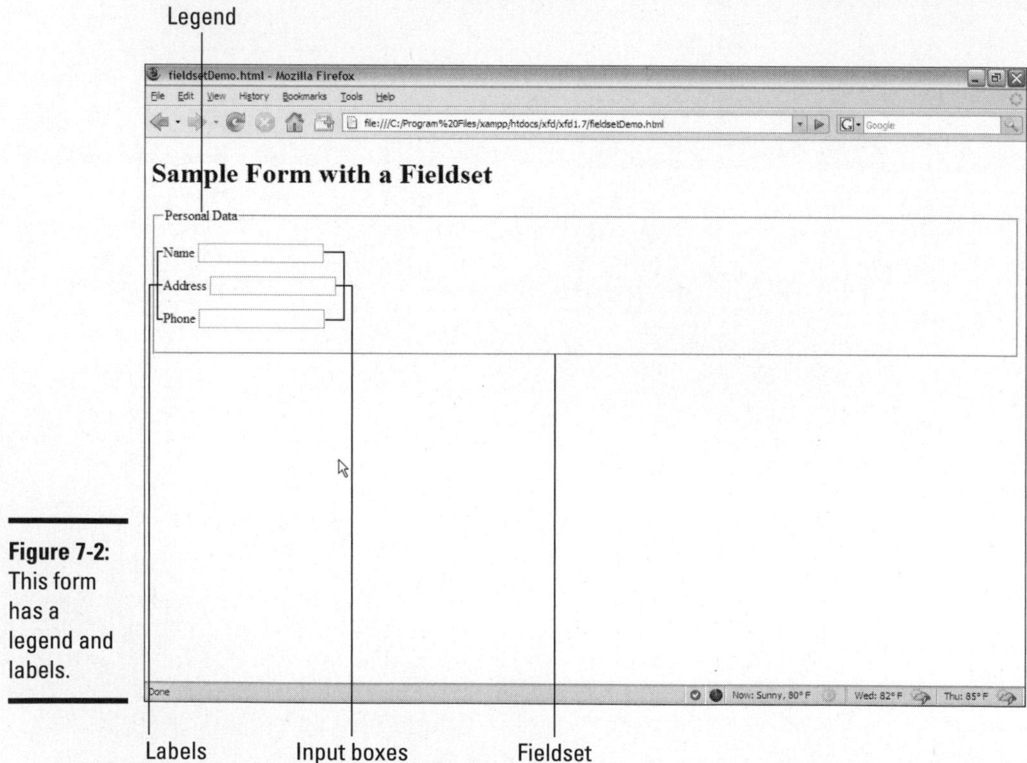

Figure 7-2: This form has a legend and labels.

Here's the code for the fieldset demo (`fieldsetDemo.html` on the CD-ROM):

```
<!DOCTYPE html PUBLIC "-//W3C//DTD XHTML 1.0 Strict//EN"
"http://www.w3.org/TR/xhtml1/DTD/xhtml1-strict.dtd">
<html lang="EN" dir="ltr" xmlns="http://www.w3.org/1999/xhtml">
  <head>
    <meta http-equiv="content-type" content="text/xml; charset=utf-8" />
    <title>fieldsetDemo.html</title>
  </head>

  <body>
    <h1>Sample Form with a Fieldset</h1>
    <form action = "">
      <fieldset>
        <legend>Personal Data</legend>
        <p>
          <label>Name</label>
          <input type = "text" />
        </p>

        <p>
          <label>Address</label>
          <input type = "text" />
        </p>

        <p>
          <label>Phone</label>
          <input type = "text" />
        </p>

      </fieldset>
    </form>
  </body>
</html>
```

The form has these elements:

- **The `<form>` and `</form>` tags:** These define the form as a part of the page. Don't forget the null `action` attribute.
- **The `<fieldset>` pair:** This pair describes the included elements as a set of fields. This element isn't necessary, but it does give you some nice organization and layout options later when you can do CSS. You can think of the fieldset as a blank canvas for adding visual design to your forms. By default, the fieldset places a border around all the contained elements.
- **The `<legend>` tag:** A part of the fieldset, this tag allows you to specify a legend for the entire fieldset. The legend is visible to the user.
- **The paragraphs:** I generally place each label and its corresponding input element in a paragraph. This provides some nice formatting capabilities and keeps each pair together.

- **The `<label>` tag:** This tag allows you to specify a particular chunk of text as a label. No formatting is done by default, but you can add formatting later with CSS.
- **The `<input>` elements:** These are the elements into which the user actually types data. For now, I'm just using very basic text inputs so the form has some kind of input. In the next section, I explain fully how to build more complete text inputs.

Building Text-Style Inputs

Most of the form elements are variations of the same tag. The `<input>` tag can be used to create single-line text boxes, password boxes, buttons, and even invisible content (such as hidden fields). Most of these objects share the same basic attributes, although the outward appearance can be different.

Making a standard text field

Figure 7-3 shows the most common form of the `input` element — a *plain text field.*

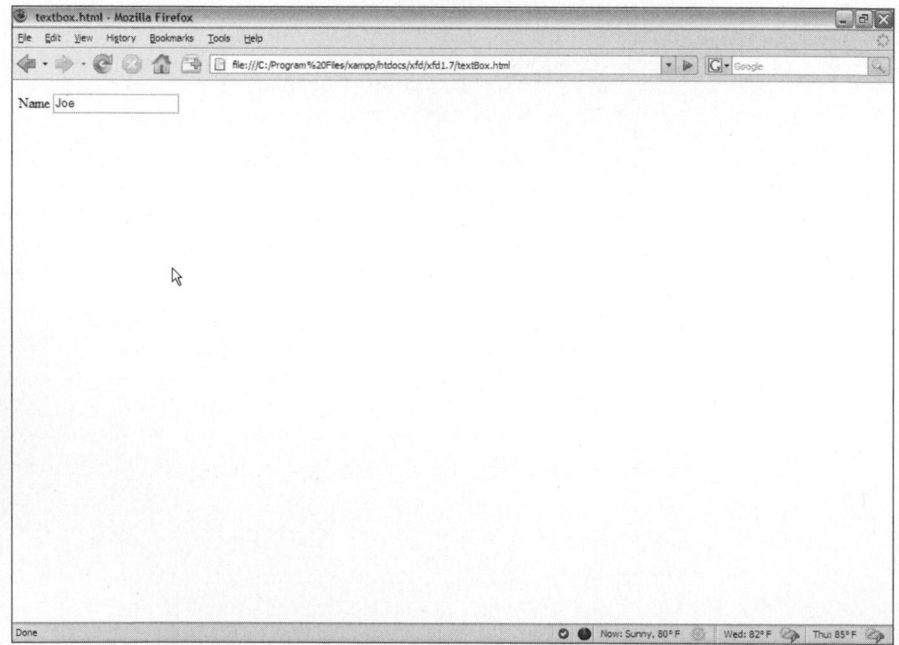

Figure 7-3: The input element is often used to make a text field.

To make a basic text input, you need a form and an `input` element. Adding a label so that the user knows what he's supposed to enter into the text box is also common. Here's the code:

```
<!DOCTYPE html PUBLIC "-//W3C//DTD XHTML 1.0 Strict//EN"
"http://www.w3.org/TR/xhtml1/DTD/xhtml1-strict.dtd">
<html lang="EN" dir="ltr" xmlns="http://www.w3.org/1999/xhtml">
  <head>
    <meta http-equiv="content-type" content="text/xml; charset=utf-8" />
    <title>textbox.html</title>
  </head>

  <body>
    <form action = "">
      <p>
        <label>Name</label>
        <input type = "text"
               id = "txtName"
               value = "Joe"/>
      </p>
    </form>

  </body>
</html>
```

The `input` element has three common attributes:

✦ **`type`:** The `type` attribute indicates the type of `input` element this is. This first example sets the `type` to `text`, creating a standard text box. Other types are used throughout this chapter to create passwords, hidden fields, check boxes, and buttons.

✦ **`id`:** The `id` attribute creates an identifier for the field. When you use a programming language to extract data from this element, use the `id` to specify which field you're referring to. `id` fields often begin with a special hint phrase to indicate the type of object it is (for instance, `txt` indicates a text box).

✦ **`value`:** This attribute determines the default value of the text box. If you leave this attribute out, the text field begins empty.

Text fields can also have other attributes, which aren't used as often, such as

✦ **`size`:** This attribute determines the number of characters that are displayed.

✦ **`maxlength`:** Use this attribute to set the largest number of characters that are allowed.

There is no `</input>` tag. Input tags are a holdover from the days when many tags did not have ending tags. You just end the original tag with a slash character (/), as shown in the preceding sample code.

Building a password field

Passwords are just like text boxes, except the text isn't displayed. Instead, a series of asterisks appears. Figure 7-4 shows a basic password field.

The following code reveals that passwords are almost identical to ordinary text fields:

```
<!DOCTYPE html PUBLIC "-//W3C//DTD XHTML 1.0 Strict//EN"
"http://www.w3.org/TR/xhtml1/DTD/xhtml1-strict.dtd">
<html lang="EN" dir="ltr" xmlns="http://www.w3.org/1999/xhtml">
  <head>
    <meta http-equiv="content-type" content="text/xml; charset=utf-8" />
    <title>password.html</title>
  </head>

  <body>
    <form action = "">
      <fieldset>
        <legend>Enter a password</legend>
        <p>
          <label>Type password here</label>
          <input type = "password"
                 id = "pwd"
                 value = "secret" />
        </p>
      </fieldset>
    </form>
  </body>
</html>
```

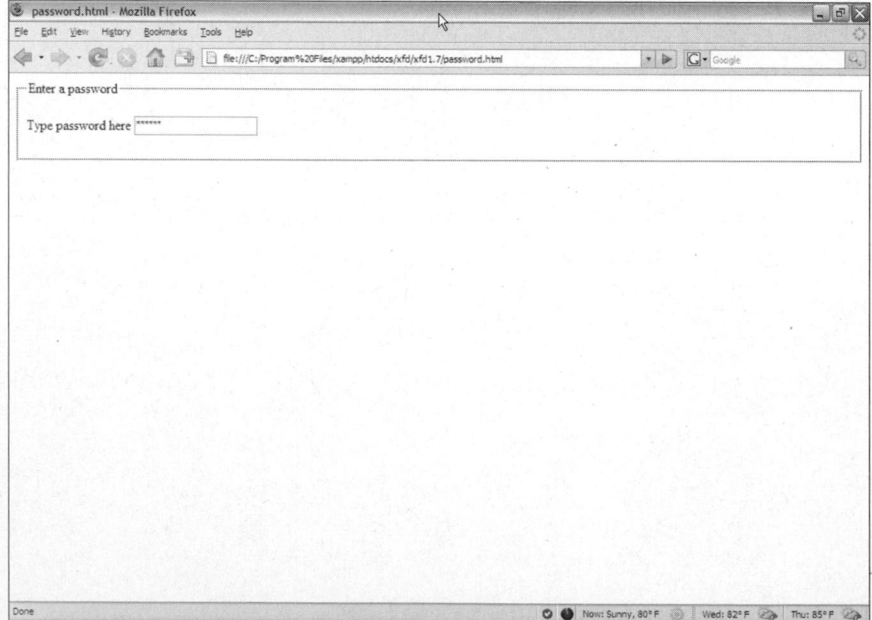

Figure 7-4: Enter the secret password. . . .

In this example, I've created a password field with the ID `pwd`. The default value of this field is `secret`. The term "secret" won't actually show up in the field but will be replaced with six asterisk characters.

The password field offers virtually no meaningful security. It protects the user from the KGB glancing over his shoulder to read a password, but that's about it. The open standards of XHTML and the programming languages mean passwords are still often passed in the open. There are solutions — like the SSL (Secure Socket Layer) technology — but for now, just be aware that the password field just isn't suitable for protecting the recipe of your secret sauce.

As usual, this example doesn't really do anything with the password, but you'll use other technologies for that.

Making multi-line text input

The single-line text field is a powerful feature, but sometimes, you want something with a bit more space. The `essay.html` program, as shown in Figure 7-5, demonstrates how you might create a page for an essay question.

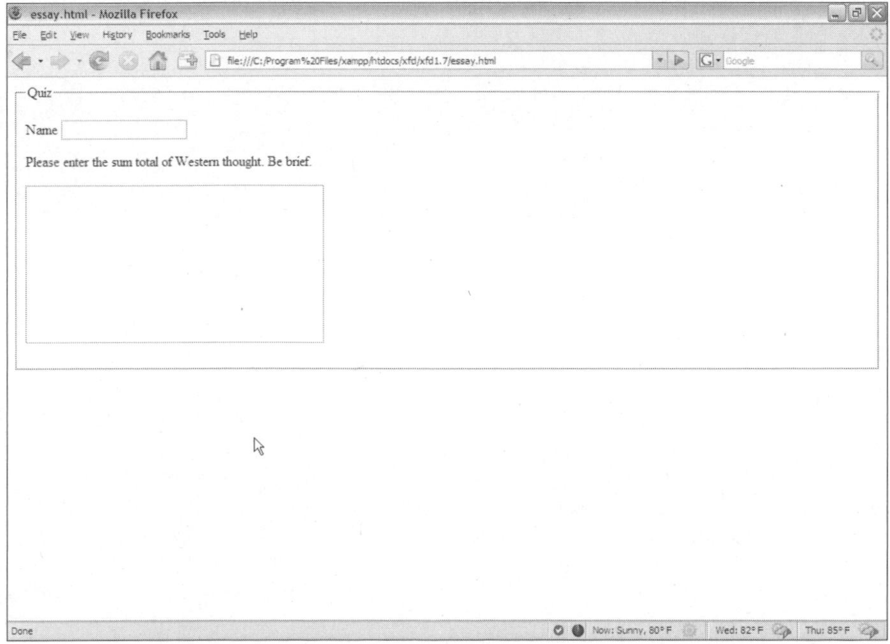

Figure 7-5: This quiz might require a multi-line response.

The star of this program is a new tag — <textarea>:

```
<!DOCTYPE html PUBLIC "-//W3C//DTD XHTML 1.0 Strict//EN"
"http://www.w3.org/TR/xhtml1/DTD/xhtml1-strict.dtd">
<html lang="EN" dir="ltr" xmlns="http://www.w3.org/1999/xhtml">
  <head>
    <meta http-equiv="content-type" content="text/xml; charset=utf-8" />
    <title>essay.html</title>
  </head>

  <body>
    <form action = "">
      <fieldset>
        <legend>Quiz</legend>

        <p>
          <label>Name</label>
          <input type = "text"
                 id = "txtName" />
        </p>

        <p>
          <label>
            Please enter the sum total of
            Western thought. Be brief.
          </label>
        </p>

        <p>
          <textarea id = "txtAnswer"
                    rows = "10"
                    cols = "40"></textarea>
        </p>
      </fieldset>
    </form>
  </body>
</html>
```

Here are a few things to keep in mind when using the <textarea> tag:

- **It needs an `id` attribute, just like the `input` element.**
- **You can specify the size with `rows` and `cols` attributes.**
- **The content goes between the tags.** The text area can contain a lot more information than the ordinary <input> tags, so rather than placing the data in the `value` attribute, the content of the text goes between the <textarea> and </textarea> tags.

Anything placed between <textarea> and </textarea> in the code ends up in the output, too. This includes spaces and carriage returns. If you don't want any blank spaces in the text area, snug up the ending tag right next to the beginning tag, as I did in the essay example.

Creating Multiple Selection Elements

Sometimes, you want to present the user with a list of choices and then have the user pick one of these elements. XHTML has a number of interesting ways to do this.

Making selections

The drop-down list is a favorite selection tool of Web developers for the following reasons:

- ✦ **It saves screen space.** Only the current selection is showing. When the user clicks the list, a series of choices drop down and then disappear again after the selection is made.
- ✦ **It limits input.** The only things the user can choose are things you've put in the list. This makes it much easier to handle the potential inputs, as you don't have to worry about typing errors.
- ✦ **The value can be different than what the user sees.** This seems like an odd advantage, but it does turn out to be very useful sometimes. I show an example as I describe color values later in this chapter.

Figure 7-6 shows a simple drop-down list in action.

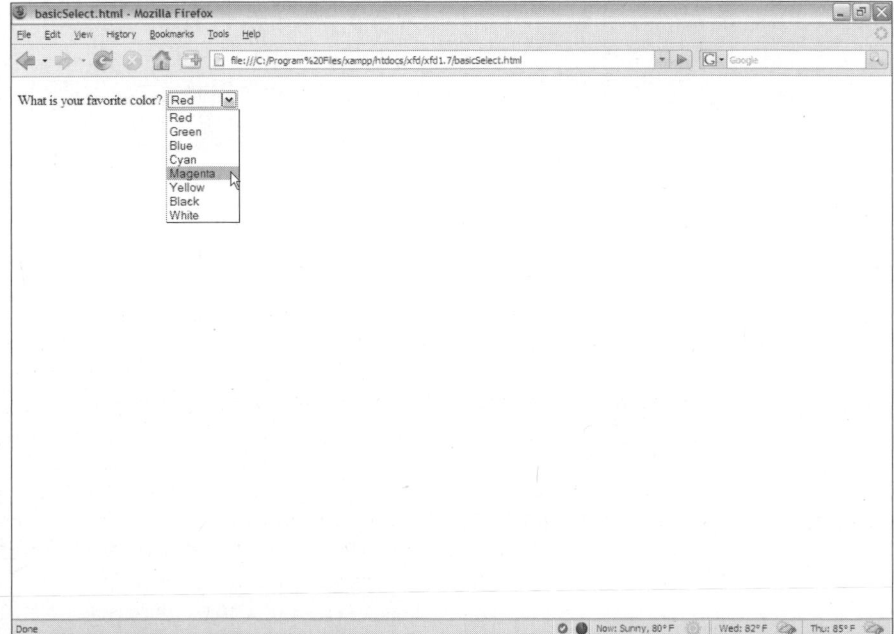

Figure 7-6: The user can choose from a list of colors.

The code for this simple drop-down list follows:

```
<!DOCTYPE html PUBLIC "-//W3C//DTD XHTML 1.0 Strict//EN"
"http://www.w3.org/TR/xhtml1/DTD/xhtml1-strict.dtd">
<html lang="EN" dir="ltr" xmlns="http://www.w3.org/1999/xhtml">
  <head>
    <meta http-equiv="content-type" content="text/xml; charset=utf-8" />
    <title>basicSelect.html</title>
  </head>

  <body>
    <form action = "">
      <p>
        <label>What is your favorite color?</label>
        <select id = "selColor">
          <option value = "#ff0000">Red</option>
          <option value = "#00ff00">Green</option>
          <option value = "#0000ff">Blue</option>
          <option value = "#00ffff">Cyan</option>
          <option value = "#ff00ff">Magenta</option>
          <option value = "#ffff00">Yellow</option>
          <option value = "#000000">Black</option>
          <option value = "#ffffff">White</option>
        </select>
      </p>
    </form>
  </body>
</html>
```

The `select` object is a bit different from some of the other `input` elements you're used to, such as

- **It's surrounded by a `<select></select>` pair.** These tags indicate the entire list.
- **The `select` object has an `id` attribute.** Although the `select` object has many other tags inside, typically only the `select` itself has an `id` attribute.
- **It contains a series of `<option></option>` pairs.** Each individual selection is housed in an `<option></option>` set.
- **Each option tag has a value associated with it.** The value is used by code. The value isn't necessarily what the user sees. (See the sidebar "What are those funky #ff00ff things?" for an example.)
- **The content between `<option></option>` is visible to the user.** The content is what the user actually sees.

Select boxes don't *have* to have the drop-down behavior. If you want, you can specify the number of rows to display with the `size` attribute. In this case, the number of rows you specify will always be visible on the screen.

What are those funky #ff00ff things?

If you look carefully at the code for `basicSelect.html`, you see that the values are all strange text with pound signs and weird characters. These are *hex codes,* and they're a good way to describe colors for computers. I explain all about how these work in Book II, Chapter 1. It's really not nearly as hard to understand as it seems. For now though, understand this is a good example of wanting to show the user one thing (the name of a color in English) and send some other value (the hex code) to a program. You see this code again when I talk about JavaScript in Book IV.

Building check boxes

Check boxes are used when you want the user to turn a particular choice on or off. For example, look at Figure 7-7.

Each check box represents a true or false value. Each can be checked or not, and the status of each check box is completely independent from the others. The user can check none of the options, all of them, or any combination.

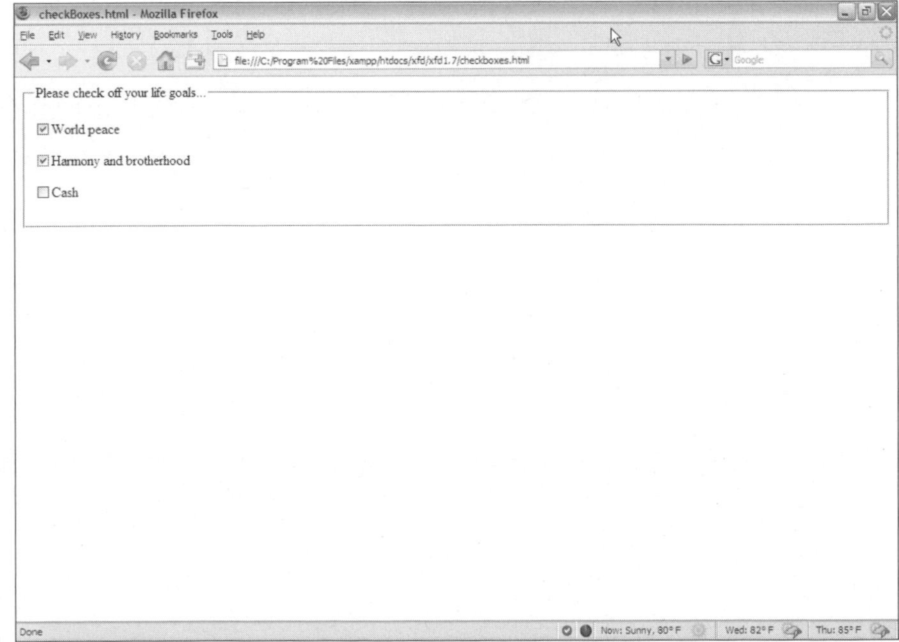

Figure 7-7: Any number of check boxes can be selected at once.

This code shows that check boxes use your old friend the `input` tag:

```
<!DOCTYPE html PUBLIC "-//W3C//DTD XHTML 1.0 Strict//EN"
"http://www.w3.org/TR/xhtml1/DTD/xhtml1-strict.dtd">
<html lang="EN" dir="ltr" xmlns="http://www.w3.org/1999/xhtml">
  <head>
    <meta http-equiv="content-type" content="text/xml; charset=utf-8" />
    <title>checkBoxes.html</title>
  </head>

  <body>
    <form action = "">
      <fieldset>
        <legend>Please check off your life goals...</legend>
        <p>
          <input type = "checkbox"
                 id = "chkPeace"
                 value = "peace" />World peace
        </p>

        <p>
          <input type = "checkbox"
                 id = "chkHarmony"
                 value = "harmony" />Harmony and brotherhood
        </p>

        <p>
          <input type = "checkbox"
                 id = "chkCash"
                 value = "cash" />Cash
        </p>

      </fieldset>
    </form>
  </body>
</html>
```

You're using the same attributes of the `input` tag, but the way they work is a little bit different than in a plain old text box:

- **The `type` is `checkbox`.** That's how the browser knows to make a check box, rather than a text field element.
- **The checkbox still requires an ID.** If you'll be writing programming code to work with this thing (and you will, eventually), you'll need an ID for reference.
- **The value is hidden from the user.** The user doesn't see the actual value. That's for the programmer (like the `select` object). Any text *following* the check box appears to be the text associated with it.

This all seems inconsistent

Sometimes, the value of a form element is visible to users, and sometimes, it's hidden. Sometimes, the text the user sees is inside the tag, and sometimes, it isn't. It's a little confusing. The standards evolved over a long time, and they honestly could have been a little more consistent. Still, this is the set of elements you have, and they're not really that hard to understand. Write forms a few times, and you'll remember. You can always start by looking over my code and borrowing it as a starting place.

Creating radio buttons

Radio buttons are used when you want to let the user pick only one option from a group. Figure 7-8 shows an example of a radio button group in action.

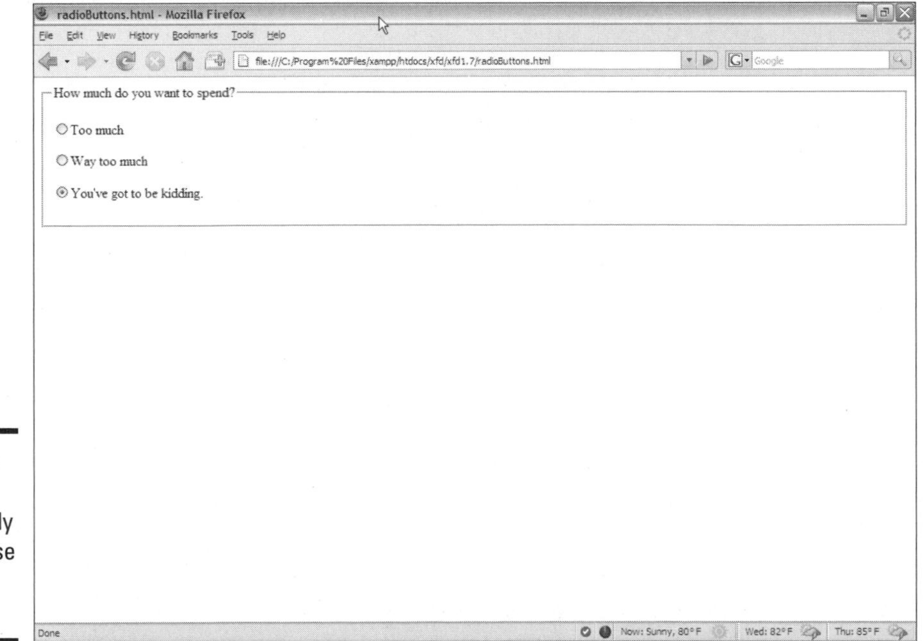

Figure 7-8: You can choose only one of these radio buttons.

Radio buttons might seem a lot like check boxes, but they have some important differences:

- **Only one can be checked at a time.** The term *radio button* came from the old-style car radios. When you push the button for one station, all the other buttons pop out. I still have one of those radios. (I guess I have a Web-design car.)
- **They have to be in a group.** Radio buttons make sense only in a group context. The whole point of a radio button is to interact with its group.
- **They all have the same name!** Each radio button has its own ID (like other `input` elements), but they also have a `name` attribute. The `name` attribute indicates the *group* a radio button is in.
- **You can have more than one group on a page.** Just use a different `name` attribute for each group.
- **One of them has to be selected.** The group should always have one value and only one. Some browsers check the first element in a group by default, but just in case, you should select the element you want selected. Add the `checked = "checked"` attribute (developed by the Department of Redundancy Department) to the element you want selected when the page appears. In this example, I pre-selected the most expensive option, all in the name of good capitalistic suggestive selling.

Here's some code that explains it all:

```
<!DOCTYPE html PUBLIC "-//W3C//DTD XHTML 1.0 Strict//EN"
"http://www.w3.org/TR/xhtml1/DTD/xhtml1-strict.dtd">
<html lang="EN" dir="ltr" xmlns="http://www.w3.org/1999/xhtml">
  <head>
    <meta http-equiv="content-type" content="text/xml; charset=utf-8" />
    <title>radioButtons.html</title>
  </head>

  <body>
    <form action = "">
      <fieldset>
        <legend>How much do you want to spend?</legend>
        <p>
          <input type = "radio"
                 name = "radPrice"
                 id = "rad100"
                 value = "100" />Too much
        </p>

        <p>
          <input type = "radio"
                 name = "radPrice"
                 id = "rad200"
                 value = "200" />Way too much
        </p>

        <p>
          <input type = "radio"
```

```
                name = "radPrice"
                id = "rad5000"
                value = "5000"
                checked = "checked" />You've got to be kidding.
        </p>
      </fieldset>
    </form>
  </body>
</html>
```

Pressing Your Buttons

XHTML also comes with several types of buttons. You use these guys to make something actually happen. Generally, the user sets up some kind of input by typing in text boxes and then selecting from lists, options, or check boxes. Then, the user clicks a button to trigger a response. Figure 7-9 demonstrates the four main types of buttons.

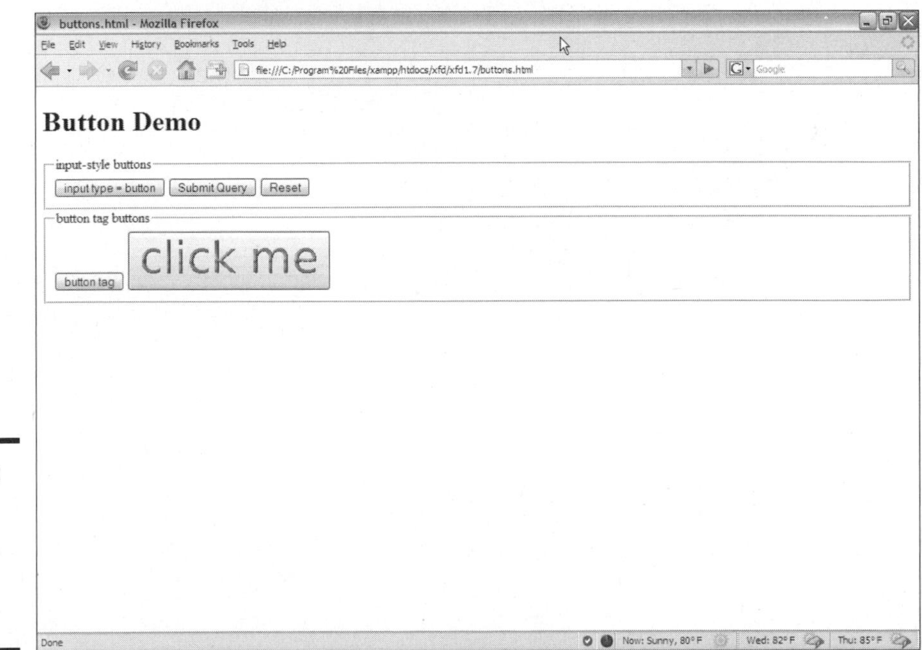

Figure 7-9: XHTML supports several types of buttons.

The code for this button example is shown here:

```
<!DOCTYPE html PUBLIC "-//W3C//DTD XHTML 1.0 Strict//EN"
"http://www.w3.org/TR/xhtml1/DTD/xhtml1-strict.dtd">
<html lang="EN" dir="ltr" xmlns="http://www.w3.org/1999/xhtml">
  <head>
    <meta http-equiv="content-type" content="text/xml; charset=utf-8" />
    <title>buttons.html</title>
  </head>

  <body>
    <h1>Button Demo</h1>
    <form action = "">
      <fieldset>
        <legend>
          input-style buttons
        </legend>

        <input type = "button"
               value = "input type = button" />

        <input type = "submit" />
        <input type = "reset" />
      </fieldset>

      <fieldset>
        <legend>button tag buttons</legend>

        <button type = "button">
          button tag
        </button>
        <button>
          <img src = "clickMe.gif"
               alt = "click me" />
        </button>
      </fieldset>
    </form>
  </body>
</html>
```

Each button type is described in this section.

Making input-style buttons

The most common form of button is just another form of your old friend, the `<input>` tag. If you set the `input`'s `type` attribute to `"button"`, you generate a basic button:

```
        <input type = "button"
               value = "input type = button" />
```

The ordinary input button has a few key features:

- **The `input type` is set to `"button"`.** This makes an ordinary button.
- **The `value` attribute sets the button's caption.** Change the `value` attribute to make a new caption. This button's caption shows how the button was made: `input type = "button"`.
- **This type of button doesn't imply a link.** Although the button appears to depress when it's clicked, it doesn't do anything. You have to write some JavaScript code to make it work.
- **Later, you'll add event-handling to the button.** After you discover Java Script in Book IV, you use a special attribute to connect the button to code.
- **This type of button is for client-side programming.** This type of code resides on the user's computer. Read how to do it in Book IV.

Building a submit button

Submit buttons are usually used in server-side programming. In this form of programming, the code is back on the Web server. In Book V, you figure out how to use PHP to create server-side code. The `input` tag is used to make a submit button, too!

```
<input type = "submit" />
```

Although they look the same, the submit button is different than the ordinary button in a couple subtle ways:

- **The `value` attribute is optional.** If you leave it out, the button says "Submit Query." Of course, you can change the `value` to anything you want, and this becomes the caption of the submit button.
- **Clicking it causes a link.** This type of button is meant for server-side programming. When you click the button, all the information in the form is gathered and sent to some other page on the Web.
- **Right now, it goes nowhere.** When you set the form's `action` attribute to null (`""`), you told the submit button it should just reload the current form. When you figure out real server-side programming, you change the form `action` to a program that works with the data.
- **Submit buttons aren't for client-side.** Although you can attach an event to the submit button (just like the regular input button), the linking behavior often causes problems. Use regular input for client-side and submit for server-side.

It's a do-over: The reset button

Yet another form of the versatile `input` tag is used to create the reset button:

```
<input type = "reset" />
```

This button has a very specific purpose. When it's clicked, it resets all the elements of its form to their default values. Like the submit button, it has a default value (`"reset"`), and it doesn't require any code.

Introducing the button tag

The button has been a useful part of the Web for a long time, but it's a bit boring. HTML 4.0 introduced the new `button` tag, which works like this:

```
<button type = "button">
  button tag
</button>
```

The `button` tag acts more like a standard XHTML tag, but it can also act like the submit button. Here are the highlights:

- **The `type` attribute determines the style.** You can set the button to be `ordinary` (by setting its type to `button`), `submit`, or `reset`. If you don't specify the type, buttons use the `submit` style. The `button type` indicates its behavior, just like the `input`-style buttons.
- **The caption goes between the `<button></button>` pair.** There's no `value` attribute. Instead, just put the intended caption inside the button pair.
- **You can incorporate other elements.** Unlike the `input` button, you can place images or styled text inside a button. This gives you some other capabilities. The second button in the `buttons.html` example uses a small GIF image to create a more colorful button.

Book II

Styling with CSS

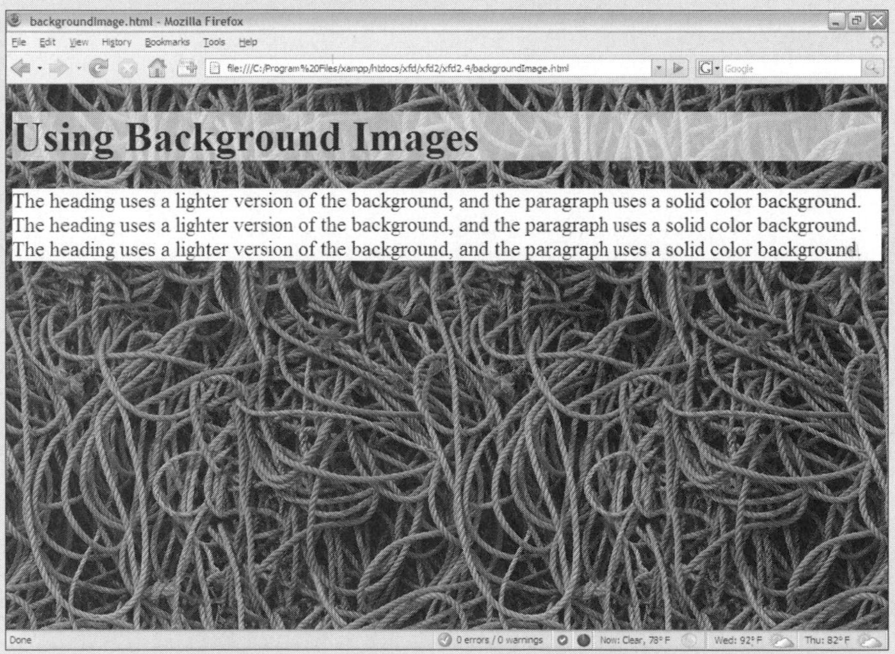

Change your fonts, colors, and backgrounds with CSS.

Contents at a Glance

Chapter 1: Coloring Your World

In This Chapter

- Introducing the style element
- Adding styles to tags
- Modifying your page dynamically
- Specifying foreground and background colors
- Understanding hex colors
- Developing a color scheme

XHTML does a good job of setting up the basic design of a page, but let's face it. The pages it makes are pretty ugly. Back in the old days, developers added a lot of other tags to HTML to make it prettier, but it was a pretty haphazard affair. Now, XHTML disallows all the tags that were used to make pages more attractive. It's not really a loss because, today, XHTML is almost always written in concert with CSS (Cascading Style Sheets). It's amazing how much you can do with CSS to beautify your XHTML pages.

CSS is used in many ways. It allows you to change the color of any image on the page. CSS lets you add backgrounds and borders. You can use CSS to change the visual appearance of elements like lists and links, as well as customize the entire layout of your page. CSS allows you to keep your XHTML simple because all the formatting is stored in the CSS. It's also very efficient because CSS allows you to reuse a style across multiple pages. If XHTML gives your pages structure, CSS gives them beauty.

This chapter gets you started by describing how to add color to your pages.

Now You Have an Element of Style

The secret to CSS is the *style sheet,* a set of rules for describing how various objects will be displayed. As an example, look at `basicColors.html` in Figure 1-1.

As always, don't take my word for it. This chapter is about color, and you need to look at these pages from the CD or Web site to see what I'm talking about.

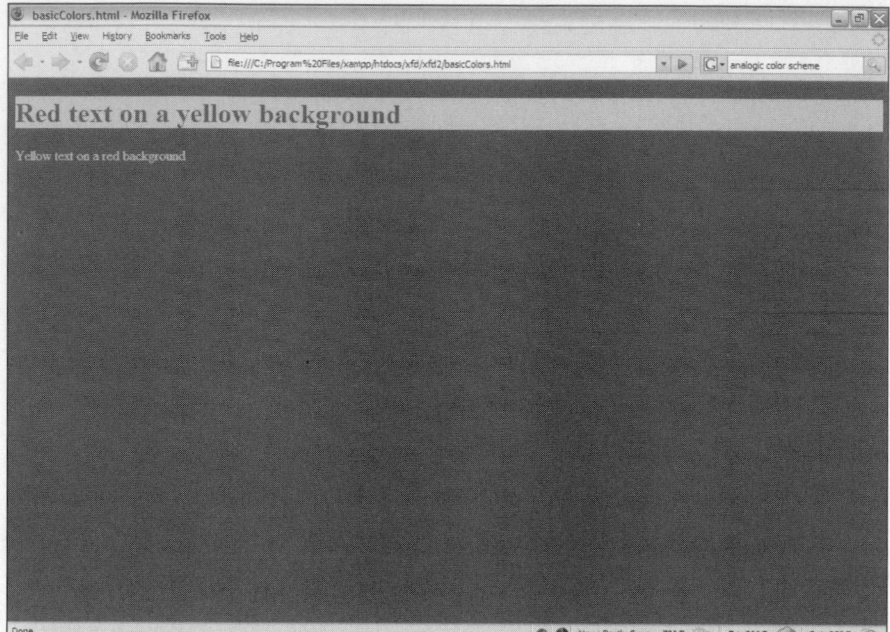

Figure 1-1: This page is in color!

Absolutely nothing in the XHTML code provides color information. What makes this page different from plain XHTML pages is a new section that I've stashed in the header. Take a gander at the code to see what's going on:

```
<!DOCTYPE html PUBLIC "-//W3C//DTD XHTML 1.0 Strict//EN"
"http://www.w3.org/TR/xhtml1/DTD/xhtml1-strict.dtd">
<html lang="EN" dir="ltr" xmlns="http://www.w3.org/1999/xhtml">
  <head>
    <meta http-equiv="content-type" content="text/xml; charset=utf-8" />
    <title>basicColors.html</title>
    <style type = "text/css">
      body {
        color: yellow;
        background-color: red;
      }

      h1 {
        color: red;
        background-color: yellow;
      }
    </style>
  </head>

  <body>
    <h1>Red text on a yellow background</h1>
    <p>
      Yellow text on a red background
    </p>
  </body>
</html>
```

As you can see, nothing is dramatically different in the XHTML code. The body simply contains an `h1` and a `p`. Although the text mentions the colors, nothing in the XHTML code makes the colors really happen.

The secret is the new `<style></style>` pair I put in the head area:

```
<style type = "text/css">
  body {
    color: yellow;
    background-color: red;
  }

  h1 {
    color: red;
    background-color: yellow;
  }
</style>
```


The `<style>` tag is an HTML tag, but what it does is special: It switches languages! Inside the `style` elements, you're not writing XHTML any more. Now you're in a whole new language — CSS. CSS has a different job than XHTML, but they're made to work well together.

It may seem that the CSS code is still part of HTML because it's inside the XHTML page, but it's best to think of XHTML and CSS as two distinct (if related) languages. XHTML describes the content, and CSS describes the layout. CSS (as you soon see) has a different syntax and style than XHTML, and it isn't always embedded in the Web page.

Setting up a style sheet

Style sheets describe presentation rules for XHTML elements. If you look at the preceding style sheet (the code inside the style tags), you can see that I've described presentation rules for two elements: the `body` and `h1` tags. Whenever the browser encounters one of these tags, it attempts to use these style rules to change that tag's visual appearance.

Styles are simply a list of *selectors* (places in the page that you want to modify). For now, I use tag names (`body` and `h1`) as selectors. But in Chapter 3 of this minibook, I show many more selectors that you can use.

Each selector can have a number of style *rules*. Each rule describes some attribute of the selector. To set up a style, keep the following in mind:

- **Begin with the style tags.** The type of style you'll be working with now is embedded directly into the page. You should describe your style in the header area.

- **Include the style type in the header area.** The style type is always `"text/css"`. The beginning style tag always looks like this:

```
<style type = "text/css">
```

- **Define an element.** Use the element name (the tag name alone) to begin the definition of a particular element's style. You can define styles for all the XHTML elements (and other things, too, but not today). The style rule for the body is designated like this:

```
body {
```

- **Use braces ({}) to enclose the style rules.** Each style's rules are enclosed in a set of braces. This is similar to many programming languages, which use braces to mark off special sections of code. It's traditional to indent inside the braces.
- **Give a rule name.** In this chapter, I'm working with two very simple rules: `color` and `background-color`. Throughout this minibook, you can read about many more CSS rules (sometimes called attributes) that you can modify. The rule name is always followed by a colon (`:`) character.
- **Enter the rule's value.** Different rules take different values. The attribute value is followed by a semicolon. Each name-value pair is traditionally put on one line, like this:

```
body {
  color: yellow;
  background-color: red;
}
```

Changing the colors

In this very simple example, I've just changed some colors around. Here are the two primary color attributes in CSS:

- **`color`:** This refers to the foreground color of any text in the element.
- **`background-color`:** The background color of the element. (The hyphen is a formal part of the name. If you leave it out, the browser won't know what you're talking about.)

With these two elements, you can specify the color of any element. For example, if you want all your paragraphs to have white text on a blue background, add the following text to your style:

```
p {
  color: white;
  background-color: blue;
}
```

Like XHTML Strict, CSS is case-sensitive. CSS styles should be written entirely in lowercase.

You'll figure out many more style elements in your travels, but they all follow the same principles illustrated by the color attributes.

Specifying Colors in CSS

Here are the two main ways to define colors in CSS. You can use color names, such as `pink` and `fuchsia`, or you can use *hex values.* (Later in this chapter, in the section "Creating Your Own Color Scheme," you find out how to use special numeric designators to choose colors.) Each approach has its advantages.

Using color names

Color names seem like the easiest solution, and, for basic colors like `red` and `yellow`, they work fine. However, here are some problems with color names that make them troublesome for Web developers:

- **Only 16 color names will validate.** Although hundreds of color names are accepted by most browsers, only 16 are guaranteed to validate in CSS and XHTML validators. See Table 1-1 for a list of those 16 colors.
- **Color names are somewhat subjective.** You'll find different opinions on what exactly constitutes any particular color, especially when you get to the more obscure colors. (I personally wasn't aware that `PeachPuff` and `PapayaWhip` are colors. They sound more like dessert recipes to me.)
- **It can be difficult to modify a color.** For example, what color is a tad bluer than `Gainsboro`? (Yeah, that's a color name, too. I had no idea how extensive my color disability really was.)
- **They're hard to match.** Let's say you're building an online shrine to your cat and you want the text to match your cat's eye color. It'll be hard to figure out exactly what color name corresponds to your cat's eyes. I guess you could ask.

Table 1-1 Legal Color Names and Hex Equivalents

Color	*Hex Value*
Black	#000000
Silver	#C0C0C0
Gray	#808080
White	#FFFFFF
Maroon	#800000

(continued)

Table 1-1 (continued)

Color	*Hex Value*
Red	#FF0000
Purple	#800080
Fuchsia	#FF00FF
Green	#008800
Lime	#00FF00
Olive	#808000
Yellow	#FFFF00
Navy	#000080
Blue	#0000FF
Teal	#008080
Aqua	#00FFFF

The mysterious hex codes are included in this table for completeness. It's really okay if you don't understand what they're about. All is revealed in the next section.

Obviously, I can't show you actual colors in this black-and-white book, so I added a simple page to the CD-ROM and Web site that displays all the named colors. Check `namedColors.html` to see the actual colors.

Putting a hex on your colors

Colors in HTML are a strange thing. The "easy" way (with color names) turns out to have a lot of problems. The method most Web developers *really* use sounds a lot harder, but it isn't as bad as it may seem at first. The *hex color* scheme uses a seemingly bizarre combination of numbers and letters to determine color values. #00FFFF is aqua. #FFFF00 is yellow. It's a scheme only a computer scientist could love. Yet, after you get used to it, you'll find the system has its own geeky charm. (And isn't geeky charm the best kind?)

Hex colors work by describing exactly what the computer is doing, so you have to know a little more about how computers work with color. Each dot (or *pixel*) on the screen is actually composed of three little tiny beams of light (or LCD diodes or something similar). Each pixel has tiny red, green, and blue beams.

The light beams work kind of like stage lights. Imagine a black stage with three spotlights (red, green, and blue) trained on the same spot. If all the lights are turned off, the stage is completely dark. If you turn on only the red light, you see red. You can turn on combinations to get new colors. For example, turning on red and green creates a spot of yellow light. Turning on all three lights makes white.

Coloring by number

You could devise a simple system to describe colors by using 1 to represent on and 0 to represent off. In this system, three digits represent each color, with one digit each for red, green, and blue. So, red would be 100 (turn on red, but turn off green and blue), and 111 would be white (turn on all three lights).

This system produces only eight colors. In a computer system, each of the little lights can be adjusted to various levels of brightness. These values measure from 0 (all the way off) to 255 (all the way on.) So, you could describe red as `rgb(255, 0, 0)` and yellow as `rgb(255, 255, 0)`.

The 0 to 255 range of values seems strange because you're probably used to base 10 mathematics. The computer actually stores values in binary notation. The way a computer sees it, yellow is actually 111111111111111100000000. Ack! There's got to be an easier way to handle all those binary values. That's why we use *hexadecimal notation*. Read on. . . .

Hex education

All those 1s and 0s get tedious. Programmers like to convert to another format that's easier to work with. It's easier to convert numbers to base 16 than base 10, so that's what programmers do. You can survive just fine without understanding base 16 (also called *hexadecimal* or *hex*) conversion, but you should understand a few key features, such as:

- ✦ **Each hex digit is shorthand for four digits of binary.** The whole reason programmers use hex is to simplify working with binary.
- ✦ **Each digit represents a value between 0 and 15.** Four digits of binary represent a value between 0 and 15.
- ✦ **We have to invent some digits.** The whole reason hex looks so weird is the inclusion of characters. This is for a simple reason: There aren't enough numeric digits to go around! Table 1-2 illustrates the basic problem.

Table 1-2 Hex Representation of Base Ten Numbers

Decimal (Base 10)	*Hex (Base 16)*
0	0
1	1
2	2
3	3
4	4
5	5

(continued)

Table 1-2 (continued)

Decimal (Base 10)	*Hex (Base 16)*
6	6
7	7
8	8
9	9
10	A
11	B
12	C
13	D
14	E
15	F

The ordinary digits 0–9 are the same in hex as they are in base 10, but the values from 10–15 (base ten) are represented by alphabetic characters in hexadecimal.

You're very used to seeing the value 10 as equal to the number of fingers on both hands, but that's not always the case when you start messing around with numbering systems like we're doing here. 10 simply means one of the current base. Up to now, you may have never used any base but base ten, but all that changes here. 10 is ten in base ten, but in base two, 10 means two. In base eight, 10 means eight, and in base sixteen, 10 means sixteen. This is important because when you want to talk about the number of digits on your hands in hex, you can't use the familiar notation 10, because in hex 10 means sixteen. We need a single-digit value to represent ten, so computer scientists legislated themselves out of this mess by borrowing letters. Ten is A, eleven is B, and fifteen is F.

If all this math theory is making you dizzy don't worry. I show in the next section some shortcuts for creating great colors using this scheme. For now, though, here's what you need to understand to use hex colors:

✦ **A color requires six digits of hex.** A pixel requires three colors, and each color uses eight digits of binary. Two digits of hex cover each color. Two digits represent red, two for green, and finally two for blue.

✦ **Hex numbers usually begin with a pound sign.** To warn the browser that a value will be in hexadecimal, the value is usually preceded with a pound sign (#). So, yellow is #FFFF00.

Working with colors in hex may seem really crazy and difficult, but it has some important advantages:

- **Precision:** Using this system gives you a huge number of colors to work with (over 16 million, if you really want to know). There's no way you could come up with that many color names on your own. Well, you could, but you'd be very very old by the time you were done.
- **Objectivity:** Hex values aren't a matter of opinion. There could be some argument about the value of *burnt sienna,* but hex value #666600 is unambiguous.
- **Portability:** Most graphic editors use the hex system, so you can pick any color of an image and get its hex value immediately. This would make it easy to find your cat's eye color for that online shrine.
- **Predictability:** After you understand how it works, you can take any hex color and convert it to a value that's a little darker, a little brighter, or that has a little more blue in it. This is difficult to do with named colors.
- **Ease of use:** This one may seem like a stretch, but after you understand the Web-safe palette, which I describe in the next section, it's very easy to get a rough idea of a color and then tweak it to make exactly the form you're looking for.

Using the Web-safe color palette

A long time ago, browsers couldn't even agree on what colors they'd display reliably. Web developers responded by working within a predefined palette of colors that worked pretty much the same on every browser. Today's browsers have no problems showing lots of colors, but the so-called *Web-safe color palette* is still sometimes used because it's an easy starting point.

The basic idea of the Web-safe palette (shown in Table 1-3) is this: Each color can have only one of the following values: 00, 33, 66, 99, AA, CC, or FF. 00 is the darkest value for each color, and FF is the brightest. The primary colors are all made of 0s and Fs: #FF0000 is red (all red, no green, no blue). A Web-safe color uses any combination of these values, so #33AA00 is Web-safe, but #112233 is not.

Table 1-3 Web-Safe Color Values

Description	*Red*	*Green*	*Blue*
Very bright	FF	FF	FF
	CC	CC	CC
	AA	AA	AA
	99	99	99
	66	66	66
	33	33	33
Very dark	00	00	00

To pick a Web-safe value from this chart, determine how much of each color you want. A bright red will have red turned on all the way (FF) with no green (00) and no blue (00), making #FF0000. If you want a darker red, you might turn the red down a little. The next darker Web-safe red is #CC0000. If that isn't dark enough, you might try #AA0000. Let's say you like that, but you want it a little more purple. Simply add a notch or two of blue: #AA0033 or #AA0066.

If you're having trouble following this, look at `colorTester.html` on the CD-ROM. It allows you to pick a Web-safe color by clicking on buttons organized just like Table 1-3.

The original problem Web-safe colors were designed to alleviate is long resolved, but they're still popular as a starting point. Web-safe colors give you a dispersed and easily understood subset of colors you can start with. You don't have to stay there, but it's a great place to start.

Choosing Your Colors

Figure 1-2 shows a program I added to the Web page and CD-ROM. This page lets you experiment with colors. I refer to it during this discussion.

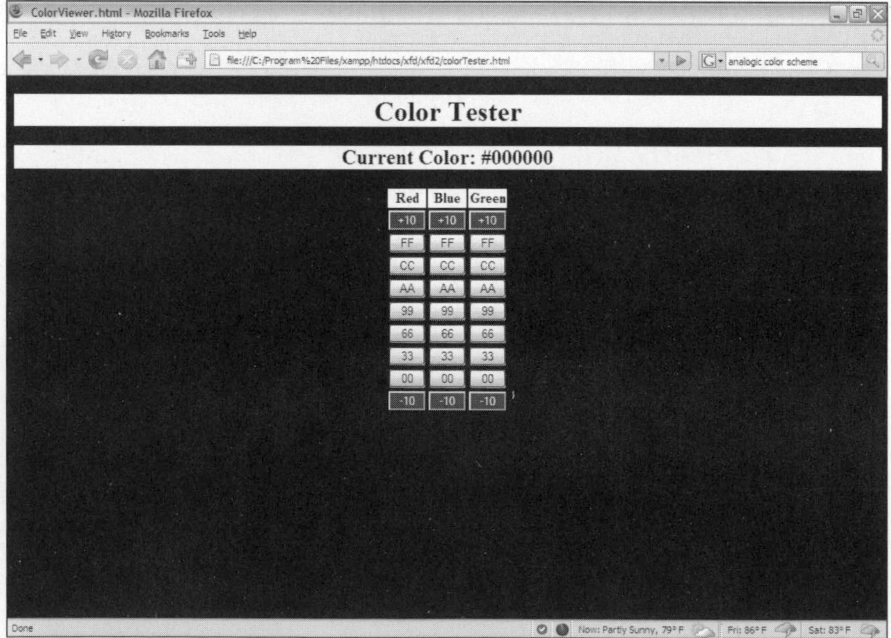

Figure 1-2: This program lets you quickly test color combinations.

The colorTester.html (as shown in Figure 1-2) page uses techniques that I describe primarily in Book IV, Chapter 5. Feel free to look over the source code to get a preview of JavaScript and Dynamic HTML concepts. By the end of Book IV, you can write this program.

The best way to understand colors is to do some hands-on experimentation. You can use the colorTester.html page to do some quick tests, or you can write and modify your own pages that use color.

Starting with Web-safe colors

The colorTester.html program works by letting you quickly enter in a Web-safe value. To make red, press the FF button in the red column. The blue and green values have the default value of 00, so the background is red.

The Web-safe colors give you a lot of room to play, and they're very easy to work with. In fact, they're so common that you can use a shortcut. Because the Web-safe colors are all repeated, you can write a repeated digit (FF) as a single digit (F). You can specify magenta as either #FF00FF or as #FOF and the browser understands, giving you a headache-inducing magenta.

To make a darker red, change the FF to the next smallest value, making #CC0000. If you want it darker yet, try #AA0000. Experiment with all the red values and see how easy it is to get several different types of red. If you want a variation of pink, raise the green and blue values together. #FF9999 is a dusty pink color; #FFAAAA is a bit brighter; and #FFCCCC is a very white pink.

Modifying your colors

The Web-safe palette is convenient, but it gives you a relatively small number of colors (216, if you're counting). Two hundred and sixteen crayons in the box are pretty nice, but you might need more. Generally, I start with Web-safe colors and then adjust as I go. If you want a lighter pink than #FFCCCC, you can jump off the Web-safe bandwagon and use #FFEEEE or any other color you wish!

In the colorTester.html program, you can use the top and bottom button in each row to fine tune the adjustments to your color.

Doing it on your own pages

Of course, it doesn't really matter how the colors look on *my* page. The point is to make things look good on *your* pages. To add color to your pages, do the following:

1. **Define the XHTML as normal.**

   The XHTML shouldn't have any relationship to the colors. Add the color strictly in CSS.

2. **Add a style tag to the page in the head area.**

   Don't forget to set the `type = "text/css"` attribute.

3. **Add a selector for each tag you want to modify.**

   You can modify any HTML tag, so if you want to change all the paragraphs, add a `p { }` selector. Use the tag name without the angle braces, so `<h1>` becomes `h1{ }`.

4. **Add color and background-color attributes.**

   You'll discover many more CSS elements you can modify throughout Books II and III but for now, stick to color and background-color.

5. **Specify the color values with color names or hex color values.**

Changing CSS on the fly

If you've installed the Web Developer toolbar to Firefox (which I describe in Book I, Chapter 3) you have some really nifty CSS tools at your disposal. I really love the CSS editor. To make it work, take any page (without CSS) and open it in Firefox. For this example, I use a list example from Book I, Chapter 4.

Be sure the Web Developer toolbar is installed and choose Edit CSS from the CSS menu. A new panel that looks like Figure 1-3 pops up.

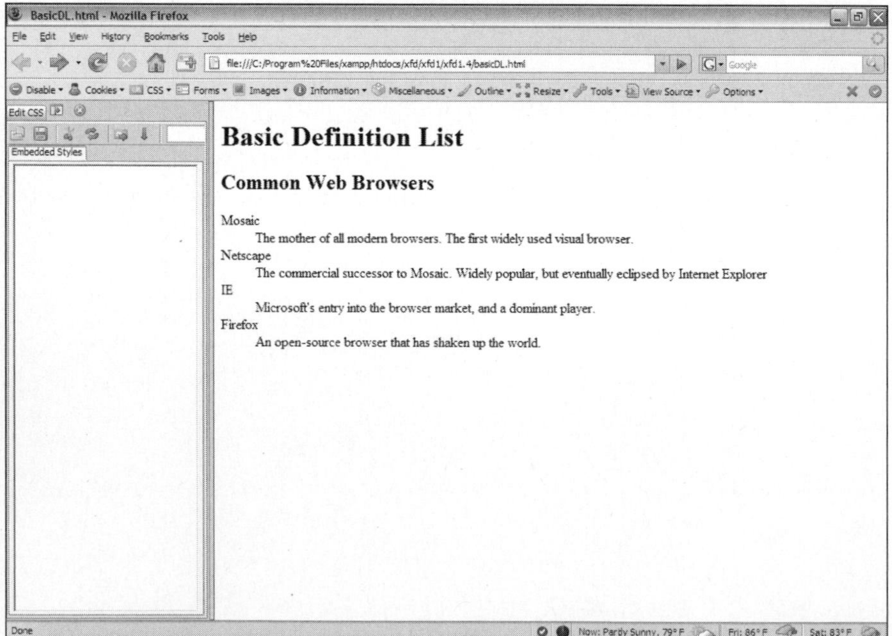

Figure 1-3: The Web Developer toolbar has a great CSS feature.

You can simply type CSS code into the little text editor, and the page is updated instantly! Figure 1-4 shows the same page after I made a few changes.

I used color to make the definition list easier to view. I changed both the foreground and background colors in the heading level 1. I set the definition terms (`dt`) to red and added a yellow background to the definitions (`dd`). Check Book I, Chapter 4 if you need a refresher on definition lists in XHTML.

The Web Developer CSS editor is great because you can see the results in real time. It's a super way to play around with your colors (and other CSS elements). You can also use it to view and modify an existing CSS document. Pull up any page you want and open the CSS editor. You can change colors all you want without making a commitment.

None of the changes made using the Web Developer CSS editor are permanent. You're making changes only in the copy in your own browser. If you really like the CSS code you've written in the editor, copy it to the clipboard and paste it into your page to make it permanent, or save it to a file for later use.

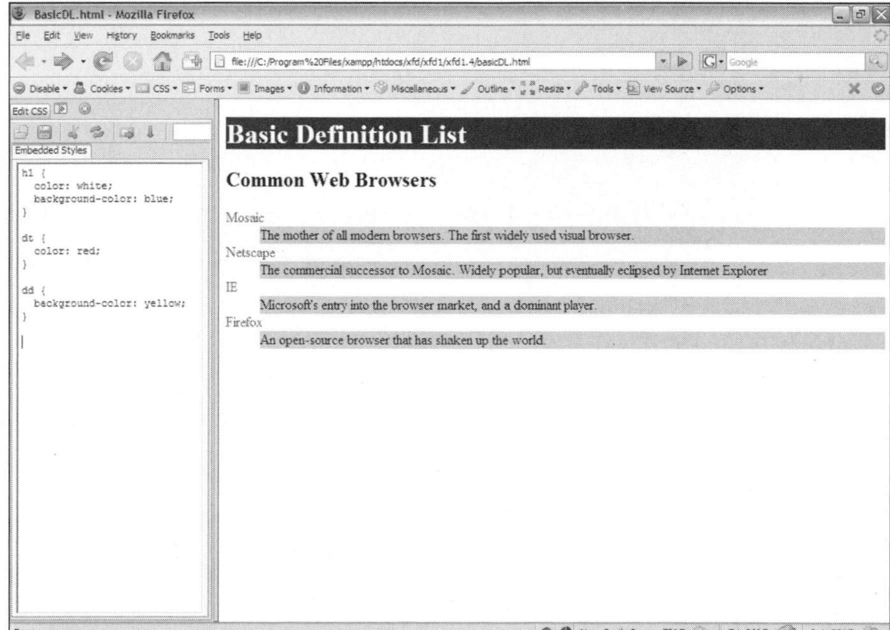

Figure 1-4: The CSS changes show immediately.

Creating Your Own Color Scheme

The technical side of setting colors isn't too difficult, but deciding *what* colors to use can be a challenge. Entire books have been written about how to determine a color scheme. A little bit of subjectivity is in the process, but a few tools and rules can get you started.

Understanding hue, saturation, and value

The RGB color model is useful because it relates directly to how computers generate color, but it's not perfect. It's a bit difficult to visualize variations of a color in RGB. For that reason, other color schemes are often used. The most common variation is *Hue, Saturation, and Value,* or *HSV.* The HSV system organizes colors in a way more closely related to the color wheel.

To describe a color using HSV, you specify three characteristics of a color using numeric values.

- **Hue:** The basic color. The color wheel is broken into a series of different hues. These are generally middle of the road colors that can be made *brighter* (closer to white) and *darker* (closer to black).
- **Saturation:** How pervasive the color is. A high saturation is very bright. A low saturation has very little color. If you reduce all the saturation in an image, the image is *grayscale,* with no color at all.
- **Value:** The brightness of the color. The easiest way to view value is to think about how the image would be when reduced to grayscale (by pulling down the saturation). All the brighter colors will be closer to white, and the darker colors will be nearly black.

The HSV model is useful because it allows you to pick colors that go well together. Use the hue property to pick the basic colors. Because there's a mathematical relationship between the various color values, it becomes easy to predict which colors work well together. After you have all the hues worked out, you can change the saturation and value to modify the overall tone of the page. Generally, all the colors in a particular scheme have similar saturation and values.

Unfortunately, you can't specify CSS colors in HSV mode. Instead, you have to use another tool to get the colors you want and convert them to RGB format.

Using the Color Scheme Generator

Some people have great color sense. Others (like me) struggle a little bit because it all seems a little subjective. If you're already confident with colors, you may not need this section — although you still might find it interesting validation of what you already know. On the other hand, if you get perplexed in a paint store, you might find it helpful to know that some really useful tools are available.

One great way to get started is with a free tool: the Color Scheme Generator, as shown in Figure 1-5. This tool created by Petr Stanicek uses a variation of the HSV model to help you pick color schemes. You can find this program at `http://wellstyled.com/tools/colorscheme2/index-en.html`.

The Color Scheme Generator has several main areas, such as:

- **The color wheel:** This tool may bring back fond memories of your elementary school art class. The wheel arranges the colors in a way familiar to artists. You can click the color wheel to pick a primary color for your page.
- **The color scheme selector:** You can pick from a number of color schemes. I describe these schemes a little later in this section.
- **A preview area:** This area displays the selected colors in action so you can see how the various colors work together.
- **Hex values:** The hex values for the selected colors are displayed on the page so you can copy them directly to your own application.

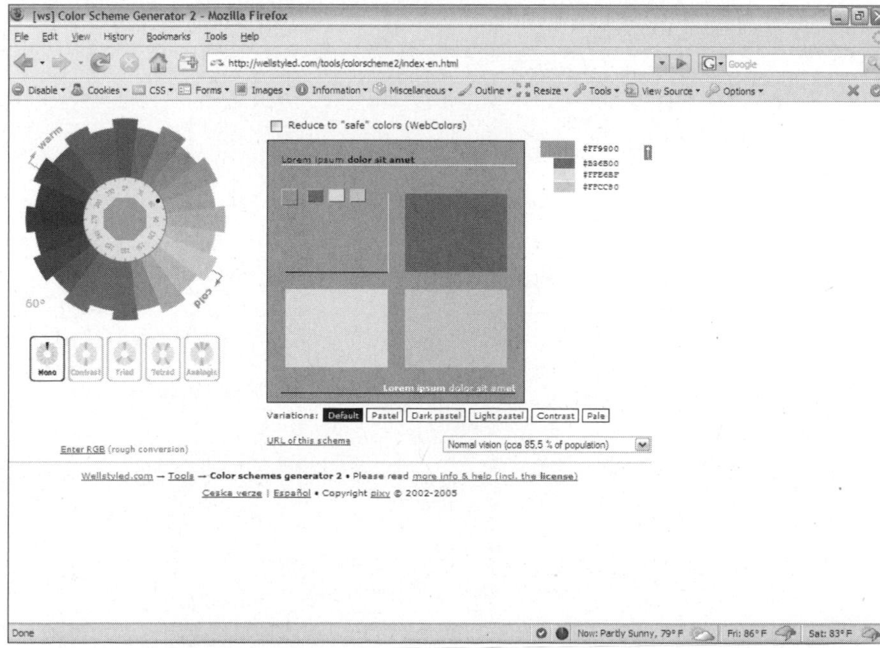

Figure 1-5: The Color Scheme Generator helps you pick colors.

- **Variations:** You can look at variations of the selected scheme. These variations are often useful because they show differences in the saturation and value without you doing the math.
- **Color-blindness simulation:** This very handy tool lets you see your color scheme as it appears to people with various types of color-blindness.

This won't make sense without experimentation. Be sure to play with this tool and see how easy it is to create colors that work well together.

Selecting a base hue

The Color Scheme Generator works by letting you pick one main hue and then uses one of a number of schemes for picking other hues that work well with the base one. To choose the base hue you want for your page, click a color on the color wheel.

The color wheel is arranged according to the traditional artist's color scheme based on HSV rather than the RGB scheme used for computer graphics. When you select a color, the closest RGB representation is returned. This is nice because it allows you to apply traditional (HSV-style) color theory to the slightly different RGB model.

When you pick a color on the color wheel, you're actually picking a hue. If you want any type of red, you can pick the red that appears on the wheel. You can then adjust the variations to modify the saturation and value of all the colors in the scheme together.

To pick a color using this scheme, follow these steps:

1. **Pick a hue.**

   The colors on the color wheel actually represent hues. Find a color you want to use as the foundation of your page.

2. **Choose a variation.**

   Rather than working directly with saturation and value, the variations (pastel, contrast, pale, and so on) pick saturations and values for you.

3. **Determine a scheme.**

   The scheme allows you to specify a number of colors related to the base color according to various mathematical relationships.

Picking a color scheme

The various color schemes use mathematical relationships around the color wheel to predict colors that work well with the primary color. Here are the basic schemes and what they do:

- **Monochramatic (mono):** Takes the base hue and offers a number of variations in saturation and value. This scheme is nice when you really want to emphasize one particular color (for example, if you're doing a Web site about rain forests and want a lot of greens). Be sure to use high contrast between the foreground and background colors so your text is readable.
- **Contrast:** Uses the base hue and the *complementary* (opposite) color. Generally, this scheme uses several variations of the base hue and a splash of the complementary hue for contrast.
- **Triad:** Selects the base hue and two opposite hues. When you select the triad scheme, you can also choose the angular distance between the opposite colors. If this distance is zero, you have the complementary color scheme. When the angle increases, you have a *split complementary* system, which uses the base hue and two hues equidistant from the contrast. Such schemes can be jarring at full contrast, but when adjusted for saturation and value, you can create some very nice color schemes.
- **Tetrad:** Generates four hues. As with the triad, when you add more hues, it becomes more difficult to keep your page unified unless you adjust the variations for lower contrast.
- **Analogic:** Schemes use the base hue and its two neighbors. Sometimes this scheme includes the complementary color as well.

Chapter 2: Styling Text

In This Chapter

- Introducing fonts and typefaces
- Specifying the font family
- Determining font size
- Understanding CSS measurement units
- Managing other font characteristics
- Using the font rule to simplify font styles

Web pages are still primarily a text-based media, so you'll want to add some formatting capabilities. XHTML doesn't do any meaningful text formatting on its own, but CSS adds a wide range of tools for choosing the typeface, font size, decorations, alignment, and much more. In this chapter, you discover how to manage text the CSS way.

A bit of semantics is in order. The thing most people dub a *font* is more properly a *typeface.* Technically, a font is a particular typeface at a particular size with a specific set of decorations (underlining, italic, and so on). The distinction is honestly not that important in a digital setting. You don't explicitly set the font in CSS. You determine the *font family* (which is essentially a typeface), and then you modify its characteristics (creating a font as purists would think of it). Still, when I'm referring to the thing most people call a font (a file in the operating system that describes the appearance of an alphabet set), I use the familiar term *font.*

Setting the Font Family

To assign a font family to part of your page, use some new CSS. Figure 2-1 illustrates a page with the heading set to Comic Sans MS.

If this page is viewed on a Windows machine, it generally displays the font correctly because Comic Sans MS is installed with most versions of Windows. If you're on another type of machine, you may get something else. More on that in a moment, but, for now, look at the simple case.

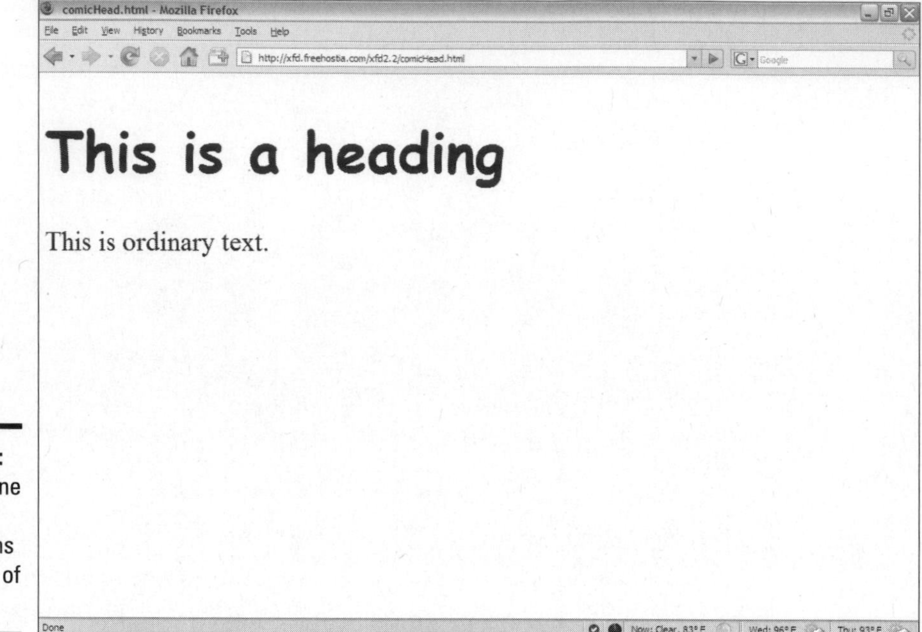

Figure 2-1: The headline is in the Comic Sans font (most of the time).

Here's the code:

```
<!DOCTYPE html PUBLIC "-//W3C//DTD XHTML 1.0 Strict//EN"
"http://www.w3.org/TR/xhtml1/DTD/xhtml1-strict.dtd">
<html lang="EN" dir="ltr" xmlns="http://www.w3.org/1999/xhtml">
  <head>
    <meta http-equiv="content-type" content="text/xml; charset=utf-8" />
    <title>comicHead.html</title>
    <style type = "text/css">
      h1 {
        font-family: "Comic Sans MS";
      }
    </style>
  </head>

  <body>
    <H1>This is a heading</H1>
    <p>
      This is ordinary text.
    </p>
  </body>
</html>
```

Applying the font-family style attribute

The secret to this page is the CSS `font-family` attribute. Like most CSS elements, this can be applied to any HTML tag on your page. In this particular case, I applied it to my level one heading.

```
h1 {
  font-family: "Comic Sans MS";
}
```

You can then attach any font name you wish, and the browser attempts to use that font to display the element.

Even though a font may work perfectly fine on your computer, it may not work if that font isn't installed on the user's machine.

If you run exactly the same page on a Linux machine, you see the result shown in Figure 2-2.

The specific font Comic Sans MS is installed on Windows machines, but the *MS* stands for Microsoft. This font isn't typically installed on Linux. (It is on some Macs, but not all.) You can't count on users having any particular fonts installed.

Using generic fonts

It's a little depressing. Even though it's easy to use fonts, you can't use them freely because you don't know if the user has them. Fortunately, you can do a few things that at least increase the odds in your favor. The first trick is to use *generic font names.* These are *virtual* font names that every compliant browser agrees to support. Figure 2-3 shows a page with all the generic fonts.

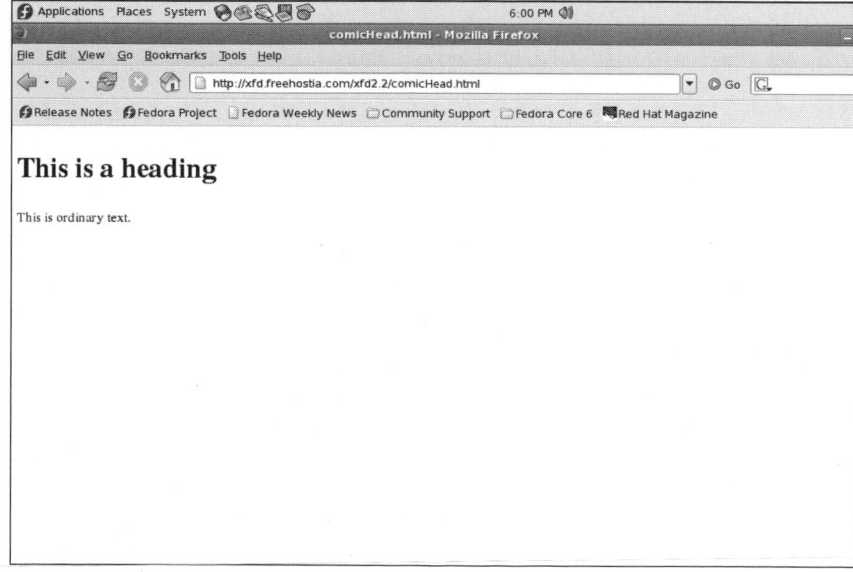

Figure 2-2: Under Linux, the heading isn't the same font!

I used browser controls to make the fonts larger than normal so you can see the details in this figure. Note that it's really handy to be able to change font size as a user. I come back to that idea later in this chapter.

The generic fonts really are families of fonts:

- **Serif:** These fonts have those little serifs (the tiny cross strokes that enhance readability). Print text (like the paragraph you're reading now) tends to use serif fonts, and they're the default font for most browsers. The most common serif typeface is Times New Roman or Times.
- **Sans-Serif:** Sans serif fonts don't have the little feet. They're generally used for headlines or other emphasis. They're sometimes seen as more modern and clean than serif fonts, so sometimes they're used for body text. Arial is the most common sans-serif font. In this book, the figure captions use a sans serif font.
- **Cursive:** These fonts look a little like handwriting. In Windows, the script font is usually Comic Sans MS. Script fonts are used when you want a less formal look. Dummies books use script fonts all over the place, for section and chapter headings.

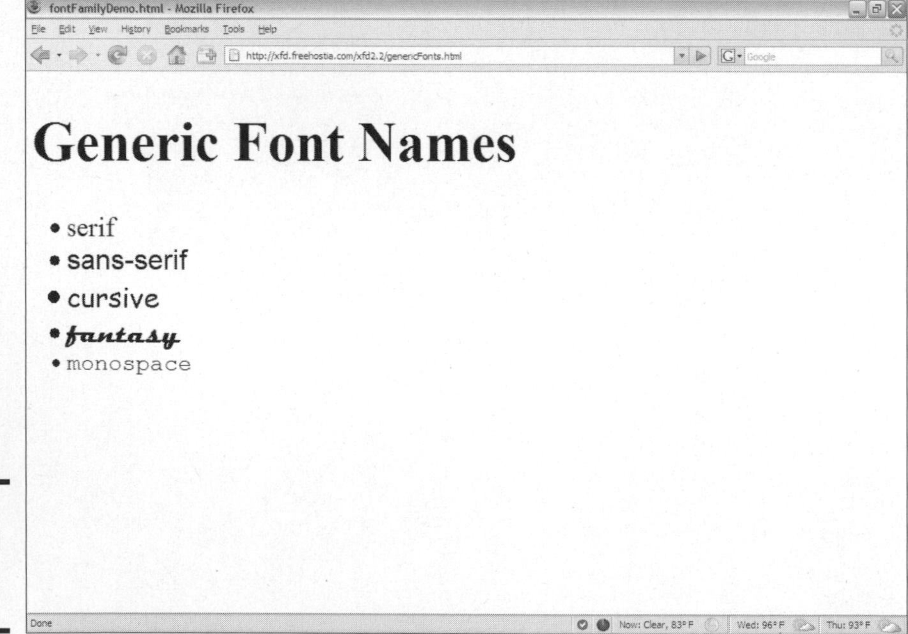

Figure 2-3: Here are all the generic fonts.

✦ **Fantasy:** Fantasy fonts are decorative. Just about any theme you can think of is represented by a fantasy font, from Klingon to Tolkien. You can also find fonts that evoke a certain culture, making English text appear to be Persian or Chinese. Fantasy fonts are best used sparingly, for emphasis, as they often trade readability for visual appeal..

✦ **Monospace:** Monospace fonts produce a fixed-width font like typewritten text. Monospace fonts are frequently used to display code. Courier is a common monospace font.

Because the generic fonts are available on all standards-compliant browsers, you'd think you could use them confidently. Well, you can be sure they'll appear, but you still might be surprised. Figure 2-4 shows the same page (as shown in Figure 2-3 in Windows) in Linux.

Macs display yet another variation. This is because the fonts listed here aren't *actual* fonts. Instead, they're *virtual* fonts. A standards-compliant browser promises to put an appropriate *stand in*. For example, if you choose sans serif, one browser may choose to use Arial. Another may choose Chicago. You can always use these font names and know the browser can make something close, but there's no guarantee exactly what font is chosen by the browser. Still, it's better than nothing. When you use these fonts, you can be assured that you get something in the right neighborhood, if not exactly what you intended.

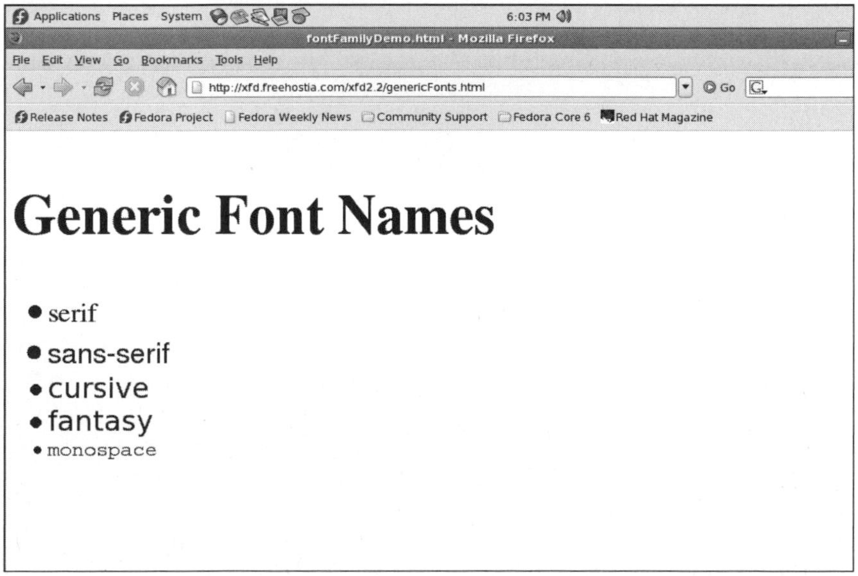

Figure 2-4: Windows and Linux disagree on fantasy.

Making a list of fonts

This uncertainty is frustrating, but you can take some control. You can specify an entire list of font names if you want. The browser tries each font in turn. If it can't find the specified font, it goes to the next and on down the line.

You might choose a font that you know is installed on all Windows machines, a font found on Macs, and finally one found on all Linux machines. The last font on your list should be one of the generic fonts, so you'll have some control over the worst-case scenario.

Table 2-1 shows a list of fonts commonly installed on Linux, Mac, and Windows machines.

Table 2-1 Font Equivalents

Windows	*Mac*	*Linux*
Arial	Arial	Nimbus Sans L
Arial Black	Arial Black	
Comic Sans MS	Comic Sans MS	TSCu_Comic
Courier New	Courier New	Nimbus Mono L
Georgia	Georgia	Nimbus Roman No9 L
Lucida Console	Monaco	
Palatino	Palatino	FreeSerif
Tahoma	Geneva	Kalimati
Times New Roman	Times	FreeSerif
Trebuchet MS	Helvetica	FreeSans
Verdana	Verdana	Kalimati

You can use this chart to derive a list of fonts to try. For example, look at the following style:

```
p {
  font-family: "Trebuchet MS", Helvetica, FreeSans, sans-serif;
}
```

This style has a whole smorgasbord of options. First, the browser tries to load Trebuchet MS. If it's a Windows machine, this font is available, so that's the one that's displayed. If that doesn't work, the browser tries *Helvetica* (a default Mac font). If that doesn't work, it tries *FreeSans,* a font frequently installed on Linux machines. If this doesn't work, it defaults to the old faithful sans-serif, which simply picks a sans-serif font.

Note that font names that take up more than one word must be encased in quotes, and the list of font names is separated by commas.

The death of the font tag

There used to be a tag in old-school HTML called the `<font>` tag. You could use this tag to change the size, color, and font family. There were also specific tags for italicizing (`<i>`), making boldface (`<b>`), and centering (`<center>`). These tags were very easy to use, but they caused some major problems. To use them well, you ended up littering your page with all kinds of tags trying to describe the markup, rather than the meaning. There was no easy way to reuse font information, so you often had to repeat things many times throughout the page, making it difficult to change. XHTML strict. no longer allows the `<font>`, `<i>`, `<b>`, or `<center>` tags. The CSS elements I show in this chapter more than compensate for this loss. You now have a more flexible, more powerful alternative.

Don't get too stressed about Linux fonts. It's true that the equivalencies are harder to find, but Linux users tend to fall into two camps: They either don't care if the fonts are exact, or they do care and they've installed equivalent fonts that recognize more common names. In either case, you can focus on Mac and Windows people for the most part, and, as long as you've used a generic font name, things work okay on a Linux box.

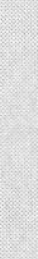

The Curse of Web-Based Fonts

Fonts seem pretty easy at first, but there are some big problems with actually using them.

Understanding the problem

The problem with fonts is this: Font resources are installed in each operating system. They aren't downloaded with the rest of the page. Your Web page can call for a specific font, but that font isn't displayed unless it's already been installed on the user's computer.

Let's say I have a cool font called *Happygeek.* (I just made that up. If you're a font designer, feel free to make a font called that. Just send me a copy. I can't wait.) It's installed on my computer, and when I choose a font in my word processor, it shows up in the list. I can create a word-processing document with it, and everything will work great.

If I send a printout of a document using Happygeek to my grandma, everything's great because the paper doesn't need the actual font. It's just ink. If I send her the digital file and tell her to open it on her computer, we'll have a problem. See, she's not that hip and doesn't have Happygeek installed. Her computer will pick some other font.

This isn't a big problem in word processing because people don't generally send around digital copies of documents with elaborate fonts in them. However, Web pages are passed around *only* in digital form. In order to know which fonts you can use, you have to know what fonts are installed on the user's machine, and that's impossible.

Part of the concern is technical (figuring out how to transfer the font information to the browser), but the real issue is digital rights management. If you've purchased a font for your own use, does that give you the right to transfer it to others, so now they can use it without paying?

Examining possible solutions

This has been a problem since the beginning of the Web. A lot of people have tried to come up with solutions. None of these solutions are good, but here are a few compromises:

- **Embedded fonts:** Netscape and IE (Internet Explorer) both came up with techniques to embed fonts directly into a Web page. Both techniques involved using a piece of software to convert the font into a proprietary format that allows it to be used for the specific page and nothing else. The two systems were incompatible, and both were a little awkward. Almost nobody used them. Firefox now completely ignores this technology, and IE can do it but with a separate tool. Until browsers come up with a compatible solution, I don't recommend this technique.
- **CSS 3 embedded fonts:** *CSS 3* (the next version of CSS on the horizon) promises a way to import a font file purely through CSS. You'll be able to specify a particular filename and pass a URL (Uniform Resource Locator) to the file on your server, and it'll be used for that particular page but not installed on the user's system. This is the way custom fonts have been handled in games for years. Unfortunately, none of the top browsers are currently using this technique. If this system becomes standard, it will be the way to handle fonts.
- **Flash:** Flash is a vector format very popular on the Web. Flash has very nice features for converting fonts to a binary format within the flash output, and most users have some kind of flash player installed. The Flash editor is expensive, somewhat challenging to figure out, and defeats many of the benefits of XHTML. These disadvantages outweigh the potential benefit of custom fonts.

I'm certainly not opposed to using Flash. I just don't think it's a good idea to build entire Web pages in Flash, or to use Flash simply to get access to fonts. If you're interested in using Flash, you might want to check out another book I wrote, *Flash Game Programming For Dummies* (Wiley Publishing, Inc.). In this book, you'll learn how to make Flash *literally* sing and dance.

- **Images:** Some designers choose to forego HTML altogether and create their pages as huge images. This requires a huge amount of bandwidth, makes the pages impossible to search, and makes them difficult to modify. This is a really bad idea. Although you have precise control of the visual layout, you lose most of the advantages of XHTML. Content in images cannot be read by search engines and is entirely inaccessible to people with screen readers. An image large enough to fill the screen will take many times longer to download than equivalent XHTML markup. The user cannot resize an image-based page, and this type of page does not scale well to phones or other portable browsers.

Using images for headlines

Generally, you should use standard fonts for the page's main content anyway, so having a limited array of fonts isn't such a big problem. Sometimes, though, you want to use fonts in your headlines. You can use a graphical editor, like GIMP, to create text-based images and then incorporate them into your pages. Figure 2-5 shows an example of this technique.

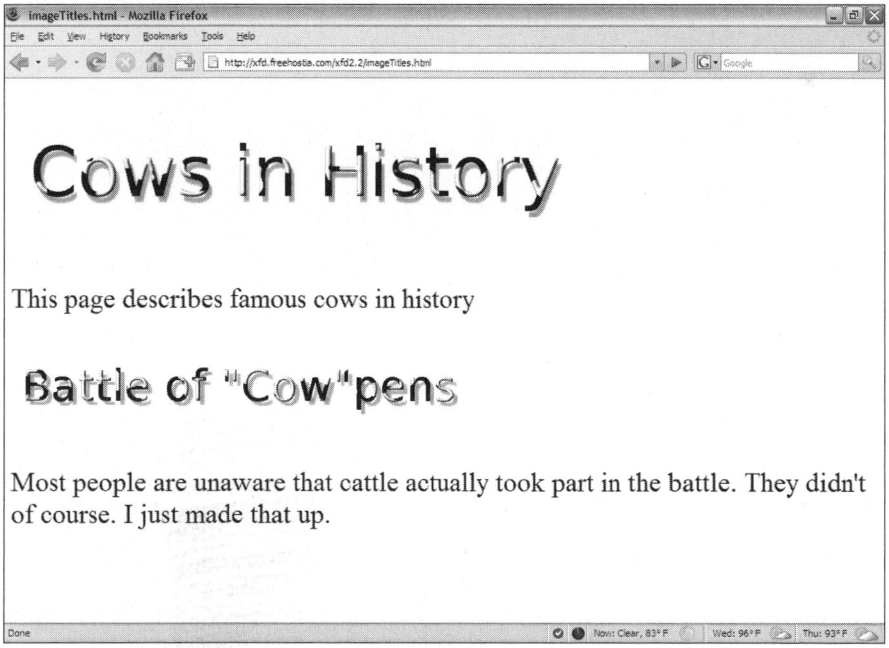

Figure 2-5: The font shows up because it's an image.

In this case, I want to use my special cow font. (I *love* my cow font.)

Here's the process:

1. **Plan your page.**

   When you use graphics, you lose a little flexibility. You'll need to know exactly what the headlines should be. You also need to know what headline will be displayed at what level. Rather than relying on the browser to display your headlines, you're creating graphics in your graphic tool (I'm using Gimp) and placing them directly in the page.

2. **Create your images.**

   I used the wonderful Logos feature in GIMP (choose Xtns➪Script-fu➪logos) to create my cow text. I built an image for each headline with the *Bovination* tool. I'm just happy to have a Bovination tool. It's something I've always wanted.

3. **Specify font sizes directly.**

   In the image, it makes sense to specify font sizes in pixels because here you're really talking about a specific number of pixels. You're creating "virtual text" in your graphic editor, so make the text whatever size you want it to be in the finished page.

4. **Use any font you want.**

   You don't have to worry about whether the user has the font because you're not sending the font itself, just an image composed with the font.

5. **Create a separate image for each headline.**

   This particular exercise has two images — a level 1 heading and a level 2. Because I'm creating images directly, it's up to me to keep track of how the image will communicate its headline level.

6. **Consider the headline level.**

   Be sure to make headline level 2 values look a little smaller or less emphasized than level 1. That is, if you have images that will be used in a heading 1 setting, they should use a larger font than images that will be used in a less emphasized heading level. This is usually done by adjusting the font size in your images.

7. **Build the page as you normally would.**

   Once you have these specialty images created, build a regular Web page. Put `<h1>` and `<h2>` tags in exactly the same places you usually do.

8. **Put `<img>` tags inside the headings.**

   Rather than ordinary text, place image tags inside the `h1` and `h2` tags. See the upcoming code `imageTitles.html` if you're a little confused.

9. **Put headline text in the `alt` attribute.**

   The `alt` attribute is especially important here because if the user has graphics turned off, the text still appears as an appropriately styled heading. People with slow connections see the text before the images load, and people using text readers can still read the image.

Here's the code used to generate the image-based headers:

```
<!DOCTYPE html PUBLIC "-//W3C//DTD XHTML 1.0 Strict//EN"
"http://www.w3.org/TR/xhtml1/DTD/xhtml1-strict.dtd">
<html lang="EN" dir="ltr" xmlns="http://www.w3.org/1999/xhtml">
  <head>
    <meta http-equiv="content-type" content="text/xml; charset=utf-8" />
    <title>imageTitles.html</title>
  </head>

  <body>
    <h1>
      <img src = "cowsHistory.png"
           alt = "Cows in History" />
    </h1>

    <p>
      This page describes famous cows in history
    </p>

    <h2>
      <img src = "cowpens.png"
           alt = "Battle of Cowpens" />
    </h2>

    <p>
      Most people are unaware that cattle actually took
      part in the battle. They didn't of course. I just
      made that up.
    </p>

  </body>
</html>
```

This technique is a pretty nice compromise between custom graphics and ordinary XHTML as follows:

- **You have great control of your images.** If you're skilled with your graphics tool, you can make any type of image you want act as a headline. There's literally no limit except your skill and creativity.
- **The page retains its structure.** You still have heading tags in place, so it's easy to see that you mean for a particular image to act as a headline. You can still see the page organization in the XHTML code.
- **You have fallback text.** The `alt` attributes will activate if the images can't be displayed.

- **The semantic meaning of image headlines is preserved.** The `alt` tags provide another great feature. If they replicate the image text, this text is still available to screen readers and search engines, so the text is not buried in the image.

This technique is great for headlines or other areas, but notice that I was careful to repeat the headline text in the `alt` tag. This is important because I don't want to lose the text. Search engine tools and screen readers need the text.

Don't be tempted to use this technique for larger amounts of body text. Doing so causes some problems:

- **The text is no longer searchable.** Search engines can't find text if it's buried in images.
- **The text is harder to change.** You can't update your page with a text editor. Instead, you have to download the image, modify it, and upload it again.
- **Images require a lot more bandwidth than text.** Don't use images if they don't substantially add to your page. You can make the case for a few heading images, but it's harder to justify having your entire page stored as an image just to use a particular font.

Specifying the Font Size

Like font names, font sizes are easy to change in CSS, but there are some hidden traps.

Size is only a suggestion!

In print media, after you determine the size of the text, it pretty much stays there. The font size in print can't be changed easily by the user. By comparison, Web browsers frequently change the size of text. A cell phone-based browser displays text differently than one on a high-resolution LCD panel. Further, most browsers allow the user to change the size of all the text on the screen. Use Ctrl++ (plus sign) and Ctrl+– (minus sign) to make the text larger or smaller. In older versions of IE (prior to IE7), use the Text Size option from the Page menu to change the text size.

The user should really have the ability to adjust the font size in the browser. When I display a Web page on a projector, I often adjust the font size so students in the back can read. Some pages have the font size set way too small for me to read. (It's probably my high-tech monitor. It couldn't possibly have anything to do with my age.)

Determining font sizes precisely is counter to the spirit of the Web. If you declare that your text will be exactly 12 points, for example, 1 of 2 things could happen:

✦ **The browser might enforce the 12-point rule literally.** This takes control from the user, so users who need larger fonts are out of luck. Older versions of IE used to do this.

✦ **The user might still change the size.** If this is how the browser behaves (and it usually is), 12 points doesn't always mean 12 points. If the user can change font sizes, the literal size selection is meaningless.

The Web developer should set up font sizes, but only in *relative* terms. Don't bother using absolute measurements (in most cases) because they don't really mean what you think. Let the user determine the base font size and specify relative changes to that size.

Using the font-size style attribute

The basic idea of font size is pretty easy to grasp in CSS. Take a look at `fontSize.html` in Figure 2-6.

This page obviously shows a number of different font sizes. The line "Font Sizes" is an ordinary `h1` element. All the other lines are paragraph tags. They appear in different sizes because they have different styles applied to them.

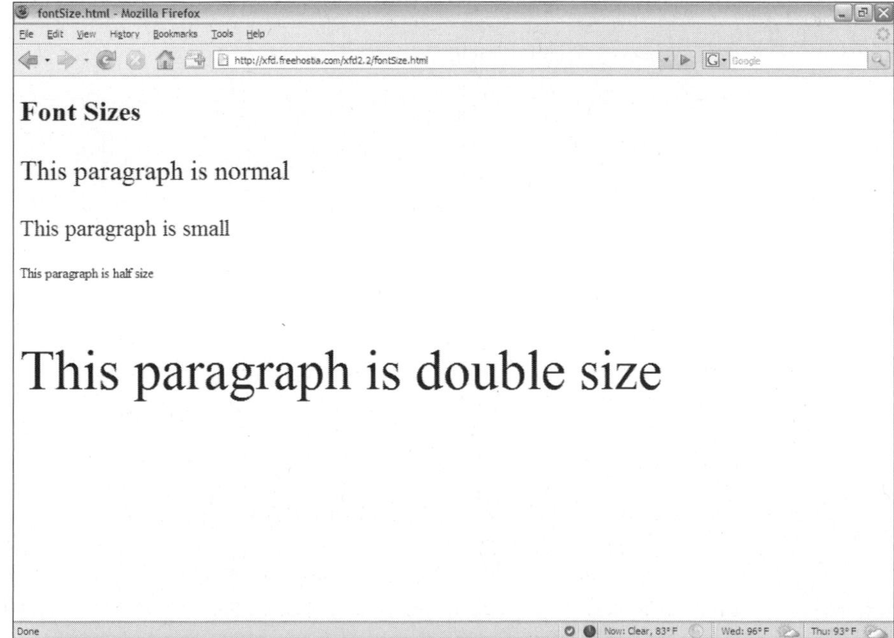

Figure 2-6: You can easily modify font sizes in your pages.

Font sizes are changed with the (cleverly named) `font-size` attribute:

```
p {
  font-size: small;
}
```

Simply indicate the `font-size` rule, and, well, the size of the font. In this example, I used the special value `small`, but there are many other ways to specify sizes in CSS.

Absolute measurement units

A lot of times you need to specify the size of something in CSS. Of course, font size is one of these cases. The different types of measurement have different implications. It's important to know there are two distinct kinds of units in CSS. *Absolute measurements* attempt to describe a particular size as in the real world. *Relative measurements* are about changes to some default value. In general, Web developers are moving toward relative measurement for font sizes.

Points (pt)

In word processing, you're probably familiar with *points* as a measurement of font size. You can use the abbreviation `pt` to indicate you're measuring in points, for example:

```
p {
  font-size: 12pt;
}
```

Note that no space is between `12` and `pt`.

Unfortunately, points aren't an effective unit of measure for Web pages. Points are an absolute scale, useful for print, but they aren't reliable on the Web because you don't know what resolution the user's screen has. A 12-point font might look larger or smaller on different monitors.

In some versions of IE, after you specify a font size in points, the user can no longer change the size of the characters. This is unacceptable from a usability standpoint. Relative size schemes (which I describe later in this chapter) prevent this problem.

Pixels (px)

Pixels refer to the small dots on the screen. You can specify a font size in pixels, although it's not usually done. For one thing, different monitors make pixels in different sizes. You can't really be sure how big a pixel will be in relationship to the overall screen size. Different letters are different sizes, so the pixel size is a rough measurement of the width and height of the average character. Use the px abbreviation to measure fonts in pixels:

```
p {
  font-size: 20px;
}
```

Traditional measurements (in, cm)

You can also use inches (in) and centimeters (cm) to measure fonts, but this is completely impractical. Imagine you have a Web page showing on your screen and also being displayed on a projection system. One inch on your own monitor may look like ten inches on the projector. Real-life measurement units aren't meaningful for the Web. The only time you might use them is if you'll be printing something and you have complete knowledge of how the printer is configured. If that's the case, you're better off using a real print-oriented layout tool than HTML.

Relative measurement units

Relative measurement is a wiser choice in Web development. Use these schemes to change sizes in relationship to the standard size.

Named sizes

CSS has a number of font size names built in:

```
xx-small
x-small
small
medium
large
x-large
xx-large
```

It may bother you that there's nothing more specific about these sizes: How big is large? Well, it's bigger than medium. That sounds like a flip answer, but it's the truth. The user sets the default font size in the browser (or leaves it alone), and all other font sizes should be in relation to this preset size. The *medium* size is the default size of paragraph text on your page. For comparison purposes, <h1> tags are usually xx-large.

Percentage (%)

The percentage unit is a relative measurement. It's used to specify the font in relationship to its normal size. Use 50% to make a font half the size it would normally appear and 200% to make it twice the normal size. Use the `%` symbol to indicate percentage, as shown here:

```
p {
  font-size: 150%;
}
```

Percentages are based on the default size of ordinary text, so an `<h1>` tag at 100% is the same size as text in an ordinary paragraph.

Em (em)

In traditional typesetting, the em is a unit of measurement equivalent to the width of the "m" character in that font. In actual Web use, it's really another way of specifying the relative size of a font. For instance, 0.5 ems is half the normal size, and 3 ems is three times the normal size. The term em is used to specify this measurement.

```
p {
  font-size: 1.5em;
}
```

Here are the best strategies for font size:

- **Don't change sizes without a good reason.** Most of the time, the browser default sizes are perfectly fine, but there may be some times when you want to adjust fonts a little more.
- **Define an overall size for the page.** If you want to define a font size for the entire page, do it in the `<body>` tag. Use a named size, percentage, or ems to avoid the side effects of absolute sizing. The size defined in the body is automatically applied to every element in the body.
- **Modify any other elements.** You might want your links a little larger than ordinary text, for example. You can do this by applying a `font-size` attribute to an element. Use relative measurement if possible.

Determining Other Font Characteristics

In addition to size and color (see Chapter 1 of this minibook), you can change fonts in a number of other ways.

Figure 2-7 shows a number of common text modifications you can make.

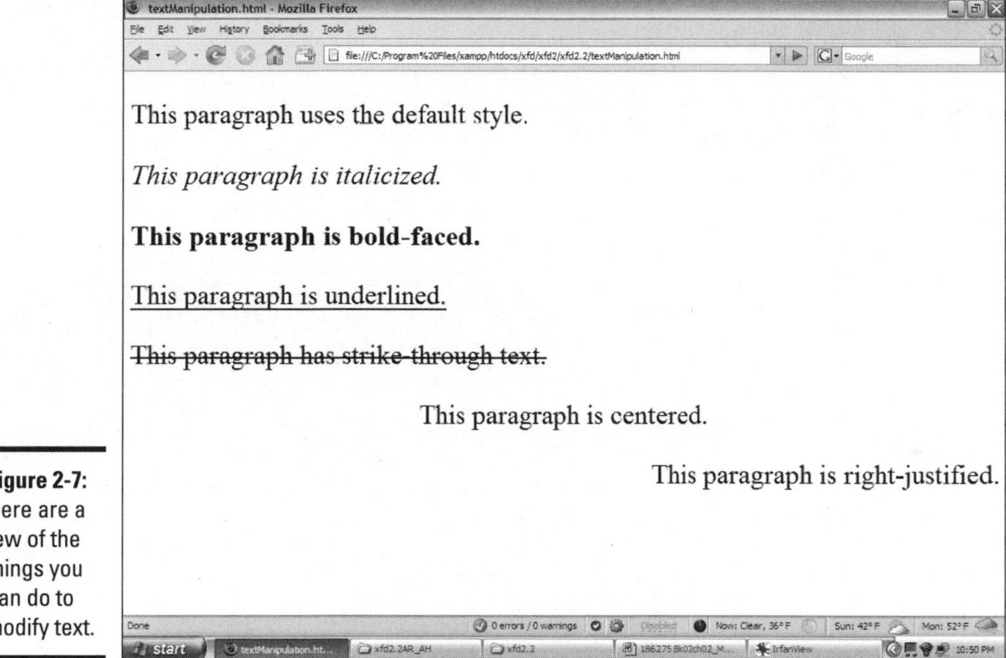

Figure 2-7: Here are a few of the things you can do to modify text.

The various paragraphs in this page are modified in different ways. You can change the alignment of the text as well as add italic, bold, underline, or strikethrough to the text.

CSS uses a potentially confusing set of rules for the various font manipulation tools. One rule is used for determining the font style, and another is used for boldness.

Each of these techniques is described in the following sections for clarity.

I used a trick I haven't shown yet to produce this comparison page. I have multiple paragraphs, each with their own style. Look to Chapter 3 of this minibook to see how to have more than one paragraph style in a particular page.

Using font-style for italics

The `font-style` attribute allows you to make italic text, as shown in Figure 2-8.

Here's some code illustrating how to add italic formatting:

```
<!DOCTYPE html PUBLIC "-//W3C//DTD XHTML 1.0 Strict//EN"
"http://www.w3.org/TR/xhtml1/DTD/xhtml1-strict.dtd">
<html lang="EN" dir="ltr" xmlns="http://www.w3.org/1999/xhtml">
  <head>
```

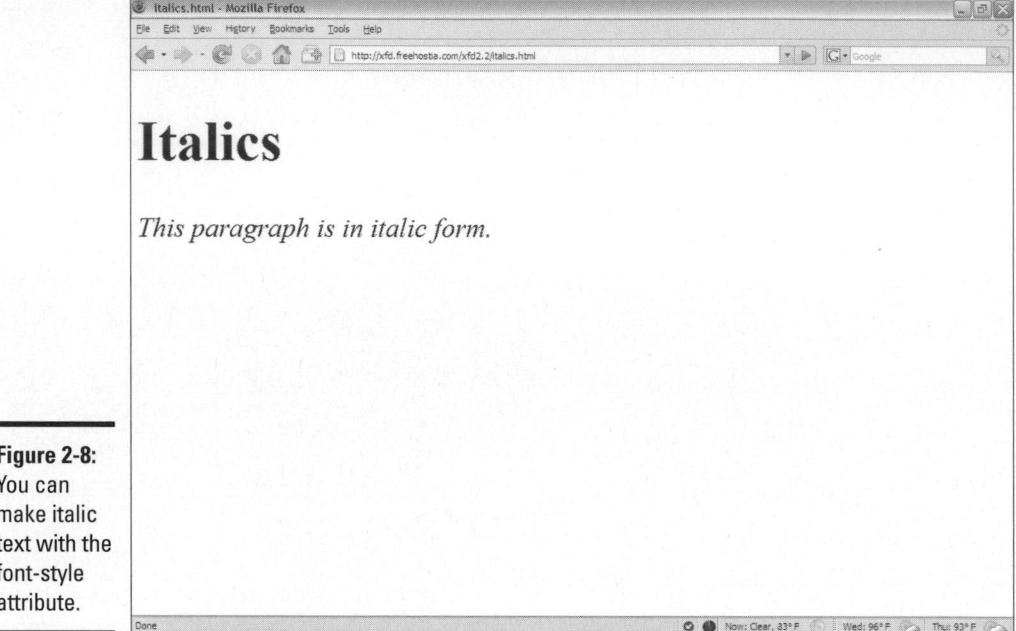

Figure 2-8: You can make italic text with the font-style attribute.

```
    <meta http-equiv="content-type" content="text/xml; charset=utf-8" />
    <title>italics.html</title>
    <style type = "text/css">
      p {
        font-style: italic;
      }
    </style>
  </head>

  <body>
     <h1>Italics</h1>
     <p>This paragraph is in italic form.</p>
  </body>
</html>
```

The `font-style` values can be `italic`, `normal`, or `oblique` (tilted toward the left).

If you want to set a particular segment to be set to italic, normal, or oblique style, use the `font-style` attribute.

Using font-weight for bold

You can make your font bold by using the `font-weight` CSS attribute, as shown in Figure 2-9.

If you want to make some of your text bold, use the `font-weight` CSS attribute, like this:

```
<!DOCTYPE html PUBLIC "-//W3C//DTD XHTML 1.0 Strict//EN"
"http://www.w3.org/TR/xhtml1/DTD/xhtml1-strict.dtd">
<html lang="EN" dir="ltr" xmlns="http://www.w3.org/1999/xhtml">
  <head>
    <meta http-equiv="content-type" content="text/xml; charset=utf-8" />
    <title>bold.html</title>
    <style type = "text/css">
      p {
        font-weight: bold;
      }
    </style>
  </head>

  <body>
    <h1>Boldface</h1>
    <p>
      This paragraph is bold.
    </p>
  </body>
</html>
```


Font weight can be defined in a couple ways. Normally, you simply indicate `bold` in the `font-weight` rule as I did in this code. You can also use a numeric value from 100 (exceptionally light) to 900 (dark bold).

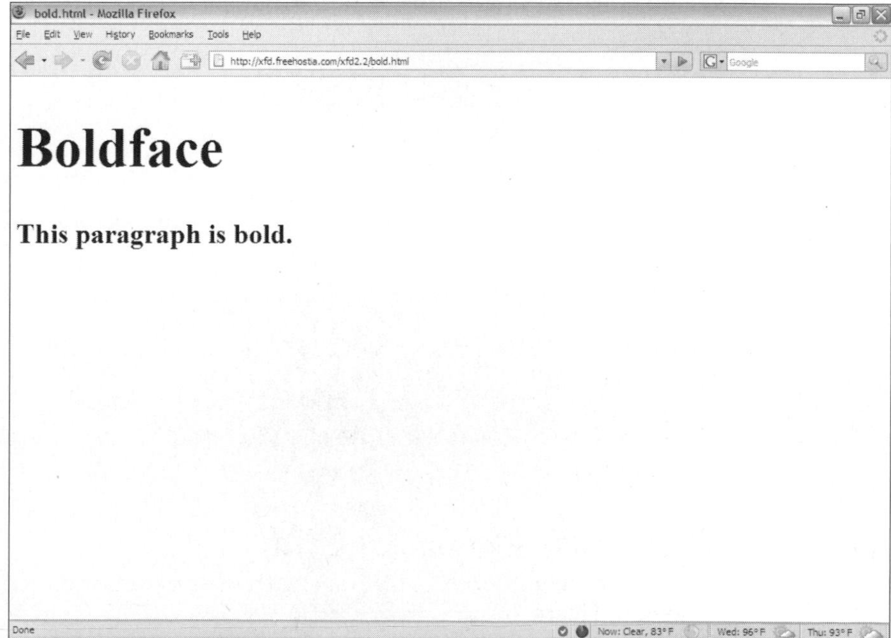

Figure 2-9: The font-weight attribute affects the boldness of your text.

Using text-decoration

`Text-decoration` can be used to add a couple other interesting formats to your text, including underline, strikethrough. overline, and blink.

For example, the following code produces an underlined paragraph:

```
<!DOCTYPE html PUBLIC "-//W3C//DTD XHTML 1.0 Strict//EN"
"http://www.w3.org/TR/xhtml1/DTD/xhtml1-strict.dtd">
<html lang="EN" dir="ltr" xmlns="http://www.w3.org/1999/xhtml">
  <head>
    <meta http-equiv="content-type" content="text/xml; charset=utf-8" />
    <title>underline.html</title>
    <style type = "text/css">
      p {
        text-decoration: underline;
      }
    </style>
  </head>

  <body>
    <h1>Underline</h1>
    <p>
      This paragraph is underlined.
    </p>
  </body>
</html>
```

Be careful using underline in Web pages. Users have been trained that underlined text is a link, so they may click your underlined text expecting it to take them somewhere.

The `underline.html` code produces a page like Figure 2-10.

You can also use `text-decoration` for other effects, like strikethrough, as shown in the following code:

```
<!DOCTYPE html PUBLIC "-//W3C//DTD XHTML 1.0 Strict//EN"
"http://www.w3.org/TR/xhtml1/DTD/xhtml1-strict.dtd">
<html lang="EN" dir="ltr" xmlns="http://www.w3.org/1999/xhtml">
  <head>
    <meta http-equiv="content-type" content="text/xml; charset=utf-8" />
    <title>strikethrough.html</title>
    <style type = "text/css">
      p {
        text-decoration: line-through;
      }
    </style>
  </head>
  <body>
    <h1>Strikethrough</h1>
    <p>
      This paragraph has strikethrough text.
    </p>
  </body>
</html>
```

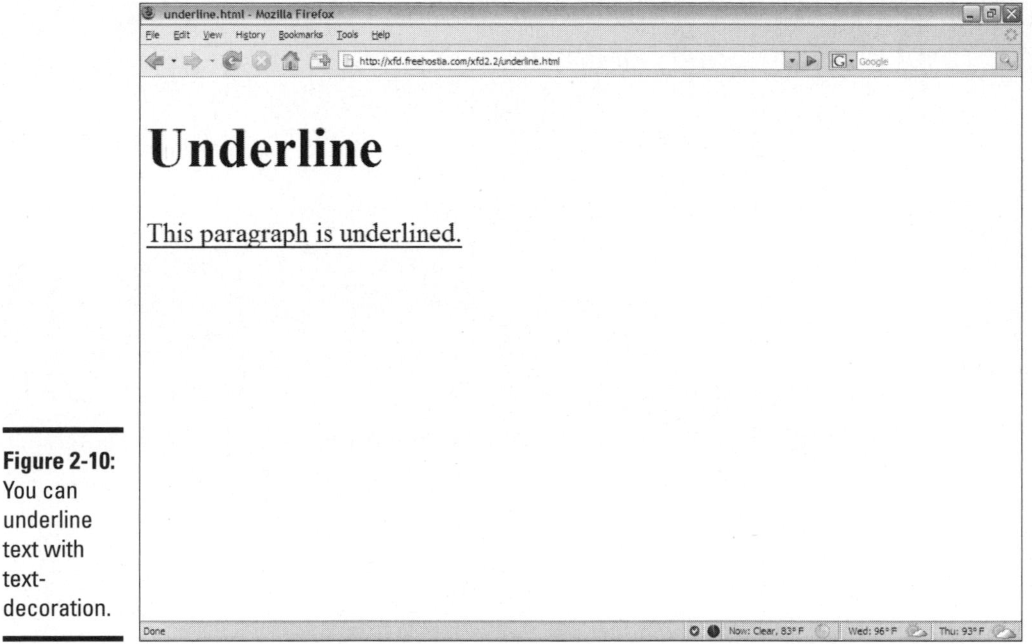

Figure 2-10: You can underline text with text-decoration.

The `strikethrough.html` code produces a page like Figure 2-11.

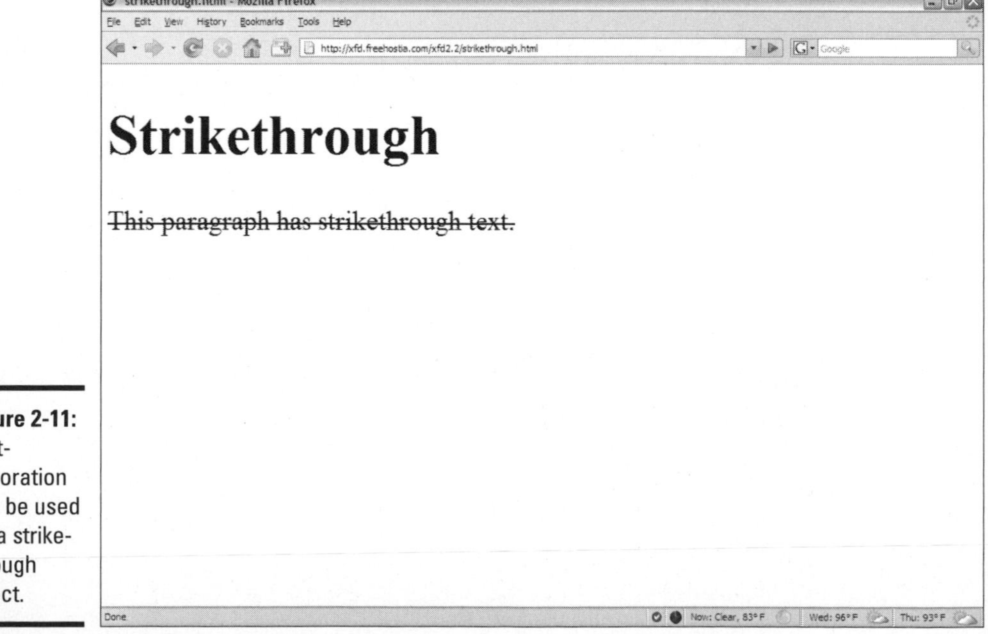

Figure 2-11: Text-decoration can be used for a strike-through effect.

`Text-decoration` has a few other rarely-used options, such as:

- **Overline:** The `overline` attribute places a line over the text. Except for a few math and chemistry applications (which would be better done in an equation editor and imported as images), I can't see when this might be used.
- **Blink:** The `blink` attribute is a distant cousin of the legendary `<blink>` tag in Netscape and causes the text to blink on the page. The `<blink>` tag (along with gratuitous animated GIFs) has long been derided as the mark of the amateur. Avoid blinking text at all costs.

There's an old joke among Internet developers: The only place to legitimately use the `<blink>` tag is in this sentence: Schroedinger's cat is `<blink>`not `</blink>` dead. Nothing is funnier than quantum mechanics illustrated in HTML.

Using text-align for basic alignment

You can use the `text-align` attribute to center, left-align, or right-align text, as shown in the following code:

```
<!DOCTYPE html PUBLIC "-//W3C//DTD XHTML 1.0 Strict//EN"
"http://www.w3.org/TR/xhtml1/DTD/xhtml1-strict.dtd">
<html lang="EN" dir="ltr" xmlns="http://www.w3.org/1999/xhtml">
  <head>
    <meta http-equiv="content-type" content="text/xml; charset=utf-8" />
    <title>center.html</title>
    <style type = "text/css">
      p {
        text-align: center;
      }
    </style>
  </head>

  <body>
    <h1>Centered</h1>
    <p>This paragraph is centered.</p>

  </body>
</html>
```

You can also use the `text-align` attribute to right- or left-justify your text.

The page shown in Figure 2-12 illustrates the `text-align` attribute.

You can apply the `text-align` attribute only to text. The old `<center>` tag could be used to center nearly anything (a table, some text, or images), which was pretty easy but caused problems. Book III explains how to position elements in all kinds of powerful ways, including centering anything. Use `text-align` to center text inside its own element (whether that's a heading, a paragraph, a table cell, or whatever).

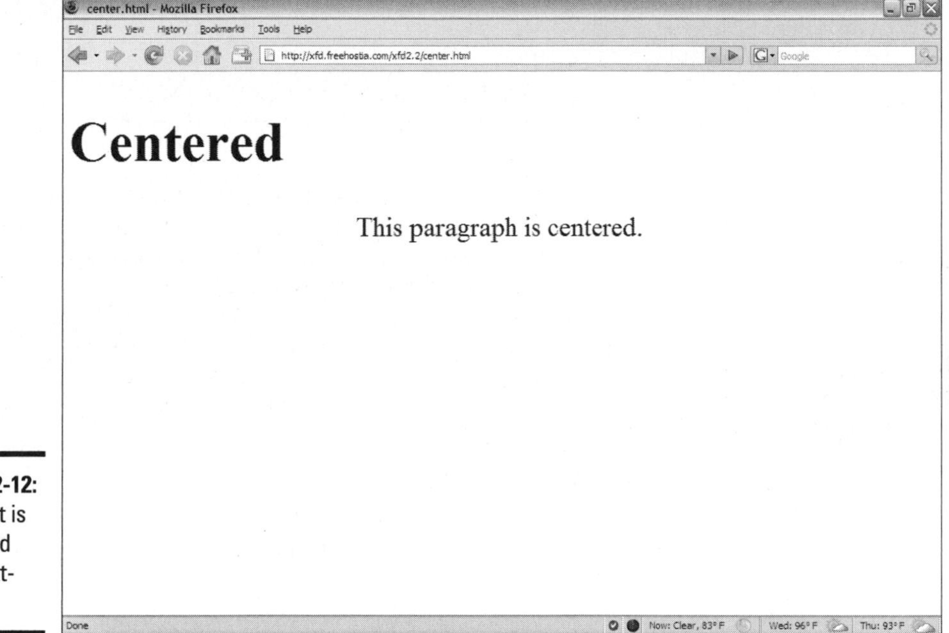

Figure 2-12: This text is centered with text-align.

Other text attributes

CSS offers a few other text manipulation tools, but they're rarely used:

- **Font-variant:** Can be set to `small-caps` to make your text use only capital letters. Lowercase letters are shown in a smaller font size.
- **Letter-spacing:** Adjusts the spacing between letters. It's usually measured in ems (see the section, "Relative measurement units," earlier in the chapter for more on ems). Fonts are so unpredictable on the Web that if you're trying to micromanage this much, you're bound to be disappointed by the results.
- **Word-spacing:** Allows you to adjust the spacing between words.
- **Text-indent:** Lets you adjust the indentation of the first line of an element. This value uses the normal units of measurement. Indentation can be set to a negative value, causing an outdent if you prefer.
- **Vertical-align:** Used when you have an element with a lot of vertical space (often a table cell). You can specify how the text behaves in this situation.
- **Text-transform:** Helps you convert text into uppercase, lowercase, or capitalized (first letter uppercase) forms.
- **Line-height:** Indicates the vertical spacing between lines in the element. Like letter and word spacing, you'll probably be disappointed if you're this concerned about exactly how things are displayed.

Using the font shortcut

It can be tedious to recall all the various font attributes and their possible values. Aptana and other dedicated CSS editors make it a lot easier, but there's another technique often used by the pros. The `font` rule provides an easy shortcut to a number of useful font attributes. The following code shows you how to use the `font` rule:

```
<!DOCTYPE html PUBLIC "-//W3C//DTD XHTML 1.0 Strict//EN"
"http://www.w3.org/TR/xhtml1/DTD/xhtml1-strict.dtd">
<html lang="EN" dir="ltr" xmlns="http://www.w3.org/1999/xhtml">
  <head>
    <meta http-equiv="content-type" content="text/xml; charset=utf-8" />
    <title>fontTag.html</title>
    <style type = "text/css">
      p {
         font: bold italic 150% "Dadhand", cursive;;
      }
    </style>
  </head>

  <body>
    <h1>Using Font shortcut</h1>
    <p>
      This paragraph has many settings.
    </p>
  </body>
</html>
```

Figure 2-13 illustrates the powerful `font` rule in action.

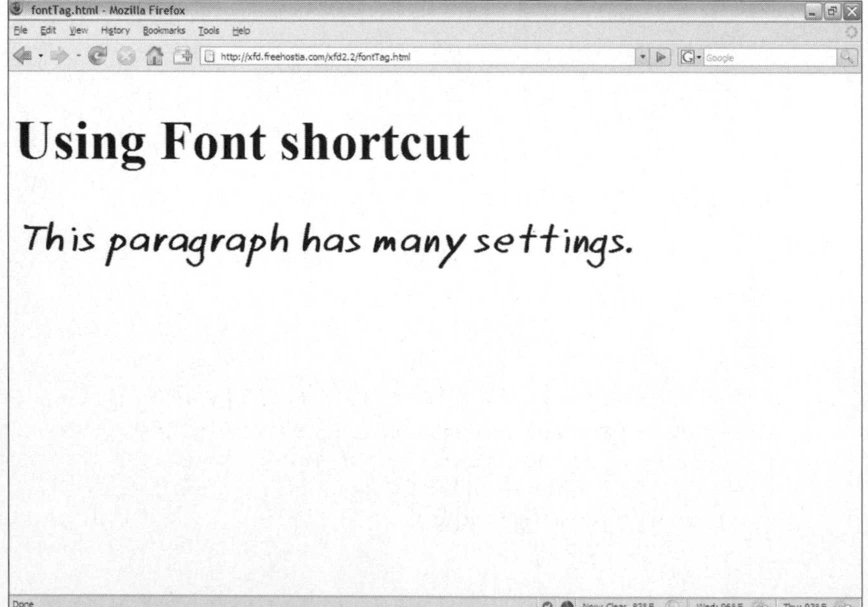

Figure 2-13: The font rule can change many things at once.

The great thing about the `font` rule is how it combines many of the other font-related rules for a simpler way to handle most text-formatting needs.

The `font` attribute is extremely handy. Essentially, it allows you to roll all the other font attributes into one. Here's how it works:

- **Specify the `font` rule in the CSS.**
- **List any `font-style` attributes.** You can mention any attributes normally used in the `font-style` rule (`italic` or `oblique`). If you don't want either, just move on.
- **List any `font-variant` attributes.** If you want small caps, you can indicate it here. If you don't, just leave this part blank.
- **List any `font-weight` values.** This can be "bold" or a font-weight number (100–900).
- **Specify the font-size value in whatever measurement system you want (but ems or percentages are preferred).** Don't forget the measurement unit symbol (`em` or `%`) because that's how the `font` rule recognizes that this is a size value.
- **Indicate a font-family list last.** The last element is a list of font families you want the browser to try. This list must be last, or the browser may not interpret the `font` attribute correctly.

The `font` rule is great, but it doesn't do everything. You still may need separate CSS rules to define your text colors and alignment. These attributes aren't included in the font shortcut.

Don't use commas to separate values in the `font` attribute list. Use commas only to separate values in the list of font-family declarations.

You can skip any values you want as long as the order is correct. For example

```
font: italic "Comic Sans MS", cursive;
```

is completely acceptable, as is

```
font: 70% sans-serif;
```

Working with subscripts and superscripts

Occasionally, you'll need *superscripts* (characters that appear a little bit higher than normal text, like exponents and footnotes) or *subscripts* (characters that appear lower, often used in mathematical notation). Figure 2-14 demonstrates a page with these techniques.

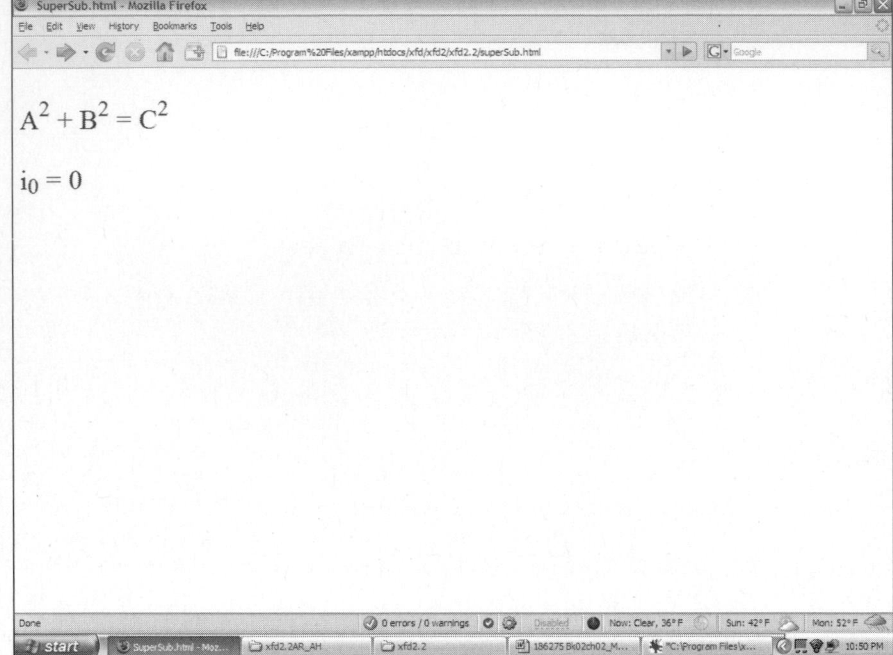

Figure 2-14: This page has superscripts and subscripts (and, ooooh, math!).

Surprisingly, you don't need CSS to produce superscripts and subscripts. These properties are managed through HTML tags. You can still style them like you can any other HTML tag.

```
<!DOCTYPE html PUBLIC "-//W3C//DTD XHTML 1.0 Strict//EN"
"http://www.w3.org/TR/xhtml1/DTD/xhtml1-strict.dtd">
<html lang="EN" dir="ltr" xmlns="http://www.w3.org/1999/xhtml">
  <head>
    <meta http-equiv="content-type" content="text/xml; charset=utf-8" />
    <title>SuperSub.html</title>
  </head>

  <body>
    <p>
      A<sup>2</sup> + B<sup>2</sup> = C<sup>2</sup>
    </p>

    <p>
      i<sub>0</sub> = 0
    </p>
  </body>
</html>
```

Chapter 3: Selectors, Class, and Style

In This Chapter

- Modifying specific named elements
- Adding and modifying emphasis and strong emphasis
- Creating classes
- Introducing spans and divs
- Using pseudo-classes and the link tag
- Selecting specific contexts
- Defining multiple styles

You know how to use CSS to change all the instances of a particular tag, but what if you want to be more selective? For example, you might want to change the background color of only one paragraph, or you might want to define some special new type of paragraph. Maybe you want to specify a different paragraph color for part of your page, or you want visited links to appear differently from unselected links. The part of the CSS style that indicates what element you want to style is a *selector.* In this chapter, you discover powerful new ways to select elements on the page.

Selecting Particular Segments

Figure 3-1 illustrates how you should refer to someone who doesn't appreciate your Web development prowess.

Defining more than one kind of paragraph

Apart from its cultural merit, this page is interesting because it has three different paragraph styles. The introductory paragraph is normal. The quote is set in italicized font, and the attribution is monospaced and right-aligned.

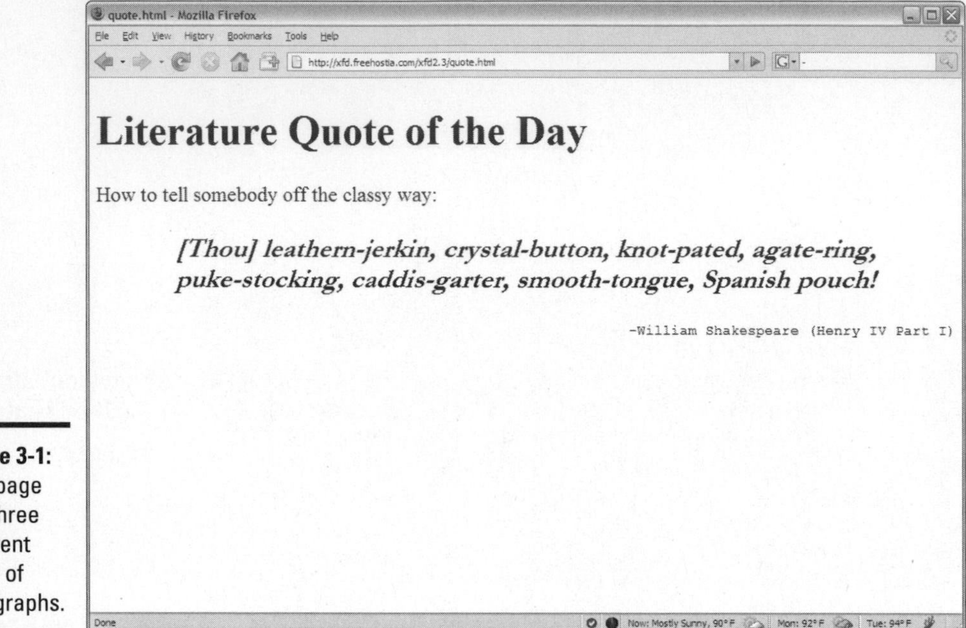

Figure 3-1: This page has three different kinds of paragraphs.

The quote in the following code was generated by one of my favorite sites on the Internet: the Shakespearean insult generator. Nothing is more satisfying than telling somebody off in iambic pentameter.

```
<!DOCTYPE html PUBLIC "-//W3C//DTD XHTML 1.0 Strict//EN"
"http://www.w3.org/TR/xhtml1/DTD/xhtml1-strict.dtd">
<html lang="EN" dir="ltr" xmlns="http://www.w3.org/1999/xhtml">
  <head>
    <meta http-equiv="content-type" content="text/xml; charset=utf-8" />
    <title>quote.html</title>
    <style type = "text/css">
      #quote {
        font: bold italic 130% Garamond, fantasy;
        text-align: center;
      }

      #attribution {
        font: 80% monospace;
        text-align: right;
      }
    </style>
  </head>

  <body>
    <h1>Literature Quote of the day</h1>
    <p>
      How to tell somebody off the classy way:
    </p>
```

```
    <p id = "quote">
      [Thou] leathern-jerkin, crystal-button, knot-pated,
      agatering, puke-stocking, caddis-garter, smooth-tongue,
      Spanish pouch!
    </p>

    <p id = "attribution">
      -William Shakespeare (Henry IV Part I)
    </p>

  </body>
</html>
```

Styling identified paragraphs

Up to now, you've used CSS to apply a particular style to an element all across the page. For example, you can add a style to the `p` tag, and that style applies to all the paragraphs on the page.

Sometimes (as in the Shakespeare insult page) you want to give one element more than one style. You can do this by naming each element and using the name in the CSS style sheet. Here's how it works:

1. **Add an `id` attribute to each HTML element you want to modify.**

   For example, the paragraph with the attribution now has an `id` attribute with the value `attribution`.

   ```
   <p id = "attribution">
   ```

2. **Make a style in CSS.**

   Use a pound sign followed by the element's ID in CSS to specify you're not talking about a tag type any more, but a specific element: For example, the CSS code contains the selector `#attribution` meaning "apply this style to an element with the attribution id."

   ```
   #attribution {
   ```

3. **Add the style.**

   Create a style for displaying your named element. In this case, I want the paragraph with the `attribution` id to be right-aligned, monospace, and a little smaller than normal. This style will be attached only to the specific element.

   ```
   #attribution {
     font: 80% monospace;
     text-align: right;
   }
   ```

The ID trick works great on any named element. IDs have to be *unique* (you can't repeat the same ID on one page), so this technique is best when you have a style you want to apply to only one element on the page. It doesn't matter what HTML element it is (it could be an h1, a paragraph, a table cell, or whatever). If it has the ID `quote`, the `#quote` style will be applied to it. You can have both ID selectors and ordinary (element) selectors in the same style sheet.

Using Emphasis and Strong Emphasis

You may be shocked to know that XHTML doesn't allow italics or bold. Old-style HTML had the `<i>` tag for italics and the `<b>` tag for bold. These seem pretty easy to use and understand. Unfortunately, they can trap you. In your XHTML, you shouldn't specify *how* something should be styled. You should specify instead the *purpose* of the styling. The `<i>` and `<b>` tags are removed from XHTML Strict and replaced with `<em>` and `<strong>`.

Adding emphasis to the page

The `<em>` tag means *emphasized.* By default, `em` italicizes your text. The `<strong>` tag stands for *strong emphasis.* It defaults to bold.

Figure 3-2 illustrates a page with the default styles for `em` and `strong`.

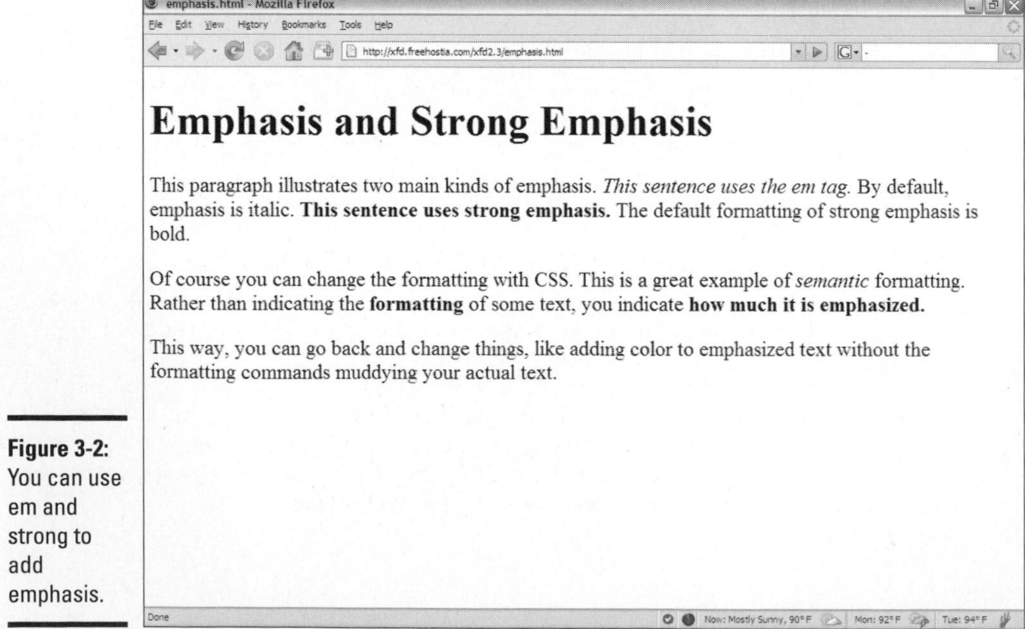

Figure 3-2: You can use em and strong to add emphasis.

The code for the `emphasis.html` page is pretty straightforward. It has no CSS at all:

```
<!DOCTYPE html PUBLIC "-//W3C//DTD XHTML 1.0 Strict//EN"
"http://www.w3.org/TR/xhtml1/DTD/xhtml1-strict.dtd">
<html lang="EN" dir="ltr" xmlns="http://www.w3.org/1999/xhtml">
  <head>
    <meta http-equiv="content-type" content="text/xml; charset=utf-8" />
    <title>emphasis.html</title>
  </head>

  <body>
    <h1>Emphasis and Strong Emphasis</h1>
    <p>
      This paragraph illustrates two main kinds of emphasis.
      <em>This sentence uses the em tag.</em>
      By default, emphasis is italic.
      <strong>This sentence uses strong emphasis.</strong>
      The default formatting of strong emphasis is bold.
    </p>

    <p>
      Of course you can change the formatting with CSS.
      This is a great example of <em>semantic</em> formatting.
      Rather than indicating the <strong>formatting</strong>
      of some text, you indicate <strong>how much it is emphasized.</strong>
    </p>

    <p>
      This way, you can go back and change things, like adding color
      to emphasized text without the formatting commands
      muddying your actual text.
    </p>
  </body>
</html>
```


It'd be improper to think that `em` is just another way to say *italic* and `strong` is another way to say *bold.* In the old scheme, after you define something as italic, you're pretty much stuck with that. The XHTML way describes the meaning, and you can define it however you want.

Modifying the display of em and strong

Figure 3-3 shows how you might modify the levels of emphasis. I used yellow highlighting (without italics) for `em` and a larger red font for `strong`.

The code for `emphasisStyle.html` (as shown in Figure 3-3) is *identical* to the code for `emphasis.html` (as shown in Figure 3-2). The only difference is the addition of a style sheet. The style sheet is embedded in the Web page between style tags. Check out Chapter 1 of this minibook for a refresher on how to incorporate CSS styles in your Web pages.

```
<style type = "text/css">
  em {
    font-style: normal;
    background-color: yellow;
  }

  strong {
    color: red;
    font-size: 110%;
  }
</style>
```

The style is used to modify the XHTML. The meaning in the XHTML stays the same — only the style changes.

The semantic markups are more useful than the older (more literal) tags because they still tell the truth even if the style has been changed. (In the XHTML code, the important thing is whether the text is emphasized, not what it means to emphasize the text. That job belongs to CSS.)

What's funny about the following sentence?

> `<strong>` is always bold.

Get it? *That's a bold-faced lie!* Sometimes I crack myself up.

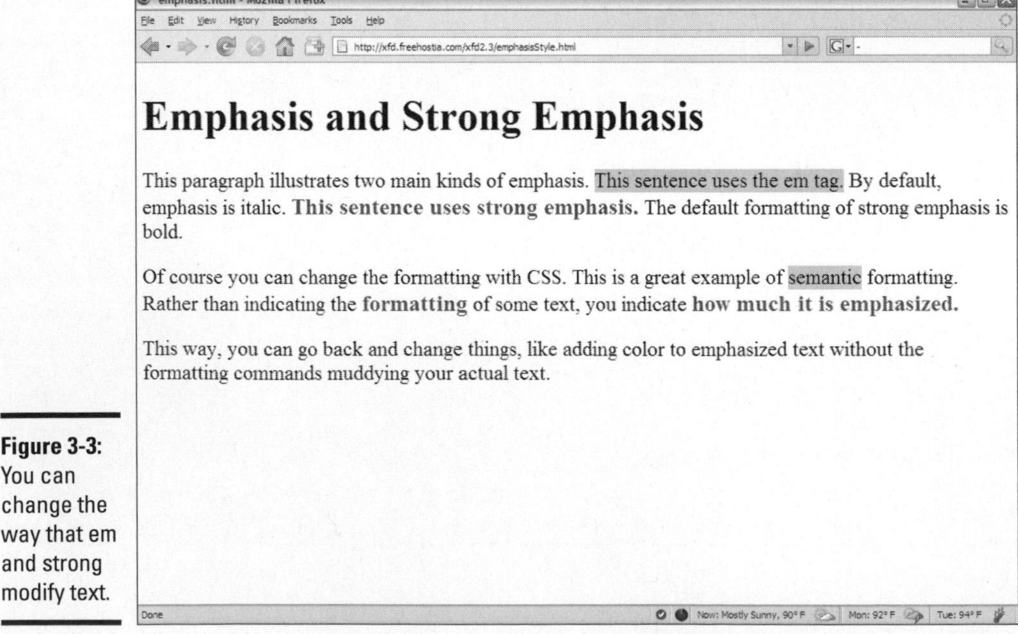

Figure 3-3: You can change the way that em and strong modify text.

Defining Classes

You can easily apply a style to all the elements of a particular type in a page, but sometimes you might want to have tighter control of your styles. For example, you might want to have more than one paragraph style. As an example, take a look at the `classes.html` page featured in Figure 3-4.

Once again, multiple formats are on this page:

- ✦ **Questions have a large italic sans serif font.** There's more than one question.
- ✦ **Answers are smaller, blue, and in a cursive font.** There's more than one answer, too.

Questions and answers are all paragraphs, so you can't simply style the paragraph because you need two distinct styles. There's more than one question and more than one answer, so the ID trick would be problematic. Two different elements can't have the same ID — you don't want to create more than one identical definition. This is where the notion of classes comes into play.

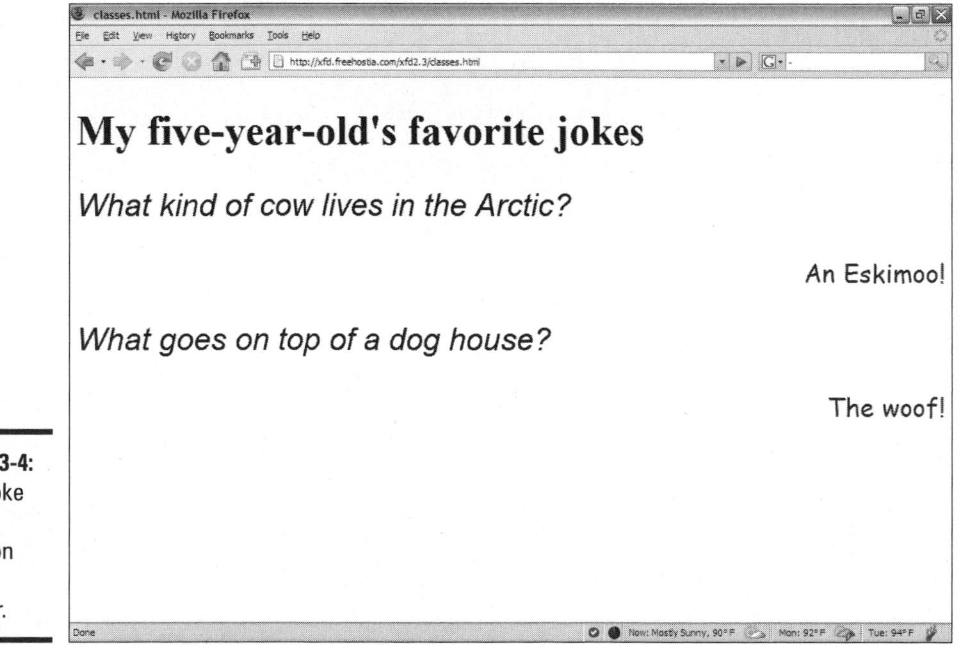

Figure 3-4: Each joke has a question and an answer.

Adding classes to the page

CSS allows you to define classes in your XHTML and make style definitions that are applied across a class. It works like this:

1. **Add the `class` attribute to your XHTML questions.**

   Unlike ID, several elements can share the same class. All my questions are defined with this variation of the <p> tag. Setting the class to `question` indicates these paragraphs will be styled as questions:

   ```
   <p class = "question">
     What kind of cow lives in the Arctic?
   </p>
   ```

2. **Add similar class attributes to the answers by setting the class of the answers to `answer`:**

   ```
   <p class = "answer">
     An Eskimoo!
   </p>
   ```

   Now you have two different subclasses of paragraph: `question` and `answer`.

3. **Create a class style for the questions.**

   The class style is defined in CSS. Specify a class with the period (`.`) before the class name. Classes are defined in CSS like this:

   ```
   <style type = "text/css">
     .question {
       font: italic 150% arial, sans-serif;
       text-align: left;
     }
   ```

   In this situation, the `question` class is defined as a large sans-serif font aligned to the left.

4. **Define the look of the answers.**

   The `answer` class uses a right-justified cursive font.

   ```
     .answer {
       font: 120% "Comic Sans MS", cursive;
       text-align: right;
       color: #00F;
     }
   </style>
   ```

Combining classes

Here's the code for the `classes.html` page, showing how to uses CSS classes:

```
<!DOCTYPE html PUBLIC "-//W3C//DTD XHTML 1.0 Strict//EN"
"http://www.w3.org/TR/xhtml1/DTD/xhtml1-strict.dtd">
<html lang="EN" dir="ltr" xmlns="http://www.w3.org/1999/xhtml">
  <head>
    <meta http-equiv="content-type" content="text/xml; charset=utf-8" />
    <title>classes.html</title>
    <style type = "text/css">
      .question {
        font: italic 150% arial, sans-serif;
        text-align: left;
      }

      .answer {
        font: 120% "Comic Sans MS", cursive;
        text-align: right;
        color: #00F;
      }
    </style>
  </head>

  <body>
    <h1>My five-year-old's favorite jokes</h1>

    <p class = "question">
      What kind of cow lives in the Arctic?
    </p>

    <p class = "answer">
      An Eskimoo!
    </p>

    <p class = "question">
      What goes on top of a dog house?
    </p>

    <p class = "answer">
      The woof!
    </p>
  </body>
</html>
```

Sometimes you see selectors, like

```
p.fancy
```

that include both an element and a class name. This style will be applied only to paragraphs with the `fancy` class attached. Generally, I like classes because they can be applied to all kinds of things, so I usually leave the element name out to make the style as reusable as possible.

Combining classes

One element can use more than one class. Figure 3-5 shows an example of this phenomenon

The paragraphs in Figure 3-5 appear to be in three different styles, but only red and script are defined. The third paragraph uses both classes. Here's the code:

```
<!DOCTYPE html PUBLIC "-//W3C//DTD XHTML 1.0 Strict//EN"
"http://www.w3.org/TR/xhtml1/DTD/xhtml1-strict.dtd">
<html lang="EN" dir="ltr" xmlns="http://www.w3.org/1999/xhtml">
  <head>
    <meta http-equiv="content-type" content="text/xml; charset=utf-8" />
    <title>redScript.html</title>
    <style type = "text/css">
      .red {
        color: white;
        background-color: red;
      }

      .script {
        font-family: cursive;
      }
    </style>
  </head>

  <body>
    <h1>Multiple Classes</h1>
    <p class = "red">
      This paragraph uses the red class
    </p>

    <p class = "script">
      This paragraph uses the script class
    </p>
```

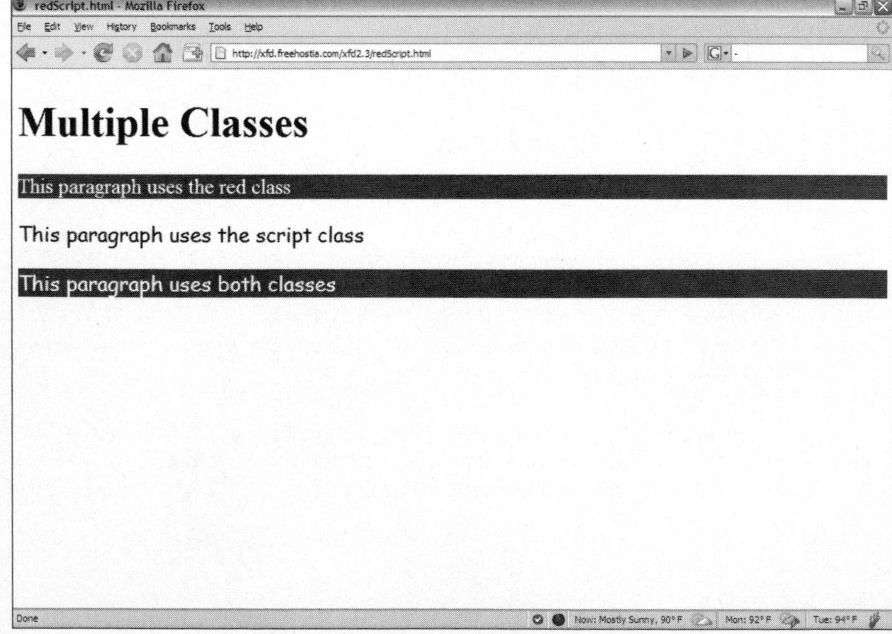

Figure 3-5: There's red, there's script, and then there's both.

```
    <p class = "red script">
      This paragraph uses both classes
    </p>
  </body>
</html>
```

The style sheet introduces two classes. The `red` class makes the paragraph red (well, white text with a red background), and the `script` class applies a cursive font to the element.

The first two paragraphs each have a class, and they act as you'd expect. The interesting part is the third paragraph, as it has two classes.

```
<p class = "red script">
```


This assigns both the `red` and `script` classes to the paragraph. Both styles will be applied to the element in the order they are written. Note that both class names occur inside quotes and no commas are needed (or allowed). You can apply more than two classes to an element if you wish. If the classes have conflicting rules (say one makes the element green and the next makes it blue), the latest class in the list will overwrite earlier values.

An element can also have an ID. The ID style, the element style, and all the class styles are taken into account when the browser tries to display the object.

Normally I don't like to use colors or other specific formatting instructions as class names. Usually, it's best to name classes based on their meaning (like `mainColorScheme`). You might decide that green is better than red, so you either have to change the class name or you have to have a `red` class that colored things green. That'd be weird.

Introducing div and span

So far, I've applied CSS styles primarily to paragraphs (with the `p` tag), but you can really use any element you want. In fact, you may want to invent your own elements. Perhaps you want a particular style, but it's not quite a paragraph. Maybe you want a particular style inside a paragraph. XHTML has two very useful elements that are designed as *generic* elements. They don't have any predefined meaning, so they're ideal candidates for modification with the `id` and `class` attributes.

- **`div`:** A block-level element (like the `p` element). It acts just like a paragraph. A `div` usually has carriage returns before and after it. Generally, you use `div` to group a series of paragraphs.

✦ **<span>:** An inline element. It doesn't usually cause carriage returns because it's meant to be embedded into some other block-level element (usually a paragraph or a `div`). A `span` is usually used to add some type of special formatting.

Organizing the page by meaning

To see why `div` and `span` are useful, take a look at Figure 3-6.

The formatting of the page isn't complete (read about positioning CSS in Book III), but some formatting is in place. Each name and phone number pair is clearly a group of things. Names and phone numbers are formatted differently. The interesting thing about this page is the code:

```
<!DOCTYPE html PUBLIC "-//W3C//DTD XHTML 1.0 Strict//EN"
"http://www.w3.org/TR/xhtml1/DTD/xhtml1-strict.dtd">
<html lang="EN" dir="ltr" xmlns="http://www.w3.org/1999/xhtml">
  <head>
    <meta http-equiv="content-type" content="text/xml; charset=utf-8" />
    <title>divSpan.html</title>
    <style type = "text/css">
      .contact {
        background-color: #CCCCFF;
      }
      .name {
        font: italic 110% arial, sans-serif;
      }
```

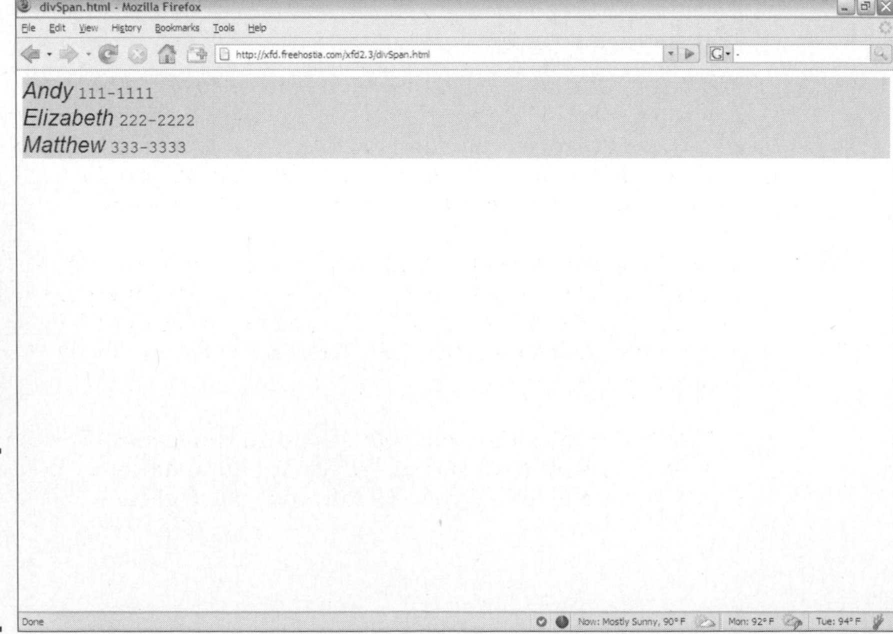

Figure 3-6: This page has names and phone numbers.

```
      .phone {
        font: 100% monospace;
      }

    </style>
  </head>

  <body>
    <div class = "contact">
      <span class = "name">Andy</span>
      <span class = "phone">111-1111</span>
    </div>

    <div class = "contact">
      <span class = "name">Elizabeth</span>
      <span class = "phone">222-2222</span>
    </div>

    <div class = "contact">
      <span class = "name">Matthew</span>
      <span class = "phone">333-3333</span>
    </div>

  </body>
</html>
```


What's exciting about this code is its clarity. When you look at the XHTML, it's very clear what type of data you're talking about because the structure describes the data. Each `div` represents a contact. A contact has a name and a phone number.

The XHTML doesn't specify how the data is displayed, just what it means.

Why not make a table?

This is where experienced HTML 4 people shake their heads in disbelief. This page seems like a table, so why not make it one? What matters here isn't that the information is in a table, but that names and phone numbers are part of contacts. There's no need to bring in artificial table elements if you can describe the data perfectly well without them.

If you still want to make the data *look* like a table, that's completely possible, as shown in Figure 3-7. See Book III to see exactly how some of the styling code works. Of course, you're welcome to look at the source code for this styled version (dubbed `divSpanStyled.html` on the CD-ROM) if you want a preview.

The point is this: After you define the data, you can control it as much as you want. Using `span` and `div` to define your data gives you far more control than tables and leaves your XHTML code much cleaner.

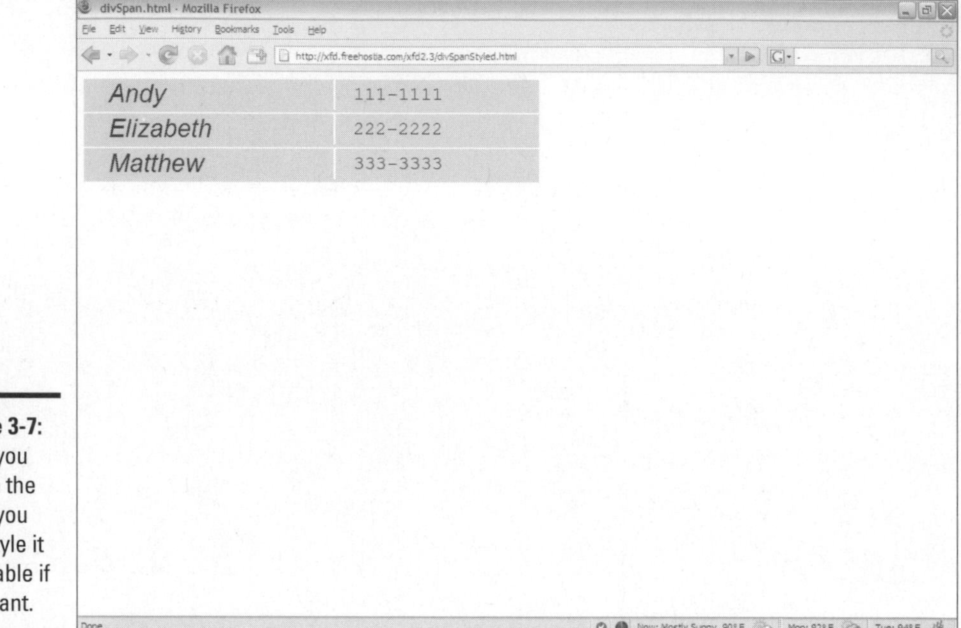

Figure 3-7: After you define the data, you can style it as a table if you want.

div and span aren't simply a replacement for tables. They're tools for organizing your page into segments based on *meaning.* After you have them in place, you can use CSS to apply all kinds of interesting styles to the segments.

Using Pseudo-Classes to Style Links

Now that you have some style going in your Web pages, you may be a bit concerned about how ugly links are. The default link styles are useful, but they may not fit with your color scheme.

Styling a standard link

It's easy enough to add a style to a link. After all, <a> (the tag that defines links) is just an XHTML tag, and you can add a style to any tag. Here's an example, where I make my links black with a yellow background:

```
a {
  color: black;
  background-color: yellow;
}
```

That works fine, but links are a little more complex than some other elements. Links actually have three different *states:*

- **Normal:** This is the standard state. With no CSS added, most browsers display unvisited links as blue underlined text.
- **Visited:** This state is enabled when the user has visited a link and returned to the current page. Most browsers use a purple underlined style to indicate that a link has been visited.
- **Hover:** The hover state is enabled when the user's mouse is lingering over the element. Most browsers don't use the hover state in their default settings.

If you apply a style to the `<a>` tags in a page, the style is applied to all the states of all the anchors.

Styling the link states

You can apply a different style to each state, as illustrated by Figure 3-8. In this example, I make ordinary links black on a white background. A link that has been visited is black on yellow, and, if the mouse is hovering over a link, it is white with a black background.

Take a look at the code and see how it's done:

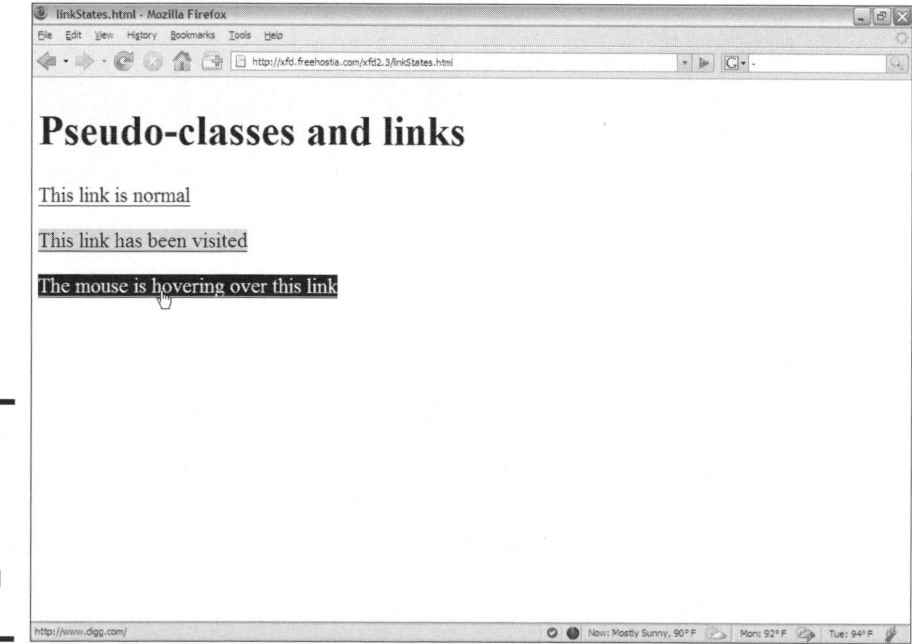

Figure 3-8: Links can have three states: normal, visited, and hover.

```
<!DOCTYPE html PUBLIC "-//W3C//DTD XHTML 1.0 Strict//EN"
"http://www.w3.org/TR/xhtml1/DTD/xhtml1-strict.dtd">
<html lang="EN" dir="ltr" xmlns="http://www.w3.org/1999/xhtml">
  <head>
    <meta http-equiv="content-type" content="text/xml; charset=utf-8" />
    <title>linkStates.html</title>
    <style type = "text/css">
      a{
        color: black;
        background-color: white;
      }

      a:visited {
        color: black;
        background-color: #FFFF33;
      }

      a:hover {
        color: white;
        background-color: black;
      }
    </style>
  </head>

  <body>
    <h1>Pseudo-classes and links</h1>

    <p>
      <a href = "http://www.google.com">This link is normal</a>
    </p>

    <p>
      <a href = "http://www.reddit.com">This link has been visited</a>
    </p>

    <p>
      <a href = "http://www.digg.com">The mouse is hovering over
      this link</a>
    </p>
  </body>
</html>
```

Nothing is special about the links in the HTML part of the code. The links change their state dynamically while the user interacts with the page. The style sheet determines what happens in the various states. Here's how you approach putting the code together:

- **Determine the ordinary link style first by making a style for the <a> tag.** If you don't define any other pseudo-classes, all links will follow this style.
- **Make a style for visited links.** A link will use this style if that site has been visited during the current browser session. The `a:visited` selector indicates links that have been visited.
- **Make a style for hovered links.** The `a:hover` style will be applied to the link only when the mouse is currently hovering over the link. As soon as the mouse leaves the link, the style reverts back to standard or visited, as appropriate.

Best link practices

Link styles have some special characteristics. You need to be a little bit careful how you apply styles to links. Consider the following issues when applying styles to list:

- **The order is important.** Be sure to define the ordinary anchor first. The pseudo-classes are based on the standard anchor style.
- **Make sure they still look like links.** It's important that users know something is intended to be a link. If you take away the underlining and the color that normally indicates a link, your users might be confused. Generally, you can change colors without trouble, but links should either be underlined text or something that clearly looks like a button.
- **Test visited links.** Testing visited links is a little tricky because, after you visit a link, it stays visited. If you have the Web Developer toolbar installed on Firefox, you can choose the Miscellaneous➪Visited Links command to mark all links as visited or unvisited. In IE, choose Tools➪Delete Browsing History and then select the Delete History button. You then need to refresh the page for the change to take effect.
- **Don't change font size in a hover state.** Unlike most styles, hover changes the page in real time. A hover style with a different font size than the ordinary link can cause problems. The page is automatically reformatted to accept the larger (or smaller) font, which can move a large amount of text on the screen rapidly. This can be frustrating and disconcerting for users. It's safest to change colors or borders on hover but not the font family or font size.

The hover pseudo-class is supposed to be supported on other elements, but browser support is spotty. You can define a hover pseudo-class for `div` and `<p>` elements with some confidence if users are using the latest browsers. Earlier browsers are less likely to support this feature, so don't rely on it too much.

Selecting in Context

CSS allows some other nifty selection tricks. Take a look at Figure 3-9 and you see a page with two different kinds of paragraphs in it.

The code for the `context-style.html` page is deceptively simple:

```
<!DOCTYPE html PUBLIC "-//W3C//DTD XHTML 1.0 Strict//EN"
"http://www.w3.org/TR/xhtml1/DTD/xhtml1-strict.dtd">
<html lang="EN" dir="ltr" xmlns="http://www.w3.org/1999/xhtml">
  <head>
    <meta http-equiv="content-type" content="text/xml; charset=utf-8" />
    <title>context-style</title>
    <style type = "text/css">
      #special p {
```

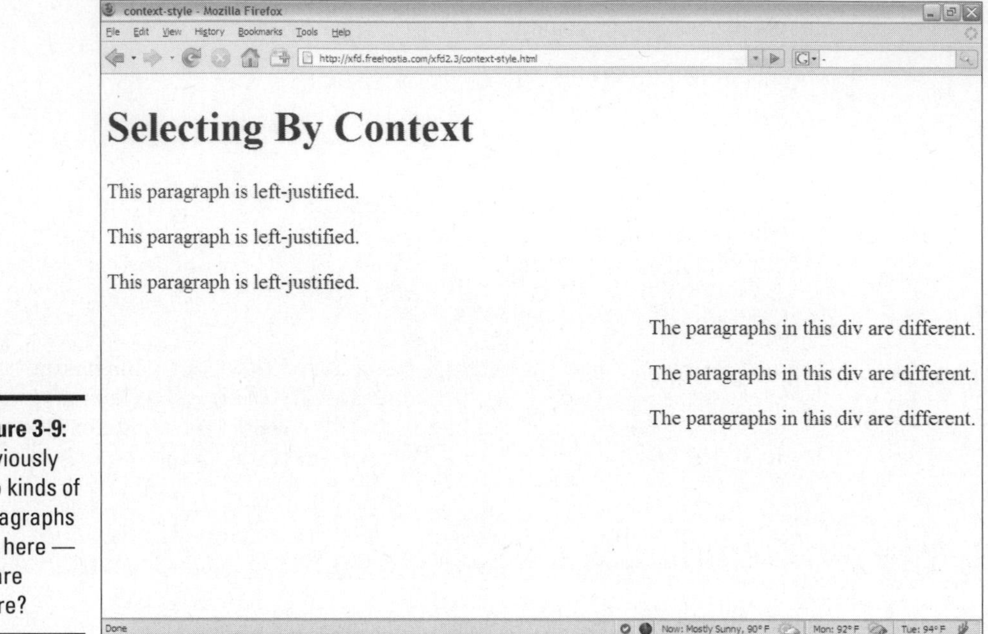

Figure 3-9: Obviously two kinds of paragraphs are here — or are there?

```
        text-align: right;
      }
    </style>
  </head>

  <body>
    <h1>Selecting By Context</h1>

    <div>
      <p>This paragraph is left-justified.</p>
      <p>This paragraph is left-justified.</p>
      <p>This paragraph is left-justified.</p>
    </div>

    <div id = "special">
      <p>The paragraphs in this div are different.</p>
      <p>The paragraphs in this div are different.</p>
      <p>The paragraphs in this div are different.</p>
    </div>
  </body>
</html>
```

If you look at the code for `context-style.html`, you see some interesting things:

- **The page has two `divs`.** One `div` is anonymous, and the other is `special`.
- **None of the paragraphs has an ID or class.** The paragraphs in this page don't have names or classes defined, yet they clearly have two different

types of behavior. The first three paragraphs are aligned to the left, and the last three are aligned to the right.

✦ **The style rule affects paragraphs inside the `special` `div`.** Take another look at the style:

```
#special p {
```

This style rule means apply this style to any paragraph appearing inside something called `special`. You can also define a rule that could apply to an image inside a list item or emphasized items inside a particular class. When you include a list of style selectors without commas, you're indicating a nested style.

✦ **Paragraphs defined outside `special` aren't affected.** This nested selection technique can help you create very complex style combinations. It becomes especially handy when you start building positioned elements, like menus and columns.

Defining Multiple Styles at Once

Sometimes you want a number of elements to share similar styles. As an example, look at Figure 3-10.

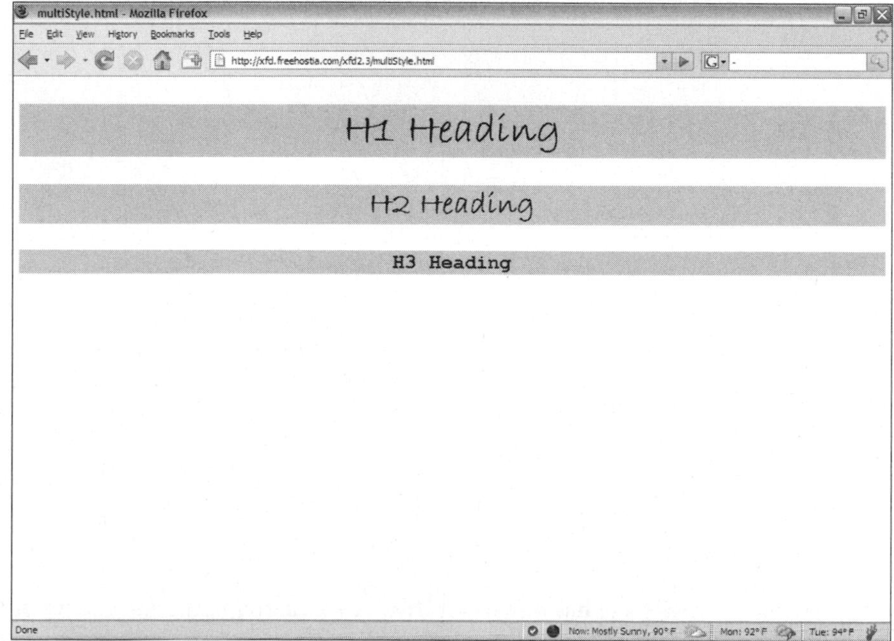

Figure 3-10: H1, H2, and H3 have similar style rules.

In this illustration, the top three headings all have very similar styles. Creating three different styles would be tedious, so CSS includes a shortcut:

```
<!DOCTYPE html PUBLIC "-//W3C//DTD XHTML 1.0 Strict//EN"
"http://www.w3.org/TR/xhtml1/DTD/xhtml1-strict.dtd">
<html lang="EN" dir="ltr" xmlns="http://www.w3.org/1999/xhtml">
  <head>
    <meta http-equiv="content-type" content="text/xml; charset=utf-8" />
    <title>multiStyle.html</title>
    <style type = "text/css">
      h1, h2, h3 {
        text-align: center;
        font-family: "Bradley Hand ITC", cursive;
        background-color: yellow;
      }

      h3 {
        font-family: monospace;
      }
    </style>
  </head>

  <body>
    <h1>H1 Heading</h1>
    <h2>H2 Heading</h2>
    <h3>H3 Heading</h3>
  </body>
</html>
```

One style element (the one that begins `h1, h2, h3`) provides all the information for all three heading types. If you include more than one element in a style selector separated by commas, the style applies to all the elements in the list. In this example, the centered cursive font with a yellow background is applied to headings level 1, 2, and 3 all in the same style.

If you want to make modifications, you can do so. I created a second `h3` rule, changing the `font-family` attribute to `monospace`. Style rules are applied in order, so you can always start with the general rule and then modify specific elements later in the style if you wish.

Remember, if you have multiple elements in a selector rule, it makes a huge difference whether you use commas. If you separate elements with spaces (but no commas), CSS looks for an element nested within another element. If you include commas, CSS applies the rule to all the listed elements.

Chapter 4: Borders and Backgrounds

In This Chapter

- Creating borders
- Managing border size, style, and color
- Using the border shortcut style
- Understanding the box model
- Setting padding and margin
- Creating background and low-contrast images
- Changing background image settings
- Adding images to list items

CSS offers some great features for making your elements more colorful. It has a flexible and powerful system for adding borders to your elements. You can also add background images to all or part of your page. This chapter describes how to use borders and backgrounds for maximum effect.

Joining the Border Patrol

You can use CSS to draw borders around any HTML element. You have some freedom in the border size, style, and color. Here are two main ways to define border properties — using individual border attributes and using a shortcut. Borders don't actually change the layout, but they do add visual separation that can be appealing, especially as your layouts get more complex.

Using the border attributes

Figure 4-1 illustrates a page with a simple border drawn around the heading.

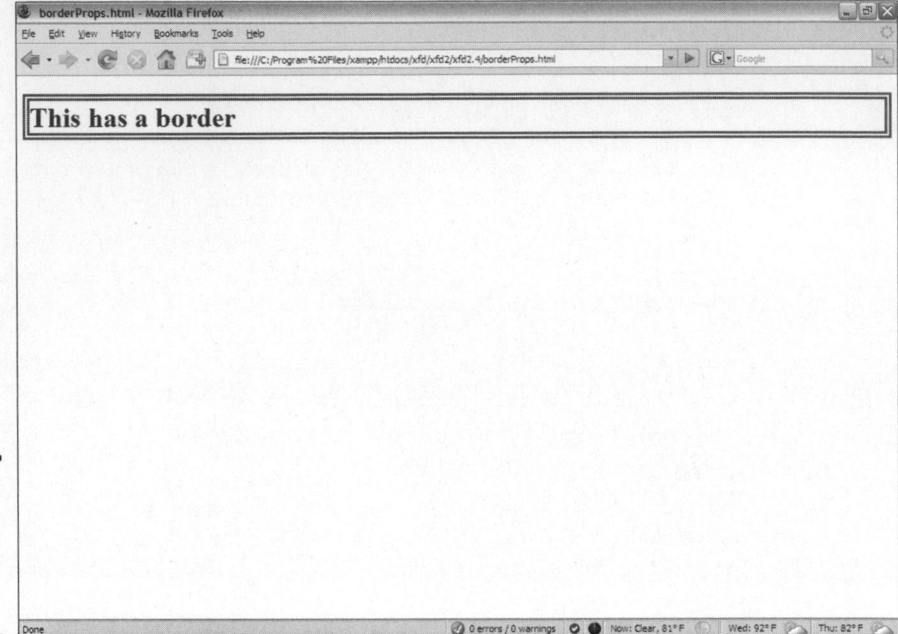

Figure 4-1: This page features a double red border.

The code for the `borderProps.html` page demonstrates the basic principles of borders in CSS:

```
<!DOCTYPE html PUBLIC "-//W3C//DTD XHTML 1.0 Strict//EN"
"http://www.w3.org/TR/xhtml1/DTD/xhtml1-strict.dtd">
<html lang="EN" dir="ltr" xmlns="http://www.w3.org/1999/xhtml">
  <head>
    <meta http-equiv="content-type" content="text/xml; charset=utf-8" />
    <title>borderProps.html</title>
    <style type = "text/css">
      h1 {
        border-color: red;
        border-width: .25em;
        border-style: double;
      }
    </style>
  </head>

  <body>
    <h1>This has a border</h1>
  </body>
</html>
```

Each element can have a border defined. Borders require three attributes:

- **`width`:** The width of the border. This can be measured in any CSS unit, but border width is normally described in pixels (`px`) or ems. (Remember, an *em* is roughly the width of the capital letter "M" in the current font.)
- **`color`:** The color used to display the border. The color can be defined like any other color in CSS, with color names or hex values.
- **`style`:** CSS supports a number of border styles. These are described in the upcoming section. For this example, I chose a double border. This draws a border with two thinner lines around the element.

You must define all three attributes if you want borders to appear properly. You can't rely on the default values to work in all browsers.

Defining border styles

After you have the three attributes defined, it's time to pick your border style. CSS has a predetermined list of border styles you can choose from. Figure 4-2 shows a page with all the primary border styles displayed.

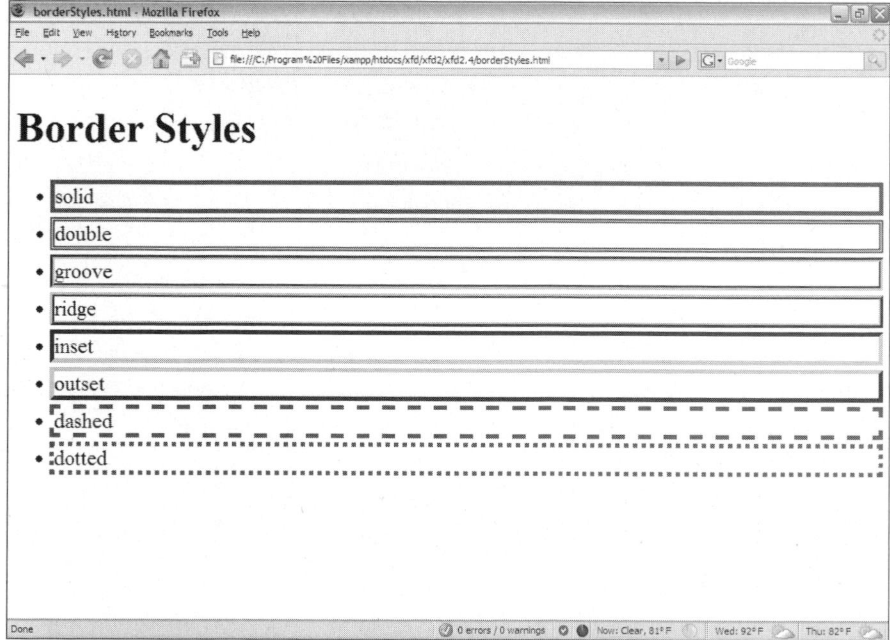

Figure 4-2: This page shows the main border styles.

You can choose any of these styles for any border:

✦ **Solid:** A single solid line around the element.

✦ **Double:** Two lines around the element with a gap between them. The border width is the combined width of both lines and the gap.

✦ **Groove:** Uses shading to simulate a groove etched in the page.

✦ **Ridge:** Uses shading to simulate a ridge drawn on the page.

✦ **Inset:** Uses shading to simulate a pressed-in button.

✦ **Outset:** Uses shading to simulate a button *sticking out* from the page.

✦ **Dashed:** A dashed line around the element.

✦ **Dotted:** A dotted line around the element.

I didn't reprint the source of `borderStyles.html` here, but it's included on the CD-ROM and Web site if you want to look it over. I added a small margin to each list item to make the borders easier to distinguish. Margins are discussed later in this chapter in the section, "Borders, margin, and padding."

Shades of danger

Several of the border styles rely on shading to produce special effects. Here are a couple things to keep in mind when using these shaded styles:

- **You'll need a wider border.** The shading effects are typically difficult to see if the border is very thin.
- **Browsers shade differently.** All the shading tricks modify the *base* color (the color you indicate with the `border-color` attribute) to simulate depth. Unfortunately, the browsers don't all do this in the same way. The Firefox/Mozilla browsers create a new color *lighter* than the base color to simulate areas in the light (the top and left sides of an outset border, for example). Internet Explorer (IE) uses the base color for the lighter regions and creates a *darker* shade to simulate areas in darkness. I show a technique to define different color schemes for each browser in Chapter 5 of this minibook. For now, avoid shaded styles if this bothers you.
- **Black shading doesn't work on IE.** IE makes colors darker to get shading effects. If your base color is black, IE can't make anything darker, so you don't see the shading effects at all. Likewise, white shading doesn't work well on Firefox.

Using the border shortcut

Defining three different CSS attributes for each border is a bit tedious. Fortunately, CSS includes a handy border shortcut that makes borders a lot easier to define, as Figure 4-3 demonstrates.

You can't tell the difference from the output, but the code for `borderShortcut.html` is extremely simple:

```
<!DOCTYPE html PUBLIC "-//W3C//DTD XHTML 1.0 Strict//EN"
"http://www.w3.org/TR/xhtml1/DTD/xhtml1-strict.dtd">
<html lang="EN" dir="ltr" xmlns="http://www.w3.org/1999/xhtml">
  <head>
    <meta http-equiv="content-type" content="text/xml; charset=utf-8" />
    <title>borderShortcut.html</title>
    <style type = "text/css">
      h1 {
        border: red 5px solid;
      }
    </style>
  </head>

  <body>
    <h1>This page uses the border shortcut</h1>
  </body>
</html>
```


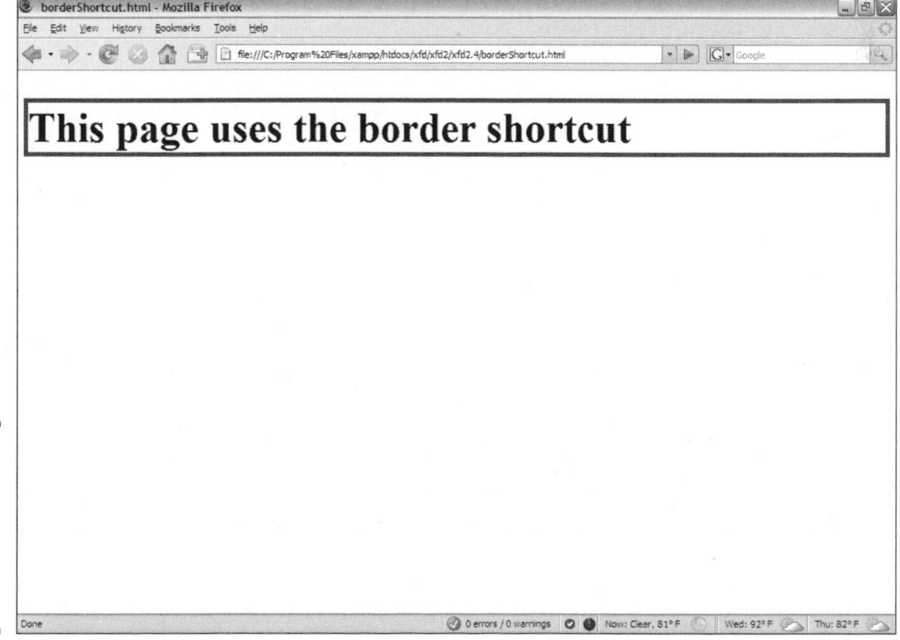

Figure 4-3: This border is defined with only one CSS rule.

The order in which you describe border attributes doesn't matter. Specify a color, a size, and a border style.

Creating partial borders

If you want, you can have more precise control of each side of a border. There are actually a number of specialized border shortcuts for each of the sub-borders. Figure 4-4 shows how you can add borders to the top, bottom, or sides of your element.

Figure 4-4 applies a border style to the bottom of the `h1` and to the left side of the paragraph. Partial borders are pretty easy to build, as you can see from the code listing:

```
<!DOCTYPE html PUBLIC "-//W3C//DTD XHTML 1.0 Strict//EN"
"http://www.w3.org/TR/xhtml1/DTD/xhtml1-strict.dtd">
<html lang="EN" dir="ltr" xmlns="http://www.w3.org/1999/xhtml">
  <head>
    <meta http-equiv="content-type" content="text/xml; charset=utf-8" />
    <title>subBorders.html</title>
    <style type = "text/css">
      h1 {
        border-bottom: 5px black double;
      }
```

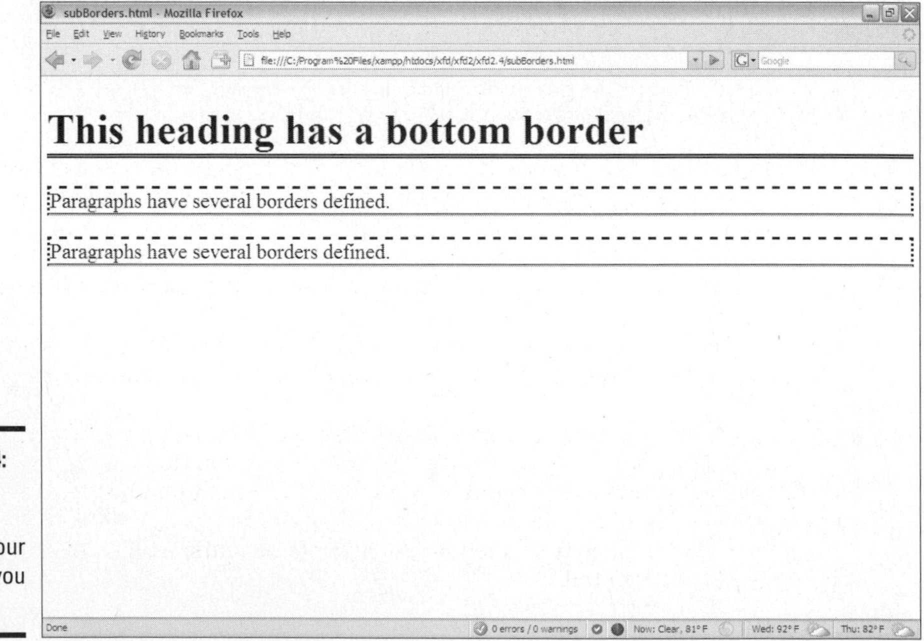

Figure 4-4: You can specify parts of your border if you want.

```
    p {
      border-left:3px black dotted;
      border-right: 3px black dotted;
      border-top: 3px black dashed;
      border-bottom: 3px black groove;
    }
  </style>
</head>

<body>
  <h1>This heading has a bottom border</h1>

  <p>
    Paragraphs have several borders defined.
  </p>

  <p>
    Paragraphs have several borders defined.
  </p>

</body>
</html>
```


Notice the border styles. CSS has style rules for each side of the border: border-top, border-bottom, border-left, and border-right. Each of these styles acts like the border shortcut, but it only acts on one side of the border.

There's also specific border attributes for each side (`bottom-border-width`), but they're almost never used because the shortcut version is so much easier.

Introducing the Box Model

XHTML and CSS use a specific type of formatting called the *box model.* Understanding how this layout technique works is important. If you don't understand some of the nuances, you'll be surprised by the way your pages flow.

The box model relies on two main types of elements, inline and block-level. `<div>` tags, paragraphs, and all headings (`h1`–`h6`) are examples of block-level elements, whereas `strong`, `a`, and `image` are examples of inline elements. Each type of element defines a rectangular box on the screen.

The main difference between inline and block-level elements is this: Block-level elements always describe their own space on the screen, whereas inline elements are allowed only within the context of a block-level element.

Your overall page is defined in block-level elements, which contain inline elements for detail.

Each block-level element (at least in the default setting) takes up the entire width of the screen. The next block-level element goes directly underneath the last element defined.

Inline elements flow differently. They tend to go immediately to the right of the previous element. If there's no room left on the current line, an inline element drops down to the next line and goes to the far left.

Borders, margin, and padding

Each block-level element has several layers of space around it, such as:

- ✦ **Padding:** The space between the content and the border.
- ✦ **Border:** Goes around the padding.
- ✦ **Margin:** Space outside the border between the border and the parent element.

Figure 4-5 shows the relationship among margin, padding, and border.

You can change settings for the margin, border, and padding to adjust the space around your elements. The `margin` and `padding` CSS rules are used to set the sizes of these elements, as shown in Figure 4-6.

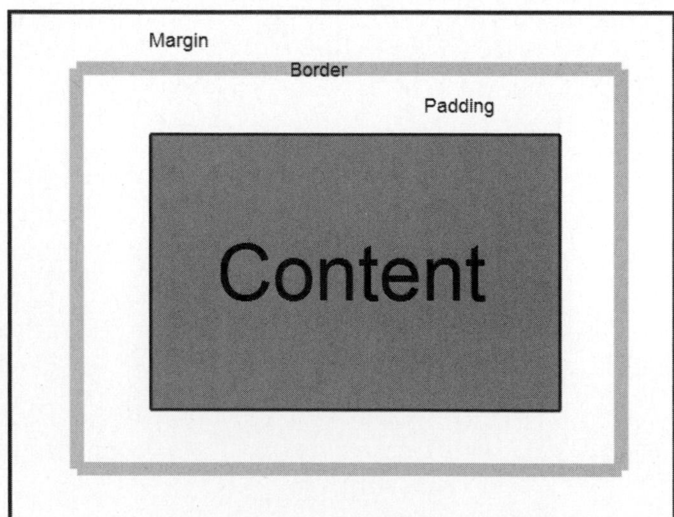

Figure 4-5: Margin is outside the border; padding is inside.

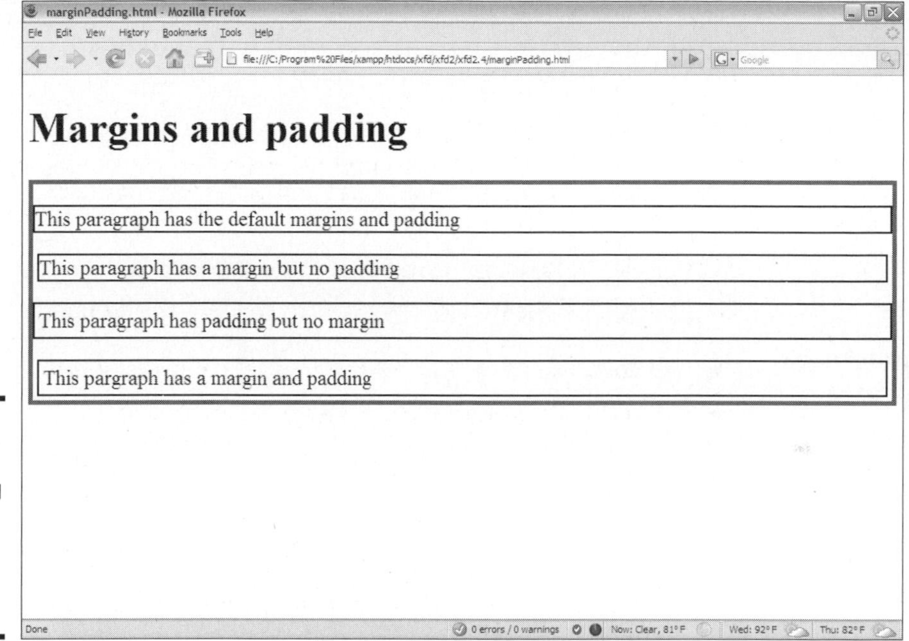

Figure 4-6: Margins and padding affect the positioning of an element.

In Figure 4-6, I applied different combinations of margin and padding to a series of paragraphs. To make things easier to visualize, I drew a border around the <div> containing all the paragraphs and each individual paragraph element. You can see how the spacing is affected.

```
<!DOCTYPE html PUBLIC "-//W3C//DTD XHTML 1.0 Strict//EN"
"http://www.w3.org/TR/xhtml1/DTD/xhtml1-strict.dtd">
<html lang="EN" dir="ltr" xmlns="http://www.w3.org/1999/xhtml">
  <head>
    <meta http-equiv="content-type" content="text/xml; charset=utf-8" />
    <title>marginPadding.html</title>
    <style type = "text/css">
      div {
        border: red 5px solid;
      }
      p {
        border: black 2px solid;
      }
      #margin {
        margin: 5px;
      }
      #padding {
        padding: 5px;
      }
      #both {
        margin: 5px;
        padding: 5px;
      }
    </style>
  </head>
```

```
<body>
  <h1>Margins and padding</h1>
  <div id = "main">
    <p>This paragraph has the default margins and padding</p>
    <p id = "margin">This paragraph has a margin but no padding</p>
    <p id = "padding">This paragraph has padding but no margin</p>
    <p id = "both">This paragraph has a margin and padding</p>
  </div>
</body>
</html>
```

You can determine margin and padding using any of the standard CSS measurement units, but the most common are pixels and ems.

Positioning elements with margins and padding

As with borders, you can use variations of the `margin` and `padding` rules to affect spacing on a particular side of the element. One particularly important form of this trick is *centering.*

In old-style HTML, you could center any element or text with the `<center>` tag. This was pretty easy, but it violated the principle of separating content from style. The `text-align: center` rule is a nice alternative, but it only works on the contents of an element. If you want to center an entire block-level element, you need another trick, as you can see in Figure 4-7.

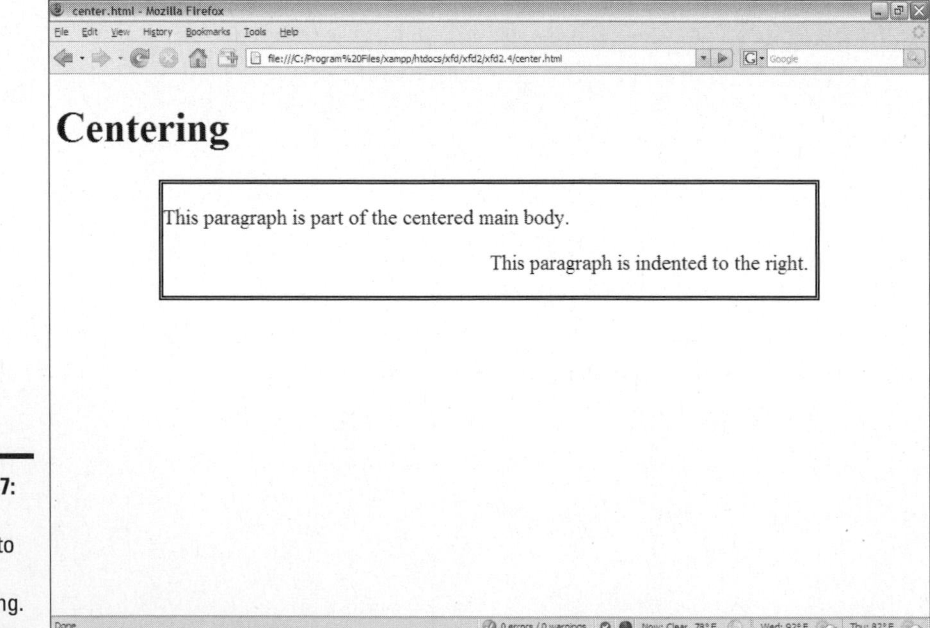

Figure 4-7: Using margins to adjust positioning.

This page illustrates a few interesting ideas:

- **You can adjust the width of a block.** The main `div` that contains all the paragraphs has its width set to 75 percent of the page body width.
- **Center an element by setting `margin-left` and `margin-right` to `auto`.** Set both the left and right margins to `auto` to make an element center inside its parent element. This trick is most frequently used to center `div`s and tables.
- **Use `margin-left` to indent an entire paragraph.** You can use `margin-left` or `margin-right` to give extra space between the border and the contents.
- **Percentages refer to percent of the parent element.** When you use percentages as the unit measurement for margins and padding, you're referring to the percentage of the parent element; so a `margin-left` of 50 percent leaves the left half of the element blank.
- **Borders help you see what's happening.** I added a border to the `mainBody div` to help you see that the `div` is centered.
- **Setting the margins to `auto` doesn't center the *text*.** It centers the *`div`* (or other block-level element). Use `text-align: center` to center text inside the `div`.

The code that demonstrates these ideas is shown here:

```
<!DOCTYPE html PUBLIC "-//W3C//DTD XHTML 1.0 Strict//EN"
"http://www.w3.org/TR/xhtml1/DTD/xhtml1-strict.dtd">
<html lang="EN" dir="ltr" xmlns="http://www.w3.org/1999/xhtml">
  <head>
    <meta http-equiv="content-type" content="text/xml; charset=utf-8" />
    <title>center.html</title>
    <style type = "text/css">
      #mainBody {
        border: 5px double black;
        width: 75%;
        margin-left: auto;
        margin-right: auto;
      }
      .indented {
        margin-left: 50%;
      }
    </style>
  </head>

  <body>
    <h1>Centering</h1>
    <div id = "mainBody">
      <p>
        This paragraph is part of the centered main body.
      </p>
```

```
      <p class = "indented">
        This paragraph is indented to the right.
      </p>
    </div>
  </body>
</html>
```

Changing the Background Image

You can use another CSS rule — *background-image* — to apply a background image to a page or elements on a page. Figure 4-8 shows a page with this feature.

Background images are easy to apply. The code for `backgroundImage.html` shows how:

```
<!DOCTYPE html PUBLIC "-//W3C//DTD XHTML 1.0 Strict//EN"
"http://www.w3.org/TR/xhtml1/DTD/xhtml1-strict.dtd">
<html lang="EN" dir="ltr" xmlns="http://www.w3.org/1999/xhtml">
  <head>
    <meta http-equiv="content-type" content="text/xml; charset=utf-8" />
    <title>backgroundImage.html</title>
    <style type = "text/css">
      body {
        background-image: url("ropeBG.jpg");
      }
```

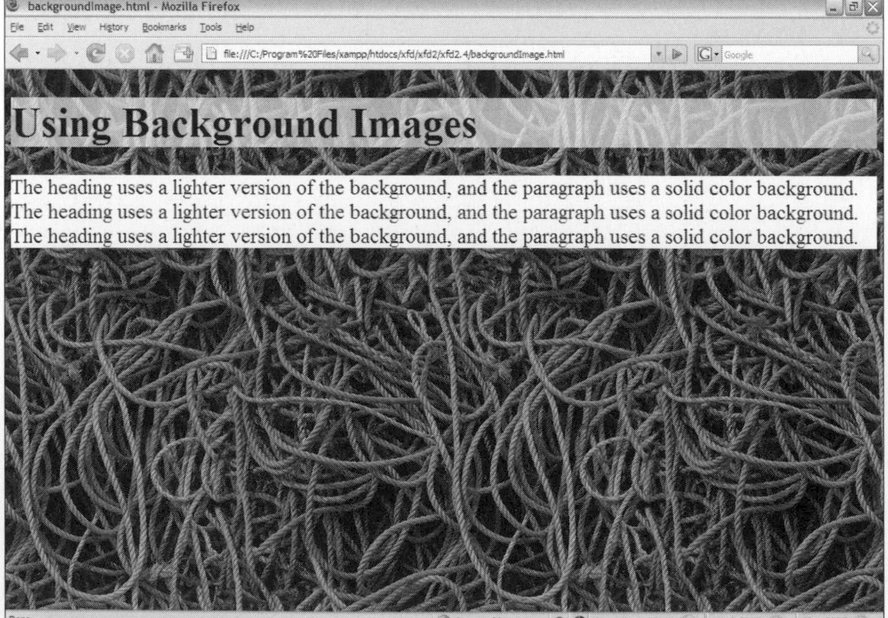

Figure 4-8: This page has a background image for the body and another for the heading.

```
      h1 {
        background-image: url("ropeBGLight.jpg");
      }
p {
        background-color: white;
      }
    </style>
  </head>

  <body>
    <h1>Using Background Images</h1>

    <p>
      The heading uses a lighter version of the background,
      and the paragraph uses a solid color background.
      The heading uses a lighter version of the background,
      and the paragraph uses a solid color background.
      The heading uses a lighter version of the background,
      and the paragraph uses a solid color background.
    </p>
  </body>
</html>
```


Attaching the background image to an element through CSS isn't difficult. Here are the general steps:

1. **Find or create an appropriate image and place it in the same directory as the page so it's easy to find.**
2. **Attach the `background-image` style rule to the page you want to apply the image to.**

   If you want to apply the image to the entire page, use the `body` element.
3. **Tell CSS where `background-image` is by adding a `url` identifier.**

   Use the keyword `url()` to indicate that the next thing is an address.
4. **Enter the address of the image.**

   It's easiest if the image is in the same directory as the page. If that's the case, you can simply type the image name. Make sure you surround the URL with quotes.
5. **Test your background image by viewing the Web page in your browser.**

   A lot can go wrong with background images. The image may not be in the right directory, you might have misspelled its name, or you may have forgotten the `url()` bit (I do all those things sometimes).

Getting a background check

It's pretty easy to add backgrounds, but background images aren't perfect. Figure 4-9 demonstrates a page with a nice background. Unfortunately, the text is difficult to read.

Figure 4-9: The text is very hard to read. Don't do this to your users!

Background images can add a lot of *zing* to your pages, but they can introduce some problems, such as:

- **Background images can add to the file size.** Images are very large, so a big background image can make your page much larger and harder to download.
- **Some images can make your page harder to read.** An image in the background can interfere with the text, so the page can be much harder to read.
- **Good images don't make good backgrounds.** A good picture draws the eye and calls attention to it. The job of a background image is to fade into the background. If you want people to look at a picture, embed it. Background images shouldn't jump into the foreground.
- **Backgrounds need to be low contrast.** If your background image is dark, you can make light text viewable. If the background image is light, dark text shows up. If your image has areas of light and dark (like nearly all good images), it'll be impossible to find a text color that looks good against it.

Solutions to the background conundrum

Web developers have come up with a number of solutions to background image issues over the years. I used several of these solutions in the `backgroundImage.html` page (the readable one shown in Figure 4-8).

Using a tiled image

If you try to create an image the size of an entire Web page, the image will be so large that dialup users will almost never see it. Even with compression techniques, a page-sized image is too large for quick or convenient loading.

Fortunately, you can use a much smaller image and fool the user into thinking it takes up the entire screen. Figure 4-10 shows the `ropeBG.jpg` that I used to cover the entire page.

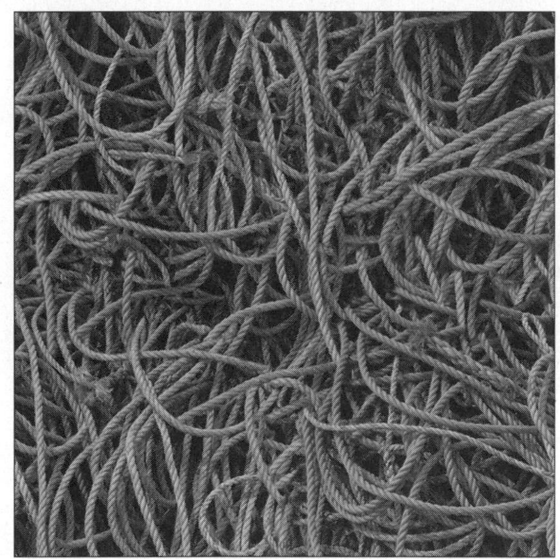

Figure 4-10: The image is only 500 x 500 pixels.

Image courtesy of Julian Burgess (Creative Commons License).

I used a specially-created image for the background. Even though it's only 500 pixels wide by 500 pixels tall, it's been carefully designed to repeat so you can't see the seams. If you look carefully, you can tell that the image repeats, but you can't tell exactly where one copy ends and the next one begins.

This type of image is a *tiled background* or sometimes a *seamless texture*.

Getting a tiled image

If you want an image that repeats seamlessly, you have two main options:

- **Find an image online.** A number of sites online have free seamless backgrounds for you to use on your site. Try a search and see what you come up with.
- **Make your own image.** If you can't find a pre-made image that does what you want, you can always make your own. All the main image editing tools have seamless background tools. In GIMP, choose Filters➪Map➪Make Seamless. You can also do it by hand by offsetting the image (choose Layer➪Transform➪Offset➪Offset by x/2, y/2) and using the Blur or Clone tools to clean up the seams.

By default, a background image repeats as many times as necessary in both the horizontal and vertical dimensions to fill up the entire page. This fills the entire page with your background, but you only have to download a small image.

Setting background colors

Background colors can be a great tool for improving readability. If you set the background color of a specific element, that background color will appear on top of the underlying element's background image. For the `backgroundImage.html` example, I set the background color of all `p` objects to white, so the text will appear on white regardless of the complex background. This is a useful technique for body text (like <p> tags) because text tends to be smaller and readability is especially important. If you want, you can set a background color that's similar to the background image. Just be sure the foreground color contrasts with the background color so the text is easy to read.

When you use a dark background image with light text, be sure to also set the `background-color` to a dark color. This way the text is readable immediately. Images take longer to load than colors and may be broken. Make sure the user can read the text immediately.

Reducing the contrast

In `backgroundImage.html`, the heading text is pretty dark, which won't show up well against the dark background image. I used a different trick for the `h1` heading. The heading uses a different version of the ropes image; this one is adjusted to be much brighter. The image is shown in Figure 4-11.

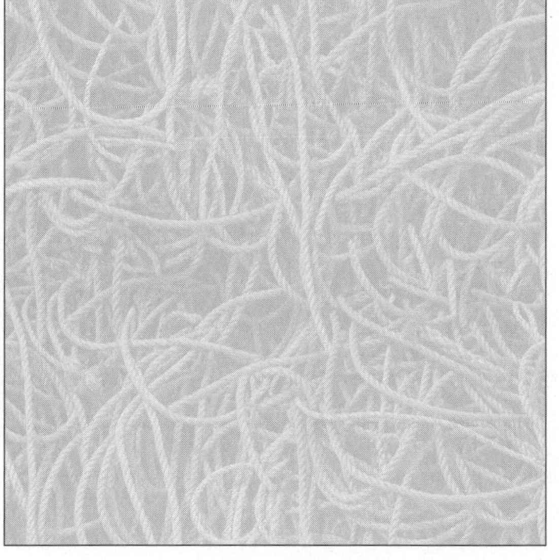

Figure 4-11: This is the ropes image with the brightness turned way up.

With this element, I kept the ropes image, but I made a much brighter background so the dark text would show up well underneath. This technique allows you to use the background image even underneath text, but here are a few things to keep in mind if you use it:

- **Make the image very dark or very light.** Use the Adjust Colors command in IrfanView or your favorite image editor to make your image dark or light. Don't be shy. If you're creating a lighter version, make it *very* light. (See Book I, Chapter 6 for details on color manipulation in IrfanView.)
- **Set the foreground to a color that contrasts with the background.** If you have a very light version of the background image, you can use dark text on it. A dark background will require light text. Adjust the text color with your CSS code.
- **Set a background color.** Make the background color representative of the image. Background images can take some time to appear, but the background color appears immediately, because it is defined in CSS. This is especially important for light text because white text on the default white background is invisible. After the background image appears, it overrides the background color. Be sure the text color contrasts with the background whether that background is an image or a solid color.
- **Use this trick for large text.** Headlines are usually larger than body text, and they can be easier to read, even if they have a background behind them. Try to avoid putting background images behind smaller body text. This can make the text much harder to read.

Manipulating Background Images

After you place your background image, you might not be completely pleased with the way it appears. Don't worry. You still have some control. You can specify how the image repeats and how it's positioned.

Turning off the repeat

Background images repeat both horizontally and vertically by default. You may not want a background image to repeat, though. Figure 4-12 is a page with the ropes image set to not repeat at all.

The code uses the `background-repeat` attribute to turn off the automatic repetition.

```
<!DOCTYPE html PUBLIC "-//W3C//DTD XHTML 1.0 Strict//EN"
"http://www.w3.org/TR/xhtml1/DTD/xhtml1-strict.dtd">
<html lang="EN" dir="ltr" xmlns="http://www.w3.org/1999/xhtml">
  <head>
    <meta http-equiv="content-type" content="text/xml; charset=utf-8" />
    <title>noRepeat.html</title>
    <style type = "text/css">
      body {
        background-image: url("ropeBG.jpg");
        background-repeat: no-repeat;
      }
```

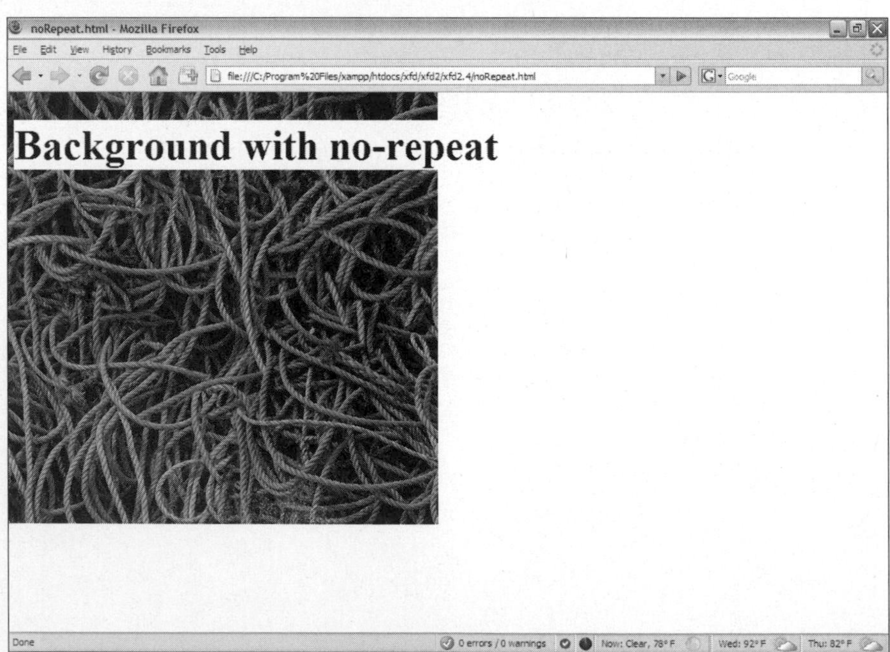

Figure 4-12: The background doesn't repeat at all.

```
      h1 {
        background-color: white;
      }
    </style>
  </head>

  <body>
    <h1>Background with no-repeat</h1>
  </body>
</html>
```

The `background-repeat` attribute can be set to one of four different values:

- **`repeat`.** The default value; the image is repeated indefinitely in both *x*- and *y*-axes.
- **`no-repeat`.** Displays the image one time; no repeat in *x*- or *y*-axis.
- **`repeat-x`.** Repeats the image horizontally but not vertically.
- **`repeat-y`.** Repeats the image vertically but not horizontally.

Making effective gradients with repeat-x and repeat-y

Gradients are images that smoothly flow from one color to another. They can have multiple colors, but simplicity is a virtue here. The `repeat-x` and `repeat-y` techniques discussed in the previous section can be combined with a special image to create a nice gradient background image that's very easy to download. Figure 4-13 shows an example of this technique.

Even though the entire page is covered in a background image, I made the actual background quite small. The outlined area in Figure 4-13 is the actual image used in the background (displayed with an `img` tag and a border). You can see that the image used is very short (5 pixels tall). I used `background-repeat: y` to make this image repeat as many times as necessary to fill the height of the page.

The code is pretty straightforward:

```
<!DOCTYPE html PUBLIC "-//W3C//DTD XHTML 1.0 Strict//EN"
"http://www.w3.org/TR/xhtml1/DTD/xhtml1-strict.dtd">
<html lang="EN" dir="ltr" xmlns="http://www.w3.org/1999/xhtml">
  <head>
    <meta http-equiv="content-type" content="text/xml; charset=utf-8" />
    <title>gradient.html</title>
    <style type = "text/css">
      body {
        background-image: url("blueGrad.jpg");
        background-repeat: repeat-y;
      }
```

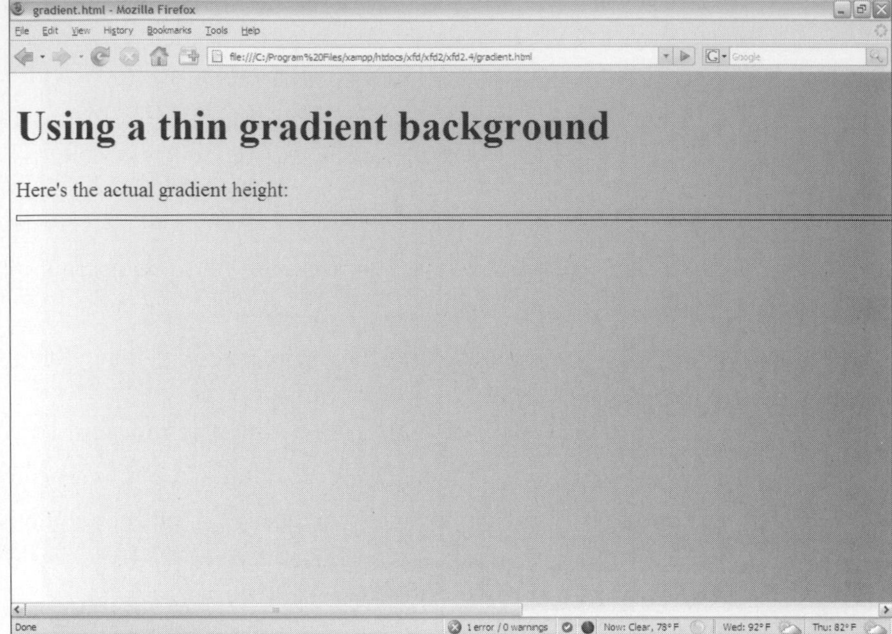

Figure 4-13: The page appears to have a large background image.

```
      img {
        border: 1px solid black;
      }
    </style>
  </head>

  <body>
    <h1>Using a thin gradient background</h1>
    <p>
    Here's the actual gradient height: <br />
    <img src = "blueGrad.jpg" />
    </p>

  </body>
</html>
```

Here's how you make a gradient background:

- **Obtain or create a gradient image.**

  Most image editing tools can make gradient fills easily. In Gimp, you simply select the gradient tool, choose an appropriate foreground and background color, and apply the gradient to the image.

- **Set the image size.**

  If you want your image to tile vertically (as I did), you'll want to make it very short (5 pixels) and very wide (I chose 1,600 pixels, so it would fill nearly any browser).

✦ **Apply the image as the background image of the body or of any other element, using the `background-image` attribute.**

✦ **Set the `background-repeat` attribute to `repeat-x` to make the image repeat as many times as necessary vertically.**

Use a vertical gradient image if you prefer. If you want to have a color that appears to change down the page, create a tall, skinny gradient and set `background-repeat` to `repeat-x`.

The great thing about this technique is how it uses a relatively small image to fill a large Web site. It looks good, but it'll still download reasonably fast.

Using Images in Lists

It's not quite a background, but you can also use images for list items. Sometimes you might want some type of special bullet for your lists, as shown in Figure 4-14.

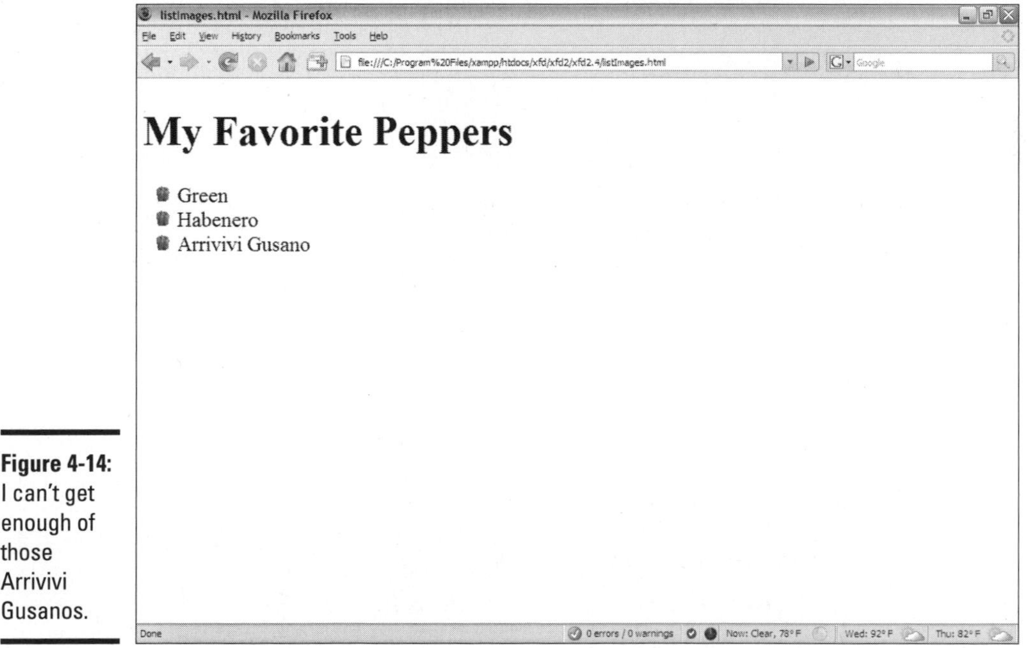

Figure 4-14: I can't get enough of those Arrivivi Gusanos.

On this page, I've listed some of my (many) favorite varieties of peppers. For this kind of list, a custom pepper bullet is just the thing. Of course, CSS is the answer:

```
<!DOCTYPE html PUBLIC "-//W3C//DTD XHTML 1.0 Strict//EN"
"http://www.w3.org/TR/xhtml1/DTD/xhtml1-strict.dtd">
<html lang="EN" dir="ltr" xmlns="http://www.w3.org/1999/xhtml">
  <head>
    <meta http-equiv="content-type" content="text/xml; charset=utf-8" />
    <title>listImages.html</title>
    <style type = "text/css">
      li {
        list-style-image: url("pepper.gif");
      }
    </style>
  </head>

  <body>
    <h1>My Favorite Peppers</h1>
    <ul>
      <li>Green</li>
      <li>Habenero</li>
      <li>Arrivivi Gusano</li>
    </ul>
  </body>
</html>
```

The `list-style-image` attribute allows you to attach an image to a list item. To create custom bullets:

1. **Begin with a custom image.**

   Bullet images should be small, so you may have to make something little. I took a little pepper image and resized it to be 25 x 25 pixels. The image will be trimmed to an appropriate width, but it will have all the height of the original image, so make it small.

2. **Specify the `list-style-image` with a `url` attribute.**

   You can set the image as the `list-style-image`, and all the bullets will be replaced with that image.

3. **Test the list in your browser.**

   Be sure everything is working correctly. Check to see that the browser can find the image, that the size is right, and that everything looks like you expect.

Chapter 5: Levels of CSS

In This Chapter

- Building element-level styles
- Creating external style sheets
- Creating a multi-page style
- Managing cascading styles
- Using conditional comments

CSS is a great tool for setting up the visual display of your pages. When you first write CSS code, you're encouraged to place all your CSS rules in a `style` element at the top of the page. CSS also allows you to define style rules inside the body of the HTML and in a separate document. In this chapter, you read about these alternative methods of applying style rules, when to use them, and how various style rules interact with each other.

Managing Levels of Style

Styles can be applied to your pages at three main levels:

- **Local styles:** Defined by specifying a style within an XHTML element's attributes.
- **Page-level styles:** Defined in the page's header area. This is the type of style used in Chapters 1 through 4 of this minibook.
- **External styles:** Defined on a separate document and linked to the page.

Using local styles

A style can be defined directly in the HTML body. Figure 5-1 is an example of this type of code. A local style is also sometimes called an *element-level* style, because it modifies a particular instance of an element on the page.

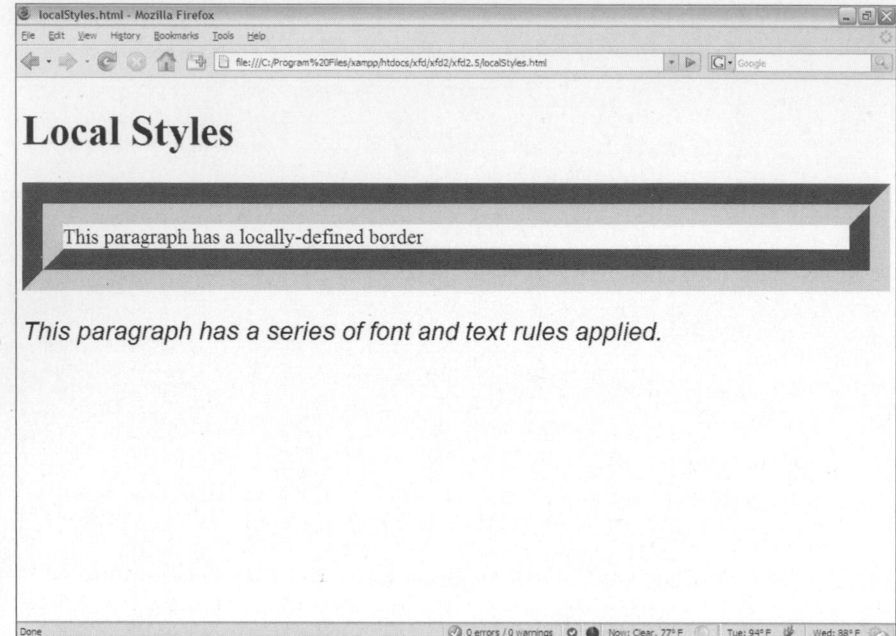

Figure 5-1: This page has styles, but they're defined differently than you've done before in this book.

You can't see the difference from Figure 5-1, but if you look over the code, you'll see it's not like style code you see in the other chapters in this minibook:

```
<!DOCTYPE html PUBLIC "-//W3C//DTD XHTML 1.0 Strict//EN"
"http://www.w3.org/TR/xhtml1/DTD/xhtml1-strict.dtd">
<html lang="EN" dir="ltr" xmlns="http://www.w3.org/1999/xhtml">
  <head>
    <meta http-equiv="content-type" content="text/xml; charset=utf-8" />
    <title>localStyles.html</title>
  </head>

  <body>
    <h1>Local Styles</h1>
    <p style = "border: 2em #FF00FF groove">
      This paragraph has a locally-defined border
    </p>

    <p style = "font-family: sans-serif;
                font-size: 1.2em;
                font-style: italic">
      This paragraph has a series of font and text rules applied.
    </p>
  </body>
</html>
```

While you look over this code, a couple things should become evident:

- **No <style> element is in the header.** Normally, you use a `<style>` section in the page header to define all your styles. This page doesn't have such a segment.
- **Paragraphs have their own style attributes.** I added a `style` attribute to each paragraph in the HTML body. All XHTML elements support the `style` attribute.
- **The entire style code goes in a single pair of quotes.** For each styled element, the entire style goes into a pair of quotes because it's one HTML attribute. You can use indentation and white space (as I did) to make things easier to understand.

When to use local styles

Local styles should not be your first choice, but they can be useful in some circumstances.

If you're writing a program to translate from a word processor or other tool, local styles are often the easiest way to make the translation work. If you use a word processor to create a page and you tell it to save as HTML, it will often use local styles because word processors often use this technique in their own proprietary format. Often when you see an HTML page with a lot of local styles, it's because an automatic translation tool made the page.

Sometimes you'll see local styles used in code examples. For example, the following code could be used to demonstrate different border styles:

```
 <!DOCTYPE html PUBLIC "-//W3C//DTD XHTML 1.0 Strict//EN"
"http://www.w3.org/TR/xhtml1/DTD/xhtml1-strict.dtd">
<html lang="EN" dir="ltr" xmlns="http://www.w3.org/1999/xhtml">
  <head>
    <meta http-equiv="content-type" content="text/xml; charset=utf-8" />
    <title>localBorders.html</title>
  </head>

  <body>
    <h1>Inline Borders</h1>
    <p style = "border: 5px solid black">
      This paragraph has a solid black border
    </p>

    <p style = "border: 5px double black">
      This paragraph has a double black border
    </p>

  </body>
</html>
```

For example purposes, it's helpful to see the style right next to the element. This code would be fine for demonstration or testing purposes (if you just want to get a quick look at some border styles), but it wouldn't be a good idea for production code.

Local styles have very high priority, so anything you apply in a local style overrides the other style rules. This can be a useful workaround if things aren't working like you expect, but it's better to get a feel for why your styles are acting as they are.

The other place you'll occasionally see local styles is in Dynamic HTML (DHTML) applications like animation and motion. This technique often involves writing JavaScript code to change various style elements on the fly. The technique is more reliable when the style elements in question are defined locally. See Book IV, Chapter 7 for a complete discussion of this topic.

The drawbacks of local styles

It's pretty easy to apply a local style, but for the most part, the technique isn't usually recommended because it has some problems, such as:

- **Inefficiency:** If you define styles at the individual element level with the `style` attribute, you're defining only the particular instance. If you want to set paragraph colors for your whole page this way, you'll end up writing a lot of style rules.
- **Readability:** If style information is interspersed throughout the page, it's much more difficult to find and modify than if it's centrally located in the header (or in an external document, as you'll see shortly).
- **Lack of separation:** Placing the styles at the element level defeats the goal of separating content from style. It becomes much more difficult to make changes, and the mixing of style and content makes your code harder to read and modify.
- **Awkwardness:** An entire batch of CSS rules has to be stuffed into a single HTML attribute with a pair of quotes. This can be tricky to read because you have CSS integrated directly into the flow of HTML.
- **Quote problems:** The XHTML attribute requires quotes, and some CSS elements also require quotes (font families with spaces in them, for example). Having multiple levels of quotes in a single element is a recipe for trouble.

Using an external style sheet

CSS supports another way to use styles, called *external style sheets.* This technique allows you to define a style sheet as a separate document and import it into your Web pages. To see why this might be attractive, take a look at the following figure.

Figure 5-2 shows a page with a distinctive style.

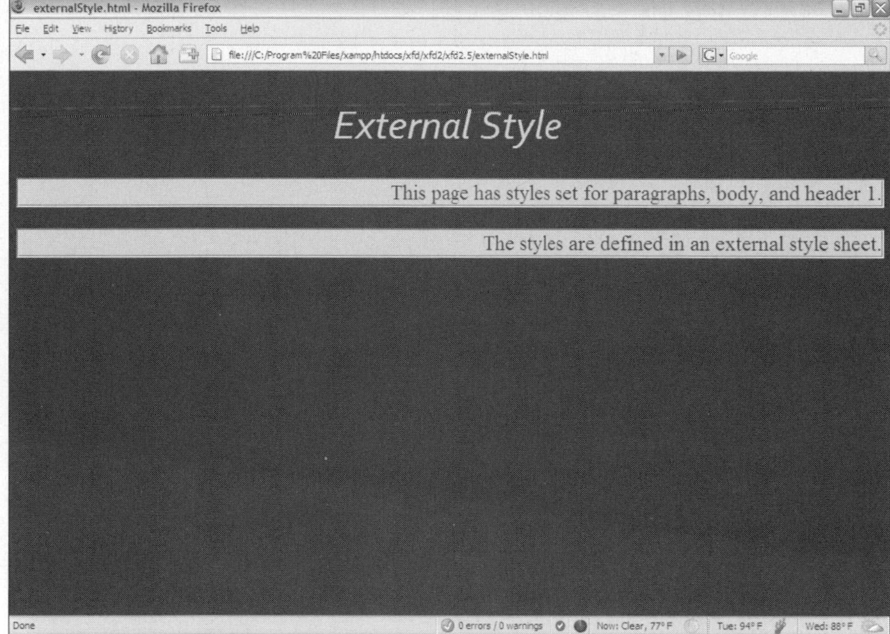

Figure 5-2: This page has styles for the body, h1, and paragraph tags.

When you look at the code for `externalStyle.html`, you might be surprised to see no obvious style information at all!

```
<!DOCTYPE html PUBLIC "-//W3C//DTD XHTML 1.0 Strict//EN"
"http://www.w3.org/TR/xhtml1/DTD/xhtml1-strict.dtd">
<html lang="EN" dir="ltr" xmlns="http://www.w3.org/1999/xhtml">
  <head>
    <meta http-equiv="content-type" content="text/xml; charset=utf-8" />
    <title>externalStyle.html</title>
    <link rel = "stylesheet"
          type = "text/css"
          href = "myStyle.css" />
  </head>

  <body>
    <h1>External Style</h1>
    <p>
      This page has styles set for paragraphs, body, and header 1.
    </p>

    <p>
      The styles are defined in an external style sheet.
    </p>
  </body>
</html>
```

Where you'd normally see style tags (in the header), there is no style. Instead, you see a `<link>` tag. This special tag is used to connect the current document with another document.

Defining the external style

When you use a page-level style, the style elements aren't embedded in the page header but in an entirely separate document.

In this case, the page is connected to a special file called `myStyle.css`. This file contains all the CSS rules:

```
/* myStyle.css */

body {
  background-color: #333300;
  color: #FFFFFF;
}

h1 {
  color: #FFFF33;
  text-align: center;
  font: italic 200% fantasy;
}

p {
  background-color: #FFFF33;
  color: #333300;
  text-align: right;
  border: 3px groove #FFFF33;
}
```

The style sheet looks just like a page-level style, except for a few key differences:

✦ **The style sheet rules are contained in a separate file.** The style is no longer part of the HTML page but is an entirely separate file stored on the server. CSS files usually end with the `.css` extension.

✦ **There are no `<style></style>` tags.** These aren't needed because the style is no longer embedded in HTML.

✦ **The code begins with a comment.** The `/* */` pair indicates a *comment* in CSS. Truthfully, you can put comments in CSS in the page level just like I did in this external file. External CSS files frequently have comments in them.

✦ **The style document has no HTML.** CSS documents contain nothing but CSS. This comes closer to the goal of separating style (in the CSS document) and content (in the HTML document).

✦ **The document isn't tied to any particular page.** The great advantage of external CSS is reuse. The CSS document isn't part of any particular page, but any page can use it.

Reusing an external CSS style

External style sheets are really fun when you have more than one page that needs the same style. Most Web sites today use multiple pages, and they should share a common style sheet to keep consistency. Figure 5-3 shows a second page using the same `myStyle.css` style sheet.

The code shows how easily this is done:

```
<!DOCTYPE html PUBLIC "-//W3C//DTD XHTML 1.0 Strict//EN"
"http://www.w3.org/TR/xhtml1/DTD/xhtml1-strict.dtd">
<html lang="EN" dir="ltr" xmlns="http://www.w3.org/1999/xhtml">
  <head>
    <meta http-equiv="content-type" content="text/xml; charset=utf-8" />
    <title>SecondPage.html</title>
    <link rel = "stylesheet"
          type = "text/css"
          href = "myStyle.css" />
  </head>

  <body>
    <h1>Second Page</h1>
    <p>
      This page uses the same style as
      <a href = "externalStyle.html">externalStyle.html</a>.
    </p>
  </body>
</html>
```


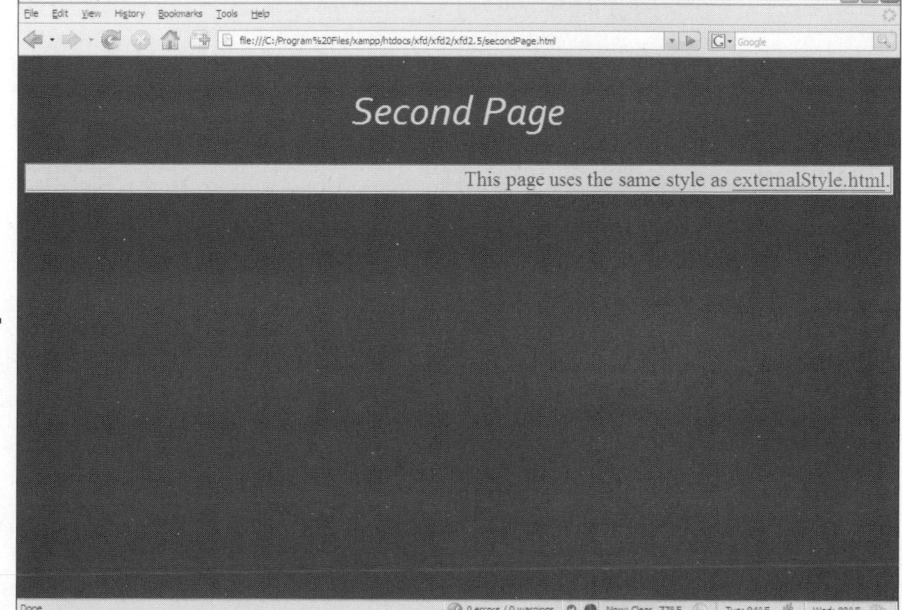

Figure 5-3: This page uses the same style as the first one, but I only defined the style once.

External style sheets have some tremendous advantages:

- **One style sheet can control many pages:** You'll generally have a large number of different pages in a Web site that all share the same general style. You can define the style sheet in one document and have all the HTML files refer to the CSS file.
- **Global changes are easier:** Let's say you have a site with a dozen pages, and you decide you want some kind of chartreuse background (I don't know why — go with me here). If each page has its own page-level style definition, you have to make the change 12 times. If you're using external styles, you make the change in one place and it's automatically propagated to all the pages in the system.
- **Separation of content and design:** With external CSS, all the design is housed in the CSS, and the data is in XHTML.
- **Easy upgrades:** Because the design parameters of the entire site are defined in one file, you can easily change the site without having to mess around with individual HTML files.

Understanding the link tag

The `link` tag is the key to adding a CSS reference to an HTML document. The `link` tag has the following characteristics:

- **The `<link>` tag is part of the HTML page.** Use a `link` tag in your HTML document to specify which CSS document will be used by the HTML page.
- **The `link` tag only occurs in the header.** Unlike the `a` tag, the `<link>` tag can occur only in the header.
- **The tag has no visual presence.** The user can't see the `link` tag, only its effects.
- **The `link` tag is used to relate the document with another document.** You use the `link` tag to describe the relationship between documents.
- **The `link` tag has a `rel` attribute, which defines the type of relationship.** For now, the only relationship you'll use is the `stylesheet` attribute.
- **The `<link>` tag also has an `href` attribute, which describes the location of the other document.**

Link tags are often used to connect a page to an externally-defined style document (more on them in the next section).

Most people refer to the hyperlinks created by the anchor (a) tag as hyperlinks or links. This can lead to some confusion, because, in this sense, the link tag doesn't create that type of links. If it were up to me, the a tag would have been called the link tag, and the tag now called link would have been called rel or something. Maybe Tim Berners-Lee meant to call me the day he named these elements, and he just forgot. That's what I'm thinking.

Specifying an external link

To use the <link> tag to specify an external style sheet, follow these steps:

1. **Define the style sheet.**

   External style sheets are very similar to the ones you already know. Just put all the styles in a separate text document without the <style> and </style> tags. In my example, I created a new text file called myStyle.css.

2. **Create a `link` element in the HTML page's head area to define the linkage between the HTML and CSS pages.**

   My link element looks like this:

   ```
   <link rel = "stylesheet"
         type = "text/css"
         href = "myStyle.css" />
   ```

3. **Set the `link`'s relationship by setting the `rel = "stylesheet"` attribute.**

   Honestly, stylesheet is almost the only relationship you'll ever use, so this should become automatic.

4. **Specify the type of style by setting `type = "text/css"` (just like you do with page-level styles).**

5. **Determine the location of the style sheet with the `href` attribute.**

Understanding the Cascading Part of Cascading Style Sheets

The *C* in CSS stands for *cascading,* which is an elegant term for an equally elegant and important idea. Styles cascade or flow among levels. An element's visual display may be affected by rules in another element or even another document.

Inheriting styles

When you apply a style to an element, you change the appearance of that element. If the element contains other elements, the style is often passed on to those containers. Take a look at Figure 5-4 for an illustration.

Figure 5-4 shows several paragraphs, all with different font styles. Each paragraph is white with a black background. All the paragraphs use a Fantasy font. Two of the paragraphs are italicized, and one is also bold. Look at the code, and you'll see how the CSS is defined.

```
<!DOCTYPE html PUBLIC "-//W3C//DTD XHTML 1.0 Strict//EN"
"http://www.w3.org/TR/xhtml1/DTD/xhtml1-strict.dtd">
<html lang="EN" dir="ltr" xmlns="http://www.w3.org/1999/xhtml">
  <head>
    <meta http-equiv="content-type" content="text/xml; charset=utf-8" />
    <title>CascadingStyles</title>
    <style type = "text/css">
      body {
        color: white;
        background-color: black;
      }

      p {
        font-family: fantasy;
      }
```

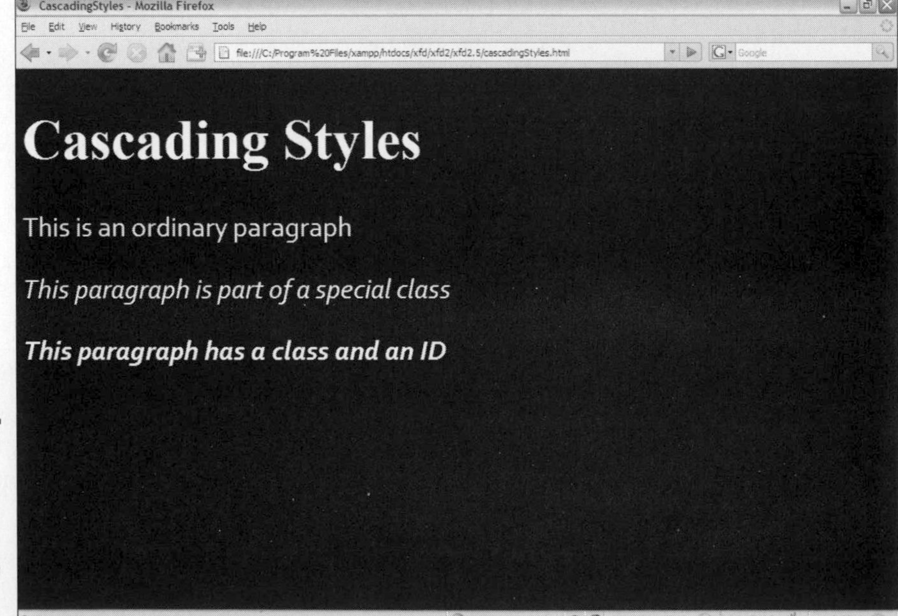

Figure 5-4: The last paragraph inherits several style rules.

```
      .italicized {
        font-style: italic;
      }

      #bold {
        font-weight: bold;
      }
    </style>
  </head>

  <body>
    <h1>Cascading Styles</h1>

    <p>This is an ordinary paragraph</p>

    <p class = "italicized">
      This paragraph is part of a special class
    </p>

    <p class = "italicized"
       id = "bold">
      This paragraph has a class and an ID</p>
  </body>

</html>
```


Take a look at the page, and you'll notice some interesting things:

- **Everything is white on a black background.** These styles were defined in the body. Paragraphs without specific colors will inherit the colors of the parent element (in this case, the `body`). There's no need to specify the paragraph colors because the `body` takes care of them.
- **Paragraphs all use the fantasy font.** I set the paragraph's `font-family` attribute to `fantasy`. All paragraphs without an explicit `font-family` attribute will use this rule.
- **A class is used to define italics.** The second paragraph is a member of the `italicized` class, which gives it italics. Because it's also a `paragraph`, it gets the paragraph font, and it inherits the color rules from the `body`.
- **The `bold` ID only identifies font weight.** The third paragraph has all kinds of styles associated with it. This paragraph displays all the styles of the second, plus the added attributes of its own ID.

In the `cascadingStyles.html` example, the final paragraph inherits the font from the generic `p` definition, italics from its class, and boldfacing from its ID. Any element can attain style characteristics from any of these definitions.

Hierarchy of styles

An element will display any style rules you define for it, but certain rules are also passed on from other places. In general, this is how style rules cascade through the page:

- **The body defines overall styles for the page.** Any style rules that you want the entire page to share should be defined in the body. Any element in the body begins with the style of the page. This makes it easy to define an overall page style.
- **A block-level element passes its style to its children.** If you define a `div` with a particular style, any elements inside that `div` will inherit the `div`'s style attributes. Likewise, defining a list will also define the list items.
- **You can always override inherited styles.** Of course, if you don't want paragraphs to have a particular style inherited from the body, you can just change them.

Not all style rules are passed on to child elements. The text formatting and color styles are inherited, but border and positioning rules are not. This actually makes sense. Just because you've defined a border around a `div` doesn't mean you'll want the same border around the paragraphs inside that `div`.

Overriding styles

The other side of inherited style is the ability to override an inherited style rule. For example, take a look at this code:

```
<!DOCTYPE html PUBLIC "-//W3C//DTD XHTML 1.0 Strict//EN"
"http://www.w3.org/TR/xhtml1/DTD/xhtml1-strict.dtd">
<html lang="EN" dir="ltr" xmlns="http://www.w3.org/1999/xhtml">
  <head>
    <meta http-equiv="content-type" content="text/xml; charset=utf-8" />
    <title>overRide.html</title>
    <style type = "text/css">
      body { color: red; }
      p {color: green; }
      .myClass { color: blue; }
      #whatColor { color: purple; }
    </style>
  </head>

  <body>
    <p class = "myClass"
       id = "whatColor">
      This paragraph is a member of a class and has an ID,
      both with style rules. It has four conflicting
      color rules!
    </p>
  </body>
</html>
```

The code listing has a different indentation scheme than I've used in the rest of the chapter. Because all the styles had one rule, I chose not to indent to save space.

The question is this: What color will the "whatColor" element display? It's a member of the body, so it should be red. It's also a paragraph, and paragraphs are green. It's also a member of the myClass class, so it should be blue. Finally, it's named whatColor, and elements with this ID should be purple.

Four seemingly conflicting color rules are all dropped on this poor element. What color will it be?

CSS has a clear ranking system for handling this type of situation. In general, more specific rules trump more general rules. Here's the precedence (from highest to lowest precedence):

1. **User preference:** The user always has the final choice about what styles are used. User's aren't required to use any styles at all, and can always change the style sheet for their own local copy of the page. If a user needs to apply a special style (for example, high contrast for people with visual disabilities), he should always have that option.
2. **local style:** A local style (defined with the style attribute in the HTML) has the highest precedence of developer-defined styles. It overrules any other styles.
3. **id:** A style attached to an element id has a great deal of weight because it overrides any other styles defined in the style sheet.
4. **class:** Styles attached to a class override the style of the object's element. So, if you have a paragraph with a color green that belongs to a class colored blue, the element will be blue because class styles outrank element styles.
5. **element:** The element style takes precedence over any of its containers. For example, if a paragraph is inside a div, the paragraph style has the potential to override both the div and the body.
6. **container element:** Divs, tables, lists, and other elements used as containers pass their styles on. If an element is inside one or more of these containers, it can inherit style attributes from them.
7. **body:** Anything defined in the body style is an overall page default, but it will be overridden by any other styles.

In the overRide.html example, the id rule will take precedence, so the paragraph will display in green.

If you want to see a more complete example, look at cascadingStyles.html on the CD-ROM. It extends the whatColor example with other paragraphs that demonstrate the various levels of the hierarchy.

Precedence of style definitions

When you have styles defined in various places (locally, page level, or externally) the placement of the style rule also has a ranking. In general, an external style has the weakest rank. You can write a page-level style rule to override an external style.

You might do this if you've decided all your paragraphs will be blue, but you have one page where you want the paragraphs green. Define paragraphs as green in the page-level style sheet, and your page will have the green paragraphs without interfering with the other page's styles.

Page-level styles (defined in the header) have medium weight. They can override external styles but are overridden by local styles.

Locally defined styles (using the HTML style attribute) have the highest precedence, but they should be avoided as much as possible. Use classes or IDs if you need to override the page-level default styles.

Using Conditional Comments

While we're messing around with style sheets, there's one more thing you should know. Every once in a while, you'll encounter a page that needs one set of style rules for most browsers and has some exceptions for Internet Explorer.

Most of what you know works equally well in any browser. I've focused on the established standards, which work very well on most browsers. Unfortunately Internet Explorer (especially before version 7) is notorious for not following the standards exactly. Internet Explorer (IE) doesn't do everything exactly right. When IE had unquestioned dominance, everybody just made things work for IE. Now you have a bigger problem. You need to make your code work for standards-compliant browsers, and sometimes you need to make a few changes to make sure that IE displays things correctly.

Coping with incompatibility

This has been a problem since the beginning of Web development, and there have been a number of solutions proposed over the years, such as:

- **"Best viewed with" disclaimers:** One common technique is to code for one browser or another and then just ask users to agree with your choice by putting up this disclaimer. This isn't a good technique because the user shouldn't have to adapt to you. Besides, sometimes the choice is out of the user's hands. More and more small devices (such as PDAs and cell phones) have browsers built in, which are difficult to change. IE isn't available on Linux machines, and not everyone can install a new browser.

✦ **Parallel pages:** You might be tempted to create two different versions of your page, one for IE and one for the standards-compliant browsers (Firefox, Netscape Navigator, Opera, Safari, and so on). This is also a bad solution because it's twice (or more) as much work. You'll have a lot of trouble keeping track of changes in two different pages. They'll inevitably fall out of synch.

✦ **JavaScript-based browser detection:** In Book IV, you see that JaveScript has features for checking on the browser. This is good, but it still doesn't quite handle the differences in style sheet implementation between the browsers.

✦ **CSS hacks:** The CSS community has frequently relied on a series of hacks (unofficial workarounds) to handle CSS compatibility problems. This approach works by exploiting certain flaws in IEs design to overcome others. The biggest problem with this is that when Microsoft fixes some flaws (as they've done with IE 7), many of the flaws you relied on to fix a problem may be gone, but the original problem is still there.

✦ **Conditional comments:** Although IE has bugs, it also has some innovative features. One of these features, *conditional comments,* lets you write code that will be displayed only in IE. Because the other browsers don't support this feature, the IE-specific code will be ignored in any browser not based on IE. This is the technique currently preferred by coders who adhere to Web standards.

Making Internet Explorer–specific code

It's a little easier for you to see how conditional comments work if I show you a simple example — and then show you how to use the conditional comment trick to fix CSS incompatibility problems.

Figure 5-5 shows a simple page with Firefox. Figure 5-6 shows the exact same page as it's displayed in IE 7.

Take a look at the code for `whatBrowser.html` and see how it works.

```
<!DOCTYPE html PUBLIC "-//W3C//DTD XHTML 1.0 Strict//EN"
"http://www.w3.org/TR/xhtml1/DTD/xhtml1-strict.dtd">
<html lang="EN" dir="ltr" xmlns="http://www.w3.org/1999/xhtml">
  <head>
    <meta http-equiv="content-type" content="text/xml; charset=utf-8" />
    <title>IEorNot.html</title>

  </head>

  <body>
    <p>
      I will now use a conditional comment to determine your
      browser. I'll let you know if you're using IE.
    </p>
```

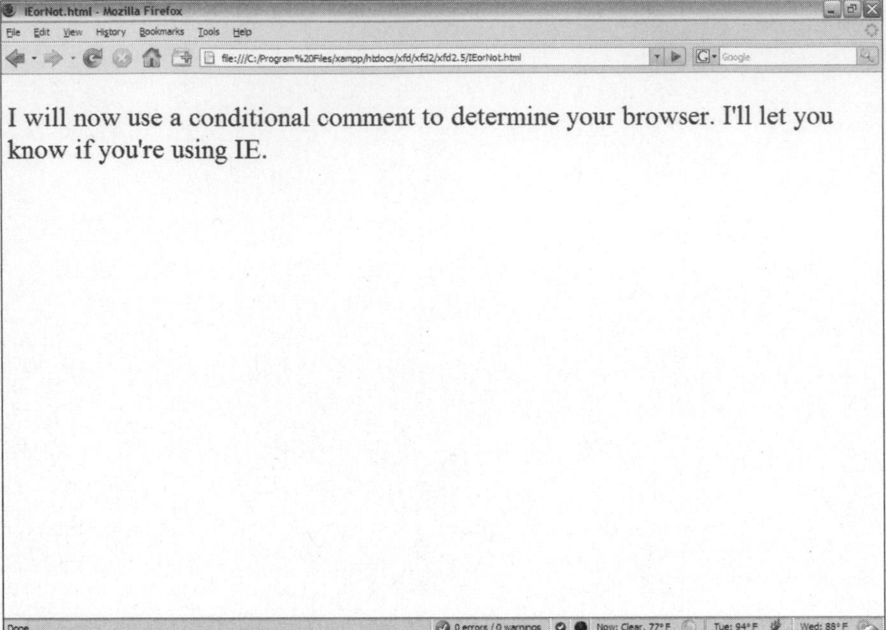

Figure 5-5: This isn't IE.

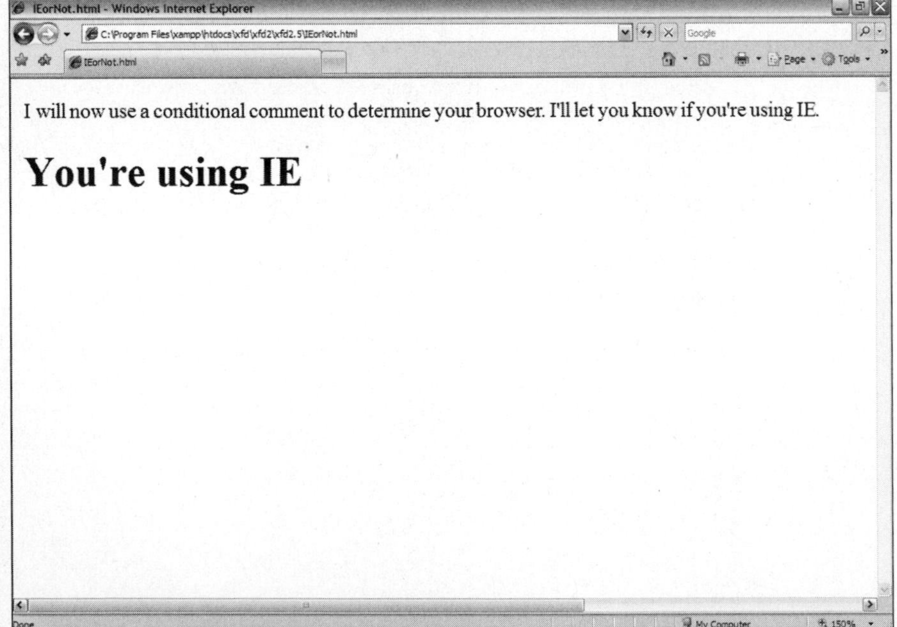

Figure 5-6: . . . And this is IE. Somehow the code knows the difference.

```
    <!--[if IE]>
      <h1>You're using IE</h1>
    <![endif]-->

  </body>
</html>
```

The only part that's new is the strange comments:

```
    <!--[if IE]>
      <h1>You're using IE</h1>
    <![endif]-->
```


Conditional comments are a special feature available only in Internet Explorer. They allow you to apply a test to your browser. You can place any XHTML code you wish between `<!-- [if IE]>` and `<![endif]-->`, but that code will only be rendered by versions of Internet Explorer. Any other browser will read the entire block as a comment and ignore it completely.

So, when you look at `whatBrowser` in IE, it sees the conditional comment, says to itself "Why yes, I'm Internet Explorer" and displays the "Using IE" headline. If you look at the same page with Firefox, the browser doesn't understand the conditional comment but sees an HTML comment (which begins with `<!--` and ends with `-->`). HTML comments are ignored, so the browser does nothing.

Using a conditional comment with CSS

Conditional comments on their own aren't that interesting, but they can be a very useful tool for creating compatible CSS. You can use conditional comments to create two different style sheets, one that works for IE and one that works with everything else. Figures 5-7 and 5-8 illustrate a simple example of this technique:

Most browsers will read a standard style sheet that creates a yellow background.

If the page is rendered in IE, it uses a second style sheet.

Look at the code and you'll see it's very similar to the `IEorNot.html` page.

```
<!DOCTYPE html PUBLIC "-//W3C//DTD XHTML 1.0 Strict//EN"
"http://www.w3.org/TR/xhtml1/DTD/xhtml1-strict.dtd">
<html lang="EN" dir="ltr" xmlns="http://www.w3.org/1999/xhtml">
  <head>
    <meta http-equiv="content-type" content="text/xml; charset=utf-8" />
    <title>WhatBrowser.html</title>
```

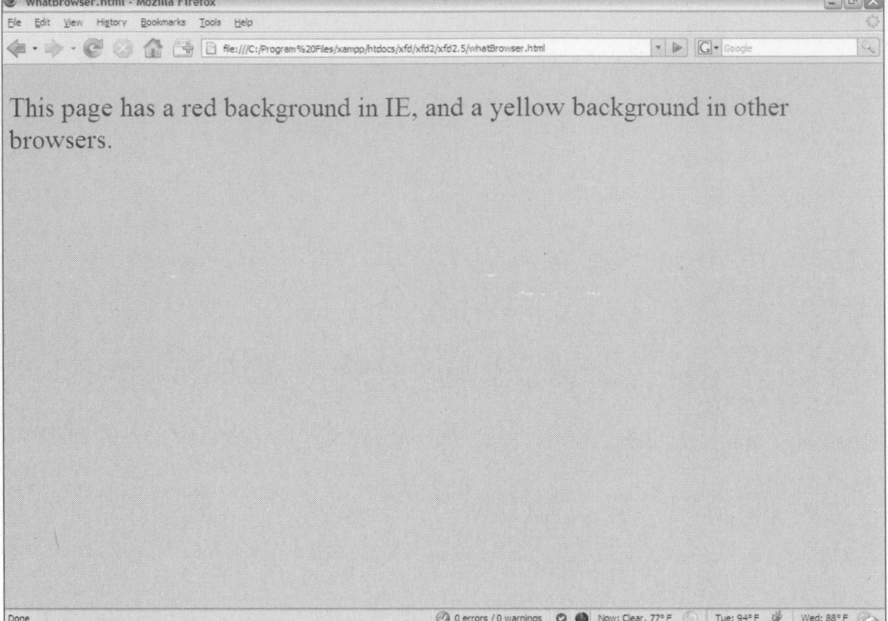

Figure 5-7: This page has a yellow background in most browsers.

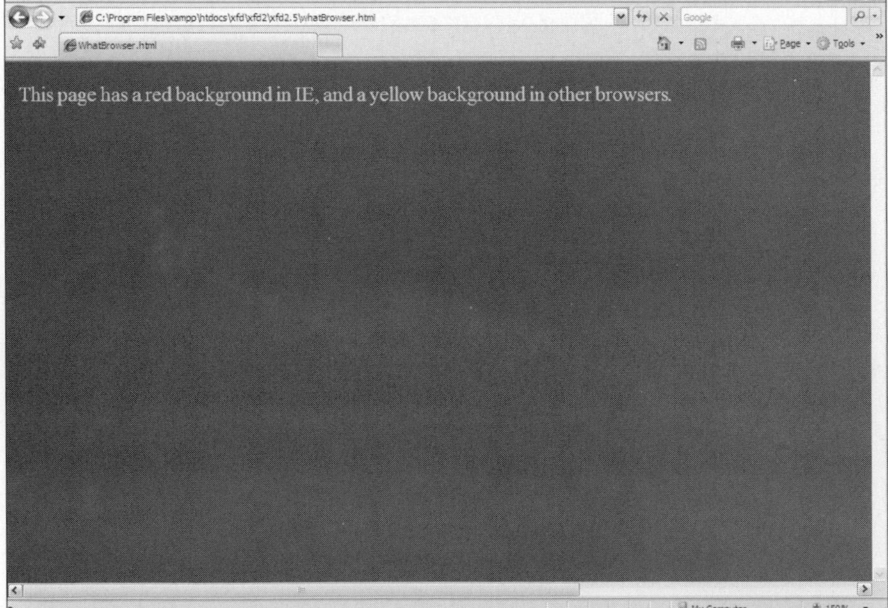

Figure 5-8: The same page uses a different style sheet in IE.

```
    <!-- default style -->
    <style type = "text/css">
      body {
        background-color: yellow;
        color: blue;
      }
    </style>

    <!-- IE only style overrides default -->
    <!--[if IE]>
      <style type = "text/css">
        body {
          background-color: red;
          color: yellow;
        }
      </style>
    <![endif]-->

  </head>

  <body>

    <p>
      This page has a red background in IE, and a yellow
      background in other browsers.
    </p>
  </body>
</html>
```


If you want a page to use different styles in IE and other browsers, do the following:

1. **Define the default style first.**

   Begin by creating the style that will work in most browsers. Most of the time, this style will also work in IE. You can create the style at the page level (with the `<style></style>` pair) or externally (with the `<link>` tag).

2. **Create a conditional comment in the header.**

   Create a conditional comment *after* the primary style, as shown in this code snippet.

   ```
   <!-- default style -->
   <style type = "text/css">
     body {
       background-color: yellow;
       color: blue;
     }
   </style>

   <!-- IE only style overrides default -->
   <!--[if IE]>

   <![endif]-->
   ```

3. **Build a new IE-specific style inside the comment.**

   The style inside the comment will be applied only to IE browsers, such as I did in the following lines:

   ```
   <!--[if IE]>
         <style type = "text/css">
           body {
             background-color: red;
             color: yellow;
           }
         </style>
       <![endif]-->
   ```

4. **The commented style can be page level or external.**

   Like the default style, you can use the `<style></style>` pair to make a page-level style, or you can use the `<link>` tag to pull in an externally-defined style sheet.

5. **Only place code that solves IE issues in the conditional style.**

   IE will read the code in both styles, so there's no need to repeat everything. Use the conditional style for only those areas where IE doesn't do what you expect.

6. **Don't forget to end the conditional comment.**

   If you leave off the end of your conditional comment (or any comment, for that matter), most of your page won't appear. That could be bad.

Checking the Internet Explorer version

So far, you haven't encountered many situations that require conditional comments, but they're handy when you need them. One more trick can be useful. You can specify which version of IE you're using. This will be important when you read about positionable CSS in Book III, as IE 7 works pretty well with standards-compliant code, but the earlier versions do not. You can use this variation to specify code only for IE 6 and earlier.

```
<!--[if lte IE 6]>
...
<[endif]-->
```

The `lte` signifies *less than or equal to,* so code inside this condition will run only on early versions of IE. Look ahead to Book III to see more examples of conditional commenting.

Book III

Using Positional CSS for Layout

Contents at a Glance

Chapter 1: Fun with the Fabulous Float

In This Chapter

- **Understanding the pitfalls of traditional layout tools**
- **Using `float` with images and block-level tags**
- **Setting the width and margins of floated elements**
- **Creating attractive forms with `float`**
- **Using the `clear` attribute with `float`**

One of the big criticisms of HTML is its lack of real layout tools. You can do a lot with your page, but it's still basically a list of elements arranged vertically on the screen. As the Web matures and screen resolutions improve, people want Web pages to look more like print matter, with columns, good-looking forms, and more layout options. CSS provides several great tools for building nice layouts. After you get used to them, you can build just about any layout you can imagine. This chapter describes the amazing `float` attribute and how it can be used as the foundation of great page layouts.

Avoiding Old-School Layout Pitfalls

Back in the prehistoric (well, pre-CSS) days, no good option was built into HTML for creating a layout that worked well. Clever Web developers and designers found some ways to make things work, but these proposed solutions all had problems.

Problems with frames

Frames were a feature of the early versions of HTML. They allowed you to break a page into several segments. Each segment was filled with a different page from the server. You could change pages independently of each other, to make a very flexible system. You could also specify the width and height of each frame.

At first glance, frames sound like an ideal solution to layout problems. In practice, they had a lot of disadvantages, such as

- **Complexity:** If you had a master page with four segments, you had to keep track of five Web pages. A *master* page kept track of the relative positions of each section but had no content. Each of the other pages had content but no built-in awareness of the other pages.
- **Linking issues:** The default link action caused content to pop up in the same frame as the original link, which isn't usually what you want. Often, you'd put a menu in one frame and have the results of that menu pop up in another frame. This meant most anchors had to be modified to make them act properly.
- **Backup nightmares:** If the user navigated to a page with frames and then caused one of the frames to change, what should the backup button do? Should it return to the previous state (with only the one segment returned to its previous state) or was the user's intent to move entirely off the master page to what came before? There are good arguments for either and no good way to determine the user's intention. Nobody ever came up with a reasonable compromise for this problem.
- **Ugliness:** Although it's possible to make frames harder to see, they did become obvious when the user changed the screen size and scroll bars would automatically pop up.

For all these reasons, frames aren't allowed in XHTML Strict documents. The layout techniques you read about in this chapter more than compensate for the loss of frames as layout tools. Read in Chapter 4 of Book VIII how to integrate content from other pages on the server with AJAX.

Problems with tables

When it became clear that frames weren't the answer, Web designers turned to tables. HTML has a flexible and powerful table tool, and it's possible to do all kinds of creative things with that tool to create layouts. Many HTML developers still do this, but you'll see that flow-based layout is cleaner and easier. Tables are meant for tabular data, not as a layout tool. When you use tables to set up the visual layout of your site, you'll encounter these problems:

- **Complexity:** Although table syntax isn't that difficult, a lot of nested tags are in a typical table definition. In order to get exactly the look you want, you probably won't use an ordinary table but tricks, like `rowspan` and `colspan`, special spacer images, and tables inside tables. It doesn't take long for the code to become bulky and confusing.
- **Content and display merging:** Using a table for layout violates the principle of separating content from display. If your content is buried inside a complicated mess of table tags, it'll be difficult to move and update.

✦ **Inflexibility:** If you create a table-based layout and then decide you don't like it, you basically have to redesign the entire page from scratch. It's no simple matter to move a menu from the left to the top in a table-based design, for example.

Tables are great for displaying tabular data. Avoid using them for layout because you have better tools available.

Problems with huge images

Some designers skip HTML altogether and create Web pages as huge images. Tools, like Photoshop, include features for creating links in a large image. Again, this seems ideal because a skilled artist can have control over exactly what is displayed. Like the other techniques, this has some major drawbacks, such as

✦ **Size and shape limitations:** When your page is based on a large image, you're committed to the size and shape of that image for your page. If a person wants to view your page on a cell phone or PDA, it's unlikely to work well, if at all.

✦ **Content issues:** If you create all the text in your graphic editor, it isn't really stored to the Web page as text. In fact, the Web page will have no text at all. This means that search engines can't index your page, and screen readers for people with disabilities won't work.

✦ **Difficult updating:** If you find an error on your page, you have to modify the image, not just a piece of text. This makes updating your page more challenging than it would be with a plain XHTML document.

✦ **File size issues:** An image large enough to fill a modern browser window will be extremely large and slow to download. Using this technique will all but eliminate users with dialup access from using your site.

Problems with Flash

Another tool that's gained great popularity is the Flash animation tool from Adobe (formerly Macromedia). This tool allows great flexibility in how you position things on a page and supports techniques that are difficult or impossible in ordinary HTML, like integrating sound and video, automatic motion tweening, and path-based animation. Flash certainly has a place in Web development (especially for embedded games — check out my earlier book *Beginning Flash Game Programming For Dummies* [Wiley Publishing, Inc.]). Even though Flash has great possibilities, you should avoid its use for ordinary Web development because of

✦ **Cost:** The Flash editor isn't cheap, and it doesn't look like it'll get cheaper. The tool is great, but if there are free or low-cost alternatives that work just as well, it's hard to justify the cost.

+ **Binary encoding:** All text in a Flash Web page is stored in the Flash file itself. It's not visible to the browser. Flash pages (like image-based pages) don't work in Web searches and aren't useful for people with screen readers.
+ **Updating issues:** If you need to change your Flash-based page, you have to have the Flash editor installed. This can make it more difficult to keep your page up to date.
+ **No separation of content:** As far as the browser is concerned, there's no content but the Flash element, so there's absolutely no separation of content and layout. If you want to make a change, you have to change the Flash application.

Adobe has recently released a very interesting tool called *Flex.* It's based on the Flash engine, and it's specifically designed to overcome some of the shortcomings I've listed in the proceeding section. It'll be interesting to see if this becomes an important technology.

Introducing the Floating Layout Mechanism

CSS supplies a couple techniques for layout. The preferred technique for most applications is a *floating layout.* The basic idea of this technique is to leave the XHTML layout as simple as possible but to provide style hints that tell the various elements how to interact with each other on the screen.

In a floating layout, you don't legislate exactly where everything will go. Instead, you provide hints and let the browser manage things for you. This insures flexibility because the browser will try to follow your intentions, no matter what size or shape the browser window becomes. If the user resizes the browser, the page will flex to fit to the new size and shape, if possible.

Floating layouts typically involve less code than other kinds of layouts because only a few elements need specialized CSS. In most of the other layout techniques, you'll need to provide CSS for every single element in order to make things work as you expected.

Using float with images

The most common place to use the `float` attribute is with images. Figure 1-1 has a paragraph with an image embedded inside.

It's more likely that you want the image to take up the entire left part of the paragraph. The text should flow around the paragraph, like Figure 1-2.

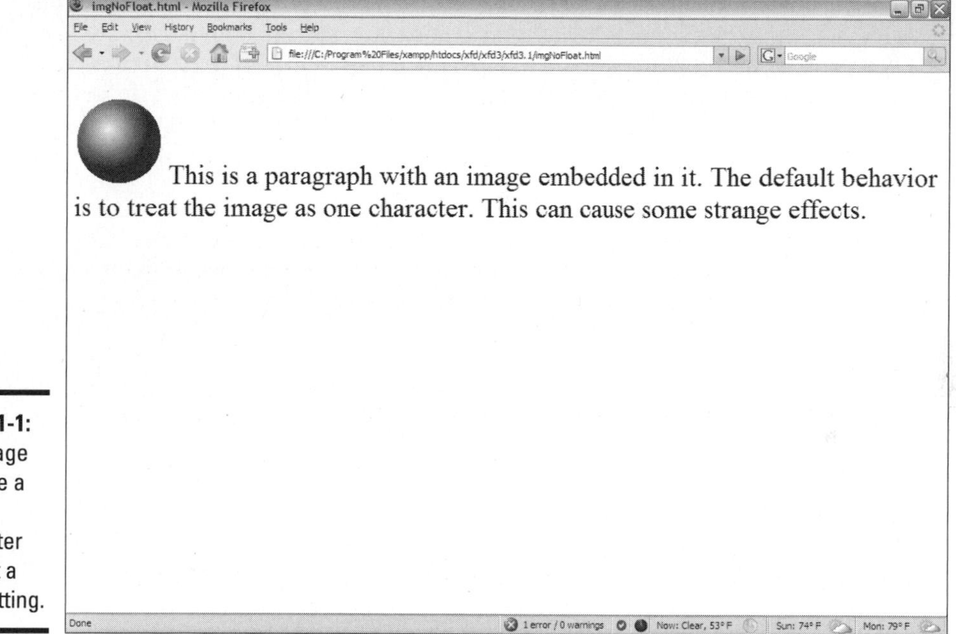

Figure 1-1: The image acts like a single character without a flow setting.

imgFloatLeft.html - Mozilla Firefox

File Edit View History Bookmarks Tools Help

file:///C:/Program%20Files/xampp/htdocs/xfd/xfd3/xfd3.1/imgFloatLeft.html

The image now has its float attribute set to left. That means that the text will flow around the image as it normally does in a magazine. The image now has its float attribute set to left. That means that the text will flow around the image as it normally does in a magazine. The image now has its float attribute set to left. That means that the text will flow around the image as it normally does in a magazine. The image now has its float attribute set to left. That means that the text will flow around the image as it normally does in a magazine. The image now has its float attribute set to left. That means that the text will flow around the image as it normally does in a magazine.

Done 0 errors / 0 warnings Now: Clear, 53° F Sun: 74° F Mon: 79° F

Figure 1-2: Now the text wraps around the image.

When you add a `float:left` attribute to the `img` element, the image tends to move to the left, pushing other content to the right. Now, the text flows around the image. The image is actually removed from the normal flow of the page layout, so the paragraph takes up all the space. Inside the paragraph, the text avoids overwriting the image.

Adding the float property

The code for adding the `float` property is pretty simple:

```
<!DOCTYPE html PUBLIC "-//W3C//DTD XHTML 1.0 Strict//EN"
"http://www.w3.org/TR/xhtml1/DTD/xhtml1-strict.dtd">
<html lang="EN" dir="ltr" xmlns="http://www.w3.org/1999/xhtml">
  <head>
    <meta http-equiv="content-type" content="text/xml; charset=utf-8" />
    <title>imgFloat.html</title>
    <style type = "text/css">
      img {
        float: left;
      }
    </style>
  </head>

  <body>
    <p>
      <img src = "ball.gif"
           alt = "ball" />
      The image now has its float attribute set to left. That means
      that the text will flow around the image as it normally does
      in a magazine.
      The image now has its float attribute set to left. That means
      that the text will flow around the image as it normally does
      in a magazine.
      The image now has its float attribute set to left. That means
      that the text will flow around the image as it normally does
      in a magazine.
      The image now has its float attribute set to left. That means
      that the text will flow around the image as it normally does
      in a magazine.
      The image now has its float attribute set to left. That means
      that the text will flow around the image as it normally does
      in a magazine.
    </p>
  </body>
</html>
```

The only new element in the code is the CSS `float` attribute. The `img` object has a `float:left` attribute. It isn't necessary to change any other attributes of the paragraph because the paragraph text *knows* to float around the image.

Of course, you don't have to simply float to the left. Figure 1-3 shows the same page with the image's `float` attribute set to the right.

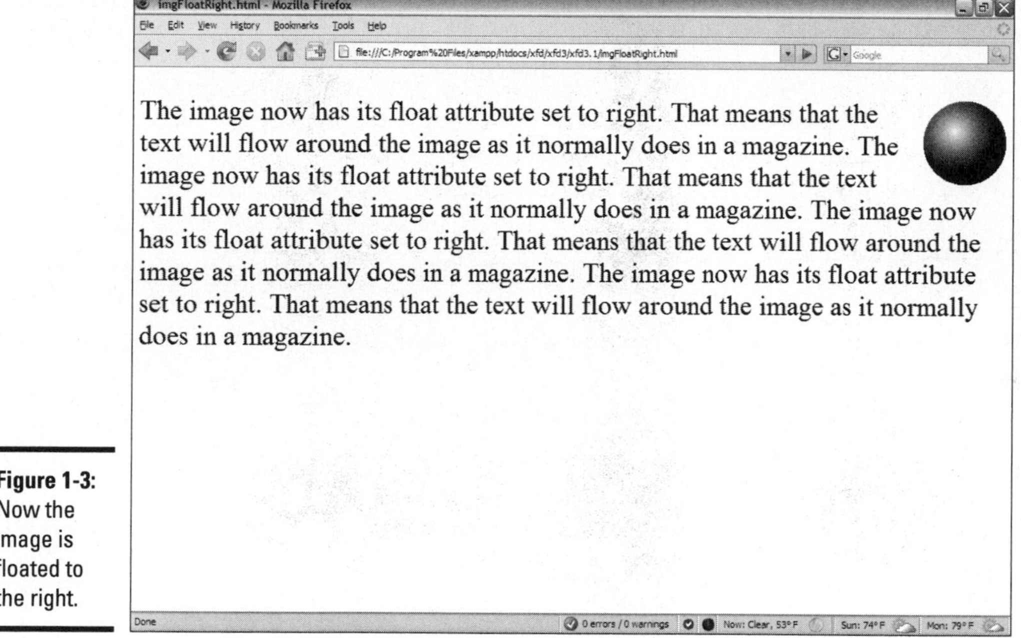

Figure 1-3: Now the image is floated to the right.

Using Float with Block-Level Elements

The `float` attribute isn't only for images. You can also use it with any block-level element (typically `p` or `div`) to create new layouts. Using the `float` attribute to set the page layout is easy after you understand how things really work.

Floating a paragraph

Paragraphs and other block-level elements have a well-defined default behavior. They take up the entire width of the page, and the next element appears below. When you apply the `float` element to a paragraph, the behavior of that paragraph doesn't change much, but the behavior of *succeeding* paragraphs is altered.

To illustrate, I take you all the way through the process of building two side-by-side paragraphs.

Begin by looking at a page with three paragraphs. Paragraph 2 has its `float` property set to `left`. Figure 1-4 illustrates such a page.

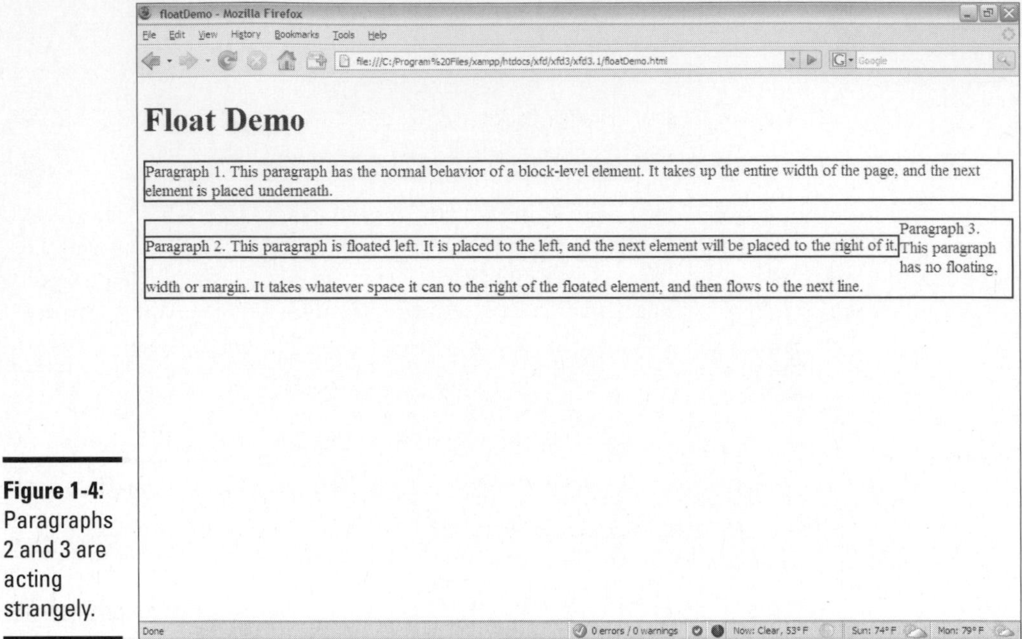

Figure 1-4: Paragraphs 2 and 3 are acting strangely.

As you can see, some strange formatting is going on here. I improve on things later to make the beginnings of a two-column layout, but for now, just take a look at what's going on:

- **The first paragraph acts normally.** The first paragraph has the same behavior you've seen in all block-style elements. It takes up the entire width of the page, and the next element will be placed below it.
- **The second paragraph is pretty normal.** The second paragraph has its `float` attribute set to `left`. This means that the paragraph will be placed in its normal position, but that other text will be placed to the left of this element.
- **The third paragraph seems skinny.** The third paragraph seems to surround the second, but the text is pushed to the right. The float parameter in the previous paragraph causes this one to be placed in any remaining space (which currently isn't much). The remaining space is on the right and eventually underneath the second paragraph.

The code to produce this is simple HTML with equally simple CSS markup:

```
<!DOCTYPE html PUBLIC "-//W3C//DTD XHTML 1.0 Strict//EN"
"http://www.w3.org/TR/xhtml1/DTD/xhtml1-strict.dtd">
<html lang="EN" dir="ltr" xmlns="http://www.w3.org/1999/xhtml">
  <head>
    <meta http-equiv="content-type" content="text/xml; charset=utf-8" />
```

```
    <title>floatDemo</title>
    <style type = "text/css">
      p {
        border: 2px black solid;
      }
      .floated {
        float: left;
      }
    </style>

  </head>

  <body>
    <h1>Float Demo</h1>
    <p>
      Paragraph 1.
      This paragraph has the normal behavior of a block-level element.
      It takes up the entire width of the page, and the next element
      is placed underneath.
    </p>

    <p class = "floated">
      Paragraph 2.
      This paragraph is floated left. It is placed to the left, and the
      next element will be placed to the right of it.
    </p>

    <p>
      Paragraph 3.
      This paragraph has no floating, width or margin. It takes whatever
      space it can to the right of the floated element, and then flows
      to the next line.
    </p>
  </body>
</html>
```


As you can see from the code, I have a simple class called `floated` with the float property set to `left`. Notice also that the paragraphs are defined in the ordinary way; even though paragraph 2 seems to be embedded inside paragraph 3 in the screen shot, the code clearly shows that this isn't the case. The two paragraphs are completely separate.

I added a black border to each paragraph so you can see that the size of the element isn't always what you'd expect.

Adjusting the width

When you float an element, the behavior of succeeding elements is highly dependant on the width of the first element. This leads to a primary principle of float-based layout:

> If you float an element, you must also define its width.

The exception to this rule is elements with a predefined width, like images and many form elements. These elements already have an implicit width, so you don't need to define width in the CSS. If in doubt, try setting the width at various values until you get the layout you're looking for.

Figure 1-5 shows the page after I adjusted the width of the floated paragraph to 50 percent of the page width.

Things look better in Figure 1-5, but paragraph 2 still seems to be embedded inside paragraph 3. The only significant change is in the CSS style:

```
<style type = "text/css">
  p {
    border: 2px black solid;
  }
  .floated {
    float: left;
    width: 50%;
  }
</style>
```

I've added a `width` property to the floated element.

Elements that have the `float` attribute enabled will generally also have a width defined, except for images or other elements with an inherent width.

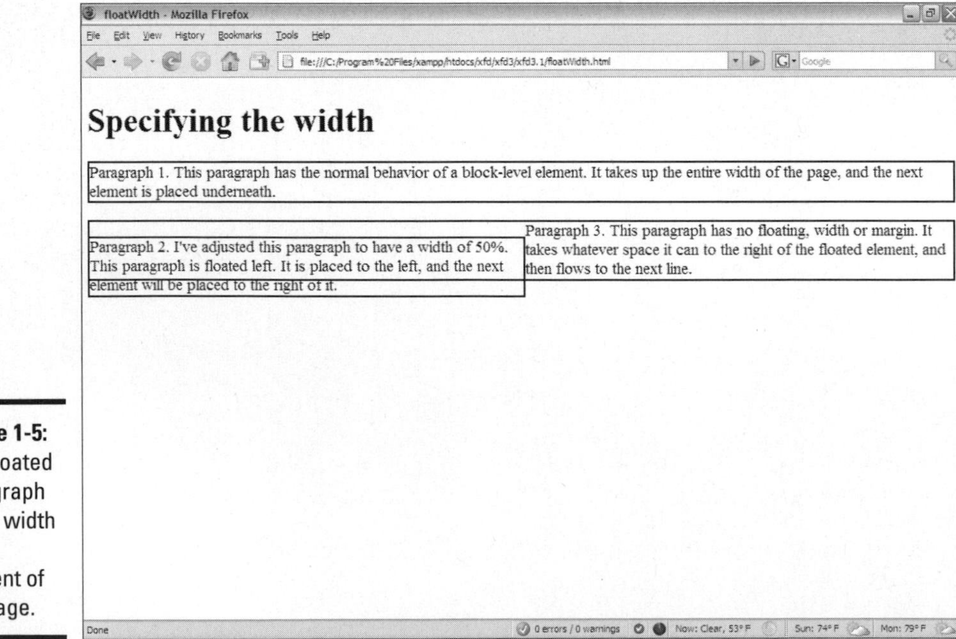

Figure 1-5: The floated paragraph has a width of 50 percent of the page.

When you use a percentage value in the context of width, you're expressing a percentage of the *parent* element (in this case, the `body` because the paragraph is embedded in the document body). Setting the `width` to `50%` means I want this paragraph to span half the width of the document body.

Setting the next margin

Things still don't look quite right. I added the borders around each paragraph so you can see an important characteristic of floating elements. Even though the text of paragraph 3 wraps to the right of paragraph 2, the actual paragraph element still extends all the way to the left side of the page. The *element* doesn't necessarily flow around the floated element, but its *contents* do. The background color and border of paragraph 3 still take up as much space as they normally would if paragraph 2 didn't exist.

This is because a floated element is removed from the normal flow of the page. Paragraph 3 has access to the space once occupied by paragraph 2, but the text in paragraph 3 will try to find its own space without stepping on text from paragraph 2.

Somehow, you need to tell paragraph 3 to move away from the paragraph 2 space. This isn't a difficult problem to solve once you recognize it. Figure 1-6 shows a solution.

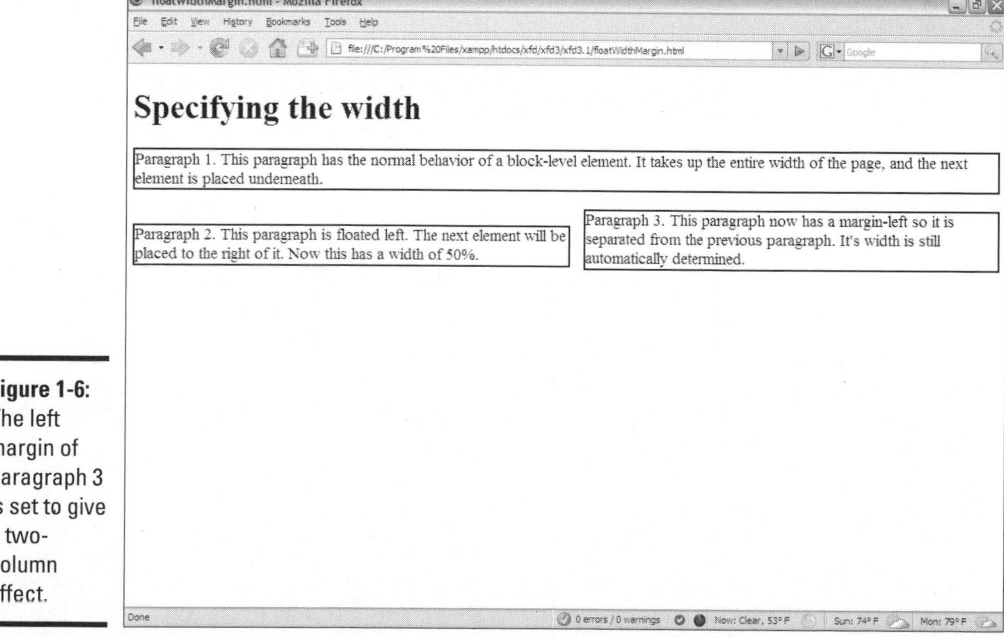

Figure 1-6: The left margin of paragraph 3 is set to give a two-column effect.

The `margin-left` property of paragraph 3 is set to 53 percent. Because the width of paragraph 2 is 50 percent, this provides a little gap between the columns. Take a look at the code to see what's going on here:

```
<!DOCTYPE html PUBLIC "-//W3C//DTD XHTML 1.0 Strict//EN"
"http://www.w3.org/TR/xhtml1/DTD/xhtml1-strict.dtd">
<html lang="EN" dir="ltr" xmlns="http://www.w3.org/1999/xhtml">
  <head>
    <meta http-equiv="content-type" content="text/xml; charset=utf-8" />
    <title>floatWidthMargin.html</title>
    <style type = "text/css">
      p {
        border: 2px black solid;
      }
      .floated {
        float: left;
        width: 50%;
      }
      .right {
        margin-left: 52%;
      }
    </style>

  </head>

  <body>
    <h1>Specifying the width</h1>
    <p>
      Paragraph 1.
      This paragraph has the normal behavior of a block-level element.
      It takes up the entire width of the page, and the next element
      is placed underneath.
    </p>

    <p class = "floated">
     Paragraph 2.
      This paragraph is floated left. The
      next element will be placed to the right of it. Now this has a width
      of 50%.
     </p>

    <p class = "right">
      Paragraph 3.
      This paragraph now has a margin-left so it is separated from the
      previous paragraph. It's width is still automatically
      determined.
    </p>

  </body>
</html>
```

Using Float to Style Forms

Many page layout problems appear to require tables. Some clever use of the CSS `float` can help elements with multiple columns without the overhead of tables.

Forms cause a particular headache because a form often involves labels in a left column followed by `input` elements in the right column. You'd probably be tempted to put such a form in a table. Adding table tags will make the HTML much more complex and isn't required. It's much better to use CSS to manage the layout.

You can float elements to create attractive forms without requiring tables. Figure 1-7 shows a form with `float` used to line up the various elements.

As page design gets more involved, it makes more sense to think of the HTML and the CSS separately. The HTML will give you a sense of the overall intent of the page, and the CSS can be modified separately. Using external CSS is a natural extension of this philosophy. Begin by looking at `floatForm.html` and concentrate on the XHTML structure before worrying about style:

```
<!DOCTYPE html PUBLIC "-//W3C//DTD XHTML 1.0 Strict//EN"
"http://www.w3.org/TR/xhtml1/DTD/xhtml1-strict.dtd">
<html lang="EN" dir="ltr" xmlns="http://www.w3.org/1999/xhtml">
  <head>
    <meta http-equiv="content-type" content="text/xml; charset=utf-8" />
    <title>floatForm.html</title>
    <link rel = "stylesheet"
          type = "text/css"
          href = "floatForm.css" />

  </head>
```


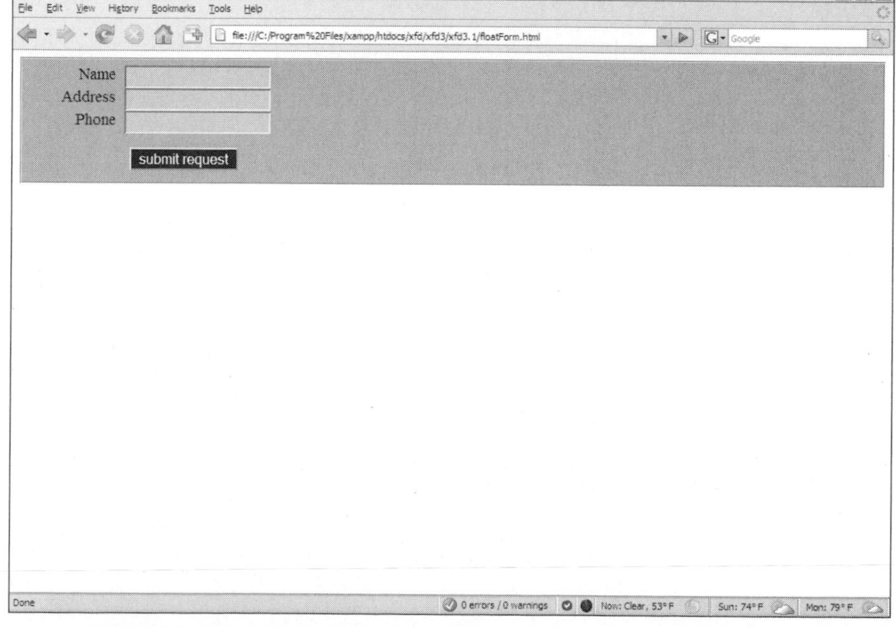

Figure 1-7: This is a nice-looking form defined without a table.

```
  <body>
    <form action = "">
      <fieldset>
        <label>Name</label>
        <input type = "text"
               id = "txtName" />
        <label>Address</label>
        <input type = "text"
               id = "txtAddress" />
        <label>Phone</label>
        <input type = "text"
               id = "txtPhone" />
        <button type = "button">
          submit request
        </button>
      </fieldset>
    </form>
  </body>
</html>
```

While you look over this code, note several interesting things about the way the page has been designed:

- **The CSS is external.** CSS is defined in an external document. This makes it easy to change the style and helps you to focus on the XHTML document in isolation.
- **The XHTML code is minimal.** The code is very clean. It includes a form with a `fieldset`. The `fieldset` contains labels, input elements, and a button.
- **There isn't a table.** There's no need to add a table as an artificial organization scheme. A table wouldn't add to the clarity of the page. The form elements themselves provide enough structure to allow all the formatting you need.
- **Labels are part of the design.** I used the `label` element throughout the form, giving me an element that can be styled however I wish.
- **Everything is selectable.** I'll want to apply one CSS style to labels, another to input elements, and a third style to the button. I've set up the XHTML so I can use CSS selectors without requiring any `id` or `class` attributes.
- **There's a `button`.** I used a `button` element instead of `<input type = "button">` on purpose. This way, I can apply one style to all the `input` elements and a different style to the `button` element.

It's wonderful when you can design a page like this one so its internal structure provides all the selectors you need. This keeps the page very clean and easy to read. Still, don't be afraid to add classes or IDs if you need them.

Figure 1-8 demonstrates how the page looks with no CSS.

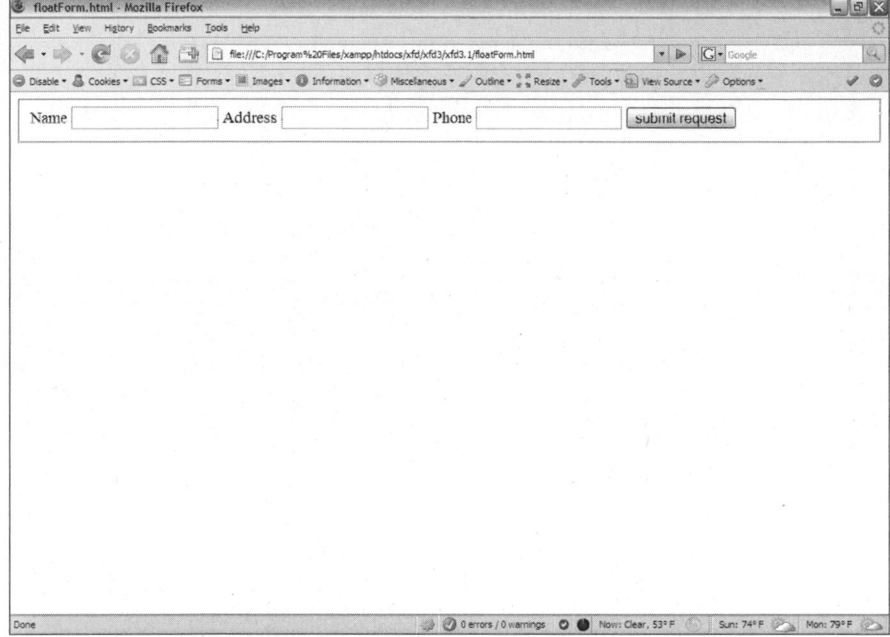

Figure 1-8: The plain XHTML is a start, but some CSS would help a lot.

It's often a good idea to look at your page with straight XHTML before you start messing around with CSS.

If you have a page with styles and you want to see how it will look without the style rules, use the Web Developer toolbar. You can temporarily disable some or all CSS style rules to see the default content underneath. This can sometimes be extremely handy.

Using float to beautify the form

It'd be very nice to give the form a tabular feel, with each row containing a label and its associated input element. My first attempt at a CSS file for this page looked like this:

```
/* floatNoClear.css
   CSS file to go with float form
   Demonstrates use of float, width, margin
   Code looks fine but the output is horrible.
*/

fieldset {
  background-color: #AAAAFF;
}
label {
  float: left;
  width: 5em;
  text-align: right;
```

```
  margin-right: .5em;
}
input {
  background-color: #CCCCFF;
  float: left;
}
button {
  float: left;
  width: 10em;
  margin-left: 7em;
  margin-top: 1em;
  background-color: #0000CC;
  color: #FFFFFF;
}
```

This CSS looks reasonable, but you'll find it doesn't quite work right. (I show the problem and how to fix it later in this chapter.) Here are the steps to build the CSS:

1. **Add colors to each element.**

   Colors are a great first step. For one thing, they help you be sure that your selectors are working correctly so that everything's where you think it is. This color scheme has a nice modern feel to it, with a lot of blues.

2. **Float the labels to the left.**

   Labels are all floated to the left, meaning they should move as far left as possible, and other things should be placed to the right of them.

3. **Set the label width to `5em`.**

   This gives you plenty of space for the text the labels will contain.

4. **Set the labels to be right-aligned.**

   Right-aligning the labels will make the text snug up to the `input` elements but give them a little `margin-right` so the text isn't *too* close.

5. **Set the `input`'s `float` to `left`.**

   This tells each `input` element to go as far to the left (toward its label) as it can. The `input` element goes next to the label if possible and on the next line, if necessary. Note that like images, `input` elements have a default width, so it isn't absolutely necessary to define the width in CSS.

6. **Float the `button`, too, but give the `button` a little top margin so it has a respectable space at the top. Set the width to `10em`.**

This seems to be a pretty good CSS file. It follows all the rules, but if you apply it to `floatForm.html`, you'll be surprised by the results shown in Figure 1-9.

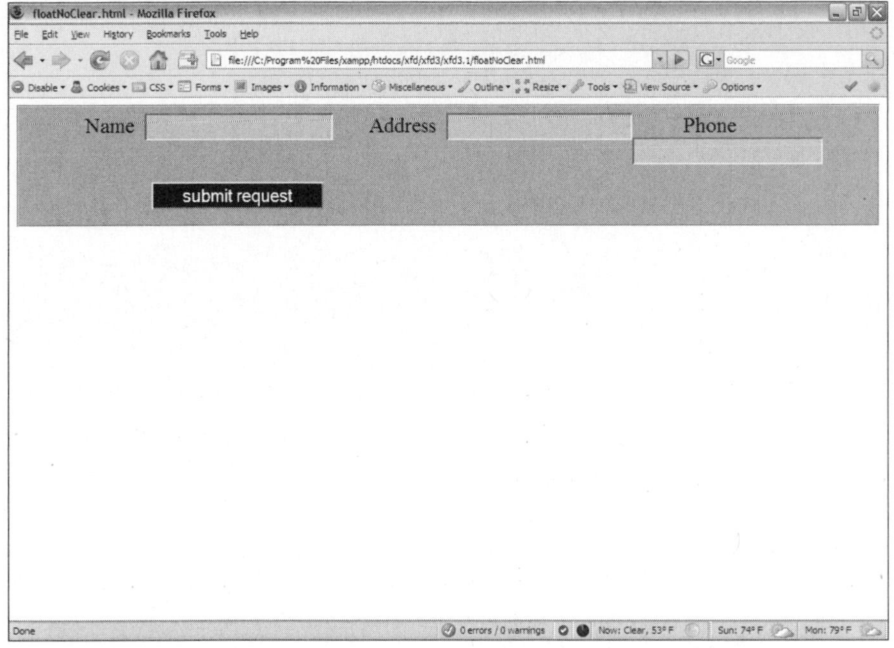

Figure 1-9: This form is — well — ugly.

After all that talk about how nice float-based layout is, you're probably expecting something a bit neater. If you play around with the page in your browser, you'll find that everything works well when the browser is narrow, but when you expand the width of the browser, it gets ugly. Figure 1-10 shows the form when the page is really skinny. (I used the CSS editor on the Web Developer toolbar to adjust the width of the page display.)

Things get worse when the page is a little wider, as you can see in Figure 1-11.

If you make the page as wide as possible, you'll get a sense of what the browser was trying to accomplish in Figure 1-12.

When CSS doesn't do what you want, it's usually acting on some false assumptions, which is the case here. Floating left causes an element to go as far to the left as possible and on the next line, if necessary. However, that's not really what you want on this page. The inputs should float next to the labels, but each label should begin its own line. The labels should float all the way to the left margin with the inputs floating left next to the labels.

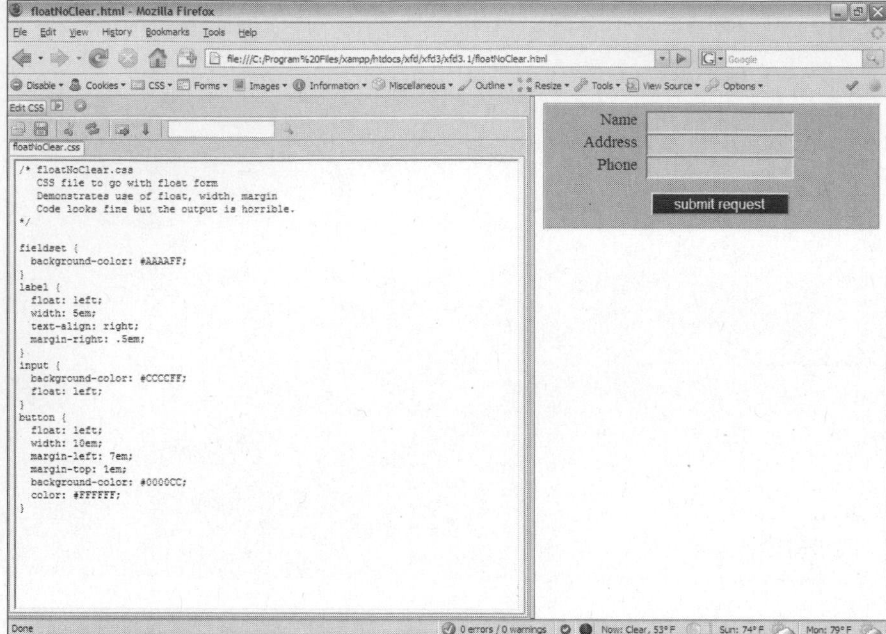

Figure 1-10: The form looks great when the page is skinny.

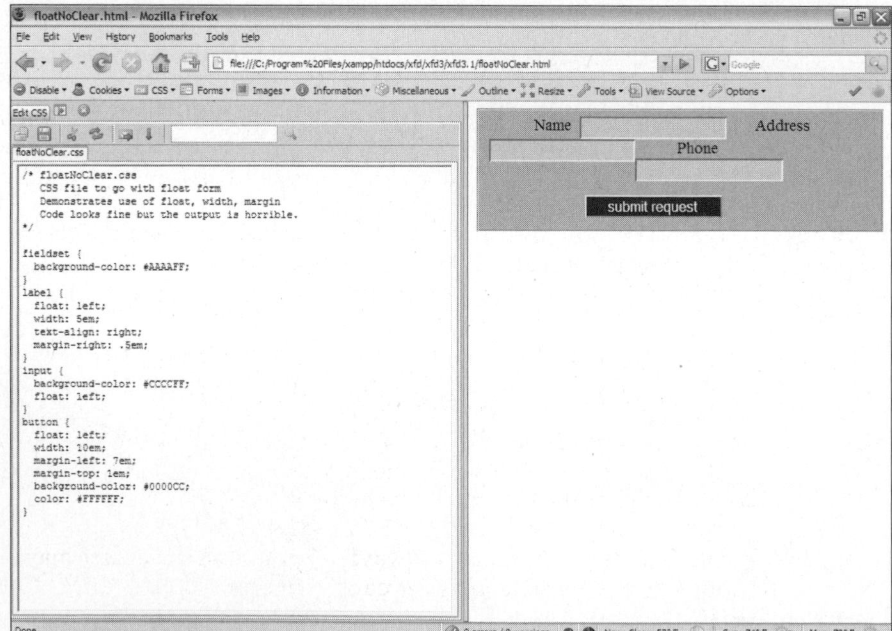

Figure 1-11: With a slightly wider browser, things get strange.

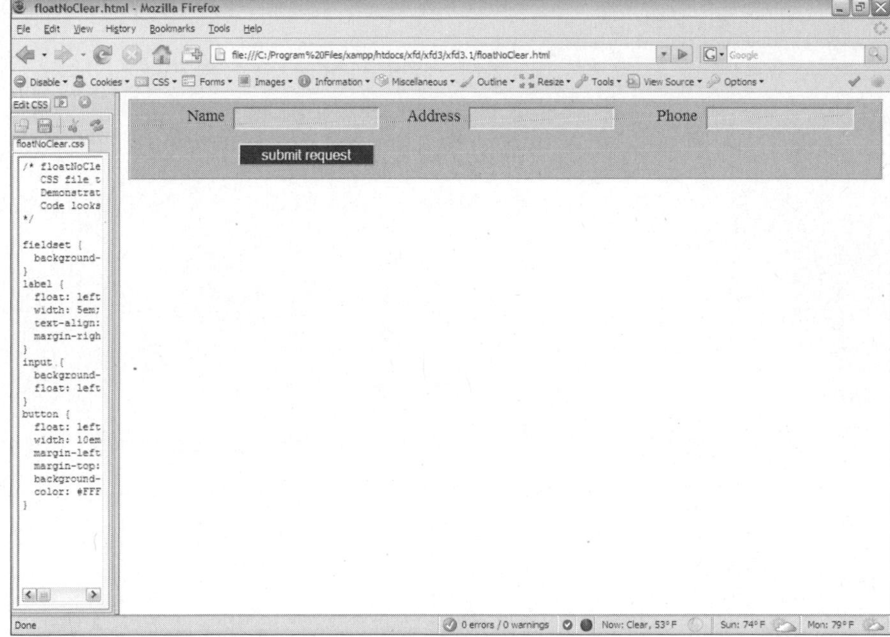

Figure 1-12: The browser is trying to put all the inputs on the same line.

Adjusting the fieldset width

One approach is to consider how well the page behaves when it's skinny because the new label and input combination will simply wrap down to the next line. You can always make a container narrow enough to force the behavior you're expecting. Because all the field elements are inside the `fieldset`, you can simply make it narrower to get a nice layout, as shown in Figure 1-13.

When you want to test changes in CSS, nothing beats the CSS editor in the Web Developer Extension. I made Figure 1-13 by editing the CSS on the fly with this tool. You can see that the new line of CSS is still highlighted.

Setting the width of the `fieldset` to `15em` does the job. Because the widths of the other elements are already determined, forcing them into a `15em`-wide box makes everything line up nicely with the normal wrapping behavior of the `float` attribute. If you don't want the width change to be so obvious, you can apply it to the `form` element, which doesn't have any visible attributes (unless you add them, like color or border).

Unfortunately, this doesn't always work because the user may adjust the font size and mess up all your careful design.

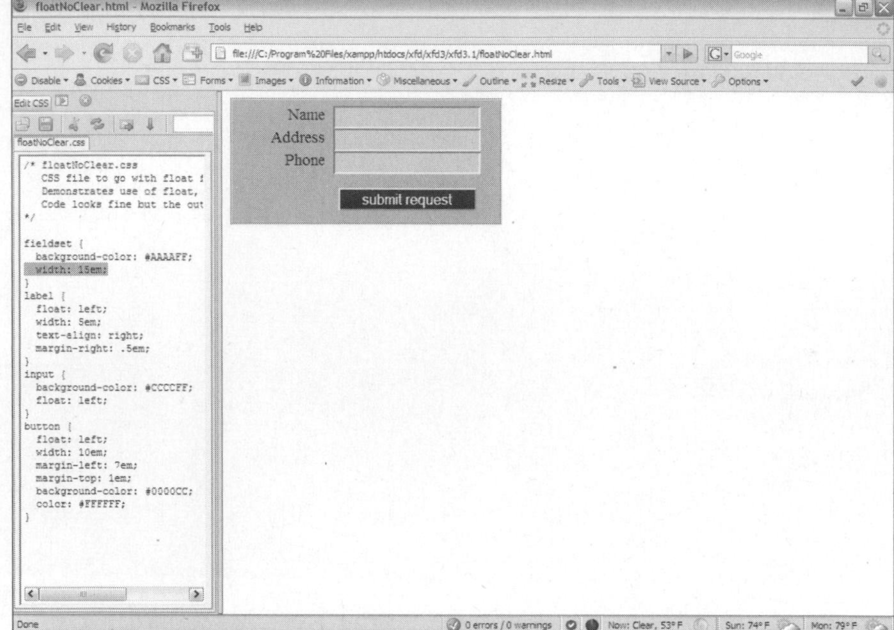

Figure 1-13: With a narrower fieldset, all the elements look much nicer.

Using the clear attribute to control page layout

Adjusting the width of the container is a suitable solution, but it does feel like a bit of a hack. There should be some way to make the form work right, regardless of the container's width. There is exactly such a mechanism.

The `clear` attribute is used on elements with a `float` attribute. The `clear` attribute can be set to `left`, `right`, or `both`. Setting the `clear` attribute to `left` means you want nothing to the left of this element. In other words, the element should be on the left margin of its container. That's exactly what you want here. Each label should begin its own line, so set its `clear` attribute to `left`.

To force the button onto its own line, set its `clear` attribute to `both`. This means that the button should have no elements to the left or the right. It should occupy a line all on its own.

If you want an element to start a new line, set both its `float` and `clear` attributes to `left`. If you want an element to be on a line alone, set `float` to `left` and `clear` to `both`.

Using the `clear` attribute allows you to have a flexible-width container and still maintain reasonable control of the form design. Figure 1-14 shows that the form can be the same width as the page and still work correctly. This version works, no matter the width of the page.

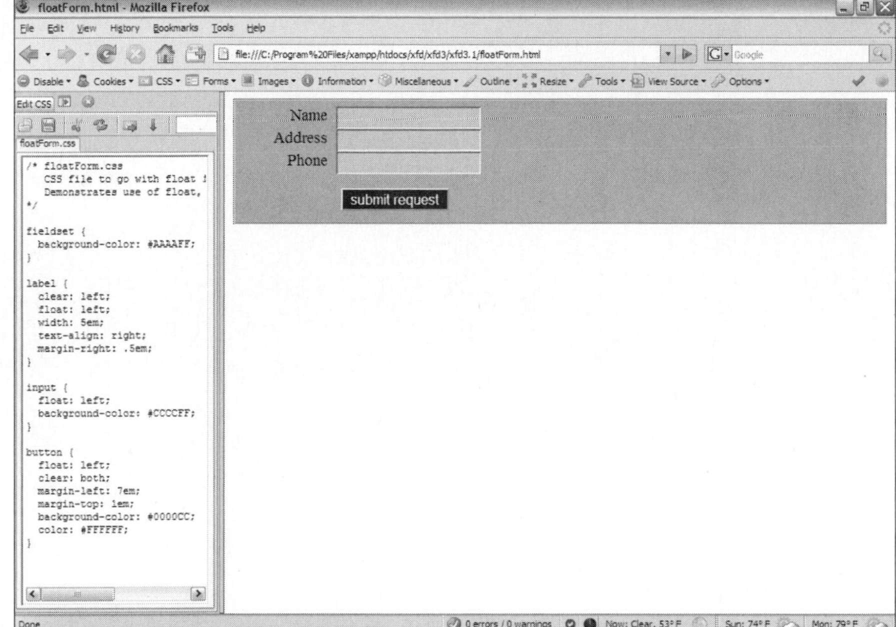

Figure 1-14: When you apply clear to floating elements, you can control the layout.

Here's the final CSS code, including `clear` attributes in the labels and button:

```
/* floatForm.css
   CSS file to go with float form
   Demonstrates use of float, width, margin, and clear
*/

fieldset {
  background-color: #AAAAFF;
}

label {
  clear: left;
  float: left;
  width: 5em;
  text-align: right;
  margin-right: .5em;
}

input {
  float: left;
  background-color: #CCCCFF;
}
```

```
button {
  float: left;
  clear: both;
  margin-left: 7em;
  margin-top: 1em;
  background-color: #0000CC;
  color: #FFFFFF;
}
```

You now have the basic tools in place to use flow layout. Look to Chapter 2 of this minibook to see how these tools are put together to build a complete page layout.

Chapter 2: Building Floating Page Layouts

In This Chapter

- ✔ **Creating a classic two-column page**
- ✔ **Creating a page-design diagram**
- ✔ **Using temporary borders**
- ✔ **Creating fluid layouts and three-column layouts**
- ✔ **Working with and centering fixed-width layouts**

The floating layout technique provides a good alternative to tables, frames, and other layout tricks formerly used. You can build many elegant multi-column page layouts with ordinary XHTML and CSS styles.

Creating a Basic Two-Column Design

Many pages today use a two-column design with a header and a footer. Such a page is quite easy to build with the techniques you read about in this chapter.

Designing the page

It's best to do your basic design work on paper, not on the computer. Here's my original sketch in Figure 2-1.

It's important to draw the sketch first so you have some idea what you're aiming for. Your sketch should include the following information:

- ✦ **Overall page flow:** How many columns do you want? Will it have a header and a footer?
- ✦ **Section names:** Each section needs a name. This will be used in both the XHTML and the CSS.
- ✦ **Width indicators:** How wide will each column be? (Of course, these widths should add up to 100 percent or less.)
- ✦ **Fixed or percentage widths:** Are the widths measured in percentages (of the browser size) or in a fixed measurement (pixels)? This has important implications. For this example, I'm using a dynamic width with percentage measurements.

✦ **Font considerations:** Do any of the sections require any specific font styles, faces, or colors?

✦ **Color scheme:** What are the main colors of your site? What will be the color and background color of each section?

This particular sketch (in Figure 2-1) is very simple because the page will use default colors and fonts. For a more complex job, you'll need a much more detailed sketch. The point of the sketch is to separate design decisions from coding problems. Solve as much of the design stuff as possible first so you can concentrate on building the design with XHTML and CSS.

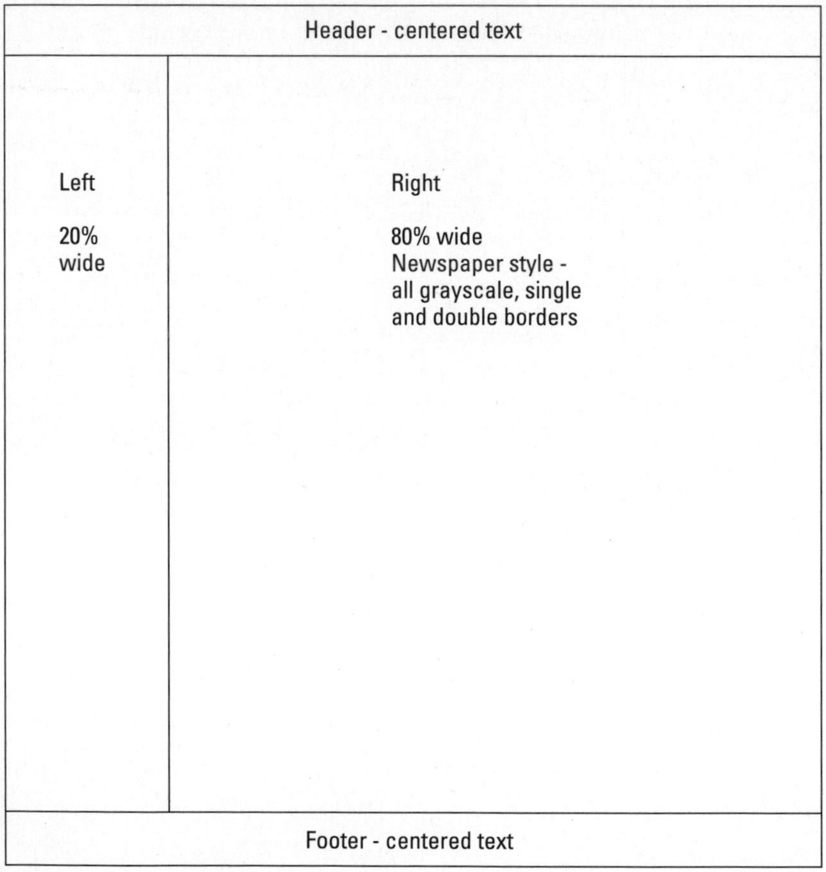

Header - centered text

Left

20%
wide

Right

80% wide
Newspaper style -
all grayscale, single
and double borders

Footer - centered text

Figure 2-1: This is a very standard two-column style.

A note to perfectionists

If you're really into detail and control, you'll find this chapter frustrating. People accustomed to having complete control of a design (as you often do in the print world) tend to get really stressed when they realize how little actual control they have over the appearance of a Web page.

Really, it's okay. This is a good thing. When you design for the Web, you give up absolute control, but you gain unbelievable flexibility. Use the ideas outlined in this chapter to get your page looking right on a standards-compliant browser. Take a deep breath and look at it on something else (like Internet Explorer 5 [IE5] if you want to suffer a heart attack!). Everything you positioned so carefully is all messed up! Take another deep breath and use conditional comments to fix the offending code without changing how it works in those browsers that do things correctly.

Building the XHTML

After you have a basic design in place, you're ready to start building the XHTML code that will be the framework. Start with basic CSS but create a div for each section that will be in your final work. You can put a placeholder for the CSS, but don't add any CSS yet. Here's my basic code (I removed some of the redundant text to save space):

```
<!DOCTYPE html PUBLIC "-//W3C//DTD XHTML 1.0 Strict//EN"
"http://www.w3.org/TR/xhtml1/DTD/xhtml1-strict.dtd">
<html lang="EN" dir="ltr" xmlns="http://www.w3.org/1999/xhtml">
  <head>
    <meta http-equiv="content-type" content="text/xml; charset=utf-8" />
    <title>twoColumn.html</title>
    <link rel = "stylesheet"
          type = "text/css"
          href = "twoCol.css" />
  </head>

  <body>
    <div id = "head">
      <h1>Two Columns with Float</h1>
    </div>

    <div id = "left">
      <h2>Left Column</h2>
    </div>

    <div id = "right">
      <h2>Right Column</h2>
    </div>

    <div id = "footer">
      <h3>Footer</h3>
    </div>
  </body>
</html>
```

What's up with the Latin?

The flexible layouts built throughout this chapter require some kind of text so the browser knows how big to make things. The actual text isn't important, but something needs to be there.

Typesetters have a long tradition of using phony Latin phrases as filler text. Traditionally, this text has begun with the words "Lorem Ipsum," so it's called *Lorem Ipsum* text.

This particular version is semi-randomly generated from a database of Latin words.

If you want, you can also use Lorem Ipsum in your page layout exercises. Conduct a search for Lorem Ipsum generators on the Web to get as much fake text as you want for your mockup pages.

Although Lorem Ipsum text is useful in the screen shots, it adds nothing to the code listings. Throughout this chapter, I remove the Lorem Ipsum text from the code listings to save space. See the original files on the CD-ROM or Web site for the full pages in all their Cesarean goodness.

Nothing at all is remarkable about this XHTML code, but it has a few important features, such as

- **It's standards-compliant.** It's good to check and make sure the basic XHTML code is well-formed before you do a lot of CSS work with it. Sloppy XHTML can cause you major headaches later.
- **It contains four divs.** The parts of the page that will be moved later are all encased in div elements.
- **Each div has an ID.** All the divs have an ID determined from the sketch.
- **No formatting is in the XHTML.** The XHTML code contains no formatting at all. That will be left to the CSS.
- **It has no style yet.** Although a `link` tag is pointing to a style sheet, the style is currently empty.

Figure 2-2 shows what the page looks like before you add any CSS to it.

Adding preliminary CSS

You can write CSS in your editor, but the Web Developer toolbar's CSS editor is an especially handy tool because it allows you to see the effects of your CSS immediately. To use this tool

1. **Use Firefox for your primary testing.**

   Firefox has much better standards support than IE. Get your code working in Firefox first. Besides, the extremely handy Web Developer isn't available for Internet Explorer.

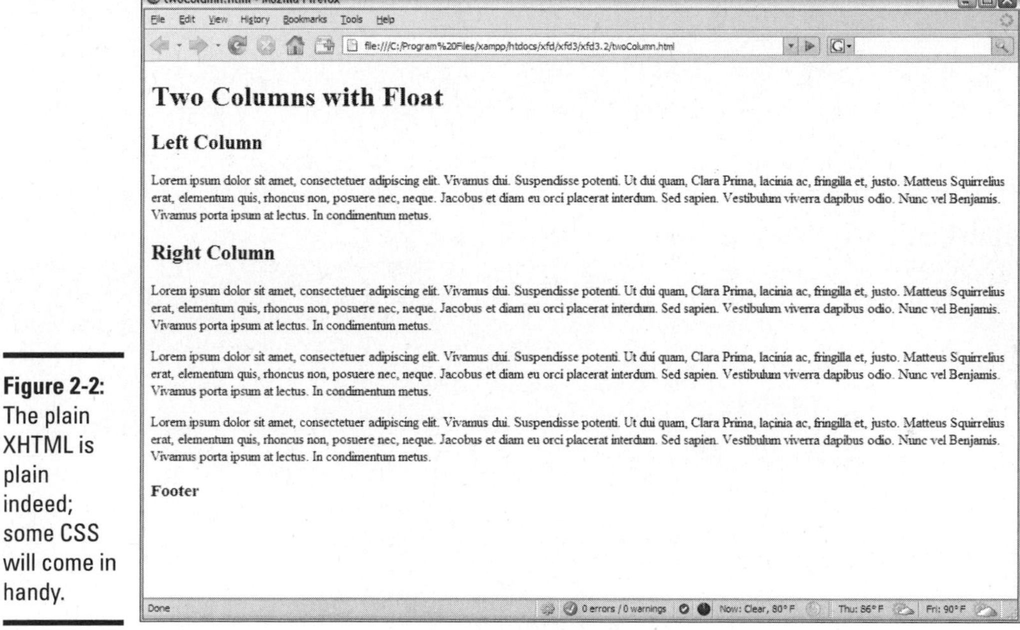

Figure 2-2: The plain XHTML is plain indeed; some CSS will come in handy.

2. **Be sure the Web Developer toolbar is installed.**

   See Chapter 3 of Book I for more information on this wonderful free tool. You'll use this tool to modify your CSS and see the results immediately in the Web browser.

3. **Activate the CSS editor by choosing Tools⇨Edit CSS or pressing Ctrl+Shift+E.**

4. **Create CSS rules.**

   Type the CSS rules in the provided window. Throughout this chapter, I show what rules you use and the order in which they go. The key thing about this editor is you can type a rule in the text window, and the page in the browser is immediately updated.

5. **Check the results.**

   Watch the main page for interactive results. As soon as you finish a CSS rule, the Web page automatically refreshes, showing the results of your work.

6. **Save your work.**

   The changes made during an edit session are temporary. If you've specified a CSS file in your document, but it doesn't exist, the Save button automatically creates and saves to that file.

Using temporary borders

And now for one of my favorite CSS tricks. . . . Before doing anything else, create a selector for each of the named divs and add a temporary border to each div. Make each border a different color. The CSS might look like this:

```
#head {
  border: 1px black solid;
}

#left {
  border: 1px red solid;
}

#right {
  border: 1px blue solid;
}

#footer {
  border: 1px green solid;
}
```

You won't keep these borders, but they provide some very useful cues while you're working with the layout:

- **Testing the selectors:** While you create a border around each selector, you can see whether you've remembered the selector's name correctly. It's amazing how many times I've written code that I thought was broken just because I didn't write the selector properly.
- **Identifying the divs:** If you make each div's border a different color, it'll be easier to see which div is which when they begin to overlap.
- **Specifying the size of each div:** The text inside a div isn't always a good indicator of the actual size of the div. The border tells you what's really going on.

Of course, you won't leave these borders in place. They're just helpful tools for seeing what's going on during the design process. Look at `borders.html` and `borders.css` on the CD-ROM or Web site to see the full code.

Figure 2-3 displays how the page looks with the color borders turned on.

It's fine that you can't see the actual colors in the black and white image in Figure 2-3. Just appreciate that when you see the page in its full-color splendor, the various colors will help you see what's going on.

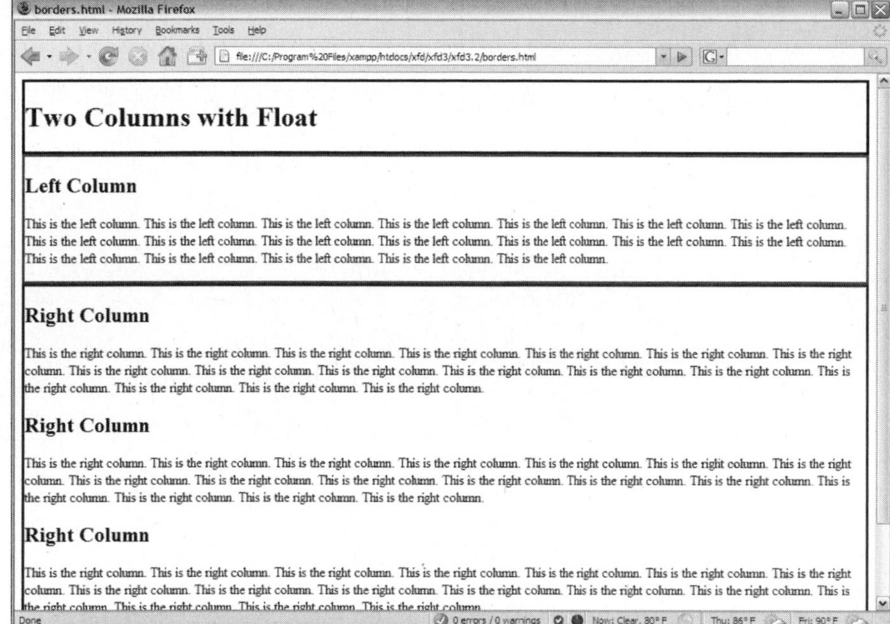

Figure 2-3: Colored borders make it easier to manipulate the divs.

Setting up the floating columns

This particular layout doesn't require major transformation. A few CSS rules will do the trick:

```
#head {
  border: 3px black solid;
}

#left {
  border: 3px red solid;
  float: left;
  width: 20%;
}

#right {
  border: 3px blue solid;
  float: left;
  width: 75%
}

#footer {
  border: 3px green solid;
  clear: both;
}
```

I made the following changes to the CSS:

- ✦ **Float the `#left` div.** Set the `#left` div's `float` property to `left` so other divs (specifically the `#right` div) are moved to the right of it.
- ✦ **Set the `#left` width.** When you float a div, you must also set its width. I've set the margin to 20 percent of the page width as a starting point.
- ✦ **Float the `#right` div, too.** The right div can also be floated left, and it'll end up snug to the left div. Don't forget to add a width. I set the width of `#right` to 75 percent, leaving another 5 percent available for padding, margins, and borders.
- ✦ **Clear the footer.** The footer should take up the entire width of the page, so set its `clear` property to `both`.

Figure 2-4 shows how the page looks with this style sheet in place (see `floated.html` and `floated.css` on the CD-ROM or Web site for complete code).

Tuning up the borders

The colored borders in Figure 2-4 point out some important features of this layout scheme. For instance, the two columns are not the same size. This can have important implications.

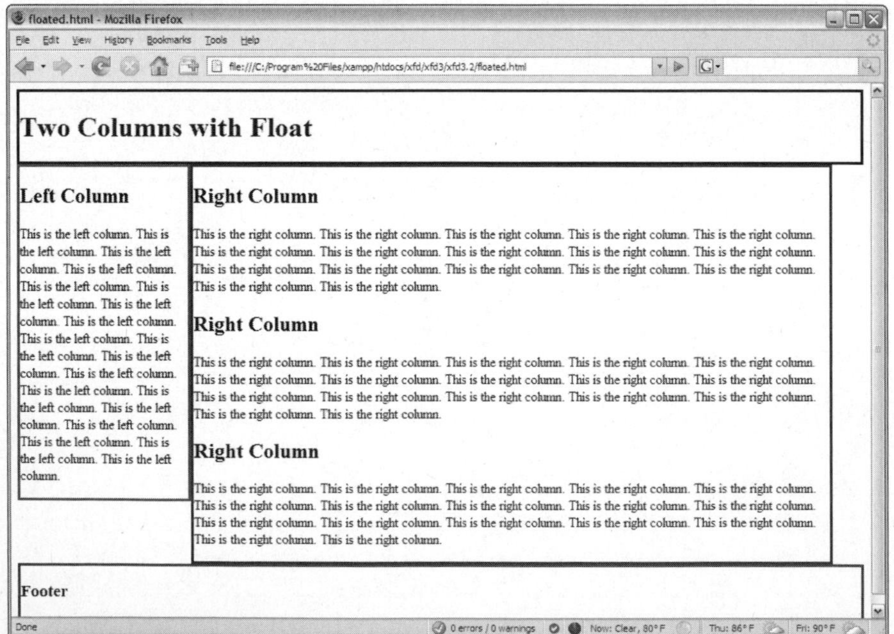

Figure 2-4: Now, the left column is floated.

You can change the borders to make the page look more like a column layout. I'm going for a newspaper-style look, so I'll use simple double borders. I put a black border under the header, a gray border to the left of the right column, and a gray border on top of the bottom column. Tweaking the padding and centering the footer complete the look. Here's the complete CSS:

```
#head {
  border-bottom: 3px double black;
}
#left {
  float: left;
  width: 20%;
}
#right {
  float: left;
  width: 75%;
  border-left: 3px double gray;
}
#footer {
  clear: both;
  text-align: center;
  border-top: 3px double gray;
}
```

The final effect is shown in Figure 2-5.

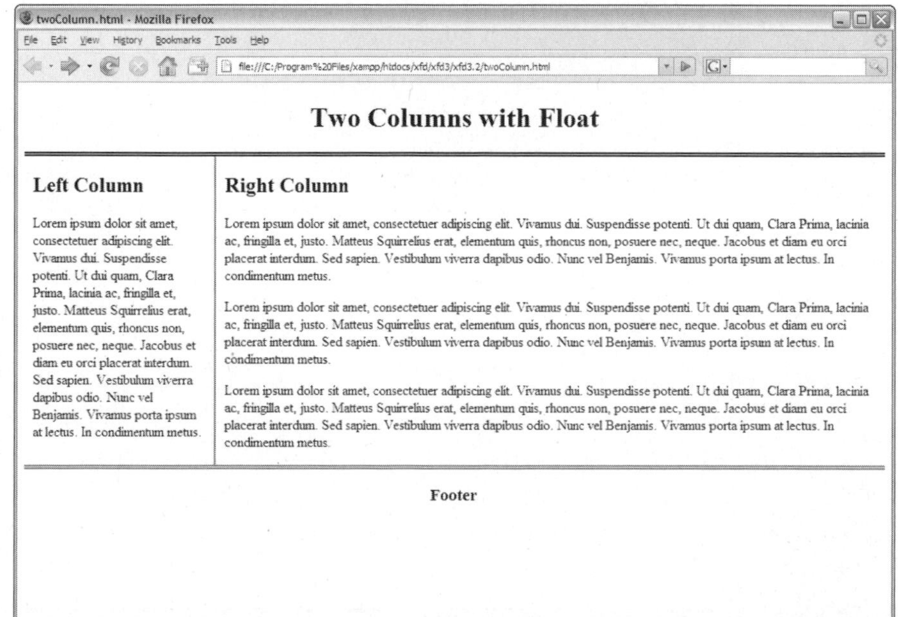

Figure 2-5: This is a decent design, which adjusts with the page width.

Advantages of a fluid layout

This type of layout scheme (with floats) is often called a *fluid* layout because it has columns but the sizes of the columns are dependent on the browser width. This is an important issue because, unlike layout in the print world, you really have no idea what size the browser window that displays your page will be. Even if the user has a widescreen monitor, the browser may be in a much smaller window. Fluid layouts can adapt to this situation quite well.

Fluid layouts (and indeed all other float-based layouts) have another great advantage. If the user turns off CSS or can't use it, the page still displays. The elements will simply be printed in order vertically, rather than in the intended layout. This can be especially handy for screen readers or devices with exceptionally small screens, like phones and PDAs.

Building a Three-Column Design

Sometimes, you'll prefer a three-column design. It's a simple variation of the two-column approach. Figure 2-6 shows a simple three-column layout.

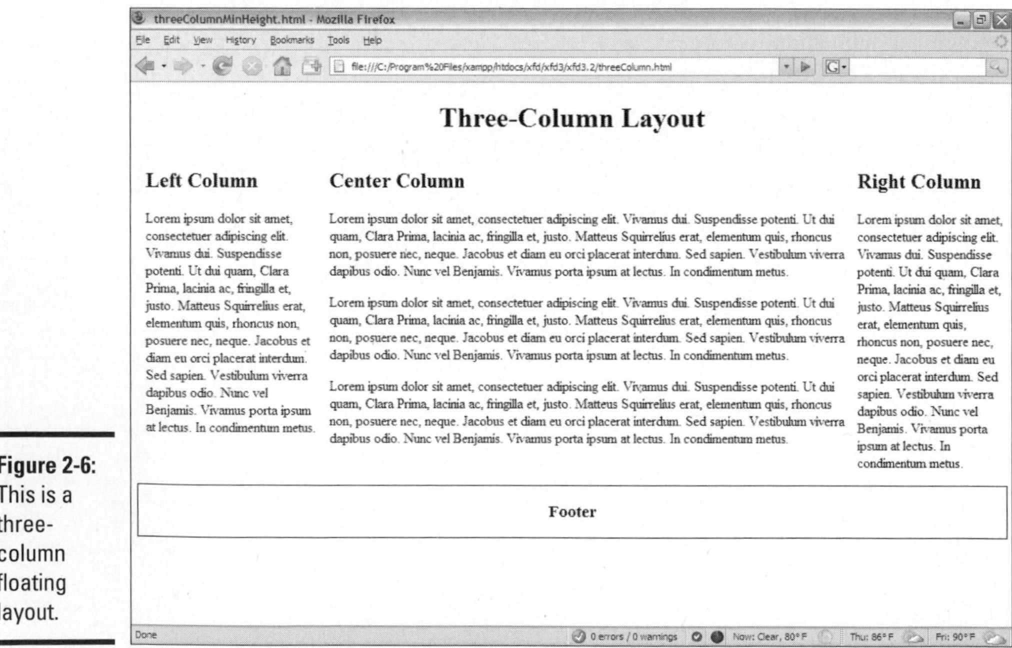

Figure 2-6: This is a three-column floating layout.

This design uses very basic CSS with five named divs. Here's the code (with the dummy paragraph text removed for space):

```
<!DOCTYPE html PUBLIC "-//W3C//DTD XHTML 1.0 Strict//EN"
"http://www.w3.org/TR/xhtml1/DTD/xhtml1-strict.dtd">
<html lang="EN" dir="ltr" xmlns="http://www.w3.org/1999/xhtml">
  <head>
    <meta http-equiv="content-type" content="text/xml; charset=utf-8" />
    <title>threeColumn.html</title>
    <link rel = "stylesheet"
          type = "text/css"
          href = "threeColumn.css" />
  </head>

  <body>
    <div id = "head">
      <h1>Three-Column Layout</h1>
    </div>

    <div id = "left">
      <h2>Left Column</h2>
    </div>

    <div id = "center">
      <h2>Center Column</h2>
    </div>

    <div id = "right">
      <h2>Right Column</h2>
    </div>

    <div id = "footer">
      <h3>Footer</h3>
    </div>
  </body>
</html>
```


Styling the three-column page

As you can see from the HTML, there isn't really much to this page. It has five named divs, and that's about it. All the really exciting stuff happens in the CSS:

```
#head {
  text-align: center;
}

#left {
  float: left;
  width: 20%;
  padding-left: 1%;
}

#center {
  float: left;
  width: 60%;
  padding-left: 1%;
}
```

```
#right {
  float: left;
  width: 17%;
  padding-left: 1%;
}

#footer {
  border: 1px black solid;
  float: left;
  width: 100%;
  clear: both;
  text-align: center;
}
```

Each element (except the head) is floated with an appropriate width. The process for generating this page is similar to the two-column layout:

1. **Diagram the layout.**

   Begin with a general sense of how the page will look and the relative width of the columns. Include the names of all segments in this diagram.

2. **Create the XHTML framework.**

   Create all the necessary divs, including `id` attributes. Add representative text so you can see the overall texture of the page.

3. **Add temporary borders.**

   Add a temporary border to each element so you can see what's going on when you start messing with `float` attributes. This also ensures you have all the selectors spelled properly.

4. **Float the leftmost element.**

   Add the `float` attribute to the leftmost column. Don't forget to specify a width (in percentage).

5. **Check your work.**

   Either work in the Web Developer CSS editor (where you can see changes on the fly) or frequently save your work and view it in a browser.

6. **Float the center element.**

   Add `float` and `width` attributes to the center element.

7. **Float the right-most element.**

   Incorporate `float` and `width` in the right element.

8. **Ensure all the widths total around 95 percent.**

   You'll want the sum of the widths to be nearly 100 percent but not quite. You'll generally need a little space for margins and padding. Final adjustments come later, but you certainly don't want to take up more than 100 percent of the available real estate.

9. **Float and clear the footer.**

   To get the footer acting right, you'll need to float it and clear it on both margins. Set its width to 100 percent, if you want.

10. **Tune up.**

    Remove the temporary borders, adjust the margins and padding, and set alignment as desired. Use percentages for margins and padding, and then adjust so all percentages equal 100 percent.

Early versions of Internet Explorer (6 and earlier) have a well-documented problem with margins and padding. According to the standards, the width of an element is supposed to be the width of the *content,* with borders, margins, and padding outside. A properly-behaved browser won't shrink your content when you add borders and margins. The early versions of Internet Explorer (IE) counted the width as *including* all borders, padding, and margin, effectively shrinking the content when you added these elements. If your page layout is looking a little off with IE, this may be the problem. Use the conditional comment technique described in Chapter 5 of Book II to make a variant style for IE if this bothers you.

Problems with the floating layout

The floating layout solution is very elegant, but it does have one drawback. Figure 2-7 shows the three-column page with the borders drawn around each element.

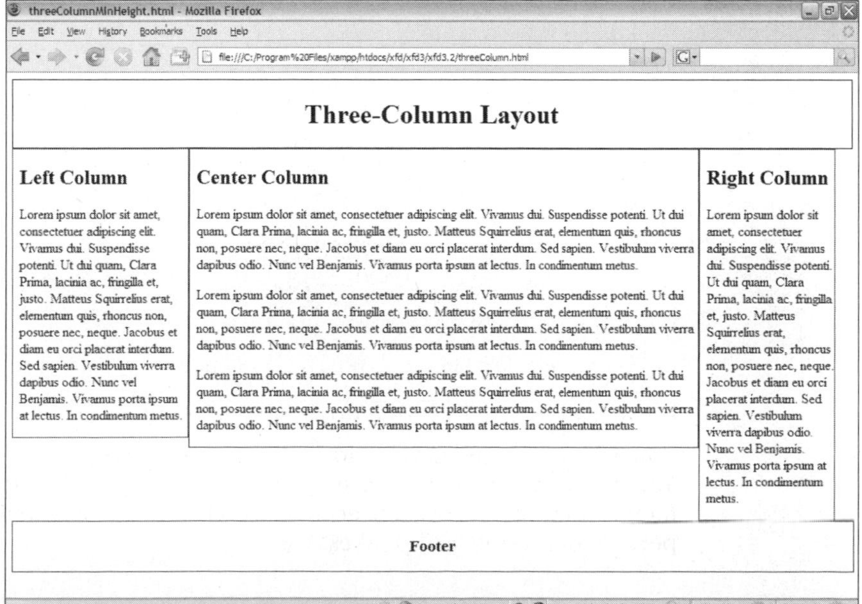

Figure 2-7: The columns aren't really columns; each is a different height.

Figure 2-7 shows an important fact about this type of layout. The columns are actually blocks, and each is a different height. Typically, I think of a column as stretching the entire height of a page, but this isn't how CSS does it. If you want to give each column a different background color, for example, you'll want each column to be the same height. This can be done with a CSS trick (at least, for the compliant browsers).

Specifying a min-height

The standards-compliant browsers (all versions of Firefox and Opera, and IE 7) support a `min-height` property. This specifies a minimum height for an element. You can use this property to force all columns to the same height. Figure 2-8 illustrates this effect.

The CSS code simply adds the `min-height` attribute to all the column elements:

```
#head {
  text-align: center;
  border-bottom: 3px double gray;
}

#left {
  float: left;
  width: 20%;
  min-height: 30em;
  background-color: #EEEEEE;
}

#center {
  float: left;
  width: 60%;
  padding-left: 1%;
  padding-right: 1%;
  min-height: 30em;
}

#right {
  float: left;
  width: 17%;
  padding-left: 1%;
  min-height: 30em;
  background-color: #EEEEEE;
}

#footer {
  border: 1px black solid;
  float: left;
  width: 100%;
  clear: both;
  text-align: center;
}
```

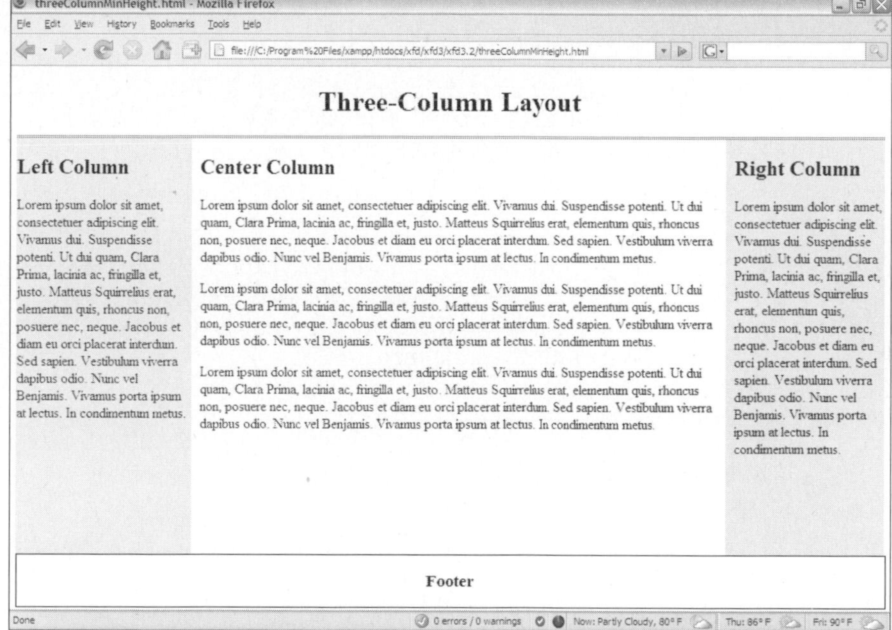

Figure 2-8: The min-height attribute forces all columns to be the same height.

Some guesswork is involved still. You have to experiment a bit to determine what the `min-height` should be. If you guess too short, one column will be longer than the `min-height`, and the columns won't appear correctly. If you guess too tall, you'll have a lot of empty space at the bottom of the screen.

Unfortunately, the `min-height` trick works only with the latest browsers. IE versions 6 and earlier don't support this attribute. For these browsers, you may need a fixed-width layout.

Building a Fixed-Width Layout

Fluid layouts are terrific. They're very flexible, and they're not hard to build. Sometimes, though, it's nice to use a fixed-width layout, particularly if you want your layout to conform with a particular background image.

The primary attribute of a fixed-width layout is the use of a fixed measurement (almost always pixels), rather than the percentage measurements used in a fluid layout.

Figure 2-9 shows a two-column page with a nicely colored background.

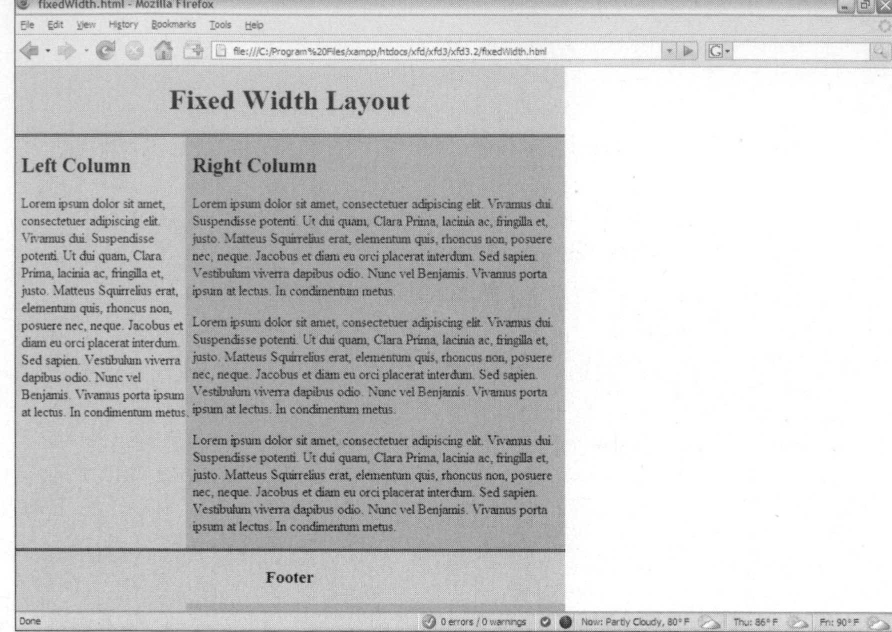

Figure 2-9: A fixed-width layout can work well with a background image.

Setting up the XHTML

As usual, the XHTML code is minimal. It contains a few named divs. (Like usual, I've removed filler text for space reasons.)

```
<!DOCTYPE html PUBLIC "-//W3C//DTD XHTML 1.0 Strict//EN"
"http://www.w3.org/TR/xhtml1/DTD/xhtml1-strict.dtd">
<html lang="EN" dir="ltr" xmlns="http://www.w3.org/1999/xhtml">
  <head>
    <meta http-equiv="content-type" content="text/xml; charset=utf-8" />
    <title>fixedWidth.html</title>
    <link rel = "stylesheet"
          type = "text/css"
          href = "fixedWidth.css" />
  </head>

  <body>
    <div id = "header">
      <h1>Fixed Width Layout</h1>
    </div>

    <div id = "left">
      <h2>Left Column</h2>
    </div>

    <div id = "right">
      <h2>Right Column</h2>
    </div>

    <div id = "footer">
```

```
      <h3>Footer</h3>
    </div>
  </body>
</html>
```

Using an image to simulate true columns

If you need to overcome the limitations of older browsers, you can use a background image to simulate colored columns. Figure 2-10 shows the basic background image I'm using for this page.

Figure 2-10: This image is repeated vertically to simulate two columns.

The image has been designed with two segments. The image is exactly 640 pixels wide, with one color spanning 200 pixels and the other 440 pixels. When you know the exact width you're aiming for, you can position the columns to exactly that size. Here's the CSS code:

```
body {
  background-image: url("fixedBG.gif");
  background-repeat: repeat-y;
}

#header {
  background-color: #e2e393;
  border-bottom: 3px double black;
  text-align: center;
  float: left;
  width: 640px;
  clear: both;
  margin-left: -8px;
  margin-top: -10px;
}

#left {
  float: left;
  width: 200px;
  clear: left;
}

#right {
  float: left;
  width: 440px;
}

#footer {
  float: left;
```

```
  width: 640px;
  clear: both;
  text-align: center;
  background-color: #e2e393;
  margin-left:-8px;
  border-top: 3px double black;
}
```

This code works a lot like the other floating layouts, except for the following changes:

- **The body has a background image attached.** I attached the two-color background image to the entire body. This will make the page look like it has two columns. Remember to set the `background-repeat` attribute to `repeat-y` so the background repeats indefinitely in the vertical *y*-axis.
- **The header and footer areas need background colors or images defined so the *fake* columns don't appear to stretch underneath these segments.**
- **Header and footer will need some margin adjustments.** The browsers tend to put a little bit of margin on the header and footer divs, so compensate by setting negative values for `margin-left` on these elements.
- **All measurements are now in pixels.** This will ensure that the layout corresponds to the image, also measured in pixels.

If you use a fixed-width layout and the user changes the font size, the results will be unpredictable. A fluid layout will change with the font size, but a fixed layout may have problems rendering a larger font in the indicated space.

Building a Centered Fixed-Width Layout

Fixed-width layouts are common, but they look a little strange if the browser isn't the width specified in the CSS. If the browser is too narrow, the layout won't work, and the second column will (usually) drop down to the next line.

If the browser is too wide, the page will appear to be scrunched onto the left margin with a great deal of white space on the right.

The natural solution would be to make a relatively narrow fixed-width design that's centered inside the entire page. Figure 2-11 illustrates a page with this technique.

Some have called this type of design (fixed-width floating centered in the browser) a *jello* layout because it's not quite fluid and not quite fixed.

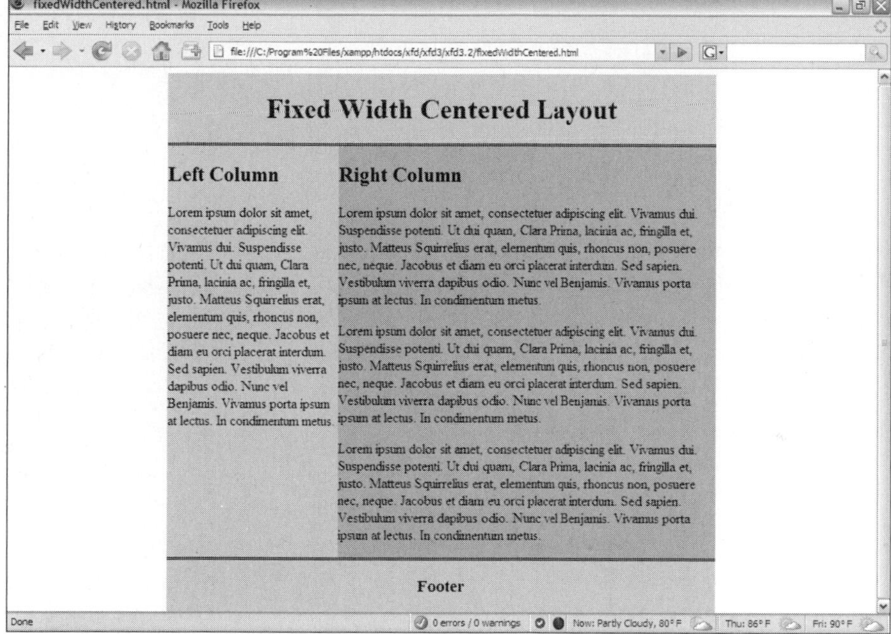

Figure 2-11: Now the fixed-width layout is centered in the browser.

Making a surrogate body with an all div

In any case, the HTML requires only one new element, an `all` div that encases everything else inside the body (as usual, I removed the placeholder text):

```
<!DOCTYPE html PUBLIC "-//W3C//DTD XHTML 1.0 Strict//EN"
"http://www.w3.org/TR/xhtml1/DTD/xhtml1-strict.dtd">
<html lang="EN" dir="ltr" xmlns="http://www.w3.org/1999/xhtml">
  <head>
    <meta http-equiv="content-type" content="text/xml; charset=utf-8" />
    <title>fixedWidthCentered.html</title>
    <link rel = "stylesheet"
          type = "text/css"
          href = "fixedWidthCentered.css" />
  </head>

  <body>
    <div id = "all">
      <div id = "header">
        <h1>Fixed Width Centered Layout</h1>
      </div>

      <div id = "left">
        <h2>Left Column</h2>
      </div>

      <div id = "right">
        <h2>Right Column</h2>
      </div>
```

```
      <div id = "footer">
        <h3>Footer</h3>
      </div>
    </div>
  </body>
</html>
```

The entire page contents are now encapsulated in a special `all` div. This div will be resized to a standard width (typically 640 or 800 pixels). The `all` element will be centered in the body, and the other elements will be placed inside `all` as if it was the body:

```
#all {
  background-image: url("fixedBG.gif");
  background-repeat: repeat-y;
  width: 640px;
  height: 600px;
  margin-left: auto;
  margin-right: auto;
}

#header {
  background-color: #e2e393;
  border-bottom: 3px double black;
  text-align: center;
  float: left;
  width: 640px;
  clear: both;
}

#left {
  float: left;
  width: 200px;
  clear: left;
}

#right {
  float: left;
  width: 440px;
}

#footer {
  float: left;
  width: 640px;
  clear: both;
  text-align: center;
  background-color: #e2e393;
  border-top: 3px double black;
}
```

How the jello layout works

This code is very similar to the `fixedWidth.css` style, but it has some important new features:

- **The background image is now applied to `all`.** The `all` div is now acting as a surrogate body element, so the background image is applied to it instead of the background.
- **The `all` element has a fixed width.** This element's width will determine the width of the fixed part of the page.
- **`all` also needs a fixed height.** If you don't specify a height, `all` will be 0 pixels tall because all the elements inside it are floated. Set the height large enough to make the background image extend as far down as necessary.
- **Center `all`.** Remember, to center divs, you set `margin-left` and `margin-right` both to `auto`.
- **Do *not* float `all`.** The `margin: auto` trick doesn't work on floated elements. `all` shouldn't have a `float` attribute set.
- **Ensure the interior widths add up to `all`'s width.** If `all` has a width of 640 pixels, be sure that the widths, borders, and margins of all the elements inside `all` add up to exactly 640 pixels. If you go even one pixel over, something will spill over and mess up the effect.

Limitations of the jello layout

Jello layouts represent a compromise between fixed and fluid layouts, but they aren't perfect:

- **Implicit minimum width:** Very narrow browsers (like cell phones) can't render the layout at all.
- **Wasted screen space:** If you make the rendered part of the page narrow, a lot of space isn't being used in higher-resolution browsers. This can be frustrating.
- **Complexity:** Although this layout technique is still far simpler than table-based layouts, it's still a bit involved. You do have to plan your divs to make this type of layout work.
- **Browser support:** Layout is an area where little differences in browser implementations can lead to big headaches. Be prepared to use conditional comments to handle inconsistencies, like IE's strange margin and padding support.

Chapter 3: Styling Lists and Menus

In This Chapter

- Using CSS styles with lists
- Building buttons from lists of links
- Dynamically displaying sublists
- Managing vertical and horizontal lists
- Building CSS-based menus

Most pages consist of content and navigation tools. Almost all pages have a list of links somewhere on the page. Navigation menus are lists of links, but lists of links in plain HTML are ugly. There has to be a way to make 'em prettier.

It's remarkably easy to build solid navigation tools with CSS alone (at least, in the modern browsers that support CSS properly). In this chapter, you rescue your lists from the boring 1990s sensibility, turning them into dynamic buttons, horizontal lists, and even dynamically cascading menus.

Revisiting List Styles

XHTML does provide some default list styling, but it's pretty dull. You'll often want to improve the appearance of a list of data. Most site navigation is essentially a list of links. One easy trick is to make your links appear as a set of buttons, as shown in Figure 3-1.

The buttons in Figure 3-1 are pretty nice. They look like buttons, with the familiar three-dimensional look of buttons. They also act like buttons, with each button *depressing* when the mouse hovers over it. When you click one of these buttons, it acts like a link, taking you to another page.

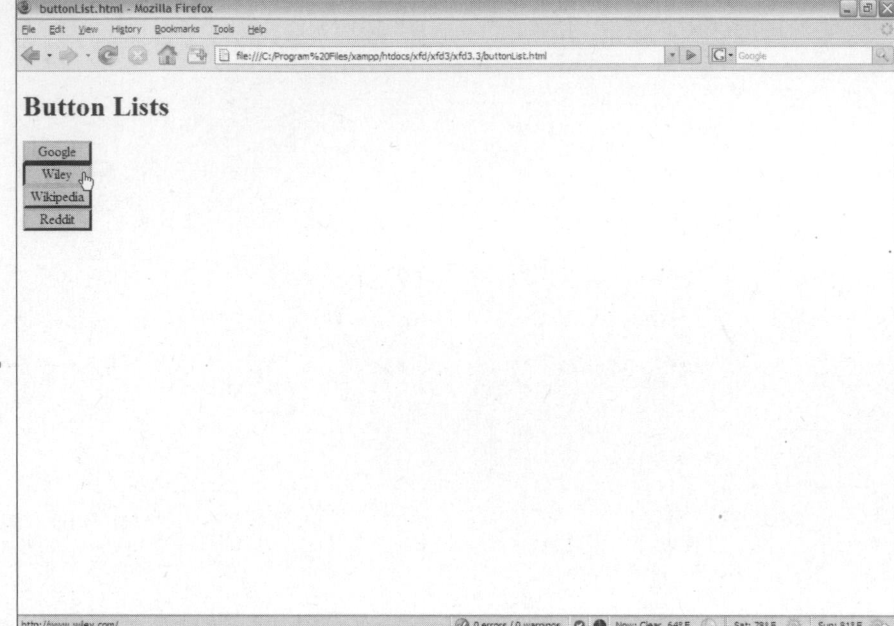

Figure 3-1: These buttons are actually a list. Note that one button is depressed.

Defining navigation as a list of links

If you look at the HTML, you'll be astonished at its simplicity:

```
<!DOCTYPE html PUBLIC "-//W3C//DTD XHTML 1.0 Strict//EN"
"http://www.w3.org/TR/xhtml1/DTD/xhtml1-strict.dtd">
<html lang="EN" dir="ltr" xmlns="http://www.w3.org/1999/xhtml">
  <head>
    <meta http-equiv="content-type" content="text/xml; charset=utf-8" />
    <title>buttonList.html</title>
    <link rel = "stylesheet"
          type = "text/css"
          href = "buttonList.css" />
  </head>

  <body>
    <h1>Button Lists</h1>
    <div id = "menu">
      <ul>
        <li><a href = "http://www.google.com">Google</a></li>
        <li><a href = "http://www.wiley.com">Wiley</a></li>
        <li><a href = "http://www.wikipedia.org">Wikipedia</a></li>
        <li><a href = "http://www.reddit.com">Reddit</a></li>
      </ul>
    </div>
  </body>
</html>
```

Turning links into buttons

As far as the XHTML code is concerned, it's simply a list of links. There's nothing special here that makes this act like a group of buttons, except the creation of a div called `menu`. All the real work is done in CSS:

```
#menu li {
  list-style-type: none;
  width: 5em;
  text-align: center;
  margin-left: -2.5em;
}

#menu a {
  text-decoration: none;
  color: black;
  display: block;
  border: 3px blue outset;
  background-color: #CCCCFF;
}

#menu a:hover {
  border: 3px blue inset;
}
```

The process for turning an ordinary list of links into a button group like this is simply an application of CSS tricks:

1. **Begin with an ordinary list that will validate properly.**

   It doesn't matter if you use an unordered or ordered list. Typically, the list will contain anchors to other pages. In this example, I'm using this list of links to some popular Web sites:

   ```
   <div id = "menu">
     <ul>
       <li><a href = "http://www.google.com">Google</a></li>
       <li><a href = "http://www.wiley.com">Wiley</a></li>
       <li><a href = "http://www.wikipedia.org">Wikipedia</a></li>
       <li><a href = "http://www.reddit.com">Reddit</a></li>
     </ul>
   </div>
   ```

2. **Enclose the list in a named div.**

   Typically, you'll still have ordinary links on a page. To indicate that these menu links should be handled differently, put them in a div named `menu`. All the CSS-style tricks described here refer to lists and anchors only when they're inside a `menu` div.

3. **Remove the bullets by setting the `list-style-type` to `none`.**

   This will take away the bullets or numbers that usually appear in a list, as these features will distract from the effect you're aiming for (a group of buttons). Use CSS to specify how list items should be formatted when they appear in the context of the menu ID:

```
#menu li {
  list-style-type: none;
  width: 5em;
  text-align: center;
  margin-left: -2.5em;
}
```

4. **Specify the width of each button:**

   ```
   width: 5em;
   ```

   A group of buttons looks best if they're all the same size. Use the CSS width attribute to set each `li` to `5em`.

5. **Remove the margin by using a negative `margin-left` value, as shown here:**

   ```
   margin-left: -2.5em;
   ```

   Lists have a default indentation of about `2.5em` to make room for the bullets or numbers. Because this list won't have bullets, it doesn't need the indentations. Overwrite the default indenting behavior by setting `margin-left` to a negative value.

6. **Clean up the anchor by setting `text-decoration` to `none` and setting the anchor's color to something static, such as black text on light blue in this example:**

   ```
   #menu a {
     text-decoration: none;
     color: black;
     display: block;
     border: 3px blue outset;
     background-color: #CCCCFF;
   }
   ```

   The button's appearance will make it clear that users can click it, so this is one place you can remove the underlining that normally goes with links.

7. **Give each button an outset border, as shown in the following:**

   ```
   border: 3px blue outset;
   ```

   The outset makes it look like a 3D button sticking out from the page. This is best attached to the anchor, so you can swap the border when the mouse is hovering over the button.

8. **Set the anchor's `display` to `block`.**

   This is a sneaky trick. Block display normally makes an element act like a block-level element inside its container. In the case of an anchor, the entire button becomes clickable, not just the text. This makes your page easier to use:

   ```
   display: block;
   ```

9. **Swap for an inset border when the mouse hovers over an anchor by using the `#menu a:hover` selector to change the border to an inset:**

```
#menu a:hover {
  border: 3px blue inset;
}
```

When the mouse hovers over the button, it appears to be pressed down, enhancing the 3D effect.

This list makes an ideal navigation menu, especially when placed inside one column of a multi-column floating layout.

Building horizontal lists

Sometimes, you want horizontal button bars. Because XHTML lists tend to be vertical, you might be tempted to think that a horizontal list is impossible. In fact, CSS provides all you need to convert exactly the same XHTML to a horizontal list. Figure 3-2 shows such a page.

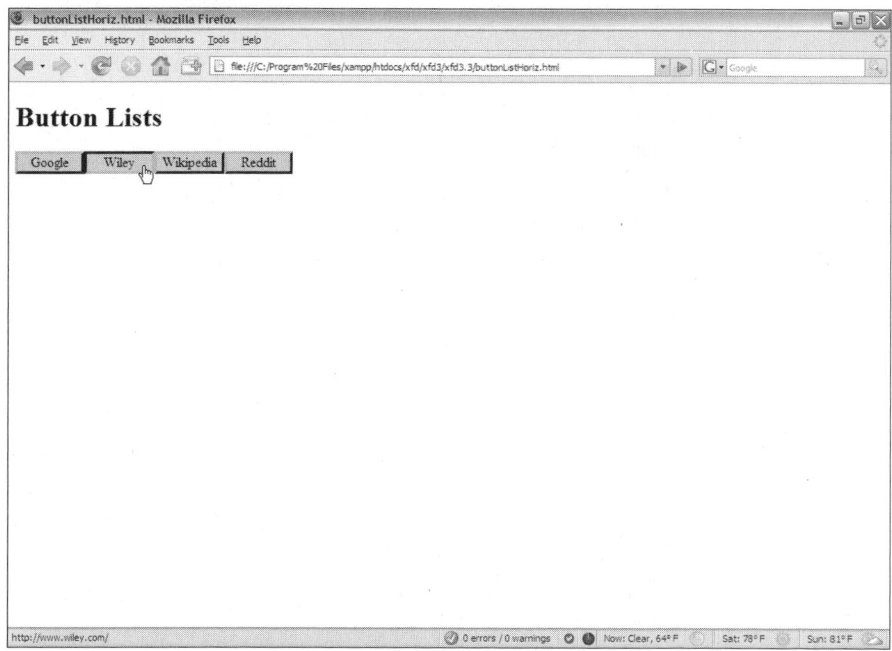

Figure 3-2: This list uses the same XHTML but different CSS.

There's no need to show the XHTML again because it hasn't changed at all (ain't CSS grand?). Even the CSS hasn't changed much:

```
#menu ul {
  margin-left: -2.5em;
}

#menu li {
  list-style-type: none;
  float: left;
  width: 5em;
  text-align: center;
}

#menu a {
  text-decoration: none;
  color: black;
  display: block;
  border: 3px blue outset;
  background-color: #CCCCFF;
}

#menu a:hover {
  border: 3px blue inset;
}
```

The modifications are incredibly simple:

1. **Float each list item by giving each `li` a `float:left` value:**

   ```
   #menu li {
     list-style-type: none;
     float: left;
     width: 5em;
     text-align: center;
   }
   ```

2. **Move the `margin-left` to the entire `ul` by taking the `margin-left` formatting from the `li` elements and transferring it to the `ul`:**

   ```
   #menu ul {
     margin-left: -2.5em;
   }
   ```

3. **Add a horizontal element.**

   Now that the button bar is horizontal, it makes more sense to put in some type of horizontal page element. For example, you may want to use this type of element inside a `heading` div.

Creating Dynamic Lists

A simple list of buttons can look better than ordinary XHTML links, but sometimes, your page needs to have a more complex navigation scheme. For example, you may want to create a menu system to help the user see the structure of your site.

When you think of a complex hierarchical organization (which is how most multi-page Web sites end up), the easiest way to describe the structure is in a set of *nested* lists. XHTML lists can contain other lists, and this can be a great way to organize data.

Nested lists are a great way to organize a lot of information, but they can be complicated. You can use some special tricks to make parts of your list appear and disappear when needed. In the sections "Hiding the inner lists" and "Getting the inner lists to appear on cue," later in this chapter, you expand this technique to build a menu system for your pages.

Building a nested list

Begin by creating a system of nested lists without any CSS at all. Figure 3-3 shows a page with a basic nested list.

No CSS styling is in place yet, but the list has its own complexities:

- **The primary list has three entries.** This is actually a multi-layer list. The top level indicates categories, not necessarily links.
- **Each element in the top list has its own sublist.** A second layer of links has various links in most elements.

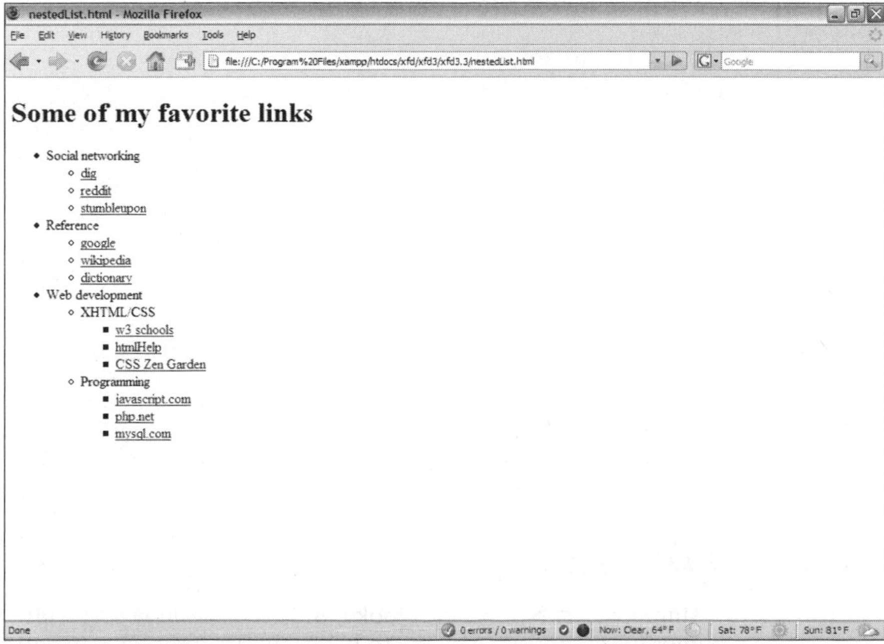

Figure 3-3: This nested list has no styles yet.

- **The Web Development element has another layer of sublists.** The general layout of this list entry corresponds to a complex hierarchy of information — like most complex Web sites.
- **The list validates to the XHTML Strict standard.** It's especially important to validate your code before adding CSS when it involves somewhat complex XHTML code, like the multi-level list. A small problem in the XHTML structure that may go unnoticed in a plain XHTML document can cause all kinds of strange problems in your CSS.

Here is the code for the nested list in plain XHTML:

```
<!DOCTYPE html PUBLIC "-//W3C//DTD XHTML 1.0 Strict//EN"
"http://www.w3.org/TR/xhtml1/DTD/xhtml1-strict.dtd">
<html lang="EN" dir="ltr" xmlns="http://www.w3.org/1999/xhtml">
  <head>
    <meta http-equiv="content-type" content="text/xml; charset=utf-8" />
    <title>nestedList.html</title>
  </head>

  <body>
    <h1>Some of my favorite links</h1>
    <ul>
      <li>Social networking
        <ul>
          <li><a href = "http://www.digg.com">dig</a></li>
          <li><a href = "http://www.reddit.com">reddit</a></li>
          <li><a href = "http://www.stumbleupon.com">stumbleupon</a></li>
        </ul>
      </li>
      <li>Reference
        <ul>
          <li><a href = "http://www.google.com">google</a></li>
          <li><a href = "http://wikipedia.org">wikipedia</a></li>
          <li><a href = "http://dictionary.com">dictionary</a></li>
        </ul>
      </li>
      <li>Web development
        <ul>
          <li>XHTML/CSS
            <ul>
              <li><a href = "http://www.w3schools.com">w3 schools</a></li>
              <li><a href = "http://htmlhelp.com">htmlHelp</a></li>
              <li><a href = "http://www.csszengarden.com">CSS Zen Garden</a></li>
            </ul>
          </li>
          <li>Programming
            <ul>
              <li><a href = "http://javascript.com">javascript.com</a></li>
              <li><a href = "http://php.net">php.net</a></li>
              <li><a href = "http://www.mysql.com">mysql.com</a></li>
            </ul>
          </li>
        </ul>
      </li>
    </ul>
  </body>
</html>
```

Take special care with your indentation when making a complex nested list like this one. Without proper indentation, it becomes very difficult to establish the structure of the page. Also note that a list item can contain text and another list. Any other arrangement (putting text between list items, for example) will cause a validation error and big headaches when you try to apply CSS.

Hiding the inner lists

The first step of creating a dynamic menu system is to hide any lists that are embedded in a list item. Add the following CSS style to your page:

```
li ul {
  display: none;
}
```

In reality, you'll usually apply this technique only to a specially marked div, like a menu system. Don't worry about that for now. Later in this chapter, I show you how to combine this technique with a variation of the button technique for complex menu systems.

Your page will undergo a startling transformation, as shown in Figure 3-4.

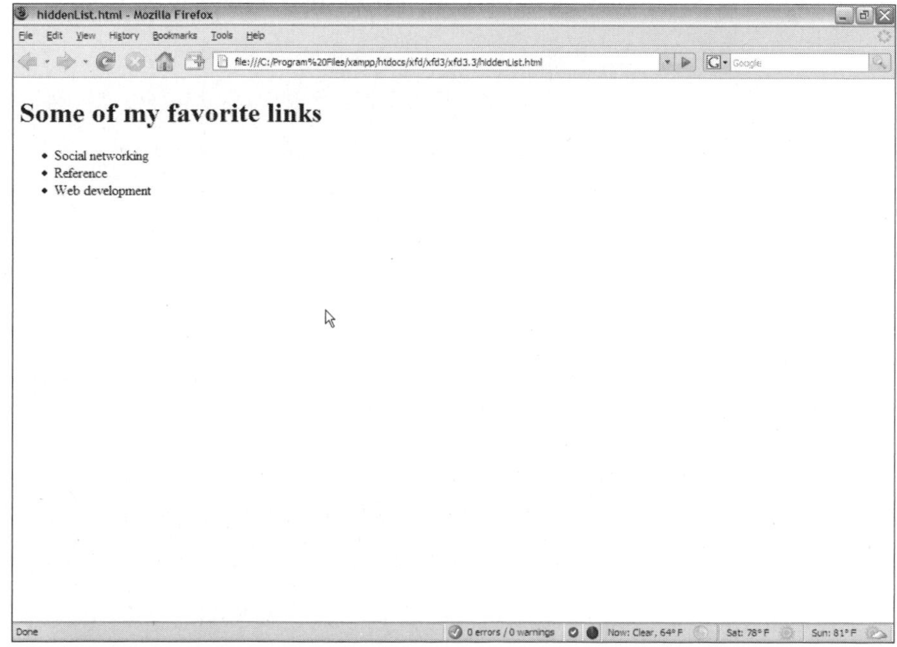

Figure 3-4: Where did everything go?

That tiny little snippet of CSS code is a real powerhouse. It does some fascinating things, such as

- **Operating on unordered lists that appear inside list items:** What this really means is the topmost list won't be affected, but any unordered list that appears inside a list item will have the style applied.
- **Using `display: none` to make text disappear:** Setting the `display` attribute to `none` tells the XHTML page to hide the given data altogether.

Note that this code works well on almost all browsers. It's pretty easy to make text disappear. Unfortunately, it's a little trickier to make all the browsers bring it back.

Getting the inner lists to appear on cue

The fun part is getting the interior lists to pop up when the mouse is over the parent element. A second CSS style can make this happen:

```
li ul {
  display: none;
}

li:hover ul {
  display: block;
}
```

The new code is pretty interesting. When the page initially loads, it appears the same as what's shown in Figure 3-4, but when you hold the mouse over the Social Networking element, you see the effect shown in Figure 3-5.

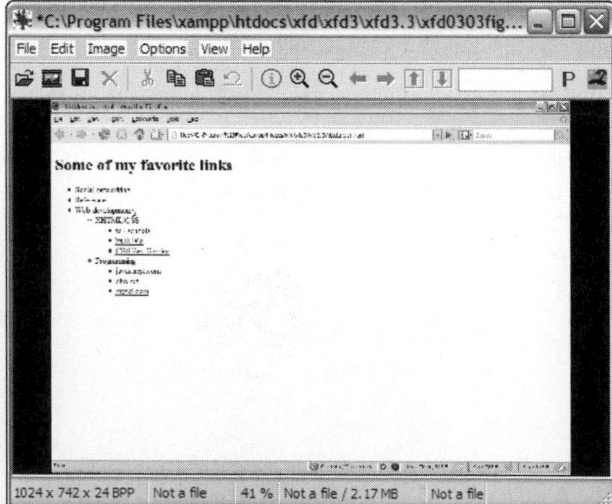

Figure 3-5: Holding the mouse over a list item causes its children to appear.

This code doesn't work on all browsers! Internet Explorer 6 (IE6) and earlier versions don't support the `:hover` pseudo-class on any element except `a`. Provide a conditional comment with an alternative style for IE.

Here's how the list-reappearing code works:

- **All lists inside lists are hidden.** The first style rule hides any list that's inside a list element.
- **`li:hover` refers to a list item that's being hovered over.** That is, if the mouse is currently situated on top of a list item, this rule pertains to it.
- **`li:hover ul` refers to an unordered list inside a hovered list item.** In other words, if some content is an unordered list that rests inside a list that currently has the mouse hovering over it, apply this rule. *(Whew!)*
- **Display the list as a block.** `display:block` overrides the previous `display:none` instruction and displays the particular element as a block. The text reappears magically.

This hide-and-seek trick isn't all that great on its own. It's actually quite annoying to have the contents pop up and go away like that. There's another more annoying problem. Look at Figure 3-6 to see what can go wrong.

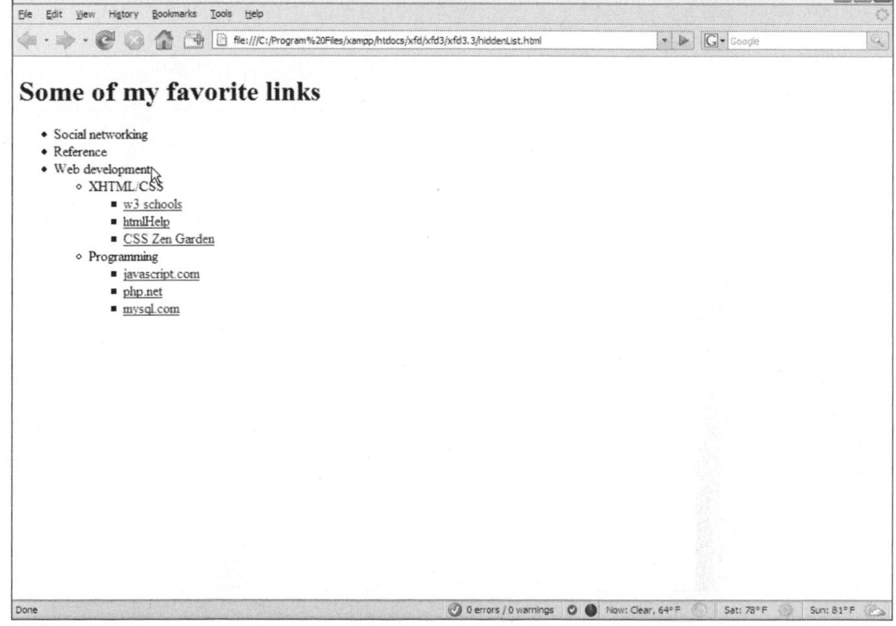

Figure 3-6: If the mouse hovers over Web Development, *both* submenus appear.

To see why this happens, take another look at the CSS code that causes the segment to reappear:

```
li:hover ul {
  display: block;
}
```

This code means set display to block for any `ul` that's a child of a hovered `li`. The problem is that the Web Development `li` contains a `ul` that contains *two more* `ul`s. All the lists under Web Development appear, not just the immediate child.

One more modification of the CSS fixes this problem:

```
li ul {
  display: none;
}

li:hover > ul {
  display: block;
}
```

The greater-than symbol (>) is a special selector tool. It indicates a direct relationship. In other words, the `ul` must be a direct child of the hovered `li`, not a grandchild or great-grandchild. With this indicator in place, the page acts correctly, as you can see from Figure 3-7.

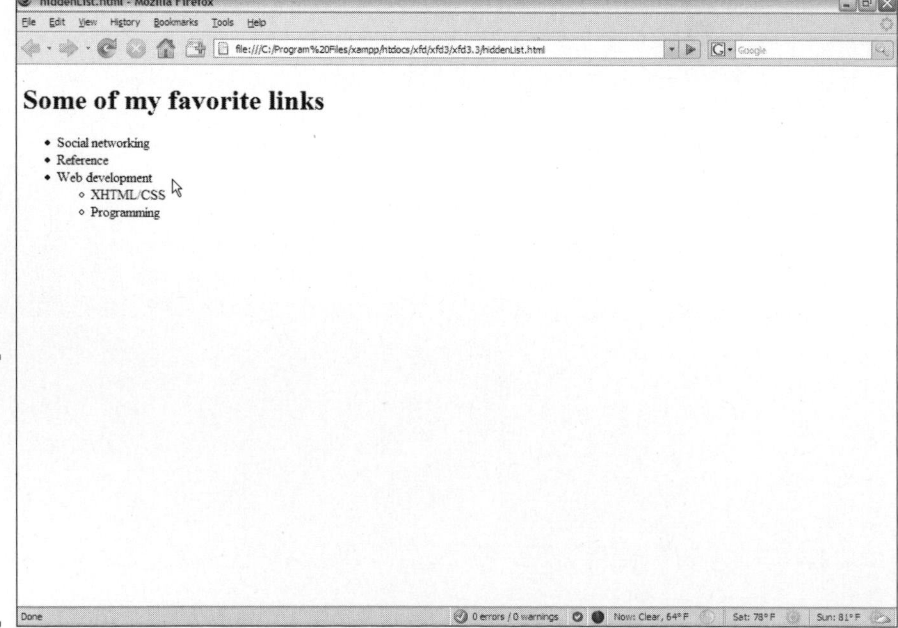

Figure 3-7: Now, only the next level of menu shows up on a mouse hover.

This trick allows you to create nested lists as deeply as you wish and to open any segment by hovering on its parent.

My current code has a list with three levels of nesting, but you can add as many nested lists as you want and use this code to make it act as a dynamic menu.

Figure 3-8 illustrates how to open the next section of the list.

I'm not suggesting that this type of menu is a good idea. Having stuff pop around like this is actually pretty distracting. With a little more formatting, you can use these ideas to make a functional menu system. I'm just starting here so you can see the hide-and-seek behavior in a simpler system before adding more details.

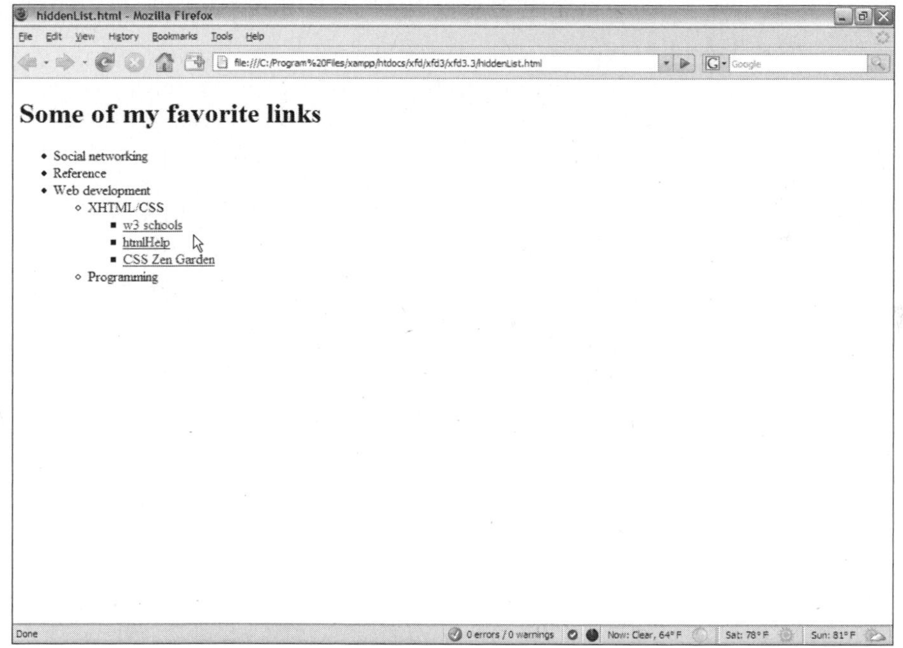

Figure 3-8: You can create these lists as deep as you wish.

Building a Basic Menu System

You can combine the techniques of buttons and collapsing lists to build a menu system entirely with CSS. Figure 3-9 shows a page with a vertically arranged menu.

When the user hovers over a part of the menu, the related sub-elements appear, as shown in Figure 3-10.

This type of menu has a couple interesting advantages, such as

- ✦ **It's written entirely with CSS.** You don't need any other code or programming language.
- ✦ **The menus are simply nested lists.** The XHTML is simply a set of nested lists. If the CSS turns off, the page is displayed as a set of nested lists, and the links still function normally.
- ✦ **The relationships between elements are illustrated.** When you select an element, you can see its parent and sibling relationships easily.

Nice as this type of menu system is, it isn't perfect. Because it relies on the `li:hover` trick, it doesn't work in versions of Internet Explorer (IE) prior to 7.0.

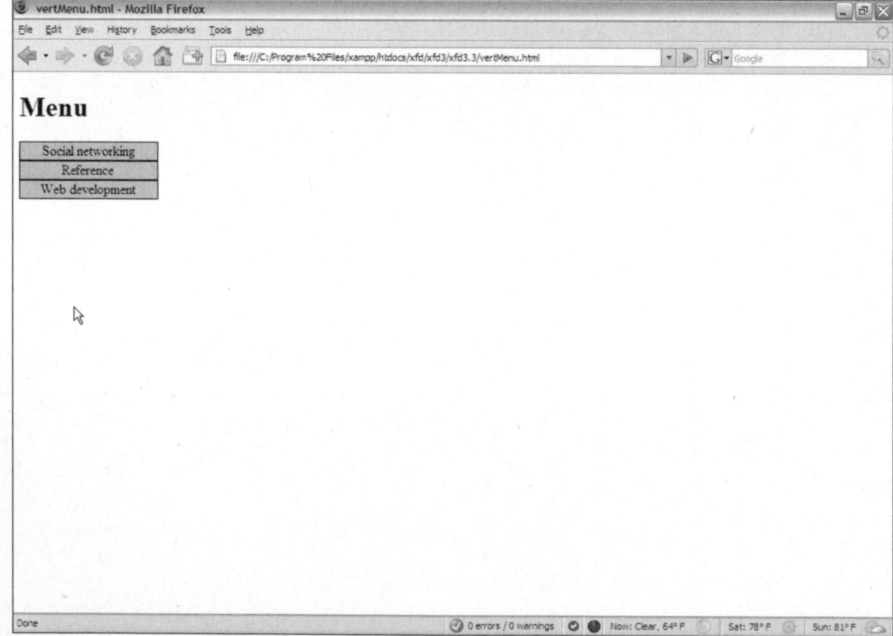

Figure 3-9: Only the top-level elements are visible by default.

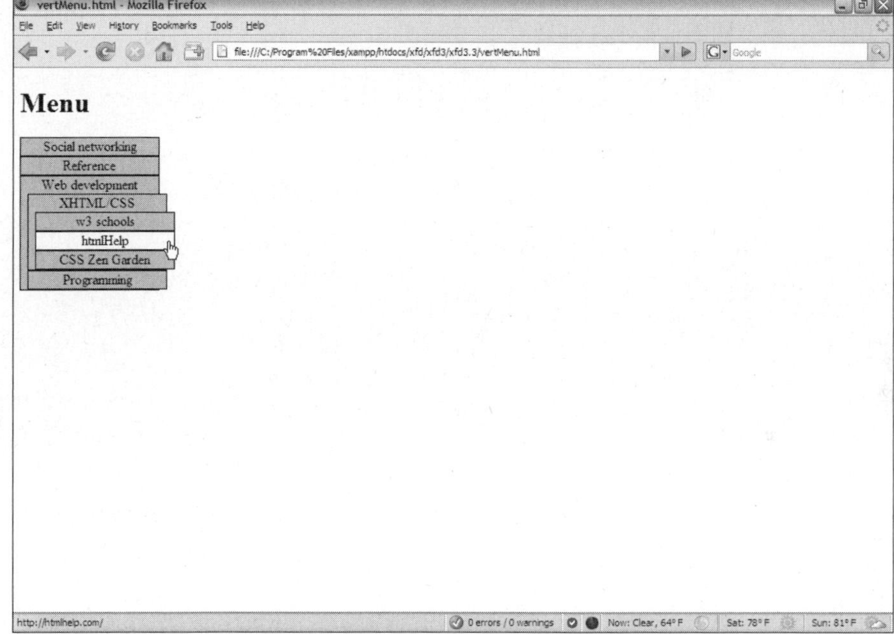

Figure 3-10: The user can select any part of the original nested list.

Building a vertical menu with CSS

The vertical menu system works with exactly the same HTML as the `hiddenList` example — only the CSS changed. Here's the new CSS file:

```
/* horizMenu.css */
/* unindent entire list */
#menu ul {
  margin-left: -2.5em;
}

/* set li as buttons */
#menu li {
  list-style-type: none;
  border: 1px black solid;;
  width: 10em;
  background-color: #cccccc;
  text-align: center;
}

/* display anchors as buttons */
#menu a {
  color: black;
  text-decoration: none;
  display: block;
}

/* flash white on anchor hover */
#menu a:hover {
  background-color: white;
```

```
}

/* collapse menus */
#menu li ul {
  display: none;
}

/* show submenus on hover */
#menu li:hover > ul {
  display: block;
  margin-left: -2em;
}
```

Of course, the CSS uses a few tricks, but there's really nothing new. It's just a combination of techniques you already know:

1. **Un-indent the entire list by setting the `ul`'s `margin-left` to a negative value to compensate for the typical indentation. `2.5em` is about the right amount.**

   Because you'll be removing the `list-style` types, the normal indentation of list items will become a problem.

2. **Format the `li` tags.**

   Each `li` tag inside the menu structure should look something like a button. Use CSS to accomplish this task:

   ```
   /* set li as buttons */
   #menu li {
     list-style-type: none;
     border: 1px black solid;;
     width: 10em;
     background-color: #cccccc;
     text-align: center;
   }
   ```

   a. **Set `list-style-type` to `none`.**

   b. **Set a border with the border attribute.**

   c. **Center the text by setting `text-align` to `center`.**

   d. **Add a background color or image, or you'll get some strange border bleed-through later when the buttons overlap.**

3. **Format the anchors as follows:**

   ```
   /* display anchors as buttons */
   #menu a {
     color: black;
     text-decoration: none;
     display: block;
   }
   ```

   a. **Take out the underline with `text-decoration: none`.**

b. **Give the anchor a consistent color.**

c. **Set display to block (so the entire area will be clickable, not just the text).**

4. **Give some indication it's an anchor by changing the background when the user hovers over the element:**

```
/* flash white on anchor hover */
#menu a:hover {
  background-color: white;
}
```

Because the anchors no longer look like anchors, you'll have to do something else to indicate there's something special about these elements. When the user moves the mouse over any anchor tag in the `menu` div, that anchor's background color will switch to white.

5. **Collapse the menus using the hidden menus trick (discussed in the section "Hiding the inner lists," earlier in this chapter) to hide all the sublists:**

```
/* collapse menus */
#menu li ul {
  display: none;
}
```

6. **Display the hidden menus when the mouse hovers over the parent element by adding the code described in the section "Getting the inner lists to appear on cue":**

```
/* show submenus on hover */
#menu li:hover > ul {
  display: block;
  margin-left: -2em;
}
```

This trick won't work on IE6 or earlier versions. You'll have to provide an alternate style sheet (with conditional commenting) or a JavaScript technique for these earlier browsers.

Building a horizontal menu

You can make a variation of the menu structure that will work along the top of a page. Figure 3-11 shows how this might look.

Notice that the submenus come straight down from their parent elements. I find a little bit of indentation helpful for deeply nested lists, as you can see in Figure 3-12.

Once again, the HTML is identical. The CSS for a horizontal menu is surprisingly close to the vertical menu. The primary difference is floating the list items:

```
/* vertMenu.css */
/* unindent each unordered list */

#menu ul {
  margin-left: -2.5em;
}

/* turn each list item into a solid gray block */
#menu li {
  list-style-type: none;
  border: black solid 1px;
  float: left;
  width: 10em;
  background-color: #CCCCCC;
  text-align: center;
}

/* set anchors to act like buttons */
#menu a {
  display: block;
  color: black;
  text-decoration: none;
}

/* flash anchor white when hovered */
#menu a:hover {
  background-color: white;
}

/* collapse nested lists */
#menu li ul {
  display: none;
}
```

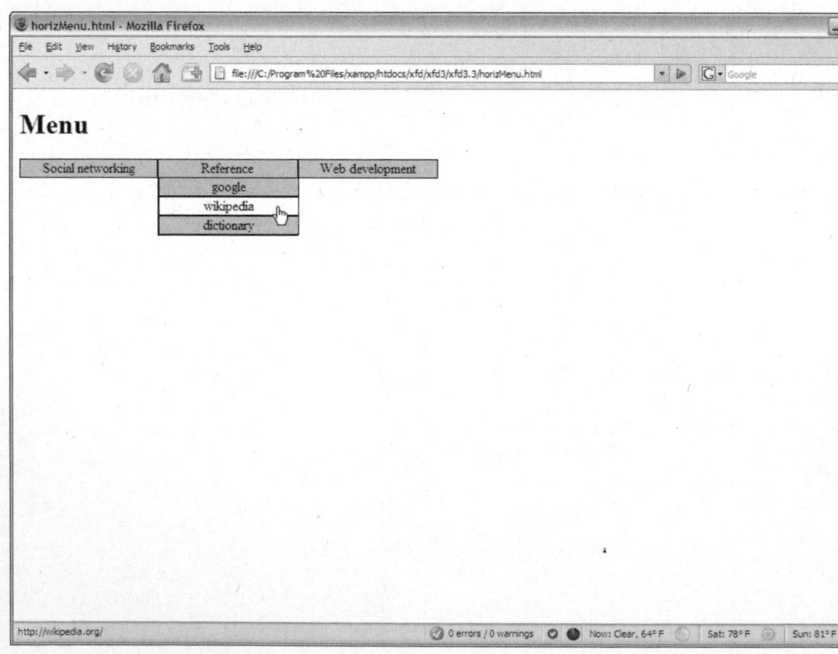

Figure 3-11: The same list is now a horizontal menu.

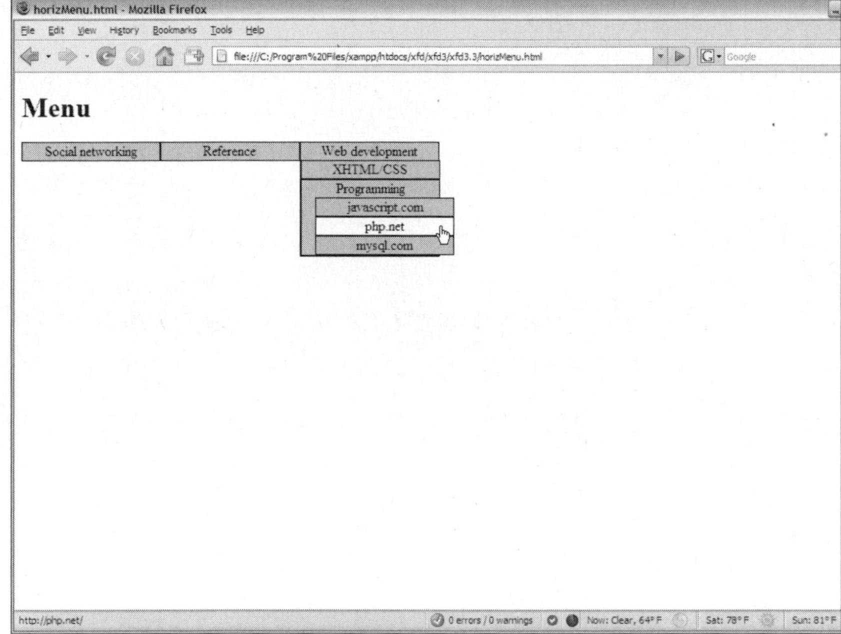

Figure 3-12: For the multi-level menus, a little bit of indentation is helpful.


```
/* display sublists on hover */
#menu li:hover > ul {
  display: block;
}

/* indent third-generation lists */
#menu li li li{
  margin-left: 1em;
}
```

The CSS code has just a few variations from the vertical menu CSS:

- Float each list item by adding `float` and `width` attributes.

  ```
  /* turn each list item into a solid gray block */
  #menu li {
    list-style-type: none;
    border: black solid 1px;
    float: left;
    width: 10em;
    background-color: #CCCCCC;
    text-align: center;
  }
  ```

  This causes the list items to appear next to each other in the same line.

- Give each list item a width. In this case, `10em` seems about right.

✦ Indent a deeply nested list by having the first-order sublists appear directly below the parent.

  A list nested deeper than its parent is hard to read. A little indentation helps a lot with clarity.

✦ Use `#menu li li li` to indent nested list items, as shown here:

```
/* indent third-generation lists */
#menu li li li{
  margin-left: 1em;
}
```

  This selector is active on an element which has `#menu` and three list items in its *family tree.* It will work only on list items three levels deep. This special formatting isn't needed at the other levels but is helpful to offset the third-level list items.

These tricks are just the beginning of what you can do with some creativity and the amazing power of CSS and HTML. You can adopt the simple examples presented here to create your own marvels of navigation.

Chapter 4: Using Alternative Positioning

In This Chapter

- **Setting position to** `absolute`
- **Managing** `z-index`
- **Creating fixed and flexible layouts**
- **Working with fixed and relative positioning**

Floating layouts (described in Chapter 2 of this minibook) are the preferred way to set up page layouts today, but some other alternatives are sometimes useful. You can use *absolute, relative,* or *fixed positioning* techniques to put all your page elements exactly where you want them. Well, *almost* exactly. It's still Web development, where nothing's exact.

Still, the techniques described in this chapter will give you even more capabilities when it comes to setting up great-looking Web sites.

Working with Absolute Positioning

Begin by considering the default layout mechanism. Figure 4-1 shows a page with two paragraphs on it.

I used CSS to give each paragraph a different color (to aid in discussion later) and to set a specific height and width. The positioning is left to the default layout manager, which positions the second (black) paragraph directly below the first (blue) one.

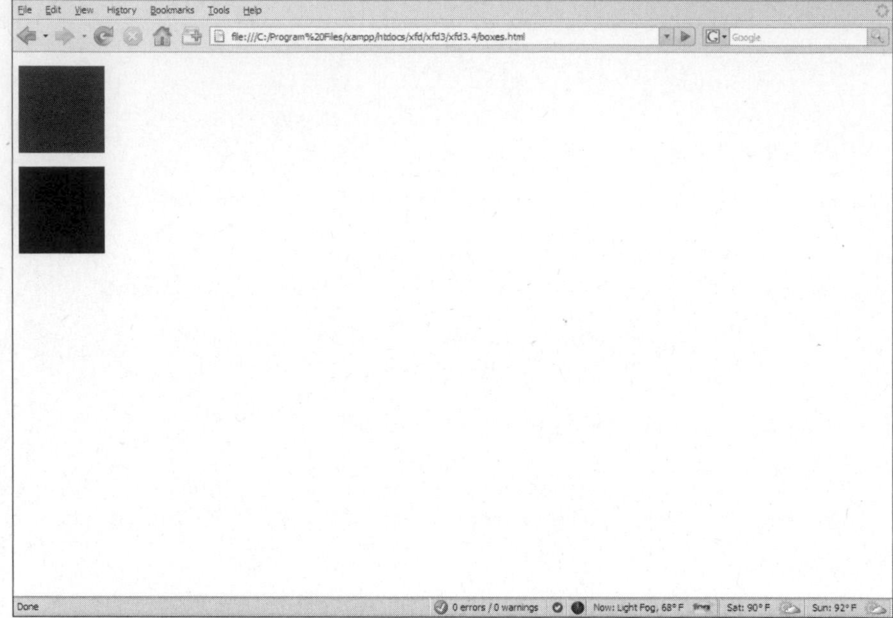

Figure 4-1: These two paragraphs have a set height and width, but default positioning.

Setting up the HTML

The code is unsurprising:

```
<!DOCTYPE html PUBLIC "-//W3C//DTD XHTML 1. 0 Strict//EN"
"http://www. w3. org/TR/xhtml1/DTD/xhtml1-strict. dtd">
<html lang="EN" dir="ltr" xmlns="http://www. w3. org/1999/xhtml">
  <head>
    <meta http-equiv="content-type" content="text/xml; charset=utf-8" />
    <title>boxes.html</title>
    <style type = "text/css">
      #blueBox {
        background-color: blue;
        width: 100px;
        height: 100px;
      }
      #blackBox {
        background-color: black;
        width: 100px;
        height: 100px;
      }
    </style>
  </head>

  <body>
    <p id = "blueBox"></p>
    <p id = "blackBox"></p>
  </body>
</html>
```

If you provide no further guidance, paragraphs (like other block-level elements) tend to provide carriage returns before and after themselves, stacking on top of each other. Note that the default layout techniques ensure that nothing ever overlaps.

Adding position guidelines

Figure 4-2 shows something new: The paragraphs are overlapping!

This feat is accomplished through some new CSS attributes:

```
<!DOCTYPE html PUBLIC "-//W3C//DTD XHTML 1. 0 Strict//EN"
"http://www. w3. org/TR/xhtml1/DTD/xhtml1-strict. dtd">
<html lang="EN" dir="ltr" xmlns="http://www. w3. org/1999/xhtml">
  <head>
    <meta http-equiv="content-type" content="text/xml; charset=utf-8" />
    <title>absPosition.html</title>
    <style type = "text/css">

      #blueBox {
        background-color: blue;
        width: 100px;
        height: 100px;
        position: absolute;
        left: 0px;
        top: 0px;
        margin: 0px;
      }
```


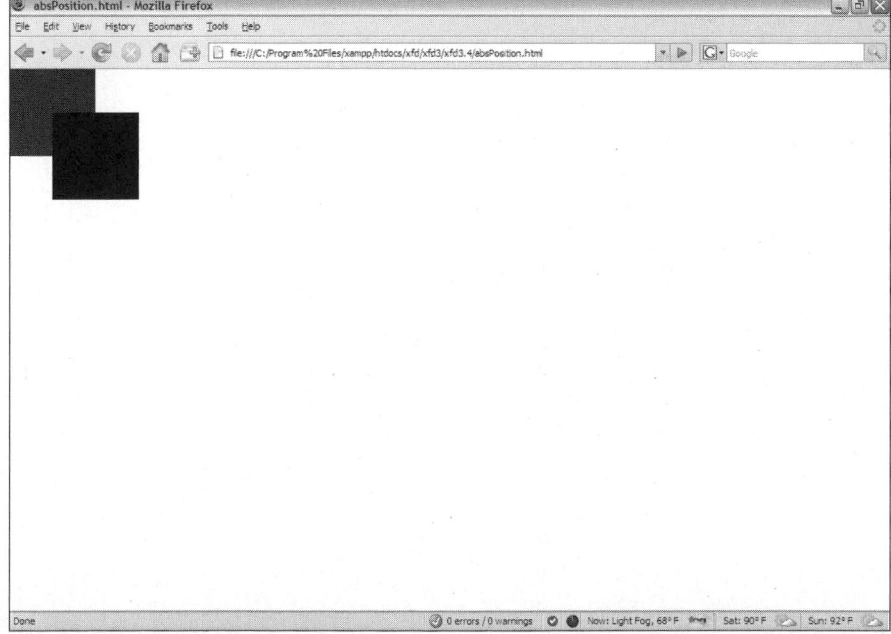

Figure 4-2: Now the paragraphs overlap each other.

```
    #blackBox {
      background-color: black;
      width: 100px;
      height: 100px;
      position: absolute;
      left: 50px;
      top: 50px;
      margin: 0px;
    }
  </style>
</head>

<body>
  <p id = "blueBox"></p>
  <p id = "blackBox"></p>
</body>
</html>
```

So, why do I care if the boxes overlap? Well, you might not care, but the interesting part is this: You can have much more precise control over where elements live and what size they are. You can even override the browser's normal tendency to keep elements from overlapping, which gives you some interesting options.

Making absolute positioning work

A few new parts of CSS allow this more direct control of the size and position of these elements. Here's the CSS for one of the boxes:

```
#blueBox {
  background-color: blue;
  width: 100px;
  height: 100px;
  position: absolute;
  left: 0px;
  top: 0px;
  margin: 0px;
}
```

1. **Set the `position` attribute to `absolute`.**

   Absolute positioning can be used to determine exactly (more or less) where the element will be placed on the screen:

   ```
   position: absolute;
   ```

2. **Specify a `left` position in the CSS.**

   After you determine that an element will have `absolute` position, it's removed from the normal flow, so you're obligated to fix its position. The `left` attribute determines where the left edge of the element will go. This can be specified with any of the measurement units, but it's typically measured in pixels:

   ```
   left: 0px;
   ```

3. **Specify a `top` position with CSS.**

   The `top` attribute indicates where the top of the element will go. Again, this is usually specified in pixels:

   ```
   top: 0px;
   ```

4. **Use the `height` and `width` attributes to determine the size.**

   Normally, when you specify a position, you'll also want to determine the size:

   ```
   width: 100px;
   height: 100px;
   ```

5. **Set the margins to 0.**

   When you're using absolute positioning, you're exercising quite a bit of control. Because browsers don't treat margins identically, you're better off setting margins to 0 and controlling the spacing between elements manually:

   ```
   margin: 0px;
   ```

Generally, you'll use absolute positioning only on named elements, rather than classes or general element types. For example, you won't want all the paragraphs on a page to have the same size and position, or you couldn't see them both. Absolute positioning works on only one element at a time.

Managing z-index

When you use absolute positioning, you can determine exactly where things are placed, so it's possible for them to overlap. By default, elements described later in HTML are positioned on top of elements described earlier. This is why the black box appears over the top of the blue box in Figure 4-2.

Handling depth

You can use a special CSS attribute called `z-index` to change this default behavior. The *z*-axis refers to how close an element appears to be to the viewer. Figure 4-3 demonstrates how this works.

The `z-index` attribute requires a numeric value. Higher numbers mean the element is closer to the user (or on *top*). Any value for `z-index` places the element higher than elements with the default `z-index`. This can be very useful when you have elements that you want to appear over the top of other elements (for example, menus that temporarily appear on top of other text).

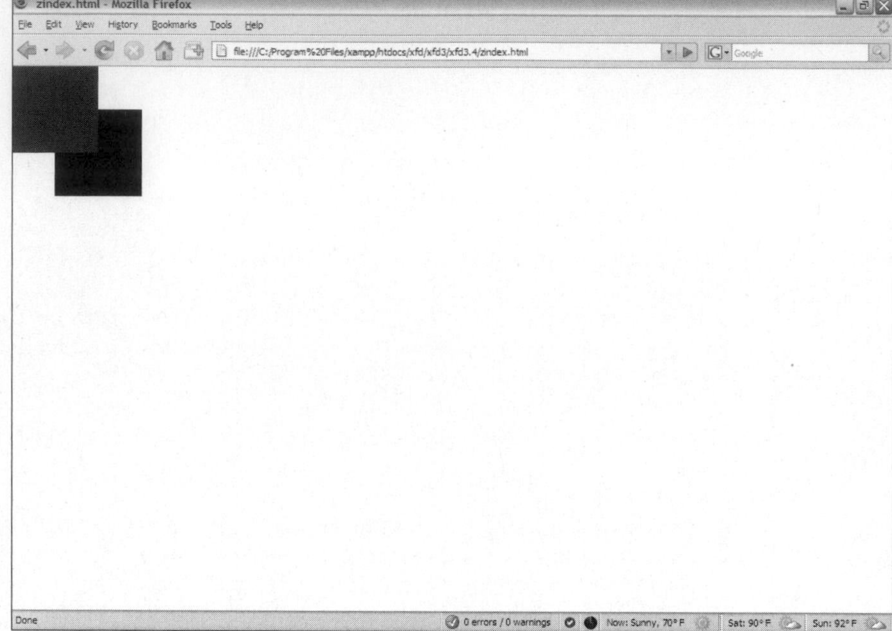

Figure 4-3: The z-index allows you to change which elements appear closer to the user.

Here's the code illustrating the `z-index` effect:

```
<!DOCTYPE html PUBLIC "-//W3C//DTD XHTML 1.0 Strict//EN"
"http://www.w3.org/TR/xhtml1/DTD/xhtml1-strict.dtd">
<html lang="EN" dir="ltr" xmlns="http://www.w3.org/1999/xhtml">
  <head>
    <meta http-equiv="content-type" content="text/xml; charset=utf-8" />
    <title>zindex.html</title>
    <style type = "text/css">

      #blueBox {
        background-color: blue;
        width: 100px;
        height: 100px;
        position: absolute;
        left: 0px;
        top: 0px;
        margin: 0px;
        z-index: 1;
      }
      #blackBox {
        background-color: black;
        width: 100px;
        height: 100px;
        position: absolute;
        left: 50px;
        top: 50px;
        margin: 0px;
      }
    </style>
```

```
  </head>
  <body>
    <p id = "blueBox"></p>
    <p id = "blackBox"></p>
  </body>
</html>
```

Working with z-index

The only change in this code is the addition of the `z-index` property. Here are a couple things to keep in mind when using `z-index`:

- **One element can totally conceal another.** When you start positioning things absolutely, one element can seem to disappear because it's completely covered by another. The `z-index` attribute is a good way to check for this situation.
- **Negative `z-index` is undefined.** The value for `z-index` must be positive. A negative value is undefined and may cause your element to disappear.
- **It may be best to give all values a `z-index`.** If you define the `z-index` for some elements and leave the `z-index` undefined for others, you have no guarantee exactly what will happen. If in doubt, just give every value its own `z-index`, and you'll know exactly what should overlap what.
- **Don't give two elements the same `z-index`.** The point of the `z-index` is to clearly define which element should appear closer. Don't defeat this purpose by assigning the same `z-index` value to two different elements on the same page.

Building a Page Layout with Absolute Positioning

You can use absolute positioning to create a page layout. This process involves some trade-offs. You tend to get better control of your page with absolute positioning (compared to floating techniques), but absolute layout requires more planning and more attention to detail. Figure 4-4 shows a page layout created with absolute positioning techniques.

The technique for creating an absolutely positioned layout is similar to the floating technique (at least, in the general sense).

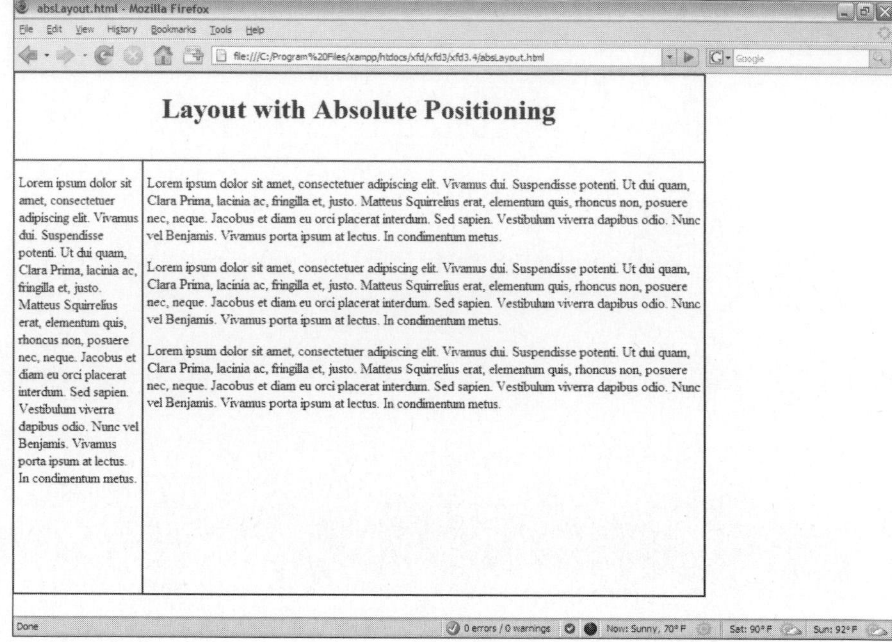

Figure 4-4: This layout was created with absolute positioning.

Overview of absolute layout

Before you begin putting your page together with absolute positioning, it's good to plan the entire process upfront. Here's an example of how the process should go:

1. **Plan the site.**

   Having a drawing specifying how your site layout will look is really important. In absolute positioning, your planning is even more important than the floating designs because you'll need to specify the size and position of every element.

2. **Specify an overall size.**

   This particular type of layout has a fixed size. Create an `all` div housing all the other elements and specify the size of this div (in a fixed unit for now, usually `px` or `em`).

3. **Create the XHTML.**

   The XHTML page should have a named div for each part of the page (so if you have headers, columns, and footers, you need a div for each).

4. **Build a CSS page.**

   The CSS page can be internal or linked, but because absolute positioning tends to require a little more markup than floating, external styles are preferred.

5. **Identify each element.**

   It's easier to see what's going on if you assign a different colored border to each element.

6. **Make each element absolutely positioned.**

   Set `position: absolute` in the CSS for each element in the layout.

7. **Specify the size of each element.**

   Set the `height` and `width` of each element according to your diagram. (You *did* make a diagram, right?)

8. **Determine the position of each element.**

   Use the `left` and `top` attributes to determine where each element goes in the layout.

9. **Tune up your layout.**

   You'll probably want to adjust margins and borders. You may need to do some adjustments to make it all work. For example, the menu is `150px` wide, but I added `padding-left` and `padding-right` of `5px` each. This means the width of the menu needs to be adjusted to `140px` to make everything still fit.

Writing the XHTML

The HTML code is pretty straightforward:

```
<!DOCTYPE html PUBLIC "-//W3C//DTD XHTML 1. 0 Strict//EN"
"http://www. w3. org/TR/xhtml1/DTD/xhtml1-strict. dtd">
<html lang="EN" dir="ltr" xmlns="http://www. w3. org/1999/xhtml">
  <head>
    <meta http-equiv="content-type" content="text/xml; charset=utf-8" />
    <title>absLayout.html</title>
    <link rel = "stylesheet"
          type = "text/css"
          href = "absLayout.css" />
  </head>

  <body>
    <div id = "all">
      <div id = "head">
        <h1>Layout with Absolute Positioning</h1>
      </div>

      <div id = "menu">
      </div>

      <div id = "content">
      </div>
    </div>
  </body>
</html>
```

Adding the CSS

The CSS code is a bit lengthy but not too difficult:

```
/* absLayout.css */
#all {
  border: 1px solid black;
  width: 800px;
  height: 600px;
  position: absolute;
  left: 0px;
  top: 0px;
}

#head {
  border: 1px solid green;
  position: absolute;
  width: 800px;
  height: 100px;
  top: 0px;
  left: 0px;
  text-align: center;
}

#menu {
  border: 1px solid red;
  position: absolute;
  width: 140px;
  height: 500px;
  top: 100px;
  left: 0px;
  padding-left: 5px;
  padding-right: 5px;
}

#content{
  border: 1px solid blue;
  position: absolute;
  width: 645px;
  height: 500px;
  top: 100px;
  left: 150px;
  padding-left: 5px;
}
```

A static layout created with absolute positioning has a few important features to keep in mind:

- **You're committed to position everything.** After you start using absolute positioning, you'll need to use it throughout your site. All the main page elements will require absolute positioning because the normal flow mechanism is no longer in place.

You can still use floating layout *inside* an element with absolute position, but all your main elements (heading, columns, and footing) need to have absolute position if one of them does.

✦ **You should specify size and position.** With a floating layout, you're still encouraging a certain amount of fluidity. Absolute positioning means you're taking the responsibility for both the shape and size of *each* element in the layout.

✦ **Absolute positioning is less adaptable.** With this technique, you're pretty much bound to a specific screen width and height. You'll have trouble adapting to PDAs and cell phones. (A more flexible alternative is shown in the next section.)

✦ **All the widths and the heights have to add up.** When you determine the size of your display, all the heights, widths, margins, padding, and borders have to add up, or you'll get some strange results. When you use absolute positioning, you're also likely to spend some quality time with your calculator, figuring out all the widths and the heights.

Creating a More Flexible Layout

You can build a layout with absolute positioning and some flexibility. Figure 4-5 illustrates such a design.

The size of this layout is attached to the size of the browser screen. It attempts to adjust to the browser while it's resized. You can see this effect in Figure 4-6.

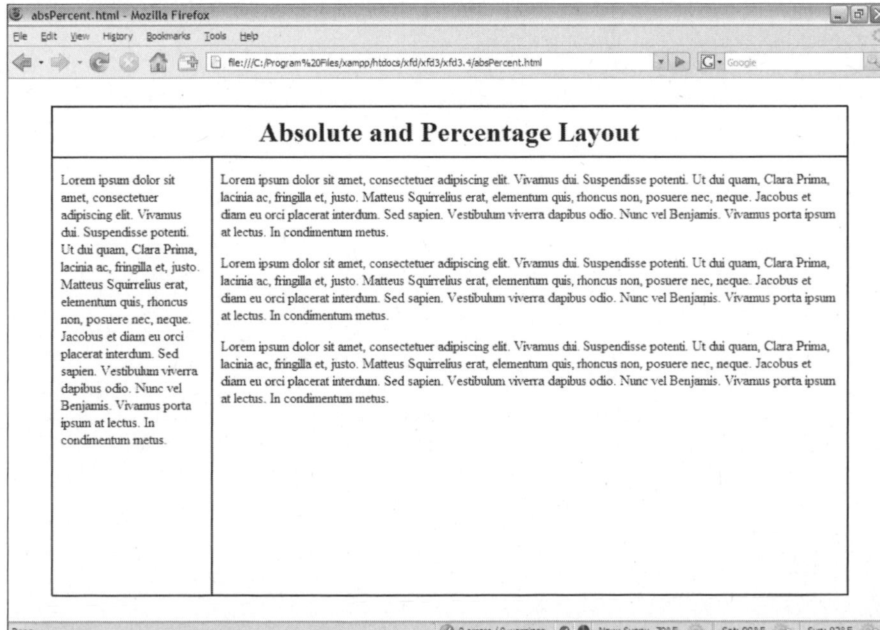

Figure 4-5: This page uses absolute layout, but it doesn't have a fixed size.

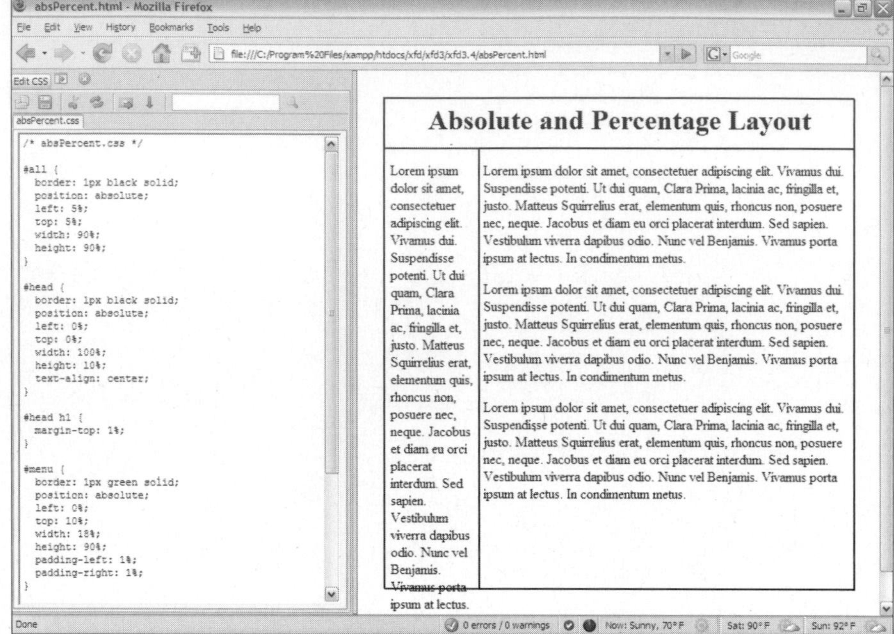

Figure 4-6: The layout resizes in proportion to the browser window.

The page simply takes up a fixed percentage of the browser screen. The proportions are all maintained, no matter what the screen size is.

Having the page resize with the browser works, but it's not a complete solution. When the browser window is small enough, the text will no longer fit without some ugly bleed-over effects.

Designing with percentages

This *absolute but flexible* trick is achieved by using percentage measurements. The position is still set to `absolute`, but rather than defining size and position with pixels, use percentages instead. Here's the CSS:

```
/* absPercent.css */

#all {
  border: 1px black solid;
  position: absolute;
  left: 5%;
  top: 5%;
  width: 90%;
  height: 90%;
}

#head {
  border: 1px black solid;
  position: absolute;
```

```
  left: 0%;
  top: 0%;
  width: 100%;
  height: 10%;
  text-align: center;
}

#head h1 {
  margin-top: 1%;
}

#menu {
  border: 1px green solid;
  position: absolute;
  left: 0%;
  top: 10%;
  width: 18%;
  height: 90%;
  padding-left: 1%;
  padding-right: 1%;
}

#content {
  border: 1px black solid;
  position: absolute;
  left: 20%;
  top: 10%;
  width: 78%;
  height: 90%;
  padding-left: 1%;
  padding-right: 1%;
}
```


The key to any absolute positioning (even this flexible kind) is math. When you just look at the code, it isn't clear where all those numbers come from. Look at the diagram for the page in Figure 4-7 to see where all these numbers come from.

Building the layout

Here's how the layout works:

1. **Create an `all` container by building a div with the `all` ID.**

   The `all` container will hold *all* the contents of the page. It isn't absolutely necessary in this type of layout, but it does allow for a centering effect.

2. **Specify the size and position of `all`.**

   I want the content of the page to be centered in the browser window, so I set its height and width to 90 percent, and its `margin-left` and `margin-top` to 5 percent. This in effect sets the `margin-right` and `margin-bottom` also to 5 percent. These percentages refer to the `all` div's container element, which is the body, with the same size as the browser window.

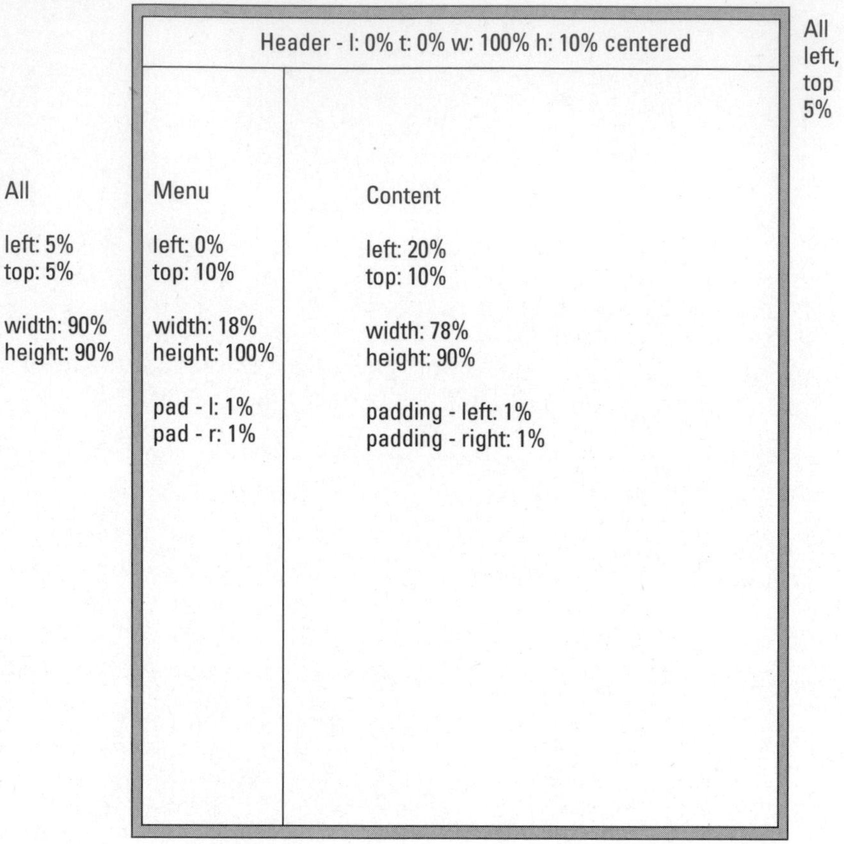

Figure 4-7: The diagram is the key to a successful layout.

3. **Other percentages are in relationship to the `all` container.**

   Because all the other elements are placed inside `all`, the percentage values are no longer referring to the entire browser window. The widths and heights for the menu and content areas are calculated as percentages of their container, which is `all`.

4. **Determine the heights.**

   Height is usually pretty straightforward because you don't usually have to change the margins. Remember, though, that the head accounts for 10 percent of the page space, so the height of both the menu and content needs to be 90 percent.

5. **Figure the general widths.**

   In principle, the width of the menu column is 20 percent, and the content column is 80 percent. This isn't entirely accurate, though. . . .

6. **Compensate for margins.**

   You'll probably want some margins, or the text looks cramped. If you want 1 percent `margin-left` and 1 percent `margin-right` on the menu column, you have to set the menu's width to 18 percent to compensate for the margins. Likewise, set the content width to 78 percent to compensate for margins.

As if this weren't complex enough, remember that Internet Explorer 6 (IE6) and earlier browsers calculate margins differently! In these browsers, the margin happens *inside* the content, so you don't have to compensate for them (but you have to remember that they make the useable content area smaller). You'll probably have to make a conditional comment style sheet to handle IE6 if you use absolute positioning.

Exploring Other Types of Positioning

If you'll use the position attribute, you're most likely to use `absolute`. However, here are other positioning techniques that can be handy in certain circumstances:

- **Relative:** Set `position: relative` when you want to move an element from its default position. For example, if you set position to `relative` and `top: -10px`, the element would be placed 10 pixels higher on the screen than normal.
- **Fixed:** Use fixed position when you want an element to stay in the same place, even when the page is scrolled. This is sometimes used to keep a menu on the screen when the contents are longer than the screen width. If you use fixed positioning, be sure you're not overwriting something already on the screen.

The real trick is to use appropriate combinations of positioning schemes to solve interesting problems.

Creating a fixed menu system

Figure 4-8 illustrates a very common type of Web page — one with a menu on the left and a number of stories or topics in the main area.

Something is interesting about this particular design. The button list on the left refers to specific segments of the page. When you click one of these buttons (say, the Gamma button), the appropriate part of the page is called up, as shown in Figure 4-9.

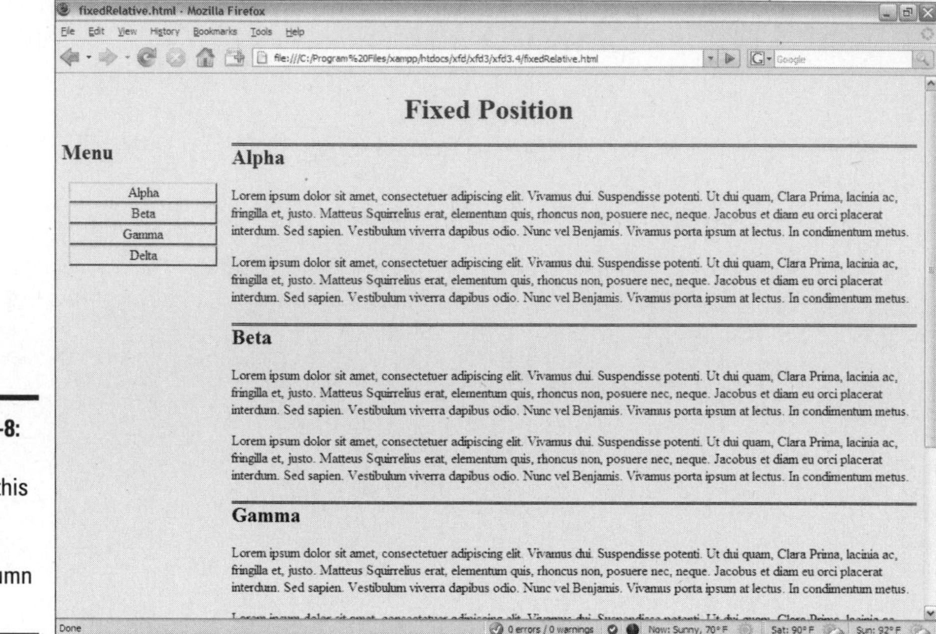

Figure 4-8: At first glance, this is yet another two-column layout.

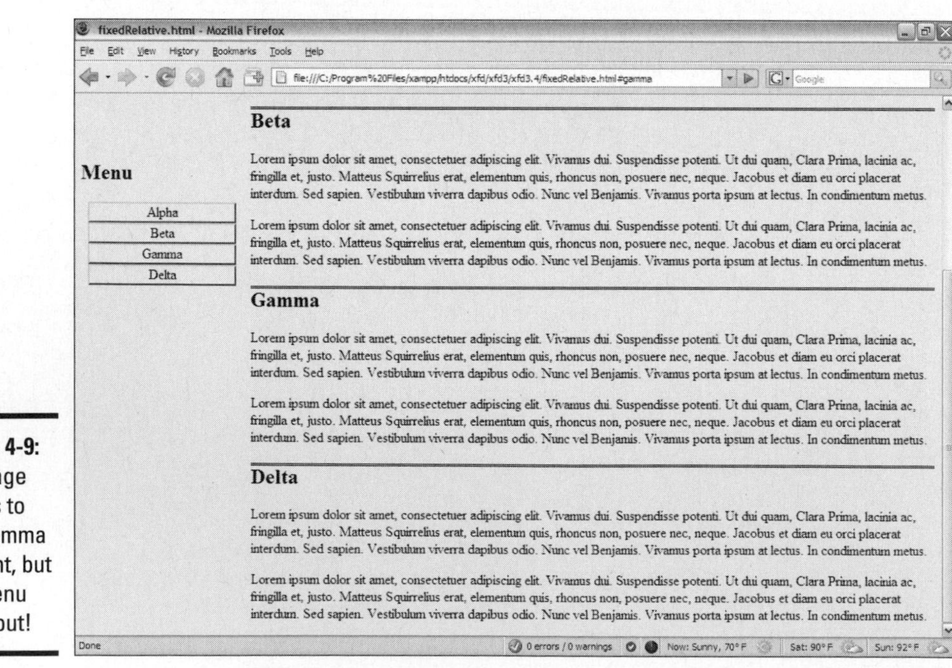

Figure 4-9: The page scrolls to the Gamma content, but the menu stays put!

Normally, when you scroll down the page, things on the top of the page (like the menu) disappear. In this case, the menu stays on the screen, even though the part of the page where it was originally placed is now off the screen.

Gamma isn't necessarily moved to the top of the page. Linking to an element ensures that it's visible but doesn't guarantee where it will appear.

You can achieve this effect using a combination of positioning techniques.

Setting up the XHTML

The HTML for the fixed menu page is simple (as you'd expect by now):

```
<!DOCTYPE html PUBLIC "-//W3C//DTD XHTML 1. 0 Strict//EN"
"http://www. w3. org/TR/xhtml1/DTD/xhtml1-strict. dtd">
<html lang="EN" dir="ltr" xmlns="http://www. w3. org/1999/xhtml">
  <head>
    <meta http-equiv="content-type" content="text/xml; charset=utf-8" />
    <title>fixedRelative.html</title>
    <link rel = "stylesheet"
          type = "text/css"
          href = "fixedRelative.css" />
  </head>

  <body>
    <h1>Fixed Position</h1>
    <div id = "menu">
      <ul>
        <li><a href = "#alpha">Alpha</a></li>
        <li><a href = "#beta">Beta</a></li>
        <li><a href = "#gamma">Gamma</a></li>
        <li><a href = "#delta">Delta</a></li>
      </ul>
    </div>

    <div class = "content"
         id = "alpha">
        <h2>Alpha</h2>
    </div>

    <div class = "content"
         id = "beta">
        <h2>Beta</h2>
    </div>

    <div class = "content"
         id = "gamma">
        <h2>Gamma</h2>
    </div>

    <div class = "content"
         id = "delta">
        <h2>Delta</h2>
    </div>

  </body>
</html>
```

The XHTML has only a few noteworthy characteristics:

- ✦ **It has a menu.** The div named `menu` contains a list of links (like most menus).
- ✦ **The menu has internal links.** A menu can contain links to external documents or (like this one) links inside the current document. The `<a href = "#alpha">Alpha</a>` code means create a link to the element in this page with the ID `alpha`.
- ✦ **The page has a series of `content` divs.** Most of the page's content appears in one of the several divs with the `content` class. This class indicates all these divs will share some formatting.
- ✦ **The `content` divs have separate IDs.** Although all the `content` divs are part of the same class, each has its own ID. This allows the menu to select individual items (and would also allow individual styling, if desired).

As normal for this type of code, I left out the filler paragraphs from the code listing.

Setting the CSS values

The interesting work happens in CSS. Here's an overview of the code:

```
/* fixedRelative.css */

body {
  background-color: #fff9bf;
}

h1 {
 text-align: center;
}

#menu {
  position: fixed;
  width: 18%;
}

#menu li {
  list-style-type: none;
  margin-left: -2em;
  text-align: center;
}

#menu a{
  display: block;
  border: 2px gray outset;
  text-decoration: none;
  color: black;
}

#menu a:hover{
  color: white;
  background-color: black;
```

```
  border: 2px gray inset;
}

#menu h2 {
  text-align: center;
}

. content {
  position: relative;
  left: 20%;
  width: 80%;
}

. content h2 {
  border-top: 3px black double;
}
```

Most of the CSS is familiar if you've looked over the other chapters in this minibook. I changed the menu list to make it look like a set of buttons, and I added some basic formatting to the headings and borders. The interesting thing here is how I positioned various elements.

Here's how you build a fixed menu:

1. **Set the menu position to `fixed` by setting the `position` attribute to `fixed`.**

   The `menu` div should stay on the same spot, even while the rest of the page scrolls. Fixed positioning causes the menu to stay put, no matter what else happens on the page.

2. **Give the menu a `width` with the `width` attribute.**

   It's important that the width of the menu be predictable, both for aesthetic reasons and to make sure the content isn't overwritten by the menu. In this example, I set the menu width to 18 percent of the page width (20 percent minus some margin space).

3. **Consider the menu position by explicitly setting the `top` and `left` attributes.**

   When you specify a fixed position, you can determine where the element is placed on the screen with the `left` and `top` attributes. I felt that the default position was fine, so I didn't change it.

4. **Set `content` position to `relative`.**

   By default, all members of the `content` class will fill out the entire page width. Because the menu needs the leftmost 20 percent of the page, set the `content` class' position to `relative`.

5. **Change `content`'s `left` attribute to 20 percent.**

   Because `content` has `relative` positioning, setting the left to 20 percent will add 20 percent of the parent element to each `content`'s `left` value. This will ensure that there's room for the menu to the left of all the content panes.

6. **Give `content` a `width` property.**

   If you don't define the width, `content` panels may bleed off the right side of the page. Use the `width` property to ensure this doesn't happen.

Determining Your Layout Scheme

All these layout options might just make your head spin. What's the right strategy? Well, that depends.

The most important thing is that you find a technique you're comfortable with that gives you all the flexibility you need.

Absolute positioning seems very attractive at first because it promises so much control. The truth is, it's pretty complicated to pull off well, it isn't quite as flexible as the floating layout techniques, and it's hard to make work right in the older browsers.

Floating layouts are generally your best bet, but it's good to know how absolute positioning works. Every once in a while, you'll find a situation where absolute positioning is a good idea. You'll see another example of absolute positioning in Chapter 7 of Book IV when you animate the position of an element on the screen.

Sometimes, fixed and relative positioning schemes are handy, as in the example introduced in the preceding section.

Sometimes, you'll find it's best to combine schemes. (It's difficult to combine absolute positioning with another scheme, but you can safely combine floating, fixed, and relative positioning techniques most of the time.)

There really aren't any set answers. CSS layout is still an art in progress, and there's plenty to find out about that I can't describe in this book. Keep practicing and keep exploring, and you'll be building beautiful and functional layouts in no time.

Book IV

Client-Side Programming with JavaScript

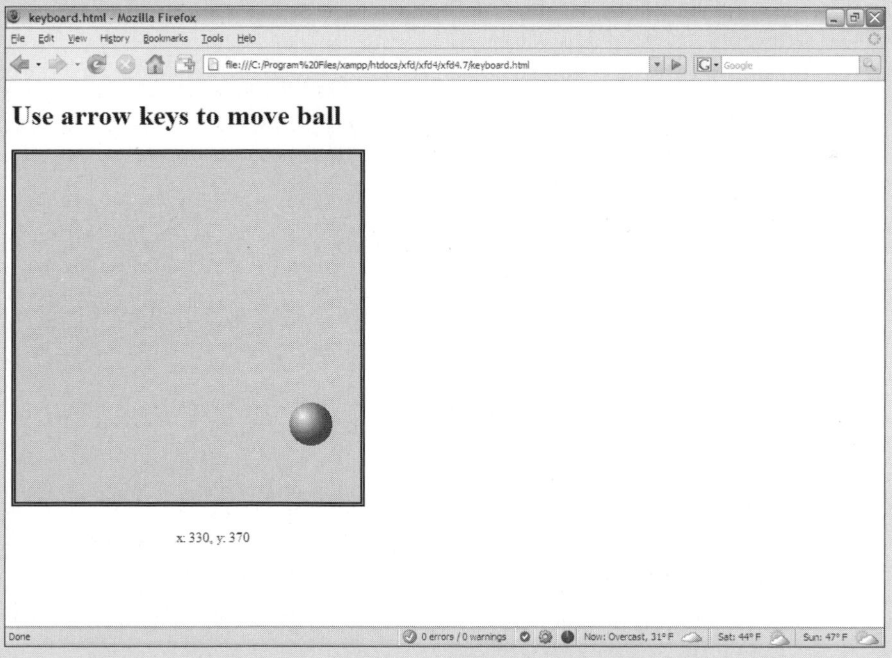

JavaScript code adds interactivity for checking input and even making games and animations.

Contents at a Glance

Chapter 1: Getting Started with JavaScript

In This Chapter

- **Adding JavaScript code to your pages**
- **Setting up your environment for JavaScript**
- **Creating variables**
- **Inputting and outputting with modal dialogs**
- **Using Concatenation to build text data**
- **Understanding data types**
- **Using string methods and properties**
- **Using conversion functions**

Web pages are defined by the XHTML code and fleshed out by CSS. But to make them move and breathe, sing, and dance, you need to add a programming language or two. If you thought building Web pages was cool, you're going to love what you can do once you do a little programming. Programming is what makes pages interact with the user. Interactivity is the "new" in "new media" (if you ask me, anyway). Learn to program, and your pages come alive.

Sometimes people are nervous about programming. It seems difficult and mysterious, and only super-geeks do it. That's a bunch of nonsense. Programming is no more difficult than XHTML and CSS. It's a natural extension, and you're going to like it.

In this chapter, you discover how to add code to your Web pages. You use a language called JavaScript, which is already built into most Web browsers. You don't need to buy any special software, compilers, or special tools, because you build JavaScript just like XHTML and CSS — in an ordinary text editor or a specialty editor like Aptana.

Working in JavaScript

JavaScript is a programming language first developed by Netscape Communications. It is now standard on nearly every browser. You should know a few things about JavaScript right away:

- **It's a real programming language.** Don't let anybody tell you otherwise. Sure, JavaScript doesn't have all the same features as a monster like C++ or VB.NET, but it's still got all the hallmarks of a complete programming language.
- **It's not Java.** Sun Microsystems developed a language called Java, which is also sometimes used in Web programming. Despite the similar names, Java and JavaScript are completely different languages. The original plan was for JavaScript to be a simpler language for controlling more complex Java applets, but that never really panned out.

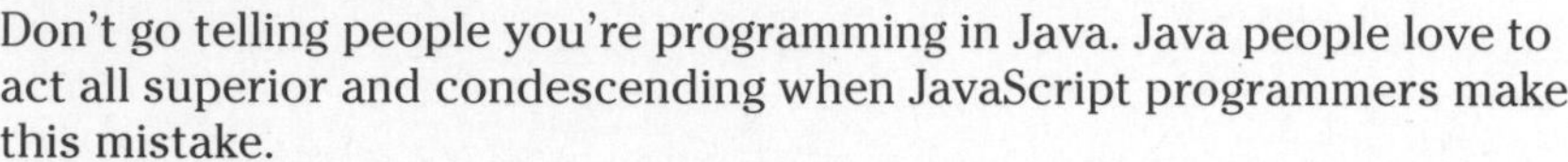

Don't go telling people you're programming in Java. Java people love to act all superior and condescending when JavaScript programmers make this mistake.

- **It's a scripting language.** As programming languages go, JavaScript's pretty friendly. It's not quite as strict or wordy as some other languages. It also doesn't require any special steps (like compilation), so it's pretty easy to use. These things make JavaScript a great first language.

Choosing a JavaScript editor

Even though JavaScript is a programming language, it is still basically text. Because it's normally embedded in a Web page, you can work in the same text editor you're using for XHTML and CSS. If you aren't already, I recommend that you use the powerful Aptana editor. Aptana is great for XHTML and CSS, but it really comes into its own when you use it to incorporate JavaScript code in your pages.

JavaScript is an entirely different language and syntax than HTML and CSS. It isn't hard to learn, but there's a lot to learning any programming language. Aptana has a number of great features that help you tremendously when writing JavaScript code:

- **Syntax highlighting:** Just like HTML and CSS, Aptana automatically adjusts code colors to help you see what's going on in your program. As you see in the sidebar "Concatenation and your editor" in this chapter, this adjustment can be a big benefit when things get complicated.
- **Code completion:** When you type the name of an object, Aptana provides you with a list of possible completions. This shortcut can be really helpful because you don't have to memorize all the details of the various functions and commands.
- **Help files**: The Start page (available from the File menu if you've dismissed it) has links to great help pages for HTML, CSS, and JavaScript. The documentation is actually easier to read than some of what you'll find on the Web.

- **Integrated help:** Hover the mouse over a JavaScript command or method, and a nifty little text box pops up to explain exactly how the feature works. Often, it even includes an example or two.
- **Error warnings:** When Aptana can tell something is going wrong, it gives you an error message and places a red squiggly (such as the one spellcheckers use) under the suspect code.

I'm unaware of a better JavaScript editor at any price, and Aptana is free, so there's just not a good reason to use anything else. Of course, you can use any text editor if you don't want or need those features. Any of the following text editors (all mentioned in Book 1, Chapter 3) are suitable for JavaScript work:

- Notepad++
- VI / VIM
- Emacs
- Scintilla
- jEdit

There's one strange characteristic I've noticed in Aptana. The Preview tab isn't as reliable a technique for checking JavaScript code as it was in XHTML and CSS. I find it better to run the code directly in my browser or use the Run button to have Aptana run it in the external browser for me.

Picking your test browser

In addition to your editor, you should think again about your browser when you're testing JavaScript code. All the major browsers support JavaScript, and the support for JavaScript is relatively similar across the browsers (at least for the stuff in this chapter). However, browsers aren't equal when it comes to testing your code.

Things will go wrong when you write JavaScript code, and the browser is responsible for telling you what went wrong. Firefox is way ahead of Internet Explorer when it comes to reporting errors. Firefox errors are much easier to read and understand, and Firefox supports a thing called the *javascript console* (described in Chapter 3 of this minibook that makes it much easier to see what's going on. If at all possible, use Firefox to test your code and then check for discrepancies in Internet Explorer.

You can discover more about finding and fixing errors in Chapter 3 of this minibook.

Hello World?

There's a long tradition in programming languages that your first program in any language should simply say, "Hello, World!" and do nothing else. There's actually a very good practical reason for this habit. Hello World is the simplest possible program you can write that you can prove works. Hello World programs are used to help you figure out the mechanics of the programming environment — how the program is written, what special steps you have to do to make the code run, and how it works. There's no point in making a more complicated program until you know you can get code to pop up and say hi.

Writing Your First JavaScript Program

The foundation of any JavaScript program is a standard Web page like the ones featured in the first three minibooks.

To create your first JavaScript program, the first thing you need to do is add JavaScript code to your pages. Figure 1-1 shows the classic first program in any language.

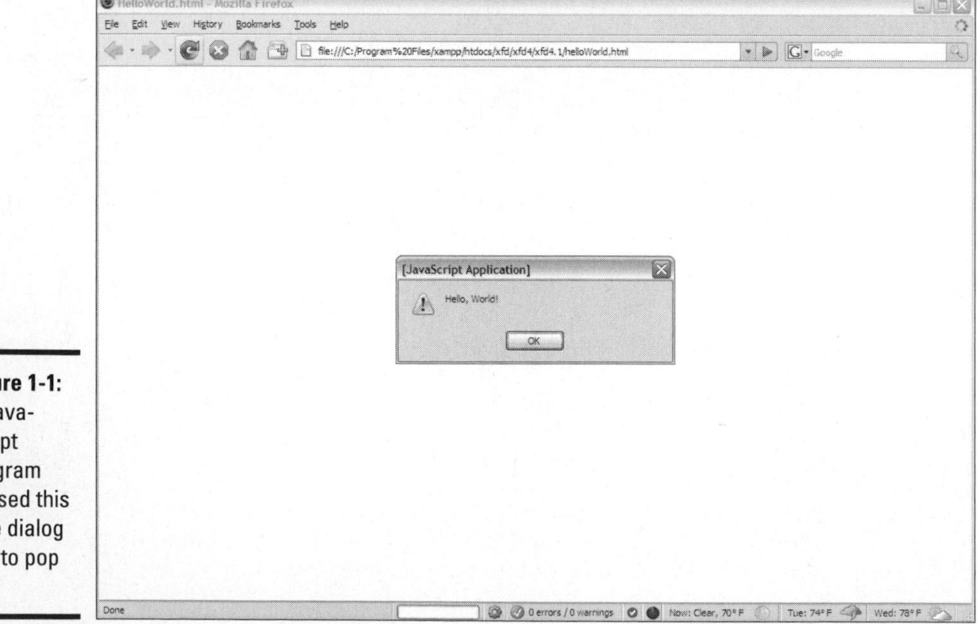

Figure 1-1: A JavaScript program caused this little dialog box to pop up!

This page has a very simple JavaScript program in it that pops up the phrase "Hello, World!" in a special element called a *dialog box*. It's pretty cool.

Here's an overview of the code:

```
<!DOCTYPE html PUBLIC "-//W3C//DTD XHTML 1.0 Strict//EN"
"http://www.w3.org/TR/xhtml1/DTD/xhtml1-strict.dtd">
<html lang="EN" dir="ltr" xmlns="http://www.w3.org/1999/xhtml">
  <head>
    <meta http-equiv="content-type" content="text/xml; charset=utf-8" />
    <title>HelloWorld.html</title>
    <script type = "text/javascript">
      //<![CDATA[
        // Hello, world!
        alert("Hello, World!");
      //]]>
    </script>
  </head>

  <body>

  </body>
</html>
```

As you can see, this page contains nothing in the HTML body. You can incorporate JavaScript with XHTML content. For now, though, you can simply place JavaScript code in the head area in a special tag and make it work.

Embedding your JavaScript code

JavaScript code is placed in your Web page via the `<script>` tag. JavaScript code is placed inside the `<script></script>` pair. The `<script>` tag has one required attribute, `type`, which will usually be `text/javascript`. (Other types are possible, but they're rarely used.)

The other funny thing in this page is that crazy CDATA stuff. Immediately inside the script tag, the next line is:

```
//<![CDATA[
```


This bizarre line is a special marker explaining that the following code is character information and shouldn't be interpreted as XHTML. The end of the script finishes off the character data marker with this code:

```
//]]>
```

In modern browsers, it's a good idea to mark off your JavaScript code as character data. If you don't, the XHTML validator will sometimes get confused and claim you have errors when you don't.

That CDATA business is bizarre. It's hard to memorize, I know, but just type it a few times, and you'll own it.

A lot of older books and Web sites don't recommend the character data trick, but it's well worth learning. You've invested too much effort into building standards-compliant pages to have undeserved error messages pop up because the browser thinks your JavaScript is badly formatted XHTML.

Creating comments

Just like XHTML and CSS, comments are important. Because programming code can be more difficult to decipher than XHTML or CSS, it's even more important to comment your code in JavaScript than it is in these environments. The comment character in JavaScript is two slashes (//).The browser ignores everything from the two slashes to the end of the line. You can also use a multi-line comment (/* */) just like the one in CSS.

Using the alert() method for output

You can output data in JavaScript in a number of ways. In this introductory chapter, I focus on the simplest to implement and understand — the `alert()`.

This technique pops up a small dialog box containing text for the user to read. The alert box is an example of a *modal dialog*. Modal dialogs interrupt the flow of the program until the user pays attention to them. Nothing else will happen in the program until the user acknowledges the dialog by clicking the OK button. The user can't interact with the page until he clicks the button.

Modal dialogs may seem a bit rude. In fact, you probably won't use them much once you discover other input and output techniques. The fact that the dialog box demands attention makes it a very easy tool to use when you start programming. I use it (and one of its cousins) throughout this chapter because it's easy to understand and use.

Adding the semicolon

Each command in JavaScript ends with a semicolon (;) character. The semicolon in most computer languages acts like the period in English. It indicates the end of a logical thought. Usually, each line of code is also one line in the editor.

To tell the truth, JavaScript will usually work fine if you leave out the semicolons. However, you should add them anyway because they help clarify your meaning. Besides, most other languages, including PHP (see Book V), requires semicolons. You may as well start a good habit now.

Introducing Variables

Computer programs get their power by working with information. Figure 1-2 shows a program that gets user data from the user to include in a customized greeting.

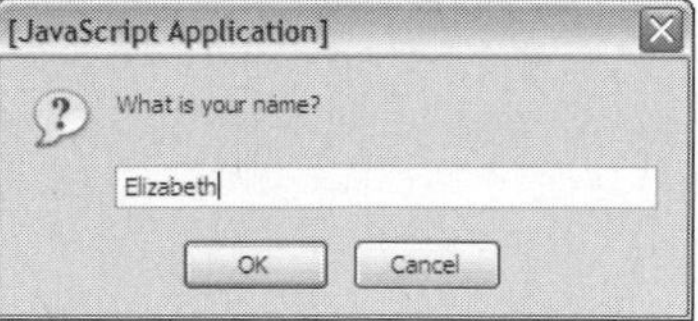

Figure 1-2: First, the program asks the user for her name.

This program introduces a new kind of dialog that allows the user to enter some data. The information is stored in the program for later use. After the user enters her name, she gets a greeting, as shown in Figure 1-3.

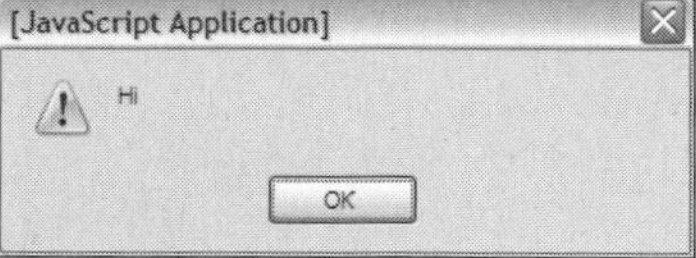

Figure 1-3: The start of the greeting. Press the button for the rest.

The rest of the greeting happens on a second alert dialog, shown in Figure 1.4. It incorporates the username supplied in the first dialog box.

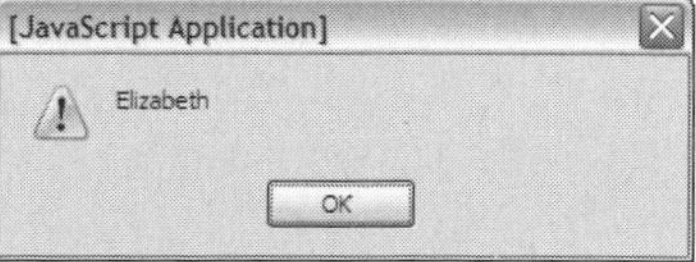

Figure 1-4: Now the greeting is complete.

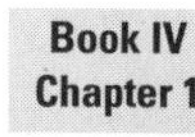

The output may not seem that incredible, but take a look at the source code to see what's happening:

```
<!DOCTYPE html PUBLIC "-//W3C//DTD XHTML 1.0 Strict//EN"
"http://www.w3.org/TR/xhtml1/DTD/xhtml1-strict.dtd">
<html lang="EN" dir="ltr" xmlns="http://www.w3.org/1999/xhtml">
  <head>
    <meta http-equiv="content-type" content="text/xml; charset=utf-8" />
    <title>prompt.html</title>
    <script type = "text/javascript">
      //<![CDATA[

      var person = "";
      person = prompt("What is your name?");
      alert("Hi");
      alert(person);

      //]]>
    </script>
  </head>

  <body>

  </body>
</html>
```

Creating a variable for data storage

This program is interesting because it allows user interaction. The user can enter a name, which is stored in the computer and then returned in a greeting. The key to this program is a special element called a *variable*. Variables are simply places in memory for holding data. Any time you want a computer program to "remember" something, you can create a variable and store your information in it.

Variables typically have the following characteristics:

- **The `var` statement:** You can indicate that you're creating a variable with the `var` command.
- **A name:** When you create a variable, you're required to give it a name.
- **An initial value:** It's useful to give each variable a value immediately.
- **A data type:** JavaScript automatically determines the type of data in a variable (more on this in the section called "Understanding Variable Types"), but you should still be clear in your mind what type of data you expect a variable to contain.

Asking the user for information

The `prompt` statement does several interesting things:

- **Pops up a dialog box.** It creates a modal dialog much like the `alert()` method does.
- **Asks a question.** The `prompt()` command expects you to ask the user a question.

- **Provides space for a response.** The dialog box contains a space for the user to type a response, as well as buttons for the user to click when he's finished or wants to cancel the operation.
- **Passes the information to a variable.** The purpose of a `prompt` is to get data from the user, so prompts are nearly always connected to a variable. When the code is finished, the variable contains the indicated value.

Responding to the user

This program uses the `alert()` statement to begin a greeting to the user. The first alert works just like the one from the `helloWorld` program, described earlier in this chapter in the section "Writing Your First JavaScript Program":

```
alert("Hi");
```

The content of the parentheses is the text you want the user to see. In this case, you want the user to see the literal value `"Hi"`.

The second alert statement is a little bit different:

```
alert(person);
```

This `alert` statement has a parameter with no quotes. Because the parameter has no quotes, JavaScript understands that you don't really want to say the text *person*. Instead, it looks for a variable named `person`, and returns the value of that variable.

The variable can take any name, store it, and return a customized greeting.

Using Concatenation to Build Better Greetings

It seems a little awkward to have a greeting and a person's name on two different lines. Figure 1-5 shows a better solution.

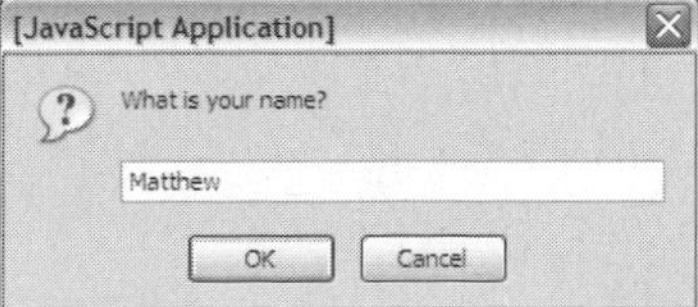

Figure 1-5: Once again, I ask the user for a name.

The program asks for a name again and stores it in a variable. This time, the greeting is combined into one alert (see Figure 1-6), and it looks a lot better.

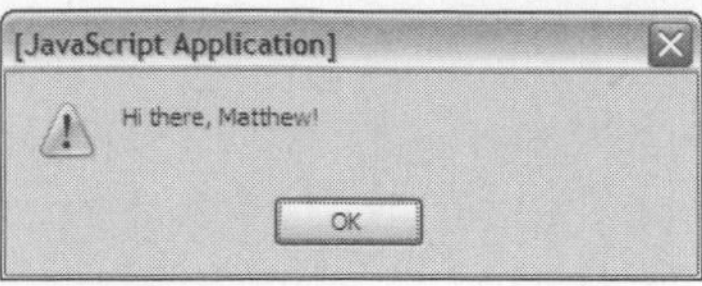

Figure 1-6: Now the user's name is integrated into the greeting.

The secret to Figure 1-6 is one of those wonderful gems of the computing world: a really simple idea with a really complicated name. The term "concatenation" is a delightfully complicated word for a basic process. Take a look at the following code, and you see that combining variables with text is not all that complicated:

```
<script type = "text/javascript">
  //<![CDATA[
  // from concat.html

  var person = "";
  person = prompt("What is your name?");
  alert("Hi there, " + person + "!");

  //]]>
</script>
```

For the sake of brevity, I include only the script tag and its contents throughout this chapter. The rest of this page is a standard blank XHTML page. As always, you can see the complete document on the Web site or CD-ROM. I do include a comment in each JavaScript snippet that indicates where you can get the entire file on the CD-ROM.

Comparing literals and variables

The program `concat.html` contains two different kinds of text. The term "Hi there, " is a *literal* text value. That is, you really mean to say "Hi there, " (including the comma and the space). `Person` is a variable. (For more on variables, see the section "Introducing Variables," earlier in this chapter.

You can combine literal values and variables in one phrase if you want:

```
alert("Hi there, " + person + "!");
```

The secret to this code is to follow the quotes. `"Hi there, "` is a literal value, because it is in quotes. On the other hand, `person` is a variable name, because it is *not* in quotes, and `"!"` is a literal value. You can combine any number of text snippets together with the plus sign.

Using the plus sign to combine text is called *concatenation*. (I told you it was a complicated word for a simple idea.)

Including spaces in your concatenated phrases

You may be curious about the extra space between the comma and the quote in the output line:

```
alert("Hi there, " + person + "!");
```

This extra space is important because you want the output to look like a normal sentence. If you don't have the space, the computer doesn't add one, and the output looks like this:

```
Hi there,Benjamin!
```

You need to construct the output as it should look, including spaces and punctuation.

Understanding the String Object

The `person` variable used in the previous program is designed to hold text. Programmers (being programmers) devised their own mysterious term to refer to text. In programming, text is referred to as *string* data.

Concatenation and your editor

The hard part about concatenation is figuring out which part of your text is a literal value and which part is a string. It won't take long before you start going cross-eyed trying to understand where the quotes go.

Modern text editors (like Aptana) have a wonderful feature that can help you here. They color different kinds of text in different colors. By default, Aptana colors variable names black and literal text dark green (at least when you're in JavaScript — in HTML, literal text is in blue).

I personally find it hard to differentiate the dark green from black, so I changed the Aptana color scheme. I have it make string literals blue whether I'm in JavaScript or HTML. I find this color more consistent and easier for me to read. With this setting in place, I can easily see what part of the statement is literal text and what's being read as a variable name. That makes concatenation a lot easier.

To change the color scheme in Aptana, choose Window⇨Preferences. An expandable outline appears in the resulting dialog box. In the section Aptana — Editors — JavaScript Editor — colors, scroll down to find color settings for any type of data. I found string (another term for text) under literals and changed the color from dark green to blue.

If you make a mistake, the "Restore Defaults" button reverts back to the default values.

Most editors that have syntax highlighting allow you to change settings to fit your needs. Don't be afraid to use these tools to help you program better.

The term *string* comes from the way text is stored in computer memory. Each character is stored in its own cell in memory, and all the characters in a word or phrase reminded the early programmers of beads on a string. Surprisingly poetic for a bunch of geeks, huh?

Introducing object-based programming (and cows)

JavaScript (and many other modern programming languages) use a powerful model called *object-oriented programming (OOP)*. This style of programming has a number of advantages. Most important for beginners, it allows you access to some very powerful objects that do interesting things out of the box.

Objects are used to describe complicated things that can have a lot of characteristics — like a cow. You can't really put an adequate description of a cow in an integer variable.

In many object-oriented environments, objects can have the following characteristics. (Imagine a cow object for the examples.)

- **Properties:** Characteristics about the object, such as `breed()` and `age()`
- **Methods:** Things the objects can do, such as `moo()` and `giveMilk()`
- **Events:** Stimuli the object responds to, such `onTip`

I describe each of these ideas throughout this minibook, as not all objects support all these characteristics.

If you have a variable of type `cow`, it describes a pretty complicated thing. This thing might have properties, methods, and events, all which can be used together to build a good representation of a cow. (Believe it or not, I've built cow programming constructs more than once in my life — and you thought programming was dull!)

Most variable types in Java are actually objects, and most JavaScript objects have a full complement of properties and methods; many even have event handlers. Master how these things work, and you've got a powerful and compelling programming environment.

Okay, before you send me any angry e-mails, I know debate abounds about whether JavaScript is a *truly* object-oriented language. I'm not going to get into the (frankly boring and not terribly important) details in this beginner book. We're going to call JavaScript object-oriented for now, because it's close enough for beginners. If that bothers you, you can refer to JavaScript as an object-based language. Nearly everyone agrees with that. You can find out more information on this topic throughout this minibook as you discover how to use HTML elements as objects in Chapter 5.

Investigating the length of a string

When you assign text to a variable, JavaScript automatically treats the variable as a string object. The object instantly takes on the characteristics of a string object. Strings have a couple of properties and a bunch of methods. The one interesting property (at least for beginners) is `length`. Look at the example in Figure 1-7 to see the `length` property in action.

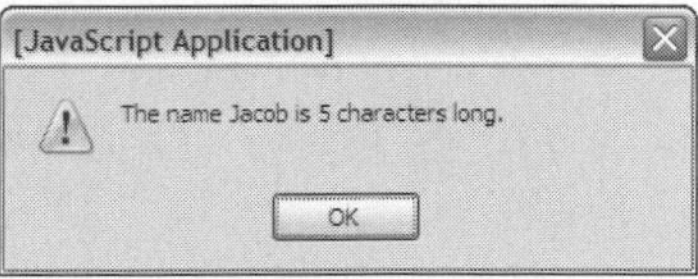

Figure 1-7: This program reports the length of any text.

That's kind of cool how the program can figure out the length of a phrase. The cooler part is the way it works. As soon as you assign a text value to a variable, JavaScript treats that variable as a string, and because it's a string, it now has a `length` property. This property returns the length of the string in characters. Here's how it's done in the code.

```
<script type = "text/javascript">
  //<![CDATA[
  //from nameLength.html

  var person = prompt("Please enter your name.");
  var length = person.length;

  alert("Hi, " + person + "!");
  alert("The name " + person + " is " + length + " characters long.");

  //]]>
</script>
```

A property is used like a special subvariable. For example, `person` is a variable in the previous example. `person.length` is the `length` property of the `person` variable. In JavaScript, an object and a variable are connected by a period (with no spaces).

The `string` object in JavaScript has only two other properties (`constructor` and `prototype`). Both of these properties are needed only for advanced programming, so I skip them for now.

Using string methods to manipulate text

The `length` property is kind of cool, but the string object has a lot more up its sleeve. Objects also have *methods* (things the object can do). Strings in JavaScript have all kinds of methods. Here are a few of my favorites:

- `toUpperCase()` makes an entirely uppercase copy of the string.
- `toLowerCase()` makes an entirely lowercase copy of the string.
- `substring()` returns a specific part of the string.
- `indexOf()` determines whether one string occurs within another.

The string object has many other methods, but I'm highlighting the preceding because they're useful for beginners. Many string methods, such as `big()` and `fontColor()`, simply add HTML code to text. They aren't used very often because they produce HTML code that won't validate, and they don't really save a lot of effort anyway. Some other methods, such as `search()`, `replace()`, and `slice()`, use advanced constructs like arrays and regular expressions that aren't necessary for beginners. (To find out more about working with arrays, see Chapter 4 of this minibook. You can find out more about regular expressions in Chapter 6.)

Don't take my word for it. Look up the JavaScript string object in the Aptana online help (or one of the many other online JavaScript references) and see what properties and methods it has.

Like properties, methods are attached to an object by the period. Methods are distinguished by a pair of parentheses, which sometimes contains special information called *parameters*.

The best way to see how methods work is to look at some in action. Look at the code for `stringMethods.html`:

```
<script type = "text/javascript">
  //<![CDATA[
  //from stringMethods.html

  var text = prompt("Please enter some text.");

  alert("I'll shout it out:");
  alert(text.toUpperCase());

  alert("Now in lowercase...");
  alert(text.toLowerCase());

  alert("The first 'a' is at letter...");
  alert(text.indexOf("a"));

  alert("The first three letters are ...");
  alert(text.substring(0, 3));

  //]]>
</script>
```

Figure 1-8 displays the output produced by this program.

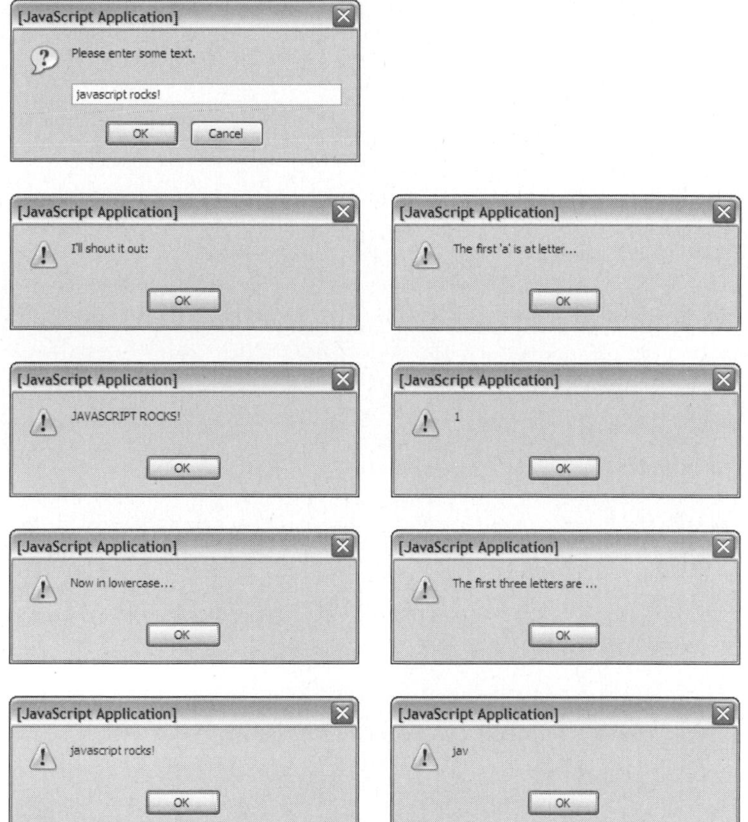

Figure 1-8: String methods can be fun.

Here's yet another cool thing about Aptana. When you type the term `text`, Aptana understands that you're talking about a string variable and automatically pops up a list of all the possible properties and methods. I wish I'd had that when I started doing this stuff!

You can see from the preceding code that methods are pretty easy to use. Once you have a string variable, you can invoke the variable name followed by a period and the method name. Some methods require more information to do their job. Here are the specifics:

✦ `toUpperCase()` and `toLowerCase()` take the value of the variable and convert it entirely to the given case. This method is often used when you aren't concerned about the capitalization of a variable.

- `indexOf(substring)` returns the character position of the substring within the variable. If the variable doesn't contain the substring, it returns the value -1.
- `substring(begin, end)` returns the substring of the variable from the beginning character value to the end.

Understanding Variable Types

JavaScript isn't too fussy about whether a variable contains text or a number, but the distinction is still important because it can cause some surprising problems. To illustrate, take a look at a program that adds two numbers together, and then see what happens when you try to get numbers from the user to add.

Adding numbers

First, take a look at the following program:

```
<script type = "text/javascript">
  //<![CDATA
  //from addNumbers.html

  var x = 5;
  var y = 3;
  var sum = x + y;

  alert(x + " plus " + y + " equals " + sum);

  //]]>
</script>
```

(As usual for this chapter, I'm only showing the script part because the rest of the page is blank.)

Why are the first three characters (0, 3)?

The character locations for JavaScript (and most programming languages) will seem somewhat strange to you until you know the secret. You may expect `text.substring(1,3)` to return the first three characters of the variable `text`, yet I used `text.substring(0,3)`. Here's why: The indices don't refer to the character numbers but to the indices *between* characters.

```
|a|b|c|d|
0 1 2 3 4
```

So, if I want the first three characters of the string "abcd", I use `substring(0,3)`. If I want the "cd" part, it's `substring(2,4)`.

This program features three variables. I've assigned the value 5 to x, and 3 to y. I then add x + y and assign the result to a third variable, sum. The last line prints the results, which are also shown in Figure 1-9.

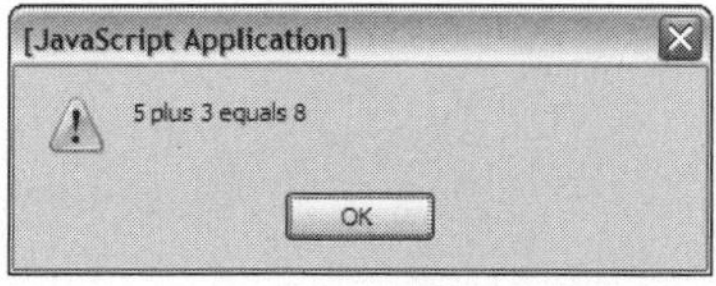

Figure 1-9: This program (correctly) adds two numbers together.

Note a few important things from this example:

- **You can assign values to variables.** It's best to read the equals sign as "gets" so that the first assignment is read as "variable x gets the value 5."

```
var x = 5;
```

- **Numeric values aren't enclosed in quotes.** When you refer to a text literal value, it's always enclosed in quotes. Numeric data, such as the value 5, isn't placed in quotes.
- **You can add numeric values.** Because x and y both contain numeric values, you can add them together.
- **You can replace the results of an operation in a variable.** The result of the calculation x + y is placed in a variable called sum.
- **Everything works as expected.** The behavior of this program works as expected. That's important because it's not always true. (You can see an example of this behavior in the next section — I love writing code that blows up on purpose!)

Adding the user's numbers

The natural extension of the addNumbers.html program is a feature that allows the user to input two values and then returns the sum. This program can be the basis for a simple adding machine. Here's the JavaScript code:

```
<script type = "text/javascript">
  //<![CDATA[
  //from addInputWrong.html

  var x = prompt("first number:");
  var y = prompt("second number:");
  var sum = x + y;
```

```
    alert(x + " plus " + y + " equals " + sum);

    //]]>
  </script>
```

This code seems reasonable enough. It asks for each value and stores them in variables. It then adds the variables up and returns the results, right? Well, look at Figure 1-10 to see a surprise.

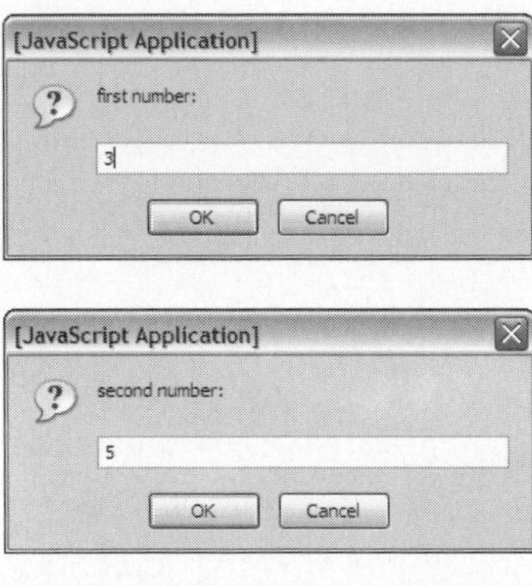

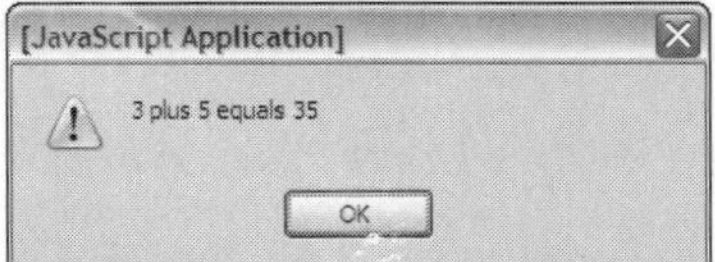

Figure 1-10: Wait a minute . . . 3 + 5 = 35???

Something's obviously not right here. To understand the problem, you need to see how JavaScript makes guesses about data types (see the next section).

The trouble with dynamic data

Ultimately, all the information stored in a computer, from music videos to e-mails, is stored as a bunch of ones and zeroes. The same value 01000001 can mean all kinds of things: It may mean the number 65 or the character `A`. (In fact, it does mean both those things in the right context.) The same binary value may mean something entirely different if it's interpreted as a real number, a color, or a part of a sound file.

The theory isn't critical here, but one point is really important: Somehow the computer has to know what kind of data is stored in a specific variable. Many languages, such as C and Java, have all kinds of rules about defining data. If you create a variable in one of these languages, you have to define exactly what kind of data will go in the variable, and you can't change it.

JavaScript is much more easygoing about variable types. When you make a variable, you can put any kind of data in it that you want. In fact, the data type can change. A variable can contain an integer at one point, and the same variable may contain text in another part of the program.

JavaScript uses the context to determine how to interpret the data in a particular variable. When you assign a value to a variable, JavaScript puts the data in one of the following categories:

- *Integers* are whole numbers (no decimal part). They can be positive or negative values.
- A *floating point number* has a decimal point — for example, 3.14. You can also express floating point values in scientific notation, such as 6.02e23 (Avagadro's number –6.02 times 10 to the 23rd). Floating point numbers can also be negative.
- A *Boolean* value can only be true or false.
- Text is usually referred to as *string* data in programming languages. String values are usually enclosed in quotes.
- *Arrays* and *objects* are more complex data types that you can ignore for now.

Most of the time, when you make a variable, JavaScript guesses right, and you have no problems. But sometimes, JavaScript makes some faulty assumptions, and things go wrong.

The pesky plus sign

I've used the plus sign in two different ways throughout this chapter. The following code uses the plus sign in one way (concatenating two string values):

```
var x = "Hi, ";
var y = "there!";

result = x + y;
alert(result);
```

In this code, `x` and `y` are text variables. The `result = x + y` line is interpreted as "concatenate x and y," and the result is `"Hi, there!"`

Here's the strange thing: The following code is almost identical.

```
var x = 3;
var y = 5;

result = x + y;
alert(result);
```

Strangely, the behavior of the plus sign is different here, even though the statement `result = x + y` is identical in the two code snippets!

In this second case, `x` and `y` are numbers. The plus operator has two entirely different jobs. If it's surrounded by numbers, it adds. If it's surrounded by text, it concatenates!

That's what happened to the first adding machine program. When the user enters data in prompt dialogs, JavaScript assumes that the data is text. When I try to add `x` and `y`, it "helpfully" concatenates instead.

There's a fancy computer science word for this phenomenon (an operator doing different things in different circumstances). Those Who Care About Such Things call this mechanism an *overloaded operator*. Smart people sometimes have bitter arguments about whether overloaded operators are a good idea because they can cause problems like this one, but they can also make things easier in other contexts. I'm not going to enter into that debate here. It's not really a big deal, as long as you can see the problem and fix it.

Changing Variables to the Desired Type

If JavaScript is having a hard time figuring out what type of data is in a variable, you can give it a friendly push in the right direction with some handy conversion functions, as shown in Table 1-1.

Table 1-1 Variable Conversion Functions

Function	*From*	*To*	*Example*	*Result*
parseInt()	String	Integer	parseInt("23")	23
parseFloat()	String	Floating point	parseFloat("21.5")	21.5
toString()	Any variable	String	myVar.toString()	*varies*
eval()	Expression	Result	eval("5 + 3")	8
Math.ceil()	Floating point	Integer	Math.ceil(5.2	6)
Math.floor()			Math.floor(5.2)	5
Math.round()			Math.round(5.2)	5

Using variable conversion tools

The conversion functions are incredibly powerful, but you only need them if the automatic conversion causes you problems. Here's how they work:

✦ `parseInt()` is used to convert text to an integer. If you put a text value inside the parentheses, the function returns an integer value. If the string has a floating point representation (4.3 for example) an integer value (4) is returned.

- `parseFloat()` converts text to a floating point value.
- `toString()` takes any variable type and creates a string representation. Note that it isn't usually necessary to use this function, because it's usually invoked automatically when needed.
- `eval()` is a special method that accepts a string as input. It then attempts to evaluate the string as JavaScript code and return the output. You can use this method for variable conversion or as a simple calculator — `eval("5 + 3")` returns the integer `8`.
- `Math.ceil()` is one of several methods of converting a floating point number to an integer. This technique always rounds *upward,* so `Math.ceil(1.2)` is `2`, and `Math.ceil(1.8)` is also `2`.
- `Math.floor()` is similar to `Math.ceil()`, except it always rounds *downward*, so `Math.floor(1.2)` and `Math.floor(1.8)` will both evaluate to `1`.
- `Math.round()` works like the standard rounding technique used in grade school. Any fractional value less than .5 rounds down, and greater than or equal to .5 rounds up, so `Math.round(1.2)` is `1`, and `Math.round(1.8)` is `2`.

Fixing the addInput code

With all this conversion knowledge in place, it's pretty easy to fix up the `addInput` program so that it works correctly. Just use `parseFloat()` to force both inputs into floating-point values before adding them. Note that you don't have to explicitly convert the result to a string. That's automatically done when you invoke the `alert()` method.

```
//<![CDATA[
// from addInput.html

var x = prompt("first number:");
var y = prompt("second number:");
var sum = parseFloat(x) + parseFloat(y);

alert(x + " plus " + y + " equals " + sum);

//]]>
```

You can see the program works correctly in Figure 1-11.

Conversion methods allow you to ensure that the data is in exactly the format you want.

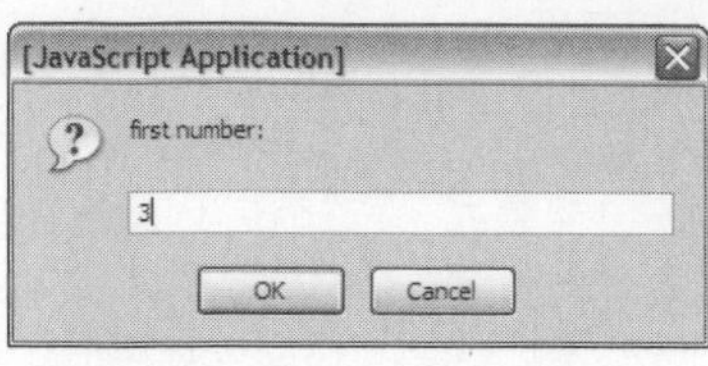

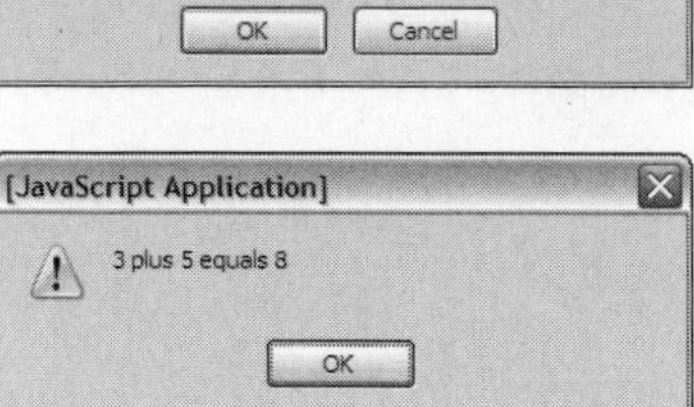

Figure 1-11: Now the program asks for input and correctly returns the sum.

Chapter 2: Making Decisions with Conditions

In This Chapter

- **Generating random numbers and integers**
- **Working with conditions**
- **Using the `if-else` and `switch` structures**
- **Handling unusual conditions**

One of the most important aspects of computers is their apparent ability to make decisions. Computers can change their behavior based on circumstances. In this chapter, you discover how to maximize this decision-making ability.

Working with Random Numbers

Random numbers are a big part of computing. They add uncertainty to games, but they're also used for serious applications, such as simulations, security, and logic. Most languages have a feature for creating random numbers, and JavaScript is no exception. The `Math.random()` function returns a random floating point value between zero and one.

Technically, computers can't create truly random numbers. Instead, they use a complex formula that starts with one value and creates a second semi-predictable value. In JavaScript, the first value (called the random *seed*) is taken from the system clock in milliseconds, so the results of a random number call seem truly random.

Creating an integer within a range

Creating a random floating point number between zero and one is easy, thanks to the `Math.random()` function. What if you want an integer within a specific range? For example, say that you want to simulate rolling a six-sided die. How do you get from the 0-to-1 floating point value to a 1-to-6 integer?

Here's the standard approach:

1. **Get a random float between 0 and 1 using the `Math.random()` function.**

2. **Multiply that value by 6.**

   This step gives you a floating point value between 0 and 5.999 (but never 6).

3. **Use `math.ceil()` to round up.**

   At this point, you need to convert the number to an integer. In Book 4, Chapter 1, I mention three functions you can use to convert from a float to an integer. `Math.ceil()` always rounds up, which means you'll always get an integer between 1 and 6.

Building a program that rolls dice

The following `RollDie.html` code helps you simulate rolling a six-sided die.

```
<!DOCTYPE html PUBLIC "-//W3C//DTD XHTML 1.0 Strict//EN"
"http://www.w3.org/TR/xhtml1/DTD/xhtml1-strict.dtd">
<html lang="EN" dir="ltr" xmlns="http://www.w3.org/1999/xhtml">
  <head>
    <meta http-equiv="content-type" content="text/xml; charset=utf-8" />
    <title>rollDie.html</title>
    <script type = "text/javascript">
      //<![CDATA[
      // from rollDie.html

      var number = Math.random();
      alert(number);

      var biggerNumber = number * 6;
      alert(biggerNumber);

      var die = Math.ceil(biggerNumber);
      alert(die);

      //]]>

    </script>
  </head>

  <body>
    <div id = "output">

    </div>
  </body>
</html>
```

As you can see, I converted the strategy from the previous section directly into JavaScript code:

1. **Create a random float.**

   The `Math.random()` function creates a random floating point number and stores it in the variable `number`.

2. **Multiply the number by 6 to move the number into the appropriate range (6 values).**

   I multiplied by 6 and stored the result in `biggerNumber`.

3. **Round up.**

   I used the `Math.ceil()` function to round the number up to the next highest integer.

Figure 2-1 shows the program running.

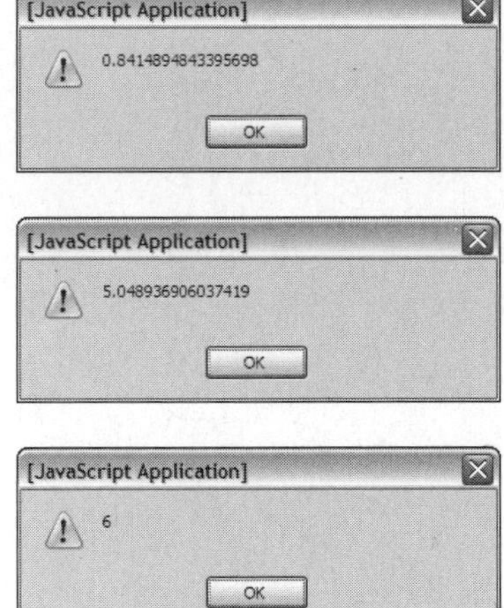

Figure 2-1: This program generates a value between 1 and 6.

You may need to run the `rollDice.html` page a few times to confirm that it works as suspected.

If you want to rerun a program you've already loaded into the browser, just hit the page refresh button on the browser toolbar.

Using if to Control Flow

If you can roll a die, you'll eventually want different things to happen based on the results of the die roll. Figure 2-2 shows two different runs of a simple game called `deuce.html`.

Okay, it's not that exciting. I promise to add dancing hippos in a later version.

In any case, the "You got a Deuce!" message happens only when you roll a 2. The code is simple but profound:

```
<script type = "text/javascript">
  //<![CDATA[
  // get a random number
  // If it's a two, you win

    var die = Math.ceil(Math.random() * 6);
```

```
        alert(die);
        if (die == 2){
          alert ("You got a Deuce!");
        } // end if

      //]]>
    </script>
```

As usual, I'm showing only the script tag and its contents here, because the rest of the page is blank.

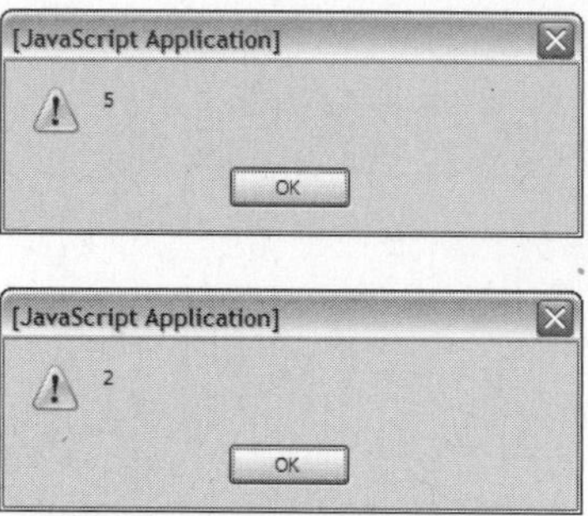

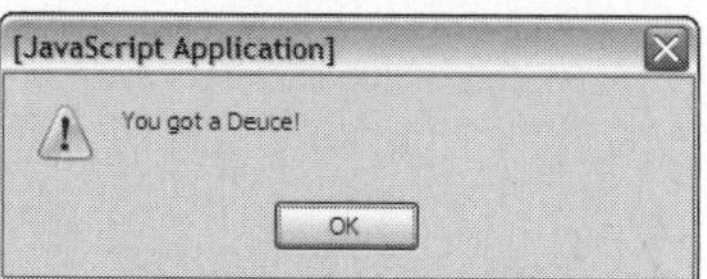

Figure 2-2: Something exciting happens when you roll a two.

The basic if statement

The key to `deuce.html` is the humble `if` statement. This powerful command does a number of important things:

- **It sets up a condition.** The main idea behind a condition is that it's a true or false question. An `if` statement always includes some type of condition in parentheses. (For more on conditions, see the next section.)
- **It begins a block of code.** An `if` statement sets up a chunk of code that doesn't always execute. The end of the `if` line includes a left brace (`{`).
- **It usually has indented code under it.** The line or lines immediately after the `if` statement are part of the block, so they're indented to indicate that they're special.
- **It ends several lines later.** The end of the `if` statement is actually the right brace (`}`) several lines down in the code. In essence, an `if` statement contains other code.
- **It's indented.** The convention is to indent all the code between the `if` statement and its ending brace.

Although not required, many programmers add a comment to indicate that the right brace ends an `if` statement. In the C-like languages, the same symbol (`}`) is used to end a bunch of things, so it's nice to remind yourself what you think you're ending here.

All about conditions

A condition is the central part of `if` and several other important structures. Conditions deserve a little respect on their own. A condition is an expression that can be evaluated to true or false. Conditions come in three main flavors:

- **Comparison:** By far the most common kind of condition. Typically, you compare a variable to a value, or two variables to each other. Table 2-1 describes a number of different types of comparisons.
- **Boolean variable:** A variable that contains only `true` or `false`. In JavaScript, any variable can be a Boolean, if you assign it `true` or `false` as a value. You don't need to compare a Boolean to anything else because it's already true or false.
- **Boolean function:** Returns a true or false value, and you can also use this type of function as a condition.

Incidentally, Boolean variables are the only variable type capitalized in most languages. They were named after a person, George Boole, a nineteenth century mathematician who developed a form of binary arithmetic. Boole died thinking his research a failure. His work eventually became the foundation of modern computing. Drop a mention of George at your next computer science function to earn mucho geek points.

Comparison operators

JavaScript supports a number of different types of comparisons summarized in Table 2-1.

Table 2-1 Comparison Operators

Name	*Operator*	*Example*	*Notes*
Equality	`==`	`(x==3)`	Works with all variable types, including strings.
Not equal	`!=`	`(x != 3)`	True if values are not equal.
Less than	`<`	`(x < 3)`	Numeric or alphabetical comparison.
Greater than	`>`	`(x > 3)`	Numeric or alphabetical comparison.
Less than or equal to	`<=`	`(x <= 3)`	Numeric or alphabetical comparison.
Greater than or equal to	`>=`	`(x >= 3)`	Numeric or alphabetical comparison.

You should consider a few things when working with conditions:

- **Be sure the variable types are compatible.** You'll get unpredictable results if you compare a floating point value to a string.
- **You can compare string values.** In JavaScript, you can use the inequality operators to determine the alphabetical order of two values. (This ability isn't possible in most other languages.)
- **Equality uses a double equal sign.** The single equal sign (=) is used to indicate assignment. When you're comparing variables, use a double equal (==) instead.

Don't confuse assignment with comparison! If you accidentally say `(x = 3)` instead of `(x == 3)`, your code won't crash, but it won't work properly. The first statement simply assigns the value 3 to the variable *x*. It returns the value `true` if the assignment was successful (which it will be). You'll think you're comparing *x* to *3*, but you're assigning *3* to *x*, and the condition will always be true. Keeping these two straight is a nightmare. I still mess it up once in a while.

Using the else Clause

The deuce game, described in the section "Using if to Control Flow," is pretty exciting and all, but it would be even better if you had one comment when the roll is a 2 and another comment when it's something else. Figure 2-3 shows a program with exactly this behavior.

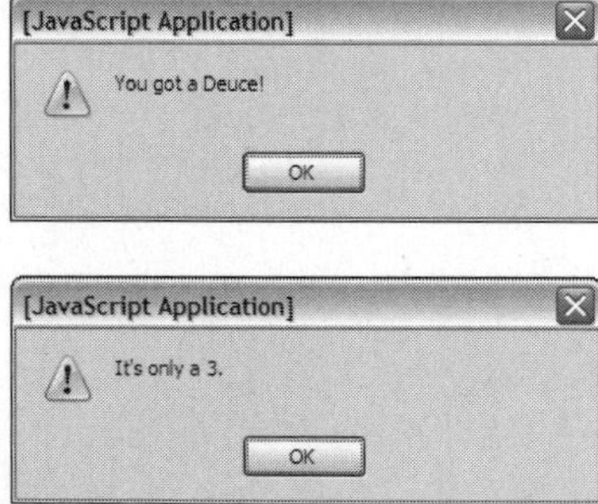

Figure 2-3: You get one message for deuces and another message for everything else.

This program uses the same type of condition as the earlier deuce game, but it adds an important section:

```
<script type = "text/javascript">
  //<![CDATA[
  // from deuceOrNot.html

  var die = Math.ceil(Math.random() * 6);
  if (die == 2){
```

```
    alert("You got a deuce!");
  } else {
    alert("It's only a " + die + ".");
  } // end if

  //]]>
</script>
```

The if statement is unchanged, but now an else clause appears. Here's how the program works:

1. **The if statement sets up a condition.**

   The if statement indicates the beginning of a code branch, and it prepares the way for a condition.

2. **The condition establishes a test.**

   Conditions are true or false expressions, so the condition indicates something that can be true or false.

3. **If the condition is true, the code between the condition and the else clause runs.**

   After this code is finished, control moves past the end of the if structure.

4. **If the condition is false, the code between else and the end of the if statement runs instead.**

The else clause acts like a fork in the road. The code goes along one path or another (depending on the condition) but never both paths at once.

You can put as much code as you want inside an if or else clause, including more if statements!

The else clause is used only in the context of an if statement. You can't use else by itself.

Using else if for more complex interaction

The if - else structure is pretty useful when you have only two branches, but what if you want to have several different options? Figure 2-4 shows a die only a geek could love. All its values are output in binary notation. (For more on binary notation, see the sidebar "Binary?")

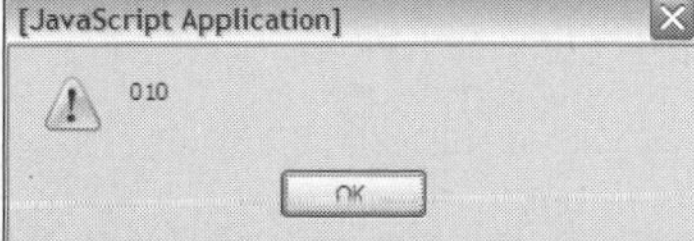

Figure 2-4: A die for the true geek gamer.

Binary?

Binary notation is the underlying structure of all data in a computer. It uses ones and zeroes to store other numbers, which you can combine to form everything you see on the computer, from graphics to text to music videos and adventure games. Here's a quick conversion chart so that you can read the dice:

Die Number	Binary Notation
1	001
2	010
3	011
4	100
5	101
6	110

You can survive just fine without knowing binary (unless you're a computer science major — then you're expected to dream in binary). Still, it's kind of cool to know how things really work.

A simple `if-else` structure isn't sufficient here because you have six different options. (`if-else` gives you only two choices.) Here's some code that uses another variation of `if` and `else`:

```
<script type = "text/javascript">
  //<![CDATA[
  // from binaryDice.html

  var die = Math.ceil(Math.random() * 6);
  if (die == 1){
    alert("001");
  } else if (die == 2){
    alert("010");
  } else if (die == 3){
    alert("011");
  } else if (die == 4){
    alert("100");
  } else if (die == 5){
    alert("101");
  } else if (die == 6){
    alert("110");
  } else {
    alert("something strange is happening...");
  } // end if

  //]]>
</script>
```

This program begins with an ordinary `if` statement, but it has a number of `else` clauses. You can include as many `else` clauses as you want if each includes its own condition.

For example, imagine the computer generates the value 3.

1. **The first condition (`die == 1`) is false, so the program immediately jumps to the next `else`.**
2. **Step 1 sets up another condition (`die == 2`), which is also false, so control goes to the next `else` clause.**
3. **This step has yet another condition (`die == 3`), which is true, so the code inside this clause executes (alerting the value `"011"`).**
4. **A condition has finally been triggered, so the computer skips all the other `else` conditions and moves to the line after the `end if`.**
5. **This step is the last line of code, so the program ends.**

Solving the mystery of the unnecessary else

When you use multiple conditions, you can (and should) still indicate an ordinary `else` clause without a condition as your last choice. This special condition sets up code that should happen if none of the other conditions is triggered. It's useful as a fallback position, in case you didn't anticipate a condition in the `else if` clauses.

If you think carefully about the binary dice program, the `else` clause seems superfluous. (I love that word.) It isn't really necessary! You went through all that trouble to create a random number scheme that guarantees you'll have an integer between 1 and 6. If you checked for all six values, why have an `else` clause? It should never be needed.

There's a big difference between what should happen and what does happen. Even if you think you've covered every single case, you're going to be surprised every once in a while. If you use a multiple `if` structure, you should always incorporate an `else` clause to check for surprises. It doesn't need to do much but inform you that something has gone terribly wrong.

Using switch for More Complex Branches

When you have one expression that may have multiple values — as is the case when rolling a die, as described in the preceding sections — you may want to take advantage of a handy tool for exactly this type of situation. Take a look at Figure 2-5, which is a variation of the die roller.

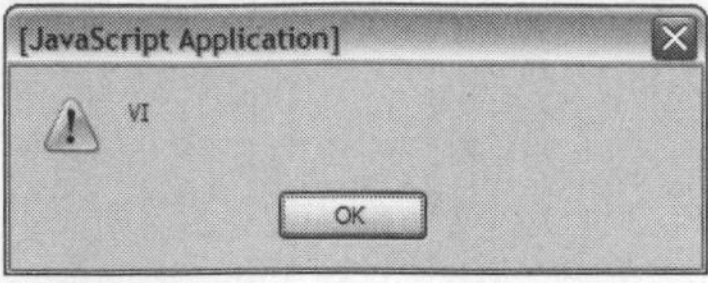

Figure 2-5: We have Roman dice. Useful if we come across any ancient Romans.

Once again, I start with an ordinary 1–6 integer and assign a new value based on the original roll. This time, I use another structure specialized for "one expression with lots of values" situations. Take a look at the following code:

```
<script type = "text/javascript">
  //<![CDATA[
  // from RomanDice.html
  var die = Math.ceil(Math.random() * 6);
  var output = "";
  switch(die){
    case 1:
      output = "I";
      break;
    case 2:
      output = "II";
      break;
    case 3:
      output = "III";
      break;
    case 4:
      output = "IV";
      break;
    case 5:
      output = "V";
      break;
    case 6:
      output = "VI";
      break;
    default:
      output = "PROBLEM!!!";
  } // end switch
```

Creating an expression

The `switch` structure in the preceding code is organized a little bit differently than the `if-else if` business.

The `switch` keyword is followed immediately by an expression in parentheses. The expression is usually a variable with several possible values. The `switch` structure then provides a series of test values and code to execute in each case.

To create a switch statement:

1. **Begin with the `switch` keyword.**

   This step sets up the structure. You'll indent everything until the right brace (}) that ends the switch.

2. **Indicate the expression.**

   The expression is usually a variable you want to compare against several values. The variable goes inside parentheses and is followed by a left brace ({).

3. **Identify the first case.**

   Indicate the first value you want to compare the variable against. Be sure the case is the same type as the variable.

4. **End the case description with a colon (:).**

   Be careful! Case lines end with a colon (indicating the beginning of a case) rather than the more typical semicolon. It's easy to forget this difference.

5. **Write code for the case.**

   You can write as many lines of code as you want. This code executes only if the expression is equal to the given case. Typically, all the code in a case is indented.

6. **Indicate the end of the case with a `break` statement.**

   This statement tells the computer to jump out of the switch structure as soon as this case has been evaluated (which is almost always what you want).

7. **Repeat with other cases.**

   Build similar code for all the other cases you wish to test.

8. **Trap for surprises with `default`.**

   The special case `default` works like the `else` in an `else if` structure: It manages any cases that haven't already been trapped. Even if you think you've got all the bases covered, you should put some default code in place just in case.

You don't need to put a `break` statement in the `default` clause, because it always happens at the end of the `switch` structure anyway.

Switching with style

The `switch` structure is powerful, but it can be tricky because the format is a little strange. Here are a few tips to keep in mind:

- **You can compare any type of expression.** If you've used another language (like C or Java), you may have learned that switches only work on numeric values. You can use JavaScript switches on any data type.

- **It's up to you to get the type correct.** If you're working with a numeric variable and you compare it against string values, you may not get the results you're looking for.
- **Don't forget the colons.** At first glance, the `switch` statement uses semicolons like most other JavaScript commands. Cases end with colons (`:`). Getting confused is easy to do.
- **Break each case.** Use the `break` statement to end each case, or you'll get weird results.

Wouldn't arrays be better? If you've got some programming experience, you may argue that another solution involving something called *arrays* is a better solution for this particular problem. I tend to agree, but for that solution, go to Chapter 4 of this minibook. Switches and `if - else if` structures do have their place, too.

Nesting if Statements

You can combine conditions in all kinds of crazy ways. One decision can include other decisions, which may incorporate other decisions. You can put `if` statements inside each other to manage this kind of (sometimes complicated) logic.

Figure 2-6 shows a particularly bizarre example. Imagine that you're watching the coin toss at your favorite sporting event. Of course, a coin can be heads or tails. Just for the sake of argument, the referee also has a complex personality. Sometimes he's a surfer, and sometimes he's a L337 94m3r (translation: elite gamer). Figure 2-6 shows a few tosses of the coin.

I don't know why the referee is sometimes a surfer and sometimes a L337 94m3r. Perhaps he faced a particularly bizarre set of childhood circumstances.

What's this L337 stuff?

Leet (L337) is a wacky social phenomenon primarily born of the online gaming community. Originally, it began as people tried to create unique screen names for multiplayer games. If you wanted to call yourself "gamer," for example, you'd usually find the name already taken. Enterprising gamers started substituting similar-looking letters and numbers (and sometimes creative spelling) to make original names that are still somewhat readable. The practice spread, and now it's combined with text messaging and online chat shortcuts as a sort of geek code. Get it? L337 94m3r is Leet Gamer, or Elite Gamer.

Figure 2-6: Heads or tails? Surfer or gamer?

This example is getting pretty strange, so you may as well look at some code:

```
<script type = "text/javascript">
  //<![CDATA[
  // from coinToss.html
  coin = Math.ceil(Math.random() * 2);
  character = Math.ceil(Math.random() * 2);
  if (character == 1){
    //It's a surfer referee
    if (coin == 1){
      alert("You got heads, Dude.");
    } else {
      alert("Dude! It's totally tails!");
    } // end coin if

  } else {
    //now it's a L337 Referee
    if (coin == 1){
      alert("h34D$ r0xx0r$");
    } else {
      alert("741L$ ruL3");
    } // end coin if
  } // end character if

  //]]>
</script>
```

Building the nested conditions

If you understand how nested `if` structures work, you can see how the code all fits together.

1. **Flip a coin.**

   I just used a variation of the die-rolling technique, described in the earlier sections. A coin can be only heads or tails, so I rolled a value that would be 1 or 2 for the `coin` variable.

2. **Flip another coin for the personality.**

   The referee's persona is reflected in another random value between 1 and 2.

3. **Check to see if you have a surfer.**

   If the `character` roll is one, we have a surfer, so set up an `if` statement to handle the surfer's output.

4. **If it's the surfer, check the coin toss.**

   Now that you know a surfer is speaking, check the coin for heads or tails. Another `if` statement handles this task.

5. **Respond to the coin toss in surfer-speak.**

   Use `alert()` statements to output the result in the surfer dialect.

6. **Handle the L337 character.**

   The outer `if` structure determines which character is speaking. The `else` clause of this case will happen if `character` is not 1, so all the LEET stuff goes in the `else` clause.

7. **Check the coin again.**

   Now that you know you're speaking in gamer code, determine what to say by consulting the coin in another `if` statement

Making sense of nested ifs

Nested `if` structures aren't all that difficult, but they can be messy, especially as you get several layers deep (as you will, eventually). The following tips help make sure that everything makes sense:

- **Watch your indentation.** Be vigilant on your indentation scheme. An editor like Aptana, which automatically indents your code, is a big plus. Indentation is a great way to tell what level of code you're on.
- **Use comments.** You can easily get lost in the logic of a nested condition. Add comments liberally so that you can remind yourself where you are in the logic. Note that I specify which `if` statement is ending.
- **Test your code.** Just because you think it works doesn't mean it will. Surprises will happen. Test thoroughly to make sure that the code does what you think it should do.

Chapter 3: Loops and Debugging

In This Chapter

- Working with `for` loops
- Building `while` loops
- Recognizing troublesome loops
- Catching crashes and logic errors
- Using the Aptana line-by-line debugger

Computers programs can do repetitive tasks easily, thanks to a series of constructs called *loops*. In this chapter, you discover the two major techniques for managing loops.

Loops are powerful, but they can be dangerous. It's possible to create loops that act improperly, and these problems are difficult to diagnose. I demonstrate several powerful techniques for identifying issues in your code.

Building Counting Loops with for

A *loop* is a structure that allows you to repeat a chunk of code. One standard type of loop — the `for` loop — repeats a chunk of code a certain number of times. Figure 3-1 Shows a `for` loop in action.

Although it looks like ten different alert statements appear, only one exists; it's just repeated ten times.

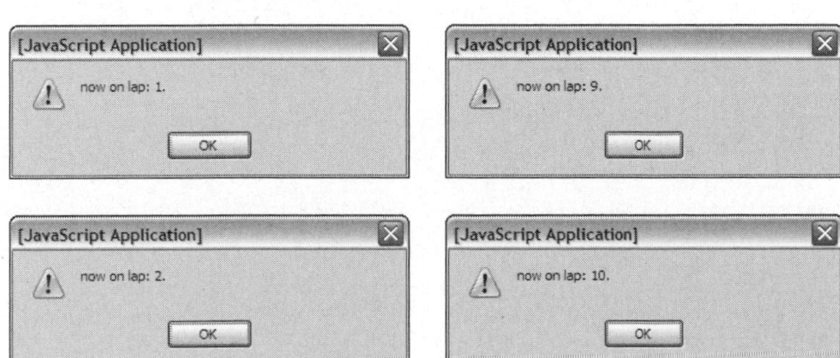

Figure 3-1: This loop repeats ten times before it stops.

I showed the first few dialogs and the last. You should be able to get the idea. Be sure to look at the actual program on the CD-ROM to see how it really works.

Building a standard for loop

You can see the structure of the `for` loop in the following code:

```
<script type = "text/javascript">
  //<![CDATA[
  //from BasicFor.html
  for (lap = 1; lap <= 10; lap++){
    alert("now on lap: " + lap + ".");
  } // end for
  //]]>
</script>
```

`for` loops are based on an integer, which is sometimes called a *sentry variable*. In this example, `lap` serves as the sentry variable. You typically use the sentry variable to count the number of repetitions through a loop.

The `for` statement has three distinct parts:

- **Initialization:** This segment (`lap = 1`) sets up the initial value of the sentry.
- **Condition:** The condition (`lap <= 10`) is an ordinary condition (although it doesn't require parentheses in this context). As long as the condition is evaluated as true, the loop will repeat.
- **Modification:** The last part of the `for` structure (`lap++`) indicates how the sentry will be modified throughout the loop. In this case, I add 1 to the `lap` variable each time through the loop.

The `for` structure has a pair of braces containing the code that will be repeated. As usual, all code inside this structure is indented. You can have as much code inside a loop as you want.

The `lap++` operator is a special shortcut. Adding 1 to a variable is common, so the `lap++` operation means "add 1 to lap." You can also write `lap = lap + 1`, but `lap++` sounds so much cooler.

When programmers decided to improve on the C language, they called the new language C++. Get it? It's one better than C! Those computer scientists are such a wacky bunch!

When you know how many times something should happen, `for` loops are pretty useful.

Counting backwards

You can modify the basic `for` loop so that it counts backwards. Figure 3-2 shows an example of this behavior.

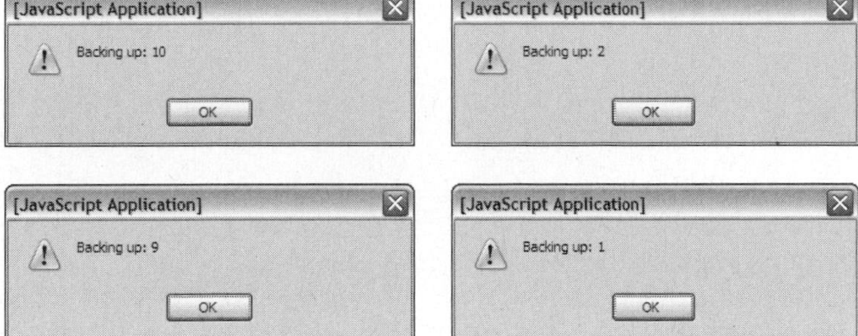

Figure 3-2: This program counts backwards.

The backward version of the `for` loop uses the same general structure as the forward version (shown in the preceding section), but with slightly different parameters:

```
<script type = "text/javascript">
  //<![CDATA[
  //from backwards.html

  for (lap = 10; lap >= 1; lap--){
    alert("Backing up: " + lap);
  } // end for

  //]]>
</script>
```

If you want to count backwards, just modify the three parts of the `for` statement:

- **Initialize the sentry to a large number.** If you're counting down, you need to start with a larger number than 0 or 1.
- **Keep going as long as the sentry is larger than some value.** The code inside the loop will execute as long as the condition is true. The number will be getting smaller, so make sure that you're doing a greater than (>) or greater than or equal to (>=) comparison.
- **Decrement the sentry.** If you want the number to get smaller, you need to subtract something from it. The `--` operator is a quick way to do so. It subtracts 1 from the variable.

Counting by 5

You can use the `for` loop to make other kinds of counting loops. If you want to count by fives, for example, you can use the following variation:

```
<script type = "text/javascript">
  //<![CDATA[

  //from byFive.html
  for (i = 5; i <= 25; i += 5){
    alert(i);
  } // end for

  //]]>

</script>
```

This code starts `i` as five, repeats as long as `i` is less than or equal to 25, and adds 5 to `i` on each pass through the loop. Figure 3-3 illustrates this code in action.

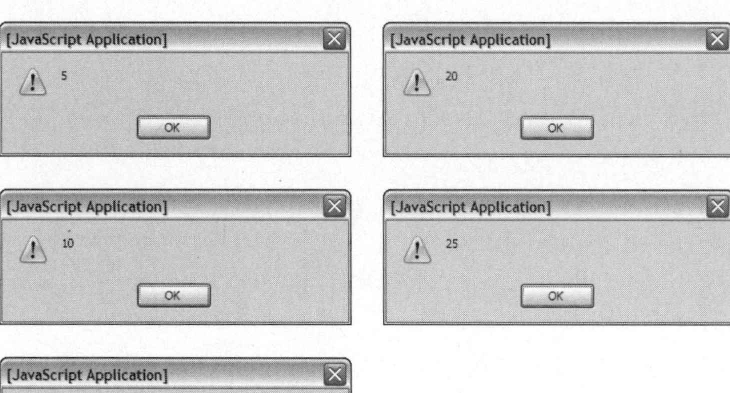

Figure 3-3: `for` loops can also skip values.

If you want a `for` loop to skip numbers, you just make a few changes to the general pattern:

- **Build a sentry variable, using a sensible initial value.** If you want the loop to start at 5, use that number as the initial value.
- **Check against a condition.** It makes sense for a 5 loop to end at a multiple of 5. If you want this loop to continue until you get to 25, continue as long as `i` is less than or equal to 25.
- **Modify the variable on each pass.** In the example, the statement `i += 5` adds 5 to i. (It's just like saying `i = i + 5`.)

Fortunately, all these elements are in the `for` loop structure, so you probably won't overlook them. Still, if you find that your loop isn't working as expected, you may need to look into the debugging tricks described in the section "Catching Logic Errors" later in this chapter.

Looping for a While

The `for` loop is useful, but it has a cousin that's even more handy, the `while` loop. A `while` loop isn't tied to any particular number of repetitions. It simply repeats as long as its condition is true.

Creating a basic while loop

The basic `while` loop is deceptively simple to build. Here's an example:

```
<script type = "text/javascript">
  //<![CDATA[
  // from while.html

  answer = "-99";
  while (answer != "5"){
    answer = prompt("What is 3 + 2?");
    if (answer == "5"){
      alert("great!");
    } else {
      alert("try again...");
    } // end if
  } // end while


  //]]>
</script>
```

This script asks the user a simple math question and keeps asking until the user responds correctly. You can see it in action in Figure 3-4.

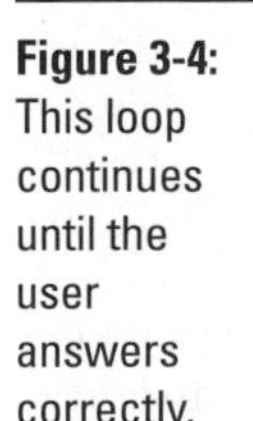

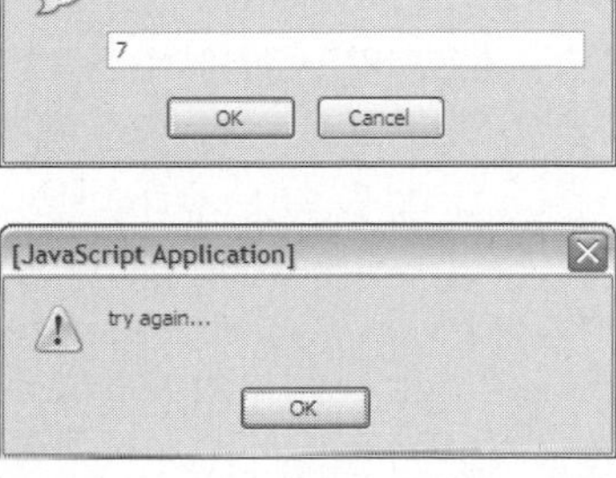

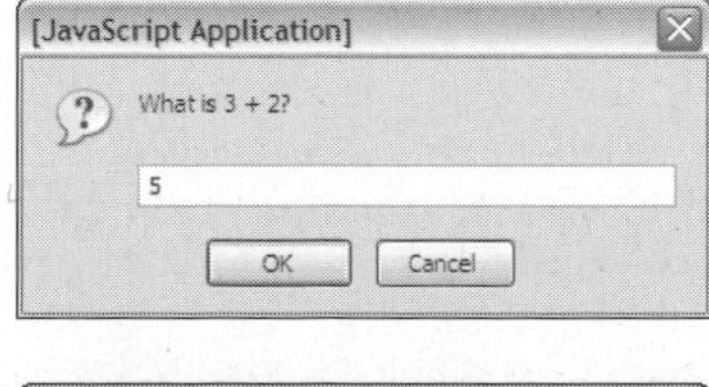

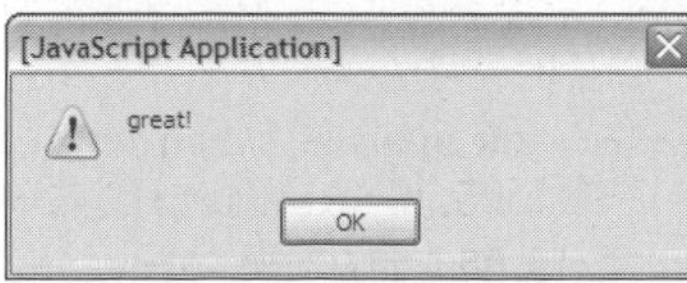

Figure 3-4: This loop continues until the user answers correctly.

The operation of a `while` loop is easy to understand. Here's how the math program works:

1. **Create a variable called `answer` to act as a sentry variable for the loop.**
2. **Initialize the variable.**

   The initial value of the variable is set to `"-99"`, which can't possibly be correct. That guarantees that the loop will execute at least one time.
3. **Evaluate the `answer`.**

   In this particular program, the correct answer is 5. If the value of `answer` is anything but 5, the loop continues. In this example, I've preset the value of `answer` to `"-99"` so that the loop happens at least once.
4. **Ask the user a challenging math question.**

   Well, a math question anyway. The important thing is to change the value of `answer` so that it's possible to get 5 in the answer and exit the loop.
5. **Give the user some feedback.**

   It's probably good to let the user know how she did, so provide some sort of feedback.

Avoiding loop mistakes

A `while` loop seems simpler than a `for` loop, but `while` has exactly the same basic requirements:

- **A critical sentry variable typically controls the loop.** Some key variable usually (but not always) controls a `while` loop.
- **The sentry must be initialized.** If the loop is going to behave properly, the sentry variable must still be initialized properly. In most cases, you'll want to guarantee that the loop happens at least one time.
- **You must have a condition.** Like the `for` loop, `while` loops are based on conditions. As long as the condition is true, the loop continues.
- **You must include a mechanism for changing the sentry.** Somewhere in the loop, you need to have a line that changes the value of the sentry. Be sure that it's possible to make the condition false, or you'll be in the loop forever!

If you forget one of these steps, the `while` loop may not work correctly. Making mistakes in your `while` loops is easy. Unfortunately, these mistakes don't usually result in a crash. Instead, the loop may either refuse to run altogether or continue on indefinitely. If your loop has that problem, you'll want to make sure that you read the next section.

Introducing Bad Loops

Sometimes loops don't behave. Even if you've got the syntax correct, your loop still may not do what you want. The following sections describe two main kinds of loop errors: Loops that never happen, and loops that never quit.

Managing the reluctant loop

You may write some code and find that the loop never seems to run, as in the following program:

```
<script type = "text/javascript">
  //<![CDATA[

  //from never.html
  //Warning! this script has a deliberate error!

  i = 1;
  while (i > 10){
    i++;
  } // end while

  //]]>
</script>
```

This code looks innocent enough, but if you run it, you'll be mystified. It doesn't crash, but it also doesn't seem to do anything. If you follow the code step by step, you'll eventually see why. I initialize `i` to `1`, and then repeat as long as `i` is greater than 10. See the problem? `i` is less than 10 right now, so the condition starts out false, and the loop never executes! I probably meant for the condition to be `(i < 10)`. It's a sloppy mistake, but exactly the kind of bone-headed error I make all the time.

I'm not showing you a screenshot of this program, because nothing happens. Likewise, I don't show you a screenshot of the one in the next section because it doesn't do anything useful either.

Managing the obsessive loop

The other kind of bad-natured loop is the opposite of the reluctant loop, described in the preceding section. This one starts up just fine, but never goes away!

The following code illustrates an endless loop:

```
<script type = "text/javascript">
  //<![CDATA[

  //from endless.html
  // Warning: this program has a deliberate
  // error! You will have to stop the browser
  // to end the loop.
```

```
  i = 0;
  j = 0;

  while (i < 10){
    j++;
    alert(j);
  } // end while

  //]]>
</script>
```

If you decide to run endless.html, be aware that it will not work properly. What's worse, the only way to stop it will be to kill your browser through the task manager. In the upcoming section "Catching Logic Errors," I show you how to run such code in a safe environment so that you can figure out what's wrong with it.

This code is just one example of the dreaded endless loop. Such a loop usually has perfectly valid syntax, but some logic error prevents it from running properly. The logical error is usually one of the following:

- **The variable wasn't initialized properly.** The initial value of the sentry is preventing the loop from beginning correctly.
- **The condition is checking for something that can't happen.** Either the condition has a mistake in it, or something else is preventing it from triggering.
- **The sentry hasn't been updated inside the loop.** If you simply forget to modify the sentry variable, you'll get an endless loop. If you modify the variable after the loop has completed, you get an endless loop. If you ask for input in the wrong format, you may also get a difficult-to-diagnose endless loop.

Debugging Your Code

If you've been writing JavaScript code, you've also been encountering errors. It's part of a programmer's life. Loops are especially troublesome because they can cause problems even if the syntax is perfect. Fortunately, you can use some really great tricks to help track down pesky bugs.

Letting Aptana help

If you're writing your code with Aptana, you already have some great help available. It gives you the same syntax-highlighting and code-completion features as you had when writing XHTML and CSS.

Also, Aptana can often spot JavaScript errors on the fly. Figure 3-5 shows a program with a deliberate error.

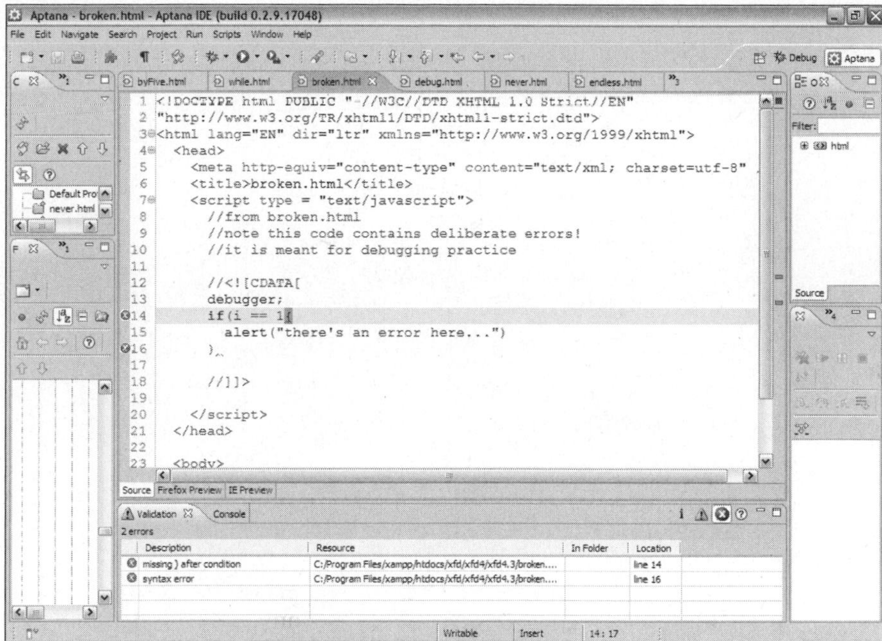

Figure 3-5: Aptana caught my error and provides some help.

Aptana notifies you of errors in your code with a few mechanisms:

- **The suspect code has a red squiggle underneath.** Just like a word-processing spell-checker.
- **A red circle indicates the troublesome line.** You can scan the margin to quickly see where the errors are.
- **The validation pane summarizes all errors.** You can see the errors and the line number for each. Double-click an error to be taken to that spot in the code.
- **You can hover over an error to get more help.** Hover the mouse over an error to get a summary of the error.

Aptana can catch some errors, but it's most useful at preventing errors with the automatic indentation and code assist features. (In the section "Using the Aptana Debug Mode," later in this chapter, I show how to use Aptana's powerful debug mode.)

Debugging JavaScript on Internet Explorer

Internet Explorer has unpredictable behavior when it comes to JavaScript errors. IE6 will take you to some type of editor, but the editors changed over the years and are modified (without your knowledge or permission) when you install new software. IE7 (at least by default) simply does nothing. You won't see an error or any indication that an error even occurred. (Denial — my favorite coping mechanism.)

You can force IE to give you a little bit of help, though. All you have to do is choose Tools⇨Internet Options and then click the Advanced tab. You see a dialog box that looks like Figure 3-6.

In the dialog box, select Display a Notification about Every Script Error. Leave all the other settings alone for now. (Yep, we're going to keep script debugging disabled, because it doesn't work very well. I show you a better technique in the section called "Finding Errors in Firefox.")

Now when you reload `broken.html` in Internet Explorer, you'll see something like Figure 3-7.

This message is actually good news, because at least you know what the problem is, and you've got some kind of clue how to fix it. In this particular case, the error message is pretty useful. Sometimes that's the case, and sometimes the error messages seem to have been written by aliens.

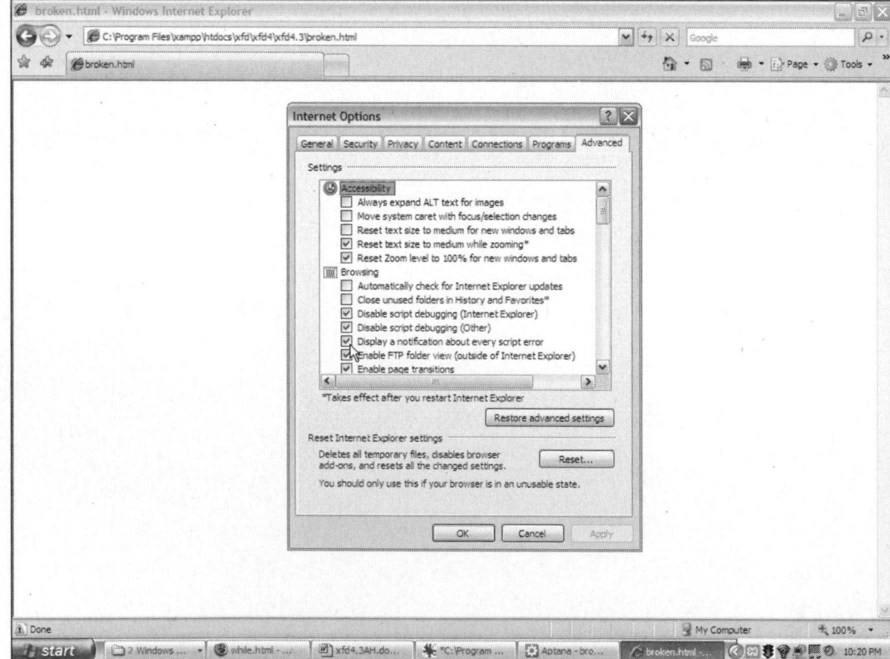

Figure 3-6: This dialog box allows you to get error warnings in Internet Explorer.

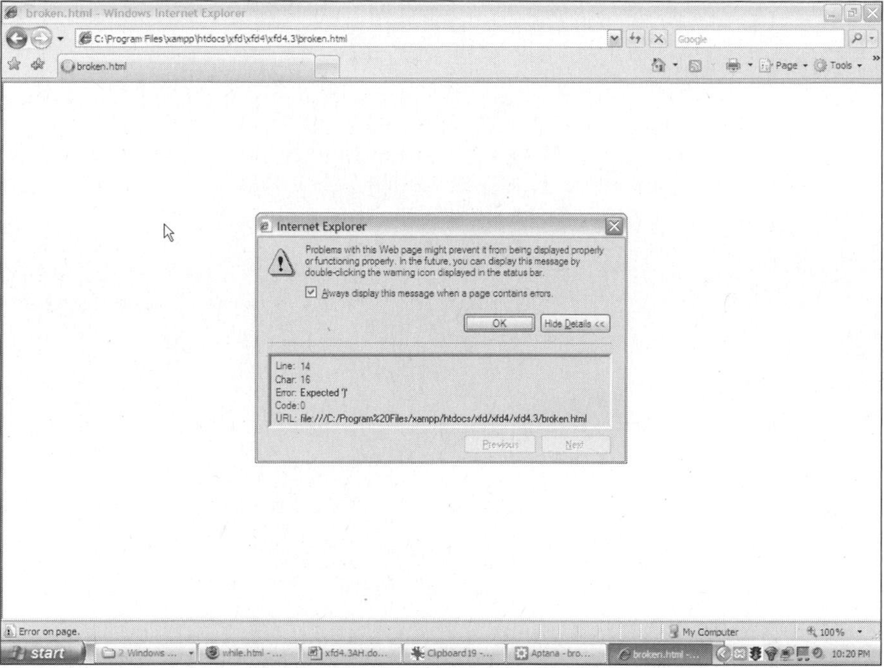

Figure 3-7: I never thought I'd be happy to see an error message.

Be sure to have the error notification turned on in IE so that you know about errors right away. Of course, you also need to check your code in Firefox, which has tons of great tools for checking out your code.

Finding errors in Firefox

Firefox has somewhat better error-handling than IE by default, and you can use add-ons to turn it into a debugging machine. At its default setting, error notification is minimal. If you suspect JavaScript errors, open up the Java Script Errors window by choosing Tools⇨Error Console or by typing **javascript:** in the location bar. Figure 3-8 shows the error console after running `broken.html`.

I generally find the error messages in the Firefox console more helpful than the ones provided by IE.

The error console doesn't automatically clear itself when you load a new page. When you open it, it may still contain a bunch of old error messages. Be sure to clear the history (with the error console's clear button) and refresh your page to see exactly what errors are happening on this page.

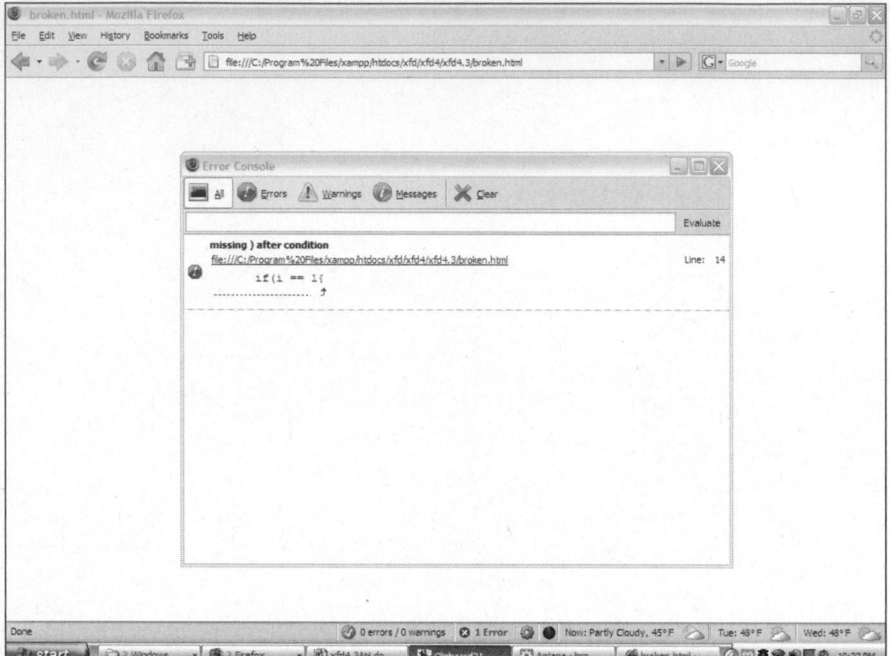

Figure 3-8: The Firefox error console is pretty useful.

Finding Errors with Firebug

One of the best things about Firefox is the add-on architecture. Some really clever people have created very useful add-ons that add wonderful functionality. Firebug is one example. This add-on (available on the CD-ROM or at `https://addons.mozilla.org/en-US/firefox/addon/1843`) adds tremendously to your editing bag of tricks.

Firebug is useful for HTML and CSS editing, but it really comes into its own when you're trying to debug JavaScript code. (For more on Firebug, see Book I, Chapter 3.)

When Firebug is active, it displays a little icon at the bottom of the browser window. If it identifies any JavaScript errors, a red error icon appear. Click this icon, and the Firebug window appears, describing the problem. Figure 3-9 shows how it works.

If you click the offending code snippet, you can see it in context — especially useful when the error isn't on the indicated line. Generally, if I'm doing any tricky JavaScript, I turn on Firebug on to catch any problems.

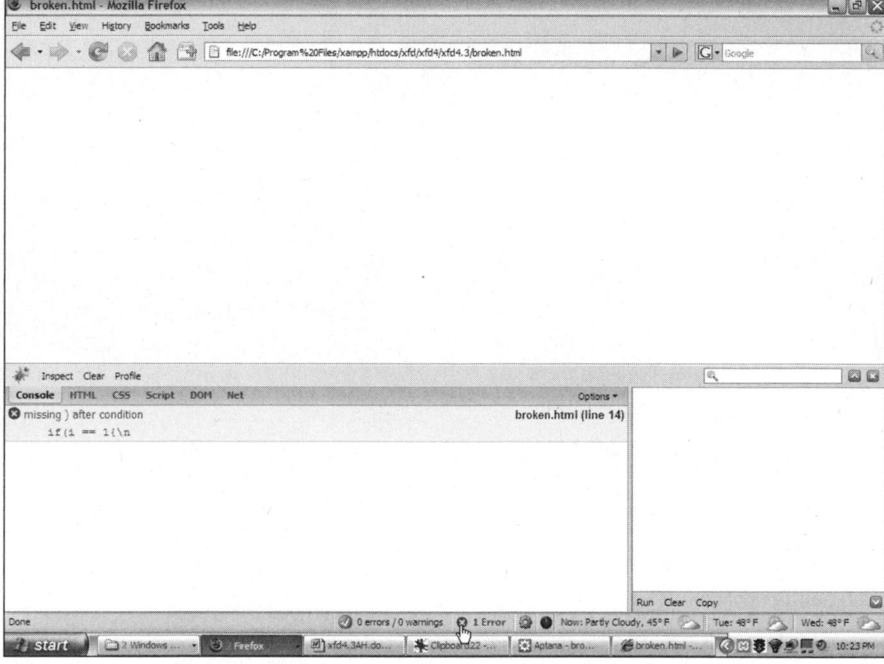

Figure 3-9: The Firebug tool shows an error. Click the error line to see it in context.

Catching Logic Errors

The dramatic kind of error you see in `broken.html` is actually easy to fix. It crashes the browser at a particular part of the code, so you get a good idea what went wrong. Crashes usually result in error messages, which generally give some kind of clue about what went wrong. Most of the time, it's a problem with syntax. You spelled something wrong, forgot some punctuation, or did something else that's pretty easy to fix once you spot it. This type of error is called a *syntax error.*

Loops and branches often cause a more sinister kind of problem, called a *logical error.* Logical errors happen when your code doesn't have any syntax problems, but it's still not doing what you want. These errors can be much harder to pin down, because you don't get as much information.

Of course, if you have the right tools, you can eventually track down even the trickiest bugs. The secret is to see exactly what's going on inside your variables — stuff the user usually doesn't see.

Logging to the console with Firebug

Firebug has another nifty trick. It allows you to send quick messages to the Firebug console. Take a look at `log.html`:

```
<script type = "text/javascript">
  //<![CDATA[
  // from log.html
  // note this program requires firebug on firefox

  Console.debug();
  for (i = 1; i <= 5; i++){
    console.log(i);
  } // end for loop

  //another loop with a fancier output
  for (i = 1; i <= 5; i++){
    console.log("i is now %d.", i);
  }

  console.info("This is info");
  console.warn("This is a warning");
  console.error("This is an error");

  //]]>
</script>
```

This code is special because it contains several references to the `console` object. This object is available only to Firefox browsers with the `FireBug` extension installed. When you run the program with Firebug and look at the console tab, you see something like Figure 3-10.

The `console` object allows you to write special messages that only the programmer in the console sees. This ability is a great way to test your code and see what's going on, especially if things aren't working like you want.

If you want to test your code in IE, there's a version of Firebug (called Firebug Lite) that works on other browsers. Check the Firebug main page (`https://addons.mozilla.org/en-US/firefox/addon/1843`) to download and install this tool if you want to use console commands on these browsers.

Looking at console output

Here's how the `console` object works:

- **The first loop prints the value of `i` to the console.** Each time through the first loop, the `console.log` function prints the current value of `i`. This information is useful whenever the loop isn't working correctly. You can use the `console.log()` method to print the value of any variable.

✦ **The second loop demonstrates a more elaborate kind of printing.** Sometimes you'll want to make clear exactly what value you're sending to the console. Firebug supports a special syntax called *formatted printing* to simplify this process.

```
console.log("i is now %d.", i);
```

The text string `"i is now %d"` indicates what you want written in the console. The special character `%d` specifies that you'll be placing a numeric variable in this position. After the comma, you can indicate the variable you want inserted into the text.

You can use other formatting characters as well. `%s` is for string, and `%o` is for object. If you're familiar with `printf` in C, you'll recognize this technique.

✦ **You can specify more urgent kinds of logging.** If you want, you can use alternatives to the `console.log` to impart more urgency in your messages. If you compare the code in `log.html` with the output of Figure 3-10, you can see how info, warning, and error are formatted.

When your program isn't working properly, try using console commands to describe exactly what's going on with each of your variables. This approach often helps you see problems and correct them.

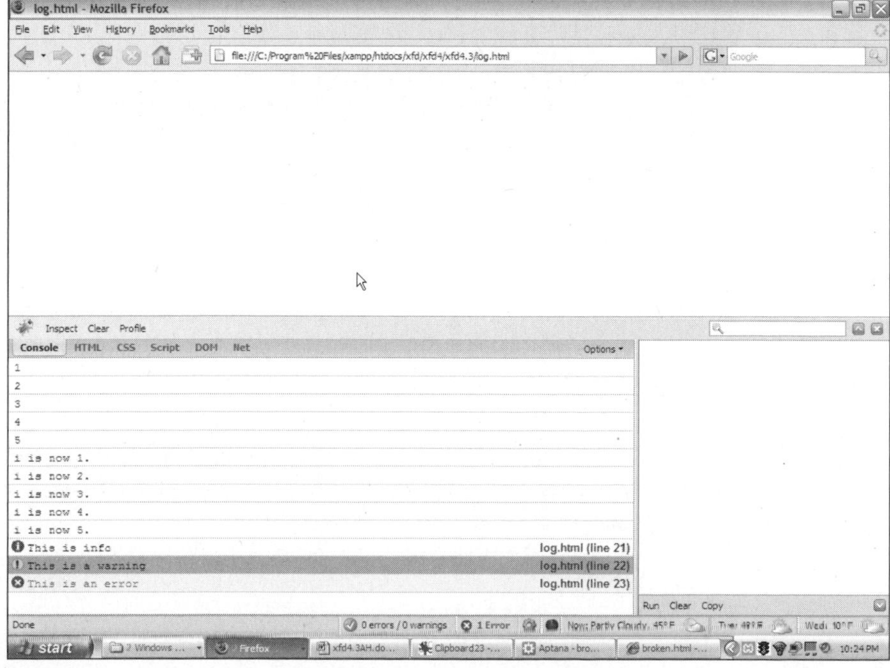

Figure 3-10: The Firebug console shows lots of new information.

When you get your program working properly, don't forget to take out the console commands! Either remove them or render them ineffective with comment characters. The console commands will cause an error in any browser that doesn't have Firebug installed. Typically, your users will not have this extension. (Nor should they need it! You've debugged everything for them!)

Using the Aptana Debug Mode

Traditional programming languages often feature a special debugging tool for fixing especially troubling problems. A typical debugger has these features:

- **The ability to pause a program as it's running.** Logic errors are hard to catch because the program keeps on going. With a debugger, you can set a particular line as a *breakpoint*. When the debugger encounters the breakpoint, the program is in a pause mode. It isn't completely running, and it isn't completely stopped.
- **A mechanism for moving through the code a line at a time.** You can normally step through code one line at a time so that you can see what's going on.
- **A way to view the values of all variables and expressions.** Knowing what's happening in your variables is important. (For example, is a particular variable changing when you think it should?) A debugger should let you look at the values of all its variables.
- **The ability to stop runaway processes.** As soon as you start creating loops, you'll find yourself accidentally creating endless loops. (For more on endless loops, see the earlier section, "Managing the obsessive loop.") In a typical browser, the only way out of an endless loop is to kill the browser with the task manager (or process manager in some operating systems). That step is a bit drastic. A debugger can let you stop a runaway loop without accessing the task manager.

Debuggers are extremely handy, and they've been very common in most programming languages. JavaScript programmers haven't had much access to debugging tools in the past because the technical considerations of an embedded language made this difficult.

Fortunately, Aptana has a wonderful debugging mode that works very well, and provides all those features. To test it, I wrote a program with a deliberate error that would be hard to find without a debugger:

```
//<![CDATA[
//from debug.html
//has a deliberate error

var i = 0;
var j = 0;
while (i <= 10){
```

```
      console.log(i);
      j++;
    } // end while


    //]]>
  </script>
```

This code is another version of the endless.html program from the “Managing the obsessive loop” section earlier in this chapter. You may be able to see the problem right away. If not, you can see it as you run the debugger, which I describe how to do in the next sections.

Aptana also supports the basic console.log() function, but not the variations (variable interpolation, errors, and warnings). I used console.log() for output in this program just to avoid jumping back and forth from the browser to the editor to handle dialog boxes.

To step through a program using the Aptana debugger, begin by loading the file into the debugger.

Adding a breakpoint

A JavaScript program can get much longer than the short examples I show in this book. You usually won't want to start the line-by-line debugging from the beginning, so you need to specify a breakpoint. When you run a program in debug mode, it runs at normal speed until it reaches a breakpoint and then it pauses so that you can control it more immediately.

To set a breakpoint, right-click a line number in the code editor.

Figure 3-11 shows me setting a breakpoint on line 12 of the debug.html code.

Running the debugger

The debugger requires you to run your program in a different way than you may be used to. Because your program is normally run by the browser (not Aptana), somehow you need a mechanism for passing information back from the browser to Aptana. Here's what you need to do:

1. **Start the debugger.**

   Click the debug icon, which looks like a little bug.

2. **Install the Aptana Firefox plugin automatically.**

   When you debug a JavaScript program for the first time, Aptana asks permission to install an additional Firefox plugin. Click Yes to complete the installation. You only need to install this feature once.

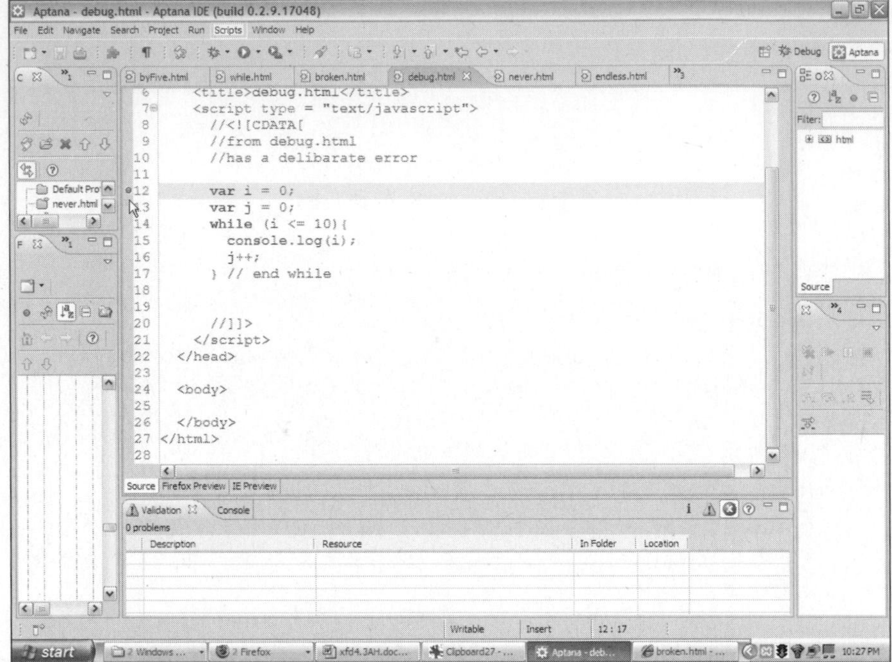

Figure 3-11: Use a breakpoint to tell the debugger where to pause.

3. **Switch to the debug perspective.**

   Aptana pops up a message box asking whether you want to switch to the debug perspective. Click Yes to (temporarily) change Aptana to debug configuration.

Using the debug perspective

When Aptana is used for debugging, it introduces a new layout (called a *perspective* in Aptana). This perspective changes the way the screen looks and optimizes the editor for debugging mode. Figure 3-12 shows the `debug.html` program in debug perspective.

The debug perspective changes the editor in the following ways to emphasize debugging:

- **The code completion window is gone.** This feature isn't needed when you're debugging, so it's removed. You need the screen space for other goodies.
- **The file management window is also missing.** Likewise, you aren't doing a lot of file manipulation in debug mode, so this window is gone, too. (Don't worry; you get it back when you return to normal edit mode.)

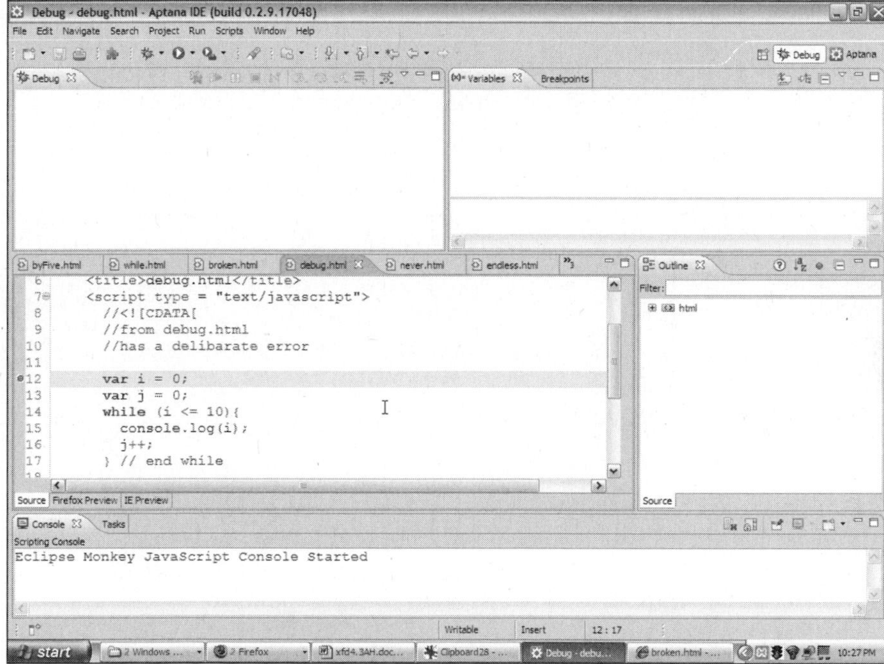

Figure 3-12: Aptana looks a little different in debug perspective.

✦ **You have a new debug window.** This window shows your active threads. The most important thing about it is the buttons along the top.

✦ **You also have a breakpoint / variables window.** This powerful new window describes the values of all your variables as the program is running.

✦ **Most of the other windows are the same.** You still have the code window, console, and outline window, but they're rearranged a little differently than normal. Of course, you can adjust them if you want.

Once you've got the debug mode running one time, a little debug icon appears in the upper-right of the Aptana interface. After this quick button is available, you can use it to switch into debug mode. Use the Aptana button to move back to ordinary editing mode.

Examining the debug mode with a paused program

When you run your code through the debugger, Aptana fires up a new instance of Firefox and loads your program into it. When your program is paused for debugging, you see a few new details, shown in Figure 3-13.

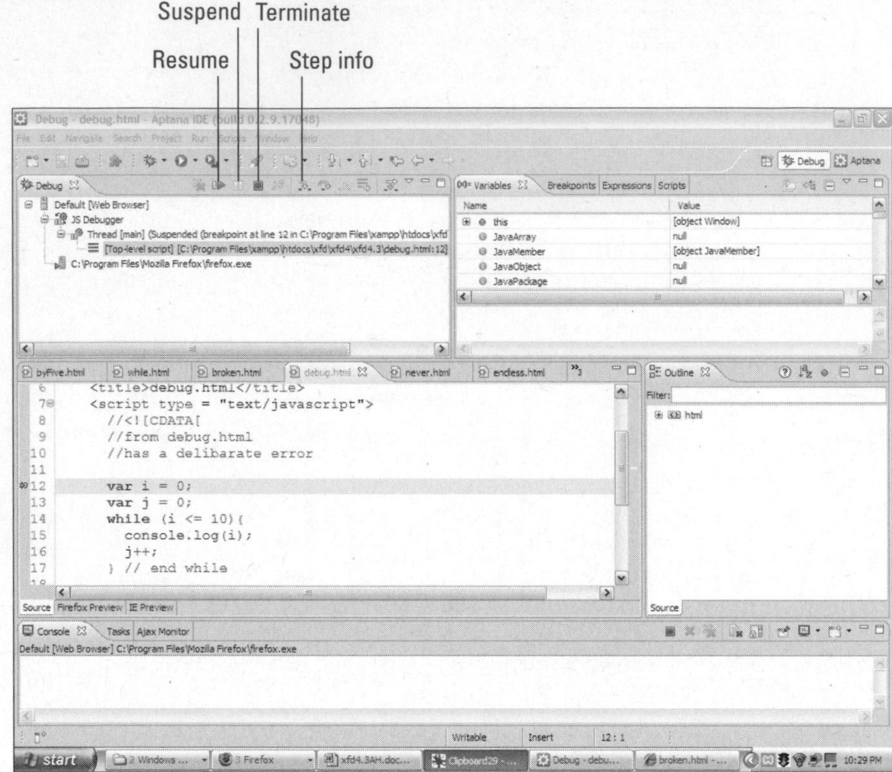

Figure 3-13: You get a few new buttons and tools when you're debugging a program.

When your program is paused, you can see several important new indicators:

- **The debug window shows which script is active.** Right now, your programs have only one script, but later you'll have more. The thread window tells you which script currently has the processor's attention.
- **The buttons in the debug window are active.** Hover the mouse over each button to see its ToolTips. I explain these buttons in the next section.
- **The Breakpoints window has more panes.** In addition to the `breakpoints` and `variables` panes, you see some new panes, `expressions` and `scripts`.
- **The `variables` panel lets you see all the variables the page knows about.** Even though this program contains only two explicitly defined variables, you can see a lot more than that. Every JavaScript program has a whole bunch of special variables built in. I explain how to use this panel in the next section ("Walking through your program").

- **The `breakpoints` panel allows you to manage your breakpoints.** This panel is a good place for you to see all the breakpoints in your project. You can enable or disable a breakpoint from this panel.
- **The `expressions` panel allows you to follow particular variables or expressions.** It's an extremely powerful tool. I demonstrate its use in the section "Viewing expression data," later in this chapter.
- **The current line of code is highlighted.** If you set a breakpoint on line 12, you'll see that line highlighted. (It may be difficult to see in Figure 3-13.) As you move through the code, this highlight moves in order to help you follow the logic.

In some versions of Aptana, a message that starts `TypeError: request.loadGroup has no properties` appears sometimes when you're debugging a program. This error isn't in your code, and it doesn't seem to cause any problems. You can safely ignore this error.

Walking through your program

Here's the best part about the Aptana debug mode. You can run your program in super slow-mo, seeing every aspect of its behavior. Here's how:

1. **Click the Step Into button on the debug panel.**

   It looks like a curved arrow pointing between two dots, or you can just use the `F5` key.

2. **Look at the code.**

   The highlighting has moved to the next line of code in your program (line 13).

3. **Mouse over the variables.**

   Hover your mouse over the two variables (`i` and `j`) in your code. You see a dialog box that describes the current value of each variable.

4. Use the Step Into button a few more times.

   Watch as the highlight moves through the program, looping.

5. **Check the variables again.**

   Take another look at the variables after a few times through the loop, and you'll begin to see what's wrong with this code: `j` is increasing, but `i` is still stuck at zero.

6. **Stop the debug session.**

   If you think you understand the problem, you can stop the debug session with the red square `terminate` button. (You'll need to do that in this program, because it's an endless loop. It will never end on its own.) Aptana then closes down the generated Firefox instance.

If the debugger isn't acting properly, be sure you've set a breakpoint. If you don't have a breakpoint, the program won't stop. Also, be sure that you've used the debug button to start the program. Using the `run` program or viewing the page directly in the browser won't activate the debugger.

Viewing expression data

The whole point of debugging is to find difficult problems. Usually, these problems are variables that aren't doing what you expect. Aptana provides a Variables tab, which shows the value of all variables in a program, but it's surprisingly difficult to use. JavaScript programs come bundled with hundreds of variables. If you dig around, you can eventually find the `i` and `j` variables. (Scroll down in the variables panel to find them.) Every time you take another step, you have to scroll down again to see the values or mouse over the variables in the code.

Fortunately, Aptana provides a much easier way. Select a variable with the mouse and right-click. In the resulting menu, choose Watch. Figure 3-14 shows the debugger after I've chosen to watch both variables and run through the loop a few times.

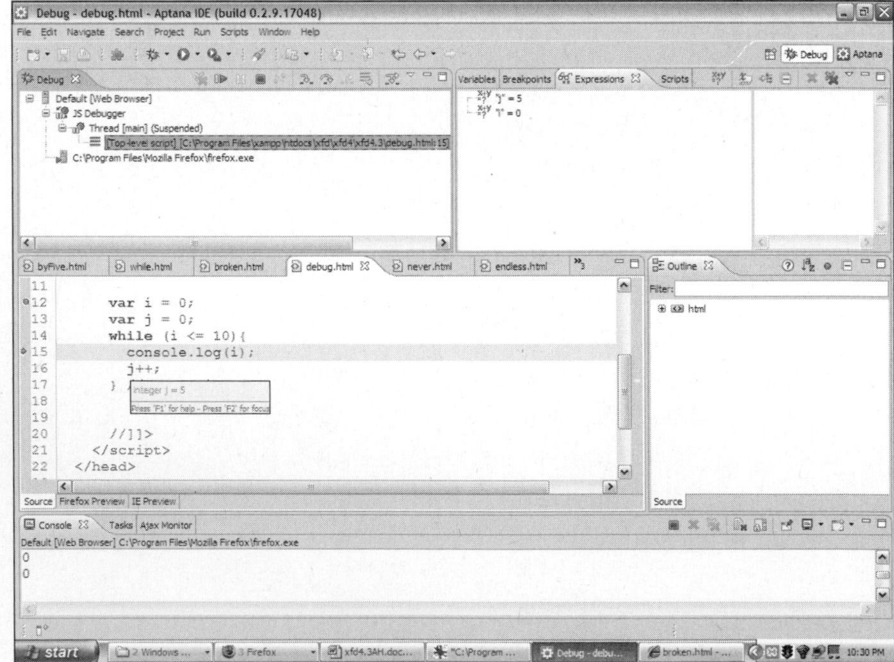

Figure 3-14: The expressions window highlights the variables I'm interested in.

In this mode, you can see the exact values of the variables you've chosen to track. When the variable changes value, you can see it happen immediately.

The expression window has one more cool trick. You can use it to watch complex expressions, not just variables. In this program, you want to know why the loop isn't exiting. Highlight the condition (`i <= 10`) and add it to the watch expressions just as you did the variables.

Now step through the program watching the variables and the condition. With all this information available to you, my coding mistake in the section "Using the Aptana Debug Mode" becomes obvious. I used the variable `i` in the condition, but I never changed it inside the loop. Instead, I changed the value of `j`, which has nothing at all to do with the loop!

Whenever you encounter a program that isn't doing what you want, fire up the debugger, watch the critical values, and step through the code a line at a time. This process often helps you find even the most difficult errors.

Chapter 4: Functions and Arrays

In This Chapter

- Getting organized with functions
- Passing parameters into functions
- Returning values from functions
- Functions and variable scope
- Producing basic arrays
- Retrieving data from arrays
- Building a multidimensional array

It doesn't take long for your code to become complex. Soon enough, you'll find yourself wanting to write more sophisticated programs. When things get larger, you need new kinds of organizational structures to handle the added complexity.

You can bundle several lines of code into one container and give this new chunk of code a name: *function*. You can also take a whole bunch of variables, put them into a container, and give it a name. That's called an *array*.

This chapter is about how to work with more code and more data without going crazy.

Breaking Code into Functions

Functions come in handy when you're making complex code easier to handle.

Functions are a useful tool for controlling complexity. You can take a large complicated program and break it into several smaller pieces. Each piece stands alone and solves a specific part of the overall problem.

You can think of each function as a miniature program. You can define variables in functions, put loops and branches in there, and do anything else you can do with a program. A program using functions is basically a program full of subprograms.

Once you have functions defined, they're just like new JavaScript commands. In a sense, when you add functions, you're adding to JavaScript.

To explain functions better, think back to an old campfire song, "The Ants Go Marching." Figure 4-1 re-creates this classic song for you in JavaScript format. (You may want to roast a marshmallow while you view this program.)

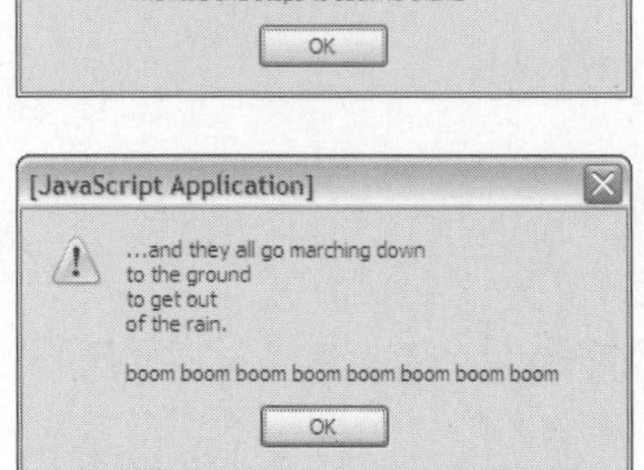

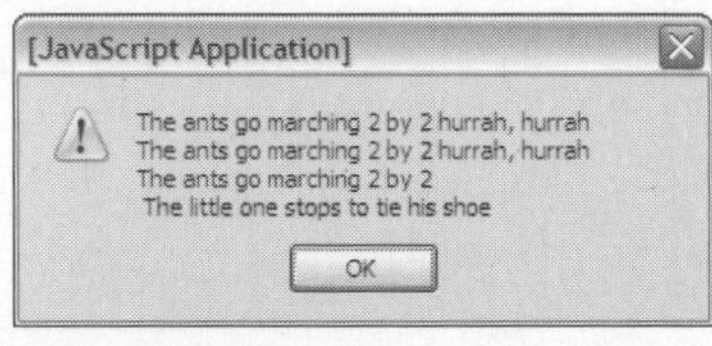

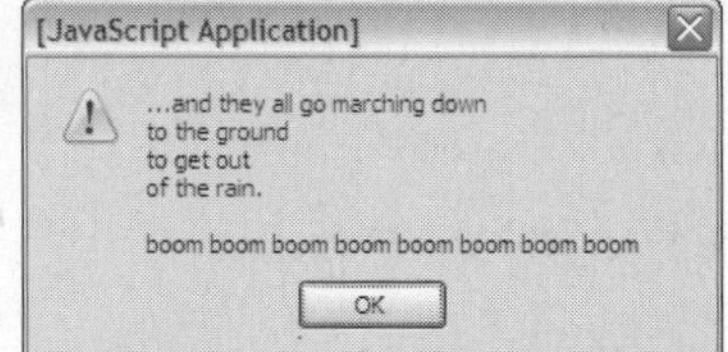

Figure 4-1: Nothing reminds me of functions like a classic campfire song.

If you're unfamiliar with this song, it simply recounts the story of a bunch of ants. The littlest one apparently has some sort of attention issues (but we love him anyway). During each verse, the little one gets distracted by something that rhymes with the verse number. The real song typically has ten verses, but I'm just doing two for the demo.

Thinking about structure

Before you look at the code, think about the structure of the song, "The Ants Go Marching." Like many songs, it has two main parts. The *chorus* is a phrase repeated many times throughout the song. The song has several *verses*, which are similar to each other, but not quite identical.

Think about the song sheet passed around the campfire. (I'm getting hungry for a S'more.) The chorus is usually listed only one time, and each verse is listed. Sometimes, you'll have a section somewhere on the song sheet that looks like the following:

Verse 1

Chorus

Verse 2

Chorus

Musicians call this thing a *road map,* and that's a great name for it. A road map is a higher level view of how you'll progress through the song. In the road map, you don't worry about the details of the particular verse or chorus. The road map shows the big picture, and you can look at each verse or chorus for the details.

Building the antsFunction.html program

Take a look at the code for `antsFunction.html` and see how it reminds you of the song sheet for "The Ants Go Marching":

```
<script type = "text/javascript">
  //<![CDATA[
  //from antsFunction.html

  function chorus() {
    var text = "...and they all go marching down\n";
    text += "to the ground \n";
    text += "to get out \n";
    text += "of the rain. \n";
    text += " \n";
    text += "boom boom boom boom boom boom boom boom \n";
    alert(text);
  } // end chorus

  function verse1(){
    var text = "The ants go marching 1 by 1 hurrah, hurrah \n";
    text += "The ants go marching 1 by 1 hurrah, hurrah \n";
    text += "The ants go marching 1 by 1 \n";
    text += " The little one stops to suck his thumb \n";
    alert(text);
  } // end verse1

  function verse2(){
    var text = "The ants go marching 2 by 2 hurrah, hurrah \n";
    text += "The ants go marching 2 by 2 hurrah, hurrah \n";
    text += "The ants go marching 2 by 2 \n";
    text += " The little one stops to tie his shoe \n";
    alert(text);
  } // end verse1

  //main code
  verse1();
  chorus();
  verse2();
  chorus();

  //>]]
</script>
```


The program code breaks the parts of the song into the same pieces a song sheet does. Here are some interesting features of `antsFunction.html`:

- **I created a function called `chorus()`.** Functions are simply collections of code lines with a name.
- **All the code for the chorus goes into this function.** Anything I want to do as part of printing the chorus goes into the `chorus()` function. Later, when I want to print the chorus, I can just call the `chorus()` function, and it will do all the code I stored there.
- **Each verse has a function, too.** I broke the code for each verse into its own function as well.

- **The main code is a road map.** Once all the details are delegated to the functions, the main part of the code just controls the order in which the functions are called.
- **Details are hidden in the functions.** The main code handles the big picture. The details (how to print the chorus or verses) are hidden inside the functions.

Passing Data into and out of Functions

Functions are logically separated from the main program. This separation is a good thing because it prevents certain kinds of errors. However, sometimes you want to send information into a function. You may also want a function to return some type of value. The `antsParam.html` page rewrites the "The Ants Go Marching" song in a way that takes advantage of function input and output.

```
<script type = "text/javascript">
  //<![CDATA[
  //from antsParam.html
```

I don't provide a figure of this program because it looks just like `antsFunction.py` to the user. One advantage of functions is that I can improve the underlying behavior of a program without imposing a change in the user's experience.

```
function chorus() {
  var text = "...and they all go marching down\n";
  text += "to the ground \n";
  text += "to get out \n";
  text += "of the rain. \n";
  text += " \n";
  text += "boom boom boom boom boom boom boom boom \n";
  return text;
} // end chorus

function verse(verseNum){
  var distraction = "";
  if (verseNum == 1){
    distraction = "suck his thumb.";
  } else if (verseNum == 2){
    distraction = "tie his shoe.";
  } else {
    distraction = "I have no idea.";
  }

  var text = "The ants go marching ";
  text += verseNum + " by " + verseNum + " hurrah, hurrah \n";
  text += "The ants go marching ";
  text += verseNum + " by " + verseNum + " hurrah, hurrah \n";
  text += "The ants go marching ";
  text += verseNum + " by " + verseNum;
  text += " the little one stops to ";
  text += distraction;
  return text;
} // end verse1
```

```
  //main code
  alert(verse(1));
  alert(chorus());
  alert(verse(2));
  alert(chorus());

  //>]]
</script>
```

This code incorporates a couple of important new ideas. (The following list is just the overview; the specifics are coming in the following sections.)

- **These functions return a value.** The functions no longer do their own `alerts`. Instead, they create a value and return it to the main program.
- **Only one verse function exists.** Because the verses are all pretty similar, using only one verse function makes sense. This improved function needs to know what verse it's working on to handle the differences.

Examining the main code

The main code has been changed in one significant way. In the last program, the main code called the functions, which did all the work. This time, the functions don't actually do the output themselves. Instead, they collect information and pass it back to the main program. Inside the main code, each function is treated like a variable.

You've actually seen this behavior. The `prompt()` method returns a value. Now the `chorus()` and `verse()` methods also return values. You can do anything you want to this value, including printing it or comparing it to some other value.

Separating the creation of data from its use as I've done here is a good idea. That way, you have more flexibility. Once a function creates some information, you can print it to the screen, store it on a Web page, put it in a database, or whatever.

Looking at the chorus

The chorus of "The Ants Go Marching" song program has been changed to return a value. Take another look at the `chorus()` function to see what I mean.

```
function chorus() {
  var text = "...and they all go marching down\n";
  text += "to the ground \n";
  text += "to get out \n";
  text += "of the rain. \n";
  text += " \n";
  text += "boom boom boom boom boom boom boom boom \n";
  return text;
} // end chorus
```

Here's what changed:

- **The purpose of the function has changed.** The function is no longer designed simply to output some value to the screen. Instead, it now provides text to the main program, which can do whatever it wants with the results.
- **There's a variable called `text`.** This variable contains all the text to be sent to the main program. (It contained all the text in the last program, but it's even more important now.)
- **The `text` variable is concatenated over several lines.** I used string concatenation to build a complex value. Note the use of newlines (`\n`) to force carriage returns.
- **The `return` statement sends `text` back to the main program.** When you want a function to return some value, simply use `return` followed by a value or variable. Note that return should be the last line of the function.

Handling the verses

The `verse()` function is quite interesting.

- It can print more than one verse.
- It takes input to determine which verse to print.
- It modifies the verse based on the input.
- It returns a value (just like `chorus()`).

To make the verse so versatile, it must take input from the primary program and return output.

Passing data to the verse() function

First, notice that the `verse()` function is always called with a value inside the parentheses. For example, the main program sets `verse(1)` to call the first verse, and `verse(2)` to invoke the second. The value inside the parentheses is called an *argument.*

The verse function must be designed to accept an argument. Look at the first line to see how I did it.

```
function verse(verseNum){
```

In the function definition, I include a variable name. Inside the function, this variable is known as a *parameter.* (Don't get hung up on the terminology. People often use the terms parameter and argument interchangeably.) The important idea is that whenever the `verse()` function is called, it automatically has a variable called verseNum. Whatever argument you send to the verse() function from the main program will become the value of the variable verseNum inside the function.

You can define a function with as many parameters as you want. Each parameter gives you the opportunity to send a piece of information to the function.

Determining the distraction

If you know the verse number, you can determine what distracts "the little one" in the song. You can determine the distraction in a couple of ways, but a simple if / else if structure is sufficient for this example.

```
var distraction = "";
if (verseNum == 1){
  distraction = "suck his thumb.";
} else if (verseNum == 2){
  distraction = "tie his shoe.";
} else {
  distraction = "I have no idea.";
}
```

I initialized the variable distraction to be empty. If verseNum is 1, set distraction to "suck his thumb." If verseNum is 2, distraction should be "tie his shoe". Any other value for verseNum is treated as an error by the else clause.

If you're an experienced coder, you may be yelling at this code. It still isn't optimal. Fortunately, in the section "Building a basic array" later in this chapter, I show an even better solution for handling this particular situation with arrays.

By the time this code segment is complete, verseNum and distraction both contain a legitimate value.

Creating the text

Once you know these variables, it's pretty easy to construct the output text:

```
  var text = "The ants go marching ";
  text += verseNum + " by " + verseNum + " hurrah, hurrah \n";
  text += "The ants go marching ";
  text += verseNum + " by " + verseNum + " hurrah, hurrah \n";
  text += "The ants go marching ";
  text += verseNum + " by " + verseNum;
  text += " the little one stops to ";
  text += distraction;
  return text;
} // end verse1
```

A whole lotta' concatenating is going on, but it's essentially the same code as the original verse() function. This one's just a lot more flexible because it can handle any verse. (Well, if the function has been preloaded to understand how to handle the `verseNum`.)

Managing Scope

A function is much like an independent mini-program. Any variable you create inside a function has meaning only inside that function. When the function is finished executing, its variables disappear! This setup is actually a really good thing. A major program will have hundreds of variables, and they can be difficult to keep track of. You can re-use a variable name without knowing it or have a value changed inadvertently. When you break your code into functions, each function has its own independent set of variables. You don't have to worry about whether the variables will cause problems elsewhere.

Introducing local and global variables

You can also define variables at the main (script) level. These variables are *global* variables. A global variable is available at the main level and inside each function. A *local* variable (one defined inside a function) has meaning only inside the function. The concept of local versus global functions is sometimes referred to as *scope*.

Local variables are kind of like local police. Local police have a limited geographical jurisdiction, but they're very useful within that space. They know the neighborhood. Sometimes you'll encounter situations that cross local jurisdictions. This situation is the kind that requires a state trooper or the FBI. Local variables are local cops, and global variables are the FBI.

In general, try to make as many of your variables local as possible. The only time you really need a global variable is when you want some information to be used in multiple functions.

Examining variable scope

To understand the implications of variable scope, take a look at `scope.html`:

```
<script type = "text/javascript">
  //<![CDATA[
  //from scope.html
  var globalVar = "I'm global!";

  function myFunction(){
    var localVar = "I'm local";
    console.log(localVar);
  }

  myFunction();

  //]]>
</script>
```

This program defines two variables. In the main code, `globalVar` is defined, and `localVar` is defined inside a function. If you run the program in debug mode while watching the variables, you can see how they behave. Figure 4-2 shows what the program looks like early in the run.

`localVar` doesn't have meaning until the function is called, so it remains undefined until the computer gets to that part of the code. Step ahead a few lines, and you see that `localVar` has a value, as shown in Figure 4-3.

Be sure to use `step into` rather than `step over` for this example. When `step over` encounters a function, it runs the entire function as one line. If you want to look into the function and see what's happening inside it (as you do here), use `step into`.

Note that `globalVar` still has a value (it's an FBI agent), and so does `localVar` because it's inside the function.

If you move a few more steps, `localVar` no longer has a value when the function ends (see Figure 4-4).

Variable scope is a good thing because it means you have to keep track of only global variables and the variables defined inside your current function. The other advantage of scope is the ability to reuse a variable name. You can have ten different functions all using the same variable name, and they won't interfere with each other because they're entirely different variables.

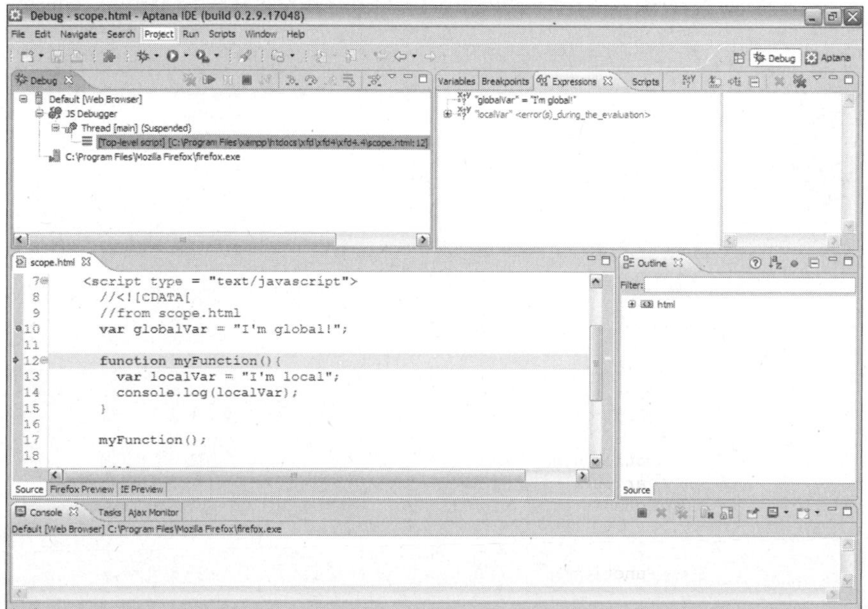

Figure 4-2: globalVar is defined, but localVar is not.

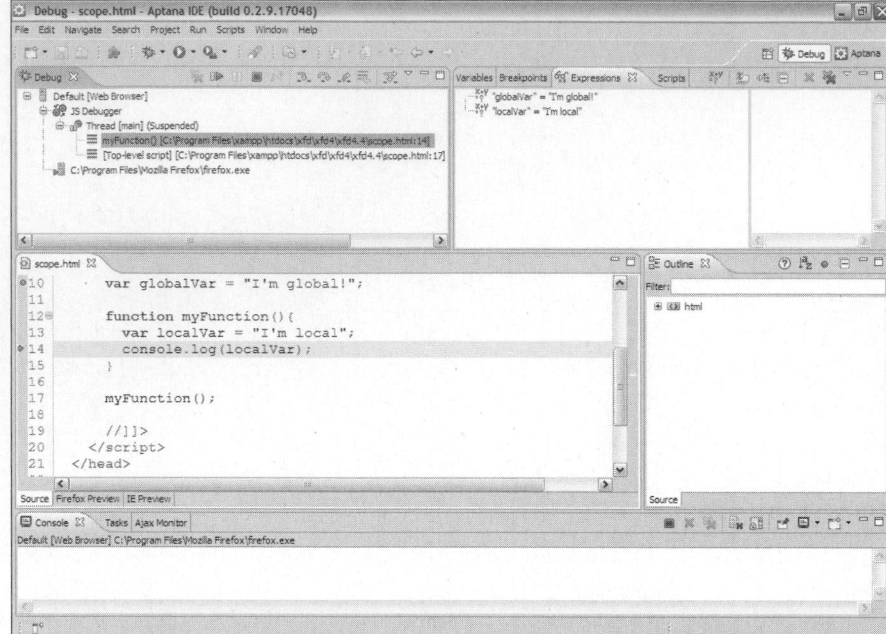

Figure 4-3: localVar has a value, because I'm inside the function.

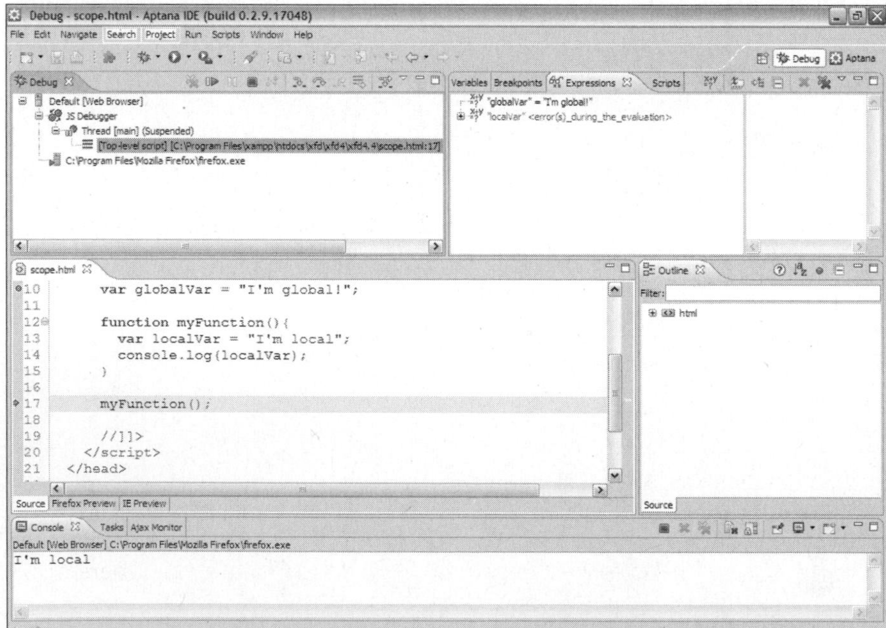

Figure 4-4: Once again, localVar has no meaning.

Building a Basic Array

If functions are groups of code lines with a name, *arrays* are groups of variables with a name. Arrays are similar to functions because they're used to manage complexity. An array is a special kind of variable. Use an array whenever you want to work with a list of similar data types.

The following code shows a basic demonstration of arrays:

```
<script type = "text/javascript">
  //<![CDATA[
  //from genres.html

  //creating an empty array
  var genre = new Array(5);

  //storing data in the array
  genre[0] = "flight simulation";
  genre[1] = "first-person shooters";
  genre[2] = "driving";
  genre[3] = "action";
  genre[4] = "strategy";

  //returning data from the array
  alert ("I like " + genre[4] + " games.");

  //]]>
</script>
```

The variable `genre` is a special variable because it contains many different values. In essence, it's a list of genres. The `new array(5)` construct creates space in memory for five variables, all named genre.

Accessing array data

Once you've specified an array, you can work with the individual elements using square brace syntax. Each element of the array is identified by an integer. The index usually begins with zero.

```
genre[0] = "flight simulation";
```


The preceding code means assign the text value `"flight simulator"` to the `genre` array variable at position `0`.

Most languages require all array elements to be the same type. JavaScript is very forgiving. You can combine all kinds of stuff in a JavaScript array. This flexibility can sometimes be useful, but be aware that this trick doesn't work in all languages. In general, I try to keep all the members of an array the same type.

Once you've got the data stored in the array, you can use the same square-bracket syntax to read the information.

The line

```
alert ("I like " + genre[4] + " games.");
```

means find element 4 of the genre array, and include it in an output message.

When `genre.html` is run, it shows Figure 4-5.

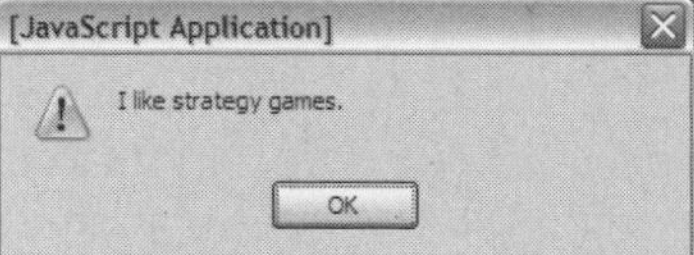

Figure 4-5: This data came from an array.

Using arrays with for loops

The main reason to use arrays is for convenience. When you have a lot of information in an array, you can write code to work with the data quickly. Whenever you have an array of data, you commonly want to do something with each element in the array. Take a look at `games.html` to see how you can do so:

```
<script type = "text/javascript">
  //<![CDATA[
  //from games.html

  //pre-loading an array
  var gameList = new Array("Flight Gear", "Sauerbraten", "Future Pinball",
      "Racer", "TORCS", "Orbiter", "Step Mania", "NetHack",
      "Marathon", "Crimson Fields");

  var text = "";
  for (i = 0; i < gameList.length; i++){
    text += "I love " + gameList[i] + "\n";
  } // end for loop
  alert(text);

  //]]>
</script>
```

Notice a couple of things in this code:

- **It features an array called `gameList`.** This array contains the names of some of my favorite freeware games.
- **The array is preloaded with values.** If you provide a list of values when creating an array, JavaScript simply preloads the array with the values you indicated. You don't need to specify the size of the array if you preload it.

- **A `for` loop steps through the array.** Arrays and for loops are natural companions. The `for` loop steps through each element of the array.
- **The array's length is used in the `for` loop condition.** Rather than specifying the value 10, I used the `length` property of the array in my `for` loop. This practice is good because the loop will automatically adjust to the size of the array if I add or remove elements.
- **Do something with each element.** Because I goes from 0 to 9 (the array indices), I can easily print each value of the array. In this example, I simply add to an output string.
- **Note the newline characters. –** `\n` combination is a special character. It tells JavaScript to add a carriage return, such as pressing the Enter key.

When `games.html` runs, it looks like Figure 4-6.

If you want to completely ruin your productivity, Google some of these game names. They're absolutely incredible, and every one of them is free. It's hard to beat that. See, even if you don't learn how to program in this book, you get something good out of it!

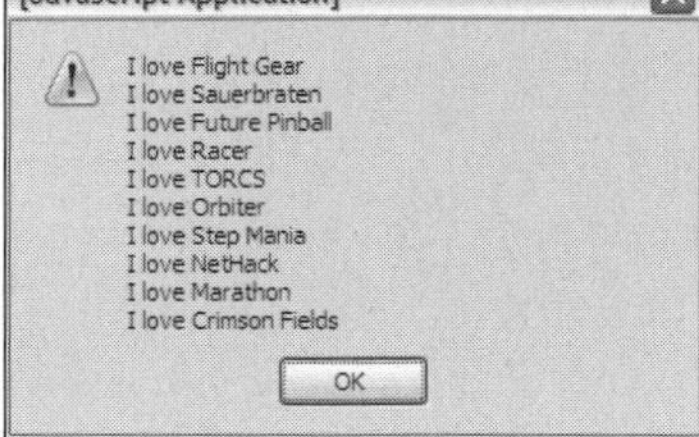

Figure 4-6: Now I've got a list of games. Arrays and loops are fun!

Revisiting the ants song

If you read the earlier sections, you had probably just gotten that marching ant song out of your head. Sorry. Take a look at the following variation, which uses arrays and loops to simplify the code even more!


```
<script type = "text/javascript">
  //<![CDATA[
  //from antsArray.html

  var distractionList = new Array("", "suck his thumb", "tie his shoe");

  function chorus() {
    var text = "...and they all go marching down\n";
    text += "to the ground \n";
    text += "to get out \n";
    text += "of the rain. \n";
    text += " \n";
    text += "boom boom boom boom boom boom boom boom \n";
```

```
      return text;
    } // end chorus

    function verse(verseNum){
      //pull distraction from array
      var distraction = distractionList[verseNum];

      var text = "The ants go marching ";
      text += verseNum + " by " + verseNum + " hurrah, hurrah \n";
      text += "The ants go marching ";
      text += verseNum + " by " + verseNum + " hurrah, hurrah \n";
      text += "The ants go marching ";
      text += verseNum + " by " + verseNum;
      text += " the little one stops to ";
      text += distraction;
      return text;
    } // end verse1

    //main code is now a loop
    for (verseNum = 1; verseNum < distractionList.length; verseNum++){
      alert(verse(verseNum));
      alert(chorus());
    } // end for loop

    //>]]
  </script>
```

This code is just a little different from the `antsParam` program shown in the section of this chapter called "Passing Data into and out of Functions."

- **It has an array called `distractionList`.** This array is (despite the misleading name) a list of distractions. I made the first one (element zero) blank so that the verse numbers would line up properly.
- **The `verse()` function looks up a distraction.** Because distractions are now in an array, you can use the `verseNum` as an index to loop up a particular distraction. Compare this function to the `verse()` function in `antsParam`. (This program can be found in the section "Passing data into and out of Functions." Although arrays require a little more planning than code structures, they can highly improve the readability of your code.
- **The main program is in a loop.** I step through each element of the `distractionList` array, printing the appropriate verse and chorus.
- **The `chorus()` function remains unchanged.** You don't need to change `chorus()`.

Working with Two-Dimension Arrays

Arrays are useful when working with lists of data. Sometimes you'll encounter data that's best imagined in a table. For example, what if you wanted to build a distance calculator that determines the distance between two cities? The original data might look like Table 4-1.

Table 4-1	Distance between Major Cities			
	0) Indianapolis	*1) New York*	*2) Tokyo*	*3) London*
0) Indianapolis	0	648	6476	4000
1) New York	648	0	6760	3470
2) Tokyo	6476	6760	0	5956
3) London	4000	3470	5956	0

Think about how you would use Table 4-1 to figure out a distance. If you wanted to travel from New York to London, for example, you'd pick out the New York row and the London column and figure out where they intersect. The data in that cell is the distance (3,470 miles).

When you look up information in any kind of a table, you're actually working with a *two-dimensional data structure* — a fancy term, but it just means table. If you want to look something up in a table, you need two indices, one to determine the row, and another to determine the column.

If this concept is difficult to grasp, think of the old game Battleship. The playing field is a grid of squares. You announce I-5, meaning column I, row 5, and the opponent looks in that grid to discover that you've sunk his battleship. In programming, you typically use integers for both indices, but otherwise it's exactly the same as Battleship. Any time you have two-dimensional data, you'll access it with two indices.

Often, we call the indices *row* and *column* to help you think of the structure as a table. Sometimes other names more clearly describe how the behavior works. Take a look at Figure 4-7, and you see that the `distance.html` program asks for two cities and returns a distance according to the data table.

Yep, you can have three, four, or more dimension arrays in programming, but don't worry about that yet. (It may make your head explode.) Most of the time, one or two dimensions are all you need.

This program is a touch longer than some of the others, so I break it into parts in the following sections for easy digestion. Be sure to look at the program in its entirety on the CD-ROM.

Setting up the arrays

The key to this program is the data organization. The first step is to set up two arrays.

```
<script type = "text/javascript">
  //<![CDATA[
  //from distance.html
```

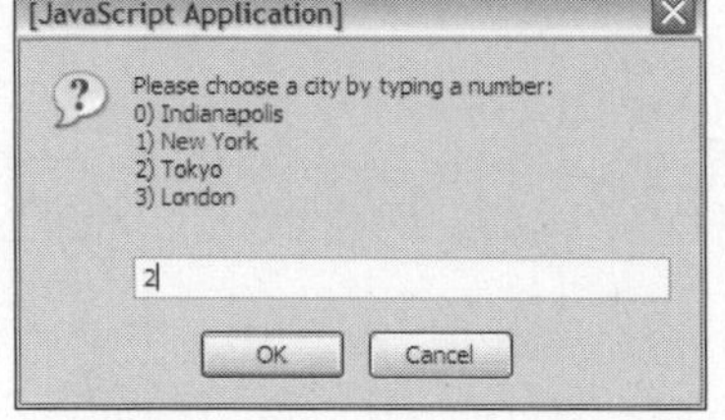

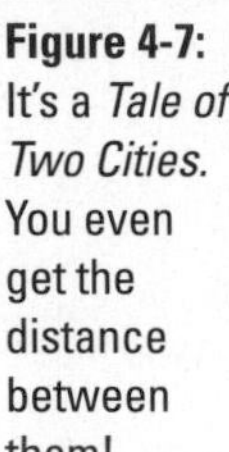

[JavaScript Application]

The distance from Indianapolis to Tokyo is 6476 miles.

OK

Figure 4-7: It's a *Tale of Two Cities.* You even get the distance between them!

```
//cityName has the names of the cities
cityName = new Array("Indianapolis", "New York", "Tokyo", "London");
//create a 2-dimension array of distances
distance = new Array (
  new Array (0, 648, 6476, 4000),
  new Array (648, 0, 6760, 3470),
  new Array (6476, 6760, 0, 5956),
  new Array (4000, 3470, 5956, 0)
);
```

The first array is an ordinary single-dimension array of city names. I've been careful to always keep the cities in the same order, so whenever I refer to city 0, I'm talking about Indianapolis (my hometown) New York is always going to be at position 1, and so on.

You have to be careful in your data design that you always keep things in the same order. Be sure to organize your data on paper before you type it into the computer, so you'll understand what value goes where.

The `cityNames` array has two jobs. First, it reminds me what order all the cities will be in, and, second, it gives me an easy way to get a city name when I know an index. For example, I know that `cityName[2]` will always be `"Tokyo"`.

The `distance` array is very interesting. If you squint at it a little bit, it looks a lot like Table 4-1, shown earlier in this chapter. That's because it *is* Table 4-1, just in a slightly different format.

distance is an array. JavaScript arrays can hold just about everything, including other arrays! That's what distance does. It holds an array of rows. Each element of the distance array is another (unnamed) array holding all the data for that row. If you want to extract information from the array, you need two pieces of information. First, you need the row. Then because the row is an array, you need the column number within that array. So, distance[1][3] means go to row one ("New York") of distance. Within that row go to element 3 ("London") and return the resulting value (3470). Cool, huh?

Getting a city

The program requires that you ask for two cities. You want the user to enter a city number, not a name, and you want to ask this question twice. Sounds like a good time for a function.

```
function getCity(){
  // presents a list of cities and gets a number corresponding to
  // the city name
  var theCity = "";  //will hold the city number

  var cityMenu = "Please choose a city by typing a number: \n";
  cityMenu += "0) Indianapolis \n";
  cityMenu += "1) New York \n";
  cityMenu += "2) Tokyo \n";
  cityMenu += "3) London \n";

  theCity = prompt(cityMenu);
  return theCity;
} // end getCity
```

The getCity() function prints up a little menu of city choices and asks for some input. It then returns that input.

You can improve getCity() in all kinds of ways. For one thing, maybe it should repeat until you get a valid number so that users can't type the city name or do something else crazy. I'll leave it simple for now. If you want to find out how to use user interface elements to help the user submit only valid input, skip ahead to Chapter 5 of this minibook.

Creating a main() function

The main() function handles most of the code for the program.

```
function main(){
  var output = "";
  var from = getCity();
  var to = getCity();
  var result = distance[from][to];
  output = "The distance from " + cityName[from];
  output += " to " + cityName[to];
  output += " is " + result + " miles.";
  alert(output);
} // end main
main();
```

The main() function controls traffic. Here's what you do:

1. **Create an output variable.**

   The point of this function is to create some text output describing the distance. I begin by creating a variable called output and setting its initial value to empty.

2. **Get the city of origin.**

   Fortunately, you've got a really great function called getCity() that handles all the details of getting a city in the right format. Call this function and assign its value to the new variable from.

3. **Get the destination city.**

   That getCity() function sure is handy. Use it again to get the city number you'll call to.

4. **Get the distance.**

   Because you know two indices, and you know they're in the right format, you can simply look them up in the table. Look up distance[from][to] and store it in the variable result.

5. **Output the response.**

   Use concatenation to build a suitable response string and send it to the user.

6. **Get city names from the cityNames array.**

   The program uses numeric indices for the cities, but they don't mean anything to the user. Use the cityNames array to retrieve the two city names for the output.

7. **Run the main() function.**

   Only one line of code doesn't appear in a function. That line calls the main() function and starts the whole thing up.

I didn't actually write the program in the order I showed it to you in the preceding steps. Sometimes it makes more sense to go "inside out." I actually created the data structure first (as an ordinary table on paper) and then constructed the main() function. This approach made it obvious that I needed a getCity() function and gave me some clues about how getCity should work. (In other words, it should present a list of cities and prompt for a numerical input.)

Chapter 5: Talking to the Page

In This Chapter

- Introducing the Document Object Model
- Responding to form events
- Connecting a button to a function
- Retrieving data from text fields
- Changing text in text fields
- Sending data to the page
- Working with other text-related form elements

JavaScript is fun and all, but it lives in Web browsers for a reason: to let you change Web pages. The best thing about JavaScript is how it helps you control the page. You can use JavaScript to read useful information from the user and to change the page on the fly.

In the first few chapters of this minibook, I concentrate on JavaScript without worrying about the HTML. The HTML code in those programs was unimportant, so I didn't include it in the code listings. This chapter is about how to integrate code with HTML, so now I incorporate the HTML as well as the JavaScript segments. Sometimes I still print code in separate blocks, so (as always) try to look at the code in its natural habitat, through your browser.

Understanding the Document Object Model

JavaScript programs usually live in the context of a Web page. The contents of the page are available to the JavaScript programs through a mechanism called the *document object model* (DOM).

The DOM is a special set of complex variables that encapsulates the entire contents of the Web page. You can use JavaScript to read from the DOM and determine the status of an element. You can also modify a DOM variable and change the page from within JavaScript code.

Navigating the DOM

The easiest way to get a feel for the DOM is to load up a page in Firefox and look at the Firebug window's DOM tab. I do just that in Figure 5-1.

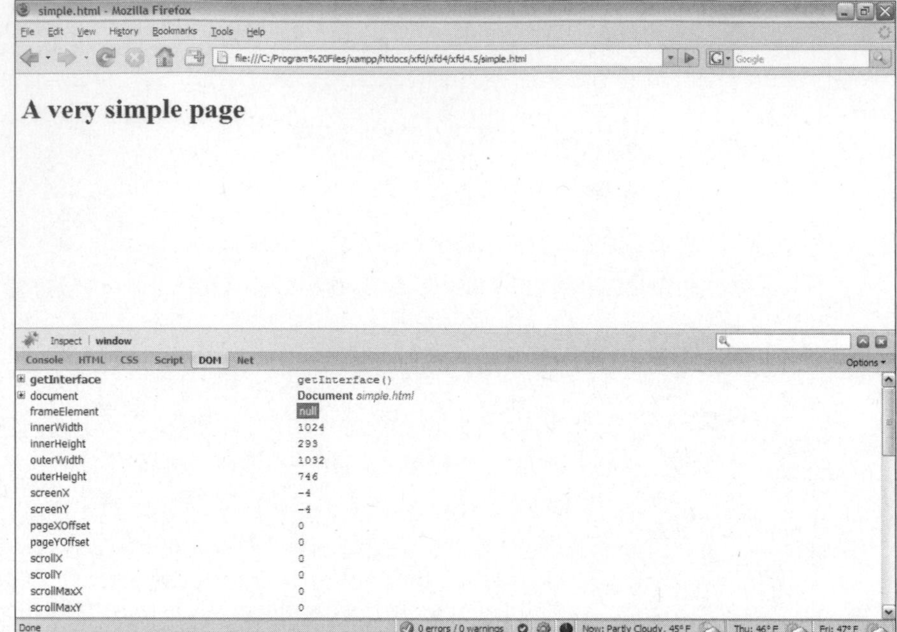

Figure 5-1: Even a very simple page has a complex DOM.

When you look over the DOM of a simple page, you can easily get overwhelmed. You'll see a lot of variables listed. Technically, these variables are all elements of a special object called `window`. The `window` object has a huge number of sub-objects, all listed in the DOM view. Table 5-1 describes a few important window variables.

Table 5-1 Primary DOM Objects

Variable	*Description*	*Notes*
document	Represents XHTML page	Most commonly scripted element
location	Describes current URL	Change location .href to move to a new page
history	A list of recently visited pages	Access this to view previous pages
status	The browser status bar	Change this to set a message in the status bar

Changing DOM properties with Firebug

To illustrate the power of the DOM, try this experiment in Firefox:

1. **Load any page.**

It doesn't matter what page you work with. For this example, I use `simple.html`, a very basic page with only an `<h1>` header.

2. **Enable the Firebug extension.**

   You can play with the DOM in many ways, but the Firebug extension is one of the easiest and most powerful tools for experimentation.

3. **Enable the DOM tab.**

   You see a list of all the top-level variables.

4. **Scroll down until you see the `status` element.**

   When you find the `status` element, double-click it.

5. **Type a message to yourself in the resulting dialog box and press Enter.**

6. **Look at the bottom of the browser.**

   The status bar at the bottom of the browser window should now contain your message.

7. **Experiment.**

   Play around with the various elements in the DOM list. You can modify many of them. Try changing `window.location.href` to any URL and watch what happens. Don't worry; you can't permanently break anything here.

Examining the document object

If the `window` object is powerful, its offspring, the `document`, is even more amazing. (If you're unfamiliar with the `window` object, see the section "Navigating the DOM," earlier in this chapter.)

Once again, the best way to get a feel for this thing is to do some exploring:

1. **Reload `simple.html`.**

   If your previous experiments caused things to get really weird, you may have to restart Firefox. Be sure the Firebug extension displays the DOM tab.

2. **Find the `document` object.**

   It's usually the second object in the `window` list. When you select this object, it expands, showing a huge number of child elements.

3. **Look for the `document.body`.**

   Somewhere in the `document` you'll see the `body`. Select this object to see what you discover.

4. **Find the `document.body.style`.**

   The document object has a `body` object, which has a `body` object, which has a style. Will it never end?

5. **Look through the style elements.**

   Some styles will be unfamiliar, but keep going, and you'll probably see some old friends.

6. **Double-click `backgroundColor`.**

   Each CSS style attribute has a matching (but not quite identical) counterpart in the DOM. Wow. Type a new color and see what happens.

7. **Marvel at your cleverness.**

   You can navigate the DOM to make all kinds of changes in the page. If you can manipulate something here, you can write code to do it, too.

If you're lost here, Figure 5-2 shows me modifying the `backgroundColor` of the style of the body of the document (on a wing on a bird on a branch on a tree in a hole in the ground). A figure can't really do this justice, though. You have to experiment for yourself. But don't be overwhelmed. You don't really need to understand all of these details, just know they exist.

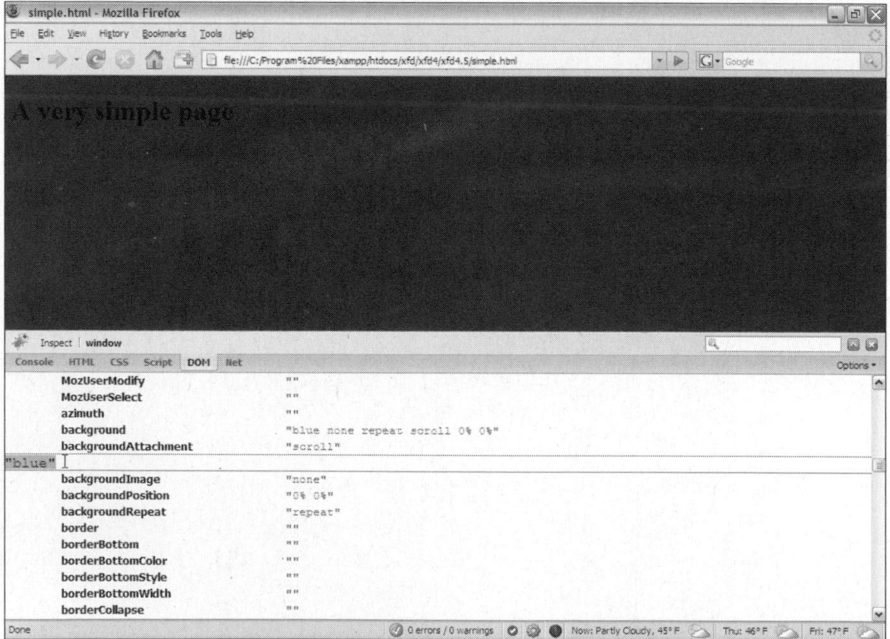

Figure 5-2: Firebug lets me modify the DOM of my page directly.

Harnessing the DOM through JavaScript

Sure, using Firebug to trick out your Web page is geeky and all, but why should you care? The whole purpose of the DOM is to provide JavaScript magical access to all the inner workings of your page.

Getting the blues, JavaScript-style

It all gets fun when you start to write JavaScript code to access the DOM. Take a look at `blue.html` in Figure 5-3.

The page has white text on a blue background, but there's no CSS! Instead, it has a small script that changes the DOM directly, controlling the page colors through code.

```
<!DOCTYPE html PUBLIC "-//W3C//DTD XHTML 1.0 Strict//EN"
"http://www.w3.org/TR/xhtml1/DTD/xhtml1-strict.dtd">
<html lang="EN" dir="ltr" xmlns="http://www.w3.org/1999/xhtml">
  <head>
    <meta http-equiv="content-type" content="text/xml; charset=utf-8" />
    <title>blue.html</title>

  </head>
  <body>
    <h1>I've got the JavaScript Blues</h1>
    <script type = "text/javascript">
      //<![CDATA[
```

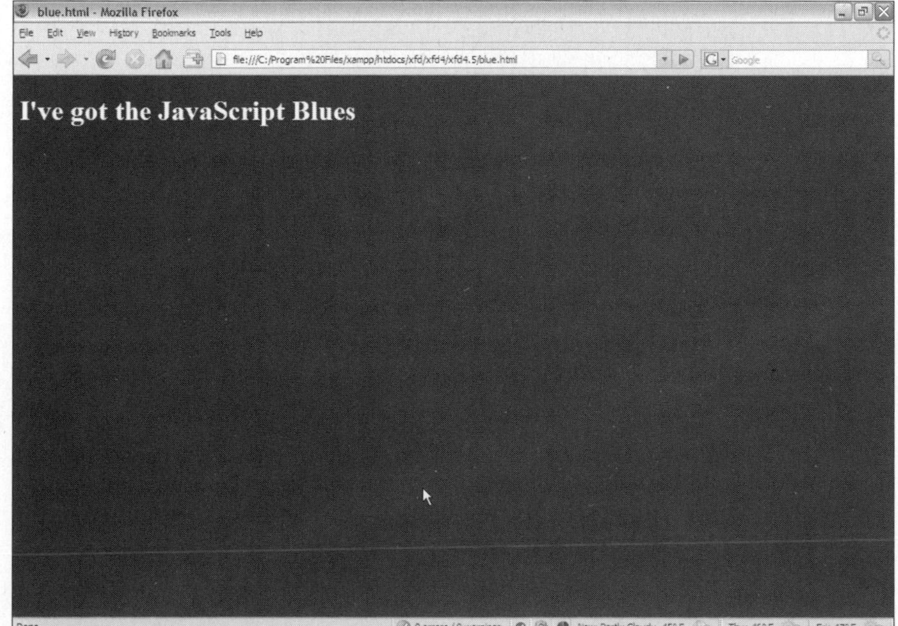

Figure 5-3: This page is blue. But where's the CSS?

```
      // use javascript to set the colors
      document.body.style.color = "white";
      document.body.style.backgroundColor = "blue";

      //]]>
    </script>
  </body>
</html>
```

Writing JavaScript code to change colors

The page shown in Figure 5-3 is pretty simple, but it has a few features not found in Chapters 1 through 4 of this minibook.

- **It has no CSS.** A form of CSS is dynamically created through the code.
- **The script is in the body.** I can't place this particular script in the header because it refers to the body.

  When the browser first sees the script, there must be a body for the text to change. If I put the script in the head, no body exists when the browser reads the code, so it gets confused. If I place the script in the body, there is a body, so the script can change it. (It's really okay if you don't get this discussion. This example is probably the only time you'll see this trick because I show a better way in the next example.)

- **Use a DOM reference to change the style colors.** That long trail of breadcrumbs syntax takes you all the way from the document through the body to the style and finally the color. It's tedious but thorough.
- **Set the foreground color to white.** You can change the color property to any valid CSS color value (a color name or a hex value). It's just like CSS, because you are affecting the CSS.
- **Set the background color to blue.** Again, this adjustment is just like setting CSS.

Shouldn't it be background-color?

If you've dug through the DOM style elements, you'll notice some interesting things. Many of the element names are familiar but not quite identical. `background-color` becomes `backgroundColor` and `font-weight` becomes `fontWeight`. CSS uses dashes to indicate word breaks, and the DOM combines words and uses capitalization for clarity. You'll find all your old favorite CSS elements, but the names change according to this very predictable formula. Still, if you're ever confused, just use the Firebug DOM inspector to look over various style elements.

Managing Button Events

Of course, there's no good reason to write code like `blue.html`, which I discuss in the section "Harnessing the DOM through JavaScript," earlier in this chapter. You will find that it's just as easy to build CSS as it is to write Java Script. The advantage comes when you use the DOM dynamically to change the page's behavior after it has finished loading.

Figure 5-4 shows a page called `"backgroundColors.html"`.

The page is set up with the default white background color. It has two buttons on it, which should change the body's background color. Click the Blue button, and you see that it works, as verified in Figure 5-5.

Some really exciting things just happened.

- **The page has a form.** For more information on form elements, refer to Book I, Chapter 7.
- **The button does something.** Plain-old XHTML forms don't really do anything. You've got to write some kind of programming code to accomplish a task. This program does it.

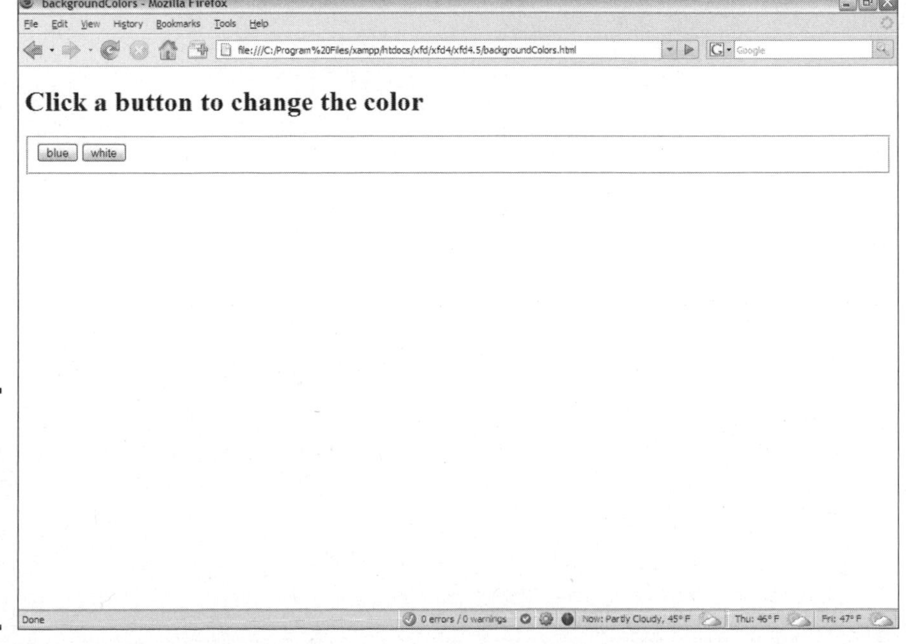

Figure 5-4: The page is white. It has two buttons on it. I've gotta click Blue.

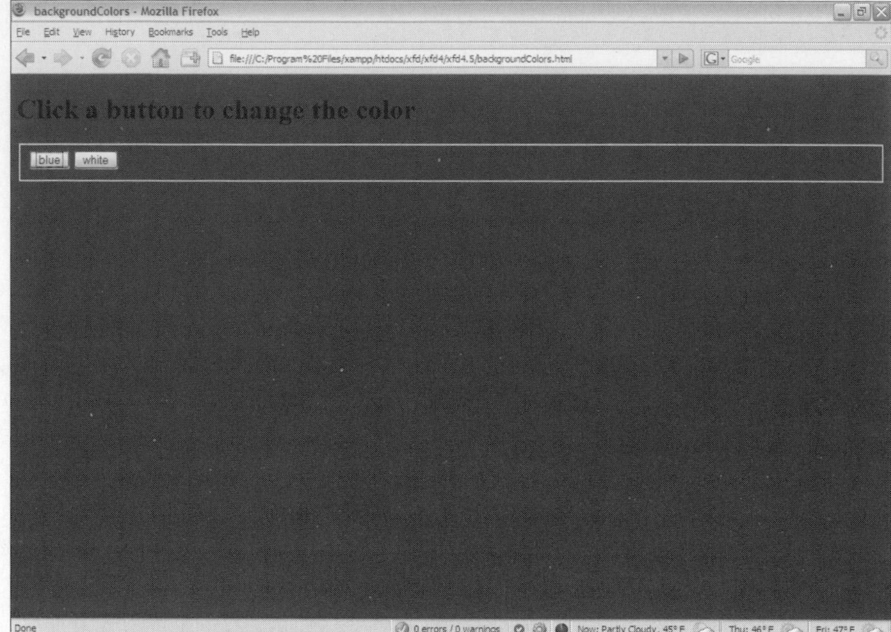

Figure 5-5: It turned blue! Joy!

- **The page has a `setColor()` function.** The page has a function that takes a color name and applies it to the background style
- **Both buttons pass information to `setColor`.** Both of the buttons call the `setColor()` function, but they each pass a different color value. That's how the program knows what color to use when changing the background.

Take a look at the code:

```
<!DOCTYPE html PUBLIC "-//W3C//DTD XHTML 1.0 Strict//EN"
"http://www.w3.org/TR/xhtml1/DTD/xhtml1-strict.dtd">
<html lang="EN" dir="ltr" xmlns="http://www.w3.org/1999/xhtml">
  <head>
    <meta http-equiv="content-type" content="text/xml; charset=utf-8" />
    <title>backgroundColors</title>
    <script type = "text/javascript">
      //<![CDATA[
      // from backgroundColors

      function changeColor(color){
        document.body.style.backgroundColor = color;
      } // end changeColor

      //]]>
    </script>
  </head>
  <body>
    <h1>Click a button to change the color</h1>
```

```
    <form action = "">
      <fieldset>
        <input type = "button"
               value = "blue"
               onclick = "changeColor('blue')"/>

        <input type = "button"
               value = "white"
               onclick = "changeColor('white')" />
      </fieldset>

    </form>
  </body>
</html>
```

Most Web pages actually treat the XHTML page as the user interface and the JavaScript as the event-manipulation code that goes underneath. It makes sense, then, to look at the HTML code that acts as the playground first:

- **It contains a form.** Note that the form's `action` attribute is still empty. You don't mess with that attribute until you work with the server in Book V.
- **The form has a `fieldset`.** The `input` elements need to be inside something, and a `fieldset` seems like a pretty natural choice.
- **The page has two buttons.** The two buttons on the page are nothing new, but they've never done anything before.
- **The buttons both have `onclick` attributes.** This special attribute can accept one line of JavaScript code. Usually, that line calls a function, as I do in this example.
- **Each button calls the same function, but with a different parameter.** Both buttons call `changeColor()`, but one sends the value `"blue"` and the other `"white"`.
- **Presumably, `changeColor` changes a color.** That's exactly what it will do. In fact, it changes the background color.

Generally, I write the XHTML code before the script. As you can see, the form provides all kinds of useful information that can help me make the script. Specifically, I need to write a function called `changeColor()`, and this function should take a color name as a parameter and change the background to the indicated color. With that kind of help, the function is half written!

Embedding quotes within quotes

Take a careful look at the `onclick` lines in the code in the preceding section. You may not have noticed one important issue:

`onclick` is an XHTML parameter, and its value must be encased in quotes. The parameter happens to be a function call, which sends a string value. String values must also be in quotes. This setup can become confusing if you use double quotes everywhere because the browser has no way to know the quotes are nested.

```
onclick = "changeColor("white")" />
```

XHTML thinks the `onclick` parameter contains the value `"changeColor("` and it will have no idea what `white")"` is.

Fortunately, JavaScript has an easy fix for this problem. If you want to embed a quote inside another quote, just switch to single quotes. The line is written with the parameter inside single quotes:

```
onclick = "changeColor('white')" />
```

Writing the changeColor function

The `changeColor()` function is pretty easy to write.

```
<script type = "text/javascript">
  //<![CDATA[
  // from backgroundColors

  function changeColor(color){
    document.body.style.backgroundColor = color;
  } // end changeColor

  //]]>
</script>
```

It goes in the header area as normal. It's simply a function accepting one parameter called `color`. The body's `backgroundColor` property is set to `color`.

I can write JavaScript in the header that refers to the body because the header code is all in a function. The function is read before the body is in place, but it isn't activated until the user clicks the button. By this time, there is a body, and there's no problem.

Managing Text Input and Output

Perhaps the most intriguing application of the DOM is the ability to let the user communicate with the program through the Web page, without all those annoying dialog boxes. Figure 5-6 shows a page with a Web form containing two textboxes and a button.

When you click the button, something exciting happens, demonstrated by Figure 5-7.

Clearly, form-based input and output is preferable to the constant interruption of dialog boxes.

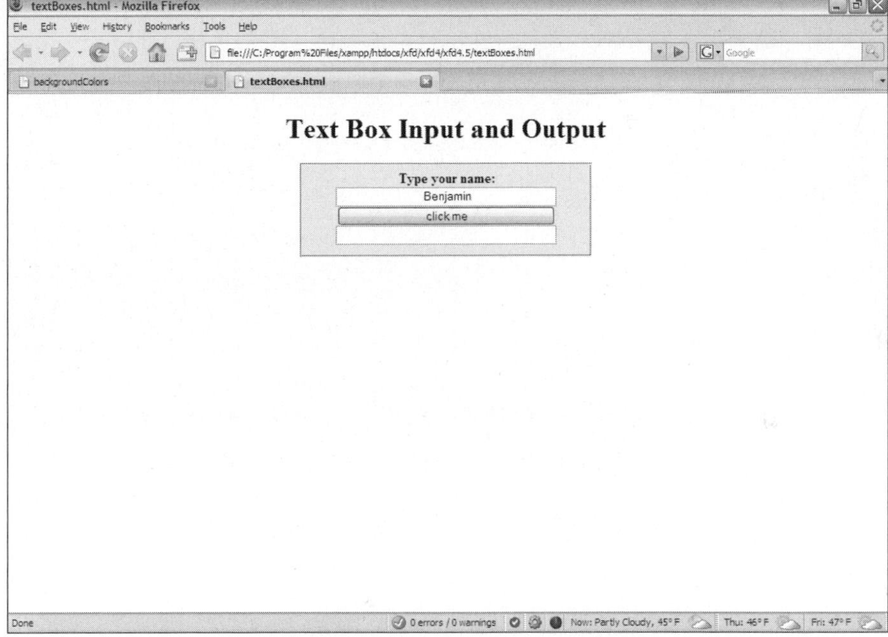

Figure 5-6: I've typed a name into the top textbox.

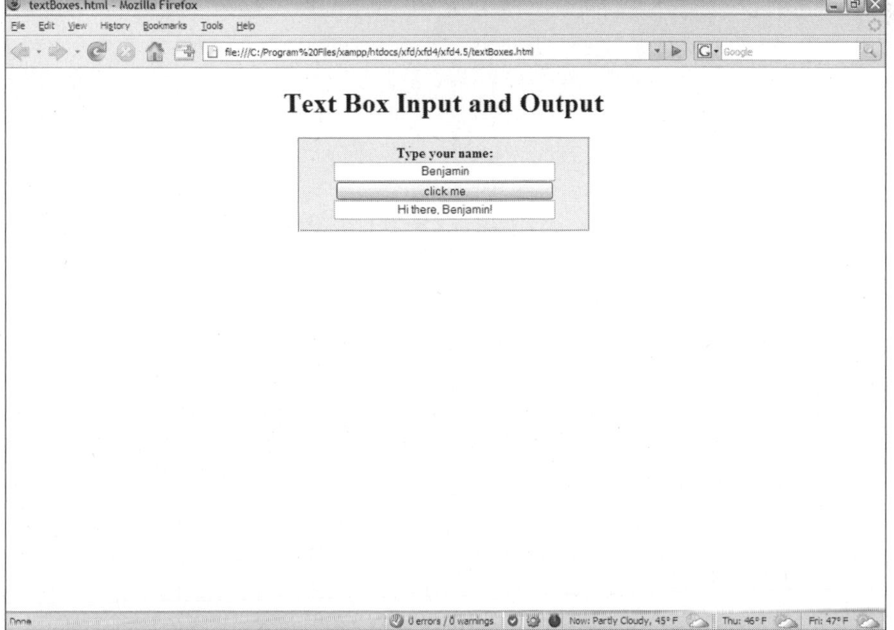

Figure 5-7: I got a greeting! With no alert box!

Introducing event-driven programming

Graphic user interfaces usually use a technique called *event-driven programming*. The idea is simple.

1. **Create a user interface.**

   In Web pages, the user interface is usually built of XHTML and CSS.

2. **Identify events the program should respond to.**

   If you have a button, users will click it. (If you want to guarantee they click it, put the text Launch the Missiles on the button. I don't know why, but it always works.) Buttons almost always have events. Some other elements do, too.

3. **Write a function to respond to each event.**

   For each event you want to test, write a function that does whatever needs to happen.

4. **Get information from form elements.**

   Now you're accessing the contents of form elements to get information from the user. You need a mechanism for getting information from a text field and other form elements.

5. **Use form elements for output.**

   For this simple example, I also use form elements for output. The output goes in a second text box, even though I don't intend the user to type any text there.

Creating the XHTML form

The first step in building a program that can manage text input and output is to create the XHTML framework. Here's the XHTML code:

```
<title>textBoxes.html</title>

<link rel = "stylesheet"
        type = "text/css"
        href = "textBoxes.css" />

</head>

<body>
  <h1>Text Box Input and Output</h1>
  <form action = "">
    <fieldset>
      <label>Type your name: </label>
      <input type = "text"
             id = "txtName" />

      <input type = "button"
             value = "click me"
             onclick = "sayHi()"/>
```

```
        <input type = "text"
               id = "txtOutput" />
      </fieldset>
    </form>

  </body>
</html>
```

As you look over the code, note a few important ideas:

- **The page uses external CSS.** The CSS style is nice, but it's not important in the discussion here. It stays safely encapsulated in its own file. Of course, you're welcome to look it over or change it.
- **Most of the page is a form.** All form elements must be inside a form.
- **A fieldset is used to contain form elements.** `input` elements need to be inside some sort of block-level element, and a `fieldset` is a natural choice.
- **There's a text field named `txtName`.** This text field contains the name. I begin with the phrase `txt` to remind myself that this field is a textbox.
- **The second element is a button.** You don't need to give the button an ID (as it won't be referred to in code), but it does have an `onclick()` event.
- **The button's `onclick` event refers to a (yet undefined) function.** In this example, it's named `"sayHi()"`.
- **A second text box contains the greeting.** This second textbox is called `txtOutput` because it's the text field meant for output.

Once you've set up the HTML page, the function becomes pretty easy to write because you've already identified all the major constructs. You know you need a function called `sayHi()`, and this function reads text from the `txtName` field and writes to the `txtOutput` field.

Using GetElementById to get access to the page

XHTML is one thing, and JavaScript is another. You need some way to turn an HTML form element into something JavaScript can read. The magical `getElementById()` method does exactly that. First, look at the first two lines of the `sayHi()` function (defined in the header as usual).

```
function sayHi(){
  var txtName = document.getElementById("txtName");
  var txtOutput = document.getElementById("txtOutput");
```

You can extract every element created in your Web page by digging through the DOM. In the old days, this approach is how we used to access form elements. It was ugly and tedious. Modern browsers have the wonderful getElementById() function instead. This beauty searches through the DOM and returns a reference to an object with the requested ID.

A *reference* is simply an indicator where the specified object is in memory. You can store a reference in a variable. Manipulating this variable manipulates the object it represents. If you want, you can think of it as making the textbox into a variable.

Note that I call the variable txtName, just like the original textbox. This variable refers to the text field from the form, not the value of that text field. Once I have a reference to the text field object, I can use its methods and properties to extract data from it and send new values to it.

Manipulating the text fields

Once you have access to the text fields, you can manipulate the values of these fields with the value property:

```
var name = txtName.value;
txtOutput.value = "Hi there, " + name + "!"
```

Text fields (and, in fact, all input fields) have a value property. You can read this value as an ordinary string variable. You can also write to this property, and the text field will be updated on the fly.

This code handles the data input and output:

1. **Create a variable for the name.**

   This is an ordinary string variable.

2. **Copy the value of the textbox into the variable.**

   Now that you have a variable representing the textbox, you can access its value property to get the value typed in by the user.

3. **Create a message for the user.**

   Use ordinary string concatenation.

4. **Send the message to the output textbox.**

   You can also write text to the value property, which changes the contents of the text field on the screen.

Text fields always return string values (like prompts do). If you want to pull a numeric value from a text field, you may have to convert it with the parseInt() or parseFloat() functions.

Writing to the Document

Form elements are great for getting input from the user, but they're not ideal for output. Placing the output in an editable field really doesn't make much sense. Changing the Web document is a much better approach.

The DOM supports exactly such a technique. Most XHTML elements feature an `innerHTML` property. This property describes the HTML code inside the element. In most cases, it can be read from and written to.

So what are the exceptions? Single-element tags (like `<img>` and `<input>`) don't contain any HTML, so obviously reading or changing their inner HTML doesn't make sense. Table elements can often be read from but not changed directly.

Figure 5-8 shows a program with a basic form.

This form doesn't have a form element for the output. Enter a name and click the button, and you see the results in Figure 5-9.

Amazingly enough, this page can make changes to itself dynamically. It isn't simply changing the values of form fields, but changing the HTML.

Figure 5-8: Wait, there's no output text field!

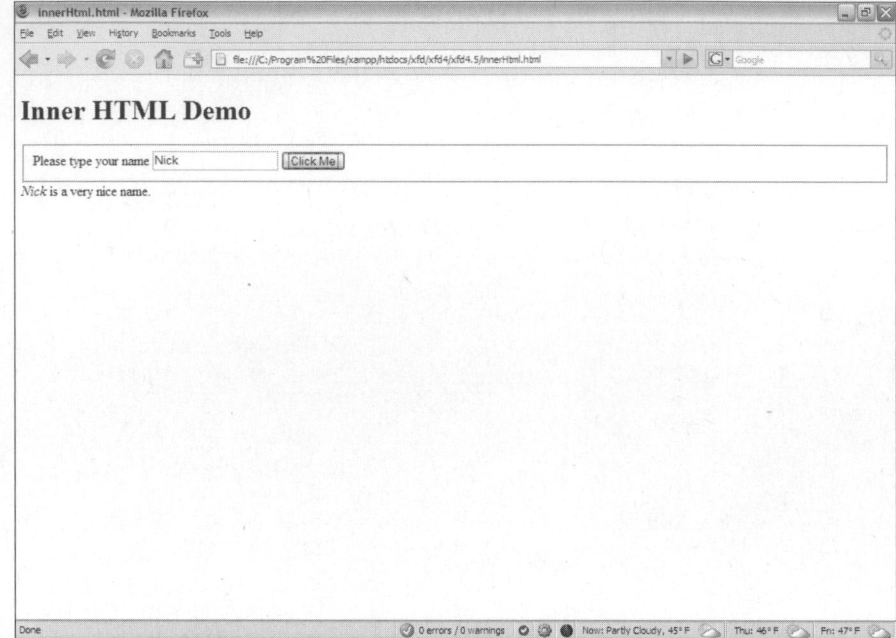

Figure 5-9: The page has changed itself.

Preparing the HTML framework

To see how the page changes itself dynamically, begin by looking at the XHTML body for `innerHTML.html`:

```
<body>
  <h1>Inner HTML Demo</h1>
  <form action = "">
    <fieldset>
      <label>Please type your name</label>
      <input type = "text"
             id = "txtName" />
      <button type = "button"
              onclick = "sayHi()">
        Click Me
      </button>
    </fieldset>
  </form>

  <div id = "divOutput">
    Watch this space.
  </div>
</body>
```

The code body has a couple of interesting features:

- **The program has a form.** The form is pretty standard. It has a text field for input and a button, but no output elements.

- **The button will call a `sayHi()` function.** The page requires a function with this name. Presumably, it says hi somehow.
- **There's a div for output.** A `div` element in the main body is designated for output.
- **The div has an ID.** The `id` attribute is often used for CSS styling, but the DOM can also use it. Any HTML elements that will be dynamically scripted should have an `id` field.

Writing the JavaScript

The JavaScript code for modifying `innerHTML` isn't very hard:

```
<script type = "text/javascript">
  //<![CDATA[
  //from innerHTML.html

  function sayHi(){
    txtName = document.getElementById("txtName");
    divOutput = document.getElementById("divOutput");

    name = txtName.value;

    divOutput.innerHTML = "<em>" + name +  "<\/em>";
    divOutput.innerHTML += " is a very nice name.";
  }
  //]]>
</script>
```

The first step (as usual with Web forms) is to extract data from the input elements. Note that I can create a variable representation of any DOM element, not just form elements. The `divOutput` variable is a JavaScript representation of the DOM div.

Finding your innerHTML

Like form elements, divs have other interesting properties you can modify. The `innerHTML` property allows you to change the HTML code displayed by the div. You can put any valid XHTML code you want inside the `innerHTML` property, even HTML tags. Be sure that you still follow the XHTML rules so that your code will be valid.

Even with the `CDATA` element in place, validators get confused by forward slashes (like the one in the `</em>` tag). Whenever you want to use a `/` character in JavaScript strings, precede it with a backslash (`<\/em>`). A backslash helps the validator understand that you intend to place a slash character at the next position.

Working with Other Text Elements

Once you know how to work with text fields, you've mastered about half of the form elements. Several other form elements work exactly like text fields, including these:

- **Password fields** obscure the user's input with asterisks, but preserve the text.
- **Hidden fields** allow you to store information in a page without revealing it to the user. (They're used a little bit in client-side coding, but almost never in JavaScript.)
- **Text areas** are a special variation of text boxes designed to handle multiple lines of input.

Figure 5-10 is a page with all these elements available on the same form.

When the user clicks the button, the contents of all the fields (even the password and hidden fields) appear on the bottom of the page, as shown in Figure 5-11.

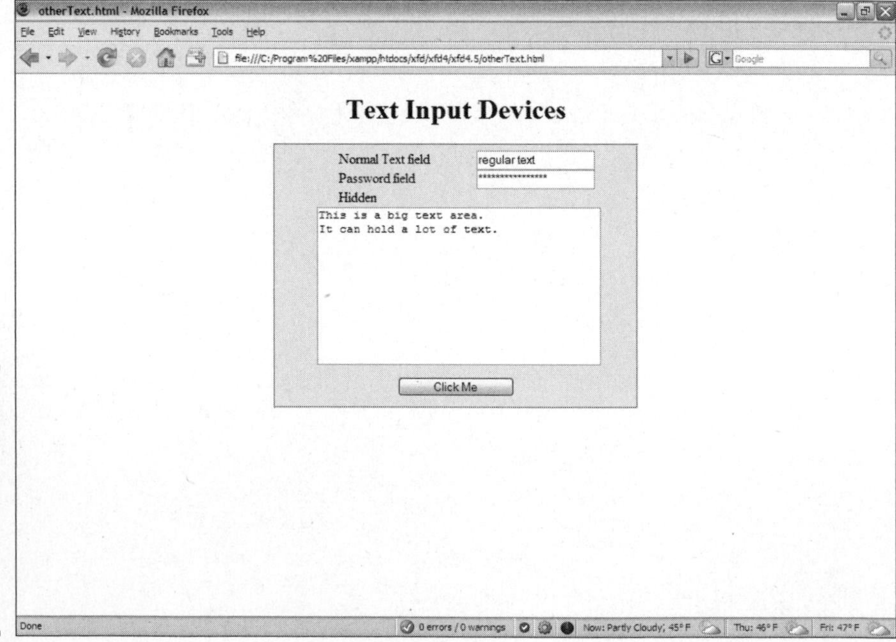

Figure 5-10: Passwords, hidden fields, and text areas all look the same to JavaScript.

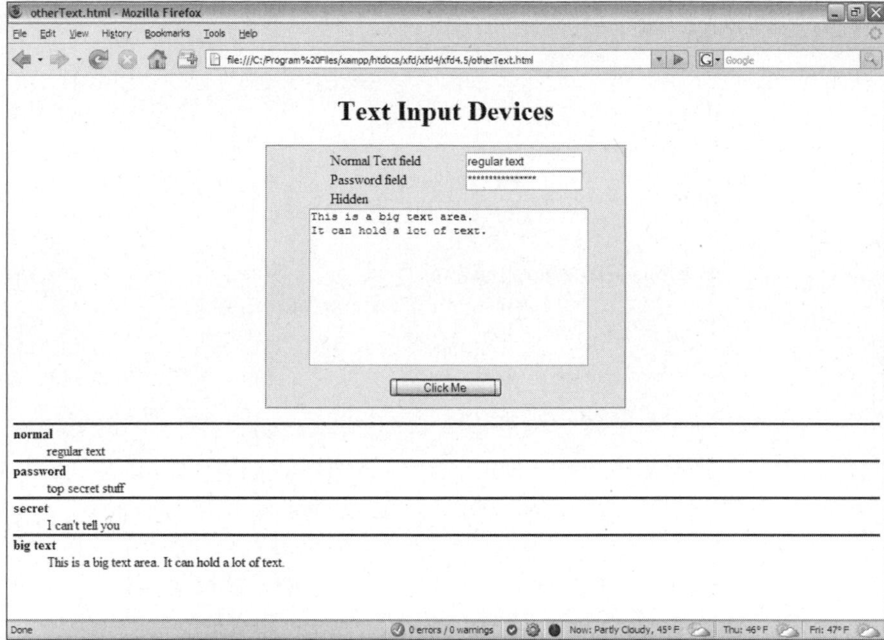

Figure 5-11: Now you can see what was in everything.

Building the form

Here's the XHTML that generates the form shown in Figures 5-10 and 5-11:

```
  <body>
    <h1>Text Input Devices</h1>
    <form action = "">
      <fieldset>
        <label>Normal Text field</label>
        <input type = "text"
               id = "txtNormal" />
        <label>Password field</label>
        <input type = "password"
               id = "pwd" />
        <label>Hidden</label>
        <input type = "hidden"
               id = "hidden"
               value = "I can't tell you" />
        <textarea id = "txtArea"
                  rows = "10"
                  cols = "40">
This is a big text area.
It can hold a lot of text.
        </textarea>
        <button type = "button"
                 onclick = "processForm()">
          Click Me
        </button>
```

```
    </fieldset>
  </form>
 <div id = "output">

 </div>
 </body>
```

The code may be familiar to you if you read about form elements in Book I, Chapter 7. A few things are worth noting for this example:

✦ **An ordinary text field appears, just for comparison purposes.** It has an `id` so that it can be identified in the JavaScript.

✦ **The next field is a password field.** Passwords display asterisks, but store the actual text that was entered. This password has an `id` of `pwd`.

✦ **The hidden field is a bit strange.** You can use hidden fields to store information on the page without displaying that information to the user. Unlike the other kinds of text fields, the user can't modify a hidden field. (She usually doesn't even know it's there.) This hidden field has an `id` of `secret` and a value (`"I can't tell you"`).

✦ **The text area has a different format.** The `input` elements are all single-tag elements, but the `textarea` is designed to contain a large amount of text, so it has beginning and end tags. The text area's `id` is `txtArea`.

✦ **A button starts all the fun.** As usual, most of the elements just sit there gathering data, but the button has an `onclick` event associated with it, which calls a function.

✦ **External CSS gussies it all up.** The page has some minimal CSS to clean it up. The CSS isn't central to this discussion, so I don't reproduce it. Note that the page will potentially have a `dl` on it, so I have a CSS style for it, even though it doesn't appear by default.

The password and hidden fields seem secure, but they aren't. Anybody who views the page source will be able to read the value of a hidden field, and passwords transmit their information in the clear. You really shouldn't be using Web technology (especially this kind) to transport nuclear launch codes or the secret to your special sauce. (Hmmm, maybe the secret sauce recipe *is* the launch code — sounds like a bad spy movie.)

When I create a text field, I often suspend my rules on indentation because the text field preserves everything inside it, including any indentation.

Writing the function

After you build the form, all you need is a function. Here's the good news: JavaScript treats all these elements in exactly the same way! The way you handle a password, hidden field, or text area is identical to the technique for a regular text field (described under "Managing Text Input and Output," earlier in this chapter). Here's the code:

```
<script type = "text/javascript">
//<![CDATA[

// from otherText.html
function processForm(){
  //grab input from form
  var txtNormal = document.getElementById("txtNormal");
  var pwd = document.getElementById("pwd");
  var hidden = document.getElementById("hidden");
  var txtArea = document.getElementById("txtArea");

  var normal = txtNormal.value;
  var password = pwd.value;
  var secret = hidden.value;
  var bigText = txtArea.value;

  //create output
  var result = ""
  result += "<dl> \n";
  result += "  <dt>normal<\/dt> \n";
  result += "  <dd>" + normal + "<\/dd> \n";
  result += " \n";
  result += "  <dt>password<\/dt> \n";
  result += "  <dd>" + password + "<\/dd> \n";
  result += " \n";
  result += "  <dt>secret<\/dt> \n";
  result += "  <dd>" + secret + "<\/dt> \n";
  result += "   \n";
  result += "  <dt>big text<\/dt> \n";
  result += "  <dd>" + bigText + "<\/dt> \n";
  result += "<\/dl> \n";

  var output = document.getElementById("output");
  output.innerHTML = result;

} // end function
```

The function is a bit longer than the others in this chapter, but it follows exactly the same pattern: It extracts data from the fields, constructs a string for output, and writes that output to the `innerHTML` attribute of a div in the page.

The code has nothing new, but it still has a few features you should consider:

- **Create a variable for each form element.** Use the `document.getElementById` mechanism.
- **Create a string variable containing the contents of each element.** Don't forget: The `getElementById` trick returns an object. You need to extract the `value` property to see what's inside the object.
- **Make a big string variable to manage the output.** When output gets long and messy like this one, concatenate a big variable and then just output it in one swoop.
- **HTML is your friend.** This output is a bit complex, but `innerHTML` is HTML, so you can use any HTML styles you want to format your code. The `return` string is actually a complete definition list. Whatever is

inside the text box is (in this case) reproduced as HTML text, so if I want carriage returns or formatting, I have to add them with code.

- **Don't forget to escape the slashes.** The validator gets confused by ending tags, so add the backslash character to any ending tags occurring in JavaScript string variables. In other words, `</dl>` becomes `<\/dl>`.
- **Newline characters (`\n`) clean up the output.** If I were writing an ordinary definition list in HTML, I'd put each line on a new line. I try to make my programs write code just like I do, so I add newline characters everywhere I'd add a carriage return in ordinary HTML.

Understanding generated source

When you run the program in the preceding section, your JavaScript code actually changes the page it lives on. The code that doesn't come from your server (but is created by your program) is sometimes called *generated source*. The generated code technique is powerful, but it can have a significant problem. Try this experiment to see what I mean:

1. **Reload the page.**

   You want to view it without the form contents showing so that you can view the source. Everything will be as expected; the source code shows exactly what you wrote.

2. **Click the Click Me button.**

   Your function runs, and the page changes. You clearly added HTML to the `output` div, because you can see the output right on the screen.

3. **View the source again.**

   You'll be amazed. The `output` div is empty, even though you can clearly see that it has changed.

4. **Check generated code.**

   Using the HTML validator extension or the W3 validator doesn't check for errors in your generated code. You have to check it yourself, but it's hard to see the code!

Figure 5-12 illustrates this problem.

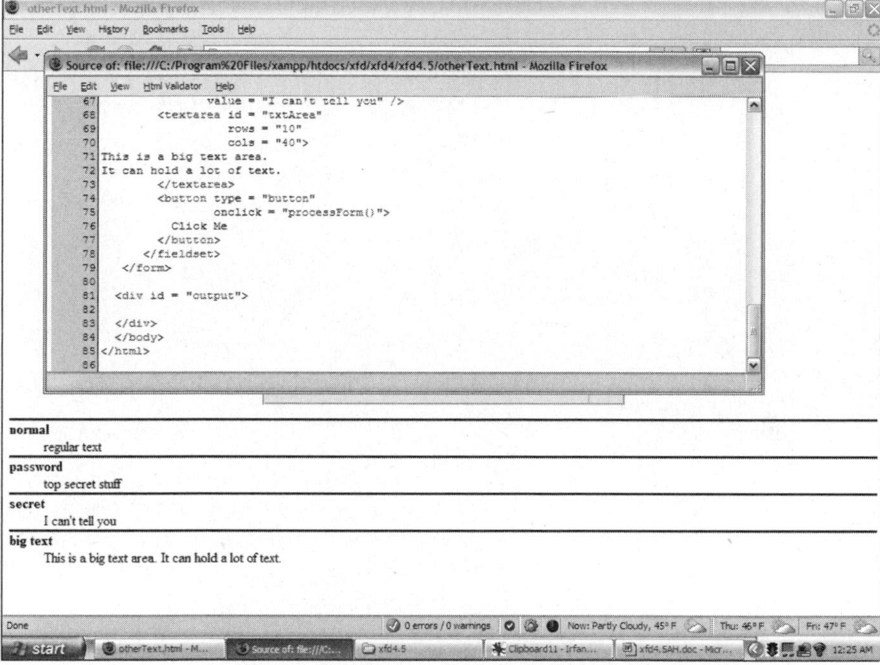

Figure 5-12: The ordinary view source command isn't showing the contents of the div!

Here's what's going on: The `view source` command (on most browsers) doesn't actually view the source of the page as it currently stands. It goes back to the server and retrieves the page, but displays it as source rather than rendered output. As a result, the `view source` command isn't useful for telling you how the page has changed dynamically. Likewise, the page validators check the page as it occurs on the server without taking into account things that may have happened dynamically.

When you build regular Web pages, this approach isn't a problem because regular Web pages don't change. Dynamically generated pages can change on the fly, and the browser doesn't expect that. If you made a mistake in the HTML, you can't simply view the source to see what you did wrong in the code generated by your script. Fortunately, Firefox plugins give you two easy solutions:

- **The Web developer toolbar:** This toolbar has a wonderful tool called `view generated source` available on the `view source` menu. It allows you to view the source code of the current page in its current state, including any code dynamically generated by your JavaScript.
- **The Firebug window**: Open this window when a page is open and browse (with the HTML tab) around your page. Firebug gives you an accurate view of the page contents even when they're changed dynamically, which can be extremely useful.

These tools keep you sane when you're trying to figure out why your generated code isn't acting right. (I wish I'd had them years ago. . . .)

Figure 5-13 shows the Firebug toolbar with the dynamically generated contents showing.

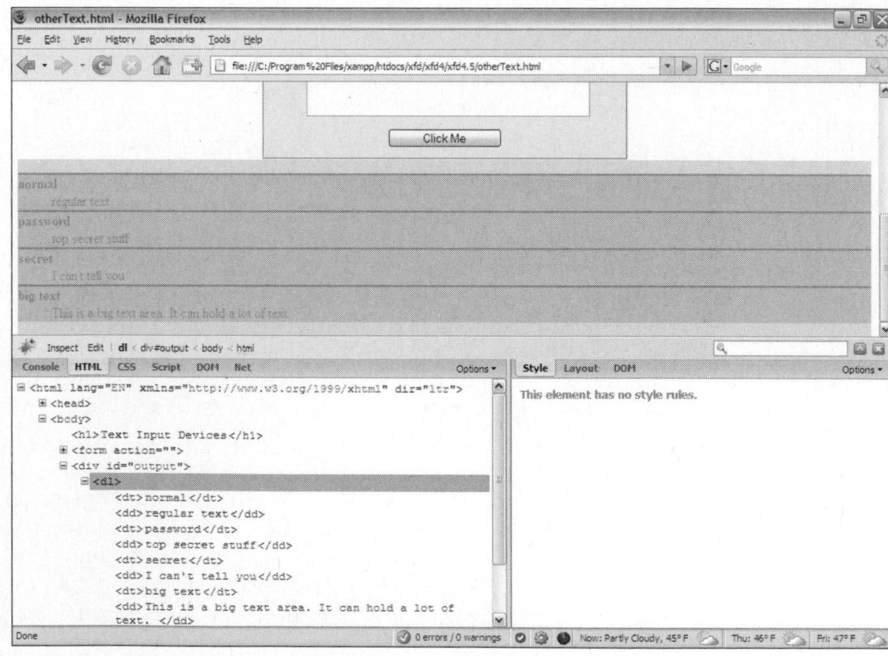

Figure 5-13: Firebug shows the current status of the page, even if it's dynamically modified.

Chapter 6: Getting Valid Input

In This Chapter

- Extracting data from drop-down lists
- Working with multiple-selection lists
- Getting data from check boxes and radio groups
- Validating input with regular expressions
- Using character, boundary, and repetition operators
- Using pattern memory

Getting input from the user is always nice, but sometimes users make mistakes. Whenever you can, you want to make the user's job easier and prevent certain kinds of mistakes.

Fortunately, you can take advantage of several tools designed exactly for that purpose. In this chapter, you discover two main strategies for improving user input: specialized input elements and pattern-matching. Together, these tools can help ensure that the data the user enters is useful and valid.

Getting Input from a Drop-Down List

The most obvious way to ensure that the user enters something valid is to supply him with valid choices. The drop-down list is an obvious and easy way to do this, as you can see from Figure 6-1.

The list-box approach has a lot of advantages over text field input:

- The user can input with the mouse, which is faster and easier than typing.
- You shouldn't have any spelling errors because the user didn't type the response.
- The user knows all the answers available because they're listed.
- You can be sure the user gives you a valid answer because you supplied the possible responses.
- User responses can be mapped to more complex values — for example, you can show the user Red and have the list box return the hex value `#FF0000`.

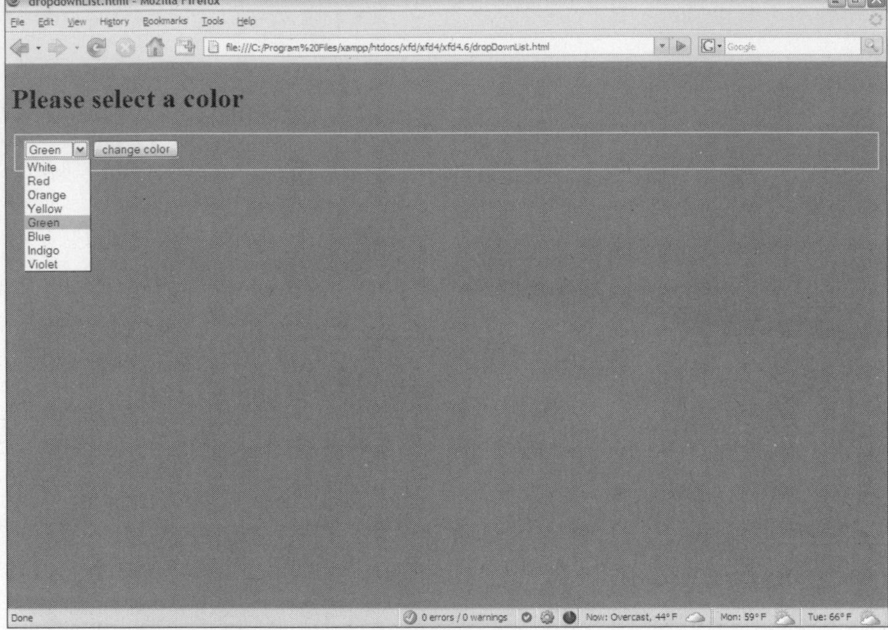

Figure 6-1: The user selects from a predefined list of valid choices.

If you want to knowhow to build a list box with the XHTML `select` object, refer to Book I, Chapter 7.

Building the form

When you're creating a predefined list of choices, create the HTML form first, because it defines all the elements you'll need for the function. The code is a standard form:

```
<body>
  <form action = "">
    <h1>Please select a color</h1>
    <fieldset>
      <select id = "selColor">
        <option value = "#FFFFFF">White</option>
        <option value = "#FF0000">Red</option>
        <option value = "#FFCC00">Orange</option>
        <option value = "#FFFF00">Yellow</option>
        <option value = "#00FF00">Green</option>
        <option value = "#0000FF">Blue</option>
        <option value = "#663366">Indigo</option>
        <option value = "#FF00FF">Violet</option>
      </select>

      <input type = "button"
             value = "change color"
             onclick = "changeColor()" />
```

```
      </fieldset>
    </form>

  </body>
</html>
```

The `select` object's default behavior is to provide a drop-down list. The first element on the list is displayed, but when the user clicks the list, the other options appear.

A `select` object that the code refers to should have an `id` field.

In this and most examples in this chapter, I add CSS styling to clean up each form. Be sure to look over the styles if you want to see how I did it.

The other element in the form is a button. When the user clicks the button, the `changeColor()` function is triggered.

Because the only element in this form is the `select` object, you may want to change the background color immediately without requiring a button click. You can do so by adding an event handler directly onto the `select` object:

```
<select id = "selColor"
        onchange = "changeColor()">
```

The event handler causes the `changeColor()` function to be triggered as soon as the user changes the `select` object's value. Typically, you'll forego the user clicking a button only when the `select` is the only element in the form. If the form includes several elements, processing doesn't usually happen until the user signals she's ready by clicking a button.

Reading the list box

Fortunately, standard drop-down lists are quite easy to read. Here's the JavaScript code:

```
<script type = "text/javascript">
  //<![CDATA[
  // from dropdownList.html

  function changeColor(){
    var selColor = document.getElementById("selColor");
    var color = selColor.value;
    document.body.style.backgroundColor = color;
  } // end function
  //]]>
</script>
```

As you can see, the process for reading the `select` object is much like working with a text-style field:

- **Create a variable to represent the `select` object.** The `document.getElementById()` trick works here just like it does for text fields.
- **Extract the `value` property of the `select` object.** The `value` property of the `select` object reflects the `value` of the currently selected `option`. So, if the user has chosen Yellow, the value of `selColor` is `"#FFFF00"`.
- **Set the document's background color.** Use the DOM mechanism to set the body's background color to the chosen value.

Managing Multiple Selections

You can use the `select` object in a more powerful way than the method I describe in the preceding section. Figure 6-2 shows a page with a multiple-selection list box.

To make multiple selection work, you have to make a few changes to both the HTML and the JavaScript code.

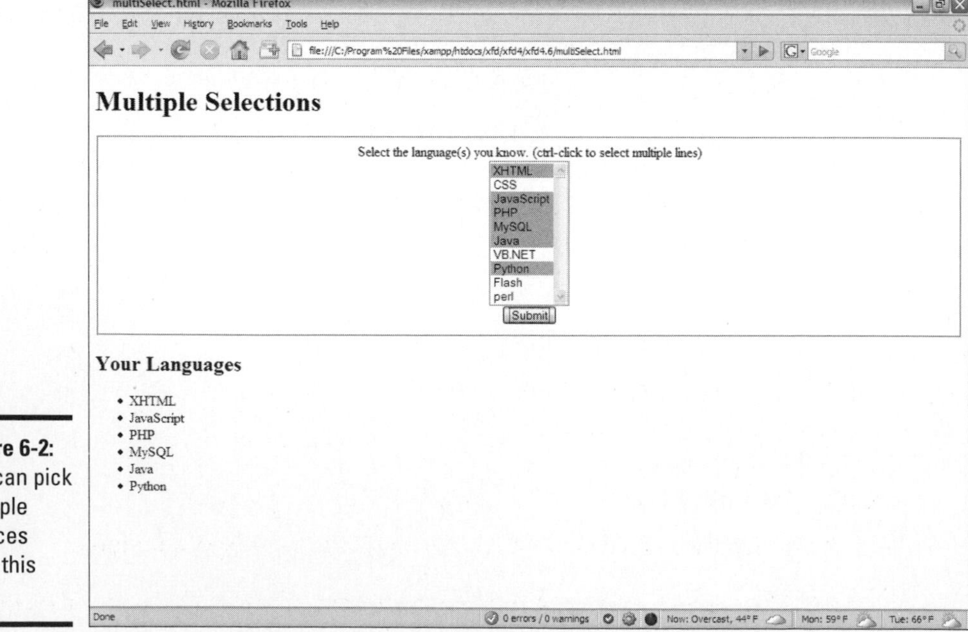

Figure 6-2: You can pick multiple choices from this list.

Coding a multiple selection select object

You modify the `select` code in two ways to make multiple selections:

- **Indicate multiple selections are allowed.** By default, `select` boxes have only one value. You'll need to set a switch to tell the browser to allow more than one item to be selected.
- **Make the mode a multiline select.** The standard drop-down behavior doesn't make sense when you want multiple selections, because the user needs to see all the options at once. Most browsers automatically switch into a multiline mode, but you should control the process directly.

The XHTML code for `multiSelect.html` is similar to the `dropdownList` page, described in the preceding section, but note a couple of changes.

```
  <body>
    <h1>Multiple Selections</h1>
    <form action = "">
      <fieldset>
        <label>
          Select the language(s) you know.
          (ctrl-click to select multiple lines)
        </label>
        <select id = "selLanguage"
                multiple = "multiple"
                size = "10">
          <option value = "XHTML">XHTML</option>
          <option value = "CSS">CSS</option>
          <option value = "JavaScript">JavaScript</option>
          <option value = "PHP">PHP</option>
          <option value = "MySQL">MySQL</option>
          <option value = "Java">Java</option>
          <option value = "VB.NET">VB.NET</option>
          <option value = "Python">Python</option>
          <option value = "Flash">Flash</option>
          <option value = "Perl">perl</option>
        </select>
        <button type = "button"
                onclick = "showChoices()">
          Submit
        </button>
      </fieldset>
    </form>

    <div id = "output">

    </div>
  </body>
</html>
```

The code isn't shocking, but it does have some important features:

- **The `select` object is called `selLanguage`.** As usual, the form elements need an `id` attribute so that you can read it in the JavaScript.

- **Add the `multiple` attribute to your `select` object.** This attribute tells the browser to accept multiple inputs using Shift+click (for contiguous selections) or Ctrl+click (for more precise selection).
- **Set the `size` to 10.** The size indicates the number of lines to be displayed. I set the size to 10 because my list has ten options.
- **Make a button.** With multiple selection, you probably won't want to trigger the action until the user has finished making selections. A separate button is the easiest way to make sure the code is triggered when you want it to happen.
- **Create an `output` div.** This code holds the response.

Writing the JavaScript code

The JavaScript code for reading a multiple-selection list box is a bit different than the standard selection code described in the section "Reading the list box" earlier in this chapter. The `value` property only returns one value, but a multiple-selection list box often returns more than one result.

The key is to recognize that a list of `option` objects inside a `select` object is really a kind of array. You can look more closely at the list of objects to see which ones are selected, which is essentially what the `showChoices()` function does:

```
<script type = "text/javascript">
  //<![CDATA[
  //from multi-select.html
  function showChoices(){
    //retrieve data
    var selLanguage = document.getElementById("selLanguage");

    //set up output string
    var result = "<h2>Your Languages<\/h2>";
    result += "<ul> \n";

    //step through options
    for (i = 0; i < selLanguage.length; i++){
      //examine current option
      currentOption = selLanguage[i];

      //print it if it has been selected
      if (currentOption.selected == true){
        result += "  <li>" + currentOption.value + "<\/li> \n";
      } // end if
    } // end for loop

    //finish off the list and print it out
    result += "<\/ul> \n";

    output = document.getElementById("output");
    output.innerHTML = result;
  } // end showChoices
  //]]>
</script>
```

At first, the code seems intimidating, but if you break it down, it's not too tricky.

1. **Create a variable to represent the entire `select` object.**

   The standard `document.getElementById()` technique works fine.

   ```
   var selLanguage = document.getElementById("selLanguage");
   ```

2. **Create a string variable to hold the output.**

   When you're building complex HTML output, working with a string variable is much easier than directly writing code to the element.

   ```
   var result = "<h2>Your Languages<\/h2>";
   ```

3. **Build an unordered list to display the results.**

   An unordered list is a good way to spit out the results, so I create one in my `result` variable.

   ```
   result += "<ul> \n";
   ```

4. **Step through `selLanguage` as if it were an array.**

   Use a `for` loop to examine the list box line by line. Note that `selLanguage` has a `length` property like an array.

   ```
   for (i = 0; i < selLanguage.length; i++){
   ```

5. **Assign the current element to a temporary variable.**

   The `currentOption` variable holds a reference to the each `option` element in the original `select` object as the loop progresses.

   ```
   currentOption = selLanguage[i];
   ```

6. **Check to see whether the current element has been selected.**

   The object `currentOption` has a `selected` property that tells you whether the object has been highlighted by the user. `selected` is a Boolean property, so it's either true or false.

   ```
   if (currentOption.selected == true){
   ```

7. **If the element has been selected, add an entry to the output list.**

   If the user has highlighted this object, create an entry in the unordered list housed in the `result` variable.

   ```
   result += "  <li>" + currentOption.value + "<\/li> \n";
   ```

8. **Close up the list.**

   Once the loop has finished cycling through all the objects, you can close up the unordered list you've been building.

   ```
   result += "<\/ul> \n";
   ```

9. Print results to the `output` div.

The `output` div's `innerHTML` property is a perfect place to print the unordered list.

```
output = document.getElementById("output");
output.innerHTML = result;
```

Something strange is going on here. The options of a select box act like an array. An unordered list is a lot like an array. Bingo! They are arrays, just in different forms. You can think of any listed data as an array. Sometimes you organize the data like a list (for display), sometimes like an array (for storage in memory), and sometimes it's a select group (for user input). Now you're starting to think like a programmer!

Check, Please: Reading Check Boxes

Check boxes fulfill another useful data input function. They're useful any time you have Boolean data. If some value can be true or false, a check box is a good tool. Figure 6-3 illustrates a page that responds to check boxes.

Check boxes are independent of each other. Although they're often found in groups, any check box can be checked or unchecked regardless of the status of its neighbors.

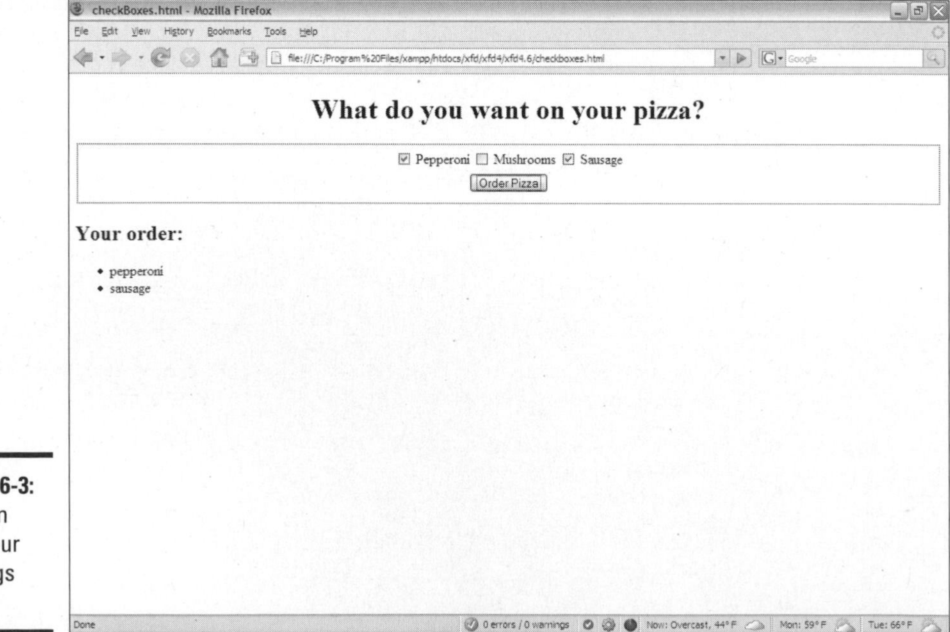

Figure 6-3: You can pick your toppings here.

Building the check box page

To build the check box page shown in Figure 6-3, start by looking at the HTML:

```
<body>
  <h1>What do you want on your pizza?</h1>
  <form action = "">
    <fieldset>
      <input type = "checkbox"
             id = "chkPepperoni"
             value = "pepperoni" />
      <label>Pepperoni</label>

      <input type = "checkbox"
             id = "chkMushroom"
             value = "mushrooms" />
      <label>Mushrooms</label>

      <input type = "checkbox"
             id = "chkSausage"
             value = "sausage" />
      <label>Sausage</label>

      <button type = "button"
              onclick = "order()">
        Order Pizza
      </button>
    </fieldset>

  </form>
  <h2>Your order:</h2>
  <div id = "output">

  </div>
</body>
```

Each check box is an individual `input` element. Note that check box values aren't displayed. Instead, a label (or similar text) is usually placed after the check box. A button calls an `order()` function.

Responding to the check boxes

Check boxes don't require a lot of care and feeding. Once you extract it, the check box has two critical properties:

- You can use the `value` property to store a value associated with the check box (just like you do with text fields in Chapter 5 of this minibook).
- The `checked` property is a Boolean value, indicating whether the check box is currently checked or not.

The code for the `order()` function shows how it's done:

```
<script type = "text/javascript">
  //<![CDATA[
  //from checkBoxes.html
  function order(){
```

```
      //get variables
      var chkPepperoni = document.getElementById("chkPepperoni");
      var chkMushroom = document.getElementById("chkMushroom");
      var chkSausage = document.getElementById("chkSausage");

      var output = document.getElementById("output");
      var result = "<ul> \n"

      if (chkPepperoni.checked){
        result += "<li>" + chkPepperoni.value + "<\/li> \n";
      } // end if

      if (chkMushroom.checked){
        result += "<li>" + chkMushroom.value + "<\/li> \n";
      } // end if

      if (chkSausage.checked){
        result += "<li>" + chkSausage.value + "<\/li> \n";
      } // end if

      result += "<\/ul> \n"
      output.innerHTML = result;
    } // end function

  //]]>
</script>
```

For each check box:

1. **Determine whether the check box is checked.**

   Use the `checked` property as a condition.

2. **If so, return the `value` property associated with the check box.**

Often, in practice, the `value` property is left out. The important thing is whether the check box is checked. If `chkMushroom` is checked, the user obviously wants mushrooms, so you may not need to explicitly store that data in the check box itself.

Working with Radio Buttons

Radio button groups appear pretty simple, but they're more complex than they seem. Figure 6-4 shows a page using radio button selection.

The most important thing to remember about radio buttons is that they must be in groups. Each group of radio buttons has only one button active. The group should be set up so that one button is always active.

You specify the radio button group in the XHTML code. Each element of the group can have an `id` (although the IDs aren't really necessary in this application). What's more important here is the `name` attribute. Look over the code, and you'll notice something interesting. All the radio buttons have the same name!

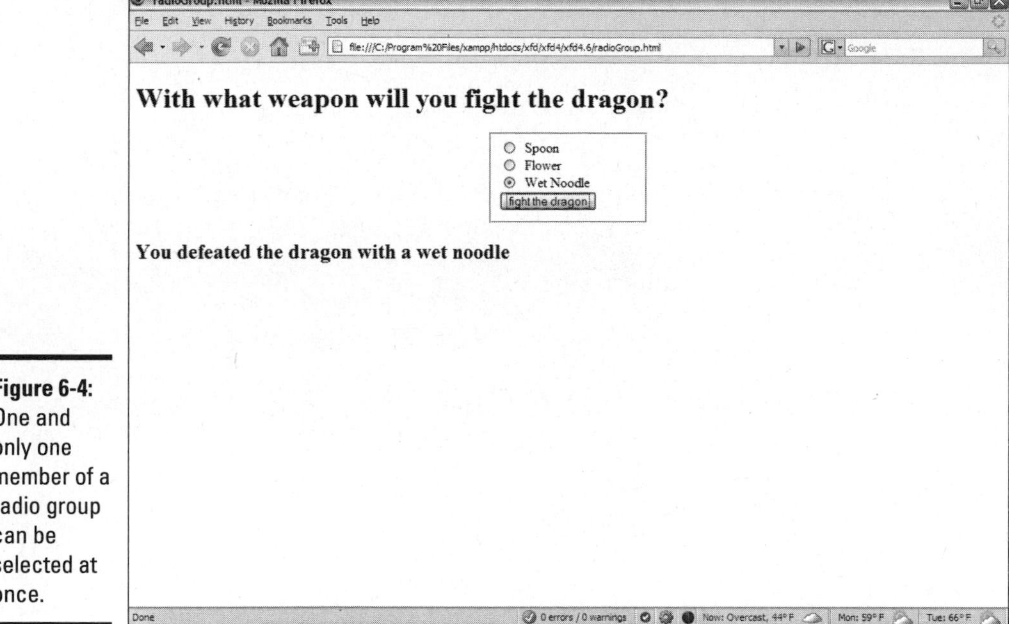

Figure 6-4: One and only one member of a radio group can be selected at once.

```
<body>
  <h1>With what weapon will you fight the dragon?</h1>
  <form action = "">
    <fieldset>
      <input type = "radio"
             name = "weapon"
             id = "radSpoon"
             value = "spoon"
             checked = "checked" />
      <label>Spoon</label>

      <input type = "radio"
             name = "weapon"
             id = "radFlower"
             value = "flower" />
      <label>Flower</label>

      <input type = "radio"
             name = "weapon"
             id = "radNoodle"
             value = "wet noodle" />
      <label>Wet Noodle</label>
      <button type = "button"
              onclick = "fight()">
        fight the dragon
      </button>
    </fieldset>
  </form>
  <div id = "output">
```

```
    </div>
  </body>
</html>
```

Using a `name` attribute when everything else has an `id` seems a little odd, but you do it for a good reason. The `name` attribute is used to indicate the *group* of radio buttons. Because all the buttons in this group have the same name, they're related, and only one of them will be selected.

The browser recognizes this behavior and automatically unselects the other buttons in the group whenever one is selected.

I added a label to describe what each radio button means.

You need to preset one of the radio buttons to true with the `checked = "checked"` attribute. If you fail to do so, you have to add code to account for the possibility that there is no answer at all.

Interpreting radio buttons

Getting information from a group of radio buttons requires a slightly different technique than most of the form elements. Unlike the `select` object, no container object can return a simple value. You also can't just go through every radio button on the page because you may have more than one group. (Imagine a page with a multiple-choice test.)

This issue is where the `name` attribute comes in. Although `id`s must be unique, multiple elements on a page can have the same `name`. If they do, you can treat these elements as an array.

Look over the code to see how it works:

```
<script type = "text/javascript">
  //<![CDATA[
  // from radioGroup.html
  function fight(){

    var weapon = document.getElementsByName("weapon");

    for (i = 0; i < weapon.length; i++){
      currentWeapon = weapon[i];

      if (currentWeapon.checked){
        var selectedWeapon = currentWeapon.value;
      } // end if

    } // end for

    var output = document.getElementById("output");
    var response = "<h2>You defeated the dragon with a ";
    response += selectedWeapon + "<\/h2> \n";
    output.innerHTML = response;
  } // end function
```

```
    //]]>
  </script>
```

This code looks much like all the other code in this chapter, but it has a sneaky difference:

- **It uses `getElementsByName` to retrieve an array of elements with this name.** Now that you're comfortable with `getElementById`, I throw a monkey wrench in the works. Note that it's plural — `getElementsByName` — because this tool is used to extract an array of elements. It returns an array of elements. (In this case, all the radio buttons in the `weapon` group.)
- **It treats the result as an array.** The resulting variable (`weapon` in this example) is an array. As usual, the most common thing to do with arrays is process them with loops. Use a `for` loop to step through each element in the array.
- **Assign each element of the array to `currentWeapon`.** This variable holds a reference to the current radio button.
- **Check to see whether the current weapon is checked.** The `checked` property indicates whether any radio button is currently checked.
- **If so, retain the value of the radio button.** If the current radio button is checked, its value is the current value of the group, so store it in a variable for later use.
- **Output the results.** You can now process the results as you would with data from any other resource.

Working with Regular Expressions

Having the right kinds of form elements can be helpful, but things can still go wrong. Sometimes, you have to let the user type things, and that information must be in a particular format. As an example, take a look at Figure 6-5.

A mechanism that checks input from a form to see whether it's in the right format would be great. You can create this feature with string functions, but it can be really messy. Imagine how many `if` statements and string methods it would take to enforce the following rules on this page:

- **An entry must appear in each field.** This one is reasonably easy — just check for non-null values.
- **The e-mail must be in a valid format.** That is, it must consist of a few characters, an "at" sign (@), a few more characters, a period, and a domain name of two to four characters. That format would be a real pain to check for.

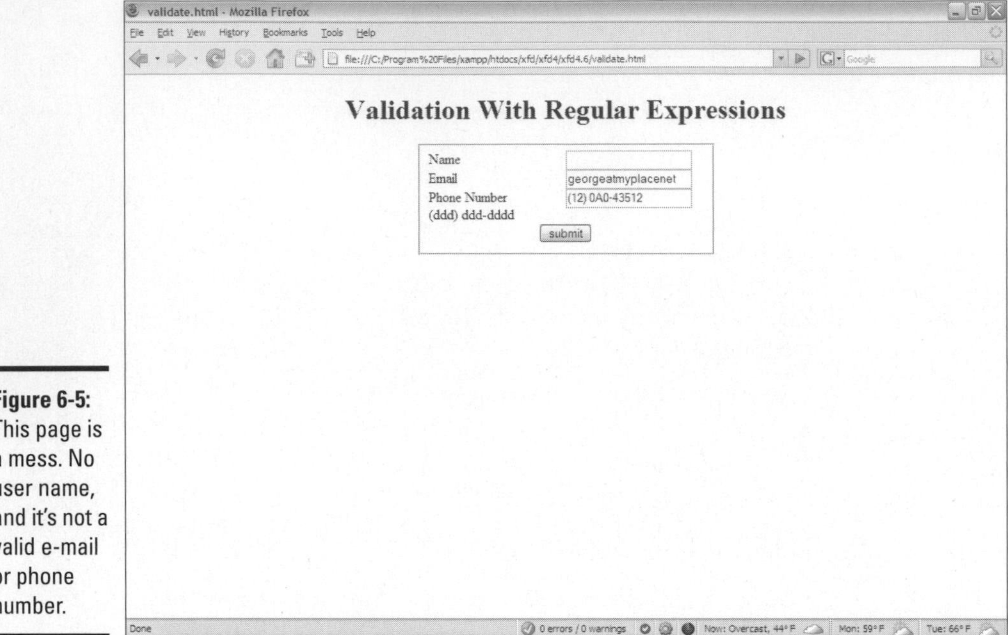

Figure 6-5: This page is a mess. No user name, and it's not a valid e-mail or phone number.

- **The phone number must also be in a valid format.** Phone numbers can appear in multiple formats, but assume that you require an area code in parentheses, followed by an optional space, followed by three digits, a dash, and four digits. All digits must be numeric.

While you can enforce these rules, it would be extremely difficult to do so using ordinary string manipulation tools.

JavaScript strings have a `match` method, which helps find a substring inside a larger string. This tool is good, but we're not simply looking for specific text, but patterns of text. For example, we want to know whether something's an e-mail address (text, an @, more text, a period, and two to four more characters).

Imagine how difficult that code would be to write; then take a look at the code for the `validate.html` page:

```
<script type = "text/javascript">
  function validate(){
    //get inputs
    name = document.getElementById("txtName").value;
    email = document.getElementById("txtEmail").value;
    phone = document.getElementById("txtPhone").value;

    //console.log("Name: " + name + ", email: " + email + ",  Phone: " +
phone);
```

```
      // name must simply exist
      if (name == ""){
        alert("Please enter a name");
      } else {
        //name is OK, now check email

        //email must include an at sign
        if (email.match("^.*\..{2,4}") == null){
          alert("That is not a valid email address");
        } else {

          //email is OK, now check phone #
          // regex is the only way to go here....

          phoneRE = /\(\d{3}\) *\d{3}-\d{4}/
          if (phone.match(phoneRE)== null){
            alert("That was not a valid phone number");
          } else {
            //everything's ok...
            alert("processing form.....");
          } // end phone if
        } // end email if
      } // end name if
    } // end function

  </script>
```

I'm only showing the JavaScript code here to save space. Look on the CD-ROM to see how the HTML and CSS are written.

The code isn't really all that difficult!

- **It extracts data from the form.** It does so in the usual way.
- **The validation is a series of nested `if` statements.** Look at the overall structure. The `if` statements go three layers deep.
- **The name check is very simple.** The only way it can go wrong is to have no name.
- **Don't check anything else if the name is wrong.** If the name isn't right, you don't need to check the other things.
- **Check the e-mail address.** This verification seems pretty simple until you look at the line that contains the `email.match("^.*\..{2,4}"` business. It looks like a cursing cartoonist in there. For now, just accept it as a magic incantation. The match will be true if it's an e-mail address or return null if it's not.
- **Check the phone number.** Once again, the phone number check is simple except the match business, which is just as mysterious: `/\(\d{3}\) *\d{3}-\d{4}/` (seriously, who makes this stuff up?).
- **If everything worked, process the form.** Usually, at this point, you call some sort of function to finish handling the form processing.

Frequently, you do validation in JavaScript before you pass information to a program on the server. This way, your server program already knows the data is valid by the time it gets there.

Introducing regular expressions

Of course, the secret of this program is to decode the mystical expressions used in the `match` statements. They aren't really strings at all, but very powerful text-manipulation techniques called *regular expression parsing.* Regular expressions have migrated from the UNIX world into many programming languages, including JavaScript.

A *regular expression* is a powerful mini-language for searching and replacing text patterns. Essentially, what it does is allow you to search for complex patterns and expressions. It's a weird-looking language, but it has a certain charm once you know how to read the arcane-looking expressions.

Regular expressions are normally used with the string `match()` method in JavaScript, but you can also use them with the `replace()` method and a few other places.

Table 6-1 summarizes the main operators in JavaScript regular expressions.

Table 6-1 Regular Expression Operators in JavaScript

Operator	*Description*	*Sample Pattern*	*Matches*	*Doesn't Match*
. (period)	Any single character except newline	.	E	\n
^	Beginning of string	^a	Apple	Banana
$	End of string	a$	Banana	Apple
[characters]	Any of a list of characters in braces	[abcABC]	A	D
[char range]	Any character in the range	[a-zA-Z]	F	9
\d	Any single numerical digit	\d\d\d-\d\d\d\d	123-4567	The-thing
\b	A word boundary	\bthe\b	The	Theater
+	One or more occurrences of the previous character	\d+	1234	Text
*	Zero or more occurrences of the previous character	[a-zA-Z]d*	B17, g	7
{digit}	Repeat preceding character *digit* times	\d{3}-\d{4}	123-4567	999-99-9999

Operator	Description	Sample Pattern	Matches	Doesn't Match
{min, max}	Repeat preceding character at least *min* but not more than *max* times	.{2,4}	Ca, com, info	watermelon
(pattern segment)	Store results in pattern memory returned with code	^(.).*\1$	gig, wallow	Bobby

Don't memorize this table! I explain in the rest of this chapter exactly how it works. Keep Table 6-1 handy as a reference.

To see how regular expressions work, take a look at `regex.html` in Figure 6-6.

The top textbox accepts a regular expression, and the second text field contains text to examine. You can practice the examples in the following sections to see how regular expressions work. They're really quite useful once you get the hang of them. As you walk through the examples, try them out in this tester. (I've included it on the CD-ROM for you, but I don't reproduce the code here.)

Figure 6-6: This tool allows you to test regular expressions.

Using characters in regular expressions

The main thing you do with a regular expression is search for text. Say that you work for the `bigCorp` company, and you ask for employee e-mail addresses. You can make a form that accepts only e-mail addresses with the term `bigCorp` in them by using the following code:

```
if (email.match("bigCorp")){
  alert("match");
} else {
  alert("no match");
} // end if
```

This match is the simplest type. I'm simply looking for the existence of the needle (bigCorp) in a haystack (the e-mail address stored in `email`). If the text `bigCorp` is found anywhere in the text, the match is true, and I can do what I want (usually process the form on the server). More often, you'll want to trap for an error and remind the user what needs to be fixed.

Marking the beginning and end of the line

You may want to improve the search, because what you really want are addresses that end with "`bigCorp.com"`. You can put a special character inside the match string to indicate where the end of the line should be:

```
if (email.match("bigCorp.com$")){
  alert("match");
} else {
  alert("no match");
} // end if
```

The dollar sign at the end of the match string indicates that this part of the text should occur at the end of the search string, so `andy@bigCorp.com` is a match, but not "bigCorp.com announces a new Web site."

If you're already an ace with regular expressions, you know this example has a minor problem, but it's pretty picky. I explain it in the upcoming section "Working with special characters." For now, just appreciate that you can include the end of the string as a search parameter.

Likewise, you can use the caret character (^) to indicate the beginning of a string.

If you want to ensure that a text field contains only the phrase `oogie boogie` (and why wouldn't you?), you can tack on the beginning and ending markers. The code `^oogie boogie$` is a true match only if nothing else appears in the phrase.

Working with special characters

In addition to ordinary text, you can use a bunch of special character symbols for more flexible matching:

- **Matching a character with the period:** The most powerful character is the period (`.`), which represents a single character. Any single character except the newline (`\n`) matches against the period. A character that matches any character may seem silly, but it's actually quite powerful. The expression `b.g` matches `big`, `bag`, and `bug`. In fact, it matches any phrase that contains `b` followed by any single character and then `g`, so `bxg`, `b g`, and `b9g` are also matches.
- **Using a character class:** You can specify a list of characters in square braces, and JavaScript matches if any one of those characters matches. This list of characters is sometimes called a *character class*. For example, `b[aeiou]g` matches on `bag`, `beg`, `big`, `bog`, or `bug`. This method is a really quick way to check a lot of potential matches.

  You can also specify a character class with a range. `[a-zA-Z]` checks all the letters.
- **Specifying digits:** One of the most common tricks is to look for numbers. The special character `\d` represents a number (0–9). You can check for a U.S. phone number (without the area code — yet) using a pattern that looks for three digits, a dash, and four digits: `\d\d\d-\d\d\d\d`.
- **Marking punctuation characters:** You can tell that regular expressions use a lot of funky characters, such as periods and braces. What if you're searching for one of these characters? Just use a backslash to indicate that you're looking for the actual character and not using it as a modifier. For example, the e-mail address would be better searched with `bigCorp\.com`, because it specifies there must be a period. If you don't use the backslash, the regular expression tool interprets the period as "any character" and allows something like `bigCorpucom`. Use the backslash trick for most punctuation, such as parentheses, braces, periods, and slashes.

  If you want to include an area code with parentheses, just use backslashes to indicate the parentheses: `\(\d\d\d\) \d\d\d-\d\d\d\d`.
- **Finding word boundaries:** Sometimes you want to know whether something is a word. Say that you're searching for the word "the" but you don't want a false positive on "breathe" or "theater." The `\b` character means "the edge of a word," so `\bthe\b` matches "the" but not words containing "the" inside them.

Conducting repetition operations

All the character modifiers refer to one particular character at a time, but sometimes you want to deal with several characters at once. Several operators can help you with this process.

- **Finding one or more elements:** The plus sign (+) indicates "one or more" of the preceding character, so the pattern `ab+c` matches on `abc`, `abbbbbbc`, or `abbbbbbbc`, but not on `ac` (there must be at least one `b`) or on `afc` (it's gotta be `b`).
- **Matching zero or more elements:** The asterisk means "zero or more" of the preceding character. So `I'm .* happy` matches on `I'm happy` (zero occurrences of any character between `I'm` and `happy`). It also matches on `I'm not happy` (because characters appear in between).

  The `.*` combination is especially useful, because you can use it to improve matches like e-mail addresses: `^.*@bigCorp\.com$` does a pretty good job of matching e-mail addresses in a fictional company.
- **Specifying the number of matches:** You can use braces ({}) to indicate the specific number of times the preceding character should be repeated. For example, you can rewrite a phone number pattern as `\(\d{3}\) *\d{3}-\d{4}`. This structure means "three digits in parentheses, followed by any number of spaces (zero or more), and then three digits, a dash, and four digits. Using this pattern, you can tell whether the user has entered the phone number in a valid format.

  You can also specify a minimum and maximum number of matches, so `[aeiou]{1, 3}` means "at least one and no more than three vowels."

  Now you can improve the e-mail pattern so that it includes any number of characters, an @ sign, and ends with a period and two to four letters: `^.*@.*\..{2,4}$`.

Working with pattern memory

Sometimes you want to remember a piece of your pattern and reuse it. You can use parentheses to group a chunk of the pattern and remember it. For example, `(foo){2}` doesn't match on `foo`, but it does on `foofoo`. It's the entire segment that's repeated twice.

You can also refer to a stored pattern later in the expression. The pattern `^(.).*\1$` matches any word that begins and ends with the same character. The `\1` symbol represents the first pattern in the string, `\2` represents the second, and so on.

After you've finished a pattern match, the remembered patterns are still available in special variables. The variable `$1` is the first, `$2` is the second, and so on. You can use this trick to look for HTML tags and report what tag was found: Match `^<(.*)>.*<\/\1>$` and then print `$1` to see what the tag was.

There's much more to discover about regular expressions, but this basic overview should give you enough to write some powerful and useful patterns.

Chapter 7: Animating Your Pages

In This Chapter

- Moving an object on the screen
- Responding to keyboard input
- Reading mouse input
- Running code repeatedly
- Bouncing off the walls
- Swapping images
- Reusing code
- Using external script files

JavaScript has a serious side, but it can be a lot of fun, too. You can easily use JavaScript to make things move, animate, and wiggle. In this chapter, you find out how to make your pages dance. Even if you aren't interested in animation, you can discover important ideas about how to design your pages and code more efficiently.

I know what you're thinking: You can use this stuff to make a really cool game. It's true. You can make games with JavaScript, but you eventually run into JavaScript's design limitations. I prefer Flash and Python as languages to learn game development. Now that you mention it, I've written other Wiley books on exactly these topics. See you there! (Check out *Beginning Flash Game Programming For Dummies* and *Game Programming: The L Line* for Python development.)

Making Things Move

You may think you need Flash or Java to put animation in your pages, but that's not the only way. You can use JavaScript to create some pretty interesting motion effects. Take a look at Figure 7-1.

Because this chapter is about animation, most of the pages feature motion. You really must see these pages in your browser to get the effect, as a static screen shot can't really do any of these programs justice.

The general structure of this page provides a foundation for other kinds of animation:

- **The HTML is pretty simple.** The page really doesn't require much HTML code. It's a couple of divs and some buttons.
- **The ball is in a special div called `sprite`.** Game developers call the little images that move around on the screen *sprites*, so I use the same term.
- **The `sprite` div has a local style.** JavaScript animation requires a locally defined style.
- **The `sprite` div has absolute positioning.** Because I'll be moving this thing around on the screen, it makes sense that it's absolutely positioned.
- **The code and CSS are as modular as possible.** Things can get a little complicated when you start animating things, so throughout this chapter, I simplify as much as I can. The CSS styles are defined externally, and the JavaScript code is also imported.
- **Code is designed to be reused.** Many programs in this chapter are very similar to each other. To save effort, I've designed things so that I don't have to rewrite code if possible.

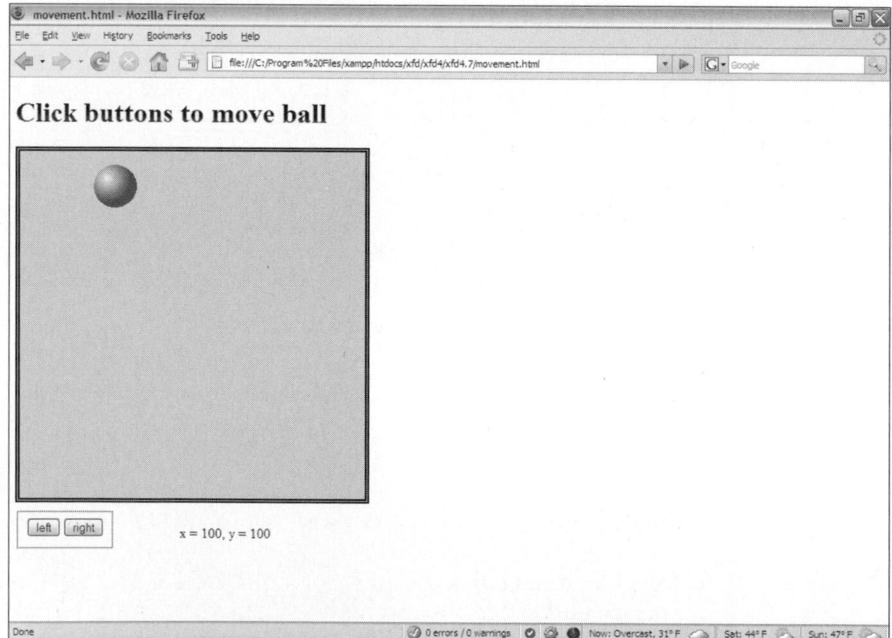

Figure 7-1: Click the buttons, and the ball moves.

Looking over the HTML

The HTML code for this program provides the basic foundation:

```
<!DOCTYPE html PUBLIC "-//W3C//DTD XHTML 1.0 Strict//EN"
```

```
"http://www.w3.org/TR/xhtml1/DTD/xhtml1-strict.dtd">
<html lang="EN" dir="ltr" xmlns="http://www.w3.org/1999/xhtml">
  <head>
    <meta http-equiv="content-type" content="text/xml; charset=utf-8" />
    <title>movement.html</title>

    <link rel = "stylesheet"
          type = "text/css"
          href = "movement.css" />

    <script type = "text/javascript"
            src = "movement.js">
    </script>
  </head>

  <body onload = "init()">
    <h1>Click buttons to move ball</h1>
    <div id = "surface">
      <div id = "sprite"
           style = "position: absolute;
           top: 100px;
           left: 100px;
           height: 25px;
           width: 25px;" >
        <img src = "ball.gif"
             alt = "ball" />
      </div>
    </div>
    <form action = ""
          id = "controls">
      <fieldset>
        <button type = "button"
                onclick = "moveSprite(-5, 0)">
          left
        </button>
        <button type = "button"
                onclick = "moveSprite(5, 0)">
          right
        </button>
      </fieldset>
    </form>
    <p id = "output">
      x = 100, y = 100
    </p>
  </body>
</html>
```


You should notice a few interesting things about this code:

- **It has an external style sheet.** Most of the CSS (the stuff that defines the surface and the forms) is moved off-stage into an external style sheet. You have to define some CSS locally, but anything that can be moved away is.

```
<link rel = "stylesheet"
      type = "text/css"
      href = "movement.css" />
```

- **The JavaScript is also outsourced.** The `script` tag has a `src` attribute, which you can use to load JavaScript code from an external file. The browser loads the specified file in and reads it as if it were directly in the code. (Note that external scripts still require a `</script>` tag.) This program gets its scripts from a file called `movement.js`.

```
<script type = "text/javascript"
        src = "movement.js">
</script>
```

✦ **The `body` tag calls a method.** In animation (and other advanced JavaScript), you commonly have some code you want to run right away. The body has an `onload` event. You can feed it the name of a function (just like you do with a button's `onclick` event). In this case, I want the function called `init()` to run as soon as the body finishes loading into the computer's memory.

```
<body onload = "init()">
```

✦ **The yellow box is a div called `surface`.** It isn't absolutely necessary, but when you have something moving around on the screen, you want some kind of boundary so that the user knows where she can move.

✦ **A `sprite` div appears inside `surface`.** This sprite is the thing that actually moves around.

```
<div id = "sprite"
     style = "position: absolute;
     top: 100px;
     left: 100px;
     height: 25px;
     width: 25px;" >
  <img src = "ball.gif"
      alt = "ball" />
</div>
```

✦ **The `sprite` div has a local style.** Your code can change only styles that have been defined locally. The `sprite` div has a local style specifying absolute position, left, and top properties.

✦ **It has buttons in a form.** This particular program uses form buttons to discern the user's intent. Those buttons are in a form.

```
<button type = "button"
        onclick = "moveSprite(-5, 0)">
  left
</button>
```

✦ **Each button calls the `moveSprite()` method.** The `moveSprite()` method is defined in the `movement.js` file. It accepts two parameters: `dx` determines how much the sprite should move in the *x* (side to side) axis, and `dy` controls how much the sprite will move in the *y* (vertical) axis.

Getting an overview of the JavaScript

The following programming concepts improve programmer efficiency, which is good as the JavaScript code becomes more complex:

- **Move code to an external file.** As with CSS code, when the JavaScript starts to get complex, it's a good idea to move it to its own file, so it's easier to manage.
- **Encapsulate code in functions.** Rather than writing a long, complicated function, try to break the code into smaller functions that solve individual problems. If you design these functions well, your code is easier to write, understand, and recycle.
- **Create a few global variables.** You can reuse a few key variables throughout your code. Create global variables for these key items, but don't make anything global that doesn't need to be.
- **Define constants for clarity.** Sometimes having a few key values stored in special variables is handy. I've created some constants to help me track the boundary of the visual surface.

Creating global variables

The first part of this document simply defines the global variables I use throughout the program:

```
//movement.js
//global variables
var sprite;
var x, y;    //position variables

//constants
var MIN_X = 15;
var MAX_X = 365;
var MIN_Y = 85;
var MAX_Y = 435;
```

The movement program has three main global variables.

- **`sprite`** represents the div that moves around on the screen.
- **`x`** is the x (horizontal) position of the sprite.
- **`y`** is the y (vertical) position of the sprite.

You don't need to give values to global variables right away, but you should define them outside any functions so that their values are available to all functions. (See Chapter 4 in this minibook for more about functions and variable scope.)

Note that in computer graphics, the *y* axis works differently than it does in math. Zero is the top of the screen, and *y* values increase as you move down the page. (This increase happens because it models the top-to-bottom pattern of most display devices.)

This program also features some special *constants*. A constant is a variable (usually global) whose value isn't intended to change as the program runs. Constants are almost always used to add clarity.

Through experimentation, I found that the ball's *x* value should never be smaller than 15 or larger than 365. By defining special constants with these values, I can make it clear what these values represent. (See the section called "Checking the boundaries" later in this chapter to see how this feature really works.)

You traditionally put constants entirely in uppercase letters. Many languages have special modifiers for creating constants, but JavaScript doesn't. If you want something to be a constant, just make a variable with an uppercase name and treat it as a constant. (Don't change it during the run of the program.)

Initializing

The `init()` function is small but mighty:

```
function init(){
  sprite = document.getElementById("sprite");
} // end init
```

It does a simple but important job: loading up the `sprite` div and storing it into a variable named `sprite`. Because `sprite` is a global variable, all other functions have access to the `sprite` variable and are able to manipulate it.

You often use the `init()` function to initialize key variables in your programs. You also can use this function to set up more advanced event handlers, as you see in the animation sections of this chapter.

Moving the sprite

Of course, the most interesting function in the program is the one that moves sprites around the screen. Take a look at the following code, which I break down for you:

```
function moveSprite(dx, dy){
  var surface = document.getElementById("surface");

  x = parseInt(sprite.style.left);
  y = parseInt(sprite.style.top);

  x += dx;
  y += dy;

  checkBounds();

  // move ball to new position
  sprite.style.left = x + "px";
  sprite.style.top = y + "px";

  //describe position
```

```
  var output = document.getElementById("output");
  output.innerHTML = "x: " + x + ", y: " + y;
} // end MoveSprite
```

The function works essentially by determining how much the sprite should be moved in x and y and then manipulating the left and top properties of its style. Here's what happens:

1. **Accept dx and dy as parameters.**

   The function expects two parameters: dx stands for delta-x, and dy is delta-y. (You can read them *difference in x* and *difference in y* if you prefer, but I like sounding like a NASA scientist.) These parameters tell how much the sprite should move in each dimension.

   ```
   function moveSprite(dx, dy){
   ```

   You may wonder why I'm working with dx and dy when this object moves only horizontally. See, I'm thinking ahead. I'm going to reuse this function in the next few programs, which I discuss in the upcoming sections. Even though I don't need to move vertically yet, I will as I continue programming, so I built the capability in.

2. **Get a reference to the surface.**

   Use the normal document.getElementById trick to extract the sprite from the page. Be sure the sprite you're animating has absolute position with top and left properties defined in a local style.

   ```
   var surface = document.getElementById("surface");
   ```

3. **Extract the sprite's x and y parameters.**

   The horizontal position is stored in the left property. CSS styles are stored as strings and include a measurement. For example, the original left value of the sprite is 100px. For the program, we need only the numeric part. The parseInt() function pulls out only the numeric part of the left property and turns it into an integer, which is then stored in x. Do the same thing to get the y value.

   ```
   x = parseInt(sprite.style.left);
   y = parseInt(sprite.style.top);
   ```

4. **Increment x and y .**

   Now that you have the x and y properties stored as integer variables, you can do math on them. It isn't complicated math. Just add dx to x and dy to y. This syntax allows you to move the object as many pixels as the user wants in both x and y axes.

   ```
   x += dx;
   y += dy;
   ```

5. **Check boundaries.**

   If you have young children, you know this rule: Once you have something that can move, it will get out of bounds. If you let your sprite move, it will leave the space you've designated. Checking the boundaries isn't difficult, but it's another task, so I'm just calling a function here. I describe `checkBounds()` in the next section, but basically it just checks to see whether the sprite is leaving the surface and adjusts its position to stay in bounds.

   ```
   checkBounds();
   ```

6. **Move the ball.**

   Changing the `x` and `y` properties doesn't really move the sprite. To do that, you need to convert the integers back into the CSS format. If `x` is `120`, you need to set `left` to `120px`. Just concatenate `"px"` to the end of each variable, and JavaScript automatically concatenates.

   ```
   // move ball to new position
   sprite.style.left = x + "px";
   sprite.style.top = y + "px";
   ```

7. **Print the position.**

   For debugging purposes, I like to know exactly where the `x` and `y` positions are, so I just made a string and printed it to an output panel.

   ```
   //describe position
   var output = document.getElementById("output");
   output.innerHTML = "x: " + x + ", y: " + y;
   ```

Checking the boundaries

You can respond in a number of ways when an object leaves the playing area. I'm going with wrapping, one of the simplest techniques. If something leaves the rightmost border, simply have it jump all the way to the left.

The code handles all four borders:

```
function checkBounds(){
  //wrap
  if (x > MAX_X){
    x = MIN_X;
  } // end if
  if (x < MIN_X){
    x = MAX_X;
  } // end if
  if (y > MAX_Y){
    y = MIN_Y;
  } // end if
  if (y < MIN_Y){
    y = MAX_Y;
  } // end if
} // end function
```

The checkBounds() function depends on the constants, which helps in a couple of ways. When you look at the code, you can easily see what's going on:

```
if (x > MAX_X){
  x = MIN_X;
} // end if
```

If x is larger than the maximum value for x, set it to the minimum value. You almost can't write it any more clearly than this. If the size of the playing surface changes, you simply change the values of the constants.

You probably wonder how I came up with the actual values for the constants. In some languages, you can come up with nice mathematical tricks to predict exactly what the largest and smallest values should be. In JavaScript, it's a little tricky because it just isn't that precise an environment.

I chose a simple but effective technique. I temporarily took out the checkbounds() call and just took a look at the output to see what the values of x and y were. I looked to see how large x should be before the sprite wraps and wrote down the value on paper. Likewise, I found the largest and smallest values for y.

Once I knew these values, I simply placed them in constants. I don't really care that the maximum value for x is 365. I just want to know that x doesn't go past the MAX_X value when I'm messing around with it.

If the size of my playing surface changes, I just change the constants, and everything works out fine.

Shouldn't you just get size values from the surface?

In a perfect world, I would have extracted the position values from the playing surface itself. Unfortunately, JavaScript / DOM is not a perfect animation framework. Because I'm using absolute positioning, the position of the sprite isn't attached to the surface (as it should be), but to the main screen. It's a little annoying, but some experimentation can help you find the right values.

Remember, once you've started using absolute positioning on a page, you're pretty much committed to it. If you're using animation like the one described in this section, you'll probably want to use absolute positioning everywhere or do some other tricks to make sure that the sprite stays where you want it to go without overwriting other parts of the page. Regardless, using constants keeps the code easy to read and maintain, even if you have to hack a little bit to find the specific values you need.

Reading Input from the Keyboard

You can use JavaScript to read directly from the keyboard. This trick is useful in a several situations, but it's especially handy in animation and simple gaming applications.

Figure 7-2 shows a program with a moving ball.

The `keyboard.html` page has no buttons because the keyboard arrows are used to manage all the input.

You know what I'm going to say. Look this thing over in your browser because it just doesn't have any charm unless you run it and mash on some arrow keys.

Building the keyboard page

The keyboard page is very much like the movement page.

```
<!DOCTYPE html PUBLIC "-//W3C//DTD XHTML 1.0 Strict//EN"
"http://www.w3.org/TR/xhtml1/DTD/xhtml1-strict.dtd">
<html lang="EN" dir="ltr" xmlns="http://www.w3.org/1999/xhtml">
  <head>
    <meta http-equiv="content-type" content="text/xml; charset=utf-8" />
    <title>keyboard.html</title>
```

Figure 7-2: You can move the ball with the arrow keys.

```
    <link rel = "stylesheet"
          type = "text/css"
          href = "keyboard.css" />

    <script type = "text/javascript"
            src = "movement.js">
    </script>
    <script type = "text/javascript"
            src = "keyboard.js">
    </script>

  </head>

  <body onload = "init()">
    <h1>Use arrow keys to move ball</h1>

    <div id = "surface">
      <div id = "sprite"
           style = "position: absolute;
           top: 100px;
           left: 100px;
           height: 25px;
           width: 25px;" >
        <img src = "ball.gif"
             alt = "ball" />
      </div>
    </div>

    <p id = "output">
      x = 100, y = 100
    </p>
  </body>
</html>
```

The preceding code is when it really pays off to build reusable code. I basically copied the movement.html page with a couple of important changes:

- **Import the movement.js script.** This page uses the same functions as the movement.html page, so just reimport the script.
- **Add another script specific to reading the keyboard.** You need a couple of modifications, which are housed in a second script file called keyboard.js.
- **Keep the rest of the page similar.** You still call init() when the body loads, and you still want the same visual design, except for the buttons. The surface and sprite divs are identical to the movement.html design.
- **Take out the form.** This page responds to the keyboard, so you no longer need a form.

This program begins with the movement.js script. As far as the browser is concerned, that entire script file has been loaded before the keyboard.js script appears. The basic foundation is already in place from movement. The keyboard script just handles the modifications to make keyboard support work.

Overwriting the init() function

Working with a keyboard still requires some initialization. I need a little more work in the `init()` function, so I make a new version to replace the version created in `movement.js`.

```
//assumes movement.js

function init(){
  sprite = document.getElementById("sprite");
  document.onkeydown = keyListener;
} // end init
```

The order in which you import scripts matters. If you duplicate a function, the browser interprets only the last script read.

Setting up an event handler

In my `init()` function, I still want to initialize the sprite (as I did in `movement.js`, described in the "Moving the Sprite" section earlier in this chapter). When you want to read the keyboard, you need to tap into the browser's *event-handling* facility. Browsers provide basic support for page-based events (such as `body.onload` and `button.onclick`), but they also provide a lower level support for more fundamental input, such as keyboard and mouse input.

If you want to read this lower level input, you need to specify a function that will respond to the input.

```
document.onkeydown = keyListener;
```

This line specifies that a special function called `keyListener` is called whenever the user presses a key. Keep a couple of things in mind when you create this type of event handler:

- **It should be called in `init()`.** You'll probably want keyboard handling to be available immediately, so setting up event handlers in the `init()` function is common.
- **The function is called as if it were a variable.** This syntax is slightly different than typically used in JavaScript. When you create function handlers in HTML, you simply feed a string that represents the function name complete with parameters (`button onclick = "doSomething()"`). When you call a function within JavaScript (as opposed to calling the function in HTML), the function name is actually much like a variable, so it doesn't require quotes.

If you want to know the truth, functions are variables in JavaScript. Next time somebody tells you JavaScript is a toy language, mention that it supports automatic dereferencing of function pointers. Then run away before they ask you what that means. (That's what I do . . .)

✦ **You need to create a function with the specified name.** If you've got this code in `init`, the browser calls a function called `keyListener()` whenever a key is pressed. (You can call the function something else, but `keyListener()` is a pretty good name for it.)

Responding to keystrokes

After you've set up an event-handler, you need to write the function to respond to keystrokes. Fortunately, this task turns out to be pretty easy.

```
function keyListener(e){
  // if e doesn't already exist, we're in IE so make it

  if (!e){
    e = window.event;
  } // end IE-specific code

  //left
  if (e.keyCode == 37){
    moveSprite(-10, 0);
  } // end if

  //up
  if (e.keyCode == 38){
    moveSprite(0, -10);
  } // end if

  //right
  if (e.keyCode == 39){
    moveSprite(10, 0);
  } // end if

  //down
  if (e.keyCode == 40){
    moveSprite(0, 10);
  } // end if

} // end keyListener
```

The `keyListener()` function is a good example of an *event handler.* These functions are used to determine what events have happened in the system, and to respond to those events. Here's how to build this one:

✦ **Event functions have event objects.** Just knowing that an event has occurred isn't enough. You need to know which key has been pressed. Fortunately, the browsers all have an event object available to tell you what's happened.

✦ **Many browsers pass the event as a parameter.** When you create an event function, the browser automatically assigns a special parameter to the function. This parameter (normally called `e`) represents the event. Just make the function with a parameter called `e`, and most browsers create `e` automatically.

```
function keyListener(e){
```

- **Internet Explorer needs a little more help.** Internet Explorer doesn't automatically create an event object for you, so you need to specifically create it.

```
// if e doesn't already exist, we're in IE so make it

if (!e){
  e = window.event;
} // end IE-specific code
```

- **You can use `e` to figure out which key was pressed.** The `e` object has some nifty properties, including `keyCode`. This property returns a number that tells you which key was pressed.

Do a quick search on *JavaScript event object* to discover other kinds of event tricks. I show the most critical features here, but this section is just an introduction to the many interesting things you can do with events.

- **Compare to known keycodes.** You can figure out the keycodes of any keys on your keyboard and use basic `if` statements to respond appropriately.

```
//left
if (e.keyCode == 37){
  moveSprite(-10, 0);
} // end if
```

- **Call appropriate variations of `moveSprite`.** If the user presses the left arrow, move the sprite to the left. You can use the `moveSprite()` function defined in `movement.js` (in the "Moving the Sprite" section of this chapter) for this task.

Deciphering the mystery of key codes

Of course, the big mystery of a keyboard handler is where all those funky key numbers came from. How did I know that the left arrow is keycode 37, for example? It's pretty simple, really. I just wrote a program to tell me. Figure 7-3 shows `readKeys.html` in action.

Run `readKeys` and press a few keys. You can then easily determine what keycode is related to which key on the keyboard. You may also want to look over this code if you're a little confused; because all the code is in one place, it may be a bit easier to read than the movement examples.

If you use a notebook or international keyboard, be aware that some of the key codes may be nonstandard, especially numeric keypad keys. Try to stick to standard keys if you want to ensure that your program works on all keyboards.

Following the Mouse

You can also create an event-handler that reads the mouse. Figure 7-4 shows such a program.

The mouse-following effect is actually quite an easy effect once you know how to read the keyboard because it works in almost exactly the same way as the keyboard approach.

Looking over the HTML

The code for `followMouse.html` is simple enough that I kept it in one file:

```
<!DOCTYPE html PUBLIC "-//W3C//DTD XHTML 1.0 Strict//EN"
"http://www.w3.org/TR/xhtml1/DTD/xhtml1-strict.dtd">
<html lang="EN" dir="ltr" xmlns="http://www.w3.org/1999/xhtml">
  <head>
    <meta http-equiv="content-type" content="text/xml; charset=utf-8" />
    <title>followMouse.html</title>
    <script type = "text/javascript">
      var sprite;

      function init(){
        sprite = document.getElementById("sprite");
        document.onmousemove = mouseListener;
      } // end init

      function mouseListener(e){
        if (!e){
          e = window.event;
        } // end IE catch

        //get width and height
        height = parseInt(sprite.style.height);
        width = parseInt(sprite.style.width);
```

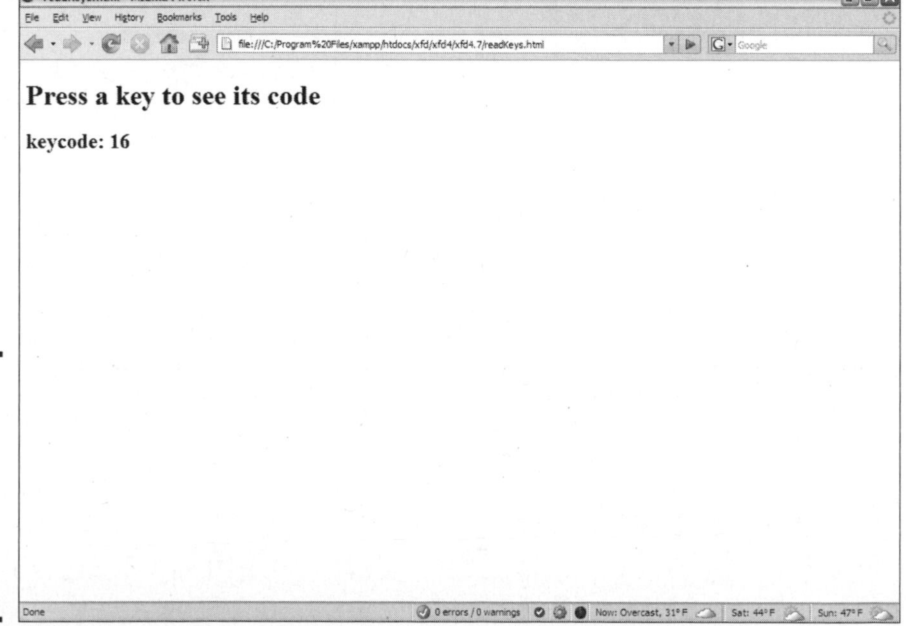

Figure 7-3: This program reads the keyboard and reports the key codes.

```
        //move center of sprite to mouse
        x = e.pageX - (width/2);
        y = e.pageY - (height/2);

        sprite.style.left = x + "px";
        sprite.style.top = y + "px";
      } // end function
    </script>
  </head>

  <body onload = "init()">
    <h1>Move the mouse and the ball will follow</h1>
    <div id = "sprite"
         style = "position: absolute;
                  left: 100px;
                  top: 100px;
                  width: 50px;
                  height: 50px;">
      <img src = "ball.gif"
           alt = "ball" />
    </div>
  </body>
</html>
```

The HTML page is simple. This time I'm letting the mouse take up the entire page. No borders are necessary because the sprite isn't able to leave the page. (If the mouse leaves the page, it no longer sends event messages.)

Just create a sprite with an image as normal and be sure to call `init()` when the body loads.

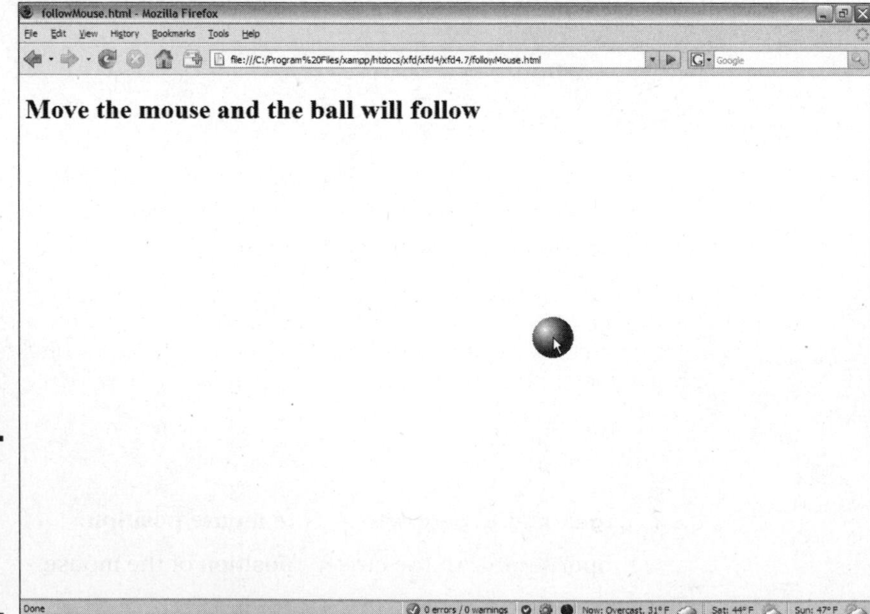

Figure 7-4: Now the sprite stays with the mouse.

Initializing the code

The initialization is also pretty straightforward:

1. **Create a global variable for the sprite.**

   Define the `sprite` variable outside any functions so that it is available to all of them.

   ```
   var sprite;
   ```

2. **Build the sprite in `init()`.**

   The `init()` function is a great place to create the sprite.

   ```
   function init(){
     sprite = document.getElementById("sprite");
     document.onmousemove = mouseListener;
   ```

3. **Set up an event handler in `init()` for mouse motion.**

   This time, you're trapping for mouse events, so call this one `mouseListener`.

   ```
     document.onmousemove = mouseListener;
   ```

Building the mouse listener

The mouse listener works much like a keyboard listener. It examines the event object to determine the mouse's current position and then uses that value to place the sprite:

1. **Get the event object.**

   Use the cross-platform technique to get the event object.

   ```
   function mouseListener(e){
     if (!e){
       e = window.event;
     } // end IE catch
   ```

2. **Determine the sprite's width and height.**

   The `top` and `left` properties point to the sprite's top-left corner. Placing the mouse in the center of the sprite looks more natural. To calculate the center, you need the height and width. Don't forget to add these values to the local style for the sprite.

   ```
     //get width and height
     height = parseInt(sprite.style.height);
     width = parseInt(sprite.style.width);
   ```

3. **Use `e.pageX` and `e.pageY` to get the mouse position.**

   These properties return the current position of the mouse.

4. **Determine x and y under the mouse cursor.**

   Subtract half of the sprite's width from the mouse's `x` (`e.pageX`) so that the sprite's horizontal position is centered on the mouse. Repeat with the `y` position.

   ```
   //move center of sprite to mouse
   x = e.pageX - (width/2);
   y = e.pageY - (height/2);
   ```

5. **Move the mouse to the new x and y coordinates.**

   Use the conversion techniques to move the sprite to the new position.

   ```
   sprite.style.left = x + "px";
   sprite.style.top = y + "px";
   ```

Another fun effect is to have the sprite influenced by the mouse. Don't make it follow the mouse directly, but check to see where the mouse is in relationship with the sprite. Have the sprite move up if the mouse is above the sprite, for example.

Creating Automatic Motion

You can make a sprite move automatically by attaching a special timer to the object. Figure 7-5 shows the ball moving autonomously across the page.

`Timer.html` is surprisingly simple because it borrows almost everything from other code.

```
<!DOCTYPE html PUBLIC "-//W3C//DTD XHTML 1.0 Strict//EN"
"http://www.w3.org/TR/xhtml1/DTD/xhtml1-strict.dtd">
<html lang="EN" dir="ltr" xmlns="http://www.w3.org/1999/xhtml">
  <head>
    <meta http-equiv="content-type" content="text/xml; charset=utf-8" />
    <title>timer.html</title>

    <link rel = "stylesheet"
          type = "text/css"
          href = "keyboard.css" />

    <script type = "text/javascript"
            src = "movement.js">
    </script>

    <script type = "text/javascript">
      function init(){
        sprite = document.getElementById("sprite");
        setInterval("moveSprite(5, 3)", 100);
      } // end init

    </script>
  </head>

  <body onload = "init()">
    <h1>Timer-based movement</h1>

    <div id = "surface">
```

```
        <div id = "sprite"
             style = "position: absolute;
             top: 100px;
             left: 100px;
             height: 25px;
             width: 25px;" >
          <img src = "ball.gif"
               alt = "ball" />
        </div>
      </div>

      <p id = "output">
        x = 100, y = 100
      </p>
    </body>
  </html>
```

The HTML and CSS is exactly the same as the `button.html` code. Most of the JavaScript comes from `movement.js`. The only thing that's really new is a tiny but critical change in the `init()` method.

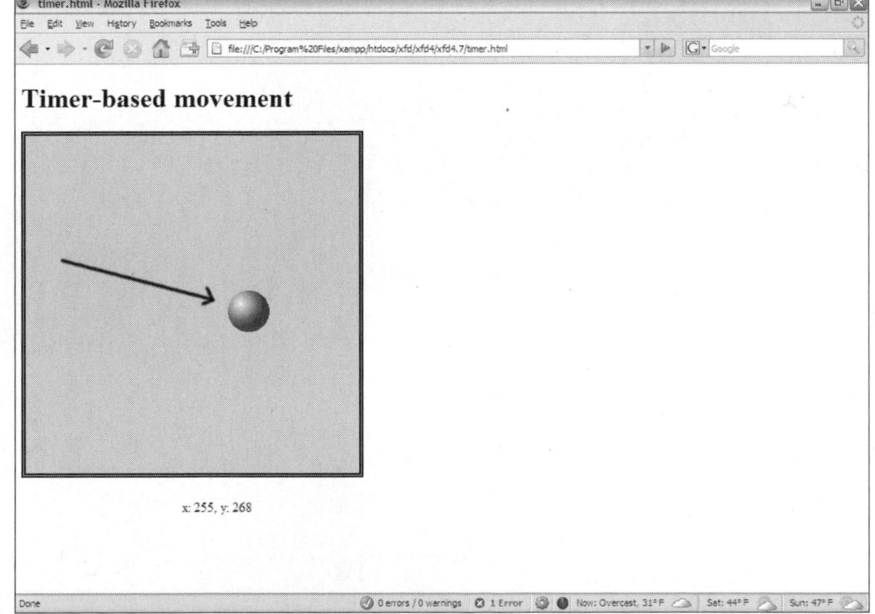

Figure 7-5: This sprite is moving on its own. (I added the arrow to show motion.)

Creating a setInterval() call

JavaScript contains a very useful function called `setInterval`. This thing takes two parameters:

- **A function call.** Create a string containing a function call including any of its parameters.

✦ **A time interval in milliseconds.** You can specify an interval in 1000ths of a second. If the interval is 500, the given function is called twice per second, 50 milliseconds is 20 times per second, and so on.

You can set the interval at whatever speed you want, but that doesn't guarantee things will work that fast. If you put complex code in a function and tell the browser to execute it 1,000 times a second, it probably won't be able to keep up (especially if the user has a slower machine than you do).

The browser will call the specified function at the specified interval. Put any code that you want repeated inside the given function.

Don't put anything in an interval function that doesn't have to go there. Because this code happens several times per second, it's called a *critical path,* and any wasteful processing here can severely slow down the entire program. Try to make the code in an interval function as clean as possible. (That's why I created the `sprite` as a global variable. I didn't want to re-create the sprite 20 times per second, making my program impossible for slower browsers to handle.)

Automatically moving objects are a great place to play with other kinds of boundary detection. If you want to see how to make something bounce when it hits the edge, look at `bounce.html` and `bounce.js` on the CD-ROM.

Building Image-Swapping Animation

The other kind of animation you can do involves rapidly changing an image. Look at Figure 7-6 to see one frame of an animated figure.

Animation is never that easy to show in a still screen shot, so Figure 7-7 shows the sequence of images used to build the kicking sprite.

You can use any series of images you want. I got these images from a site called Reiner's Tilesets (`http://reinerstileset.4players.de/englisch.htm`). It includes a huge number of sprites, each with several animations. These animations are called Freya.

Preparing the images

You can build your own images, or you can get them from a site like Reiner's. In any case, here are a few things to keep in mind when building image animations:

✦ **Keep them small.** Larger images take a long time to download and don't swap as smoothly as small ones. My images are 128 by 128 pixels, which is a good size.

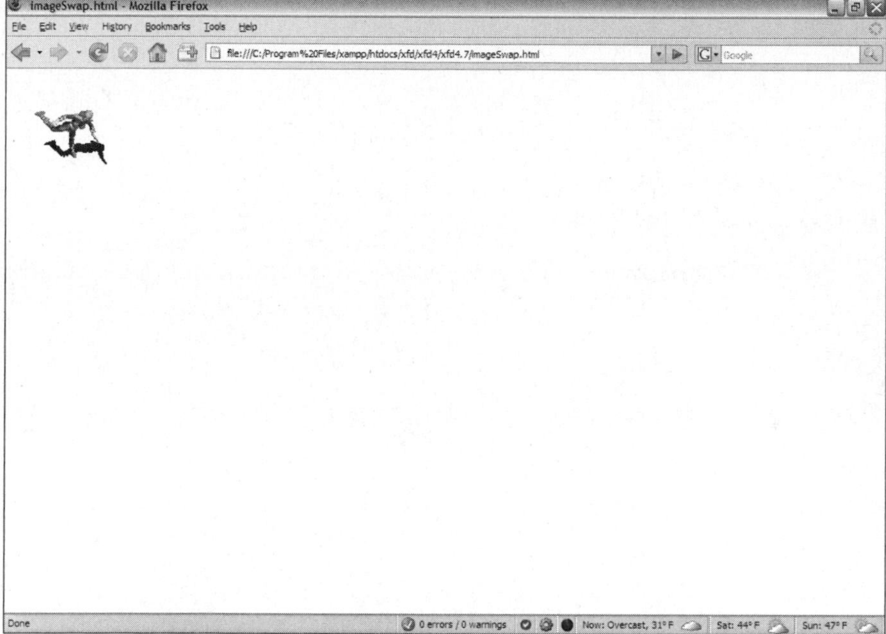

Figure 7-6: This sprite is kicking!

Figure 7-7: I used this series of images to build the animation.

✦ **Consider adding transparency.** The images from Reiner have a brown background. I changed the background to transparent using my favorite graphics editor (Gimp).

✦ **Change the file format.** The images came in `.bmp` format, which is inefficient and doesn't support transparency. I saved them as `.gif` images to make them smaller and enable the background transparency.

- **Consider changing the names.** I renamed the images to make the names simpler and to eliminate spaces from the filenames. I called the images `kick00.gif` to `kick12.gif`.
- **Put animation images in a subdirectory.** With ordinary page images, I often find a subdirectory to be unhelpful. When you start building animations, you can easily have a lot of little images running around. A large number of small files is a good place for a subdirectory.

Building the page

The code for animation just uses variations of techniques described throughout this chapter: a `setInterval` function and some DOM coding.

```
<!DOCTYPE html PUBLIC "-//W3C//DTD XHTML 1.0 Strict//EN"
"http://www.w3.org/TR/xhtml1/DTD/xhtml1-strict.dtd">
<html lang="EN" dir="ltr" xmlns="http://www.w3.org/1999/xhtml">
  <head>
    <meta http-equiv="content-type" content="text/xml; charset=utf-8" />
    <title>imageSwap.html</title>
    <script type = "text/javascript">
      //<![CDATA[
      var imgList = new Array (
        "freya/kick00.gif",
        "freya/kick01.gif",
        "freya/kick02.gif",
        "freya/kick03.gif",
        "freya/kick04.gif",
        "freya/kick05.gif",
        "freya/kick06.gif",
        "freya/kick07.gif",
        "freya/kick08.gif",
        "freya/kick09.gif",
        "freya/kick10.gif",
        "freya/kick11.gif",
        "freya/kick12.gif"
      );

      var frame = 0;
      var spriteImage

      function init(){
        setInterval("animate()", 100);
        spriteImage = document.getElementById("image");
      } // end init

      function animate(){
        frame += 1;
        if (frame > imgList.length){
          frame = 0;
        } // end if
        spriteImage.src = imgList[frame];
      }
      //]]>
    </script>
  </head>

  <body onclick = "init()">
    <div id = "sprite">
```

```
      <img id = "image"
           src = "freya/kick00.gif"
           alt = "kicking sprite" />
    </div>
  </body>
</html>
```

The HTML is incredibly simple:

1. **Set up the body with an `init()` method.**

   As usual, the body's `onclick` event calls an `init()` method to start things up.

2. **Create a `sprite` div.**

   Build a div named `sprite`. Because you aren't changing the position of this div (yet), you don't need to worry about the local style.

3. **Name the `img`.**

   In this program, you animate the `img` inside the div, so you need to give it an `id`.

Building the global variables

The JavaScript code isn't too difficult, but it requires a little bit of thought.

1. **Create an array of image names.**

   You have a list of images to work with. The easiest way to support several related images is with an array of image names. Each element of the array is the filename of an image. Put them in the order you want the animation frames to appear.

   ```
   var imgList = new Array (
     "freya/kick00.gif",
     "freya/kick01.gif",
     "freya/kick02.gif",
     "freya/kick03.gif",
     "freya/kick04.gif",
     "freya/kick05.gif",
     "freya/kick06.gif",
     "freya/kick07.gif",
     "freya/kick08.gif",
     "freya/kick09.gif",
     "freya/kick10.gif",
     "freya/kick11.gif",
     "freya/kick12.gif"
   );
   ```

2. **Build a `frame` variable to hold the current frame number.**

   Because this animation has 12 frames, the `frame` variable goes from 0 to 11.

   ```
   var frame = 0;
   ```

3. **Set up `spriteImage` to reference to the `img` tag inside the `sprite` tag.**

```
var spriteImage
```

Setting up the interval

The `init()` function attaches the `spriteImage` variable to the image object and sets up the `animate()` method to run ten times per second.

```
function init(){
  setInterval("animate()", 100);
  spriteImage = document.getElementById("image");
} // end init
```

Animating the sprite

The actual animation happens in the (you guessed it...) `animate()` function. The function is straightforward:

1. **Increment frame.**

   Add one to the frame variable.

   ```
   frame += 1;
   ```

2. **Check for bounds.**

   Any time you change a variable, you should consider whether it may go out of bounds. I'm using `frame` as an index in the `imgList` array, so I check to see that `frame` is always less than the length of `imgList`.

   ```
   if (frame > imgList.length){
     frame = 0;
   } // end if
   ```

3. **Reset `frame`, if necessary.**

   If the frame counter gets too high, reset it to zero and start the animation over.

4. **Copy the image filename over from the array to the `src` property of the `spriteImage` object.**

   This step causes the given file to display.

   ```
   spriteImage.src = imgList[frame];
   ```

JavaScript is not an ideal animation framework, but it will do. You do get some delays on the first pass as all the images load. (Making the images smaller and in the GIF or PNG formats will help with this issue.) Most browsers store images locally, so the images animate smoothly after the first pass.

If you want smoother animation, you can either preload the images or combine all the frames into a single image and simply change what part of the image is displayed.

Even if you don't like animation, these techniques can be useful. You can use the `setInterval()` technique for any kind of repetitive code you want, including the dynamic display of menus or other page elements. In fact, before CSS became the preferred technique, most dynamic menus used JavaScript animation.

Movement and Swapping

Finally, you can combine motion effects with image-swapping to have an image move around on the screen with animated motion. Figure 7-8 tries to show this effect (but you need to use a browser to really see it).

Making this program requires nothing at all new. It's just a combination of the techniques used throughout this chapter. Figure 7-9 shows the list of images used to make Freya run. (I added the arrow again just so you can see how the movement works.)

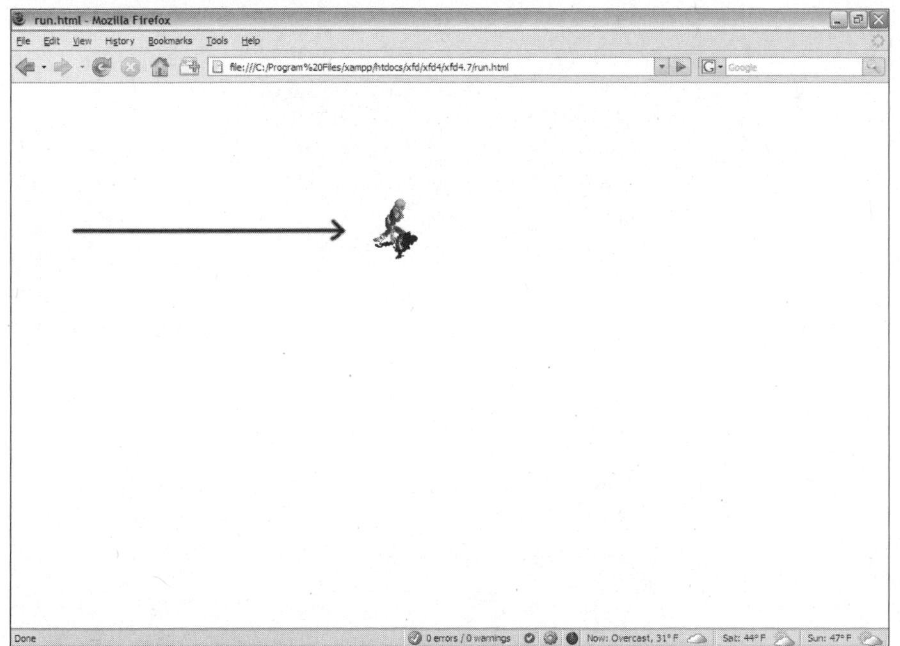

Figure 7-8: Now Freya's running around the screen. Run, Freya, Run!

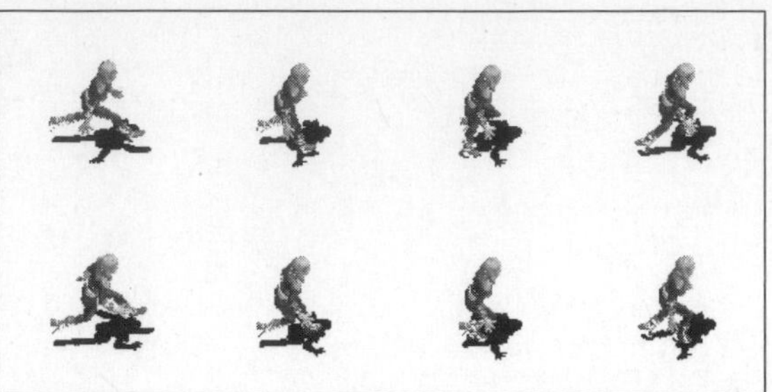

Figure 7-9: These are the running images from Reiner's Tilesets.

The HTML is (as usual) pretty minimal here:

```
<!DOCTYPE html PUBLIC "-//W3C//DTD XHTML 1.0 Strict//EN"
"http://www.w3.org/TR/xhtml1/DTD/xhtml1-strict.dtd">
<html lang="EN" dir="ltr" xmlns="http://www.w3.org/1999/xhtml">
  <head>
    <meta http-equiv="content-type" content="text/xml; charset=utf-8" />
    <title>run.html</title>
    <script type = "text/javascript"
            src = "run.js">
    </script>
  </head>

  <body onload = "init()">
    <div id = "sprite"
         style = "position: absolute;
                  top: 100px;
                  left: 100px;">
      <img src = "freya/run0.gif"
           id = "image"
           alt = "running image" />
    </div>
  </body>
</html>
```

When you want to create a moving image-swap animation:

1. **Import the script.**

   You can build the script locally (as I did in the last example), but any time the script gets complex, it may be better in an external file.

2. **Call an `init()` method.**

   Most animation requires an `init()` method called from `body.onload()`, and this one is no exception.

3. **Name the sprite.**

   The sprite is a div that moves, so it needs absolute position, top and left all defined as local styles.

4. **Name the image.**

   You also animate the image inside the sprite. The only property you change here is the `src`, so no local styles are necessary.

Building the code

The JavaScript code is familiar because all the elements can be borrowed from previous programs. Here's the code in its entirety:

```
//run.js

var frame = 0;
var imgList = new Array(
  "freya/run0.gif",
  "freya/run1.gif",
  "freya/run2.gif",
  "freya/run3.gif",
  "freya/run4.gif",
  "freya/run5.gif",
  "freya/run6.gif",
  "freya/run7.gif"
);

var sprite;
var spriteImage;
var MAX_X = 500;

function init(){
  sprite = document.getElementById("sprite");
  spriteImage = document.getElementById("image");

  setInterval("animate()", 100);
} // end init

function animate(){
  updateImage();
  updatePosition();
} // end animate

function updateImage(){
  frame++;
  if (frame > imgList.length){
    frame = 0;
  } // end if
  spriteImage.src = imgList[frame];
} // end updateImage

function updatePosition(){
  sprite = document.getElementById("sprite");
  var x = parseInt(sprite.style.left);
  x += 10;
  if (x > MAX_X){
    x = 0;
  } // end if
  sprite.style.left = x + "px";
} // end function
```

Defining global variables

You'll have a few global variables in this code:

- **`Frame`** is the frame number. It is an integer from 0 to 11, which serves as the index for the `imgList` array.
- **`imgList`** is an array of filenames with the animation images.
- **`sprite`** is the div that moves around the screen.
- **`spriteImage`** is the `img` element of `sprite` and the image that is swapped.
- **`MAX_X`** is a constant holding the maximum value of X. In this program, I'm only moving in one direction, so the only boundary I'm worried about is `MAX_X`. If the sprite moved in other directions, I'd add some other constants for the other boundary conditions.

Initializing your data

The `init()` function performs its normal tasks: setting up sprite variables and calling the `animate()` function on an interval.

```
function init(){
  sprite = document.getElementById("sprite");
  spriteImage = document.getElementById("image");
setInterval("animate()", 100);
} // end init
```

When you move and swap images, sometimes you have to adjust the animation interval and the distance traveled each frame so that the animation looks right. Otherwise, the sprite may seem to skate rather than run.

Animating and updating the image

I really have two kinds of animation happening at once, so in the grand tradition of encapsulation, the `animate()` function passes off its job to two other functions:

```
function animate(){
  updateImage();
  updatePosition();
} // end animate
```

The `updateImage()` function handles the image-swapping duties:

```
function updateImage(){
  frame++;
  if (frame > imgList.length){
    frame = 0;
  } // end if
  spriteImage.src = imgList[frame];
} // end updateImage
```

Moving the sprite

The sprite is moved in the `updatePosition()` function:

```
function updatePosition(){
  sprite = document.getElementById("sprite");
  var x = parseInt(sprite.style.left);
  x += 10;
  if (x > MAX_X){
    x = 0;
  } // end if
  sprite.style.left = x + "px";
} // end function
```

Book V

Server-Side Programming with PHP

"Okay, I think I forgot to mention this, but we now have a Web management function that automatically alerts us when there's a broken link on The Aquarium's Web site."

Contents at a Glance

Chapter 1: Setting Up Your Server

In This Chapter

- **Introducing server-side programming**
- **Installing and starting your server**
- **Testing the installation**
- **Inspecting** `phpinfo()`

Welcome to the server-side programming portion of the book. In this minibook, you discover all the basics of PHP and how you can use PHP to make your pages dynamic and relevant in today's Internet.

In this chapter, you read about getting your server set up and ready to go. I walk you through the process as painlessly as possible, and by the end, you'll be up and running, and ready to serve up your own Web pages in a test environment. (I talk about making them available to the rest of the world in Book VIII.)

Introducing Server-Side Programming

I begin with an introduction to server-side programming. If you already know how this all works, you can safely skip ahead to the section "Installing Your Web Server," later in this chapter.

Programming on the server

Server-side programming is what you'd use to create pages dynamically on the server before sending them to the client. Whereas client-side programming is executed on the client's machine, server-side programming all happens on the server before the Web page is even sent to the user.

Client-side programming (as done in JavaScript) does most of the work on the individual user's machine. This has advantages because those machines have doohickeys, like mice and graphics cards. Client-side programs can be interactive in real-time.

The client has a big problem, though. Programs written on the client usually have a form of forced amnesia (no long term memory). For security reasons, client-side applications can't store information in files and can't interact with other programs on the computer. Also, you never know exactly what kind of setup the user has, so you can't really be sure if your program will work.

This is where server-side programming comes in. In a pure server-side programming environment, all the action happens on the Web server. The user thinks she's asking for a Web page like normal, but the address really goes to a computer program. The program does some magic and produces a Web page. The user sees a Web page, perhaps never knowing that an ordinary program was in the mix.

A program running on a Web server has some really nice advantages, such as

- **A server-side program can access the local file system.** Asking a server program to load and save files on the server is no problem at all.
- **A server-side program can call external programs.** This is a very big deal because many Web applications are really about working with data. Database programs are very important to modern Web development. See Book VI for much more on this.
- **All the user sees is ordinary XHTML.** You can set up your program to do whatever you want, but the output is regular XHTML. You don't have to worry about what browser the user has or whether he has a Mac. Any browser that can display XHTML can be used with PHP.

Serving your programs

When using a browser to retrieve Web pages, you send a request to a server. The server then looks at the extension (`.html`, `.php`, `.js`, and so on) at the end of your requested file and decides what to do. If the server sees `.html` or `.js`, it says, "Cool, nothing doing here, just gotta send her back as is." When the server sees `.php`, it says, "Oh boy, they need PHP to build something here."

The server takes the page and hollers for PHP to come along and construct the requested Web page on the fly. Usually, PHP goes through and looks at the programmer's blue print, and then constructs the working page out of XHTML.

The server then takes that page from PHP and sends it back to the client for the browser to display to the user.

When you write ordinary (non-PHP) documents, your pages can go just anywhere because the browser does all the processing. When you write PHP programs, a Web server must process the form before the browser can see it. This means you have to have a Web server available and place the file in a specific place on your computer for the server to serve it. You can't run a PHP file directly from your Desktop. It must be placed in the `htdocs` directory under the server.

Picking a language

There are all sorts of different ways to go about dynamically creating Web pages with server-side programming. Back in the day when the Internet was still in diapers, people used things like Perl and CGI scripting to handle all their server-side programming. Eventually, people placed more and more demand on their Web sites, and soon these languages just weren't enough.

The prevalent languages today are

- ✦ **ASP.NET:** Microsoft's contender
- ✦ **Java:** The heavyweight offering from Sun Microsystems
- ✦ **PHP:** The popular language described in this minibook

ASP.NET

ASP.NET is event-driven, compiled, and object-oriented. ASP.NET replaced the '90s language ASP in 2002. Microsoft repurposed it for use with their .NET framework to facilitate cross-compatibility with their Desktop applications (apps) and integration into Visual Studio (although you can write ASP.NET apps from any text editor). ASP.NET runs on Microsoft's IIS Web server, which isn't free. I don't recommend it to cost-conscious users.

Object-oriented (OO) versus procedural

What is the difference between object-oriented programs and procedural programs?

A *procedural* program normally has all the code contained in one file. You start at the top and go to the bottom, possibly calling functions on variables, but ultimately running through the whole thing, start to finish, just as you see it.

Object-Oriented Programming (OOP) allows you to create objects and call methods on them (a method is just a function; but in OOP, functions are sometimes dubbed methods). Each object gets its own text file and contains all its own methods. An object is like a mold that you can cast multiple copies from.

The great thing about PHP is that you can choose if you want OOP or procedural programming. This book covers both. When it makes sense, I utilize the object-oriented capabilities, and for the simple stuff, I use the procedural approach. Don't worry if you don't understand this right now. You'll get the hang of it later when you begin using OOP in your PHP.

Compile versus interpret?

What's the difference between an interpreted language and a compiled language? A *compiled* language is compiled one time into a more computer-friendly format for faster processing when called by the computer. Compiled languages are typically very fast but not very flexible. *Interpreted* languages have to be interpreted on the spot by the server *every time* they're called, which is slower but provides more flexibility. With blazing fast servers these days, interpreted languages can normally stand under the load, and the ability to handle changes without recompiling can be an advantage in the fast-paced world of Web development.

Java

Java's been a strong contender for a long time now. The language is indeed named after coffee. If you work for a banking company or insurance company, or need to build the next eBay or Amazon.com, you might want to consider Java. However, Java can consume a lot of time, and it's hard to figure out. You may have to write up to 16 lines of code to do in Java what it could take a mere 4 lines of code in PHP. Java is absolutely free, as is the Apache Tomcat Web server that it uses to serve its Web components. Java was originally created to write Desktop applications and is still very good at doing that. If you're comfortable with C/C++, you'll be very comfortable with Java because it's very similar. It's fully object-oriented, and it's compiled. Java is powerful, but it can be challenging for beginners. It'd be a great second language to work with.

PHP

PHP was born from a collection of modifications for Perl and has boomed ever since (in a way, replacing Perl, which was once considered the duct tape and bubble gum that held the Internet together).

PHP works great for your server-side Web development purposes. *MediaWiki* (the engine that was written to run the popular Internet encyclopedia Wikipedia) runs on PHP, as do many other popular large-, medium-, and small-scale Web sites. PHP's a solid, easy-to-learn, well-established language (it's 13 years old). PHP can be object-oriented or procedural (you can take your pick!). PHP is interpreted rather than compiled.

Installing Your Web Server

In order for PHP to work usefully, you have to have some other things installed on your computer, such as

- **A Web server:** This is a special program that enables a computer to process files and send them to Web browsers. I'll use Apache because it's free, powerful, and works very well with PHP.
- **A database backend:** Modern Web sites rely heavily on data, so a program that can manage your data needs is very important. I'll use MySQL (a free and powerful tool) for this. Book VI is entirely dedicated to creating data with MySQL and some related tools.
- **A programming language:** Server-side programming relies on a language. I'll use PHP because it works great, and it's free.

Setting up a server-side programming environment can be a daunting task. That's a lot of software to download and install, and each piece needs to know how to work with all the others.

Thanks to friends at `www.apachefriends.org`, it's now easier than ever to install all those things in the list. Apachefriends.org bundles them all into one little program — *XAMPP.* Here's how you load it up:

1. **Go to `www.apachefriends.org`.**
2. **Scroll down and click XAMPP.**
3. **Scroll down and click XAMPP for Windows.**
4. **Scroll down and click XAMPP under the Download heading.**

   At this point, you can take your pick. I always click the EXE for no other reason than it's the smallest. I use that one for this example.
5. **Click EXE (7-Zip).**

   This takes you to a SourceForge.net page. (You won't need the 7-Zip software. This program is simply an archive created with 7-Zip.)
6. **Click Save File (Firefox).**

   If you're in Internet Explorer, you might get the annoying yellow bar at the top of the page letting you know it didn't download the file. Click the yellow bar and choose to download the file, and then click Save in the File Download pop-up. Go ahead and save the file to your Desktop.
7. **Double-click the `xampp-win....exe` file on your Desktop.**

   Windows might ask you at this point if it's okay to run the file. Click Run.

8. **Pick a place to extract the program to.**

   I chose `C:\` because that's the easiest place to find it.

9. **Click Extract, and you're done!**

   At this point, it's safe to delete the EXE file from your Desktop.

   Okay, great, you've installed XAMPP. See? Easy as pie, just like I said!

Starting your server

Okay, so you've installed XAMPP, and you're ready to get your server up and running. Here's how:

1. **Browse to the folder where you unzipped XAMPP.**
2. **Run the XAMPP Controller (`xampp-control.exe`).**

   You may want to put a shortcut to this program on your Desktop, as you'll use it frequently to manage the various parts of the XAMPP system.

   At this point, a little utility opens with all sorts of buttons, like some sort of crazy universal remote for your server. This program looks like Figure 1-1.

Figure 1-1: The XAMPP Control Panel lets you turn on the various parts of XAMPP.

3. **Under Modules and to the right of Apache, click the Start button.**

   You'll probably get a Windows Security Alert that asks if you want to keep blocking the Apache HTTP Server program. Click Unblock.

4. **Check to see that your server is running correctly.**

If all is working well, the Start button (in the Control Panel, not the Windows Start button) should change to read Stop, and to the left of it, you should see a green area containing Running. The server doesn't have a graphic interface like most programs, so without this indication, you might not know it's running.

You can also start Apache (and MySQL) by clicking `xampp_start.exe`. This opens a command or console window telling you that `### APACHE + MYSQL IS STARTING NOW ###`. You can stop them by clicking `xampp_stop.exe`. I personally prefer the XAMPP Control Panel because it's more user-friendly and pretty.

For now, Apache is the only thing you need to have running. See more details about the other parts of XAMPP in Book VIII, Chapter 1.

Testing the installation

How do you know if your server really is working? Follow these steps:

1. **Open a Web browser.**
2. **Browse to `http://localhost`.**

You should get a XAMPP page with a congratulatory message on it that looks like Figure 1-2.

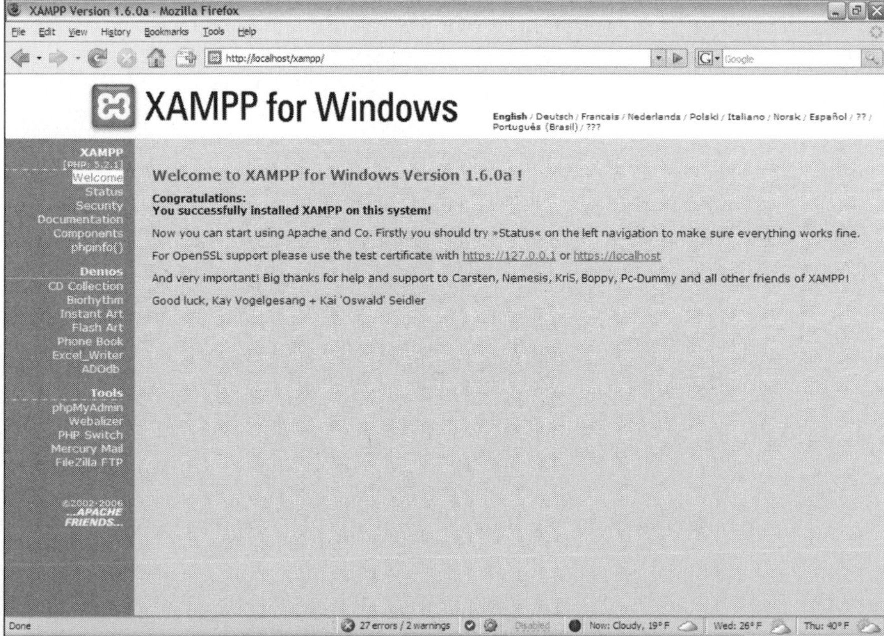

Figure 1-2: The server is installed!

Great job, you're now officially a Server Admin! Don't put that on your resume just yet, though. . . .

What do you do if it doesn't work? Check `www.apachefriends.org/en/faq-xampp-windows.html` to see if it addresses your problem. Otherwise, try Googling the specific problem you're having. Lastly, you could try posting on `www.apachefriends.org/f/?language=english` to see if anyone can help you.

Inspecting phpinfo()

Using your shiny new server is really quite simple, but a lot of beginners can get confused at this point.

One thing you have to remember is that anything you want the server to serve must be located in the server's file structure. If you have a PHP file on your Desktop and you want to view it in your browser, it won't work because it isn't in your server. Although, yes, technically it is on the same *machine* as your server (XAMPP), it is not *in* the server.

So, to serve a file from the server, it must be located in the `htdocs` directory of your server install. Go to the folder where you installed XAMPP (probably either `c:/xampp` or `c:/Program Files/xampp`) and locate the `htdocs` directory. This is where you'll put all your PHP files. Make note of it now.

To get the hang of placing your files in the correct place and accessing them through localhost, create a test file that will display all your PHP, Apache, and MySQL settings.

The following numbered list creates a file in Aptana Studio that will test your XAMPP configuration to ensure that Apache is up and running:

1. **Open Aptana Studio.**

   As always, you can use any text editor you want, but Aptana is optimized for working with PHP code, so that's the one I use for this example.

2. **From the File menu, choose New⇨Other.**

   This will take you to a list of file types Aptana knows how to handle.

3. **Pick Untitled PHP File from the resulting dialog box.**

   This tells Aptana you want to write a PHP file, and it automatically creates a very simple but powerful PHP sample program.

4. **Save the file as `test.php`.**

   It's important that you save the file in the `htdocs` directory.

5. **Open your browser.**

   Point your browser to `http://localhost/test.php`. You'll see a page like Figure 1-3.

This phpinfo page that you're looking at is critical in inspecting your server configuration. It displays all the different settings for your server, describing what version of PHP is running and what modules are currently active. This can be very useful information.

You generally should not have a page with all the `phpInfo()` information running on a live server because it tells the bad guys information they might use to do mischief.

This `test.php` program shows one of the most interesting things about PHP. The program itself is just a few lines long, but when you run it, the result is a complex Web page. If you view the source on the Web page, you'll see a lot of code you didn't write. That's the magic of PHP. You write a program, and it creates a Web page for you.

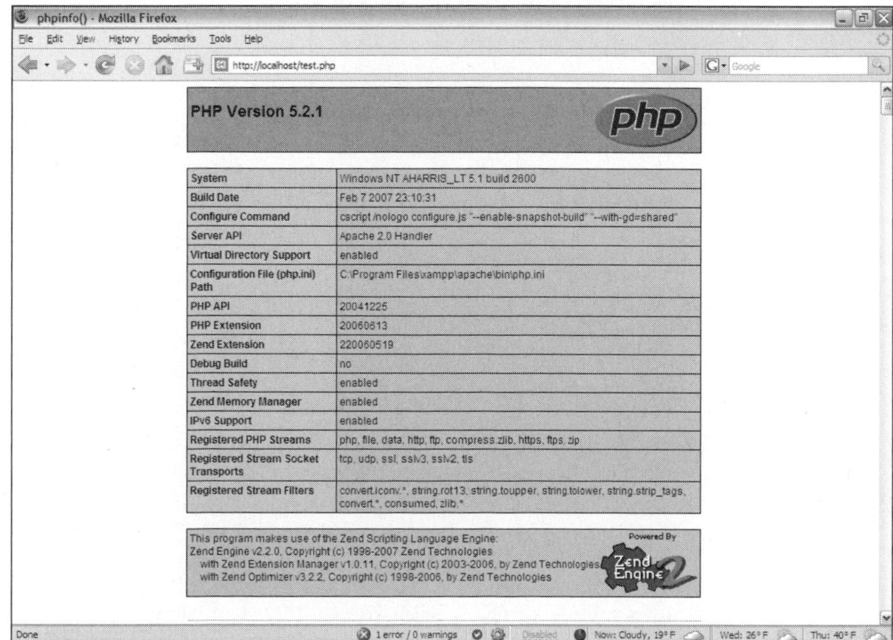

Figure 1-3: That tiny PHP program sure puts a lot of information on the screen.

By default, Apache will load `index.html` or `index.php` automatically if you type a directory path into the Web browser. There's already a program in htdocs called `index.php`. Rename it `index.php.off`. Now, if you navigate to `http://localhost/`, you'll see a list of directories and files your server can run, including `test.php`. When you have a live site, you'll typically name one file `index.html` or `index.php` so the user doesn't have to type the entire filename.

To reveal line numbers in Aptana, right-click in the margin to the left of the document body (where you'd expect line numbers to be).

Chapter 2: Generating HTML with PHP

In This Chapter

- **Creating your first PHP program**
- **Using quotation marks**
- **Working with variables PHP style**
- **Interpolating variables into text**
- **Creating heredocs**

In PHP, you aren't actually printing anything to the user; you're building an HTML document that will be sent to the browser, which will interpret the HTML and then print *that* (the HTML) out to the user. Therefore, all your code gets interpreted twice; first on the server to generate the HTML and then on the user's machine to generate the output display.

If you've used XHTML, CSS, and JavaScript, you might have been frustrated because all of these environments run on the client, and you have no control of the client environment. You don't know what browser the user will have, and thus you don't know exactly how XHTML, CSS, and JavaScript will run there. When you program in PHP, you're working on a machine (the server) that you actually control. You know exactly what the server's capabilities are because (in many cases) you configured it yourself.

It's still not a perfect situation, though, because your PHP code will generate XHTML/CSS pages (sometimes even with JavaScript), and those pages still have to contend with the wide array of client environments.

Creating Your First PHP Program

The first program you ever write in any language is invariably the `"Hello World!"` program or some variant thereof. Follow these steps:

1. **Create a new PHP file in Aptana Studio.**

   See Chapter 1 of this minibook for instructions on creating a PHP file in Aptana.

If you're using some other text editor, just open a plain text file however you normally do that (often File⇨New) and be sure to save it under `htdocs` with a `.php` extension.

2. **Enter the following code:**

```
<?php
print "Hello World!";
?>
```

Depending on your installation of Apache, you may be able to use the shorter `<? ?>` version of the PHP directive (instead of `<?php ?>`).

3. **Save the file by pressing Ctrl+S, choosing File⇨ Save from the menu, or clicking the picture of the computer disk.**

Remember to save directly into `htdocs` or a subdirectory of htdocs.

4. **View the file in a Web browser, as shown in Figure 2-1.**

The address of a Web page begins with the `http://` protocol and then the server name. Since this page is on the local machine, the server name is `localhost`, which corresponds directly to your `htdocs` directory. If you have a file named `thing.php` in the `htdocs` directory, the address would be `http://localhost/thing.php`. Likewise, if it's in a subdirectory of `htdocs` called `project`, the address would be `http://localhost/project/thing.php`.

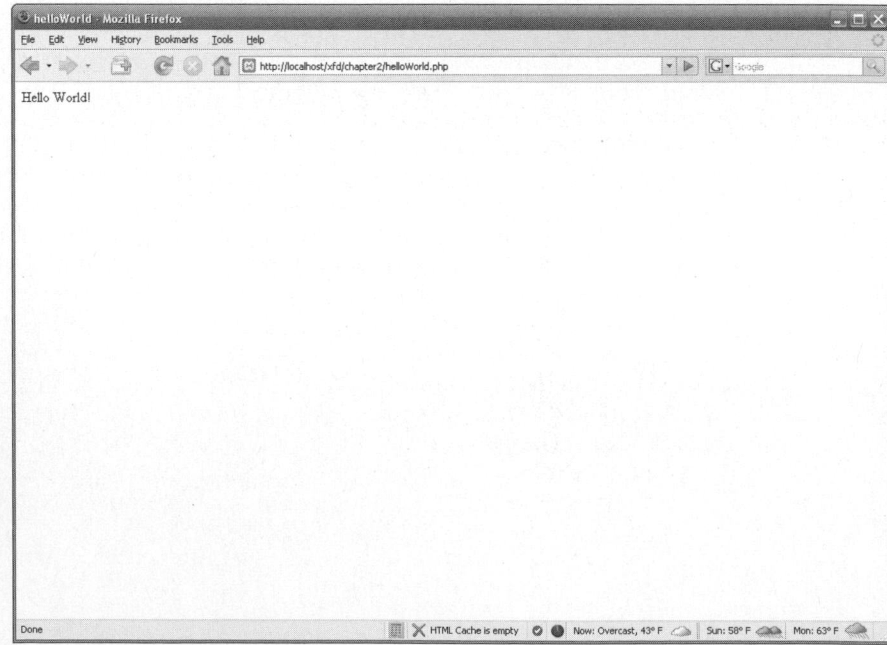

Figure 2-1: The "Hello World!" program example.

echo or print?

`echo` is another way to generate your code for the browser. In almost all circumstances, you use `echo` exactly like you use `print`. Everyone knows what `print` does, but `echo` sounds like I should be making some sort of dolphin noise.

The difference is that `print` returns a value and `echo` doesn't. `print` can be used as part of a complex expression and `echo` can't. It really just comes down to the fact that `print` is more dynamic, whereas `echo` is slightly (and I'm talking very slightly here) faster.

I prefer `print` because there's nothing that `echo` can do that `print` can't.

To see a more detailed discussion go here: `www.faqts.com/knowledge_base/view.phtml/aid/1/fid/40`.

So, what is it that you've done here? You've figured out how to use the `print` statement. This allows you to spit out any text you want to the user.

Note that each line ends with a semicolon (`;`). There may be times when your program throws an error that you just can't figure out. In these cases, I recommend looking first for missing semicolons. It seems obvious, but time and time again, it turns out to be a missing semicolon (same goes with brackets and parentheses). Aptana will give you a red squiggly if you forget the semicolon.

Coding with Quotation Marks

There are many different ways to use `print`. The following are all legal ways to print text, but they have subtle differences:

```
print ("<p>Hello World!</p>");
print ("<p>Hello World!<br />
Hello Computer!</p>");
print '<p><a href="http://www.google.com">Hello Google!</a></p>';
```

Any way you cut it, you have to have some form of quotations around text that you want printed.

What if you want to print double quotation marks inside a `print` statement surrounded by double quotation marks? You *escape* them (you tell PHP to treat them as literal characters, rather than the end of the string) with a backslash, like this:

```
print "<a href=\"link.html\">A Link</a>";
```

This can get tedious, so a better solution is discussed in the "Generating output with heredocs" section, later in this chapter.

Escape sequences

In the first section of this chapter, "Creating Your First PHP Program," you see that you can escape double quotation marks with a backslash. Quotation marks aren't the only thing you can escape, though. You can give a whole host of other special escape directives to PHP.

The most common ones are

`\t` (creates a tab in the resulting HTML)

`\n` (creates a new line in the resulting HTML)

`\$` (creates a dollar sign in the resulting HTML)

`\"` (creates a double quote in the resulting HTML)

`\'` (creates a single quote in the resulting HTML)

`\\` (creates a backslash in the resulting HTML)

PHP can take care of this for you automatically if you're receiving these values from a form. To read more, go here: `http://us3.php.net/types.string`.

This backslash technique works only with text encased inside double quotes. Single quotes tell PHP to take everything inside the quotes exactly as is. Double quotes give PHP permission to analyze the text for special characters, like escaped quotes (and variables, which you learn about in the next section of this chapter).

Working with Variables PHP Style

Variables are extremely important in any programming language and no less so in PHP.

A variable in PHP always begins with a `$`.

A PHP variable can be named almost anything. There are some reserved words that you can't name a variable (like `print`, which already has a meaning in PHP), so if your program isn't working and you can't figure out why, try changing some variable names or looking at the reserved words list (in the online help at `http://www.php.net`) to find out if your variable name is one of these illegal words.

PHP is very forgiving about the type of data in a variable. When you create a variable, you simply put content in it. PHP automatically makes the variable whatever type it needs. This is called *loose typing*. The same variable can hold numeric data, text, or other more complicated kinds of data. PHP determines the type of data in a variable on-the-fly by examining the context.

Even though PHP is cavalier about data types, it's important to understand that data is still stored in one of several standard formats based on its type. PHP supports several forms of integers and floating-point numbers. PHP also has great support for text data. Programmers usually don't say "text," but call text data *string* data. This is because the internal data representation of text reminded the early programmers of beads on a string. You rarely have to worry about what type of information you're using in PHP, but you do need to know that PHP is quietly converting data into formats it can use.

Concatenation

Concatenation is the process of joining smaller strings together to form a larger string. (See Book IV, Chapter 1 for a description of concatenation as it's applied in JavaScript.) PHP uses the period (`.`) symbol to concatenate two string values, so the following code returns the phrase "oogie boogie":

```
$word = "oogie ";
$dance = "boogie";

Print $word . $dance
```

If you already know some JavaScript or another language, most of the ideas transfer, but details can trip you up. JavaScript uses the + sign for concatenation, and PHP uses the period. These are annoying details, but with practice, you'll be able to keep it straight.

When PHP sees a period, it treats the values on either side of the period as strings (text) and concatenates (joins) them together. If PHP sees a plus sign, it treats the values on either side of the plus sign as numbers and attempts to perform mathematical addition on them. The operation helps PHP figure out what type of data it is working with.

The following program illustrates the difference between concatenation and addition (see Figure 2-2 for the output):

```
<?php
    $output = "World!";

    print "<p>Hello " . $output . "</p>";

    print "<p>" . $output + 5 . "</p>";
?>
```

The previous code takes the variable `output` with the value `World` and concatenates it to `Hello` when printed. Next, it adds the variable `output` to the number `5`. When PHP sees the plus sign, it interprets the values on either side of it as numbers. Because `output` has no logical numerical value, PHP assigns it the value of `0`, which it adds to `5`, resulting in the output of `<p>5</p>` being sent to the browser.

Figure 2-2: The difference between addition and concatenation.

Interpolating variables into text

If you have a bunch of text to print with variables thrown in, it can get a little tedious to use concatenation to add in the variables. Luckily, you don't have to!

With PHP, you can include the variables as follows (see Figure 2-3 for the output):

```
<?php
    $firstName = "John";
    $lastName = "Doe";

    print "Hello $firstName $lastName!";
?>
```

This process is called *interpolation.* Since all PHP variables begin with quotes, you can freely put variables right inside your string values, and when PHP sees a variable, it will automatically replace that variable with its value.

Interpolation only works with double-quoted strings because double quotes indicate PHP should process the string before passing it to the user.

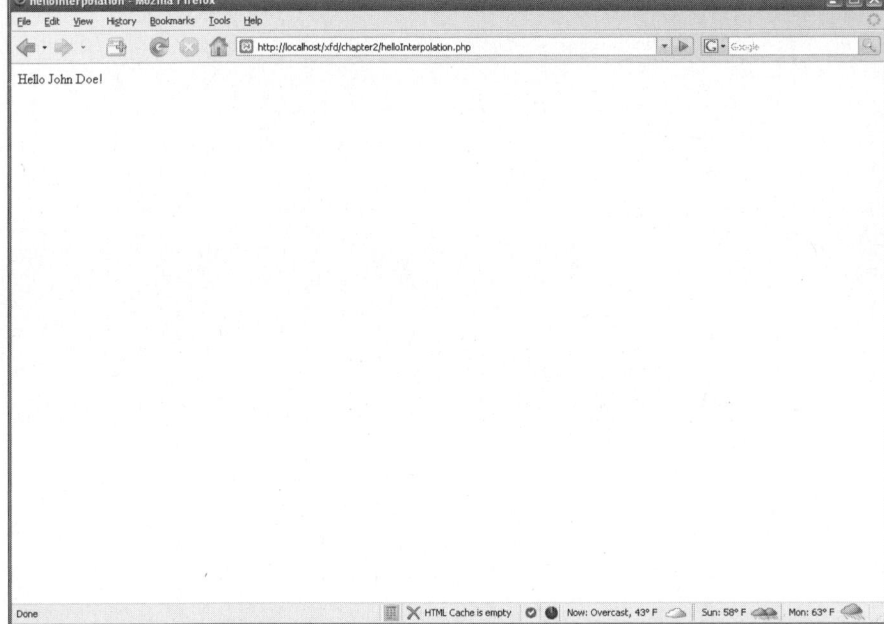

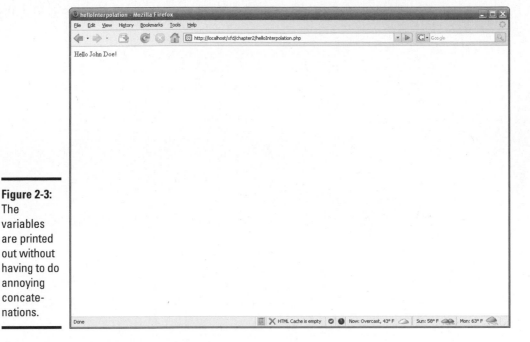

Figure 2-3: The variables are printed out without having to do annoying concatenations.

Building XHTML Output

The output of a PHP program is usually an XHTML page. As far as PHP is concerned, XHTML is just string data, so your PHP program often has to do a lot of string manipulation. You'll often be writing long chunks of text (XHTML code) with several variables (generated by your PHP program) interspersed throughout the code. This type of text (XHTML output) will often stretch over several lines, requires carriage returns to be preserved, and often contains special characters like quotes and <> symbols. The ordinary quote symbols are a little tedious if you want to use them to build a Web page. Here's an example.

Say you wanted to create a program which could take the value of the `$name` and `$address` variables and put them into a table like this:

```
<table style = "border: 1px solid black">
   <tr>
    <td>name</td>
    <td>John</td>
  </tr>
  <tr>
    <td>address</td>
    <td>123 Main St.</td>
  </tr>
</table>
```

There are a few ways to combine the PHP and XHTML, code as shown in the following sections.

Using double quote interpolation

Using regular double quotes, the code would look something like this:

```
$name = "John";
$address = "123 Main St.";
$output = "";
$output .= "<table style = \"border: 1px solid black\"> \n";
$output .= "   <tr> \n";
$output .= "     <td>name</td> \n";
$output .= "     <td>$name</td> \n";
$output .= "   </tr> \n";
$output .= "   <tr> \n";
$output .= "     <td>address</td> \n";
$output .= "     <td>$address</td> \n";
$output .= "   </tr> \n";
$output .= "</table> \n";

print $output
```

However, using quotes to generate XHTML output is inconvenient for the following reasons:

- **The `$output` variable must be initialized.** Before adding anything to the `$output` variable, give it an initial null value.
- **You must repeatedly concatenate data onto the `$output` variable.** The .= operator allows me to append something to the end of a string variable.
- **All quotes must be escaped.** Because double quotes indicate the end of the string, all internal double quotes must be preceded with the backslash (\).
- **Every line must end with a newline (`\n`) sequence.** PHP creates XHTML source code. Your PHP-derived code should look as good as what you write by hand, so you need to preserve carriage returns. This means you need to end each line with a newline.
- **The XHTML syntax is buried inside PHP syntax.** The example shows PHP code creating HTML code. Each line contains code from two languages interspersed. This can be disconcerting to a beginning programmer.

Generating output with heredocs

PHP uses a clever solution called heredocs to resolve all these issues. A *heredoc* is simply a type of multi-line quote, usually beginning and ending with the word `HERE`.

The best way to understand heredocs is to see one in action, so here's the same example written as a heredoc:

```
<?
$name = "John";
$address = "123 Main St.";
print <<<HERE
<table style = "border: 1px solid black">
   <tr>
     <td>name</td>
     <td>$name</td>
   </tr>
   <tr>
     <td>address</td>
     <td>$address</td>
   </tr>
</table>
HERE;
?>
```

Heredocs have some great advantages:

- **All carriage returns are preserved.** There's no need to put in any newline characters. Whatever carriage returns are in the original text will stay in the output.
- **Heredocs preserve quote symbols.** There's also no need to escape your quotes because the double quote is not the end-of-string character for a heredoc.
- **Variable interpolation is supported.** You can use variable names in a heredoc, just like you do for an ordinary quoted string.
- **The contents of a heredoc feel like ordinary XHTML.** When you're working inside a heredoc, you can temporarily put your mind in XHTML mode, but with the ability to interpolate variables.

The following are some things to keep in mind about heredocs:

- A heredoc is opened with three less-than symbols (<<<) followed by a heredoc symbol that will act as a "superquote" (instead of single or double quotation marks, you make your own custom quotation mark out of any value that you want).
- A heredoc symbol can be denoted by almost any text, but `HERE` is the most common delimiter (thus, heredoc). You can make absolutely anything you want serve as a heredoc symbol. You probably should just stick to `HERE` because that's what other programmers are expecting.
- You need only one semicolon for the whole heredoc. Technically, the entire heredoc counts as one line. That means the only semicolon you need is after the closing symbol.

Printing shortcut

When switching in and out of PHP, if you have just one variable you want to print, depending upon your server setup, you may be able to do print the variable like this:

```
<?= $name ?>
```

You don't have to actually write `print`. Note that this doesn't work if you have to type **php** after the question mark in the opening PHP tag.

- A heredoc must be closed with the same word it was opened with.
- The closing word for the heredoc must be on its own line.
- You can't indent the closing word for the heredoc; there can't be any spaces or tabs preceding the closing word.

By far the most common problem with heredocs is indenting the closing token. The `HERE` (or whatever other symbol you're using) must be flush with the left margin of your editor, or PHP will not recognize it. This usually means PHP interprets the rest of your program as part of a big string and never finishes executing it.

Heredocs have one disadvantage: They tend to mess up your formatting because you have to indent heredocs differently than the rest of the code.

When writing a heredoc, don't put a semicolon after the first `<<<HERE` and don't forget that the last `HERE;` can't have any whitespace before it — it must be alone on a new line without any spaces preceding it.

Switching from PHP to XHTML

There's one more way to combine PHP and XHTML code. The server treats a PHP document mainly as an XHTML document. Any code not inside the `<?php ?>` symbols is treated as XHTML, and anything inside the PHP symbols is interpreted as PHP.

This means you can switch in and out of PHP, like the following example:

```
<?php
    $name = "John";
    $address = "123 Main St.";
    // switch 'out' of PHP temporarily
?>
<table style = "border: 1px solid black">
   <tr>
```

```
    <td>name</td>
    <td><?php print $name; ?></td>
  </tr>
  <tr>
    <td>address</td>
    <td><?php print $address; ?></td>
  </tr>
</table>
<?php
  //I'm back in PHP
?>
```

This option (switching back and forth) is generally used when you have a lot of XHTML code with only a few simple PHP variables.

Chapter 3: PHP and XHTML Forms

In This Chapter

- **Understanding the relationship between XHTML and PHP**
- **Using the `date()` function**
- **Formatting date and time information**
- **Creating XHTML forms designed to work with PHP**
- **Choosing between `get` and `post` data transmission**
- **Retrieving data from your XHTML forms**
- **Working with XHTML form elements**

PHP is almost never used on its own. PHP is usually used in tight conjunction with XHTML. Many languages have features for creating input forms and user interfaces, but with PHP, the entire user experience is based on XHTML. The user never really sees any PHP. Most of the input to PHP programs comes from XHTML forms, and the output of a PHP program is an XHTML page.

In this chapter, you discover how to integrate PHP and XHTML. You explore how PHP code is embedded into XHTML pages, how XHTML forms can be written so they will send information to a PHP program, how to write a PHP program to read that data, and how to send an XHTML response back to the user.

Exploring the Relationship between PHP and XHTML

PHP is a different language than XHTML, but they are very closely related. It may be best to think of PHP as an extension that allows you to do things you cannot do easily in XHTML. See Figure 3-1 for an example.

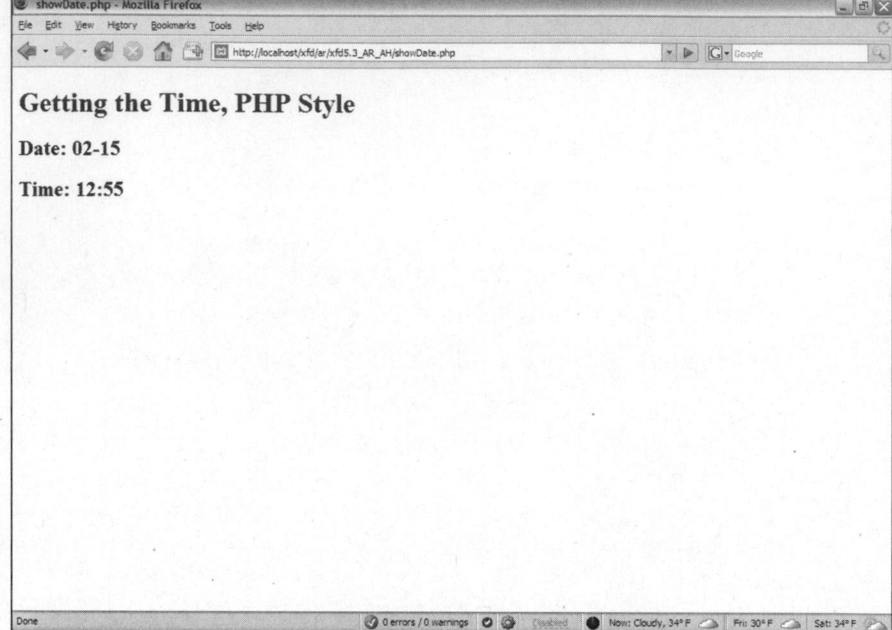

Figure 3-1: This program gives me the current date and time.

Every time you run `getTime.php`, it generates the current date and time, and returns these values to the user. This would not be possible in ordinary XHTML because the date and time (by definition) always change. While you could make this page using JavaScript, the PHP approach is useful for demonstrating how PHP works. First, take a look at the PHP code:

```
<!DOCTYPE html PUBLIC "-//W3C//DTD XHTML 1.0 Strict//EN"
"http://www.w3.org/TR/xhtml1/DTD/xhtml1-strict.dtd">
<html lang="EN" dir="ltr" xmlns="http://www.w3.org/1999/xhtml">
  <head>
    <meta http-equiv="content-type" content="text/xml; charset=utf-8" />
    <title>showDate.php</title>
  </head>

  <body>
    <body>
    <h1>Getting the Time, PHP Style</h1>
    <?php

print "      <h2>Date: ";
print date("m-d");
print "</h2> \n";

print "      <h2>Time: ";
print date("h:i");
print "</h2>";
```

```
  ?>

 </body>
</html>
```

Embedding PHP inside XHTML

The PHP code has some interesting characteristics:

- **It's structured mainly as an XHTML document.** The doctype definition, document heading, and initial H1 heading are all ordinary XHTML. Begin your page as you do any XHTML document. A PHP page can have as much XHTML code as you wish. (You might have no PHP at all!) The only thing the PHP designation does is inform the server that PHP code may be embedded into the document.
- **PHP code is embedded into the page.** You can switch from XHTML to PHP with the `<?php` tag. Signify the end of the PHP code with the `?>` symbol.
- **The PHP code creates XHTML.** PHP is usually used to create XHTML code. In effect, PHP takes over and prints out the part of the page that can't be created in static XHTML. The result of a PHP fragment is usually XHTML code.
- **The `date()` function returns the current date with a specific format.** The format string indicates how the date should be displayed. (See the sidebar "Exploring the date( ) format function," in this chapter, for more information about date formatting.)
- **The result of the PHP code will be an XHTML document.** When the PHP code is finished, it will be replaced by XHTML code.

Viewing the results

If you view `showDate.php` in your browser, you won't see the PHP code. Instead, you'll see an XHTML page. It's even more interesting when you use your browser to view the page source. Here's what you'll see:

```
<!DOCTYPE html PUBLIC "-//W3C//DTD XHTML 1.0 Strict//EN"
"http://www.w3.org/TR/xhtml1/DTD/xhtml1-strict.dtd">
<html lang="EN" dir="ltr" xmlns="http://www.w3.org/1999/xhtml">
  <head>
    <meta http-equiv="content-type" content="text/xml; charset=utf-8" />
    <title>showDate.php</title>
  </head>

  <body>
    <h1>Getting the Time, PHP Style</h1>
    <h2>Date: 02-13</h2>
    <h2>Time: 10:02</h2>
  </body>
</html>
```

Exploring the date() format function

The `showDate.php` program takes advantage of one of PHP's many interesting and powerful functions to display the date. The PHP `date()` function returns the current date. Generally, you'll pass the `date()` function a special format string that indicates how you want the date to be formatted. Characters in the date string indicate a special code. Here are a few of the characters and their meanings:

- `d`: day of the month (numeric)
- `D`: three character abbreviation of weekday ("Wed")
- `m`: month (numeric)
- `M`: three character abbreviation of month ("Feb")
- `F`: text representation of month ("February")
- `y`: two-digit representation of the year ("08")
- `Y`: four-digit representation of the year ("2008")
- `h`: hour (12 hours)
- `H`: hour (24 hours)
- `i`: minutes
- `s`: seconds

You can embed standard punctuation in the format, as well, so `d/m/y` will include the slashes between each part of the date. There are many more symbols available. Check the PHP documentation at `http://us3.php.net/manual/en/function.date.php` for more information about date and time formatting.

The remarkable thing is what you don't see. When you look at the source of `showDate.php` in your browser, the PHP is completely gone! This is one of the most important points about PHP: The browser never sees any of the PHP. The PHP code is converted completely to XHTML before anything is sent to the browser. This means that you don't need to worry about whether a user's browser understands PHP. Because the user never sees your PHP code (even if he views the XHTML source), PHP code will work on any browser.

Sending Data to a PHP Program

You can send data to a PHP program from an HTML form. For an example of this technique, see `askName.html` in Figure 3-2.

XHTML forms (described fully in Book I, Chapter 7) allow the user to enter data onto a Web page. However, XHTML cannot respond to a form on its own. You need some sort of program to respond to the form. Book IV describes how to use JavaScript to respond to forms, but you can also write PHP code to handle form-based input. When the user submits the form, the `askName.html` disappears completely from the browser and is replaced with `greetUser.php`, as shown in Figure 3-3.

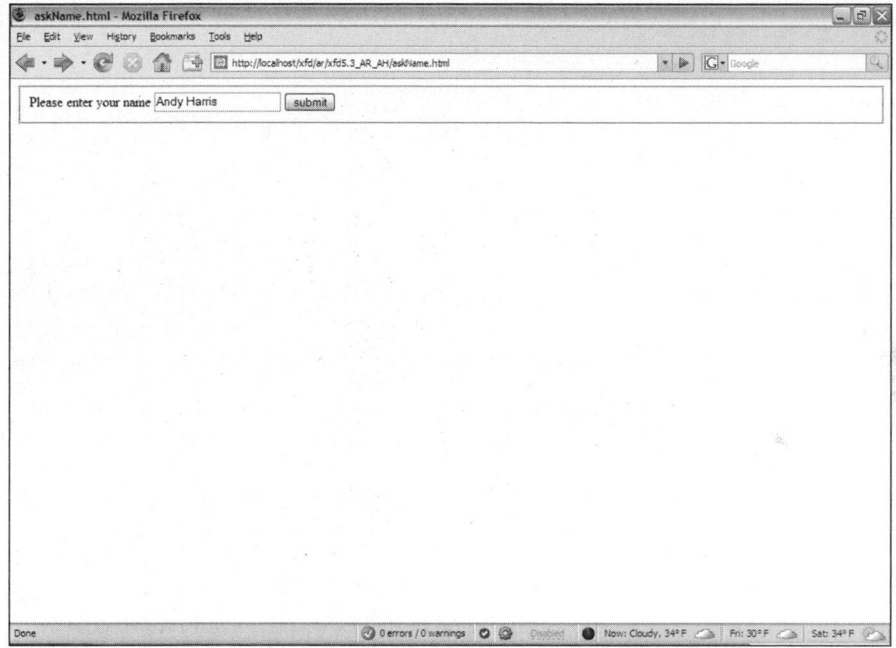

Figure 3-2: This XHTML page has a simple form.

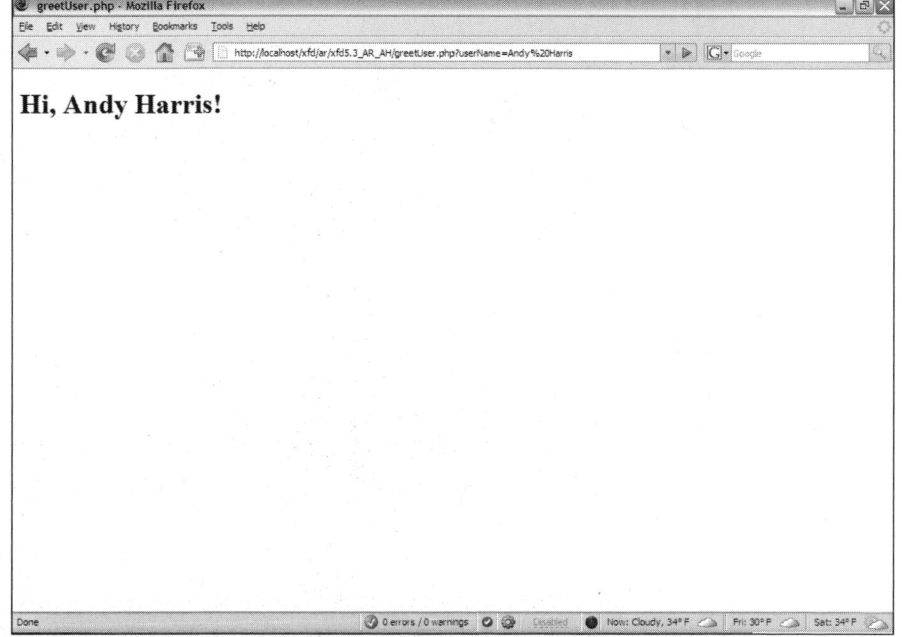

Figure 3-3: This program uses the entry from the previous form.

The `greetUser.php` program retrieves the data from the previous page (`askName.html`, in this case) and returns an appropriate greeting.

Creating a form for PHP processing

The `askName.html` program is a standard XHTML form, but it has a couple of special features which make it suitable for PHP processing. (See Book I, Chapter 7 for more information about how to build XHTML forms.) Here is the XHTML code:

```
<!DOCTYPE html PUBLIC "-//W3C//DTD XHTML 1.0 Strict//EN"
"http://www.w3.org/TR/xhtml1/DTD/xhtml1-strict.dtd">
<html lang="EN" dir="ltr" xmlns="http://www.w3.org/1999/xhtml">
  <head>
    <meta http-equiv="content-type" content="text/xml; charset=utf-8" />
    <title>askName.html</title>
  </head>

  <body>
    <form action = "greetUser.php"
          method = "get">
      <fieldset>
        <label>Please enter your name</label>
        <input type = "text"
               name = "userName" />
        <button type = "submit">
          submit
        </button>
      </fieldset>

    </form>
  </body>
</html>
```

To build a form designed to work with PHP, there are a few special steps to take:

1. **Write an XHTML page as the framework.**

   This page is a regular XHTML page. Begin with the same XHTML framework you use for building your standard XHTML pages. You can use CSS styles, if you wish (but I'm leaving them out of this simple example).

   Normally, you can create an XHTML document anywhere you want, but this is not so when your page will be working with PHP. This page is meant to be paired with a PHP document. PHP documents will run only if they are in a server's file space, so you should save your XHTML document under `htdocs` to be sure it will be able to call the PHP form correctly.

2. **Set the form's `action` property to point to a PHP program.**

   The form element has an attribute called `action`. The `action` attribute is used to determine which program should receive the data transmitted by the form. I want this data to be processed by a program called greetUser.php, so I set greetUser.php as the action:

```
<form action = "greetUser.php"
      method = "get">
```

3. **Set the form's method attribute to get.**

   The method attribute indicates how the form data will be sent to the server. For now, use the get method. See the section "Choosing the Method of Your Madness," later in this chapter, for information on the various methods available:

```
<form action = "greetUser.php"
      method = "get">
```

4. **Add any input elements your form needs.**

   The point of a form is to get information from the user and send it to a program on the server. Devise a form to ask whatever questions you want from the server. My form is as simple as possible, with one text field, but you can use any XHTML form elements you want:

```
<form action = "greetUser.php"
      method = "get">
  <fieldset>
    <label>Please enter your name</label>
    <input type = "text"
           name = "userName" />
    <button type = "submit">
      submit
    </button>
  </fieldset>
```

5. **Give each element a name attribute.**

   If you want a form element to be passed to the server, you must give it a name attribute (note this is a different attribute than id, which is used in client-side processing):

```
    <input type = "text"
           name = "userName" />
```

   The name attribute will be used by the PHP program to extract the information from the form.

   A form element can have both a name and an ID, if you wish. The name attribute will be used primarily by server-side programs, and the id attribute is mainly used for CSS and JavaScript. The name and ID can (and probably should) have the same value.

6. **Add a submit button to the page**

   The most important difference between a client-side form and a form destined for processing on the server is the button. A special submit button packages all the data in the form and passes it to the program indicated in the `action` property. Submit buttons can be created in two forms:

```
<input type = "submit" value = "click me"/>
```

Or

```
<button type = "submit">click me</button>
```

Specify `submit` as the button's `type` attribute to ensure the button sends the data to the server.

If your form has a submit button and a blank `action` attribute, the current page will be reloaded.

Receiving data in PHP

PHP code is usually a two-step process. First, you create an XHTML form, and then you send that form to a PHP program for processing. Be sure you've read the previous section on "Creating a form for PHP processing" because now I show you how to read that form with a PHP program.

The XHTML form in the last section pointed to a program named `greetUser.php`. This tells the server to go to the same directory that contained the original XHTML document (`askName.html`) and look for a program named `greetUser.php` in that directory. Because greetUser is a PHP program, the server passes it through PHP, which will extract data from the form. The program then creates a greeting using data that came from the form. Look over all the code for `greetUser.php` before I explain it in more detail:

```
<!DOCTYPE html PUBLIC "-//W3C//DTD XHTML 1.0 Strict//EN"
"http://www.w3.org/TR/xhtml1/DTD/xhtml1-strict.dtd">
<html lang="EN" dir="ltr" xmlns="http://www.w3.org/1999/xhtml">
  <head>
    <meta http-equiv="content-type" content="text/xml; charset=utf-8" />
    <title>greetUser.php</title>
  </head>

  <body>
    <?php
    $userName = $_REQUEST["userName"];
    print "<h1>Hi, $userName!</h1>"
    ?>

  </body>
</html>
```

`greetUser.php` is not a complex program, but it shows the most common use of PHP: retrieving data from a form. Here's how you build it:

1. **Build a new PHP program.**

   This program should be in the same directory as `askName.html`, which should be somewhere the server can find (usually under the `htdocs` or `public_html` directory).

2. **Start with ordinary XHTML.**

   PHP programs are usually wrapped inside ordinary XHTML, so begin the document as if it were plain XHTML. Use whatever CSS styling and ordinary HTML tags you want. (I'm keeping this example as simple as possible, although I'd normally add some CSS styles to make the output less boring.)

3. **Add a PHP segment.**

   Somewhere in the page, you'll need to switch to PHP syntax so you can extract the data from the form. Use the `<?php` symbol to indicate the beginning of your PHP code:

   ```
   <?php
   $userName = $_REQUEST["userName"];
   print "<h1>Hi, $userName!</h1>";
   ?>
   ```

4. **Extract the username variable.**

   PHP stores all the data sent to the form inside a special variable called `$_REQUEST`. This object contains a list of all the form elements in the page that triggered this program. In this case, I want to extract the value of the `userName` field and store it in a PHP variable called `$userName`:

   ```
   $userName = $_REQUEST["userName"];
   ```

   See the section called "Getting data from the form," later in this chapter, for more information on the `$_REQUEST` object and some of the other tools that are available for retrieving information.

5. **Print the greeting.**

   Now, your PHP program has a variable containing the user's name, so you can print a greeting to the user. Remember that all output of a PHP program is XHTML code, so be sure to embed your output in a suitable XHTML tag. I'm putting the greeting inside a level-one heading:

   ```
   print "<h1>Hi, $userName!</h1>";
   ```

The `greetUser.php` script is not meant to be run directly. It relies on `askName.html`. If you provide a direct link to `greetUser.php`, the program will run, but it will not be sent the username, so it will not work as expected. Do not place links to your PHP scripts unless you've designed them to work without input.

Choosing the Method of Your Madness

The key to server-side processing is adding `method` and `action` properties to your XHTML form. You have two primary choices for the `method` property:

- **get:** The get method gathers the information in your form and appends it to the URL. The PHP program extracts form data from the address. The contents of the form are visible for anyone to see.
- **post:** The post method passes the data to the server through a mechanism called *environment variables.* This mechanism makes the form elements slightly more secure because they aren't displayed in public as they are with the get method.

Using get to send data

The get method is easy to understand. View getRequest.php after it has been called from askName.html in Figure 3-4. Pay careful attention to the URL in the address bar.

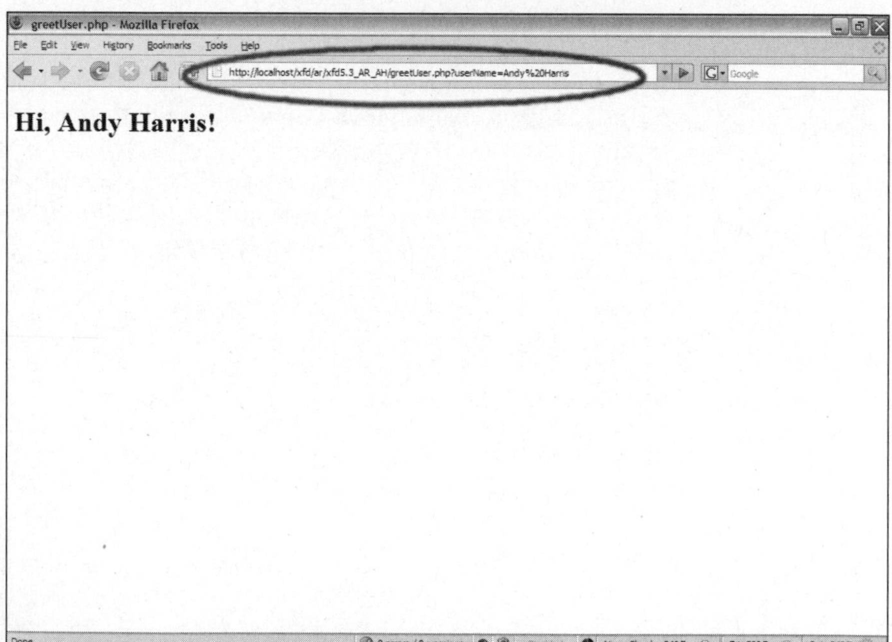

Figure 3-4: The address has been modified!

The address sent to the PHP program has additional material appended to the end:

```
http://localhost/xfd/ar/xfd5.3_AR_AH/greetUser.php?userName=Andy%20Harris
```

Most of this address is the (admittedly convoluted) address of the page on my test server. The interesting part is the section after greetUser.php:

```
greetUser.php?userName=Andy%20Harris
```

This line shows exactly how the `get` method passes information to the program on the server:

+ **The URL is extracted from the form `action` property.** When the submit button is activated, the browser automatically creates a special URL beginning with the `action` property of the form. The default address is the directory as the original XHTML file.
+ **A question mark indicates form data is on the way.** The browser appends a question mark to the URL to indicate form data follows.
+ **Each field/value pair is listed.** The question mark is followed by each field name and its associated value in the following format:

  ```
  URL?field1=value1&field2=value2
  ```

+ **An equal sign (=) follows each field name.** Each field name is separated by the value of that field with an equal sign (and no spaces).
+ **The field value is listed immediately after the equal sign.** The value of each field follows the equal sign.
+ **Spaces are converted to hexadecimal symbols.** `get` data is transmitted through the URL, and URLS are not allowed to have spaces or other special characters in them. The browser will automatically convert all spaces in field names or values to the `%20` symbol. Other special characters (like ampersands and equal signs) are also automatically converted to special symbols.

  Sometimes, the spaces are converted to + signs, rather than `%20`. It isn't really that important, as the conversion is done automatically. Just know that URLs can't contain spaces.

+ **Ampersand (&) is used to add a new field name/value pair.** This particular example (the URL created by `askName.html`) has only one name/value pair. If the form had more elements, they would all be separated by ampersands.

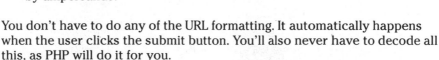

You don't have to do any of the URL formatting. It automatically happens when the user clicks the submit button. You'll also never have to decode all this, as PHP will do it for you.

If you understand how the `get` method works, you can take advantage of it to send data to programs without the original form. For example, take a look at this address:

```
http://www.google.com/search?q=dramatic%20chipmunk
```

If you type this code into your browser's location bar, you'll get the Google search results for a classic 5-second video. (If you haven't seen this video, it's worth viewing.) If you know a particular server-side program (like Google's search engine) uses the `get` protocol, and you know which fields are needed (q stands for the query in Google's program), you can send a request to a program as if that request came from a form.

You can also write a link with a pre-loaded search query in it:

```
<a href = "http://www.google.com/search/q=dramatic%20chipmunk">
  Google search for the dramatic chipmunk
</a>
```

If a user clicks on the resulting link, he would get the current Google search for the dramatic chipmunk video. (Really, it's a prairie dog, but "dramatic chipmunk" just sounds better.)

Of course, if you can send requests to a program without using the intended form, others can do the same to you. You can never be 100-percent sure that people are sending requests from your forms. This can cause some problems. Look at the next section for a technique to minimize this problem by reading only data sent via the post method.

Using the post method to transmit form data

The get method is easy to understand because it sends all data directly in the URL. This makes it easy to see what's going on, but there are some downsides to using get:

- **The resulting URL can be very messy.** Addresses on the Web can already be difficult without the added details of a get request. A form with several fields can make the URL so long it is virtually impossible to follow.
- **All form information is user-readable.** The get method displays form data in the URL, where it can easily be read by the user. This may not be desired, especially when the form sends potentially sensitive data.

How did I know how to write the Google query?

You might wonder how I knew what fields the Google engine expects. If the program uses get, just use the intended form to make a search and look at the resulting URL. Some practice and experience told me that only the q field is absolutely necessary.

This trick (bypassing the form) could be considered rude by some because it circumvents safety features that may be built into the form. Still, it can be helpful for certain very public features, like pre-loaded Google searches, or looking up weather data for a particular location through a hard-coded link.

✦ **The amount of information that can be passed is limited.** The Apache server (in its default form) will not accept URLs longer than 4,000 characters. If you have a form with many fields or with fields that contain a lot of data, you will easily exceed this limit.

The answer to the limitations of the `get` method is another form of data transmission: the `post` method.

Here's how it works:

✦ **You specify that the form's method will be `post`.** You create the XHTML form in exactly the same way. The only difference is the form `method` attribute. Set it to `post`:

```
<form action = "greetUser.php"
      method = "post">
```

✦ **Data is gathered and encoded, just like it is in the `get` method.** When the user clicks the submit button, the data is encoded in a format similar to the `get` request, but it is not attached to the URL.

✦ **The form data is sent directly to the server.** The PHP program can still retrieve the data (usually through a mechanism called *environment variables*), even though the data is not encoded on the URL. Again, you will not be responsible for the details of extracting the data. PHP makes it pretty easy.

The `post` method is often preferable to `get` because

✦ **The URL is not polluted with form data.** The data is no longer passed through the URL, so the resulting URL is a lot cleaner than one generated by the `get` method.

✦ **The data is not visible to the user.** Since the data is not presented in the URL, it is slightly more secure than `get` data.

✦ **There is no practical size limit.** The size of the URL is not a limiting factor. If your page will be sending a large amount of data, the `post` method is preferred.

With all these advantages, you might wonder why anybody uses `get` at all. Really, there are two good reasons. The `get` approach allows you to embed requests in URLs (which can't be done with `post`). Also, `get` is sometimes a better choice for debugging because it's easier to see what is being passed to the server.

Getting data from the form

PHP includes a number of special built-in variables that give you access to loads of information. Each of these variables is stored as an associative array (see Chapter 5 of this minibook for more on associative arrays). These special variables are available anywhere in your PHP code, so they're called *superglobals*. Here's a few of the most important ones:

- **$_GET:** A list of variables sent to this program through the `get` method
- **$_POST:** A list of variables sent to this program through the `post` method
- **$_REQUEST:** A combination of `$_GET` and `$_POST`

You can use these variables to look up information posted in the form. For example, the `askName.html` page contains a field called `userName`. When the user views this page, it sends a request to `greetUser.php` via the `get` method. `greetUser.php` can then check its `$_GET` variable to see if a field named `userName` exists:

```
$userName = $_GET["userName"];
```

This line checks all the data sent via `get`, looks for a field named `userName`, and copies the contents of that field to the variable `$userName`.

If you want to retrieve a value sent through the `post` method, use this variation:

```
$userName = $_POST["userName"];
```

If you don't care whether the data was sent via `get` or `post`, use `$_REQUEST`:

```
$userName = $_REQUES["userName"];
```

The `$_REQUEST` superglobal grabs data from both `get` and `post` requests, so it works, no matter how the form was encoded. Many programmers use the `$_REQUEST` technique because then they don't have to worry about the encoding mechanism.

If you don't like the idea of somebody accessing your data without a form, use `$_POST` in your PHP program. If data is encoded in the URL, your program ignores it because you're only responding to `post` data, and data encoded in the URL is (by definition) `get` data.

This solution is far from foolproof. There's nothing to prevent a bad guy from writing his own form using the `post` method and passing data to your program that way. You can never be 100-percent safe.

Retrieving Data from Other Form Elements

It's just as easy to get data from drop-down lists and radio buttons as it is to get data from text fields. In PHP (unlike JavaScript), you use exactly the same technique to extract data from any type of form element.

Can't I just have automatic access to form variables?

The earliest forms of PHP had a feature called `register_globals` which automatically did the `$_REQUEST` extraction for you. If your program comes from a `userName` field, the program will "magically" just have a `$userName` variable pre-loaded with the value of that field. While this was a very convenient option, evildoers soon learned how to take advantage of this behavior to cause all kinds of headaches. Convenient as it may be, the `register_globals` feature is now turned off on most servers and isn't even available on the next version of PHP. The `$_REQUEST` approach is safer and not much harder. If you want even more control of how information is passed to your programs, investigate the `filter` functions that are in the latest versions of PHP. They are not quite complete (as of this writing), but by the time PHP6 rolls around, they'll probably become an even better way to extract data from forms.

Building a form with complex elements

For an example of a more complex form, look over `monty.html` in Figure 3-5. This program is a tribute to my favorite movie of all time. (You might just have to rent this movie if you're really going to call yourself a programmer. It's part of the culture.)

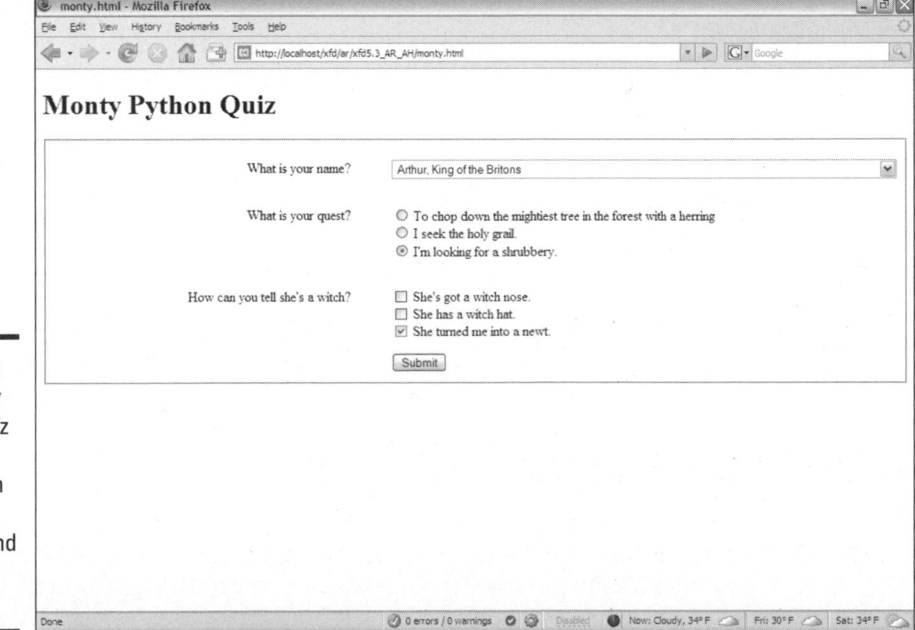

Figure 3-5: The Monty Python quiz features a drop-down list, radio buttons, and check boxes.

The XHTML form poses the questions. (Check out Book I, Chapter 7 for a refresher on XHTML forms, if you need it.) Here's the code:

```
<!DOCTYPE html PUBLIC "-//W3C//DTD XHTML 1.0 Strict//EN"
"http://www.w3.org/TR/xhtml1/DTD/xhtml1-strict.dtd">
<html lang="EN" dir="ltr" xmlns="http://www.w3.org/1999/xhtml">
  <head>
    <meta http-equiv="content-type" content="text/xml; charset=utf-8" />
    <title>monty.html</title>
    <link rel = "stylesheet"
          type = "text/css"
          href = "monty.css" />
  </head>

  <body>
    <h1>Monty Python Quiz</h1>
    <form action = "monty.php"
          method = "post">
      <fieldset>
        <p>
          <label>What is your name?</label>
          <select name = "name">

            <option value = "Roger">
              Roger the Shrubber
            </option>
            <option value = "Arthur">
              Arthur, King of the Britons
            </option>
            <option value = "Tim">
              Tim the Enchanter
            </option>
          </select>
        </p>

        <p>
          <label>What is your quest?</label>
          <span>
            <input type = "radio"
                   name = "quest"
                   value = "herring" />

            To chop down the mightiest tree in the forest
            with a herring
          </span>
          <span>
            <input type = "radio"
                   name = "quest"
                   value = "grail" />

            I seek the holy grail.
          </span>
          <span>
            <input type = "radio"
                   name = "quest"
                   value = "shrubbery" />
            I'm looking for a shrubbery.
          </span>
        </p>

        <p>
```

```
        <label>How can you tell she's a witch?</label>
        <span>
          <input type = "checkbox"
                 name = "nose"
                 value = "nose"/>
          She's got a witch nose.
        </span>
        <span>
          <input type = "checkbox"
                 name = "hat"
                 value = "hat"/>
          She has a witch hat.
        </span>
        <span>
          <input type = "checkbox"
                 name = "newt"
                 value = "newt" />
          She turned me into a newt.
        </span>
      </p>
        <button type = "submit">
          Submit
        </button>
    </fieldset>
  </form>
 </body>
</html>
```

There's nothing too crazy about this code. Please note the following features:

- **The `action` attribute is set to `monty.php`.** This page (`monty.html`) will send data to `monty.php`, which should be in the same directory on the same server.
- **The `method` attribute is set to `post`.** All data on this page will be passed to the server via the `post` method.
- **Each form element has a `name` attribute.** The `name` attributes will be used to extract the data in the PHP program.
- **All the radio buttons have the same `name` value.** The way you get radio buttons to work together is to give them all the same `name`. While they all have the same name, each has a different value. When the PHP program receives the request, it will get only the value of the currently selected radio button.
- **Each check box has an individual name.** Check boxes are a little bit different. Each check box has its own name, but the value is sent to the server only if the check box is currently checked.

I don't cover text areas, passwords fields, or hidden fields here because, to PHP, they are just like text boxes. Retrieve data from these elements just like you do for text fields.

Responding to a complex form

The monty.php program is designed to respond to monty.html. You can see it respond when I submit the form in monty.html, as shown in Figure 3-6.

It's no coincidence that monty.html uses monty.css and calls monty.php. I deliberately gave these files similar names so it will be easy to see how they fit together.

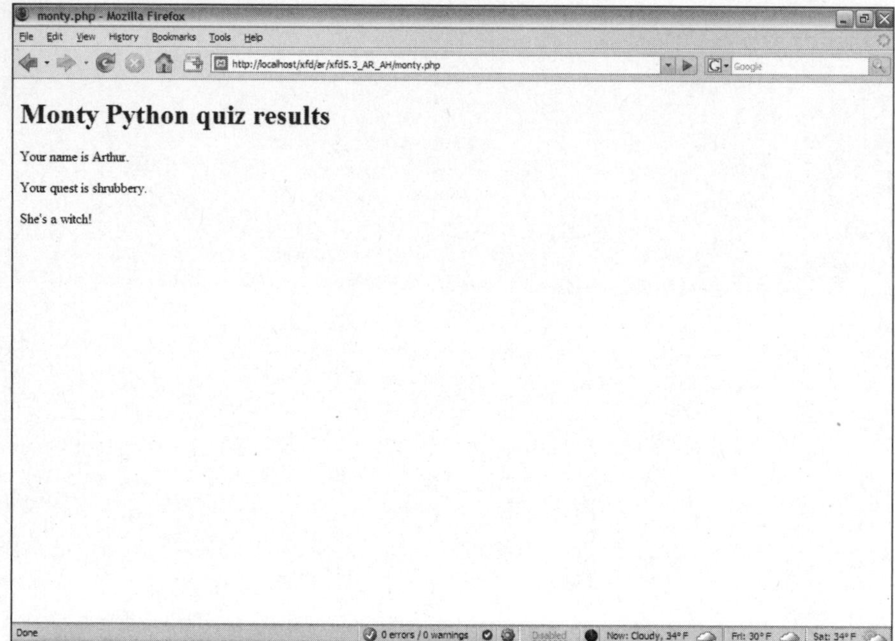

Figure 3-6: The monty.php program responds to the Monty Python quiz.

This program works like most PHP programs: It loads data from the form into variables and assembles output based on those variables. Here's the PHP code:

```
<!DOCTYPE html PUBLIC "-//W3C//DTD XHTML 1.0 Strict//EN"
"http://www.w3.org/TR/xhtml1/DTD/xhtml1-strict.dtd">
<html lang="EN" dir="ltr" xmlns="http://www.w3.org/1999/xhtml">
  <head>
    <meta http-equiv="content-type" content="text/xml; charset=utf-8" />
    <title>monty.php</title>
    <!-- Meant to run from monty.html -->
  </head>

  <body>
    <h1>Monty Python quiz results</h1>
    <?php
      //gather the variables
      $name = $_REQUEST["name"];
```

```
      $quest = $_REQUEST["quest"];
      $nose = $_REQUEST["nose"];
      $hat = $_REQUEST["hat"];
      $newt = $_REQUEST["newt"];

      //send some output
      $reply = <<< HERE
    <p>
      Your name is $name.
    </p>

    <p>
      Your quest is $quest.
    </p>

HERE;
      print $reply;

      //determine if she's a witch
      $witch = false;
      if ($nose != ""){
        $witch = true;
      } // end if

      if ($hat != ""){
        $witch = true;
      } // end if

      if ($newt != ""){
        $witch = true;
      } // end if

      if ($witch == true){
        print "<p>She's a witch!</p> \n";
      } // end if
    ?>

  </body>
</html>
```

If you want to respond to a form with multiple types of data, here's how it's done:

1. **Begin with the XHTML form.**

   Be sure you know the names of all the fields in the form, as your PHP program will need this information.

2. **Embed your PHP inside an XHTML framework.**

   Use your standard XHTML framework as the starting point for your PHP documents, too. The results of your PHP code should still be standards-compliant XHTML. Use the `<?php` and `?>` symbols to indicate the presence of PHP code.

3. **Create a variable for each form element.**

Use the `$_REQUEST` technique described in the "Receiving data in PHP" section of this chapter to extract form data and store it in local variables:

```
//gather the variables
$name = $_REQUEST["name"];
$quest = $_REQUEST["quest"];
$nose = $_REQUEST["nose"];
$hat = $_REQUEST["hat"];
$newt = $_REQUEST["newt"];
```

4. **Build your output in a heredoc.**

   PHP programming almost always involves constructing an XHTML document influenced by the variables that were extracted from the previous form. The heredoc method (described in Chapter 2 of this minibook) is an ideal method for packaging output:

```
    //send some output
    $reply = <<< HERE
  <p>
    Your name is $name.
  </p>

  <p>
    Your quest is $quest.
  </p>

HERE;
    print $reply;
```

5. **Check for the existence of each check box.**

   Check boxes are the one exception to the "treat all form elements the same way" rule of PHP. The important part of a check box isn't really its value. What you really need to know is whether the check box is checked or not. Here's how it works: If the check box is checked, a name and value are passed to the PHP program. If the check box is not checked, it's like the variable never existed:

   a. **Create a variable called `$witch` set to `false`. (We'll assume innocent until proven guilty in *this* witch hunt.)**

      Each check box, if checked, would be proof that she's a witch. If the field was not passed (which will happen if the check box is not checked), the resulting variable will be empty (`""`).

   b. **Check each check box variable. If it's not empty, the corresponding check box was checked, so she must be a witch (and she must weigh the same as a duck — you've *really* got to watch this movie).**

      After testing for the existence of all the check boxes, the `$witch` variable will still be `false` if none of the check boxes were checked. If any combination of check boxes is checked, `$witch` will be `true`:

```
//determine if she's a witch
$witch = false;
if ($nose != ""){
  $witch = true;
} // end if

if ($hat != ""){
  $witch = true;
} // end if

if ($newt != ""){
  $witch = true;
} // end if

if ($witch == true){
  print "<p>She's a witch!</p> \n";
} // end if
```

Chapter 4: Control Structures

In This Chapter

- **Getting familiar with `if-else` conditionals**
- **Using `switch` structures**
- **Working with `while` and `for` loops**
- **Using comparison operators**

Control structures allow you to make decisions or control the order of execution of your program. `if-else` conditionals, `case` statements, `for` loops, and `while` loops are all control structures.

Introducing if-else Conditionals

If you have two or more courses of action to choose from in your program, a perfect way to handle this is through `if-else` conditionals.

if conditionals

The simplest form of a control statement is the `if` conditional, also known as an `if` statement or an `if` construct.

An `if` conditional evaluates an expression down to its `True` or `False` value. If the value is equal to `True`, some code will be executed. If the value is `False`, the code won't be executed.

Here's how you construct an `if` conditional:

1. **Start with `if`.**
2. **Follow this with a condition expression in parentheses, `()`.**
3. **Follow this with the code to be executed if the expression is met.**

This code must be surrounded by curly braces.

The simplest form of an `if` conditional uses a variable that you expect to contain the value `True` or `False` (known as a Boolean variable) as the expression to be evaluated by the `if` statement:

```
$expression = true;

if($expression){
    print "true!";
}
```

This code would print `true!`.

If you wanted to check `$expression` to see if it was equal to `False`, you could precede it with an exclamation point:

```
$expression = true;

if(!$expression){
    print "false!";
}
```

In this case, nothing would print as a result of the execution of this code because `$expression` is set to `True`.

The `if` conditional also evaluates to `True` if a variable simply exists and isn't equal to the Boolean values `True` or `False`. So, the following code would evaluate to `True` because I'm using the string `"false"` instead of the Boolean `False`:

```
$expression = "false";

if($expression){
    print "true";
}
```

Be careful when setting Booleans to `True` or `False`. If you put quotes around either `True` or `False`, the value won't be treated as a Boolean, but rather as a string.

Beyond checking to see whether variables exist or are equal to the Boolean values `True` and `False`, you can use an `if` statement to compare two or more variables.

The most common form of comparison is the check for equality. When checking for equality, use a double equal sign (==), not a single one (=). Single equal signs *assign* (a sign assigns!), whereas double equal signs *compare* (one sign for each value!).

So, this code would always evaluate to `True` and print `2`, even though it's obvious to you that that is not what you intended:

```
<?
$var = 1;
if($var = 2){
    print "$var";
}
?>
```

Here's a dice-rolling game where the user tries to roll a six. You'll use an `if` conditional to make sure the `$userNumber` variable exists and another to determine whether the user wins (see Figure 4-1 for the output):

```
<h1>Dice Rolling Game</h1>
<p>Welcome to the dice rolling game. See if you can roll a six!</p>

<?php

$userNumber = rand(1,6);

if($userNumber){
    print "<p><img src=\"die$userNumber.png\" /></p>";

    if($userNumber == 6){
        print "<p>You rolled a six!</p>";
    }
}

?>

<p><a href="ifConditional.php">Try Again!</a></p>
```

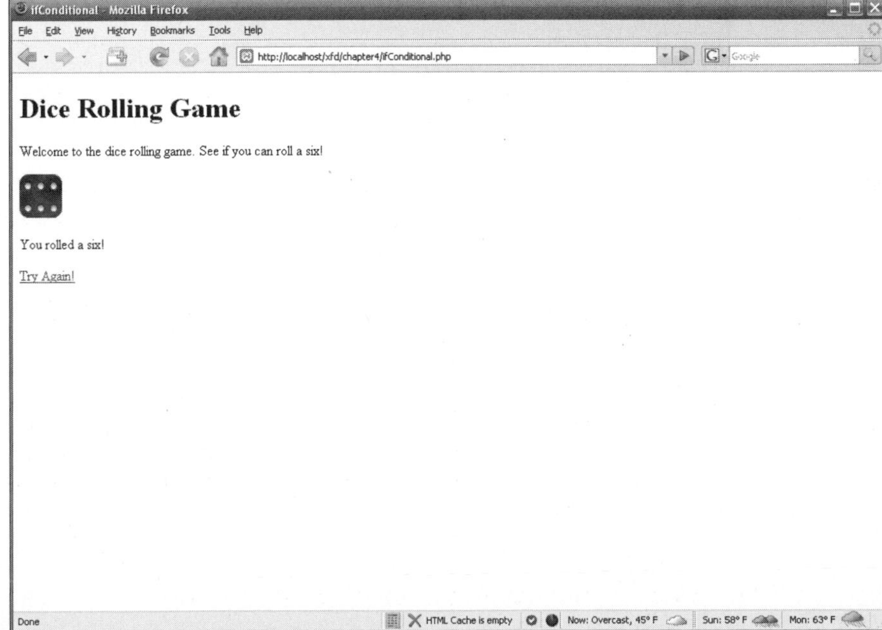

Figure 4-1: If a six is rolled, a special message is shown.

Each time you come to the page, it chooses a random number from `1` to `6` and then evaluates that number to see if you rolled a six. If you did roll a six, it displays the special `"You rolled a six!"` message.

Notice that the code inside the curly braces runs *only* if the condition inside the parentheses is met. Otherwise, it just skips right to the closing curly brace and resumes from there.

In this case, checking whether the `$userNumber` variable existed isn't really necessary because you set it immediately before you checked it. However, if the `$userNumber` variable came from a form submitted to this page, ensuring that the `$userNumber` variable was submitted successfully would be a good idea.

else conditionals

When writing `if` conditionals, it's good practice to always include at least one `else` conditional.

When evaluating a Boolean to see if it equals `True`, the `else` conditional would function as the code that would execute if the Boolean is equal to `False`:

```
$expression = false;

if($expression){
    print "true";
}else{
    print "false";
}
```

This code would print `false` because the expression is equal to the Boolean value `False`.

Conversely, just as you checked for the variable to equal `False` instead of `True`, the `else` conditional would function as the check for `True` in the following statement:

```
$expression = true;

if(!$expression){
    print "false";
}else{
    print "true";
}
```

This code would print `true`.

else and errors

Note the last `else` conditional in the 8-ball program. This should never execute; but if it did for some reason, you're letting the user know what to do. In this case, you're giving the user an error code to send back to you that you can recognize. In this example, `8BIC` stands for *8-ball if conditional.* It's followed by the value `$yourNumber` so that you'll have enough information to begin your investigation into why the error occurred.

It's really up to you as to what you want to happen here, and it wouldn't be very good practice to print an error code to the user every time things didn't go the way you expected. However, for the 8-ball program — because the `if` statement really *is* the entire program — you might consider printing the error code. More realistically, however, you'd probably want to arbitrarily hard code a valid number and print the picture for that number. Who cares if it isn't the number that got rolled?

When printing errors to the user, think about how important it is that the user lets you know the error occurred. Is there some default value you could've shown the user or some default behavior you could've executed, leaving the user none the wiser and ultimately happy? Errors degrade faith in your program. How excited would you be about making a credit card purchase on a site that constantly spit errors every time a tiny thing happened that you didn't care about?

A good solution for this 8-ball program may be to *swallow* the error and never let the user know anything went wrong. Instead, you can have the program e-mail an error report with relevant information to you. Even this solution is extreme overkill, though, because it really doesn't matter how many times that `else` runs, as long as the user doesn't realize it. It only becomes a problem if `else` runs *every* time, but you'd probably notice that during your testing phase.

`else` conditionals can be stacked with `if`s, so you can include as many as you want. If you're following an `else` with an `if`, you can write the `else` statement as `elseif` or `else if`. I prefer `else if` over `elseif` simply because it looks better to me.

Here are basically the two rules to remember with `else`:

- ✦ The `else` conditional goes right after the closing curly brace and can be immediately followed by a new `if` conditional.
- ✦ The final `else` conditional can simply be followed by another opening curly brace. This `else` is executed only if none of the `if` conditionals are met.

Here's a magic 8-ball game that gives you a different outcome dependent upon a random number (see Figure 4-2 for the output):

```
<?php

$yourNumber = rand(1,8);
```

```
if($yourNumber == 1){
    print "<p><img src=\"8ball1.png\" /></p>";
}else if($yourNumber == 2){
    print "<p><img src=\"8ball2.png\" /></p>";
}else if($yourNumber == 3){
    print "<p><img src=\"8ball3.png\" /></p>";
}else if($yourNumber == 4){
    print "<p><img src=\"8ball4.png\" /></p>";
}else if($yourNumber == 5){
    print "<p><img src=\"8ball5.png\" /></p>";
}else if($yourNumber == 6){
    print "<p><img src=\"8ball6.png\" /></p>";
}else if($yourNumber == 7){
    print "<p><img src=\"8ball7.png\" /></p>";
}else if($yourNumber == 8){
    print "<p><img src=\"8ball8.png\" /></p>";
}else{
    print "An error has occurred. Please try again, or contact
     support@somesite.com for assistance. Error code: 8BIC:$yourNumber";
}

?>

<a href="ifElse.php">Ask another question!</a>
```

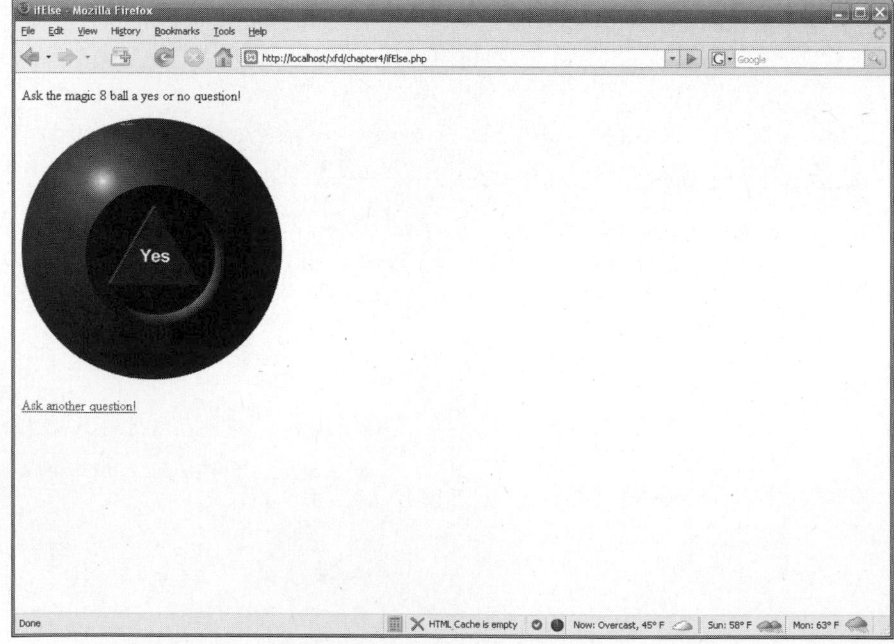

Figure 4-2: The results of the ifElse.php code. A simple 8-ball simulator.

Comparison operators

There are many ways to test variables to see if they're equal to, less than, greater than, or not equal to certain text, numbers, or even other variables, as shown in the following:

- **==:** Checks for equality
- **!=:** Checks for inequality
- **<:** Checks to see if the value on the left is less than the value on the right
- **>:** Checks to see if the value on the left is greater than the value on the right
- **<=:** Checks to see if the value on the left is less than or equal to the value on the right
- **>=:** Checks to see if the value on the left is greater than or equal to the value on the right

Remember, these comparisons work on any sort of data, not just numbers. You can compare letters from the alphabet, as shown here:

```
if("a" < "b")
```

This would evaluate to `True` because *a* comes before *b* in the alphabet, and thus is smaller.

Here's a program that rolls two ten-sided dice to get a percentile. Through a series of `if-else` statements, the program determines what happens, based on your roll, by using comparison operators (feel free to get the code from the CD-ROM, rather than typing it all — Figure 4-3 shows the output):

```
<?php

$tensDie = rand(1,10);
$onesDie = rand(1,10);

print "<p><img src=\"10sided$tensDie.png\" /><img src=\"10sided$onesDie.png\"
    /><br />";

if($onesDie == 10)
    $onesDie = 0;//if ones die == 10, make it zero.

if($tensDie == 10){
    if($onesDie != 0){
        print "You rolled a $onesDie</p>";
    }else{
        print "You rolled 100!</p>";
    }
}else{
    print "Your rolled $tensDie$onesDie</p>";
}
```

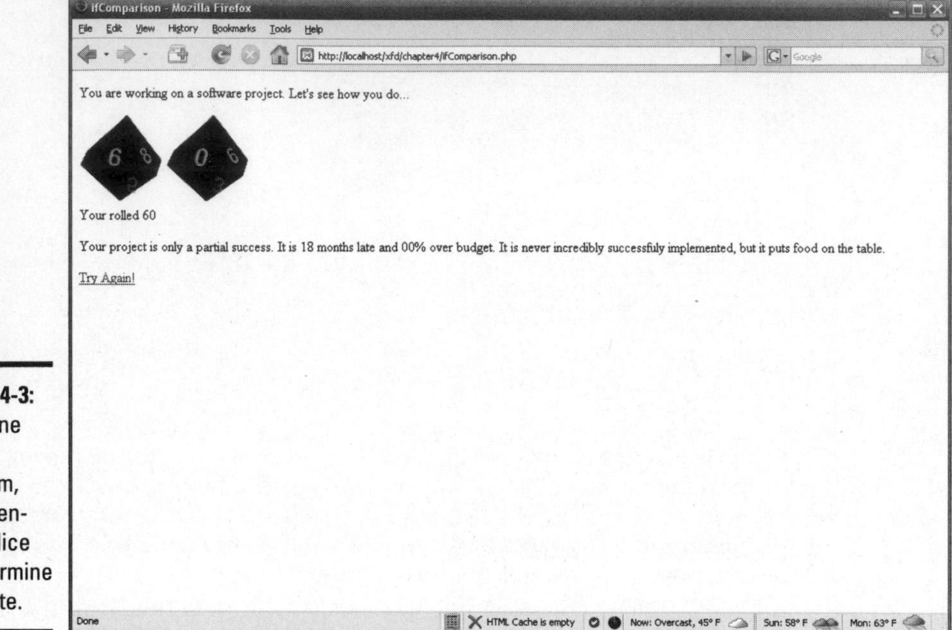

Figure 4-3: A fortune teller program, using ten-sided dice to determine your fate.

```
print "<p>";
if($tensDie != 10){
    if($tensDie <= 4){
            print "Your project is a failure. It is $tensDie years late and " .
    $onesDie .
        "00% over budget before it finally gets canceled. All of your co-workers
    are
        disgruntled and send each other's code to worsethanfailure.com";
    }else if($tensDie <= 7){
        print "Your project is only a partial success. It is " . $tensDie * 3 . "
    months
        late and " . $onesDie . "0% over budget. It is never incredibly
    successfully
        implemented, but it puts food on the table.";
    }else if($tensDie < 9){
        print "Your project is a success. It is only $tensDie weeks late and has
    " .
        $onesDie . "% of the features originally planned, but it survives through
    " .
        ($tensDie + $onesDie) . " more releases before it is obsolete.";
    }else{
        print "Your project is a huge success! ";
        if($onesDie == 9){
            print " It is purchased by Google, and you are snatched up along with
    it. You
            lucky entrepreneur you...";
        }else{
            print " It remains an industry standard for the next $onesDie years,
    making
            you filthy rich.";
        }
```

```
        }
    } else {
        if($onesDie == 0){
                print "When you were born, your mother christened you \"William
        Gates\", and the
                rest is history.";
        }else{
                print "Someone burns your office down and you lose your job. Better
        luck next
                time.";
        }
    }
    print "</p>";

    ?>

    <a href="ifComparison.php">Try Again!</a>
```

Logical operators

You can cram as many comparisons as you want into the `if` statement. You simply need to separate the comparisons with logical operators, such as the following:

- **AND or &&:** Either can be placed between two conditionals to make sure both conditions are met.
- **OR or ||:** Either can be placed between two conditionals to make sure at least one is met.
- **XOR:** Can be placed between two conditionals to make sure at least one is not met.

These logical operators go right inside the parentheses with the expressions:

```
if("a" < "b" || 1 == 2)
```

Because you need only one of the expressions to evaluate to `True` (with an `OR` logical operator), this code evaluates to `True` because even though `1` is not equal to `2`, `a` is less than `b`. However, if I replaced `OR` with `AND`:

```
if("a" < "b" && 1 == 2)
```

This would evaluate to `False` because both expressions on either side of `AND` don't evaluate to `True`.

You can go pretty crazy with all the logical operators if you want (using parentheses to organize them), much the way you would an equation in math, as shown in the following (see Figure 4-4 for the output):

```
<h1>Spacewar!</h1>
<p>It is 1962. You are Steve Russell hard at work on your DEC PDP-1 Computer
    trying to invent the very first computer game, "Spacewar!"</p>
```

```
<p>Everything would be going great if only you could get the Cathode-Ray Tubes to
    work. There are two that are giving you trouble. They are getting either too
    much, or too little power, but you just need one to work to play the game.
    Try restarting until one works!</p>
<?php

//set random power level
$crt1 = rand(1,10);
$crt2 = rand(1,10);

print <<<HERE
<p>Your CRTs (need one to be green):<br />
<img src="crt$crt1.png" />
<img src="crt$crt2.png" /></p>
HERE;

//see if one crt's power levels is between 4 and 6 (inclusive)...
if(($crt1 >= 4 && $crt1 <= 6) || ($crt2 >= 4 && $crt2 <= 6)){
    print"<p>SPACEWAR!<br /><img src=\"computerOn.png\" /></p>";
}else{
    print"<p>No Go... <a href=\"ifLogical.php\">Try again</a>...<br /><img
    src=\"computerOff.png\" /></p>";
}
?>
```

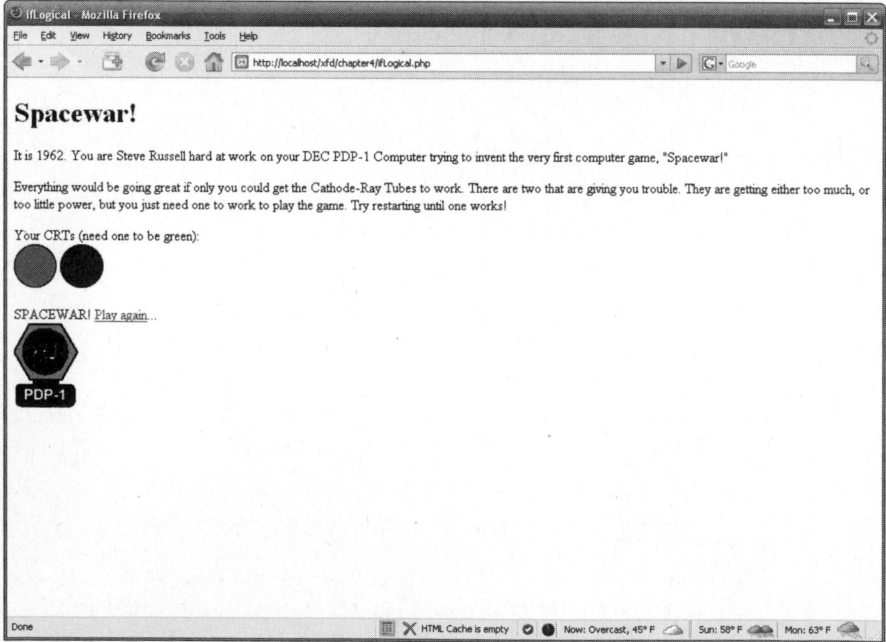

Figure 4-4: The first computer game. Can you get it to work?

This really optimizes your `if` statements. Without the logical operators, this same code would've taken about five `if` statements:

```
xif($crt1 >= 4){
    if($crt1 <= 6){
        print"<p>SPACEWAR!<br /><img src=\"computerOn.png\" /></p>";
    }else if($crt2 >= 4){
        if($crt2 <= 6){
        print"<p>SPACEWAR!<br /><img src=\"computerOn.png\" /></p>";
        }else{
            print"<p>No Go... <a href=\"ifLogical.php\">Try again</a>...<br
    /><img
            src=\"computerOff.png\" /></p>";
        }
    }
}
```

Comparing with switch Structures

The `switch` statement is a great replacement for an `if` conditional if you have a single variable that you want to compare to a set number of values by using the double equal sign (==) comparison.

Here's how you construct the `switch` statement:

1. **Start with the keyword `switch`.**
2. **Add the variable you wish to evaluate in parentheses, `()`.**

   In this example, `$theVar` is the variable.
3. **Insert a pair of curly braces (`{}`).**
4. **Put the `case` statements inside the curly braces, beginning with `case`.**
5. **Add the value to test the variable against.**

   In this example, `1`, `b`, and `False` are all values to test the variable against. These values are like the value on the right side of an `if` comparison, whereas the variable (`$theVar`, in this example) is like the variable on the left side of an `if` comparison.
6. **Enter the code to run if the variable test evaluates to `True`.**
7. **Add the `break` statement to exit the `switch` structure.**
8. **Put as many `case` statements as you want until you've exhausted all of the reasonable possibilities you think might occur.**

   If you are rolling a six-sided die, for example, you would test for numbers `1` to `6` because those are reasonable possibilities.
9. **(Optional) Include a default clause.**

Loose comparisons with switch

The `switch` statement uses loose comparisons to check for equality. Basically, this means that it's a lot less strict about whether the two values are equal. For instance, with loose comparison, the following:

```
true == 1
```

evaluates to `True`. Whereas with strict comparisons, the same statement would evaluate to `False`.

For more on strict versus loose comparisons, see `http://us2.php.net/manual/en/types.comparisons.php#types.comparisions-loose`.

You can compare against numbers, text, Booleans, or all three:

```
switch($theVar){
    case 1:
        //do something
        break;
    case "b":
        //do something
        break;
    case false:
        //do something
        break;
    default:
        //do something
}
```

Don't forget the `break` statement, or every single line following the first statement that evaluates to `True` will run! Try commenting the `break` statements out of the magic 8-ball code following the next paragraph to see for yourself.

Look at this modified version of the 8-ball program from earlier in this chapter to see how the `case` statement can simplify your programs:

```
<p>Ask the magic 8 ball a yes or no question!</p>

<?php

$yourNumber = rand(1,8);

switch($yourNumber){
case 1:
    print "<p><img src=\"8ball1.png\" /></p>";
    break;
case 2:
    print "<p><img src=\"8ball2.png\" /></p>";
    break;
```

if statements considered harmful

If you've followed along so far, you simplified the 8-ball program with `case` statements instead of `if-else` statements. Is there anything else you could do that would simplify it more?

The most efficient version of the 8-ball program functions without `ifs` or `cases` and is only two lines of PHP code:

```
$yourNumber = rand(1,8);
print "<p><img
        src=\"8ball$yourNumber.png\"
        /></p>";
```

Often, you'll find that if you're doing something extremely complicated with lots of nested `ifs`, you're probably doing something wrong. Many new programmers use `if` statements for everything because if your only tool is a hammer, everything looks like a nail.

After you expand your toolbox with tools such as arrays, multidimensional arrays, and simple solutions like the one shown in this sidebar, you'll find that you write fewer and fewer `if` statements. Very rarely do you write long, complex `if` statements like the ones shown in this chapter.

Note: `if` statements aren't really considered harmful, that was just a catchy title based on a common phrase in computer science popularized by a 1968 letter written about GOTO statements. For more on this topic, see `http://blog.chomperstomp.com/?p=110`.

```
case 3:
    print "<p><img src=\"8ball3.png\" /></p>";
    break;
case 4:
    print "<p><img src=\"8ball4.png\" /></p>";
    break;
case 5:
    print "<p><img src=\"8ball5.png\" /></p>";
    break;
case 6:
    print "<p><img src=\"8ball6.png\" /></p>";
    break;
case 7:
    print "<p><img src=\"8ball7.png\" /></p>";
    break;
case 8:
    print "<p><img src=\"8ball8.png\" /></p>";
    break;
default:
    print "An error has occurred. Please try again, or contact
     support@somesite.com for assistance. Error code: 8BIC:$yourNumber";
}

?>

<a href="switch.php">Ask another question!</a>
```

Looping It Up with Loops

Many times, you'll find that you want the computer to repeat a certain task. The way to do this is through loops.

while loops

Loop structures rely heavily on `if` statements. In fact, the `while` loop looks exactly like an `if` statement with the word *if* replaced with the word *while.* The only difference is that whereas `if` executes only once, `while` continues to repeat until it evaluates to `False`.

So, this code could go on forever unless something inside the curly braces set `$theVar` to `False`:

```
$theVar = true;

while($theVar){
    //do something
}
```

Look back at the dice-rolling program earlier in this chapter (refer to Figure 4-1). Instead of clicking Try Again! for every roll, you could easily modify this program to simply roll the dice until you get a six (see Figure 4-5 for the output):

```
<h1>Dice Rolling Game 2</h1>
<p>Welcome to the dice rolling game. See how many rolls it takes to get a
    six!</p>

<?php
while ($userNumber != 6){
    $userNumber = rand(1,6);
    print "<p><img src=\"die$userNumber.png\" /></p>";
}

    print "<p>You rolled a six!</p>";
?>

<p><a href="while.php">Try Again!</a></p>
```

for loops

A `for` loop is really just a convenient `while` loop. With `while` loops, you have to initialize the variable, create the `while` loop with the `if` expression, and then remember to make the expression evaluate to `True`:

```
$theVar = 0;

while($theVar < 10){
    //do something
    $theVar++;
}
```

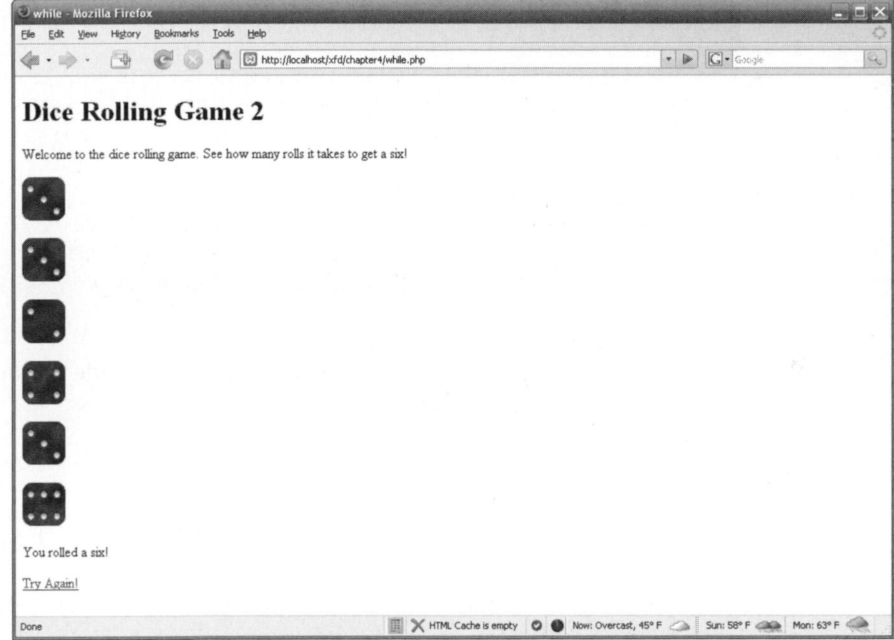

Figure 4-5: The dice keep rolling until you get a six!

`for` loops take care of all this in a nice succinct, compact way in the expression area of the loop:

```
for($theVar = 0; $theVar < 10; $theVar++){
    //do something
}
```

Each time PHP gets to the end of the loop (the last curly brace), it jumps right back to the beginning if the expression still evaluates to `False`, and it increments `$theVar` by `1`.

Here's what the `for` loop is doing:

```
$theVar = 0;
if ($theVar < 10){
     //do something
     $theVar++;
}
//go back to the first if
```

So, you can see it's basically just a conveniently structured `while` loop.

You can make the loop increment by any value you like; it doesn't have to just be by `1`.

If you made the dice-rolling game for the `while` loop in the preceding section, you made it keep rolling until it rolled a six. What if, instead, you wanted it simply to roll the dice 100 times and see how many times you rolled a six? This would be extremely easy to do with a `for` loop (see Figure 4-6 for the output):

```
<h1>Dice Rolling Game 2</h1>
<p>Welcome to the dice rolling game. See how many rolls it takes to get a
    six!</p>
<p>
<?php
$sixCount = 0;

for ($i = 0; $i < 100; $i++){
    $userNumber = rand(1,6);
    print "<img src=\"die$userNumber.png\" />";
    if($userNumber == 6){
        $sixCount++;
    }
}

    print "<p>You rolled $sixCount six(es)!</p>";
?>
</p>
<p><a href="for.php">Try Again!</a></p>
```

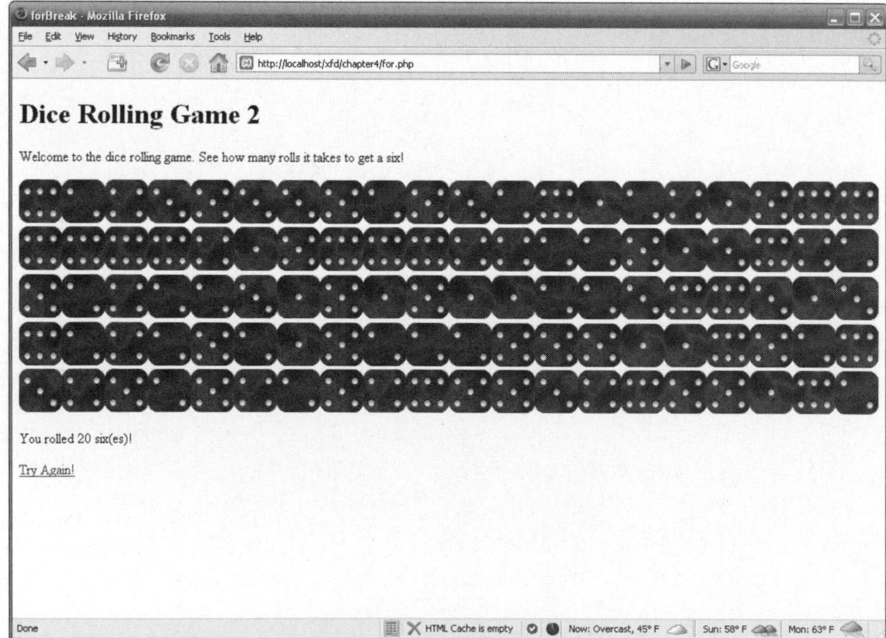

Figure 4-6: 100 dice rolls with a count of the number of sixes rolled.

TIP

More on control structures

Here are a few more control structures that I haven't discussed yet in this chapter:

- **`do-while`:** Exactly like `while`, except that the `if` conditional is evaluated at the end of the loop, rather than at the beginning. This ensures that the loop executes at least once, whereas with `while`, there's a chance it won't execute at all.
- **`foreach`:** This works only on arrays; I cover this in Chapter 5 of this minibook.
- **`continue`:** This is used within the loop structure to skip the remaining code and move to the next iteration of the loop.
- **`declare`:** `declare` constructs are used to set an execution directive for blocks of code. You'll probably won't use this often.
- **`return`:** Called from within a function.
- **`require`:** Includes and evaluates a specific file and kills the program if the file doesn't exist.
- **`include`:** Includes and evaluates a specific file.
- **`require_once`:** Same as `require`, except that if the file has already been included, it won't be included again.
- **`include_once`:** Same as `include`, except that if the file has already been included, it won't be included again.

These control structures aren't quite as prevalent as the ones covered in this chapter, but you may still run across them every now and then.

For more detail and alternative syntaxes for control structures, check out the PHP manual online at `http://us2.php.net/manual/en/language.control-structures.php`.

As you can see, the structure of the `for` loop is

```
for (expression1; expression2; expression3)
    //do something
```

Here's what each part of the code is doing:

- ✦ **First expression:** Executes exactly once at the beginning of the `for` loop. This is where you initialize variables.
- ✦ **Second expression:** Evaluates at the beginning of each iteration of the loop until it evaluates to `False`, at which point, the loop ends.
- ✦ **Third expression:** Executes at the end of each iteration of the loop.

Within each of these expressions, you can place multiple expressions separated by commas. In this way, you can modify your dice-rolling program to simplify the six count by putting the initialization of the `$sixCount` variable inside the `for` loop in the `expression1` place:

```
for ($i = 0, $sixCount = 0; $i < 100; $i++){
```

All the expressions places are optional. If you leave them empty, the loop will still work. Leaving `expression2` empty simply causes the loop to run forever unless you exit it with a `break` directive. Take a look at this modified version of the dice-rolling program. I leave the `expression2` slot empty and manually exit the loop if either the dice-roll count exceeds 100 or you roll more than 20 sixes (see Figure 4-7 for the output):

```
<h1>Dice Rolling Game 3</h1>
<p>Welcome to the dice rolling game. See how many rolls it takes to get 20 sixes.
    You can roll the dice up to 100 times!</p>
<p>
<?php
for ($i = 0, $sixCount = 0; ; $i++){
    $userNumber = rand(1,6);
    print "<img src=\"die$userNumber.png\" />";

    if($userNumber == 6){
        $sixCount++;
    }

    if($i > 99 || $sixCount > 19){
        break;
    }
}

    print "<p>You rolled the dice $i times, and rolled $sixCount six(es)!</p>";
    if($sixCount < 20){
        print "<h2>You failed to roll 20 sixes!!!</h2>";
    }
?>
</p>
<p><a href="forBreak.php">Try Again!</a></p>
```

You can do some amazing things with loops, and they'll be one of the most important tools in your toolbox, especially when using arrays (see Chapter 5 of this minibook for more about working with arrays).

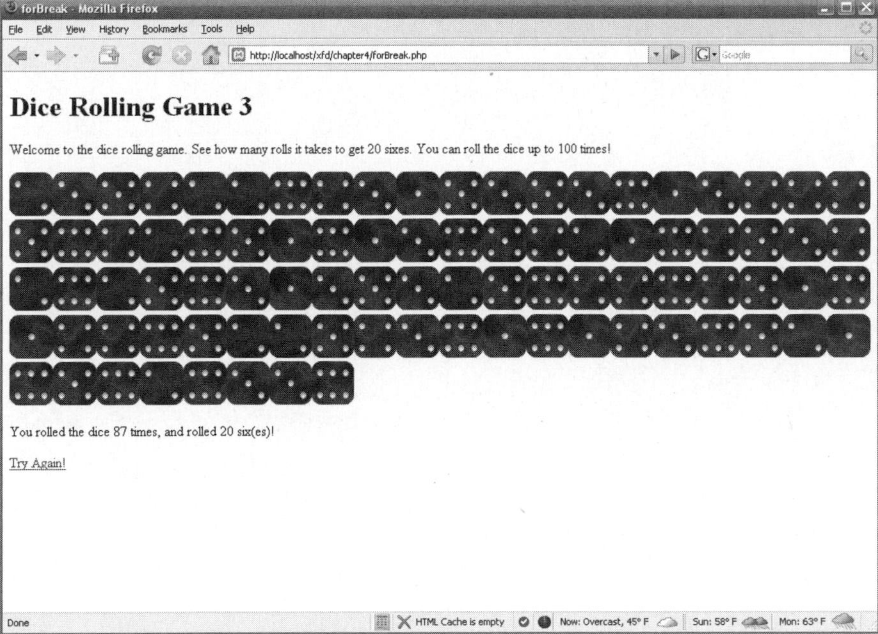

Figure 4-7: Roll the dice 100 times and try to get more than 20 sixes.

Chapter 5: Working with Arrays

In This Chapter

- **Creating one-dimensional arrays**
- **Making the most of multidimensional arrays**
- **Using `foreach` loops to simplify array management**
- **Breaking a string into an array**

In time, arrays will become one of the most important tools in your toolbox. They can be a bit hard to grasp for beginners, but don't let that stop you. Arrays are awesome because they allow you to quickly apply the same instructions to a large number of items.

In PHP, an *array* is a variable that holds multiple values that are mapped to keys. Think of a golfing scorecard. You have several scores, one for each hole on the golf course. The hole number is the key, and the score for that hole is the value. Keys are usually numeric, but values can be any type. You can have an array of strings, numbers, or even objects.

Using One-Dimensional Arrays

The most basic array is a *one-dimensional array.* It's just one container with slots, and each slot has only one variable in it. In this section, you find out how to create this type of array and fill it.

Creating an array

Array creation is pretty simple. First, you need to create a variable and then tell PHP that you want that variable to be an array:

```
$theVar = array();
```

Now, `$theVar` is an array. However, it's an empty array waiting for you to come along and fill it.

Technically, you can skip the variable creation step. It's still a good idea to explicitly define an array because it helps you remember the element is an array, and there are a few special cases (such as passing an array into a function) where the definition really matters.

Filling an array after creation

An array is a wonderful thing after you put something in it. Here are the three ways you can fill an array after you create it:

- Reference a numerical index and place something in that slot of the array.
- Specify an index and place something in that slot of the array.
- Take the next highest available numerical index greater than zero.

Take a look at the following:

```
$theVar[0] = "something";
$theVar[] = 4;
```

If you were paying close attention, you'll notice that I used `0` as my first array index. That's because computers start counting from zero, and now you do, too! So, in the example, index `0` holds the value `something` and index `1` holds the value `4`.

When filling an array, if you don't specify an index, it simply takes the next highest index equal to or greater than zero and places the value there. Because I didn't specify an index for the number `4`, it looked at the current numbered indices it had (which was index `0`) and took the next highest numbered index (which was index `1`) and placed `4` inside that index. If you had indices `0`, `5`, `6`, and `27`, the next highest numbered index would be `28`.

Filling an array upon creation

You can fill an array upon creation by placing values, separated with commas, inside the parentheses, as shown here:

```
$theVar = array("one", $two, 3);
```

This creates an array whose 0th index is filled with the string `one`, the 1st index is filled with the variable `$two`, and the 2nd index is filled with the integer `3`. You can explicitly define which index gets what by using little arrows:

```
$theVar = array(2 => "one", 0 => $two, 4 => 3);
```

Now, you have an array with the 0th index equal to the variable `$two`, the 2nd index equal to the string `one` (note that there's no 1st index, or rather, the first index is `null`), and the index `4` equal to the number `3`.

Why => instead of <=?

The arrows (=>) can be a little bit confusing. Some might think they should go the other way (<=) so that it'd be like placing the value into the index:

```
$anArray["anIndex"] <= "the value I'm
        putting in the index";
```

However, because of the way that `if` statements function, if they had the arrow the more logical way, PHP would get confused (the following code doesn't work):

```
if(0 <= 1){
    $anArray["anIndex"] <= "the value I'm
        putting in the index";
}
```

PHP will get really confused if you do this. Are you trying to do a comparison or place a value into an index? Instead of looking at the arrow as placing a value into a slot, look at it as placing a pointer from the slot to the variable. Also, note that in OO PHP (see Chapter 1 of this minibook), you assign values to an object's properties with the pointer arrow (=>). So, at least it is consistent.

Accessing an array index

To access one of the indices in an array (to get to the egg in a slot), call it by name:

```
print $anArray[0];
```

This would print whatever was in the 0th index of the array. It's as simple as that. If you wanted to, you could even use a variable equal to the name of the index you wanted to call, as shown here:

```
$anArray = array(0=>"first egg", "second egg", "bazaar"=>"third egg");
$aVar = 0;

print $anArray[$aVar];
```

In this case, `first egg` would be printed because `$aVar` is equal to `0`, and `first egg` is in the 0th index. Changing `$aVar` to `1` would cause `second egg` to be printed, and changing `$aVar` to `bazaar` would cause `third egg` to be printed.

So, now take a look at all this in action:

```
<h1>Random Computer Quotes</h1>
<?

$theVar = array();
```

```
$theVar[] = "<p>If at first you don't succeed; call it version 1.0 and ship it
    anyways...</p>";
$theVar[] = "<p>Some things Man was never meant to know. For everything else,
    there's Google.</p>";
$theVar[] = "<p>SUPERCOMPUTER: what it sounded like before you bought it.</p>";
$theVar[] = "<p>My software never has bugs. It just develops random
    features.</p>";
$theVar[] = "<p>If you give someone a program, you will frustrate them for a day;
    if you teach them how to program, you will frustrate them for a
    lifetime.</p>";
$theVar[] = "<p>It is easier to change the specification to fit the program than
    vice versa.</p>";
$theVar[] = "<p>Programmers are tools for converting caffeine into code.</p>";
$theVar[] = "<p>Always program as if the person who will be maintaining your
    program is a violent psychopath that knows where you live.</p>";

print $theVar[rand(0,7)];

?>

<p><a href="quotes.php">See Another!</a></p>
```

In this program, you fill an array with eight different quotes and then get and print a random array with the `print()` and `rand()` functions.

Debugging with print_r

A very useful tool when working with arrays is the `print_r()` function. With this function, you can print every index and its value in an array.

When building the `quotes.php` program (see the previous section), if you accidentally called the `rand()` function with `1` and `8` instead of `0` and `7`, you'd get a blank quote every now and then. A quick way to figure out the problem if you didn't catch your mistake immediately would have been to call `print_r()` on the array and then capture and print the random value you were trying to use to call the array with:

```
<h1>Random Computer Quotes</h1>
<p>"
<?

$theArray = array();

$theArray[] = "If at first you don't succeed; call it version 1.0 and ship it
    anyways...<br />";
$theArray[] = "Some things Man was never meant to know. For everything else,
    there's Google.<br />";
$theArray[] = "SUPERCOMPUTER: what it sounded like before you bought it.<br />";
$theArray[] = "My software never has bugs. It just develops random features.<br
    />";
$theArray[] = "If you give someone a program, you will frustrate them for a day;
    if you teach them how to program, you will frustrate them for a lifetime.<br
    />";
$theArray[] = "It is easier to change the specification to fit the program than
    vice versa.<br />";
$theArray[] = "Programmers are tools for converting caffeine into code.<br />";
```

```
$theArray[] = "Always program as if the person who will be maintaining your
    program is a violent psychopath that knows where you live.<br />";

$randNumber = rand(1,8);

print $theArray[$randNumber];

print "<br />Trying to get $randNumber in array:";
print_r($theArray);

?>
"</p>

<p><a href="quotesDebug.php">See Another!</a></p>
```

Introducing Associative Arrays

You can use string values as keys. For example, you might create an array like this:

```
$myStuff = array();
$myStuff["name"] = "andy";
$myStuff["email"] = "andy@aharrisbooks.net";

Print $myStuff["name"];
```

Associative arrays are different than normal (numeric-indexed) arrays in some subtle but important ways:

- **The order is undefined.** Regular arrays are always sorted based on the numeric index. You don't know what order an associative array will be because the keys aren't numeric.
- **You must specify a key.** If you're building a numeric-indexed array, PHP can always guess what key should be next. This isn't possible with an associative array.
- **Associative arrays are best for name-value pairs.** Associative arrays are used when you want to work with data that comes in name/value pairs. This comes up a lot in PHP and XHTML. XHTML attributes are often in this format, as are CSS rules and form input elements.
- **Some of PHP's most important values are associative arrays.** The `$_REQUEST` variable (described in Chapter 3 of this minibook) is an important associative array. So are `$_GET`, `$_POST`, and several others.

Make sure to include quotation marks if you're using a string as an array index. It will probably work if you don't, but it's bad programming practice and may not work in the future.

Expanding to Multidimensional Arrays

A *multidimensional array* is an array that holds arrays. You can put as many arrays inside as many arrays as you could possibly want.

Some uses for these are to group things or to use as lookup tables. See Book IV, Chapter 4 for one possible use of lookup tables — using multidimensional arrays to hold the distances between cities.

Another use of a multidimensional array is to store and group items. For example, think of a deck of cards. You could use a multidimensional array to simultaneously store the cards, which suit they belong to, and even whether the cards are in the deck or dealt to a player or players.

Creating and filling multidimensional arrays

Multidimensional arrays are created exactly the same way a normal array is created. If you desire, you initialize the parent array:

```
$yourArray = array();
```

The sub-arrays are created on the fly by PHP while you fill them.

Take a look at this program (also shown in Figure 5-1) that uses multidimensional arrays to build a deck of cards:

```
<p>
<?
//set up arrays
$cardLocation = array();
$suits = array("heart", "diamond", "spade", "club");

//fill deck
for($rank=0; $rank<13; $rank++){
    //print "<br />";
    for($suit=0; $suit<4; $suit++){
        $cardLocation[$rank][$suit] = "deck";
            print '<img style="width: 150px;" src="' . $suits[$suit] . ($rank+1)
    . '.png" />';
    }
}

print "</p>";
```

The program uses an array to hold all the cards. The first dimension of the array is the card ranks (1–13). Each rank has four possible suits (hearts, diamonds, spades, and clubs). The program uses nested `for` loops to cycle through the array, filling the rank indices with `suit` arrays. The `suit` arrays have four indices each, which contain the value `deck` to begin with, indicating that these cards are all located in the deck (as opposed to a player's hand).

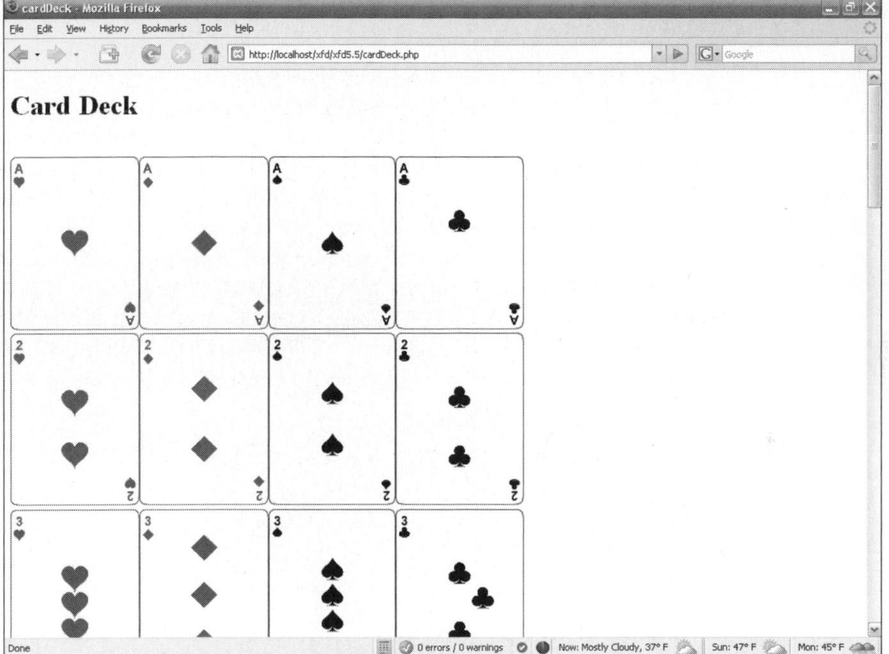

Figure 5-1: Behold. An entire deck of cards built from a mere eight lines of code!

The program also uses a `suits` array to hold the name values of each suit to aid in printing the correct pictures to the user.

You can look at multidimensional arrays as tables. The card deck array could look something like this, if represented in tabular format:

0	0	"deck"
1	"deck"	
2	"deck"	
3	"deck"	
1	0	"deck"
1	"deck"	
2	"deck"	
3	"deck"	
2	0	"deck"
1	"deck"	
2	"deck"	

3	"deck"	
3	0	"deck"
1	"deck"	
2	"deck"	
3	"deck"	
4	0	"deck"
1	"deck"	
2	"deck"	
3	"deck"	
5	0	"deck"
1	"deck"	
2	"deck"	
3	"deck"	
6	0	"deck"
1	"deck"	
2	"deck"	
3	"deck"	
7	0	"deck"
1	"deck"	
2	"deck"	
3	"deck"	
8	0	"deck"
1	"deck"	

2	"deck"	
3	"deck"	
9	0	"deck"
1	"deck"	
2	"deck"	
3	"deck"	
10	0	"deck"
1	"deck"	
2	"deck"	
3	"deck"	
11	0	"deck"
1	"deck"	
2	"deck"	
3	"deck"	
12	0	"deck"
1	"deck"	
2	"deck"	
3	"deck"	

The entire table is the multidimensional array. The far-left column in each set represents the indices of the parent array, which in this example is the card ranks. Each index in the parent array contains its own sub-array, which in this example is the card suits. Each index in the sub-array contains a value, which in this example is the location of the card. All the cards are located in the deck in this example (you deal five to the player in the next section).

Accessing a value in a multidimensional array

Using the table in the previous example as a guide representing the `$cardLocation` array, which holds your deck of cards, if you wanted to access the queen of diamonds, you'd do so like this:

```
$cardLocation[11][1];
```

The first number in this example represents the card you want to access, the queen, which is stored in the indice 11. The next number in this example represents the rank you want to access, the diamonds, which are stored in the indice `1`. So, the first number represents the indice in the parent array, and the second number is the indice for the child array in that spot in the parent array.

A longer, less convenient representation of this would be:

```
$queenSuits = $cardLocation[11];
$ownerOfCard = $queenSuits[1];
```

The value of `$ownerOfCard` in the latter example and `$cardLocation[11][1]` in the former example, is `deck`.

Now, try dealing five cards to the player (see Figure 5-2 for the output):

```
<h1>Card Hand</h1>
<p>
<?
//set up arrays
$cardLocation = array();
$suits = array("heart", "diamond", "spade", "club");

//fill deck
for($rank=0; $rank<13; $rank++){
    for($suit=0; $suit<4; $suit++){
        $cardLocation[$rank][$suit] = "deck";
    }
}

print "</p><p>";

//deal hand
for($i=0; $i<5; $i++){
    $duplicate = true;

    while($duplicate){
        $suit = rand(1,4);
        $rank = rand(1,13);
        if($cardLocation[$rank][$suit] == "deck"){
            $cardLocation[$rank][$suit] = "player";
            $duplicate = false;
                print '<img style="width: 150px;" src="' . $suits[$suit] . ($rank
    + 1) . '.png" />';
        }
    }
```

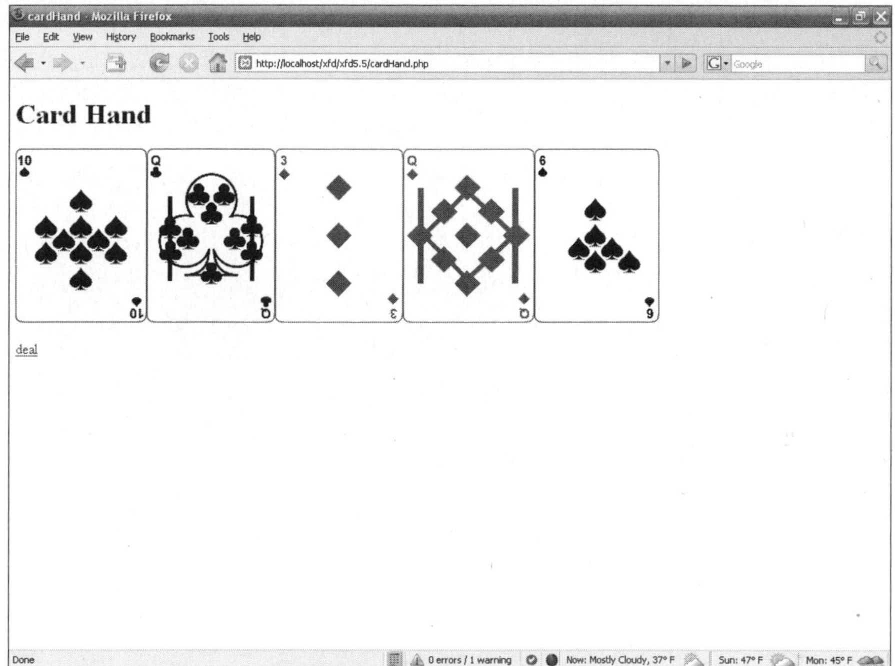

Figure 5-2: A hand of cards dealt to the player.

```
}
?>
</p>

<p><a href="cardHand.php">deal</a></p>
```

Here, you generate two random numbers to pick a card rank and suit. Then, you check to see if that card is in the player's hand or in the deck. If the card's in the deck, give it to the player by setting the value at that index to `player` instead of `deck`. You do this until five different indices are set to `player`.

It's a bit beyond the scope of this chapter, but you can use all this to make a PHP poker game. See the CD-ROM for the source code and the start of an algorithm for scoring poker hands.

Using foreach Loops to Simplify Array Management

`foreach` loops are great for when you want to step through all elements of an array one by one and do something with them. They work like a `for` loop, except they're much simpler:

1. **Start with the `foreach()` function.**
2. **Plug in the array (`$languages`, in this case) you want to use, followed by . . .**
3. **The keyword `as`, followed by . . .**
4. **The variable you want to store the value of the current array indices in (`$language`, in this case), followed by . . .**
5. **The code you want to execute upon each iteration inside brackets (if more than one line long).**

Take a look (see Figure 5-3 for the output):

```
<h1>Ancestry of PHP</h1>
<ul>
<?
$languages = array("FORTRAN", "ALGOL58", "ALGOL60", "CPL", "BCPL", "B", "C",
    "sh", "awk", "PERL", "PHP");

foreach($languages as $language){
    print "<li>$language</li>";
}
?>
</ul>
<p><a href="http://www.oreilly.com/news/graphics/prog_lang_poster.pdf">Reference:
    History of Programming Languages Timeline from O'Reilly's website</a></p>
```

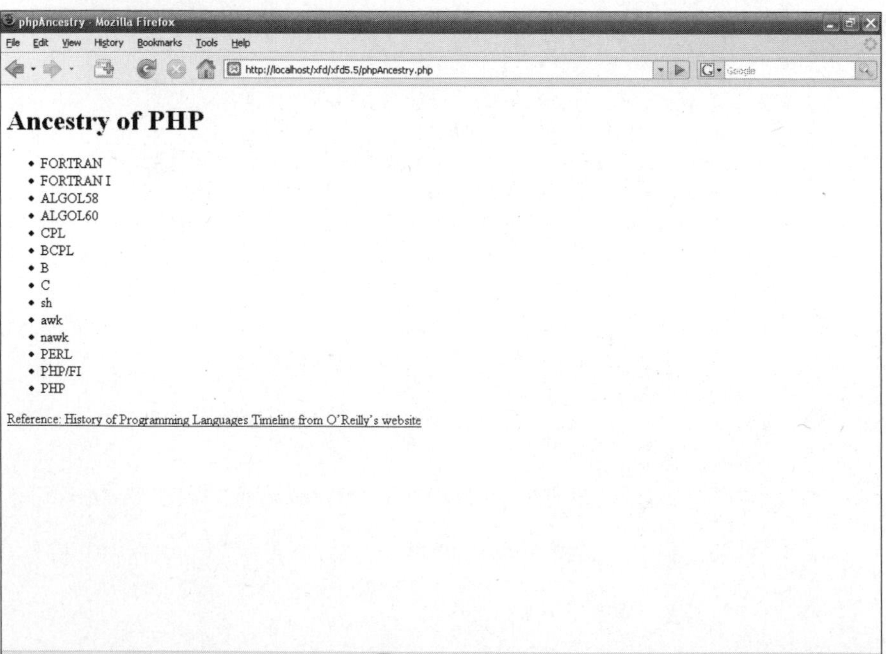

Figure 5-3: PHP's family tree, condensed.

The `foreach` loop allows you to just step through each array element one by one and print it or do anything else you may want with it.

The `foreach` loop can be used just as easily with multidimensional arrays (you don't have to type all this; just look on the CD-ROM for the code and view Figure 5-4 for the output):

```
<h1>Ancestry of PHP Expanded</h1>
<ul>
<?
$languageDetails["FORTRAN"] = array("1954", "FORmula TRANslation", "John W.
    Backus", "IBM", "<a href=\"http://en.wikipedia.org/wiki/Fortran\">Read
    More</a>");
$languageDetails["ALGOL58"] = array("1958", "ALGOrithmic Language", "Friedric L.
    Bauer", "Hermann Bottenburch", "Heinz Rutishauser", "Klaus Samelson", "John
    Backus", "Charles Katz", "Alan Perlis", "Joseph Henry Wegstein", "<a
    href=\"http://en.wikipedia.org/wiki/ALGOL_58\">Read More</a>");
$languageDetails["ALGOL60"] = array("1960", "ALGOrithmic Language", "Friedrich L.
    Bauer", "Peter Naur", "Heinz Rutishauser", "Klaus Samelson", "Bernard
    Vauguois", "Adriaan Van Wijngaarden", "Michael Woodger", "John W. Backus",
    "Julien Green", "Charles Katz", "John McCarthy", "Alan J. Perlis", "Joseph
    Henry Wegstein", "<a href=\"http://en.wikipedia.org/wiki/ALGOL\">Read
    More</a>");
$languageDetails["CPL"] = array("1963", "Combined Programming Language",
    "Christopher Strachey", "University of Cambridge", "University of London",
    "<a href=\"http://en.wikipedia.org/wiki/Combined_Programming_Language\">Read
    More</a>");
$languageDetails["BCPL"] = array("1967", "Basic Combined Programming Language",
    "Martin Richards", "University of Cambridge", "<a
    href=\"http://en.wikipedia.org/wiki/BCPL\">Read More</a>");
$languageDetails["B"] = array("1969", "Ken Thomspon", "Dennis Ritchie", "Bell
    Labs", "<a href=\"http://en.wikipeadia.org/B_programming_language\">Read
    More</a>");
$languageDetails["C"] = array("1972", "Dennis Ritchie", "Bell Labs", "<a
    href=\"http://en.wikipedia.org/wiki/C_programming_language\">Read
    More</a>");
$languageDetails["sh"] = array("1971", "tompson SHell", "Ken Thompson", "<a
    href=\"http://en.wikipedia.org/wiki/Thompson_shell\">Ream More</a>");
$languageDetails["awk"] = array("1978", "Accronym for first letters of author's
    last names", "Alfred Aho", "Peter Weinberger", "Brian Kernighan", "<a
    href=\"http://en.wikipedia.org/wiki/AWK\">Read More</a>");
$languageDetails["PERL"] = array("1987", "Doesn't actually stand for anything",
    "Larry Wall", "<a href=\"http://en.wikipedia.org/wiki/PERL\">Read
    More</a>");
$languageDetails["PHP"] = array("1995", "PHP: Hypertext Preprocessor (originally:
    Personal Home Page tools)", "Rasmus Lendorf", "<a
    href=\"http://en.wikipedia.org/wiki/php\">Read More</a>");

foreach($languageDetails as $language => $details){
    print "<li>$language</li>";
    print "<ul>";
    foreach($details as $detail){
        print "<li>$detail</li>";
    }
   print "</ul>";
}
?>
</ul>
```

```
<p><a href="http://www.oreilly.com/news/graphics/prog_lang_poster.pdf">Reference:
    History
 of Programming Languages Timeline from O'Reilly's website</a></p>
```

The nested `foreach` loops work great for the nested arrays. In the main `foreach` loop, each child array of the parent array is extracted into an array variable `$details` with each iteration of the loop. Then, in the nested `foreach` loop, each value of the extracted child `$details` array is stored in the `$detail` variable and printed to the user.

Note that because I wanted to print the name of the language being detailed, I used a variant of the `foreach` loop that extracted and stored not only the value, but also the index. Because I'm using an associative array for the parent array, each index is a word instead of a number. In this case, the word is the programming language name. I store the index in the `$language` variable and the value of the index (which, in this case, is an array) in the `$detail` variable.

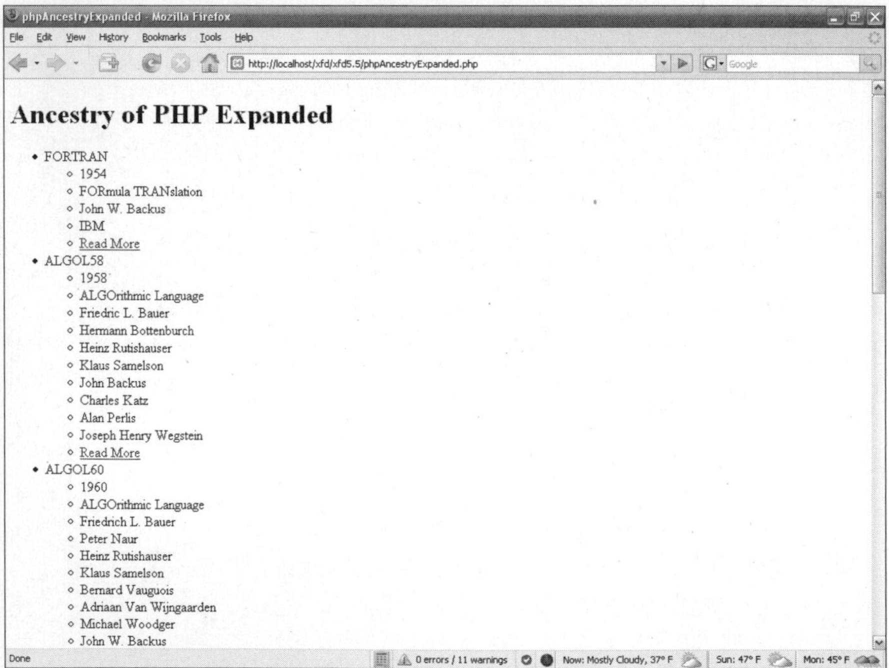

Figure 5-4: An expanded PHP family tree.

Associative arrays

When you use a string instead of an integer for your array indices, this is an associative array. It behaves the same as a normal array, but it gets a special name because it is special (in that it uses strings instead of integers as the array indices).

One thing worth mentioning about associative arrays is that although using strings without quotes around them will work as array indices, it is a big code-writing no-no. So don't do this:

```
$myArray[blah] = "the stuff you want to
        store";
```

Instead, do this:

```
$myArray["blah"] = "the stuff you want to
        store";
```

Forgetting to include quotes creates an undefined constant `blah` as the indices, rather than the string `blah`. This may seem like no big deal, but it can lead to subtle errors. The most simple scenario to explain is

```
$myArray[blah] = "the stuff you want to
        store";
$myArray["blah"] = "stuff you are trying
        to replace the original stuff
        you stored with";
Print $myArray[blah];
```

You can see that your program would print the wrong thing. Your `$myArray` array would now have two separate indices, `"blah"` and `blah`, which each hold a different value. See the manual at `http://php.net` for a more detailed discussion on this, if you're interested. Best practices state that you use quotes around the strings, which I also encourage you to do.

Using foreach with associative arrays

It's very common to have a large associative array that you want to evaluate. For example, PHP includes a very useful array called `$_SERVER` that gives you information about your server configuration (things like your hostname, PHP version, and lots of other useful stuff). The following code snippet runs through the entire `$_SERVER` array and prints each key/value pair:

```
foreach ($_SERVER as $key => $value){
  print "<p> \n";
  print "  $key: $value \n";
  print "<\p>";
} // end foreach
```

Here's how it works:

1. **Begin the `foreach` loop as normal.**

   The associative form of the `foreach` loop begins just like the regular one:

   ```
   foreach ($_SERVER as $key => $value){
   ```

2. Identify the associative array.

The first parameter is the array name:

```
foreach ($_SERVER as $key => $value){
```

3. Create a variable for the key.

Each element of an associative array has a key and a value. I put the key in a variable named `$key`:

```
foreach ($_SERVER as $key => $value){
```

4. Use the => symbol to indicate the associative relationship.

This symbol helps PHP recognize you're talking about an associative array lookup:

```
foreach ($_SERVER as $key => $value){
```

5. Assign the value of the element to a variable.

The `$value` variable holds the current value of the array item:

```
foreach ($_SERVER as $key => $value){
```

6. Use the variables inside your loop.

Each time PHP goes through the loop, it pulls another element from the array, puts that element's key in the `$key` array, and puts the associated value in `$value`. You can then use these variables inside the loop however you wish:

```
print "  $key: $value \n";
```

The `$_SERVER` variable is extremely useful for checking your environment, but you shouldn't make this program available on a publicly-accessible server. Doing so gives the bad guys information they could use to cause you headaches. Use it for testing and debugging, then remove it.

Breaking a String into an Array

Many times, it can be useful to break a string into an array programmatically, especially when reading input from a file.

Here are the two different ways of doing this:

- **`explode`:** `explode` takes one parameter as a delimiter and splits the string into an array based upon that one parameter.
- **`split`:** If you require regular expressions, `split`'s the way to go. `split` allows you to take complicated chunks of text, look for multiple different delimiters, and break it into an array based on the delimiters you specify.

`explode` works well with comma-separated value (CSV) files and the like, where all the parameters you wish to break the text on are the same. `split` works better for when there are many different parameters that you wish to break the text on or when the parameter you're looking for is complex.

Creating arrays with explode

Array creation with `explode` is very straightforward:

```
explode(" ", $theString);
```

The first value is the parameter on which you're splitting up the string. The second value is the string you would like to split into an array. In this example, the string would be split up on each space. You can put anything you want as the `split` parameter.

So, if you have the string that you want to store each word as a value in, enter the following code (see Figure 5-5 for the output):

```
<?
$theString = "PARC (Palo Alto Research Center) was one of the single most
    important hubs of invention for modern computing";

$theArray = explode(" ", $theString);

print_r($theArray);
?>
```

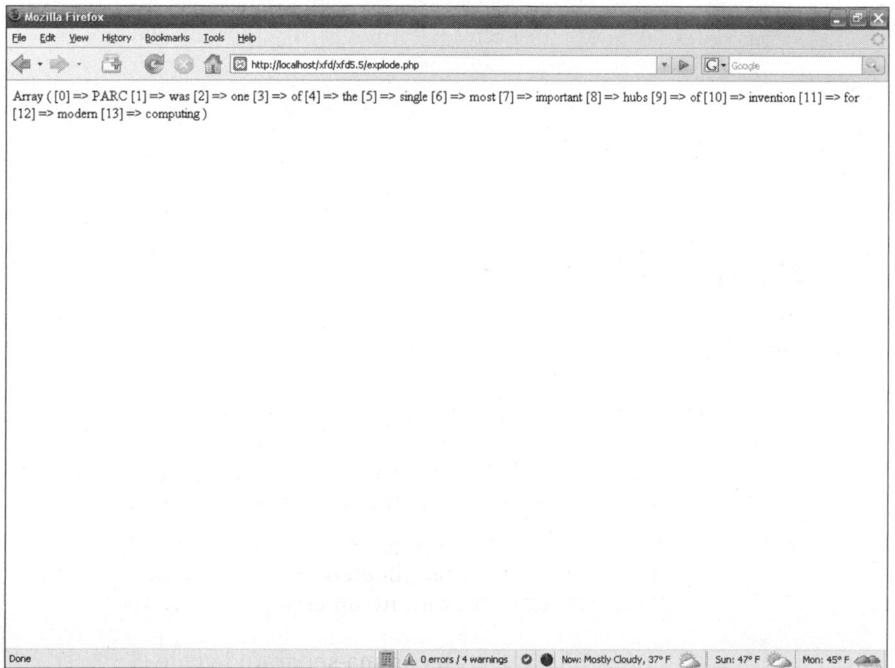

Figure 5-5: The string exploded into an array.

More on split and regex

If you're more comfortable with PERL-style regular expressions, use `preg_split()` instead of `split()`.

If you're looking for a character that can be in either lower- or uppercase, you can use `split()`, which is case-insensitive.

`split` can get really complicated, especially after you really start using regular expressions. I've only touched on the surface here. Other functions, such as `ereg()` and `ereg_replace()`, use regular expressions to make sure that strings have certain elements in them (to do things like make sure a user entered a valid e-mail address) and even to replace certain elements in a string. Also, you can see `http://us2.php.net/manual/en/ref.regex.php` for more on `split` and other regular expression functions.

The delimiter can be anything you want. If you're dealing with a comma-separated value (CSV) file, where each value is separated by a comma, your `explode` method might look like this:

```
$theArray = explode(",", $theString);
```

Creating arrays with split

`split` is a bit more complicated. `split` uses regular expressions to split a string into an array, which can make it a bit slower than `explode`, in some instances.

`split` looks exactly like `explode`, but instead of one character inside quotations, you can cram all the characters you want to split on into brackets inside the quotations.

An instance where you'd want to use `split` instead of `explode` could be when processing an e-mail address. A basic e-mail address has dots (`.`) and an at sign (`@`). So, to split on both of these, you could do the following (see Figure 5-6 for the output):

```
<?
$theString = "joe@somebody.net";

$theArray = split("[@.]", $theString);

print_r($theArray);
?>
```

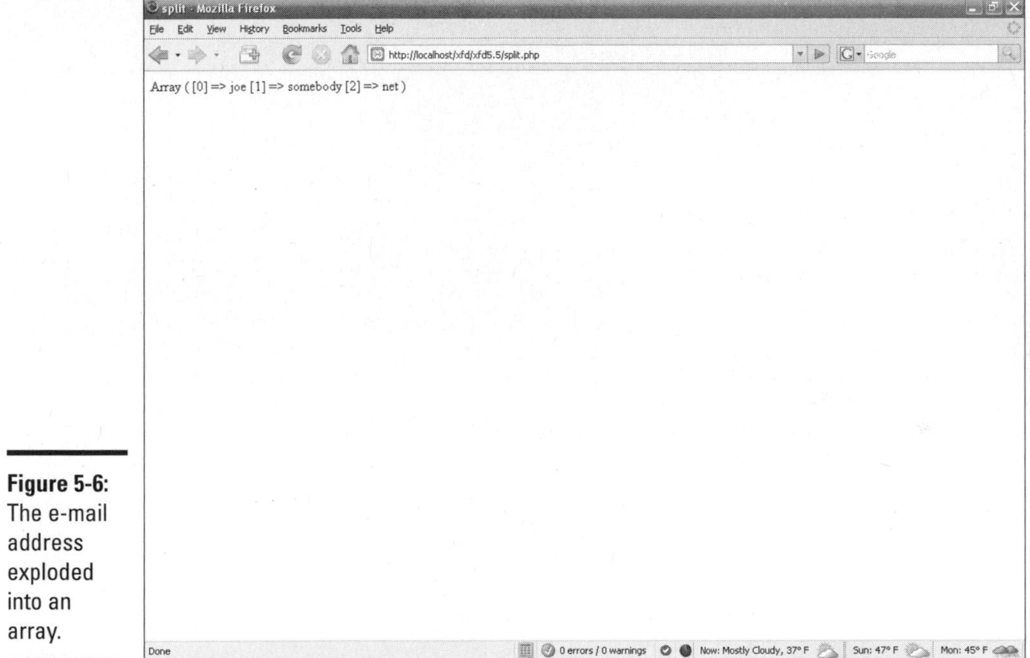

Figure 5-6: The e-mail address exploded into an array.

`split` works well for timestamps, e-mail addresses, and other things where there's more than just one unique delimiter that you wish to split the string on.

Chapter 6: Using Functions and Session Variables

In This Chapter

- Creating functions to manage your code's complexity
- Enhancing your code by using functions
- Working with variable scope
- Getting familiar with session variables
- Incorporating session variables into your code

PHP programs are used to solve interesting problems, which can get quite complex. In this chapter, you explore ways to manage this complexity. You discover how to build functions to encapsulate your code. You also learn how to use session variables to make your programs keep track of their values, even when the program is called many times.

Creating Your Own Functions

It won't take long before your code starts to get complex. Functions are used to manage this complexity. As an example, take a look at Figure 6-1.

Rolling dice the old-fashioned way

Before I show you how to improve your code with functions, look at a program that doesn't use functions, so you have something to compare with.

The `rollDice.php` program creates five random numbers and displays a graphic for each die. Here's the code:

```
<!DOCTYPE html PUBLIC "-//W3C//DTD XHTML 1.0 Strict//EN"
"http://www.w3.org/TR/xhtml1/DTD/xhtml1-strict.dtd">
<html lang="EN" dir="ltr" xmlns="http://www.w3.org/1999/xhtml">
  <head>
    <meta http-equiv="content-type" content="text/xml; charset=utf-8" />
    <title>rollDice1.php</title>
  </head>

  <body>
    <h1>RollDice 1</h1>
    <h2>Uses Sequential Programming</h2>
```

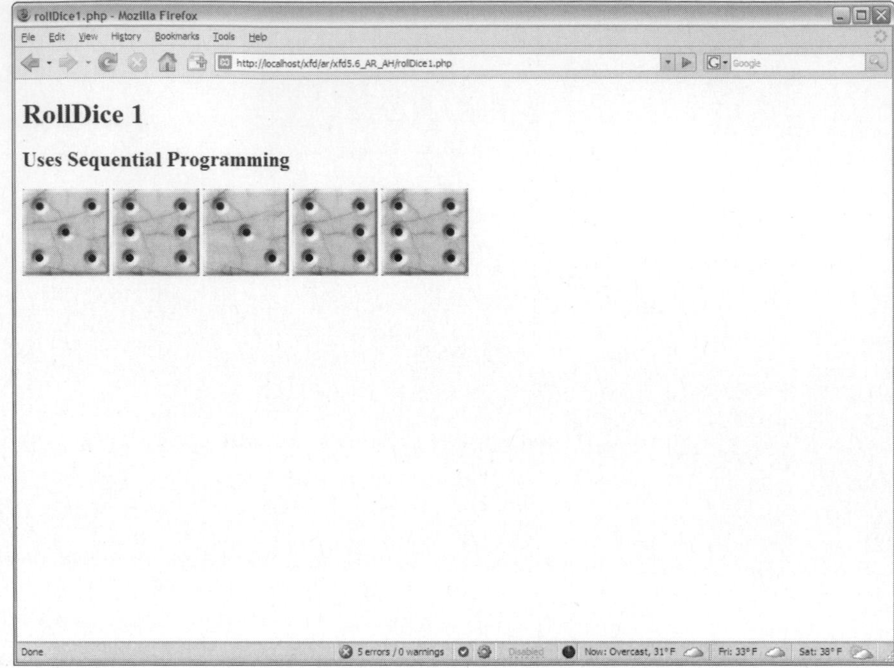

Figure 6-1: This program rolls five dice.

```
    <?php

$roll = rand(1,6);
$image = "die$roll.jpg";
print <<< HERE
    <img src = "$image"
         alt = "roll: $roll" />

HERE;

$roll = rand(1,6);
$image = "die$roll.jpg";
print <<< HERE
    <img src = "$image"
         alt = "roll: $roll" />

HERE;

$roll = rand(1,6);
$image = "die$roll.jpg";
print <<< HERE
    <img src = "$image"
         alt = "roll: $roll" />

HERE;

$roll = rand(1,6);
$image = "die$roll.jpg";
print <<< HERE
```

```
    <img src = "$image"
         alt = "roll: $roll" />

HERE;

$roll = rand(1,6);
$image = "die$roll.jpg";
print <<< HERE
    <img src = "$image"
         alt = "roll: $roll" />

HERE;
    ?>
  </body>
</html>
```

There are some interesting features of this code:

- **The built-in `rand()` function rolls a random number.** Whenever possible, try to find functions that can help you. The `rand()` function produces a random integer. If you use two parameters, the resulting number will be in the given range. To roll a standard six-sided die, use `rand(1,6)`:

  ```
  $roll = rand(1,6);
  ```

- **I have created an image for each possible roll.** To make this program more visually appealing, I created an image for each possible die roll. The images are called `die1.jpg`, `die2.jpg`, and so on. All these images are stored in the same directory as the PHP program.
- **The `img` tag is created based on the die roll.** Once I have a die roll, it's easy to create an image based on that roll:

  ```
  $image = "die$roll.jpg";
  print <<< HERE
      <img src = "$image"
           alt = "roll: $roll" />

  HERE;
  ```

- **The die-rolling code is repeated five times.** If you can roll one die, you can easily roll five. It's as easy as copying and pasting the code. This seems pretty easy, but it leads to problems. What if I want to change the way I roll the dice? If so, I'll have to change the code five times. What if I want to roll 100 dice? The program will quickly become unwieldy. In general, if you find yourself copying and pasting code, you can improve the code by adding a function.

Improving code with functions

Functions are pre-defined code fragments. Once you define a function, you can use it as many times as you wish. The outward appearance of this program is identical to `rollDice1.php`, but the internal organization is quite different:

```
<!DOCTYPE html PUBLIC "-//W3C//DTD XHTML 1.0 Strict//EN"
"http://www.w3.org/TR/xhtml1/DTD/xhtml1-strict.dtd">
<html lang="EN" dir="ltr" xmlns="http://www.w3.org/1999/xhtml">
  <head>
    <meta http-equiv="content-type" content="text/xml; charset=utf-8" />
    <title>rollDice2.php</title>
  </head>

  <body>
    <h1>RollDice 2</h1>
    <h2>Uses Functions</h2>
    <?php

function rollDie(){
  $roll = rand(1,6);
  $image = "die$roll.jpg";
  print <<< HERE
    <img src = "$image"
         alt = "roll: $roll" />

HERE;
} // end rollDie

for ($i = 0; $i < 5; $i++){
  rollDie();
} // end for loop

    ?>

  </body>
</html>
```

Here's how things have changed in this version:

1. **Use the `function` keyword to define a function.**

   The `function` keyword indicates that a function definition will follow. The code inside the definition won't be run immediately, but instead, PHP will "remember" the code inside the function definition and play it back on demand:

   ```
   function rollDie(){
   ```

2. **Give the function a name.**

   The function name should indicate what the function does. I call my function `rollDie()` because that's what it does (rolls a die):

   ```
   function rollDie(){
   ```

3. **Specify arguments with parentheses.**

   You can send *arguments* (special variables for your function to work with) by indicating them in the parentheses. This function does not need arguments, so I leave the parentheses empty:

   ```
   function rollDie(){
   ```

For more information on functions, arguments, and the `return` statement, turn to Book IV, Chapter 4. Functions in PHP act almost exactly like their cousins in JavaScript.

4. **Begin the function definition with a left brace ({).**

   The left brace is used to indicate the beginning of the function code.

5. **Indent the code that makes up your function.**

   Use indentation to indicate which code is part of your function. In this case, the function generates the random number and prints an image tag based on that random number:

```
function rollDie(){
  $roll = rand(1,6);
  $image = "die$roll.jpg";
  print <<< HERE
    <img src = "$image"
         alt = "roll: $roll" />

HERE;
} // end rollDie
```

6. **Denote the end of the function with a right brace (}).**
7. **Call the function by referring to it.**

   Once the function is defined, you can use it in your code as if it were built into PHP. In this example, I call the function inside a loop:

```
for ($i = 0; $i < 5; $i++){
  rollDie();
} // end for loop
```

Naming functions and variables

It can be hard to come up with a good naming scheme for your variables and functions. Doing so is very important because when you come back to your program, if you haven't named your functions and variables consistently, you'll have a hard time understanding what you wrote. Here are two common naming schemes to make this simple: underscores "_" between words or camel-casing.

Using underscores is as straightforward as `separating_each_word_with_an_underscore`. It's readable, but it's ugly and can cause the variable names to get awfully lengthy.

The method I prefer and use throughout this book is *camel-casing* — each new word after the first word gets capitalized `justLikeThis`. It takes up less space than the underscore method and makes reading the code quicker, and after you get used to it, you won't even notice it anymore.

Tons of naming schemes are out there, and even if you don't use either of these, picking one and being consistent is important. Searching for *naming variables* in Google returns over a million hits, so plenty of resources are out there if you want to find more.

Because the code is defined in a function, it's a simple matter to run it as many times as I want. Functions also make your code easier to read because the details of rolling the dice are hidden in the function.

Managing variable scope

Two kinds of scope are in PHP: global and local.

If you define a variable outside a function, it has the potential to be used inside any function. If you define a variable inside a function, you can access it only from inside the function in which it was created. See Book IV, Chapter 4 for more on variable scope.

So, if you have a variable that you want to access and modify from within the function, you either need to pass it through the parentheses or access it with the global modifier.

The following code will print "hello world!" only once:

```
<?php
$output = "<p>hello world!</p>";

function helloWorld(){
    global $output;

    print $output;
}

function helloWorld2(){
    print $output;
}

helloWorld();
helloWorld2();
?>
```

I left the global keyword off in the `helloWorld2()` function, so it didn't print at all because inside the function, the local variable `$output` is undefined. By putting the global keyword on in the `helloWorld()` function, I let it know I was referring to a global variable defined outside the function.

PHP defaults to local inside variables because it doesn't want you to accidentally access or overwrite other variables throughout the program. For more information about global and local scoping, check out `http://us3.php.net/global`.

Returning data from functions

At the end of the function, you can tell the function to return one (and only one) thing. The return statement should be the last statement of your function. The return statement isn't required, but it can be handy.

The `getName()` function in the following code example will return `world` to be used by the program. The program will print it once and store the text in a variable to be printed multiple times later, as shown in the following code and Figure 6-2:

```
<?php
function getName(){
    return "world";
}

print "<h1>Hello" . getName() . "</h1>";

$name = getName();

print <<<HERE
<p>$name, welcome to our site. We are so very happy to have you here.</p>
<p>If you would like to contact us $name, just use the form on the contact
    page.</p>
HERE;
?>
```

For more on `return` statements see `http://de3.php.net/return`.

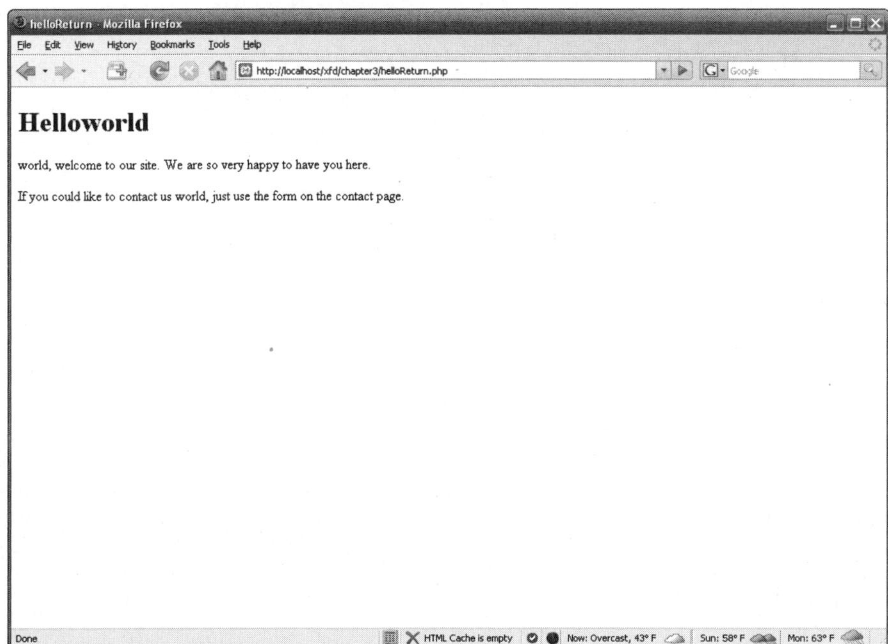

Figure 6-2: An example of a function with a return statement.

Managing Persistence with Session Variables

Server-side programming is very handy, but it has one major flaw. Every connection to the server is an entirely different transaction. Sometimes, you'll want to reuse a variable between several calls of the program. As an example, take a look at `rollDice3.php` in Figure 6-3.

The interesting feature of `rollDice3.php` happens when you reload the page. Take a look at Figure 6-4. This is still `rollDice3.php`, after I refreshed the browser a few times. Take a look at the total. It increases with each roll.

The `rollDice3.php` program is interesting because it defies normal server-side programming behavior. In a normal PHP program, every time you refresh the browser, the program starts over from scratch. Every variable starts out new.

Understanding session variables

The `rollDice3.php` program acts differently. It has a mechanism for keeping track of the total rolls and number of visits to the page.

When a visitor accesses your Web site, she's automatically assigned a unique session `id`. The session `id` is either stored in a cookie or in the URL. *Sessions* allow you to keep track of things for that specific user during her time on your site and during future visits if she's not cleared her cache or deleted her cookies.

Any mundane hacker can sniff out your session `id`s if you allow them to be stored in the URL. To keep this from happening, use the `session.use_only_cookies` directive in your PHP configuration file. This may be inconvenient to users who don't want you to have a cookie stored on their machine, but it's necessary if you're storing anything sensitive in their session.

Sessions are great because they are like a big box that the user carries around with him that you can just throw stuff into. Even if the user comes back to the site multiple times, the variables stored in the session retain their values. If you have hundreds of users accessing your site at the same time, each one will still have access to only their own versions of the variable.

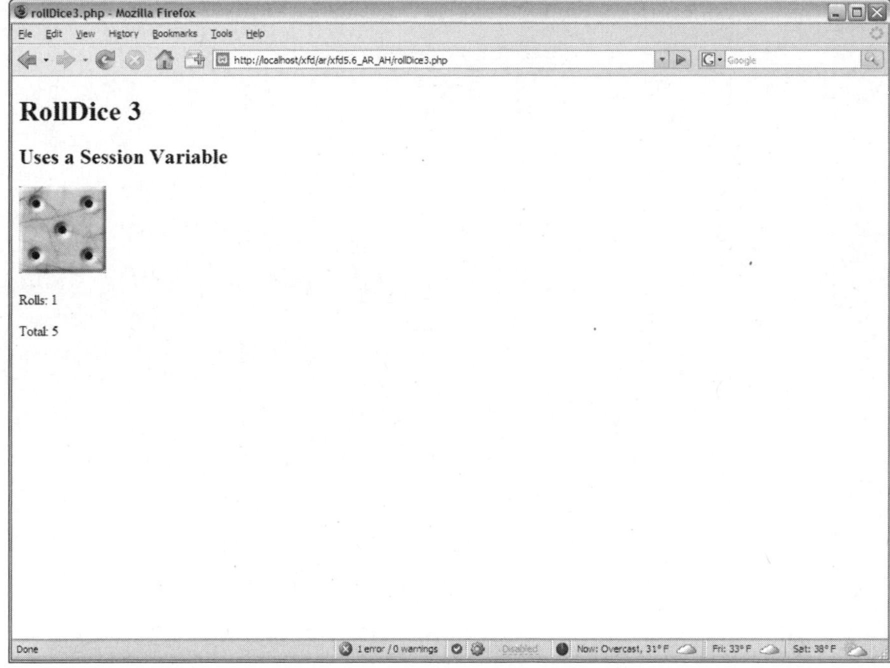

Figure 6-3: This page displays a roll, the number of rolls, and the total rolls so far.

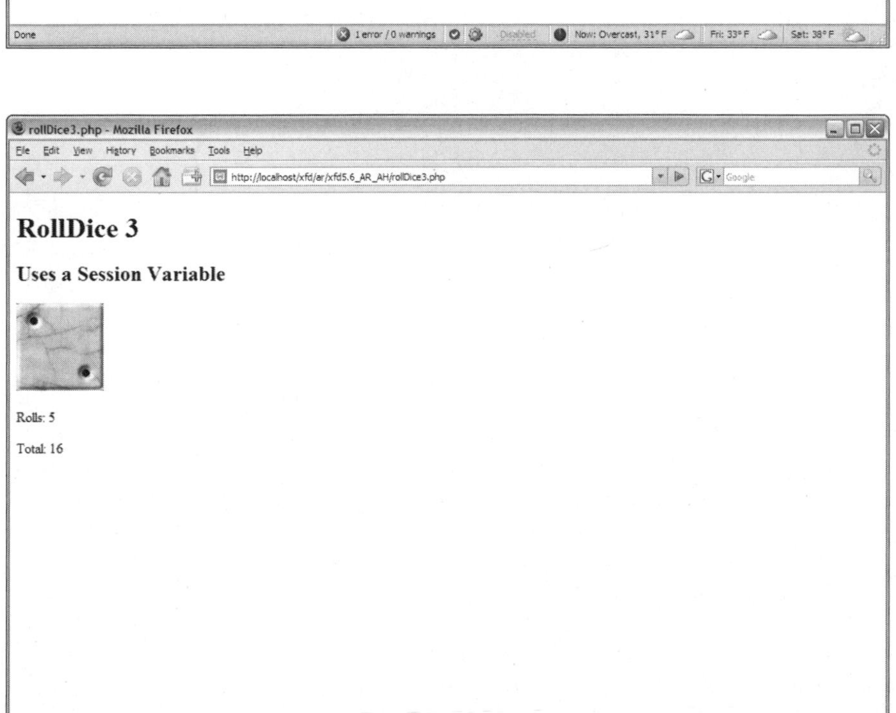

Figure 6-4: The count and total values keep on growing.

Here's the code for `rollDice3.php`:

```
<?php
  session_start();
?>

<!DOCTYPE html PUBLIC "-//W3C//DTD XHTML 1.0 Strict//EN"
"http://www.w3.org/TR/xhtml1/DTD/xhtml1-strict.dtd">
<html lang="EN" dir="ltr" xmlns="http://www.w3.org/1999/xhtml">
  <head>
    <meta http-equiv="content-type" content="text/xml; charset=utf-8" />
    <title>rollDice3.php</title>
  </head>

  <body>
    <h1>RollDice 3</h1>
    <h2>Uses a Session Variable</h2>

    <?php

function rollDie(){
  global $total;

  $roll = rand(1,6);
  $image = "die$roll.jpg";
  print <<< HERE
    <img src = "$image"
         alt = "roll: $roll" />

HERE;
  $total = $_SESSION["total"];
  $total += $roll;
  $_SESSION["total"] = $total;

} // end rollDie

$count = $_SESSION["count"];
$count++;
$_SESSION["count"] = $count;

rollDie();

print "    <p>Rolls: $count</p> \n";
print "    <p>Total: $total</p> \n";

    ?>
  </body>
</html>
```

This program rolls a die, but it uses session variables to keep track of the number of rolls and total value rolled. The session variable is updated every time the same user (using the same browser) visits the site.

Adding session variables to your code

Here's how to incorporate sessions into your programs:

1. **Begin your code with a call to `session_start()`.**

   If you want to use session variables, your code must begin with a `session_start()` call, even before the DOCTYPE definition. I put a tiny `<?php ?>` block at the beginning of the program to enable sessions:

   ```
   <?php
     session_start();
   ?>
   ```

2. **Load session variables from the `$_SESSION` superglobal.**

   `$_SESSION` is a superglobal array (much like `$_REQUEST`). Create a local variable and extract the current value from the `$_SESSION` associative array:

   ```
   $total = $_SESSION["total"];
   ```

   If there is no `total` element in the `$_SESSION` array, a null value is assigned to the variable, instead (which evaluates to 0 in a numeric context).

Sessions and security

The session mechanism is powerful and easy to use. It isn't quite foolproof, though. Sessions are automatically handled through a browser mechanism called *cookies.* Cookies aren't inherently good or evil, but they've gotten a bad reputation because some programs use them maliciously. You'll occasionally run across a user who's turned cookies off, but this is not a major problem, as PHP can automatically use other options when cookies are not available. There's rarely a need to work with cookies directly in PHP, as sessions are a higher-level abstraction of the cookie concept.

Like all data passed through the HTTP protocol, session and cookie information is passed entirely in the clear. A person with evil intent can capture your session information and use it to do bad things.

Generally, you should stay away from sensitive information (credit card data, Social Security numbers, and so on) unless you're extremely comfortable with security measures. If you must pass potentially sensitive data in your PHP program, investigate a technology called TLS (Transport Layer Security), which automatically encrypts all data transferred through your site. TLS replaces the older SSL technology and is available as a free plugin to Apache servers.

3. **Store session variables in the `$_SESSION` superglobal.**

   You can manipulate the local variable, but if you want to use the value the next time the program runs for this user, you need to store the value back into the session after you change it.

   For example, the following code loads the variable `$count` from the session, adds one to it, and stores it back into the session:

   ```
   $count = $_SESSION["count"];
   $count++;
   $_SESSION["count"] = $count;
   ```

If you want to reset your sessions for testing purposes, you can write a quick program to set the variables to 0, or you can use the Web Developer toolbar: Cookies ⇨ Clear Session Cookies. Note that the session data itself isn't stored in the cookie. The cookie just contains a reference number so the server can look up the session data in a file stored on the server.

Chapter 7: Working with Files and Directories

In This Chapter

- ✔ **Saving to text files**
- ✔ **Reading from text files**
- ✔ **Reading a file as an array**
- ✔ **Parsing delimited text data**
- ✔ **Working with file and directory functions**

An important part of any programming language is file manipulations. Whether you need to create a comma-separated value (CSV) file or generate a dynamic list of files in a directory, or just need a semi-permanent place to log records on the server, file manipulation functions are an indispensable part of your PHP toolbox.

Text File Manipulation

Work with text files is split into two basic categories: writing and reading. Writing and reading come down to six basic functions. See the following bullet list for a brief explanation of the six basic file functions. Each of these six functions has an entire sub-section in the following "Writing text to files" and "Reading from text files" sections:

- **`fopen()`:** Stores a connection to a file you specify in a variable you specify
- **`fwrite()`:** Writes text you specify to a file you specify
- **`fclose()`:** Closes the connection to a file you specify that you created with `fopen()`
- **`fgets()`:** Reads a line from a file you specify
- **`feof()`:** Checks to see if you have hit the end of a file you specify during a file read
- **`file()`:** Puts the entire contents of a file you specify into an array

Writing text to files

This section details the functions needed to access and write to a file, such as how to request access to a file from PHP with the `fopen()` function, write to the file using the `fwrite()` function, and let PHP know you are done with the file with the `fclose()` function.

fopen()

In order to do any file manipulations, you must tell PHP about the file you would like to manipulate and tell PHP how you would like to manipulate that file.

The `fopen()` function has two required parameters that you must pass to it; the path to the file and the type of file manipulation you would like to perform (called the *mode*).

The `fopen()` function returns a connection to the requested file if it is successful (the connection is called a *pointer* — see the "Official file manipulation terminology" sidebar for more information). If there is an error, the `fopen()` function returns `False`. Whatever the `fopen()` function returns (the connection or `False`), it should be assigned to a variable (called a *stream*).

Here is an example of the `fopen()` function (see the "Creating a CSV file" section, later in this chapter, for an example of the `fopen()` function in action):

```
$fileConnection = fopen($theFile, $theMode);
```

In the preceding example, the file connection returned by the `fopen()` function is assigned to the variable `$fileConnection`. The variable `$theFile` would contain the path to a file (for example, both `C:\\xampp\\htdocs\\inc\\info.txt` and `/inc/log.txt` are valid file paths). The file must be in a place the server can access, meaning that you can put the file anywhere you could put a PHP page for the server to serve. For example, you couldn't normally try to serve the file from your `My Documents` folder. It has to be a folder under the `htdocs` directory on your server. The variable `$theMode` would contain one of the values from the following list:

- **r:** Grants read-only access to the file.
- **w:** Grants write access to the file. Be careful, though, if you specify this mode for the `fopen()` function and use the `fwrite()` function, it will completely overwrite anything that may have been in the file. Don't use `w` if there's anything in the file you want to keep.
- **a:** Grants the right to append text to the file. When you specify this mode for the `fopen()` function and use the `fwrite()` function, the `fwrite()` function appends whatever text you specify to the end of the existing file.

✦ **`r+` or `w+`:** Grants read and write access to the file. I don't talk about `r+` and `w+` in this book, except to say that they're a special way of accessing the file. This special file access mode is called *random access.* This allows you to simultaneously read and write to the file. If you require this type of access, you probably should be using something more simple and powerful, like relational databases.

fwrite ()

After you have opened a file with the `fopen()` function and assigned the file connection to a variable (see the "fopen()" section, earlier in this chapter, for more information), you can use the file in your PHP code. You can either read from the file, or you can write to the file with the `fwrite()` function.

Depending on what mode you specified when you opened the file with the `fopen()` function, the `fwrite()` function will either overwrite the entire contents of the file (if you used the `w` mode), or it will append the text you specify to the end of the file (if you used the `a` mode).

Official file manipulation terminology

If you look at the documentation for `fopen()`, or any of the file manipulation functions, you will see some funny terminology. I decided, to keep things simple, I would use more recognizable, easily understandable terms. I wanted you to know that I switched things up a little bit and give you a quick primer to help you out if you did happen to look at the official documentation or talk to a more seasoned programmer who might use the official terms.

According to the official online PHP documentation, the `fopen()` function *returns a file pointer, and binds a named resource to a stream.*

What this means is that when you use the `fopen()` function, it opens a file (much like you would do if you opened the file in Notepad) and returns a pointer to that file.

The pointer is like if you put your mouse arrow at the beginning of the file and clicked there to create the little blinky-line cursor telling Notepad where you are focusing (where you would like to begin editing the text). The pointer is PHP's focus on the file.

With the `fopen()` function, PHP's focus is *bound to a stream,* which means that it is attached to a variable. When you use the `fopen()` function, you associate the file with a variable of your choosing. This variable is how PHP keeps track of the location of the file and keeps track of where PHP's cursor is in the file. Normally, when you think of a stream, you might think of a one-way flow. But, in this case, the stream can either be read into the program character by character, line by line, or you can move the cursor around to any point in the file that you want. So, rather than being just a one-way flow, the stream is really an open connection to a file.

See `http://us.php.net/manual/en/function.fopen.php` for more detail on the `fopen()` function.

The fwrite() function has two required parameters you must pass to it; the connection to the file that was established by the fopen() function and the text you wish to write to the file. The fwrite() function returns the number of bytes written to the file on success and False on failure.

Here is an example of the fwrite() function (see the "Creating a CSV file" section, further in this chapter, for an example of the fwrite() function in action):

```
$writeResults = fwrite($fileConnection, $text);
```

The fwrite() function can also be written fputs(). fwrite() and fputs() both do the exact same thing. fputs() is just a different way of writing fwrite() (fputs() is referred to as an *alias* of fwrite()).

fclose()

After you are finished working with the file, it's important to close the file connection.

To close the connection to a file you have been working with, you must pass the connection to the file you wish to close to the fclose() function. The fclose() function will return True if it is successful in closing the connection to the file and False if it is not successful in closing the connection to the file.

Here is an example of the fclose() function:

```
fclose($fileConnection);
```

Creating a CSV file

The most common reason to write to text files from PHP is to create comma-separated value (CSV) files. CSV files are usually opened in a spreadsheet program, such as Microsoft Excel. This section is an example of how to use the functions from previous sections in this chapter (fopen(), fwrite(), and fclose()) to create a CSV file from a database table. (See Chapter 8 in this minibook for more on working with databases in PHP.)

You can think of a CSV file as a big table. Each column is separated by commas, and each row is separated by newline characters (\n). So, the following text

```
row1 item1, row1 item2\n
row2 item1, row2 item2
```

would generate the following cells if opened in a spreadsheet program (such as Excel):

```
row1 item1          row1 item2
row2 item1          row2 item2
```

When reading items back into PHP from a CSV file, you use the commas and newlines to parse the data so that it can be used by the program. (See the "Reading from a CSV file" section, later in this chapter.)

REMEMBER

Don't forget to end each line with a newline (`\n`) character.

str_replace ()

While commas are the most common delimiter, you can use tabs (`\t`), pipes (`|`), tildes (~), or anything else you want to separate the text. Whatever you decide to use as the delimiter, make sure errant occurrences of the delimiting character don't appear in the text and throw off the scheme. To protect against this, you can run the `str_replace()` function on the text before adding the delimiters and inserting it into the file; this replaces unwanted occurrences of the delimiting character with an empty string.

The `str_replace()` function takes three parameters; the string to be replaced, the string to replace it with, and the string the replacing is to be done in:

```
$text = str_replace(",", "", $text);
```

Escaping with HTML entities

If you're planning on displaying the user's input to the screen, escape all the special characters before saving the user's input to a file or sending it to the browser. Otherwise, some malicious user could use some simple CSS and HTML to replace your entire Web page with one of his choosing. Remember, paranoia is your friend. The simplest way to guard against this is to use the `htmlentities()` function:

```
$userInput =
    htmlentities($userInput);
```

This function converts any HTML characters the user may have entered into the character's HTML entities equivalent. That is, if the user entered `<div>`, it'd be converted to `<div>`. When you display it back to the page, instead of creating a new HTML div, the browser will simply output the literal string `<div>` to the user.

If, for some reason, you want to decode these entities, use the `html_entity_decode()` function. This works exactly like its `htmlentities()` counterpart, just in reverse.

Because you may not want all of the commas removed from your text, you might consider using something that is not likely to occur in your text as the delimiter, such as a pipe (|) or tilde (~), or even just a custom multi-character delimiter like `~myDelimiter|`. The problem with the multi-character delimiter method is that if you plan on using the text file in a spreadsheet program (such as Excel), the spreadsheet program may not support multi-character delimiters. The multi-character delimiter method is best for storing text that you only plan on reading back into PHP and not for text you plan on using in a spreadsheet program.

The CSV file creation example

This CSV file creation example performs the following tasks:

1. Opens a connection to a file
2. Connects to a database
3. Gets the desired information out of a database table
4. Writes information from the table to the file
5. Builds an HTML table showing what was written to the file
6. Closes the connection to the file

See Chapter 8 of this minibook for more on database connection and manipulation. The CD-ROM contains the full code for this example, as well as the SQL to generate the table used in this example. Figure 7-1 shows the HTML and CSV file generated by this example.

Here is the PHP code for the CSV file creation example:

```
  <body>
<?
//This is the CSV file we want to create
$theFile = "employees.csv";
//We want to completely over-write the file, so use "w".
$theMode = "w";
//prepare the string to be filled with employees and printed to the file.
$employees = "";

/*
* If we successfully connect to the file, do all of the file operations.
* Otherwise, print an error.
*/
if($fileConnection = fopen($theFile, $theMode)){

  //connect to the database
  $conn = mysql_connect("localhost", "xfd", "xfd123") or die(mysql_error());
  mysql_select_db("file_manipulation", $conn) or die(mysql_error());

  //get the employees out of the employee table
  $sql = "SELECT * FROM employees";
  $result = mysql_query($sql, $conn);

  /*
```

```
 * for each employees row, print a new table row,
 * and add the employee to the text string to be printed to the file.
 */
 print "<table>";
 while($row = mysql_fetch_array($result, MYSQL_ASSOC)){
   print "<tr>\n";

   foreach($row as $col=>$val){
     print "\t<td>$val</td>\n";

     //escape commas in string
     $val = str_replace(",", "\,", $val);

     $employees .= $val . ",";
   }
   print "</tr>\n\n";

   //go to the next line in the CSV file to prepare for the next record.
   $employees .= "\n";
 }
 print "</table>";

 //print the employees to the file
 if(fwrite($fileConnection, $employees)){
   print "<p>$employees successfully written to the file.</p>";
 }else{
   print "<p>There was an error while attempting to write $employees to the
    file.</p>";
 }

 //close the file
 if(fclose($fileConnection)){
   print "<p>Closed the file connection successfully.</p>";
 }else{
   print "<p>Unable to close the file connection.</p>";
 }
}else{
 print "<p>Unable to connect to the file.</p>";
}

?>
 </body>
```

In the CSV file creation example, the text file was written to only once, at the very end of the program. If the `a` mode had been used, instead of the `w` mode, each record could have been written to the file as it was read from the database, but that would have put much more strain on the server and made the program slower. File reads and writes are very expensive in terms of processing time and memory for the server, in comparison to simple string concatenation in a PHP program.

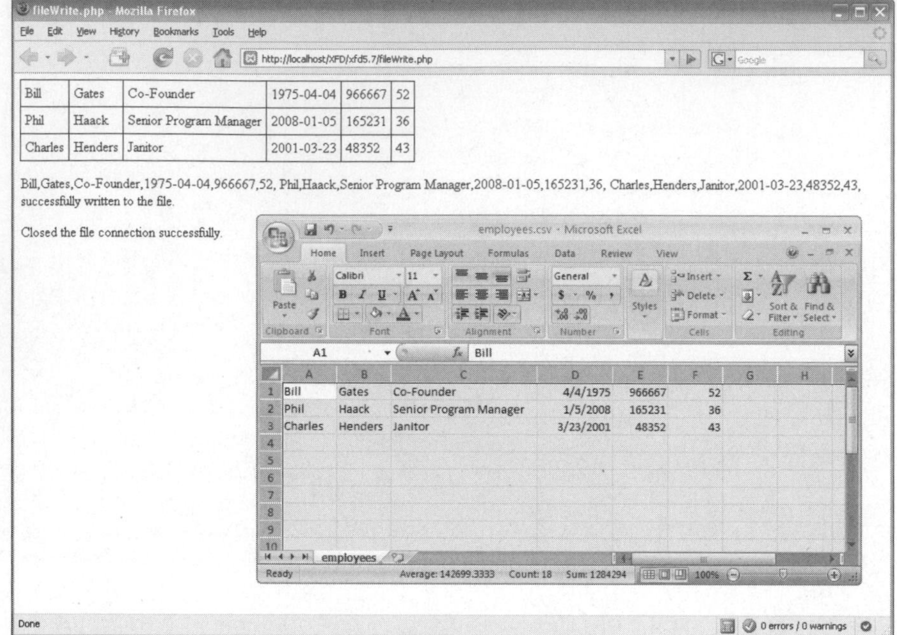

Figure 7-1: The HTML file contains the raw text to be written to the file; the CSV file (opened in Excel) renders as a spreadsheet.

Reading from text files

This section details the functions needed to read from a text file. Requesting access to a file from PHP with the `fopen()` function (See the "fopen()" section, earlier in this chapter) grants you access to the file. When you have access to the file, you can read from the file one line at a time with the `fgets()` function. With a combination of the `fgets()` function and the `feof()` function, you can iterate through the entire file, reading the file into a PHP program one line at a time. With the `file()` function, you can read the entire file into an array in a PHP program.

fgets()

After you have opened a file with the `fopen()` function and assigned the file connection to a variable, you can use the file in your PHP code. You can either write to the file, or you can read from the file. One method of reading from the file is to use the `fgets()` function. The `fgets()` function reads one line from the file. You can combine the `fgets()` function with the `feof()` function to read each line of the file, starting with the first line. (See the "feof()" section and the "file()" section, both later in this chapter).

In order to be able to read from the file, you must have specified either the `r`, `r+`, or `w+` mode when using the `fopen()` function.

To use the `fgets()` function, you must pass it a variable containing the connection to the file that you established with the `fopen()` function. The `fgets()` function returns the string read from the file on success and `False` on failure.

Here is an example of the `fgets()` function (See the "Reading from a CSV file" section, later in this chapter, for an example of the `fgets()` function in action):

```
$line = fgets($fileConnection);
```

If you know exactly how much of each line you want to read from a file, you can pass the `fgets()` function an optional length parameter after the file connection. See the online PHP documentation for more information (`http://us.php.net/fgets`).

feof()

The `feof()` function tests to see if you have hit the end of a file when you are reading from a file. When you combine the `feof()` function with the `fgets()` function, you can read the contents of a file into your PHP program one line at a time.

To use the `feof()` function, you must pass it a variable containing a connection to the file that you established with the `fopen()` function. (See the "fopen()" section, earlier in this chapter, for more information.) The `feof()` function will return `True` if the end of the file has been reached (or if an error occurs), otherwise it returns `False`.

Here is an example of the `feof()` function. This example will print a specified file, line by line, to the screen:

```
while(!feof($fileConnection)){
  print fgets($fileConnection);
}
```

The actual `feof()` function itself is `feof($fileConnection)`.

file()

The `file()` function allows you to read the entire file at once and load it into an array. Using the `file()` function is convenient because, whereas the `fgets()` function requires you to open the file, read it line by line, and then close the file, when you use the `file()` function, it loads the file into an array, which you can do whatever you want with. You do not have to use the `fopen()` function or the `fclose()` function with the `file()` function. The `file()` function performs the file open and close on it's own.

The only problem with the `file()` function is that when a file is particularly large, loading the entire file into memory can be bad for your server. The bigger the file, the more memory it takes up. Therefore, it isn't recommended you use the `file()` function for very large files. Instead, for large files, it is better to read them in one line at a time with the `fgets()` function.

The `file()` function has only one parameter you must pass to it — the path to the file you wish to read. This path can be relative to the PHP file calling it, or it can be a URL. If successful, the `file()` function will return an array containing the contents of the file. Each line of the file will include the newline character (`\n`) and will be a separate element in the array. (See Book IV, Chapter 4 for more on arrays.) If it fails, the `file()` function will return `False`.

Here is an example of the `file()` function. This function stores the entire contents of a file named `log.dat` in an array called `$logData`:

```
$logData = file("log.dat");
```

Reading from a CSV file

The most common reason to read from text files with PHP is to extract data from comma-separated value (CSV) files. CSV files are usually created with a spreadsheet program, such as Microsoft Excel. This section is an example of how to use the functions explained in previous sections in this chapter (`fopen()`, `fgets()`, `feof()`, and `fclose()`) to read from a CSV file and insert the data from the file into a database table. (See Chapter 8 in this minibook for more on working with databases in PHP.)

Bringing text back in and parsing it is a little bit trickier than saving it to the file (refer to the "Creating a CSV file" section, earlier in this chapter). For parsing data, you have to expand the code to include the actual parsing.

split()

When you retrieve the text with the `fgets()` function, it's all just one big line. In order to use the text, you need to split it up by whatever you used as the delimiter.

The `split()` function takes two parameters, the delimiter you wish to split the text on and the text you wish to split. The `split()` function returns an array of the split-up text if it is successful and `False` if it fails.

Here is an example of the `split()` function. This function stores the contents of the `$line` variable split into an array on the pipe (`|`) delimiter in the `$lineArray` variable:

```
$lineArray = split("|", $line);
```

stripslashes()

If you're receiving the text to be split from a form submitted by the user, you may end up with some funny results from the `split()` function, especially if you used tabs to delimit your data. Sometimes, PHP will add slashes before single quotes ('), double quotes ("), and backslashes (\). This is because the PHP directive `magic_quotes_gpc` is on by default (in your `php.ini` file). This causes PHP to run `addslashes()` on all text sent through `post`, `get`, or cookies, which means that ', ", and \ will turn into \', \", and \\ when they're submitted through a form. To reverse this for when you're printing to the page (so that you don't have funny output), run the `stripslashes()` function on the line before you split it:

```
$line = stripslashes($line);
```

Now, you have an array containing the split elements of the line to do whatever you want with.

list()

The `list()` function will take an array and distribute its contents to variables you specify. This makes it perfect for using with the `split()` function and anything where you want to print the contents of an array out to the screen or insert them into a database.

The `list()` function is different from most functions because it can take a large number of parameters. To use the `list()` function, you need to know exactly how many items your array has and pass a different parameter to the `list()` function for each array item. The list function doesn't return anything. It assigns the array elements to the variables you specify. Normally, functions return `False` if they fail, but if the `list()` function fails, PHP just errors out and crashes. The `list()` function (like `array()`), technically speaking, isn't a function at all, but rather is a *language construct.*

Here is an example of the `list()` function. This function takes an array with three items and stores each of the three items in a separate variable:

```
list($var1, $var2, $var3) = $anArray;
```

The `list()` function works only on numerical arrays and assumes that the array index begins at `0`. If you want to use the `list()` function with associative arrays, surround the array variable with the `array_values()` function. (See `http://us3.php.net/list` for more information on the `list()` function.)

Using split() and list() together

You can combine the `split()` and the `list()` functions to get one powerful, concise result:

```
list($fname, $lname, $position, $startDate, $salary, $age) = split(",", $line);
```

The `split()` generates an array that the `list()` catches and distributes to variables. You can then take those variables and easily print them to the screen (or do anything else you might want with them):

```
print "<p>$name<br /> $phone<br /> $email<br /> $comments</p>";
```

Without the `list()` function, you'd be stuck doing something like this:

```
print "<p>" . $lineArray[0] . "<br />";
print $lineArray[1] . "<br />";
print $lineArray[2] . "<br />";
print $lineArray[3] . "</p>";
```

Not very convenient, is it?

The CSV file read example

This CSV file read example performs the following tasks:

1. Opens a connection to a file
2. Reads the text from the file, line by line
3. Closes the connection to the file
4. Connects to a database
5. Builds an HTML table showing what was read from the file
6. Builds a SQL statement to insert the data from the file into the database
7. Inserts the data from the file into the database

See Chapter 8 in this minibook for more on database connection and manipulation. The CD-ROM contains the full code, as well as the text file, used in this example. Figure 7-2 shows the HTML generated by this example. (See the "Creating a CSV file" section for this example's counterpart.)

Here is the PHP code for the CSV file read example:

```
<?
//This is the CSV file we want to create
$theFile = "employees.csv";
//We want to read from the file, so use "r".
$theMode = "r";
//prepare the employees array to hold the contents of the file
$employees = array();
```

```
//prepare the sql string for insert
$sql = "INSERT INTO employees VALUES";

/*
* If we successfully connect to the file, do all of the file operations.
* Otherwise, print an error.
*/
if($fileConnection = fopen($theFile, $theMode)){
  print "<p>Opened file successfully</p>";

  while(!feof($fileConnection)){
    $line = fgets($fileConnection);

    $employees[] = split(",", $line);
  }

  //close the file
  if(fclose($fileConnection)){
    print "<p>Closed the file connection successfully.</p>";
  }else{
    print "<p>Unable to close the file connection.</p>";
  }

  //connect to the database
  $conn = mysql_connect("localhost", "xfd", "xfd123") or die(mysql_error());
  mysql_select_db("file_manipulation", $conn) or die(mysql_error());

  /*
  * prepare sql for insertion of data into employees table, and generate a table
  * showing the contents of the file
  */
  print "<table>";
  for($i = 0; $i < (count($employees)-1); $i++){
    $sql .= "(";
    $sql .= $employees[$i][0] . ", ";
    $sql .= $employees[$i][1] . ", ";
    $sql .= $employees[$i][2] . ", ";
    $sql .= $employees[$i][3] . ", ";
    $sql .= $employees[$i][4] . ", ";
    $sql .= $employees[$i][5];
    $sql .= ")";

    if(($i + 1) < (count($employees)-1)){
      $sql .= ", ";
    }

    print "<tr>\n";
    foreach($employees[$i] as $index=>$val){
      print "\t<td>$val</td>\n";
    }
    print "</tr>\n\n";
  }
  print "</table>";

  //insert data into database
  $result = mysql_query($sql, $conn);

}else{
  print "<p>Unable to connect to the file.</p>";
}

?>
```

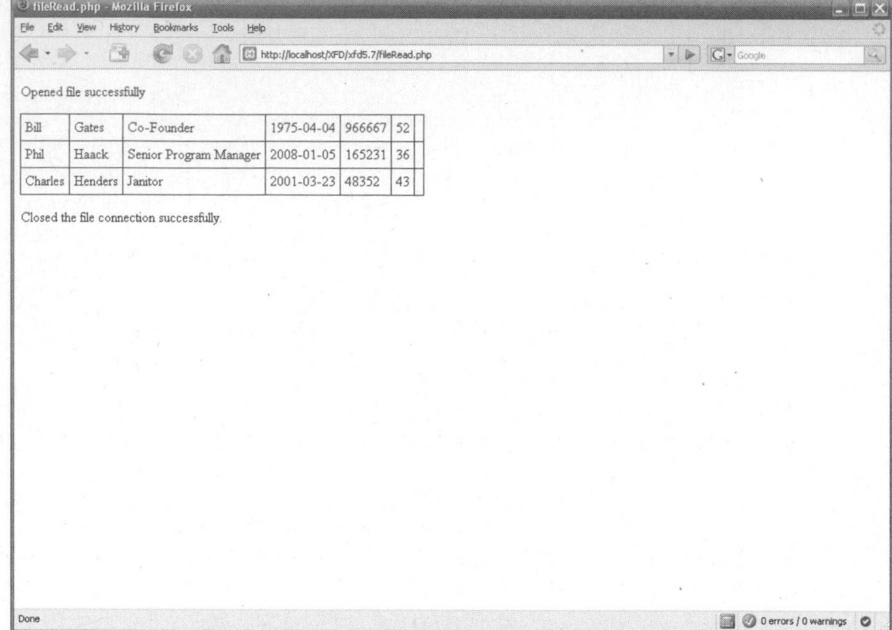

Figure 7-2: The HTML file contains a table of the data read from the file.

In the CSV file read example, the database was only written to once, at the very end of the program. The program could have written to the database as it read each line in, but that would have put much more strain on the server and made the program slower. Database reads and writes are very expensive in terms of processing time and memory for the server, in comparison to simple string concatenation in a PHP program.

Working with File and Directory Functions

Sometimes, you may need PHP to work with files in a directory. Say you have a reporting tool for a client. Each week, you generate a new report for the client and place it in a directory. You don't want to have to alter the page each time you do this, so instead, make a page that automatically generates a list of all the report files for the client to select from. This is the kind of thing you can do with functions like `openddir()` and `readdir()`.

opendir()

Using the `opendir()` function, you can create a variable (technically speaking, this type of variable is called a *handle*) that allows you to work with a particular directory.

The `opendir()` function takes one parameter: the path to the directory you want to work with. The `opendir()` function returns a directory handle (kind of like a connection to the directory) on success and `False` on failure.

Here is an example of the `opendir()` function (see the "Generating the list of file links" section to see the `opendir()` function in action). This function stores a directory handle to the `C:\xampp\htdocs\XFD\xfd5.7` directory in the `$directoryHandle` variable:

```
$directoryHandle = opendir("C:\xampp\htdocs\XFD\xfd5.7");
```

readdir()

After you've opened the directory with the `opendir()` function, you have a cursor pointed at the first file. At this point, you can read the filenames one by one with a `while` loop. To do this, you'll use the `readdir()` function.

The `readdir()` function takes one parameter; the variable containing the directory handle created with the `opendir()` function. The `readdir()` function returns the name of a file currently being focused on by the cursor on success and `False` on failure.

Here is an example of the `readdir()` function. This function iterates through each file in the directory specified by `$dp` and assigns the filename of the current file to a new index in `$fileArray` array:

```
while($currentFile !== false){
    $currentFile = readDir($dp);
    $filesArray[] = $currentFile;
}
```

The actual `readdir()` function itself is `readdir($dp)`. For more on the `readdir()` function, see the official PHP online documentation at `http://us.php.net/function.readdir`.

In some circumstances, the `readdir()` function might return non-Boolean values which evaluate to `False`, such as `0` or `""`. When testing the return value of the `readdir()` function, use === or !==, instead of == or !=, to accommodate these special cases.

chdir()

If you want to create a file in a directory other than the directory that the PHP page creating the file is in, you need to change directories. You change directories in PHP with the `chdir()` function.

If you want to be absolutely sure you're in the right directory before writing the file, you can use an `if` statement with the `getcwd()` function. This is usually a bit of overkill, but I wanted to at least make you aware of the function. Check out the PHP manual for more info on the `getcwd()` function.

The `chdir()` function takes one parameter; the path to the directory you wish to work with. The `chdir()` function returns `True` on success and `False` on failure.

Here is an example of the `chdir()`. This function changes to the `C:\xampp\htdocs\XFD\xfd5.7` directory:

```
chdir("C:\xampp\htdocs\XFD\xfd5.7");
```

When you change to a directory; you're then free to write to it with the `fwrite()` function (see the "fwrite()" section, earlier in this chapter).

Generating the list of file links

Using the `opendir()` and `readdir()` functions, you can generate a list of links to the files in a directory.

The file links list example performs the following tasks:

1. Opens a directory
2. Reads each filename in the directory into an array
3. Prints a link to each file in the directory

Here is the PHP code for the file links list example (see Figure 7-3 for the HTML generated by this example):

```
<?
$dp = opendir("C:\\xampp\\htdocs\\XFD\\xfd5.7\\");

while($currentFile !== false){
    $currentFile = readDir($dp);
    $filesArray[] = $currentFile;
}

$output = "";
foreach($filesArray as $aFile){
    $output .= "<a href=\"$aFile\">$aFile</a><br />";
}

print "<p>$output</p>";
?>
```

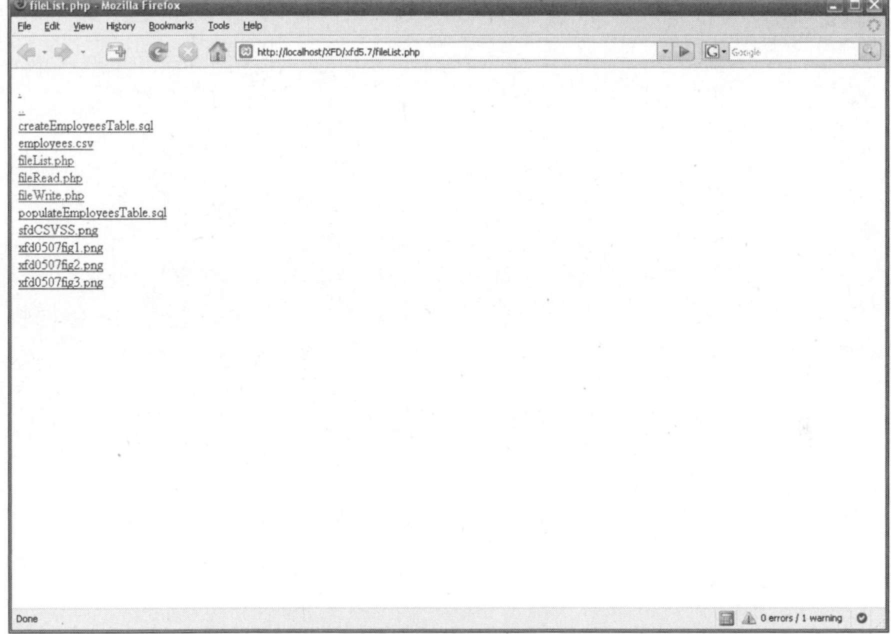

Figure 7-3: A list of links to all files in the directory specified by the opendir() function.

On a Windows server, you have to escape the backslashes in the file path. You do this by adding a backslash before the backslashes in the file path. (So you would write `C:\\xampp\\htdocs\\XFD\\xfd5.7\\` instead of `C:\xampp\htdocs\XFD\xfd5.7\`.) On a UNIX server, you don't have to do this because file paths use forward slashes (/) instead of backslashes (\).

If you wanted just one particular file type, you could use regular expressions to filter the files. If I had wanted only the `.txt` and `.dat` files from the directory, I could've run the files array through this filter to weed out the unwanted file types:

```
$filesArray = preg_grep("/txt$|dat$/", $filesArray);
```

For more on regular expressions, check out the online PHP manual at `http://us.php.net/preg_grep`.

Chapter 8: Connecting to a MySQL Database

In This Chapter

- Building the connection string
- Sending queries to a database
- Retrieving data results
- Formatting data output
- Allowing user queries
- Cleaning user-submitted data requests

Data has become the prominent feature of the Web. As you build more sophisticated sites using XHTML and CSS, you will eventually feel the need to incorporate data into your Web sites. You can do a certain amount of data work with the basic data structures built into PHP. Increasingly, Web sites turn to relational database management systems (RDBMSs) to handle their data needs. The RDBMS is a special program which accepts requests, processes data, and returns results.

This chapter assumes you already have a database available, and you have some basic knowledge of how SQL (the language of databases) works. If you are unfamiliar with these topics, please look over Book VI, which describes using data in detail.

Retrieving Data from a Database

PHP programmers frequently use MySQL as their preferred data back end. There are a number of good reasons for this:

- **MySQL is open source and free.** Like PHP, MySQL is open source, so PHP and MySQL can be used together (with Apache) to build a very powerful low-cost data solution.
- **MySQL is very powerful.** MySQL's capability as a data program has improved steadily, and it is now nearly as capable as commercial tools costing thousands of dollars. (And it is better than many that cost hundreds of dollars.)

- **PHP has built-in support for MySQL.** PHP includes a number of functions specifically designed to help programmers maintain MySQL databases.
- **You probably already have MySQL.** If you installed XAMPP, you probably already have an installation of MySQL ready to go.
- **MySQL was designed with remote control in mind.** MySQL is meant to be managed from some other program (like the code you write in PHP). It's not designed with a user interface (like Access has), but it's designed from the beginning to be controlled through a programming language like PHP.

Before diving into details, here's an overview of how you get information to and from a MySQL database:

1. **Establish a connection.**

   Before you can work with a database, you must establish a relationship between you PHP program and the database. This process involves identifying where the database is and passing it a username and password.

2. **Formulate a query.**

   Most of the time, you'll have some sort of query or request you want to pass to the database. You may want to see all the data in a particular table, or you may want to update a record. In either case, you use Structured Query Language (SQL) to prepare a request to pass to the database.

3. **Submit the query.**

   Once you've built the query, you pass it (through the connection) to the database. Assuming the query is properly formatted, the database will process the request and return a result.

4. **Process the result.**

   The database returns a special variable containing the results of your query. You'll generally need to pick through this complex variable to find all the data it contains. (For example, it can contain hundreds of records.)

5. **Display output to the user.**

   Most of the time, you'll process the query results and convert them to some sort of XHTML display the user can view.

As an example, take a look at `contact.php` in Figure 8-1.

The `contact.php` program contains none of the actual contact information. All the data was extracted from a database. Here's an overview of the code:

```
<!DOCTYPE html PUBLIC "-//W3C//DTD XHTML 1.0 Strict//EN"
"http://www.w3.org/TR/xhtml1/DTD/xhtml1-strict.dtd">
<html lang="EN" dir="ltr" xmlns="http://www.w3.org/1999/xhtml">
  <head>
    <meta http-equiv="content-type" content="text/xml; charset=utf-8" />
    <title>showContact.php</title>
```

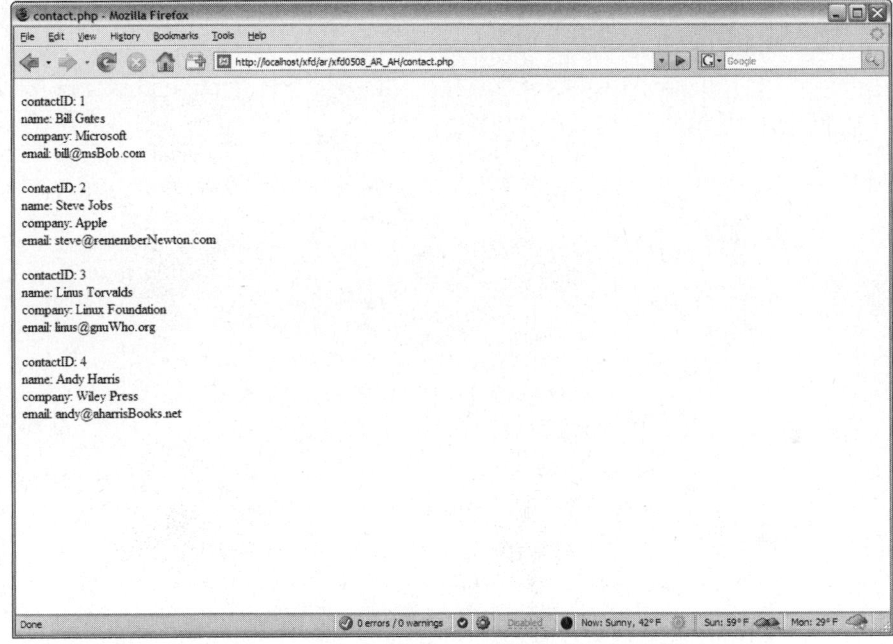

Figure 8-1: This program gets all the contact data from a database.

```
  </head>

  <body>
  <p>
  <?php

$conn = mysql_connect("localhost","user","password") or die(mysql_error());
mysql_select_db("xfd");

$sql = "SELECT * FROM contact";
$result = mysql_query($sql, $conn) or die(mysql_error());

while($row = mysql_fetch_assoc($result)){
  foreach ($row as $name => $value){
    print "$name: $value <br />\n";
  } // end foreach
  print "<br /> \n";
} // end while

  ?>
  </p>
  </body>
</html>
```

If you want to try this program at home, begin by running the `buildContactAutoIncrement.sql` script (available in Book VI, Chapter 2) in your copy of MySQL. This will ensure you have the database created. See Book VI, Chapter 2 if you need more information on creating databases.

Understanding data connections

The key to all database work is the connection. Database connections remind me of the pneumatic tubes at some bank drive-through locations. There's a little container you can stick your request into. You press a button, and the container shoots through a tube to the teller, who processes your request and sends you the results back through the tube.

In data programming, the connection is like that tube. It's the pipeline between your program (your car) and the data (the bank). To establish a data connection, you need to know four things:

- **The hostname (where the server is):** Often, the data server will be housed on the same physical machine as the Web server and PHP program. In these cases, you can use `localhost` as the server name. Test servers using XAMPP almost always use `localhost` connections. If you're working in a production environment, you may need to ask your service provider for the server address of your database.
- **Your database username:** Database programs should always have some type of security enabled. (See Book VI, Chapter 1 for information on setting up database users and passwords.) Your program needs to know the username it should use for accessing the data. (I often create a special username simply for my programs. Chapter 1 of Book VI outlines this process.)

  When you first install MySQL through XAMPP, it allows root access with no password. These settings allow anybody to do anything with your data. Obviously, that's not a good solution, security-wise. Be sure to set up at least one username and password combination for your database. If you're using an online hosting service, you probably don't have root access. In this case, you typically have a new user created for each database you build. Book VI explains all.
- **A password for the database:** The username is not secure without a password. Your PHP program also needs a password. This is established when you create the database.

  If you're going to make your source code available (as I do on the CD and Web site), be sure to change the username and password so people can't use this information to hack your live data.
- **The database name:** A single installation of MySQL can have many databases available. You'll typically have a separate database designed for each project you build. MySQL needs to know which particular database houses the information you're seeking.

Building a connection

The data connection is created with the `mysql_connect()` function. Here's how to do it:

1. **Create a variable to house the connection.**

   When you build a connection, a special variable is created to house information about that variable. I usually call my connection `$conn`:

   ```
   $conn = mysql_connect("localhost","user","password") or
       die(mysql_error());
   ```

2. **Invoke the `mysql_connect()` function.**

   This function (usually built into PHP) attempts to build a connection to the database given all the connection information:

   ```
   $conn = mysql_connect("localhost","user","password") or
       die(mysql_error());
   ```

3. **Pass the hostname, username, and password to `mysql_connect()`.**

   These three values are required parameters of the `mysql_connect()` function:

   ```
   $conn = mysql_connect("localhost","user","password") or
       die(mysql_error());
   ```

   You'll need to supply your own username and password. My values here are just samples.

4. **Prepare for a graceful crash.**

   It's very possible that something will go wrong when you attempt a data connection. The `or die()` clause tells PHP what to do if something goes wrong while making the connection:

   ```
   $conn = mysql_connect("localhost","user","password") or
       die(mysql_error());
   ```

   How many times in your life have you heard that phrase? "Prepare for a graceful crash." You've got to love programming.

5. **Invoke `mysql_error()` if something goes wrong.**

   If there's a problem with the MySQL connection, the error message will come from MySQL, not PHP. To ensure that you see the MySQL error, use the `mysql_error()` function. If you made a mistake (like misspelling the username), MySQL will report this error to PHP. Use `mysql_error()` to print out the last error from MySQL:

   ```
   $conn = mysql_connect("localhost","user","password") or
       die(mysql_error());
   ```

6. **Specify the particular database.**

   Once you're connected to the server, you need to specify which database on the server will be used for your transaction. I'm using a database called `xfd` for all the examples in this book. The `mysql_select_db()` function is used to handle this task:

   ```
   mysql_select_db("xfd");
   ```

Passing a query to the database

The reason for connecting to a database is to retrieve data from it (or to add or modify data, but the basic approach is always the same). In any case, you need to pass instructions to the database in SQL. (If you're unfamiliar with SQL, it is described in Book VI, Chapter 1.)

Your PHP program usually constructs an SQL statement in a string variable and then passes this value to the database. For this basic example, I specify the entire query. See the section "Processing the input," later in this chapter, for some warnings about how to incorporate user information in data queries.

The `showContact.php` program simply asks for a list of all the values in the `contact` table of the `xfd` database. The SQL query for displaying all the data in a table looks like this:

```
SELECT * FROM contact;
```

To use an SQL statement, package it into a string variable, like this:

```
$sql = "SELECT * FROM contact";
```

Note that you don't need to include the semicolon inside the string variable. You can call the variable anything you wish, but it's commonly called `$sql`. SQL queries can get complex, so if the SQL requires more than one line, you may want to encase it in a heredoc. (See Chapter 2 of this minibook for information on using heredocs.)

Pass the request to the database using the `msql_query()` function:

```
$result = mysql_query($sql, $conn) or die(mysql_error());
```

The `mysql_query()` function has a lot going on. Here's how you put it together:

1. **Create a variable to house the results.**

   When the query is finished, it will send results back to the program. The `$result` variable will hold that data:

   ```
   $result = mysql_query($sql, $conn) or die(mysql_error());
   ```

2. **Invoke `mysql_query()`.**

   This function passes the query to the database:

   ```
   $result = mysql_query($sql, $conn) or die(mysql_error());
   ```

3. **Send the query to the database.**

   The first parameter is the query. Normally, this is stored in a variable called `$sql`:

   ```
   $result = mysql_query($sql, $conn) or die(mysql_error());
   ```

4. **Specify the connection.**

   The second parameter is the connection object created when you ran `mysql_connect()`. If you leave out the connection object, PHP uses the last MySQL connection that was created:

   ```
   $result = mysql_query($sql, $conn) or die(mysql_error());
   ```

5. **Handle errors.**

   If there's an error in your SQL request, MySQL will send back an error message. Prepare for this with the `or die()` clause (just like you used for `mysql_connect()`):

   ```
   $result = mysql_query($sql, $conn) or die(mysql_error());
   ```

6. **Return the MySQL error if there was a problem.**

   If something went wrong in the SQL code, have your program reply with the MySQL error so you'll at least know what went wrong:

   ```
   $result = mysql_query($sql, $conn) or die(mysql_error());
   ```

Processing the results

The results of an SQL query are usually data tables, which are a complex data structure. The next step when you work with a database is to get all the appropriate information from the `$request` object and display it in a XHTML output for the user to understand.

This process is a little involved because SQL results are normally composed of two-dimensional data. A query result typically consists of multiple *records* (information about a specific entity — sometimes also called a row). Each record consists of a number of *fields* (specific data about the current record).

I'm tossing a bunch of database terms at you here. Databases deserve (and have) a minibook of their own. If nothing in this chapter makes sense to you, build your own copy of the `contact` database following the instructions in Book VI and then come back here to have your program present that data through your Web site.

The `$request` variable has a lot of data packed into it. You get that data out by using a pair of nested loops:

1. **The outer loop extracts a record at a time.**

   The first job is to get each record out of the request, one at a time.

2. **Use another loop to extract each field from the record.**

   Once you've got a record, you'll need to extract each field from the record.

Here's all the code for this segment (I explain it in detail in the following sections):

```
while($row = mysql_fetch_assoc($result)){
  foreach ($row as $name => $value){
    print "$name: $value <br />\n";
  } // end foreach
  print "<br /> \n";
} // end while
```

Extracting the rows

The first task is to break the `$result` object into a series of variables that each represent one record (or row). Here's the line that does the job:

```
while($row = mysql_fetch_assoc($result)){
```

To break a result into its constituent rows, follow these steps:

1. **Begin a `while` loop.**

   This code will continue as long as more rows are available in the result object:

   ```
   while($row = mysql_fetch_assoc($result)){
   ```

2. **Extract the next row as an associative array.**

   Every time through the loop, you'll extract the next row from the result. There are several functions available for this task, but I use `mysql_fetch_assoc()` because I think it's easiest to understand (see the sidebar "MySQL fetch options" for some other options and when you might choose them):

   ```
   while($row = mysql_fetch_assoc($result)){
   ```

3. **Pass the resulting object to a variable called `$row`.**

   The output of `mysql_fetch_assoc` is an array (specifically, an associative array). Copy that value to a variable called `$row`:

   ```
   while($row = mysql_fetch_assoc($result)){
   ```

4. **Continue as long as there are more rows to retrieve.**

   `mysql_fetch_assoc()` has an important side effect. In addition to extracting an associative array from `$result`, the function returns the value `false` if no more records are left. Because I'm using this statement inside a condition, the loop will continue as long as there is another row available. When there are no rows left, the assignment will evaluate to `false`, and the loop will exit.

   ```
   while($row = mysql_fetch_assoc($result)){
   ```

MySQL fetch options

You can extract data from a MySQL result in four different ways:

- mysql_fetch_row() creates an ordinary (numeric index) array from the current row.
- mysql_fetch_assoc() creates an associative array from the current row, with the field name as the key and field value as the value in each key/value pair.
- mysql_fetch_array() can be used to get numeric or associative arrays, based on a parameter.
- mysql_fetch_object() returns a PHP object corresponding to the current row. Each field in the row is a property of the object.

In general, the mysql_fetch_assoc() provides the best combination of ease-of-use and information. Use mysql_fetch_array() when you don't need the field names (for example, you're using an XHTML table for output, and you're getting the field names from the mysql_fetch_field() function). The mysql_fetch_object() technique is useful if you're going to build a complete object based on a query row, but that is beyond the scope of this book.

Extracting fields from a row

Each time you go through the while loop described in the previous section, you'll have a variable called $row. This will be an associative array containing all the field names and values from the current form. If you know a field name, you can access it directly. For example, I know the contact table has a field named company, so you can use an associative array lookup to see the current company name:

```
print $row["company"];
```

This will print the company name of the current record.

More often, you will want to print out all the information in the row, so you can use the special form of foreach() loop used with associative arrays:

```
foreach ($row as $name => $value){
```

Here's how it works:

1. **Set up the foreach loop.**

   This form of for loop automatically loads variables with members of the array:

   ```
   foreach ($row as $name => $value){
   ```

2. **Analyze the `$row` array.**

   The `$row` variable contains an associative array, so it's a perfect candidate for this type of loop:

   ```
   foreach ($row as $name => $value){
   ```

3. **Assign each key to `$name`.**

   On each pass of the loop, assign the current key of the array (which will contain the current field name) to the variable `$name`:

   ```
   foreach ($row as $name => $value){
   ```

4. **Indicate the relationship between `$name` and `$value` with the `=>` operator.**

   This indicates that `$name` is the key and `$value` is the value in this relationship:

   ```
   foreach ($row as $name => $value){
   ```

5. **Assign the value to `$value`.**

   The value of the current element will be placed in the `$value` variable:

   ```
   foreach ($row as $name => $value){
   ```

When you use a `foreach` loop with an associative array, you assign each element to two variables because each element in an associative array has a name and a value. Check Chapter 5 of this minibook for more information about associative arrays and the `foreach` loop.

Inside this loop, you'll have the name of the current field in a variable called `$name` and its value in a variable called `$value`. This loop will continue for each field in the current record.

Printing the data

For this simple example, I'm using the simplest way I can think of to print out the contents:

```
print "$name: $value <br />\n";
```

This line simply prints out the current field name, followed by a colon and the current field value. Because this simple line is inside the complex nested loops, it ends up printing the name and value of every field in the query result. Here's the whole chunk of code again:

```
while($row = mysql_fetch_assoc($result)){
  foreach ($row as $name => $value){
    print "$name: $value <br />\n";
  } // end foreach
  print "<br /> \n";
} // end while
```

The result isn't the most elegant formatting on the Internet, but it gets the job done, and it's easy to understand. Note I added a `<br />` tag at the end of each line, so each field will appear on its own line of XHTML output. I also added a final `<br />` at the end of each `for` loop. This will cause a line break between each record, so the records are separated.

Improving the Output Format

Using `<br />` tags for output is a pretty crude expedient. It's fine for a basic test, but `<br />` tags are usually a sign of sloppy XHTML coding. Take a look at this variation called `contactDL.php` in Figure 8-2.

Building definition lists

Definition lists are designed for name/value pairs, so they're often a good choice for data in associative arrays. It's not too difficult to convert the basic data result program into a form that uses definition lists:

```
<!DOCTYPE html PUBLIC "-//W3C//DTD XHTML 1.0 Strict//EN"
"http://www.w3.org/TR/xhtml1/DTD/xhtml1-strict.dtd">
<html lang="EN" dir="ltr" xmlns="http://www.w3.org/1999/xhtml">
  <head>
    <meta http-equiv="content-type" content="text/xml; charset=utf-8" />
    <title>contactDL.php</title>
    <style type = "text/css">
      dt {
        float: left;
        width: 7em;
        font-weight: bold;
        clear: left;
      }

      dd {
        float: left;
      }

      dl {
        float: left;
        clear: left;
      }

    </style>
  </head>

  <body>
  <?php

$conn = mysql_connect("localhost","user","password") or die(mysql_error());
mysql_select_db("xfd");

$sql = "SELECT * FROM contact";
$result = mysql_query($sql, $conn) or die(mysql_error());


while($row = mysql_fetch_assoc($result)){
```

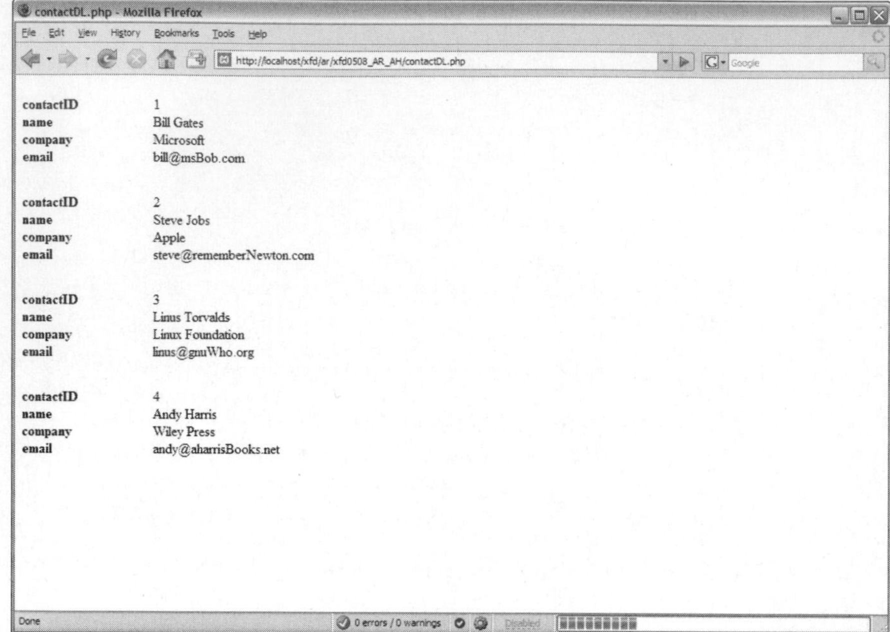

Figure 8-2: Now, the output of the query is in a nice definition list.

```
  print "     <dl> \n";
  foreach ($row as $name => $value){
    print "       <dt>$name</dt> \n";
    print "       <dd>$value</dd> \n";
  } // end foreach
  print "     </dl> \n";
} // end while

  ?>
  </body>
</html>
```

The general design is copied from `contact.html`, with the following changes:

1. **Add CSS styling for the definition list.**

   Definition lists are great for this kind of data, but the default style is pretty boring. I added some float styles to make the data display better. (See Book III, Chapter 1 for how to use floating styles.)

2. **Put each record in its own definition list.**

   The `while` loop executes once per record, so begin the definition list at the beginning of the `while` loop. The `</dl>` tag goes at the end of the `while` loop. Each pass of the `while` loop will create a new definition list.

3. **Display the field names as `<dt>` elements.**

   The field name maps pretty well to the concept of a definition term, so put each `$name` value in a `<dt></dt>` pair.

4. **Place the values inside `<dd>` tags.**

   The values will be displayed as definition data. Now, you have the contents of the data set up in a form that can be easily modified with CSS.

Using XHTML tables for output

The basic unit of structure in SQL is called a *table* because it's usually displayed in a tabular format. XHTML also has a table structure, which is ideal for outputting SQL data. Figure 8-3 shows `contactTable.php`, which displays the `contact` information inside an XHTML table.

Tables are a very common way to output SQL results. There's one big difference between table output and the techniques that have been shown elsewhere in this chapter. In a table, you have a separate row containing field names. Here's the code:

```
<!DOCTYPE html PUBLIC "-//W3C//DTD XHTML 1.0 Strict//EN"
"http://www.w3.org/TR/xhtml1/DTD/xhtml1-strict.dtd">
<html lang="EN" dir="ltr" xmlns="http://www.w3.org/1999/xhtml">
  <head>
    <meta http-equiv="content-type" content="text/xml; charset=utf-8" />
    <title>contactTable.php</title>
    <style type = "text/css">
      table, th, td {
        border: 1px solid black;
      }
    </style>
  </head>

  <body>
    <h1>My Contacts</h1>
  <?php
$conn = mysql_connect("localhost", "user", "password");
mysql_select_db("xfd");
$sql = "SELECT * FROM contact";
$result = mysql_query($sql, $conn);

print "  <table> \n";

//get field names first
print "      <tr> \n";
while ($field = mysql_fetch_field($result)){
  print "        <th>$field->name</th> \n";
} // end while
print "      </tr> \n";

while ($row = mysql_fetch_assoc($result)){
  print "      <tr> \n";
  foreach ($row as $name => $value){
    print "        <td>$value</td> \n";
  } // end foreach
```

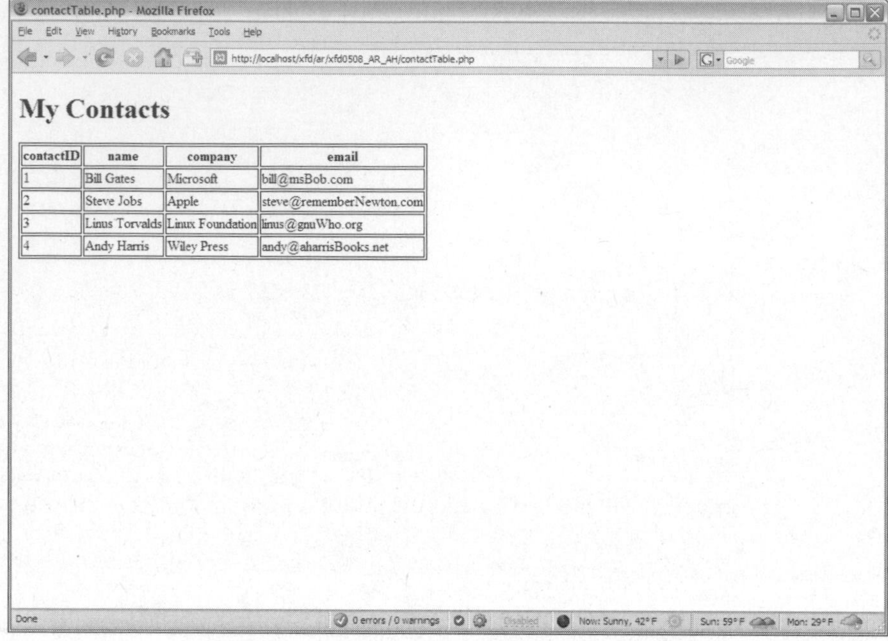

Figure 8-3: The contact information displayed in an XHTML table.

```
  print "       </tr> \n";

} // end while loop

print "    </table> \n";

  ?>
  </body>
</html>
```

This code is still very similar to the basic `contact.php` program. It extracts data from the database in exactly the same way. The main difference is the way field names are treated. The field names will go in table headings, and only the values are printed from each row. To make this work, follow these steps:

1. **Build a normal MySQL connection.**

   Begin with the standard connection. Don't worry about formatting until you're reasonably certain you can read data from the database.

2. **Print the `table` tag before extracting any results.**

   All the query data will be displayed inside the table, so print the `table` tag before you start printing anything that should go inside the table.

3. **Print the table header row first.**

   The table headers must be printed before you can worry about the other data:

   ```
   //get field names first
   print "      <tr> \n";
   while ($field = mysql_fetch_field($result)){
     print "          <th>$field->name</th> \n";
   } // end while
   print "      </tr> \n";
   ```

4. **Extract metadata from the result set with `mysql_fetch_field()`.**

   After you've gotten a result from a data query, you can learn a lot about the data by using the `mysql_fetch_field()` function:

   ```
   while ($field = mysql_fetch_field($result)){
   ```

   This function (`mysql_fetch_field()`) extracts the next field object from the result and passes it to a variable called `$field`. It returns `false` if there are no more fields in the result, so it can be used in a `while` loop, like `mysql_fetch_assoc()`.

5. **Print the field's name.**

   The field is an object, so you can extract various elements from it easily. In this case, I'm interested in the field name. `$field->name` yields the name of the current field (see the sidebar, in this chapter, "More about metadata" for more information about information you can extract from field objects):

   ```
     print "          <th>$field->name</th> \n";
   ```

6. **Print each row's data as a table row.**

   Each row of the data result maps to a table row. Use the preceding variation of nested loops to build your table rows.

7. **Finish off the table.**

   The `table` tag must be completed. Don't forget to print `</table>` when you're done printing out all the table information.

8. **Clean up your XHTML.**

   Check your code in a browser. Make sure it looks right, but don't stop there. Check with a Validator to make sure that your program produces valid XHTML code. View the source and ensure that the indentation and white space are adequate. Even though a program produced this code, it needs to be XHTML code you can be proud of.

Allowing User Interaction

If you've got a large database, you probably want to allow users to search the database. For example, the form in Figure 8-4 allows the user to search the My Contacts database.

There's a couple of interesting things about the form in Figure 8-4:

- **The search value can be anything.** The first field is an ordinary text field. The user can type absolutely anything here (so you should expect some surprises).
- **The user selects a field with a drop-down menu.** You don't expect the user to know exactly what field names you are using in your database. Whenever possible, supply this type of information in a format that's easier for the user and less prone to error.
- **This form is built to fill in a query.** The back-end program (`search.php`) will be constructing a query from data gathered from this form. The point of the form is to request two pieces of information from the user: a field to search in and a value to look for in that field. `search.php` will use the data gleaned from this form to construct and submit that query to the database.

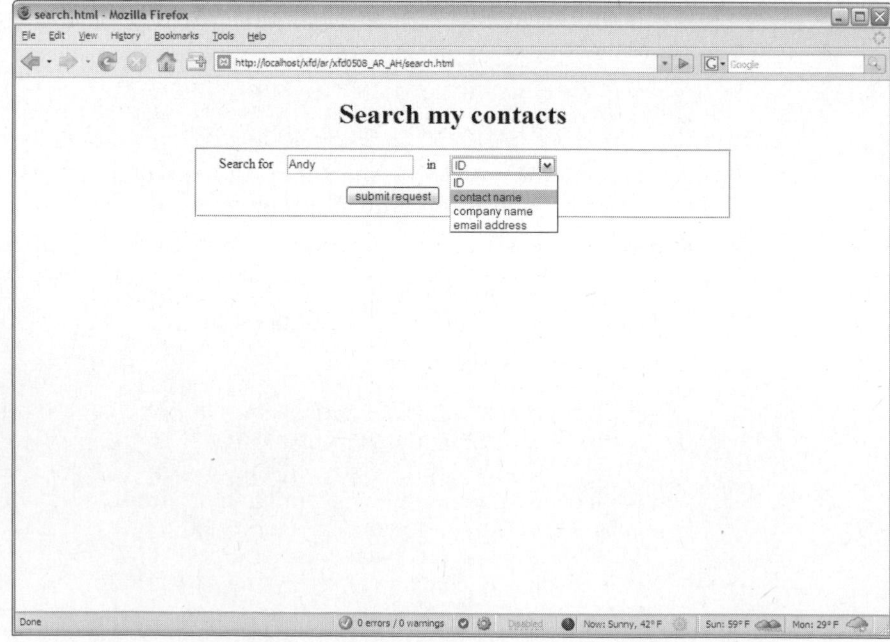

Figure 8-4: The user can check for any value in any field.

More about metadata

You can find out all sorts of information about the table you're querying with the `mysql_fetch_field()` function.

This function returns an object that has the following properties:

- **`table`**: The name of the table the field (column) belongs to
- **`name`**: The field's name
- **`type`**: The field's datatype
- **`primary_key`**: If the field is a primary key, will return a `1`
- **`unique_key`**: If the field is a unique key, will return a `1`
- **`max_length`**: The field's maximum length
- **`def`**: The field's default value (if any)
- **`not_null`**: If the field can't be `NULL`, will return a `1`
- **`multiple_key`**: If the field is a non-unique key, will return a `1`
- **`numeric`**: If the field is numeric, will return a `1`
- **`blob`**: If the field is a `blob`, will return a `1`
- **`unsigned`**: If the field is unsigned, will return a `1`
- **`zerofill`**: If the field is zero-filled, will return a `1`

You'll probably end up using `table`, `name`, `type`, `primary_key`, and `max_length` the most. Refer to any of these values using object-oriented syntax, so if you've got a field named `$field`, get its name with `$field->name`.

- **The user doesn't know SQL.** Even if the user does know SQL, don't let him use it. The SQL query should always be built on the server side. Get enough information to build an SQL query, but don't send a query to the PHP. (Doing so exposes your database to significant abuse.)
- **The form uses the `post` mechanism.** From the XHTML perspective, it isn't important whether the form uses `get` or `post`, but when you're using forms to construct SQL queries, `post` is a bit safer because it makes the bad guys work a little bit harder to spoof your site and send bogus requests to your database.

Building an XHTML search form

Here's the XHTML code for `search.html`:

```
<!DOCTYPE html PUBLIC "-//W3C//DTD XHTML 1.0 Strict//EN"
"http://www.w3.org/TR/xhtml1/DTD/xhtml1-strict.dtd">
<html lang="EN" dir="ltr" xmlns="http://www.w3.org/1999/xhtml">
  <head>
    <meta http-equiv="content-type" content="text/xml; charset=utf-8" />
    <title>search.html</title>
    <link rel = "stylesheet"
          type = "text/css"
          href = "search.css" />
```

```
  </head>

  <body>
    <h1>Search my contacts</h1>

    <form action = "search.php"
          method = "post">
      <fieldset>

        <label>Search for</label>
        <input type = "text"
               name = "srchVal" />

        <label>in</label>
        <select name = "srchField">
          <option value = "contactID">ID</option>
          <option value = "name">contact name</option>
          <option value = "company">company name</option>
          <option value = "email">email address</option>
        </select>

        <button type = "submit">submit request</button>
      </fieldset>

    </form>
  </body>
</html>
```

It's really a pretty basic form. The interesting stuff happens in the `search.php` program that's triggered when the user submits this form.

Responding to the search request

When the user submits `search.html`, a page like Figure 8-5 appears, created by `search.php`.

The `search.php` program isn't really terribly different from `contactTable.php`. It takes an SQL query, sends it to a database, and returns the result as an XHTML table. The only new idea is how the SQL query is built. Rather than pre-loading the entire query into a string variable, as I did in all other examples in this chapter, I used input from the form to inform the query. As usual, I provide the code in its entirety here, then I point out specific features. Look at the big picture first:

```
<!DOCTYPE html PUBLIC "-//W3C//DTD XHTML 1.0 Strict//EN"
"http://www.w3.org/TR/xhtml1/DTD/xhtml1-strict.dtd">
<html lang="EN" dir="ltr" xmlns="http://www.w3.org/1999/xhtml">
  <head>
    <meta http-equiv="content-type" content="text/xml; charset=utf-8" />
    <title>search.php</title>
    <style type = "text/css">
      table, th, td {
        border: 1px solid black;
      }
    </style>
  </head>
```

```
<body>
  <h1>My Contacts</h1>
<?php

$sql = processInput();
printResults($sql);

function processInput(){
  //extract information from previous form and build a safe query
  $srchVal = $_POST["srchVal"];
  $srchField = $_POST["srchField"];
  $srchVal = mysql_real_escape_string($srchVal);
  $srchField = mysql_real_escape_string($srchField);

  $sql = "SELECT * FROM contact WHERE $srchField LIKE '%$srchVal%'";
  return $sql;

} // end processInput

function printResults($sql){
  $conn = mysql_connect("localhost", "user", "password");
  mysql_select_db("xfd");

  $result = mysql_query($sql, $conn);

  print "  <table> \n";
```

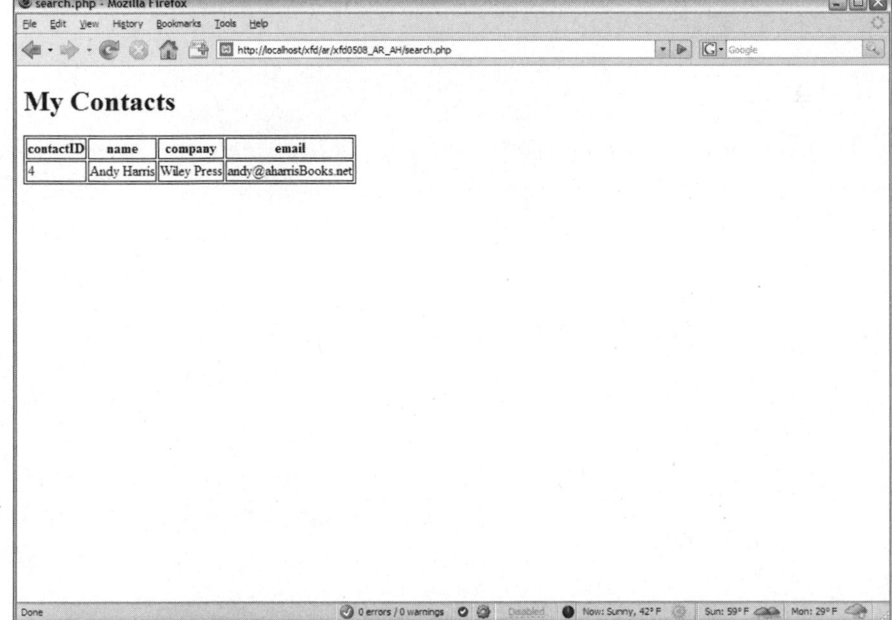

Figure 8-5: The program searches the database according to the parameters in search.html.

```
    //get field names first
    print "      <tr> \n";
    while ($field = mysql_fetch_field($result)){
      print "         <th>$field->name</th> \n";
    } // end while
    print "      </tr> \n";

    while ($row = mysql_fetch_assoc($result)){
      print "      <tr> \n";
      foreach ($row as $name => $value){
        print "         <td>$value</td> \n";
      } // end foreach
      $count++;
      print "      </tr> \n";

    } // end while loop

    print "    </table> \n";
  } // end printResults
  ?>
  </body>
</html>
```

Breaking the code into functions

This code is complex enough to deserve functions. The program has two main jobs, so it's not surprising that a function is designated to perform each major task. Here's the main section of the PHP code:

```
$sql = processInput();
printResults($sql);
```

This code fragment nicely summarizes the entire program (as well-designed main code ought to do). Here's the overview:

1. **Designate a variable called `$sql` to hold a query.**

   The central data for this program is the SQL query.

2. **Create the query with `processInput()`.**

   The job of `processInput()` is to get the data from the `search.html` form and create a safe, properly-formatted query, which will be passed to the `$sql` variable.

3. **Process the query with the `printResults()` function.**

   This function will process the query and format the output as an XHTML table.

Processing the input

The `processInput()` function does just what it says — processes input:

```
function processInput(){
  //extract information from previous form and build a safe query
```

```
   $srchVal = $_POST["srchVal"];
   $srchField = $_POST["srchField"];

   $conn = mysql_connect("localhost", "user", "password");
   $srchVal = mysql_real_escape_string($srchVal, $conn);
   $srchField = mysql_real_escape_string($srchField, $conn);

   $sql = "SELECT * FROM contact WHERE $srchField LIKE '%$srchVal%'";
   return $sql;

 } // end processInput
```

It works by doing several small but important tasks:

1. **Retrieve values from the form.**

   The key values for this program are `$srchVal` and `$srchField`. They both come from the previous form. Note that I used `$_POST` rather than `$_REQUEST` because `post` requests are mildly harder to hack than `get`, and I really don't want anybody spamming my database:

   ```
   $srchVal = $_POST["srchVal"];
   $srchField = $_POST["srchField"];
   ```

2. **Filter each field with `mysql_real_escape_string()`.**

   You never want to use input from a form without passing it through a security check. It's quite easy for a bad guy to post additional text in the query that could cause you a lot of headaches. This bit of nastiness is commonly called a *SQL injection attack.* Fortunately, PHP provides a very useful function for preventing this sort of malice. The `mysql_real_escape_string()` function processes a string and strips out any potentially dangerous characters, effectively minimizing the risks of SQL injection ickiness. The second parameter of `mysql_real_escape_string()` is the name of the data connection, so I make a connection and pass it as a parameter:

   ```
   $conn = mysql_connect("localhost", "xfd", "xfdaio");
   $srchVal = mysql_real_escape_string($srchVal, $conn);
   $srchField = mysql_real_escape_string($srchField, $conn);
   ```

   TIP

   For more on database security and preventing SQL injection attacks, a good place to start is this document in the PHP online manual:

   ```
   http://us3.php.net/manual/en/security.database.sql-injection.php
   ```

3. **Embed the cleaned-up strings in the `$sql` variable.**

   Now, you can build the query comfortably. Note that a `LIKE` clause is more likely to provide the kinds of results your user is expecting. Also, don't forget that SQL often requires single quotes (see Book VI, Chapter 2 for more on building `LIKE` clauses):

   ```
   $sql = "SELECT * FROM contact WHERE $srchField LIKE '%$srchVal%'";
   ```

4. Return the final `$sql` variable.

The query is now ready to be sent back to the main code segment, which will pass it on to the next function:

```
return $sql;
```

Generating the output

Now that query is complete, the job of `printResults()` is quite easy. This code is really just a copy of the `contactTable.php` code packaged into a function:

```
function printResults($sql){
  $conn = mysql_connect("localhost", "user", "password");
  mysql_select_db("xfd");

  $result = mysql_query($sql, $conn);

  print "  <table> \n";

  //get field names first
  print "      <tr> \n";
  while ($field = mysql_fetch_field($result)){
    print "        <th>$field->name</th> \n";
  } // end while
  print "      </tr> \n";

  while ($row = mysql_fetch_assoc($result)){
    print "      <tr> \n";
    foreach ($row as $name => $value){
      print "        <td>$value</td> \n";
    } // end foreach
    $count++;
    print "      </tr> \n";

  } // end while loop

  print "    </table> \n";
} // end printResults
```

There's only one twist here: SQL is now a parameter. This function won't create the `$sql` variable itself. Instead, it accepts `$sql` as a parameter. I took out the line that created `$sql` as a hard-coded query because now I want to implement the query created by `processInput()`. Otherwise, the code in this function is a direct copy of `contactTable.php`.

Book VI

Databases with MySQL

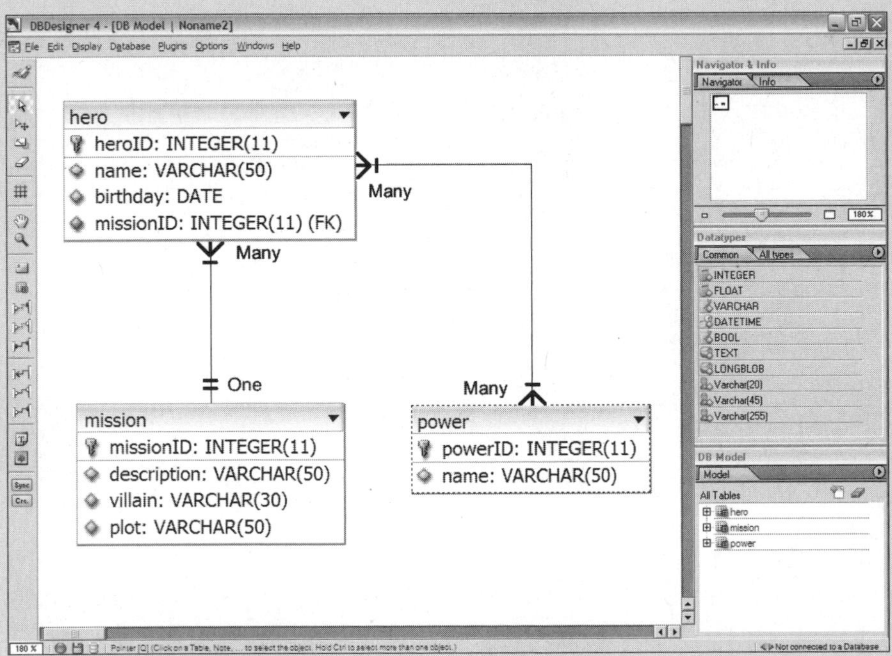

Well-defined data is the central element in most commercial Web sites.

Contents at a Glance

Chapter 1: Getting Started with Data

In This Chapter

- **Understanding databases, tables, records, and fields**
- **Introducing the relational data model**
- **Introducing a three-tier model**
- **Understanding MySQL data types**
- **Getting started with MySQL and phpMyAdmin**
- **Adding a password to your MySQL root account**
- **Creating new MySQL users**
- **Designing a simple table**
- **Adding data to the table**

Most programs and Web sites are really about data. Data drives the Internet, so you really need to understand how data works and how to manage it well if you want to build high-powered modern Web sites.

The trend in Web development is to have a bunch of specialized languages that work together. XHTML describes page content, CSS manages visual layout, JavaScript adds client-side interactivity, and PHP adds server-side capabilities. You're probably not surprised when I tell you that yet another language, SQL (Structured Query Language), specializes in working with data.

In this minibook, you discover how to manage data. Specifically, you find out how to create databases, add data, create queries to retrieve data, and create complex data models to solve real-world problems. In this chapter, I show you some automated tools that automate the process of creating a data structure and adding data to it. In later chapters in this minibook, I show how to control the process directly through SQL.

Examining the Basic Structure of Data

Data has been an important part of programming from the beginning. Many languages have special features for working with data, but through the years, a few key ideas have evolved. A system called *relational data modeling* has become the primary method for data management, and a standard language for this model, called SQL (Structured Query Language), has been developed.

SQL has two major components:

- *Data Definition Language* (DDL) is a subset of SQL that helps you create and maintain databases. You use DDL to build your databases and add data to them.
- *Data Query Language* (DQL) is used to pull data out of a database after it's been placed there. Generally, your user input is converted to queries to get information from an existing database.

The best way to think about data is to simply look at some. The following table contains some basic contact information:

Name	Company	E-mail
Bill Gates	Microsoft	bill@msBob.com
Steve Jobs	Apple	steve@rememberNewton.com
Linus Torvalds	Linux Foundation	linus@gnuWho.org
Andy Harris	Wiley Press	andy@aharrisBooks.net

All these e-mail addresses are completely made up (except mine). Bill Gates hasn't given me his actual e-mail address. He doesn't answer my calls, either. . . . (sniff).

It's very common to think of data in the form of tables. In fact, the fancy official database programmer name for this structure is *table.* A table (in database terms) is just a two-dimensional representation of data. Of course, some fancy computer-science words describe what's in a table:

- **Each row is a *record.*** A record describes a discrete entity. In this table, each record is a person in an e-mail directory.
- **A record is made of *fields.*** All the records in this table have three fields: name, company, and e-mail. Fields are a lot like variables in programming languages; they can have a type and a value. Sometimes, fields are also called *columns.*
- **A collection of records is a *table.*** All records in a table have the same field definitions but can have different values in the fields.
- **A bunch of tables makes a *database.*** Real-world data doesn't usually fit well in one table. Often, you'll make several different tables that work together to describe complex information. The database is an aggregate of a bunch of tables. Normally, you restrict access to a database through a user and password system.

Determining the fields in a record

If you want to create a database, you need to think about what entity you're describing and what fields that entity contains. In the table in the preceding section, I'm describing e-mail contacts. Each contact requires three pieces of information:

- **Name:** Gives the name of the contact, in 50 characters or less.
- **Company:** Describes which company the contact is associated with, in 30 characters or less.
- **E-mail:** Lists the e-mail address of the contact, in 50 characters or less.

Whenever you define a record, begin by thinking about what the table represents and then think of the details associated with that entity. The topic of the table (the kind of thing the table represents) is the record. The fields are the details of that record.

Before you send me e-mails about my horrible data design, know that I'm deliberately simplifying this table. Sure, it should have separate fields for first and last name, and it should also have a primary key. If you don't know about that stuff yet, I talk about them later in this minibook, as well as in the section "Defining a primary key," later in this chapter. If you do know about them already, you probably don't need to read this section. For the rest of you, you should start with a simple data model, and I promise to add all those goodies soon.

Introducing SQL data types

Each record contains a number of fields, which are much like variables in ordinary languages. Unlike scripting languages, such as JavaScript and PHP (which tend to be free-wheeling about data types), databases are particular about the type of data that goes in a record.

Table 1-1 illustrates several key data types in MySQL (the variant of SQL used in this book).

Table 1-1 MySQL Data Types

Data Type	*Description*	*Notes*
INT (INTEGER)	Positive or negative integer (no decimal point)	Ranges from about –2 billion to 2 billion. Use BIGINT for larger integers.
DOUBLE	Double precision floating point	Holds decimal numbers in scientific notation. Use for extremely large or extremely small values.

(continued)

Table 1-1 *(continued)*

Data Type	*Description*	*Notes*
DATE	Date stored in YYYY-MM-DD format.	Can be displayed in various formats.
TIME	Time stored in HH:MM:SS format	Can be displayed in various formats.
CHAR(*length*)	Fixed-length text	Always same length. Shorter text is padded with spaces. Longer text is truncated.
VARCHAR(*length*)	'variable'-length text	Still fixed length, but trailing spaces are trimmed. Limit 256 characters.
TEXT	Longer text	Up to 64,000 (roughly) characters. Use LONGTEXT for more space.
BLOB	Binary data	Up to 64K of binary data. LONGBLOB for more space.

I list only the most commonly used data types in Table 1-1. These data types handle most situations, but check the documentation of your database package if you need some other type of data.

Specifying the length of a record

Data types are especially important when you're defining a database. Relational databases have an important structural rule: Each record in a table must take up the same amount of memory. This rule seems arbitrary, but it's actually very useful.

Imagine that you're looking up somebody's name in a phone book, but you're required to go one entry at a time. If you're looking for Aaron Adams, things will be pretty good, but what if you're looking for Zebulon Zoom? This sequential search would be really slow because you'd have to go all the way through the phone book to find Zebulon. Even knowing that Zeb was in record number 5,379 wouldn't help much because you don't know exactly when one record ends and another begins.

If you're name is really Zebulon Zoom, you have a very cool name — a good sign in the open source world, where names like Linus and Guido are really popular. I figure the only reason I'm not famous is my name is too boring. I'm thinking about switching to a dolphin name or something. (Hi, my name is "Andy Squeeeeeeek! Click Click Harris.")

Relational databases solve this problem by forcing each record to be the same length. Just for the sake of argument, imagine that every record takes exactly 100 bytes. You would then be able to figure out where each record is on the disk by multiplying the length of each record by the desired record's index. (Record 0 would be at byte 0, record 1 is at 100, record 342 is at 34200, and so on.) This mechanism allows the computer to keep track of where all the records are and jump immediately to a specific record, even if hundreds or thousands of records are in the system.

My description here is actually a major simplification of what's going on, but the foundation is correct. You should really investigate more sophisticated database and data structures classes or books if you want more information. It's pretty cool stuff.

The length of the record is important because the data types of a record's fields determine its size. *Numeric data* (integers and floating point values) have a fixed size in the computer's memory. Strings (as used in other programming languages) typically have *dynamic length.* That is, the amount of memory used depends on the length of the text. In a database application, you rarely have dynamic length text. Instead, you generally determine the number of characters for each text field.

Defining a primary key

When you turn the contact data into an actual database, you generally add one more important field. Each table should have one field that acts as a *primary key.* A primary key is a special field that's

- **Unique:** You can't have two records in a table with the same primary key.
- **Guaranteed:** Every record in the table has a value in the primary key.

Primary key fields are often (though not always) integers because you can easily build a system for generating a new unique value. (Find the largest key in the current database and add one.)

In this book, each table has a primary key. They are usually numeric and are always the first field in a record definition. I also end each key field with the letters ID to help me remember it's a primary key.

Primary keys are useful because they allow the database system to keep a Table of Contents for quick access to the table. When you build multitable data structures, you can see how you can use keys to link tables together.

Defining the table structure

When you want to build a table, you begin with a definition of the *structure* of the table. What are the field names? What is each field's type? If it's text, how many characters will you specify?

The table definition for the e-mail contacts table may look like this:

Field Name	*Type*	*Length (Bytes)*
ContactID	INTEGER	11
Name	VARCHAR	50
Company	VARCHAR	30
E-mail	VARCHAR	50

Look over the table definition, and you'll notice some important ideas:

- **There's now a contactID field.** This field serves as the primary key. It's an INTEGER field.
- **INTEGERs are automatically assigned a length.** It isn't necessary to specify the size of an INTEGER field (as all INTEGERs are exactly 11 bytes long in MySQL).
- **The text fields are all VARCHARs.** This particular table consists of a lot of text. The text fields are all stored as VARCHAR types.
- **Each VARCHAR has a specified length.** Figuring out the best length can be something of an art form. If you make the field too short, you aren't able to squeeze in all the data you want. If you make it too long, you waste space.

VARCHAR isn't quite variable length. The length is fixed, but extra spaces are added. Imagine that I had a VARCHAR(10) field called `userName`. If I enter the name 'Andy', the field contains `"Andy      "` (that is, 'Andy' followed by six spaces). If I enter the value 'Rumplestiltskin', the field contains the value `"Rumplestil"` (the first 10 characters of 'Rumplestiltskin').

The difference between CHAR and VARCHAR is what happens to shorter words. When you return the value of a CHAR field, all the padding spaces are included. A VARCHAR automatically lops off any trailing spaces.

In practice, programmers rarely use CHAR because VARCHAR provides the behavior you almost always want.

Introducing MySQL

Programs that work with SQL are usually called relational database management systems (RDBMS). A number of popular RDBMSs are available:

- **Oracle** is the big player. Many high-end commercial applications use the advanced features of Oracle. It's powerful, but the price tag makes it primarily useful for large organizations.

- **MS SQL Server** is Microsoft's entry in the high-end database market. It's usually featured in Microsoft-based systems integrated with .NET programming languages and the Microsoft IIS server. It can also be quite expensive.
- **MS Access** is the entry-level database system installed with most versions of Microsoft Office. While Access is a good tool for playing with data design, it has some well-documented problems handling the large number of requests typical of a Web-based data tool.
- **MySQL** is an open-source database that has made a big splash in the open-source world. While it's not quite as robust as Oracle or SQL Server, it's getting closer all the time. The latest version has features and capabilities that once only belonged to expensive proprietary systems.
- **SQLite** is another open-source database that's really showing some promise. This program is very small and fast, so it works well in places you wouldn't expect to see a full-fledged database (think cell phones and PDAs).

The great news is that almost all these databases work in the same general way. They all read fairly similar dialects of the SQL language. No matter which database you choose, the basic operation is roughly the same.

Why use MySQL?

This book focuses on MySQL because this program is

- **Very accessible:** If you've already installed XAMPP (see Book VIII), you already have access to MySQL. Many hosting accounts also have MySQL access built in.
- **Easy to use:** You can use MySQL from the command line or from a special program. Most people manipulate SQL through a program called `phpMyAdmin` (introduced in the section "Setting Up phpMyAdmin," later in this chapter). This program provides a graphical interface to do most of the critical tasks.
- **Reasonably typical:** MySQL supports all the basic SQL features and a few enhancements. If you understand MySQL, you'll be able to switch to another RDBMS pretty easily.
- **Very powerful:** MySQL is powerful enough to handle typical Web server data processing for a small to mid-size company. Some extremely large corporations even use it.
- **Integrated with XAMPP and PHP:** PHP has built-in support for MySQL, so you can easily write PHP programs that work with MySQL databases.

Understanding the three-tier architecture

Modern Web programming often uses what's called the *three-tiered architecture,* as shown in Table 1-2.

Table 1-2 The Three-Tiered Architecture

Tier	*Platform (Software)*	*Content*	*Language*
Client	Web browser (Firefox)	Web page	XHTML/CSS/JS
Server	Web server (Apache)	Business rules and logic	PHP (or other similar language)
Data	Data server (MySQL)	Data content	SQL (through MySQL or another data server)

The user talks to the system through a Web browser, which manages XHTML code. CSS and JavaScript may be at the user tier, but everything is handled through the browser. The user then makes a request of the server, which is sometimes passed through a server-side language like PHP. This program then receives a request and processes it, returning HTML back to the client. Many requests involve data, which brings the third (data) tier into play. The Web server can package up a request to the data server through SQL. The data server manages the data and prepares a response to the Web server, which then makes HTML output back for the user.

Figure 1-1 provides an overview of the three-tier system.

Practicing with MySQL

MySQL is a server, so it must be installed on a computer in order to work. To practice with MySQL, you have a few options:

- **Run your own copy of MySQL from the command line.** If you have MySQL installed on your own machine, you can go to the command line and execute the program directly. This task isn't difficult, but it is tedious.
- **Use phpMyAdmin to interact with your own copy of MySQL.** This solution is often the best. phpMyAdmin is a set of PHP programs that allow you to access and manipulate your database through your Web browser. If you've set up XAMPP, you've got everything you need. (See Book VIII for more information about XAMPP.) You can also install MySQL and phpMyAdmin without XAMPP, but you should really avoid the headaches of manual configuration, if you can. In this chapter, I do all MySQL through phpMyAdmin, but I show other alternatives in Book V (where you can connect to MySQL through PHP) and Chapter 2 of this minibook.
- **Run MySQL from your hosting site.** If you're using Free Hostia or some other hosting service, you generally access MySQL through phpMyAdmin.

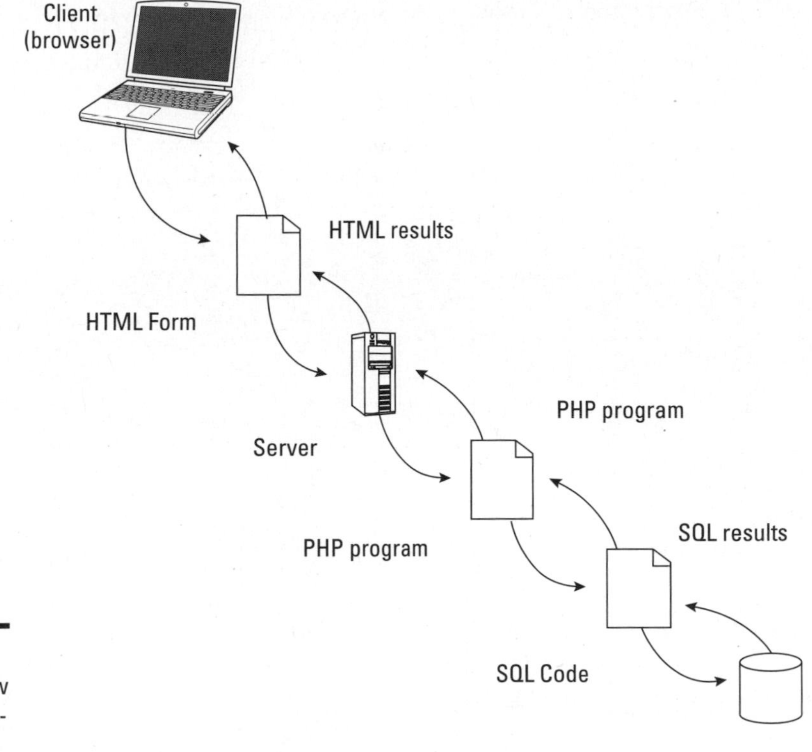

Figure 1-1: An overview of the three-tier data model.

Setting Up phpMyAdmin

By far the most common way to interact with MySQL is through phpMyAdmin. If you've installed XAMPP, you already have phpMyAdmin. Here's how you use it to get to MySQL:

1. **Turn on MySQL with the XAMPP Control Panel, shown in Figure 1-2.**

   You also need Apache running (because XAMPP runs through the server). You don't need to run MySQL or Apache as a service, but you must have them both running.

2. **Go to the XAMPP main directory in your browser.**

   If you used the default installation, you can just point your browser to `http://localhost/xampp`. It should look like Figure 1-3.

   WARNING!

   Don't just go through the regular file system to find the XAMPP directory. You must use the `localhost` mechanism so that the PHP code in php MyAdmin is activated.

3. **Find phpMyAdmin in the Tools section of the menu.**

   The phpMyAdmin page looks like Figure 1-4.

4. **Create a new database.**

   Type the name for your database in the indicated text field. I call my database `xfd`. (Xhtml For Dummies — get it?)

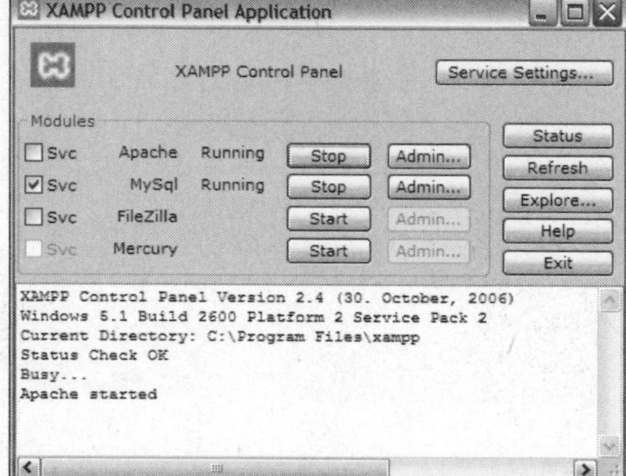

Figure 1-2: Turning on MySQL and Apache.

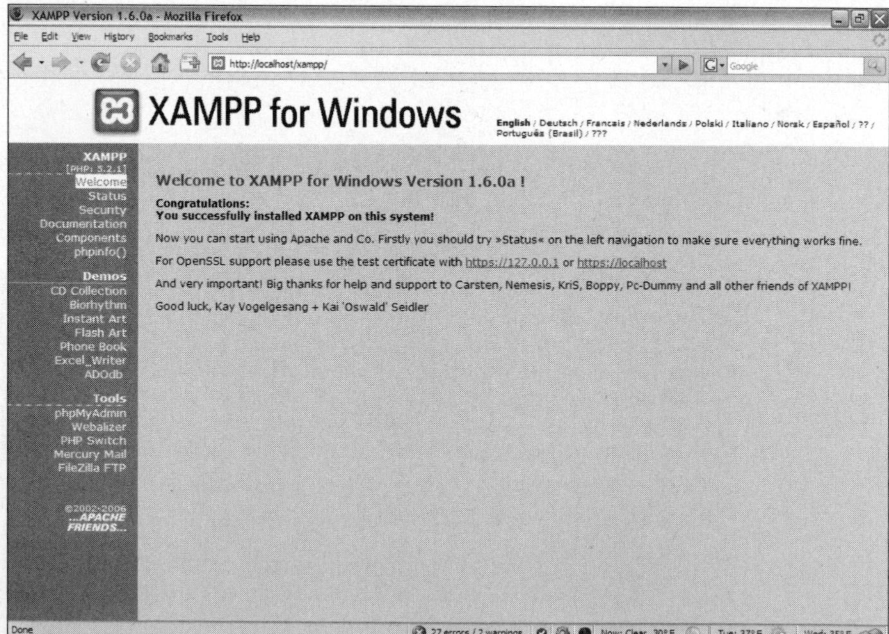

Figure 1-3: Locating the XAMPP subdirectory through localhost.

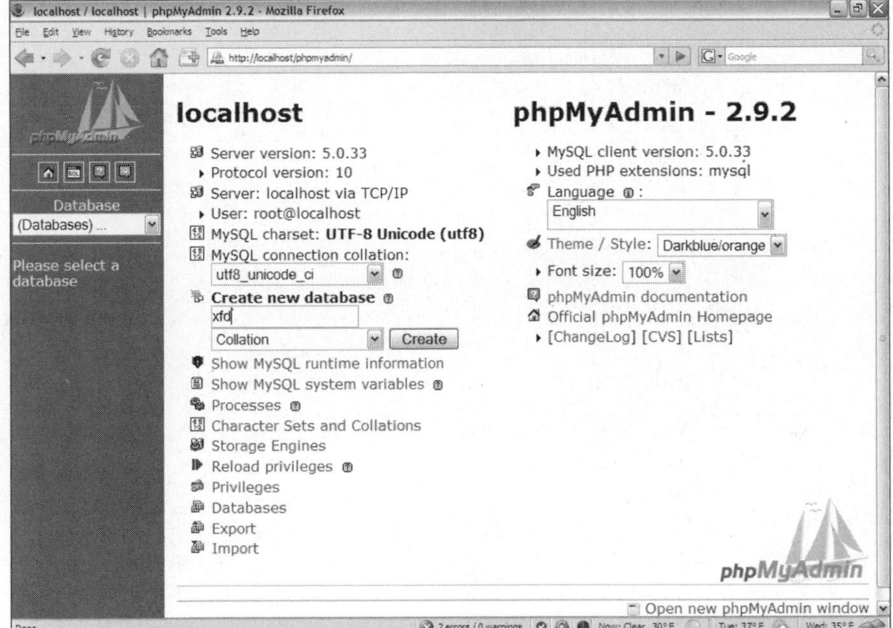

Figure 1-4: The php-MyAdmin main page.

Changing the root password

MySQL is a powerful system, which means it can cause a lot of damage in the wrong hands. Unfortunately, the default installation of MySQL has a security loophole you could drive an aircraft carrier through. The default user is called root and has no password whatsoever. Although you don't have to worry about any pesky passwords, the KGB can also get to your data without passwords, either.

Believe me, the bad guys know that root is the most powerful account on MySQL and that it has no password by default. They're glad to use that information to do you harm (or worse, to do harm in your name). Obviously, giving the root account a password is a very good idea. Fortunately, it's not difficult to do. . . .

1. **Log into phpMyAdmin as normal.**

   The main screen looks like Figure 1-5. Note the scary warning of gloom at the bottom. You're about to fix that problem.

2. **Click the Privileges link to modify user privileges.**

   The new screen looks something like Figure 1-6.

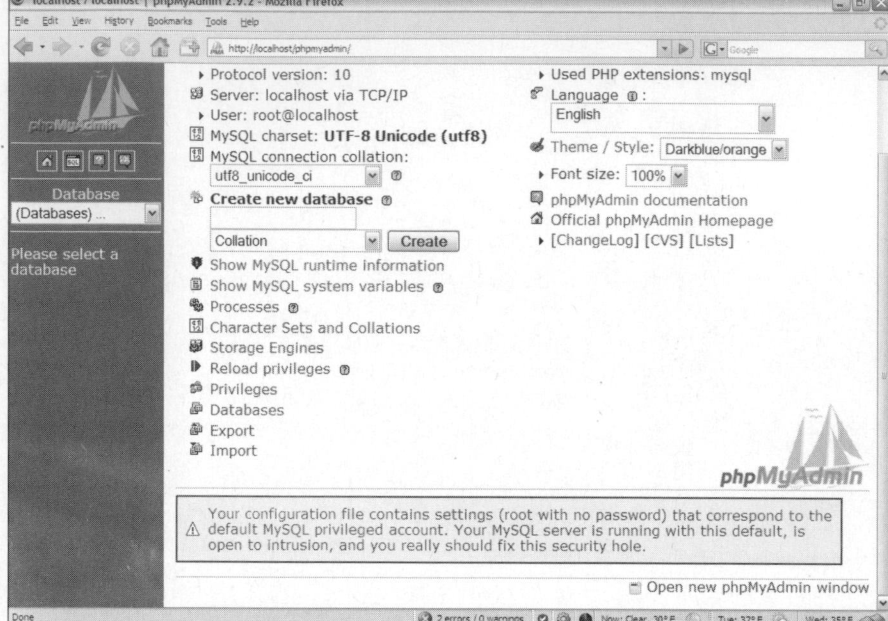

Figure 1-5: Here's the main phpMyAdmin screen with a privileges link.

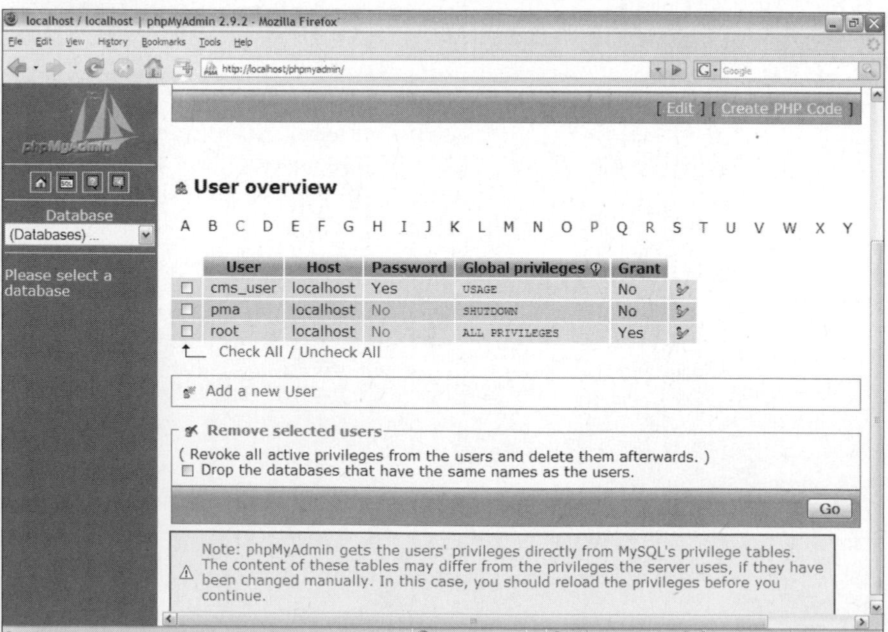

Figure 1-6: The various users are stored in a table.

3. **Edit the root user.**

   Chances are good that you have only one user, called root, and the `Password` field says `No`. You'll be adding a password to the root user. The icon at the right allows you to edit this record. (Hover your mouse over the small icon to see ToolTips if you can't find it.) The edit screen looks like Figure 1-7.

4. **Examine the awesome power of the root administrator.**

   Even if you don't know what all these things are, root can clearly do lots of things, and you shouldn't let this power go unchecked. (Consult any James Bond movie for more information on what happens with unfettered power.) You're still going to let root do all these things, but you're going to set a password so that only you can be root on this system. Scroll down a bit on the page until you see the segment that looks like Figure 1-8.

5. **Assign a password.**

   Simply click the box that says `Password` and then type the password in this box and the next one. Be sure that you type the same password twice. Follow all your typical password rules (six or more characters long, no spaces, case-sensitive).

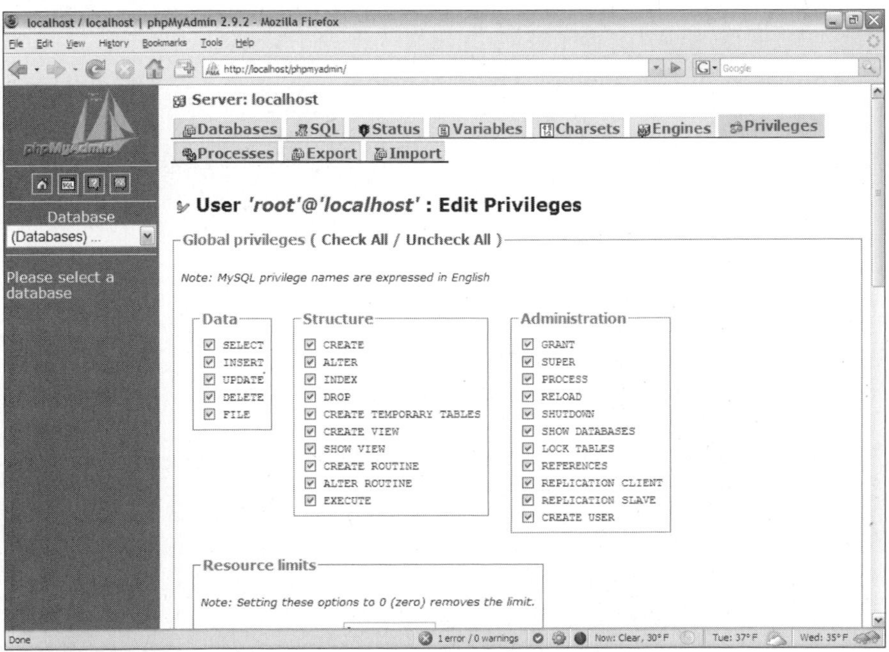

Figure 1-7: You can use this tool to modify the root user's permissions.

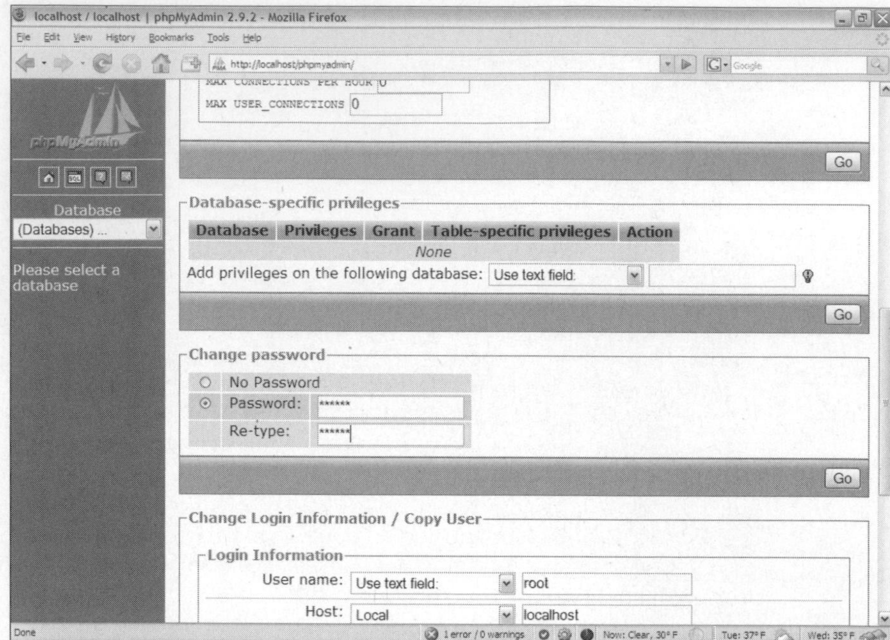

Figure 1-8: This area is where you add the password.

6. **Hit the Go button.**

   If all went well, the password changes.

7. **Recoil in horror.**

   Try to go back to the phpMyAdmin home (with the little house icon), and something awful happens, as shown in Figure 1-9.

Don't panic about the error in Figure 1-9. Believe it or not, this error is good. Up to now, phpMyAdmin was logging into your database as root without a password (just like the baddies were going to do). Now, phpMyAdmin is trying to do the same thing (log in as root without a password), but it can't because now root has a password.

What you have to do is tell phpMyAdmin that you just locked the door and give it the key. (Well, the password, but I was enjoying my metaphor.)

1. **Find the phpMyAdmin configuration file.**

   You have to let phpMyAdmin know that you've changed the password. Look for a file in your phpMyAdmin directory called `config.inc.php`. (If you used the default XAMPP installation, the file is in `C:\Program Files\xampp\phpMyAdmin\config.inc.php`.)

Figure 1-9: That message can't be good. Maybe I should have left it vulnerable.

2. **Find the root password setting.**

   Using the text editor's search function. I found it on line 70, but it may be someplace else in your editor. In Notepad++, it looks like Figure 1-10.

3. **Change the root setting to reflect your password.**

   Enter your root password. For example, if your new password is myPassword, change the line so that it looks like

   ```
   $cfg['Servers'][$i]['password']      = 'myPassword';     // MySQL password
   ```

   Of course, myPassword is just an example. It's really a bad password. Put your actual password in its place.

4. **Save the `config.inc.php` file.**

   Save the configuration file and return to phpMyAdmin.

5. **Try getting into phpMyAdmin again.**

   This time, you don't get the error, and nobody is able to get into your database without your password. You shouldn't have to worry about this issue again, but whenever you connect to this database, you do need to supply the username and password.

Notepad++ - C:\Program Files\xampp\phpMyAdmin\config.inc.php

```
                                                                    // features (pmadb)
$cfg['Servers'][$i]['auth_type']       = 'config';       // Authentication method (config, http or
cookie based)?
$cfg['Servers'][$i]['user']            = 'root';         // MySQL user
$cfg['Servers'][$i]['password']        = '';             // MySQL password (only needed
                                                         // with 'config' auth_type)
$cfg['Servers'][$i]['only_db']         = '';             // If set to a db-name, only
                                                         // this db is displayed in left frame
                                                         // It may also be an array of db-names,
where sorting order is relevant.
$cfg['Servers'][$i]['verbose']         = '';             // Verbose name for this host - leave
blank to show the hostname

$cfg['Servers'][$i]['pmadb']           = 'phpmyadmin';              // Database used for
Relation, Bookmark and PDF Features
                                                         // (see scripts/create_tables.sql)
                                                         //   - leave blank for no support
                                                         //     DEFAULT: 'phpmyadmin'
$cfg['Servers'][$i]['bookmarktable'] = 'pma_bookmark';             // Bookmark table
                                                         //   - leave blank for no bookmark support
                                                         //     DEFAULT: 'pma_bookmark'
$cfg['Servers'][$i]['relation']        = 'pma_relation';            // table to describe the
relation between links (see doc)
                                                         //   - leave blank for no relation-links
support
```

PHP Hypertext Preprocessor file | nb char : 38176 | Ln : 70 Col : 41 Sel : 0 | Dos\Windows | ANSI | INS

Figure 1-10: Here's the username and configuration information.

Adding a user

Changing the root password is the absolute minimum security measure, but it's not the only one. You can add various virtual users to your system to protect it further.

You're able to log into your own copy of MySQL (and phpMyAdmin) as root because you're the root owner. (If not, then refer to the preceding section.) It's your database, so you should be allowed to do anything with it.

You probably don't want your programs logging in as root because that can allow malicious code to sneak into your system and do mischief. You're better off setting up a different user for each database and allowing that user access only to the tables within that database.

I'm really not kidding about the danger here. A user with root access can get into your database and do anything, including creating more users or changing the root password so that you can no longer get into your own database! You generally shouldn't write any PHP programs that use root. Instead, have a special user for that database. If the bad guys get in as anything but root, they can't blow up everything.

Fortunately, creating new users with phpMyAdmin isn't a difficult procedure:

1. **Log into phpMyAdmin with root access.**

   If you're running XAMPP on your own server, you'll automatically log in as root.

2. **Activate the Privileges tab to view user privileges.**

3. **Add a new user using the Add a New User link on the Privileges page.**

4. **Fill in user information on the new user page (see Figure 1-11).**

   Be sure to add a username and password. Typically, you use `'localhost'` as the host.

5. **Create a database, if it doesn't already exist.**

   If you haven't already made a database for this project, you can do so automatically with the Create Table Automatically radio button.

6. **Do not assign global privileges.**

   Only the root user should have global privileges. You want this user to have the ability to work only within a specific database.

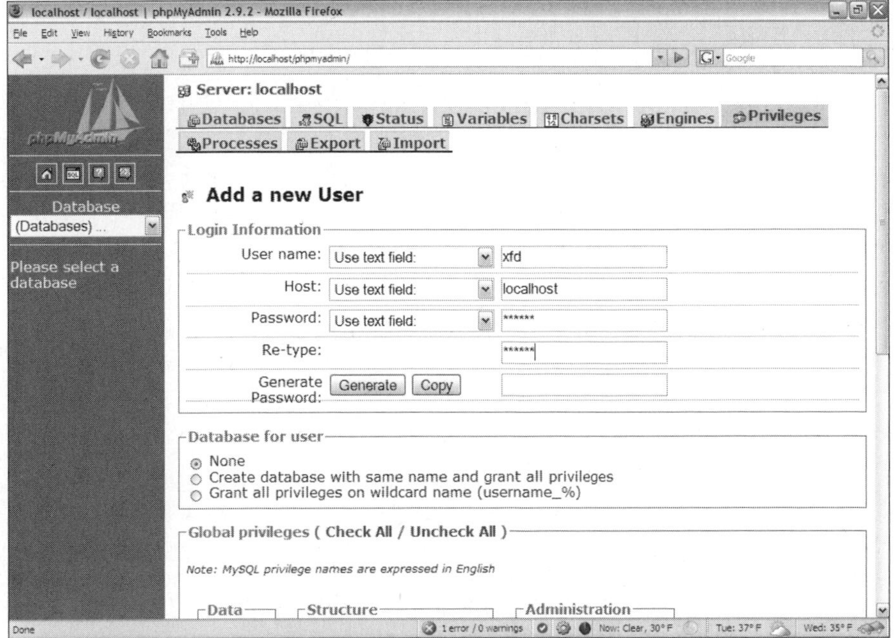

Figure 1-11: Here's the new xfd user being created.

7. **Create the user by clicking the Go button.**

   You see a new screen like Figure 1-12 (you need to scroll down a bit to see this part of the page).

8. **Specify the user's database.**

   Select the database in the drop-down list. This user (`xfd`) will have access only to tables in the `xfd` database. Note that you probably don't have many databases on your system when you start out.

9. **Apply most privileges.**

   You generally want your programs to do nearly everything within their own database so that you can apply almost all privileges (for now, anyway). I typically select all privileges except grant, which allows the user to allow access to other users. Figure 1-13 shows the Privileges page.

As you're starting out, your programs have access to one database and are able to do plenty with it. As your data gets more critical, you'll probably want to create more restrictive user accounts so that those programs that should only be reading your data don't have the ability to modify or delete records. This change makes it more difficult for the bad guys to mess up your day.

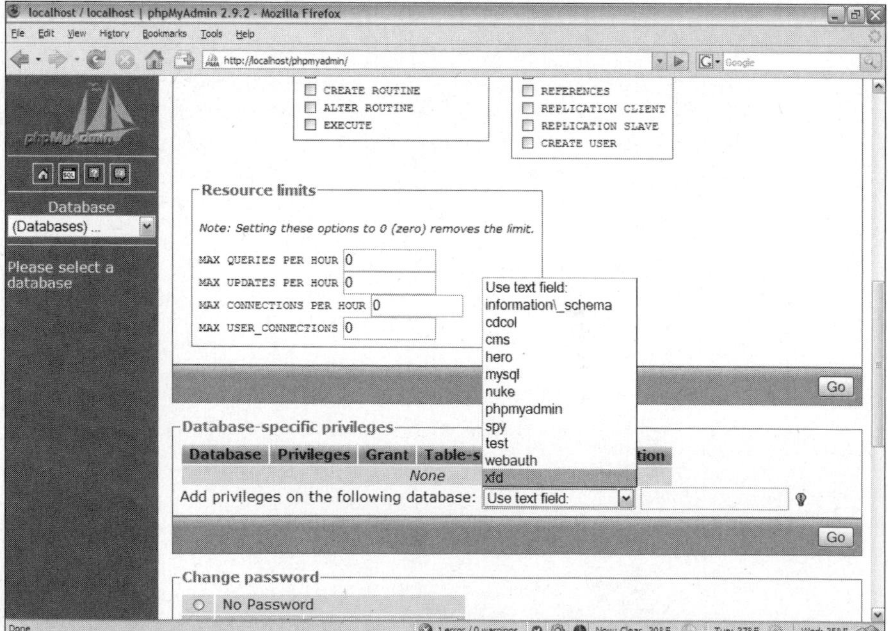

Figure 1-12: You can specify a specific database for this user.

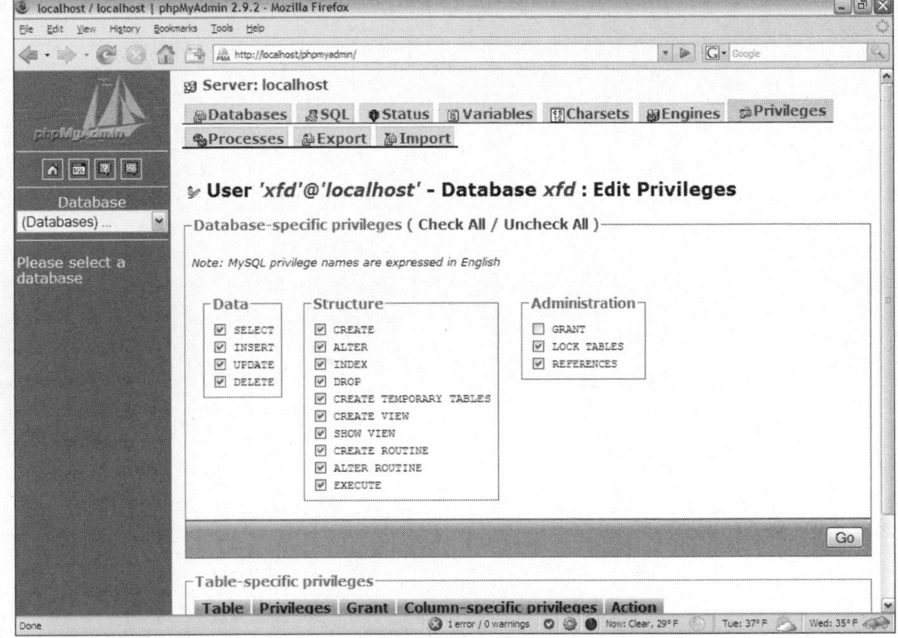

Figure 1-13: The xfd user can do everything but grant other privileges on this database.

Your database users won't usually be people. This idea is hard, particularly if you haven't used PHP or another server-side language yet. The database users are usually programs you have written that access the database in your name.

Using phpMyAdmin on a remote server

If you're working on some remote system with your service provider, the mechanism for managing and creating your databases may be a bit different. Each host has its own quirks, but they're all pretty similar. As an example, here's how I connect to the system on Free Hostia at `http://freehostia.com` (where I post the example pages for this book):

1. **Log onto your service provider using the server login.**

   You usually see some sort of control panel with the various tools you have as an administrator. These tools often look like Figure 1-14.

2. **Locate your database settings.**

   Not all free hosting services provide database access, but some (like Free Hostia — at least, as of this writing) do have free MySQL access. You usually can access some sort of tool for managing your databases. (You'll probably have a limited number of databases available on free servers, but more with commercial accounts.) Figure 1-15 shows the database administration tool in Free Hostia.

Figure 1-14: The Free Hostia site shows a number of useful administration tools.

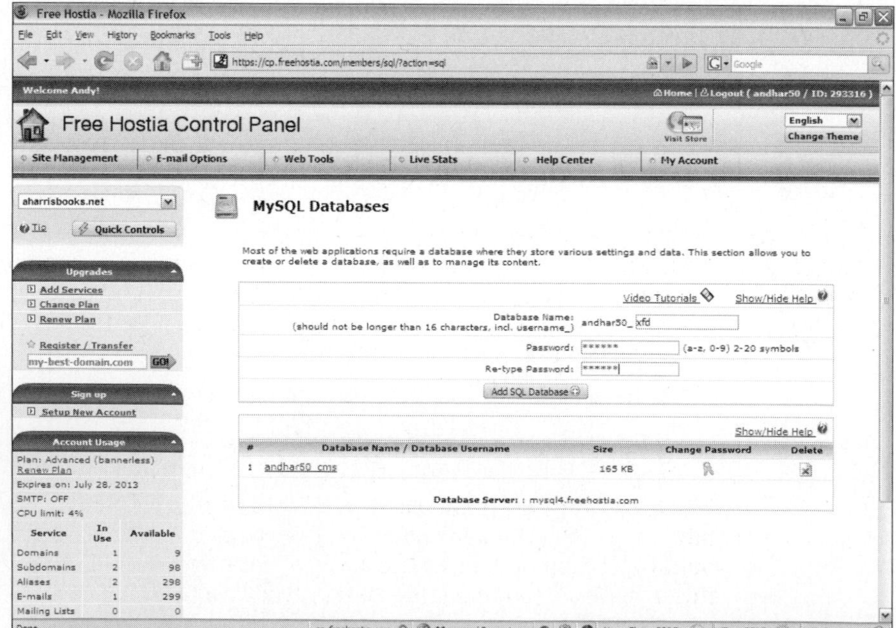

Figure 1-15: The database administration tool lets me create or edit databases.

3. **Create a database according to the rules enforced by your system.**

   Sometimes, you can create the database within phpMyAdmin (as I did in the last section), but more often, you need to use a special tool like the one shown in Figure 1-15 to create your databases. Free Hostia imposes a couple of limits: The database name begins with the system username, and it can't be more than 16 characters long.

   Don't freak out if your screen looks a little different than Figure 1-15. Different hosting companies have slightly different rules and systems, so things won't be just like this, but they'll probably be similar. If you get stuck, be sure to look at the hosting service's Help system. You can also contact the support system. They're usually glad to help, but they're (understandably) much more helpful if you've paid for the hosting service. Even the free hosting systems offer some online support, but if you're going to be serious, paying for online support is a good deal.

4. **Create a password for this database.**

   You probably need a password (and sometimes another username) for your databases to prevent unauthorized access to your data. Because the database is a different server than the Web server, it has its own security system. On Free Hostia, I must enter a password, and the system automatically creates a MySQL username with the same name as the database. Keep track of this information because you need it later when you write a program to work with this data.

5. **Use phpMyAdmin to add tables to your database.**

   Once you've defined the database, you can usually use phpMyAdmin to manipulate the data. With Free Hostia, you can simply click a database name to log into phpMyAdmin as the administrator of that database. Figure 1-16 shows the new database in phpMyAdmin, ready for action.

Typically, a remote server doesn't give you root access, so you don't have to mess around with the whole root password mess described in the "Changing the root password" section of this chapter. Instead, you often have either one password you always use in phpMyAdmin, or you have a different user and password for each database.

Making a Database with phpMyAdmin

When you've got a database, you can build a table. When you've defined a table, you can add data. When you've got data, you can look at it. Begin by building a table to handle the contact data described in the first section of this chapter, "Examining the Basic Structure of Data":

1. **Be sure you're logged into phpMyAdmin.**

   The phpMyAdmin page should look something like Figure 1-17, with your database name available in the left column.

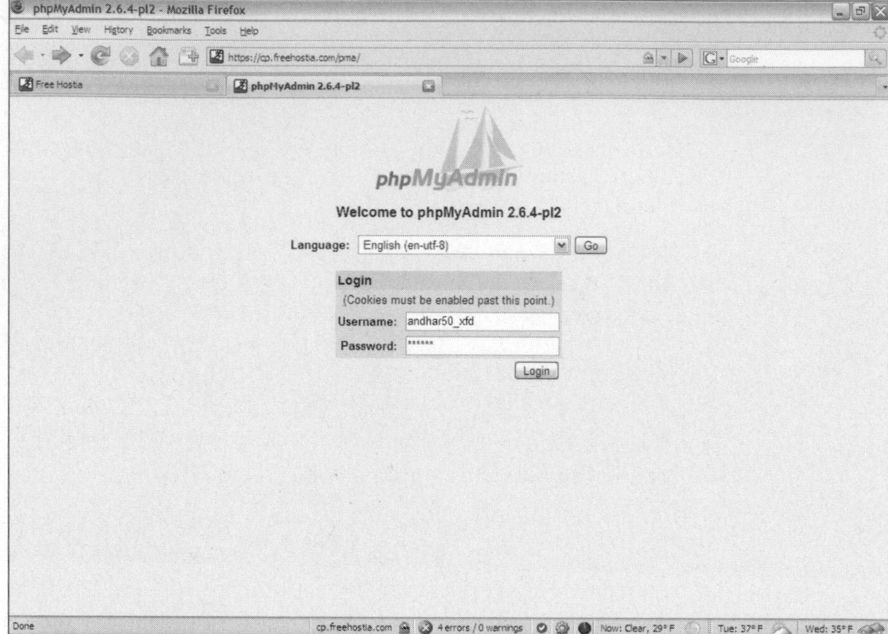

Figure 1-16: Now, I can edit the database in php-MyAdmin.

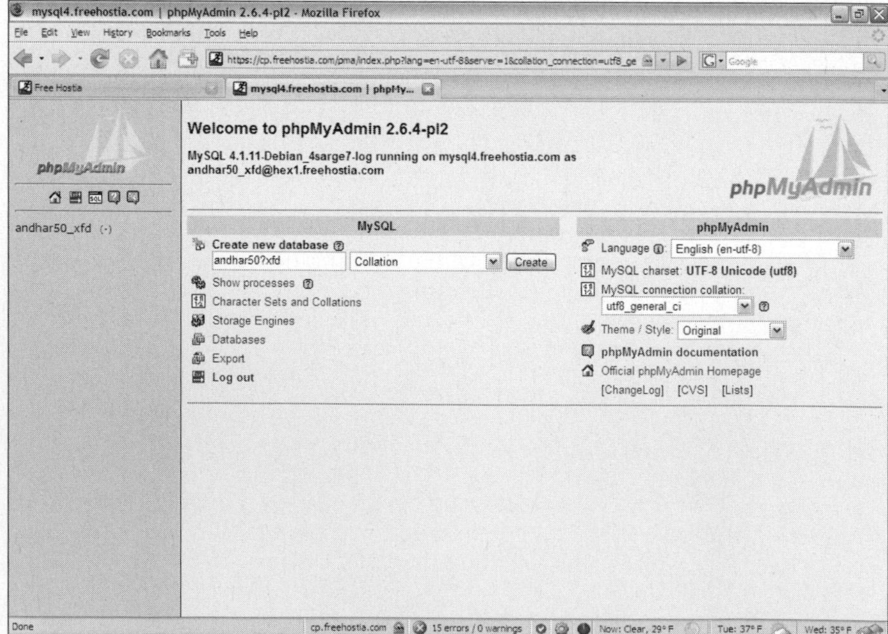

Figure 1-17: The main screen of the php-MyAdmin system.

2. **Activate the database by clicking the database name in the left column.**

   If the database is empty, an Add Table page, shown in Figure 1-18, appears.

3. **Create a new table using the phpMyAdmin tool.**

   Now that you have a database, add the contacts table to it. The contacts database has four fields, so type a 4 into the box and let 'er rip. A form like Figure 1-19 appears.

4. **Enter the field information.**

   Type the field names into the grid to create the table. It should look like Figure 1-20.

   In Figure 1-20, you can't see it, but a radio button appears to the far right that you can use to set the contactID as a primary key. Be sure to add this indicator.

5. **Click the Save button and watch the results.**

   phpMyAdmin automatically writes some SQL code for you and executes it. Figure 1-21 shows the code and the new table.

   Now, the left panel indicates that you're in the `xfd` database, which has a table called contact.

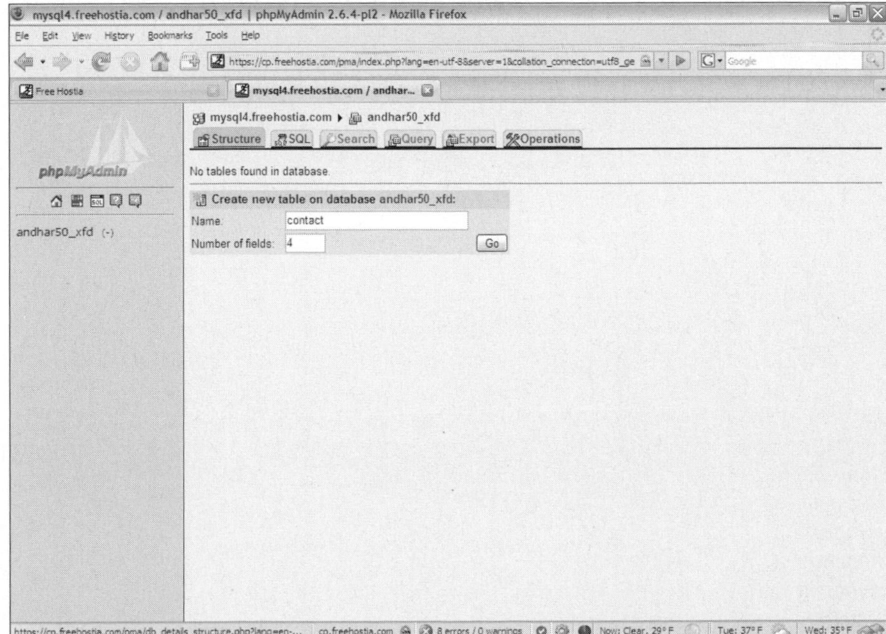

Figure 1-18: Type a table name to begin adding a table.

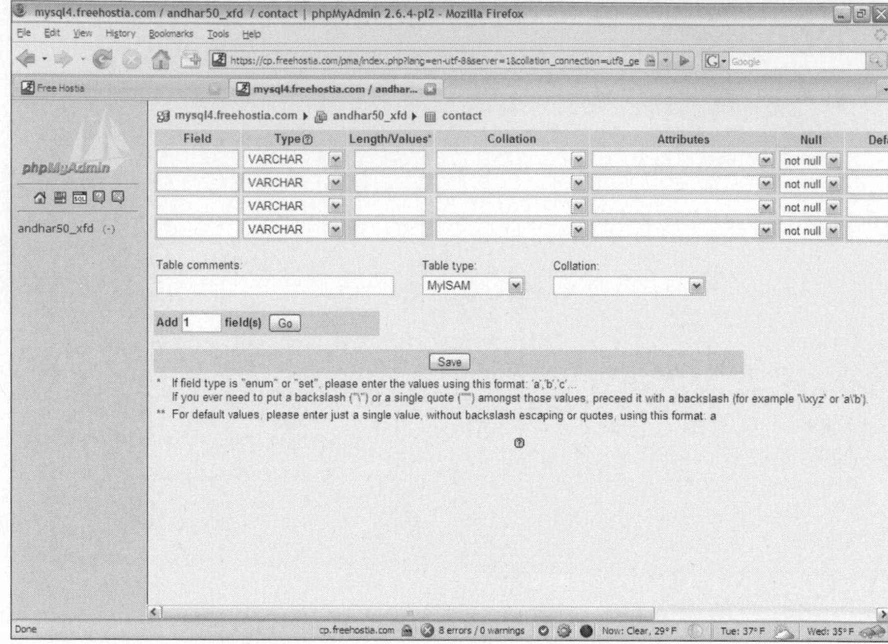

Figure 1-19: Creating the contacts table.

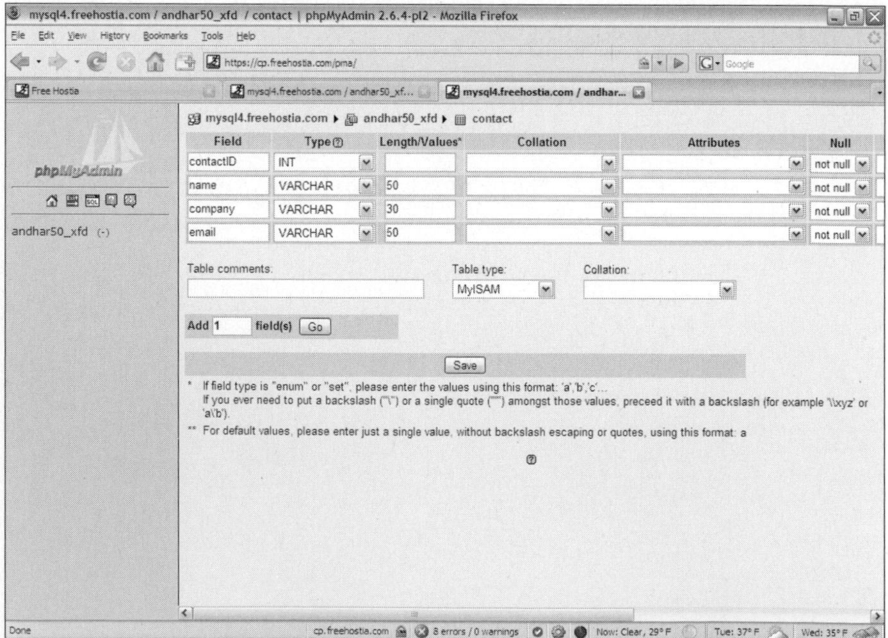

Figure 1-20: Enter field data on this form.

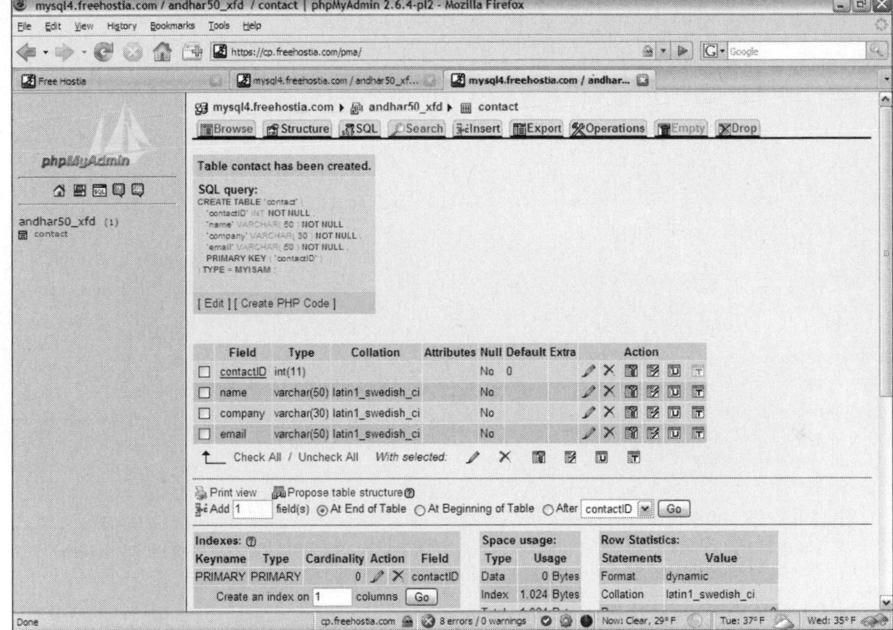

Figure 1-21: phpMyAdmin created this mysterious code and built a table.

After you define a table, you can add data. Click contact in the left column, and you see the screen for managing the contact table, as shown in Figure 1-22.

You can add data with the Insert tab, which gives a form like Figure 1-23, based on your table design.

After you add the record, choose Insert Another Row and click the Go button. Repeat until you've added all the contacts you want in your database.

After you add all the records you want to the database, you can use the Browse tab to see all the data in the table. Figure 1-24 shows my table after I added all my contacts to it and browsed.

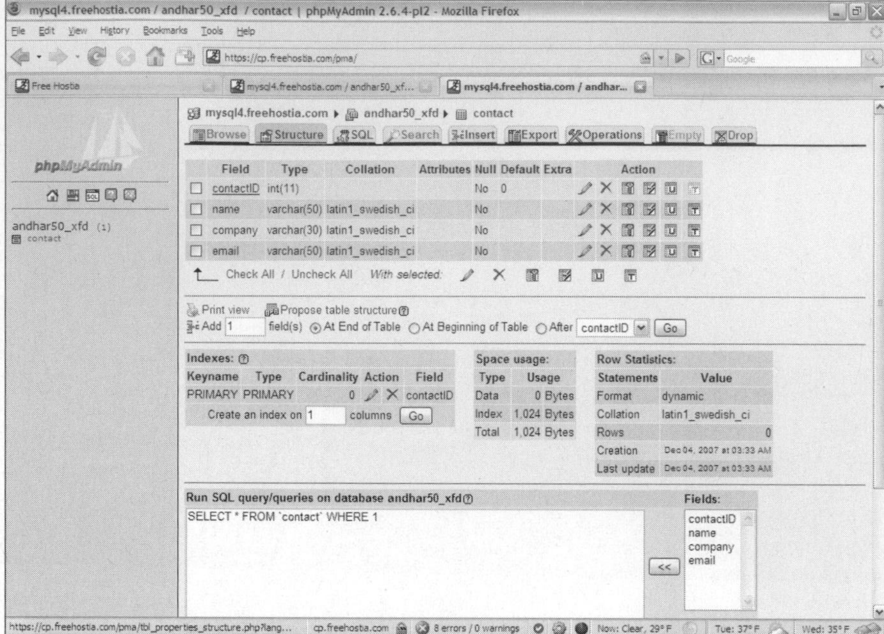

Figure 1-22: I've added the fields.

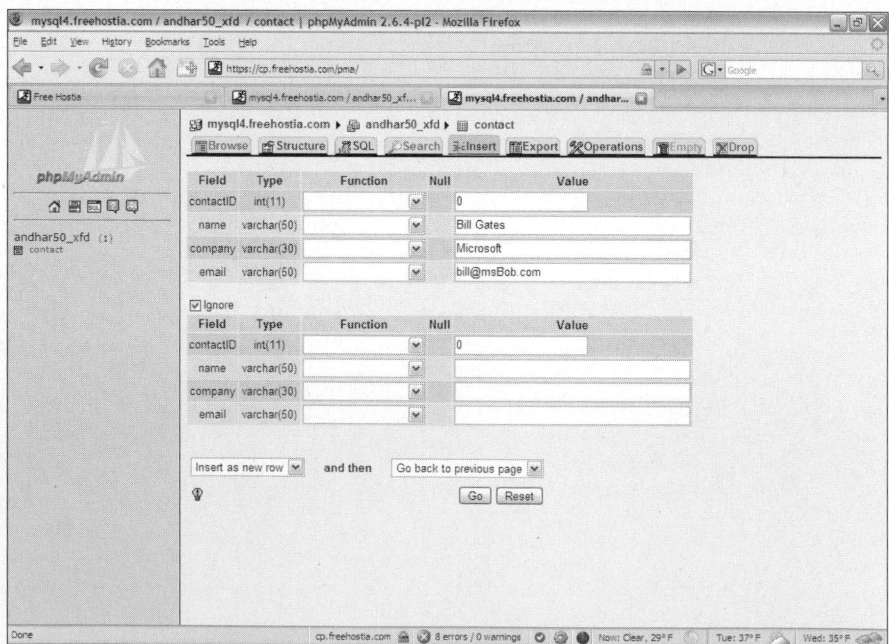

Figure 1-23: Adding a record to the table.

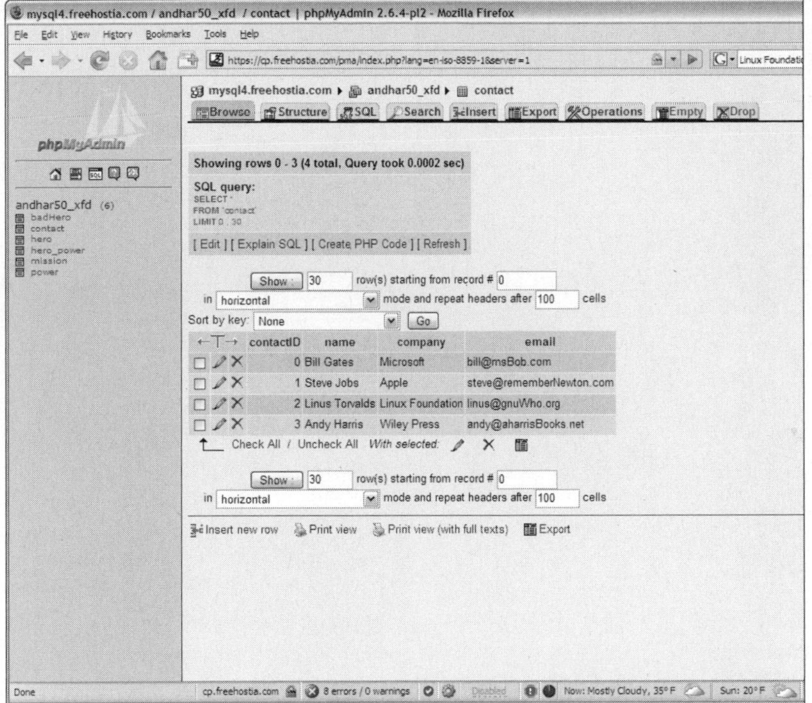

Figure 1-24: Viewing the table data in phpMy-Admin.

Chapter 2: Managing Data with SQL

In This Chapter

- ✔ **Working with SQL script files**
- ✔ **Using** `AUTO_INCREMENT` **to build primary key values**
- ✔ **Selecting a subset of fields**
- ✔ **Displaying a subset of records**
- ✔ **Modifying your data**
- ✔ **Deleting records**
- ✔ **Exporting your data**

Although we tend to think of the Internet as a series of interconnected documents, the Web is increasingly about data. The HTML and XHTML languages are still used to manage Web documents, but the SQL (Structured Query Language) — the language of data — is becoming increasingly central. In this chapter, you discover how SQL is used to define a data structure, add data to a database, and modify that data.

Writing SQL Code by Hand

Although you can use phpMyAdmin to build databases, all it really does is write and execute SQL code for you. You should know how to write SQL code yourself for many reasons:

- ✦ **It's pretty easy.** SQL isn't terribly difficult (at least, to begin with — things do get involved later). The basics are actually probably easier to code yourself than to create them using phpMyAdmin.
- ✦ **You need to write code in your programs.** You probably run your database from within PHP programs. You need to be able to write SQL commands from within your PHP code, and phpMyAdmin doesn't help much with that job.
- ✦ **You can't trust computers.** You should understand any code that has your name on it, even if you use a tool like phpMyAdmin to write it. If your program breaks, you have to fix it eventually, so you really should know how it works.

✦ **SQL scripts are portable.** Moving an entire data structure to a new server is difficult, but if you have a script that creates and populates the database, that script is just an ASCII file. You can easily move a complete database (including the data) to a new machine.

✦ **SQL scripts allow you to quickly rebuild a corrupted database.** As you're testing your system, you'll commonly make mistakes that can harm your data structure. It's very nice to have a script that you can use to quickly reset your data to some standard test state.

Understanding SQL syntax rules

SQL is a language (like XHTML, JavaScript, CSS, and PHP), so it has its own syntax rules. The rules and traditions of SQL are a bit unique because this language has a different purpose than more traditional programming languages:

✦ **Keywords are in uppercase.** Officially, SQL is not case-sensitive, but the tradition is to make all reserved words in uppercase and the names of all your custom elements camel-case. Some variations of SQL are case-sensitive, so you're safest assuming that they all are.

✦ **One statement can take up more than one line in the editor.** SQL statements aren't usually difficult, but they can get long. Having one statement take up many lines in the editor is common.

✦ **Logical lines end in semicolons.** Like PHP and JavaScript, each statement in SQL ends in a semicolon.

✦ **White space is ignored.** DBMS systems don't pay attention to spaces and carriage returns, so you can (and should) use these tools to help you clarify your code meaning.

✦ **Single quotes are used for text values.** MySQL usually uses single quotes to denote text values, rather than the double quotes used in other languages. If you really want to enclose a single quote in your text, backslash it.

Examining the buildContact.sql script

Take a look at the following code:

```
-- buildContact.sql

DROP TABLE IF EXISTS contact;

CREATE TABLE contact (
  contactID int PRIMARY KEY,
  name VARCHAR(50),
  company VARCHAR(30),
  email VARCHAR(50)
);
```

```
INSERT INTO contact VALUES
  (0, 'Bill Gates', 'Microsoft', 'bill@msBob.com');
INSERT INTO contact VALUES
  (1, 'Steve Jobs', 'Apple', 'steve@rememberNewton.com');
INSERT INTO contact VALUES
  (2, 'Linus Torvalds', 'Linux Foundation', 'linus@gnuWho.org');
INSERT INTO contact VALUES
  (3, 'Andy Harris', 'Wiley Press', 'andy@aharrisBooks.net');

SELECT * FROM contact;
```

This powerful code is written in SQL. I explain each segment in more detail throughout the section, but here's an overview:

1. **Delete the contact table, if it already exists.**

   This script completely rebuilds the contact table, so if it already exists, it is temporarily deleted to avoid duplication.

2. **Create a new table named `contact`.**

   As you can see, the table creation syntax is spare but pretty straightforward. Each field name is followed by its type and length (at least, in the case of VARCHARs).

3. **Add values to the table by using the `INSERT` command.**

   Use a new `INSERT` statement for each record.

4. **View the table data using the `SELECT` command.**

   This command displays the content of the table.

Dropping a table

It may seem odd to begin creating a table by deleting it, but there's actually a good reason. As you experiment with a data structure, you'll often find yourself building and rebuilding the tables.

The line

```
DROP TABLE IF EXISTS contact
```

means "look at the current database and see whether the table `contact` appears in it. If so, delete it." This syntax ensures that you start over fresh, as you are rebuilding the table in the succeeding lines. Typical SQL scripts begin by deleting any tables that will be over-written to avoid confusion.

Creating a table

You create a table with the (aptly named) `CREATE TABLE` command. The specific table creation statement for the `contact` table looks like

```
CREATE TABLE contact (
  contactID int PRIMARY KEY,
  name VARCHAR(50),
  company VARCHAR(30),
  email VARCHAR(50)
);
```

Creating a table involves several smaller tasks:

1. **Specify the table name.**

   The `CREATE TABLE` statement requires a table name. Specify the table name. Table names (like variables and filenames) should generally not contain spaces or punctuation without good reason.

2. **Begin the field definition with a parenthesis.**

   The left parenthesis indicates the beginning of the field list. You traditionally list one field per line, indented as in regular code, although that format isn't required.

3. **Begin each field with its name.**

   Every field has a name and a type. Begin with the field name, which should also be one word.

4. **Indicate the field type.**

   The field type immediately follows the field name (with no punctuation).

5. **Indicate field length, if necessary.**

   If the field is a VARCHAR or CHAR field, specify its length in parentheses. You can specify the length of numeric types, but I don't recommend it because MySQL automatically determines the length of numeric fields.

6. **Add special modifiers.**

   Some fields have special modifiers. For now, note that the primary key is indicated on the contactID field.

7. **End the field definition with a comma.**

   The comma character indicates the end of a field definition.

8. **End the table definition with a closing parenthesis and a semicolon.**

   Close the parenthesis that started the table definition and end the entire statement with a semicolon.

Adding records to the table

You add data to the table with the `INSERT` command. The way this command works isn't too surprising:

```
INSERT INTO contact VALUES
  (0, 'Bill Gates', 'Microsoft', 'bill@msBob.com');
```

Follow these steps:

1. **Begin with the `INSERT` keyword.**

   Use `INSERT` to clarify that this instruction is a data insertion command.

2. **Specify the table you want to add data to.**

   In my example, I have only one table, so use `INTO contact` to specify that that's where the table goes.

3. **(Optional) Specify field names.**

   You can specify a list of field names, but this step is unnecessary if you add data to all fields in their standard order. (Normally, you don't bother with field names.)

4. **Use the `VALUES` keyword to indicate that a list of field values is coming.**

5. **Enclose the values in parentheses.**

   Use parentheses to enclose the list of data values.

6. **Put all values in the right order.**

   Place values in exactly the same order the fields were designated.

7. **Place text values in single quotes.**

   MySQL uses single quotes to specify text values.

8. **End the statement with a semicolon, as you do with all SQL commands.**

9. **Repeat with other data.**

   Add as many `INSERT` commands as you want to populate the data table.

Viewing the sample data

Once you've created and populated a table, you'll want to look it over. SQL provides the `SELECT` command for this purpose. `SELECT` is amazingly powerful, but its basic form is simplicity itself:

```
SELECT * FROM contact;
```

This command simply returns all fields of all records from your database.

Running a Script with phpMyAdmin

phpMyAdmin provides terrific features for working with SQL scripts. You can write your script directly in phpMyAdmin, or you can use any text editor.

Aptana Studio is fine for editing SQL files, but it doesn't have built-in SQL support, such as syntax checking and coloring. You can download a plugin to add these features (search for eclipse SQL plugins); use another editor like Notepad++, which does have syntax coloring for SQL; or just do without syntax coloring in Aptana (which is what I do).

If you've written a script in some other editor, you'll need to save it as a text file and import it into phpMyAdmin.

To run a script in phpMyAdmin

1. **Connect to phpMyAdmin.**

   Be sure that you're logged in and connected to the system.

2. **Navigate to the correct database.**

   Typically, you use a drop-down list to the left of the main screen to pick the database. (If you haven't created a database, see the instructions in Chapter 1 of this minibook.) Figure 2-1 shows the main phpMyAdmin screen with the `xfd` database enabled.

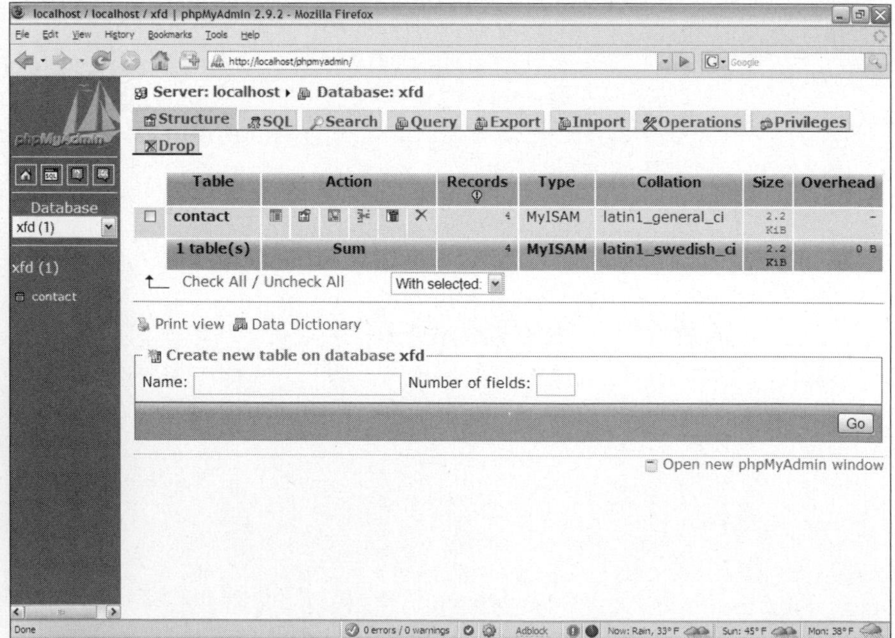

Figure 2-1: The xfd database is created and ready to go.

3. **Activate the SQL pop-up window.**

   You can do so by clicking the small SQL icon in the left-hand navigation menu. The resulting window looks like Figure 2-2.

Figure 2-2: The SQL script window.

4. **(Optional) Type your SQL code directly into this dialog box.**

   This shortcut is good for making quick queries about your data, but generally, you create and initialize data with prewritten scripts.

5. **Move to the Import Files tab.**

   In this tab, you can upload the file directly into the MySQL server. Figure 2-3 shows the resulting page. Use the Browse button to locate your file and the Go button to load it into MySQL.

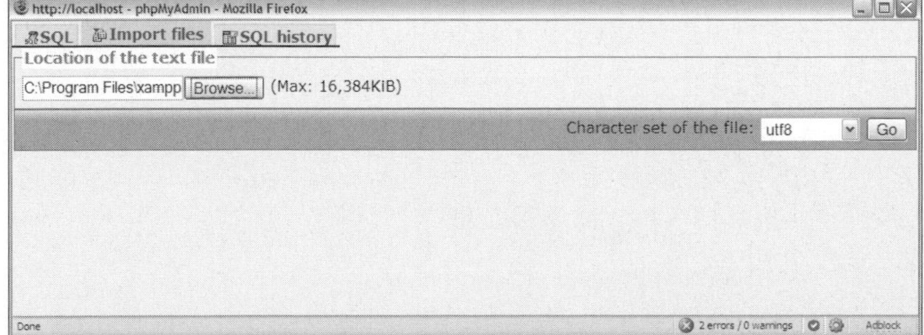

Figure 2-3: Importing an externally defined SQL script.

If you've already created the contact database by following the instructions in Chapter 1 of this minibook, you may be nervous that you'll overwrite the data. You will, but for this stage in the process, that's exactly what you want. The point of a script is to help you build a database and rebuild it quickly. After you've got meaningful data in the table, you won't be rebuilding it so often, but during the test and creation stage, it's a critical skill.

6. **Examine your handiwork.**

   Look back at the phpMyAdmin page, and you see something like Figure 2-4. It shows your script and, if you ended with a `SELECT` statement, an output of your table.

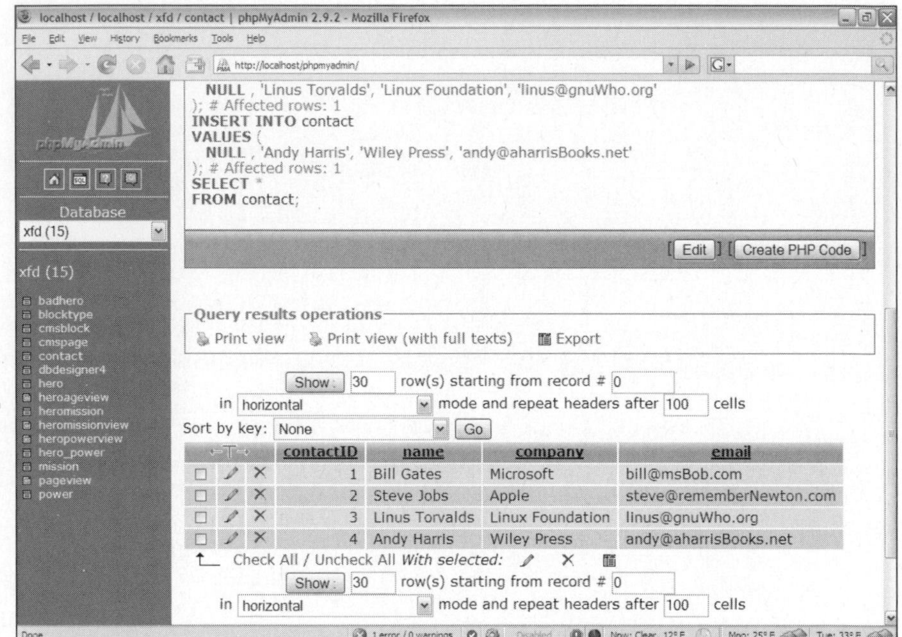

Figure 2-4: Here's the script and its results, shown in phpMyAdmin.

Using AUTO_INCREMENT for Primary Keys

Primary keys are important because you use them as a standard index for the table. The job of a primary key is to uniquely identify each record in the table. Remember that primary keys have a few important characteristics:

- **It must exist.** Every record must have a primary key.
- **It must be unique.** Two records in the same table can't have the same key.
- **It should not be null.** There must be a value in each key.

When you initially create a table, you have all the values in front of you, but what if you want to add a field later? Somehow, you have to ensure that the primary key in every record is unique.

Over the years, database developers have discovered that integer values are especially handy as primary keys. The great thing about integers is that you can always find a unique one. Just look for the largest index in your table and add one.

Fortunately, MySQL (like most database packages) has a wonderful feature for automatically generating unique integer indices.

Take a look at this variation of the `buildContact.sql` script:

```
-- buildContactAutoIncrement.sql

DROP TABLE IF EXISTS contact;

CREATE TABLE contact (
  contactID int PRIMARY KEY AUTO_INCREMENT,
  name VARCHAR(50),
  company VARCHAR(30),
  email VARCHAR(50)
);

INSERT INTO contact VALUES
  (null, 'Bill Gates', 'Microsoft', 'bill@msBob.com');
INSERT INTO contact VALUES
  (null, 'Steve Jobs', 'Apple', 'steve@rememberNewton.com');
INSERT INTO contact VALUES
  (null, 'Linus Torvalds', 'Linux Foundation', 'linus@gnuWho.org');
INSERT INTO contact VALUES
  (null, 'Andy Harris', 'Wiley Press', 'andy@aharrisBooks.net');

SELECT * FROM contact;
```


Here are the changes in this script:

- **Add the `AUTO_INCREMENT` tag to the primary key definition.** This tag indicates that the MySQL system will automatically generate a unique integer for this field. You can apply the `AUTO_INCREMENT` tag to any field, but you most commonly apply it to primary keys.
- **Replace index values with `null`.** When you define a table with `AUTO_INCREMENT`, you should no longer specify values in the affected field. Instead, just place the value `null`. When the SQL interpreter sees the value `null` on an `AUTO_INCREMENT` field, it automatically finds the next largest integer.

You may wonder why I'm entering the value `null` when I said primary keys should never be null. Well, I'm not really making them null. The `null` value is simply a signal to the interpreter: "Hey, this field is `AUTO_INCREMENT`, and I want you to find a value for it."

Latin-Swedish?

phpMyAdmin is a wonderful tool, but it does have one strange quirk. When you look over your table design, you may find that the `collation` is set to `latin1_swedish_ci`. This syntax refers to the native character set used by the internal data structure. Nothing is terribly harmful about this set (Swedish is a wonderful language), but I don't want to incorrectly imply that my database is written in Swedish.

Fortunately, it's an easy fix. In phpMyAdmin, go to the Operations tab and look for Table Options. You can then set your collation to whatever you want. I typically use `latin1_general_ci` as it works fine for American English, which is the language used in most of my data sets. (See the MySQL documentation about internationalization if you're working in a language that needs the collation feature.)

I've only run into this problem with phpMyAdmin. If you create your database directly from the MySQL interpreter or from within PHP programs, the collation issue doesn't seem to be a problem.

Selecting Data from Your Tables

Creating a database is great, but the real point of a database is to extract information from it. SQL provides an incredibly powerful command for retrieving data from the database. The basic form looks like

```
SELECT * FROM contact;
```

The easiest way to practice SQL commands is to use phpMyAdmin. Figure 2-5 shows phpMyAdmin with the SQL tab open.

Note that you can enter SQL code in multiple places. If you're working with a particular table, you can invoke that table's SQL tab (as I do in Figure 2-5). You can also always enter SQL code into your system with the SQL button on the main phpMyAdmin panel (on the left panel of all phpMyAdmin screens).

If you have a particular table currently active, the SQL dialog box shows you the fields of the current table, which can be handy when you write SQL queries.

Try the `SELECT * FROM contact;` code in the SQL dialog box, and you see the results shown in Figure 2-6.

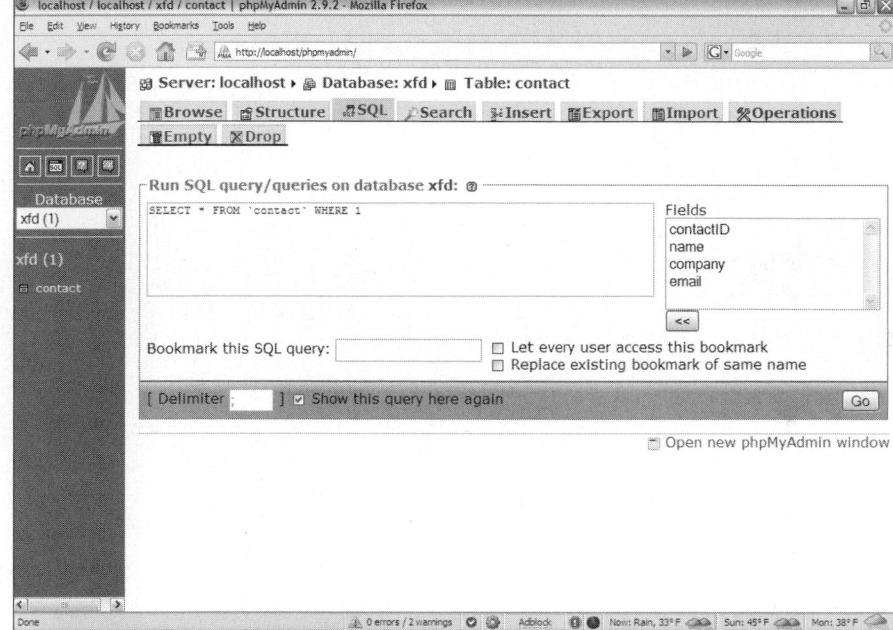

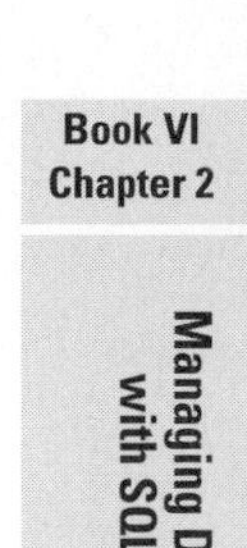

Figure 2-5: You can easily test queries in phpMyAdmin.

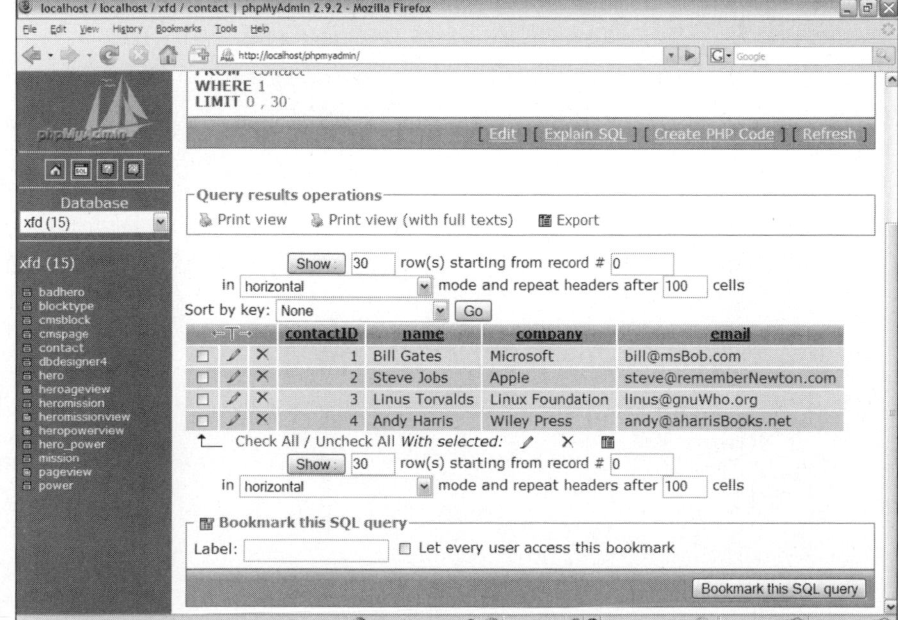

Figure 2-6: The standard `SELECT` statement returns the entire table.

Selecting only a few fields

As databases get more complex, you'll often find that you don't want everything. Sometimes, you only want to see a few fields at a time. You can replace the * characters with field names. For example, if you want to see only the names and e-mail addresses, use this variation of the `SELECT` statement:

```
SELECT name, email FROM contact;
```

Only the columns you specify appear, as you can see in Figure 2-7.

Here's another really nice trick you can do with fields. You can give each column a new virtual field name:

```
SELECT
  name as 'Person',
  email as 'Address'
FROM contact;
```

This code also selects only two columns, but this time, it attaches the special labels Person and Address to the columns. You can see this result in Figure 2-8.

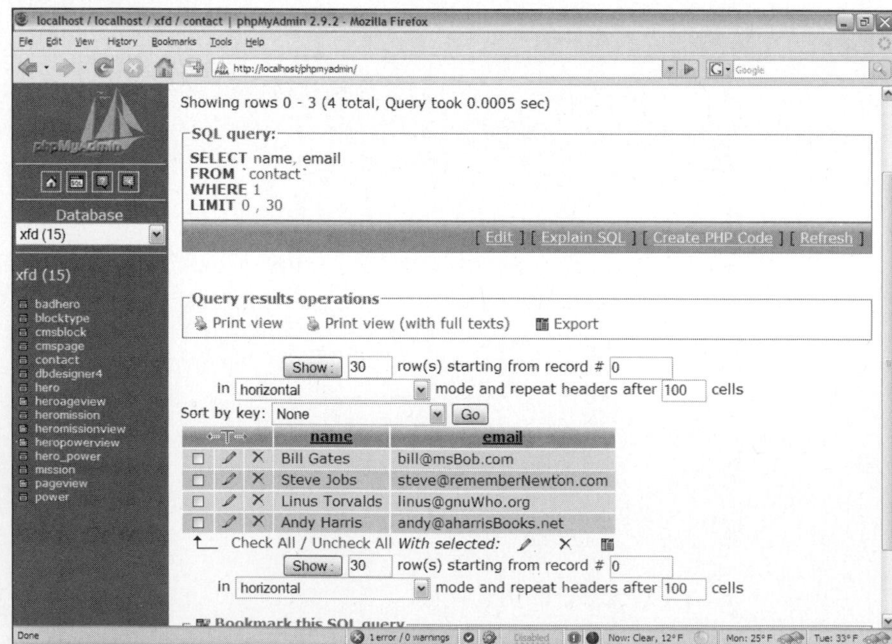

Figure 2-7: Now, the result is only two columns wide.

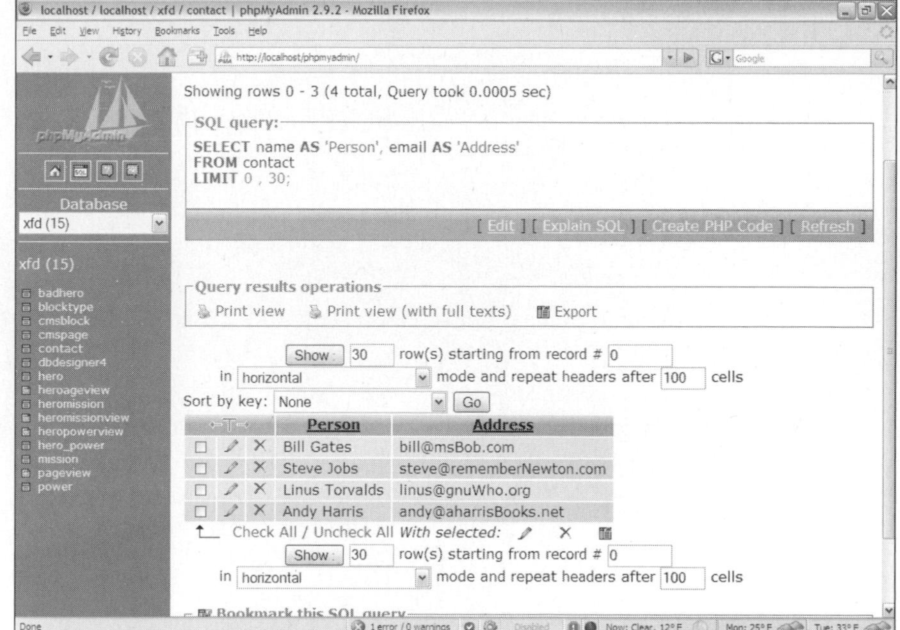

Figure 2-8: You can create virtual titles for your columns.

The capability to add a virtual name for each column doesn't seem like a big deal now, but it becomes handy when your database contains multiple tables. (For example, you may have a table named `pe` and another table named `owner` that both have a `name` field. The virtual title feature helps keep you (and your users) from being confused.

Selecting a subset of records

One of the most important jobs in data work is returning a smaller set of the database that meets some kind of criterion. For example, what if you want to dash off a quick e-mail to Steve Jobs? Use this query:

```
SELECT *
FROM contact
WHERE
  name = 'Steve Jobs';
```

This query has a few key features:

- **It selects all fields.** This query selects all the fields (for now).
- **A `WHERE` clause appears.** The `WHERE` clause allows you to specify a condition.

- **It has a condition.** SQL supports conditions, much like ordinary programming languages. MySQL returns only the records that match this condition.
- **The condition begins with a field name.** SQL conditions usually compare a field to a value (or to another field).
- **Conditions use single equals signs.** You can easily get confused on this detail because SQL uses the single equal sign (=) in conditions, where most programming languages use double equals (==) for the same purpose.
- **All text values must be in single quotes.** I'm looking for an exact match on the text string `'Steve Jobs'`.
- **It assumes that searches are case-sensitive.** Different databases have different behavior when it comes to case-sensitivity in `SELECT` statements, but you're safest assuming that case matters.

Figure 2-9 shows the result of this query.

SQL is pretty picky about the entire text string. The following query doesn't return any results in the contact database:

```
SELECT *
FROM contact
WHERE
  name = 'Steve';
```

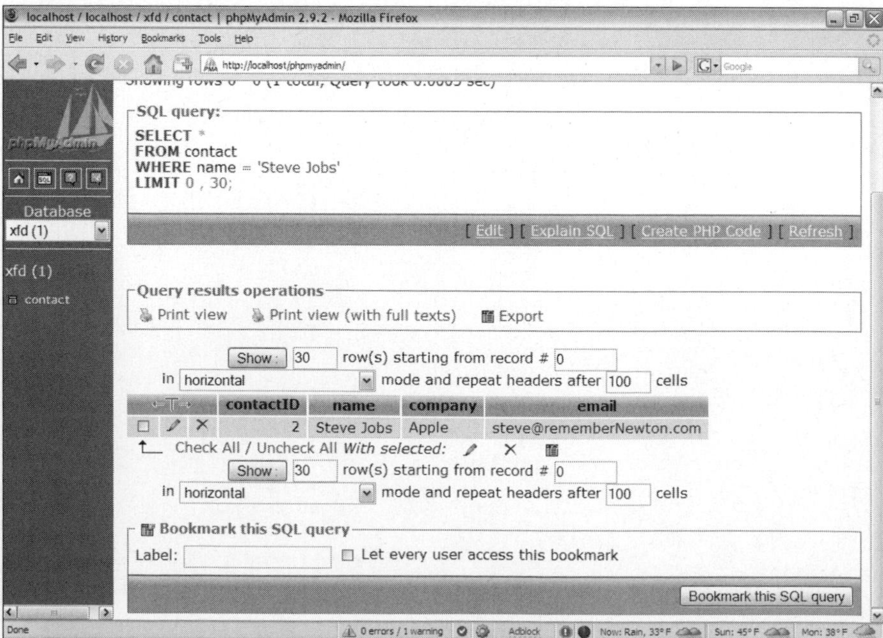

Figure 2-9: Here's a query that returns the result of a search.

The contact table doesn't have any records with a `name` field containing Steve (unless you added some records when I wasn't looking). Steve Jobs is not the same as Steve, so this query returns no results.

Searching with partial information

Of course, sometimes all you have is partial information. Take a look at the following variation to see how it works:

```
SELECT *
FROM contact
WHERE
  company LIKE 'L%';
```


This query looks at the `company` field and returns any records with a company field beginning with L. Figure 2-10 shows how it works.

The `LIKE` clause is pretty straightforward:

- **The keyword `LIKE` indicates a partial match is coming.** It's still the `SELECT` statement, but now it has the `LIKE` keyword to indicate an exact match isn't necessary.
- **The search text is still in single quotes, just like the ordinary `SELECT` statement.**
- **The percent sign (%) indicates a wildcard value.** A search string of `'W%'` looks for W followed by any number of characters.
- **Any text followed by % indicates that you're searching the beginning of the field.** So, if you're looking for people named Steve, you can write `SELECT * FROM contact WHERE name LIKE 'Steve%';`.

Searching for the ending value of a field

Likewise, you can find fields that end with a particular value. Say that you want to send an e-mail to everyone in your contact book with a `.com` address. This query does the trick:

```
SELECT *
FROM contact
WHERE
  email LIKE '%.com';
```

Figure 2-11 shows the results of this query.

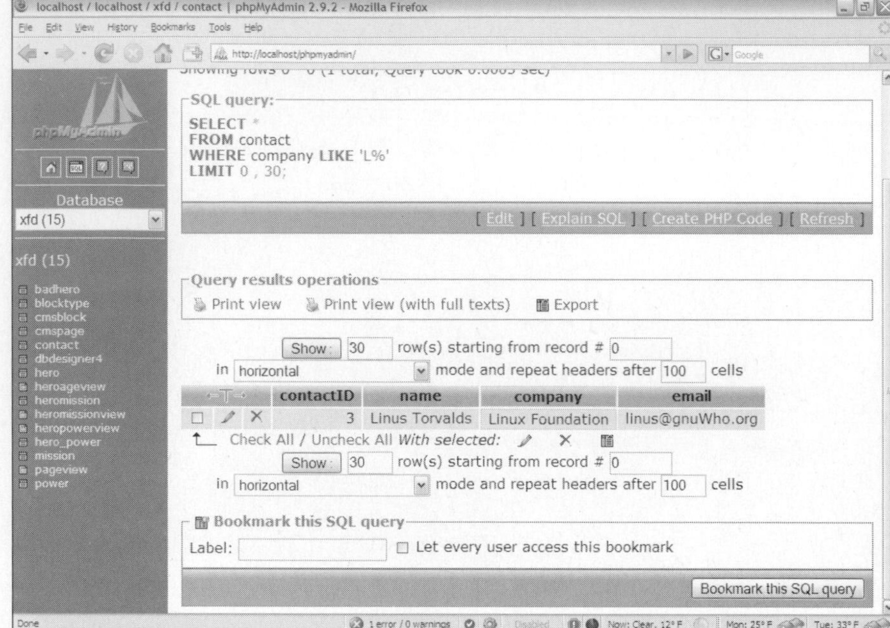

Figure 2-10: This query returns companies that begin with L.

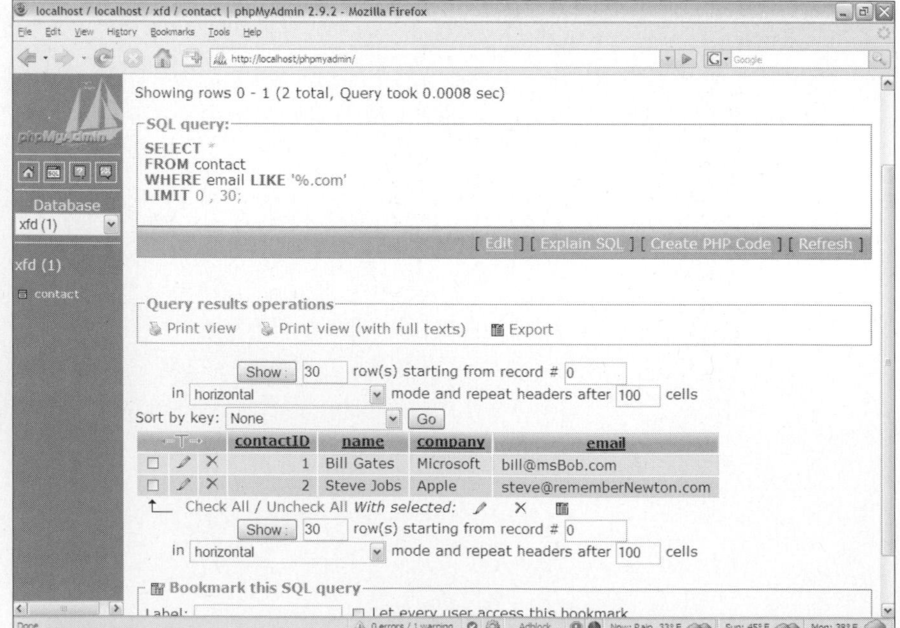

Figure 2-11: You can build a query to check the end of a field.

Searching for any text in a field

One more variant of the LIKE clause allows you to find a phrase anywhere in the field. Say that you remember somebody in your database writes books, and you decide to search for e-mail addresses containing the phrase book:

```
SELECT *
FROM contact
WHERE
  email LIKE '%book%';
```

The search phrase has percent signs at the beginning and the end, so if the phrase book occurs anywhere in the specified field, you get a match. And what do you know? Figure 2-12 shows this query matches on the record of a humble yet lovable author!

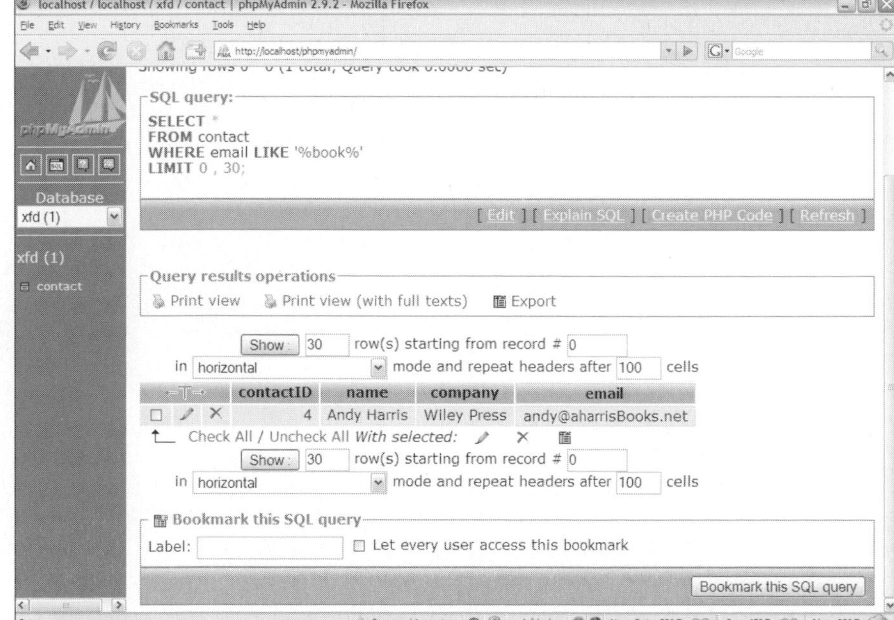

Figure 2-12: This query searched for the phrase 'book' anywhere in the e-mail string.

Searching with regular expressions

If you know how to use regular expressions, you know how great they can be when you need a more involved search. MySQL has a special form of the `SELECT` keyword that supports regular expressions:

```
SELECT *
FROM contact
WHERE
  company REGEXP '^.{5}$';
```

The `REGEXP` keyword lets you search using powerful regular expressions. (Refer to Book IV, Chapter 6 for more information on regular expressions.) This particular expression checks for a company field with exactly five letters. In this table, it returns only one value, shown in Figure 2-13.

Unfortunately, not all database programs support the `REGEXP` feature, but `MySQL` does, and it's really powerful if you understand the (admittedly arcane) syntax of regular expressions.

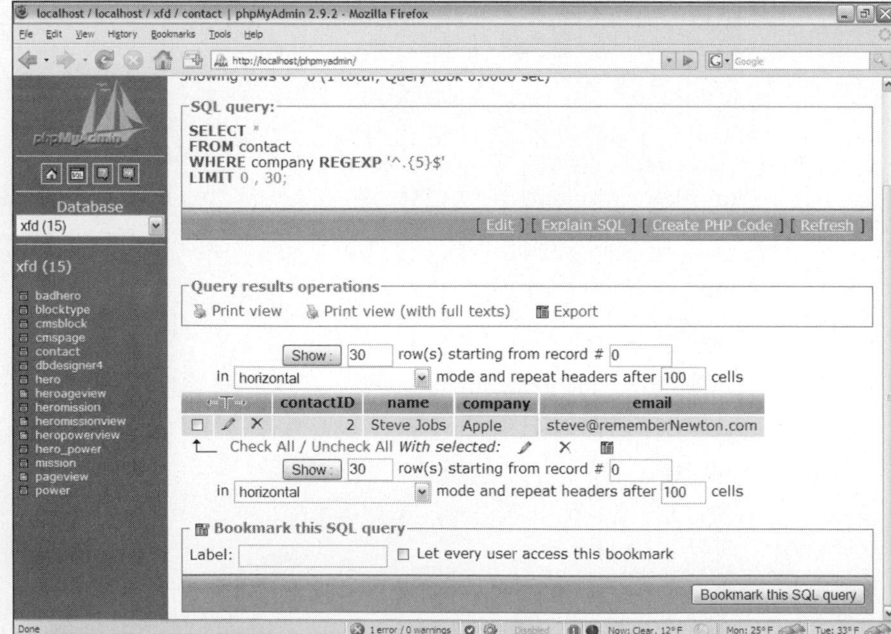

Figure 2-13: Regular expressions are even more powerful than the standard LIKE clause.

Sorting your responses

You can specify the order of your query results with the `ORDER BY` clause. It works like

```
SELECT *
FROM contact
ORDER BY email;
```

The `ORDER BY` directive allows you to specify a field to sort by. In this case, I want the records displayed in alphabetical order by e-mail address. Figure 2-14 shows how it looks.

By default, records are sorted in ascending order. Numeric fields are sorted from smallest to largest, and text fields are sorted in standard alphabetic order.

Well, not quite standard alphabetic order . . . SQL isn't as smart as a librarian, who has special rules about skipping "the" and so on. SQL simply looks at the ASCII values of the characters for sorting purposes.

You can also invert the order:

```
SELECT *
FROM contact
ORDER BY email DESC;
```

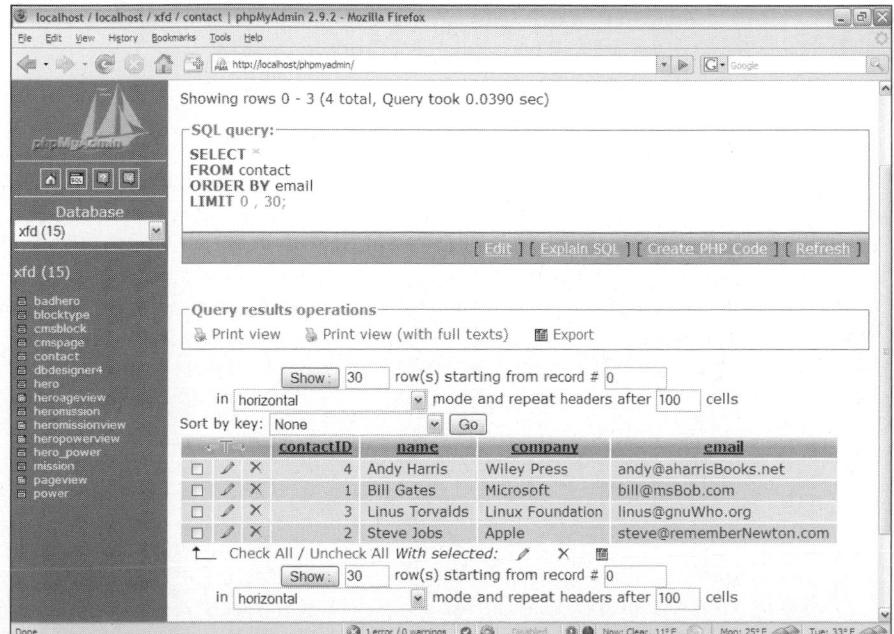

Figure 2-14: Now, the result is sorted by e-mail address.

Inverting the order causes the records to be produced in reverse alphabetic order by e-mail address. DESC stands for descending order. ASC stands for ascending order, but because it's the default, it isn't usually specified.

Editing Records

Of course, the purpose of a database is to manage data. Sometimes, you want to edit data after it's already in the table. SQL includes handy commands for this task: UPDATE and DELETE. The UPDATE command modifies the value of an existing record, and the DELETE command removes a record altogether.

Updating a record

Say that you decide to modify Bill Gates' address to reinforce his latest marketing triumph. The following SQL code does the trick:

```
UPDATE contact
SET email = 'bill@vistaRocks.com'
WHERE name = 'Bill Gates';
```

The UPDATE command has a few parts:

- **The UPDATE command.** This indicates which table you will modify.
- **The SET command.** This indicates a new assignment.
- **Assign a new value to a field.** This uses a standard programming-style assignment statement to attach a new value to the indicated field. You can modify more than one field at a time. Just separate the `field = value` pairs with commas.
- **Specify a WHERE clause.** You don't want this change to happen to all the records in your database. You want to change only the e-mail address in records where the name is Bill Gates. Use the WHERE clause to specify which records you intend to update.

More than one person in your database may be named Bill Gates. Names aren't guaranteed to be unique, so they aren't really the best search criteria. This situation is actually a very good reason to use primary keys. A better version of this update looks like

```
UPDATE contact
SET email = 'bill@vistaRocks.com'
WHERE contactID = 1;
```

The contactID is guaranteed to be unique and present, so it makes an ideal search criterion. Whenever possible, UPDATE (and DROP) commands should use primary key searches so that you don't accidentally change or delete the wrong record.

Deleting a record

Sometimes, you need to delete records. SQL has a command for this eventuality, and it's pretty easy to use:

```
DELETE FROM contact
WHERE contactID = 1;
```

This command deletes the entire record with a contactID of 1.

Be very careful with this command, as it is destructive. Be absolutely sure that you have a `WHERE` clause, or you may delete all the records in your table with one quick command! Likewise, be sure that you understand the `WHERE` clause so that you aren't surprised by what gets deleted. You're better off running an ordinary `SELECT` using the `WHERE` clause before you `DELETE`, just to be sure that you know exactly what you're deleting. Generally, you should `DELETE` based on only a primary key so that you don't produce any collateral damage.

Exporting Your Data and Structure

After you've built a wonderful data structure, you probably will want to export it for a number of reasons:

- **You want a backup.** Just in case something goes wrong!
- **You want to move to a production server.** It's smart to work on a local (offline) server while you figure things out, but eventually, you'll need to move to a live server. Moving the actual database files is tricky, but you can easily move a script.
- **You want to perform data analysis.** You may want to put your data in a spreadsheet for further analysis or in a comma-separated text file to be read by programs without SQL access.
- **You want to document the table structure.** The structure of a data set is extremely important when you start writing programs using that structure. Having the table structure available in a word-processing or PDF format can be extremely useful.

MySQL (and thus phpMyAdmin) have some really nice tools for exporting your data in a number of formats.

Figure 2-15 shows an overview of the Export tab, showing some of the features.

The different styles of output are used for different purposes:

- **CSV (comma-separated value) format:** A plain ASCII comma-separated format. Each record is stored on its own line, and each field is separated by a comma. CSV is nice because it's universal. Most spreadsheet programs can read CSV data natively, and it's very easy to write a program to read CSV data, even if your server doesn't support MySQL. If you want to back up your data to move to another server, CSV is a good choice. Figure 2-16 shows some of the options for creating a CSV file.

The data file created using the specified options looks like

```
'contactID','name','company','email'
'1','Bill Gates','Microsoft','bill@msBob.com'
'2','Steve Jobs','Apple','steve@rememberNewton.com'
'3','Linus Torvalds','Linux Foundation','linus@gnuWho.org'
'4','Andy Harris','Wiley Press','andy@aharrisBooks.net'
```

The CSV format often uses commas and single quotes, so if these characters appear in your data, you may encounter problems. Be sure to test your data and use some of the other delimiters if you have problems.

- **MS Excel and Open Document Spreadsheet:** These are the two currently supported spreadsheet formats. Exporting your data using one of these formats gives you a spreadsheet file that you can easily manipulate, which is handy when you want to do charts or data analysis based on your data. Figure 2-17 shows an Excel document featuring the contact table.
- **Word-processing formats:** Several are available to create documentation for your project. Figure 2-18 shows a document created with this feature. Typically, you use these formats to describe your format of the data and the current contents. LaTeX and PDF are special formats used for printing.

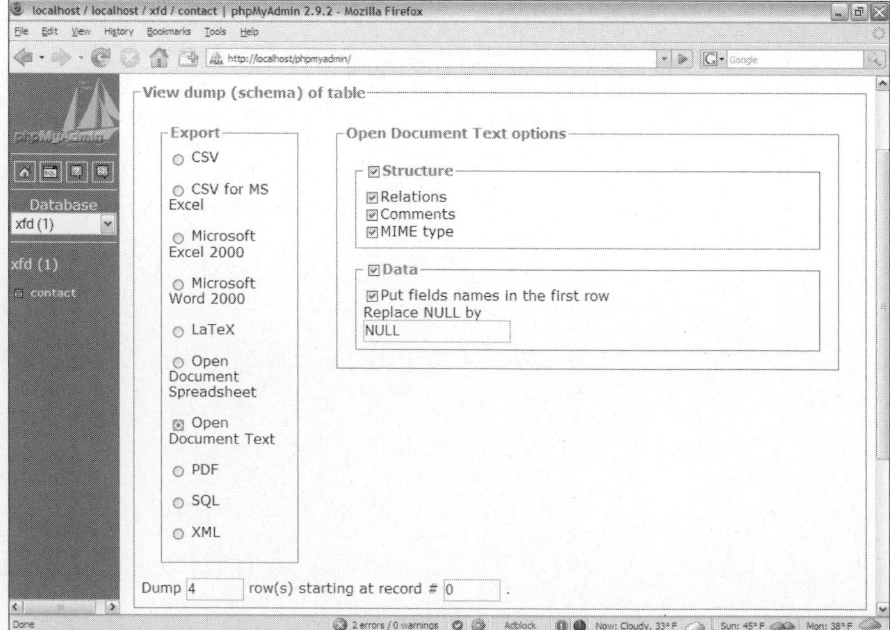

Figure 2-15: These are some of the various output techniques.

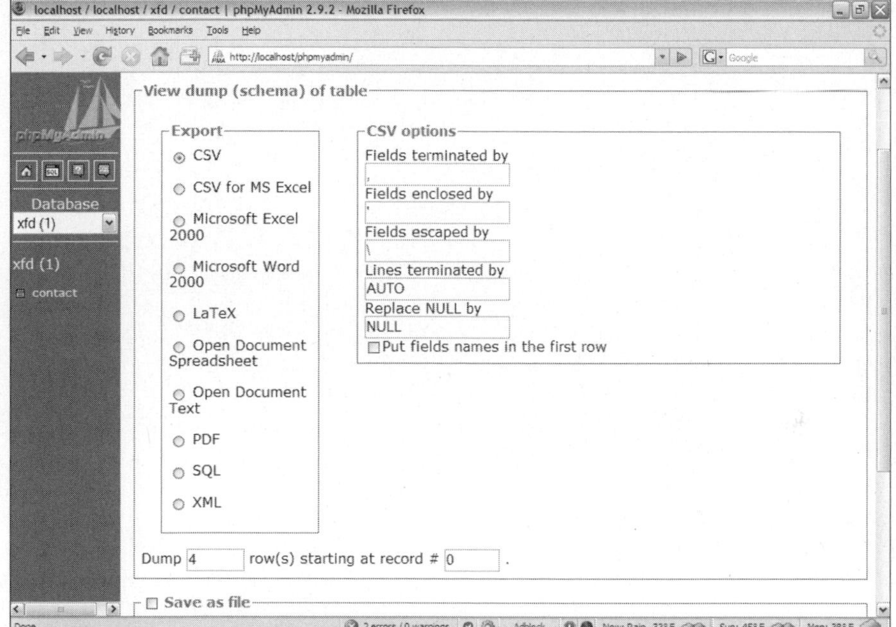

Figure 2-16: You have several options for creating CSV files.

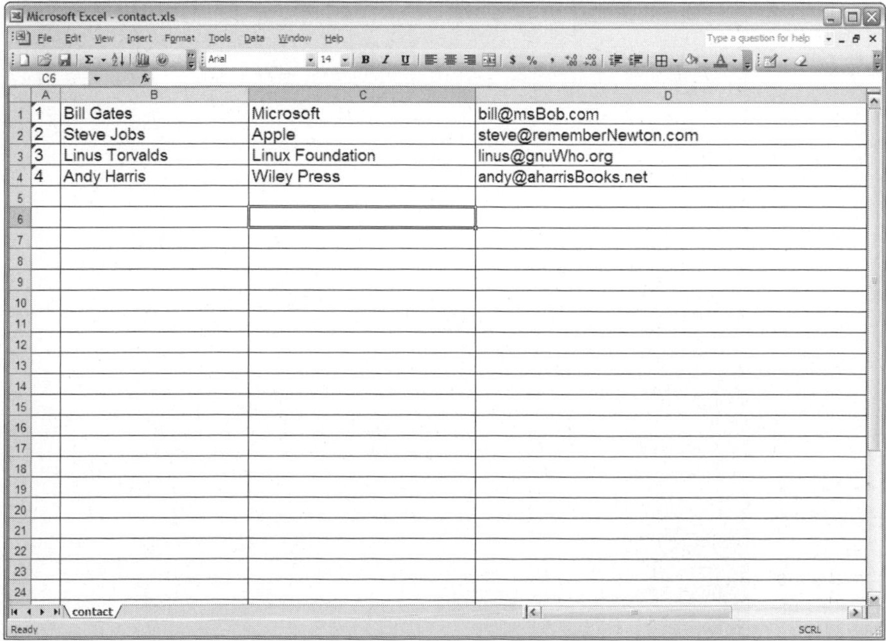

Figure 2-17: This Excel spreadsheet was automatically created.

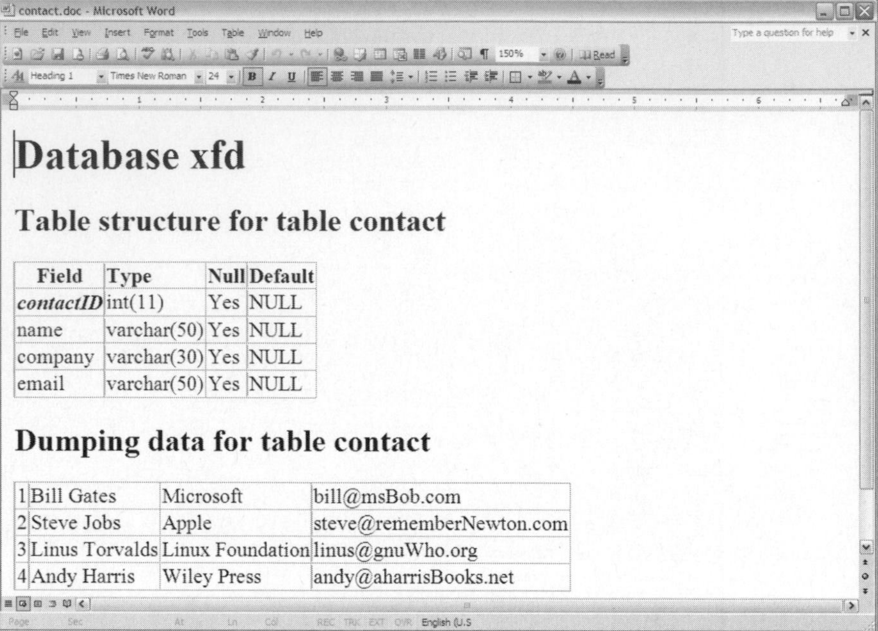
Database xfd

Table structure for table contact

Field	Type	Null	Default
contactID	int(11)	Yes	NULL
name	varchar(50)	Yes	NULL
company	varchar(30)	Yes	NULL
email	varchar(50)	Yes	NULL

Dumping data for table contact

1	Bill Gates	Microsoft	bill@msBob.com
2	Steve Jobs	Apple	steve@rememberNewton.com
3	Linus Torvalds	Linux Foundation	linus@gnuWho.org
4	Andy Harris	Wiley Press	andy@aharrisBooks.net

Figure 2-18: Word-processing, PDF, and LaTeX formats are great for documentation.

Exporting SQL code

One of the neatest tricks is to have phpMyAdmin build an entire SQL script for re-creating your database. Figure 2-19 shows the available options.

The resulting code looks like

```
-- phpMyAdmin SQL Dump
-- version 2.9.2
-- http://www.phpmyadmin.net
--
-- Host: localhost
-- Generation Time: Dec 08, 2007 at 12:15 PM
-- Server version: 5.0.33
-- PHP Version: 5.2.1
--
-- Database: `xfd`
--

-- --------------------------------------------------------

--
-- Table structure for table `contact`
--

CREATE TABLE `contact` (
  `contactID` int(11) NOT NULL auto_increment,
  `name` varchar(50) collate latin1_general_ci default NULL,
  `company` varchar(30) collate latin1_general_ci default NULL,
  `email` varchar(50) collate latin1_general_ci default NULL,
  PRIMARY KEY  (`contactID`)
```

```
) ENGINE=MyISAM  DEFAULT CHARSET=latin1 COLLATE=latin1_general_ci
    AUTO_INCREMENT=5 ;

--
-- Dumping data for table `contact`
--

INSERT INTO `contact` VALUES (1, 'Bill Gates', 'Microsoft', 'bill@msBob.com');
INSERT INTO `contact` VALUES (2, 'Steve Jobs', 'Apple',
    'steve@rememberNewton.com');
INSERT INTO `contact` VALUES (3, 'Linus Torvalds', 'W3C', 'linus@gnuWho.org');
INSERT INTO `contact` VALUES (4, 'Andy Harris', 'Wiley Press',
    'andy@aharrisBooks.net');
```

You can see that phpMyAdmin made a pretty decent script that you can use to re-create this database. You can easily use this script to rebuild the database if it gets corrupted or to copy the data structure to a different implementation of MySQL.

Generally, you use this feature for both purposes. Copy your data structure and data every once in a while (just in case Godzilla attacks your server or something).

Typically, you build your data on one server and want to migrate it to another server. The easiest way to do it is by building the database on one server. You can then export the script for building the SQL file and load it into the second server.

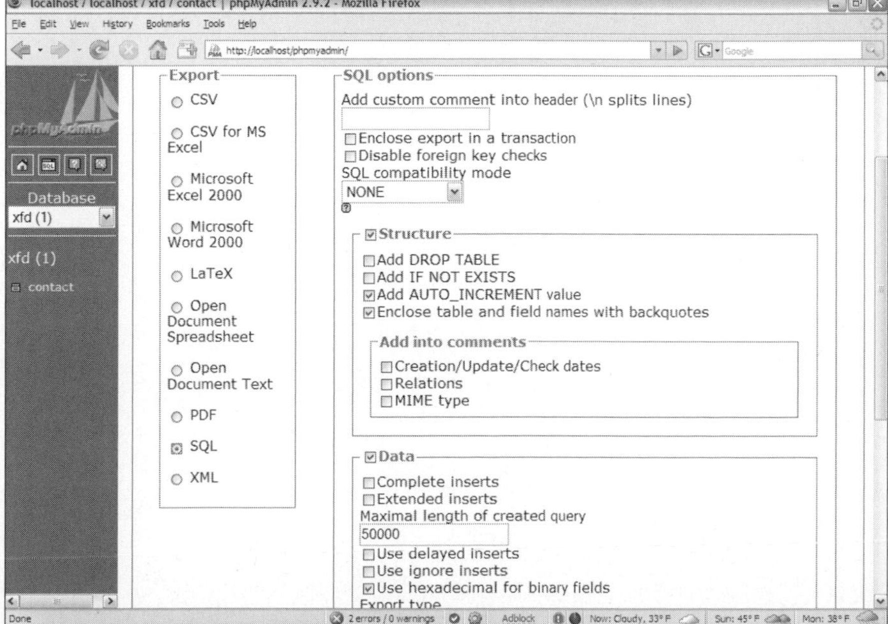

Figure 2-19: You can specify several options for outputting your SQL code.

Creating XML data

One more approach to saving data is through XML. phpMyAdmin creates a standard form of XML encapsulating the data. The XML output looks like

```
<?xml version="1.0" encoding="utf-8" ?>
<!--
-
- phpMyAdmin XML Dump
- version 2.9.2
- http://www.phpmyadmin.net
-
- Host: localhost
- Generation Time: Dec 08, 2007 at 08:16 PM
- Server version: 5.0.33
- PHP Version: 5.2.1
-->

<!--
- Database: 'xfd'
-->
<xfd>
  <!-- Table contact -->
    <contact>
        <contactID>1</contactID>
        <name>Bill Gates</name>
        <company>Microsoft</company>
        <email>bill@msBob.com</email>
    </contact>
    <contact>
        <contactID>2</contactID>
        <name>Steve Jobs</name>
        <company>Apple</company>
        <email>steve@rememberNewton.com</email>
    </contact>
    <contact>
        <contactID>3</contactID>
        <name>Linus Torvalds</name>
        <company>W3C</company>
        <email>linus@gnuWho.org</email>
    </contact>
    <contact>
        <contactID>4</contactID>
        <name>Andy Harris</name>
        <company>Wiley Press</company>
        <email>andy@aharrisBooks.net</email>
    </contact>
</xfd>
```

XML is commonly used as a common data language, especially in AJAX applications.

Chapter 3: Normalizing Your Data

In This Chapter

- Understanding why single-table databases are inadequate
- Recognizing common data anomalies
- Creating entity-relationship diagrams
- Using DBDesigner to create data diagrams
- Understanding the first three normal forms
- Defining data relationships

Databases can be deceptive. Even though databases are pretty easy to create, beginners usually run into problems as soon as they start working with actual data.

Computer scientists (particularly a gentleman named E.F. Codd in the 1970s) have studied potential data problems and defined techniques for organizing data. This scheme is called *data normalization.* In this chapter, you discover why single-table databases rarely work for real-world data and how to create a well-defined data structure according to basic normalization rules.

On the CD-ROM, I include a script called `buildHero.sql` that builds all the tables in this chapter. Feel free to load that script into your MySQL environment to see all these tables for yourself.

Recognizing Problems with Single-Table Data

Packing everything you've got into a single table is tempting. Although you can do it pretty easily (especially with SQL) and it seems like a good solution, things can go wrong pretty quickly.

Table 3-1 shows a seemingly simple database describing some superheroes.

Table 3-1 A Sample Database

Name	*Powers*	*Villain*	*Plot*	*Mission*	*Age*
The Plumber	Sewer snake of doom, unclogging, ability to withstand smells	Septic Slime Master	Overcome Chicago with slime	Stop the Septic Slime	37
Binary Boy	Hexidecimation beam, obfuscation	Octal	Eliminate the numerals 8 and 9	Make the world safe for binary representation	19
The Janitor	Mighty Mop	Septic Slime Master	Overcome New York with slime	Stop the Septic Slime	41

It seems that not much can go wrong here because the database is only three records and six fields. The data is simple, and there isn't that much of it. Still, a lot of trouble is lurking just under the surface. The following sections outline potential problems.

The identity crisis

What's Table 3-1 about? At first, it seems to be about superheroes, but some of the information isn't about the superhero as much as things related to the superhero, such as villains and missions. This issue may not seem like a big deal, but it causes all kinds of practical problems later on. A table should be about only one thing. When it tries to be about more than that, it can't do its job as well.

Every time a beginner (and, often, an advanced data developer) creates a table, the table usually contains fields that don't belong there. You have to break things up into multiple tables so that each table is really about only one thing. The process for doing so solves a bunch of other problems, as well.

The listed powers

Take a look at the `powers` field. Each superhero can have more than one power. Some heroes have tons of powers. The problem is, how do you handle a situation where one field can have a lot of values? You frequently see the following solutions:

- **One large text field:** That's what I did in this case. I built a massive (255 character) `VARCHAR` field and hoped it would be enough. The user just has to type all the possible skills.
- **Multiple fields:** Sometimes, a data designer just makes a bunch of fields, such as `power1`, `power2`, and so on.

Both these solutions have the same general flaw. You never know how much room to designate because you never know exactly how many items will be in the list. Say that you choose the large text field approach. You may have a really clever hero with a lot of powers, so you fill up the entire field with a list of powers. What happens if your hero learns one more power? Should you delete something just to make things fit? Should you abbreviate?

If you choose to have multiple power fields, the problem doesn't go away. You still have to determine how many skills the hero can have. If you designate ten skill fields and one of your heroes learns an eleventh power, you've got a problem.

The obvious solution is to provide far more room than anybody needs. If it's a text field, make it huge, and if it's multiple fields, make hundreds of them. Both solutions are wasteful. Remember, a database can often have hundreds or thousands of records, and each one has to be the same size. If you make your record definition bigger than it needs to be, this waste is multiplied hundreds or thousands of times.

You may argue that this is not the 1970s. Processor power and storage space are really cheap today, so why am I worrying about saving a few bytes here and there? Well, cheap is still not free. Programmers tend to be working with much larger data sets than they did in the early days, so efficiency still matters. And here's another important change. Today, data is much more likely to be transmitted over the Internet. The big deal today isn't really processor or storage efficiency. Today's problem is transmission efficiency, which comes down to the same principle: Don't store unnecessary data.

When databases have listed fields, you tend to see other problems. If the field doesn't have enough room for all the data, people will start abbreviating. If you're looking for a hero with invisibility, you can't simply search for "invisibility" in the `powers` field because it may be "inv," "in," or "invis" (or even "can't see"). If you desperately need an invisible hero, the search can be frustrating, and you may miss a result because you didn't guess all the possible abbreviations.

If the database uses the listed fields model, you have another problem. Now, your search has to look through all ten (or hundred) power fields because you don't know which one holds the "invisible" power. This problem makes your search queries far more complicated than they would have been otherwise.

Another so-called solution you sometimes see is to have a whole bunch of Boolean fields: Invisibility, Super-speed, X-ray vision, and so on. This fix solves part of the problem because Boolean data is small. It's still troublesome, though, because now the data developer has to anticipate every possible power. You may have an `other` field, but it then re-introduces the problem of listed fields.

Listed fields are a nightmare.

Repetition and reliability

Another common problem with data comes with repetition. If you allow data to be repeated in your database, you can have some really challenging side effects. Refer to Table 3-1, earlier in this chapter, and get ready to answer some questions about it. . . .

What is the Slime Master's evil plot?

This question seems simple enough, but Table 3-1 provides an ambiguous response. If you look at the first row (The Plumber), the plot is Overcome Chicago with slime. If you look at The Janitor, you see that the plot is to Overcome New York with slime. Which is it? Presumably, it's the same plot, but in one part of the database, New York is the target, and elsewhere, it's Chicago. From the database, you can't really tell which is correct or if it could be both. I was required to type in the plot in two different records. It's supposed to be the same plot, but I typed it differently. Now, the data has a conflict, and you don't know which record to trust.

Is it possible the plots were supposed to be different? Sure, but you don't want to leave that assumption to chance. The point of data design is to ask exactly these questions and to design your data scheme to reinforce the rules of your organization.

Here's a related question. What if you needed to get urgent information to any hero fighting the Septic Slime Master? You'd probably write a query like

```
SELECT * FROM hero WHERE villain = 'Septic Slime Master'
```

That query is a pretty reasonable request, but it wouldn't work. The villain in The Janitor record is the Septic *Slim* Master. Somebody mistyped something in the database, and now The Janitor doesn't know how to defeat the Slime Master.

If your database allows duplication, this type of mistake will happen all the time.

In general, you don't want to enter anything into a database more than once. If you had a way to enter in the Septic Slime Master one time, that should eliminate this type of problem.

Fields that change

Another kind of problem is evident in the `Age` field. (See, even superheroes have a mandatory retirement age.) Age is a good example of a field that shouldn't really be in a database because it changes all the time. If you have age in your database, how are you going to account for people getting older? Do you update the age on each hero's birthday? (If so, you need to store that birthday, and you need to run a script every day to see whether it's anybody's birthday.) You could just age everybody once a year, but this solution doesn't seem like a good option, either.

Whenever possible, you want to avoid fields that change regularly and instead use a formula to generate the appropriate results when you need them.

Deletion problems

Another kind of problem is lurking right under the surface. Say that you had to fire the Binary Boy. (With him, everything is black and white. You just can't compromise with him.) You delete his record, and then you want to assign another hero to fight Octal. When you delete Binary Boy, you also delete all the information about Octal and his nefarious scheme.

In a related problem, what if you encounter a new villain, and you haven't yet assigned a hero to this villain? The current data design doesn't allow you to add villains without heroes. You have to make up a fake hero, and that just doesn't seem right.

Introducing Entity-Relationship Diagrams

You can solve all the problems with the database shown in Table 3-1 by breaking the single table into a series of smaller, more specialized tables.

The typical way of working with data design is to use a concept called an *Entity-Relationship (ER) diagram.* This form of diagram usually includes

- **Entities:** Typically, a table is an entity, but you see other kinds of entities, too. An entity is usually drawn as a box with each field listed inside.
- **Relationships:** Relationships are drawn as lines between the boxes. As you find out about various forms of relationships, I show you the particular symbols used to describe these relationship types.

Using DBDesigner 4 to draw ER diagrams

You can create ER diagrams with anything (I typically use a whiteboard), but some very nice free software can help. One particularly nice program is called DBDesigner 4. This software has a number of really handy features:

- **Visual representation of database design:** DBDesigner allows you to define a table easily and then see how it looks in ER form. You can create several tables and manipulate them visually to see how they relate.
- **An understanding of ER rules:** DBDesigner is not simply a drawing program. It's specialized for drawing ER diagrams, so it creates a standard

design for each table and relationship. Other data administrators can understand the ER diagrams you create with this tool.

- **Integration with MySQL:** Once you've created a data design you like, you can have DBDesigner create a MySQL script to create the databases you've defined. In fact, you can even have DBDesigner look at an existing MySQL database and create an ER diagram from it.
- **Ability to manipulate data:** You can connect to an actual MySQL database and use DBDesigner as a front end. You can view queries, and add and edit data, all through the tool.

Creating a table definition in DBDesigner

Creating your tables in DBDesigner is a fairly easy task:

1. **Create a new model.**

   Choose File⇨New to create a new model. Figure 3-1 shows DBDesigner in action.

2. **Create a new table.**

   You can use the icons along the left border to control the diagram. The New Table icon looks like two grids. It's near the center of the icon strip. You see a blank table like Figure 3-2.

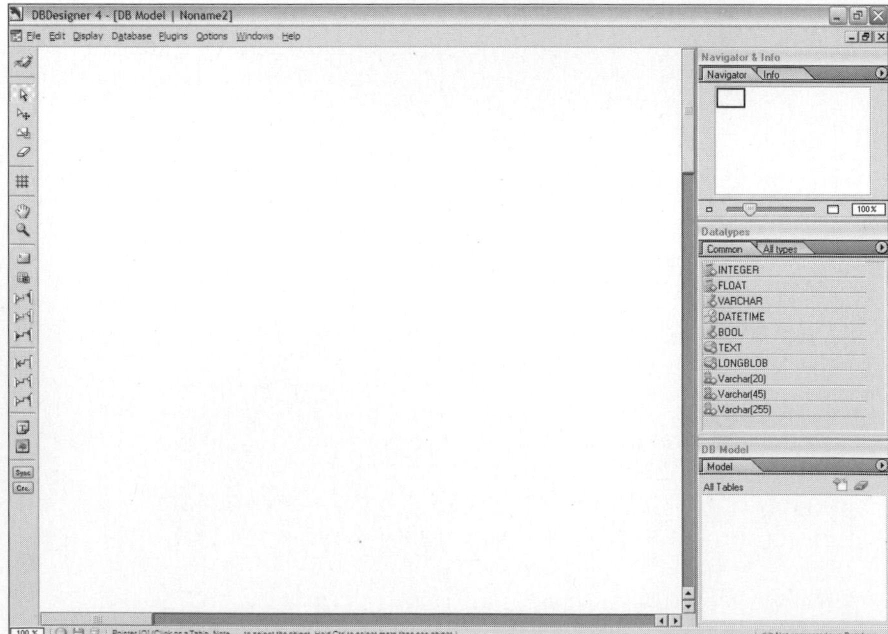

Figure 3-1: The DB-Designer main screen.

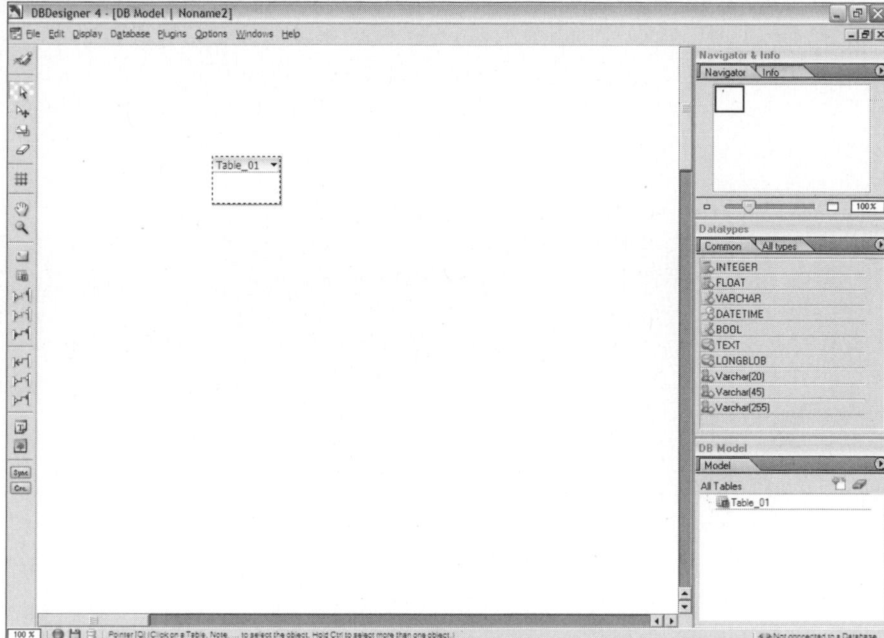

Figure 3-2: Now, your model has a table in it.

3. **Edit the table.**

   Right-click the table and choose Edit Object to define the table's characteristics. You get a screen that looks something like Figure 3-3. Add the fields as I've done in the example. Note that the first field is automatically the primary key.

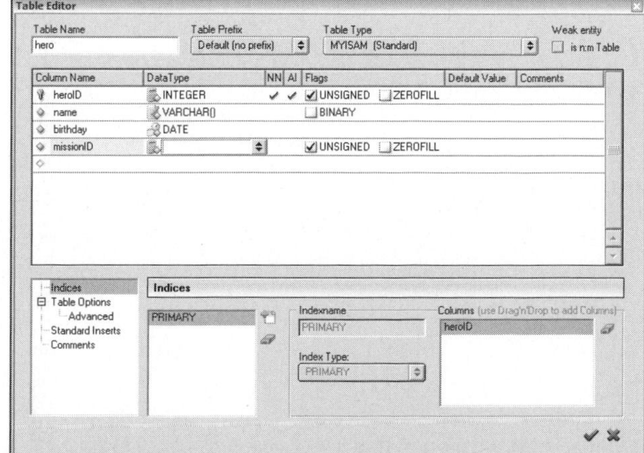

Figure 3-3: Editing the table definition.

4. **Extract the code.**

   If you want, you can see the SQL code used to create the table you just designed. Simply right-click the table and choose Copy SQL Table Create. The `CREATE` statement for this table is copied to the Clipboard, and you can paste it to your script. Figure 3-4 shows the `hero` table in ER form.

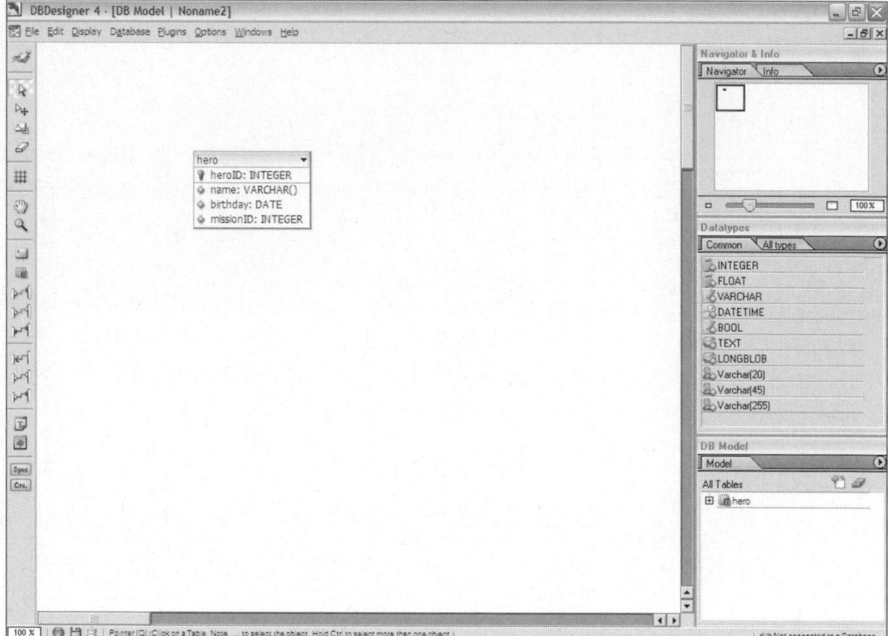

Figure 3-4: Now, the diagram of the hero table is visible.

Connecting to a database with DBDesigner

You don't ever have to connect to a database using DBDesigner, but it can be useful. If you've already got MySQL running on your local machine, here's how you connect DBDesigner to your database:

1. **Make sure that MySQL is running.**

   DBDesigner is looking for a running version of MySQL.

2. **Connect to the database.**

   Choose Data➪Connect to Database. Selecting this tool creates a dialog box like Figure 3-5.

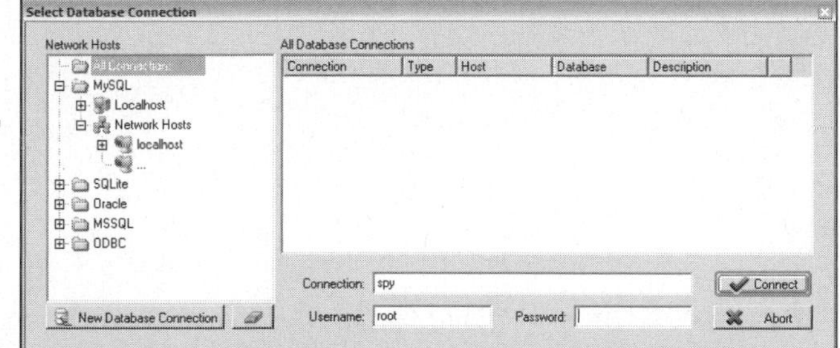

Figure 3-5: This is the database connection dialog box.

3. **Navigate to MySQL Localhost.**

   You'll be connecting to a MySQL database on the local server (most likely), so highlight Localhost under MySQL. Click the plus sign to see the list of databases under Localhost. You'll probably be prompted for a username and password.

4. **Select the database you want to work with.**

   Each diagram should be about only one database (at least, in this stage of your career.) Find the database you want to use and select it, as shown in Figure 3-6.

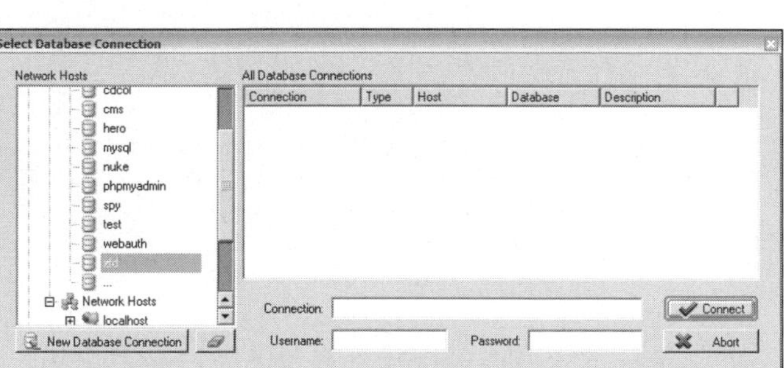

Figure 3-6: I'm selecting the xfd database.

5. **Create a new database connection.**

   The New Database Connection button appears on the bottom of the screen. You see the Database Connection Editor dialog box, shown in Figure 3-7.

6. **Enter connection details.**

   Give the connection a name and specify the username and password used to access that database. (Check Chapter 2 of this minibook for more details on assigning users and passwords to databases.)

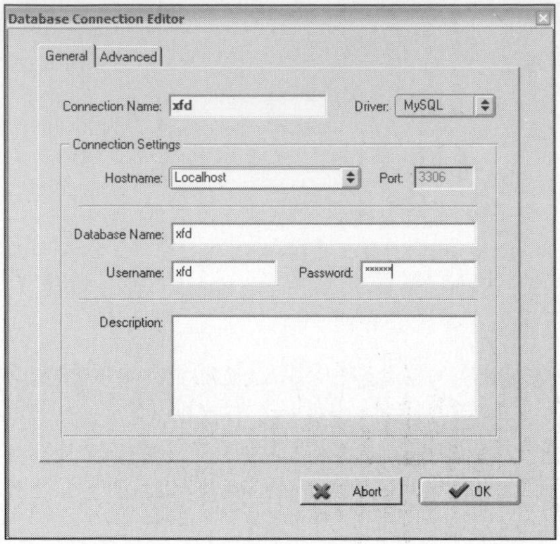

Figure 3-7: Enter the name of your database, the username, and password.

7. **Test your connection.**

   Go back to the Localhost entry in the Select Database Connection window, and you should now see your new connection, as shown in Figure 3-8. Select the connection, check the username and password, and click Connect.

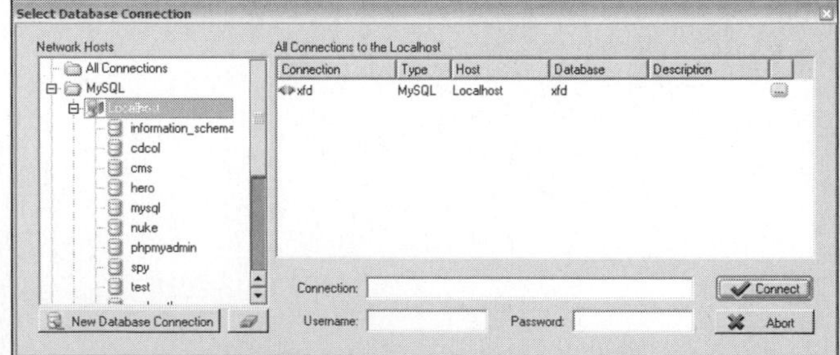

Figure 3-8: Now, the xfd connection is available.

8. **Verify your connection.**

   If nothing went wrong, it probably worked. When you get back to the DBDesigner screen, you see text in the lower-right corner saying Connected to Database. Now, your changes in the diagram can be reflected in the actual database.

Manipulating your data from DBDesigner

You can use DBDesigner to view and manipulate your database, as well. You can copy data from your modeling software to the database with the Synchronization command, or extract data from the database and bring it into the model with the Reverse Engineer command. Both are found on the Database menu.

I've found the Reverse Engineer command to be more reliable. I still like to build scripts in a text editor and then have the DBDesigner show me what it sees, but DBDesigner doesn't always write code as well as I can.

The easiest way to work with your data is to type commands in Query mode:

1. **Be sure you're connected to your database.**

   Queries are pretty silly without a database.

2. **Get DBDesigner into Query mode.**

   The top button toggles between Design and Query mode. Query mode looks like Figure 3-9.

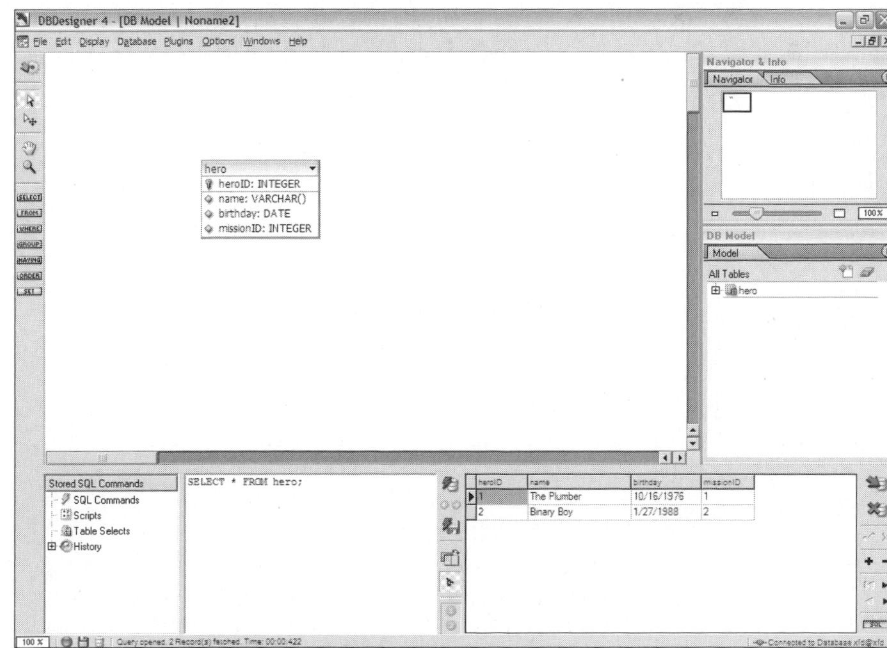

Figure 3-9: DBDesigner in query mode. Note that I'm connected to xfd.

3. **Type a query into the query box.**

   The bottom-center panel allows you to enter queries.

4. **Execute the query.**

   An icon next to the query window looks like a barrel with lightning. This icon executes whatever query you've just entered. The query results appear in the bottom-right panel.

5. **Use Query mode shortcuts.**

   If you click the mouse over a table and drag, you see a little context menu of SQL commands, similar to Figure 3-10. Use this menu to get a quick SQL query started in the query window. You still need to edit the query, but this shortcut is a really handy timesaver.

6. **Edit data.**

   If you have a table query available, you can add and modify records in the database. Experiment with the buttons on the right-hand panel to see how this function works.

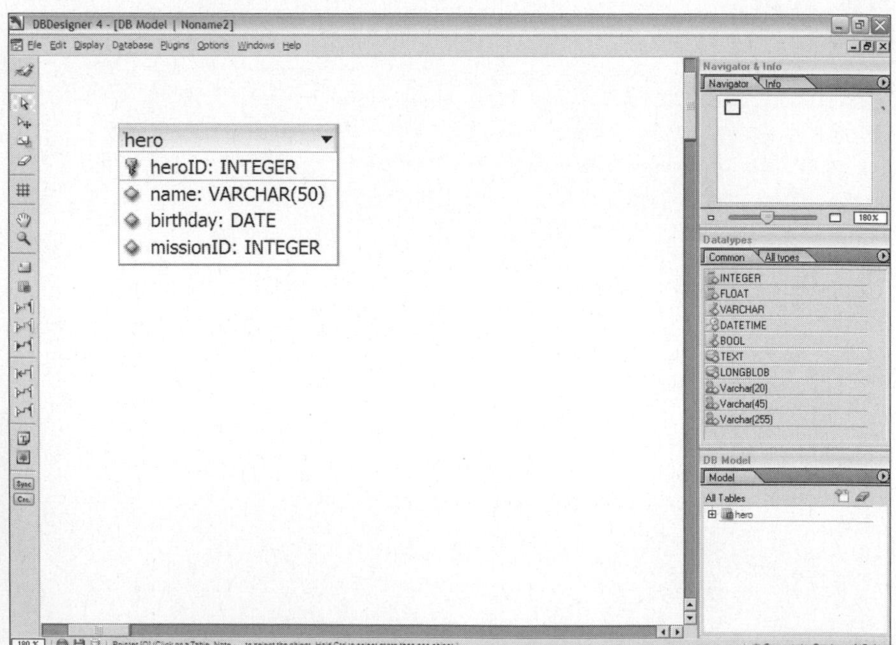

Figure 3-10: DBDesigner can help you build queries.

Introducing Normalization

Trying to cram all your data into a single table usually causes problems. The process for solving these problems is called *data normalization.* Normalization is really a set of rules. When your database follows the first rule, it's said to be in *first normal form.* For this introductory book, you get to the third normal form, which is suitable for most applications.

First normal form

The official definitions of the normal forms sound like the offspring of a lawyer and a mathematician. Here's an official definition of the first normal form:


```
A table is in first normal form if and only if it represents a relation. It does
    not allow nulls or duplicate rows.
```

Yeah, whatever.

Here's what it means in practical terms:

```
Eliminate listed fields.
```

A database is in first normal form if

- **It has no repeating fields.** Take any data that would be in a repeating field and make it into a new table.
- **It has a primary key.** Add a primary key to each table. (Some would argue that this requirement isn't necessarily part of first normal form, but it'll be necessary in the next step, anyway.)

In a practical sense, the first normal form means getting rid of listed fields and making a new table to contain powers. Figure 3-11 shows an ER diagram of the data in first normal form.

A couple of things happen here:

1. **Make a new table called `power`.**

   This table contains nothing but a key and the power name.

2. **Take the `power` field away from the `hero` table.**

   The `hero` table no longer has a `power` field.

3. **Add a primary key to both tables.**

   Both tables now have an integer primary key. Looking over my tables, there are no longer any listed fields, so I'm in first normal form.

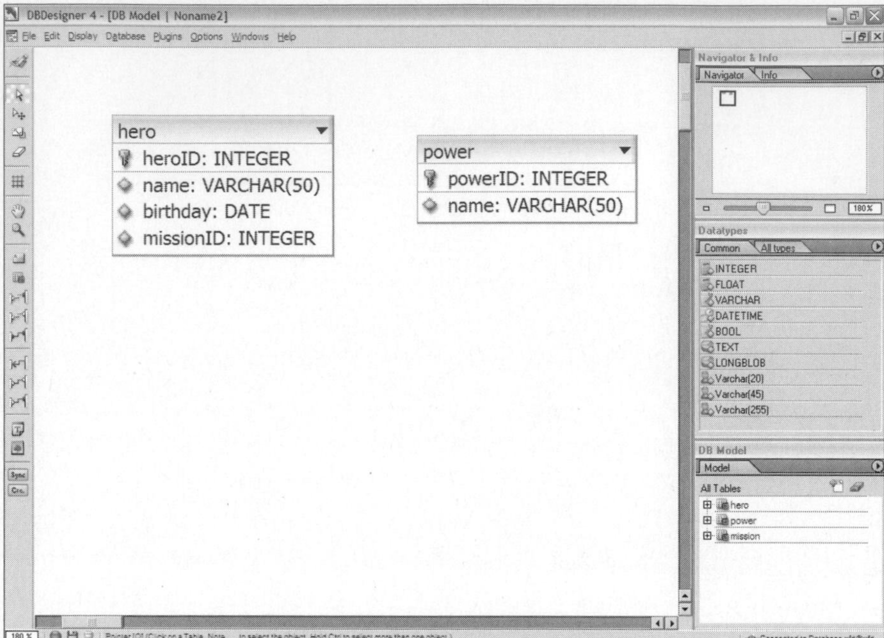

Figure 3-11: Now, I have two tables.

All this is well and good, but the user really wants this data connected, so how do you join it back together? For that answer, see Chapter 4 of this minibook.

Second normal form

The official terminology for the second normal form is just as baffling as the first normal form:

```
A table is in second normal form (2NF) only if it is in 1NF and all nonkey fields
    are dependant entirely on the entire candidate key, not just part of it.
```

Huh? You've gotta love these computer scientists.

In practical terms, second normal form is pretty easy, too. It really means

Eliminate repetition.

Look at all those places where you've got duplicated data and create new tables to take care of them.

In the heroes data (shown in Table 3-1, earlier in this chapter), you can eliminate a lot of problems by breaking the hero data into three tables. Figure 3-12 illustrates one way to break up the data.

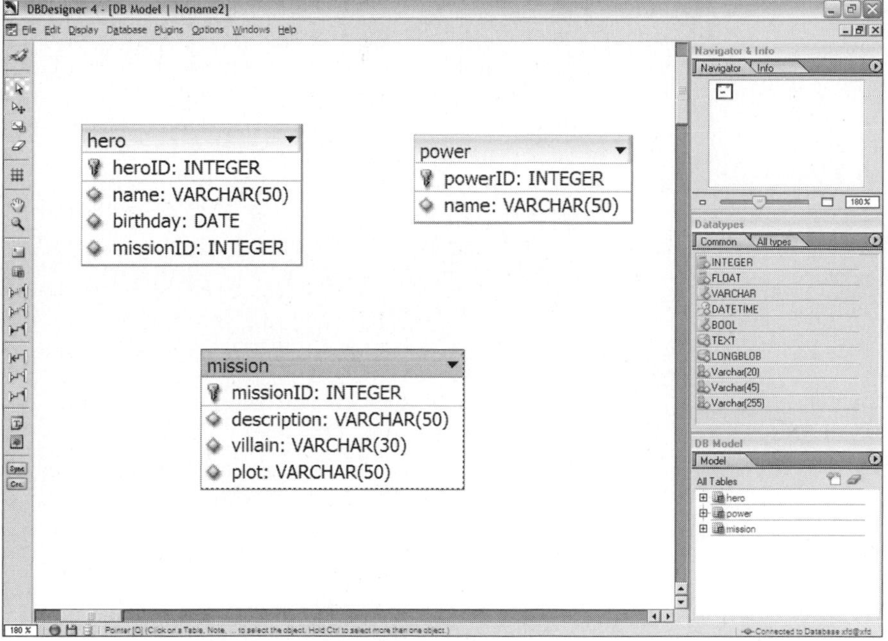

Figure 3-12: Now, I have three tables: hero, power, and mission.

Many of the problems in the `badHero` design happen because apparently more than one hero can be on a particular mission, and thus the mission data gets repeated. By separating mission data into another table, I've guaranteed that the data for a mission is entered only once.

Note that each table has a primary key, and none of them has listed fields. The same data won't ever be entered twice. The solution is looking pretty good!

Notice that everything related to the mission has been moved to the `mission` table. I added one field to the `hero` table, which contains an integer. This field is called a *foreign key reference.* You can find out much more about how foreign key references work in Chapter 4 of this minibook.

Third normal form

The third normal form adds one more requirement. Here is the official definition:

```
A table is in 3NF it is in 2NF and has no transitive dependencies on the candi-
    date key.
```

Wow. These definitions get better and better. Once again, it's really a lot easier than it sounds:

```
Ensure functional dependency.
```

In other words, check each field of each table and ensure that it really describes what the table is about. For example, is the plot related to the mission or the hero? What about the villain?

The tricky thing about functional dependency is that you often don't really know how the data is supposed to be connected. Only the person who uses the data really knows how it's supposed to work. (Often, they don't know, either, when you ask them.) You have to work with the client to figure out exactly what the *business rules* (the rules that describe how the data really works) are. You can't really tell from the data itself.

The good news is that, for simple structures like the hero data, you're often already in third normal form by the time you get to second normal form. Still, you should check.

Once a database is in third normal form, you've reduced the possibility of several kinds of anomalies, so your data is far more reliable than it was in the past. Several other forms of normalization exist, but third normal form is enough for most applications.

Identifying Relationships in Your Data

After you normalize the data (see the preceding section), you've created the entities (tables). Now, you need to investigate the relationships between these entities.

Three main types of data relationships exist (and of these, only two are common):

- **One-to-one relationships:** Each element of table A is related to exactly one element of table B. This type of relationship isn't common because if a one-to-one relationship exists between two tables, the information can be combined safely into one table.
- **One-to-many relationship:** For each element of table A, there could be many possible elements in table B. The relationship between mission and hero is a one-to-many relationship, as each mission can have many heroes, but each hero has only one mission. (My heroes have attention issues and can't multitask very well.) Note that hero and mission are not a one-to-many relationship, but a many-to-one. The order matters.
- **Many-to-many relationship:** This type of relationship happens when an element of A may have many values from B, and B may also have many values of A. Usually, listed fields turn out to be many-to-many relationships. In the hero data, the relationship between hero and power is a many-to-many relationship because each hero can have many powers, and each power can belong to multiple heroes.

You can use an ER tool to diagram the various relationship types. Figure 3-13 shows this addition to the `hero` design.

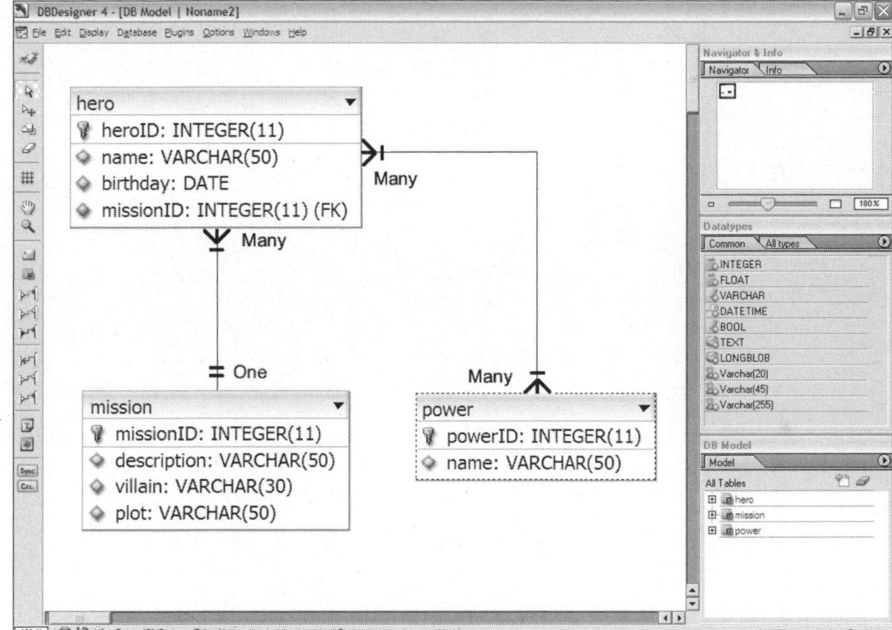

Figure 3-13: Now, I've added relationships.

Note that DBDesigner doesn't actually allow you to draw many-to-many joins. I drew that into Figure 3-13 to illustrate the point. In the next chapter, I show how to emulate many-to-many relationships with a special trick called a *link table.*

ER diagrams use special symbols to represent different kinds of relationships. The line between tables indicates a *join,* or relationship, but the type of join is indicated by the markings on the ends of the lines. In general, the crow's feet or filled-in circle indicate many, and the double lines indicate 1.

ER diagrams get much more complex than the simple ones I show here, but for this introduction, the one and many symbols are enough to get you started.

Chapter 4: Putting Data Together with Joins

In This Chapter

- ✓ **Using SQL functions**
- ✓ **Creating calculated fields**
- ✓ **Working with date values**
- ✓ **Building views**
- ✓ **Creating inner joins and link tables**

Single tables aren't sufficient for most data. If you understand the rules of data normalization (see Chapter 3 of this minibook), you know how to break your data into a series of smaller tables. The question remains, though: How do you recombine all these broken-up tables to make something the user can actually use?

In this chapter, you discover several techniques for combining the data in your tables to create useful results.

I wrote a quick PHP script to help me with most of the figures in this chapter. Each SQL query I intend to look at is stored in a separate SQL file, and I can load up the file and look at it with the PHP code. Feel free to look over the code for `showQuery` on the CD-ROM. If you want to run this code yourself, be sure to change the username and password to reflect your data settings. I also include a script called `buildHero.sql` that creates a database with all the tables and views I mention in this chapter. Feel free to load that script into your database so that you can play along at home.

Calculating Virtual Fields

Part of data normalization means that you eliminate fields that can be calculated. In the hero database described in Chapter 3 of this minibook, data normalization meant that you don't store the hero's age, but his or her birthday instead (see Chapter 3 of this minibook). Of course, if you really want the age, you should be able to find some way to calculate it. SQL includes support for calculating results right in the query.

Begin by looking over the improved hero table in Figure 4-1.

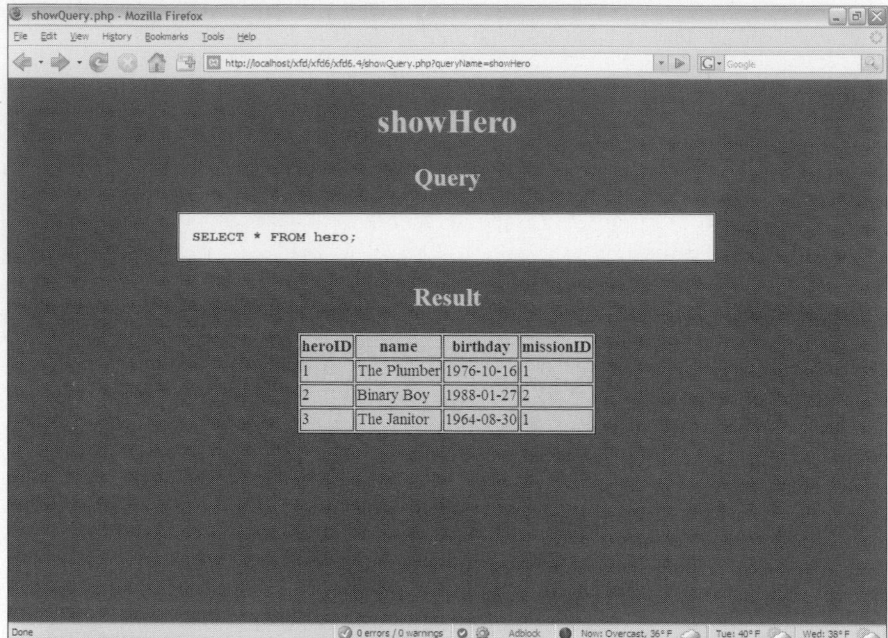

Figure 4-1: The hero table after normalization.

The original idea for the database, introduced in Table 3-1 in Chapter 3 of this minibook, was to keep track of each hero's age. This idea was bad because the age changes every year. Instead, I stored the hero's birthday. But what if you really do want the age?

Introducing SQL Functions

It turns out SQL supports a number of useful functions that you can use to manipulate data. Table 4-1 shows especially useful MySQL functions. Many more functions are available, but these functions are the most frequently used.

Table 4-1 Useful MySQL Functions

Function	*Description*
`CONCAT(A, B)`	Concatenates two string results. Can be used to create a single entry from two or more fields. For example, combine `firstName` and `lastName` fields.
`FORMAT(X, D)`	Format the number X to the number of digits D.
`CURRDATE(), CURRTIME()`	Return the current date or time.
`NOW()`	Return the current date and time.

Function	Description
`MONTH(), DAY(), YEAR(), WEEK(), WEEKDAY()`	Extract the particular value from a date value.
`HOUR(), MINUTE(), SECOND()`	Extract the particular value from a time value.
`DATEDIFF(A, B)`	Frequently used to find the time difference between two events (age).
`SUBTIMES(A, B)`	Determine the difference between two times.
`FROMDAYS(INT)`	Converts an integer number of days into a date value.

Typically, you use a programming language, such as PHP, to manage what the user sees, and programming languages tend to have a much richer set of functions than the database. Still, it's often useful to do certain kinds of functionality at the database level.

Knowing when to calculate virtual fields

You calculate data in these situations:

- **You need to create a single field from multiple text fields.** You might need to combine first, middle, and last name fields to create a single name value. You can also combine all the elements of an address to create a single output.
- **You want to do a mathematical operation on your data.** Imagine that you're writing a database for a vegetable market, and you want to calculate the value from the `costPerPound` field plus the `poundsPurchased` field. You can add the mathematical operation in your query.
- **You need to convert data.** Perhaps you stored weight information in pounds, and you want a query to return data in kilograms.
- **You want to do date calculations.** Often, you need to calculate ages from specific days. Date calculations are especially useful on the data side because databases and other languages often have different date formats.

Calculating Date Values

The birthday value is stored in the hero table, but what you really want to know is the hero's age. It's very common to have an age stored in a database. You often need to output this age in years, or perhaps in years and months. Functions can help you do this calculation.

Begin by looking at a simple function that tells you the current date and time, as I do in Figure 4-2.

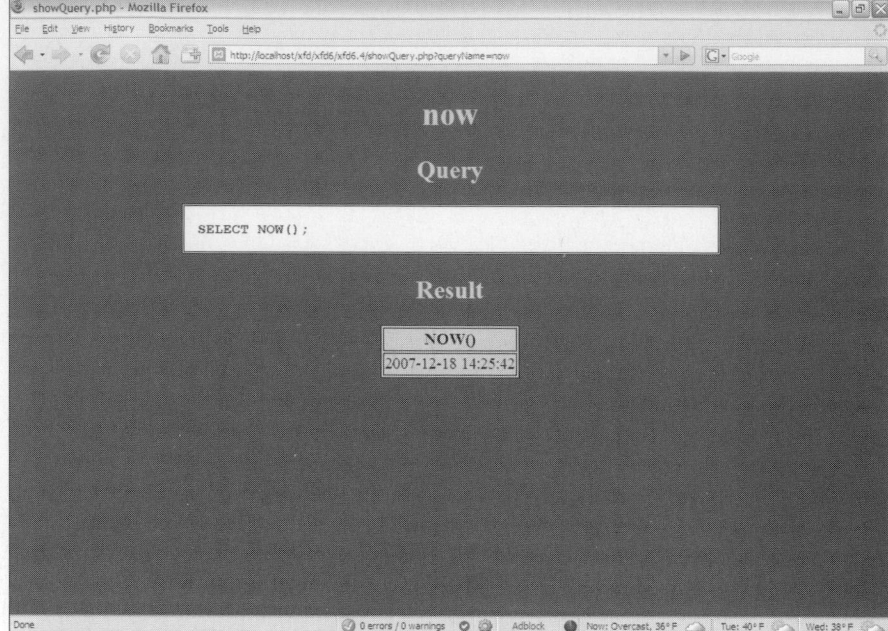

Figure 4-2: The NOW() function returns the current date and time.

The current date and time by themselves aren't that important, but you can combine this information with other functions, described in the following sections, to do some very interesting things.

Using DATEDIFF to determine age

The `NOW()` function is very handy when you combine it with the `DATEDIFF()` function, as shown in Figure 4-3.

This query calculates the difference between the current date, `NOW()`, and each hero's birthday. The `DATEDIFF` function works by converting both dates into integers. It can then subtract the two integers, giving you the result in number of days.

You normally name the fields you calculate because, otherwise, the formula used to calculate the results becomes the virtual field's name. The user doesn't care about the formula, so use the `AS` feature to give the virtual field a more useful name.

Adding a calculation to get years

Of course, most people don't think about age in terms of days. Age (at least, of people) is typically measured in years. One simple solution is to divide the age in days by 365 (the number of days in a year). Figure 4-4 shows this type of query.

Figure 4-3: The DATEDIFF function determines the difference between dates.

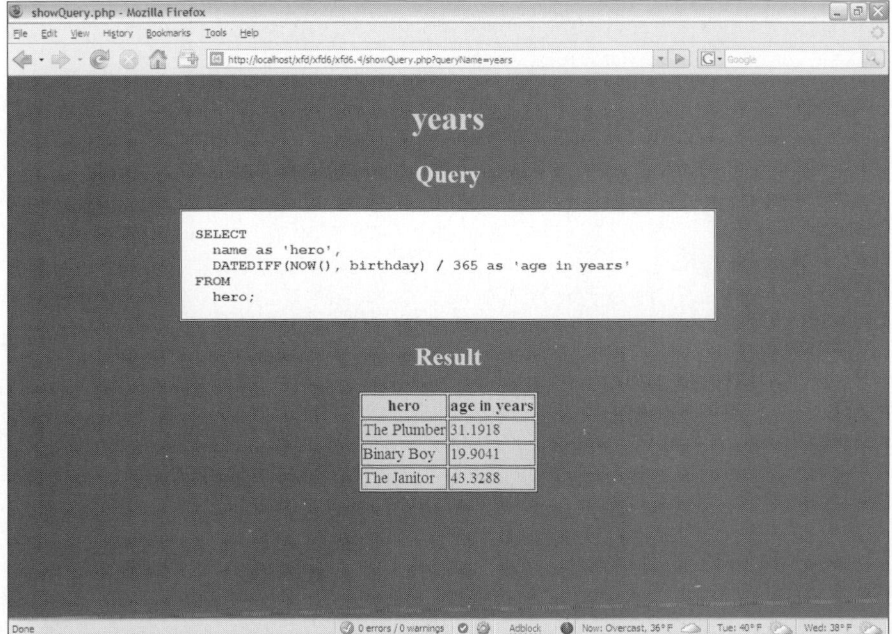

Figure 4-4: You can divide by 365 to determine the number of years.

This code is almost like the query shown in Figure 4-3, except it uses a mathematical operator. You can use most of the math operators in queries to do quick conversions. Now, the age is specified in years, but the decimal part is a bit odd. Normally, you either go with entire year measurements or work with months, weeks, and days.

Converting the days integer into a date

The `YEAR()` function extracts only the years from a date, and the `MONTH()` function pulls out the months, but both these functions require a `date` value. The `DATEDIFF()` function creates an integer. Somehow, you need to convert the integer value produced by `DATEDIFF()` back into a `date` value. (For more on this function, see the section "Using DATEDIFF to determine age," earlier in this chapter.)

Figure 4-5 is another version of a query that expresses age in terms of years and months.

This query takes the `DATEDIFF()` value and converts it back to a date. The actual date is useful, but it has some strange formatting. If you look carefully at the dates, you'll see that they have the age of each hero, but it's coded as if it was a particular date in the ancient world.

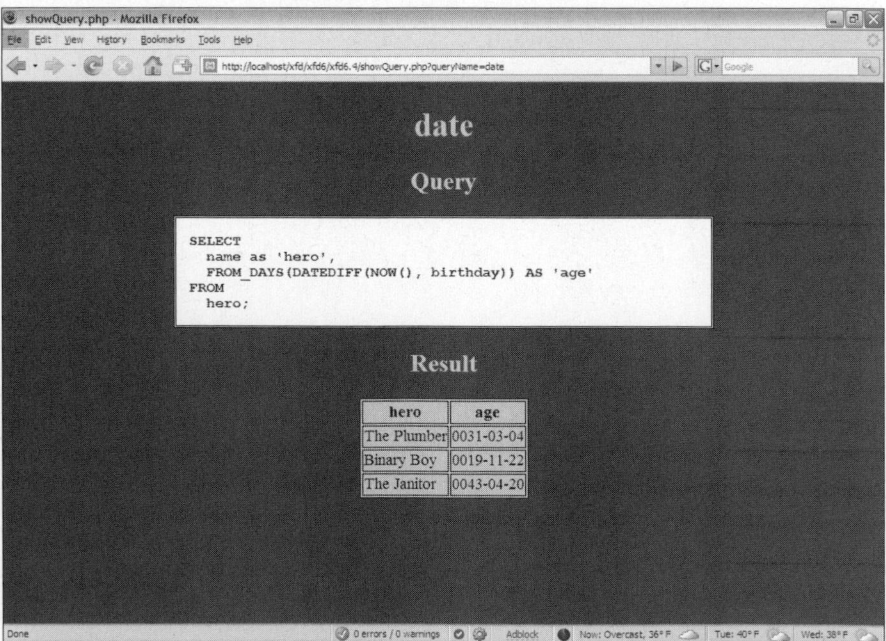


```
SELECT
  name as 'hero',
  FROM_DAYS(DATEDIFF(NOW(), birthday)) AS 'age'
FROM
  hero;
```

hero	age
The Plumber	0031-03-04
Binary Boy	0019-11-22
The Janitor	0043-04-20

Figure 4-5: The age is now converted back to a date.

Using YEAR() and MONTH() to get readable values

After you've determined the age in days, you can use the `YEAR()` and `MONTH()` functions to pull out the hero's age in a more readable way, as illustrated by Figure 4-6.

The query is beginning to look complex, but it's producing some really nice output. Still, it's kind of awkward to have separate fields for year, month, and day.

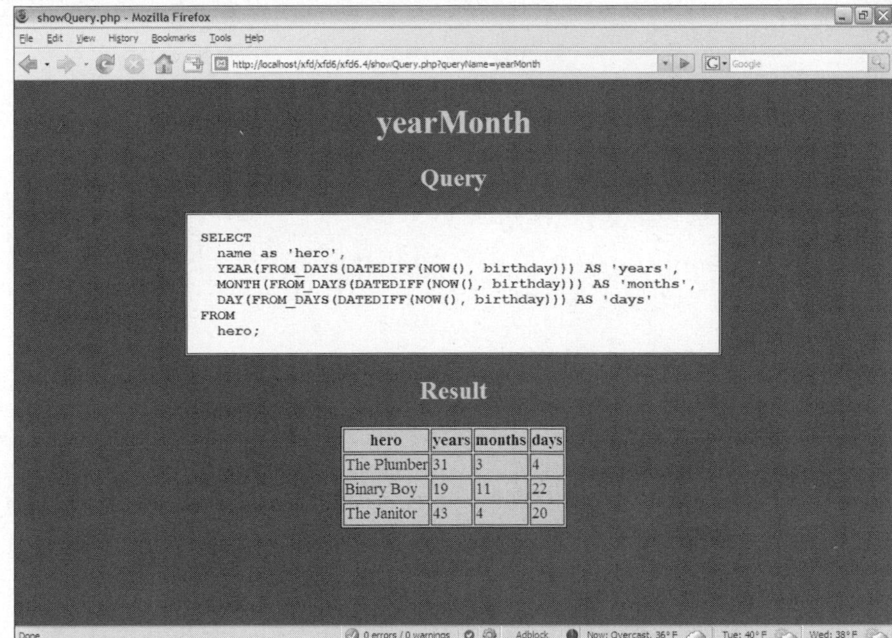

Figure 4-6: The YEAR(), MONTH(), and DAY() functions return parts of a date.

Concatenating to make one field

If you have year, month, and day values, it would be nice to combine some of this information to get a custom field, as you can see in Figure 4-7.

This query uses the `CONCAT()` function to combine calculations and literal values to make exactly the output the user is expecting. Even though the birthday is the stored value, the output can be the age.

There's no way I'm writing that every time. . . .

I know what you're thinking. All this fancy function stuff is well and good, but there's no stinkin' way you're going to do all those function gymnastics every time you want to extract an age out of the database. Here's the good news: You don't have to. It's okay that the queries are getting a little tricky because you'll write code to do all the work for you. You write it only once, and then your code does all the heavy lifting. Generally, you write PHP code to manage each query inside a function. Once you've tested it, you run that function and off you go. . . . You can also use a little gem called the view, described in the "Creating a View" section. Views allow you to store complex queries right in your database.

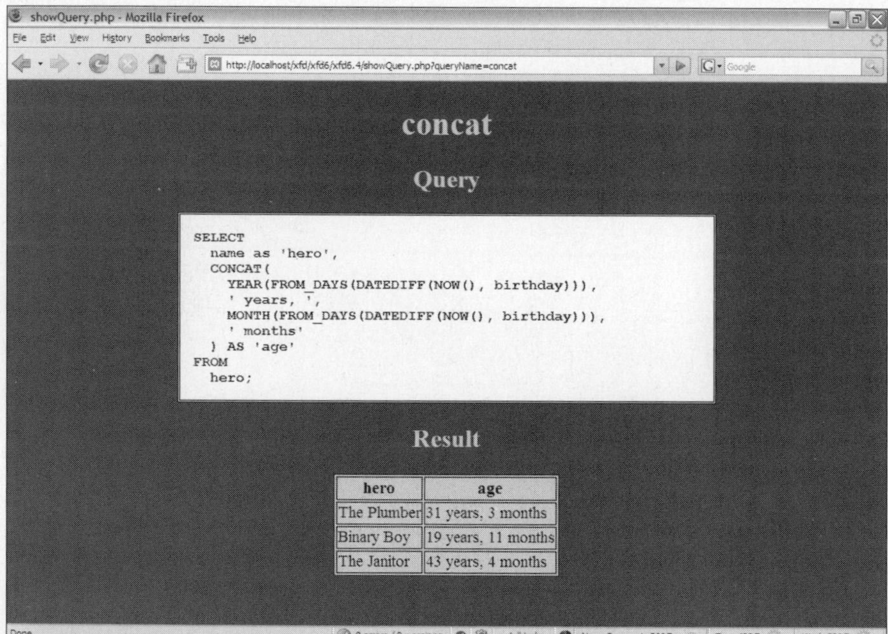

Figure 4-7: Now, the age is back in one field, as originally intended.

Creating a View

The query that converts a birthday into a formatted age is admittedly complex. Normally, you'll have this query predefined in your PHP code so that you don't have to think about it any more. If you have MySQL 5.0 or later, though, you have access to a wonderful tool called the `VIEW`. A *view* is something like a virtual table.

The best way to understand a view is to see a sample of it in action. Take a look at this SQL code:

```
CREATE VIEW heroAgeView AS
  SELECT
    name as 'hero',
    CONCAT(
      YEAR(FROM_DAYS(DATEDIFF(NOW(), birthday))),
      ' years, ',
      MONTH(FROM_DAYS(DATEDIFF(NOW(), birthday))),
      ' months'
    ) AS 'age'
  FROM
    hero;
```


If you look closely, it's exactly the same query used to generate the age from the birth date, just with a `CREATE VIEW` statement added. When you run this code, nothing overt happens, but the database stores the query as a view called `heroView`. Figure 4-8 shows the cool part.

This code doesn't look really fancy, but look at the output. It's just like you had a table with all the information you wanted, but now the data is guaranteed to be in a decent format.

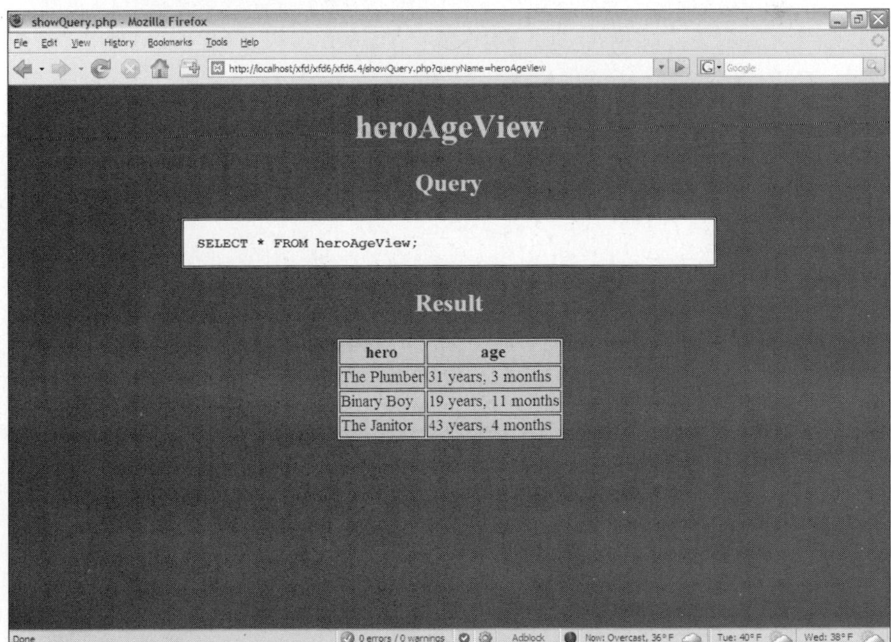

Figure 4-8: This simple query hides a lot of complexity.

So what if I'm stuck with MySQL 4.0?

Views are so great that it's hard to imagine working with data without them. However, your hosting service may not have MySQL 5.0 or later installed, which means you aren't able to use views. All is not lost. You can handle this issue in two ways.

The most common approach is to store all the queries you're likely to need (the ones that would be views) as strings in your PHP code. Execute the query from PHP, and you've essentially executed the view. This method is how most programmers did it before views were available in MySQL.

Another approach is to create a new table called something like `storeQuery` in your database. Put the text of all your views inside this table, and then you can extract the view code from the database and execute it using a second pass at the data server.

After you create a view, you can use it in subsequent `SELECT` statements as if it were a table! Here are a couple of important things to know about views:

- **They aren't stored in the database.** The view isn't really data; it's just a stored query. It looks and feels like a table, but it's created in real time from the tables.
- **You can't write to a view.** Because views don't contain data (they reflect data from other tables), you can't write directly to them. You don't use the `INSERT` or `UPDATE` commands on views, as you do ordinary tables
- **They're a relatively new feature of MySQL.** Useful as they are, views weren't added to MySQL until Version 5.0. If your server uses an earlier version, you'll have to do some workarounds, described in the sidebar "So what if I'm stuck with MySQL 4.0?".
- **You can treat views as tables in `SELECT` statements.** You can build `SELECT` statements using views as if they were regular tables.

Some database packages make it appear as if you can update a view, but that's really an illusion. Such programs reverse-engineer views to update each table. This approach is far from foolproof, and you should probably avoid it.

Using an Inner Join to Combine Tables

When I normalized the hero database in Chapter 3 of this minibook, I broke it up into several tables. Take a quick look at the hero table in Figure 4-9.

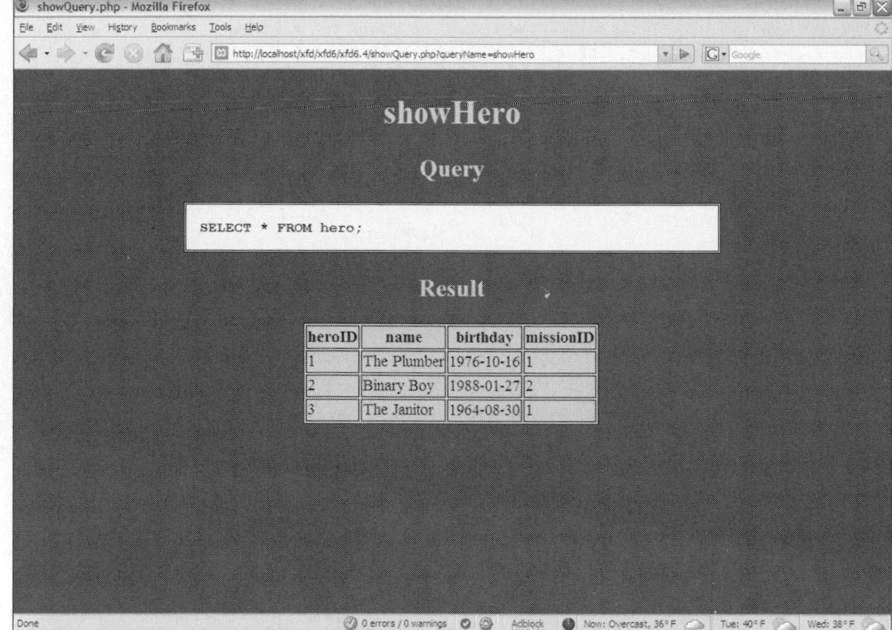

Figure 4-9: The hero table has a link to the mission table.

You probably noticed that most of the mission information is now gone from this table, except one important field. The `missionID` field is an integer field that contains the primary key of the mission table. A *foreign key* is a field that contains the primary key of another table. Foreign keys are used to reconnect tables that have been broken apart by normalization.

Look at the mission table in Figure 4-10, and it begins to make sense.

The mission table doesn't have a link back to the hero. It can't because any mission can be connected to any number of heroes, and you can't have a listed field.

Building a Cartesian join and an inner join

Compare the hero and mission tables, and you see how they fit together. The `missionID` field in the hero table identifies which mission the hero is on. None of the actual mission data is in the `hero` field, just a link to which mission the player is on.

Creating a query with both tables, as in Figure 4-11, is tempting. This query appears to join the tables, but it obviously isn't doing the right thing. You have only three heroes and two missions, yet this query returns six rows! What's happened here is called a *Cartesian join*. It's a combination of all the possible values of hero and mission, which is obviously not what you want.

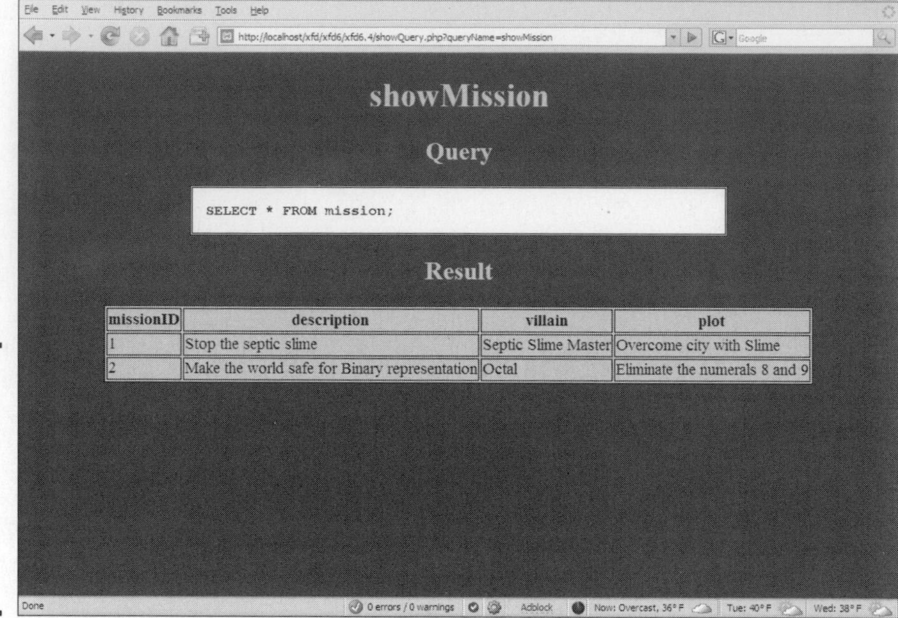

Figure 4-10: The mission table handles mission data but has no link to the hero.

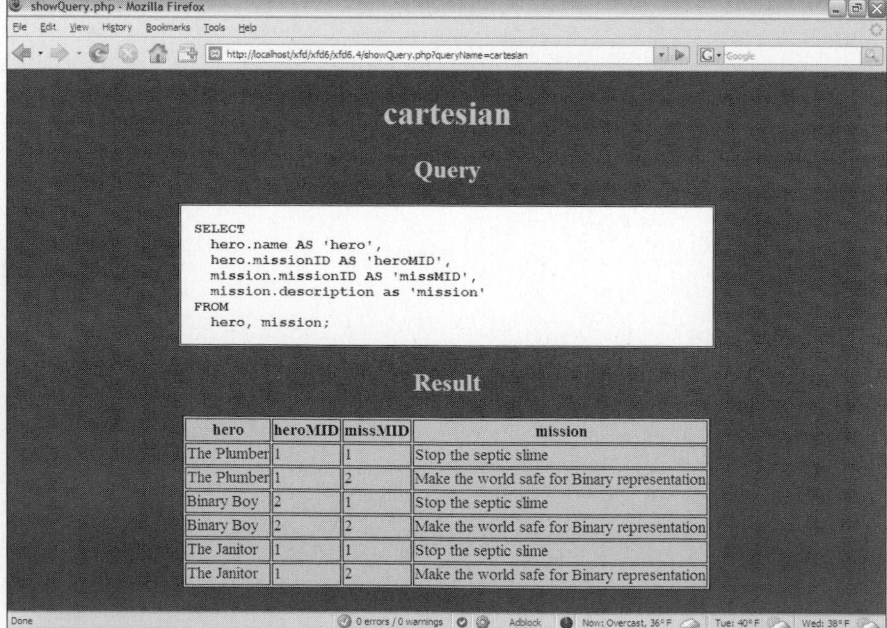

Figure 4-11: This query joins both tables, but it doesn't seem right.

You don't really want all these values to appear; you want to see only the ones where the hero table's `missionID` matches up to the `missionID` field in the mission table. In other words, you want a query that says only return rows where the two values of `missionID` are the same. That query may look like Figure 4-12. It's almost identical to the last query, except this time, a `WHERE` clause indicates that the foreign key and primary key should match up.

This particular setup (using a foreign key reference to join up two tables) is called an inner join. Sometimes, you see the syntax like

```
SELECT
  hero.name AS 'hero',
  hero.missionID AS 'heroMID',
  mission.missionID AS 'missMID',
  mission.description as 'mission'
FROM
  hero INNER JOIN mission
ON
  hero.missionID = mission.missionID;
```

Some of Microsoft's database offerings prefer this syntax, but it really does the same thing: join up two tables.

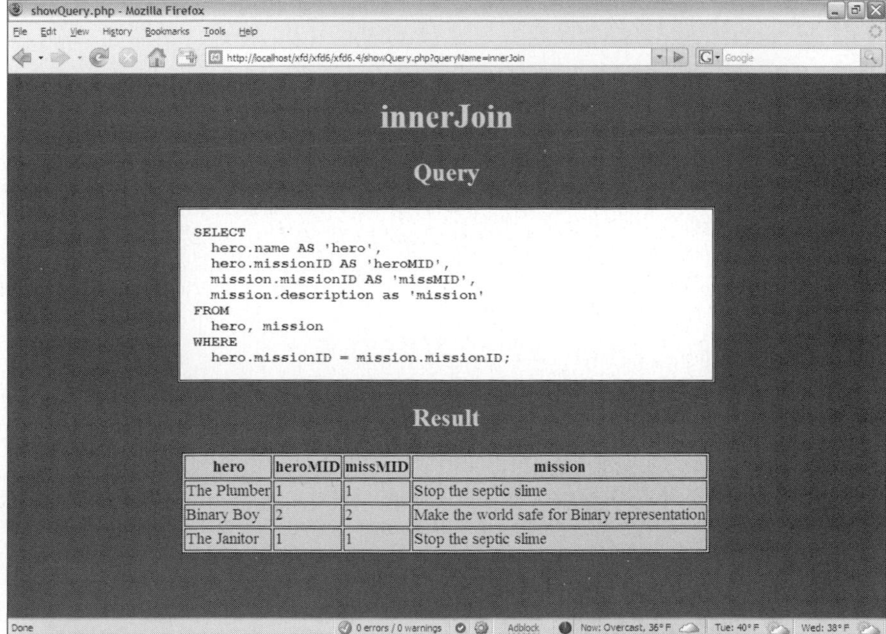

Figure 4-12: Now, you have an inner join.

Enforcing one-to-many relationships

Whenever your ER diagram indicates a many-to-one relationship, you generally use an inner join (see the preceding section). Here's how you do it:

1. **Start with the ER diagram.**

   No way are you going to get this right in your head! Make a diagram. Use a tool like DBDesigner, some other software, pencil and paper, lipstick on a mirror, whatever. You need a sketch.

2. **Identify one-to-many relationships.**

   You may have to talk with people who use the data to determine which relationships are one-to-many. In the hero data, a hero can have only one mission, but each mission can have many heroes. Thus, the hero is the many side, and the mission is the one side.

3. **Find the primary key of the one table and the many table.**

4. **Make a foreign key reference to the one table in the many table.**

   Add a field to the table on the many side of the relationship that contains only the key to the table on the one side.

   You don't need a foreign key in the one table. This concept confuses most beginners. You don't need (or want) a link back to the many table because you don't know how many you'll need.

If the preceding steps are hard for you to understand, think back to the hero example. Each hero (according to the business rules) can be on only one mission. Thus, it makes sense to put a link to the mission in the hero table because you have only one mission. Each mission can be related to many heroes, so if you try to link missions to heroes, you have listed fields in the mission table, violating the first normal form. (For information on the types of normal forms, see Chapter 3 of this minibook.) Figure 4-13 shows how it works in action. The result of this join looks a lot like the original intention of the database, but now it's normalized!

Counting the advantages of inner joins

Even though the table in Figure 4-13 contains everything in the original non-normalized data set (except for the repeated field), the new version is considerably better for several reasons:

- **No data is repeated.** The plot is stored only one time in the database. Even though it may appear several times in this output, each value is stored only once.
- **Searching is much more efficient.** Because the data is stored only one time, you no longer have to worry about spelling and typing errors. If the entry is wrong, it is universally wrong, and you can repair it in only one place.

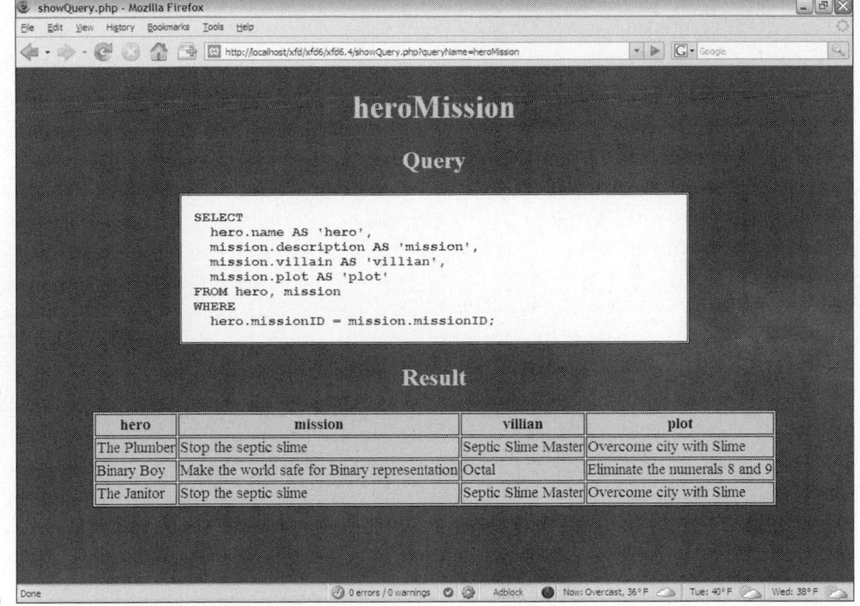

Figure 4-13: Here's a nice join of the hero and mission tables.

- **The data is organized correctly.** Although the user can't see it from this output, the tables are now separated so that each type of data goes where it belongs.
- **The output still looks like what the user wants.** Users don't care about the third normal form. (For more on forms, see Chapter 3 of this minibook.) They just want to get to their data. This table gives them a query that returns the data they're looking for, even though the underlying data structure has changed dramatically.

Building a view to encapsulate the join

The inner join query is so useful, it's a dandy place for a view. I created a view from it:

```
CREATE VIEW heroMissionView AS
  SELECT
    hero.name AS 'hero',
    mission.description AS 'mission',
    mission.villain AS 'villian',
    mission.plot AS 'plot'
  FROM hero, mission
  WHERE
    hero.missionID = mission.missionID;
```

Having a view means that you don't have to recreate the query each time. You can treat the view as a virtual table for queries:

```
SELECT * FROM heroMissionView;
```

Managing Many-to-Many Joins

Inner joins are a perfect way to implement one-to-many relationships. If you look at ER diagrams, you often see many-to-many relationships, too. Of course, you also need to model them. Here's the secret: You can't really do it. It's true. The relational data model doesn't really have a good way to do many-to-many joins. Instead, you fake it out. It isn't hard, but it's a little bit sneaky.

You use many-to-many joins to handle listed data, such as the relationship between hero and power. Each hero can have any number of powers, and each power can belong to any number of heroes (see the table in Figure 4-14).

The inner join was easy because you just put a foreign key reference to the one side of the relationship in the many table. (See the section "Using an Inner Join to Combine Tables," earlier in this chapter.) In a many-to-many join, there is no 'one' side, so where do you put the reference? Leave it to computer scientists to come up with a sneaky solution.

First, review the hero table in Figure 4-14.

Note that this table contains no reference to powers. Now, look at the power table in Figure 4-15. You see a lot of powers, but no reference to heroes.

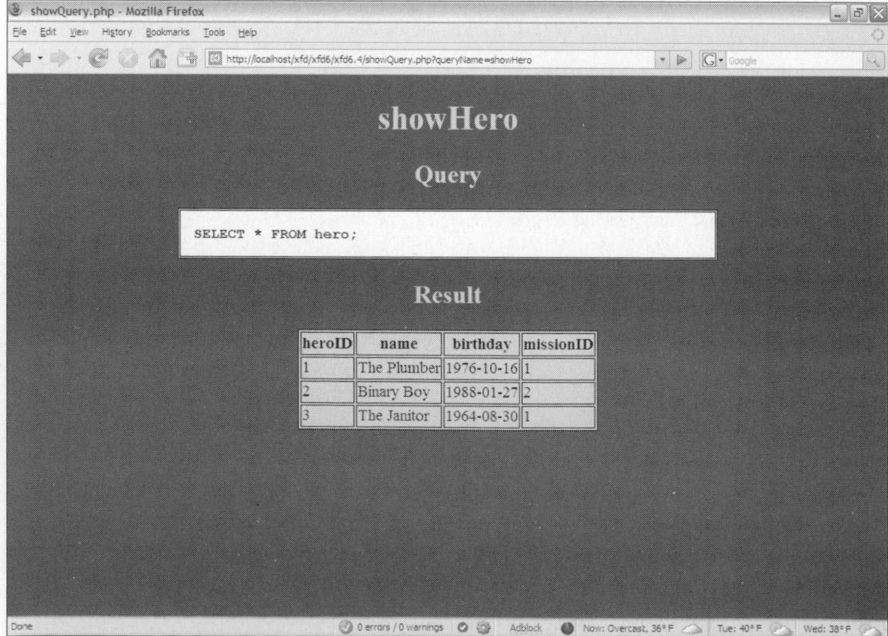

heroID	name	birthday	missionID
1	The Plumber	1976-10-16	1
2	Binary Boy	1988-01-27	2
3	The Janitor	1964-08-30	1

Figure 4-14: The hero table has no reference to powers.

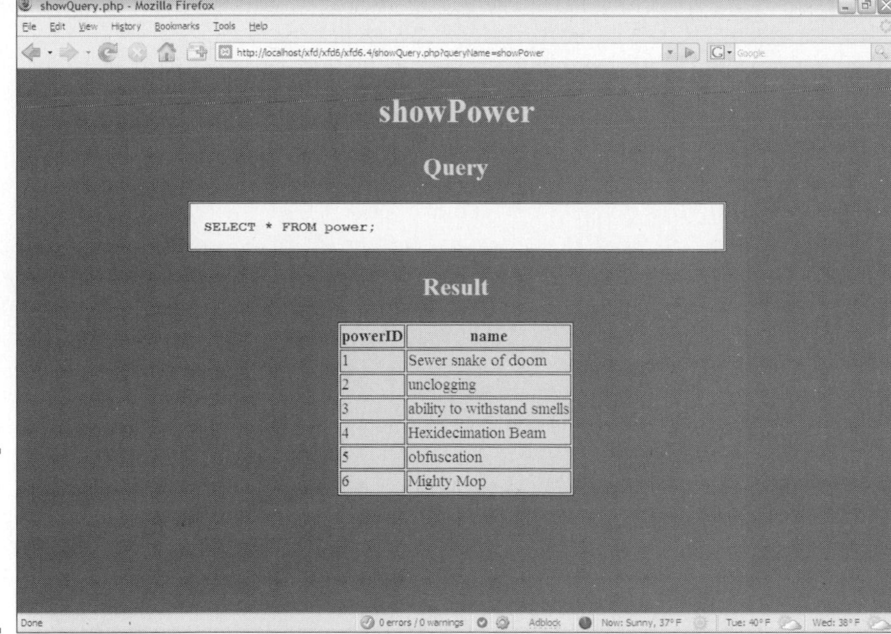

powerID	name
1	Sewer snake of doom
2	unclogging
3	ability to withstand smells
4	Hexidecimation Beam
5	obfuscation
6	Mighty Mop

Figure 4-15: The power table has no reference to heroes.

Here's the tricky part. Take a look at a new table in Figure 4-16.

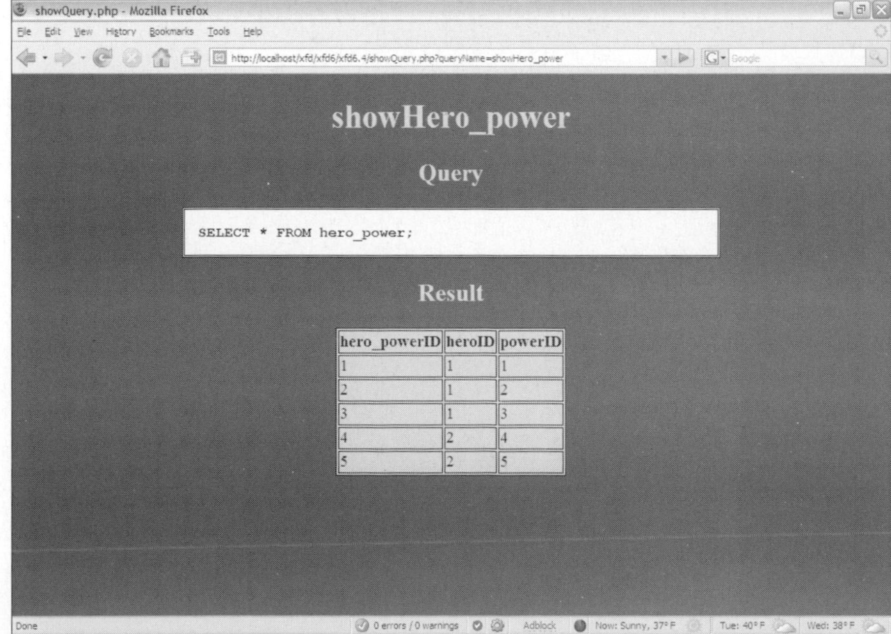

hero_powerID	heroID	powerID
1	1	1
2	1	2
3	1	3
4	2	4
5	2	5

Figure 4-16: This new table contains only foreign keys!

The results of this query may surprise you. The new table contains nothing but foreign keys. It doesn't make a lot of sense on its own, yet it represents one of the most important ideas in data.

Understanding link tables

The hero_power table shown in Figure 4-16 is a brand new table, and it's admittedly an odd little duck:

- **It contains no data of its own.** Very little appears inside the table.
- **It isn't about an entity.** All the tables shown earlier in this chapter are about entities in your data. This one isn't.
- **It's about a relationship.** This table is actually about relationships between hero and power. Each entry of this table is a link between hero and power
- **It contains two foreign key references.** Each record in this table links an entry in the hero table with one in the power table.
- **It has a many-to-one join with each of the other two tables.** This table has a many-to-one relationship with the hero table. Each record of hero_power connects to one record of hero. Likewise, each record of hero_power connects to one record of power.
- **The two many-to-one joins create a many-to-many join.** Here's the magical part: By creating a table with two many-to-one joins, you create a many-to-many join between the original tables!
- **This type of structure is called a *link table.*** Link tables are used to create many-to-many relationships between entities.

Using link tables to make many-to-many joins

Figure 4-17 displays a full-blown ER diagram of the hero data.

Link tables aren't really useful on their own because they contain no actual data. Generally, you use a link table inside a query or view:

```
SELECT
  hero.name AS 'hero',
  power.name AS 'power'
FROM
  hero, power, hero_power
WHERE
  hero.heroID = hero_power.heroID
AND
  power.powerID = hero_power.powerID;
```

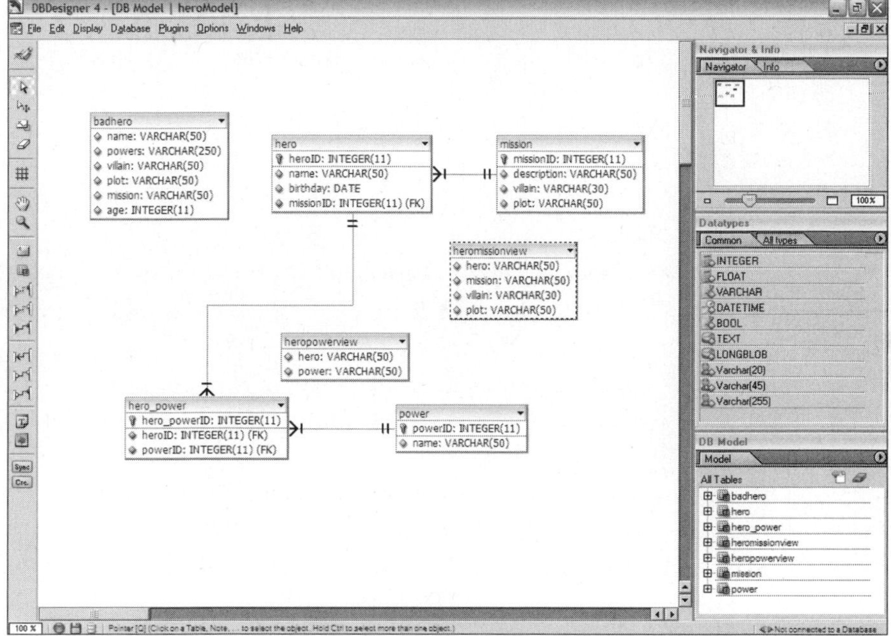

Figure 4-17: Here's the actual ER diagram of the hero data.

Here are some thoughts about this type of query:

- **It combines three tables.** That complexity seems scary at first, but it's really fine. The point of this query is to use the hero_power table to identify relationships between hero and power. Note that the `FROM` clause lists all three tables.
- **The `WHERE` clause has two links.** The first part of the `WHERE` clause links up the hero_power table with the hero table with an inner join. The second part links up the power table with another inner join.
- **You can use another `AND` clause to further limit the results.** Of course, you can still add other parts to the `AND` clause to make the results solve a particular problem, but I leave that alone for now.

Figure 4-18 shows the result of this query. Now, you have results you can use.

Once again, this query is an obvious place for a view:

```
CREATE VIEW heroPowerView AS
  SELECT
    hero.name AS 'hero',
    power.name AS 'power'
  FROM
    hero, power, hero_power
```

```
WHERE
  hero.heroID = hero_power.heroID
AND
  power.powerID = hero_power.powerID;
```

Typically, you won't do your results exactly like this view. Instead, you display information for, say, Binary Boy, and you want a list of his powers. It isn't necessary to say Binary Boy three times, so you tend to use two queries (both from views, if possible) to simplify the task. For example, look at these two queries:

```
SELECT * FROM heroMissionView WHERE hero = 'binary boy';
SELECT power FROM heroPowerView WHERE hero = 'binary boy';
```

The combination of these queries give you enough data to describe everything in the original table. Typically, you attach all this data together in your PHP code. Figure 4-19 shows a PHP page using both queries to build a complete picture of Binary Boy.

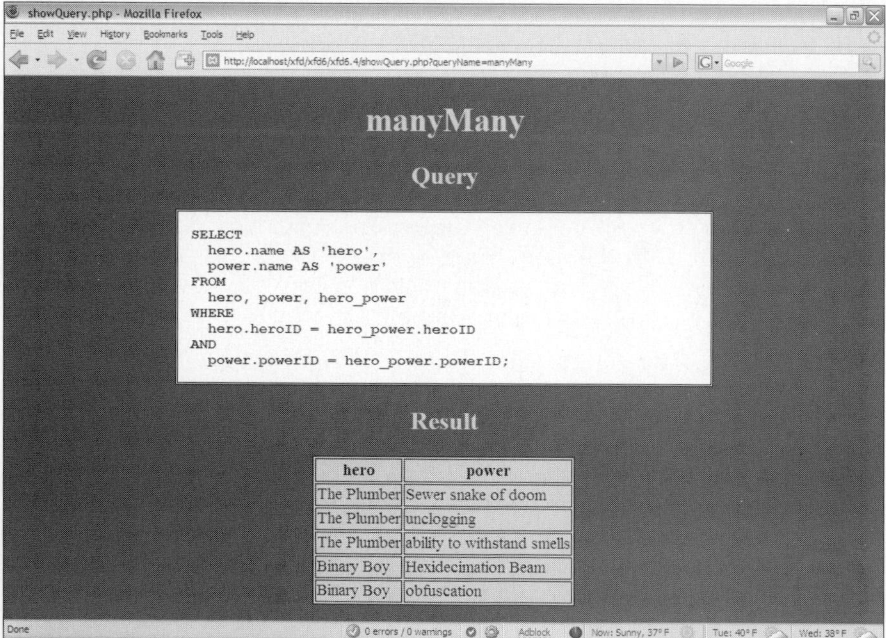

Figure 4-18: The Link Query joins up heroes and powers.

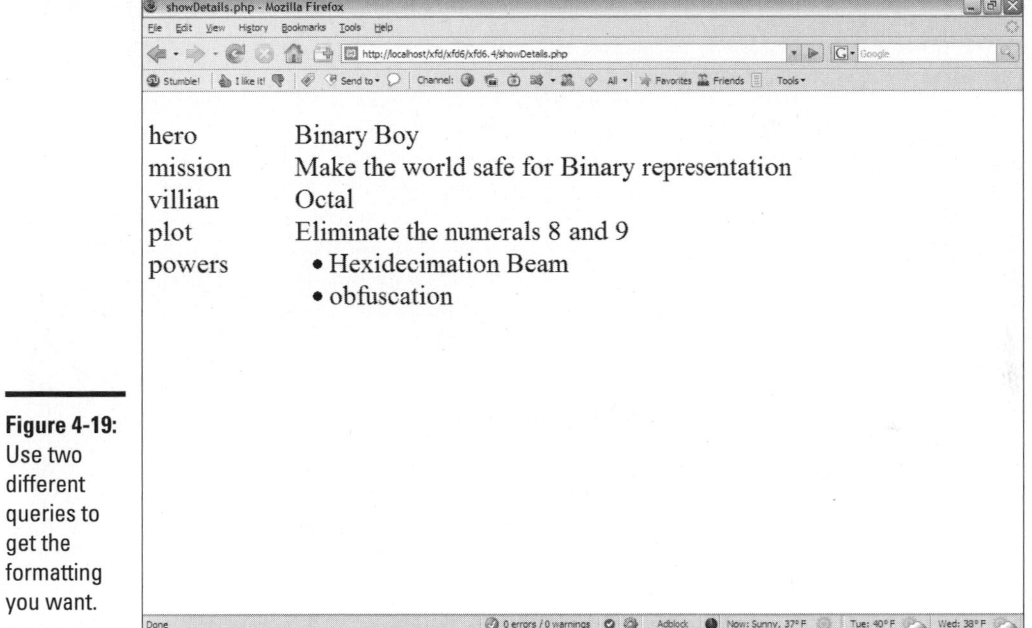

Figure 4-19: Use two different queries to get the formatting you want.

The code is standard PHP data access, except it makes two passes to the database:

```
<!DOCTYPE html PUBLIC
"-//W3C//DTD XHTML 1.0 Strict//EN"
"http://www.w3.org/TR/xhtml1/DTD/xhtml1-strict.dtd">
<html lang = "EN" xml:lang = "EN" dir = "ltr">
<head>
<meta http-equiv="content-type" content="text/xml; charset=iso-8859-1" />
<title>showDetails.php</title>
<style type = "text/css">
  dt {
    float: left;
    width: 4em;
    clear: left;
  }

  dd {
    float: left;
    width: 20em;
  }
</style>

</head>

<body>
<?php
```

```
//connect
$conn = mysql_connect("localhost", "xfd", "password");
//change this password and username to work on your system
mysql_select_db("xfd");

//get most information for requested hero
$hero = "binary boy";
$query = <<<HERE
SELECT
  *
FROM
  heroMissionView
WHERE
  hero = '$hero'
HERE;

print "<dl> \n";
$result = mysql_query($query, $conn);
$row = mysql_fetch_assoc($result);
foreach ($row as $field => $value){
  print <<<HERE
  <dt>$field</dt>
  <dd>$value</dd>

HERE;
} // end foreach
print "  <dt>powers</dt> \n";
print "  <dd> \n";
print "    <ul> \n";

//create another query to grab the powers
$query = <<<HERE
SELECT
  power
FROM
  heroPowerView
WHERE hero = '$hero'
HERE;

//put powers in an unordered list
$result = mysql_query($query, $conn);
while ($row = mysql_fetch_assoc($result)){
  foreach ($row as $field => $value){
    print "    <li>$value</li> \n";
  } // end foreach
}  // end while looop
print "  </ul> \n";
print "</dd> \n";
print "</dl> \n";
?>
</body>
</html>
```

Refer to Book V to read more on PHP and how it's used to access databases.

Book VII

Into the Future with AJAX

"Evidently he died of natural causes following a marathon session animating everything on his personal Web site. And no, Morganstern – the irony isn't lost on me."

Contents at a Glance

Chapter 1: AJAX Essentials

In This Chapter

- Understanding AJAX
- Using JavaScript to manage HTTP requests
- Creating an XMLHttpRequest object
- Building a synchronous AJAX request
- Retrieving data from an AJAX request
- Managing asynchronous AJAX requests

If you've been following the Web trends, you've no doubt heard of AJAX. This technology has generated a lot of interest. Depending on who you listen to, it's either going to change the Internet or it's a lot of overblown hype. In this minibook, I show you what AJAX really is, how to use it, and how to use a particular AJAX library to supercharge your Web pages.

The first thing is to figure out exactly what AJAX is and what it isn't. It isn't:

- **A programming language:** It isn't one more language to learn along with the many others you encounter.
- **New:** Most of the technology used in AJAX isn't really all that new; it's the way the technology's being used that's different.
- **Remarkably different:** For the most part, AJAX is about the same things you'll see in the rest of this book: building compliant Web pages that interact with the user.

So you've got to be wondering why people are so excited about AJAX. It's a relatively simple thing, but it has the potential to change the way people think about Internet development. Here's what it really is:

- **Direct control of client-server communication:** Rather than the automatic communication between client and server that happens with Web sites and server-side programs, AJAX is about managing this relationship more directly.
- **Use of the `XMLHttpRequest` object:** This is a special object that's been built into the DOM of all major browsers for some time, but it wasn't used heavily. The real innovation of AJAX was finding creative (perhaps unintentional) uses for this heretofore virtually unknown utility.

- **A closer relationship between client-side and server-side programming:** Up to now, client-side programs (usually JavaScript) did their own thing, and server-side programs (PHP) operated without too much knowledge of each other. AJAX helps these two types of programming work together better.
- **A series of libraries that facilitate this communication:** AJAX isn't that hard, but it does have a lot of details. Several great libraries have sprung up to simplify using AJAX technologies. You'll find AJAX libraries for both client-side languages like JavaScript, and server-side languages like PHP.

Let's say you're making an online purchase with a shopping cart mechanism.

In a typical (pre-AJAX) system, an entire Web page is downloaded to the user's computer. There may be a limited amount of JavaScript-based interactivity, but anything that requires a data request needs to be sent back to the server. For example, if you're on a shopping site and you want more information about that fur-lined fishbowl you've had your eye on, you might click on the "more information" button. This causes a request to be sent to the server, which builds an entire new Web page for you containing your new request.

Every time you make a request, the system builds a whole new page on the fly. The client and server have a long-distance relationship.

In the old days when you wanted to manage your Web site's content, you had to refresh each Web page — time-consuming to say the least. But with AJAX, you can update the content on a page without refreshing the page. Instead of the server sending an entire page response just to update a few words on the page, the server *just sends the words you want to update and nothing else.*

If you're using an AJAX-enabled shopping cart, you might still click on the fish bowl image. An AJAX request goes to the server and gets information about the fish bowl, which is immediately placed in the current page, without requiring a complete page refresh.

AJAX technology allows you to send a request to the server, which can then change just a small part of the page. With AJAX, you can have a whole bunch of smaller requests happening all the time, rather than a few big ones that rebuild the page in large distracting flurries of activity.

To the user, this makes the Web page look more like traditional applications. This is the big appeal of AJAX: It allows Web applications to act more like desktop applications, even if these Web applications have complicated features like remote database access.

Google's Gmail was the first major application to use AJAX, and it blew people away because it felt so much like a regular application inside a Web browser.

AJAX Spelled Out

Technical people love snappy acronyms. There's nothing more intoxicating than inventing a term. AJAX is one term which has taken on a life of its own. Like many computing acronyms, it may be fun to say, but it doesn't really mean much. AJAX stands for Asynchronous JavaScript And XML. Truthfully, these terms were probably chosen to make a pronounceable acronym rather than for their accuracy or relevance to how AJAX works.

A is for asynchronous

An *asynchronous* transaction (at least in AJAX terms) is one in which more than one thing can happen at once. For example, you can make an AJAX call process a request while the rest of your form is being processed. AJAX requests do not absolutely have to be asynchronous, but they usually are.

When it comes to Web design, *asynchronous* means that you can independently send and receive as many different requests as you want. Data may start transmitting at any time without having any effect on other data transmissions. You could have a form that saves each field to the database as soon as it's filled out. Or perhaps a series of drop-down lists that generates the next drop-down list based upon the value you just selected. (It's OK if this doesn't make sense right now. It's not an important part of understanding AJAX, but vowels are always nice in an acronym.)

In this chapter, I show you how to do both synchronous and asynchronous versions of AJAX.

J is for JavaScript

If you want to make an AJAX call, you simply write some JavaScript code that simulates a form. You can then access a special object hidden in the DOM (the `XMLHttpRequest` object) and use its methods to send that request to the user. Your program acts like a form, even if there was no form there. In that sense, when you're writing AJAX code, you're really using JavaScript. Of course, you can also use any other client-side programming language that can speak with the DOM, including Flash and (to a lesser extent) Java. JavaScript is the dominant technology, so it's in the acronym.

A lot of times, you also use JavaScript to decode the response from the AJAX request.

A is for . . . and?

I think it's a stretch to use "and" in an acronym, but AJX just isn't as cool as AJAX. I guess they didn't ask me.

And X is for . . . data

The *X* is for *XML,* which is one way to send the data back and forth from the server.

Since the object we're using is the `XMLHttpRequest` object, it makes sense that it requests XML. It can do that, but it can also get any kind of text data. You can use AJAX to retrieve all kinds of things:

- **Plain old text:** Sometimes you just want to grab some text from the server. Maybe you have a text file with a daily quote in it or something.
- **Formatted HTML:** You can have text stored on the server as a snippet of HTML/XHTML code and use AJAX to load this page snippet into your browser. This gives you a powerful way to build a page from a series of smaller segments. You can use this to reuse parts of your page (say headings or menus) without duplicating them on the server.
- **XML data:** XML is a great way to pass data around. (That's what it was invented for.) You might send a request to a program that goes to a database, makes a request, and returns the result as XML.
- **JSON data:** A new standard called JSON (JavaScript Object Notation) is emerging as an alternative to XML for formatted data transfer. It has some interesting advantages.

Making a Basic AJAX Connection

AJAX uses some pretty technical parts of the Web in ways that may be unfamiliar to you. Read through the rest of this chapter so you know what AJAX is doing, but don't get bogged down in the details. *Nobody does it by hand!* (Except people who write AJAX libraries or books about using AJAX.) In Chapter 2 of this minibook I show a library that does all the work for you. If all these details are making you misty-eyed, just skip ahead to the next chapter and come back here when you're ready to see how all the magic works.

The `basicAJax.html` program shown in Figure 1-1 illustrates AJAX at work.

When the user clicks on the link, a small pop-up shown in Figure 1-2 appears.

If you don't get the joke, you need to go rent *Monty Python and the Holy Grail.* It's part of the geek culture. Trust me. In fact, you should really own a copy.

It's very easy to make JavaScript pop up a dialog, but the interesting thing here is where that text comes from. The data is stored on a text file on the server. Without AJAX, there is no easy way to get data from the server without reloading the entire page.

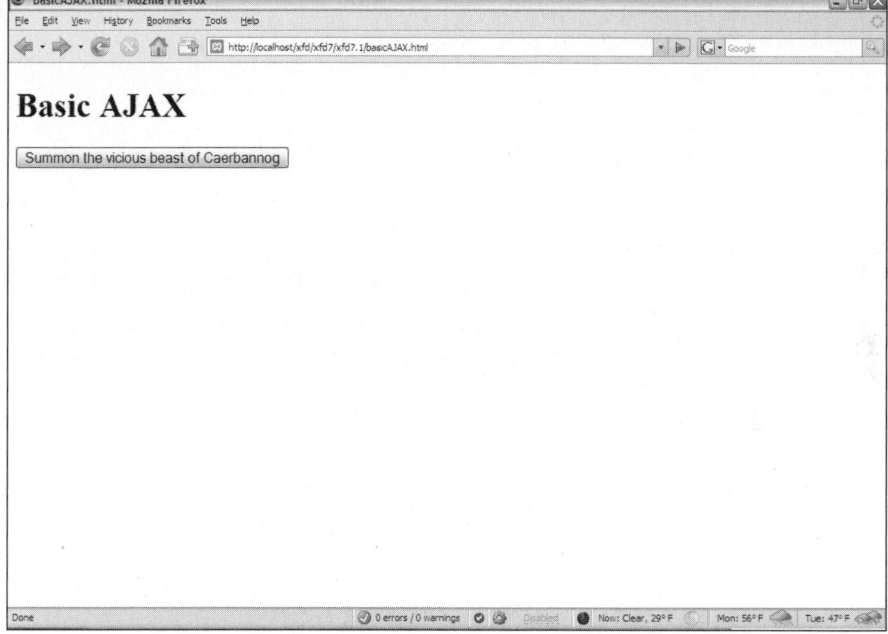

Figure 1-1: Click on the link and you'll see some AJAX magic.

Figure 1-2: This text came from the server.

You might claim that HTML frames allow you to pull data from the server, but frames have been deprecated in XHTML because they cause a lot of other problems. You can use a frame to load data from the server, but you can't do all the other cool things with frame-based data that you can with AJAX. Even if frames were allowed, AJAX is a much better solution most of the time.

You won't be able to run this example straight from the CD-ROM. Like PHP, AJAX requires a server to work properly. If you want to run this program, put it in a subdirectory of your server and run it through `localhost` as you do for PHP programs.

This particular example uses a couple of shortcuts to make it easier to understand:

- **It isn't fully asynchronous.** The program will pause while it retrieves data. As a user, you won't even notice this, but as you'll see, this can have a serious drawback. It's a bit simpler, so I start with this example and then extend it to make the asynchronous version.
- **It isn't completely cross-browser-compatible.** The AJAX technique I use in this program works fine for IE 7 and all versions of Firefox (and most other standards-compliant browsers). It does not work correctly in IE 6 and earlier. I recommend you use jQuery or another library (described in Chapter 2 of this minibook) for cross-browser compatibility.

Look over the code, and you'll find it reasonable enough:

```
<!DOCTYPE html PUBLIC
"-//W3C//DTD XHTML 1.0 Strict//EN"
"http://www.w3.org/TR/xhtml1/DTD/xhtml1-strict.dtd">
<html lang = "EN" xml:lang = "EN" dir = "ltr">
<head>
<meta http-equiv="content-type" content="text/xml; charset=utf-8" />

<title>Basic AJAX</title>
<script type = "text/javascript">
//<![CDATA[

function getAJAX(){
  var request = new XMLHttpRequest();
  request.open("GET", "beast.txt", false);
  request.send(null);

  if (request.status == 200){
    //we got a response
    alert(request.responseText);
  } else {
    //something went wrong
    alert("Error- " + request.status + ": " + request.statusText);
  } // end if
} // end function
//]]>
```

```
</script>


</head>

<body>
<h1>Basic AJAX</h1>

<form action = "">
  <p>
    <button type = "button"
            onclick = "getAJAX()">
      Summon the vicious beast of Caerbannog
    </button>
  </p>
</form>


</body>
</html>
```

Building the HTML form

You don't absolutely need an HTML form for AJAX, but I have a simple one here. Note that the form is not attached to the server in any way.

```
<form action = "">
  <p>
    <button type = "button"
            onclick = "getAJAX()">
      Summon the vicious beast of Caerbannog
    </button>
  </p>
</form>
```


This code uses a button, and the button is attached to a JavaScript function called `getAJAX()`.

All you really need is some kind of structure that can trigger a JavaScript function.

AJAX isn't a complex technology, but it does draw on several other technologies. You may need to look over the JavaScript chapters in Book IV if this material is unfamiliar to you. Although these examples don't require PHP, they do involve server-side responses like PHP does, so AJAX is usually studied by people already familiar with both JavaScript and PHP.

Creating an XMLHttpRequest object

The key to AJAX is a special object called the `XMLHttpRequest` object. All the major browsers have it, and knowing how to use it in code is what makes AJAX work. It's pretty easy to create:

```
var request = new XMLHttpRequest();
```

Internet Explorer 5 and 6 had an entirely different way of invoking the `XMLHttpRequest` object involving a technology called ActiveX. If you want to support these older browsers, use one of the libraries mentioned in Chapter 2 of this minibook. I've decided not to worry about them in this introductory chapter.

This line makes an instance of the `XMLHttpRequest` object. You'll use methods and properties of this object to control a request to the server.

AJAX is really nothing more than HTTP, the protocol that your browser and server quietly use all the time to communicate with each other. You can think of an AJAX request like this: Imagine you have a basket with a balloon tied to the handle and a long string. As you walk around the city, you can release the basket under a particular window and let it rise up. The window (server) will put something in the basket, and you can then wind the string to bring the basket back down and retrieve the contents.

Don't worry about all the details in this Table 1-1. I describe these things as you need them in the text. Also, some of these elements only pertain to asynchronous connections, so you won't always need them all.

Table 1-1 Useful Members of the XMLHttpRequest Object

Member	*Description*	*Basket analogy*
`open(protocol, URL, synchronization)`	Opens up a connection to the indicated file on the server.	Stand under a particular window.
`send(parameters)`	Initiates the transaction with given parameters (or null).	Release the basket but hang onto the string.
`status`	Returns the HTTP status code returned by the server (200 is success).	Check for error codes ("window closed," "balloon popped," "string broken," or "everything's great").
`statusText`	Text form of HTTP status.	Text form of status code.
`responseText`	Text of the transaction's response.	Get the contents of the basket.
`readyState`	Describes current status of the transaction (4 is complete).	Is the basket empty, going up, coming down, or here and ready to get contents?
`onReadyState Change`	Event handler. Attach a function to this parameter, and when the `ready State` changes, the function will be called automatically.	What should I do when the state of the basket changes? For example, should I do something when I've gotten the basket back?

Opening a connection to the server

The XMLHttpRequest object has several useful methods. One of the most important is the open() method.

```
request.open("GET", "beast.txt", false);
```

The open() method opens up a connection to the server. As far as the server is concerned, this connection is identical to the connection made when the user clicks a link or submits a form. The open() method takes the following three parameters:

- **Request method:** The request method describes how the server should process the request. The values are identical to the form method values described in Chapter 3 of Book V. Typical values are GET and POST.
- **A file or program name:** The second parameter is the name of a file or program on the server. This is usually a program or file in the same directory as the current page.
- **A synchronization trigger:** AJAX can be done in synchronous or asynchronous mode. (Yea, I know, then it would just be JAX, but stay with me here.) The synchronous form is easier to understand, so I use it first. The next example (and all the others in this book) will use the asynchronous approach.

For this example, I use the GET mechanism to load a file called beast.txt from the server in synchronized mode.

Sending the request and parameters

Once you've opened up a request, you need to pass that request to the server. The send() method performs this task. It also provides you a mechanism for sending data to the server. This only makes sense if the request is going to a PHP program (or some other program on the server). Since I'm just requesting a regular text document, I send the value null to the server.

```
request.send(null);
```

This is a synchronous connection, so the program pauses here until the server sends the requested file. If the server never responds, the page will hang. (This is exactly why you'll usually use asynchronous connections.) Since this is just a test program, assume everything will work OK and motor on.

Returning to the basket analogy, the send() method releases the basket, which floats up to the window. In a synchronous connection, we're assuming the basket is filled and comes down automatically. The next step won't happen until the basket is back on earth. (But, if something went wrong, the next step may *never* happen, because the basket will never come back.)

Checking the status

The next line of code won't happen until the server passes some sort of response back. Any HTTP request is followed by a numeric code. Normally, your browser checks these codes automatically, and you don't see them. Occasionally, you will run across an HTTP error code, like 404 (file not found) or 500 (internal server error). If the server was able to respond to the request, it will pass a status code of 200. The `XMLHttpRequest` object has a property called `status` that returns the HTTP status code. If the status is 200, everything went fine and you can proceed. If the status is some other value, some type of error occurred.

You'll want to make sure that the status of the request is successful before you run the code that's dependant upon the request. You can check for all the various status codes if you wish, but for this simple example I'm just ensuring that the status is 200.

```
if (request.status == 200){
  //we got a response
  alert(request.responseText);
} else {
  //something went wrong
  alert("Error- " + request.status + ": " + request.statusText);
} // end if
```

The `request.status` property will contain the server response. If this value is 200, I want to do something with the results. In this case, I simply display the text in an alert box. If the request is anything but 200, I use the

Fun with HTTP response codes

Just like the post office stamping success/error messages on your envelope, the server sends back status messages with your request. You can see all the possible status codes on the World Wide Web Consortium's Web site at `www.w3.org/Protocols/rfc2616/rfc2616-sec10.html`, but the important ones to get you started are as follows:

- **`200 = OK`:** This is a success code. Everything went okay, and your response has been returned.
- **`400 = Bad Request`:** This is a client error code. It means that something went wrong on the user side. The request was poorly formed and couldn't be understood.
- **`404 = Not Found`:** This is a client error code. The page the user requested doesn't exist or couldn't be found.
- **`408 = Request Timeout`:** This is a client error code. The server gave up on waiting for the user's computer to finish making its request.
- **`500 = Internal Server Error`:** This is a server error code. It means that the server had an error and couldn't fill the request.

statusText property to determine what went wrong and pass that information to the user in an alert.

The status property is like looking at the basket after it returns. It might have the requested data in it, or it might have some sort of note. ("Sorry, the window was closed. I couldn't fulfill your request.") There's not much point in processing the data if it didn't return successfully.

Of course, I could do a lot more with the data. If it's already formatted as HTML code, I can use the innerHTML DOM tricks described in Book IV to display the code in any part of my page. It might also be some other type of formatted data (XML or JSON) that I can manipulate with JavaScript and do whatever I want with.

All Together Now — Making the Connection Asynchronous

The synchronous AJAX connection described in the previous section is easy to understand, but it has one major drawback. The client's page completely stops processing while waiting for a response from the server. This doesn't seem like a big problem, but it is. If aliens attack the Web server, it won't make the connection, and the rest of the page will never be activated. The user's browser will hang indefinitely. In most cases, the user will have to shut down the browser process with Ctl+Alt+Del (or the similar procedure on other OSs). Obviously, it would be best to prevent this kind of error.

That's why most AJAX calls use the asynchronous technique. Here's the big difference: When you send an asynchronous request, the client keeps on processing the rest of the page. When the request is complete, an event handler processes the event. If the server goes down, the browser will not hang (although the page probably won't do what you want).

In other words, the readyState property is like looking at the basket's progress. The basket could be sitting there empty, because you haven't begun the process. It could be going up to the window, being filled, coming back down, or it could be down and ready to use. You're only concerned with the last state, because that means the data is ready.

I didn't include a figure of the asynchronous version, because to the user, it looks exactly the same as the synchronous connection. Be sure to put this code on your own server and check it out for yourself.

The asynchronous version looks exactly the same on the front end, but the code is structured a little differently.

```
<!DOCTYPE html PUBLIC
"-//W3C//DTD XHTML 1.0 Strict//EN"
"http://www.w3.org/TR/xhtml1/DTD/xhtml1-strict.dtd">
<html lang = "EN" xml:lang = "EN" dir = "ltr">
<head>
<meta http-equiv="content-type" content="text/xml; charset=utf-8" />

<title>asynch.html</title>
<script type = "text/javascript">
//<![CDATA[

var request;  //make request a global variable

function getAJAX(){
  request = new XMLHttpRequest();
  request.open("GET", "beast.txt");
  request.onreadystatechange = checkData;
  request.send(null);
} // end function

function checkData(){
  if (request.readyState == 4) {
    // if state is finished
    if (request.status == 200) {
      // and if attempt was successful
      alert(request.responseText);
    } // end if
  } // end if
} // end checkData

//]]>

</script>

</head>

<body>
<h1>Asynchronous AJAX transmission</h1>
<form action = "">
  <p>
    <button type = "button"
            onclick = "getAJAX()">
      Summon the beast of Caerbannogh
    </button>
  </p>
</form>
</body>
</html>
```

Setting up the program

The general setup of this program is just like the earlier AJAX example. The HTML is a simple button which calls the `getAJAX()` function.

The JavaScript code now has two functions. The `getAJAX()` function sets up the request, but a separate function (`checkData()`) responds to the request. In an asynchronous AJAX model, you typically separate the request and the response in different functions.

Note that in the JavaScript code, I made the XMLHttpRequest object (request) a global variable by declaring it outside any functions. I generally avoid making global variables, but it makes sense in this case because I have two different functions that require the request object.

Building the getAJAX() function

The getAJAX() function sets up and executes the communication with the server.

```
function getAJAX(){
  request = new XMLHttpRequest();
  request.open("GET", "beast.txt");
  request.onreadystatechange = checkData;
  request.send(null);
} // end function
```

The code in this function is pretty straightforward:

1. **Create the request object.**

   The request object is created exactly as it was in the first example under "Creating an XMLHttpRequest object" earlier in this chapter.

2. **Call request's open() method to open a connection.**

   Note that this time I left the synchronous parameter out, which creates the (default) asynchronous connection.

3. **Assign an event handler to catch responses.**

   You can use event handlers much like the ones in the DOM. In this particular case, I'm telling the request object to call a function called checkData whenever the state of the request changes.

   You can't easily send a parameter to a function when you call it using this particular mechanism. That's why I made request a global variable.

4. **Send the request.**

   As before, the send() method begins the process. Since this is now an asynchronous connection, the rest of the page will continue to process. As soon as the request's state changes (hopefully because there's been a successful transfer), the checkData function will be activated.

Reading the response

Of course, you now need a function to handle the response when it comes back from the server. This works by checking the *ready state* of the response. Any HTTP request has a ready state, which is a simple integer value describing what state the request is currently in. There are many ready states, but the only one we're concerned with is 4, meaning the request is finished and ready to process.

Ready, set, ready state!

The readyState property of the request object indicates the ready state of the request. It has five possible values:

- 0 = **Uninitialized:** The request object has been created, but the open() method hasn't been called on.
- 1 = **Loading:** The request object has been created, the open() method has been called, but the send() method hasn't been called.
- 2 = **Loaded:** The request object has been created, the open() method has been called, the send() method has been called, but the response isn't yet available from the server.
- 3 = **Interactive:** The request object has been created, the open() method has been called, the send() method has been called, the response has started trickling back from the server, but not everything has been received yet.
- 4 = **Completed:** The request object has been created, the open() method has been called, the send() method has been called, the response has been fully received, and the request object is finished with all its request/response tasks.

Each time the readyState property of the request changes, the function you map to readyStateChanged is called. In a typical AJAX program, this will happen four times per transaction. There's no point in reading the data until the transaction is completed, which will happen when readyState is equal to 4.

The basic strategy for checking a response is to check the ready state in the aptly-named request.readyState property. If the ready state is 4, check the status code to ensure there's no error. If ready state is 4 and status is 200, you're in business, so you can process the form. Here's the code:

```
function checkData(){
  if (request.readyState == 4) {
    // if state is finished
    if (request.status == 200) {
      // and if attempt was successful
      alert(request.responseText);
    } // end if
  } // end if
} // end checkData
```

Once again, you can do anything you want with the text you receive. I'm just printing it out, but the data can be incorporated into the page or processed in any way you wish.

Chapter 2: Improving JavaScript with jQuery

In This Chapter

- **Downloading and including the jQuery library**
- **Using component selectors**
- **Handling events**

When building AJAX-enabled Web sites, it can be extremely tedious to write all the JavaScript you need to do even the simplest things. A good way around this is to use a JavaScript library. These are simply JavaScript code fragments with a number of useful functions built in.

Many JavaScript libraries are out there, and none of them write the code for you. What JavaScript libraries do is make complex JavaScript tasks easier to perform. They give you functions to encapsulate complex code into simpler function calls.

JavaScript libraries will vastly increase your productivity and allow you to do a lot more fun and impressive things in much less time. They'll also make it much easier for you to maintain your code because you don't have to rebuild basic functionality. You can concentrate instead on creating a program that solves a particular problem.

jQuery is a JavaScript library, so to use it, you must be familiar with JavaScript and DOM programming. Check out Book IV if you need a refresher on these topics.

Introducing jQuery

For this minibook, I use the jQuery JavaScript library to enhance JavaScript. jQuery has good documentation, high community involvement, and is easy to use.

JavaScript libraries

There are many other JavaScript libraries besides jQuery. I chose jQuery for this book because of its good documentation, ease of use, shallow learning curve, and large following. After you get the hang of jQuery, check out some other JavaScript libraries:

- **Prototype** (`www.prototypejs.org`): AJAX and form functions.
- **Script.aculo.us** (`http://script.aculo.us`): Add-on to Prototype that gives you basic animation and effects.
- **Moo Tools** (`http://demos.mootools.net`): Complete AJAX and user interface tools.
- **Moo.fx** (`http://moofx.mad4milk.net`): Add-on to Prototype and Moo Tools allows you to add special effects to Moo.fx.
- **MochiKit** (`www.mochikit.com`): Complete (but complex) AJAX and user interface library.

Getting acquainted with jQuery

To start with, go to the jQuery Web site at `www.jquery.com`, as shown in Figure 2-1. You'll find links to download the library as well as links to the documentation, plugins, tutorials, discussion mailing lists, and a blog. The Web site tends to change with some frequency, so don't be surprised if you go back in a week and it looks completely different.

Downloading the jQuery library

The first thing you need to do is download the jQuery library, by following these steps:

1. **With a browser, navigate to the jQuery Web site at `www.jquery.com`.**
2. **On the jQuery main page under Download jQuery, click the Download link.**

   This takes you to a wiki-style page containing the different jQuery releases. You're presented with three options for downloading:

   - **Minified — Gzipped:** A version of the file packed in a special format called gzip. This makes the file much smaller than it normally would be.
   - **Uncompressed:** Normally formatted JavaScript code. This is the easiest version to read, but it will take a little bit longer for your users to download.
   - **Packed:** Another file format that works with nearly every browser.

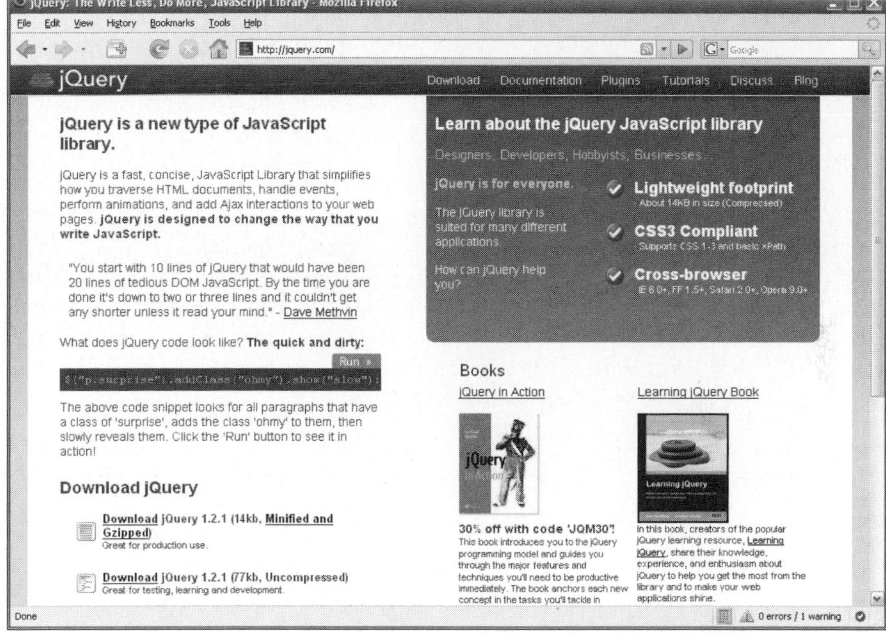

Figure 2-1: The jQuery Web site gives you an idea what this package can do.

3. **For this example, select Minified.**

Most modern browsers can read the gzip version with no problems, but occasionally you'll run across an older browser which can't handle this format. These browsers are going to have trouble with most of jQuery's other features, too. By the time you're working in AJAX, you're going to have to assume the user is using a reasonably recent browser.

4. **Download the latest version and save it to your computer somewhere you can find it easily.**

If you're using Aptana, all the most popular JavaScript libraries are already on your computer, so you probably already have the jQuery library, but you may not have the most recent version.

Using the documentation

There are several different helpful documentation options for jQuery. The official documentation can be found on the Web site (`http://jquery.com`); it appears in a wiki-style and is constantly updated and improved. There are also tutorials, mailing lists, and IRC (chat) channels. One more interesting piece of jQuery documentation is Visual jQuery.

The official documentation

When using the jQuery documentation (`http://docs.jquery.com`), the main points of interest are the API (Application Programming Interface) reference and the UI (user interface) reference. At first, you'll just use the API, but eventually after you get the hang of things, you'll use the UI to start adding nifty effects to your site to really make it shine.

Two places in the jQuery API where you'll probably spend most your time starting off are the Attributes and Manipulation sections, followed closely by the CSS section after you start dabbling in some effects. Here's some more information about each section:

- **Attributes:** Allows you to set the values of different HTML elements for your AJAX calls and functions.
- **Manipulation:** Allows you to build and remove different page elements entirely.
- **CSS:** Allows you to change the look and feel of the page on the fly.

Becoming familiar with these three sections of the documentation is a good way to get up and running with jQuery and the jQuery documentation. After you have these sections under your belt, you'll be more comfortable branching out into the rest of the documentation.

Tutorials

Many tutorials are on the jQuery Web site to get you started. After you master these and are eager to dive in and discover more, check out the tutorials at `http://docs.jquery.com/Tutorials`.

The tutorials are great but can be a little confusing for non-programmers just starting out with JavaScript, HTML, and CSS. Luckily for you, you have this chapter to take you through the basics of jQuery, but if you need more info, these tutorials are a great place to go.

Visual jQuery

Visual jQuery is a neat reference tool for the jQuery library. It provides a drill-down view of the documentation, which is great for beginners who don't know exactly where to find what they're looking for in jQuery.

With the official documentation, it can take a while to actually remember where the thing you're looking for is and then find it. If you click Selectors and you're looking for something that's really in the Manipulation section, you have to wade through the Selectors page, realize it's not there, and guess where it might be. Obviously, this can take valuable development time away, get you out of the *zone,* and can be frustrating.

Visual jQuery puts all the documentation on one page in an easy-to-navigate view (see Figure 2-2). No reloading the entire page and wading through text just to realize the thing you're looking for is somewhere else.

Unfortunately, Visual jQuery is still at jQuery 1.1.2, whereas jQuery has moved all the way on to jQuery 1.2.1, so it's five versions behind (and hasn't been updated at the time of this writing). However, the library hasn't changed that drastically in the last five versions, so the Visual jQuery documentation is still relevant. After you've been using jQuery for a month or so, you won't need Visual jQuery because you'll know exactly where everything is within the official documentation.

Getting started with jQuery

After you download jQuery, you're ready to go. No installation or compilation is required.

You can place jQuery in any directory you wish, but since you will frequently use jQuery with AJAX and PHP, it makes sense to place jQuery somewhere in your main server path, which is usually under `xampp/htdocs`. (PHP and AJAX only work through the server, which requires all files to be in this path.) Look at Book VIII, Chapter 1 for more information on configuring your server.

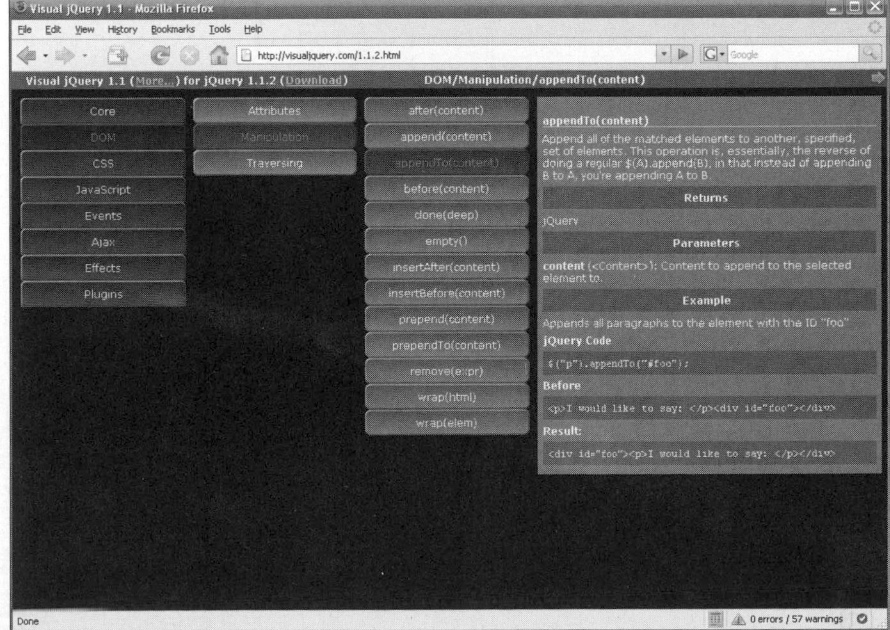

Figure 2-2: Visual jQuery is a useful documentation system for jQuery.

Copy the library you downloaded from the jQuery Web site into the directory you'll be using for this chapter's Web site examples.

Including the library

You include the library just like you would any other JavaScript code:

```
<script type="text/javascript" src="inc/jquery-1.2.1.min.js">
</script>
```

This is a special variation of the `script` tag introduced in Book IV. This tag is different because rather than including script directly, the script is loaded from the indicated JavaScript file.

Including the JavaScript code does increase page-loading times for your users, so don't include the jQuery library if you don't intend to use it. The gzip version of the library is quite small. It takes as long to download as a small image does.

Hello World, jQuery-style

The best way to understand any technology is to put it in action. Figure 2-3 shows a jQuery version of the famous Hello World program.

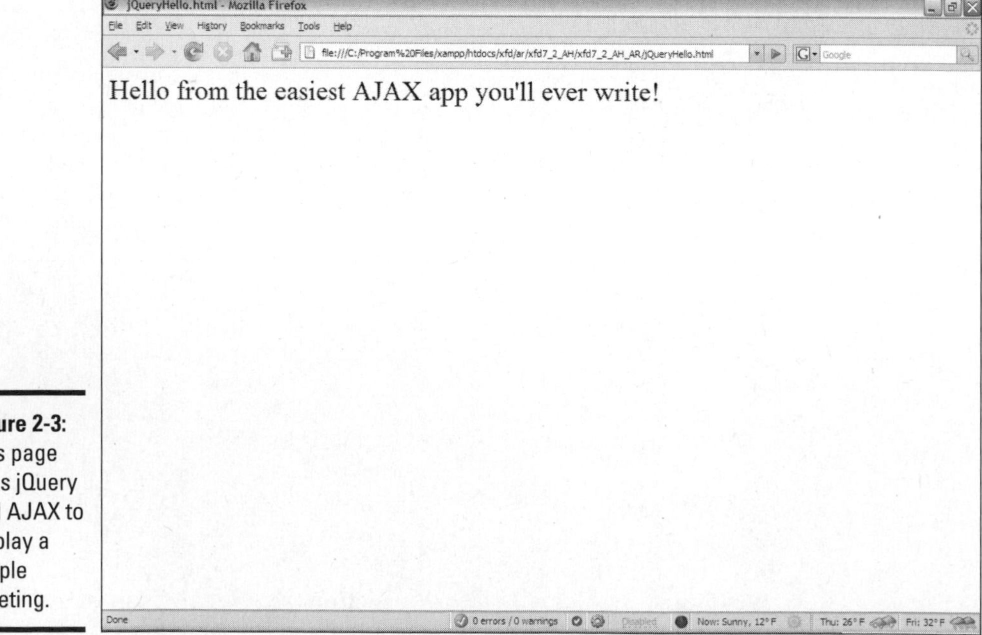

Figure 2-3: This page uses jQuery and AJAX to display a simple greeting.

Aptana's easy setup

If you're using Aptana, you don't have to set up the library. Simply start a new project; to do so:

1. **Choose Ajax Projects ⇨Ajax Library Project.**
2. **Save your project with an appropriate name.**
3. **Choose jQuery as your Ajax library.**

   A sample jQuery page is generated that you can use as reference for using or including the jQuery library. (Aptana calls this subdirectory `lib` and places jQuery in yet another subdirectory called `jQuery`.)

If you have looked over Chapter 1 of this minibook, you know that AJAX calls can be used to insert text into your pages. You also know that AJAX requires a little bit of work to get working correctly. The `jQueryHello.html` page uses jQuery to make AJAX incredibly easy. Here's the code:

```
<!DOCTYPE html PUBLIC "-//W3C//DTD XHTML 1.0 Strict//EN"
"http://www.w3.org/TR/xhtml1/DTD/xhtml1-strict.dtd">
<html lang="EN" dir="ltr" xmlns="http://www.w3.org/1999/xhtml">
  <head>
    <meta http-equiv="content-type" content="text/xml; charset=utf-8" />
    <title>jQueryHello.html</title>
    <script type = "text/javascript"
            src = "jquery-1.2.3.min.js"></script>

    <script type = "text/javascript">
      //<![CDATA[
      $(document).ready(getAJAX);

      function getAJAX(){
        $("#output").load("hello.txt");
      }
      //]]>
    </script>

  </head>

  <body>
    <div id = "output"></div>
  </body>
</html>
```


This code has a number of interesting features:

✦ **It imports jQuery.** The first `script` tag imports the jQuery library.

```
<script type = "text/javascript"
        src = "jquery-1.2.3.min.js"></script>
```

✦ **It contains regular a JavaScript section.** The second pair of `script` tags contains the actual JavaScript code. I describe the code in detail in the section called "Coding with jQuery" later in this chapter.

```
<script type = "text/javascript">
  //<![CDATA[
  $(document).ready(getAJAX);

  function getAJAX(){
    $("#output").load("hello.txt");
  }
  //]]>
</script>
```

- **It has an empty div named `output`.** This element will contain text extracted from a file called `hello.txt` after the document runs.

```
<div id = "output"></div>
```

- **The actual greeting is not in this file.** When you run this program, you'll see a greeting, but the text of that greeting is not in this page. It will be loaded into the `output` div with an AJAX call.

Coding with jQuery

The JavaScript code in this section illustrates several primary features of jQuery.

```
//<![CDATA[
$(document).ready(getAJAX);

function getAJAX(){
  $("#output").load("hello.txt");
}
//]]>
```

Here's how it works:

1. **Place code in a CDATA section.**

   Like all JavaScript code, this example should go inside a CDATA block to ensure the XHTML validator doesn't try to check this code as XHTML.

2. **Specify a function to trigger when the document is ready.**

   Most jQuery code is designed to run as soon as the page is finished loading. The `$(document).ready()` syntax means "when the document is ready, run the following function." In this case, I want to run the `getAJAX` function as soon as the document has finished loading.

   ```
   $(document).ready(getAJAX);
   ```

3. **Create a function.**

   Use an ordinary JavaScript function to perform the AJAX call.

   ```
   function getAJAX(){
     $("#output").load("hello.txt");
   }
   ```

4. **Identify the output div.**

> **What if it isn't working?**
>
> If the test page doesn't work, try these solutions:
>
> - **Did you include the jQuery file correctly?** The most common error is misspelling the jQuery library name.
> - **Is the jQuery library where you actually told the page it'd be?** Make sure the library is where you say it is.
> - **Is the correct version being used?** The minified version will usually work, but, if it doesn't, try one of the other versions.
> - **Is JavaScript working at all?** Try some JavaScript code that doesn't rely on jQuery. It's possible that JavaScript is turned off in your browser or you've made a fundamental JavaScript error. (Don't feel bad, I still do that.)

jQuery has a great feature for working with parts of the page. It uses most of the same selectors you're already familiar with in CSS. `$("#output")` is shorthand for `document.getElementById("output")`. See the section called "Selecting elements in jQuery" for more on how to selector elements.

```
$("#output").load("hello.txt");
```

5. **Load a file into the div using AJAX.**

   The `load()` function sets up an AJAX connection with the specified file or program and loads the results into the indicated element. In this case, I want to load the contents of the `hello.txt` file into the `output` div.

   ```
   $("#output").load("hello.txt");
   ```

If you compare this code to the AJAX code in Chapter 1 of this minibook, you can see right away that jQuery makes AJAX much simpler. If that was all jQuery did, that would be exciting enough. jQuery has a lot more surprises up its sleeve.

Putting jQuery to Work

jQuery is fairly straightforward and easy to use. There are just a few concepts you need to know to get you started:

- The jQuery node object
- Component selection
- The enhanced event mechanism

The key to jQuery is the *jQuery object.* This is a special object that jQuery uses to describe any XHTML element. It works a little bit like the classic `getElementById` found in ordinary JavaScript, but the jQuery approach builds a more interesting and capable object around each element.

- **Any XHTML element can become a jQuery object.** You can turn any part of an XHTML page into a jQuery object.
- **Multiple selection options.** You determine which XHTML element you want to turn into a jQuery object using the same general rules as selection in CSS. That is, you can identify all the objects of a specific type, all the objects with a specific class, or an object with a particular ID.
- **jQuery objects have methods**. Once you have a jQuery object, you can tell it to do things. jQuery objects have many useful methods which allow you to manipulate them on the fly, add new event handlers, animate them, load AJAX content, and much more.
- **jQuery events can be chained**. Each jQuery method returns another jQuery object, so you can *chain* your commands together (write a complex command that does several things to one element in one line).

Most of jQuery's functionality is handled in the following format:

```
$([component selector]).function([optional function
   variables]);
```

Selecting elements in jQuery

If you want a JavaScript program to interact with part of your Web page, you have to somehow select the element from the DOM (Document Object Model) hierarchy. The most common way to do this in plain JavaScript is with code like this:

```
var myThing = document.getElementById("elementId");
```

jQuery allows you to do the same thing in a much shorter syntax.

```
var myThing = $("#elementId");
```

Here's how this line works:

1. **Create a JavaScript variable.**

   You can place a jQuery object in an ordinary JavaScript variable.

2. **The dollar sign indicates a jQuery object.**

   Use the dollar sign symbol followed by a pair of parentheses to indicate you are constructing a jQuery object.

3. **Use a CSS-style selector to indicate which object you are referring to.**

In CSS syntax, you can use `#myThing` to indicate an element with the `myThing` ID. You can also use `p` to indicate all paragraphs, or `.myClass` to indicate all elements with the `myClass` class defined.

4. **The resulting object can do more than a regular DOM object.**

   Because the `$` function creates a special jQuery object, your resulting variable can do anything jQuery objects can do.

The jQuery code is shorter and easier to read, is more flexible, and creates a more powerful object than the JavaScript original.

Selecting all elements of a specific type

You may find that you want to do something interesting with all the elements of a particular type of tag. As an example, look at the `modList.html` program in Figure 2-4.

Although there is a border element around the list, the page has no CSS! The border was added dynamically through jQuery.

There's another surprise: Click on any list item, and the contents of that item appear in a dialog box, as shown in Figure 2-5.

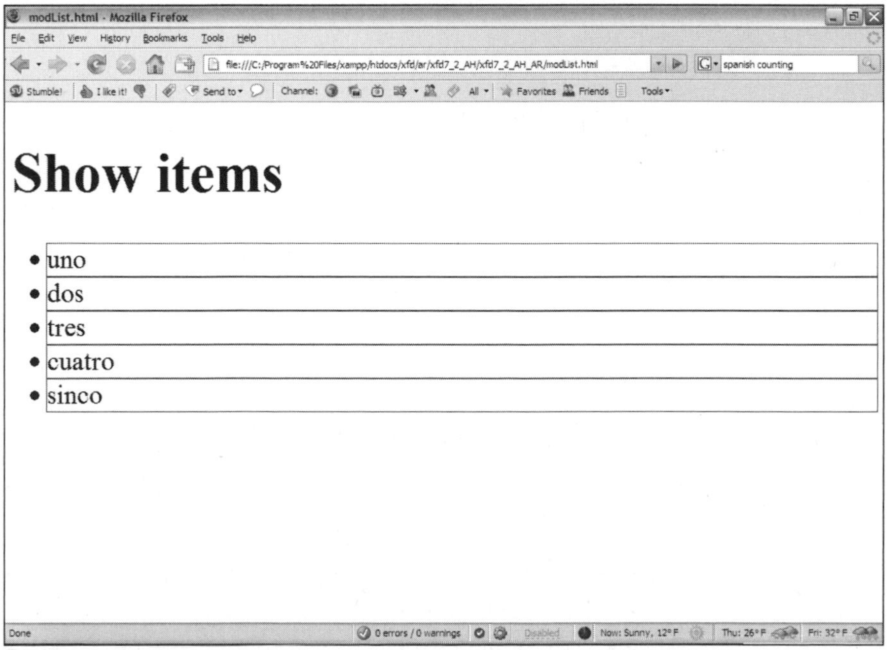

Figure 2-4: Each element of this list has a border.

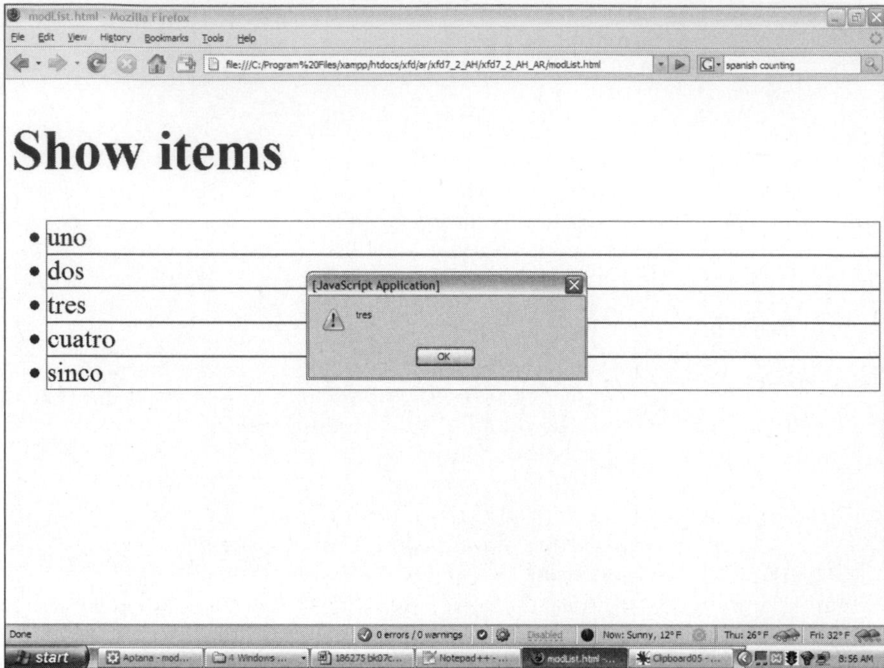

Figure 2-5: The list items all now have a click() method.

These features can be added in plain JavaScript, but they would be tedious. jQuery makes it very easy to manipulate all the elements of a particular type. Here's the code for `modList.html`:

```
<!DOCTYPE html PUBLIC "-//W3C//DTD XHTML 1.0 Strict//EN"
"http://www.w3.org/TR/xhtml1/DTD/xhtml1-strict.dtd">
<html lang="EN" dir="ltr" xmlns="http://www.w3.org/1999/xhtml">
  <head>
    <meta http-equiv="content-type" content="text/xml; charset=utf-8" />
    <title>modList.html</title>

    <script type = "text/javascript"
            src = "jquery-1.2.3.min.js"></script>

    <script type = "text/javascript">
      //<![CDATA[
      $(document).ready(modifyListItems);

      function modifyListItems(){
        var items = $("li");
        items.css("border", "1px red solid");
        items.click(sayValue);
      } // end modifyListItems

      function sayValue(){
        alert($(this).html());
      } // end sayValue

      //]]>
```

```
    </script>
  </head>

  <body>
    <h1>Show items</h1>

    <ul>
      <li>uno</li>
      <li>dos</li>
      <li>tres</li>
      <li>quatro</li>
      <li>sinco</li>
    </ul>

  </body>
</html>
```

The overall structure isn't too hard to see:

- **There is no CSS style.** No internal or external CSS is defined for this page. Any CSS is generated dynamically by the JavaScript/jQuery code.
- **The XHTML document contains a list.** For this example, I add some functionality to all the `li` elements on the page, but I could just as easily add functionality to any other element — all `p` tags or headers, for example.
- **The jQuery library is included.** The jQuery library adds the functionality required for this project.
- **The `modifyListItems()` method is called when the document is ready.** Like most jQuery programs, much of the action happens once the page is ready for processing. In this case, I call the `modifyListItems()` method as soon as the DOM object is ready. (See the upcoming section, "Modifying the list items," for details on how to write this function.)
- **The `sayValue()` method will be used to indicate the text associated with a specific element.** This function is used to output the value of an element. Its use is explained in the next section.

Modifying the list items

The main purpose of the jQuery code in this page is to illustrate how to change the appearance and behavior of all instances of a particular element (in this case, all `li` elements).

```
function modifyListItems(){
  var items = $("li");
  items.css("border", "1px red solid");
  items.click(sayValue);
} // end modifyListItems

function sayValue(){
  alert($(this).html());
} // end sayValue
```

Here's how it works:

1. **Create a jQuery object called items.**

   Use the `$("li")` selector to refer to every `li` element on the page. All `li` items will now be encased in a special variable called `items`.

   ```
   var items = $("li");
   ```

2. **Add a CSS style to `items`.**

   The `css()` function lets you apply a CSS style to all the elements associated with this jQuery object. The CSS style requires two parameters: a style rule and its associated value. In this case, I apply a thin red border to all list items.

   ```
   items.css("border", "1px red solid");
   ```

3. **Add a click event to `items`.**

   The `click()` method allows you to call a specified function whenever any element in the `items` object is clicked. In effect, this adds an event handler to all the list items with one line of code. In this particular case, I run the `sayValue()` function if any `li` is clicked.

   ```
   items.click(sayValue);
   ```

   Note that when I called the `sayValue()` function from within the jQuery click events, I left off the parentheses. It won't work with the parentheses.

4. **The `sayValue()` function returns the text associated with the current element.**

   `$(this)` refers to the current element. The `.html()` function returns the code associated with that item. In the case of the `li` elements, the text of the `li` will be repeated.

   ```
   function sayValue(){
     alert($(this).html());
   } // end sayValue
   ```

You don't have to call an outside function from your event if you don't want to. If you know for sure that the event on the element in question is the only place you'll be doing whatever it is you'll be doing, you can simply insert the function right there during the event bind:

```
$("#clickButton").click(function(){
   //insert your functionality here
});
```

You can use ordinary JavaScript code to achieve all these effects, but once you understand how to use jQuery, you'll find it extremely easy to manipulate all the elements of a specific type in your page.

Selecting elements by class name

Often you'll want to perform some sort of task with all the elements having a specific class name. It's surprising that JavaScript doesn't have an easy way to do this. Fortunately, jQuery overcomes this oversight quite easily. Figure 2-6 illustrates with a simple program called `showSurprise.html`.

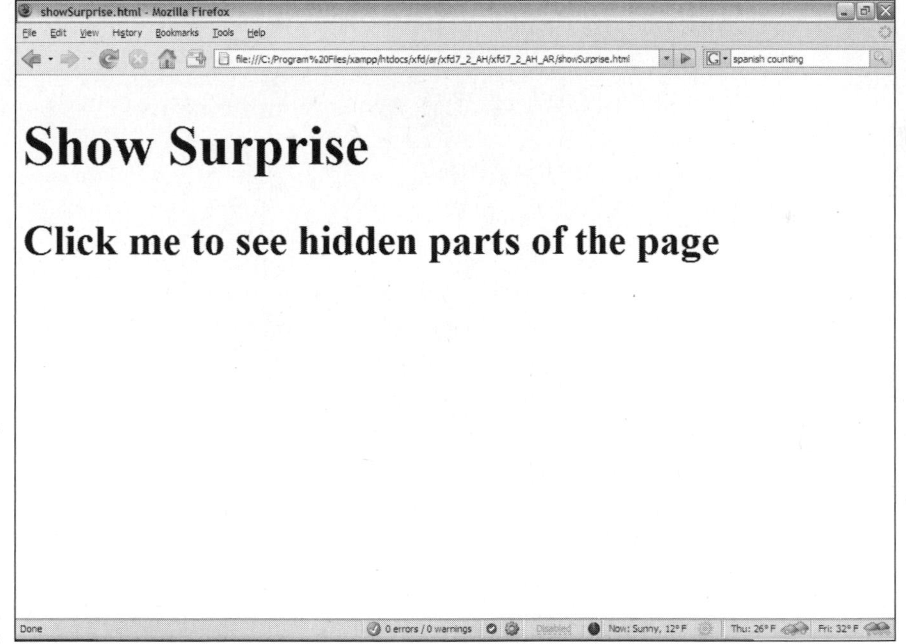

Figure 2-6: The page looks simple — click for a surprise.

Some of the page elements are hidden when the page is initially loaded. When you click on the indicated heading, these hidden elements are revealed, as shown in Figure 2-7.

jQuery makes it quite simple to hide and show page elements. In this case, all the elements of the `surprise` class are hidden when the page loads, and revealed when the user clicks on the indicated `h2` element.

The code reveals all:

```
<!DOCTYPE html PUBLIC "-//W3C//DTD XHTML 1.0 Strict//EN"
"http://www.w3.org/TR/xhtml1/DTD/xhtml1-strict.dtd">
<html lang="EN" dir="ltr" xmlns="http://www.w3.org/1999/xhtml">
  <head>
    <meta http-equiv="content-type" content="text/xml; charset=utf-8" />
    <title>showSurprise.html</title>
    <script type = "text/javascript"
            src = "jquery-1.2.3.min.js"></script>
```

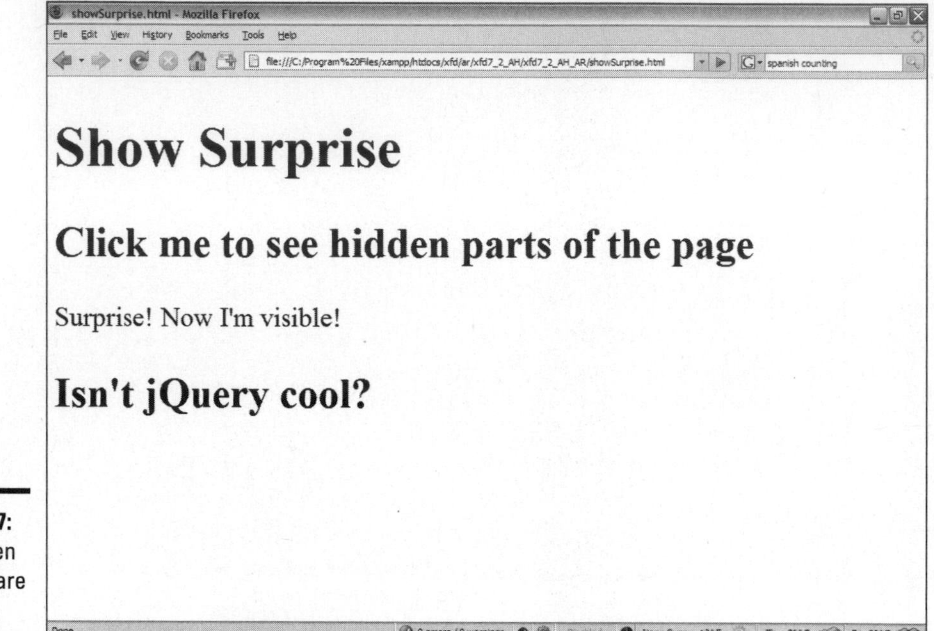

Figure 2-7: The hidden features are revealed.

```
    <script type = "text/javascript">
      //<![CDATA[
      $(document).ready(setupTrigger);

      function setupTrigger(){
        $(".surprise").hide();
        $(".trigger").click(showSurprise);
      } // end setupTrigger

      function showSurprise(){
        $(".surprise").show();
      } // end showSurprise

      //]]>
    </script>
  </head>

  <body>
    <h1>Show Surprise</h1>
    <h2 class = "trigger">
      Click me to see hidden parts of the page
    </h2>
    <p class = "surprise">
      Surprise!  Now I'm visible!
    </p>

    <h2 class = "surprise">Isn't jQuery cool?</h2>
  </body>
</html>
```

Building this program requires a few new jQuery tricks, but nothing terribly difficult:

1. **Import jQuery as usual.**

   The jQuery library makes the task of identifying elements by class name much easier than standard JavaScript.

   ```
   <script type = "text/javascript"
           src = "jquery-1.2.3.min.js"></script>
   ```

2. **Create the XHTML framework.**

   I use two classes in the XHTML. The `trigger` class is applied to the `h2` element that will make the hidden features appear when clicked. The `surprise` class is applied to any element that will begin life hidden and appear on demand.

   ```
   <body>
     <h1>Show Surprise</h1>
     <h2 class = "trigger">
       Click me to see hidden parts of the page
     </h2>
     <p class = "surprise">
       Surprise!  Now I'm visible!
     </p>

     <h2 class = "surprise">Isn't jQuery cool?</h2>
   </body>
   ```

3. **Call the `setupTrigger()` function when the page is ready.**

   This function will do all the necessary setup.

   ```
   $(document).ready(setupTrigger);
   ```

4. **In `setupTrigger()`, hide all elements with the `surprise` class.**

   The `(".surprise")` selector is used to make a jQuery object containing all the elements with the `surprise` class attached. (Check Book II to see that CSS uses the same technique to indicate class elements.) The `hide()` method makes each element of the class invisible. Since this code is called when the document is ready, the user will not initially see any `surprise` elements on the screen.

   ```
   function setupTrigger(){
     $(".surprise").hide();
     $(".trigger").click(showSurprise);
   } // end setupTrigger
   ```

5. **Attach a click event to the `trigger` class.**

   The `trigger` class is selected using the class selection technique. In this case, the `click()` method is used to indicate the `showSurprise()` method should run whenever the user clicks on an element of the `trigger` class.

   ```
   $(".trigger").click(showSurprise);
   ```

6. **Show the `surprise` elements on demand.**

   When the `showSurprise()` method is activated, it selects all elements with the `surprise` class attached, and makes them visible.

```
function showSurprise(){
  $(".surprise").show();
} // end showSurprise
```

If you prefer, you can use the following variation to make the `surprise` elements toggle between visible and invisible:

```
function showSurprise(){
  $(".surprise").toggle();
} // end showSurprise
```

Managing Events through jQuery

You can easily add an event handler to a jQuery object using the `click()` method. This is not the only event handler that jQuery recognizes. You can add the following events to any `jQuery` object:

- **Change:** The content of the element changes.
- **Click:** The user has clicked on the element.
- **Dblclick:** The user has double-clicked on the element.
- **Focus:** The user has selected the element.
- **Keydown:** The user has pressed a key while the element has the focus.
- **Hover:** The mouse is over the element, but has not been clicked.
- **Mousedown:** A mouse button has been pressed while the element has the focus.
- **Select:** The user has selected text in a text-style input.

These are the most commonly used events, but not all. Check the jQuery documentation for other events you can trap.

Using bind to bind events to elements

You can use the jQuery `bind` function to attach events to elements, as shown here:

```
$("#clickButton").bind("click", changeColors);
```

When you call a function through the bind event, you can't include parentheses after the function to be called.

Just like when attaching events by their name (see the preceding section), you can insert your function during the event binding rather than calling an external function if you want:

```
$("#clickButton").bind("click", function(){
    alert("here");
});
```

Unbinding

You can unbind event functions from elements if you want:

```
$("#rollDiv").unbind();
```

This particular version of unbind (with empty parentheses) unbinds all events attached to the specified element. If there's a specific function you want to unbind, you can specify it:

```
$("#rollDiv").unbind("mouseover");
```

If you've bound events to an element through some sort of nonspecific binding (like if you've bound events to a whole class or by tag names), attempting to unbind the event from just one sub-element of the element group won't work:

```
$("#clickButton").bind("click", function(){
    //this does absolutely nothing in this case
    $("#rollDiv").unbind();
});

//ultimate jQuery bind
$("*").mouseover(changeColors);
```

Check out `eventComparrison.php` on the CD to see all these examples side-by-side in working code.

Chapter 3: Animating with jQuery

In This Chapter

- Adding jQuery effects
- Getting familiar with the jQuery user interface
- Working with Interface Elements for jQuery

In this chapter, you work with some slightly more advanced jQuery selectors, as well as discover how to use neat effects and other user Interface Elements, such as draggable items and custom dialog boxes.

jQuery's Special Effects

After you're comfortable with the jQuery library, you can start doing fun and flashy things that really add a little zing to your Web site. When used correctly, effects can take your site from an amateur-looking homepage to a professionally done Web site.

Predefined animations

All the jQuery effects really come down to showing and hiding elements in slightly different ways. Showing and hiding elements gives you a perfect way to make custom pop-ups, drop-down navigation menus, and many other nifty-looking page elements. The effects are broken down into four different categories:

- **Show:** Make a hidden element appear.
- **Slide:** The element slides into place.
- **Fade:** Change the transparency.
- **Custom animations:** Move the element along a specified path.

The most basic form of showing and hiding elements is done through the Show effect. Simply indicate the hidden page element you wish to show and tell it to show itself by entering the following code:

```
$("#hiddenElement").show();
```

You can hide it again with the `hide` function:

```
$("#visibleElement").hide();
```

You can indicate the speed at which the element should be shown or hidden, as well as implement a `callback` function to be executed after the showing or hiding is complete. You indicate speed in increments of `slow`, `medium`, `fast`, or thousandths of a second (1000 = 1 second):

```
$("p").show(1000, anyFunction());
```

The `callback` function doesn't always run when it's supposed to, and most of the time, it actually executes before the `show` or `hide`, so don't rely on this too much. You can skip it, if you prefer:

```
$("p").show(1000);
```

You can even leave the timing out if you're okay with the default timing:

```
$("p").show();
```

With the `show()` and `hide()` functions, if you specify a length of time for the animation to execute, the Slide and Fade effects combine to form one graceful effect.

All the other effects follow the same format as the Show and Hide effects, except that with the other elements, you must specify a speed. All the possible effects are

- **`slideDown`:** The element appears to slide down into place.
- **`slideUp`:** The element appears to slide up into place.
- **`slideToggle`:** The element slides into place if it was invisible or slides away if it's currently visible.
- **`fadeIn`:** The element transitions from transparent to opaque.
- **`fadeOut`:** The element transitions from opaque to transparent.
- **`fadeTo`:** This effect requires you to specify not only the speed but the opacity to stop at.

You can do some really nifty things with these effects. Take a look at Figure 3-1, which uses special selectors to show the section you hover over and to hide all other sections:

```
<head>
    <meta http-equiv="Content-type" content="text/html; charset=utf-8" />
    <title>helloAJAX</title>
    <style type="text/css">
        div{
            border: solid black;
            border-width: 2px 4px;
            padding-left: 15px;
            width: 400px;
        }
```

```
        h2{
            text-decoration: underline;
        }
    </style>
</head>
<body>
    <div class="section" id="home">
        <h2 id="homeHeader">Home</h2>
        <p>Welcome to Fake Website Inc. LLC. We hope you find everything you need
    here.</p>
    </div>
    <div class="section" id="news">
        <h2 id="newsHeader">News</h2>
        <p>We have recently added a FAQ section to this page!</p>
    </div>
    <div class="section" id="faq">
        <h2 id="faqHeader">FAQ</h2>
        <p>Q. Is this a FAQ section?</p>
        <p>A. Yes, it most certainly is! Thanks for asking!</p>
    </div>
<script type="text/javascript" src="inc/jquery-1.2.1.min.js"></script>
<script type="text/javascript">
    $(".section p").hide();

    $(".section h2").mouseover(function(){
        $("#" + $(this).attr("id") + " ~ p").slideDown(300);
        $("h2:not(#" + $(this).attr("id") + " ~ p) ~ p").hide(300);
    });
</script>
</body>
```


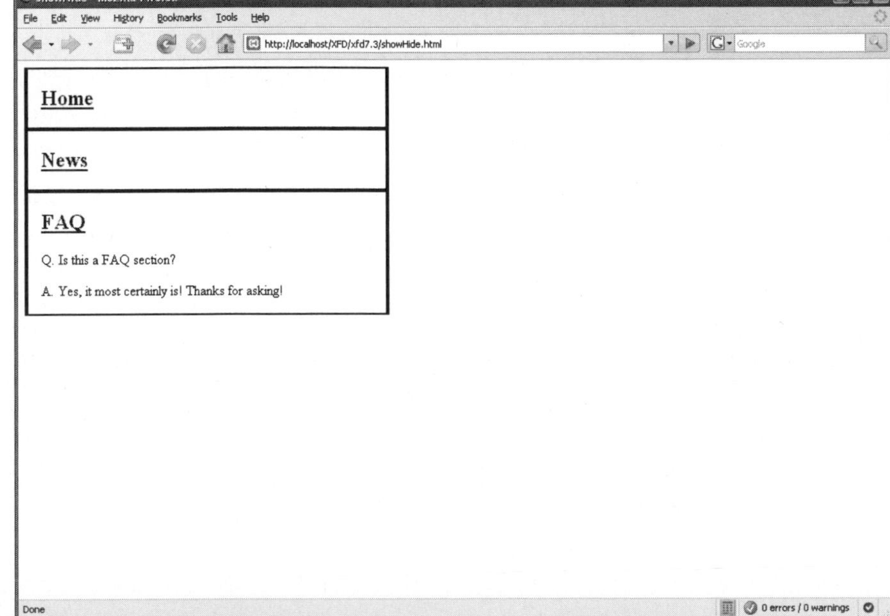

Figure 3-1: The contents of each box pop up when you hover over the titles.

Several advanced selector functions are here. The tilde (~) selects all siblings after the specified element. The `this` keyword specifies the current element that triggered the function. The `:not` selector excludes all elements found by the selector.

After hiding all paragraphs with the class type of `"section"`, the jQuery code adds a `mouseover` event to each `"section"` header (the h2s). When this event is triggered, the code finds all paragraph siblings following the triggering `h2` and shows them. It then finds all `h2` elements that aren't the triggering `h2` element and hides the paragraph siblings that follow them.

Custom animations

You can create your own custom effects. Any style that takes a numeric value can be manipulated through the `animate` function.

The `animate()` function takes four values:

- **Parameters that indicate the elements to be animated.**
- **The intended duration of the animation.**
- **Easing specifies the style of the animation (this requires a plugin).** Easing indicates how an animation will begin and end. Some animations start slowly to imply the element has mass.
- **Callback specifies a function to be executed upon completion of animation for each element.**

```
animate({"width": "100"}, 1000, "linear", someFuntion())
```

CSS selectors are indicated using the standard `DOM` style, so border width would be `borderWidth`. (Check Book IV, Chapter 5 for more on referring to CSS elements through the `DOM`.)

Easing has two built-in functions that don't require plugins: `linear` and `swing`. It appears that `swing` starts slow, speeds up, and then slows down again; and `linear` is steady throughout.

You can specify an absolute value to animate to or add/subtract values with -= and +=.

This program expands the width of divs when they're rolled over by the user. With some clever CSS backgrounds, these functions can turn some simple HTML and a few lines of JavaScript into a worm race (see Figure 3-2):

```
<head>
    <meta http-equiv="Content-type" content="text/html; charset=utf-8" />
    <title>animate</title>
    <style type="text/css">
        div{
```

```
            background: #FFF url("worm.gif") right no-repeat;
            width: 50px;
            height: 25px;
        }
    </style>
</head>
<body>
    <h1>Worm Race!</h1>
    <p>Roll your cursor wildly randomly over the worms to spur them along...</p>
    <div></div>
    <div></div>
    <div></div>
    <p>Rolled over worms: <span id="counter">0</span> times.</p>
<script type="text/javascript" src="inc/jquery-1.2.1.min.js"></script>
<script type="text/javascript">
    var counter = 0;

    function countUp(){
        counter++;
        $("#counter").text(counter);
    }

    $("div").mouseover(function(){
        $(this).animate({"width": "+=10"}, 500, "linear", countUp());
    });
</script>
</body>
```

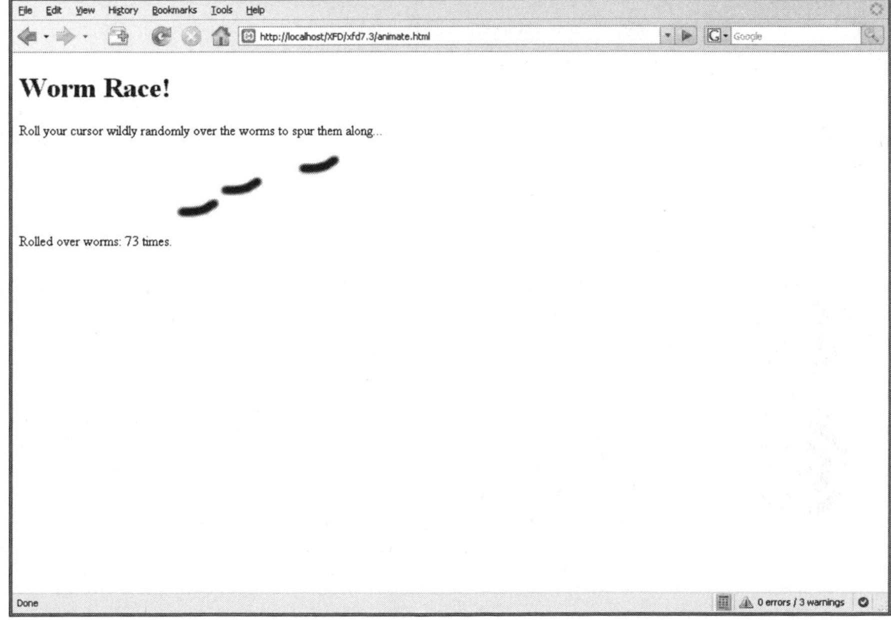

Figure 3-2: It's a worm-racing page! Who doesn't love worm racing?

Beyond these animations, there are also many plugins available on the jQuery Web site. Also, a few more effects functions allow you to access the animation queue, as well as to completely stop animations in their tracks.

Interfacing with the Official UI Plugin

jQuery's official user interface (UI) library is somewhat incomplete. As of this writing, many of the demos on the Web site don't work. Probably the most promising of them all seems to be the `draggable()` and `droppable()` functions.

I describe how to use the drag and drop features, as well as the custom dialog boxes and table sorting, but then I move on to the much more robust, well-documented, and coded plugin — *Interface Elements* (see the section "Interface Elements for jQuery," later in this chapter).

Dragging and dropping

If you were building an online store, it'd be nice to allow the user to pick what item he wanted and drop it into the shopping cart. You could do this with jQuery through the `draggable` and `droppable` UI functions.

The draggable() function

You need the `ui.mouse.js`, `ui.draggable.js`, and `ui.draggable.ext.js` libraries to implement draggable functionalities. You should download these from `http://ui.jquery.com` and include them in your file, like this:

```
<script type="text/javascript" src="inc/ui.mouse.js"></script>
<script type="text/javascript" src="inc/ui.draggable.js"></script>
<script type="text/javascript" src="inc/ui.draggable.ext.js"></script>
```

Making an element draggable is as easy as specifying an element(s) with a selector and then making it draggable:

```
$(".dragMe").draggable();
```

You can specify many different things when making an element draggable. The full list of these options is available at `http://docs.jquery.com/UI/Draggables/draggable#options`.

Options are placed inside the parentheses after the `draggable` function call and are separated by commas:

```
    $(".draggableElements").draggable({
        opacity: .5,
        start: function(){
```

```
            $("#statusText").append("dragging Item");
        },
        stop: function(){
            $("#statusText").append("dragged Item");
            $(this).draggableDisable();
            $(this).fadeOut(400);
        }
    });
```

The helper option is very commonly used. This allows you to specify another element entirely as the element that attaches to the cursor when you begin dragging the target element. This option also allows you to clone the target element and use that as the object being dragged:

```
$(".dragMe").draggable({
    helper: "clone",
});
```

You can also create an HTML element on the fly and return that to be used as the helper:

```
$(".dragMe").draggable({
    helper: function() {
        return $(document.createElement('div')).css({
            'background': 'url(worm.gif)',
            'width': '50px',
            'height': '25px'
        }).appendTo("body")[0];
    }
}
```


Dropping with the droppable() function

The counterpart to draggable is droppable. If you don't have a draggable element, there's no point in having a droppable one.

With droppable, you specify the element to be made droppable, as well as which draggable elements it'll accept:

```
$(".dragTarget").droppable({
    accept: ".dragMe",
});
```

Just like draggable, droppable has many different options you can specify. Among the most useful of these is the drop option, which fires twice each time something is dropped into it or fires once if only an object's clone is dropped into it. The way to fix this is to set the greedy option to True:

```
$(".dragTarget").droppable({
    accept: ".dragMe",
```

```
    greedy: true,
    drop: function(){
        alert("dropped!");
    }
});
```

For a full list of options, see `http://docs.jquery.com/UI/Droppables/droppable#options`.

Playing the Catch the Worms game

Listing 3-1 shows a little game that makes three worms crawl out onto the screen and allows you to drag and drop them into a bucket (see Figure 3-3). This sort of drag-and-drop effect would be fine for shopping carts or any page where you're adding items to a collection.

Listing 3-1: The Catch the Worms Game

```
<head>
    <meta http-equiv="Content-type" content="text/html; charset=utf-8" />
    <title>draggable</title>
    <style type="text/css">
        .dragMe{
            cursor: move;
            position: absolute;
            top: 0px;
            left: 0px;
            background-image: url("worm.gif");
            width: 50px;
            height: 25px;
        }

        .dragTarget{
            position: absolute;
            top: 50px;
            left: 500px;
            width: 100px;
            height: 100px;
            background: #bbb;
            border: 3px inset black;
        }
    </style>
</head>
<body>
    <h1>Worm Catcher!</h1>
    <p id="wormsCaught">Catch the worms, and place them in the worm bucket.</p>
    <div class="dragTarget" id="wormBucket">Worm Bucket. Put Worms Here!</div>
    <div class="dragMe" id="worm1"></div>
    <div class="dragMe" id="worm2"></div>
    <div class="dragMe" id="worm3"></div>

<script type="text/javascript" src="inc/jquery-1.2.1.min.js"></script>
<script type="text/javascript" src="inc/ui.mouse.js"></script>
<script type="text/javascript" src="inc/ui.draggable.js"></script>
<script type="text/javascript" src="inc/ui.draggable.ext.js"></script>
<script type="text/javascript" src="inc/ui.droppable.js"></script>
<script type="text/javascript" src="inc/ui.droppable.ext.js"></script>
```

```
<script type="text/javascript">
    $(".dragMe").each(function(){
        $("#" + this.id).animate({"top": Math.ceil(Math.random() * 400)},
    {duration: 1000, queue: false});
    $("#" + this.id).animate({"left": Math.ceil(Math.random() * 400)}, {duration:
    1000, queue: false});
    });

    var wormsCaught = 0;
    var whichWorm = null;

    $(".dragTarget").droppable({
        accept: ".dragMe",
        greedy: true,
        drop: function(){
            $("#" + whichWorm).draggableDisable().appendTo(this).css({"left":
    Math.random() * 50 + "px", "top": Math.random() * 75 + "px"});
            $("#wormsCaught").append("<br />You caught a worm!");

            wormsCaught++;

            if(wormsCaught == 3){
                $("#wormsCaught").append("<br /><em>You caught all of the
    worms!</em>");
            }
        }

    });

    $(".dragMe").draggable({
        start: function(){
            whichWorm = $(this).attr("id");
        }
    })
</script>
</body>
```


Sorting with the table sorter

jQuery comes with a table sorter that helps you enhance your XHTML tables.

The `tablesorter()` function can be attached to any table to make it sortable by its header rows. It requires the inclusion of two extra files, the JavaScript plugin, and a CSS theme.

Making a basic table

The code for making a table sortable is surprisingly short and concise:

```
$("#tableToBeSorted").tablesorter();
```

Specify the element for the table sorter to be applied to and call the function.

Figure 3-3: In this program, you pick up the worms and drop them on a div.

You need to include the library and theme for this to work properly:

```
<link rel="stylesheet" href="inc/themes/flora/flora.all.css"
   type="text/css" media="screen" title="Flora (Default)">
<script  src="inc/ui.tablesorter.js"></script>
```

If you have multiple tables on the page, you can apply the `tablesorter()` function to the `tablesorter` class.

Your table has to have the class of `tablesorter` in order for the theme to be applied to it.

See Listing 3-2 for an example of two sortable tables. A sortable table is shown in Figure 3-4.

Sorting options

There are currently 11 different options for the `tablesorter()` function. Two of them are pretty useful on a regular basis. The empty `tablesorter()` function call does its job pretty well so that you probably won't even need options, but these two are actually pretty useful.

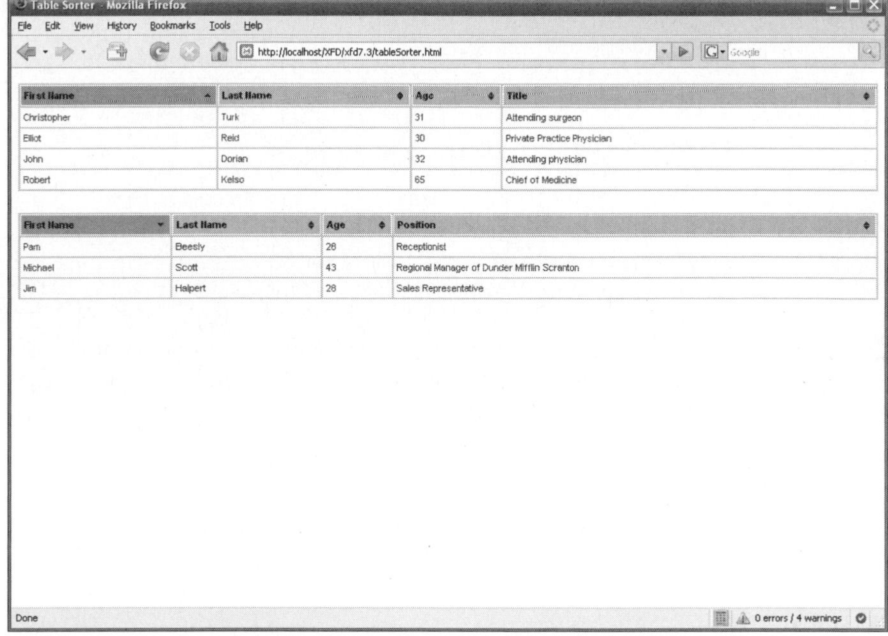

Figure 3-4: Click on any table heading to sort by that value.

sortList

The `sortList` option allows you to specify columns to be sorted by default. You pass this option a two-dimension array (multidimensional arrays are described in Chapter 5 in Book V):

```
$(".tablesorter").tablesorter({
    sortList: [[0, 1], [1, 1], [2, 0]]
});
```

The first number in each array specifies the column — starting with zero (0) for the first column — you want the sort to be forced on. The second number can be either zero (0) or one (1) and specifies the sort direction. The sort direction can be set to either 0 for ascending or 1 for descending.

Make sure to use camel-casing for this option.

sortForce

The `sortForce` option's functionality is a little bit more subtle. It prevents the table from appearing to have a random secondary sort when the user's sorting. When applied to a column, it forces that column to sort secondarily when the user sorts another column.

For example, if you put a `sortForce` on the last name column and the user sorted by the first name column, a secondary sort would be placed on the last name column so that if you had eight people with the same first name, their last names would be in alphabetical order:

```
$(".tablesorter").tablesorter({
    sortForce: [[0, 1], [1, 1], [2, 0]]
});
```

This options syntax is nearly identical to `sortList`, and the sub-arrays function the same way.

This function is a little buggy. Be careful when you use it to make sure that it's functioning as you expect. Sometimes, the force overrides the user-selected sort.

Listing 3-2: Two Tables Sorted by the Table Sorter

```
<table id="scrubsCharacters" class="tablesorter">
    <thead>
        <tr>
            <th>First Name</th>
            <th>Last Name</th>
            <th>Age</th>
            <th>Title</th>
        </tr>
    </thead>
    <tbody>
        <tr>
            <td>Robert</td>
            <td>Kelso</td>
            <td>65</td>
            <td>Chief of Medicine</td>
        </tr>
        <tr>
            <td>John</td>
            <td>Dorian</td>
            <td>32</td>
            <td>Attending physician</td>
        </tr>
        <tr>
            <td>Christopher</td>
            <td>Turk</td>
            <td>31</td>
            <td>Attending surgeon</td>
        </tr>
        <tr>
            <td>Elliot</td>
            <td>Reid</td>
            <td>30</td>
            <td>Private Practice Physician</td>
```

```
        </tr>
    </tbody>
</table>

<table id="officeCharacters" class="tablesorter">
    <thead>
        <tr>
            <th>First Name</th>
            <th>Last Name</th>
            <th>Age</th>
            <th>Position</th>
        </tr>
    </thead>
    <tbody>
        <tr>
            <td>Michael</td>
            <td>Scott</td>
            <td>43</td>
            <td>Regional Manager of Dunder Mifflin Scranton</td>
        </tr>
        <tr>
            <td>Pam</td>
            <td>Beesly</td>
            <td>28</td>
            <td>Receptionist</td>
        </tr>
        <tr>
            <td>Jim</td>
            <td>Halpert</td>
            <td>28</td>
            <td>Sales Representative</td>
        </tr>
    </tbody>
</table>
<script type="text/javascript" src="inc/jquery-1.2.1.min.js"></script>
<link rel="stylesheet" href="inc/themes/flora/flora.all.css" type="text/css"
    media="screen" title="Flora (Default)">
<script  src="inc/ui.tablesorter.js"></script>
<script type="text/javascript">
    $(".tablesorter").tablesorter({
        sortList: [[0, 1], [1, 1], [2, 0]]
    });
</script>
```


Creating dialog boxes

Custom dialog boxes have long been a desire for Web developers. Who wants that nasty alert box that comes standard with browsers? With the dialog function, you can turn any page element (normally a div) into a dialog box.

Figure 3-5 shows a custom dialog box.

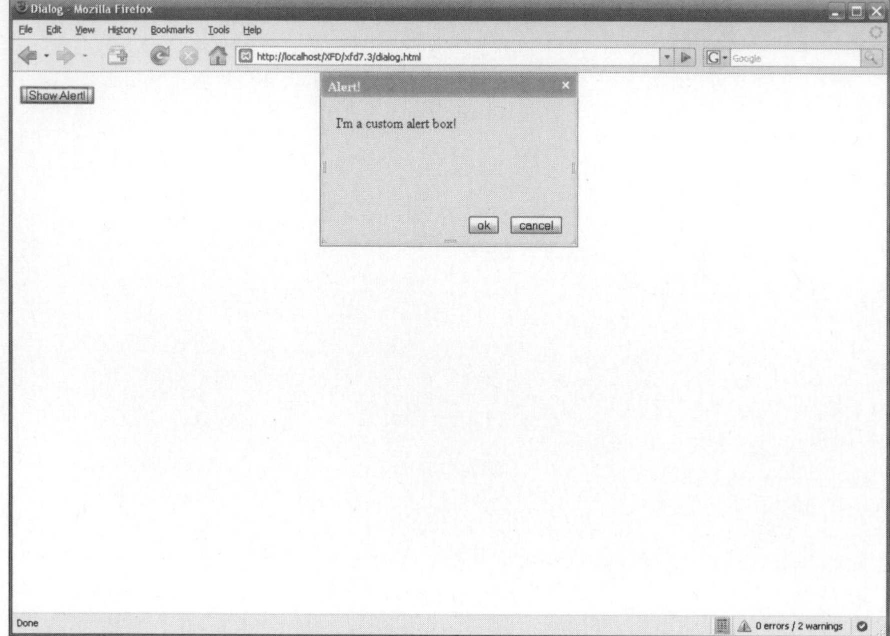

Figure 3-5: This dialog box was created from a special div in the page.

Basic dialog box

The basics you need to know about the `dialog` function are the `creation` function, the `open` function, and the `close` function. With these three functions, you can completely replace the standard browser dialog box and alert pop-ups.

For the `dialog()` function, in addition to including the jQuery library, you need to include the dialog, the dimensions, the mouse, the draggable and resizable libraries, and a theme style package:

```
<link rel="stylesheet" href="inc/themes/flora/flora.all.css"
   type="text/css" media="screen" title="Flora (Default)">
<script type="text/javascript"
   src="inc/jquery.dimensions.js"></script>
<script type="text/javascript"
   src="inc/ui.dialog.js"></script>
<script type="text/javascript"
   src="inc/ui.resizable.js"></script>
<script type="text/javascript"
   src="inc/ui.mouse.js"></script>
<script type="text/javascript"
   src="inc/ui.draggable.js"></script>
```

dialog()

Making a custom dialog box is as simple as creating a div, giving it the class specified by your theme (default is `flora`), giving it a title, and then calling the `dialog()` function on it:

```
<div id="alertBox" class="flora" title="Alert!">
    I'm a custom alert box!
</div>

<script type="text/javascript">
    $("#alertBox").dialog();
</script>
```

Don't forget to apply the correct class to the div. Also, make sure you put the title in there, or else the title bar of the dialog box will be empty.

dialogClose()

This is how you close the dialog box:

```
$("#yourDiv").dialogClose()
```

You can call this from an event within another block of JavaScript or jQuery, or even just through a button:

```
<div id="alertBox" class="flora" title="Alert!">
    <p>I'm a custom alert box!</p>
    <p><button id="hideAlert" type="button">Ok</button></p>
</div>
$("#hideAlert").click(function(){$("#alertBox").dialogClose()
    });
```

You might also consider calling this function on the dialog box immediately after you create the dialog so that it doesn't begin visible to the user.

Use the `button` option to specify OK, Cancel, Save, and other buttons.

dialogOpen()

You trigger the appearance of the dialog box with the following line:

```
$("#yourDiv").dialogOpen()
```

You can call this from an event within another block of JavaScript or jQuery, or even with a button:

```
<p><button id="showAlert" type="button">Show Alert!
    </button></p>
$("#showAlert").click(function(){$("#alertBox").dialogOpen()}
    );
```

Dialog box options

jQuery provides many options for customizing your dialog box. A few of them are as follows.

buttons

With the buttons option, you can create custom buttons for your dialog box:

```
$("#alertBox").dialog({
    buttons: {
        'ok': function(){$("#alertBox").dialogClose();},
        'cancel':
function(){$("#alertBox").dialogClose();}
    }
});
```

As of this writing, there's a bug with the buttons option. You're supposed to be able to use this keyword instead of having to re-specify the div. Perhaps this will be fixed soon.

draggable

With the draggable option, you can specify with a Boolean (True or False; don't surround with quotes) whether the dialog box can be moved around. As of this writing, this option doesn't actually work, though, but at least it defaults to True.

position

This function allows you to specify a position where your dialog box pops up. It'll take 'center', 'top', 'right', 'bottom', or 'left' values and allows you to choose where the dialog box should appear on the page:

```
$("#alertBox").dialog({
    position: 'top'
});
```

Other options

There are many other options for the dialog box, including:

- **height**
- **maxHeight**
- **minHeight**
- **maxWidth**
- **minWidth**
- **resizable**

- **`title`**
- **`width`**

In addition to these, there are also `callback` methods.

Listing 3-3 shows a page that allows you to click a button to view a custom dialog box, which can be closed by clicking either OK or Cancel.

Listing 3-3: A Custom Dialog Box

```
<div id="alertBox" class="flora" title="Alert!">
    <p>I'm a custom alert box!</p>
</div>
<p><button id="showAlert" type="button">Show Alert!</button></p>
<script type="text/javascript" src="inc/jquery-1.2.1.min.js"></script>
<link rel="stylesheet" href="inc/themes/flora/flora.all.css" type="text/css"
    media="screen" title="Flora (Default)">
<script type="text/javascript" src="inc/jquery.dimensions.js"></script>
<script type="text/javascript" src="inc/ui.dialog.js"></script>
<script type="text/javascript" src="inc/ui.resizable.js"></script>
<script type="text/javascript" src="inc/ui.mouse.js"></script>
<script type="text/javascript" src="inc/ui.draggable.js"></script>

<script type="text/javascript">
    $("#alertBox").dialog({
        height: 200,
        position: 'top',
        buttons: {
            'ok': function(){$("#alertBox").dialogClose();},
            'cancel': function(){$("#alertBox").dialogClose();}
        }
    });
    $("#alertBox").dialogClose();
    $("#showAlert").click(function(){$("#alertBox").dialogOpen()});
</script>
```

Unlike a normal alert box (the kind you build with regular JavaScript), this dialog box doesn't actually cancel any action when closed by clicking Cancel.

Interface Elements for jQuery

When you're ready to really get into making some swell user interfaces for jQuery, you might want to move away from the standard effects library and check out some plugins, like Interface Elements.

You can access Interface Elements' documentation and demos at `http://interface.eyecon.ro`. This is also where you'll download the library. Just like with the jQuery standard UI library, clicking the Download link takes you to a page that allows you to select which UI effects you desire and then to download the library packages for those effects. You can also just download everything by clicking the link under the Download heading in the navigation pane on the left side of the page.

Download everything as one big package and unzip it into the directory you're building your site from. All you have to do to implement these elements for any page, no matter which effect you want, is include the `interface.js` file in your page, as shown here:

```
<script type="text/javascript" src="inc/interface1.2/
   interface.js"></script>
```

Make sure the `src` attribute in your `<script>` tag points to the location of your `interface.js` file. I placed mine under `inc/interface1.2/`, but you may have placed yours somewhere else.

Getting to know the Interface Elements

Most of the Interface Elements functions follow the same sort of structure. I'll take a bit of an in-depth look at the sorting function and then give you an overview of two other major ones.

Super dragging and dropping with the sortables interface

The sortables interface is extremely easy to implement. It's sort of a super drag-and-drop. Like most of the Interface Elements, a basic function can take options and trigger an event the elements controlled by the event change.

Basic sorting

The sortable interface requires that you have containers (which are *droppables*) and items (which are *draggables*). After you've set up these, you specify the container class as `Sortable` and then specify the item class as the element that the container class can accept:

```
<div class="container">
    <p>container 1</p>
    <div class="item">the item</div>
</div>
<div class="container">
    <p>container 2</p>
</div>
<script type="text/javascript">
    $('.container').Sortable({
        accept: 'item'
    });
</script>
```

Options

Most of the Interface Elements functions take options. A few of the major options for the sortables function are as follows:

- **`accept`:** This one's required. Use it to specify the class names of the sortable items.
- **`activeclass`:** Use this to specify the CSS class to be used for all the valid drop points of a sortable item whenever an item is being dragged for sorting.
- **`hoverclass`:** Use this to specify the CSS class to be used for a valid drop point when a sortable item is hovering over it while being dragged for sorting.
- **`helperclass`:** Use this to specify the CSS class to be used for the exact spot a sortable item will be placed in when it's being dragged for sorting. This is sort of like a target area; it shows exactly where the item would fall if you released it at any moment during a drag.
- **`opacity`:** This should be a number between zero (`0`) and one (`1`), where `1` is completely visible and `0` is completely transparent. For instance, `.5` would be half invisible and would look ghostlike.
- **`ghosting`:** This is a Boolean. If you set it to `True`, the current drop target for the sortable item will contain a copy of the element being dragged. Be careful when using this because it's buggy and may not work properly. When I used it, upon releasing my dragged item, it and its ghost both disappeared.
- **`containment`:** This confines the element to its parent container. The only acceptable value here is `'parent'`. Its implementation is slightly buggy.
- **`axis`:** This confines the element's draggability to one axis or the other. It accepts `'vertically'` or `'horizontally'`. Although it confines the element being dragged to only one axis, it can't confine your mouse, and therefore, it doesn't really change the functionality of where you can drop the element — it only *appears* to. Your mouse cursor decides where the element gets dropped.

Don't forget to surround the string values for the options with quotes (either single or double are accepted). It's also best to remember to separate options with commas (`,`) instead of semi-colons (`;`).

If your `active`, `hover`, and/or `helper` classes seem to not be working, check the order of your rules in your style sheet. Because they cascade, if you put the `active` rule after the `hover` rule, the `hover` rule will be over-written by the `active` rule and thus be rendered useless. This can be extremely frustrating if you don't realize what's going on because it just silently fails. So, make sure you place the rules in the order that the options are written above and in the documentation. (This is the order: `normal base` rule, `active`, `hover`, and finally `helper`.)

Note that these options are not camel-cased. So, `helperclass` really is `helperclass` and not `helperClass`. Camel-casing will break these options.

onchange

In order for this to be useful as a user input device, you have to be able to detect which elements were changed. Sortable allows you to detect this with the `onchange` option.

The `onchange` option returns an array of the container elements that were changed by their ID.

Make sure you have a unique ID for every container and item. Otherwise, this option won't work. It won't give you any errors if you don't have IDs; it just won't do anything. This is the worst kind of failure because it's not immediately apparent that it isn't working, and it'll leave you very frustrated.

The basic `onchange` function looks like this:

```
onchange: function(arrayOfChangedContainers){}
```

You can name the function `arrayOfChangedContainers` or anything you want. In the documentation, they call the function `"ser"`. This is an array of the container elements that were changed. Normally, this array will have a length of either one or two because you'll either be dragging an item from one container to another or within one container.

You can serialize the container into a `$_REQUEST`-friendly hash through the `$.SortSerialize()` function in conjunction with the `.hash()` function:

```
onchange: function(ser){
    var changedItems = "";
    for(var i=0; i<ser.length; i++){
        changedItems += ($.SortSerialize(ser[i])).hash;
        changedItems += "&"
    }
    alert(changedItems);
}
```

The `$.SortSerialize()` and `.hash` function combination returns a string containing the container element's IDs, as well as the item element's IDs. It'll look something like this:

```
container1[]=item1&container2[]=item3&container2=item2&
```

This allows you to send the new order for each element to the server for saving. Just replace the alert with a call to an AJAX function that saves the new order. See Chapter 1 and Chapter 4 of this minibook for more on sending, receiving, and processing requests.

Listing 3-4 shows a sample program that allows you to arrange four tasks over a three-day period. It could easily be expanded to allow for adding custom tasks and removing unwanted tasks.

Listing 3-4: The Day Planner

```
<head>
    <meta http-equiv="Content-type" content="text/html; charset=utf-8" />
    <title>sortables</title>
    <style type="text/css">
        .task{
            border: 3px dotted #090;
            background-color: #AFA;
            width: 200px;
            padding: 0px 10px;
        }

        .taskDrag{
            border: 3px dashed #900;
        }

        .day{
            border: 2px solid #009;
            background-color: #AAF;
            width: 250px;
            padding: 10px 10px;
            float: left;
        }

        .taskHover{
            background-color: #F00;
        }
    </style>
</head>
<body>
<h1>Day Planner</h1>
<div id="monday" class="day">
    <h2>Monday</h2>
    <div id="laundry" class="task">
        <h3 class="taskTitle">Laundry</h3>
        <p class="taskDescription">Do all of the laundry for the week.</p>
    </div>
    <div id="food" class="task">
```

(continued)

Listing 3-4 ***(continued)***

```
            <h3 class="taskTitle">Make Food</h3>
            <p class="taskDescription">Make all of the Food for the week and freeze
        it.</p>
        </div>
</div>
<div id="tuesday" class="day">
    <h2>Tuesday</h2>
    <div id="shopping" class="task">
        <h3 class="taskTitle">Grocery Shopping</h3>
        <p class="taskDescription">Go grocery shopping for the week.</p>
    </div>
</div>
<div id="wednesday" class="day">
    <h2>Wednesday</h2>
    <div id="randr" class="task">
        <h3 class="taskTitle">R &amp; R</h3>
        <p class="taskDescription">Sit around, play video games and read.</p>
    </div>
</div>

<script type="text/javascript" src="inc/jquery-1.2.1.min.js"></script>
<script type="text/javascript" src="inc/interface1.2/interface.js"></script>
<script type="text/javascript">
    $('.day').Sortable({
        accept: 'task',
        helperclass: 'taskDrag',
        hoverclass: 'taskHover',
        opacity: '.5',
        onchange: function(ser){
            var changedItems = "";
            for (var i = 0; i < ser.length; i++) {
                changedItems += serialize(ser[i]) + "&";
            }
            save(changedItems);
        }
    });

    function serialize(theContainer){
        serial = $.SortSerialize(theContainer);
        return serial.hash;
    }

    function save(changedItems){
        $.ajax({
            type: "POST",
            url: "saveSchedule.php",
            data: changedItems,
            success: function(msg){
                alert("Data Saved: " + msg);
            }
        });
    }
</script>
```

The day planner is shown in Figure 3-6.

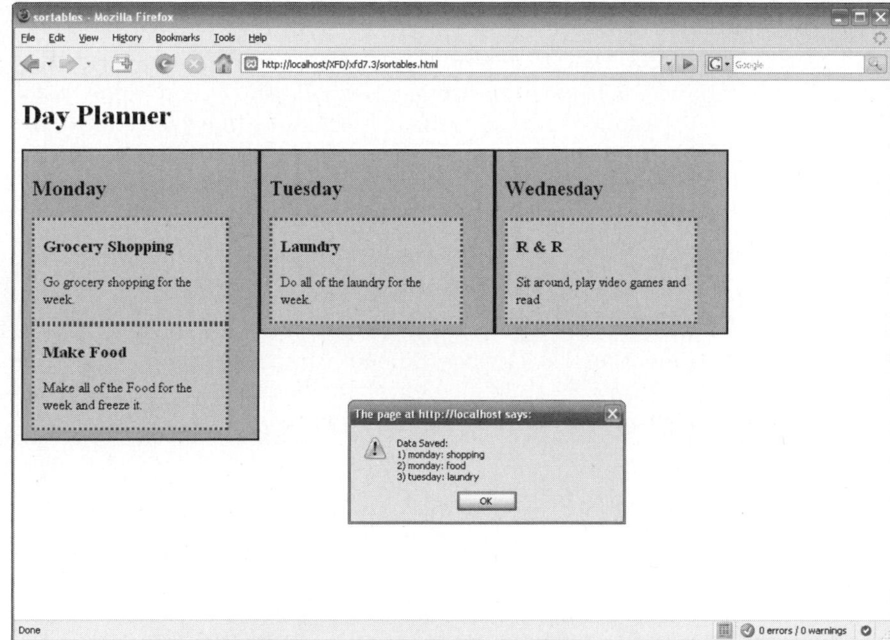

Figure 3-6: The user can drag the tasks to a different day!

See Chapter 4 in this minibook for more on sending and receiving AJAX requests with jQuery. This program has just enough of a back-end setup to make it look like it's working, although it doesn't really do anything. It could be easily modified to save to a text file or a database. The current code in `saveSchedule.php`, which is just enough to give some sort of meaningful response, consists of two `foreach` loops and a `print` statement:

```
<?
$i = 1;

foreach($_POST as $day => $task){
    foreach($task as $task){
        print $i . ") " . $day . ": " . $task . "\n";
        $i++;
    }
}
?>
```

See Book V, Chapter 3 for more on request/response processing with PHP and Book V, Chapter 5 for more on `foreach` loops.

Every container and item needs to have its own ID. Otherwise, you get subtle errors without any error messages. It's possible you could go for quite some time without realizing you forgot an ID on an element.

Selectables

The `selectables` function allows you to select items by dragging a box around them. It can return an array of the selected items that you can use in an AJAX function to save the chosen items however you wish.

For a more in-depth look at an Interface Elements function, see the "Getting to know the Interface Elements" section, earlier in this chapter. This is a basic overview to get you started.

Basic selectables

This function takes a page element (probably a div) and denotes it as being *selectable* — the child elements specified by the function's mandatory accept option are selectable (see Figure 3-7):

```
<head>
<style type="text/css">
    .item{
        width: 100px;
        height: 100px;
        background-color: black;
        border: 1px solid white;
    }
    .selectedItem{
        background-color: blue;
        border: 1px solid #888;
    }
    .selectionHelper{
        border: 3px double red;
    }
</style>
</head>
<body>
<div id="container">
    <div id="item1" class="item"></div>
    <div id="item2" class="item"></div>
    <div id="item3" class="item"></div>
</div>
<script type="text/javascript" src="inc/jquery-
   1.2.1.min.js"></script>
<script type="text/javascript"
   src="inc/interface1.2/interface.js"></script>
<script type="text/javascript">
    $('#container').Selectable({
        accept : 'item',
        selectedclass : 'selectedItem',
        helperclass : 'selectionHelper'
    });
</script>
</body>
```

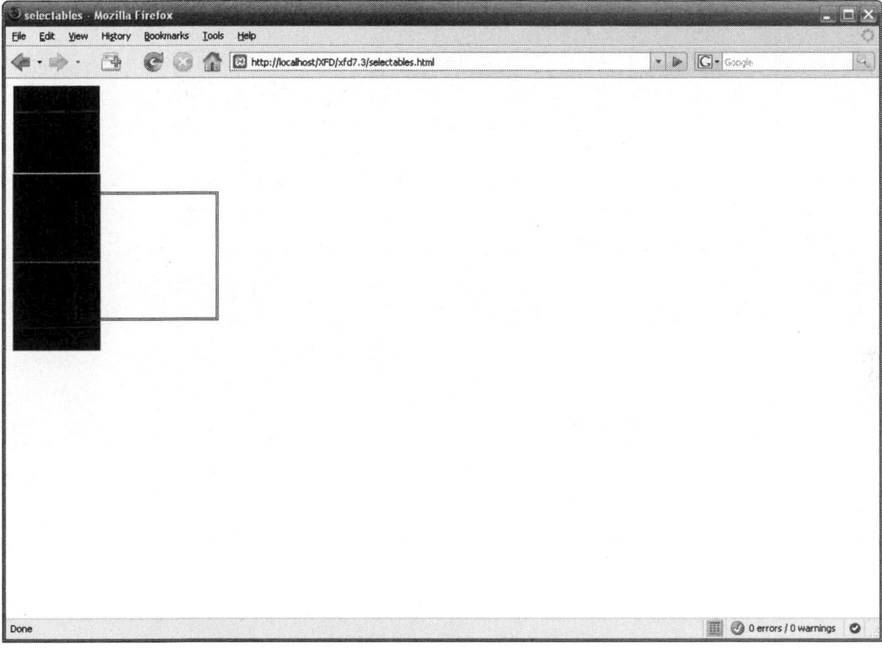

Figure 3-7: These items can be individually selected.

Although `accept` is the only required option, this function appears to not be working if you don't specify at least the `selectedclass` option.

Hold down the Ctrl or Shift key to help with multiple item selection.

Selectables options

The selectables have very few options, as follows:

- `accept`: This option is mandatory. It specifies the classes within the parent element that are actually selectable.
- `selectedclass`: This might as well be mandatory. It specifies the class that will be applied to the selected items.
- `helperclass`: This specifies the CSS rule for the box that you use to select items.
- `opacity`: This specifies the opacity for the box that you use to select items.
- `onselect`: This is the function that's called upon selection completion. It receives an array of the selection elements that can be used to call an AJAX function, as in the sortables example, above.

See http://interface.eyecon.ro/docs/select for more information about this function.

Making a slider

One of my favorite Interface Elements is the slider. With a little work, it can function like a radio button group.

For a more in-depth look at an Interface Elements function, see the "Getting to know Interface Elements" section, earlier in this chapter. This is a basic overview to get you started.

Basic slider

The basic slider consists of a container element, which functions as the track that the indicator slides on, and an indicator that slides along the track (see Figure 3-8). Listing 3-5 shows a sample of a basic slider.

Listing 3-5: The Basic Slider

```
<head>
    <title>slider</title>
    <style type="text/css">
        #track{
            top: 20px;
            left: 10px;
            height: 100px;
            width: 20px;
            background-color: #00F;
        }

        .indicator{
            height: 25px;
            width: 20px;
            background-color: black;
        }
    </style>
</head>
<body>
<div id="track">
    <div id="indicator" class="indicator"></div>
</div>
<script type="text/javascript" src="inc/jquery-
   1.2.1.min.js"></script>
<script type="text/javascript"
   src="inc/interface1.2/interface.js"></script>
<script type="text/javascript">
```

```
    $("#track").Slider({
        accept: '.indicator',
    });
</script>
</body>
```

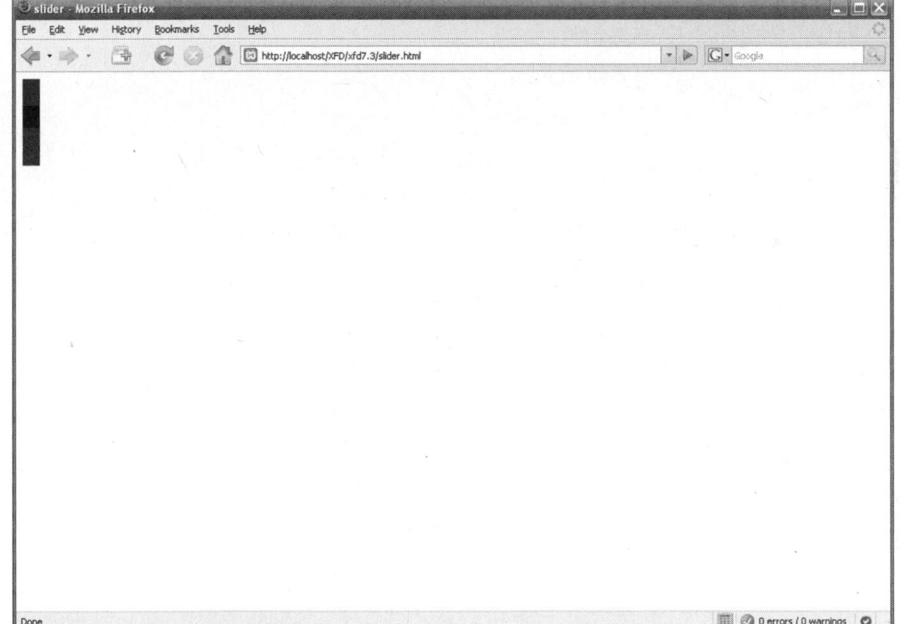

Figure 3-8: This item is a little slider.

You can have multiple indicators on the same track. You can also go horizontal instead of vertical. I suppose you could have a horizontal and vertical slider, but unless done very carefully, that could be a usability nightmare.

Slider options

Unlike other Interface Elements functions, the slider function's options *do* use camel-casing. Don't forget to camel case them (`onSlide()` instead of `onslide()`).

The slider has very few options, which are as follows:

- **`accept:`** This option is mandatory. It accepts a CSS class, indicating the *indicators* (what you move along the slider track) inside the slider.
- **`fractions:`** This is a number (don't put it inside quotes). This divides the slider along into fractions based on the number you specify. Note

that it starts counting at 0, so 3 is really 4, 4 is 5, and so on. Think of it as making however many slices you indicate into the slider.

✦ **`onSlide`:** This is a callback function. It executes while you're sliding the indicator. It returns four parameters belonging to the indicator at any given moment:

  - *x*-percentage
  - *y*-percentage
  - *x*-coordinate
  - *y*-coordinate

✦ **`onChange`:** This is a callback function. It executes when you stop sliding the indicator. It returns the final result of the same four parameters returned on the `onSlide()` function.

✦ **`values`:** This allows you to specify where the indicator(s) should start on the slider bar. It accepts an array of arrays (one inner array for each indicator's start position):

```
[[20,20],[50,100]]
```

✦ **`restricted`:** This requires a Boolean value (don't surround it with quotes). If `restricted` is set to `True` and there are multiple indicators, the indicators won't pass each other on the slider bar.

See `http://interface.eyecon.ro/docs/slider` for more information about this function.

Chapter 4: Sending and Receiving Data

In This Chapter

- Summarizing XML
- Generating an XML response
- Traversing XML with JavaScript
- Introducing JSON

AJAX can be used to send information to the client from the server. Elsewhere in Book VII, I concentrate on using complete XHTML code that can be integrated directly into the page. There's another powerful way to work with AJAX. You can pass data around in a specialized format and let the JavaScript/jQuery code manipulate the data on the client. The data is usually packed in XML format, but JSON is an increasingly popular technique. Both systems are introduced in this chapter.

Working with XML

eXtensible Markup Language (XML) is an extremely useful tool for sending and receiving data. XML data is easy to read and understand, even by humans. It's not too difficult to write programs that can read XML data, and the structure of the data is preserved by the tags. When you create your own XML format, you define custom tags to describe the data as follows:

```
<person>
    <name>
        <first>John</first>
        <middle>L</middle>
        <last>Doe</last>
    </name>
    <age>25</age>
    <gender>Male</gender>
</person>
```

XML is nothing new if you've read any other part of this book. XHTML is simply a form of HTML that also follows XML rules. The new idea is this: Rather than having to conform to somebody else's list of tags, you can invent your own and transmit information using your custom XML syntax.

These tags can be parsed with JavaScript and generated with PHP fairly easily.

Every XML element must have an opening and closing tag. (This is just like the XHTML rule.)

XML is a little bulky. Just look at the previous example: You have to use all those tags just to get that little bit of data back to the browser. See the section "Introducing JSON," later in this chapter, for an alternative to XML.

Generating XML with PHP

When you send an AJAX request to the server, the server then generates a response. This response can be plain text, an HTML fragment, or some code generated by a PHP program. If you're using PHP, you have to decide whether that response is an XML response or a plain XHTML response. If you want PHP to generate XML, you have to set the content type of the response.

Setting the content type

The first thing you need to do to send an XML response is to set the content type in your response header. When the browser receives the response, it checks the header to see what kind of data you're sending so that it can have a better idea of what to do with the data. Here's how you let the browser know that you're sending XML:

```
<? header('Content-Type: text/xml'); ?>
```

You must set the content type at the beginning of your response generation page. If you don't set the content type explicitly, the content type will be automatically set to `text/html`. The browser will try to read the data as XHTML, when the data should be read as XML.

If you forget to set the content type, you'll get weird errors in Internet Explorer. Firefox works just fine whether or not you set the content type.

The XML declaration

Besides specifying your content type in the header, you also need to declare your document type as XML in the text of the response. The tag for declaring the document type as XML is sort of like the tag for declaring the document type as HTML:

```
<?xml version="1.0" encoding="UTF-8" standalone="yes"?>
```

The document type declaration for XML is similar to the one for XHTML because XHTML is a subset of XML

This `xml` declaration specifies the XML version as 1.0 and the encoding as `UTF-8`, and that the XML document is a standalone, with no external DTD (document type declaration). You don't need to worry about what all this means because it never changes throughout all the XML documents you generate. Just copy and paste this into your header.

Note the PHP-friendly `<? ?>` tags surrounding the XML declaration. Those make it impossible to place this tag inside a PHP document without putting it inside a `print` or `echo` statement surrounded with single quotes (`'`):

```
print '<?xml version="1.0" encoding="UTF-8" standalone=
   "yes"?>';
```

See Book V, Chapter 2 for more on `print` and `echo` statements in PHP.

Populating the XML document with data

Generating your XML with PHP is exactly like generating text with PHP. Use `print` and `echo` statements to print your XML response to be sent back to the browser:

```
print <<<HERE
<person>
    <name>
        <first>$fname</first>
        <middle>$mname</middle>
        <last>$lname</last>
    </name>
    <age>$age</age>
    <gender>$gender</gender>
</person>
HERE;
```

See Book V, Chapter 2 for more on `print` and `heredocs` with PHP.

I can't stress this enough. You absolutely must have one almighty, super one-to-rule-them-all element that contains all other elements. Note that in the XML code in this section, I've used one super-person element that contains all the other elements. If I was to add a new person, I'd then have to surround the two separate person elements with one super-people element. If you don't set it up this way, you'll get a parse error.

Handling the XML response with jQuery

Because XHTML and XML are nearly identical at their roots, JavaScript can parse XML just like it parses XHTML.

The easiest way to parse the XML is by tag name. You can read more about accessing page elements by tag name in Book IV, Chapter 5, but the basic JavaScript and jQuery code for this is as follows:

JavaScript

```
document.getElementsByTagName("desiredTagNameHere");
```

jQuery

```
$("desiredTagNameHere");
```

Getting the XML from the server

The PHP page that generates the XML and the HTML page that uses this XML need a way to talk to each other. That's where AJAX comes in. You can see how to send and receive a basic text request with AJAX in Chapter 1 in this minibook. In this section, you see how to use jQuery to do the same thing and then parse the XML.

Sending the request with jQuery

The code in Chapter 1 of this minibook that you used to send the request to the PHP page was a horrible, confusing, ridiculous monster compared to the code I'm about to show you:

```
$.ajax({
    type: "POST",
    url: "page.php",
    dataType: "xml",
    success: pageUpdate
});
```

This little bit of jQuery packs a wallop. It replaces the `request` object creation required in normal JavaScript, as well as replaces the code that does the request generating and sending. You can specify many options with this function, but the important ones are as follows:

- **`type`:** This specifies what type of request you want to use. Possible types include
  - `"POST"`
  - `"GET"`
  - `"PUT"`
  - `"DELETE"`

  If the `type` option isn't specified, it defaults to `"GET"`, so the main reason to use this is if you want to use `"POST"` (which you should make a habit of doing).

Inserting foreign HTML with jQuery

What if you just want to insert an external HTML page directly into the current HTML page and have no reason to process anything before the insertion?

jQuery has an extremely convenient function for you! Check out the jQuery `load()` function. With it, you specify a page element to have the foreign HTML inserted into and then call the `load()` function, into which you pass a parameter indicating the page you wish to be loaded:

```
$("#localElement").load
    ("foreignHtml.php");
```

You can pass data through to the foreign page if it needs data in order to generate a dynamic response. You can also specify a callback function to be executed upon the completion of the load. Check out `http://docs.jquery.com/Ajax/load#urldatacallback` for more information.

- **`url`:** This specifies the page you want to send the request to. In most cases, this is the PHP page that you're using to process the request and generate a response. You can also specify a page in XML, JavaScript, ASP, or a Java resource.
- **`dataType`:** This specifies the type of data you're expecting to receive back in the response. In Chapter 1 of this minibook, you received text with a `responseText` object when processing the plain text response. In plain JavaScript, a sister object, `responseXML`, is used to process XML responses, so you can traverse the response with `DOM` (Document Object Model) techniques. Here, you can specify which of these you want jQuery to use. If you don't specify this here, jQuery usually figures it out for itself. The different values you can specify are
    - `"xml"`
    - `"html"`
    - `"script"`
    - `"json"`
    - `"jsonp"`
    - `"text"`

Specifying `"script"` will override your type specification with `"GET"` if you tried to use `"POST"`.

- **`error`:** This specifies the function to be called if the request fails. The function will automatically be passed through three parameters: The `XMLHttpRequest`, an error string, and optionally (if one occurred) an exception object.

- **success:** This specifies the function to be called if the request succeeds. The function will automatically be passed through two parameters: the data returned by the response (formatted according to your specification in the `dataType` option) and the status.
- **complete:** This specifies a function to be called upon completion, whether or not the request was successful.

Receiving the response with jQuery

In Chapter 1 of this minibook, you can see how you'd normally handle the response with JavaScript. Make sure the response is finished and successful, and then access the response. Finally, you can parse and do something with it.

jQuery vastly simplifies this. In the previous section, you can see how to specify a function to be called upon a successful response (as well as an error response).

This function can be placed right there in the `send` function:

```
$.ajax({
    url: "page.php",
    success: pageUpdate = function (data, statusText){

    },
    error: errorHandler = function(request, error){

    }
});
```

Or it can be referenced from the `success` option in the `send` function:

```
$.ajax({
    url: "page.php",
    success: pageUpdate,
    error: errorHandler
});

function pageUpdate(data, statusText){

}
```

Remember *not* to put the parentheses on the function reference for the success, error, or completion options in the `send` function. So, if you want to call the `pageUpdate()` function on success, you'd put `"pageUpdate"` and *not* `"pageUpdate()"`.

The XML, text, or whatever it is that you happened to request from the server is contained in that `"data"` parameter in the `success` function. You can name this parameter anything you want, like `"theXML"` or `"responseText"` or `"josh"`.

Parsing the XML

After you have your XML, you're ready to make the AJAX magic happen.

The most important thing you need to know right off is how to access the XML with the selector techniques. The easiest way to handle the XML is by tag name. In Chapter 3 of this minibook, you can see how to access page elements by tag name with jQuery. For instance, if you wanted to access all the paragraph (`<p>`) tags in the page, you could do so like this:

```
$("p")
```

Accessing the returned XML elements by tag name is almost exactly the same. In your `success` function, access the tag name that you want by using the tag name function and passing on the XML object you want it to search through instead of the current page:

```
function testUpdate(data, statusText){
    $("desiredTag", data);
}
```

Retrieving a table of data and printing it to the screen is a common task. Normally, you send some search terms to a PHP page. The PHP program would perform some SQL magic on those terms, generate some XML representing the data it retrieved from the database, and then send the data back to the browser as an XML response. Then, you'd take the XML response and parse it, turning it into your table.

Here's an example of code where the PHP page sends the XML back to the browser:

```
<?php
header('Content-Type: text/xml');

print <<<HERE
<?xml version="1.0" encoding="utf-8"?>
<characters>
<character>
    <first>Robert</first>
    <last>Kelso</last>
    <age>65</age>
    <occupation>Chief of Medicine</occupation>
</character>
<character>
    <first>John</first>
    <last>Dorian</last>
    <age>32</age>
    <occupation>Attending physician</occupation>
</character>
<character>
    <first>Christopher</first>
    <last>Turk</last>
    <age>31</age>
    <occupation>Attending surgeon</occupation>
```

```
</character>
<character>
    <first>Elliot</first>
    <last>Reid</last>
    <age>30</age>
    <occupation>Private Practice Physician</occupation>
</character>
</characters>
HERE;
?>
```

Here's the page that turns the XML into a table and displays it to the user:

```
<div id="response"></div>
<button id="getCharacters">Get The Characters!</button>

<script type="text/javascript" src="inc/jquery-1.2.1.min.js"></script>
<link rel="stylesheet" href="inc/themes/flora/flora.all.css" type="text/css"
    media="screen" title="Flora (Default)">
<script src="inc/ui.tablesorter.js"></script>
<script type="text/javascript">
$("#getCharacters").click(function(){
    $.ajax({
        type: "POST",
        url: "characters.php",
        dataType: "xml",
        success: pageUpdate,
        error: pageError = function(request, error){
            alert(error);
        },
        complete: pageComplete = function(){
            alert("done");
        }
    })
});

function pageUpdate(data, statusText){
    var character = $("character", data);
    var theTable = '<table class="tablesorter"><thead><tr><td>First
    Name</td><td>Last
    Name</td><td>Age</td><td>Occupation</td></tr></thead><tbody>';
    jQuery.each(character, function(i, val){
        theTable += "<tr>";
        attr = $(character[i]).children();
        jQuery.each(attr, function(ii, val){
            theTable += "<td>" + $(attr[ii]).text() + "</td>";
        });
        theTable += "</tr>";
    });
    theTable += "</table>";
    $("#response").html(theTable);

    $(".tablesorter").tablesorter();
}
</script>
```

Figure 4-1 shows this program in action, translating the XML response to a data query to an XHTML table.

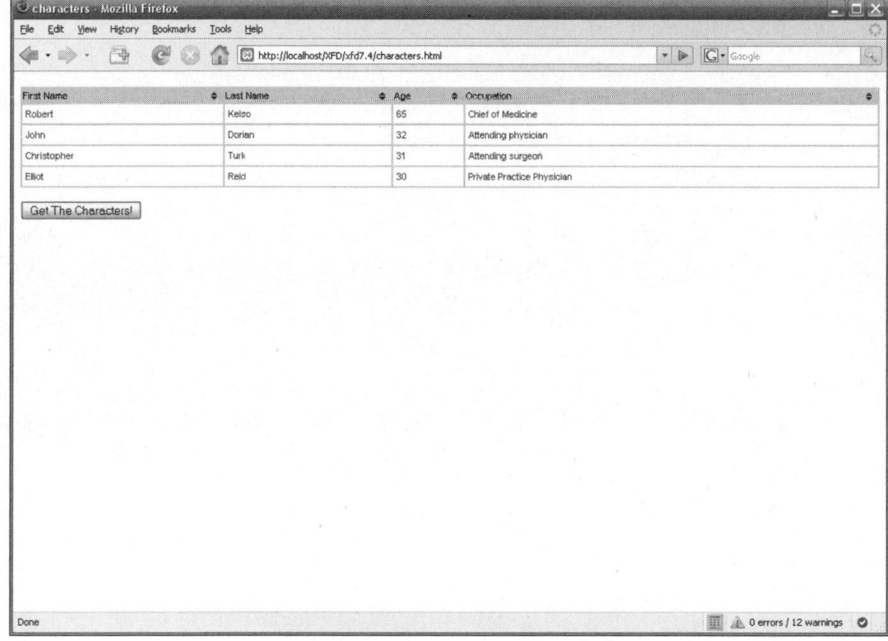

Figure 4-1: The data in this table came from an XML response.

You can use the `jQuery.each()` function to easily iterate through an object or array. See `http://docs.jquery.com/Utilities/jQuery.each#objectcallback` for more info on this function and `http://docs.jquery.com/Utilities` for more on other useful utility functions.

Introducing JSON

XML is easy to understand; you can look at it and know exactly what you're dealing with, but it's still just a bit bloated. You have to have at least two tags (a tag opener and close) for one piece of data.

It'd be nice if there was a leaner way to describe data without having to use this fat, chunky data structure. Well there is — it's JavaScript Object Notation (JSON). It's been gaining popularity over the last few years, especially as AJAX has become more prevalent.

Overview of JSON

JSON is basically just object-oriented JavaScript, which is an enhanced form of multidimensional JavaScript arrays:

```
var character = {
    "first" : "John",
```

```
    "last" : "Dorian",
    "age" : 32,
    "occupation" : "Attending Physician"
};
```

Looks familiar, doesn't it? It's almost the exact same syntax you've been using for all jQuery functions:

```
$.ajax({
    url: "somePage.php",
    dataType: "text",
    success: pageUpdate
});
```

You can access the different elements of your JSON data with ease. Say you wanted to access the first name index of the character array in the same JSON data. You could do this with JavaScript syntax, like so:

```
character.first
```

It doesn't get any simpler than that. You can even iterate through the data as you would with a JavaScript array:

```
jQuery.each(character, function(){
    alert(this);
});
```

The above code sample would alert the value of each array index, so you'd get four alert boxes ("John", "Dorian", "32", and "Attending Physician") while it cycled through the array and alerted what it found.

See Book IV, Chapter 4 for more on working with JavaScript objects and arrays.

If you give JSON a chance, I guarantee you'll find it easier to use than XML after you get used to it.

Using JSON with PHP

As of version 5.2, PHP can natively encode and decode JSON, which means that there's nothing extra you have to do to be able to use JSON instead of XML. JSON also speeds up your AJAX because it makes your already-small data calls even leaner.

You only need to know two new PHP functions to use JSON with PHP.

json_encode ()

You can use the `json_encode()` function in PHP to generate JSON to be sent back to the browser in response to an AJAX request.

First, create your array as normal with PHP:

```
$jd => array(
    "first" => "John",
    "last" => "Dorian",
    "age" => 32,
    "occupation" => "Attending Physician");
```

Then, use the `json_encode()` function to turn the PHP array into JSON:

```
$jd = json_encode($jd);
```

After it's encoded, it could be printed to the page the same way you'd print XML or text to be sent back to the browser as the response to an AJAX request. Check out `http://us.php.net/manual/en/function.json-encode.php` for more on the `json_encode()` function.

json_decode ()

You use the `json_decode()` function in PHP to generate a PHP object or associative array from JSON:


```
$jd = json_decode($jd);
```

This code takes the JSON that you encoded (in the `json_encode()` example) and turns it into a PHP object:

```
$jd = json_decode($jd, true);
```

The next line takes the JSON that you encoded (in the `json_encode()` example) and turns it right back into a PHP associative array.

Check out `http://us.php.net/manual/en/function.json-decode.php` for more on `json_decode()`.

Using JSON with AJAX

There are some differences when using JSON with AJAX instead of XML. You need to send the request a little bit differently, and parsing the response is much simpler.

Sending the request

When sending the request with jQuery, you can specify that you're expecting to receive back JSON by setting the `dataType` to `"json"`:

```
$.ajax({
    url: "somePage.php",
    dataType: "json",
    success: pageUpdate
});
```

This lets jQuery know that you expect to get back JSON instead of XML or just plain text. This way, you can just jump right into your JSON processing.

Receiving the response

If you're using jQuery and you specify the `dataType` as JSON, you don't have to do anything special when you receive the response before you can dive in and start using the data.

If you're not using jQuery, you'll need to evaluate the text returned from the PHP in the response:

```
var theJSON = eval('(' + response.responseText + ')');
```

Evaluating the `responseText` will take it from some plain text and turn it into `JSON` recognized by JavaScript.

Generating tables with JSON

At the end of the "Parsing the XML" section, earlier in this chapter, the example uses XML and AJAX to create a characters table. This time, I take the same code and show you how to use JSON and AJAX to do the same thing.

Here's the PHP that sends back the JSON to the browser:

```
<?php

$characters = array(
    "jd" => array(
        "first" => "John",
        "last" => "Dorian",
        "age" => 32,
        "occupation" => "Attending Physician"),
    "elliot" => array(
        "first" => "Elliot",
        "last" => "Reid",
        "age" => 30,
        "occupation" => "Private Practice Physician"),
    "turk" => array(
```

```
        "first" => "Christopher",
        "last" => "Turk",
        "age" => 31,
        "occupation" => "Attending Surgeon"),
    "bob" => array(
        "first" => "Robert",
        "last" => "Kelso",
        "age" => 65,
        "occupation" => "Chief of Medicine")
);

print (json_encode($characters));

?>
```

The following is the page that turns the JSON into a table and displays it to the user (see Figure 4-2):

```
<div id="response"></div>
<button id="getCharacters">Get The Characters!</button>

<script type="text/javascript" src="inc/jquery-1.2.1.min.js"></script>
<link rel="stylesheet" href="inc/themes/flora/flora.all.css" type="text/css"
    media="screen" title="Flora (Default)">
<script src="inc/ui.tablesorter.js"></script>
<script type="text/javascript">
$("#getCharacters").click(function(){
    $.ajax({
        url: "json.php",
        dataType: "json",
        success: pageUpdate,
        error: pageError = function(request, error){
            alert(error);
        },
        complete: pageComplete = function(){
            alert("done");
        }
    })
});

function pageUpdate(data, statusText){
    var theTable = '<table class="tablesorter"><thead><tr><td>First
    Name</td><td>Last
    Name</td><td>Age</td><td>Occupation</td></tr></thead><tbody>';
    jQuery.each(data, function(){
        theTable += "<tr>";
        jQuery.each(this, function(){
            theTable += "<td>" + this + "</td>";
        });
        theTable += "</tr>";
    });
    theTable += "</table>";
    $("#response").html(theTable);

    $(".tablesorter").tablesorter();
}
</script>
```

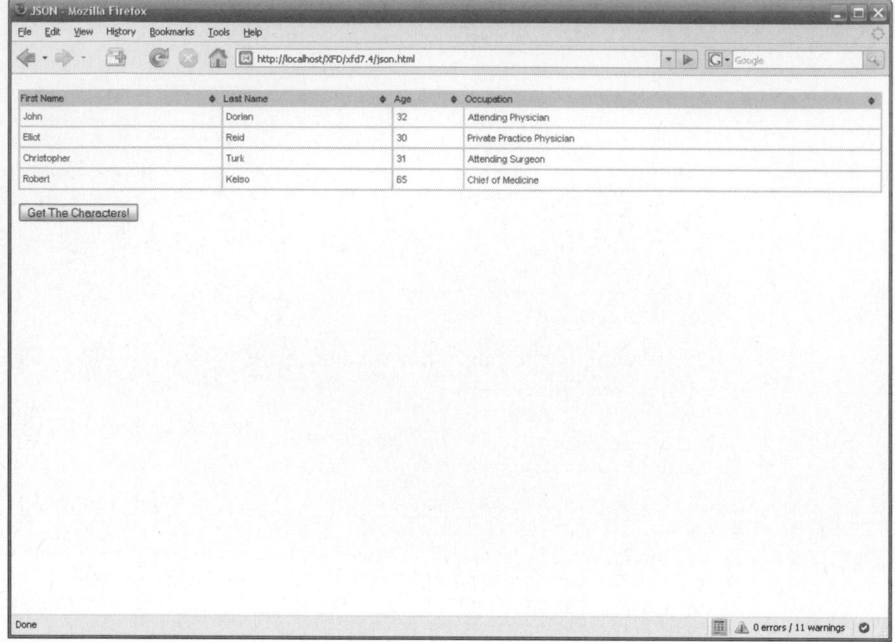

Figure 4-2: This version of the program uses JSON data.

Note the double-nested `each` loop. In the outer `each` loop, `"this"` represents the main array for each character that's taken out of the response data while the loop iterates through all the characters. In the inner `each` loop, `"this"` represents each element of the character array. It can be confusing to have two `this` keywords that each contain different data, but try not to let it mix you up. If you want, instead of having an `each` loop inside the outer `each` loop, you could access each element individually by hand because you know the structure of the data you are getting back:

```
jQuery.each(data, function(){
    theTable += "<tr>";
    theTable += "<td>" + this.first + "</td>";
    theTable += "<td>" + this.first + "</td>";
    theTable += "<td>" + this.age + "</td>";
    theTable += "<td>" + this.occupation + "</td>";
    theTable += "</tr>";
});
```

With the two previous examples, there's about a 30-percent decrease in the non-data code that's sent back to the browser in the request (the XML response has about 400 non-data characters, and the JSON response has about 270). That means that with JSON, the response time with AJAX will be at least 30-percent faster, and you type 30-percent less code.

Book VIII

Moving from Web Pages to Web Sites

"Look into my Web site, Ms. Carruthers. Look deep into its rotating spiral, spinning, spinning, pulling you deeper into its vortex, deeper...deeper..."

Contents at a Glance

Chapter 1: Managing Your Servers

In This Chapter

- **Understanding the client-server relationship**
- **Reviewing tools for client-side development**
- **Gathering server-side development tools**
- **Installing a local server with XAMPP**
- **Setting essential security settings**
- **Choosing a remote server**
- **Managing the remote servers**
- **Choosing and registering a domain name**

Web pages are a complex undertaking. The basic Web page itself isn't too overwhelming, but Web pages are unique because they have meaning only in the context of the Internet — a vastly new undertaking with unique rules.

Depending where you are on your Web development journey, you may need to understand the entire architecture, or you may be satisfied with a smaller part. Still, you should have a basic idea of how the Internet works and how the various technologies described in this book fit in.

Understanding Clients and Servers

A person using the Web is a *client*. You can also think of the user's computer or browser as the client. Clients on the Internet have certain characteristics:

- **Clients are controlled by individual users.** You have no control over what kind of connection or computer the user has. It may not even be a computer, but may be instead a cellphone or (I'm not kidding) refrigerator.
- **Clients have temporary connections.** Clients typically don't have permanent connections to the Internet. Even if a machine is on a permanent network, most machines used as clients have temporarily assigned addresses that can change.
- **Clients might have wonderful resources.** Client machines may have multimedia capabilities, a mouse, and real-time interactivity with the user.

- **Clients are limited.** Web browsers and other client-side software are often limited so that programs accessed over the Internet can't make major changes to the local file system. For this reason, most client programs operate in a sort of "sandbox" to prevent malicious coding.
- **Clients can be turned off without penalty.** It doesn't really cause anybody else a problem if you turn off your computer. Generally, client machines can be turned off or moved without any problems.

Servers are the machines that typically host Web pages. They have a much different set of characteristics:

- **Servers are controlled by server administrators.** A server administrator is responsible for ensuring that all data on the server is secure.
- **Servers have permanent connections.** The purpose of a server is to allow requests. For this reason, a server needs to have an IP number permanently assigned to it.
- **Servers usually have names, too.** To make things easier for users, server administrators usually register domain names to make their servers easier to find.
- **Servers can access other programs.** Web servers often talk to other programs or computers (especially data servers).
- **Servers must be reliable.** If a Web server stops working, anybody trying to reach the pages on that server is out of luck. This is why Web servers frequently run Unix or Linux because these operating systems tend to be more stable.
- **Servers must have specialized software.** The element that truly makes a computer a server is the presence of Web server software. Although several options are available, only two dominate the market: Apache and Microsoft IIS.

Parts of a client-side development system

A development system is made up of several components. If you're programming on the client (using XHTML, CSS, and JavaScript), you need the following tools:

- **Web browsers:** You need at least a couple of browsers so that you can see how your programs behave in different ones. Firefox is especially useful for Web developers because of its numerous available extensions.
- **Browser extensions:** Consider adding extensions to Firefox to improve your editing experience. Web Developer, Firebug, and HTML Validator are extremely helpful.
- **Text editor:** Almost all Web development happens with plain text files. A standard text editor should be part of your standard toolkit. I prefer

Notepad++ for Windows and prefer VI or emacs for other operating systems.

- **Integrated Development Environment:** Aptana Studio is a specialized text editor with added features for Web programming. It understands all the main Web languages and has syntax help, code coloring, and preview features.

For client-side development, you don't necessarily need access to a server. You can test all your programs directly on your own machine with no other preparation. Of course, you'll eventually want a server so that you can show your pages to everyone.

The client-side development tools listed here are described in more detail in Book I, Chapter 3.

Parts of a server-side system

When you start working on the server side (with PHP, MySQL, and AJAX), you need a somewhat more complex setup. In addition to everything you need for client-side development, you also need these items:

- **A Web server:** This piece of software allows users to request Web pages from your machine. You must either sign on to a hosting service and use its server or install your own. (I show you both techniques in this chapter.) By far the most common server in use is Apache. Web server software usually runs all the time in the background because you never know when a request will come in.
- **A server-side language:** Various languages can be connected to Web servers to allow server-side functionality. PHP is the language I chose in this book because it has an excellent combination of power, speed, price (free), and functionality. PHP needs to be installed on the server machine, and the Web server has to be configured to recognize it.
- **A data server:** Many of your programs work with data, and they need some sort of application to deal with that data. The most common data server in the open-source world is MySQL. This data package is free, powerful, and flexible. The data server is also running in the background all the time. You have to configure PHP to know that it has access to MySQL.
- **A mail server:** If your programs send and receive e-mail, you need some sort of e-mail server. The most popular e-mail server in the Windows world is Mercury Mail, and Sendmail is popular in the world of Unix and Linux. You probably won't bother with this item on a home server, but you should know about it when you're using a remote host.
- **An FTP server:** Sometimes, you want the ability to send files to your server remotely. The FTP server allows this capability. Again, you

probably don't need this item for your own machine, but you definitely should know about it when you use a remote host.

- **phpMyAdmin:** There's a command-line interface to MySQL, but it's limited and awkward. The easiest way to access your MySQL databases is to use the phpMyAdmin program. Because it's a series of PHP programs, it requires a complete installation of PHP, MySQL, and Apache.

Creating Your Own Server with XAMPP

If the requirements for a Web hosting solution seem intimidating, that's because they are. It's much more difficult to set up a working server system by hand than it is to start programming with it.

I don't recommend setting up your own system by hand. It's simply not worth the frustration because very good options are available.

XAMPP is an absolutely wonderful open-source tool. It has the following packages built in:

- **Apache:** The standard Web server and the cornerstone of the package
- **PHP:** Configured and ready to start with Apache and MySQL
- **MySQL:** Also configured to work with Apache and PHP
- **phpMyAdmin:** A data management tool that's ready to run
- **Mercury Mail:** A mail server
- **FileZilla FTP server:** An FTP server
- **PHP libraries:** A number of useful PHP add-ons, including gd (graphics support), Ming (Flash support), and more
- **Additional languages:** Perl, another extremely popular scripting and server language, and SQLite, another useful database package
- **Control and configuration tools:** A Control Panel that allows you to easily turn various components on and off.

This list is a description of the Windows version. The Mac and Linux versions have all the same types of software, but the specific packages vary.

Considering the incredible amount of power in this system, the download is remarkably small. The installer is only 34MB. A copy is included on the CD-ROM that accompanies this book.

XAMPP installation is pretty painless: Simply download the installer and respond to all the default values.

If you're using Vista, you may want to change where the package is installed because the program files directory is causing problems for some users.

Running XAMPP

After you install XAMPP, you can manage your new tools with the XAMPP Control Panel. Figure 1-1 shows this program in action.

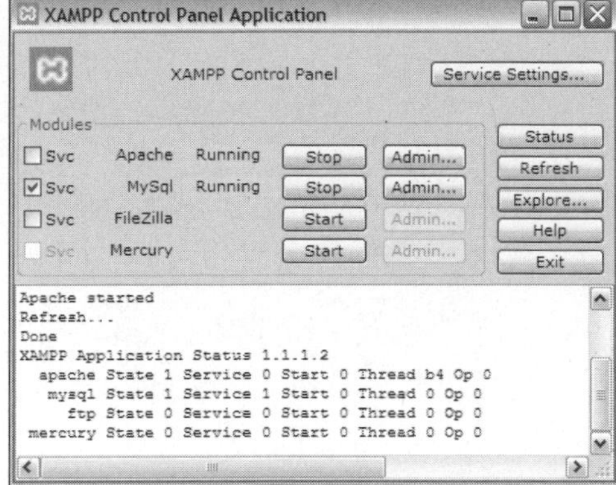

Figure 1-1: The XAMPP Control Panel allows you to turn features on and off.

Some components of XAMPP (PHP, for example) run only when they're needed. Some other components (Apache and MySQL) are meant to run constantly in the background. Before you start working with your server, you need to ensure that it's turned on.

You can choose to run Apache and MySQL as a service, which means that the program is always running in the background. This arrangement is convenient, but it slightly reduces the performance of your machine. I generally turn Apache on and off as I need it and leave MySQL running as a service because I have a number of other programs that work with MySQL.

Leaving server programs open on your machine constitutes a security hazard. Be sure to take adequate security precautions. See the section "Setting the security level," later in this chapter, for information on setting up your security features.

Testing your XAMPP configuration

Ensure that Apache and MySQL are running, and then open your Web browser. Set the address to `http://localhost`, and you see a screen like the one shown in Figure 1-2.

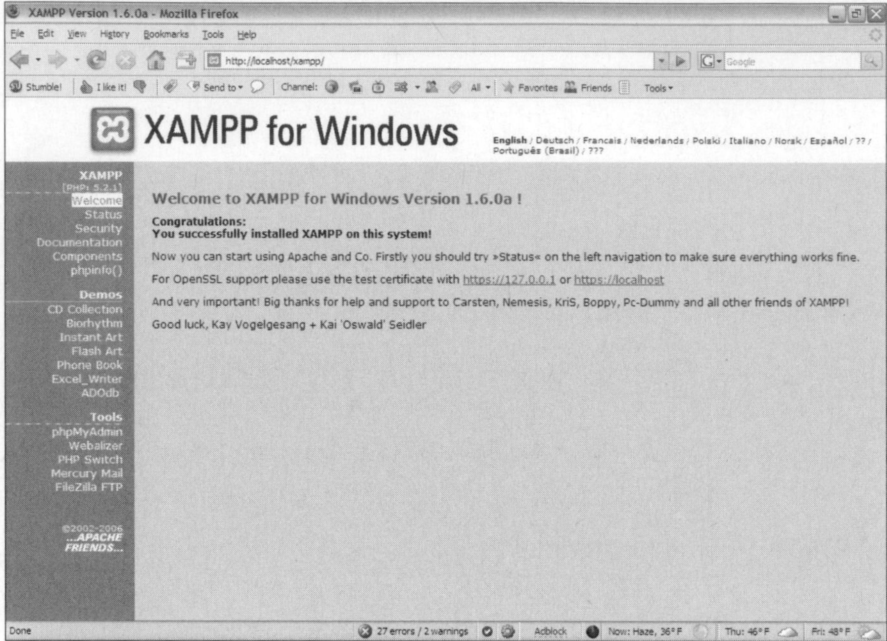

Figure 1-2: The XAMPP main page.

This page indicates that XAMPP is installed and working. Feel free to experiment with the various items in the Demos section. Even though you may not know yet what they do, you should know what some of their capabilities are.

Adding your own files

Of course, the point of having a Web server is to put your own files in it. Use your file management tool to find the XAMPP directory in your file system. Right under the XAMPP directory is the `htdocs` folder, the primary Web directory. Apache serves only files that are in this directory or under it. (That way, you don't have to worry about your love letters being distributed over the Internet.)

All the files you want Apache to serve must be in `htdocs` or in a subdirectory of it.

When you specified `http://localhost` as the address in your browser, you were telling the browser to look on your local machine in the main `htdocs` directory. You didn't specify a particular file to load. If Apache isn't given a filename and it sees the file named `index.html` or `index.php`, it displays that file, instead. So, in the default `htdocs` directory, the `index.php` program is immediately being called. Although this program displays the XAMPP welcome page, you don't usually want that to happen.

Rename `index.php` to `index.php.old` or something similar. It's still there if you want it, but now there's no index page, and Apache simply gives you a list of files and folders in the current directory. Figure 1-3 shows my `localhost` directory as I see it through the browser.

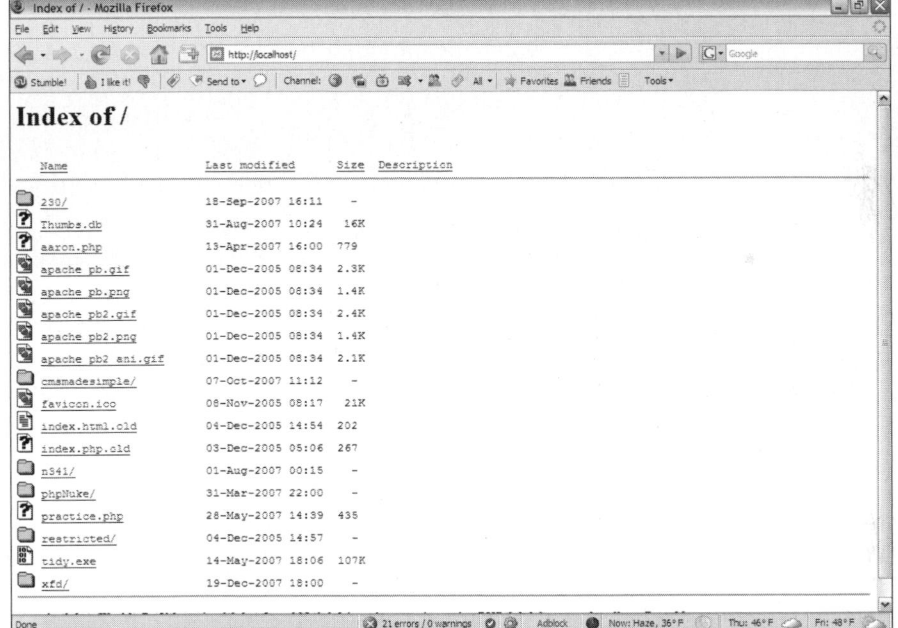

Figure 1-3: After disabling index.php, I can see a list of files and directories.

You typically don't want users to see this ugly index in a production server, but I prefer it in a development environment so that I can see exactly what's on my server. After everything is ready to go, I put together `index.html` or `index.php` pages to generate more professional directories.

Generally, you want to have subdirectories to all your main projects. I added a few others for my own use, including `xfd`, which contains all the code for this book.

If you want to display the XAMPP welcome screen after you remove the `index.php` program, simply point your browser to `http://localhost/xampp`.

Setting the security level

When you have a Web server and a data server running, you create some major security holes. You should take a few precautions to ensure that you're reasonably safe:

- **Treat your server only as a local asset.** Don't run a home installation of Apache as a production server. Use it only for testing purposes. Use a remote host for the actual deployment of your files. It's prepared for all the security headaches.
- **Run a firewall.** You should run, at an absolute minimum, the Windows firewall that comes with all recent versions of Windows. You might also consider an open-source or commercial firewall. Block incoming access to all ports by default and open them only when needed. There's no real need to allow incoming access to your Web server. You only need to run it in localhost mode.

If you want to see which ports XAMPP uses for various tools, they are listed on the security screen shown in Figure 1-4.

- **Run basic security checks.** The XAMPP package has a handy security screen. Figure 1-4 shows the essential security measures. I've already adjusted my security level, so you'll probably have a few more "red lights" than I do. Click the security link at the bottom of the page for some easy-to-use security utilities.
- **Change the MySQL root password.** If you haven't already done so, use the security link to change the MySQL root password, as shown in Figure 1-5. (I show an alternative way to change the password in Book VI, Chapter 1.)

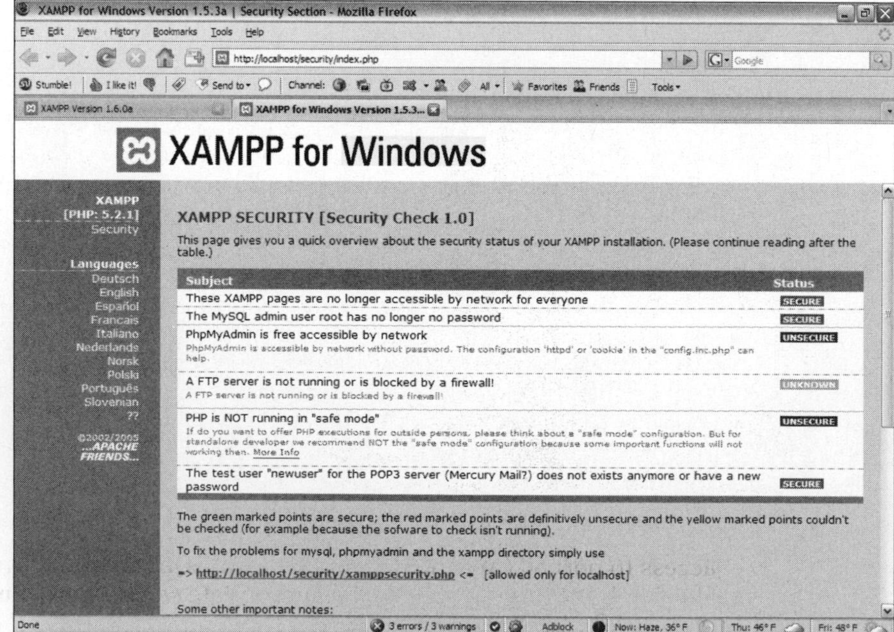

Figure 1-4: The XAMPP Security panel shows a few weaknesses.

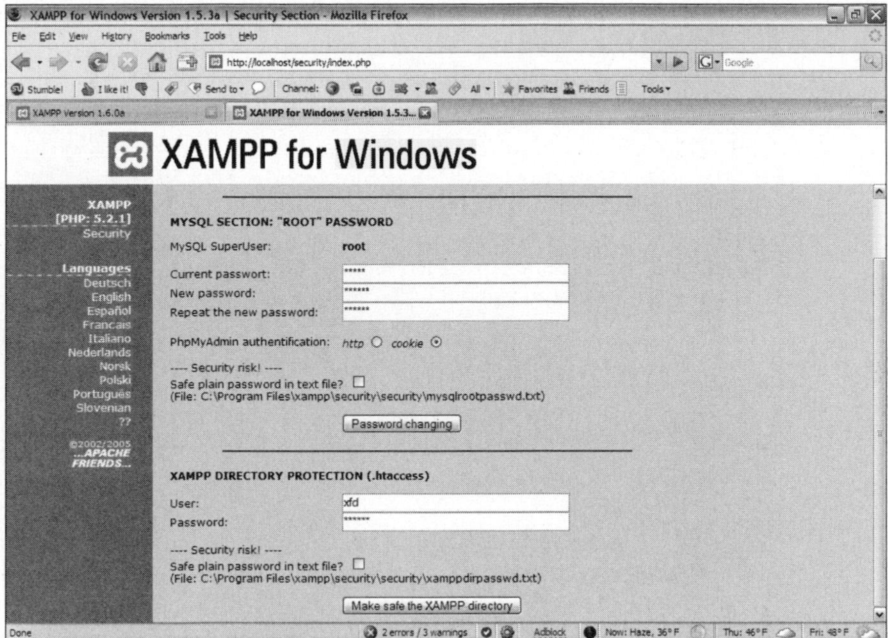

Figure 1-5: Changing the MySQL root password.

✦ **Add an XAMPP Directory password.** Type a password into the lower half of the security form to protect your xampp directory from unauthorized access. When you try to go to the xampp directory, you're prompted for this password.

Security is always a compromise. When you add security, you often introduce limits in functionality. For example, if you changed the root password for MySQL, some of the examples (and phpMyAdmin) may not work any more because they're assuming that the password is blank. You often have to tweak. See Chapter 1 in Book VI for a complete discussion of password issues in MySQL and phpMyAdmin.

Compromising between functionality and security

You may be shocked that my example still has a couple of security holes. It's true, but it's not quite as bad as it looks:

✦ **The firewall is the first line of defense.** If your firewall blocks external access to your servers, the only real danger your system faces is from yourself. Begin with a solid firewall and ensure that you don't allow access to port 80 (Apache) or port 3306 (MySQL) unless you're absolutely sure that you have the appropriate security measures in place.

- **I left phpMyAdmin open.** phpMyAdmin needs root access to the MySQL database, so if anybody can get to phpMyAdmin through the Web server, they can get to my data and do anything to it. Because my firewall is blocking port 80 access, you can't get to phpMyAdmin from anything other than localhost access, and it's not really a problem.
- **I'm not running PHP in secure mode.** Secure mode turns off several PHP features to make the connection a bit more secure. Unfortunately, this process also removes some important functionality. For localhost access, I normally leave the default PHP configuration in place.

Choosing a Web Host

Creating a local server is useful for development purposes because you can test your programs on a server you control and you don't need a live connection to the Internet.

However, you should avoid running a production server on your own computer, if you can. A typical home connection doesn't have the guaranteed IP number you need. Besides, you probably signed an agreement with your broadband provider that you won't run a public Web server from your account.

This situation isn't really a problem because thousands of Web hosting services are available that let you easily host your files. You should consider an external Web host for these reasons:

- **The host, not you, handles the security headaches.** This reason alone is sufficient. Security isn't difficult, but it's a never-ending problem (because the bad guys keep finding new loopholes).
- **The remote server is always up.** Or, at least, it should be. The dedicated Web server isn't doing anything other than serving Web pages. Your Web pages are available, even if your computer is turned off or doing something else.
- **A dedicated server has a permanent IP address.** Unlike most home connections, a dedicated server has an IP address permanently assigned to it. You can easily connect a domain name to a permanent server so that users can easily connect.
- **Ancillary services usually exist.** Many remote hosting services offer other services, like databases, FTP, and e-mail hosting.
- **The price can be quite reasonable.** Hosting is a competitive market, which means that some good deals are available. Decent hosting is available for free, and improved services are extremely reasonable.

You can find a number of free hosting services at sites like `http://free-webhosts.com`.

Finding a hosting service

When looking for a hosting service, ask yourself these questions:

- **Does the service have limitations on the types of pages you can host?** Some servers are strictly for personal use, and some allow commercial sites. Some have bandwidth restrictions and close your site if you draw too many requests.
- **How much space are you given?** Ordinary Web pages and databases don't require a huge amount of space, but if you do a lot of work with images, audio, and video files, your space needs will increase dramatically.
- **Is advertising forced on you?** Many free hosting services make money by forcing advertisements on your pages. This practice can create a problem because you might not always want to associate your page with the company being advertised. (A page for a day care center probably should not have advertisements for dating services, for example.)
- **Which scripting languages (if any) are supported?** Look for PHP support.
- **Does the host offer prebuilt scripts?** Many hosts offer a series of prebuilt and preinstalled scripts. These can often include content management systems, message boards, and other extremely useful tools. If you know that you're going to need Moodle, for example (a course management tool for teachers), you can look for hosting services that have it built in.
- **Does the host provide access to a database?** Is phpMyAdmin support provided? How many databases do you get? What is the size limit?
- **What sort of Control Panel does the service provide?** Does it allow easy access to all the features you need?
- **What type of file management is used?** For example, determine how you upload files to the system. Most services use browser-based uploading. This system is fine for small projects, but it's quite inconvenient if you have a large number of files you want to transfer. Look for FTP support to handle this.
- **Does the host have an inactivity policy?** Many free hosting services automatically shut down your site if you don't do anything with it (usually after 30 to 90 days of inactivity). Be sure you know about this policy.
- **Do you have assurances that the server will remain online?** Are backups available? What sort of support is available? Note that these services are much more likely on a paid server.

- **How easily can you upgrade if you want?** Does a particular hosting plan meet your needs without being too expensive?
- **Does the service offer you a subdomain, and can you register your own?** You may also want to redirect a domain that you didn't get through the service. (See the section "Naming Your Site," later in this chapter, for information on domain names.)

Connecting to a hosting service

The sample pages for this book are hosted on Freehostia.com, an excellent, free hosting service. You can find many great hosting services, but the rest of the examples in this chapter use Free Hostia. I chose this service for the examples because

- **Its free account is terrific.** At the time of this writing, the features of the free account at Free Hostia are as good as they are at many paid accounts.
- **The pages have no forced advertising.** Free Hostia doesn't place any ads on your pages (a major selling point for me).
- **PHP, phpMyAdmin, and MySQL are supported — all on the free account.** Often, you have to upgrade to a paid service to get these features.
- **You get enough space to start with.** The free account comes with 250MB of space. This amount is fine for ordinary Web pages, PHP, and database needs. You need more, though, if you do a lot of image or video hosting.
- **You can have a subdomain for free.** Even if your site doesn't have a domain name, you can choose a subdomain so that your site has a recognizable address, like `http://myStuff.freehostia.com`.
- **It has a good list of script installers.** It comes with a nice batch of scripts that you can install effortlessly.
- **The upgrade policy is reasonable.** Free Hostia makes money on commercial Web hosting. It offers an excellent free service that, ideally, gets you hooked so that you then upgrade to a commercial plan. It has a number of good upgrade packages for various sizes of businesses.
- **You get a nice batch of extras.** The free service comes with FTP and e-mail support and also a MySQL database.
- **Customer support is excellent.** Most free hosting services offer no customer support. Free Hostia provides good support, even to the free services. (I asked a couple of questions before anyone there knew that I was writing this book, and I was impressed with the speed and reliability of the responses.)

Choose whichever hosting service works for you. If you find a free hosting service that you really like, upgrade to a paid service. Hosting is a reasonably cheap commodity, and a quality hosting service is well worth the investment.

Managing a Remote Site

Obviously, having a hosting service isn't much fun if you don't have pages there. Fortunately, there are a lot of ways to work with your new site.

Using Web-based file tools

Most of the time, your host has some sort of Control Panel that looks like the one shown in Figure 1-6.

There's usually some sort of file management tool that might look like the one shown in Figure 1-7.

In this particular case, all my Web files are in the `www/aharrisbooks.net` directory, so I click to see them. Figure 1-8 shows what you might see in an actual directory.

Figure 1-6: This Control Panel allows you to manage your site remotely.

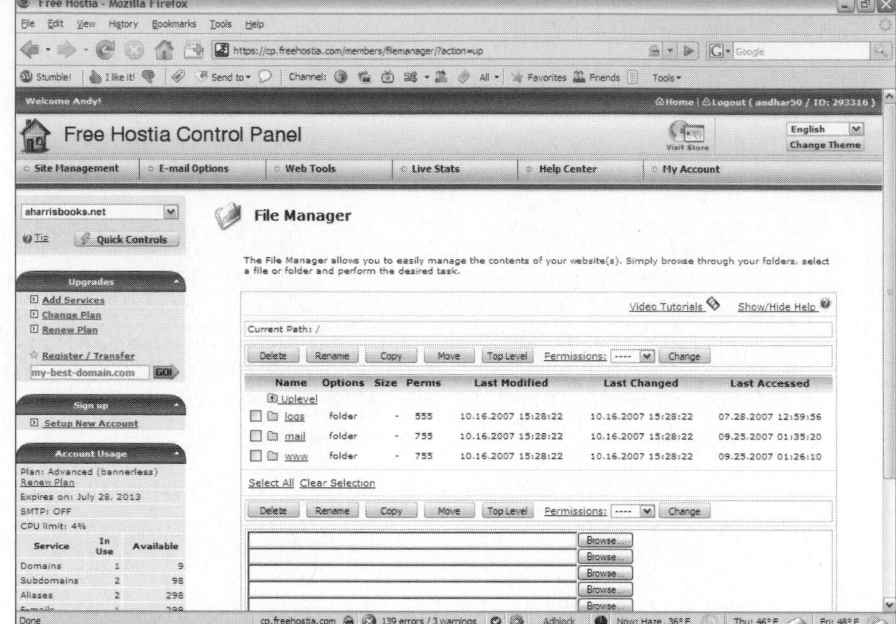

Figure 1-7: This file management tool allows you to manipulate the files on your system.

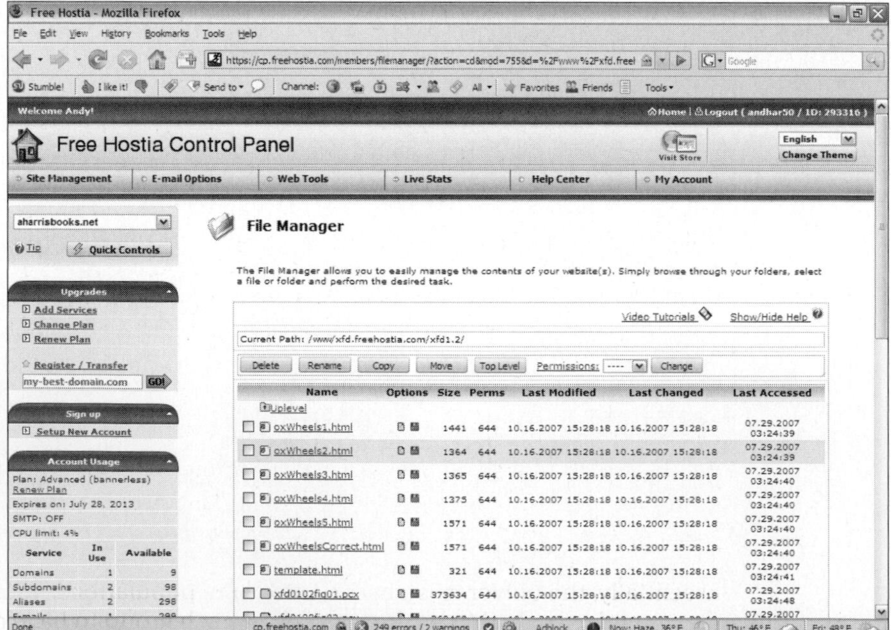

Figure 1-8: Now, you can see some files here.

This page allows you to rename, upload, and edit existing files and change file permissions.

You can create a new file directly, with the Create File button. Type a filename into the text area and click the button, and you see the text editor shown in Figure 1-9.

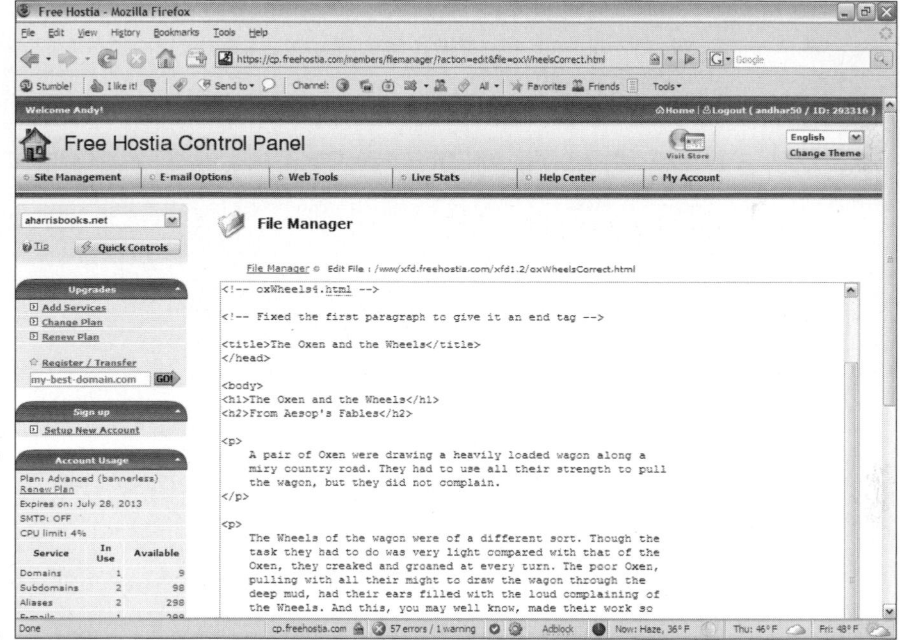

Figure 1-9: The hosting service has a limited text editor.

You can write an entire Web site using this type of editor, but the Web-based text editing isn't helpful, and it's kind of awkward. More often, you create your files on your own XAMPP system and upload them to the server when they're basically complete. Use server-side editing features for quick fixes only.

Understanding file permissions

Most hosting services use Linux or Unix. These operating systems have a more sophisticated file permission mechanism than the Windows file system does. At some point, you may need to manipulate file permissions.

Essentially, the universe is divided into three populations: Yourself, your group, and everybody else. You can allow each group to have different kinds of permission for each file. Each of the permissions is a Boolean (true or false) value:

What's with all the permissions?

Permissions are typically treated as binary numbers: 111 means "read, write, execute." This (111 value) is also a 7 permission because 111 binary translates to 7 in base ten (or base eight, but let's skip that detail for now).

A permission is read as three digits, each one a number indicating the permissions, so 644 permission means `rw- r-- r--`. This example can be translated as "The owner should be able to read and write this file. Everyone else can read it. Nobody can execute it."

If you don't understand this concept, don't worry about it. The guidelines are very simple: Make sure that each of your files has 644 permission and that each directory has 755 permission. That's all you really need to know.

- **Read permission:** The file can be read. Typically, you want everybody to be able to read your files, or else you wouldn't put them on the Web server.
- **Write permission:** The file can be written, changed, and deleted. Obviously, only you should have the ability to write to your files.
- **Execute permission:** Indicates that the file is an executable program or a directory that can be passed through. Normally, none of your files is considered executable, although all your directories are.

Using FTP to manage your site

Most of the work is done on a local machine and then sent to the server in a big batch. (That's how I did everything in this book.) The standard Web-based file management tools are pretty frustrating when you want to efficiently upload a large number of files.

Fortunately, most hosts have the FTP (File Transfer Protocol) system available. *FTP* is a client/server mechanism for transferring files efficiently. To use it, you may have to configure some sort of FTP server on the host to find out which settings, username, and password you should use. Figure 1-10 shows the Free Hostia Control Panel with this information displayed.

You also need an FTP client. Fortunately, many free clients are available. I like FireFTP, for a number of reasons:

- **It's free and open source.** That's always a bonus.
- **It works as a Firefox plugin.** I always know where it is.
- **It's easy to use.** It feels just like a file manager.

Figure 1-11 shows FireFTP running in my browser.

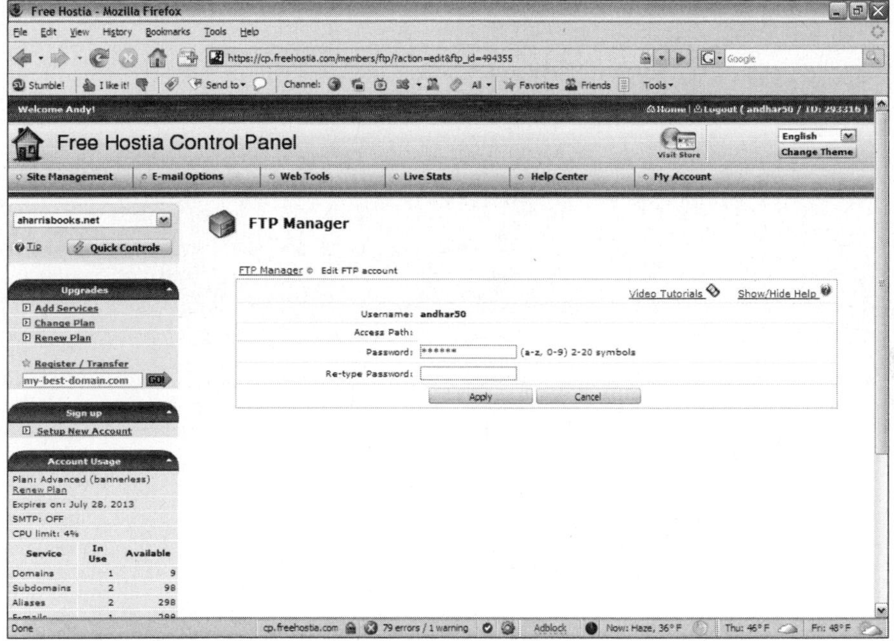

Figure 1-10: Configuring the FTP server.

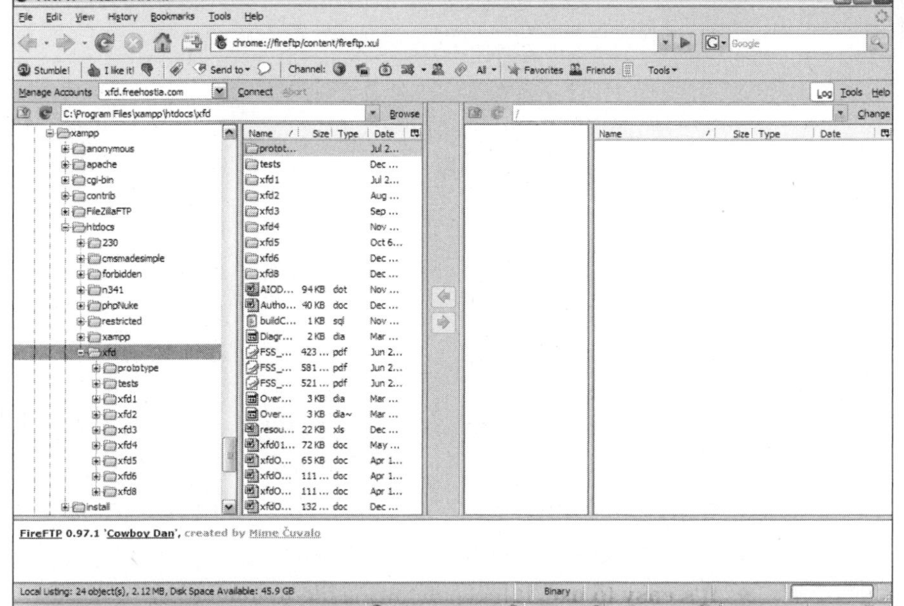

Figure 1-11: FireFTP is a complete FTP program that runs inside Firefox.

If you want to connect to your server with FTP, follow these steps:

1. **Look up the configuration settings.**

   You may have to dig around in the server documentation, but you should find the server name, username, and password to access your server. Sometimes, you have to configure these elements yourself.

2. **Create a profile for your server.**

   Use the Manage Accounts feature to create a profile using the FTP settings. Figure 1-12 shows a profile for my aharrisbooks account.

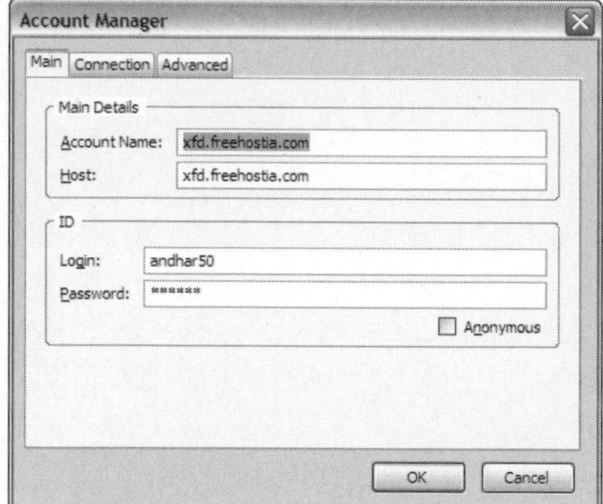

Figure 1-12: The profile editor for FireFTP.

3. **Connect to the remote server.**

   FTP programs look a lot like the Windows Explorer you might have on your machine, except that they usually have two file panels. The left panel represents the files on your local system, and the right panel shows files on the remote system.

4. **Navigate to the directories you're interested in.**

   If you want to move a file from the local system to the remote one, use the two file explorers to find the appropriate directory on each system.

5. **Drag the file to transfer it.**

   FireFTP automatically determines the type of transfer you need to make.

6. **Wait for the transfer to complete.**

   It usually takes some time to transfer a large number of files. Be sure the transfer is complete before you close the FTP window.

7. **Manipulate remote files.**

   You can right-click on the remote file system to display a context menu. This menu has commands for changing permissions, creating directories, and performing other handy tasks.

FTP is a completely unsecure protocol. Anything you transfer with FTP is completely visible to any bad guys sniffing the Internet. For this reason, some servers use a different protocol: Secure FTP (SFTP). FireFTP doesn't support this protocol, but search Google for open-source SFTP clients, and you'll find plenty.

Naming Your Site

After you have a site up and running, you need to give it an address that people can remember. The Domain Name System (DNS) is sort of an address book of the entire Internet. DNS is the mechanism by which you assign a name to your site.

Understanding domain names

Before creating a domain name, you should understand the basics of how this system works:

- **Every computer on the Internet has an IP (Internet Protocol) address.** When you connect to the Internet, a special number is assigned to your computer. This *IP address* uniquely identifies your computer. Client machines don't need to keep the same address. For example, my notebook has one address at home and another at work. The addresses are dynamically allocated. A server needs a permanent address that doesn't change.
- **IP addresses are used to find computers.** Any time you request a Web page, you're looking for a computer with a particular IP address. For example, the Google IP address is `66.102.9.104`. Type it into your browser address bar, press Enter, and you see the Google main page.
- **DNS names simplify addressing.** IP numbers are too confusing for human users. The Domain Name System (DNS) is a series of databases connecting Web site names with their associated IP numbers. When you type `http://www.google.com`, for example, the DNS system looks up the text `www.google.com` and finds the computer with the associated IP.
- **You have to register a DNS name.** Of course, to ensure that a particular name is associated with a page, you need to register that relationship.

Registering a domain name

In this section, I show you how to register a domain using Freehostia.com. Check the documentation on your hosting service. Chances are that the main technique is similar, even if the details are different.

To add a domain name to your site, follow these steps:

1. **Log in to the service.**

   Log in to your hosting service administration panel. You usually see a Control Panel something like the one shown in Figure 1-13.

2. **Find the domain manager.**

   In Free Hostia, the domain manager is part of the regular administration panel.

3. **Pick a subdomain.**

   In a free hosting service, the main domain (`freehostia.com`, for example) is often chosen for you. Sometimes, you can set a subdomain (like `mystuff.freehostia.com`) for free. The page for managing this process might look like Figure 1-14.

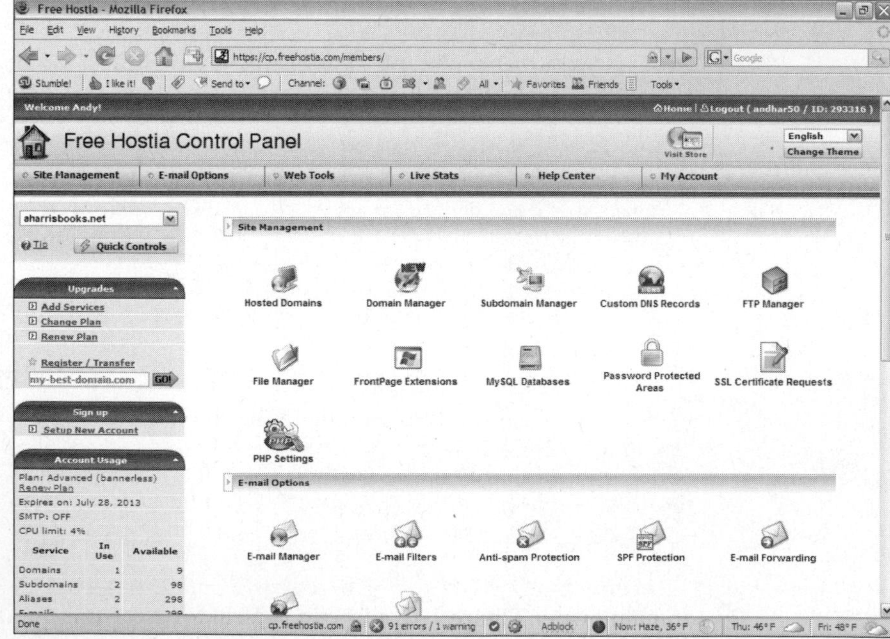

Figure 1-13: This Control Panel shows all the options, including domain and subdomain tools.

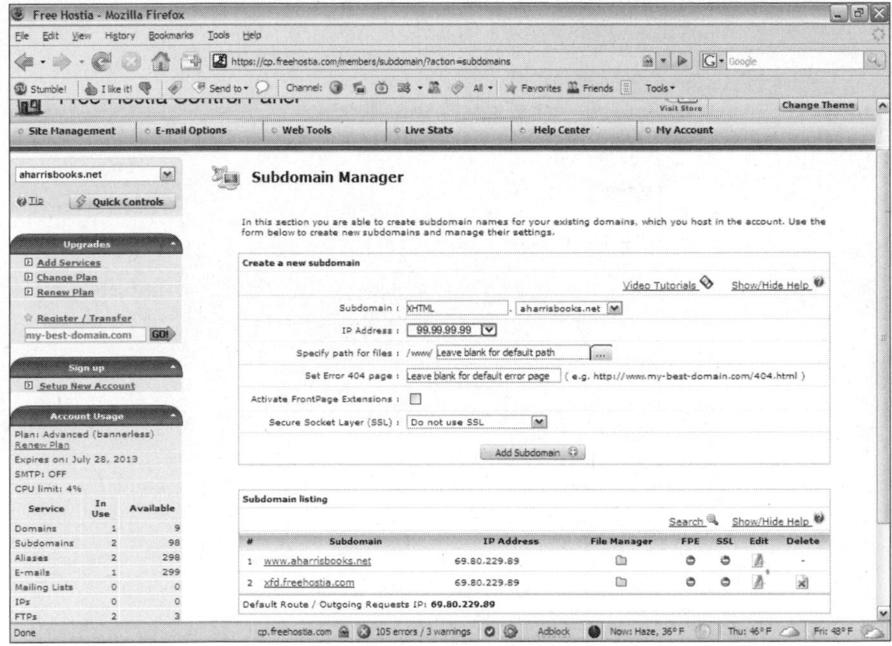

Figure 1-14: Use this page to create a subdomain for your account.

4. **Look for a domain search tool.**

   Often, you have a tool, like the one shown in Figure 1-15, that allows you to search for a domain.

5. **Search for the domain name you want.**

   You can type a domain name to see whether it's available.

6. **If the domain name is available to register and you want to own it, purchase it immediately.**

   If a domain is available to transfer, it means that somebody else probably owns it.

   Don't search for domains until you're ready to buy them. Unscrupulous people on the Web look for domains that have been searched and then buy them immediately, hoping to sell them back to you at a higher price. If you search for a domain name and then go back the next day to buy it, you often find that it's no longer available and must be transferred.

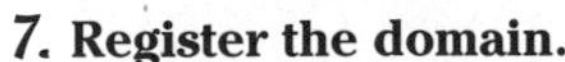

7. **Register the domain.**

   The domain-purchase process involves registering yourself as the domain owner. Figure 1-16 shows a typical form for this transaction. WHOIS information provides your information to people inquiring about the domain name.

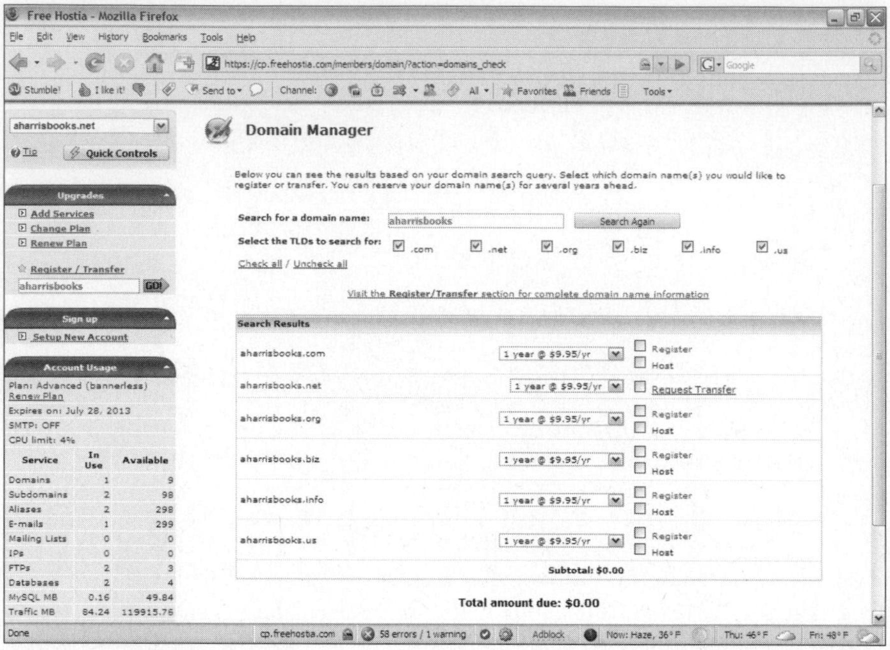

Figure 1-15: I'm searching for aharrisbooks.net — it seems like a good domain name!

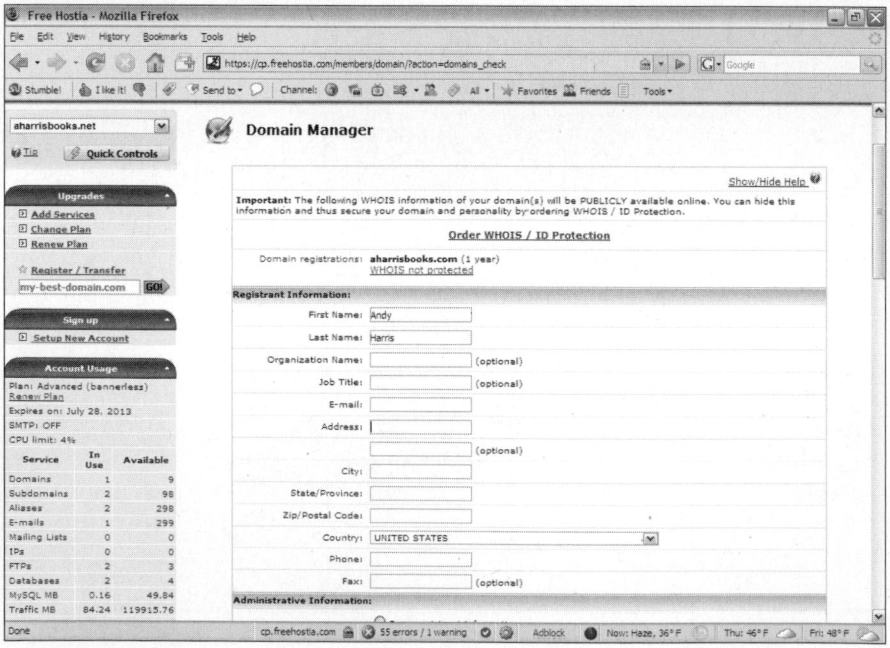

Figure 1-16: Registering the domain name.

8. **Wait a day or two.**

   Your new domain name won't be available immediately. It takes a couple of days for the name to be registered everywhere.

9. **Remember to renew your domain registration.**

   Domain-name registration isn't expensive (typically about $10 per year), but you must renew it or risk losing it.

Managing Data Remotely

Web sites often work with databases. Your hosting service may have features for working with MySQL databases remotely. You should understand how this process works because it's often slightly different from working with the database on your local machine.

Creating your database

Often, a tool like the one shown in Figure 1-17 allows you to pick a defined database or create a new one.

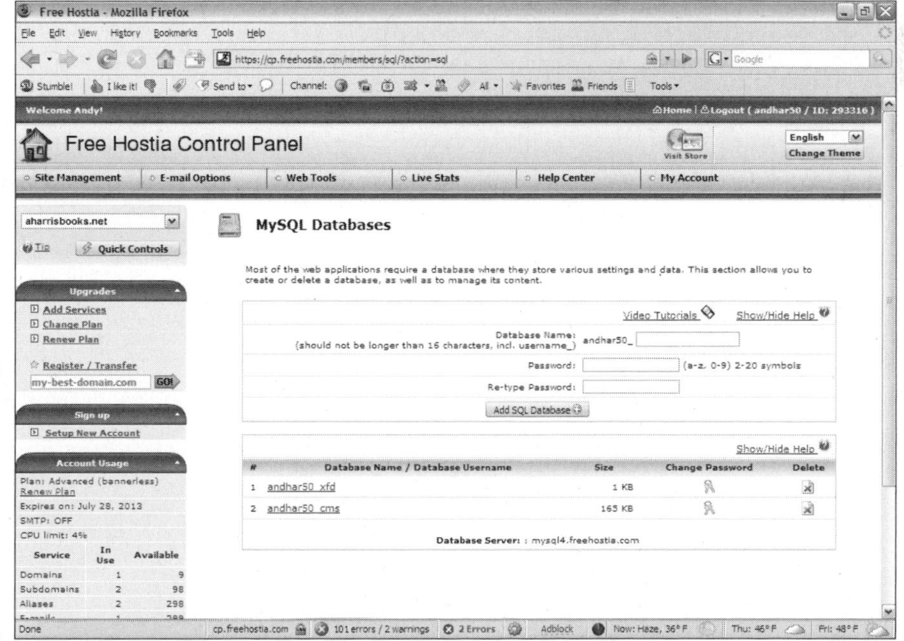

Figure 1-17: You often have to create a database outside of phpMy-Admin.

This database creation step happens because you don't have `root` access to MySQL. (If everybody had `root` access, chaos would ensue.) Instead, you usually have an assigned username and database name enforced by the server. On Free Hostia, all database names begin with the username and an underscore. To create a new database, you need to provide a database name and a password. Usually, a MySQL user is created with the same name as the database name.

After you create the database, you can select it to work with the data in MySQL. Figure 1-18 shows the MySQL screen for my database on Free Hostia.

If you look carefully, you see that Free Hostia is still using MySQL 4. Therefore, not all SQL scripts in this book work correctly. The only significant problem is views because this feature wasn't included in MySQL 4. I include a version of the `buildHero4.sql` script on the CD-ROM that eliminates all references to views. Otherwise, the script is the same.

You can see from Figure 1-18 that phpMyAdmin is somewhat familiar if you read Book VI. Often, public servers remove the Privileges section because you aren't logged in as `root`. Everything else is basically the same. See Book VI for details on how to use PHPMyAdmin to work with your databases.

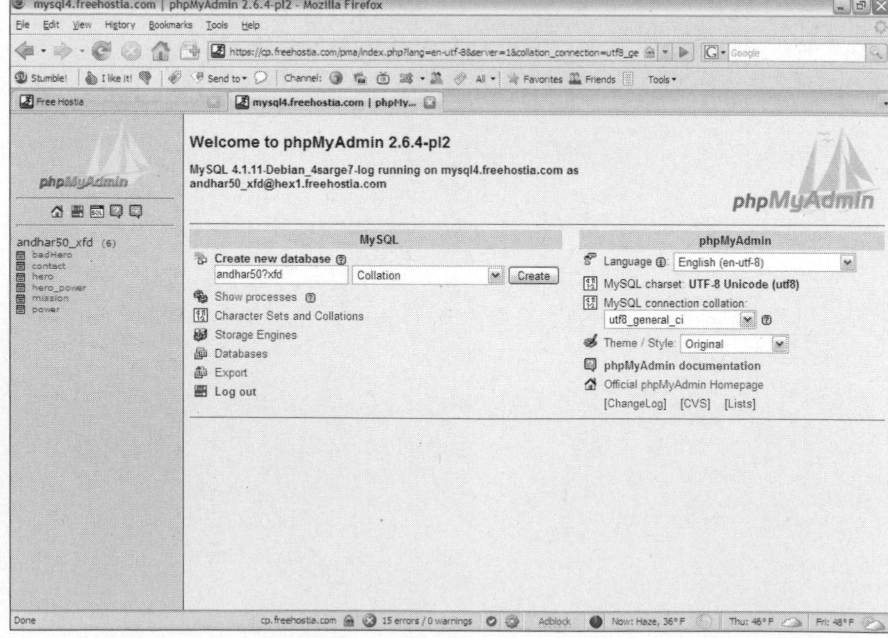

Figure 1-18: phpMyAdmin is just like the one on your home machine!

Finding the MySQL server name

Throughout Book VI, I assume that the MySQL server is on the same physical machine as the Web server. This situation is common in XAMPP installations, but commercial servers often have separate servers for data. You may have to dig through the documentation or find a Server Statistics section to discover how your PHP programs should refer to your server.

By far the biggest problem when moving your programs to a remote server is figuring out the new connection. Make sure that you know the right combination of server name, username, and password. Test on a simple PHP application before working on a complex one.

Chapter 2: Moving from Pages to Sites

In This Chapter

- Planning multipage Web sites
- Working with the client
- Analyzing the audience
- Building a site plan
- Creating XHTML and CSS templates
- Fleshing out the project

At some point, your Web efforts begin to grow. Rather than think about single Web documents, you begin to build more complex systems. Most real-life Web problems require a lot more than a single page to do their work. How do you make the transition to a site with many different but interconnected pages? How do you think through the process of creating a site that serves a specific purpose?

You might even be thinking about doing commercial Web development work. If so, it's definitely time to think about how to put together a plan for a customer.

Creating a Multipage Web Site

A complete Web site has these characteristics:

- **A consistent theme:** All the pages in a Web site should be about something — a product, a shop, a hobby. It doesn't matter much what the theme is, but the pages should be unified around it.
- **Consistent design:** The site should have a unified color scheme. All pages should have the same (or similar) layout, and the font choices and images should all use a similar style.
- **A navigation scheme:** Users must have a clear method to move around from page to page. The organization of the pages and their relationships should be clear.
- **A common address:** Normally, all pages in a site are on the same server and have a common DNS name so that they're easy to distinguish.

Obviously, the skills of Web design are critical to building a Web site, but another, broader skill set is required when creating something larger than individual pages.

If you're starting to build a more complicated Web site, you need to have a plan, or else you won't succeed. This plan is even more important if you're building a site for somebody else.

Planning a Larger Site

Here are some questions you need to ask yourself when designing a larger Web site:

- **What's the point of the site?** The site doesn't have to be serious, but it does have to have a theme. If you don't know what your site is about, neither do your users (and they'll leave in a hurry).
- **Who am I talking to?** Web sites are a form of communication, and you can't communicate well if you don't understand your audience. Who is the primary target audience for this site?
- **Which resources do I have available?** Resources involve a lot more than money (but it helps). How much time do you have? Do you have access to a solid technical framework? Can you get help if you need it? Do you have all the copy and raw materials?
- **What am I trying to say?** Believe it or not, this question often poses a huge problem. Somebody says, "I need a Web site." When you ask what she wants on the site, she says, "Oh, lots of things." When you try to pin down the answers, though, people often don't know *what* they want their Web site to say.
- **What are the visual design constraints?** If you're building a page for a small business, it probably already has some kind of visual identity (through brochures or signage, for example). The business owner often wants you to stick within the company's current branding, which may involve negotiation with graphic artists or advertisers the business has worked with.
- **Where will I put this thing?** Does the client already have a domain name? Will moving the domain name cause a problem? Does content that's already on the Web need to be moved? Do you already have hosting space and a DNS name in mind?

Understanding the Client

Often, a larger site is created at the behest of somebody else. Even if you're making a site for your own purposes, you should consider yourself a client.

If the project is going to be successful, you need to know a few things about the client, as described in the following sections.

Ensuring that the client's expectations are clear

The short answer to the question of whether a client's expectations are clear is "Not usually."

A client who truly understands the Internet and knows what it takes to realize her vision for the site probably doesn't need you. Most of the time, a client's own concepts of what should happen on the site are vague, at best. Here are some introductory questions you can ask to get a sense of your client's expectations:

- **What are you trying to say with this site?** If the Web site has a single message that can be boiled down to one phrase or sentence, find out what that message is.
- **Who are you trying to reach with this site?** Determine who the client expects to be the typical users of the site. Find out whether she expects others and whether the site has more than one potential type of user. (For example, customers and employees may need different things.)
- **What problem is this site trying to solve?** Sometimes, a Web site is envisioned as a solution to a particular problem (getting the schedule online or keeping an online newsletter updated, for example).
- **What kind of design framework is already in place?** Determine whether the organization already has some sort of branding and design strategy or whether you have freedom in this arena.
- **What is the time constraint?** Find out how quickly the client needs the site completed. Does the client want the entire project at one time, or can it be phased in?
- **Do you already have a technical framework in place?** Determine whether the project needs to work with an existing database, Web server, Web site, or domain name and whether you have complete access to those resources.
- **Are there security concerns?** First ask whether you will be asked to post data (personal information, credit card numbers, or Social Security numbers, for example) on the Internet that shouldn't be there. Run from any project that requires you to work with this potentially dangerous data, unless you're extremely comfortable with security measures.
- **How will you get the copy?** Any professional Web developer can tell you that the client usually promises to make the copy available immediately but rarely delivers it without a lot of pleading. If the content is available, it's often incomplete or incorrect. You need to have some plan

for getting the material from the client, or else you cannot proceed past a certain point.

- **Does the client have a remuneration strategy?** If you will be paid for your work, find out how you will be paid and whether it's hourly or by the project. If you have a business arrangement, treat it as such and write out a contract. Even if the page is written for free for a friend, a written contract is a good idea because you don't want to ruin a friendship over something as silly as a Web site.

Delineating the tasks

Building a Web site can involve a lot of different tasks. Your contract should indicate which of these tasks is expected. This list describes the potential scope of the project:

- **Site layout:** Determine which pages the site has and how they're connected to each other.
- **XHTML coding:** Some projects simply require XHTML coding and CSS. Presumably, the copy has already been provided, and you simply need to convert it to XHTML format. This work isn't difficult, but it's tedious. Use a text editor with macro capability — after you create an XHTML template.
- **XHTML template design:** Devise an overall page design. The content isn't important here, but the general page design is the issue. This task requires sample data and an editor. It's normally done in conjunction with CSS templating.
- **CSS design:** After you have an XHTML template or two (so that you know the logical structure of the pages), you can work on the visual design. Start with sketches on paper and maybe images from a paint program. After you have a layout approved, write the CSS to implement it.
- **Data design:** If the project will have a database component, take some time to analyze (and, often, rebuild) the data structure to follow the normalization rules. Data work is difficult because it doesn't have a visual result, yet it's critical to the overall site. This step is usually put off until the end, and that decision often dooms Web projects. If you need data design, start it early.
- **Data implementation:** If the project has a data component, write and test the SQL code to build the database, including tables, views, and sample queries. You need time to write PHP code to connect the database to the XHTML front end.
- **Site integration and implementation:** It takes some effort to fit all the pieces back together and make them work. Usually, this process is ongoing. The site needs to be set up on a production server and then tested and launched.

✦ **Testing:** Testing your work with live users is critical. You can use formal usability studies, but failing that, you still learn a lot by asking people to use your system and watching them do it (with your mouth shut). This method is the best way to see whether your assumptions are correct and the site is doing what it needs to do.

Understanding the Audience

Understanding your audience is one of the trickiest parts of Web planning. You need to anticipate the audience in a number of ways, as described in the following sections.

Determining whom you want to reach

Before you make a lot of design decisions, you need to think carefully about the type of person you're trying to reach in the Web site.

Try to anticipate the mindset that people have when they use a particular site. For example, one of my students simultaneously worked on two sites: one for a graduate program at a university and another for a spa and salon. She had to think quite differently about the users of the two sites, which had implications for how she approached each step of the process.

The graduate program page was part of a Web site for a university. The university already had its own style and branding guidelines, official colors, and a number of (evolving) standards. The potential users of this site were graduate students seeking online degrees. The focus of this site was all business. People were there to learn about the graduate program and set up their schedules. They wanted information about classes, instructors, and schedules, but they didn't want anything that interfered with the problem at hand. The writing was efficient and official, the color scheme was standard, and the layout was also official.

The spa and salon page had an entirely different feel. The owner loves design and spent long hours picking exactly the right paint color for the walls in the physical space. She's really happy with her brochure, and although she's not sure exactly what she wants, she knows when something isn't right. She wants to give her customers information about the salon, but more importantly, she wants them to get a sense of how invigorating, relaxing, and feminine the experience of visiting her salon can be. The salon now has a site that was hastily created by somebody's cousin.

These two sites, although they require the same general technical skills, demand vastly different visual and technical designs because the clients and their users are vastly different.

Ironically, one person could simultaneously be a graduate student and a patron of the salon, but the same person would still have a different identity in these different sites. If you're going to a university site, you're in a student mindset, and you want quick, reliable information. After you sign up for classes, if you're looking for a salon, you want to be pampered.

Web sites are experiences. The design of the site should reflect the experience you're trying to give the user when he visits your site.

Finding out the user's level of technical expertise

Understanding the user isn't just an exercise in psychology. You also need to estimate the users' technical proficiency because it can have a major impact on your site. Consider these issues for the typical user:

✦ **Whether the user has broadband access:** University students, hard-core gamers, and Web developers often have high-speed Internet access, so they don't mind a page with lots of video, multimedia assets, and large file sizes. (In fact, they may *expect* a page like this.) Lots of people still use dialup connections. If your audience has slower connections, every image creates a delay. Audio and video assets are completely unavailable to this group — and even make your site unattractive to them.

✦ **Whether the user has a recent browser:** You have no way to predict which browser a user has, but think about whether your target audience has a reason to install any of the current browsers. By and large, grandmothers use whichever browsers were on their machines when they purchased them. (I do know some L337 H@XX0R grandmas, however.) If most people in your audience are still using the AOL browser — believe it or not, it's still used a lot — using advanced CSS and JavaScript tricks on your page may not be the best choice.

✦ **Whether the user has a recent computer:** As technical people, we tend to assume that everyone else keeps up-to-date on technology. That's not necessarily an accurate assumption.

✦ **Whether the user has certain proficiencies:** If you include a Flash animation, for example, the user might not have the right version of Flash installed. You have to decide whether it's reasonable to expect the user to install a plugin.

This process isn't about stereotyping, but you *must* consider the user as you're building a site. You want to match users' expectations and capabilities, if possible.

Of course, you're making assumptions here, and you may well be wrong. I once did some work for a club for retired faculty members, and I based my expectations on their being retired. I should have based my assumptions on their being professors. And they let me have it! Be willing to adjust your expectations after you meet real users. (For professional work, you *must* meet and watch real users use your site.)

Building a Site Plan

Often, the initial work on a major site involves creating a plan for the site design. I like to do this step early because it helps me see the true scope of the project. A *site plan* is an overview of a Web site. Normally, it's drawn as a hierarchy chart.

I was asked to help design a Web site for an academic department at a major university. The first question I asked was, "What do you want on the Web site?" I wrote down everything on a whiteboard, with no thought of organization. Figure 2-1 shows a (cleaned-up) version of that sketch.

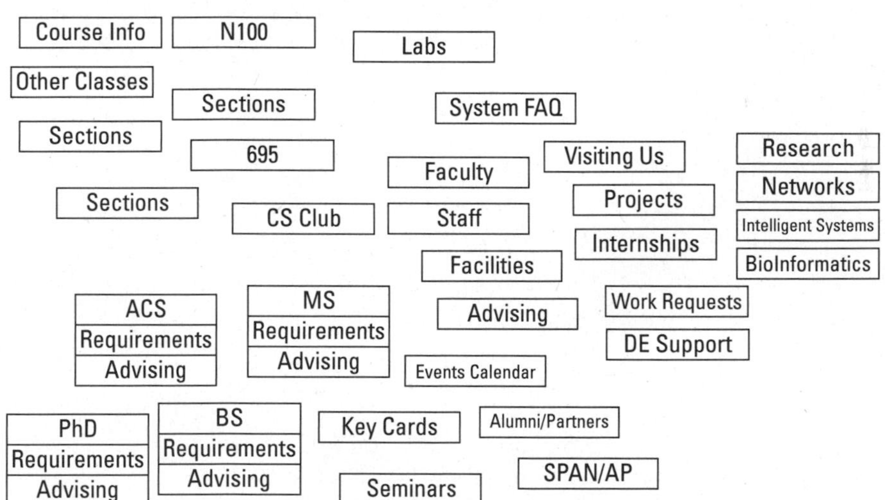

Figure 2-1: We need a lot of stuff on this site. Good grief!

For all the sketches in this chapter, I used *Dia,* the open-source drawing tool. An excellent tool for this kind of work, it's included on the CD-ROM so that you can play with it.

After all participants suggested everything they thought their site needed, I shooed them out of the room. Using only paper and pencil, I created a more organized sketch based on how *I* thought the information should be organized. My diagram looked like the one shown in Figure 2-2.

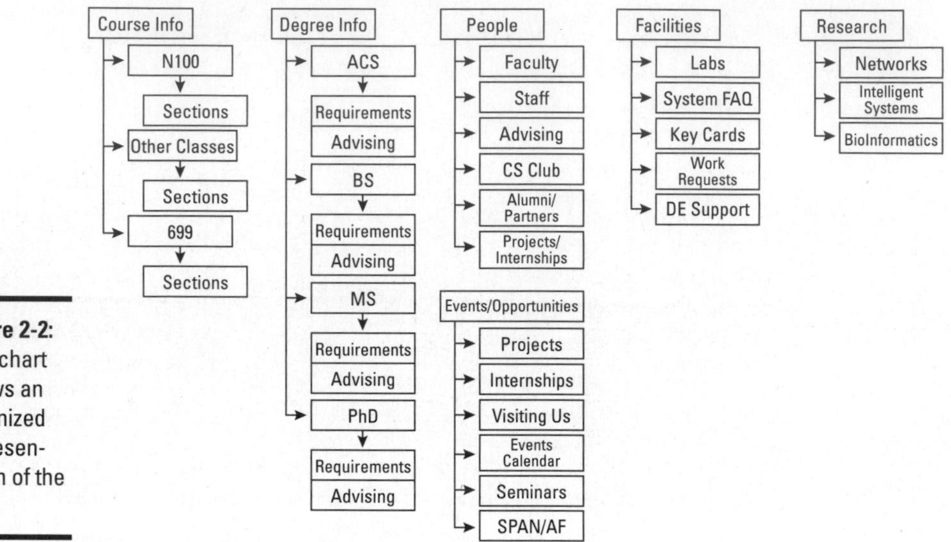

Figure 2-2: This chart shows an organized representation of the data.

Creating a site overview

Keep these suggestions in mind while creating a site overview diagram:

- **Use the Law of Seven.** This law suggests that people generally can't handle more than seven choices at a time. Try not to have more than seven major segments of information at any level. Each of these can be separated into as many as seven chunks, and each of these can have seven chunks.

  Note: Even this book uses the Law of Seven! (Well, sorta — this book has eight minibooks.) The monster you're holding is too intimidating to look at as just one book, but if you break it into smaller segments, it becomes easier to manage. Clever, huh?

- **Identify commonalities.** As you look over the data, general groupings emerge. In the university example, I could easily see that we had a lot of course data, degree information, information about faculty, and research. I wanted to consider a few other topics that didn't fit as well, until I realized that they could be grouped as events and opportunities.

- **Try to assign each topic to a group.** If you read Book VI already, you probably recognize that I'm doing a form of *data normalization* here. This data structure isn't necessarily a formal one, but I'm using the same sort of thinking, so it could be. Clearly, I'm using the principle of functional dependency.

- **Arrange a hierarchy.** Group the topics from most general to most specific. For example, the term *course info* is very broad. N100 is a specific course, and it may have many sections (specific date, time, and instructor combinations). Thus, it makes sense to group sections under N100 and to group N100 under courses.
- **Provide representative data.** Not every single scrap of information is necessary here. The point is to have enough data so you can see the relationships among data.
- **Keep in mind that this diagram does *not* represent the site design.** When I showed this diagram to people, many assumed that I was setting up a menu structure, and they wanted a different kind of organization or menu. That's not the point yet. The purpose of this type of diagram is to see how the data itself fits together. Of course, it usually turns out to reflect the page setup and the menu structure, but it doesn't have to.
- **Not each box is a page.** It might be, but it doesn't have to be. Later in the process, you can decide how to organize the parts of the site. For example, we decided to put all sections of N100 on one page with the N100 information using AJAX.

Building this sort of site diagram is absolutely critical for larger sites, or else you never really grasp the scope of the project. Have the major stakeholders look it over to see whether it accurately reflects the *information* you're trying to convey.

Building the site diagram

The site diagram is a more specific version of the site overview. At this point, you make a commitment about the particular pages you want in the system and their organizational relationship. Figure 2-3 shows a site diagram for the department site.

The site diagram is a bit different from the overview, for these reasons:

- **Each box represents a page.** Now, you have to make some decisions about how the pages are organized. Determine at which level of the overview you have separate pages. For example, are all the course sections on one page, or all the sections of N100? Does each section of each course have a different page? These decisions will help you determine which technologies to use in constructing the page.
- **The site diagram still doesn't need every single page.** If you have 30 classes, you still don't need to account for each one, as long as you know where they go and that they all have the same general purpose and design.

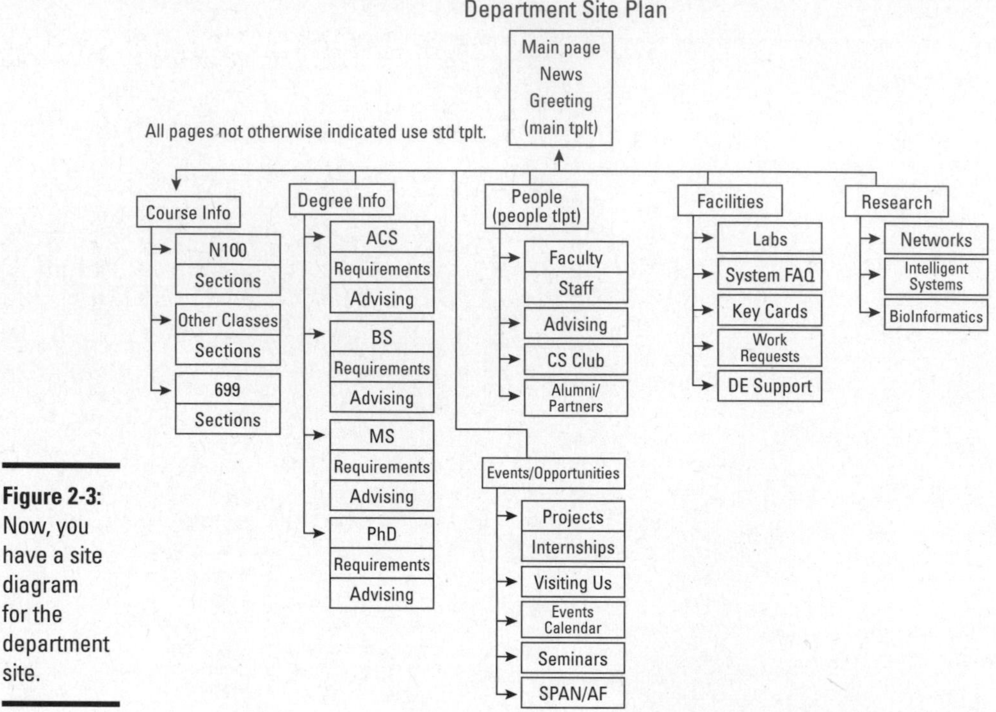

Figure 2-3: Now, you have a site diagram for the department site.

- ✦ **The navigation structure should be clear.** The hierarchy should give you a clear navigation structure. (Of course, you can, and often should, add a secondary navigation structure. See the sidebar "Semantic navigation.")
- ✦ **Name each box.** Each page should have a name. These box names translate to page titles and help you form a unified title system. This arrangement is useful for your navigation scheme.
- ✦ **Identify overall layout for each box.** Generally, a site uses only a few layouts. You have a standard layout for most pages. Often, the front page has a different layout (for news and navigation information). You may have specialty layouts, as well. For example, the faculty pages all have a specific layout with a prominent image. Don't plan the layout here — just identify it.
- ✦ **Sort out the order.** If the order of the pages matters, the site diagram is the place to work it out. For example, I organized the degrees from undergraduate to PhD programs.

Semantic navigation

One idea that has been popular in Web design circles is the notion of *semantic navigation,* where you set up your menu structure so that it reflects the jobs people are trying to do, rather than reflect the hierarchy of your sites.

This idea is a good one that can be quite helpful if done properly, but don't try to set up your entire site this way because it involves too much duplication of data. Instead, set up your site in a normalized way, and then put another menu system on your site that allows users to choose the section of the site they want based on problems they're trying to solve. Then, you create the best of both worlds.

The goal for this part of the site-planning process is to have a clear understanding of what each page requires. This information should make it easy for you to complete the data and visual design steps. The site diagram is an absolutely critical document. After you have it approved, print it and tape it to your monitor.

Creating Page Templates

If you've developed a site diagram, you should have a good feel for the overall requirements of the Web development project. You should know how many layouts you need and the general requirements for each one. Your next task is to think about the visual design. Here are some guidelines:

- **Get help if you need it.** Visual design is a skill that requires insight and experience. If you "design like a programmer" (I sure do!), don't be afraid to get help from a person who has design sensibility. You still need to translate the design into code, however.
- **Identify unifying design goals.** All pages on the site have certain characteristics in common. Find out the overall color scheme, whether you will have a logo, and whether all pages will have the same header and retain the same fonts throughout.
- **Identify a primary layout.** Generally, a Web site requires one major layout that's repeated throughout the site. Often, the main page does not use this primary layout, but most internal pages do. Determine, for example, which broad design elements can be shared by most of the pages, whether every page has a headline, whether you need columns, and how important images are.
- **Identify specialty designs.** The main page is often a bit different from the other pages because it serves as an overview to the site. Likewise, if you have a certain kind of page that will be repeated (the course pages and faculty pages in my university example), you have to know how

these designs differ from the primary layout. Keep design elements as consistent as you can because unity makes your job easier and ties the site pages together.

Sketching the page design

Do not write even a single line of code before sketching out some design ideas. Figure 2-4 shows a page sketch for my sample site.

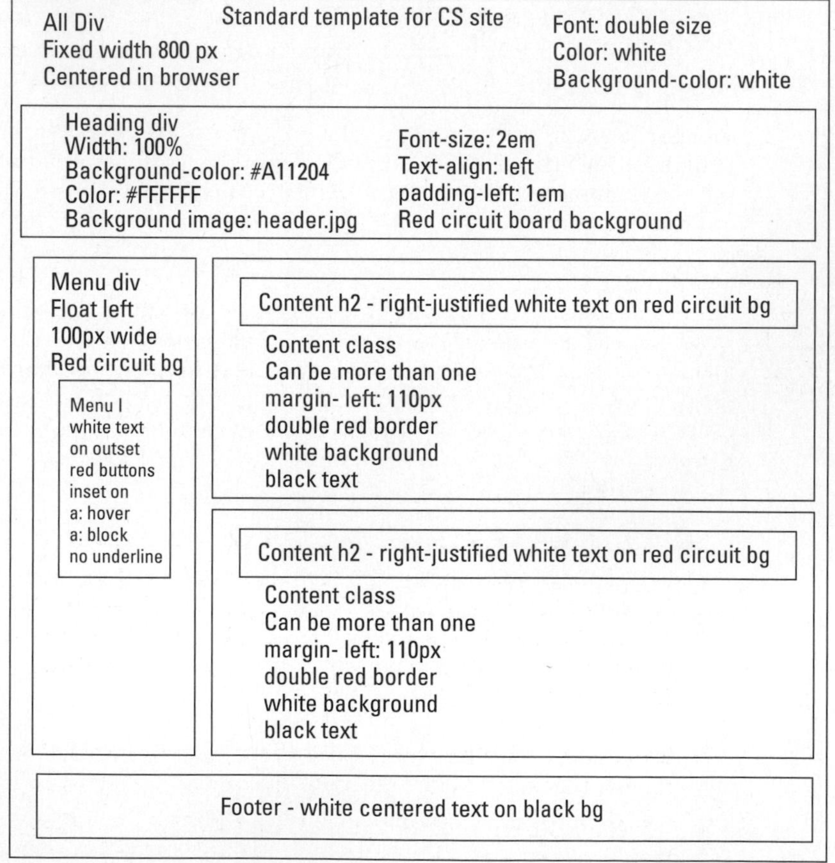

Figure 2-4: Here's a sample sketch for the standard template on this site.

Your page sketch gives you enough information to create XHTML and CSS code. It needs to start showing some detail, such as the following details:

✦ **Draw out each element on the page.** Any major page element (headlines, menus, columns) must be delineated.

- **Include the class or ID identifier for each element.** If you have a segment that will be used as a menu, name it "menu," for example. If you have a content area, identify that name now. Write all names directly on the diagram so that you're clear about what belongs where.
- **Include all relevant style information.** Describe every font, the width of every element (including measurement units), the foreground and background colors (with hex codes), the background images (including sizes), and anything else you might need in order to code CSS styles for the page.
- **Build a page sketch following these guidelines for each page template in your site.** If you have three page designs, for example, you need three separate diagrams.

These diagrams are finished only if they give you everything you need to build the XHTML and CSS templates. The idea is to do all your design work on paper and then implement and tweak your project with code. If you plan well, the coding is easy.

The design sketch isn't a page mock-up. It's not meant to look exactly like the page. Instead, it's a sketch that explains with text all the various details you need to code in XHTML and CSS. Often, designers produce beautiful mock-ups that aren't helpful in development because you need to know sizes and colors, for example. If you want to produce a mock-up, by all means do so, but also make a design sketch that includes things like actual font names and hex color codes so that you can re-create the mock-up with live code.

Building the XHTML template framework

With a page layout in place, you can finally start writing some code. Begin with your standard page layout diagram and create an XHTML template to implement the diagram in working code. The XML template is quite simple because most of the design should happen in the CSS. Keep these guidelines in mind:

- **Remember that the template is simply a framework.** The XHTML is mainly blank. It's meant to be duplicated and filled in with live data.
- **It has a reference to the style sheet.** External CSS is critical for large Web projects because many pages refer to the same style sheet. Make a reference to the style sheet, even though it may not actually exist yet.
- **Include all necessary elements.** The elements themselves can be blank, but if your page needs a list for a menu, add an empty list. If you need a content div, put it in place.
- **Create a prototype from the template.** You use the template quite a bit, but you need sample data in order to test the CSS. Build a prototype page that contains typical data. The amount of data should be typical of the actual site so that you can anticipate formatting problems.

It's very possible that you'll never manually put code in your template. There are several options for automating this process, which can be found in Chapter 4 of this minibook.

The XHTML template should be easy to construct because everything you need is in the page template diagram. Figure 2-5 shows an XHTML prototype.

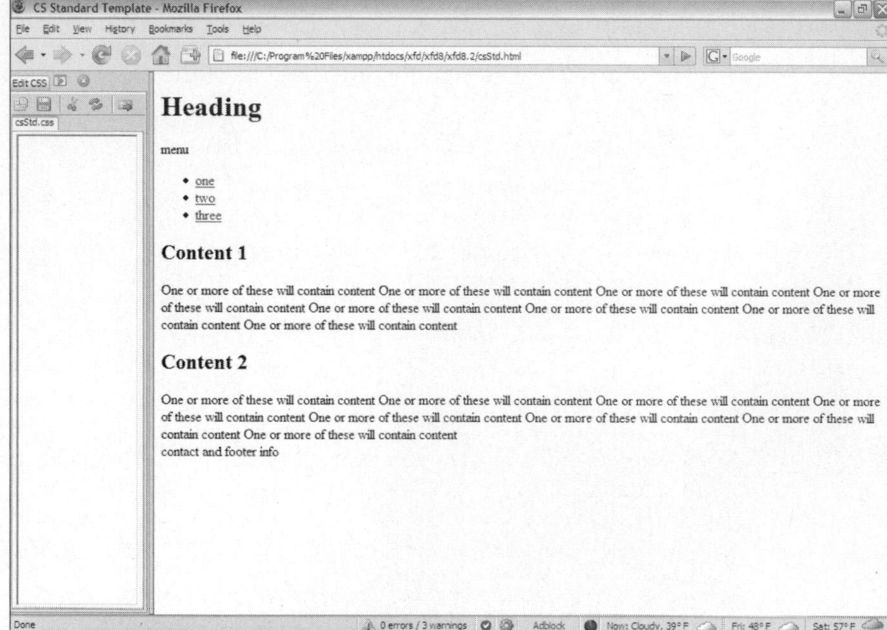

Figure 2-5: An XHTML prototype for my site (with no CSS attached yet).

Here's the XHTML code for my prototype:

```
<!DOCTYPE html PUBLIC "-//W3C//DTD XHTML 1.0 Strict//EN"
"http://www.w3.org/TR/xhtml1/DTD/xhtml1-strict.dtd">
<html lang="EN" dir="ltr" xmlns="http://www.w3.org/1999/xhtml">
  <head>
    <meta http-equiv="content-type" content="text/xml; charset=utf-8" />
    <title>CS Standard Template</title>
    <link rel = "stylesheet"
          type = "text/css"
          href = "csStd.css" />
  </head>

  <body>
    <div id = "all">
      <!-- This div centers a fixed-width layout -->
      <div id = "heading">
        <h1>Heading</h1>
      </div><!-- end heading div -->
```

```
      <div id = "menu">
        menu
        <ul>
          <li><a href = "">one</a></li>
          <li><a href = "">two</a></li>
          <li><a href = "">three</a></li>
        </ul>
      </div> <!-- end menu div -->

      <div class = "content">
        <h2>Content 1</h2>
        One or more of these will contain content
        One or more of these will contain content
        One or more of these will contain content
        One or more of these will contain content
        One or more of these will contain content
        One or more of these will contain content
        One or more of these will contain content
        One or more of these will contain content
      </div> <!-- end content div -->

      <div class = "content">
        <h2>Content 2</h2>
        One or more of these will contain content
        One or more of these will contain content
        One or more of these will contain content
        One or more of these will contain content
        One or more of these will contain content
        One or more of these will contain content
        One or more of these will contain content
        One or more of these will contain content
      </div> <!-- end content div -->

      <div id = "footer">
        contact and footer info
      </div> <!-- end footer div -->
    </div> <!-- end all div -->
  </body>
</html>
```

People commonly start writing pages at this point, but that's a dangerous idea. Don't use any real data until you're certain of the general XHTML structure. You can always change the style later, but if you create 100 pages and then decide that each of them needs another `<div>` tag, you have to go back and add 100 divs.

Creating page styles

With an XHTML framework in place, you can start working on the CSS. The best way to incorporate CSS is by following these steps:

1. **Begin with the page template diagram.**

   It should have all the information you need.

2. **Load your XHTML prototype into Firefox.**

   Nothing beats Firefox with the Web Developer CSS editor for CSS design because it lets you see your changes in real time. Honestly, you can use any browser you wish, but if you use another browser, you'll need to create the CSS file in a text editor and check it frequently in the browser. (Check Books II and III to see how FireFox and Web Developer simplify this task.)

3. **Implement the CSS from your diagram.**

   You should be *implementing* the design you already created, not *designing* the page. (That already happened in the diagramming process.)

4. **Save the design.**

   If you're using the Web Developer CSS editor, you can save your CSS directly into a file. If your XHTML template had an external style definition, this is the default save file. If you're editing CSS in a text editor, save it in the normal way so the browser will be able to read it. (See Book II for information on implementing external style sheets.)

5. **Test and tweak.**

   Things are never quite what they seem with CSS because browsers don't conform to standards equally. You need to test and tweak on other browsers, and you probably have to write a secondary style for IE exceptions.

6. **Repeat for other templates.**

   Repeat this process for each of the other templates you identified in your site diagram.

The result of this process should be a number of CSS files that you can readily reuse across your site.

Here's the CSS code for my primary page:

```
body {
  background-color: #000000;
}

#all {
  background-color: white;
  border: 1px solid black;
  width: 800px;
  margin-top:2em;
  margin-left: auto;
  margin-right: auto;
  min-height: 600px;
}

#heading {
  background-color: #A11204;
  color: #FFFFFF;
```

```
  height: 100px;
  font-size: 2em;
  padding-left: 1em;
  border-bottom: 3px solid black;
  margin-top: -1.5em;
}

#menu {
  background-color: #A11204;
  color: #FFFFFF;
  float: left;
  width: 100px;
  min-height: 500px;
}

#menu li {
  list-style-type: none;
  margin-left: -2em;
  margin-right: .5em;
  text-align: center;
}

#menu a {
  color: #FFFFFF;
  display: block;
  border: #A11204 3px outset;
  text-decoration: none;
}
#menu a:hover {
  border: #A11204 3px inset;
}

.content {
  border: 3px double #A11204;
  margin: 1em;
  margin-left: 110px;
  padding-left: 1em;
  padding-bottom: 1em;
  padding-right: 1em;
}

.content h2 {
  background-color: #A11204;
  color: #FFFFFF;
  text-align: right;
}

#footer {
  color: #FFFFFF;
  background-color: #000000;
  border: 1px solid #A11204;
  float: left;
  clear: both;
  width: 100%;
  text-align: center;
}
```

Figure 2-6 shows the standard template with the CSS attached.

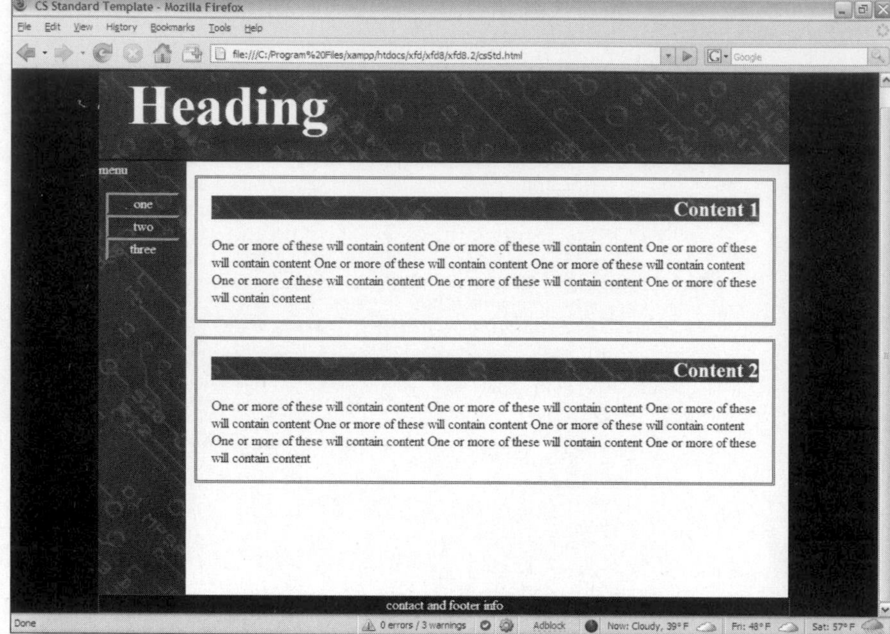

Figure 2-6: The XHTML template looks good with the CSS attached.

Building a data framework

The examples throughout this chapter assumed that a large Web project can be done in straight XHTML and CSS. That's always a good starting point, but if your program needs data or interactivity, you probably have a data back end.

Most data-enabled site plans fail.

The reason is almost always that the data normalization wasn't incorporated into the plan early enough, and the other parts of the project inevitably depend on a well-planned data back end.

If you suspect your project will involve a database, you should follow these steps early in the process (during the early site-planning phase):

1. **Identify the true data problem to be solved.**

   Data gets complicated in a hurry. Determine why exactly you need the data on the site. Keep the data as simple as you can, or else you'll become overwhelmed.

2. **Identify data requirements in your site diagram.**

   Find out where on the site diagram you're getting data. Determine which data you're retrieving and record this information on the site diagram.

3. **Create a third normal form ER diagram.**

   Don't bother building a database until you're sure that you can create an ER diagram in third normal form. Check Book VI, Chapter 3 for details on this process.

4. **Implement the data structure.**

   Create an SQL script that creates all the necessary data structures (including tables and views) and includes sample data.

5. **Create PHP middleware.**

   After the database is in place, you usually need PHP code to take requests, pass them to the database, and return the results. Most of the PHP code for the main site consists of simple queries from the database. If you can use AJAX or SSI, it simplifies the process because your PHP code doesn't have to create entire pages — it simply creates snippets of code.

   See Chapter 4 of this minibook for help on implementing these technologies.

6. **Consider update capabilities.**

   Usually, when you have a database, you need another part of the site to allow the client to update information. It's often an administrative site with password access. An administrative site is much more complex than the main site because it requires the ability to add, edit, and update records.

Fleshing Out the Project

If you completed all the steps in the preceding section, it becomes relatively easy to create the page: It's simply a matter of forming the copy into the templates you created, tying it all together, and launching on the site.

Making the site live

Typically, you do the primary development on a server that isn't in public view. Follow these steps to take the site to production:

1. **Test your design.**

   Do some usability testing with real users. Watch people solve typical problems on the site and see what problems they encounter.

2. **Proofread everything.**

   Almost nothing demolishes credibility as quickly as sloppy writing. Get a quality proofreader or copy editor to look over everything on the site to check for typos and spelling errors. Have another expert check the site for factual or content errors.

3. **Prepare the online hosting environment.**

   Be sure that you have the server space to handle your requirements. Make a copy of your database and test it. Check the domain name to be sure that you have no legal encumbrances.

4. **Move your site online.**

   Move the files from your development server to the main server.

5. **Test everything again.**

   Try a *beta* test, where your page is available to only a few people. Get input and feedback from these testers and incorporate the best suggestions.

6. **Take a vacation. You earned it!**

Contemplating efficiency

As you start working with the site, you'll probably encounter repeated code. For example, each page may have exactly the same title bar. You obviously don't want to write exactly the same code for 100 different pages because it might change, and you don't want to make the change in 100 different places. You have three major options in this case:

- **Use AJAX to import the repeated code.** Follow the AJAX instructions in Chapter 4 of this minibook to import your header (or other repeated code).
- **Use Server-Side Includes (SSI) to import code on the server.** If your server allows it, you can use the SSI technology to import pages on the server without using a language like PHP. SSI is explained in Chapter 4 of this minibook.
- **Build the pages with PHP.** Put all segments in separate files and use a PHP script to tie them together. When you do this, you're creating a content management system, which is the topic of Chapters 3 and 4 of this minibook.

Chapter 3: Introducing Content Management Systems

In This Chapter

- Understanding the need for content management systems
- Previewing typical content management systems
- Installing a content management system
- Adding content to a content management system
- Setting up the navigation structure
- Adding new types of content
- Changing the appearance with themes

If you've ever built a large Web site, you'll probably agree that the process can be improved. Experienced Web developers have discovered the following maxims about larger projects:

- **Duplication should be eliminated whenever possible.** If you find yourself repeatedly copying the same XHTML code, you have a potential problem. When (not if) that code needs to be changed, you have a lot of copying and pasting to do.
- **Content should be separated from layout.** You've already heard this statement, but it's taken to a new level when you're building a large site. Separating *all* content from the layout would be helpful so that you could create the layout only one time and change it in only one place.
- **Content is really data.** At some point, the content of the Web site is really just data. It's important data, to be sure, but the data can — and should — be separated from the layout code, and should be, if possible.
- **Content belongs to the user.** Developing a Web site for somebody can become a long-term commitment. If the client becomes dependent on the site, he frequently pesters you for changes. It would be helpful if the client could change his own content and ask you only for changes in structure or behavior.
- **A Web site isn't a collection of pages — it's a framework.** If you can help the client own the data, you're more concerned with the framework for manipulating and displaying that data. It's a good deal for you and the client.

A content management system (CMS) is designed to address exactly these issues, as this chapter will show you.

Overview of Content Management Systems

CMSs are used in many of the sites you use every day. As you examine these CMSs, you start to recognize them all over the Web. If you have your own server space, a little patience, and a little bit of knowledge, you can create your own professional-looking site using a CMS.

This list describes the general characteristics of a CMS:

- **It's written in a server-side language.** The language is usually PHP, but CMSs are sometimes written in other languages. Stick with PHP for now because it's described in this book, it's easy to use, and it's the most frequently used CMS language.
- **All content is treated as data.** Almost all the content of the CMS is stored in text files or (more commonly) a MySQL database. A CMS usually has few HTML files.
- **The layout consists of data, too.** The CSS and XHTML templates, and everything else the CMS needs, are also stored as data, in either text files or the database.
- **All pages are created dynamically.** When a user logs in to a CMS, she is normally talking to a PHP program. This program analyzes the current situation and generates an HTML document on the fly.
- **There are different levels of access.** Most CMSs allow anonymous access (like regular Web pages) but also allow users to log in for increased access.
- **The content can be modified from within the system.** Users with the appropriate access can modify the content of the CMS without knowing anything about PHP or databases. Often, you don't even need HTML or CSS.
- **The layout can be often modified from within the system, too.** Most CMSs allow you to change the layout and design from within the system, although the process is usually more involved.
- **CMSs can be expanded.** Most CMSs are easily modified with hundreds of visual themes, add-in modules, and new capabilities available for free. In most cases, if you need something that isn't there, you can make it yourself.
- **Many of the best CMSs are open source.** CMSs are a shocking value. When you consider how much they can contribute to your online presence, it's amazing that most CMS programs are absolutely free.

Previewing Common CMSs

To get a true feel for the power of CMSs, you should test-drive a few. The wonderful resource `www.opensourcecms.com` allows you to log in to hundreds of different CMSs as a user and as an administrator to see how they work. I show you a few typical CMSs so that you can get a feel for how they work.

Moodle

Often, you have a special purpose in mind. For example, I wanted to teach an online course without purchasing an expensive and complicated course management system. I installed the special-purpose CMS Moodle. Figure 3-1 shows the Moodle screen for one of my courses.

Moodle has a lot of features that lend themselves to the educational setting:

- **Student and instructor management:** The system already understands the roles of student and instructor, and makes appropriate parts of the system available.
- **Online assignment creation and submission:** One of the biggest problems with online courseware is getting assignments to and from students. Moodle has a complete system for handling this problem.

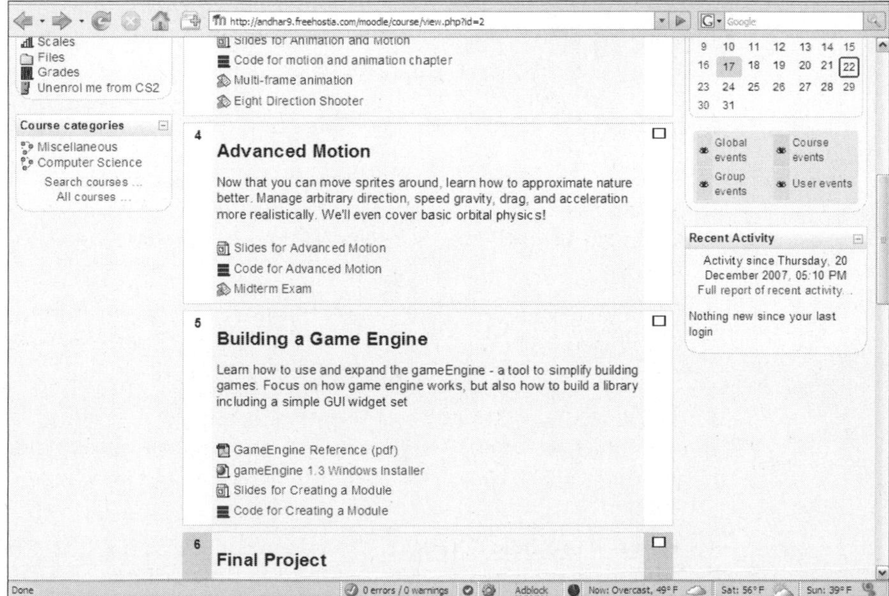

Figure 3-1: Moodle is useful for managing online courses.

- **Online grade book:** When a teacher grades an assignment (online through Moodle), the student's grades are automatically updated.
- **Online testing support:** Moodle has built-in modules for creating, managing, and scoring online quizzes and exams.
- **Communication tools:** Moodle includes a *wiki* (a collaborative documentation tool), online chat, and forum tools you can set up for improved communication with your students.
- **Specialized educational content:** Moodle was put together by hundreds of passionate (and geeky) teachers, so it has all kinds of support for various teaching methodologies.

Community-created software can be very good (as Moodle is) because it's built by people who know exactly what they want, and anybody with an idea (and the skills to carry them out) can add or modify the features. The result is an organic system that can often be better than the commercial offerings.

I personally find Moodle easier to use and more reliable than the commercial course management system that my university uses. I keep a Moodle backup for my classes because, when the "official" system goes down, I can always make something available for my students.

WordPress

WordPress is another specialty CMS, meant primarily for blogging (short for We*b logging,* or keeping an online public diary). WordPress has become the dominant blogging tool on the Internet. Figure 3-2 shows a typical WordPress page.

WordPress takes one simple idea (blogging) and pushes it to the limit. Unregistered users see the blog output, but if you log in, you gain access to a complete set of tools for managing your online musings.

Figure 3-3 illustrates the administrator view of WordPress.

Of course, you can change the layout and colors, add new templates, and do much more, as you would do in a more traditional CMS.

Of course, hundreds of other specialized CMSs are out there. Before you try to build your own CMS from the ground up, take a look at the other available offerings and see whether you can start by using the work of somebody else.

Figure 3-2: Woot! I'm blogging!

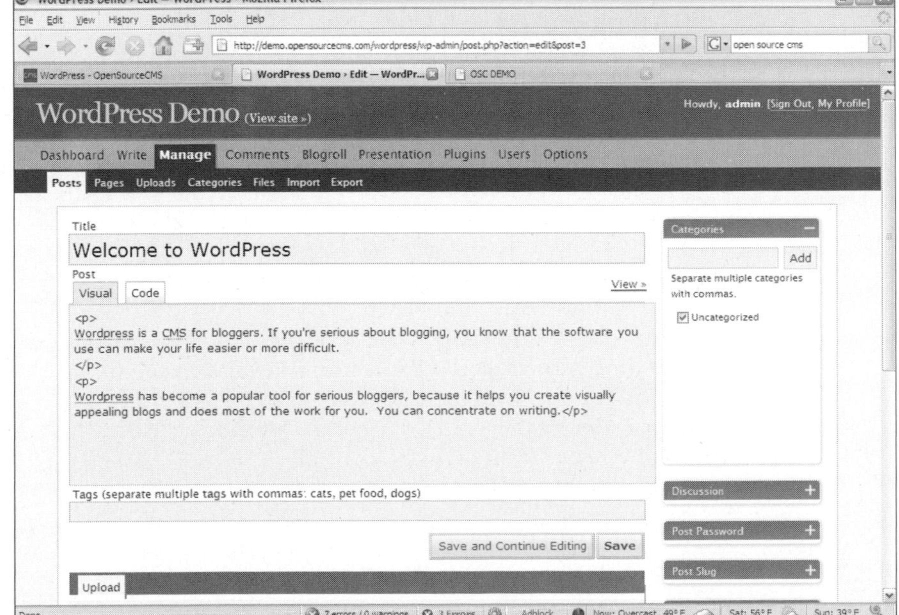

Figure 3-3: You can easily get started with WordPress — just start writing.

Drupal

Drupal is one of the most popular multipurpose CMSs out there. Intended for larger sites, it's more involved than the specialty CMSs — although it can do almost anything.

Figure 3-4 shows a basic site running Drupal.

Drupal is meant to be community Web sites. It is commonly used in the following types of sites:

- ✦ **Gaming sites:** Many game communities are based around a CMS like Drupal because it allows opportunities for users to share information, opinions, news, and files.
- ✦ **Software sites:** A CMS like Drupal is an ideal place to post information about your software, including downloads, documentation, and user support.
- ✦ **Forums:** Although you can find many dedicated forum packages, Drupal supports several good forum sites.
- ✦ **Blogging:** You can also use Drupal as a news site and place to post your blog. You can add community features as you want or need them.

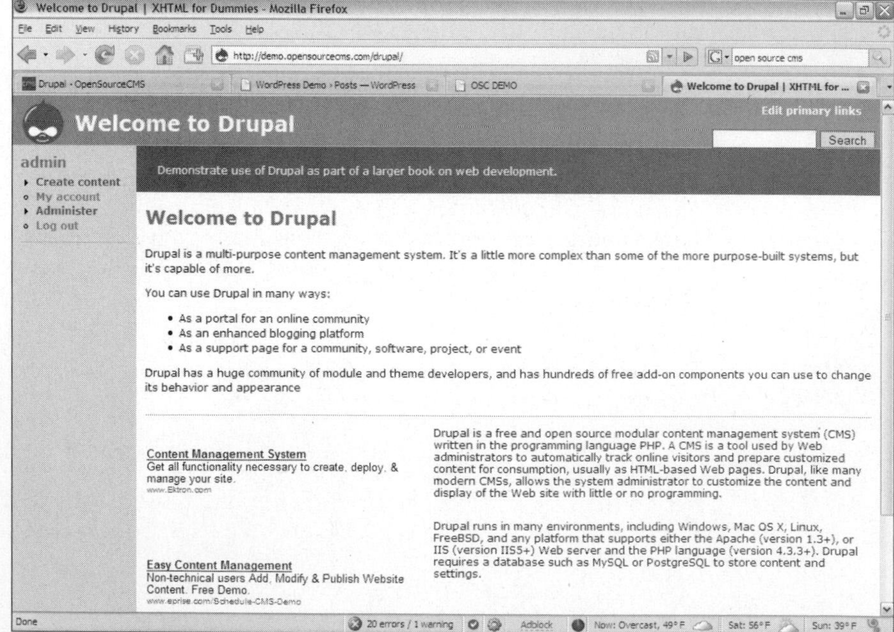

Figure 3-4: Drupal is intended to support online communities.

As you experiment with Drupal (in upcoming sections of this chapter) and look over its themes, you'll probably recognize it or one of its cousins as the foundation of many of your favorite sites.

Installing a Content Management System

Content management systems usually require both PHP and MySQL access. Installing a CMS usually involves following these steps (I'm using Drupal on my localhost as an example, but the concept is much the same for all CMSs):

1. **Download the CMS files.**

   Most CMSs are in plain PHP form, so they're multiplatform. In this example, I use Drupal 5.5, but other versions are similar.

2. **Copy the files to your `htdocs` path.**

   Usually, you need to put the various files in a subdirectory of `htdocs` because the CMS is a Web application. Check for any installation notes that come with the CMS. If it has none, simply drag the entire directory to `htdocs`.

3. **Access the CMS through the server.**

   Use your browser to point to the CMS main page. (Don't forget to use a localhost reference so the program runs through your server.) Normally, if a CMS hasn't yet been initialized, you get some sort of database prompt, like the one shown in Figure 3-5.

4. **Create a MySQL database.**

   CMSs often require a MySQL database. If possible, create a new database for each CMS to avoid table name conflicts. Make a database with a user and password. See Book VI, Chapter 1 for information on creating databases and users. Remember your database name, username, and password. In Figure 3-6, I'm creating a database, user, and password for Drupal.

   It's a common occurrence to create a username and database name that are the same. If you're on a remote server, you may find restrictions on creating the database name.

   If you set up a new user in phpMyAdmin (the Privileges table), you can also have phpMyAdmin set up a database with the same name and assign the new user rights for only that database using the Database for User panel (shown in Figure 3-6). That's exactly what you want to happen.

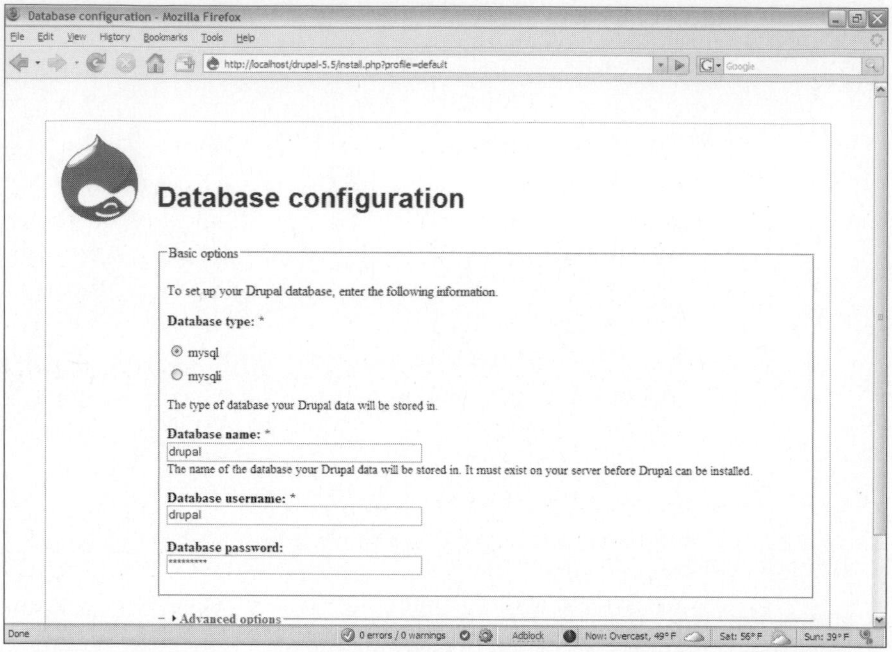

Figure 3-5: The CMS complains if you haven't yet connected to a database.

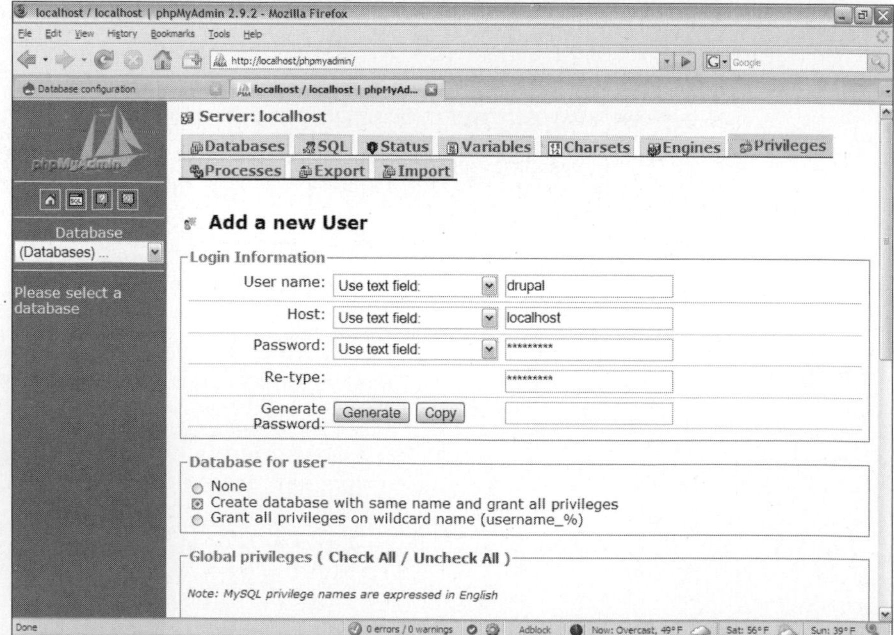

Figure 3-6: Use phpMyAdmin to set up the required database.

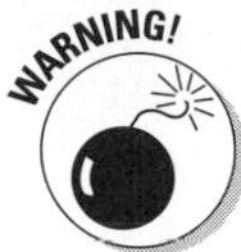

Do not set up a CMS to use the root database user, especially if you haven't set up a root password. The results can be disastrous because anybody using the CMS can potentially destroy all your databases. (That's a bad thing!)

5. **Specify the database, username, and password.**

   Go back to the CMS site and try to run the CMS again. Usually, the installation script logs in to MySQL using the information you provided, and then it runs an SQL script to create all the various tables and joins required by that CMS.

6. **Run the installation script.**

   Normally, the CMS runs a few more magical scripts, creating various files and directories, and changing permissions. You see a welcome screen indicating that the script was run successfully and an invitation to visit your new site, which looks like Figure 3-7.

7. **Create an administrator login.**

   There's usually some way to create an administrative account. The technique for creating an admin account varies from system to system. In Drupal, the first account you create is automatically an admin account. Create a username and password for this account, as shown in Figure 3-8.

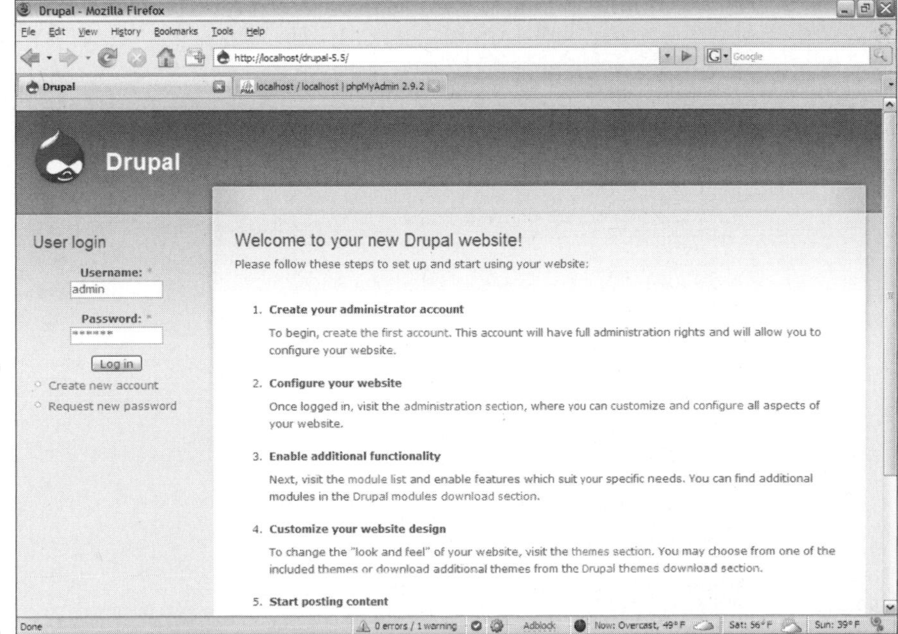

Figure 3-7: Congratulations! You're the proud parent of a bouncing baby CMS!

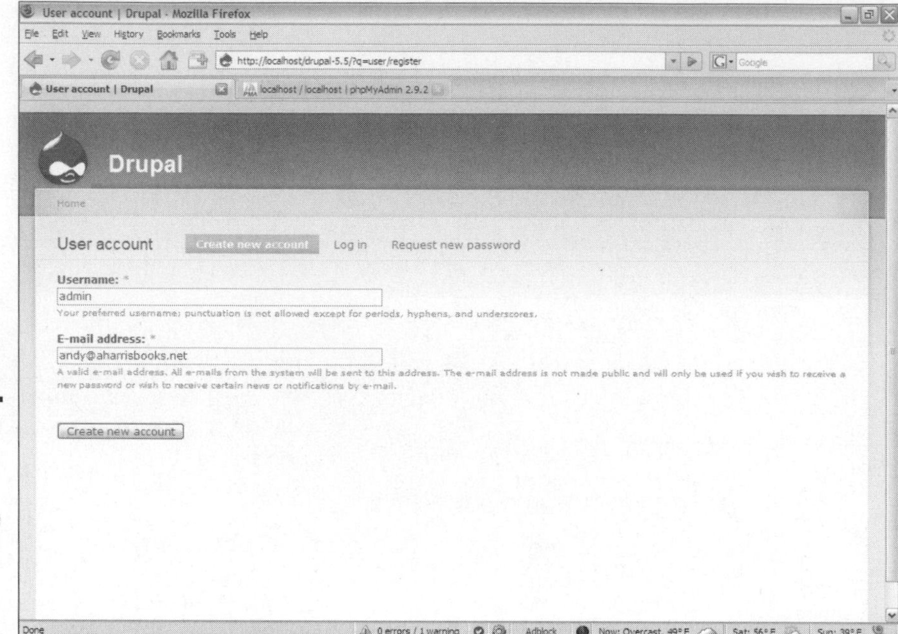

Figure 3-8: CMSs almost always have a special admin account.

The admin login is different from the database login. The database user is used by the CMS. You don't use this (database) account directly, but it's stored in the CMS data. You use the admin account to make changes to the database.

8. **Test the installation.**

   You should be able to test the installation by logging back in to the CMS main directory. This time, rather than see the installation screen, you should see the guest access screen.

Adding content

Before you can do anything interesting with a CMS, you need to dig around to see how things work. Follow these steps to define some structure and add various types of content:

1. **Log in as the administrator.**

   Use your new admin account to log in to the system. You need to be the administrator to change content. Figure 3-9 shows the default screen for Drupal administration.

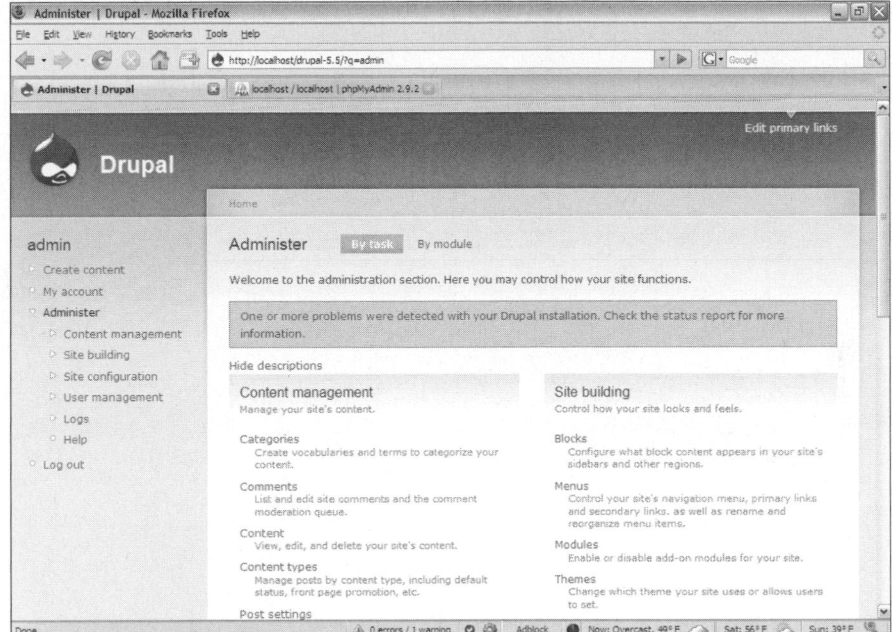

Figure 3-9: The administration screen for Drupal is functional.

In this installation, Drupal lets me know that I didn't configure an e-mail server (a program that sends e-mail) properly. That's because I'm running this test installation on my personal machine, and I'm not running an e-mail server.

2. **Find the "create content" tool.**

   Most CMSs have a tool that allows you to create content. In Drupal, it's the Create Content link, which is available if you log in as administrator. Clicking this link displays a screen like the one shown in Figure 3-10.

3. **Create a new page by choosing Page from the simple menu shown in Figure 3-10.**

   Drupal offers hundreds of types of content, but the two main ones are stories and pages. Begin by making a new page. You see a page like the one shown in Figure 3-11.

Note that you're allowed to use XHTML tags in your pages. Different CMSs have different rules about how much control you have over content. Drupal lets you choose how much control you want to have, from automatically creating all XHTML code for you to allowing you to write the code by hand.

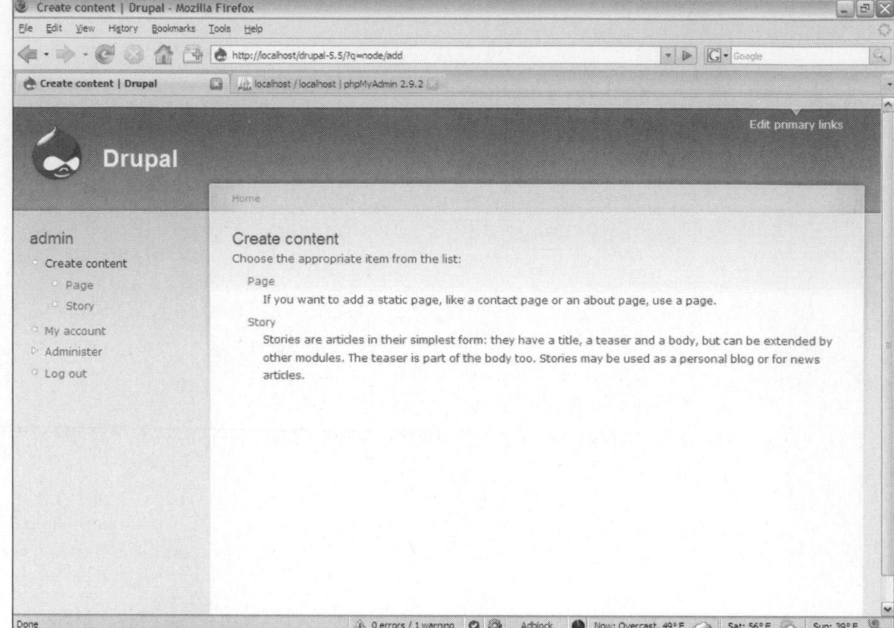

Figure 3-10: Building content is a big part of using a CMS.

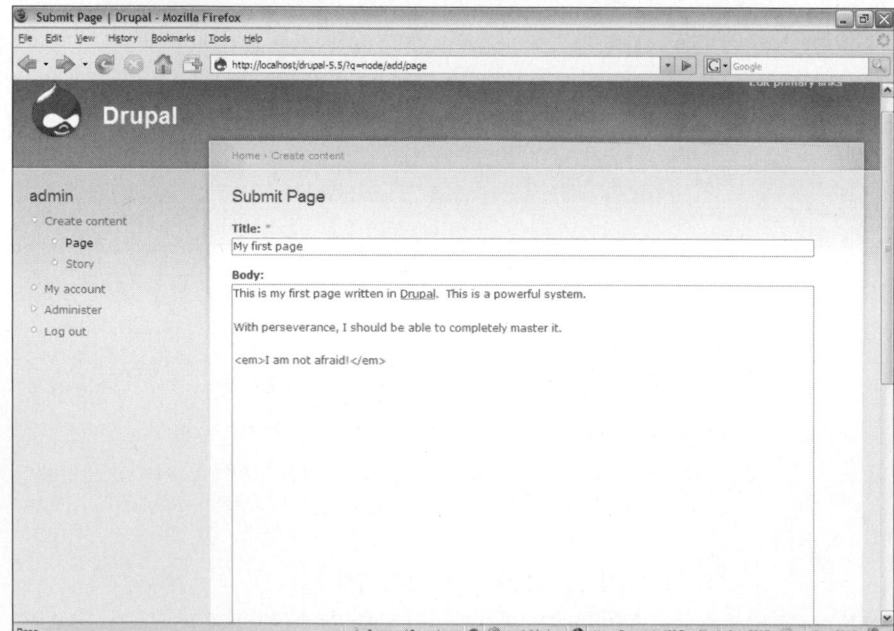

Figure 3-11: The page editor is the mainstay of all CMS work.

4. Submit the page.

Use the Submit button to commit this page to the database. At this point, it has been created, but you want it to be the new front page when someone enters the system.

5. Promote your page.

Click the Administration – Content Management link to see various options for pages. This page looks like Figure 3-12.

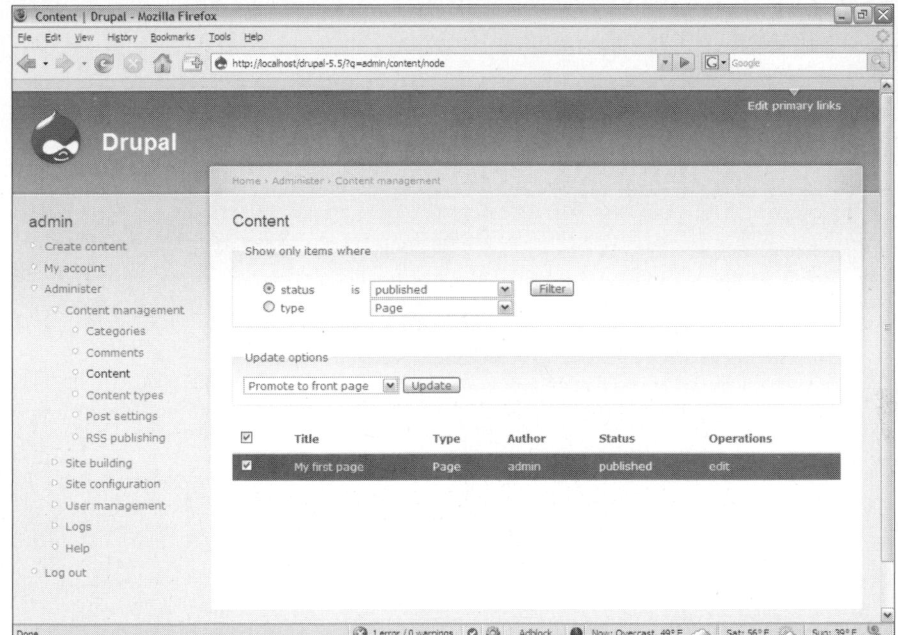

Figure 3-12: You have to specify a page as the front page in Drupal.

Find the Content link and select it to see a page like the one shown in Figure 3-12. Select the page and choose Promote to Front Page from the drop-down list. Finally, click Update to update the page's settings.

6. Click the title in the upper-left corner.

In admin mode, this is a special link that lets you see how the page looks from a guest perspective. Now, your page is the front page of the CMS.

Building a menu system

You can add more pages easily. Just repeat the process: Be sure you're logged in as the administrator, navigate to the "Create content" page, and edit your new page.

When you have a lot of pages, you'll definitely want to add some sort of navigation system. When you create or edit a page, you can add it to Drupal's menu system. Figure 3-13 shows the menu settings for a new page.

To set a page's place in the menu structure, follow these steps:

1. **Modify the menu settings.**

   The page creation screen has a section called "Menu settings" (shown in Figure 3-13).

2. **Give the page a title.**

   The page will be displayed in the menu only if it has a title.

3. **Provide a description for the page.**

   The description text will automatically appear when you hover over the menu. This can be used to provide additional text to explain the page's contents.

4. **Specify a parent item.**

   Typically, you'll use "content" for the parent because this will cause a link to appear on the primary navigation menu of the system.

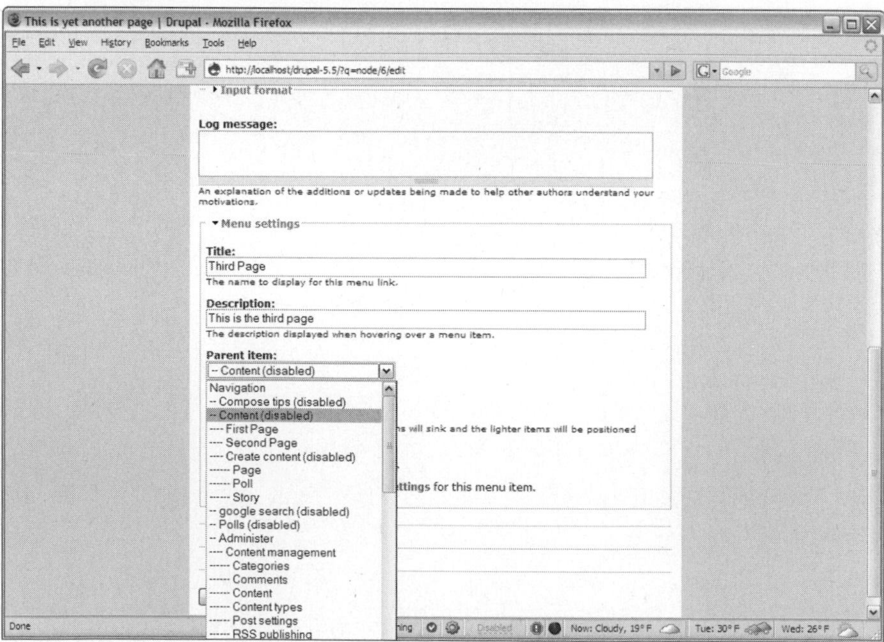

Figure 3-13: Designate your page's place in the menu system.

5. **Submit the page.**

   Use the Submit button to save changes to your page.

6. **Test the menu.**

   Your page should now appear on the left-side menu, as shown in Figure 3-14.

   If you want to modify the menu placement of a page after it has been created, you can either edit the page (see the next section) or modify the menu structure itself. Menus can be modified through the Administer menu: Administer ⇨ Site building ⇨ Menus.

Editing your pages

You may want to change a page once you've added it to the system. You can change the content to your heart's content if you're logged in as the administrator. Here's how:

1. **Log in as the administrator.**

   Only the administrator (or someone given special privileges by the administrator) can change the content of a page.

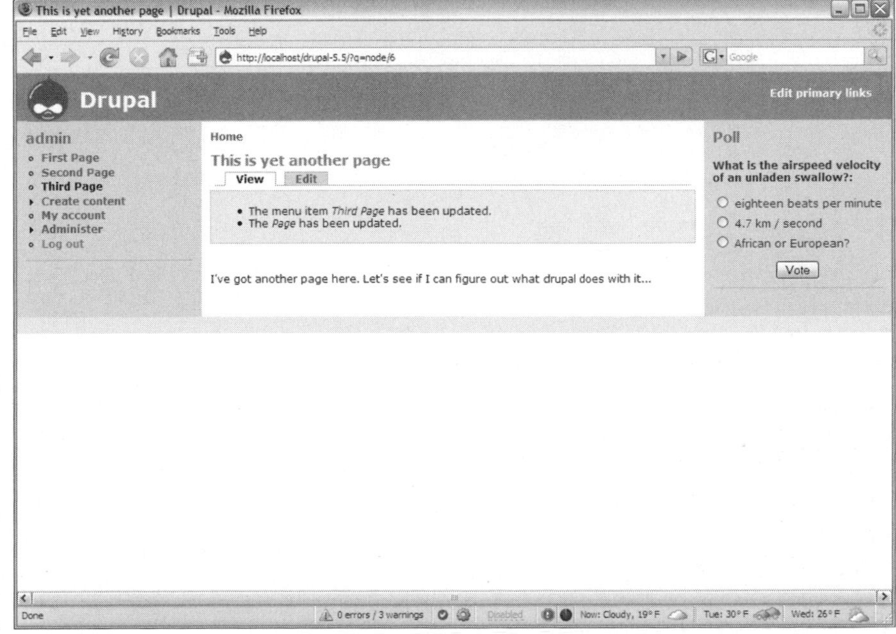

Figure 3-14: Now, the new page (Third Page) shows in the menu structure.

2. **Navigate to the Administer page.**

   The administrator has access to a special menu item called "Administer." Click this link to view the page shown in Figure 3-15.

Drupal uses the word "administrate" in a lot of different ways. Here's the rundown: The *administrator* is a person with special privileges. The account you use as the administrator is sometimes called the *admin account.* When you're logged in as the administrator, you have access to a special page called the *Administer page.*

Adding a new content block

You may want to add a new type of content to your page. Drupal comes with several modules already, and you can choose from hundreds more. To begin by adding a poll, follow these steps:

1. **Log in as admin (if you haven't already).**

   You'll change the site design again.

2. **Find the Modules page.**

   It's in the Administer – Site Building section. You see a screen like the one shown in Figure 3-16.

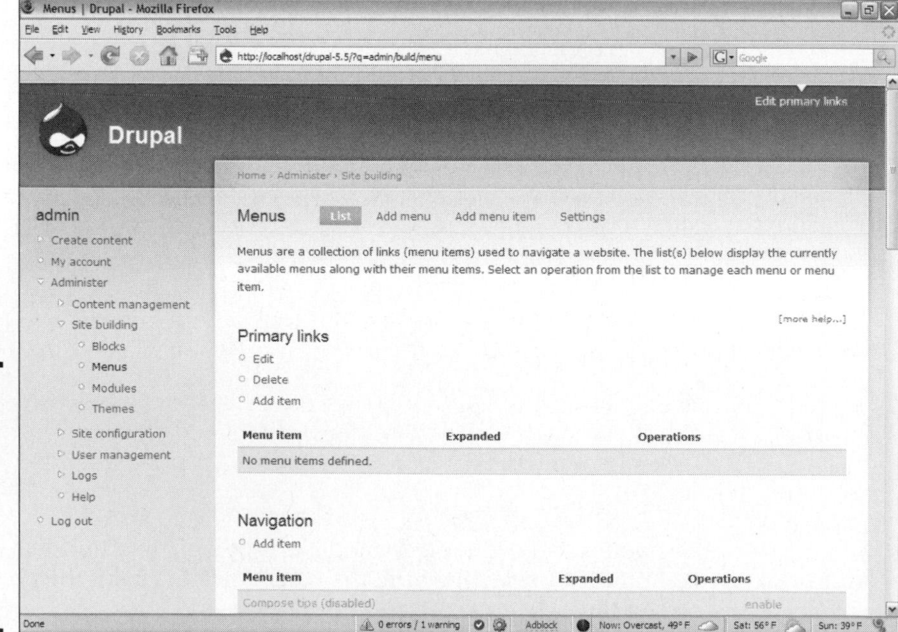

Figure 3-15: The Administer page allows you to modify various parts of the system.

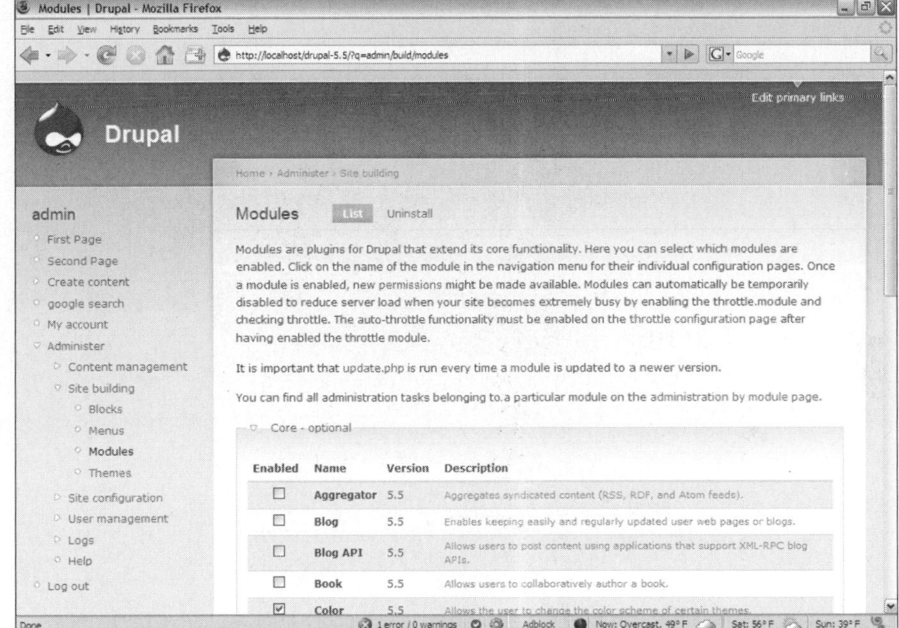

Figure 3-16: You add a new module with the Modules page.

3. **Look for the Poll module.**

   The Poll module allows you to ask a question and track user responses to it. Select the Enabled check box for this module and click the Save Configuration button.

4. **Create a poll.**

   A poll is interesting only if you ask a question. You find the poll configuration on the Create Content page, in the Submit Poll section (see Figure 3-17).

5. **Edit the poll.**

   Click the Edit button to add a new poll.

6. **Display the Poll module.**

   Even though the Poll module is enabled, it hasn't been placed in the site. Use the Administer – Site Building – Blocks page, shown in Figure 3-18, to make the poll visible.

7. **Place the poll.**

   The poll is listed in the Disabled block by default. Choose another placement for it by selecting from the drop-down list. I put the poll in the sidebar on the right.

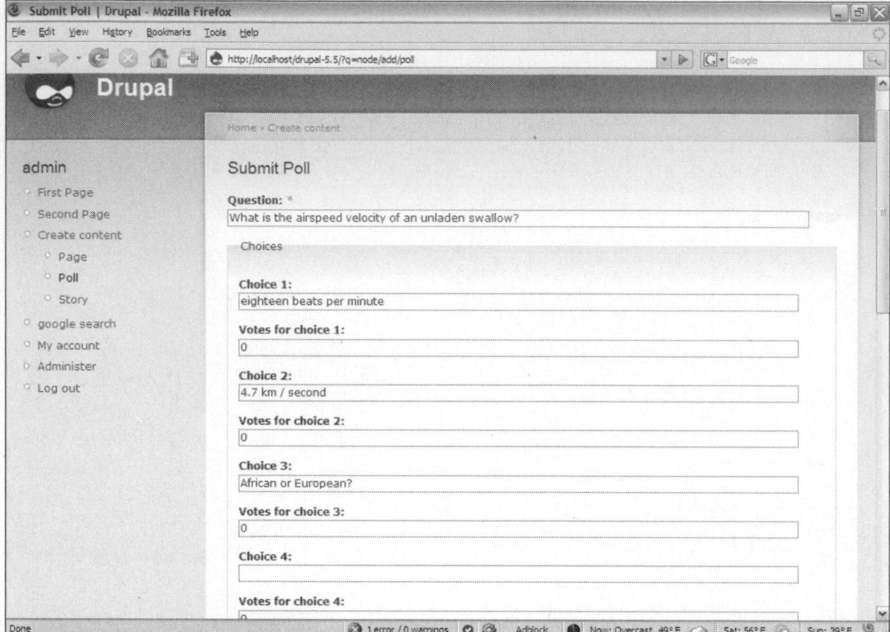

Figure 3-17: Creating a new poll object.

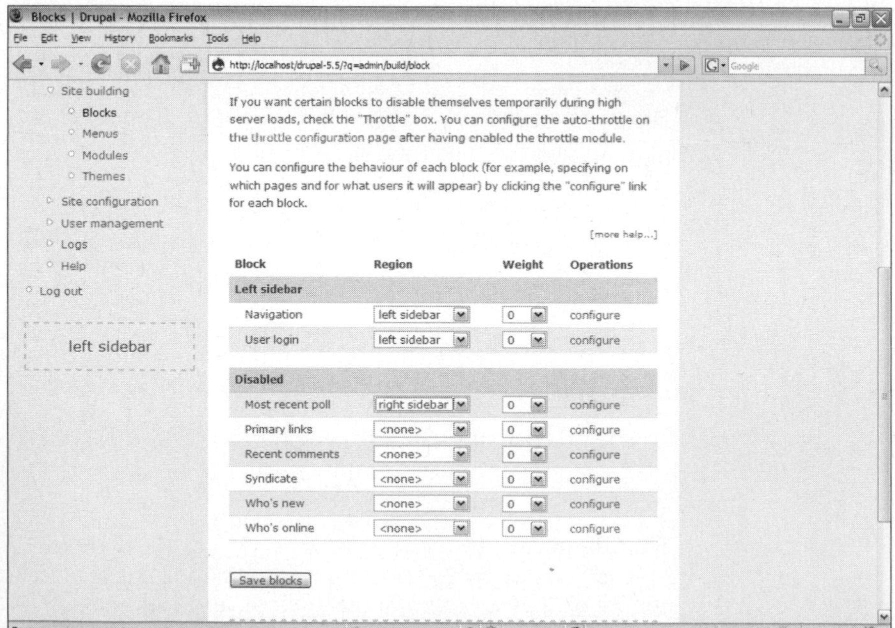

Figure 3-18: Of course, you want the new poll to be visible.

8. **Test the poll.**

   You want to see whether it looks the way you expect. Figure 3-19 shows my site with the new poll in place.

By default, users can create their own polls. You may want to disable this feature for anonymous users, or else you'll get spammed.

Of course, the poll is not the only module available. Drupal has several interesting modules available to experiment with in the default package, with hundreds more available for free download.

Almost all CMSs have plugin modules available. You can usually find a list of modules on the CMS's home page, or you can search for it at `www.google.com`. Of course, modules are usually nothing more than PHP code, so you can always write your own.

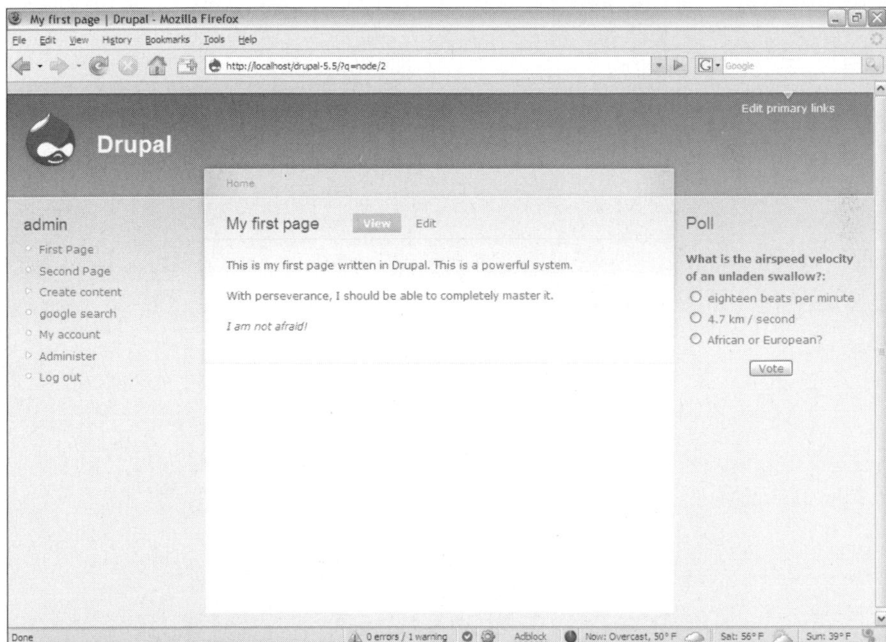

Figure 3-19: I've added a new module!

Changing the look

You can easily change the look and feel of Drupal. It uses (like most CMSs) the concept of themes to organize the look and feel of a site. A *theme* is a prepackaged layout and visual display configuration. To try one of the other default themes, just go to Administer – Sitebuilding – Themes in Admin mode and select a new theme.

You'll see a list of all the installed themes. Each theme can be enabled or disabled, and one theme can be set as the default theme.

Enabling a theme makes it available for users to choose, and setting a theme as the default makes it the primary theme of your account. Figure 3-20 shows the site using the Pushbutton theme.

Of course, you probably want more exciting options than the one in my example. Hundreds of themes are available, so you should find one that suits your needs. Follow these steps:

1. **Download a theme from the Internet.**

   Nearly every CMS has a community of theme builders. Do a quick search for Drupal themes to find the theme you're looking for. Most Drupal themes are saved as Zip files containing a single directory.

2. **Copy the theme to the `themes` directory.**

   I found an attractive theme, named Aberdeen, so I copied the entire directory found in the Zip file to the `themes` directory under the Drupal main directory.

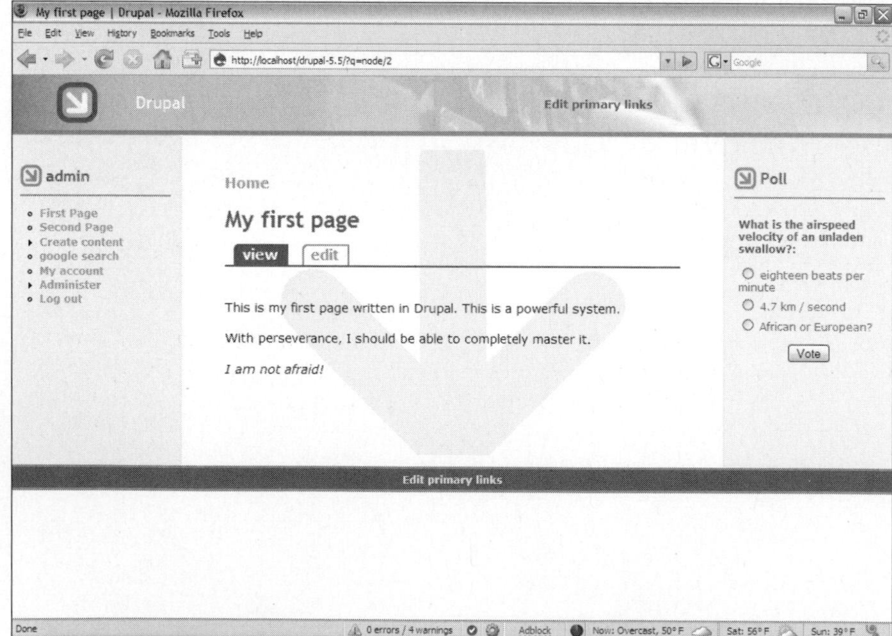

Figure 3-20: I changed the theme with one quick setting.

3. **Refresh or re-navigate to the `themes` directory.**

   If you're already in the `themes` directory, refresh the browser. If you're not there, find the directory to see the new theme.

4. **Select the theme and test it.**

   Figure 3-21 shows my Drupal site with the Aberdeen theme. It's amazing how easy it is to change the look and feel.

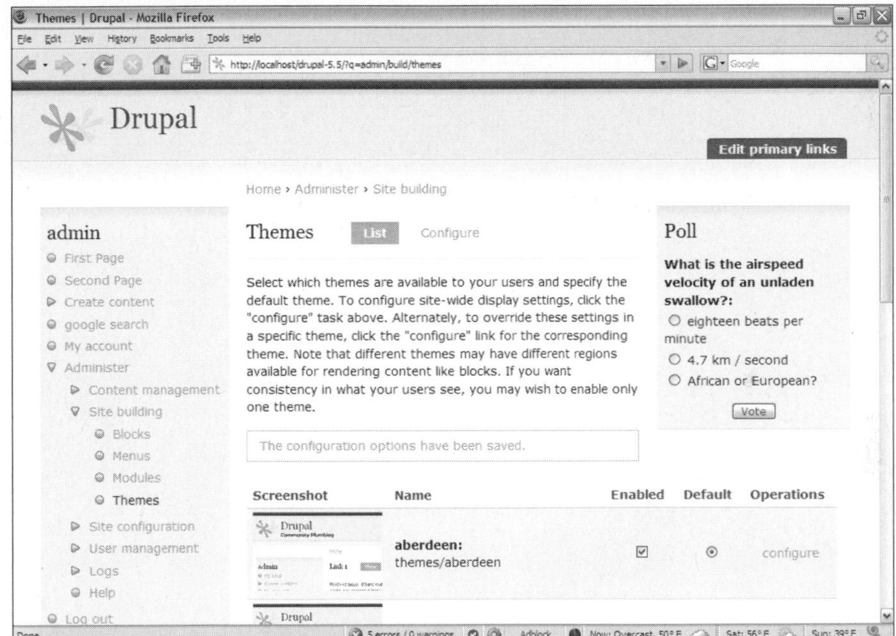

Figure 3-21: You can download themes easily to most CMSs.

Of course, you can also create your own themes. In most cases, the CMS themes are simply PHP files organized in a specific way. Check the documentation for your specific theme system.

Chapter 4: Taking Control of Content

In This Chapter

- **Using CMS Made Simple (CMSMS)**
- **Adding new pages in CMSMS**
- **Adding themes**
- **Working with templates**
- **Approximating CMS with SSI and AJAX**
- **Creating a CMS with PHP and MySQL**

The idea of a content management system (CMS) is very appealing because it gives you a great deal of additional control of your site and allows the user to manage his own content. Of course, when you use a content management system, you're somewhat at the mercy of that system's designers. In this chapter, I show you how to customize a relatively simple CMS, including adding new styles and layouts.

I also show you several ways to approximate a CMS with your own code using technologies introduced throughout this book. Finally, I develop a rudimentary CMS using PHP and MySQL. Even if you don't end up building your own CMS, looking through this code helps you see how "real world" CMSs work.

Getting Started with CMSMS

Content management systems are certainly useful, but it's no fun to be stuck with somebody else's design. You probably have your own design ideas you'd like to implement in the CMS. Of course, you can build new themes for any CMS, but that's not always as easy as you might think. You have to be comfortable with using most CMSs before you can write your own themes.

I show you CMSMS (or CMS Made Simple), a CMS that's so simple you should be able to customize your site with it completely in just a couple of days. For small to medium-size projects, it's a good blend of simplicity and capability (and now my favorite CMS).

Installing CMSMS

The installation of CMSMS is similar to any other CMS installation. Follow these steps:

1. **Download the package from the CD-ROM (or get the latest version from the Web site).**

   The CMS itself is mainly a series of PHP files with a few images and other materials.

2. **Copy it to your `htdocs` directory.**

   Like other CMSs, CMSMS needs to be in your `htdocs` path because it uses PHP.

3. **Run CMSMS through localhost.**

   The first time CMSMS runs, it checks for the existence of a script named `config.php`. You need to create an empty file of this name and put it in the directory requested by the script.

4. **Create an administration account when prompted by CMSMS.**

   This account sets up an administrator for CMSMS (not for the database).

5. **Define the data configuration.**

   Figure 4-1 illustrates how CMSMS expects the data to be configured. Define the database, username, and password you will use for the database relating to this CMS.

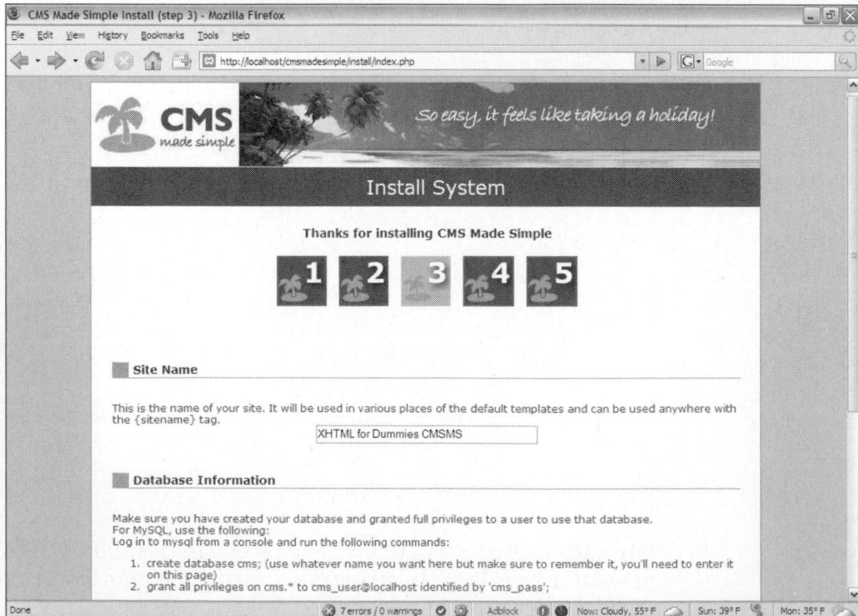

Figure 4-1: How the database will be configured.

Data configuration is easier if you create a database and a user with the same name.

6. **Create a dedicated database.**

   Use phpMyAdmin to create a database with the settings you specified in Step 5.

Playing around with the default package

CMSMS is unique because the default setup is the documentation! Most of what you need to know is already available within CMSMS itself. Don't worry, though: The documentation is still available, even after you replace it with your own content, and CMSMS isn't that hard to use (much easier than Drupal, in my opinion). The default setup of CMSMS is shown in Figure 4-2.

Before you change anything, take a look around and make sure to read the default pages because they're full of helpful information about how the system is designed.

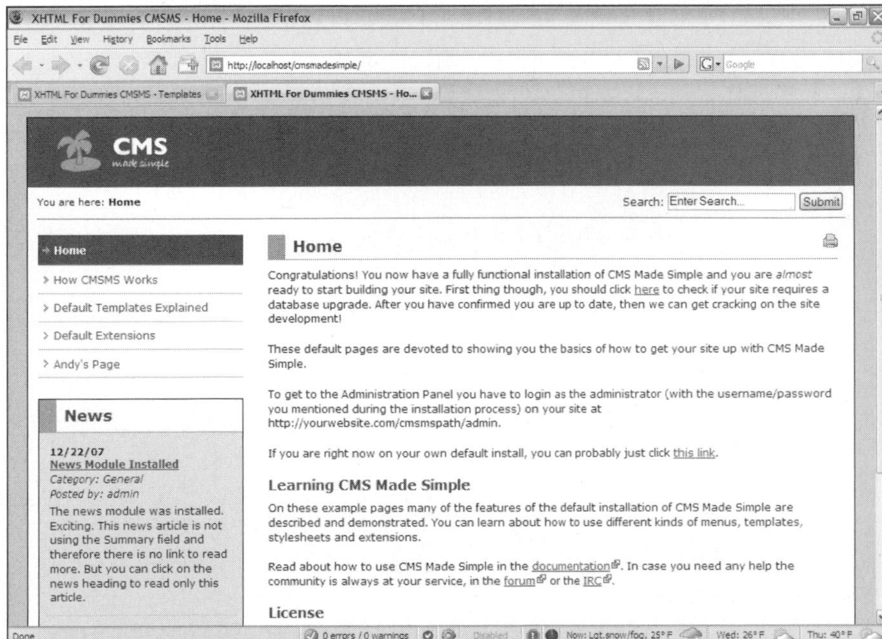

Figure 4-2: CMS Made Simple is clean-looking.

The philosophy of CMSMS is straightforward:

✦ **Templates define structure.** Templates are basically XHTML pages. If you want a new XHTML structure, you simply modify or create a new XHTML page.

- **Templates include smarty tags.** Templates contain XHTML structure, but no content. You put special markers in the templates to indicate where the content is placed. I tell you more on that topic as I describe how to modify templates, later in this chapter.
- **CSS describes layout.** As always, use CSS to define the look and feel. The CSS for CMSMS isn't really any different than it is for regular XHTML, except that a lot of it is already done for you (and done very well).
- **Content is defined within the system.** When you want to create content, you specify a layout, and CMSMS provides a WYSIWYG editor to let you type in the content.

Adding a new page

The easiest way to understand how CMSMS does its magic is to simply add a new page. Here's how it's done:

1. **Log in as admin.**

   Point your browser to the `admin` directory, under the `cmsms` directory, and the login screen for administrative privileges is displayed. The default screen looks like the one shown in Figure 4-3.

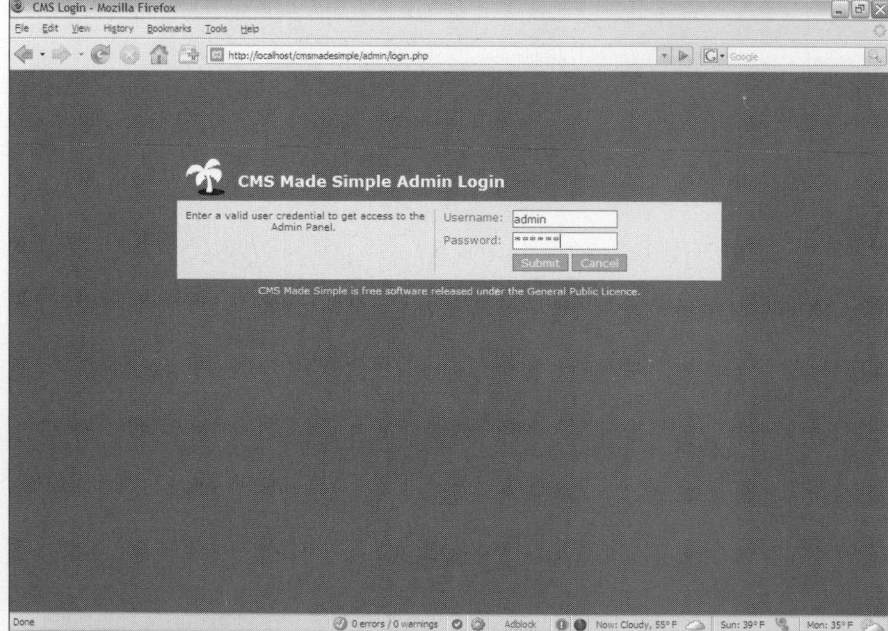

Figure 4-3: As always, you need to log in as admin to do anything *really* dangerous.

2. **Examine the main administration screen to see all your options.**

   After you click the Submit button, you'll see a screen like Figure 4-4.

   The first time you see this page, you see a warning that the install directory is still in place. Delete the install directory (you don't need it any more), and then you don't see the error any more.

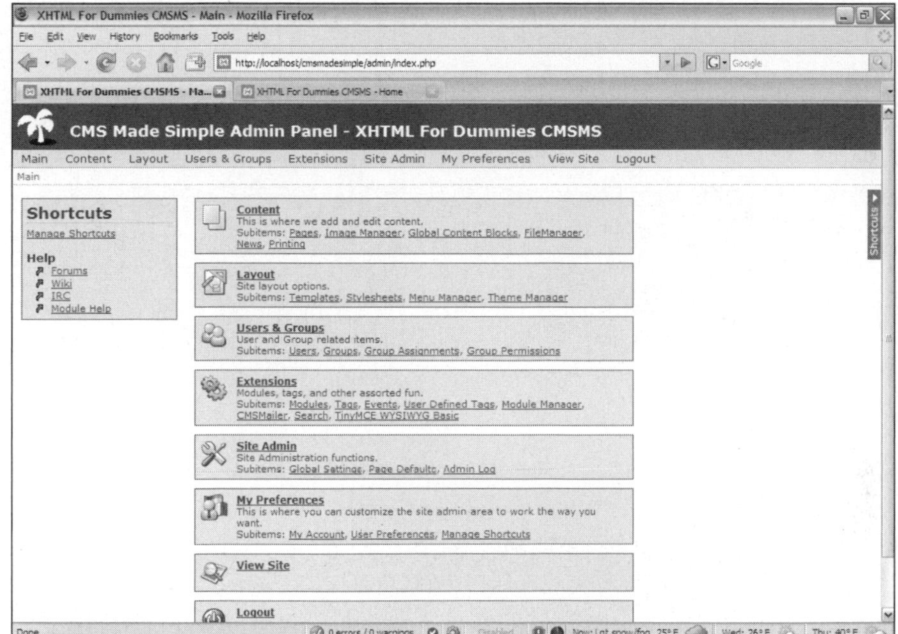

Figure 4-4: The main Control Panel for CMSMS.

3. **Go to the Content section and pick pages. You can go directly to the pages section by clicking the pages link.**

   This page, shown in Figure 4-5, is where you create and modify the pages in your system.

4. **Create a new page by clicking the Add New Content link.**

   You see a page editor like the one shown in Figure 4-6.

5. **Edit the page.**

   CMSMS features a handy editor that feels a lot like a word processor. People with no skill in using HTML are still reasonably comfortable creating content with this tool. Of course, if you prefer HTML, you can click the HTML button and type your own XHTML text. (For basic editing, I let the editor do the work, but when I want things a particular way, I write my own HTML.)

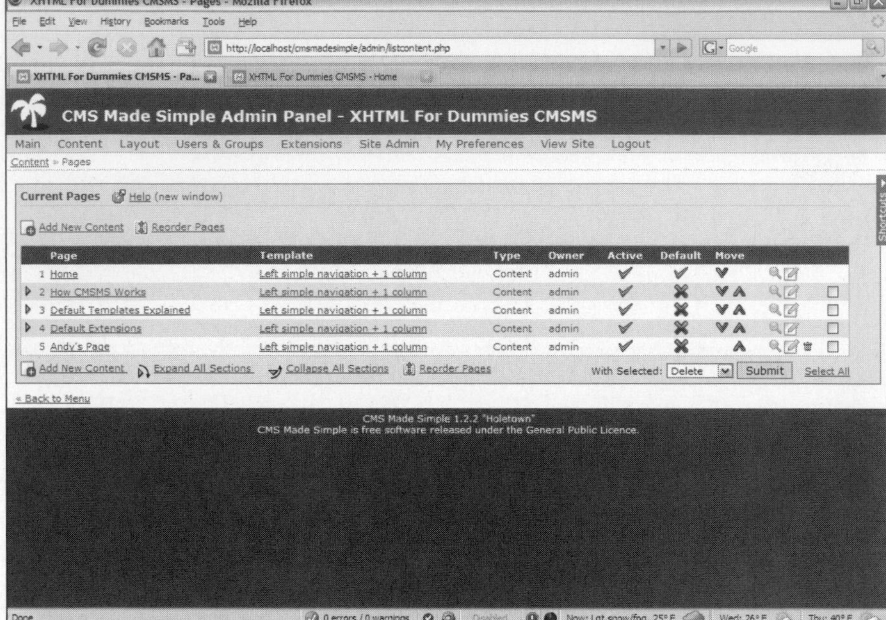

Figure 4-5: You spend a lot of time managing your pages here.

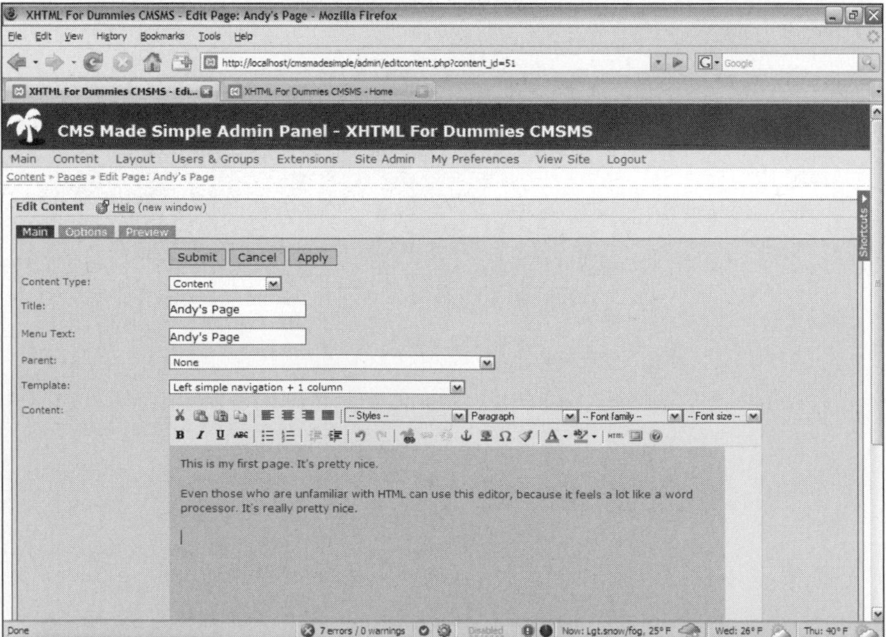

Figure 4-6: The page editor.

6. **Choose a template from the provided drop-down list.**

   By default, CMSMS has five template choices. Of course, you can choose many more, but this number is plenty to start with. Be aware that some templates have more text areas than others, so your template choice may be based on the type of text you want to incorporate.

   TIP

   The CSS style is integrated into the template, but you can change it later, if you want.

7. **Test the page by clicking the Preview button.**

   Go back and fix your page if there's anything you want to change.

8. **Click the Submit button to accept the changes to your page.**

   You return to the Pages section.

9. **Modify your page settings.**

   Although the page is automatically linked to the menu system, you can easily change each page's position and settings. You can move a page up or down in the menu system, and you can assign it a parent, making the page a submenu of any other page.

Feel free to experiment by adding and manipulating pages and changing the page styles.

Customizing CMSMS

Of course, you have the most fun working with a CMS when you totally change the way it looks. Fortunately, CMSMS is easier to customize than most CMSs.

Adding a theme

Begin by finding a theme online that you want to modify. CMSMS has an active and dynamic community of theme builders. Follow these steps:

1. **Find a theme you like.**

   Search `http://themes.cmsmadesimple.org`, and you're bound to find something you like. It doesn't have to be perfect. Find something close, and then you can modify it with your own graphics and colors.

2. **Download the theme.**

   Most CMSMS themes are XML files. You download the file, rather than open it directly. You need to store the XML file somewhere on a disk.

3. **Log into CMSMS in admin mode.**

4. **Find the theme manager on the Layout menu. It looks like Figure 4-7.**

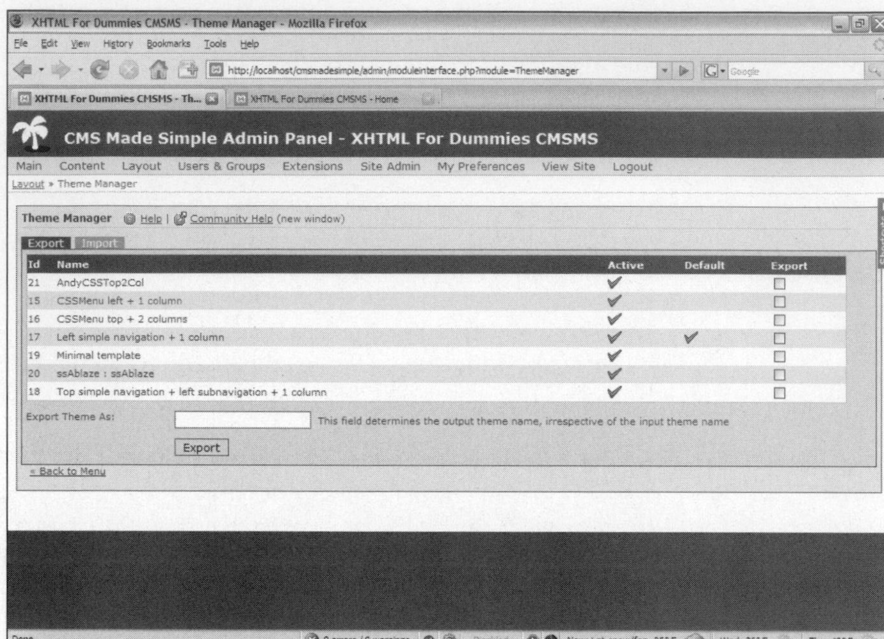

Figure 4-7: The theme manager in CMSMS.

5. **Import the theme.**

   You see the Import tab near the top of the theme manager. Navigate to the XML file you just downloaded and click the Import button. The Theme Manager returns, and your new theme should be available.

   The theme is just the packaging of a template and some CSS files (and sometimes images and other resources).

6. **Activate the template by clicking the X to change it to a green check mark.**

   To activate the theme, go to the Template Manager on the Layout menu. It looks like Figure 4-8.

   Your new template is listed as Inactive by default so that you can test it before you make it available.

7. **Set all pages to use the new template by clicking the appropriate link.**

   Because this is just a test, try setting all your pages to use the template.

8. **View the site with the new template in place.**

   Your site now follows the standards of the new template. Figure 4-9 demonstrates the site with a new template in place.

The new template, named `ssAblaze`, was ported from an earlier style at `www.styleshout.com`. Take a look at this site to see some excellent CSS styles.

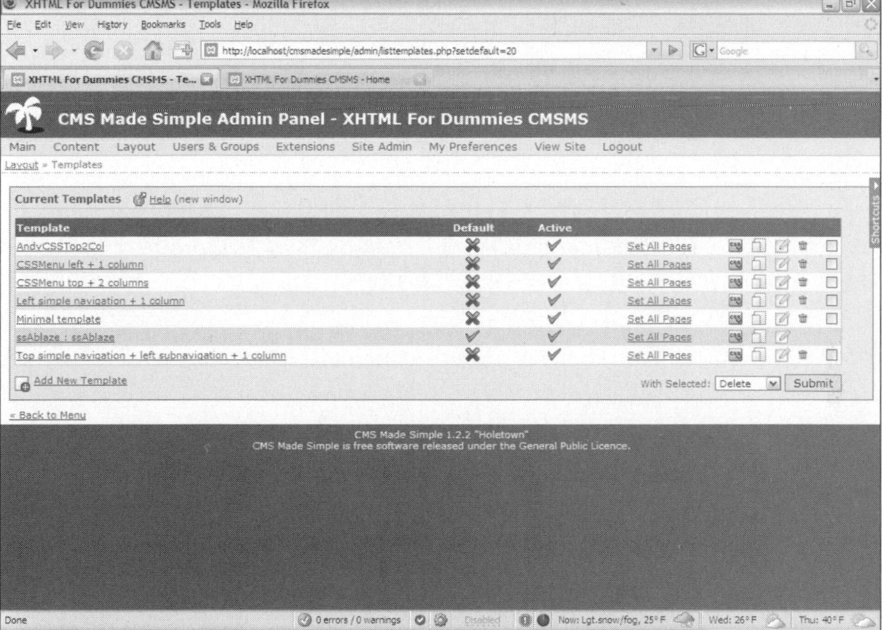

Figure 4-8: The Template Manager manages templates.

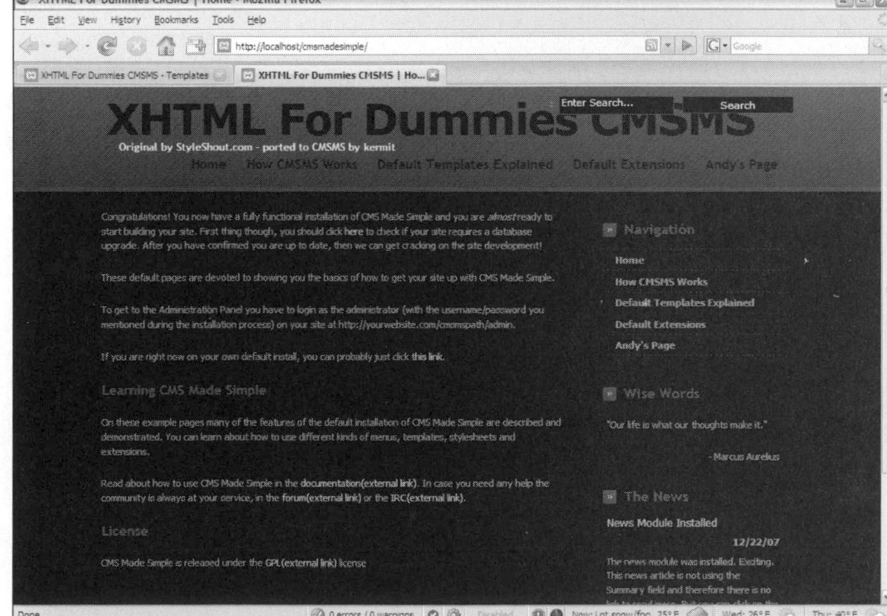

Figure 4-9: The look and feel have changed, but the content is unchanged.

Working with templates

You can create a template from scratch if you want, but it may be easier to modify an existing template. Here's how:

1. **Choose a template you like.**

   We recommend that you start with an existing template so that you can take advantage of the previous coder's skill. Identify a template you want to modify and locate it in the Template Manager.

2. **Duplicate the template.**

   Locate the small Duplicate button on the right side of the Template Manager. Duplicate the template and work on a copy so that you don't risk breaking the original.

3. **Assign the duplicated template a new name.**

   I named mine `andyCSSTop2Col` because it's based on the `CSSMenu top 2 col` template.

4. **Edit the template.**

   You click the small Edit icon to edit the template. You won't make a lot of changes to it, but look over the code. Figure 4-10 shows a simple template in the editor.

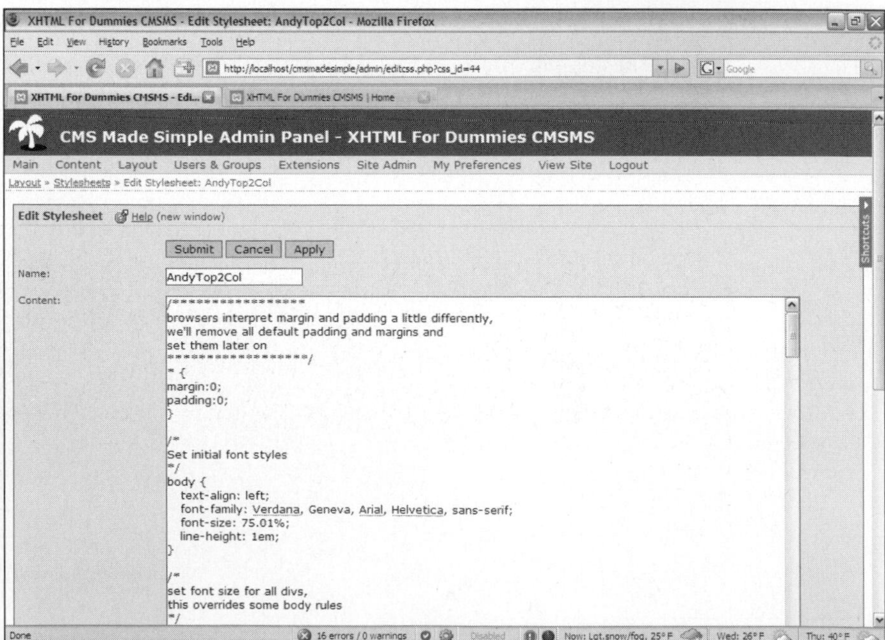

Figure 4-10: In this basic template, notice the { } tags.

5. **Notice the smarty tags.**

   A template is just an XHTML framework, but it has special smarty tags. The Smarty template engine, which is included with CMSMS, allows for server-side replacement. The `{ content }` tag is replaced with whichever content has been added to that page, for example.

6. **Make changes and close the Template Manager.**

   You can add boilerplate code, if you want. I thought that the left column looked bare, for example, so I added a Quote of the Day feature.

7. **Attach a style sheet or two.**

   You use the Attach Stylesheets button to attach one or more style sheets to this template. Whenever the template is invoked, the indicated style sheet is automatically loaded by the CMS. You can add more than one style sheet (for example, the print style sheet already handles creating a print layout). Figure 4-11 shows the style-sheet linking tool.

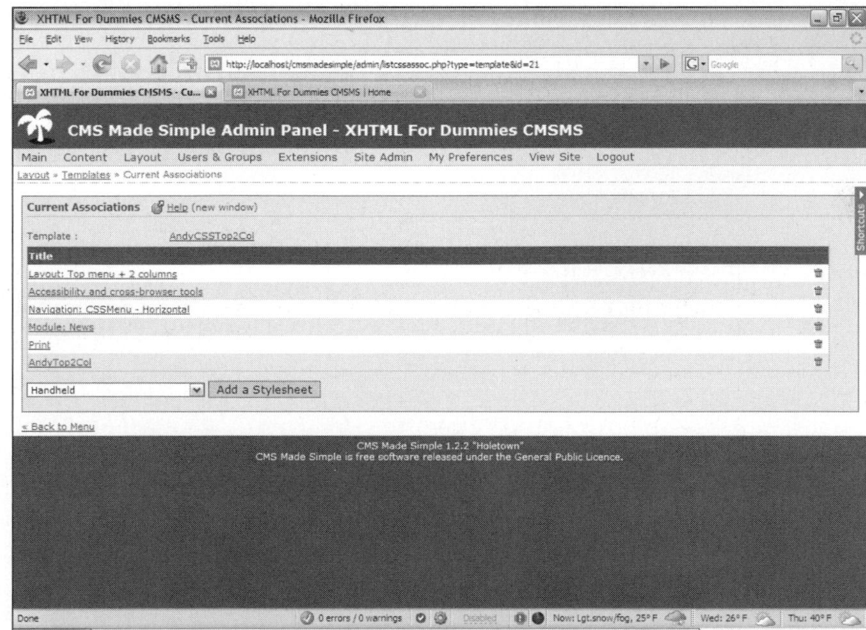

Figure 4-11: The style-sheet linking tool connects one or more style sheets to a template.

Changing a style

Of course, you probably want to add your own styles, which is pretty easy to do in CMSMS. Follow these steps:

1. **Check the Assign Styles dialog box to see which styles are attached.**

   If your template was copied from another template, it probably inherited some styles from the parent template. Identify any styles your template is already using.

2. **Duplicate a style before changing it.**

   Adjust one of the already existing styles. As with templates, never change the original, but instead make a copy and then modify the copy. Duplicate the style sheet and give it a new name.

3. **Edit the new style sheet.**

   The new style sheet is simply a CSS document. Look it over to see which changes you want to make. (As always, the Web Developer toolbar can be a godsend for modifying styles.) Begin with basic changes, such as colors, before doing the more dramatic stuff.

4. **Attach the new style sheet to the template.**

   Tell the template that you want to use the new style sheet with your changes by adjusting the CSS assignments. Also, remove the style sheet that your new style replaces.

Adding a custom tag

One of the coolest features of CMSMS is also one of the easiest to use. You can easily create custom tags that do anything you can do in PHP. Here's how it works:

1. **Open the User-Defined Tags page in the Extensions menu.**
2. **Add a new user-defined tag by clicking the appropriately named link.**
3. **Insert some PHP code in the resulting text editor.**

   Just for fun, I added a simple loop, as shown in Figure 4-12.

4. **Name and save the tag.**

   I named my new tag `count` because it creates an unordered list with a `for` loop. Use the Submit button to save your tag.

   This counting script is a completely made-up example. Normally, you'll use custom scripts for things like database lookup or other more advanced PHP not already handled by the CMS.

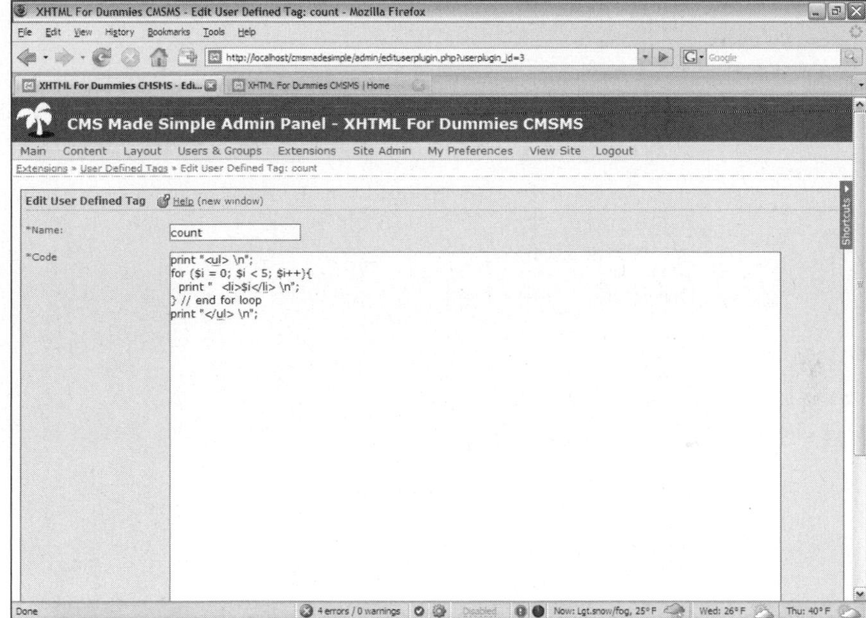

Figure 4-12: This quick PHP script is about to become a smarty tag.

5. **Edit a page or template.**

   I'm adding the counter to "Andy's Page," for this example.

6. **Add the `count` tag to the page.**

   Figure 4-13 shows a page with the new `{ count }` tag included in the source.

   Figure 4-13 also illustrates my customized style on my custom page. Slick, huh?

7. **View the page and be amazed.**

   When you view the page, you see the tag replaced by the results of executing the code.

The custom tag feature is incredibly useful because you can use it to do anything you can do with ordinary PHP, which is quite a lot.

Even better, your PHP is in short snippets, which are usually easier to write and understand than huge applications that create mounds of XHTML code.

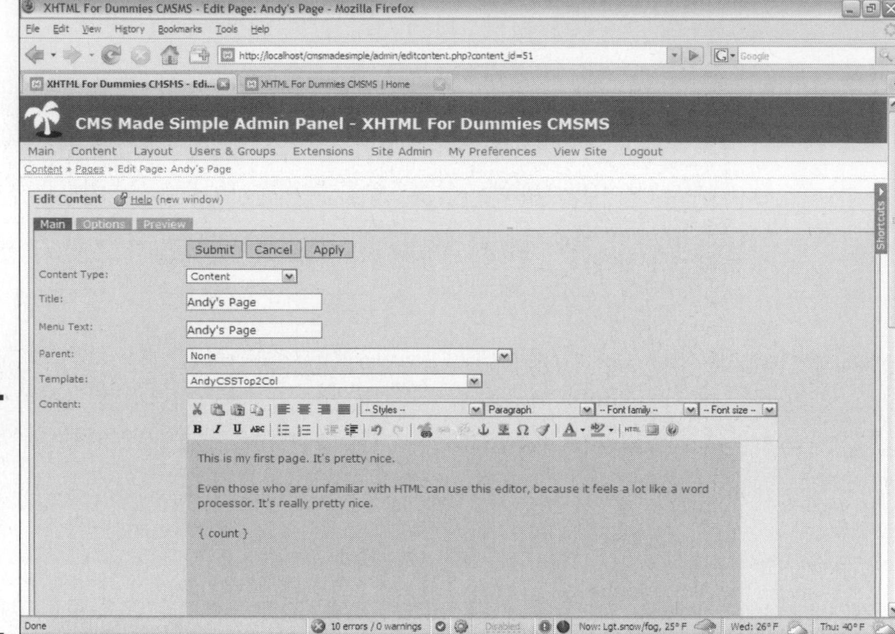

Figure 4-13: Now, whenever I use the { count } tag, the PHP code executes.

Building a "Poor Man's CMS" with Your Own Code

The benefits of using a CMS are very real, but you may not want to make the commitment to a full-blown CMS. For one thing, you have to learn each CMS's particular way of doing things, and most CMSs force you into a particular mindset. For example, you think differently about pages in Drupal than you do in CMSMS. You can still get some of the benefits of a CMS with some simpler development tricks, as described in the following sections.

Using Server-Side Includes (SSIs)

Web developers have long used the simple SSI (Server-Side Include) trick as a quick and easy way to manage content. It involves breaking the code into smaller code segments and a framework that can be copied. For example, Figure 4-14 shows a variation of the Web site developed in Chapter 2 of this minibook.

Even if you view the source code, you don't find anything unusual about the page.

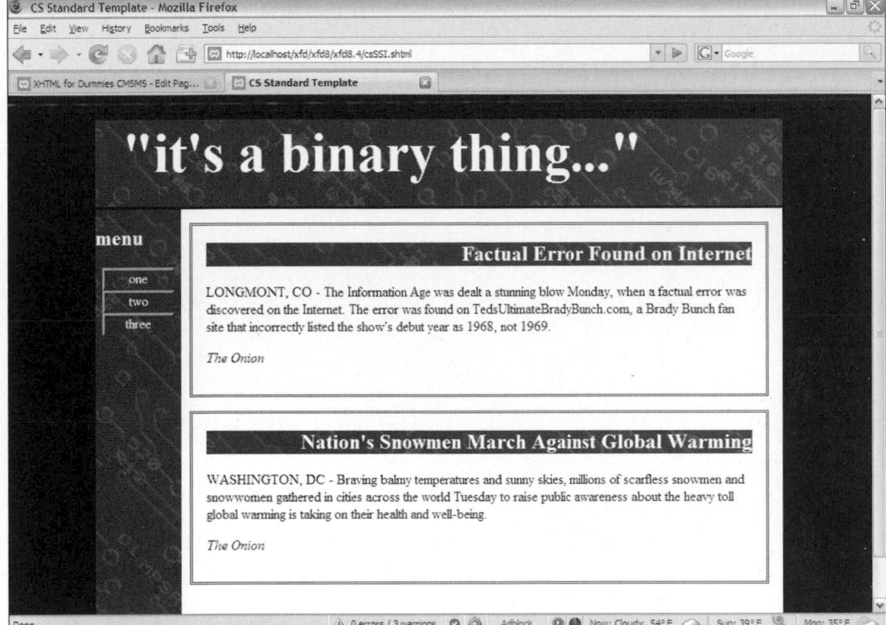

Figure 4-14: This Web page appears to be a standard page.

However, if you look at the code in a text editor, you find some interesting discoveries:

```
<!DOCTYPE html PUBLIC "-//W3C//DTD XHTML 1.0 Strict//EN"
"http://www.w3.org/TR/xhtml1/DTD/xhtml1-strict.dtd">
<html lang="EN" dir="ltr" xmlns="http://www.w3.org/1999/xhtml">
  <head>
    <meta http-equiv="content-type" content="text/xml; charset=utf-8" />
    <title>CS Standard Template</title>
    <link rel = "stylesheet"
          type = "text/css"
          href = "csStd.css" />
  </head>


  <body>
    <div id = "all">
      <!-- This div centers a fixed-width layout -->
      <div id = "heading">
        <!--#include virtual = "head.html" -->
      </div><!-- end heading div -->

      <div id = "menu">
        <!--#include virtual = "menu.html" -->
      </div> <!-- end menu div -->

      <div class = "content">
        <!--#include virtual = "story1.html" -->
      </div> <!-- end content div -->
```

```
      <div class = "content">
        <!--#include virtual = "story2.html" -->
      </div> <!-- end content div -->

      <div id = "footer">
        <!--#include virtual = "footer.html" -->
      </div> <!-- end footer div -->
    </div> <!-- end all div -->
  </body>
</html>
```

Some interesting things are happening in this code snippet:

- **The page has no content!** All the actual content (the menus and the phony news stories) are gone. This page, which contains only structural information, is the heart of any kind of CSS — the structure is divorced from the content.
- **A funky new tag is in place of the content.** In each place that you expect to see text, you see an `<!--#include -->` directive, instead. This special instruction tells the server to go find the specified file and put it here.
- **The filename is unusual.** The server doesn't normally look for include tags (because most pages don't have them). Typically, you have to save the file with the special extension `.shtml` to request that the server look for include directives and perform them.
- **Servers don't always allow SSI technologies.** Not every server is configured for Server-Side Includes. You may have to check with your server administrator to make this work.

The nice thing about Server-Side Includes is the way that it separates the content from the structure. For example, look at the code for the first content block:

```
<!--#include virtual = "story1.html" -->
```

This code notifies the server to look for the file `story1.html` in the current directory and place the contents of the file there. The file is a vastly simplified HTML fragment:

```
<h2>Factual Error Found on Internet</h2>

<p>
LONGMONT, CO - The Information Age was dealt a stunning blow Monday,
when a factual error was discovered on the Internet. The error
was found on TedsUltimateBradyBunch.com, a Brady Bunch fan site
that incorrectly listed the show's debut year as 1968, not 1969.
</p>

<p><em>The Onion</em></p>
```

This approach makes it very easy to modify the page. If I want a new story, I simply make a new file, `story1.html`, and put it in the directory. Writing a program to do this automatically is easy.

Like PHP code, SSI code doesn't work if you simply open the file in the browser or drag the file to the window. SSI requires active participation from the server; to run an SSI page on your machine, therefore, you need to use localhost, as you do for PHP code.

Using AJAX/JQuery for client-side

If you don't have access to Server-Side Includes, you can use AJAX to get the same effect.

Figure 4-15 shows what appears to be the same page, but all is not what it appears to be.

Figure 4-14 and 4-15 look identical, but they're not. I used totally different means to achieve exactly the same output, from the user's point of view.

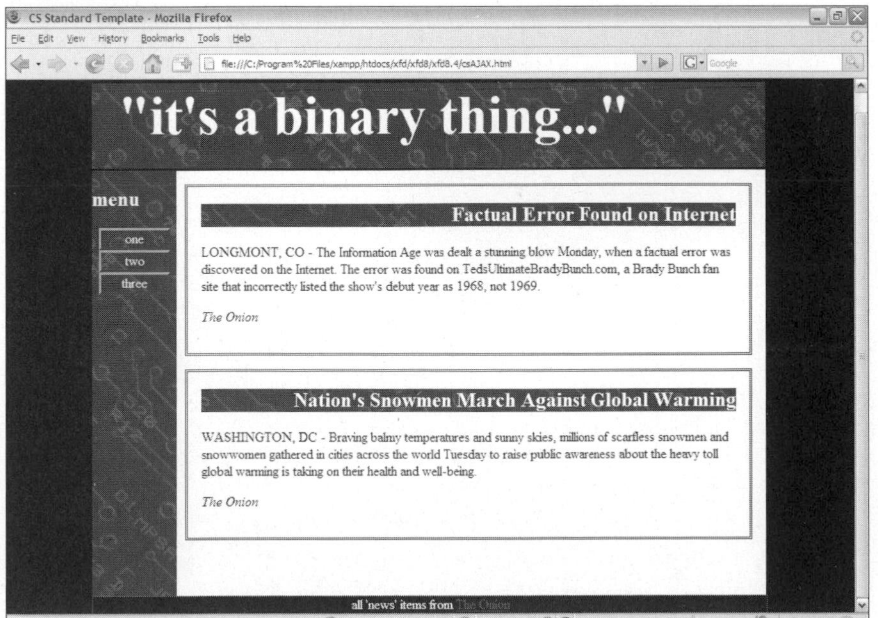

Figure 4-15: This time, I grabbed content from the client side.

The code reveals what's going on:

```
<!DOCTYPE html PUBLIC "-//W3C//DTD XHTML 1.0 Strict//EN"
"http://www.w3.org/TR/xhtml1/DTD/xhtml1-strict.dtd">
<html lang="EN" dir="ltr" xmlns="http://www.w3.org/1999/xhtml">
  <head>
    <meta http-equiv="content-type" content="text/xml; charset=utf-8" />
    <title>CS Standard Template</title>
    <link rel = "stylesheet"
          type = "text/css"
          href = "csStd.css" />
    <script type = "text/javascript"
            src = "jquery-1.2.1.js"></script>
    <script type = "text/javascript">
    //<![CDATA[
      $(document).ready(function() {
        $("#heading").load("head.html");
        $("#menu").load("menu.html");
        $("#content1").load("story1.html");
        $("#content2").load("story2.html");
        $("#footer").load("footer.html");
      });
    //]]>
    </script>
  </head>

  <body>
    <div id = "all">
      <!-- This div centers a fixed-width layout -->
      <div id = "heading">
      </div><!-- end heading div -->

      <div id = "menu">
      </div> <!-- end menu div -->

      <div class = "content"
           id = "content1">
      </div> <!-- end content div -->

      <div class = "content"
           id = "content2">
      </div> <!-- end content div -->

      <div id = "footer">
      </div> <!-- end footer div -->

    </div> <!-- end all div -->
  </body>
</html>
```

Once again, the page content is empty. All the contents are available in the same text files as they were for the Server-Side Includes example. This time, though, I used a jQuery AJAX call to load each text file into the appropriate element.

The same document structure can be used with very different content by changing the JavaScript. If you can't create a full-blown CMS (because the server doesn't allow SSI, for example) but you can do AJAX, this is an easy way to separate content from layout.

Building a page with PHP includes

Of course, if you have access to PHP, it's quite easy to build pages dynamically.

The `csInclude.php` program shows how this is done:

```
!DOCTYPE html PUBLIC "-//W3C//DTD XHTML 1.0 Strict//EN"
"http://www.w3.org/TR/xhtml1/DTD/xhtml1-strict.dtd">
<html lang="EN" dir="ltr" xmlns="http://www.w3.org/1999/xhtml">
  <head>
    <meta http-equiv="content-type" content="text/xml; charset=utf-8" />
    <title>CS PHP Includes</title>
    <link rel = "stylesheet"
          type = "text/css"
          href = "csStd.css" />
  </head>

  <body>
    <div id = "all">
      <!-- This div centers a fixed-width layout -->
      <div id = "heading">
        <?php include("head.html"); ?>
      </div><!-- end heading div -->

      <div id = "menu">
        <?php include("menu.html"); ?>
      </div> <!-- end menu div -->

      <div class = "content">
        <?php include("story1.html"); ?>
      </div> <!-- end content div -->

      <div class = "content">
        <?php include("story2.html"); ?>
      </div> <!-- end content div -->
      <div id = "footer">
        <?php include("footer.html"); ?>
      </div> <!-- end footer div -->
    </div> <!-- end all div -->
  </body>
</html>
```

As you can see, using PHP is almost the same as using the SSI and AJAX approaches from the last two sections of this chapter:

1. **Start by building a template.**

   The general template for all three styles of page inclusion is the same. There's no need to change the general design or the CSS.

2. **Create a small PHP segment for each inclusion.**

   In this particular situation, it's easiest to write XHTML code for the main site and write a small PHP section for each segment that needs to be included.

3. **Include the HTML file.**

   Each PHP snippet does nothing more than include the appropriate HTML.

Creating Your Own Data-Based CMS

Of course, if you've come this far in the chapter, you ought to go all the way and see how a relational database can add flexibility to a page-serving system. If you really want to turn the corner and make a real CMS, you need a system that stores all the data in a data structure and compiles the pages from that structure dynamically. *That* sounds like a project. It's not nearly as intimidating as it sounds, though.

Using a database to manage content

The first step is to move from storing data in files to storing it a relational database. Each page in a content management system is often the same structure, and only the data is different. What happens if you move away from text files altogether and store all the content in a database?

The data structure might be defined like this in SQL:

```
DROP TABLE IF EXISTS cmsPage;
CREATE TABLE cmsPage (
  cmsPageID INTEGER PRIMARY KEY AUTO_INCREMENT,
  title VARCHAR(30)
);

DROP TABLE IF EXISTS cmsBlock;
CREATE TABLE cmsBlock (
  cmsBlockID INTEGER PRIMARY KEY AUTO_INCREMENT,
  blockTypeID INTEGER,
  title VARCHAR(50),
  content TEXT,
  pageID INTEGER

);

DROP TABLE IF EXISTS blockType;
CREATE TABLE blockType (
  blockTypeID INTEGER PRIMARY KEY AUTO_INCREMENT,
  name VARCHAR(30)
);

DROP VIEW IF EXISTS pageView;
CREATE VIEW pageView AS
  SELECT
    blockType.name as 'block',
    cmsBlock.title as 'title',
    cmsBlock.content as 'content',
    cmsPage.cmsPageID as 'pageID',
    cmsPage.title as 'page'
  FROM
    cmsBlock, blockType, cmsPage
  WHERE
    cmsBlock.blockTypeID = blockType.blockTypeID;
```

This structure has three tables and a view:

- **The `cmsPage` table:** Represents the data about a page, which currently isn't much. A fuller version might put menu information in the page data so that the page would "know" where it lives in a menu structure.
- **The `cmsBlock` table:** Represents a block of information. Each block is the element that would be in a miniature HTML page in the other systems described in this chapter. This table is the key table in this structure because most of the content in the CMS is stored in this table.
- **The `blockType` table:** Lists the block types. This simple table describes the various block types.
- **The pageView view:** Ties together all the other information. After all the data is loaded, the pageView view ties it all together, as shown in Figure 4-16.

Some of the data (the menu information and the link to *The Onion*) is being read as HTML, but it's still text data. I included the entire SQL file, including the `INSERT` statements, on the CD-ROM as `buildCMS.sql`.

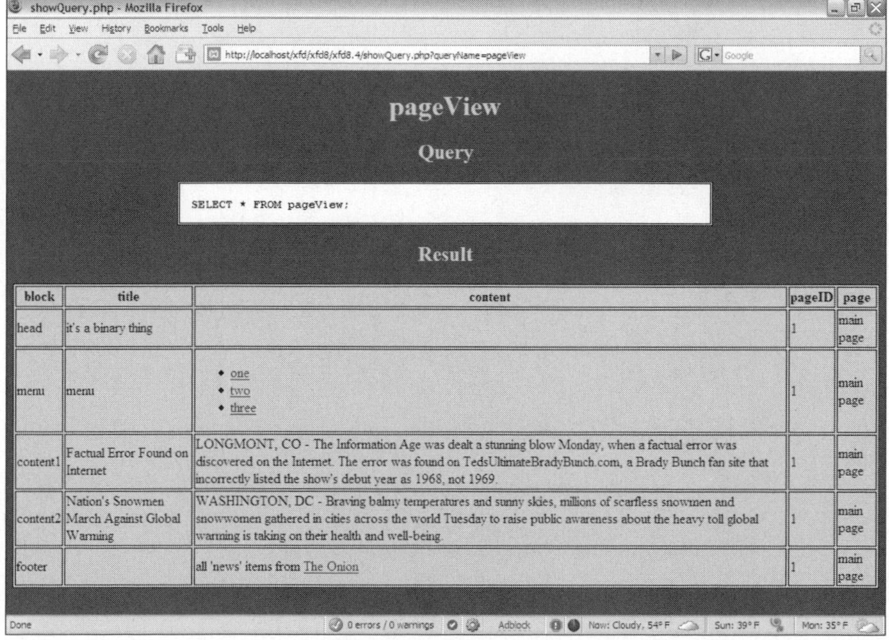

Figure 4-16: This view describes all the data needed to build a page.

Writing a PHP page to read from the table

The advantage of using a data-based approach is scalability. In using all the other models in this chapter, I had to keep copying the template page. If you decide to make a change in the template, you have to change hundreds of pages. If you use data, you can write one PHP program that can produce any page in the system. All this page needs is a page-number parameter. Using that information, it can query the system, extract all the information needed for the current page, and then display the page. Here's the (simplified) PHP code for such a system:

```
<!DOCTYPE html PUBLIC "-//W3C//DTD XHTML 1.0 Strict//EN"
"http://www.w3.org/TR/xhtml1/DTD/xhtml1-strict.dtd">

<html lang="EN" dir="ltr" xmlns="http://www.w3.org/1999/xhtml">
  <head>
    <meta http-equiv="content-type" content="text/xml; charset=utf-8" />
    <title>dbCMS.php.</title>
    <link rel = "stylesheet"
          type = "text/css"
          href = "csStd.css" />
  </head>
<?php

//get pageID from request if possible
$pageID = $_REQUEST["pageID"];
$pageID = mysql_real_escape_string($pageID, $conn);
if ($pageID == ""){
  $pageID = 1;
} // end if

//read current page information from the db
$conn = mysql_connect("localhost", "xfd", "xfdaio");
mysql_select_db("xfd");
$sql = "SELECT * FROM pageView WHERE pageID = 1";
$result = mysql_query($sql, $conn);

//populate local variables from db result
while ($row = mysql_fetch_assoc($result)){
  if ($row["block"] == "head"){
    $head = $row["title"];
  } else if ($row["block"] == "menu"){
    $menu = $row["content"];
  } else if ($row["block"] == "content1"){
    $c1Title = $row["title"];
    $c1Text = $row["content"];
  } else if ($row["block"] == "content2"){
    $c2Title = $row["title"];
    $c2Text = $row["content"];
  } else if ($row["block"] == "footer"){
    $footer = $row["content"];
  } // end if
} // end while

?>

  <body>
    <div id = "all">
      <!-- This div centers a fixed-width layout -->
```

```
      <div id = "heading">
        <h1>
          <?php print $head; ?>
        </h1>
      </div><!-- end heading div -->

      <div id = "menu">
        <?php print $menu; ?>
      </div> <!-- end menu div -->

      <div class = "content">
        <h2>
          <?php print $c1Title; ?>
        </h2>
        <p>
          <?php print $c1Text; ?>
        </p>
      </div> <!-- end content div -->

      <div class = "content">
        <h2>
          <?php print $c2Title; ?>
        </h2>
        <p>
          <?php print $c2Text; ?>
        </p>
      </div> <!-- end content div -->

      <div id = "footer">
        <?php print $footer; ?>
      </div> <!-- end footer div -->
    </div> <!-- end all div -->
  </body>
</html>
```

Here's the cool thing about dbCMS. This page is all you need! You won't have to copy it ever. The same PHP script is used to generate every page in the system. If you want to change the style or layout, you do it in this one script, and it works automatically in all the pages.

Looking at all the code at once may seem intimidating, but it's quite easy when you break it down, as explained in these steps:

1. **Pull the `pageID` number from the request.**

   If possible, extract the `pageID` number from the GET request. If the user has sent a particular page request, it has a value. If there's no value, get page number 1:

   ```
   //get pageID from request if possible
   $pageID = $_REQUEST["pageID"];
   $pageID = mysql_real_escape_string($pageID, $conn);
   if ($pageID == ""){
     $pageID = 1;
   } // end if
   ```

Don't forget to escape the `pageID` data! Whenever you extract data from a page to use in a query, remember to escape the data to prevent injection attacks.

2. **Query `pageView` to get all the data for this page.**

   The `pageView` view was designed to give you everything you need to build a page with one query.

   If you're using MySQL 4 (without views), just copy the query from the view definition and insert it into your PHP code. The view is just a shortcut — it's never absolutely necessary.

3. **Pull values from the query to populate the page.**

   Look at each response of the query. Then, look at the `block` value to see which type of query it is and populate local variables:

```
//read current page information from the db
$conn = mysql_connect("localhost", "xfd", "password");
mysql_select_db("xfd");
$sql = "SELECT * FROM pageView WHERE pageID = $pageID";
$result = mysql_query($sql, $conn);
```

4. **Write out the page.**

   Go back to HTML and generate the page, skipping into PHP to print the necessary variables.

Improving the dbCMS design

Although the simple PHP/MySQL combination described in the last section is a suitable starting point, you probably want to do a bit more to make a complete CMS because a better CMS might have the following features:

- **Automatic menu generation:** The menu system in dbCMS is too static as it is. Your database should keep track of where each page is located in the system, and your menu code should be dynamically generated based on this information.
- **Error-checking:** This program isn't nearly robust enough for real use (yet). It crashes if the data isn't complete. Before you can use this system in a real application, you need a way to improve its "crashworthiness."
- **Data input:** What would truly improve this system is a mechanism for adding new data to the data tables. Allow the user to create new pages and content. Provide a form for creating a new page. When the user adds information, it's passed to the database, where it's immediately available as a new page.

Appendix A: What's on the CD

In This Appendix:

- **System requirements**
- **Using the CD with Windows and Mac**
- **What you'll find on the CD**
- **Troubleshooting**

System Requirements

Make sure that your computer meets the minimum system requirements shown in the following list. If your computer doesn't match up to most of these requirements, you may have problems using the software and files on the CD. For the latest and greatest information, please refer to the ReadMe file located at the root of the CD-ROM.

- A PC running Microsoft Windows 98, Windows 2000, Windows NT4 (with SP4 or later), Windows Me, Windows XP, or Windows Vista.
- A Macintosh running Apple OS X or later.
- A PC running a version of Linux with kernel 2.4 or greater.
- An Internet connection
- A CD-ROM drive

If you need more information on the basics, check out these books published by Wiley Publishing, Inc.: *PCs For Dummies,* by Dan Gookin; *Macs For Dummies*, 9th Edition, by Edward C. Baig; *iMac For Dummies,* 5th Edition, by Mark Chambers; *Windows 95 For Dummies, Windows 98 For Dummies, Windows 2000 Professional For Dummies, Microsoft Windows ME Millennium Edition For Dummies, Windows Vista For Dummies,* all by Andy Rathbone.

Using the CD

To install the items from the CD to your hard drive, follow these steps.

1. **Insert the CD into your computer's CD-ROM drive. The license agreement appears.**

Note to Windows users: The interface won't launch if you have autorun disabled. In that case, click Start⇨Run (For Windows Vista, Start⇨All Programs⇨Accessories⇨Run). In the dialog box that appears, type D:\Start.exe. (Replace D with the proper letter if your CD drive uses a different letter. If you don't know the letter, see how your CD drive is listed under My Computer.) Click OK.

Note for Mac Users: The CD icon will appear on your desktop, double-click the icon to open the CD and double-click the "Start" icon.

2. **Read through the license agreement, and then click the Accept button if you want to use the CD.**

   The CD interface appears. The interface allows you to install the programs and run the demos with just a click of a button (or two).

What You'll Find on the CD

The following sections are arranged by category and provide a summary of the software and other goodies you'll find on the CD. If you need help with installing the items provided on the CD, refer back to the installation instructions in the preceding section.

Shareware programs are fully functional, free, trial versions of copyrighted programs. If you like particular programs, register with their authors for a nominal fee and receive licenses, enhanced versions, and technical support.

Freeware programs are free, copyrighted games, applications, and utilities. You can copy them to as many PCs as you like @md for free @md but they offer no technical support.

GNU software is governed by its own license, which is included inside the folder of the GNU software. There are no restrictions on distribution of GNU software. See the GNU license at the root of the CD for more details.

Trial, demo, or *evaluation* versions of software are usually limited either by time or functionality (such as not letting you save a project after you create it).

Author-created material

For Windows and Mac.

All the examples provided in this book are located in the Author directory on the CD and work with Macintosh, Linux, Unix and Windows 95/98/NT and later computers. These files contain the sample code from the book. The structure of the examples directory is

```
Author/Book1/Chapter1
```

Aptana Studio 1.1, Community Edition

Open source.

For Windows and Mac OS. A full-featured programmer's editor that greatly simplifies creating Web pages, CSS documents, and code in multiple languages.

CMS Made Simple 1.2.2

Open source.

For Windows and Mac OS. A content management system that's easy to run and modify.

DBDesigner 4.0.5.6

Open source.

For Windows. A visual database designer for building complex database models.

Dia 0.96.1

Open source.

For Windows. A drawing tool suitable for site diagrams, flow diagrams, and other vector-drawing applications.

FireFox 2.0.0.12 and Extensions

Open source.

For Windows and Mac OS. I've included several extensions to the Firefox Web browser that turn it into a thoroughbred Web development platform. Web Developer Toolbar 1.1.4 adds all kinds of features for creating and testing pages; HTML Validator 0.840 checks your pages for standards-compliance; the FireBug 1.05 extension adds incredible features for JavaScript and AJAX debugging; and FireFTP, Mozilla's FTP client program.

GIMP 2.4.4

Open source.

For Windows. A professional-level graphics editor in a free package. It does everything the expensive graphics editors do.

IrfanView 4.10

Freeware.

For Windows. A useful graphics viewer program.

jQuery 1.2.1

Open source.

For Windows and Mac OS. A JavaScript Library that helps you transfer HTML documents, handle events, and include AJAX features in your Web pages.

Nvu 1.0

Open source.

For Windows and Mac OS. A visual HTML editor that lets you see changes as you make them.

prototype 1.6

Open source.

For Windows and Mac OS. A JavaScript library that simplifies form handling and AJAX.

SQLite 303.5.6

Open source.

For Windows and Mac OS. A powerful software library as well as SQL database engine.

WinSCP 4.0.5

Open source.

For Windows. WinSCP is an SFTP client and FTP client for Windows used to secure file transfers between local and remote computers.

Vim 7.1

Open source.

For Windows and Mac OS. A venerable text editor with modern enhancements.

XAMPP 1.6.4

GNU version.

For Windows and Mac OS. XAMPP is a complete server package that's easy to install and incredibly powerful. This package includes the incredible Apache Web server, the PHP programming language, the MySQL database manager, and tons of useful utilities.

Troubleshooting

I tried my best to compile programs that work on most computers with the minimum system requirements. Alas, your computer may differ, and some programs may not work properly for some reason.

The two likeliest problems are that you don't have enough memory (RAM) for the programs you want to use, or you have other programs running that are affecting installation or running of a program. If you get an error message such as `Not enough memory` or `Setup cannot continue`, try one or more of the following suggestions and then try using the software again:

- **Turn off any antivirus software running on your computer.** Installation programs sometimes mimic virus activity and may make your computer incorrectly believe that it's being infected by a virus.
- **Close all running programs.** The more programs you have running, the less memory is available to other programs. Installation programs typically update files and programs; so if you keep other programs running, installation may not work properly.
- **Have your local computer store add more RAM to your computer.** This is, admittedly, a drastic and somewhat expensive step. However, adding more memory can really help the speed of your computer and allow more programs to run at the same time.

Customer Care

If you have trouble with the CD-ROM, please call the Wiley Product Technical Support phone number at (800) 762-2974. Outside the United States, call 1(317) 572-3994. You can also contact Wiley Product Technical Support at **http://support.wiley.com**. John Wiley & Sons will provide technical support only for installation and other general quality control items. For technical support on the applications themselves, consult the program's vendor or author.

To place additional orders or to request information about other Wiley products, please call (877) 762-2974.

Index

Symbols

A

B

D

E

G

H

I

J

K

L

M

N

O

P

Q

R

U

V

W

BUSINESS, CAREERS & PERSONAL FINANCE

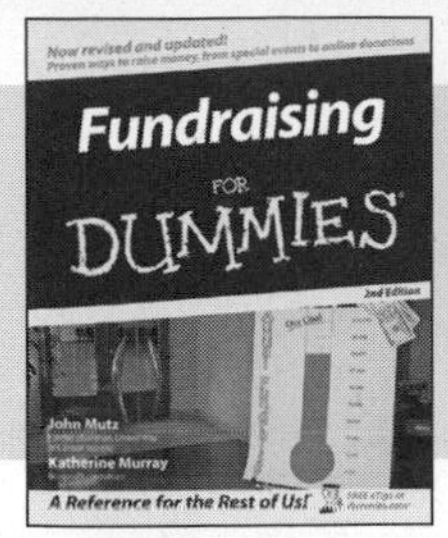

0-7645-9847-3

0-7645-2431-3

Also available:

- Business Plans Kit For Dummies 0-7645-9794-9
- Economics For Dummies 0-7645-5726-2
- Grant Writing For Dummies 0-7645-8416-2
- Home Buying For Dummies 0-7645-5331-3
- Managing For Dummies 0-7645-1771-6
- Marketing For Dummies 0-7645-5600-2
- Personal Finance For Dummies 0-7645-2590-5*
- Resumes For Dummies 0-7645-5471-9
- Selling For Dummies 0-7645-5363-1
- Six Sigma For Dummies 0-7645-6798-5
- Small Business Kit For Dummies 0-7645-5984-2
- Starting an eBay Business For Dummies 0-7645-6924-4
- Your Dream Career For Dummies 0-7645-9795-7

HOME & BUSINESS COMPUTER BASICS

0-470-05432-8

Windows Vista
FOR
DUMMIES
A Reference for the Rest of Us!

0-471-75421-8

Also available:

- Cleaning Windows Vista For Dummies 0-471-78293-9
- Excel 2007 For Dummies 0-470-03737-7
- Mac OS X Tiger For Dummies 0-7645-7675-5
- MacBook For Dummies 0-470-04859-X
- Macs For Dummies 0-470-04849-2
- Office 2007 For Dummies 0-470-00923-3
- Outlook 2007 For Dummies 0-470-03830-6
- PCs For Dummies 0-7645-8958-X
- Salesforce.com For Dummies 0-470-04893-X
- Upgrading & Fixing Laptops For Dummies 0-7645-8959-8
- Word 2007 For Dummies 0-470-03658-3
- Quicken 2007 For Dummies 0-470-04600-7

FOOD, HOME, GARDEN, HOBBIES, MUSIC & PETS

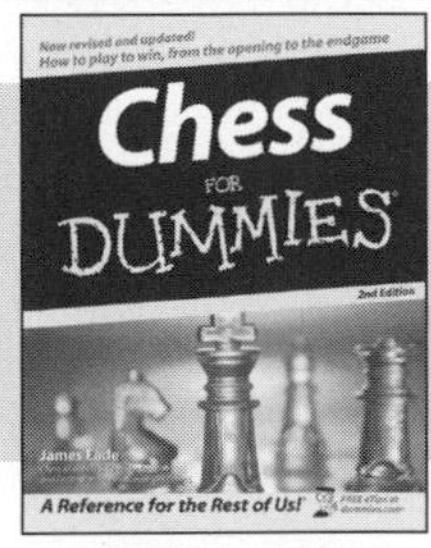

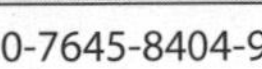

0-7645-8404-9

0-7645-9904-6

Also available:

- Candy Making For Dummies 0-7645-9734-5
- Card Games For Dummies 0-7645-9910-0
- Crocheting For Dummies 0-7645-4151-X
- Dog Training For Dummies 0-7645-8418-9
- Healthy Carb Cookbook For Dummies 0-7645-8476-6
- Home Maintenance For Dummies 0-7645-5215-5
- Horses For Dummies 0-7645-9797-3
- Jewelry Making & Beading For Dummies 0-7645-2571-9
- Orchids For Dummies 0-7645-6759-4
- Puppies For Dummies 0-7645-5255-4
- Rock Guitar For Dummies 0-7645-5356-9
- Sewing For Dummies 0-7645-6847-7
- Singing For Dummies 0-7645-2475-5

INTERNET & DIGITAL MEDIA

0-470-04529-9

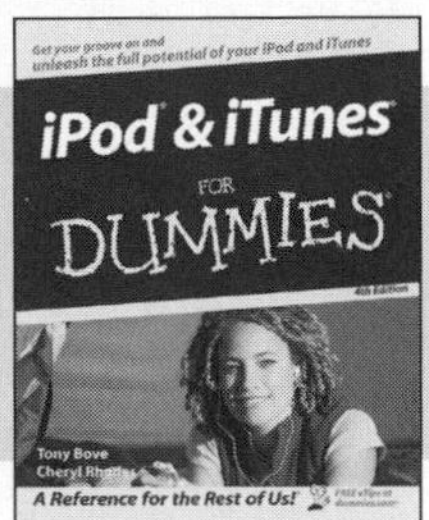

0-470-04894-8

Also available:

- Blogging For Dummies 0-471-77084-1
- Digital Photography For Dummies 0-7645-9802-3
- Digital Photography All-in-One Desk Reference For Dummies 0-470-03743-1
- Digital SLR Cameras and Photography For Dummies 0-7645-9803-1
- eBay Business All-in-One Desk Reference For Dummies 0-7645-8438-3
- HDTV For Dummies 0-470-09673-X
- Home Entertainment PCs For Dummies 0-470-05523-5
- MySpace For Dummies 0-470-09529-6
- Search Engine Optimization For Dummies 0-471-97998-8
- Skype For Dummies 0-470-04891-3
- The Internet For Dummies 0-7645-8996-2
- Wiring Your Digital Home For Dummies 0-471-91830-X

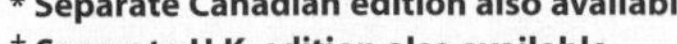

*** Separate Canadian edition also available**
† Separate U.K. edition also available

Available wherever books are sold. For more information or to order direct: U.S. customers visit www.dummies.com or call 1-877-762-2974. U.K. customers visit www.wileyeurope.com or call 0800 243407. Canadian customers visit www.wiley.ca or call 1-800-567-4797.

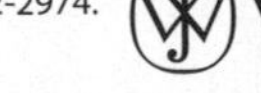

SPORTS, FITNESS, PARENTING, RELIGION & SPIRITUALITY

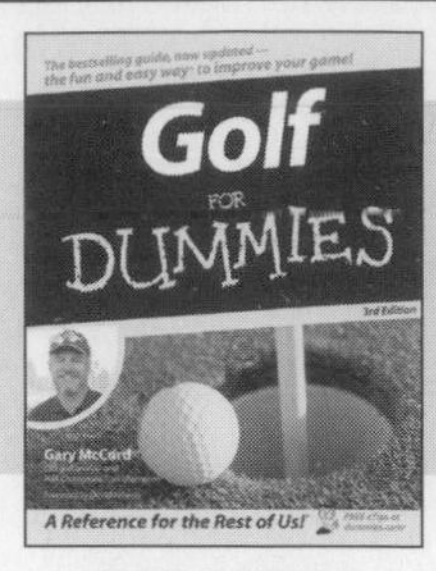

0-471-76871-5

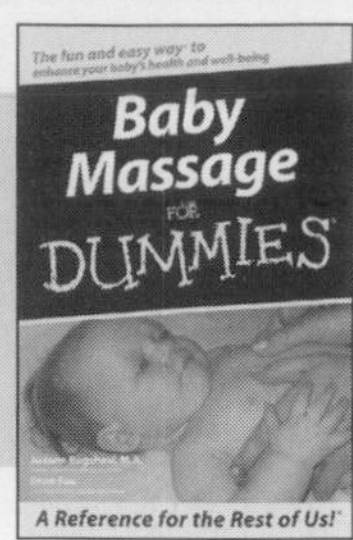

0-7645-7841-3

Also available:

- Catholicism For Dummies 0-7645-5391-7
- Exercise Balls For Dummies 0-7645-5623-1
- Fitness For Dummies 0-7645-7851-0
- Football For Dummies 0-7645-3936-1
- Judaism For Dummies 0-7645-5299-6
- Potty Training For Dummies 0-7645-5417-4
- Buddhism For Dummies 0-7645-5359-3
- Pregnancy For Dummies 0-7645-4483-7 †
- Ten Minute Tone-Ups For Dummies 0-7645-7207-5
- NASCAR For Dummies 0-7645-7681-X
- Religion For Dummies 0-7645-5264-3
- Soccer For Dummies 0-7645-5229-5
- Women in the Bible For Dummies 0-7645-8475-8

TRAVEL

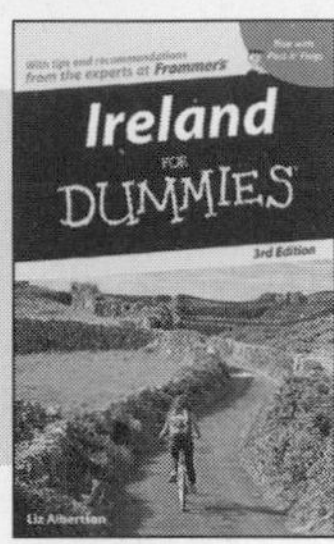

0-7645-7749-2

0-7645-6945-7

Also available:

- Alaska For Dummies 0-7645-7746-8
- Cruise Vacations For Dummies 0-7645-6941-4
- England For Dummies 0-7645-4276-1
- Europe For Dummies 0-7645-7529-5
- Germany For Dummies 0-7645-7823-5
- Hawaii For Dummies 0-7645-7402-7
- Italy For Dummies 0-7645-7386-1
- Las Vegas For Dummies 0-7645-7382-9
- London For Dummies 0-7645-4277-X
- Paris For Dummies 0-7645-7630-5
- RV Vacations For Dummies 0-7645-4442-X
- Walt Disney World & Orlando For Dummies 0-7645-9660-8

GRAPHICS, DESIGN & WEB DEVELOPMENT

0-7645-8815-X

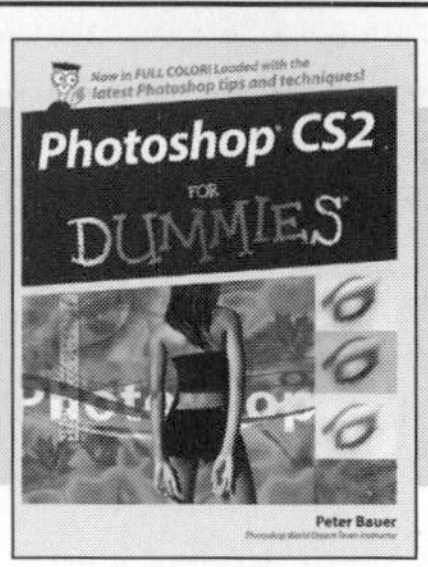

0-7645-9571-7

Also available:

- 3D Game Animation For Dummies 0-7645-8789-7
- AutoCAD 2006 For Dummies 0-7645-8925-3
- Building a Web Site For Dummies 0-7645-7144-3
- Creating Web Pages For Dummies 0-470-08030-2
- Creating Web Pages All-in-One Desk Reference For Dummies 0-7645-4345-8
- Dreamweaver 8 For Dummies 0-7645-9649-7
- InDesign CS2 For Dummies 0-7645-9572-5
- Macromedia Flash 8 For Dummies 0-7645-9691-8
- Photoshop CS2 and Digital Photography For Dummies 0-7645-9580-6
- Photoshop Elements 4 For Dummies 0-471-77483-9
- Syndicating Web Sites with RSS Feeds For Dummies 0-7645-8848-6
- Yahoo! SiteBuilder For Dummies 0-7645-9800-7

NETWORKING, SECURITY, PROGRAMMING & DATABASES

0-7645-7728-X

0-471-74940-0

Also available:

- Access 2007 For Dummies 0-470-04612-0
- ASP.NET 2 For Dummies 0-7645-7907-X
- C# 2005 For Dummies 0-7645-9704-3
- Hacking For Dummies 0-470-05235-X
- Hacking Wireless Networks For Dummies 0-7645-9730-2
- Java For Dummies 0-470-08716-1
- Microsoft SQL Server 2005 For Dummies 0-7645-7755-7
- Networking All-in-One Desk Reference For Dummies 0-7645-9939-9
- Preventing Identity Theft For Dummies 0-7645-7336-5
- Telecom For Dummies 0-471-77085-X
- Visual Studio 2005 All-in-One Desk Reference For Dummies 0-7645-9775-2
- XML For Dummies 0-7645-8845-1

Wiley Publishing, Inc. End-User License Agreement

READ THIS. You should carefully read these terms and conditions before opening the software packet(s) included with this book "Book". This is a license agreement "Agreement" between you and Wiley Publishing, Inc. "WPI". By opening the accompanying software packet(s), you acknowledge that you have read and accept the following terms and conditions. If you do not agree and do not want to be bound by such terms and conditions, promptly return the Book and the unopened software packet(s) to the place you obtained them for a full refund.

1. **License Grant.** WPI grants to you (either an individual or entity) a nonexclusive license to use one copy of the enclosed software program(s) (collectively, the "Software") solely for your own personal or business purposes on a single computer (whether a standard computer or a workstation component of a multi-user network). The Software is in use on a computer when it is loaded into temporary memory (RAM) or installed into permanent memory (hard disk, CD-ROM, or other storage device). WPI reserves all rights not expressly granted herein.

2. **Ownership.** WPI is the owner of all right, title, and interest, including copyright, in and to the compilation of the Software recorded on the physical packet included with this Book "Software Media". Copyright to the individual programs recorded on the Software Media is owned by the author or other authorized copyright owner of each program. Ownership of the Software and all proprietary rights relating thereto remain with WPI and its licensers.

3. **Restrictions on Use and Transfer.**

   (a) You may only (i) make one copy of the Software for backup or archival purposes, or (ii) transfer the Software to a single hard disk, provided that you keep the original for backup or archival purposes. You may not (i) rent or lease the Software, (ii) copy or reproduce the Software through a LAN or other network system or through any computer subscriber system or bulletin-board system, or (iii) modify, adapt, or create derivative works based on the Software.

   (b) You may not reverse engineer, decompile, or disassemble the Software. You may transfer the Software and user documentation on a permanent basis, provided that the transferee agrees to accept the terms and conditions of this Agreement and you retain no copies. If the Software is an update or has been updated, any transfer must include the most recent update and all prior versions.

4. **Restrictions on Use of Individual Programs.** You must follow the individual requirements and restrictions detailed for each individual program in the "About the CD" appendix of this Book or on the Software Media. These limitations are also contained in the individual license agreements recorded on the Software Media. These limitations may include a requirement that after using the program for a specified period of time, the user must pay a registration fee or discontinue use. By opening the Software packet(s), you agree to abide by the licenses and restrictions for these individual programs that are detailed in the "About the CD" appendix and/or on the Software Media. None of the material on this Software Media or listed in this Book may ever be redistributed, in original or modified form, for commercial purposes.

5. **Limited Warranty.**

   (a) WPI warrants that the Software and Software Media are free from defects in materials and workmanship under normal use for a period of sixty (60) days from the date of purchase of this Book. If WPI receives notification within the warranty period of defects in materials or workmanship, WPI will replace the defective Software Media.

   (b) **WPI AND THE AUTHOR(S) OF THE BOOK DISCLAIM ALL OTHER WARRANTIES, EXPRESS OR IMPLIED, INCLUDING WITHOUT LIMITATION IMPLIED WARRANTIES OF MERCHANTABILITY AND FITNESS FOR A PARTICULAR PURPOSE, WITH RESPECT TO THE SOFTWARE, THE PROGRAMS, THE SOURCE CODE CONTAINED THEREIN, AND/OR THE TECHNIQUES DESCRIBED IN THIS BOOK. WPI DOES NOT WARRANT THAT THE FUNCTIONS CONTAINED IN THE SOFTWARE WILL MEET YOUR REQUIREMENTS OR THAT THE OPERATION OF THE SOFTWARE WILL BE ERROR FREE.**

   (c) This limited warranty gives you specific legal rights, and you may have other rights that vary from jurisdiction to jurisdiction.

6. **Remedies.**

   (a) WPI's entire liability and your exclusive remedy for defects in materials and workmanship shall be limited to replacement of the Software Media, which may be returned to WPI with a copy of your receipt at the following address: Software Media Fulfillment Department, Attn.: *HTML, XHTML, and CSS All-in-One Desk Reference For Dummies*, Wiley Publishing, Inc., 10475 Crosspoint Blvd., Indianapolis, IN 46256, or call 1-800-762-2974. Please allow four to six weeks for delivery. This Limited Warranty is void if failure of the Software Media has resulted from accident, abuse, or misapplication. Any replacement Software Media will be warranted for the remainder of the original warranty period or thirty (30) days, whichever is longer.

   (b) In no event shall WPI or the author be liable for any damages whatsoever (including without limitation damages for loss of business profits, business interruption, loss of business information, or any other pecuniary loss) arising from the use of or inability to use the Book or the Software, even if WPI has been advised of the possibility of such damages.

   (c) Because some jurisdictions do not allow the exclusion or limitation of liability for consequential or incidental damages, the above limitation or exclusion may not apply to you.

7. **U.S. Government Restricted Rights.** Use, duplication, or disclosure of the Software for or on behalf of the United States of America, its agencies and/or instrumentalities "U.S. Government" is subject to restrictions as stated in paragraph (c)(1)(ii) of the Rights in Technical Data and Computer Software clause of DFARS 252.227-7013, or subparagraphs (c) (1) and (2) of the Commercial Computer Software - Restricted Rights clause at FAR 52.227-19, and in similar clauses in the NASA FAR supplement, as applicable.

8. **General.** This Agreement constitutes the entire understanding of the parties and revokes and supersedes all prior agreements, oral or written, between them and may not be modified or amended except in a writing signed by both parties hereto that specifically refers to this Agreement. This Agreement shall take precedence over any other documents that may be in conflict herewith. If any one or more provisions contained in this Agreement are held by any court or tribunal to be invalid, illegal, or otherwise unenforceable, each and every other provision shall remain in full force and effect.